THE DOPE CHRONICLES

1850-1950

THE DOPE CHRONICLES
1850-1950

Editor
GARY SILVER
Head of Yellow Press

Art Direction, Assemblage
RAY WARD
Assemblage West

Introduction and Commentary
MICHAEL R. ALDRICH, Ph.D.
Curator of
Fitz Hugh Ludlow Memorial Library

1817

Published in San Francisco by
HARPER & ROW, PUBLISHERS
New York, Hagerstown, San Francisco, London

Front cover graphic by Rodney Thomson, which first appeared in *Hearst's International* magazine, February 1923.

The following is a partial list of such writers, correspondents, artists, cartoonists, photo sources, newspapers, magazines, syndicates, research institutions—and those who offered valuable assistance to help prepare this book:

Ace Books, Acme, A.P. Adams, *American Examiner*, American Periodical Archives, *American Weekly,* And/Or Press, Alfred Andriola, Arnold Magazines, Associated Press, Avon Publishing Co., Winifred Black, Bill Blackbeard, *Boston Daily Record, Boston Globe,* Brassai, Arthur Brisbane, *The Bulletin,* W.A. Byrnes, California State Library, Frank G. Carpenter, *The Call,* Cattell Press, The Century Co., *Chicago Examiner, Chicago Herald-Examiner, Chicago Tribune,* Chopin, Clarathorn Publishing Co., C.R. Clark, Kenneth Clark, *Click,* Coll, Lee Conres, Country Press Inc., Cravath, Culver, *The Daily Graphic,* Dell Publishing Co., Detective House, *Down Beat,* Enright, *Everyweek Magazine,* Field Newspaper Syndicate, Film Services of San Francisco, Bud Fisher, Fitz Hugh Ludlow Memorial Library, *Frank Leslie's Illustrated,* Foulsham & Banfield of London, Gale, Chester Gould, Government Printing Office, Guevin, Fred Harman, Harper & Brothers, *Hartford Courant,* J.L. Hearn, *Hearst's International,* John Held Jr., Hoban, *Hollywood Life,* E.O. Hoppe of London, *Hush-Hush,* International Feature Service, International News Service, International Newsreel, J.B. Publishing Co., Burris Jenkins, Kadel & Herbert, Kerr, Keystone View Co., King Features Syndicate, Knickerbocker Press, Library of Congress, *Life,* J.B. Lippincott Co., *The Literary Digest,* Joe Little, *The London Times, Los Angeles Examiner, Los Angeles Express, Los Angeles Times, Look,* Jack Lustig, MacMillan Co., T.D. McAvoy, Winsor McCay, McNaught Syndicate, *The Medical Times,* Metropolitan Newspaper Service, Midwest Distributors, Multnomah County Library, Harry Murphy, *New York American, New York Herald, New York Sun, New York World,* Newspaper Enterprise Association, Newspaper Feature Service, North American Newspaper Alliance, Northland Publishing House, *Oakland Tribune,* F. Opper, Packer, *Pictorial Review,* Picture Magazines Inc., Photo-Arts, Rolf Pielke, *Portland Oregonian,* Press Publishing Co., Public Ledger, Publishers Newspaper Syndicate, Alex Raymond, *Reader's Guide to Periodical Literature,* Robert Ripley, Frank Robbins, *Sacramento Bee,* San Francisco Academy of Comic Art, *San Francisco Call-Bulletin, San Francisco Chronicle, San Francisco Examiner,* San Francisco Public Library, Science Service, *Seattle Post-Intelligencer,* M. Shaw, *Shock, Signs of the Times, Simplicissimus,* Dan Smith, Dorman H. Smith, Neville Spearman Ltd., Sponagel & Herrmann, *St. Louis Post Dispatch,* Stanford Library, Star Co., *Sunset, Syracuse Post Standard, Time,* Underwood & Underwood, United Feature Service, United Feature Syndicate, United Press, Universal Publishing & Distributing Corp., Universal Service, University of California, Berkeley Library; University of Pennsylvania Press, Vail & Co., Cornelius Vanderbilt Jr., Carol Wald, *Washington Herald,* Wheelan, James Whitaker, *Wichita Eagle,* O.P. Williams.

Special thanks to Geoffrey Turner, curator of American Periodical Archives, for editorial assistance and use of magazines and other ephemera; and to Judith Freeman, journalist, Washington, D.C., for research and guidance.

The original collection of approximately 2500 full newspaper pages which were torn apart, cut up, edited, pasted down and collaged together to make this book has been permanently preserved on microfilm for scholars and researchers. For information contact:

Yellow Press, Box 14141, San Francisco 94114.

FIRST EDITION
Designed by Ray Ward
ISBN 0-06-250790-7
Library of Congress Catalogue Card Number: 78-15835

79 80 81 82 83 10 9 8 7 6 5 4 3 2 1

Contents

Introduction

Dope is a dirty word, as Aldous Huxley once said. How it got that way is the subject of this scrapbook collage of drug history. Headlines, cartoons, clippings, and full pages from a century of newspapers re-create American attitudes toward drugs with astonishing immediacy. Here we see history in process, from the days of opium clippers plying the seas, through the "noble experiment" with alcohol prohibition in the Jazz Age, to the great crusades that made cocaine, heroin, and marijuana illegal throughout the world. Sometimes funny, sometimes tragic, always fascinating, these pages evoke a time when there were no social drugs, just social menaces—an era of black and white starkness, the rich opposition of good and evil painted bold.

Most of the periodical material comes from the major metropolitan dailies of 1850 to 1950, supplemented by appropriate books, magazines, and ephemera of each period. Three giants of journalism are represented. James Gordon Bennett's *New York Herald* offered its upper-middle-class readers a unique brand of genteel muckraking (now called investigative reporting) that can be seen, for instance, in a superb 1891 series on Puget Sound opium smuggling. Joseph Pulitzer's *New York World* and *St. Louis Post-Dispatch* set the style of yellow journalism (so named for "yellow kid" cartoons he published to spice up the news pages) that revolutionized reporting throughout the world during the newspaper circulation wars of the 1880s. After Pulitzer's death in 1911 his successors adopted a somewhat tamer but still shocking style, like that of a 1913 article on heroin pushers debauching high school kids in New York. Thirdly, there are copious selections from the Hearst newspapers and magazines, which will be discussed below. To round it off, there are sprinklings from independent or home-owned papers, such as the *Boston Globe, Portland Oregonian, Sacramento Bee, Los Angeles Express, San Francisco Chronicle, Wichita Eagle,* and others, with a few tattered remnants from the *London Times* for good measure. The available material, including dime novels and scandal sheets, has thus weighted the book heavily on the side of the sensational press—but after all, that's where dope was chronicled most vividly.

This book is, in many ways, a tribute to the genius of William Randolph Hearst. Fresh from the *Harvard Lampoon* when he took over his father's *San Francisco Examiner* in 1887, Hearst became a media mogul who eventually controlled some thirty major metropolitan papers, several magazines, feature syndicates, newsreels, and a movie company. The key to his success was that his pages were never boring. He had a brilliant flair for plucking out the most exciting elements of a story, splashing them across the pages in banner headlines, and inventing new twists to milk the story serially for days or weeks, keeping readers begging for more.

If something sufficiently electrifying could not be found in news events, Hearst would arrange it. A perfect example is pointed out by W.A. Swanberg in his book *Citizen Hearst:* when Sarah Bernhardt visited San Francisco shortly after Hearst took over the *Examiner,* other papers waited patiently for interviews, covered her performances, and prattled about her private life. Hearst sent a reporter clear to Nevada to insinuate himself into her entourage, and when she arrived in San Francisco he hustled her off to Chinatown. The result: a scoop about the greatest actress in the world scrounging through an opium den. *"C'est horrible!"* gasped the ladies. *"C'est magnifique!"* exclaimed the Divine Sarah. ("Great circulation builder!" chortled Hearst.)

Hearst was grand master of the art of crusading because he had the money to buy the best talent and the creative imagination to push that talent to its limit. Three of his hirelings deserve special mention, as their work permeates this book.

Underpinning each crusade was an overall editorial policy that carefully selected the news, editorials, and graphics for that campaign. Arthur Brisbane, editor of the *New York American,* set the tone for all Hearst's papers, usually with the boss peering over his shoulder. His pompous messages (not only editorials and a front-page column but also syndicated essays like one on Samuel Taylor Coleridge and opium: "long years of pitiful struggle against the drug that ruled him, with occasional moments of achievement") seem overblown in our day, but his skill in weaving together various journalistic elements to build a pitch to a purpose is still widely imitated.

Winifred Black, who wrote under the name Annie Laurie in the West Coast papers, was the original "sob sister." Possessed of tremendous energy, she spewed forth columns in Hearst's papers almost daily for over twenty years—and dope was one of her favorite topics. She put heart and soul into dope-fiend imagery, as in her rendition of an instant metamorphosis caused by cocaine: "A harmless, good-natured boy of 17 will take two or three 'sniffs' of 'snow' and turn into a cold-blooded, cruel, blood-thirsty bandit, ready to hold up his own father and kill his own mother to get enough money to go out and buy some more 'snow'." Black's style of peppy punch lines and gushy rhetorical questions is no longer fashionable in the newspapers, but turn on any television news commentator to see it in action today.

Hearst hired excellent artists to create editorial cartoons and graphics for his crusades: Dorman H. Smith, O.P. Williams, D.J. Enright, Hoban, Murphy, Chopin, Gale, Packer, and others. Surpassing them all was the inimitable Winsor McCay, who had drawn "Little Nemo" for Bennett before Hearst stole him away to help spruce up his Sunday comic page. McCay created the immortal visions of "Little Nemo in Slumberland," "Dreams of Rarebit Fiend," and roughly a dozen other comic strips; drew perhaps 3,000 editorial cartoons; pioneered film animation with *Gertie the Dinosaur* and ten other films; and somehow found time to roam the vaudeville circuit doing a quick-sketch act.

McCay's meticulous pen-and-ink drawings are distinguished by frequent use of crowd scenes and a foreshortened perspective gained from his film work. He involves us directly in his allegories, making us part of the fantasy so it strikes us as real. He occasionally uses popular songs to make a point, as in the Jazz Age figure of Death (gangsterism) dancing through a throng singing "East Side, West Side, All Around the Town." Even at their most surreal, McCay's cartoons are imbued with a gentleness and a keen understanding of human failings that makes them as freshly luminous now as when they first touched newsprint sixty years ago.

Hearst was hardly alone in creating anti-drug crusades to jolt circulation. The entire book is filled with shockers and boners, pointers and surprises. Though most came from big-city papers, there was plenty of small-town coverage as dope swept across Middle America. For example:

1896—South Manchester, Connecticut: "Whole Town Mad for Cocaine" after going dry in a fit of temperance fever.

1923—Summerset, Kentucky: Population less than 5,000, fills 4,000 prescriptions for morphine and cocaine in 2 years.

1934—Lawrence, Kansas: Two or three hundred university students "addicted" to marijuana, "known also as Peyote."

1941—Grand Forks, North Dakota: "Tea" parties, black men jitterbugging with white women, holding bags over their heads to keep the pot smoke in.

Some of these stories, like the sordid mobster dramas of prohibition, are familiar to us from fiction and films as well as the popular press. Even so, items such as "1,550 Killed by Fanatic Dry Agents in Decade" will make us sit up and ponder. And many will inspire a sense of *déjà vu,* like the clipping about nonsmokers trying to ban Lady Nicotine from public cars in 1913. Those who thought the government started growing pot in the 1960s will be astonished to learn of the 1904 federal poison farm near Washington, D.C., where the government planted fields of marijuana, opium, coca, and other drugs, with an eye to commercial production, so we wouldn't have to import so much!

Throughout this period of dope history, figures of almost mythic proportions recur. The Trembling Addict Full of Contrition Confessing His Woes to the World. The Pusher. The Wily Nark and the Beefy Commissioner. The Do-Gooder in the Slums. The Self-Experimenters, like Arthur Symons tracing "the very course of madness as it ravaged his remarkable mind," or the "doctor who watched himself die" of cocaine. The Prohibitionists, going back to those in the nineteenth century who railed against the "Sunday vice" of opium and

Sunday bars for beer. The Grand Ranters who, in good times, used drugs as an excuse to castigate celebrities who indulged and, in bad times, used drugs as a means to deport aliens. Likewise, there have always been proponents of what might be called the leper theory of treatment, isolating addicts in camps or treating them as insane. There will always be frivolous youth, worried mamas, and indignant dads in the endless universe of drugs.

Subtlety is rare in these pages. Dope inspires extremes, even absurdities. 1908: "Within six months it will be impossible for the average Chinese to secure opium in San Francisco." 1928: "Mussolini Leads Way in Crushing Dope Evil." 1935: "World Victory Over Dope" declared by the YMCA.

Scholars who look closely will find many interesting tidbits, for instance, identification of the ancient Persian drug *homa* as hemp. Legislators will recognize the kaleidoscope of crises—and the impact of crusades—that produce our laws. Photographers will notice some extraordinary pictures, like the Brassai photo of a Parisian opium *femeuse* that illustrates a 1938 Portland junkie tale. Anthropologists will unearth a treasure trove of American peyote rites, Syrian hemp harvests, Chinese opium campaigns. And even the most casual reader will be amazed at some of the long-forgotten tales revealed here, such as the gangland slaying behind the creation of the Federal Bureau of Narcotics in 1930 or the fascinating account of the expedition that first brought *caapi,* the Amazon visionary vine, into the United States in 1922.

One way to read this book is to decade-hop across the material for a sense of what's happening:

1883—Women take lunch breaks in Chinatown opium dens.
1893—Use of stimulants (alcohol, opium) blamed on doctors; *Health Reader* warns against giving "soothing syrups" to children.
1903—Missionaries in the Philippines oppose selling government opium monopoly to private interests.
1913—"Drug Crazed Negroes" shoot up a Mississippi town; San Francisco opium murders revealed; New York girls doped and kidnapped for white-slave trade.
1923—Crusades: Wally Reid and Juanita Hansen stir Hollywood; "World War on Drugs Launched" in Geneva; Paris addicts claim right to die from drugs.
1933—Ratifications: Twenty-first Amendment repeals prohibition; Geneva Convention ratified by League of Nations; Uniform Narcotics Laws signed in most states.
1943—Marijuana blamed for "Flaming Youth"; Gene Krupa busted.

What's *not* here is significant too, in terms of what the papers chose to emphasize or not among peripheral news items. (1943—a Swiss chemist discovered LSD-25.) There was hardly any coverage of the Harrison Act when it passed in 1914—pathetic stories of addicts flocking to hospitals had to wait until the effects of the law were felt. The same was true of the Marijuana Tax Act of 1937, though by then it was mostly ghetto teenagers herded into addict-crowded jails. Throughout a century of reporting there was very little in the way of strictly accurate scientific information about drugs, free of anti-drug fervor. and, of course, little defense of drug use (except alcohol). The masters of confessional addict literature were rarely mentioned except to be clucked at. Even medical prescription was suspicious, the newspapers vascillating between blaming doctors for spreading addiction, and gushing over addicts as sick souls needing treatment.

A visitor from a far planet would wonder why people used these substances at all, given the plethora of stories about the perils involved. There is never an indication that people might *choose* to use drugs for various purposes; instead, it's usually "they fell into it by accident" (medical addiction), or "the pusher led them into it"—a curious vision of a world untroubled by free will.

Michael R. Aldrich, Ph.D.
October, 1978

WARD
pium Traffic Back
China's Unrest
ERE can be little doubt that the opium
raffic underlies all the disturbance now
oing on in China.
unt Michimasa Soyeshima
DOPE

Opium

Thou only givest these gifts to man;
and thou has the keys of Paradise,
oh, just, subtle, and mighty opium!
—Thomas De Quincy, 1822

According to these newspaper accounts, opium use was the crime of the century between the Opium Wars and the World Wars. Britain forced China to open its ports to Western trade in the first Opium War (1839-1842), fought while fast clippers exchanged opium for tea, silk, and cash. Reformers were aghast, but Britain had a virtual world monopoly on the drug grown in Bengal; it was a mainstay of the Empire, yielding nearly a fifth of India's total revenue. Another Opium War (1856-1858) legalized opium in China and added to its burgeoning addict population.

And at just this time, thousands of Chinese were brought to America to work on the transcontinental railroad. Although use of morphine was already rampant in the United States (during the Civil War it was called the "soldier's disease," and opiated medicines splashed addiction throughout all social classes), the Chinese were blamed for opium's rapid spread across the country. Do-gooders prowled the squalid slums of Chinatowns, decrying the gambling, prostitution; and opium dens they found. Ever-higher tariffs on opium imports led only to increased smuggling of both opium and Chinese from Canada.

In 1898—as the Bayer Company marketed a new cough syrup with the brand name *Heroin*—the end of the Spanish-American War in the Philippines sent droves of missionaries to the Far East. Scandalized by native opium use (and liquor consumption, promoted by Yankee traders), Bishop Charles H. Brent urged President Theodore Roosevelt to call a conference of opium-bloc nations which met at Shanghai in 1909. The United States banned opium prepared for smoking; at the same time doctors freely prescribed heroin.

Meanwhile, China reached a Ten Years' Agreement with India (1907) to reduce opium cultivation and imports by ten percent a year until the trade ceased. The result? "Human heads in baskets and ears skewered on sticks"; thousands of addicts fleeing to French Indochina; a partial takeover of the trade by Japan (discovered when the liner *America Maru* was seized in 1911); and, ultimately, increased opium production in Szechuan, China. Now all four giants of Asia, including British India, were involved.

The Hague Convention (1912) outlawed nonmedical opiate use worldwide, as the Harrison Act (1914) did in America. World War I interrupted the prohibition process, but in 1920 the League of Nations set up an import certificate system requiring opium importers to certify that all supplies of the drug were for medical use only.

Such restrictions made little difference in a vastly changed world between wars. Opium was the rage from the parlors of Paris to the dives of Saigon. Japan encouraged it in China; Britain, France, Holland, and Portugal sold it openly through government monopolies in their respective colonies; Turkey began producing it in quantity, and the French Connection through Marseille to New York slowly evolved.

American police had their hands full pursuing bootleggers, catching only an occasional millionaire dope dealer. Heroin ousted morphine from the black market when a 1924 law made its import illegal. By 1929, while Police Commissioner Carleton Simon was chasing small fry in Harlem, legitimate international suppliers produced 10,000 tons of opium, more than twice the world's medical needs. That same year the wife of the Chinese vice-consul in San Francisco was charged with opium smuggling; she begged not to be deported, for Chinese troops were executing addicts and peddlers as enemies of the state.

In the late 1930s, as the Nazis gathered strength in Europe (Hermann Goering, Hitler's Gestapo chief, was a morphine addict), Japan invaded China and flooded it with dope, exactly as Britain had done a century before. A powerful tong in Shanghai dealt heroin to the world, with Sicilian and Corsican mobsters running a close second and Mexican smugglers moving up fast. American papers ran juicy junkie tales replete with glossaries of slang.

Japanese troops overran eastern China on the eve of World War II, forcing Chiang Kai-shek into Szechuan, where he, in turn, drove opium-growing hill tribes south into the Golden Triangle—that borderless and lawless region in north Burma, Thailand, and Laos where most opium originates today.

The Times.

LONDON, FRIDAY, JANUARY 1, 1858.

THERE is NO LETTER for you at the Post-office.—K. D.

M. D.—The request shall be immediately complied with.

M. S. A.—I beg most gratefully to ACKNOWLEDGE from M. S. A. £5, (second donation,) on behalf of the Destitute Poor of Bethnal-green, and for missionary work in that locality; and from E. Gosnell, Esq., £5, for the same objects; also from Captain — £1 10s., and from M. F. 2s. 6d., which will be distributed to the special cases referred to as requested. Through the mercy of our God the cry "Come over and help us" has not been raised in vain. He knows the greatness of the need and will supply.—D. WARDLAW SCOTT, 9, Palestine-place, Cambridge-heath-gate, Bethnal-green, N.E.

ROYAL FREE HOSPITAL, Gray's-inn-road.—Messrs. Nisbet and Co. beg to ACKNOWLEDGE the receipt of a DONATION of £10 (No. U-B 58,67...

BOMBAY direct (having the greater portion of her cargo engaged, and will meet with prompt despatch), the splendid copper ship McLEOD, A 1, 1,365 tons register, J. L. GALBRAITH, Commander; loads in the Victoria Docks. Has excellent accommodation for passengers. For terms of freight, &c., apply to G. and A. Herring and Co., 12, Old Broad-street, E.C.

BOMBAY direct, has the greater part of her cargo engaged, the clippership ADRIATIC, 824 tons register, DAVID SCOTT, Commander; to load in St. Katharine's Docks. The fast sailing properties of this fine ship render her an eligible opportunity for shippers desirous of despatch. Apply to David C. Thomas, Lombard-street-chambers, Clement's-lane, E.C.

BOMBAY, Calcutta, and Australia.—First-class fast-sailing SHIPS, 1,000 tons, ably commanded, loading in London, sail monthly for the above presidencies. For freight or passage (having superior accommodation for passengers) apply to Bishop, Fairbridge, and Braham, 63, Cornhill, E.C. Midshipmen and Apprentices Wanted.

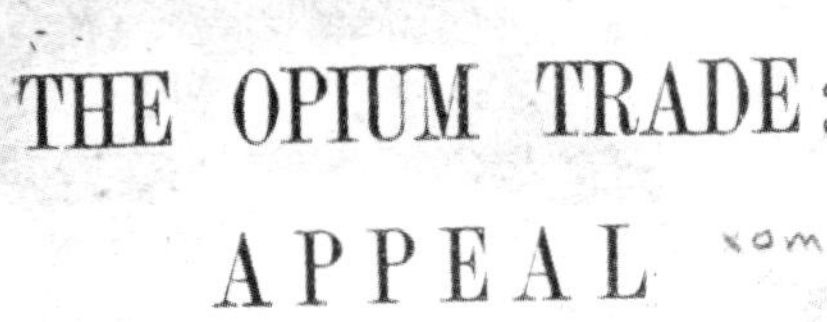

Rev M. Hall

THE OPIUM TRADE:

APPEAL

TO THE

BRITISH NATION

AGAINST IT,

ON RELIGIOUS, MORAL, & COMMERCIAL GROUNDS.

BY THE REV. W. TAIT.

I.—Its Iniquity.
II.—Its Folly
III.—Miseries which it Entails.
IV.—Free Trade—No Apology for it.

London:
...M AND MACINTOSH.
...KINGDOM RAGGED SCHOOL INDUSTRIAL
...TORIA STREET, WESTMINSTER.

1858.

...ice Sixpence.

PREPARATIONS FOR THE ROYAL MARRIAGE.

It is a long time since the ordinary operations of bricklaying, carpentering, and house-decorating generally have excited so much attention as those which are now going forward daily in the precincts of old St. James's. That dingy mausoleum of departed grandeur resounds with the note of preparation, and there are such symptoms of animation amid the ponderous magnificence of its halls and chambers as would almost lead one to the belief that it was really inhabited and about to be once more used by men. Acres of brown Holland sufficient to keep all Belgravia from the dust are being removed; ceilings being dusted, gilding retouched, washing, painting, and papering all going forward at once, with such a din of saws and hammers, such a dusting of carpets, uncovering of chairs, and general putting on of a rich and festive appearance that the imagination can quite realize the aspect it must have presented when the building was really a palace, and when St. James's rivalled in wealth and splendour even the magnificent Court of the *Grand Monarque*. There is scarcely a room of importance in which some alteration or decoration is not going forward—nay, even beyond the rooms themselves, down into corridors and courtyards, the workmen are busy erecting stages and seats for the few, the very few comparatively who can be allowed to witness the bridal procession in its different stages of advance towards the Chapel Royal. Just now these preparations are all in their earliest stages—so early, indeed, that half of them are going forward provisionally as it were, and without any one knowing whether they are to be carried out ultimately or not. In fact, the greater portion of the details of the programme for the important day are still to be resolved on, so that, beyond such general features...

...thought of, so St. James's ... chosen on the same principle as "Hobson" is asserted to have made his choice. Outside the Queen's private...

XVO

[PRICE ONE SHILLING.]

THE

RISE AND PROGRESS

OF

BRITISH OPIUM SMUGGLING:

THE

ILLEGALITY OF THE EAST INDIA COMPANY'S MONOPOLY OF THE DRUG;

AND

ITS INJURIOUS EFFECTS UPON INDIA, CHINA, AND THE COMMERCE OF GREAT BRITAIN.

Five Letters

ADDRESSED TO THE RIGHT HONOURABLE THE EARL OF SHAFTESBURY.

BY

MAJOR-GENERAL R. ALEXANDER,

MADRAS ARMY.

THIRD EDITION REVISED AND ENLARGED.

LONDON:
JUDD AND GLASS, 21 PATERNOSTER ROW,
AND AT THE OFFICES OF THE SOCIETY FOR "SUPPRESSING OPIUM SMUGGLING," 13 BEDFORD ROW, HOLBORN.

1856.

BRITISH MANUFACTURES AND THE OPIUM TRADE.

TO THE EDITOR OF THE TIMES.

Sir,—When I wrote yesterday commenting on some remarks in the letter of your China correspondent I had not then seen the second part of that letter in *The Times* of the 28th inst. Allow me to add a few lines, therefore, to what I have already written.

The main object of your correspondent in the second half of this letter is to show that the true remedy for the languishing condition of our export trade to China and for the inconvenient drain of our silver to pay for silk is to be found in pushing into consumption British manufactures. Here I am quite at one with him. He has put his finger on the real remedy, but meanwhile, like the too indulgent physician prescribing for a self-indulgent patient, while he proposes the means of cure he allows the man to continue certain bad habits which feed the disease. Your correspondent states as one reason why our manufactures do not find their way into China, that the British merchants there do not care to cultivate that branch of trade. The bulky and comparatively unremunerative bales of piece goods have no attraction to those who are making large profits in opium. There is much truth in this, and we have an apt illustration of it in the spirit trade at home. A shopkeeper who holds a license to retail spirits counts upon this branch of his business as his mainstay, and becomes indifferent to the bulkier and less valuable commodities on his premises; while another who has no such license, by giving his whole attention to the less valuable articles, is enabled to make a business out of them which was despised by the other. But if the opium trade thus confessedly stands in the way of British manufactures, why does not your correspondent go a step further? The British merchant will never have any greater liking for such heavy goods while the opium trade continues to allure by its larger profits. The brilliant imaginary voyage of your correspondent up the Yang-tse-Kiang opens a magnificent vista to the British manufacturer; but if these virgin regions are first to be spoliated and demoralized by opium what is the prospect for our manufactures? And if, in addition to this argument against the opium trade, appealing so powerfully to the manufacturing interests, we have the far higher one, that it is utterly indefensible in a moral and a Christian point of view, surely our common sense, as well as our common Christianity, urge upon this nation as the first step in the process the abandonment of that opium trade in India hitherto maintained and fostered by the East India Company.

Your correspondent ingeniously enough observes, under shelter of a banter at John Chinaman, that he smokes opium at the rate of only 6d. per head per annum, or but one-fifth of what we consume in gin and whisky. Your readers exclaim, "Oh, if that's all, let the opium trade flourish!" But stay—we find from another paragraph that some of the labouring classes in China spend out of 8d. per day of wages as much as 6d. per day on opium, or 9l. per head per annum. The only difference between these two calculations is, that in the one case the drug is theoretically diluted into a harmless dose by being divided among the whole 360,000,000; in the other case, it is proved to be a cruel devastating poison by being confined at the most to 10,000,000, though probably much fewer. In the one case any attempt to stop the universal habit might be thought hopeless, but in the other it becomes hopeful, and was, indeed, all but accomplished in 1839, but for the want of any countenance or support from foreign Powers. To say, as your correspondent does, that no power on earth can stop opium-smoking is a bold statement; but it is bolder still to say, and may well make the reader shudder as he joins in saying it, that because things must be so, therefore we (Britons) shall continue to administer the poison. Well may we expect in such case a righteous retribution for our deeds.

I am, Sir, your most obedient servant,
AN OLD RESIDENT IN CHINA.

Dec. 30, 1857.

...for the effective selection of the points from which they are taken, and we cannot doubt that the publishers and the artist, Mr. Frith, will be rewarded for the enterprise and skill which they have displayed in so novel an undertaking.

STAFF APPOINTMENTS.

TO THE EDITOR OF THE TIMES.

Sir,—I have had a good deal of communication lately with officers who are anxious to qualify for staff appointments or Ordnance surveyors, and many of them would at once commence their preparation for the competitive examination which should decide their fitness for admission to the Staff College on the 1st of February, 1858, or a year hence; or their fitness, in 1860, for the duties required without entering the college, if time were allowed to refresh what they have learnt, and acquire what is necessary besides. My experience enables me to judge with considerable accuracy of what is required for these examinations; and several whom I know would, I am certain, be well prepared, but time for preparation they have not. This complaint is universal. A part of the day is spent on regimental duty; of this no officer complains, but a great part is spent, or rather misspent, upon parade, where the whole duty is to shout, "Fall in," "Rear rank take open order," "March," "Port arms," "Half cock arms," &c. A certain amount of this duty is necessary for young officers; and there is, I believe, quite a sufficient number of them in all ... for the drill the soldiers require ...

...use of the Corps Diplomatique as on the occasion of the celebration of Her Majesty's nuptials. There is not the least foundation for what has been stated as to foreign musical artistes and vocal ce...

The Society for Suppressing Opium Smuggling.

OFFICE:—13 BEDFORD ROW, HOLBORN, LONDON.

President:

The Right Honourable the EARL OF SHAFTESBURY.

Vice-Presidents:

The Right Honourable the LORD CALTHORPE.
The Honourable A. KINNAIRD, M.P.
SIR E. N. BUXTON, BART.
JOSEPH FERGUSON, ESQ., M.P.
THOMAS CHAMBERS, ESQ., M.P.

Committee:

The Rev. Henry Venn, B.D.,	Church Missionary Society.
" Rev. Joseph Ridgway, M.A.,	Church Missionary Society.
" Rev. J. Chapman, B.D.,	Church Missionary Society.
" Rev. W. Knight,	Church Missionary Society.
" Rev. Dr. Tidman,	London Missionary Society.
" Rev. W. Arthur,	Wesleyan Missionary Society.
" Rev. F. Trestrail,	Baptist Missionary Society.
" Rev. S. B. Bergne,	British and Foreign Bible Society.
Captain Fishbourne, R.N.	Royal Patriotic Fund.
G. H. Davis, Esq.,	Religious Tract Society.
" Honble F. Maude, R.N.,	Eaton Square.
... Hughes,	Strangers' Home, Temple Bar.
	Strangers' Home, Temple Bar.

FOLLY
OF THE
OPIUM TRADE.

"We are drugging to death the man whom we hope to see enter our shop daily, purse in hand."
NORTH BRITISH REVIEW, Feb., 1857.

FELLOW COUNTRYMEN,

Listen to a simple parable. There were three brothers, among whom a wealthy father had divided his fortune. Having determined to invest it in trade, they settled together in a small town. One commenced as A DRAPER AND CLOTHIER; his window was fill… …ith shawls, muslins, and every … The second commenced …NT, displaying admirable …d tools, fitted for the …y and the tradesman. … as to how he should …e opened A GIN PALACE. …rything which could …pend their time and …as brilliantly illumi- … to the shops of his … time. The draper

MISERIES
OF THE
OPIUM TRADE:

"The use of Opium in China, is attended with MISERIES deeper and more widely spread than those which sprang from the Slave Trade."
NORTH BRITISH REVIEW, Feb. 1857.

FELLOW COUNTRYMEN,

IT would ill become any one who pretends to human feeling to underrate the miseries produced by the Slave Trade. It makes the heart sick even to think of them. The cruel wars fomented by the Slave Dealer—the firing of the peaceful village—the tearing of the able-bodied from their homes, with the murder of the aged and of the helpless babes—the horrors of the middle passage—the hopeless, life-long bondage to which the miserable victims are consigned, rise before us at once in dark perspective. Well might the illustrious CHARLES FOX exclaim, when as Prime Minister of England he signed the act which decreed its abolition, "Thank God, I have not lived in vain!"

Can any miseries be conceived deeper and more wide-spread than these? The facts of the Opium Trade must answer this Appeal.

L'OPIUM.

EXTRAIT DE L'ŒUVRE ÉPUISÉE "L'ANGLETERRE, LA CHINE, ET L'INDE,"

PAR DON SINIBALDO DE MAS,

Envoyé Extraordinaire et Ministre Plénipotentiaire de la Reine d'Espagne…

PARIS, 1858.

L'opium a été incontestablem…
celle qui a lieu présentement n'…
d'importance pour que nous n…
spécial. Je n'ai jamais, ni comm…
été intéressé dans ce commerce; …
peut-être les seuls dont on puisse …
en Chine une seule caisse d'opium. …
à Calcutta, Singapour, Pinang, M…
localités de la Chine, où je suis p…
manière à pouvoir converser av…
naître la matière et me trouv…
entièrement impartial.

On a beaucoup déclamé contre …
poison, et on a trouvé par co…
un objet de commerce et de …
un mémoire rédigé dans ce …
appuyé par le comte de Ch…
philanthropes antiopistes, …
dans le même sens que …
président du comité form…
président est le comte …
le mémoire. Enfin, d…
et de lords se sont é…
mercants chrétiens é…
E. Davis, et d'autr…

The following, from a Hindoo, dated Calcutta, August 1839, is particularly forcible and striking:—

"The opium question is next treated by ———. If from what was before known in England one book has been published 'On the Iniquities of the Opium Trade,' there will be dozens when the people in England know as much of this trade as we now know. The latter circumstance I will relate myself. The Red Rover and Sir Edward … lately arrived from China, and they have both sailed within these … days, the former with about one thousand chests, and the … seven hundred chests of opium. The agents of the former … of the latter are ———. They are armed to … They have thus sailed out of a British … British Government, with the avowed … it at all hazards on the east … that British merchants … the world, without a … and piratical

INIQUITY
OF THE
OPIUM TRADE.

"The Slave Trade was merciful, compared with the Opium Trade. The English murderer and Chinese suicide vie with each other in their offerings at this Moloch's shrine."—MR. MONTGOMERY MARTIN.

FELLOW COUNTRYMEN,

You have heard many times of the wrongs of Africa. She had Wilberforce, and Clarkson, and Buxton, to proclaim them on the house-tops, till the attention of the whole nation was roused. Would to God that their mantle might descend on some in this generation to proclaim to you the wrongs of China! If China hates the name of England, if her people maltreat us whenever they have opportunity, if they conspire to poison English residents in their cities, if they insult the English flag, we are to blame; it is we who have taught them so to do. More than sixty years ago China forbad the introduction of Opium. In defiance of this prohibition we contrived, in the year 1800, to introduce into her ports 2,000 chests of opium; and this quantity was year by year increased, till, in 1820, it reached 5,… The Government of Ch… most earnestly …

OPIUM IN CHINA.

(FROM OUR CORRESPONDENT.)

SHANGHAI, FEB. 12.

It has been observed by residents in the Far East that during the late Parliamentary recess the Society for the Suppression of the Opium Trade has been more than usually active and the speeches delivered by its leaders have been more than usually violent. The British public is told that England taught China to smoke opium, and thereafter insisted upon supplying her with the drug at a handsome profit to the Government of India, at first whether the Chinese Government would or not, and latterly by virtue of a tariff rule legalizing its importation attached to the Treaty of Tientsin, which was extorted from the terrified Chinese commissioners by force of arms; that Lord Elgin, in extorting the permission through his secretaries, was simply carrying out the brutal and bullying policy of the English Government of the day, whose servant he was, but that the policy itself was to him distasteful and to the Chinese plenipotentiaries odious; that the production and consumption of opium by its subjects have always been abhorred by the Chinese Government, and that they have shown this by their persistent and consistent efforts, at all times and in all provinces, to root up the poppy crops; that, deeply sensible of the evils which opium-smoking entails on the country, they have ever been vigilant to minimize the mischief by limiting the consumption to the amount of the Indian drug imported; that the whole policy and the only policy of the Chinese Government with regard to native opium has been and is one of hostility, prohibition, and punishment; that these efforts are rendered futile and this policy is paralyzed by the increased importation of the Indian drug; and that, in sum, Christian England, turning a deaf ear alike to the prayers of the Chinese Government and the groans of the people, is directly responsible for the slow poisoning of heathen China.

Now the instincts of an ordinary Englishman, whether with regard to his family, his country, or the world generally, are in the main those of the *bonus paterfamilias* of the Roman Law, and an accusation of this kind brought against his country, especially when reiterated with all the fervour of religion and the vehemence of burning truth, will certainly arrest his attention. Neither the fervour nor the vehemence has of late been wanting. The proceedings of the society whose gospel I have just given are rapidly reaching the stage of organized agitation, and as public opinion in England, given the initial impetus, forms and shapes itself with dangerous rapidity, this question of the Indian opium revenue may come prominently before Parliament and the country at any time. To help my countrymen to decide whether we are as a nation the immoral wretches the anti-opium Society say we are, I have been at some pains to collate certain broad facts regarding the production and consumption of opium in China, a knowledge of which will tend to illumine the question by the light of common sense.

The habit of opium-smoking is common all over China, but it is in the West, in the comparatively unknown half of China west of the 110th meridian, that it is most prevalent. In some parts of Western Hu Pei and Eastern Szechuen it is all but universal; there are few adults in any station of life who do not take an occasional whiff, and the very streets of the towns and villages reek with opium fumes. The practice is there indulged in in the most open manner, and no more stigma or disgrace attaches to it than to smoking tobacco. Mr. Watters, Her Majesty's Consul at Ichang, made careful inquiries last year into the origin of the practice, and he found that it had been indulged in for several hundred years, long before either the present reigning dynasty or foreign merchants and their opium were ever dreamt of. The custom generations ago passed into the family *Sacra*, and at funerals in the West of China, among other gifts which are transmitted into the next world, by burning paper fac-similes of them in this, for the solace of the departed, is a complete set of opium smoking requisites—pipe, lamp, needle, &c. By the people themselves the habit, so far from being regarded as a curse, is looked on as *sine quâ non* for a Chinaman who wishes to make the best of both worlds. The whole of the opium consumed in the West is locally produced, and Indian opium does not come higher up the Yangtsze than the districts contiguous to the port of Hankow, nor is it imported by any channel into Western Hu Pei, Szechuen, or the other provinces of the West. Above and beyond the enormous quantity there grown for local use there is a large trade in the drug, mostly contraband, from West to East. Indian opium is consumed in the provinces adjacent to the treaty ports, and, being an expensive article as compared with native opium, is mostly smoked by the well-to-do classes. The common people in these provinces smoke the native drug, which is either grown on the borders of Kiang Su and Ho Nan or is smuggled overland from the West. All Western China, therefore, and the lower classes in Eastern China smoke native-grown opium, and it is most important for English people who are asked at meetings to say whether they think Indian opium is forced by our Government on the Chinese or not to know to what extent and under what official conditions the production of native opium is carried on.

Regarding the opium districts of Eastern China—that is, the borderland of Chih Li, Ho Nan, Shantung, and Kiang Su—I have no personal knowledge. But with the West, and especially the section of it I have mentioned as the centre both of consumption and production of the native drug, I have not only had some acquaintance myself, but I have lately been able to avail myself of the experience of the two Englishmen who have had the best opportunities and means of procuring information regarding the native opium of the West—Mr. Colborne Baber, who was for four years Consular Agent in Szechuen watching the trade there; and Mr. Watters, who was our Consul at Ichang, the port of Western Szechuen, until the other day. I can, therefore, speak with authority and confidence. The production of opium in Szechuen has been exceedingly under-estimated hitherto. Mr. Davenport gives it as 50,000 chests for 1878, basing his estimate probably on Chinese official information. But all such statistical information on this point is misleading. I have been assured by officials both of Szechuen and Kweichow that for every *picul* (133lb.) of opium returned to the Government, 2½ to 3 *piculs* are produced and sold contraband. Mr. Baber, living and travelling among the Szechuen people, has been able to hear and see for himself, and he has obtained ample evidence that the production of Chinese opium in this one province is greater than the whole Indian crop, Malwa, Patna, and Benares, put together. Of the amount produced in the hill country of Hu Pei Mr. Watters has not been able to give me any figures, but he says that in Ichang alone there is an opium restaurant to every 13 inhabitants, where nothing is consumed except the native drug, produced in one or other of the four western provinces, and that in the outlying parts of the two adjacent prefectures the officials admit of a production on which they receive revenue of 2,000 *piculs*. All over Western China the conditions of poppy culture, as far as the officials are concerned, are those of perfect freedom, and even open encouragement. All the grower has to think of is his profit. Opium is a more risky crop than cereals, but it pays seven times as well. If he chooses to run the risk of a failure in the crop, or of inability to buy rice with the money he gets for his opium, he is at liberty to grow opium if he likes. In ordinary circumstances a poppy crop subjects the grower to no interference on the part of his officials beyond paying the customary taxes; and in many districts where opium in manufacture or transit is the sole source of revenue its culture is encouraged.

There is one risk, however, which the native grower of the poppy must take into account, although it is a small one, and that is the risk of destruction of his crop by an official in some part of whose jurisdiction there may be a famine. When cereals fail in China the places which have cannot come to the relief of those which have not, and neither money nor opium can be exchanged for bread, owing to the defective means of inter-communication in the country. It is customary in such circumstances to order the rooting up of the poppy crop, and the orders are carried out in proportion to the sincerity and energy of the official. But as soon as the time of scarcity is past the poppy is allowed to bloom over the land again, and the reforming official, whose thoroughgoing patriotism has in the meantime been reported to and dilated on by the anti-opium society, reaps the usual reward in an enhanced revenue. Proclamations against the culture of the poppy, whether emanating from high or low officials, the grower may at all times disregard, or "contract" himself out of by valuable consideration in the shape of bribes. During the past 12 years I can only recollect one case where a crusade against the poppy was carried on by an honest and a determined reformer with a single eye to the good of his country, and being honest and determined he was thoroughly successful, as a local official in China must be in any legitimate scheme of local government he may choose to enforce with energy.

Regarding the effect of opium on the Chinese nation, there is by no means a consensus of opinion that it is thoroughly bad. That it enslaves, enfeebles, and may kill all who take it in excess is incontestable. That it impoverishes all except the well-to-do is equally incontestable. But there are two things that may be said in favour of it. As it is a pleasure (or a vice) which it is quite possible to enjoy moderately, the vast majority of smokers take their opium as most Scotchmen do their whisky—in moderation; and a Chinaman stupefied is a much less terrible person than a Scotchman drunk.

Be this as it may, so long as the Chinese do not interfere with the production of opium within their own borders in any manner which can be considered either genuine in purpose or effective in deed, the question of the supply by India to China of opium hardly comes within the domain of practical politics. So long as the Chinese not only allow the free cultivation of the poppy by their people, whether in the west or the east of China, but regard native-grown opium as a valuable and legitimate source of revenue, the cry that England is forcing opium on China is unfair and untrue, and statements such as that made by a now responsible member of the present Government, that "the opium traffic gravely imperils our friendly relations with the Chinese Empire," are unmeaning. The present attitude of the central and provincial Governments of China regarding native opium, as judged by their acts and forbearances, not their words, and the present state of poppy cultivation in Western China, must be taken into account by any one who wishes to decide for himself the question which the Society for the Suppression of the Opium Trade is placing before the country, and the society itself, in not fully informing itself of either one or the other, seems to be basing its case more on the sands of prejudice than on the rocks of truth.

GREECE.

(FROM OUR CORRESPONDENT.)

ATHENS, MARCH 24.

The gravity of the last step in the Greek preparations for war will hardly have been conveyed by the brief telegram which told that the Chamber had passed (after a discussion so hot and prolonged that it was clear that the decision was not only an honestly contested, but a very earnestly taken one) the Bill for the enrolling of all the hitherto exempted citizens between 20 and 30 in the active army. It meant that many a widow's only son, the only means of support of many an old and dependent father and mother, the only protector of the young and even more helpless, is now to be dragged away by the conscription, leaving a degree of misery and deprivation, should war actually ensue, which Greece has never experienced or even conceived. No doubt many exemptions have been fraudulently obtained, the last call not having produced the quarter of its expected result; but, even as a remedy against such frauds the measure is a severe one, and the passing of it with general public approbation is a proof of the unfaltering decision of the nation to risk all on the die. Had any doubt existed in the public mind that the Ministry fully intended the speedy resort to the

IN THE OPIUM SMUGGLING TRADE IN THE FIFTIES.

ATTACKED BY CHINESE PIRATES

By CAPTAIN GEORGE NAUNTON.

MOST of the old-time mariners of fifty and sixty years ago will remember the saucy little topsail schooners so numerous about that period plying between the eastern ports of our Atlantic coast and the Mediterranean for fruit, they were mostly built in Baltimore and their principal merit was speed and ability to stand up well under a stiff breeze. They were always looked upon with a sort of affection by deep-water men, who appreciated the hardships the poor fellows underwent, in comparison with their own vessels so high out of water.

In many ways they were the prototypes of our modern racing yachts, especially in the long heel they were all built with and having a very liberal depth of keel were enabled to hold their own much better than a common merchantman, and I heard their captains and mates aver that they could lay within four and a half points of the wind and make it good, and that they would be carrying all sail when an East Indiaman would be under single reefs. I know that there is not much exaggeration in this, but very few deep-water ships (square riggers) can lay within six points of the wind and seldom if ever make good.

In August, 1858, I was lying in the little harbor of Dartmouth having just arrived as mate of the bark Shelburne from Rio Janeiro, loaded with coffee and sugar and as the captain was a Dartmouth man, also the owner, he inserted in the charter party at Rio that the vessel should proceed to Dartmouth for orders as to what port her cargo was to be discharged. He had a double motive in this, one was to be near his family, and the other to get all the necessary repairs done by his own crew and also to benefit the mechanics and tradespeople of his native town, and very worthy motives they were.

The west coast of England in the summer and fall has been termed the garden spot of the world, and at this particular time the harbor was the rendezvous of numerous costly yachts who would come and go as they pleased and made a lively picture in their clean white canvas and glittering brass work in the sun. There were no motor boats in those days and the scores of dingeys, punts and gigs pulling about in all directions still further enlivened the scene. The principal place on shore where we went to spend a jolly evening was at the Marine Hotel just at the head of the wharf and kept by mine host Tipper. At this time of year we could easily see well enough to have a game or two of skittles or ten pins before it got dark and afterward retire to the large commercial room and exchange yarns with each other. At these evenings there would be quite a number of the captains and mates of the yachts, and on occasions the owners themselves would join us for an hour or two, and they especially enjoyed the singing of those good old sea songs which I hope some enterprising manager of the present day will resuscitate and give to the public among his other vaudeville.

Lying in the bay a few yards from the Shelburne were two of the sauciest looking schooners, spoken of in the beginning, named respectively the Game Cock and the Chanticleer, but among so many smart vessels in the bay they attracted no particular attention, which they otherwise would have done. The captains and mates of these two schooners, a few others and myself made quite a little coterie of our own, and I found that we had many friends in common.

In a Congenial Trade.

The captain of the Game Cock was about 25 years old, Charles Fyfe by name, and had been educated at the Blue Coat School in London, which accounted in a measure for his daredevil proclivities, and this life he was engaged in just suited him. He was a fair musician and played the cornet well. The Chanticleer had for her commander a young Scotchman named James Park, a native of Glasgow and about 24 or 25, slightly the junior of Fyfe, but as stanch a friend in a hard fight as a man wants to have. They had been shipmates in several clippers to India and China and had been selected by their present owners as the fittest for their purpose among all their old officers and as proof of their appreciation they paid them the same salary as the commanders of the deep-water clippers.

Now, a word or so about the vessels themselves. They were practically the same tonnage, 175 tons each, and were, in fact, sister ships, being built on the same lines and by the same builder. They had been owned by a gentleman in Boston, who operated them very successfully from the time of their launching in conjunction with the captains who were always expected to have a one-fourth interest. Their usual voyages commenced at Boston, where they loaded with ice and took it to New Orleans. There they purchased as much tobacco as their finances permitted, had it all made up into cigars, duly packed in cases; thence sailed for Havana, where the captain paid both the import and export duty and had every case branded with a large Spanish name from Havana. The vessel then proceeded usually to St. Petersburg, in Russia, where the cigars were sold at a goodly profit.

Sometimes the captain would here purchase a cargo of hemp and sheet-iron and return home to Boston, or, if it happened to be the fruit season, he would sail away for the Mediterranean with Smyrna as his objective point. This was the great entrepot for figs in those days, and the first figs in the market netted the captain generally from 1 to 2 cents a pound for his celerity.

The great addition to the fleet of merchant steamers in all the maritime ports of the world in the middle fifties caused such a reduction in the profits of all sailing vessels and was even more keenly felt by vessels of this class, so that the owners decided that they had better sell them at once, as they were too deep-draughted to be used as coasters and had no carrying capacity to speak of. Therefore, the owner of these two sent them over to England, thinking he could get a better price for them there, and where they would be used as "opium clippers," which was eventually done, and they were bought by their present owners, and sent to lay up in Dartmouth harbor and await orders.

The opium trade on the coast of China was a very extensive and profitable one, and while not exactly connived at or encouraged by the British Government, it did not appear to put any obstacles in its way. The agents of our vessels were among the highest in China, kept up large establishments and were renowned all over Christendom for their great and generous hospitality. It is unnecessary to mention their names, for some of their descendants are in the city at present, and probably would not care to have their names made public.

Somehow during our stay in Dartmouth Captain Fyfe had become a frequent vistor on board the Shelburne and on more than one occasion suggested that he would like to have me go with him as mate; that he would pay me £9 a month. I was only getting £6 10s where I was. He explained the high wages by saying that our voyage would be more or less dangerous, but the extra profit we could make would compensate for our risk. I thought the matter over day and night, and probably would have decided right away, but the mate he had on board had been sent by the overlooker and invariably in such cases is a thorn in the captain's side, and moreover disinclined to leave his vessel. Therefore the matter was dropped.

Our lay days waiting for orders having expired our captain came on board and told me to have everything ready to get under way next morning and we were to proceed to Bristol to discharge our cargo of coffee and sugar. In the morning promptly at 6 o'clock our two boats went ashore and brought back one of the owners and the captain, his wife and little girl of 4. They were going round to Bristol for the fun of the thing, and expected to be at least a week in making the passage, but the wind happening to be favorable we arrived there in a little less than three days, to their great disappointment.

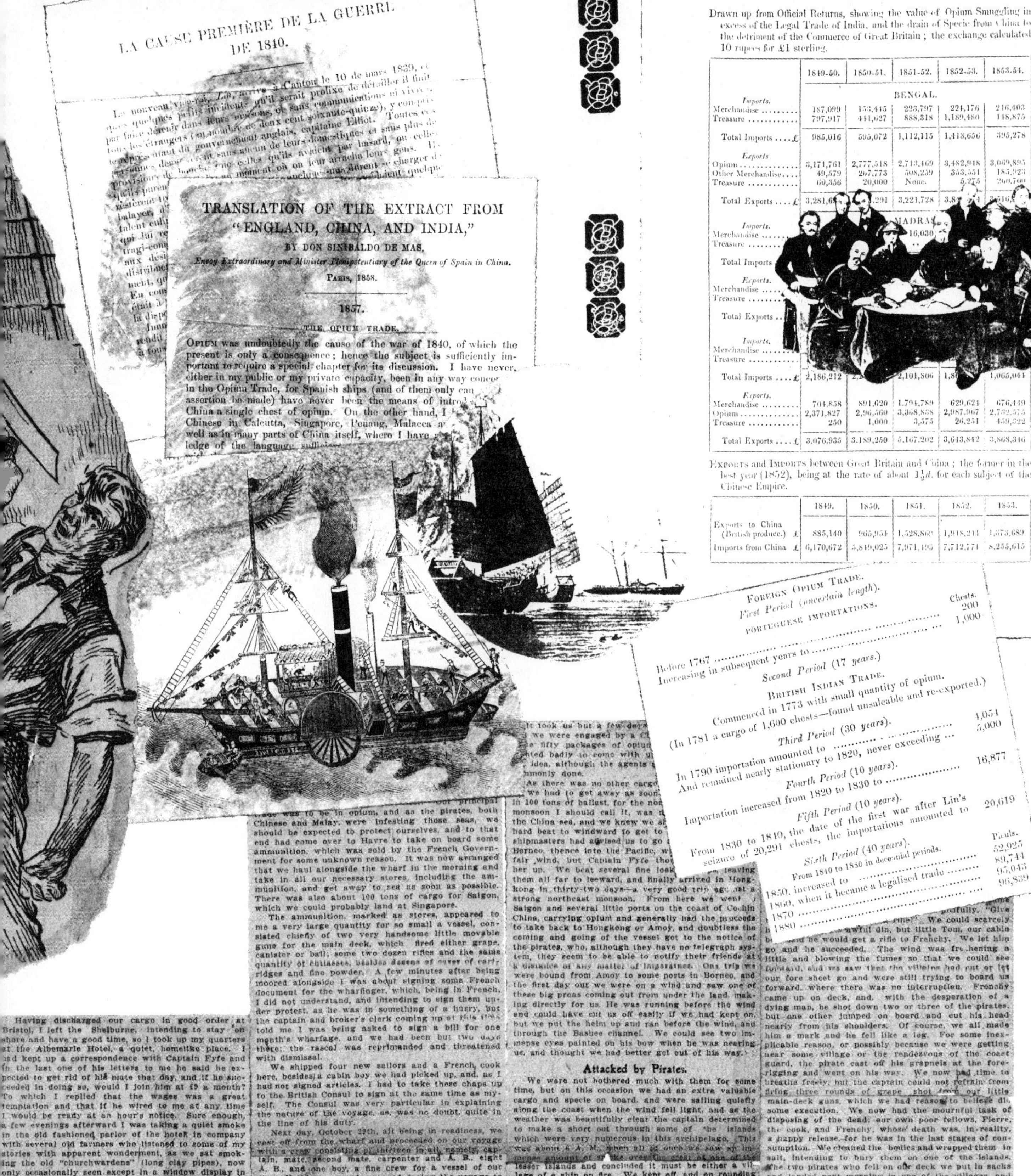

LA CAUSE PREMIÈRE DE LA GUERRE DE 1840.

Le nouveau vice-roi, *Lin*, arrive à Canton le 10 de mars 1839, ... qu'il serait prolixe de détailler il finit par faire détenir dans leurs maisons, et sans communications ni vivres, tous les étrangers (au nombre de deux cent soixante-quinze), y compris le représentant du gouvernement anglais, capitaine Elliot. Toutes ces personnes demeurèrent sans aucun de leurs domestiques et sans plus de provisions ... que celles qu'ils avaient par hasard, ou celles ... moment où on leur arracha leurs gens. ...

TRANSLATION OF THE EXTRACT FROM "ENGLAND, CHINA, AND INDIA,"

BY DON SINIBALDO DE MAS,

Envoy Extraordinary and Minister Plenipotentiary of the Queen of Spain in China.

PARIS, 1858.

1857.

THE OPIUM TRADE.

OPIUM was undoubtedly the cause of the war of 1840, of which the present is only a consequence; hence the subject is sufficiently important to require a special chapter for its discussion. I have never, either in my public or my private capacity, been in any way conce[rned] in the Opium Trade, for Spanish ships (and of them only can [this] assertion be made) have never been the means of intro[ducing into] China a single chest of opium. On the other hand, I h[ave ...] Chinese in Calcutta, Singapore, Penang, Malacca a[nd ...] well as in many parts of China itself, where I have ... ledge of the language sufficient ...

TABLE

Drawn up from Official Returns, showing the value of Opium Smuggling in excess of the Legal Trade of India, and the drain of Specie from China to the detriment of the Commerce of Great Britain; the exchange calculated 10 rupees for £1 sterling.

	1849-50.	1850-51.	1851-52.	1852-53.	1853-54.
	BENGAL.				
Imports.					
Merchandise	187,099	153,445	223,797	224,176	216,403
Treasure	797,917	441,627	888,318	1,189,480	148,875
Total Imports ....£	985,016	595,072	1,112,115	1,413,656	395,278
Exports.					
Opium	3,171,761	2,777,518	2,713,469	3,482,918	3,069,895
Other Merchandise....	49,579	267,773	508,259	353,551	185,923
Treasure	60,356	20,000	None.	5,275	260,700
Total Exports ....£	3,281,6[illegible]	[illegible],291	3,221,728	3,8[illegible]	3,516,[illegible]
	MADRAS.				
Imports.					
Merchandise	[illegible]	[illegible]	16,030	[illegible]	[illegible]
Treasure	[illegible]	[illegible]	..	[illegible]	[illegible]
Total Imports	[illegible]	[illegible]	[illegible]	[illegible]	[illegible]
Exports.					
Merchandise	[illegible]	[illegible]	[illegible]	[illegible]	[illegible]
Treasure	[illegible]	[illegible]	[illegible]	[illegible]	[illegible]
Total Exports ..	[illegible]	[illegible]	[illegible]	[illegible]	[illegible]
Imports.					
Merchandise	[illegible]	[illegible]	[illegible]	[illegible]	[illegible]
Treasure	[illegible]	[illegible]	[illegible]	[illegible]	[illegible]
Total Imports ....£	2,186,212	2,[illegible]	2,101,806	1,8[illegible]	1,065,044
Exports.					
Merchandise	704,858	891,620	1,794,789	629,624	676,449
Opium	2,371,827	2,96[illegible],560	3,368,838	2,987,967	2,732,575
Treasure	250	1,000	3,575	26,251	459,322
Total Exports ....£	3,076,935	3,189,250	5,167,202	3,643,842	3,868,346

EXPORTS and IMPORTS between Great Britain and China; the former in the best year (1852), being at the rate of about $1\frac{1}{2}d.$ for each subject of the Chinese Empire.

	1849.	1850.	1851.	1852.	1853.
Exports to China (British produce.) £	885,140	965,954	1,528,869	1,918,211	1,373,689
Imports from China £	6,170,672	5,849,025	7,971,195	7,712,771	8,255,615

FOREIGN OPIUM TRADE.

First Period (uncertain length).

PORTUGUESE IMPORTATIONS.

	Chests.
Before 1767	200
Increasing in subsequent years to	1,000

Second Period (17 years.)

BRITISH INDIAN TRADE.

Commenced in 1773 with small quantity of opium.

(In 1781 a cargo of 1,600 chests—found unsaleable and re-exported.)

Third Period (30 years).

In 1790 importation amounted to	4,054
And remained nearly stationary to 1820, never exceeding ...	5,000

Fourth Period (10 years).

Importation increased from 1820 to 1830 to	16,877

Fifth Period (10 years).

From 1830 to 1840, the date of the first war after Lin's seizure of 20,291 chests, the importations amounted to	20,619

Sixth Period (40 years).

From 1840 to 1850 in decennial periods.

	Piculs.
1850, increased to	52,925
1860, when it became a legalised trade	89,744
1870	95,043
1880	96,839

Having discharged our cargo in good order at Bristol, I left the Shelburne, intending to stay on shore and have a good time, so I took up my quarters at the Albemarle Hotel, a quiet, homelike place. I had kept up a correspondence with Captain Fyfe and in the last one of his letters to me he said he expected to get rid of his mate that day, and if he succeeded in doing so, would I join him at £9 a month? To which I replied that the wages was a great temptation and that if he wired to me at any time I would be ready at an hour's notice. Sure enough, a few evenings afterward I was taking a quiet smoke in the old fashioned parlor of the hotel in company with several old farmers who listened to some of my stories with apparent wonderment, as we sat smoking the old "churchwardens" (long clay pipes), now only occasionally seen except in a window display in a tobacconist shop, when of a sudden a messenger boy appeared at my side and handed me the following telegram:

"HAVRE, France—Come over at once; will explain all; keep mum. FYFE."

I immediately turned round and sent a reply to the effect that I would leave by first opportunity, and on consulting "Bradshaw" found that I had time to catch the midnight mail train for Plymouth, and thence to Havre by steamer. Our smoker was continued for another hour or so and I had to gather up the rest of my baggage and start for the train. Everything went well and we arrived at the pier at Havre just at dusk. I soon spied Captain Fyfe in his gig close by the steamer's berth, but I had to have all my baggage researched, which the customs officials said would have to be postponed till daylight, but I had had some experience with these chaps in other parts of the world and found them pretty much like "chips off the same block" and calling one of them aside told him that I must join my vessel to-night, and that I had stuff in my chest which would spoil if kept over night. He consented to open my chest

... Our principal trade was to be in opium, and as the pirates, both Chinese and Malay, were infesting those seas, we should be expected to protect ourselves, and to that end had come over to Havre to take on board some ammunition, which was sold by the French Government for some unknown reason. It was now arranged that we haul alongside the wharf in the morning and take in all our necessary stores, including the ammunition, and get away to sea as soon as possible. There was also about 100 tons of cargo for Saigon, which we could probably land at Singapore.

The ammunition, marked as stores, appeared to me a very large quantity for so small a vessel, consisted chiefly of two very handsome little movable guns for the main deck, which fired either grape, canister or ball; some two dozen rifles and the same quantity of cutlasses, besides dozens of cases of cartridges and fine powder. A few minutes after being moored alongside I was about signing some French document for the wharfinger, which, being in French, I did not understand, and intending to sign them under protest, as he was in something of a hurry, but the captain and broker's clerk coming up at this time told me I was being asked to sign a bill for one month's wharfage, and we had been but two days there; the rascal was reprimanded and threatened with dismissal.

We shipped four new sailors and a French cook here, besides a cabin boy we had picked up, and, as I had not signed articles, I had to take these chaps up to the British Consul to sign at the same time as myself. The Consul was very particular in explaining the nature of the voyage, as, was no doubt, quite in the line of his duty.

Next day, October 29th, all being in readiness, we cast off from the wharf and proceeded on our voyage with a crew consisting of thirteen in all, namely, captain, mate, second mate, carpenter and A. B., eight A. B., and one boy, a fine crew for a vessel of our size. Nothing unusual occurred during the voyage to Colombo, Ceylon; we had the usual trade winds, and here is where this kind of schooner proved her superiority, being bound round the Cape of Good Hope, of course, the southeast trades were almost directly against us, and we were close-hauled all through.

After losing the southeast trades we prepared for the westerly winds by getting our square sail ready, which contained as many square yards of canvas as nearly all the other sails, and we soon had use for it. We bowled off 250 to 280 miles a day for about twenty days, and had variable winds and weather till we arrived at Colombo, December 23d, 86 days from Havre.

The agents, as usual, paid a visit on board and were delighted with the vessel; thought she was the equal of anything they had in the East, and as we had a massive bank safe built in under the cabin table, which by the way, was fastened to the bulkhead by a large brass hinge and was easily lifted to get access to the safe, they decided that as they had a large quantity of sycee they would ship it with us for Hongkong.

It took us but a few days ... we were engaged by a Ch... fifty packages of opium ... wanted badly to come with us ... idea, although the agents ... commonly done.

As there was no other cargo ... we had to get away as soon ... in 100 tons of ballast, for the nor... monsoon I should call it, was ... the China sea, and we knew we sh... hard beat to windward to get to ... shipmasters had advised us to go ... Borneo, thence into the Pacific, wh... fair wind, but Captain Fyfe tho... her up. We beat several fine look... ...s, leaving them all far to leeward, and finally arrived in Hongkong in thirty-two days—a very good trip against a strong northeast monsoon. From here we went to Saigon and several little ports on the coast of Cochin China, carrying opium and generally had the proceeds to take back to Hongkong or Amoy, and doubtless the coming and going of the vessel got to the notice of the pirates, who, although they have no telegraph system, they seem to be able to notify their friends at a distance of any matter of importance. One trip we were bound from Amoy to some ports in Borneo, and the first day out we were on a wind and saw one of these big proas coming out from under the land, making directly for us. He was running before the wind and could have cut us off easily if we had kept on, but we put the helm up and ran before the wind, and through the Bashee channel. We could see two immense eyes painted on his bow when he was nearing us, and thought we had better get out of his way.

Attacked by Pirates.

We were not bothered much with them for some time, but on this occasion we had an extra valuable cargo and specie on board, and were sailing quietly along the coast when the wind fell light, and as the weather was beautifully clear the captain determined to make a short cut through some of the islands which were very numerous in this archipelago. This was about 8 A. M., when all at once we saw an immense amount of smoke over the crest of one of the lesser islands and concluded it must be either a village of a ship on fire. We kept off, and on rounding the point came directly in view of what had been a handsome bark; her masts and rigging all gone and there was little but the outside planking left. On passing her stern we could read the last four letters of her name, which appeared to have been "rida" and "port." The rest was all burned away. We had barely got around the point and saw this when all at once a big piratical proa came out from another point and was making directly for us. He came so suddenly that we were caught and before he reached us we could see there had been a bloody fight, for his sides and parts of his dirty decks gave every evidence of such. We were all alarmed and got up our rifles in good order and called all hands aft for instructions, which had to be short and quick.

"Let every man of us pick out his man and take good aim. It is the only chance for our lives." The cook was ordered to keep a boiler full of scalding water to throw on them. On they came and grappled our fore rigging and hung on while they threw several of their stink pots on board. These are most terrible things to deal with. They are pots made of clay

... pitifully, "Give ... rifle!" We could scarcely h... awful din, but little Tom, our cabin b... said he would get a rifle to Frenchy. We let him go and he succeeded. The wind was freshening a little and blowing the fumes so that we could see forward, and we saw that the villains had cut or let our fore sheet go and were still trying to board us forward, where there was no interruption. Frenchy came up on deck, and, with the desperation of a dying man, he shot down two or three of the pirates, but one other jumped on board and cut his head nearly from his shoulders. Of course, we all made him a mark and he fell like a log. For some inexplicable reason, or possibly because we were getting near some village or the rendezvous of the coast guard, the pirate cast off his grapnels at the fore-rigging and went on his way. We now had time to breathe freely, but the captain could not refrain from firing three rounds of grape shot from our little main-deck guns, which we had reason to believe did some execution. We now had the mournful task of disposing of the dead; our own poor fellows, Pierre, the cook, and Frenchy, whose death was, in reality, a happy release, for he was in the last stages of consumption. We cleaned the bodies and wrapped them in salt, intending to bury them on one of the islands. The two pirates who fell on our deck we put in sacks and landed next morning in one of the villages, and also notified the Taotai of the attack of the pirates the day before.

As we were now a long way out of our course, owing to our having had to run away from the pirate, and finding that we should now have to go south and through the Sooloo archipelago to get into the China sea, where Borneo is situated, we had the bodies of the two Frenchmen put into coffins and we bore up for a Spanish village on one of the small islands of Luzon, and buried them in one grave, paying $5 for the privilege. We arrived in Borneo in due course and made a full report of all our troubles, and the British Consul assured us that a man-of-war would be sent at once to try and capture the pirate.

ROVING COMMISSION WITH A MILLIONAIRE OPIUM EATER AS A PASSENGER

(Many of the incidents narrated in the following story happened under my personal observation, and therefore I can vouch for their accuracy, and "I tell the tale as 'twas told to me"):

IN THE summer of 1863 I had just returned to New York from a Mediterranean voyage in a ship which had been put under the Swedish flag on account of the war, and as the owners meantime had sold the vessel to a Russian firm I found myself temporarily out of employment. The wharves and piers on both sides of the North and East river were congested with ships unable to get employment on account of the depredations of the Confederate cruisers and privateers. I had previously entertained the idea of joining Uncle Sam's Navy, and had already made application to the authorities to that end, but the reply I received was not satisfactory, mainly that I would have to accept a subordinate position and at a very modest salary.

In a Fifth-Avenue Mansion

The appointed time found me at the door of a Fifth-avenue mansion, and the liveried servant had hardly taken my card in his hand, when O'Brien came into the hall, and, taking both my hands, almost dragged me into a magnificently furnished reception room. He said:

"By Jove, old fellow, I am glad to see you; but what are you doing?" I told him I had just resigned the command of the old Metropolis, as she had been sold to the Russians on account of the war, and was at present a gentleman of leisure. He again expressed his delight, though for the life of me I could not understand why he should be so exuberant at what I considered my misfortune. He continued: "By Jove, you are the very man," and was about to unfold to me his ideas, when we were interrupted by the advent of his two sisters into the room, and there was no need of any introduction. The eight years since I last saw them had added greatly to their good looks. They were much interested in what I had been doing since we last met, but, as dinner was soon announced, we withdrew to the dining-room. I found there were about six other people besides the family, among whom were Henry Burmester of the firm of Burmester & Co. of 44 Maiden lane, who was accompanied by his wife and only son, Henry.

After the cloth was removed, the ladies still remaining, the conversation became general, mostly referring to my different adventures at sea. I noticed that Burmester paid great attention to what I said, and questioned me closely on matters of discipline and generally as to the relations between the passengers and the master of the ship. At length, calling his wife to his side, he said: "My dear, I want you to be present at this interview (the other members of the party having left the dining-room). I think we have got the right man for our purpose, but I wish for your opinion." I was anxious to know what it all meant. He said:

"My son, whom I have taken into partnership, is a most exemplary young man in every respect, but for one failing, and that is that he has, unfortunately, fallen into the morphine habit, which he contracted just after leaving Harvard. He has just come into a fortune of nearly half a million dollars, and as Wall street has a great infatuation for him, these weaknesses combined determined me to consult one of the most eminent physicians in New York, who, after carefully watching him for some months, strongly urged my sending him if possible on a long sea voyage in a sailing ship with a few choice companions, who would assist him in breaking away from this pernicious habit he himself was trying to break, but the surroundings were fatal to any cure.

Plans for the Voyage.

"Now, sir, my project is this: Henry is now 26 years old, graduated four years ago from Harvard, is a good business man, and has an excellent constitution, is beloved by all his associates, generous to a fault, in short, though as his father I may be pardoned for thus extolling his virtues. Were it not for that cursed habit which is slowly but surely leading him to destruction, we should not wish to lose sight of him for a day.

"In the first place, let me send for my son to be present at this interview." This was quickly done, and Henry joined us. "My idea," continued the father, "is that Henry, with his own money, shall purchase a suitable ship and fit her out with every comfort and take with him as companions a college chum, Professor Bliss, who is a scientist and wants to add to his collection of curiosities from all parts of the world, a member of our firm named Anderson, who is suffering from overwork in the office, and Doctor Benjamin F. Hammond, just graduated from the University of Pennsylvania, and who will render his services when required, as it is necessary that Henry should have proper medical attendance in order, if possible, to get rid of the disease.

… prisoners both made abject apologies … after a … duct, they were discharged from custody after a severe reprimand had been given them. When sober they were decent enough chaps, but drink got the better of them and made them temporarily insane.

Arrival at Panama.

We arrived at Panama on the 10th of July, and were soon taken across the isthmus on the train, and found the steamer awaiting us on the Atlantic side. In nine days we arrived in New York. Our arrival having been announced by telegraph from Sandy Hook, we found several of our friends awaiting us on the pier, and we lost no time in getting our lig… acks and were driven to our de… that I accompa…

… ove from … Beatley of Dickson, de Wolf … to put myself in the hands of Messrs. … & Co., as they were the agents for the Hudson Bay Company, and I had already had correspondence with them on a former voyage.

As I was very busy the first few days I saw our quartet safely landed at the Union Club, which was at that day one of the most hospitable and luxurious on the Coast, renowned for its warm-hearted reception accorded to all visiting strangers. The older members were of a class who have long since passed away.

At Market-Street Wharf.

Having deposited my papers at the Consulate and made the acquaintance of the Consul … glass … Booker, I set about the selling … Burmester had the … says, quietly: "Gentlemen" … introduction to W… the civilized … by the officers and guests all follow suit … to the Queen. Then cigars, pipes and toddies are indulged in, and with a good song and general conversation the evening is spent.

Sailed for Honolulu.

On the 5th of April we were all ready for our start for Honolulu, but there was not a breath of wind to enable us to sail out of the harbor. The Scout sent two boats' crews, ten men in each boat, to assist in towing us clear of the Heads, and with our own two boats we soon had a good offing from the island, and shaped our course for Honolulu. I had intended to take a run over to Tahiti, but on account of putting into the Marqueres islands it took us so far north of Tahiti that I considered it better to try and get to San Francisco as quickly as possible, where I h… our people in New York to send mail to m… ised our … Henry was … ther reason was that …

After dinner I noticed that Mr. Henry was acting in a strange and boisterous manner, and trying to quarrel with all of us. We were very patient with him for some time, but at last consulted with Dr. Hamond as to what was the best thing to do to keep him quiet. The doctor then admitted that while at the hotel for an hour or so this afternoon he had noticed Mr. Henry at the bar, and found him drinking brandy, which he had forbidden him to do, but we would induce him to go to bed and put one of the seamen to guard him all night.

In the morning he was more quiet, but still suffering from a slight attack of delirium tremens. After this experience he was always under surveillance when on shore. I found that there was a good supply of ice in the market, and as there was an ice manufacturing plant in course of erection in the city which was expected to be ready for business in a few weeks the prospect for a good sale was poor. I could get an offer of only $20 per ton, but concluded to wait a few days, as we had plenty of work to do … used only $50 of the $100 I left for him in Barbados.

Bound for Bahia.

On the 5th day of October Mr. Henry was pronounced well enough to be returned to the ship. We hoisted him on board from a stretcher lent by the hospital and carried him carefully to his own stateroom, where he soon recovered his strength. We then got under way and started our long beat down the Caribbean sea, bound for Bahia. This part of the passage was tedious, for the reason that it was made against the trade wind, and we were twenty days getting to the longitude of Barbados, which we accomplished in seven days going the other way. We were in company with several vessels, who were desirous to get news of the war. One ste… the American flag (this was a bold … in and out of port every …

After leaving the Cormorant we had a succession of light winds and calms and had to resort to games of cards to while away the time. The doctor and Mr. Anderson soon got to be inveterate cribbage players, while the rest of us indulged in a quiet game of poker when these two could be weaned away from their favorite game and induced to join us. As for Henry, poor fellow, he seldom played; he was suffering terribly from the deprivation of the opium, and if he did join in he would prevaricate and cheat to such an extent that it was simply impossible to continue playing. Whether the doctor occasionally gave him a small dose to taper off with was only known to himself; possibly he did; but the lying and cheating were only symptoms of the disease.

… and others in the … to prepare for the worst. There is a record that in one of these hurricanes, in 1780, a twelve-pounder cannon was taken from its position and carried by the force of the wind and sea a distance of 140 yards. My second mate, Mr. Reid, not having returned from his shore liberty, I left $100 with the Collector of Customs for his expenses and passage money, and instructions for him to follow us to Jamaica by the first mail boat going in that direction.

A West India Hurricane.

However, I could not afford to lose a minute, and the Customs officials very kindly gave me my papers. I lost no time in getting under way and made sail directly between the islands of St. Lucia and St. Vincent. I think every vessel in port got away about the same time as we did, and the procession reminded me of the Straits of Gibraltar after a long spell of westerly winds, when large fleets of ships of all flags and sizes are compelled to lay under the rock wind-bound. If any vessel remained in port it … she was unseaworthy or had no ballast … driven on the beach and …

… ailed mo… the Heads we… and learned it was the … bound to San Francisco, and we were … with this ship for several days. The day … Rio it fell calm, and the weather became … sultry. We all got our mattresses on deck and slept under the poop awnings. The atmosphere, though heated, was beautifully clear.

Almost a Tragedy.

On this particular evening everybody seemed in high spirits, the whole sky was illuminated with myriads of stars, among which the constellation of the Southern Cross shone with resplendent grandeur. The sea was a mass of phosphorescence, and we occasionally got a light air, or catspaw, which lasted but a few minutes. The wake of the ship appeared literally aflame with the myriads of animalcula, which is supposed to cause that brilliant appearance … phosphorescence.

Next day the surgeons decided to put the patient under an anesthetic and replace the dislocation, and Dr. Schmeltz quietly came to Mr. Henry and insisted on his taking a pill which contained morphine or opium, so as to deaden the pain. The patient was suffering intensely, but fought them off, and said:

"By —— I will shoot the man as soon as I get out who will force me to take that drug. I am man enough to come this voyage to cure myself, and I will not give in now. Go ahead and perform your operation." Those who were present said afterward that they had never seen such an exhibition of sheer grit and courage. Dr. Schmeltz, however, on advice from our own doctor, gave him a good stiff drink of brandy. We left Dr. Hamond at the hospital as the guest of Dr. Schmeltz, and he assured us that he was royally entertained.

… except that we employed a… the masts and painting the yards and mas… in a general way making the ship as spick … as possible. On the 17th of May we made the Fa… lon islands and hove to for the pilot who took charge and sailed us into San Francisco harbor. This pilot was Captain William Jolliffe.

Arrival in San Francisco.

Our arrival in San Francisco had been signaled from the station at Point Lobos, so that as soon as we were abreast of Fort Point a boat was alongside with our mail, forwarded by Messrs. Falkner, Bell & Co., who also requested me to call on them as soon as convenient, and offering … services in any way that was found desirable. … ere not allowed to read our letters undisturbed. … for the ship was beset by tradesmen, butch… clerks and the usual horde of sailor …

On the morning of the seventh day after leaving Bermuda the lookout reported:

"A sail on port bow, under jury masts, standing this way, sir."

The first officer, Mr. Cousins, who was on watch, got his spyglass, but was unable to make out any more than it appeared to be a long, low schooner of three masts, but had only the fore and mizzen masts standing. He reported it to me and, after partaking of my usual cup of coffee, came on deck. The wind was very light from the southeast and we could barely lay our course and making about three knots an hour. I was naturally curious to find out about this craft and kept all our sails shaking so as not to get ahead of her too quickly, as it might be … distress.

… Bay… pose… runn… be r… aston… once… Bird… of Ja… rative… interes… It w… civilize… would… Great… in diff… owned… were op… the purp… their ex… blockade… of sophis… matter of… it might… the large… It was… Golconda w… my friend… mand her… steamship… ered to lo… Nassau, New… on board as… the very ag… tance below… Lord Palm…

NATIVE GROW…

FROM THE "CHINA OVE…

As might have been anticipat… vation in China, transmitted … ment of India, has attracted a … country. So large a portion of … article, that Indian statesmen … leave it out of their calculatio… much of the soil, and utilizes … ference with the outturn of th… interests. As more especially c… into China, Mr. Gubbay's view … however be classed as extreme. … for beneficial effects from opium … arguments in favour of the tra… amount of injury inflicted by t… *circumstances of the Chinese peop… certainly the listless and hopeless … ment forces them to pass their lives … become a matter of necessity to a h… or other certainly must influence the … sistible devotion to opium, the result … ting policy of the Government, there … China a quantity of opium rivalling t… the assertion is ventured that, if this … cut off, there would not be one smoke…* circumstances, it is urged that the … economic. We are powerless to h… degree affect the other. In fact, t… tion has assumed much the same as… countries. Bass, Allsopp, and Gui… Commons as respected members, yet … Great Britain, from fiscal as well as … of toba… In the United Kingdom, … d over to public detest… d over again as to the p… able. Vices there are … more disastrous than th… an open question how… bbay should place the … be anticipated from th… d though our own i…

A DEFENCE OF OPIUM SMOKING.

FROM THE "PALL MALL GAZETTE," NOVEMBER 13TH, 1879.

OPIUM smoking is viewed with such horror by a large class of persons that anything said in its favour is not likely to raise the practice in general estimation; Consul Gardner, nevertheless, in his trade report on Chefoo, for the past year, boldly comes forth to defend it. As the question of the morality of the opium trade in China seems, he says, to be exciting much attention at home, and as influential persons have expressed opinions on the subject founded, he conceives, on misinformation and misconception, a few facts may not be out of place.

Opium smokers are of three classes:—1st, occasional smokers; 2nd, habitual smokers who smoke in moderation but have not got a craving; 3rd, habitual smokers who smoke in excess and have a craving. When it is said of a Chinaman that he smokes opium, it is meant that he belongs to the third class, just as with us the expression that a man "drinks" means that he drinks too much. Sir Thomas Wade is stated to have estimated the number of opium-smokers in China to be five per cent. of the adult population. If this estimate includes the first and second class, Consul Gardner thinks it is too low; if it refers only to the third class, he would say it was too high. The average amount of Indian opium consumed in China is about 12,000,000 lbs. per annum, and probably 5,000,000 lbs. more of native opium is produced. In smoking only a portion of the opium is consumed; the ash is re-prepared, and yields fifty per cent. of opium. It is this ash that enables the opium saloon to sell the preparation apparently at cost price, the ash paying for the light, attendance, house-rent and profit. Deducting the unconsumed opium, few moderate smokers consume more than a pound and a-half a year, while the most immoderate smoker does not consume more than four pounds; and it would probably be about correct to reckon half a pound per head as the average annual consumption of all classes of smokers. This would bring the number of smokers up to about half the adult population. Then the question arises, "If opium smoking is the great evil it is represented to be, how is it that after so many years no inherited ill effects are visible?" Most of our medical knowledge has been obtained empirically, and the greatest achievements in the sciences of chemistry and physiology often consist in merely giving the reason for facts already known by experience. Physiology teaches us that the length of the intestines in an animal is correlated with its diet; vegetable feeders have long, and animal feeders have short intestines. The length of the intestines in man shows that a due admixture of animal and vegetable food is the diet best suited to him. In China the population lives almost entirely on vegetables. Opium smoking "slows" the processes of digestion, and, … fact has the same effect as long intestines, and, consequently, is

M 2

REIGN OPIUM.

DE REPORT," MAY, 1874.

bay's report on Opium culti-
. Medhurst to the Govern-
amount of attention in that
revenue depends on this one
eir views, cannot afford to
the cultivation occupies so
our, that any serious inter-
uld affect large and varied
ith the import of the drug
guessed at. They cannot
t put in that strange claim
brought ridicule on some
he attempt to state the
the pipe. "*The peculiar
the nature of the climate,
hich the system of Govern-
the use of the opium pipe to
of the nation. Some cause
this their strange and irre-
ut, assisted by the vacilla-
more than one province in
p of British India; and
British India were entirely
n China.*" Under these
stion has merged in the
but we can to a certain
pect of the opium ques-
similar points in other
n the British House of
is susceptible of abuse,
ons, forbids the

ADVERTISEMENTS.

I.

fter having fearlessly introduced myself in the Preface as a merchant dealing in much despised drug, I hope that as a practical business man I may be excused remarking here that, at times this article is particularly suited for a safe speculation, may be fairly inferred from the second paragraph on page 136. Should anyone be sirous to hear more about the commercial merits of the article, *i.e., so soon as circumstances may render it worth my while to issue a circular to that effect*, he is hereby vited to send me his address by means of a ready addressed and stamped envelope, be simply enclosed in another stamped envelope, directed as follows:—

MERCHANT, Ridge Mount, Anerley, London, S.E.

II.

On the other hand, should any kindly-disposed reader of this little volume be in possession of additional information respecting the article opium, I would feel greatly obliged by his sending me the particulars thereof, in order to enable me to make use of the same *pro bono publico* in a possible second edition which, naturally enough, I flatter myself may become necessary before long.

Any such communication should be addressed

EDITOR, Ridge Mount, Anerley, London, S.E.

THE CULTIVATION OF OPIUM IN TURKEY AND PERSIA.

I.—TURKEY OPIUM.

As, notwithstanding my thirty years' experience in this particular growth of the drug, I never had the good luck to fall in with any proper descriptive account of it, I must try to say a few about it myself as best I can.

Perfectly ignorant as to the time at which Turkey opiu become an article of export, I simply begin by stating that i I entered this trade, from 1,500 to 2,000 chests were con average crop, the bulk of which quantity was shipped to America, then chiefly, if not exclusively, for pharmaceut while the rest found its way to the Straits Settlements ar in the East.

At that time Asia Minor was the only part of Tur opium, and Smyrna was the only market for the dru Constantinople always received a small portion of it fr producing districts as are either bordering on the Bl situate closer to the metropolis than to Smyrna—the reaching Constantinople until recently was far too smal market, and therefore was thence shipped to London f sent to Smyrna for still speedier realisation.

The compulsory examination of every single ch before its leaving Smyrna rendered the business in t comparative safety, because as a natural consequence tion the quality of the drug was kept up to as regu was practically possible from season to season, an security no doubt contributed a great deal towards t sion of the trade. Importers here and in America what they were going to receive for their money, an desire to try other qualities. The business of those that of our present time was a very smooth one, re knowledge of the article, since the examiner was t the well-established reputation of the Smyrna mar important functionary was appointed I never coul it mentioned several times that it was even an h and since the export duty on the article was collec of the examination, this functionary partook som ment official, besides acting as a perfectly inde between buyer and seller, who treated with each respective brokers.

This almost absolute security of former times a

L 2

OPIUM SMOKING AT THE EAST END OF LONDON.

COPIED FROM THE "DAILY NEWS" OF 1864.

WHO "Palmer" was, and why he committed his "Folly," are questions we will not attempt to answer. It is as needless to speculate upon his appearance or character, to figure him with staff, scrip and sandalled shoon, expiating early sins by life-long penance, as it is to ask why a court of disreputable houses should be called a Folly, or bear his name. It is enough to know that through an iron gate, and up a low-roofed tunnel leading from Ratcliff-highway, stands the place we have come to see, and that it is known as Palmer's Folly by every dweller in or periodical visitor to this section of the East. A dreadful ... Shocking in the squalid vice, making itself felt in the air ... the sounds you hear, and the sights you see; ... reputation for deeds of lawless violence, for ... its houses are put, and for the open ... the dwellers within its gates ... are peeped at by ... open doors, ... as if ...

After these facts—which speak with such sad significance of the tone and custom of the place—are hastily gathered, we become conscious of a peculiar smell of burning, the aroma from which is not unpleasant. Following this odd scent, and half recognising the drug from which it comes, we push at a half-open front door, and at once find ourselves in a small, half-lit, shabby room on the ground floor, in which a large French bedstead occupies the most conspicuous place. The smell has grown in intensity as we neared this house, and, once here, it becomes trying both to eyes and head. First, as to the company we meet. On the bed, which is devoid of sheets or counterpane, and has its pillows and bolster placed lengthwise along its sides, are three Chinamen sprawled round a small japan tray, in the centre of which is a tumbler half full of a thick brown syrup, of the consistency of treacle, some brass thimbles, one or two bits of wire about the size known as "blankets;" a burning taper, and some pipes, which look like big walking stick, well-worn air-guns, or rude musical instruments. An old Chinaman on the end of the bed nearest the window seems in a half trance, though he smokes vigorously, and in his cadaverous face, painfully-hollow cheeks, deeply-sunken eyes, open vacuous mouth, teeth discoloured, decayed, and, as it seems, loose as castanets, you read the penalties of opium smoking. This is the proprietor of the house, whose preparation of the drug is so exceptionally good that Chinamen come from all parts of London to patronise his you hastily form a judgment as to the wreck of vitality ... see, learn that the old man is seventy-five years old, and quite alone, and is his own housemaid, scullion, and ... is diligent in his business, such as it is; rises daily at 5 a.m. ... celebrated throughout his dingy neighbourhood for the energetic ... ticularity with which he scrubs and washes pots, pans, and house, and the scrupulous care wherewith he purchases and prepares his Miss Dorothy Tear-sheet bears testimony to this as she leans ... Inspector's face, as he sits with back to door, ... Brown, and assumes a confidential air ... playfully appeals to memory and ... "trying it on;" and as the ... wish to repulse more

... have ... figure ... to you ... action ... remember ... tion to ... treated. and it is ... poor debos ... Hence the ... heart, and a ... has been no ... dressed prosp ... next. The p ... strictness, and ... proved. Braw ... outrages on dece ... any form of duty ... secure the palpab ... robbed and beaten. ... called "respectable

THE CULTIVATION OF OPIUM IN INDIA.

ALTHOUGH the foregoing two chapters already contain some information on this particular subject from two different aspects, I deem it necessary to say a few words about it from a third point of view.

Unlike the valorous gentleman, who addressed to me the letter as at foot,* I always made it my particular study not only to read whatever comes within my reach in the shape of publications on the part of my opponents, but also to attend their meetings whenever able to do so.

Thus it happened that, from one of the speakers at the last May meeting at Exeter Hall, I gathered some particulars, which, to a certain extent, make up for Don Sinibaldo de Mas' inability to give us his own figures respecting the quantity of food that could be grown on a given extent of land, as compared with its production of opium.

In the course of his speech at the above named meeting, Mr. David McLaren stated that "the Government grant licenses to persons who apply for them, or who can be induced to apply for them, to grow the poppy in land that is fit for the purpose; and with the license which the Government give there is an advance of money without interest; and not a farthing do they give for any other agricultural purpose. The condition is that every drop of poppy-juice, which the cultivator extracts from the poppy-head must be delivered up to the Government agent, under a very heavy penalty, and that, at a price not fixed by mutual bargaining, but fixed by the Government. At this time it is five shillings for the pound-weight. He accordingly brings it to the Government, and the Government manufacture the opium, and pack it in chests of 140 lb. weight, and then sell it by their broker at Calcutta. The cost to the Government of a chest of opium, on the average of the last ten years, has been £41 10s., of which £35 or more goes to the cultivator. The balance is the expense of manufacture and sale. For that chest of opium, costing £41 10s., they have obtained on the average £127. The profit of £85 upon £41 10s. constitutes the Bengal branch of the opium revenue." And towards the end of his speech he further remarked that, "an acre of the best land in India, plentifully irrigated and highly cultivated, produces—what do you think? Less than 13 lbs. weight of opium. I turn up a volume issued by the Government of India itself on 'The Opium Question,' and I find there a statement that if an acre of such land had been devoted to the growth of cotton, it would have produced 285 lbs. of cotton and 706 lbs. of cotton seed. If planted with potatoes, it would have produced nearly three and a half tons of potatoes. The exact quantity is 7,680 lbs. The quantity of wheat is not given, but from calculations, which I

* Upper Clapton, 10 m. 30, 1883.

Sir,—I have been out for a few days, and find thy letter now. I am an active and ardent member of the Anti-Opium League, and do not of course wish to read thy book, which I fear may do harm.

Respectfully,

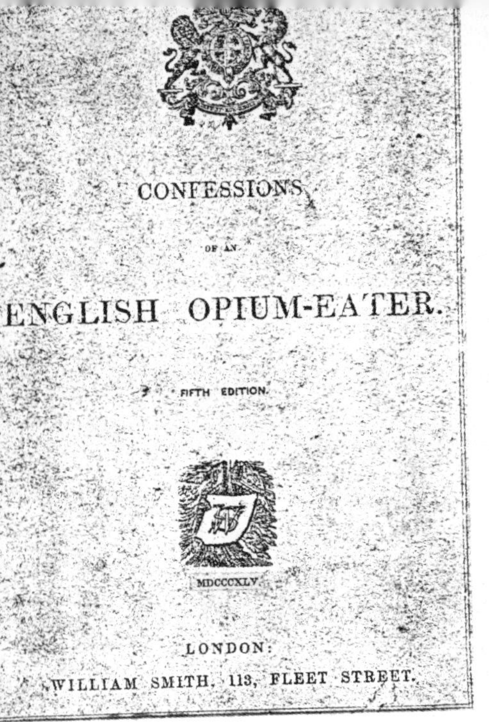

CONFESSIONS

OF AN

ENGLISH OPIUM-EATER.

FIFTH EDITION.

MDCCCXLV.

LONDON:

WILLIAM SMITH, 113, FLEET STREET.

THOMAS DE QUINCEY, Englishman and Opium-Eater, has left us his *Confessions* to afford insight upon the cosmic fantasies of a keen intellect, and they secure him his office as priest and prophet of unbridled reverie. Brilliant imagery seethed in De Quincey's brain, and he multiplied and manifolded his faculties by the use of laudanum in such amounts as "eight, ten, or twelve thousand drops daily." He entered London chemists' shops and called for "a glass of laudanum negus, warm, and without sugar"—then his fancy crept among the green grass blades of the English lake country and spun in another instant to the furthest frayed ravelings of the universe. His soul flowed and swept in one flight from the sweet charm of Englishwomen to the hideous hypnosis of Asia's nightmare deities. In his study he read German metaphysics beside a quart decanter of ruby-colored laudanum, and dreams and speculation whirled him from lamp-lit London streets to the deep cavern under the weight of twenty Atlantics.

...seven, he published anonymously his first book, *The Confessions of an Opium-Eater.* From 1821 to 1824 he was on the staff of the "London Magazine," and in 1825 he published the sham Waverley novel, *Walladmor*, the English adaptation of a German forgery. In 1826 he began to write for "Blackwood," and to alternate his dwelling-

JUNE 14, 1891.

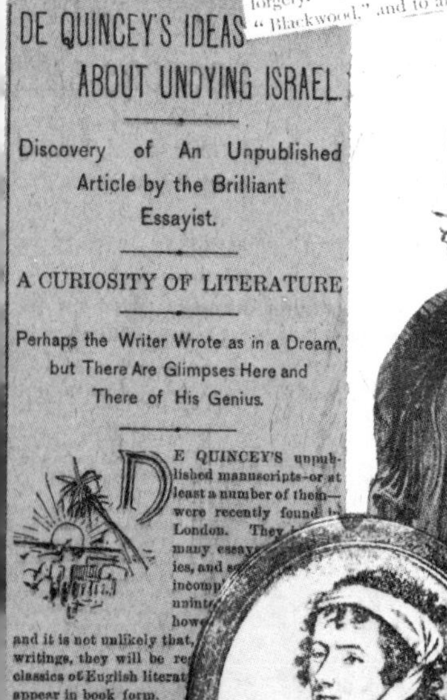

DE QUINCEY'S IDEAS ABOUT UNDYING ISRAEL.

Discovery of An Unpublished Article by the Brilliant Essayist.

A CURIOSITY OF LITERATURE

Perhaps the Writer Wrote as in a Dream, but There Are Glimpses Here and There of His Genius.

DE QUINCEY'S unpublished manuscripts—or at least a number of them—were recently found in London. They ... many essay... ies, and s... incomp... uninte... howe... and it is not unlikely that, ... writings, they will be re... classics of English literat... appear in book form.

The HERALD has obta... one of the essays. It is ... this time because it relat... the children of Israel, bu... that it is not sufficiently ... ab... except as a curiosit... essay follows.

THE PLEASURES OF OPIUM.

IT is so long since I first took opium, that if it had been a trifling incident in my life, I might have forgotten its date: but cardinal events are not to be forgotten; and from circumstances connected with it, I remember that it must be referred to the autumn of 1804. During that season I was in London, having come thither for the first time since my entrance at college. And my introduction to opium arose in the following way. From an early age I had been accustomed to wash my head in cold water at least once a day: being suddenly seized with toothache, I attributed it to some relaxation caused by an accidental intermission of that practice; jumped out of bed; plunged my head into a basin of cold water; and with hair thus wetted went to sleep. The next morning, as I need hardly say, I awoke with excruciating rheumatic pains of the head and face, from which I had hardly any respite for about twenty days. On the twenty-first day, I think it was, and on a Sunday, that I went out into the streets; rather to run away, if possible, from my torments, than with any distinct purpose. By accident I met a college acquaintance who recommended opium. Opium! dread agent of unimaginable pleasure and pain! I had heard of it as I had of manna or of ambrosia, but no further: how unmeaning a sound was it at that time! what solemn chords does it now strike upon my heart! what heart-quaking vibrations of sad and happy remembrances! Reverting for a moment to these, I feel a mystic importance attached to the minutest circumstances connected with the place and the time, and the man (if man he was) that first laid open to me the Paradise of Opium-eaters. It was a Sunday afternoon, wet and cheerless: and a duller spectacle this earth of ours has not to show than a rainy Sunday in London. My road homewards lay through Oxford-street; and near "the *stately* Pa...heon" (as Mr. Wordsworth has obligingly ... I saw a druggist's shop. The drug-... is minister of celestial pleasures!

THE PAINS OF OPIUM.

——— as when some great painter dips
His pencil in the gloom of earthquake and eclipse.
Shelley's Revolt of Islam.

Reader, who have thus far accompanied me, I must request your attention to a brief explanatory note on three points:

1. For several reasons, I have not been able to compose the notes for this ... of my narrative into any regular and ... I give the notes disjointed ... have now drawn them ... Some of them point to the ... I have dated; and some a... ever it could answer my p... them from the natural or... I have not scrupled to ... speak in the present, s...

however, which the opium-eater will find, in the end, as oppressive and tormenting as any other, from the sense of incapacity and feebleness, from the direct embarrassments incident to the neglect or procrastination of each day's appropriate duties, and from the remorse which must often exasperate the stings of these evils to a reflective and conscientious mind. The opium-eater loses none of his moral sensibilities, or aspirations: he wishes and longs, as earnestly as ever, to realise what he believes possible, and feels to be exacted by duty; but his intellectual apprehension of what is possible infinitely outruns his power, not of execution only, but even of power to attempt. He lies under the weight of incubus and nightmare: he lies in sight of all that he would fain perform, just as a man forcibly confined to his bed by the mortal langour of a relaxing disease, who is compelled to witness injury or outrage offered to some object of his tenderest love:—he curses the spells which chain him down from motion:—he would lay down his life if he might but get up and walk; but he is powerless as an infant, and cannot even attempt to rise.

I now pass to what is the main subject of these latter confessions, to the history and journal of what took place in my dreams; for these were the immediate and proximate cause of my acutest suffering.

The first notice I had of any important change going on in this part of my physical economy, was from the re-awakening of a state of eye generally incident to childhood, or exalted states of irritability. I know not whether my reader is aware that many chil...n, perhaps most, have a power of painting, ... were, upon the darkness, all sorts of ...oms: in some, that power is simply a ...nic affection of the eye; others have a ...ry, or a semi-voluntary power to dis... or to summon them; or, as a child once ... me when I questioned him on this ...r, "I can tell them to go, and they go; ... sometimes they come, when I don't tell ... to come." Whereupon I told him that ... had almost as unlimited a command over ...itions, as a Roman centurion over his ...—In the middle of 1817, I think it ... this faculty became positively dis... ... me: at night, when I lay awake in

De Quincey

ATE A POUND OF OPIUM A DAY!

(ENOUGH TO KILL 1100 PEOPLE)

Poetry Will Make His Name Live Through Centuries

The Opium Ruined His Life

The evil that men do lives after them;
The good is oft interred with their bones.

THIS sounds well in Shakespeare; fortunately, it is not true in real life. The evil that men do is buried with them, or forgotten soon after they go. The good that they do lives on.

Samuel Taylor Coleridge proves it. A man of genius, a truly great writer with marvelous imagination, he went through life, the better part of it, struggling vainly against the curse of opium. That deadly drug, in the early part of the last century, and before, was sold as freely as milk or any commodity; the world did not know its dangers. It was so cheap that workmen sometimes bought it because its deadly, sedative effects could be purchased more cheaply than the exhilaration of alcohol.

No satisfactory life of Coleridge has been written. It would show long years of pitiful struggle against the drug that ruled him, with occasional moments of achievement, in a life "embittered by recurring agonies of self-reproach," tormented by

"Sense of past youth, and manhood come in vain,
And genius given, and knowledge won in vain."

AT the age of thirty Coleridge had "enslaved himself to that fatal drug which was to remain his tyrant for the rest of his days."

His story is that of every drug victim, hopeless effort, resolutions made and broken, friends lost, death at last, the only sure relief. De Quincey, another drug victim, telling his story in the **"Confessions of an Opium Eater,"** with little sympathy for a fellow sufferer, accuses Coleridge of taking up opium deliberately for pleasure. The truth is that, ignorant of the frightful danger, Coleridge sought in opium relief for physical pain. **When the habit was formed**, it was too late, opium had seized control of a man of genius. Millions of drug victims could re-write Coleridge's life and his struggles from their own experience. A sufficient account of them will be found in a brief biography by H. D. Traill, **"English Men of Letters,"** your book dealer might procure from Macmillan and Company.

Like De Quincey and others of his day, Coleridge took his drug in the liquid form of laudanum. With sorrow and frankness he tells of his downfall and slavery:

"In an evil hour I procured it (the opium); it worked miracles—the swellings disappeared, the pains vanished. I was all alive, and all around me being as ignorant as myself, nothing could exceed my triumph. I talked of nothing else, prescribed the newly-discovered panacea for all complaints, and carried a little about with me not to lose any opportunity of administering 'instant relief and speedy cure' to all complainers, stranger or friend, gentle or simple. Alas! it is with a bitter smile, a laugh of gall and bitterness, that I recall this period of unsuspecting delusion, and how I first became aware of the maelstrom, the fatal whirlpool to which I was drawing, just when the current was beyond my strength to stem."

LIKE millions of other drug victims, Coleridge spread the opium habit among friends. Later, enlightened, Coleridge tells how opium punishes its victims:

"A grief without a pang, void, dark and drear,
A stifled, drowsy, unimpassioned grief,
Which finds no natural outlet, no relief,
In word, or sigh, or tear."

One who knows Coleridge well declares that:

"In 1814, when Coleridge was 42 years of age, he had been long in the habit of taking from two quarts of laudanum a week to a pint a day, and on one occasion he had been known to take in the twenty-four hours a whole quart of laudanum."

Such a quantity of the devastating drug was sufficient to kill several men, not accustomed to it. At forty-five, when it was too late to save the genius that opium had destroyed, Coleridge found relief, putting himself, almost a prisoner, in the hands of a

"Mr. Gillman, of Highgate, hoping and believing with a soothing confidence that he would leave this retreat restored in mind and body."

He left in his coffin, happier than he had been, having found peace and rest at last.

Every public library, every seller of books, has Coleridge's poems.

ARTHUR BRISBANE.

"In Xanadu did Kubla Khan
A stately pleasure-dome decree;
Where Alph, the sacred river, ran
Through caverns measureless to man,
Down to a sunless sea.

But oh that deep romantic chasm which slanted
Down the green hill athwart a cedar cover!
A savage place! as holy and enchanted
As e'er beneath a waning moon was haunted
By woman wailing for her demon-lover!

* * *

The shadow of the dome of pleasure
Floated midway on the waves;
Where was heard the mingled measure
From the fountain and the caves.

It was a miracle of rare device,
A sunny pleasure-dome with caves of ice!

That sunny dome! those caves of ice!
And all who heard should see them there,
And all should cry, Beware! Beware!
His flashing eyes, his floating hair!
Weave a circle round him thrice,
And close your eyes with holy dread,
For he on honey-dew hath fed
And drank the milk of Paradise."

HARPER'S NEW MONTHLY MAGAZINE.

No. CCV.—JUNE, 1867.—Vol. XXXV.

CONTENTS OF VOLUME XXXV.

JUNE TO NOVEMBER, 1867.

WHAT SHALL THEY DO TO BE SAVED?

I HAVE just returned from forty-eight hours' friendly and professional attendance at a bedside where I would fain place every young person in this country for a single hour before the Responsibilities of Life have become the sentinels and Habit the jailer of his Will.

My patient was a gentleman of forty, who for several years of his youth occasionally used opium, and for the last eight has habitually taken it. During these eight years he has made at least three efforts to leave it off, in each instance diminishing his dose gradually for a month before its entire abandonment, and in the most successful one holding the enemy at bay for but a single summer. In two cases he had no respite of agony from the moment he dropped till he resumed it. In the third case, a short period of comparative repose succeeded the first fiery battle, but in the midst of felicitations on his victory he was attacked by the most agonizing hemicranial headaches (resulting from what I now fear to have been already permanent disorganization of the stomach), and went back to his nepenthe in a state of almost suicidal despair, only after the torture had continued for weeks without a moment's mitigation.

He had first learned its seductions, as happens with the vast majority of Anglo-Saxon opium-eaters, through a medical prescription. The amount of it which my friend had taken during his month's eclipse represents an ounce of dry gum opium—in rough measurement a piece as large as a French billiard ball. I thus particularize because he had never previously been addicted to the drug; had inherited a sound constitution, and differed from any other fresh subject only in the intensity of his nervous temperament. I wish to emphasize the fact that the system of a mere neophyte, with nothing to neutralize the effects of the drug save the absorbency, so to speak, of the pain for which it was given, could so rapidly adapt itself to them as to demand an increase of the dose in such an alarming ratio. There are certain men to whom opium is as fire to tow, and my friend was one of these. On the 1st of October he sensibly perceived the trifling dose of fifty drops; on the first of November he was taking, without increased sensation, an ounce vial of "M'Munn" daily.

WHAT IS OPIUM?

It is the most complicated drug in the Pharmacopœia. Though apparently a simple gummy paste, it possesses a constitution which analysis reveals to contain no less than 25 elements, each one of them a compound by itself, and many of them among the most complex compounds known to modern chemistry. Let me concisely mention these by classes.

First, at least three earthy salts—the sulphates of lime, alumina, and potassa. Second, two organic and one simpler acid—acetic (absolute vinegar), meconic (one of the most powerful irritants which can be applied to the intestines through the bile), and sulphuric. All these exist uncombined in the gum, and free to work their will on the mucous tissues. A green extractive matter, which comes in all vegetal bodies developed under sunlight, next deserves a place by itself, because it is one of the few organic bodies of which no rational analysis has ever been pretended. Though we can not state the constitution of this chlorophyl, we know that, except by turning acid in the stomach, it remains inert on the human system, as one might imagine would happen if he swallowed a bunch of green grass. *Lignin*, with which it is always associated, is mere woody fibre, and has no direct physical action. In no instance has any stomach been found to *digest* it save an insect's—some naturalists thinking that certain beetles make their horny wing-cases of that. I believe one man did think he had discovered a solvent for it in the gastric juice of the beaver, but that view is not widely entertained. So far as it exists in opium it can only act as a foreign substance and a mechanical irritant to the human bowels. Next come two inert, indigestible, and very similar gummy bodies, *mucilagin and bassorine*. Sugar, a powerfully active volatile principle, and a fixed oil (probably allied to turpentine) are the only other invariable constituents of opium belonging to the great organic group of the hydro-carbons.

The remainder, five in number, are the opium alkaloids, which act generally upon the whole system, but particularly, in their immediate phenomena, upon the brain. I mention them in the ascending order of their nervine power: narcotin; codein; opianin; metamorphia, and morphia.

The first of these the poppy shares in common with many other narcotic plants—tobacco the most conspicuous among the number. In its anti-periodic effects on the human system it has been found similar to quinia, and it is an undoubted narcotic poison acting on the nerves of organic life, though, compared with its associates in the drug, comparatively innocent.

The remaining four act very much like morphia, differing only in the size of the dose in which they prove efficient. Most perfectly fresh constitutions feel a grain of morphia powerfully; metamorphia is soporific in half-grain doses;* opianin in its physical effects closely approximates morphia; codeia is about one-fifth as powerful; a new subject may not get sleep short of six grains; its main action is expended on the sympathetic system. It does not seem to congest the brain as morphia does; but its action on the biliary system is probably little less deadly than that of the more powerful narcotic.

"One by one you have paralyzed all the excretory functions of the body. Opium, aiming at all those functions for their death, first attacked the kidneys, and with your experimental doses you experienced a slight access of *dysouria*. As you went on, the same action, progressively paralytic to organic life, involved the liver. Flatulence, distress at the epigastrium, irregularity of bowels, indicated a spasmodic performance of the liver's work which showed it to be under high nervous excitement. Your mouth became dry through a cessation of the salivary discharge. Your lachrymal duct was parched, and your eye grew to have an *arid* look in addition to the dullness produced by opiate contraction of the pupil.

"About this time you may have had some temporary gastric disturbance, accompanied with indescribable distress, loathing at food, and nausea. This indicated that the mucous lining of the stomach had been partially removed by the corrosions of the drug, or that nervous power had suddenly come to a standstill, which demanded an increase of stimulus.

"Since that time you have been taking your daily dose only to preserve the *status in quo*. The condition both of your nervous system and your stomach indicate that you must always take some anodyne to avoid torture, and *your* only anodyne is opium.

"The rest of your life must be spent in keeping comfortable, not in being happy."

Opium-eaters enjoy a strange immunity from other disease. They are not liable to be attacked by miasma in malarious countries; epidemics or contagions where they exist. They almost always survive to die of their opium itself. And an opium death is usually in one of these two manners:

The opium-eater either dies in collapse through nervous exhaustion (with the blood poisoning and delirium above-mentioned), sometimes after an overdose, but oftener seeming to occur spontaneously; or in the midst of physical or mental agony, as great and irrelievable as men suffer in hopeful abandonment of the drug, and with a colliquative diarrhea, by which—in a continual, fiery, acrid discharge—the system relieves itself during a final fortnight of the effete matters which have been accumulating for years.

Either of these ends is terrible enough; let us draw a curtain over their details.

Opium is a corrosion and paralysis of all the noblest forms of life. The man who voluntarily addicts himself to it would commit in cutting his throat a suicide only swifter and less ignoble. The habit is gaining fearful ground among our professional men, the operatives in our mills, our weary sewing women, our fagged clerks, our disappointed wives, our former liquor-drunkards, our very day-laborers, who a generation ago took gin; all our classes, from the highest to the lowest, are yearly increasing their consumption of the drug. The terrible demands, especially in this country, made on modern brains by our feverish competitive life, constitute hourly temptations to some form of the sweet, deadly sedative. Many a professional man of my acquaintance, who twenty years ago was content with his *tri-diurnal* "whisky," ten years ago, drop by drop, began taking stronger "laudanum cock-tails," until he became what he is now—an habitual opium-eater. I have tried to show what he will be. If this article shall deter any from an imitation of his example, or excite an interest in the question—"*What he shall do to be saved?*"—I am content.

HASHEESH EATER:

BEING PASSAGES FROM THE

LIFE OF A PYTHAGOREAN.

NEW YORK:
HARPER & BROTHERS, PUBLISHERS,
FRANKLIN SQUARE.
1857.

"Weave a circle round him thrice,
And close your eyes with holy dread,
For he on honey-dew hath fed,
And drunk the milk of Paradise."

KUBLA KHAN.

Fitz Hugh Ludlow

DOCTOR JUDAS

A PORTRAYAL OF THE OPIUM HABIT

COBBE

CHICAGO
S. C. GRIGGS AND COMPANY
1895

from Bondage to Freedom

AMERICAN OPIUM EATER CONFESSIONS

BOSTON
JAMES H. EARLE
178 Washington Street
1895

BERNHARDT DISCOURSES.

She is Interviewed by the "Examiner's" Special Correspondent.

CAR "SARAH BERNHARDT," NEAR HUMBOLDT, Saturday, May 14.—Just where the Nevada desert blooms into a little oasis I met the Bernhardt party.

I had a voyage of over 340 miles from San Francisco and arrived at Humboldt two hours before the west-bound train pulled up at the station.

An "Examiner" Expedition About Chinatown.

HOW SHE SPENT HER FIRST DAY.

On the train that brought Madame Sarah Bernhardt to San Francisco yesterday the universal comment was that the enterprise of the EXAMINER in sending a special correspondent 374 miles into the Nevada desert was unprecedented.

The fact had got abroad through the train dispatchers and conductors of the road, and the EXAMINER was eagerly looked for at Benicia, where the daily papers were served at 9:30 A.M.

UNDERGROUND HORRORS.

Madame Bernhardt Visits the Opium and Other Dens.

Emerging from the side entrance of the theater the party filed across the street to a narrow alleyway.

"It is frightening!" said Madame Sarah, glancing around at the dark, sinister rookeries as if fascinated by the horrors they might contain.

"It is a place for bravos with long daggers!" she exclaimed, presently, as the way became more black and tortuous.

Detective Martin and the Chinese interpreter being informed of her remark, hastened to explain, through the medium of the EXAMINER representative, that that very spot was a favorite execution ground for the dreadful brotherhood of highbinders.

"Ah!" cried Madame Sarah, "so they have the bravo after all! How droll! How delightful! Can they be seen—these bravos!"

The mysterious ways of the highbinders were explained to her, and Detective Martin assured her that her only chance to look upon a real, live highbinder would be to visit him in his cage at the County Jail.

OPIUM SMOKERS.

A sharp turn was made into a little passage leading to a cavernous courtyard. Then a long flight of stairs led the party to a cellar, where the ladies clutched desperately at the gentle-

MADAME SARAH

Her Arrival in the Western City of the Continent.

men's arms to keep from stumbling, and suddenly they all found themselves in a little ten by twelve apartment, in which a dim candle burned.

On the low bunks around the room lay Chinamen, whose faces stood out in the cloud of smoke with ghastly pallor.

"*C'est horrible!*" gasped the ladies.

"*C'est magnifique!*" exclaimed Madame Sarah, pushing into the room with eager curiosity.

A victim lay in a stupor before her. He was evidently marked for an early death. The tight skin seemed green and moldy.

His fingers were mechanically preparing a ball of opium for his pipe.

His muscles seemed to act without the control of nerves.

It was a sort of living death.

"HE DREAMS!"

"*Il rêve!*" exclaimed Bernhardt, leaning over him and peering into his countenance, as if to read his dreams.

Then breaking away with a shudder she hurried to the door and out from the cloud of smoke to the cold air of the street.

THE RESTAURANT.

Bernhardt Drinks Tea and Sips Sam

SAFE AFTER CRISIS, Sarah Bernhardt, great French tragedienne, was reported out of danger yesterday following her collapse during rehearsal. Though seventy-eight, "Divine Sarah" fought off heart attack by sheer strength of will and physique.

OPIUM

The Diary of an Addict

By JEAN COCTEAU

MANIA FOR MORPHINE.

Grave Charges That Have Been Made Against Physicians of Paris.

A SPECIALIST'S OPINIONS.

Fifty Thousand Persons in the Capital Use the Drug Every Day.

A TABLE OF THE "FIENDS."

Physicians and Their Wives Found To Be at the Top of the Heaviest Users.

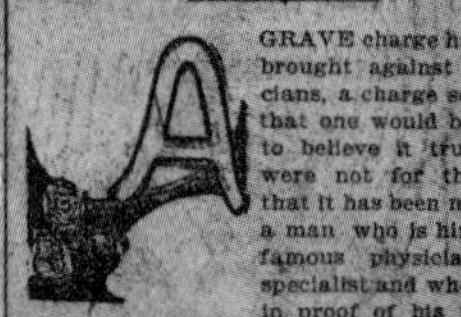

GRAVE charge has been brought against phy[...]cians, a charge so gr[...] that one would be [...] to believe it true [...] were not for the fact that it has been made by a man who is himself a famous physician and specialist and who offers in proof of his terrible statements an array of statistics which certainly seem to be conclusive.

When Aubert was arrested in Paris the other day on the charge of assassinating the young philatelist, Delahaeff, it soon became apparent that he was a confirmed morphine fiend. During his trial he suffered agonies for lack of the deadly drug, and at last the public prosecutor, fearing that he would utterly collapse, instructed a physician to administer a timely injection. This in itself, the prisoner being on trial, was a remarkable proceeding, but what surprised the public more than the fact that a poverty stricken fellow like Aubert should have become addicted to the use of such an expensive drug as morphine. Hitherto the popular opinion has been that only the comparatively well-to-do could afford a luxury of this kind, but now this opinion has been shown to be baseless.

The question, then, which the French people are asking is, How are we to account for this strange epidemic, which is evidently spreading among all classes of society? To this question a startling reply has been given by this eminent French specialist and physician. Here is what he says:—

"I do not desire my name to be mentioned," he began, "because what I have to say is not very flattering to a certain number of my colleagues, and while I have nothing to conceal I have neither the time nor the inclination to take part in any paper war on the subject."

It may be stated here that this specialist is one of the best known living authorities on nervous diseases.

"The mania for morphine," he continued, "is growing daily and among all classes. Statistics on the subject are not easily obtainable, because morphine fiends are very crafty, and because no exterior symptoms condemn them in public, as is the case with drunkards and epileptics. From what a number of druggists and physicians have told me, however, I estimate that there are not less than fifty thousand persons in Paris who use morphine secretly and almost constantly. Most of these who belong to this army of degenerates are women; indeed, I should put their number at not less than thirty thousand.

Instructive Statistics.

"More instructive, however, than this general statement are the following statistics, which have been carefully compiled, and which show how the vice has spread among persons of the various professions. Here is a table of 230 morphine fiends who belong to twenty-two different professions or trades. You will see—and this is the most startling point—that the first rank on the list is occupied by physicians and their wives, the number of victims among them being sixty nine. In the second rank we find army officers and their wives, the number of victims among them being twenty; in the third, druggists and their families, and in the fourth workingmen and working women, the number of victims among them being eighteen. Among members of the other professions, namely college professors, magistrates, literary men, artists and others, the number of victims varies from two to ten.

"Now, the amazing fact is that physicians, who, from their knowledge of the danger, ought to be most of all beyond the reach of contamination, should actually be at the head of the list of morphine fiends. To many the reason will seem obvious. Their explanation is that physicians become addicted to the drug through weariness and through their disgust with the most ungrateful of all professions. In other words, being often disappointed and obliged to struggle unsuccessfully for their daily bread, they have sought in the discreet and comparatively silent intoxication of morphine that oblivion which the workingman finds in raw brandy.

Druggists Also Blamed.

"I tell you the physicians who act thus are incurring a terrible responsibility, and perhaps the time is not far distant when there will be applied to such practices that article of the Civil Code which says that every one shall be held responsible for whatever harm he may do, not only by his own act, but also by his own negligence or imprudence.

"Druggists are quite as often to blame as physicians. If they were to strictly obey that law which prohibits them from selling drugs except on a regular prescription, which must be renewed at the time of each purchase, the facilities for obtaining morphine would be much diminished. Certainly, those persons who could not get physicians to help them out of their difficulty would find it very hard to get the drug. A druggist was recently punished for having sold in one month 1,500 grammes of morphine without any formality to one of his lady customers.

"It is just as easy to procure syringes as it is to procure the drug itself. Any one who wants them can buy them at stores where [sur]gical instruments are sold, and also at cer[tain] second hand stores. Jewellers even deal in them. I know one who was on the point of becoming a bankrupt when he conceived the happy idea of manufacturing these deadly little weapons. His customers were mostly women, and he knew well what they wanted. Instead of filling his store windows with bare, unadorned syringes, he hid them deftly in scent bottles, fans, bracelets, and even in parasol handles. The result was that he soon paid his debts and is now on the high road to fortune.

"There are four periods in the evolution of the disease—that of initiation, that of hesitation, that of morphinomania, and that of cachexia, the end of which is death. How long does it take to pass from the initiatory stage to that of morphinomania? That depends on the temperament, those persons who are most nervous being most amenable to the disease. As a rule, however, after a month and a half of injections at the rate of from two to five centigrammes per dose a desire is created which is horribly difficult to conquer.

"Many so-called remedies for the disease are being tried. In Germany, where the scourge rages with even more intensity than in France, special asylums have been established, in which are employed different methods of treatment, such as the Levinstein or abrupt method, the slow or progressive method, and the Erlenmeyer or semi-rapid method. This last seems to have given the best results. Here in France we still use the individual and persuasive treatment. Do what we will, however, the incontestable fact remains—and it is a sad confession—that of all known voluntary diseases for which a treatment has been found morphinomania is one of those, if not the one, which is

SLAVE TO MORPHINE DIES FROM DRUG

Mary J Holmes Passed from Dee[p] Sleep to Death While a Friend Watched Beside Her.

POLICE SAY A SUICIDE.

Two Companions Allowed Her to Slumber All Afternoon Before They Became Alarmed.

IN RICHLY FURNISHED ROOMS

Was Handsome, Dressed Expensively and Was Visited by a Man Who Always Came in a Carriage.

DIED OF MORPHINE.

Why Young Nelson B. Reynolds Killed Himself Remains a Mystery.

WROTE OF HIS INTENTION.

Two Young Women Called to Learn Whether He Had Carried Out His Resolve.

BROKER MARTINEZ A SUICIDE.

He Was Worried About Financial Affairs and Inhaled Gas Through a Tube.

TRIES TO DIE BY MORPHINE AND GAS

Henry Carleton Jones, Interior Decorator, Attempts Suicide After Trip for Health.

INHALED GAS AS SHE WROTE.

Mrs. Stowe Sat at a Table, in Her Mouth a Tube Connected with the Jet.

VICTIM OF MORPHINE HABIT.

Had Been in Several Institutes, but the Cure Guaranteed Did Not Last.

HER DEATH IN THE FOURTH.

APRIL 11, 1893

FOUND MORPHINE IN HER CORPSE.

Professor Rudolph A. Witthaus Thinks Poison Killed Mrs. Anna B. Buchanan.

ALSO SAW SIGNS OF ATROPINE.

But the Expert Would Not Positively Declare That the Body Contained This Drug.

DR. PRUDDEN AS A WITNESS.

SHOCKS ENLIVEN BUCHANAN'S TRIAL.

Quick Poisons, a Fresh Brain and Defiant Witnesses Among the Surprises.

WELLMAN'S SNEER MET IN KIND.

Dr. Wolff Persists That Mrs. Buchanan Died of Uraemia or Cirrhosis of the Liver.

POISON TESTS BEFORE THE JURY.

Professor Vaughan in the Buchanan Trial Ridicules the Witthaus Methods.

REACTIONS IN PRETTY COLORS.

Opposing Experts Grow Sulky and Refuse Invitations to Help in the Experiments

Contradicted Himself When Explaining Why He Thought His Wife Saw That Doctor.

COULDN'T WORRY DR. SCHEELE

Prisoner Did Not Say of Her, "If They Dig Her up They'll Find Her Full of Morphine."

DR. BUCHANAN FOUND GUILTY.

Murder in the First Degree Was the Verdict Brought in by the Jurymen.

ONE JUROR FALLS IN A FAINT.

Twenty-Eight Hours of Foul Air and Earnest Argument Too Much for His Strength.

PRISONER CALM AS EVER.

His First and Third Wife Goes Into Hysterics When She Learns Her Husband's Fate.

BACK TO HIS CELL IN THE TOMBS.

TOXICOLOGICAL EXPERTS DOUBT.

Professor Witthaus Not Sure He Found Atropine in Mrs. Buchanan's Body.

DR. DOREMUS IS SHAKY ON CATS.

Poured Some Stuff in a Kitten's Eye and Drew Results from the Pupil's Dilation.

PROSECUTION SOON TO END.

Dr. Robert W. Buchanan was out of sight yesterday, so far as the attention of persons in the General Sessions Court room was concerned. Everybody appeared to have forgotten that the pale, little, weak eyed man was on trial for having murdered his wife with morphine.

What interested for awhile and then bored the jury was the battle of the toxicological experts. After the smoke of legal battle had drifted away

DR. C. A. DOREMUS.

two facts stood out clearly—that Professor Witthaus was not positive he had found atropine in Mrs. Buchanan's body, and that Dr. Doremus was not so familiar as he might be with the dilation of the pupils of cats' eyes.

This was important, because without this knowledge he had tested some of the stuff found in the woman's body, thought to be atropine, by dropping it into a kitten's eye at two o'clock in the afternoon. The pupil did not become dilated for two hours, and Dr. O'Sullivan sought to show inferentially that the dilation was due to the approach of twilight. Dr. Doremus and Professor Witthaus ascribed the enlargement of the pupil to the action of atropine.

PAMPHLET EXCLUDED.

Professor Rudolph A. Witthaus looked [...] when Dr. O'Sulli[van] [...]

[...] of pugilists, [...] continued Professor Witt[haus'] cross-examination.

Q. Are not the crystals of morphine like crystals of some other poisons? A. They are.

Q. (Handing up a little box filled with vials of white crystals). Can you, by looking, tell me what these are? A. I cannot—by mere looking.

MORPHINE FOUND.

Q. How much morphine did you find in this woman? A. I infer from the intensity of the reaction that we found not less than one-tenth of a grain.

Q. I asked you how much morphine you found—not what the intensity of the reaction of your experiments indicated. A. I believe we found ten grains.

Q. Did you isolate it? A. We separated it.

Q. Did you isolate it? A. No.

Q. If you found one-tenth of a grain of morphine let me see it. A. Why, I told you yesterday what we did with it.

"You cannot show me any of the morphine you say you found in this woman's body!" exclaimed Dr. O'Sullivan. "You say you did not isolate the morphine you think you found in the residue of the stomach, in which you say it was. Now, how do you know it was morphine?"

Professor Witthaus carefully explained at great length the chemical reactions and physiological tests which convinced him that he had found morphine.

Q. Could you isolate as small an amount as 1-180 of a grain of morphine? A. Yes.

Q. Why didn't you isolate this substance, then, as morphine?

NOT SURE OF ATROPINE.

Professor Witthaus entered into a dissertation on the true meaning in chemistry of the word isolate.

Q. Could you isolate 1-180 of a grain of morphine? A. I don't know.

Q. Now, did you find any atropine in this woman's body. A. I do not know, sir.

"That will do, then," cried Dr. O'Sullivan.

"What?" cried the District Attorney, "is that all?"

Everybody was surprised, the jury gratefully so.

"You do not ordinarily find morphine in a dead body by weighing or isolating it?" asked the District Attorney.

"Certainly not," replied the great chemist.

"You established the presence of morphine here by the use of the proper tests?"

"Yes."

Dr. O'Sullivan had another innings with Professor Witthaus.

Q. You have testified that when you dropped part of one of the residues from Mrs. Buchanan's body into the eye of a kitten it dilated the pupil, and that therefore you thought that residue contained atropine. Are there not substances resulting from the decay of the human body which will produce the enlargement of the eye as you say this residue did? A. There are.

Q. Then why do you say that there was atropine in that residue? A. I did not say so; I inferred so.

Q. You have testified to the effect of the residue, you say contained morphine, on frogs? Is the effect of morphine the same on frogs and human beings? A. It is not.

Q. Are there not substances resulting from the decay of the human body which will act on frogs as morphine does? A. (After a pause). No.

MORPHINE CRAZED HE ATTACKS TO R[OB]

Louis Hays, of Wealt[hy] Family, Temporarily In[sane], Fells Aged Bank Messenger.

STRIKES HIM WITH A HEAVY IRON BA[R]

George F. Mellert Stunned Wh[ile] Attempting to Resist Assailan[t] Who Is Captured.

WAS ONCE IN AN ASYLU[M]

"There Was No Need of His Resorti[ng] to Robbery to Obtain Money," Said Father.

Temporarily insane through the habit[ual] use of morphine originally prescribed [for] him by a physician during a serious illn[ess] seven years ago, Louis Hays, one of six so[ns] of Simon Hays, a millionnaire real est[ate] man, tried to rob a bank messenger in Ha[r]lem yesterday, after atacking the old m[an] with a heavy iron bar. He was arrested a[nd] gave an assumed name, but later told t[he] police who he was. He was held for e[x]amination to-day, and the bank he tried [to] rob will press the case, despite the you[ng] man's conections and the family theory th[at] he was not responsible for what he did.

Because of the fact that no money w[as] found in his pockets when he was search[ed] at the police station, and his haggard fa[ce] and hungry glare, the police believe th[at] having no money to buy morphine, he we[nt] to the bank with the intention of robbi[ng] some one, so that he could get the dru[g].

Deed of a Crazed Man.

"We cannot understand this act of m[y] brother's in any other light than that it [is] the deed of a man temporarily crazed [by] morphine. My brother has a good positi[on] and a comfortable salary. He was not [in] need of money. He knows also that his rel[a]tives would not see him want for anythin[g]. Seven years ago he was seriously ill and o[ur] family doctor prescribed morphine. Lou[is] became addicted to its use. He was cured [of] the habit at that time, but a year and a ha[lf] ago his craving for morphine returned."

"My son is a morphine fiend," said th[e] [...] when seen at his residence, at No. [...] 125th street. "That accounts for th[e] [...] thing. He has been addicted to th[e] [...] for several years, and it has finall[y] [...]red his mind, so that he has, at last, be[come] crazy. He was placed in an asylum [...] [...]yn for a long time, a few years ag[o] [...] treatment there failed to cure him. [The]re was no need of his reporting t[o] [...] to obtain money. We shall emplo[y] [...] and make a nendeavor to have h[im] [...] and made an endeavor to have hi[m] [...] insane, for he is clearly so. H[e] [...] bad habits outside of that one grea[t] [...] far as we know. His associate[s] [...] vicious, and he was around hi[s] [...]st of the time when he was no[t] [...]

EXPERIMENTED ON A DOG.

Successful Application of an Antidote for Morphine Poisoning by Dr. Guilfoy on a Homeless Cur.

An interesting example of the efficacy of permanganate of potassium as an antidote for opium poisoning was recently given by Dr. W. H. Guilfoy, of the Bureau of Vital Statistics, before a class of the New York Evening High School, in West Thirtieth street. A full account of the dramatic demonstration of the virtues of the permanganate by Dr. Moor, the discoverer of the treatment, was recently given in the HERALD. On that occasion Dr. Moor fearlessly offered himself as a subject by swallowing three grains of morphine, the effects of which he immediately neutralized by taking in the presence of a dozen physicians a dose of four grains of the antidote.

Two of the witnessing physicians were so fearful of the result of the experiment that they immediately left the room rather than place themselves, as they expressed it, in the attitude of particeps criminis, but the trial was abundantly successful, and the fearless demonstrator experienced no ill effects whatever.

Dr. Guilfoy's experience was for the purpose of confirming the result of Dr. Moor's test, and the subject selected was a small dog which had been picked up in the street by one of the students of the class.

To test the efficacy of the antidote to the most extreme limit Dr. Guilfoy administered to the animal on Monday night a hypodermic injection of four grains of morphine, the equivalent of many times that amount administered to a human subject. In the case of Dr. Moor the antidote was administered immediately, but in the experiment on the dog several minutes were permitted to elapse to give the poison time to take effect.

In the case of the dog an effect directly contrary to that produced on the human subject was observed, for the respiration immediately increased rapidly and the action of the pulse was greatly accelerated. Finally the animal frothed furiously at the mouth, and evidences of the approach of dissolution became apparent.

At this stage five grains of the permanganate were administered hypodermically. The effect was not immediately apparent, but within one hour after the administration of the morphine the animal began to show symptoms of rallying from the effects of the poison.

It staggered to its feet, walked a few steps and then fell over on its side. No further treatment was used, and in the morning the dog seemed to be in as good health as ever. Under ordinary conditions the quantity of morphine administered would have resulted fatally in less than an hour.

One of the students has adopted the dog and

AS BAD AS MORPHINE OR LIQUOR.

A New Drug Which Is Coming Into Use as a Narcotic and Is Denounced by Physicians as Injurious.

KILLED BY MORPHINE TAKEN BY MISTAKE.

Sad Death of Martin Mundt, Due, His Family Allege, to a Drug Clerk's Blunder.

THOUGHT IT WAS QUININE.

That Was What Martin Asked for, and the Package He Received Was Labelled Quinine.

HIS BROTHER FALLS IN A FIT.

Clerk Thomas Nichols, Who Sold the Powder, Gives Himself up to the Police—Differing Statements of Sigmund Mundt and Clerk Beitman.

Martin Mundt, twenty-seven years old, died of morphine poisoning at half past five o'clock yesterday morning at his residence, No. 206 West 121st street.

His family say that his death is due to a blundering drug clerk, who, they claim, put up morphine in a package labelled quinine.

The package was obtained in William Glokner's drug store, at Eighth avenue and 120th street. Thomas Nichols, about twenty-three years old, whose family live in Pennsylvania, is the clerk accused of making the terrible mistake. He has been employed in the drug store only three days, and but little is known about him there. He is said to have worked as drug clerk for six years.

Martin Mundt was unmarried. He lived with his father, who was engaged up to three years ago in the manufacture of skirts, at Nos. 123 and 127 Franklin street. After his wife's death he retired from the business, which is now conducted by his eldest son, Sigmund M. Mundt, at the same place. Another son, Arthur, thirty-one years old, has an interest in the concern, which gives him a handsome income, and Martin also had an interest.

COMPLAINED OF A HEADACHE.

Martin and Arthur went out driving Saturday evening and returned to the stables in 120th street about nine o'clock. Martin complained of a headache, and said he had some fever. Arthur suggested that he get some quinine, and they walked to Glokner's drug store.

Arthur says that Martin asked for ten grains of quinine, and that the clerk handed him an envelope marked quinine. The brothers then went home. They slept together, and retiring to their room on the top floor a few moments after entering the house they went to sleep.

Arthur was awakened about three o'clock yesterday morning by his brother's heavy breathing and moaning. He sat up in bed, called to Martin and tried to arouse him, but could not. Then Arthur jumped from the bed, lit the gas and seeing that Martin's condition was serious he ran from the room, awakened his brother Sigmund, who slept [...] back room, and his father. All three returned [...] bedside and tried to awaken him. [...] availing and the entire house- [...] carried out for

[...] Mundt was [...] tery, going out as soon as [...] there was no conversation betwe[...] man showed Coroner Schultz the cash book [...] which all sales are recorded. There was marked in one place, in lead pencil, "Sulphate quinine, ten cents, No. 3."

This, Beitman stated, was Mundt's purchase. The clerks are numbered. Beitman is No. 1, a young lady is No. 2 and Nichols is No. 3. Coroner Schultz examined the book in which all poisons sold are required to be registered, but he could not find any recent entry of morphine.

Clerk Beitman, when he heard of the death of Mundt, analyzed the quinine and found it perfect. He also tested the morphine to see if there were any impurities in it, but could find none. Coroner Schultz took away with him one spoonful of the quinine and one of the morphine. He intends to analyze them.

Beitman declared it as his [...] committed suicide and wanted to have it [...] that his death was due to an error. The clerk surmised that Mundt had purchased quinine in his place and morphine at another druggist's and had then put the morphine in the quinine envelope, thrown away the morphine envelope and the quinine and swallowed the morphine.

But the relatives of Martin Mundt are positive that he did not commit suicide. They place the entire blame for his death on the drug clerk.

NICHOLS SURRENDERS.

Nichols, accompanied by Mrs. Glokner and Clerk Beitman, went to the West One Hundred and [...]

MORPHINE POISON MADE HARMLESS.

FEBRUARY 12, 1894

Dr. Moor Advances Another Step with His Antidote to the Salts of Opium.

EXPERIMENTS UPON RABBITS.

Permanganate of Potash Restored Them After Hypodermic Injections of Morphine.

VALUE OF THE DISCOVERY.

The discovery of Dr. William Moor, of the staff of the West Side German Clinic in West Forty-second street, of a sure antidote for morphine, as exclusively published in the HERALD of January 21, was advanced a step yesterday in a series of experiments performed in the laboratory of the West Side Dispensary, by which it was conclusively demonstrated that the permanganate of potassium is equally effective as an antidote in cases where the morphine poison has been absorbed into the blood vessels.

It will be recalled that the chief objection raised by the medical faculty to the value of the experiment which Dr. Moor made upon himself in swallowing three grains of morphine, which he followed immediately with a dose of four grains of his antidote, was that the poison had not had sufficient time to become absorbed into the system. It was argued that the antidote would be powerless in any case in which the poison had been absorbed by the blood vessels.

It was for the purpose of demonstrating that the permanganate of potassium would attack and neutralize the activity of morphine previously injected into the veins of an animal that yesterday's experiments were prosecuted. The experiments were entirely successful, and Dr. Moor and his associates feel satisfied that their discovery is bound to prove of incalculable value in the treatment of cases of chronic morphine poisoning. Five healthy rabbits were operated upon by Dr. Moor and his assistants with entirely satisfactory results. Dr. Edward Von Donhoff inoculated the animals, and the effects of the poison and its antidote were observed and noted by Drs. Moor, M. M. Weill and J. Mount Bleyer and Expert Chemists Goelet, Dittrich and Lesser.

HOW THE RABBITS WERE TREATED.

Rabbit No. 1 was treated with one grain of morphine introduced through the mouth into the stomach by means of a flexible tube. A gastric fistula was established and thirty minutes after the operation the animal's respiration had risen to 152. Examination with the ophthalmoscope showed that the pupil of the eye was much contracted. The rabbit failed gradually and died in about three hours after the experiment.

Rabbit No. 2 was treated hypodermically with one grain of sulphate of morphia and fifteen minutes later three-quarters of a grain of permanganate of potassium was injected into his jugular. After the lapse of another quarter of an hour one-third of a grain more of the antidote was injected into the vein. It was observed that shortly after the hypodermic injection of morphine the normal respiration, which in rabbits is 140, had dropped down to 14. Upon the injection of the permanganate it rose quickly to 46. In two hours the animal was quite comfortable and, though sluggish, was capable of moving around the operating table.

Rabbit No. 3 was given two grains of morphine through the mouth at eight minutes to five o'clock. Respiration had dropped to 14 at half-past five, and at a quarter to seven o'clock had fallen to 12. An intra-venous injection of two grains of the permanganate of potassium was then administered, with the result that in ten minutes the respiration had risen to 26. It fell again, however, to 20, but became stronger after the lapse of half an hour, when it was registered at 34. The animal was then pronounced to be out of danger, and after an interval of an hour was apparently as well as ever.

Rabbit No. 4 received an intra-venous injection of one grain of morphine, and exhibited almost exactly similar symptoms to those observed in rabbit No. 1, who received the same quantity of poison through the mouth.

Rabbit No. 5 was made the piece de resistance of the day. He received a dose of five grains of morphine through the mouth. This was administered at twelve minutes to six o'clock. He was sinking rapidly by seven o'clock, when he was treated with a solution of six grains of permanganate of potassium, injected through the veins. Within half an hour he began to show signs of improvement and by eight o'clock was almost entirely recovered.

VALUE OF THE EXPERIMENTS.

"What we seek to show by these experiments," said Dr. Weill, "is that the permanganate of potassium will attack the morphia in the blood just as readily as when the poison is taken into the stomach. We also claim that morphia, if given hypodermically, sends a good part of the alkaloid poison to the stomach. In other words the tendency of morphia is to get into the stomach. Dr. Hetzig, of Germany, discovered that when morphia is injected hypodermically into the [...] that about fifty per cent of the poison [...] finds its way into the stom[...] absurd to insist that [...] himself was val[...]

SURE ANTIDOTE FOR MORPHINE.

Dr. Williams Describes It in Permanganate of Potassium and Demonstrates the Fact.

FOR HE SWALLOWED THE DRUG.

Three Grains of Morphine Would Have Killed Him but He Applied His Remedy.

ACTS THE SAME AS OPIUM.

Several of the Doctors Who Were to Witness the Experiment Left the Room.

THOUGHT IT SUICIDAL.

They Afterward Watched Dr. Moore for Five Hours, but He Was Unaffected

Dr. William Moor, a specialist on therapeutics, who is a member of the staff of the West Side German Clinic, in West Forty-second street, has discovered that permanganate of potassium is an antidote for morphine poisoning, and that it will counteract within a reasonable lapse of time the effects of any of the salts of opium.

Dr. Moor, in the presence of twelve members of the clinic who assembled on January 9, swallowed what is ordinarily a fatal dose of morphine.

His fellow physicians attempted to dissuade him. Some of them left the room, declaring that they would not countenance such madness by their presence.

But Dr. Moor persisted in committing "suicide" with the utmost cheerfulness. Then he swallowed his new found antidote.

Deadly languor and death must have followed ordinarily, for Dr. Moor swallowed three grains of the drug, a positively fatal dose in his case, as he is super-sensitive to the effect of narcotics. But the permanganate of potassium did its work well. In the business of the meeting which followed the experiment no head was clearer than Dr. Moor's, and when it came to eating, drinking and making merry some hours afterward he was quoted as active a participant as there was in the party.

PROOF CONCLUSIVE.

The experiment was so bold, the physician's faith in his discovery so absolute and the proof so conclusive that the physicians present were at once absorbed and delighted.

The experiment, although its complete bearing upon the saving of life is not yet known, proved conclusively that the effect of an ordinarily fatal dose of morphine, opium, paregoric or laudanum may be counteracted by a remedy at once simple, harmless and easily obtainable upon all occasions.

Of its importance in the treatment of the morphine and opium habits it is too early to speak authoritatively, but if Dr. Moor's opinion is correct its usefulness in this direction will prove incalculable.

Dr. Moor has been experimenting with his new antidote since early spring, but it was not until the meeting of the West Side German Clinic on January 9 that he felt that he had advanced far enough to permit of an experiment which would instantly establish the importance of his discovery in the eyes of his colleagues.

THEY WITNESSED THE EXPERIMENTS.

Among the physicians who were present on the occasion in question were Dr. Valentine, president of the clinic; Dr. Egbert A. Grandin, Dr. F. W. Warner, Dr. Herman L. Collyer, Dr. William Gottheil, Dr. J. M. Bleyer, Dr. Robert A. Murray, Dr. Augustive H. Goelet and Dr. William J. Brickelmaier.

The experiment, which was as unexpected as it was startling, took place at eight o'clock in the evening. Dr. Gottheil ordered Druggist Lesser to weigh out three grains of morphine.

"Here, gentlemen," he said, "are three grains of morphine which Dr. Moor wishes to take in our presence to-night in order to show the efficacy of the antidote which he has discovered it. He takes it in our presence so that he may refer to us as witnesses in the scientific report regarding it which he proposes to make public shortly."

Dr. Gottheil held the powder out in his hand and said:—

"Gentlemen, do you wish to see Dr. Moor make this experiment?"

Dr. Grandin and Dr. Murray displayed some uneasiness, and both finally said they did not care to witness any such attempt as that proposed.

President Valentine agreed with them. "I, for [...]," he said, "do not wish to be [...]"

[...] the question was [...] decided that Mr. [...] dose weighed out [...]

[...] that case I'll take [...] self, and I will do it [...] sibility."

[...] three grains of mor[...] water and immedi[...] ation of four grains [...] in four ounces of [...]

Merck's Merits in the Manufacture of Morphine

THE work of Seguin (1804), of Serturner (1805), of Dumas and Pelletier (1823) was scientific to the highest degree. For the sake of knowledge they investigated perseveringly until MORPHINE was thoroughly defined.

E. MERCK, personally acquainted as he was with investigators, shared their enthusiasm. In addition to their erudition, he had the foresight to recognize the importance of MORPHINE to medicine and, despite the advice of more conservative friends, he undertook the manufacture of MORPHINE as early as 1827.

The clearness of his foresight and the wisdom of his step were quickly proved by the host of other manufacturers, who, after witnessing his success, could without risk to themselves follow MERCK'S lead.

Specify MERCK'S on your prescriptions for **MORPHINAE SULPHAS**

SAN FRANCISCO
San Francisco, California.
STOCKTON ST.
SACRAMENTO ST.
CLAY
WASHINGTON
JACKSON ST.
PACIFIC ST.
CALIFORNIA ST.
BROOKLYN PLACE
SPOFFORD ST.
WAVERLY PLACE
CHURCH COURT
ROSS ST.
DUPONT ST.
LOZIER ST. (BARTLETT ALLEY)
WASHINGTON PLACE
BRENHAM PLACE
KEARNEY ST.
MONTGOMERY
Official Map of
Chinatown San Francisco
Prepared under the supervision
of the Special Committee of the
Board of Supervisors, July, 1885
W. B. Farwell
John E. Kunkler
E. B. Pond
The colors indicate as follows:
General Chinese Company
Chinese Gambling Houses
Chinese Prostitution
Chinese Opium Resorts
Chinese Joss Houses
White Prostitution
The map and colors show only the first or
street floor of Chinatown and the occupancy
of same.
VOL. III.
JULY, 1899.

FIFTH SECTION. THE NEW YORK HERALD. PAGES 1 TO 16.

NEW YORK, SUNDAY, OCTOBER 10, 1897.—[COPYRIGHT, 1897, BY JAMES GORDON BENNETT.] PRICE FIVE CENTS.

SISTER LILY'S VISIT TO DARKEST NEW YORK.

LUMS OF NEW YORK,

Bad as We May Think Them,

DON'T EQUAL LONDON'S

ister Lily, the English Rescue Worker, Gives the Herald Her Impressions of Gotham's Purlieus.

ER VISIT TO AN OPIUM JOINT.

Miss Lily Dewhurst, known in London as Sister Lily, is a familiar figure in ...um" districts of the modern Babylon. For ten years she has been active in "res... work," principally among the degraded and fallen of her own sex in that great ..., and her noble efforts in that direction, which have been in connection with the ...est London Mission, of which the Rev. Hugh Price Hughes is the guiding spirit, ...e met with signal success.

Sister Lily is now in this country on her way to attend an international conven...n of "rescue workers" to be held at Toronto next month. She spent a week in New ...rk, during which she paid a visit of inspection to our "slums" with a view to com...ing them with the "slums" of her own city. After devoting an afternoon and night ...the purpose, Sister Lily prepared exclusively for the HERALD an account of the ...ces and persons and things she saw. That she was agreeably disappointed is evi...t in every paragraph of her paper. New York, she says, is far in advance of Lon...n in its general moral tone. Indeed, she asserts that the conditions and atmosphere ...the London "slums" do not, as far as she can observe, exist here.

Sister Lily's impressions, as she gives them to the HERALD, will certainly be very ...couraging to philanthropic minded men and women of this city whose zeal has con...buted so much toward the betterment of the lower stratum of New York's popula...n.

By Lily Dewhurst.

I HAVE just returned from a visit to your slums, and, contrasting them with the sights our London slums present, I find it hard to believe that we have really visited the worst quarters in your city.

"Have I really seen ...ur slums?" said I. "It seems impossible."

...here was a statement made in one of your ...rnals the other day to the effect that I ...d come here to try and reform the rescue ...rk in this great capital. Nothing has been ...rther from my thought. I have been a sis... in the West London Mission, of which the ...v. Hugh Price Hughes is superintendent, ... ten years. In that capacity I have touched ...e at many points. "Slum" life is one of the ...any, and I confess that I shrink very much ...m expressing any opinion which is based ...on such a superficial glance as a ride ...rough the slums affords. It seems to me ...is an opinion of no value.

Where Is Crime's Lurking Place?

...hear and read of the miseries of New ...rk, of the drink and gambling, of social ...e and wicked competition, of the bitter ...rife, the love of fight, the lust of gold, the ...rit that would as soon kill as injure.

...Where is it? All out of sight.

...For three hours we have been driving slowly through these lowest quarters. "Hell's Kitchen" is as utterly unlike its name as can be imagined; quiet, clean, orderly; neither want nor strife nor misery to be seen. Thence to the "Tenderloin," where we were most kindly received by the officers of police. We were introduced to the Captain, who told us that in this Nineteenth precinct there were 182 police on duty, and in it were all the principal theatres, hotels, clubs, &c., which brought a great variety of arrests.

The matron showed us the cells, &c., and then we were privileged to see the "Rogues' Gallery," which contains the photographs and histories of all the—I was going to say, graduated—scoundrels of the United States. One fine looking man of forty-five years of age has spent twenty-two years in prison.

Then we quickly passed into Broadway, where we saw elegantly dressed women busy shopping, and for a moment we lingered on the contrasts of life.

Through the Bowery.

Our next locality was the Bowery, which was comfortably busy with what seemed an artisan population. Grand street brought us into a foreign quarter—mostly Jews along Allen street and Canal street. Being a Jewish holiday we saw in the synagogues men robed and reading their sacred books, the women and children thronged the streets, all so happy and bright; rounds of games and groups of gossip.

Are these the city slums?

What a power there is in music, even in a street organ!

Our guide told us a sweet little story here. In one of the streets we were passing there lived a street sweeper, with only one little child of two summers, who was passionately fond of music. Listening at the window one cold, bitter day, she caught a chill, pneumonia set in and the little one died. The father was almost heartbroken, and the expression of his grief was found in the only tribute he could pay to the love of his darling for music. He took all his savings, and when the child was laid to rest a band of fifteen performers accompanied her to the grave, that the last offering and service might accord with the spirit of music in the little child.

A Peep at Baxter Street.

Next we passed through the Chinese quarter to Five Points, round Mulberry Bend and Paradise Park, everywhere noticing space and leisure. Baxter street holds a strange reputation as to the weakness or feebleness of men. They say this street is occupied by Jewish tailors who are so keen in their business that sometimes five men will seize an innocent passerby, tear off his coat, put him in a new one and insist upon his taking it and paying for it. The first, by a great effort of imagination, I might accept, but I cannot believe that a New Yorker has become so feeble as to fulfil the latter.

Catherine street soon brought us to Cherry Hill, where we saw a few poorer people in the streets. Then we passed "Newspaper Row," the leather factories, Varick street, West Broadway, Greenwich village and Sullivan street. Here we saw the negro quarter and Thompson street. At the corner of Bleecker street and Sullivan street we noted one of the finest model tenement blocks I have seen, here or in England. It is most striking, and if the interior equals the exterior, it may be truly a "model." We went through Washington square, and soon reached the Metropolitan Temple, from which we started.

And here, may I say, one word in appreciation of the great work Dr. Cadman is doing. From seven thousand to eight thousand people attend the various lectures and services every week. There is a breadth and tone about his organization which indicate a healthy, wholesome Christian life. I do not wonder that there have been accessions to the church of more than eight hundred members since Dr. Cadman became pastor, two and a half years ago.

A Nocturnal Excursion.

At eleven o'clock in the evening a small party, including Dr. Cadman, gave me the opportunity of seeing a little of the "fast" or "tough" life of your city.

Again I was struck with the quietness of the streets. The contrast between West London and New York at midnight was very great. I am ashamed to acknowledge that where we met one doubtful looking woman last night we should have met fifty in Piccadilly. We are so degraded that we permit our streets to be thronged by women loitering and lingering for "trade."

The "Haymarket," they said, was unusually quiet. So we went along Broadway into the noted "gardens," where I saw the vice which has been shunted out of sight. Here is where you meet this terrible evil, and here you find that in order to maintain it saloons where drink may be obtained are necessary.

People may sneer at the bigotry of narrow temperance reformers, but the man who holds the loosest views would admit that such a sight as the crowded, hilarious, gay company at the Broadway gardens last night would be impossible if drink were not supplied. At the bottom of nine-tenths of our social misery is drink. It provides and maintains almost every other vice.

Visit to an Opium Joint.

Then we visited Chinatown. Passing along the Bowery, through the courtesy of a friend of one in the party, we gained an entrance into one of the "opium joints." Outside quiet, order and peace prevailed. Inside a perfect hell.

A long, low room, clouds of smoke, men, out of whom opium had eaten their last trait of manhood. Reclining on a wooden platform at the end of the room was a Chinaman, cooking his opium. Life for him centred round that pill. He turned and fondled it. His dull eye glistened as he watched the process. Then, when the right moment arrived, literally "done to a turn," he drew in the poisonous drug with slow, long breath, then gave it out, in clouds of smoke and satisfaction to himself and of offensiveness and sadness to us.

It was told that he had been lying there the whole day; that he neither eats nor moves, but lies, like a pig, with no thought above the fodder—for him there is no care, for as long as he has breath he will have opium.

Sister Lily's First Impressions.

My first general impressions are these:—

First—That in New York the outer conditions under which the poor live do not approach the conditions of the London poor.

Your streets are broader, there is more space, there is not the apparent overcrowding, nor the number of congested buildings. There did not seem a street through which a carriage could not pass.

If I were to take a visitor through our London slums we should have to leave the carriage and walk—some of our courts and alleys are so narrow that you might shake hands from opposite windows.

And yet, I read that the result of the investigations of your Tenement House Committee proved that a condition of congestion and misery prevails such as even the older cities of Europe cannot parallel. These are the actual figures:—

"The committee found 15,726 families, numbering 67,897 persons, with an average of four and one-third persons to 234.4 square feet of floor area. Some idea of these figures can be obtained by remarking that one room, 12x24, contains 288 square feet in floor area."

Second—That you cannot have the same kind of poverty.

I most carefully observed the faces of the people. There was no hunger written upon them.

Those who know our poor easily detect the lines which starvation prints upon the faces of those who are chronically underfed.

Apparent Spirit of Happiness.

Third—That there is a spirit of happiness in your slums which is absent in ours.

The women appear brighter. They have not the hard, beaten, haggard look that ours have. If it be true that "the English take their pleasures sadly" it is infinitely more true that they bear the heavier burdens of life more sadly.

Fourth—That there was an absence of rags.

But one child was only partially clothed. In three hours we saw only five children without shoes or stockings.

Fifth—That there was an absence of drunkenness.

Though we passed many—and I carefully watched every saloon—I only saw one woman inside and only one man really drunk.

These visits have been to me full of interest. The result of the one in the afternoon gave me great pleasure. ... true it is that evil exist... and not in the environme...

In many ... you a...

HYPNOTIC HOTBED.

Philadelphia Has Established a Cult in the Mystic Art.

THE LEADER IS A WOMAN

PHILADELPHIA is a veritable hotbed of hypnotism. The staid old city, over which William Penn casts his benign influence from his lofty perch atop the great marble City Hall, has developed a strange mania for the study and practice of the occult science, if so it may be called. Noted surgeons have not only become converts to hypnotism, but almost daily employ it in their work.

The most remarkable member of this cult—for it really amounts to a cult in Philadelphia—is Mrs. K. D. S. Armbruster. Only last Tuesday evening, in the presence of several of the Quaker City's leading psychological authorities, she performed a feat in hypnotism which proved her remarkable powers to be little less than supernatural. A man and a woman were both hypnotized by Mrs. Armbruster, who succeeded in accomplishing a feat in pictorially descriptive telepathy. The subjects were Edward Simmonds and a Mrs. Joynes.

Mrs. K. D. S. Armbruster was formerly Miss Kismet Guyer. Never but once has she been hypnotized, but she has since possessed a wonderful hypnotic power over others. She is looked upon with something akin to rever... by those who have witnessed and bear testimony to her strange power.

Mrs. Armbruster First Hypnotized.

The first and only person who ever hypnotized Mrs. Armbruster was Michael Kegrize, Jr., who is professor of music at Ogontz Seminary, the fashionable school for young ladies, and which was formerly the country residence of Jay Cooke in his palmy days. Kegrize wields tremendous magnetic power over his pupils, and his great success as a teacher of piano playing is said to be due to this. Eight years ago he hypnotized Mrs. Armbruster and communicated to her the post-hypnotic suggestion that she would never afterward be hypnotized by any one else.

MIDNIGHT IN A RESTAURANT

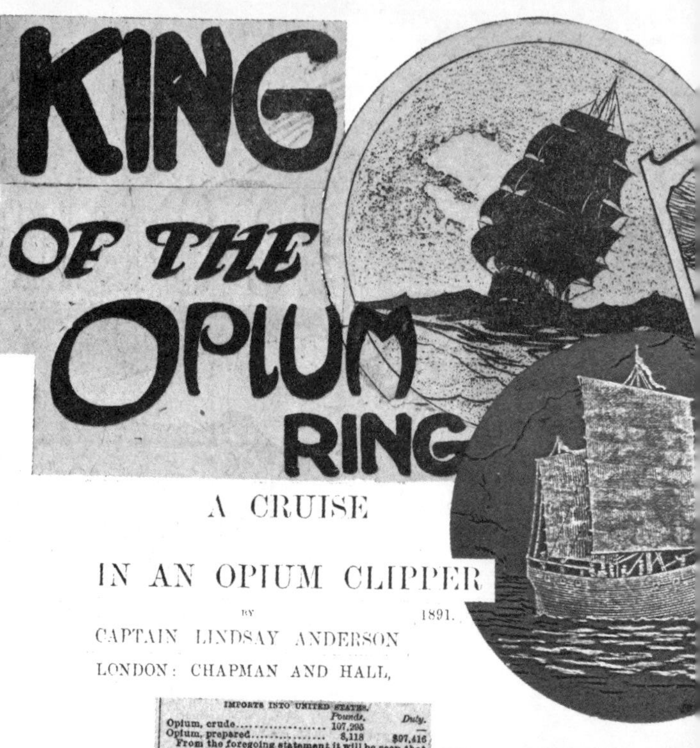

KING OF THE OPIUM RING
A CRUISE
IN AN OPIUM CLIPPER
BY
1891.
CAPTAIN LINDSAY ANDERSON
LONDON: CHAPMAN AND HALL,

By J. GORDON SMITH.

Died at sea, July 29th, W. W. Whaley, an indigent citizen from Manila. Remains were buried at sea.—Extract from log of U. S. Army transport Thomas.

SCANT epitaph for the King of the Opium Ring, is it not? Old-timers on the Pacific Coast will recall Whaley and his fleet schooner Halycon, built at Benicia for the late Hugh Tevis, millionaire of San Francisco, who decided he did not want the craft when a salt sea swept her deck off the Golden Gate. In his day Whaley was notorious enough, and so too was the Halycon, now lying among the sealing schooners anchored at Victoria, B. C., and known as the sealing schooner Vera. It is many years, though, since the King of the Opium Ring decamped from Honolulu, leaving the Halcyon swinging at her anchor until a new master was sent from Victoria, B. C., Whaley taking with him $50,000 profits of a cargo of opium landed on Oahu, Hawaiian islands. He took passage on a Pacific Mail liner and was in Yokohama before news reached Victoria by mail—there were no Pacific cables in those days. At Yokohama he bought an interest in a prominent hotel, not a hundred yards from the hatoba and with his gay cummerbund about his waist, his white drill clothes and pith helmet he was for some years one of the notables of Yokohama's colony of exiles. He was an adventurer still, and prospered. With the occupation of the Philippine islands by the United States he went to Manila where he bought a saloon and cafe, known as the Merchants' Club and situated on the Pasig river. The Merchants' Club was the rendezvous of many adventurers and many a tale was to be heard there of gun-running and other contraband enterprizes which governments frown upon. With the passing of years, however, Whaley's ill-gotten gains vanished quickly, for he was an open-handed spender, and for the last few years he has been tampering with the free lunch coutner where he once was proprietor. Then some months ago, broke and broken in health, he applied to the Quartermaster-General at Manila for passage to the place of his birth in California, as an indigent citizen—and died on the way home.

One of Whaley's Partners.

Living in Victoria now is a companion of Whaley in some of his enterprises of his palmy days when he was King of the Opium Ring, and from him the writer learned of details of some exciting opium-running trips of the smuggler Halycon.

"When I left home in July, 1887," said Captain Felix—that name will do as well as any other—"I went to San Francisco and ran across Whaley. He was an ex-customs officers of California. 'Hello,' says he, 'I'm going to send a vessel trading to the Arctic, do you want to go?' He took me over to Sausalito and we watched a schooner being provisioned; but she didn't belong to Whaley. He was giving me a steer, and to cut the story short, he was trying me out to see if I was in for a smuggling cruise. I was on.

"He bought the schooner Halycon from Robert Morrow for $6000. She was dirt cheap. Hugh Tevis owned her, but he got cold feet when a sea came over her deck when he took her out, and, although he paid $25,000 to have her built at Benicia, he was willing to give her away. It was August 9, 1887, when we left the Golden Gate to start our smuggling trips which soon made the Halycon notorious and secured for Whaley the title of 'King of the Opium Ring.' We came to Victoria and when we sailed into the straits came to anchor off Sooke, where Johnnie Cottsford and E. W. McLean came off with a sloop.

"They gave us the sign as they came off, and we replied. Then we put into Sooke harbor and anchored in shelter behind the spit, where we transhipped the 'coal oil.' There were 1600 pounds of opium in those coal oil cases, all that could be supplied from Victoria and Vancouver opium factories. The local dope factories were unable to supply us with as much opium as we wanted, and Li Hop & Co. of 505 Dupont street, sent to China for a supply. We were ten days at Sooke and then we beat out of the straits and made a fast run down to Drake's bay in four days.

"Things had been well fixed, and we had some of our men waiting at Drake's bay for us. They pretended to be fishermen, going out now and then with the sloop Flora, a forty-ton craft. With the Flora the man we called "Jack," and Manuel, a Greek, came off to the Halcyon and took the dope ashore. The cases of 'coal oil' were transferred at night and taken to a cache we had arranged on the San Bruno road in a Chinese vegetable garden. Wagons were brought there and we hauled the stuff right into Chinatown at San Francisco. We made a good thing of it, though, for all we paid was from $6 to $6 50 a pound, and it sold for $12 per pound at San Francisco.

Did Not Connect.

"Some one tipped the thing to the Collector, but in the meantime we had sailed from Drake's bay on our way back to Victoria for another load of dope. This time we took 1900 pounds and would have made a big profit, but we didn't make connections. The Flora met us in Bodega bay with Jack and Manuel. We made a leisurely trip, having learned at Victoria that the Collector was watching for us at San Francisco, and we got between fifty and sixty sealskins, so that it would seem that we were sealing and had put in for water. We managed to get the dope transferred to a fishing boat Jack brought and it was put off as coal oil at a fishing station where it was transferred overland to a Sacramento-river boat. We ran in then and landed our sealskins. In November we tied up at Antioch and laid there until April.

"Somebody started something in San Francisco at that time, and numbers of newspaper reporters, customs men and others came down and looked us over—but there was nothing dc ng. The dope reached Chinatown again all right, but the expenses were greater this time and although we made a fair profit, it was not as large as we anticipated. We got ready to sail north in April, 1888, and told the reporters who came aboard that we had been fortunate in getting the boat from Mr. Tevis, and intended to take her to Victoria and fit her out as a sealer. They made columns under the caption, "Fine Yacht Becomes a Sealer."

"Whaley concluded at that time it was better to take a layoff for a while, and when we were ready to sail we got a tugboat and towed out. We really became a sealer then. Metcalf was captain and Johnnie Cottsford mate, and when we cast about for a crew we were overwhelmed with applications for berths. Men left their work ashore and came aboard, thinking we were going on another dope-running cruise. When they found that we were really going sealing, they were disgusted, and there was lots of trouble on board. After a cruise of six or eight weeks we dropped anchor in Victoria harbor with thirteen skins on board.

Over a Ton of Opium.

"We were tied up at Victoria several months, and then, in August, 1889, we started business again. Whaley as usual planned the cruise thoroughly. We got 2400 pounds of opium from the factories in Chinatown at Victoria and sent the lot cased in coal oil tins to Prevost island on a sloop. I went to Prevost island first to arrange for landing the opium, and ran short of grub. I shot some pigs eventually and got some pork, which I used until the sloop came. The schooner cleared from Victoria in ballast, clearing for sealing. She put into San Juan and we boated the dope to her, and she went off loaded with 2400 pounds. We had no crew. After the previous trip everyone seemed to fight shy of us, and we couldn't go around with a brass band to let them know we were running opium.

"Whaley put into Dodge's cove, Berkeley sound, to get Indians as sailormen. They were suspicious of us, especially when Whaley offered $30 and then $40 a month. We told them we were taking coal oil to a lighthouse. Finally we got some Indians and started. We were jolly near swamped in a storm, encountered off the Columbia river that voyage. It was a terrible gale, and we suffered. Water was deep in the cabin, and we sat on the bunks to keep clear of it. It was at that time that the big hurricane took place at Apia.

"This was our hoodoo trip. Whaley had made arrangements for Galloway and Manuel to meet us as usual, but the storm delayed us, and when we got into Drake's bay and made our signals there were none in response. We fooled around there six weeks, and no one came off to meet us. I left the schooner and went to San Francisco, where I stayed at the Baldwin. I couldn't find Jack and Manuel, and sent word to Whaley asking him to come in and get a sloop. He brought the Halcyon off the Farallones and wanted to sink the opium there, but found that scheme was not practical. We waited for some time, and then Whaley and an Indian came ashore. We were unable to do anything, and then went to Drake's bay, where we again landed. It began to blow hard after we left the schooner, and we were capsized on the beach, losing our grub, except some soaked soda crackers. We had a long walk to get to the station, and we had an awful night—hungry, fatigued and with blistered feet. I draw a curtain over that night, but I shall never forget it.

Had Schooner Scared Away.

"It seems that the Halycon had started north without landing the opium, Laing having been afraid of being seized after Whaley left. She went to Village island, Dodge's cove, where we got the Indians, and when she arrived with one of the Indians missing the natives raised a row. Laing took the opium and hid it in a cache he made on one of the islands of Barkley sound. The fact
Indians was missing from the Halyc
however, raised no end of a row. T
father and some others took a big
for Victoria. They arrived soon afte
San Francisco, and there was quit
father and son met.

"After a while we got the sch
again and went to Barkley sound to
Jim Harvey and Bill Johnson, wh
drowned, came out and joined us
Sooke with a sloop, which brought n
ing our total on board 2650 pounds.
Bodega bay with this and transferr
isfactorily this time to Jack and Ma
landed the stuff on the beach, thir
capsized when a Whitehall boat turr
fore dawn. Daylight came before
stuff away, and people came along
the stuff was. Some people stopped
to ask about the cases, and I sai
what it was.

"'Opium,' they said, and I didn't
good guess they made. I got a bugg
and went to get wagons. Didn't we
ing of those wagons? I went to see
been made of the landing. As far
no report had been made, but I didn
We hid in the tules for five days
and finally put it in boats, covered w
ran down into San Francisco bay
Angel island at sundown, and then s
bay. Two wagons were ready waitir
customs man and a Chinese be
them. We got a fright before we
A cutter started in our direction
in it, but they didn't come near. I
only our guilty conscience that ma
that they were headed for us.

The Last Trip.

"After we landed that lot of o
came too warm for us in San Fr
framed up that Honolulu trip, whi
Whaley made. We got a lot of p
interested and bought a big carg
got it down to Honolulu all right a
to an anchor with the Halycon off th
He went ashore and made quite a s
lulu. He was put up at the club
ways able to put up a swell front
with any one, could Whaley. He
old King Kalakaua and was quite
waiian society. How he fixed thing
but this I do know, he had fires
shores at the time arranged and w
load of dope ashore to a ranch ow
lishman. We cached it there unt
sent, and it was carted to Chinato
Then Whaley went back to the clu

"He lived pretty high then, and
messages to him wanting to know
home was to be made, when they
pay, etc. To all such messages W
that he had not yet effected a settlem
one fine morning that, with $50,000,
mail steamer for Yokohama. We w
by the Canadian-Australian steamer
tain was sent from Victoria for the
was sold on arrival to Captain J. G.
and she became a sealing schoone
such to the present time.

"There was a mad crowd in Vic
who had put up money found how W
them. He, however, lived a lotus l
spending freely. He bought an int
nent hotel, and was one of the A
Yokohama, prominent in every hap
Spanish-American War he drifted
and was proprietor of the Merchant
Pasig at Manila. Of late years he
both in wealth and health, until a
became a dock walloper at Manila, a
year got a free passage home as an
the Army trnsport Thomas. He
verely from Bright's disease, and
died and was buried at sea.

OPIUM HABIT NOW FOSTERED.

SEPTEMBER 19, 1891.

How the McKinley Law Has Stimulated the Smuggling of the Drug from Canada.

AN IMMENSE TRAFFIC.

Brought Across the Border in Steamers, Canoes or Light Spring Wagons.

NO QUESTIONS ASKED.

[SPECIAL CORRESPONDENCE OF THE HERALD.]

WINNIPEG, Man., Sept. 11, 1891.—The good citizens of the United States will be surprised to learn that one of the provisions of the most important law enacted by their late Billion Dollar Congress—the McKinley tariff I refer to—has opened the way for the perpetration of a fraud upon the revenues of their government amounting to considerably over a million dollars annually.

They will be shocked to know that this particular clause of that same law is fostering and encouraging one of the most horrible and deadly vices of the century—a vice that is rapidly fastening itself upon thousands of the people in the great cities of the Union.

They will be amused at the spectacle presented of a great branch of the Internal Revenue Service, created by that same law, with rules, regulations and preparations galore, and—

Not one dollar's worth of business transacted within the year under the law!

At the time of the passage of the McKinley bill this particular clause of the act appeared unreasonable and inexplicable.

Its enactment has resulted in a fraud upon the Treasury and an outrage upon the morals of the nation.

It has caused the smuggling of hundreds of thousands of dollars' worth of prepared opium into the United States.

It has turned every Chinese laundry into a manufactory and every pigtailed and almond-eyed Celestial in the United States into a manufacturer of prepared opium for smoking purposes in violation of law.

The fraud upon the revenue can be approximated in dollars and cents; the effect upon the morals of the people can be but vaguely guessed—surmised—with a shudder of horror for its possible extent.

Prior to the enactment of the McKinley tariff the law relating to the importation of opium placed a duty upon that drug as follows:—

"Opium, crude, containing nine per cent and over of morphia, $1 per pound.

"Opium, prepared for smoking, $10 per pound."

Under this law the imports were extensive. For comparison I will call your attention to the figures for the three months ending September 30, 1890, and immediately preceding the taking effect of the McKinley law:—

IMPORTS INTO UNITED STATES.

	Pounds.	Duty.
Opium, crude	77,015	$77,015
Opium, prepared	16,652	166,520

As changed by the late Billion Dollar Congress the law now reads:—

"Opium, crude, free of duty.

"Opium, prepared, $12 per pound."

Under this law the imports for the three months ending March 30, 1891, were:—

IMPORTS INTO UNITED STATES.

	Pounds.	Duty.
Opium, crude	107,295	—
Opium, prepared	8,118	$97,416

From the foregoing statement it will be seen that during the year there will be legally brought into the United States for consumption by the inhabitants thereof nearly five hundred thousand pounds of crude opium.

But that is not all. Customs officers of the Dominion government estimate that at least one hundred thousand pounds of prepared opium, worth $2,000,000 in the United States, will be smuggled from Canada and British Columbia across the border into the States.

This state of affairs is due directly to the McKinley bill and the Billion Dollar Congress.

The only explanation—which in no sense explains—that the tariff tinkers offered for this most remarkable legislation is conveyed in a brief note, which may be found in the report of the Ways and Means Committee accompanying the presentation of the McKinley bill to the House of Representatives. It is as follows:—

"If crude opium be put on the free list, as is proposed, it is presumed that opium will be manufactured in the United States for smoking purposes. Sections 34 to 38 inclusive contemplate such manufacture and provide for an internal tax thereon with necessary safeguards."

A NEW INDUSTRY.

After thus "presuming" that opium would be manufactured in the United States for smoking purposes and create a "home industry," the committee found it necessary to levy an internal revenue tax upon the manufactured article, so the following provisions were included in the bill to regulate the "new industry:"—

"SECTION 36.—That an internal revenue tax of $10 per pound shall be levied and collected upon all opium manufactured in the United States for smoking purposes, and no person shall engage in such manufacture who is not a citizen of the United States, and who has not given the bond required by the Commissioner of Internal Revenue.

"SEC. 37.—That every manufacturer of such opium shall file with the Collector of Internal Revenue of the district in which his manufactory is located such notices, inventories and bonds, shall keep such books and render such returns of material and products, shall put up such signs and affix such number to his factory, and conduct his business under such surveillance of officers and agents as the Commissioner of Internal Revenue, with the approval of the Secretary of the Treasury, may by regulation require. But the bond required of such manufacturer shall be with sureties satisfactory to the Collector of Internal Revenue and in a penal sum of not less than $5,000, and the sum of said bond may be increased from time to time and additional sureties required at the discretion of the Collector or under instructions of the Commissioner of Internal Revenue.

"SEC. 38.—That all prepared smoking opium imported into the United States shall, before removal from the Custom House, be duly stamped in such manner as to denote that the duty thereon has been paid, and that all opium manufactured in the United States for smoking purposes before being removed from the place of manufacture, whether for consumption or storage, shall be duly stamped in such permanent manner as to denote the payment of the internal revenue tax thereon.

"SEC. 39.—That the provisions of existing laws governing the engraving, issue, sale, accountability, effacement, cancellation and destruction of stamps relating to tobacco and snuff, as far as applicable, are hereby made to apply to stamps provided for by the preceding section.

"SEC. 40.—That a penalty of not more than $1,000 or imprisonment not more than one year, or both, in the discretion of the Court, shall be imposed for each and every violation of the preceding sections of this act relating to opium by any person or persons, and all prepared smoking opium, wherever found within the United States without stamps required by this act, shall be forfeited."

The committee were right in presuming that opium would be manufactured for smoking purposes in the United States. It is being manufactured at the rate of 500,000 pounds a year.

But when they calculated to collect an internal revenue tax of $10 per pound on it they reckoned without their host.

What has been the result of this legislation?

The Honorable Commissioner of Internal Revenue at the Treasury Department in Washington will tell you:—

"**Not a single application has been made to this bureau for license to manufacture opium, and not a dollar has been collected from that source.**"

Yet, in the space of three months, there has been brought into the United States, duty free, through the United States custom houses, under sanction of law, 107,295 pounds of crude opium.

Every pound of it has been made into smoking opium in the United States in violation of law.

The special agents of the Treasury Department will tell you that thousands of pounds of it have been prepared in Mott street, New York city; vast quantities in San Francisco, New Orleans, Denver, Galveston, Seattle, Tacoma, Portland, St. Paul, Chicago, the mining towns of the Rockies and the Pacific coast—in fact, everywhere that there is a group of Chinamen.

The Billion Dollar Congress could hardly have enacted a happier law than they did for the benefit and delight of the men and women who "hit the pipe" and the Chinese population, to whom opium is more than bread.

NOBODY WANTED A CHANGE.

Why was the law made thus? No one outside of that charmed circle of tariff tinkers who conceived the bill can tell. There is no record of it. While the Ways and Means Committee were hatching the bill they gave audience to manufacturers and patrons of "home industries," of every class and character. These men went before the commit
and gave the reasons why the tariff should
raised. The testimony of these gentlemen w
afterward printed by the committee and fills
volume of over a thousand pages.

There is not one word about opium, however,
the thousand and odd pages. Nobody advocat
the change in the tariff on opium.

I will now describe the process of manufact
ing opium for smoking purposes, and the mann
in which it is smuggled into the United States fr
British Columbia and Canada.

The opium is brought in its crude form fro
China and India to Vancouver, B. C., consigned
the Chinese merchants and opium boilers at th
place and at Moose Jaw, Northwest Territor
There are twelve or fifteen extensive boiling esta
lishments in Vancouver and several down the li
of the Canadian Pacific Railroad engaged in redu
ing great quantities of opium to a prepared st
for smoking.

When the opium is prepared it resembles a thic
dark colored paste. It is packed in five tael c
per cans holding half a pound each. This form
packing is adopted to render the transport of t
"stuff" easy.

In Vancouver there are organized syndicat
of men, with considerable capital invested, e
gaged solely in smuggling opium into the Unit
States.

Her Majesty's Customs officers advise me that
least $2,000,000 worth of opium is "handled" b
these syndicates annually.

That represents a fraud of $1,200,000 upon th
revenues of the United States governme
annually.

My informers base their estimate upon th
annual imports of crude opium and the output
the British Columbia boilers.

The smuggling syndicates have agents in Sa
Francisco, Seattle, Denver, Helena, Montrea
Toronto, Chicago, Detroit, New York, St. Paul an
in all of the border towns, as Grand Forks, Bott
neau, St. Johns, Crookston Halleck, Fort Benton
&c.

They also have agents in Winnipeg, Regina, Cal
gary and all of the stations on the Canadian Pacifi
Railway and its branch lines that form points o
departure for "the States."

THE SMUGGLING.

The most popular mode of smuggling is to pac
$3,000 worth of prepared opium in an ordinar
trunk, which one of the agents checks as his bag
gage. To avoid suspicion he will check it as far a
Calgary, where he calls for it. It is then checked
the next day by another agent and carried to Win
nipeg. This is called "breaking the checks" and i
a good scheme, as it prevents a trunk being fol
lowed or "spotted" while *en route*.

The Winnipeg agent takes the trunk down one of
the three lines of railroad and unloads at a station
a few miles from the United States border. Here
he communicates with another agent, who has a
light spring wagon and a double team of flyers.

The trunk next makes its appearance at a railway station in North Dakota or Minnesota, from whence it goes to the distributing depot at St. Paul or Chicago.

That is the quick route, what might be called "the Smuggler's Fast Express." This route is used for quick delivery of small quantities.

In a previous letter I described to you the unprotected condition of the border on the American side, which renders such traffic possible and profitable.

I am informed that immense quantities of opium are now being packed in convenient shape ready to be smuggled into the United States during the coming fall and winter in wheat and grain shipped in bulk, when the great wheat crop is moved. The greater portion of this, I am told, will enter the United States at lake ports.

A heavy traffic is done in the aggregate of small lots of opium smuggled across the border from Toronto, Montreal, Windsor and eastern Canadian points. The "stuff" is shipped in 100 pound cases to those cities, broken into small lots and sneaked across.

The porters of Pullman cars running between Canada and the United States take over many thousand pounds during the year, and make a tidy profit from it. They can easily secrete five or ten pounds every trip in their cars.

The most open traffic in opium smuggling is carried on in the region of the Lake of the Woods and the Rainy Lake River. Absolutely no objection is interposed by the United States government to the traffic in this section.

The "stuff" is unloaded from the Canadian Pacific Railroad at Rat Portage and carried aboard a small steamboat which plies the Lake of the Woods and the Rainy Lake River. An agent accompanies it and simply throws a tarpaulin over it. No other concealment is necessary.

It is transported to Fort Francis at the head of navigation on the Rainy Lake River. It's go-as-you-please here. Revenue duties are not thought of—that is, on the American side. On the Canadian side a vigilant force of officers prevent American whiskey and tobacco from coming over.

A fleet of canoes manned by half-breeds and French Canadians now meet the agent. The "stuff" is quickly transferred, and in charge of another agent commences a canoe journey up the Rainy Lake River to Vermillion River, thence to Vermillion Lake and across the lake to the town of Tower, Minn., terminus of the Duluth and Iron Range Railway.

There is nothing to hinder. There are no United States Customs officers to ask embarrassing questions, not even an occasional mounted patrolman to dodge. The traffic goes on and will continue until the United States government adopts measures such as Canada enforces.

BURIED AT SEA
AS AN
INDIGENT

A PARADISE FOR SMUGGLERS.

Over One Million Dollars' Worth of Opium Annually Brought Into the United States from British Columbia.

CHINAMEN COMING IN DROVES.

Utterly Useless Precautions of the Treasury Department Against an Organized and Lucrative Business.

HOW IT IS MANAGED.

Tortuous Inland Channels Offering Scores of Paths for the Adventurers from Victoria to the State of Washington.

CANADA PROFITS AT OUR EXPENSE.

A Large Fleet of Vessels Maintained, Good Telegraphic Service for the Law Breakers—One Steamer and Slow Wires for the Government.

(From the Special Correspondent of the New York Herald.)

VICTORIA, B. C., Oct. 1, 1891.—The question of the smuggling of Chinese and opium across the Northwestern border of the United States will undoubtedly be one of the first to receive the attention of the coming Congress and will take its place among the most important subjects of legislation.

There are three pre-eminent questions which must be taken up by Congress:—

First—The abuses of the pension system, which the HERALD has so fully exposed.

Second—The fraudulent census that Mr. Porter and his aids have foisted upon the country at a cost of so many millions of dollars.

Third—The evasions of the Revenue and Anti-Chinese laws by the wholesale smuggling of opium and coolies across the border from British Columbia, causing a loss of revenue to the United States of over ONE MILLION DOLLARS annually.

A petty handful of brave men placed by the Treasury Department are exerting to their utmost to check the traffic, but they are as a corporal's guard confronting a regiment.

One revenue cutter with a crew of only eight men plies night and day on the Sound under command of a vigilant and energetic captain, who realizes the situation and does his best to cope with it, but the distance to be covered is so great that it is impossible to protect more than a small portion of the waterway, while a dozen routes available for the smugglers are necessarily left unguarded.

OPIUM SMUGGLING.

I will give you an idea of the amount of the traffic in prepared opium alone which is carried on by smugglers in these waters. The city of Victoria is the headquarters of the opium manufacturers. There are ten opium manufactories in this city, running night and day, working up the crude opium into a state necessary for smoking purposes. These factories are owned by rich Chinese merchants and return enormous profits to their owners annually.

In company with one of the principal Chinese merchants engaged in manufacturing prepared opium I went to Her Majesty's Custom House at Victoria and made application for a statement of the amount of crude or raw opium imported into Victoria from China during the last fiscal year.

Following is the statement, official, copied from the records of Her Majesty's customs:—

Importations crude opium, fiscal year ending June 30:—

	Pounds.	Value.
July, August, September	26,019	$60,942
October, November, December	37,499	89,029
January, February, March	39,186	91,554
April, May, June	22,607	55,239
Total	125,311	$296,764

When I read this statement I asked the customs officer who had kindly furnished it to tell me what use was made of this large amount of opium.

"It was probably all manufactured into smoking opium by the Chinese firms in Victoria engaged in that business," he replied.

Then I asked my friend, the Chinese merchant who had accompanied me, to tell me how much prepared or smoking opium could be manufactured from this amount of the crude material.

"About seventy thousand pounds," he replied.

"How much of these seventy thousand pounds of prepared opium was legally entered for export at Her Majesty's Custom House?" I asked the customs officer.

"Not one pound!" he promptly replied.

"What became of it, then?" I asked.

"It was smuggled into the United States," he replied, in an offhand way.

"Just so," remarked my Chinese friend, with a corroborative nod of his head and a smile of gratification.

The customs duty on these seventy thousand pounds of opium, if legally entered into the United States, would have been $840,000.

Therefore, the smugglers stole exactly $840,000 from the United States government.

I am aware that this word "stole" will grate upon the feelings of some estimable people of Victoria, Tacoma, Seattle, Port Townsend and other cities, who are said to be engaged in aiding the smugglers, but stole is the legal interpretation of their transaction.

It will be remembered that the foregoing figures relate only to the city of Victoria. There are opium manufactories in Nanaimo, Vancouver, New Westminster and other towns in British Columbia, all engaged in preparing opium for the American market.

The fraud upon the United States customs revenues will, therefore, amount to at least one million five hundred thousand dollars per year and is increasing every year.

SMUGGLING OF CHINAMEN.

Every incoming ship from China, which touches at Victoria or Vancouver brings on an average about three hundred Chinamen, who pay the British government $50 apiece for the privilege of landing.

Over ninety per cent of them eventually find their way into the United States in violation of the Chinese Exclusion act. The majority of the intruders find entrance into the United States through the Puget Sound district. In the mining camps of Idaho and Montana, along the lines of new railroads building in Washington, I have seen these fellows at work in the very garb they had worn less than a month previous in China, showing every indication of having but recently entered this country.

Glance for a moment at the map of Puget Sound and vicinity published herewith and let me explain to you the happy physical conditions which exist to make this section a paradise for smugglers. Notice what a vast extent of shore line the State of Washington presents upon Puget Sound and the Strait of Juan de Fuca. It is a shore line of some twelve hundred miles. Perceive how the coast is indented with bays, inlets and coves, furnishing anchorage and hiding places for the smugglers.

NATURAL OPPORTUNITIES.

What better natural advantage could the smugglers ask than the numerous islands in the northern part of the sound that make an almost continuous land highway between the British Island of Vancouver, upon which is situated Victoria, and the mainland of Washington.

The islands are separated by narrow, winding

glers upon the hills and at night, when an outfit is to be smuggled, their signal lights can be seen flashing from headland to headland.

The mainland of Washington is also heavily pine clad, but traversed by numerous trails and easily travelled. On the line of the railroad which skirts the eastern shore of Puget Sound, between the cities of Tacoma and Seattle on the south and the town of Blaine on the international boundary at the north, are many small towns easily reached from the water. Chinamen are found in all of them and the smugglers have agents in those places to hide the cargoes and ship them to their destination.

West of Port Townsend along the Strait of Juan de Fuca, on the peninsula, are several small towns and between them numerous safe landing places for the smugglers. A great many Chinamen are employed cutting timber in the pine belt of the peninsula and their huts are scattered all along the trails.

To sum up the situation, the only thing necessary for the smugglers to do is to cross a strip of water, ranging in width from one and one-half miles to ten miles, at any chosen point on a water front of several hundred miles.

Having gained the mainland the opium is easily spirited away, the Chinamen mingle with their countrymen, it being impossible to distinguish the newcomers from the old ones, and another fraud upon the government is consummated.

THE HEADQUARTERS.

The city of Victoria is the headquarters of the smugglers and their point of departure for the American shore. No secret is made of the traffic here. Every one knows about it and outside of the customs officials the majority of the citizens countenance it. The sentiment of the people of the town is favorable to the traffic and they will lend aid to a smuggler before they will give information to the officers. It has not been a week since preparations for carrying over a schooner load of one hundred Chinamen to the American side were carried on so openly that the British Collector of Customs was constrained to take cognizance of the fact and warned the captain of the schooner that he would seize his schooner if he made a false clearance from Victoria.

The smuggling fleet of Victoria consists of some forty or more clipper sloops and small schooners. They all carry a great breadth of canvas, are good sea boats and swift as the wind. Their navigators are men who are thoroughly familiar with every rock and passage in Puget Sound, the set of the tide, and could pick up a given point in a thick night without the variation of a boat's length.

The smuggling fleet is ostensibly engaged in fishing. Every one of them carries a bundle of nets piled up forward of the foremast, with a bucket handy to wet them down occasionally. As a rule the men who run the cargoes of opium do not own the opium, but handle it for another man, getting a compensation by the pound for smuggling it.

The opium ring in Victoria maintains a perfect system of communication between the mainland of Washington and the smuggling fleet. Every movement of the United States revenue cutter and of the special agents of the customs service is watched at Port Townsend, Seattle and Tacoma and reported by telegraph to Victoria. The opium ring has its spies in all of the towns along Puget Sound, and they are aware of the movements of the United States officers as soon as they are attempted. The telegraph works promptly for them. On the other hand, the Collector of Customs at Port Townsend tells me that telegrams from Americans in Victoria giving information of intended raids of smugglers frequently reach his office several hours after the hour had passed in which the expedition landed on the American shore.

HOW IT IS DONE.

The United States revenue cutter Walcott usually makes her anchorage at Port Townsend. When she weighs anchor and steams away in a given direction the information is flashed over the wires to Victoria, and the next day comes rumor of an expedition landed somewhere in an opposite direction from the scene of her cruising.

When the word reaches Victoria that a favorable opportunity exists for landing a smuggling expedition, the sloops that are to be engaged in it stand out of the harbor in the afternoon, with their nets displayed, "going after fish." They work their way around to the eastward, and before nightfall come to anchor in the little bay back of Discovery Island or in Finley Inlet. Before sundown a man on Discovery Island headland sweeps the sound with a powerful glass for sight of a suspicious sail.

In the meantime the cargo of Chinamen or opium has been shipped out of Victoria and carried overland to the appointed rendezvous. It is quickly loaded aboard, and then the anchor is weighed, the big mainsail set and the clipper little craft fills away and stands off down the sound with the speed of a race horse before the fresh night breeze that comes booming in from the Pacific.

Refer to the map now and you will see there are twenty different routes to follow and as many points of destination. They can follow the straits between the islands and land in Bellingham Bay, near the towns of Whatcom, Fairhaven or Anacortes, finding easy access to the railroad; they can bear away to the southeastward and after threading Deception Pass make a landing in Skagitt Bay or up the Skagitt River, or they can fill away to the southward

dives.

Information of the intended landing reached the Collector of Customs at Port Townsend late in the evening. He immediately detailed two of his officers to patrol the beach and keep a sharp lookout for the expedition.

It was a bright moonlight night, clear and calm, with no surf running on the beach to imperil a small boat. For several hours the officers tramped the beach without observing any signs of smugglers. Finally about three o'clock in the morning they caught sight of a little steamer slipping out of a cove in Port Discovery Bay and making off under a full head of steam.

TOO LATE.

The officers rushed down the beach, but the Chinamen had clambered up the cliffs and were safe in the timber. The only traces of them were footprints in the sand and a small ladder standing against the cliff.

The revenue cutter had gone to Tacoma the previous day, and of course her departure was known in Victoria before she cleared the harbor of Port Townsend.

The smugglers have caches and huts in the interior of San Juan Island, Lopez Island and Orcas Island, where they secrete their contraband goods and Chinamen, until safe opportunities occur for putting them ashore on the mainland.

These islands are less than two miles distant from the islands on the British side of the international boundary line, and are the favorite haunts of smugglers. They are halfway stations on the smugglers' route between Vancouver Island and the landing places in Bellingham Bay and Skagitt Bay, on the coast of Washington.

The United States revenue cutter Walcott is the laughing stock and butt of derision of the smugglers of Victoria. They all know what a slow thing she is, and they only avoid her for the reason that they know she can send away a small boat full of fighting jack tars, and that Captain Tozier is not a man to be trifled with at close range.

Upon a calm night they hear the old craft while she is several miles away. Her screw sets well up out of the water, and in revolving makes a peculiar noise that can be heard a long distance—long enough to afford the smugglers ample time to seek shelter in one of the many bays or coves indenting the islands.

Smuggling on Puget Sound is not confined to the men who go out in small boats. A great business is done on the steamers that ply between Victoria and Seattle and Tacoma. Steamers leave Victoria morning and evening for Seattle and Tacoma. They are handsome, big propeller steamers, and carry large crews.

I am told by the United States Customs officials at Port Townsend that these steamers occasion them a great deal of trouble and annoyance, that they have to be constantly watched, and, despite the utmost endeavors of the customs officials to prevent it, a large amount of opium is smuggled on these steamers.

It is the practice of the opium ring to secure positions for their agents as members of the crew of the steamers. The opium is brought quietly aboard by these men while the steamer is lying at her wharf in Victoria, and is hidden away in the hold to be landed at Seattle or Tacoma. Of course a customs inspector goes through the steamer when she touches at Port Townsend en route, but he cannot search every portion of the ship, and a ton of opium could be scattered around the vessel in small lots, hidden away where it would require a month to find it.

Although it is known that thousands of pounds of opium are smuggled into the United States annually on these steamers, no action can be taken against the vessel until it is proven that the captain is privy to the transactions and an accomplice.

A Seattle newspaper just received gives an account of a unique case of smuggling which occurred this week. It says:—

"A gentleman from Victoria who is now in this city met two men on the street whom he had known in Victoria. They told him they had just brought a load of opium from Victoria in an Indian canoe, at a profit of $400 to themselves."

It was an easy feat. It is only eighty-seven miles from Victoria to Seattle, and an inland passage between the islands can be found all the way. Of course no attention would be paid by customs officials to a couple of duck hunters paddling around in a siwash canoe with a bundle of fish nets piled up in the bottom.

Another item in the same paper referred casually to the fact that thirty Chinamen were believed to have been smuggled into Seattle the previous night.

The newspapers pay but little attention to these occurrences. They have become so common as to cease to be of interest to the readers. Everybody knows what is going on, and a bold, bad smuggler with a cargo of opium or a bunch of Chinamen is not a novelty to them.

A humiliating feature to Americans of this great evil of smuggling is the fact that the Canadian government is constantly profiting at our discomfiture. Canada levies an import duty of $1 per pound upon the importations of crude opium which are brought to British Columbia to be manufactured into prepared opium. This means a great source of income annually. They also get $50 per head from the Chinamen who land, and this foots up a round sum at the end of the year. Both the opium and the Chinamen find their way into the United States without bringing us one cent of revenue.

There is another strange feature of the situation. It was claimed in Congress that the import duty of $12 per pound imposed upon prepared opium and the internal revenue tax of $10 per pound upon its domestic manufacture were intended to act as a prohibitory tax to keep the vile stuff out of the country. The opium habit was extending among the lower classes in the great cities to an alarming degree, and the price of the deadly drug must be enhanced to place it beyond the reach of the multitude.

Yet when the government seizes a cargo of smuggled opium, does it burn the stuff or destroy it? Not much!

It is put up at auction and sold to the highest bidder! Of course it is always bought by the opium ring, the very men who had tried to smuggle it.

It usually brings from $5 to $6 per pound. It is stamped and put on the market to compete with the opium legally imported by some honest merchant, whose opium represents a cost to him, with duty paid, of $18 to $20. The opium ring is still ahead of the game. They paid $6 per pound for it originally, they added $5 or $6 to its cost when they bought it again from the government, and it has still been obtained for $6 per pound less than the opium which has paid duty.

No more conclusive proof of the extent of the smuggling can be brought than the market price of the stuff. Let me give you an instance.

Prepared opium in Victoria costs $6 per pound. The customs duty is $12; allow a margin for profit of $4 per pound, which will include the cost of handling it, and you have a cost of $22 per pound. You cannot buy it for less from honest dealers.

I will make a contract to furnish you ten thousand pounds within twenty-four hours at $14 per pound. I will obtain it in Tacoma, Seattle, Port Townsend and Portland and make enough on the deal to pay for the trouble.

The recent ruling of the Treasury Department, in accordance with a decision of the courts, to the effect that Chinamen found to be unlawfully in the United States must be returned to China, is being taken advantage of by the wily Celestials in a peculiar way. They have discovered a means of returning to China at no expense to themselves. They simply make a bluff at crossing into the United States, allow themselves to be caught, and when brought before the United States Commissioner for trial, acknowledge that they are unlawfully in the United States, and are forthwith shipped back to their native country at the expense of the United States.

USE AND ABUSE OF STIMULANTS.

SUNDAY, MAY 7, 1893.

Doctors Are Largely Responsible for Drunkenness and the Opium Habit.

SOME TERRIBLE STATISTICS.

Alcohol and Opiates Are Too Frequently and Carelessly Prescribed by Medical Men

USEFUL AGENTS PERVERTED.

SK any conscientious, competent doctor which two of all the remedies in the pharmacopœia he regards as most useful to mankind, and he will in all probability say opium and alcohol—opium first, alcohol a close second.

But should you press him further with the question which two drugs are most dangerous to mankind, he will surely reply opium and alcohol, or alcohol and and opinion, so save him elf from being paradoxical.

At any rate, it is an unquestionable fact that these two drugs have done incalculable good and immeasurable mischief.

But how the mischief? Simply because they have been prescribed without rhyme or reason, at times when there wasn't the slightest indication that their use was necessary, and by doctors, too, many of them in practice long enough to know the danger of such medication. And what has been the consequence?

Thousands and thousands of opium fiends and drunkards to-day got the first taste of what must be their ultimate destruction from the hands—yes, from the hands of their doctors.

This is a sweeping accusation to make, but, nevertheless, it is borne out by facts, borne out by statistics, and, more than that, a large minority of the doctors in the city and, for that matter, elsewhere in the country will admit that the reckless and what may be termed the unprofessional use of alcohol, of opium and its alkaloids has much to answer for.

Opium and alcohol have few, if any, curative properties. Both are palliatives, tonics, valuable assistants to weakened nature in her effort to regain her lost strength. But that is all. If administered with calm, good judgment they do a world of good and often tide over a sufferer in his struggle for health who would otherwise die. Yet, somehow or other, physicians have fallen into the habit of prescribing them for all conceivable manner of ailments from consumption to alopecia.

EXAMINING PRESCRIPTIONS.

Not long ago I took several druggists into my confidence and they allowed me to look over their files of prescriptions—those long worms of dusty papers strung on wires that are found in the back of every chemist's shop where prescriptions are compounded.

Listen to these few figures, doctors, and then explain them if you can. To me they are an enigma. I ceased trying to classify and study out long ago.

In a little drug shop in the very heart of the most populous district in the east side less than a week ago I saw over three hundred odd prescriptions. Most of them were combinations such as are used by us in our every day practice. By actual count forty-nine of them contained opium in one or other of its forms. The prescriptions were not sorted out; they were taken in rotation just as they came in to be filled, and twelve of them contained such large quantities that only could be prescribed for one long accustomed to the use of the narcotic.

Further down, where poverty and misery are more prevalent, in that part of the city where tall, badly ventilated tenements are still allowed to be inhabited by human beings, I opened another of these wire worms that had gathered dust in a remote corner for two years and told off three hundred prescriptions as they ran and looked them over. It was at once evident that opium is still too dear for the pocketbook of the poor man. Here only thirty-four contained opium and the doses were ever so much smaller.

Curiosity then took me up town where a dollar is not turned over so often before it is spent. The prescriptions were carefully numbered and pasted into a big scrap book for ready reference. It was less of a task to read them over, and the signatures were those of our better doctors who charge $2 or more for a consultation.

Think of it! Fifty-one in a string of three hundred had opium as their chief ingredient. The other drugs written for were mainly menstrums, or better vehicles to carry the drug and give it a disguise.

But this is not all.

Of the total number of prescriptions that were compounded a second time in nine drug stores forty per cent were those that had opium in them. In the same establishments sixty-three per cent of all that were refilled a third time had opium or morphine in them.

STARTLING FIGURES.

These figures ought to set every honest doctor to thinking.

One druggist, who kept a record of his prescriptions for several years, assured me that nearly two thousand out of sixteen thousand prescriptions he had counted called for opium.

But that is not all. When the patent medicines that go to make up three-fourths of the merchantable stock of the chemist are gone over we run across more opium. With few exceptions, the patented cough balsams all contain opium. That's why they are so dear. The more expensive the preparation the larger the amount of opium it contains. It almost seems as if they were a cloak under which the unrestricted sale of opium is carried on in open violation of the law.

The figures given here were rather difficult to obtain, but anybody can verify them. It would pay legislators to ponder over them, now that they have given us laws to regulate the practice of medicine and surgery in this State.

Many fiends carry a doctor's prescription calling for half an ounce or more of opium in their pockets for years and have it replished as often as they like. When the paper becomes old and faded they have it copied by an obliging druggist's assistant and it lasts for another year or so of daily use. They are the persons who sooner or later go to fill up our insane asylums and private retreats. If they are poor they become burdens upon the community. If they have influential friends they find a home in some retired retreat where the hope is kept green that they have not passed beyond human aid.

By this time they are physical and moral wrecks, for nothing like opium will undermine a noble character and a strong will.

All this is the pernicious side of opium. Now what good can be said of it?

A great deal.

It is beyond question a valuable drug, and no doctor can afford to be without it for a moment. To relieve excruciating pain, which of itself may kill a person, it has no equal as a sedative, a sleep producer and a tonic. If wakeful nights have sapped a sufferer's vital force until there is little left nothing like opium will bring on rest and freedom from pain. There are many kindred conditions in which the use of opium is indicated, yes, demanded, but rarely has it any other value in the therapy for the cure of disease. It is seldom more than a remedy of expediency. As a rule it disguises the very symptoms that enable a thoughtful, competent doctor to strike at the root of the evil, as he should, and it is precisely for this reason that its apparent haphazard use is so much to be condemned in medical practice.

HOW TO ADMINISTER OPIUM.

Perhaps it is because a patient in pain always feels better after a dose of opium that the doctor who is weak in diagnosis, physiology and pathology, but strong in therapy, requires such a large amount of it in treating the diseases human flesh is heir to. Countless thousands of opium habitués can trace their addiction to the drug to doctors.

I know dozens of physicians who, like myself, make it a rule never to let a patient know when opium is given and who mark their prescriptions with a cabalistic sign which says to the apothecary "Not to be duplicated except upon instructions."

As long as the apothecary has a soul above money the possible evil is kept under control. The only justification for the unrestricted dosage of opium that medical science can sanction is where a person is afflicted with a painful incurable disease which has resisted all known forms of treatment. Then opium serves a useful purpose in easing suffering. To quickly educate such persons to become opium eaters is only humane.

And now a word about alcohol. Of all the substances that enter into the dietary of man that are used for stimulation, to check waste and promote repair none are superior to alcohol. So great is its reconstructive power that strictly speaking it must be classed as a food. Whenever the powers of life are waning, be the cause whatever it may, alcohol ranks first among remedies to check it.

Like opium it is good if properly used and baneful if abused. It is scarcely necessary to say much for or against alcohol. It is too well known to all of us to need much comment and I shall confine myself to speaking of its use medicinally by those who never tasted it before a physician prescribed it for some disease.

Alcohol is unquestionably par excellence a food adjunct in the severe forms of fever where nutriment is urgently required to keep up life, but where the digestive organs have lost their assimilative function.

Here as long as the actual waste is compensated for alcohol does good. Beyond that it is worse than useless. Unfortunately such restricted dosage does not satisfy the careless doctor of easy conscience. He gives it by the oft repeated tablespoonfuls without stopping to discover that the result wished for has been attained in the slower, fuller pulse and stronger heart.

CONTRACTING TIPPLING HABITS.

Hundreds and hundreds of men and women in all walks of society contracted their tippling habit by regarding as unrestricted the advice of their physicians that wine or stimulants of some kind are necessary for them to take. The advice in itself is justinable, but the lack of restriction is culpable. And so these poor deluded convalescents go on taking stimulants, which they find not only agreeable but desirable, until they become slaves to drink.

Bear in mind that these remarks have no bearing on the temperance question. Those who of themselves have a liking for alcohol are perfectly entitled to do so and no doctor ought to attempt to correct his patients' habit of eating and drinking as long as they do not interfere with or originate the ailment for which he is consulted.

Many old topers who have been so for half a century or more are in good health at ninety, and others regularly partake of their stimulants who are all the better for it.

It is for the uninitiated that the doctor should be careful with the use of alcohol. Patients have been known to acquire the alcohol habit, but none of them willingly habituate themselves to the use of ipecac without positive instructions from their medical advisers.

Medical literature teems with diseases like hardened liver, decaying kidney, alcoholic consumption and the like, which are directly caused by a too liberal consumption of alcohol.

DR. GERMAIN-SEE'S ADVICE.

I have before me a most excellent treatise on the subject by Dr. Germain-See, of Paris, in which he says:—"It is only when the dose of alcohol is considerable and long continued that the eliminations of the solids is increased. Thus we may say alcohol is a means of economy for the organism, a verification of the doctrine of Von Voit on the conservative action of certain substances in common use."

Thus we possess in alcohol a most useful agent by the use of which the intake and output of the body may be balanced when all other means fail. Intelligently prescribed by physicians it has saved many human lives, but when medicinally applied it should not be left to the pleasure of the patient, but should be kept under the careful observation of the doctor, lest the sufferer become cured of one disease only to contract a far graver one.

It is in the judicious use of these two valuable remedies that the doctor owes much of his high repute and by it he may become a benefactor or curse to his fellow beings.

SUICIDE MADE EASY.

Scientific Research Has at Length Perfected the Art of Self-Destruction.

SMUGGLING OPIUM AND OPIUM SMOKERS.

Clever Devices Adopted by the Smugglers to Elude Detection and Revenue Officers.

A HYDRA HEADED GANG.

The Government Loses Nearly Two Millions Yearly, but It Cannot Cope with the Law Breakers.

[FROM OUR REGULAR CORRESPONDENT.]

HERALD BUREAU,
CORNER FIFTEENTH AND G STREETS, N. W.,
WASHINGTON, Oct. 12, 1890.

During the year 1889 something like 180,000 pounds of prepared or smoking opium was smuggled into the United States, and this government thereby deprived of a revenue tax of $1,800,000.

In the space of twenty months from March, 1887, until December, 1889, there were landed in British Columbia 6,818 Chinamen, four-fifths of whom were smuggled into the United States.

These figures are derived from the agents of the United States and from estimates based upon reports and statistics of importations furnished by the British customs officers at the ports of British Columbia.

Congress several years ago enacted a law placing an import duty of $10 per pound upon smoking opium brought into this country. Notwithstanding this heavy duty the regular importation of opium through legal channels and upon which duty was paid amounted to $1,600,000 last year. The estimated amount of opium smuggled added to this sum will just about reach the amount of yearly importations at the time the tax was enforced.

Congress also passed a law prohibiting the entry of Chinese laborers into this country, but the contraband traffic goes on in spite of it.

For several months past United States officers have been engaged in making a thorough and silent investigation of the amount of the traffic, the modes of carrying it on and the remedy for the evil. The Treasury Department is astounded at the extent of the smuggling, as shown by the investigations of the officers. The department has reason to believe that the evil is even greater than is shown by the figures presented.

WHERE SMUGGLERS OPERATE.

There are two routes which smugglers use to get Chinamen and opium into the United States. One of them is overland and the other is by water, on Puget Sound. The routes are used as the exigencies of the occasion demand—the destination of the cargo or as the presence of officers necessitates, such presence always being made known to the smugglers by their principals in town. The start in either case is from the same point—Vancouver or Victoria. Vancouver is on Puget Sound, British Columbia, and is the western terminus of the Canadian Pacific Railway, which runs eastward to the Dominion of Canada. About three times a month steamships arrive at Vancouver from China with cargoes of Chinamen. The average cargo of opium is 25,000 pounds, and sometimes larger. A portion of the opium is retained for the use of the Chinese population of the district, and the remainder, nine-tenths of the whole importation, is smuggled into the United States, so the British customs officers say. Of the Chinamen who land ninety-five out of every hundred are bound for the United States, and get there.

HOW THE HEATHEN GET THERE.

Upon arriving at Vancouver the Chinamen are taken in charge by their resident countrymen in the Chinese portion of the city. In a few days they take passage for Victoria, just across the Sound, on Vancouver Island. Here they remain, quietly biding their time for an opportunity to get across to the American shore. They are divided into little squads of a dozen or fifteen and are in charge of some crafty old Celestial who "knows the ropes." Each man has put up from $25 to $50 passage money. The guide keeps his countrymen well out of sight. Their craft are at anchor in the harbor—trim, clipper built little sloops, with a great spread of canvas, but looking innocent enough with the bundle of fish nets drying on the roof of the cabin, and a lazy waterman stretched on the deck smoking his pipe. The master and his men are up town looking out for bargains. If all is propitious and the wind fair the Chinese padrone makes a bargain for the transportation of so many men across the Sound that night.

Shortly after dark the Chinamen steal quietly out of town, and, striking off to the southwest, begin an all night tramp across the rugged country, following in single file narrow trails through the woods, heading for some landlocked bay or inlet in the Straits of San Juan de Fuca, which connects Puget Sound with the Pacific Ocean. About the time when all is quiet in the harbor and there is no sound but the brawling and revelry from the dance houses along the shore the sloop silently steals out of the harbor. Before day breaks the smuggler has dropped anchor in some quiet cove, the sloop resumes her appearance of a fishing smack, while the captain goes ashore to consult with his Chinese friend, after posting a man with a glass on the headland at the mouth of the cove to watch for the possible coming of the only revenue cutter in those waters, the Walcott, a wheezy old craft that can be outrun by any smuggling sloop in the business.

About sundown the Chinamen come aboard and settle themselves in the sloop for the night's run. All hands keep on the lookout, while the poor Chinamen crouch together in the bottom of the vessel. If the wind fails or if there are indications of revenue officers around the sloop puts into one of the numerous islands dotting the Sound, where there are huts and hiding places, and waits for another opportunity. Then they watch their chance to make a landing on the American shore, where the Chinamen are tumbled out, turned over to another guide and hurried back up the country on their way to the numerous towns in Washington.

OTHER ENTRANCES INTO THE UNITED STATES.

Other consignments of Chinamen land at Westminster, in British Columbia, just north of the border. From this place to within sixty miles east their are twenty trails, good for eight months in the year, by which the men can get into the United States. There are huts and hiding places all along the route. The native inhabitants usually belong to the "ring," and every facility is furnished the smugglers, while every obstacle is thrown in the way of the customs officers.

There is still another route of entry for the contrabandists. Taking the Canadian Pacific Railroad at Vancouver the Chinamen proceed east until they are north of the border of the States of Dakota, Montana or Minnesota. Thence they make for the American border, which is only from forty to eighty miles away. They have their well worn trails, their huts and rendezvous, and the smugglers are always on hand to guide them across the border.

The larger part of the smuggled opium comes into the United States by way of the Canadian Pacific, while nearly every week some little band of Mongolians steals into the land of promise from the railroad stations.

Probably the heaviest traffic in both opium and Chinamen is carried on in the neighborhood of the Lake of the Woods, a large body of water lying pa[illegible] British Columbia and the United States, no[illegible] Minnesota, on the numerous freight and passenger steamers and lumber boats and smaller sailing craft which ply these waters. Once safely landed on the Minnesota shore the men and their cargoes easily make their way into Chicago, St. Paul or any railroad centre.

A great many Chinamen cross the border into

OPIUM SMUGGLING ON OUR WESTERN COASTS.

Great Temptations to Illicit Trade, Consequent Upon the High Rate of Duty.

LARGE PROFITS IN THE BUSINESS.

How the Drug Is Brought Into Washington Ports Almost Daily.

CONCEALED IN MANY WAYS.

Chinamen Carry Queer Balls, and the Partitions of Steamers Are Padded with Strange Packages.

[SPECIAL CORRESPONDENCE OF THE HERALD.]

SEATTLE, Wash., Dec. 20, 1890.—Opium smuggling has become very profitable in the Northwest, and few persons have any conception of the immense traffic that is being carried on in Seattle, Tacoma and other Puget Sound ports, where this costly drug is smuggled in from British Columbia points. Victoria is the great shipping point, and since the passage of the McKinley bill the business has assumed gigantic proportions, and has become so lucrative that a number of new dealers have established themselves in that city, where prepared opium is manufactured in large quantities and is openly sold to all who wish to purchase, there being no law against its sale in the British provinces. The duty on prepared opium is $12 a pound, and as it sells for $7 a pound in Victoria smuggling is a big temptation to a poor man, for by bringing the drug across the line he can readily find a market for it at from $15 to $17 a pound, where it is bought by wholesale dealers, who ship it to New York, Chicago and other Eastern cities and to San Francisco.

In Victoria there are several Chinese firms who make a business of preparing the crude opium for smoking and putting it up in various kinds of packages so that it will not excite the suspicion of customs officers. Packages are put up like Chinese laundry bundles, with laundry marks on the outside, and in tin boxes and in many other ways to deceive the officers. That the shrewd Chinese have succeeded very well is evidenced by the large quantity of opium that finds its way to these ports. Although a violation of the law to handle smuggled goods, many dealers here are willing to assume the risk for the profits to be derived from the illegitimate traffic, and [illegible] the customs officers cannot or dare not op[illegible] charge certain persons to whom suspicion po[illegible] most strongly, there can be no doubt as to th[illegible] fact that business men of wealth and influ[illegible] and other Sound ports are extensively [illegible] the opium traffic. The Chinese dealers [illegible] only ones in the business, although [illegible] Chinese laundry and junk shop is a place [illegible] safety for concealing smuggled goods. Th[illegible] known to the officers, but the ingen[illegible] smugglers enables them to save their good[illegible] seizure.

BIG PROFITS [illegible]

If the customs officer[illegible] only as shrewd as those who violate the [illegible] some startling disclosures would be ma[illegible] pr[illegible]inent business men in Seattle, Tac[illegible] and San Francisco would be arres[illegible] in smuggled opium and other artic[illegible] which the duty is so high as to make the [illegible] justify the risk. These who carry the good[illegible] across the line are not the only ones who reap a rich harvest from smuggling and whose profits are enormous by reason of the high tariff imposed by the McKinley bill on prepared opium, fine silks, laces and other goods of great value that constitute the smuggler's stock in trade. Their profits are shared with the dealers who receive these goods, the shippers and the Eastern firms to whom the goods are consigned. The high duty is not paid, and those who transgress the laws are enriched by the profits derived from a traffic in goods that should be a profitable source of revenue.

DUTIES TOO HIGH TO PAY.

During the past three months there have been about two hundred pounds of smuggled opium seized to every pound that came in through the customs office, to say nothing of the immense quantities that were smuggled in and escaped detection. At Port Townsend, which until a few days ago was the only port of entry in Puget Sound, the Custom House records show receipts for duty on only about twelve pounds of prepared opium. A recent ruling of the Secretary of the Treasury that vessels may enter and clear from Seattle and Tacoma as well as Port Townsend by making two more ports of entry will add to the facilities for smuggling and give those engaged in that business such excellent opportunities for escape that the customs officers will be powerless to check the growing tendency of this profitable traffic. There is no doubt but that the Treasury officials would never have put such a construction upon the Sub-Port of Entry bill if they had been familiar with the geographical position of this section, and they would have hesitated before giving either Seattle or Tacoma power to enter and clear foreign vessels. This new construction of the law will make it an easy matter for such ships as feel inclined to smuggle thousands of dollars' worth of merchandise into the United States and defraud the government of duties by sailing past Port Townsend, where they were formerly searched, without interference. Captains of vessels are now enabled to land smuggled goods at any of the islands in the upper Sound without the customs officers being any the wiser.

A NAVAL OFFICER'S VIEWS.

In an interview with Captain Glover, of the revenue cutter Oliver Wolcott, he said:—"There is no doubt that the heavy duty on opium has led to an increase in smuggling. Various seizures have been made, but it is almost impossible to search the steamers thoroughly in the short time they stop at the ports, especially such large vessels as the Olympian. The best thing the government could do would be to admit crude opium free and put a lower duty on the prepared drug. Then we should get the duty and have the manufacturing done in this country. That is what Canada does, and she manufactures large quantities at Victoria. The great mistake was the repeal of the Fines, Forfeiture and Moiety act in 1874. It gave the informer one-third of the value of the seizure, and provided that his name and that of the officer making the seizure should not be disclosed. Thus some inducements as well as protection were furnished to men who gave information, but now the man has to bear the odium of being an *informer* and then trust to the Secretary of the Treasury to get a reward.

"As to Chinamen, it is almost as difficult to keep them out of the United States as it is to catch them after they get in. You may find plenty of Chinamen in the woods around Port Townsend, and be absolutely certain that they have been smuggled

arrested here for smuggling for many months was the case of Mrs. Abdelnour, alluded to above. She had been noticed by customs officers making frequent trips between Victoria and Seattle, always carrying a large valise. A twelve-year-old boy was her constant companion. She was shadowed and found to be a pedler of fine laces and embroidery, and had sold a large quantity of these costly articles to Seattle ladies. A warrant was issued for her arrest, but there being no evidence to show that she had smuggled the goods she was released.

SMUGGLING ON PUGET SOUND STEAMERS.

On the steamer Olympian alone there have been 720 five tael cans of prepared opium seized within the past four weeks, all of which was smuggled across the line from Victoria. A few days ago, on the Olympian's arrival at Port Townsend, inspecting officers noticed that the baseboard in the storeroom of that ship was fastened by means of screws and presented the appearance of having been recently removed. Their suspicions were aroused and upon the board's being removed a search resulted in the finding of 160 pounds of opium concealed between the partition walls. The night watchman, who had endeavored to throw the officers off the track, was arrested.

On the Olympian's next trip two hundred pounds of opium were found concealed in the coal room among the coal. The chief steward and three other members of the crew are now under arrest for smuggling, and detectives are at work trying to implicate some of the officers of that ship, and insist that it is unreasonable to suppose that such large quantities of opium should be shipped on board a vessel without the knowledge of some one in authority.

Quite a number of officers of vessels plying between British Columbia ports and Seattle and Tacoma have grown comparatively rich within the past few months, although their salaries are not large. During this time great quantities of prepared opium and several thousand Chinamen have been smuggled across the line, and as most of the smuggling is done on the water this sudden accumulation of wealth is somewhat suspicious, to say the least of it. Opium is found on these vessels stowed away in closets, between decks, under coal and put up in all sorts of deceptive packages. A few days ago a large quantity of opium was found carefully concealed in a bundle of soiled clothes sent from a steamer to a Chinese laundry here, and every imaginable device is resorted to to deceive the customs inspectors.

A SCHOONER RUN DOWN.

While the swift steam vessels are able to escape from the revenue cutters occasionally a slow craft is overtaken and captured. The latest capture is that of a small schooner, owned by two French-Canadians, which was sighted by the revenue cutter near Victoria at an early hour in the morning. She immediately made for the rocks, where the cutter could not follow in pursuit, but there being no wind her progress was slow, and after firing two shots the cutter put on full steam with the intention of heading off the smuggler, for it was evident when the schooner was first sighted that she was engaged in smuggling, but seeing that could not be done the cutter gave chase and the light schooner ran over the rocks and landed on one of the islands. A boat was sent ashore to secure the smuggler and her cargo, but when the vessel was reached the men who owned it had disappeared and left to their fate twenty Chinamen. The frightened Celestials seemed completely bewildered and made no attempt to escape. They were arrested and taken to McNeil's Island, where United States prisoners are confined, until their case could be investigated. The testimony showed that these Chinese were new arrivals and had just been brought from China through the instrumentality of a British agent there who undertook to land them safely at Vancouver, whence they could be smuggled by persons familiar with the methods into the United States. The scheme failed because the wind was not favorable and the schooner could not land her cargo before daylight. The Chinese were ordered back to China, and their transportation must be paid for by the United States government. An attempt was first made to land them at Vancouver, but the British customs officials declined to permit Chinese laborers to be sent there from this country.

Another smuggler was less fortunate in attempting to escape among the rocks and shoals around the islands, and while dodging the revenue cutter ran into the rocks and was lost. A number of Chinese ornaments and articles of wearing apparel were recently found washed ashore on the islands by the tide, and the supposition is that a boat containing smuggled Chinese goods must have been wrecked among the breakers.

SEATTLE POLICE AS OPIUM SELLERS.

To-day eleven opium smugglers were arraigned in the United States Court for offences committed within the past two months, and several others are awaiting the action of the Grand Jury. The indictments charge them with importing, concealing, selling and attempting to sell prepared opium upon which no duty had been paid. Among those now under indictment are two Seattle police officers, Charles Raymond and Nelson Clouett, who used their official position to secure fifty pounds of opium from a smuggler and then sold the captured booty. The history of this case shows how the business in smuggled opium is generally conducted in the Northwest. In the latter part of September Joseph Manseau, a member of the Canadian mounted police, seeing the big profits that were being derived from smuggling opium into the United States, resigned from the force and embarked in that business. With $350 he purchased fifty pounds of prepared opium at Victoria, which he sent to Seattle by an accomplice and followed on the next steamer. In Seattle he took charge of the valise containing his opium, and being green and unaccustomed to the business he sought advice as to its disposition to the best advantage. His conversation was with a Seattle liquor dealer in the French language, and Officer Clouett, who was in an adjoining room, overheard the plans for disposing of the opium and arranged with Officer Charles Raymond, who was unknown to Manseau, to arrest the latter and secure the valise. The plans were carried out, and Manseau was so badly frightened that in order to get away he did as the officer directed, dropped the valise and hastily departed. Raymond took possession of the valise, but instead of reporting the matter to the customs authorities he and Clouett disposed of the opium and kept the proceeds, about $900. Manseau finally recovered from his fright and tried to compromise with the police officers, but they refused to give him any share of the booty, so he reported the matter to the customs officers and became prosecuting witness in the case against these men, who have been suspended from the police force and are now on bail awaiting trial.

CURIOUS CHINESE ORNAMENTS.

The impression prevails generally that many police officers and others whose duties should prompt them to assist in suppressing the opium traffic are secretly aiding and permitting the business to go on, for it is impossible that so much opium selling should be carried on continually and the officers know nothing about it. Even the Chinese here who earn but $1 a day and less have their opium, and the heavy duty does not seem to affect them in the least, for the great numbers of their countrymen who are smuggled into the country come well supplied with smoking opium, which is furnished them at cost price—$7 a pound. Among the many ornaments that Chinese are partial to are little wax balls, closely resembling marbles. They have been seen by the thousands in the wash houses and stores of Chinamen for months, but their contents were never suspected until a short time ago, when a small sloop with forty smuggled Mongolians aboard came right into the harbor here from Victoria and safely landed during a heavy fog, which effectually concealed them and enabled them to escape detection. Fourteen of these new arrivals were subsequently captured, however, in a Chinese laundry, and when searched a large number of these wax balls were found in their pockets. One of the balls was broken open and was found to be filled with prepared opium. The balls taken from the pockets of the entire gang contained nearly ten pounds of the drug, and it is probable that the other twenty-six of their countrymen were also well supplied. These mysterious little balls are made so perfectly and skilfully that no one would ever suspect their contents. The fondness of the Chinese for those wax marbles is thus explained, but as they are aware of the exposure of their ingenious little device they will doubtless invent some other method for deceiving the customs inspectors and supplying themselves with the drug to which they are so devoted and the effect of which has tended so largely to degenerate their race.

HOW CHINAMEN ARE SMUGGLED IN.

Another feature of the smuggling business, and one out of which large profits are made by officers and owners of vessels on Puget Sound, is the smuggling of Chinamen into the United States. Chinese laborers are brought to Victoria in great numbers by British ships and there they are taken charge of by agents, who for sums varying, according to circumstances, from $10 to $50 a head, undertake to land Chinamen safely into or within convenient distance of Port Townsend, Seattle, Tacoma or some other city where their countrymen are numerous. The Chinese Exclusion act cannot

SMUGGLERS' PATHS FROM CANADA.

Over a Thousand Miles of Boundary Line with Few Customs Officers to Guard It.

OPIUM TRAFFIC FLOURISHING.

Development of a Lively Business in Running Chinamen and Contraband Goods Into the States.

AROUND THE TURTLE MOUNTAINS.

[SPECIAL CORRESPONDENCE OF THE HERALD.]

WINNIPEG, Man., Sept. 19, 1891.—When the Secretary of the Treasury submits to the next Congress of the United States, as he will, a statement of the unprotected condition of the northwestern boundary of this country, from Lake Superior to the Rocky Mountains, and describes the enormous amount of smuggling and consequent fraud upon the revenues which is being carried on in that quarter by reason of the unprotected boundary, he will throw that august body into a state of proper surprise and consternation.

If the Secretary of the Treasury describes in full the existing condition of affairs, if he transmits with his description the reports of his special agents and customs officers upon the subject—piles upon piles of them on file in the department—if he tells the tale as it is known by every man in this section, Congress will doubtless emerge from its surprise and enter into a state of activity to correct the evil.

ORGANIZED BANDS.

Few people in the United States are aware that organized bands of smugglers lurk upon the northern frontiers and make a business of cheating the revenues of the government to the extent of vast sums annually. They are not the swashbuckling smugglers of olden times, with piratical beards and armed to the teeth, living in caves and holding a brotherhood of blood. On the contrary, they are a set of keen, shrewd citizens, men who pass well in the community, who own houses and teams of fast horses. Men upright in other respects, but who do

SMUGGLERS ON THE LAKE OF THE WOODS.

not hesitate to break the law of the land regarding customs duties and who think they have a perfect right to gouge Uncle Sam out of every dollar they can.

Their business is rendered possible and profitable by the neglect of the United States government to protect its own—culpable, inexcusable neglect of the government to provide the means to prevent its own pocket from being picked of many hundred thousand dollars annually.

I have just returned from a trip which I made for the HERALD along the northern boundary of Minnesota and North Dakota, adjoining the Province of Manitoba and the Lake of the Woods and Rainy Lake River.

The condition of affairs as I found them seems almost inexplicable.

From the Red River of the North, which forms the dividing line between Minnesota and North Dakota, eastward along the boundary line of Minnesota to the Lake of the Woods, a distance of about one hundred miles, the United States government has one mounted officer to patrol the country and prevent smuggling. The port of entry for this district is at St. Vincent, near the junction of the Red River of the North and the international boundary line. There are only two men stationed here, a deputy collector and his assistant. While one stays in the office the other is out on patrol duty.

The mounted officer goes once in every twenty-four hours to a point fourteen miles east. Probably once a week he extends his trip to the Roseau River, thirty-six miles away. The other sixty-five miles to the Lake of the Woods is left entirely unguarded. It is rather an inhospitable country, and the government trusts to this fact for immunity from smugglers. You can perceive what an opportunity for smuggling exists.

It would be impossible to find a country presenting more natural advantages to smugglers than does this section. It would almost appear that the country was made for their especial benefit.

Even the government has contributed to their safety by locating the customs station in the most out of the way place, and advantageous—for the smugglers.

ABUNDANT OPPORTUNITY.

Imagine a great stretch of prairie, level as a floor, extending twenty-five miles in every direction, the dull monotony broken by frequent belts of timber and thick brush, offering the securest shelter and concealment. No streams to ford, nothing to prevent a quick trip with fast teams

NO QUESTIONS ASKED ABOARD THIS BOAT.

over the firm roads of the hundreds of trails which gridiron the prairie and wind in and out among the timber and brush.

On the north of the boundary line and within half a dozen miles three or four Canadian towns along the railroad, where no questions are asked of outfits starting for "the States." On the south, within six or eight miles, the Minnesota towns of Hallock, Stevens and Argyle, where railroad communication is obtained with all parts of the State

point where Rainy Lake River emp[illegible] into the Lake of the Woods, but he is a useless fixture, for the steamboats and smugglers' canoes simply follow the Canadian side of the river, eighty miles east, to Fort Francis, where there is no officer.

OPIUM, TOO.

At Fort Francis, which is the head of navigation, everything is "wide open" on the American side. There is no restraint whatever. There is a large amount of commerce on the waterways, and no questions are asked about cargoes destined for the United States. Prepared opium, which is dutiable at the rate of $12 per pound, is unloaded from the steamer, packed in Indian canoes and transported up Rainy Lake River to Vermilion River, thence to Vermilion Lake and across to the town of Tower, Minn., which is the terminus of the Duluth and Iron Range Railway. No attempt is made by the United States government to prevent it.

From Fort Francis to Lake Superior, a distance of 350 miles along the greatest smugglers' highway in the world, there is not one United States Customs officer to be found.

The Lake of the Woods is dotted with hundreds of small islands with wooded shores and separated by deep, winding channels. Many of the smugglers live on these islands, and when not running a cargo of contraband goods they engage in the fisheries industry, which flourishes hereabouts.

The smugglers of the Lake of the Woods and the Rainy Lake River are half-breeds, Indians and French Canadians of the lower order. They are a brave, reckless set, and very handy with the trigger. The Canadian government keeps a detachment of mounted police with canoes at their command in the neighborhood, and by their vigilance prevent the smugglers bringing whiskey or American goods over the Canadian border; but, of course, they cannot prevent the smuggling of merchandise from Canada across the border into the United States.

ALONG NORTH DAKOTA.

The North Dakota frontier is a little better protected, but the force of men employed in the duty is ridiculously small when the great area of country is considered, and is entirely inadequate for the necessities of the case. The bulk of the smuggling done from Manitoba into the United States is carried on upon the North Dakota frontier.

The officers on duty will tell you that very little smuggling is done. Well, they are sincere in that belief.

Canadian officers, however, and the Canadian mounted police will tell a different tale. They know that many a lovely cargo, the aggregate duty upon which would be a very considerable drop in the bucket recently emptied by the late billion dollar Congress, is hustled across the Dakota prairies after nightfall, when the smugglers know that the solitary American patrolman is at the other end of his fifteen mile beat.

The first Custom House in North Dakota, after you cross the Red River of the North from Minnesota, is Pembina. This is a station on the branch of the Northern Pacific Railroad, which runs between St. Paul and Winnipeg. The Custom House is at the railroad depot, a few yards from the Canadian line. The force at present consists of a deputy collector of customs, two assistants, an immigration inspector and a mounted patrolman, who rides west toward Neche. Special Agents Stone and Day, of the Chicago Custom House force, are also stationed there temporarily, looking out for opium and Chinamen.

Every incoming train from Canada is boarded at the line by the officers, who make an examination of the coaches and the passengers' baggage. Everything moves along smoothly at this point. It is very seldom any one tries to smuggle right under the Collector's nose.

When a cargo is to be run into the United States the operators simply leave the train at some station north of the line and drive around Pembina at night, boarding the train again at one of the lower stations the next day.

About seventeen miles due west of Pembina is Neche. This station is on the Great Northern Railroad, a mile or more below the Canadian line. The country between Neche and Pembina is a beautiful prairie, with numberless trails crossing it from the Canadian border to the lower countries. One officer patrols these seventeen miles of smugglers' paradise—one lone man, jogging wearily along night and day, trying to protect the revenues of a great country from a gang of shrewd, energetic law breakers who have fleet teams and dozens of men to watch and wait and strike when the opportunity comes.

There are many settlers along the route who not only advise their friends of the movements of the lone patrolman but who will lend friendly shelter and a helping hand to hoist the cargo into a haymow in case of dire necessity.

The next fifty-five miles to the westward is pretty much the same country and conditions. From Neche to Walhalla, a distance of twenty miles, there is one mounted patrolman. From Walhalla to Elkwood, twenty miles, one mounted patrolman. From Elkwood to St. Johns, fifteen miles, one mounted patrolman. St. Johns is the terminus of one of the branch lines of the Great Northern Railway, and the patrolman has to give considerable of his attention to affairs immediately in the neighborhood of the station, which leaves a tolerably fair field for the smugglers on the prairie.

THE BEST SMUGGLING GROUND.

Bottineau, thirty miles west, is also the terminus of a branch of the Great Northern. Bottineau is at the base of the Turtle Mountains. Between Bottineau and St. Johns lies the hardest and most dangerous country, yet the best country for the smugglers. This section has long been a kind of Botany Bay, where fugitives from justice have congregated ready to step across the line upon a moment's notice. To while away the time and make a living they have engaged in smuggling, doing a nice little business in that line, especially in handling prepared opium, which is the most profitable cargo to run.

I know of one firm that was in a legitimate business in Bottineau which made $5,000 in a few months handling smuggled opium. They lost their nerve, however, moved out and are now respected merchants in Winnipeg.

The Turtle Mountain Indians lend a hand to the smugglers—for a consideration—and guide many a rich cargo through the bad lands in the mountains. The country is admirably adapted for the business. A level prairie stretches away to the north and rolls its green surface to the foot of the hills, which open into a hundred devious defiles to secrete the smugglers.

You will remember that a branch of the Canadian Pacific Railroad runs east and west, parallel with the international boundary line and but a few miles north of it. There are numerous stations and from half a dozen different points the smugglers take their departure down into Bottineau and St. Johns.

Through all this country you ask one mounted patrolman, in the face of such odds, to protect our revenue!

I cannot refrain from uttering a word of admiration for this handful of brave men who patrol the lonely prairie between the Roseau River and the Turtle Mountains. They are conscientious workers for an unappreciative government, taking their lives in their hands, facing death in the blinding, howling Dakota blizzards or at the muzzle of the smuggler's rifle, suffering hunger and cold, fatigue and exposure.

More like them, enough like them, and smuggling can be crushed from the northern border.

Your Canadian neighbors make great sport at the expense of your feeble customs service. Theirs is a perfect system of patrol which does not leave a foot of the border untrodden between the Lake of the Woods and the Rocky Mountains.

If the United States had a customs service one-half as good as Canada's her revenues would be greater to the extent of several hundred thous[illegible] dollars annually.

A BLOODTHIRSTY OPIUM EATER.

HE KILLS TWO PEOPLE, WOUNDS TWO OTHERS AND THEN COMMITS SUICIDE.

ST. LOUIS, Mo., Dec. 7, 1889.—Casper Clispy, an opium eater, walked into the home of John Anson this morning, said a few angry words and shot him through the head. He then fired at Agnes Anson, inflicting a fatal wound. Next he shot at Mary Anson, but the bullet glanced round the scalp, causing only a flesh wound. Michael Anson, a boy of sixteen, grappled with the madman and was shot in the wrist. Clispy then shot himself three times in the head and fell dead. John Anson died in a few hours after he was shot and Agnes is on her death bed. The murderer was in love with Mary and committed the crimes mentioned above because John Anson had forbidden him to pay attention to his daughter.

MADE GOOD HIS DEFICIENCY.

[BY TELEGRAPH TO THE HERALD.]

BOSTON, Dec. 7, 1889.—It is understood that John

OPIUM SMUGGLING BY WHOLESALE.

Prominent Citizens of the State of Washington Engaged in the Business of Defrauding the Government.

WHY THE DUTY WAS IMPOSED.

Influence with Congress to Raise the Tariff in Order to Prohibit Importations by Legitimate Dealers.

TWO SENATORS IMPLICATED.

Custom House Officials Bribed and if They Prove Too Honest Efforts Made to Secure Their Removal.

YEARLY PROFITS, HALF A MILLION.

[FROM THE SPECIAL CORRESPONDENT OF THE NEW YORK HERALD.]

PORT TOWNSEND, Wash., Oct. 2, 1891.—The opium ring of Puget Sound is a fearful, shadowy, impalpable something; shadowy in form, but most substantial in fact. It makes its presence known, yet is itself unknown. The subordinate members of it obey a system—they work in unison—yet they know not what is the motor power of this immense machine that is taking opium from British Columbia into America with almost mechanical regularity—this giant octopus that is sucking in the revenues rightly due the United States and diverting them to its own enrichment.

For years the secret agents of the United States government have been trying to legally locate the leaders of the opium ring. They know that men with brain direct the movements of the subordinate workers; that men with money provide the opium; that men with influence must be in it to accomplish the wonders which are accomplished when one of the gang is released who happens to have been caught.

Rumor gives them a clew which they trace, and lo! it ends with some prominent citizen whose reputation in the commercial and social world of the community is untainted. They are baffled, and watch as they will they cannot find evidence enough to bring the man to justice. Frequently they are satisfied in their own minds from circumstantial evidence their man is guilty, that he is putting his money into the game and raking off big profits, yet they could not take the stand

SMUGGLERS' PASS.

in a court of justice and make their impressions clear enough to a jury to secure a conviction.

HOW THE M'KINLEY TARIFF WORKS.

The leaders of the opium ring are powerful enough to control Congressional legislation. They induced the Billion Dollar Congress to impose a duty of $12 per pound upon opium, knowing that this would enhance the value of the drug, keep out legal importations and swell their profits on the smuggled opium. They persuaded the same Congress to enact legislation which places such a high license and heavy internal revenue tax upon manufacturers of opium in the United States as to effectually and absolutely keep out all manufacturers of the drug and leave the market entirely at the mercy of the supply furnished by the smugglers.

They control Senators and dictate the appointment of customs officers. When a customs officer proves too efficient, makes too many seizures and keeps too bright a lookout they simply have him removed. This is especially the case with the Puget Sound customs district. This district has given the Treasury Department more trouble than any other district in the United States.

Within two weeks the Collector of Customs for this district, appointed by President Harrison at the beginning of the administration, has been removed without a word of warning or explanation. He has been seizing too many Chinamen and too much opium belonging to the ring.

A son of the late Henry Ward Beecher was appointed Collector of this district by President Cleveland. Almost the first thing the young man did was to trace and seize one lot of opium, valued at $40,000, which had been smuggled from British Columbia into Alaska and was awaiting shipment to the United States in salmon cans marked "Alaska Salmon." Within a few months he had seized $130,000 worth of opium and was treading heavily upon the toes of the opium ring.

The ring went to Washington and prevented the [illegible]

When the opium ring finds it cannot corrupt an official it proceeds to get him removed. Many an unfortunate official has been blarneyed into granting some small "favor" to the ring, which, while unimportant, was a technical violation of the law, and thereby placed himself in the power of the unscrupulous gang, who, threatening to inform upon him, have led the poor fellow deeper into violations of law until it was too late to stop and he continued until caught and disgraced.

I am aware of an incident which happened in recent years to a Collector of Customs of this Puget Sound district. He was approached by a stranger who frankly admitted that he was agent for other persons and acting for them. The stranger said his clients had thirty-two tons of fine British Columbia wool on Vancouver Island, which, if passed through the Custom House, would be dutiable at eleven cents per pound. It was proposed, he said, to slip the wool across to the islands of San Juan and Lopez and the other islands on Puget Sound where there there are petty farmers, and then ship it from there as domestic wool, which, being raised in American territory, would, of course, be duty free. All that was asked of the Collector was that he should withdraw his officers in that neighborhood for a day, and he should share the profits. The Collector indignantly refused and informed the agent that extra vigilance would be exercised in that neighborhood. The Collector was surprised a day later to be approached by a prominent business man, who urged him to consent to the scheme, but without avail.

Within six months from that time the Collector was removed. He was too honest for the Port Townsend district.

An agent of the Puget Sound opium ring has been in Port Townsend this week making negotiations to carry out a scheme of wholesale fraud upon the revenues. He has made no secret of his mission, and I can state accurately the intentions of the ring.

WAYS OF THE OPIUM RING.

The ring will soon close a contract for the building of a small, swift steamer at a cost of $20,000, to be used exclusively in smuggling opium and Chinamen from Victoria into the United States. The specifications call for a steamer low in the water, nothing showing above board but pilot house and smokestack. She will be built to stand a heavy sea and for the greatest possible speed attainable in a craft of her tonnage.

I understand she will have Herreshoff engines of high power, sufficient to drive her through the heaviest seas.

The agent is at present looking for a competent Puget Sound steamboat man to run the vessel. A compensation of $1 per pound is offered for said service for every pound of opium landed.

The business which a vessel of this character could do in Puget Sound would be enormous. Under present conditions and with ordinary precautions she would be absolutely safe. She could make a trip every night between sunset and sunrise and land unlimited quantities of opium and innumerable Chinamen. The fare for landing Chinamen is $50 to $60 per head, and the profit on opium ranges from $5 to $7 per pound.

If the opium ring carries out its present intentions with regard to the building and operation of this steamer, the Chinese population of British Columbia will be transferred to the United States within a twelvemonth.

ORGANIZED FOR FRAUD.

The opium ring rejoices in an admirable organization and works under a system almost faultless. The point of distribution of the stuff is Portland, Ore. The opium that is brought across Puget Sound is landed at all of the towns along the eastern shore of the sound from Tacoma northward to Blaine. It is turned over by the carrier to an accredited agent at the point of delivery. The carrier, who brings it from Victoria, knows nothing of the destination of his cargo beyond the man to whom he delivers it. This agent in turn packs the opium in some form which renders it safe from discovery and ships it direct to Portland. He knows nothing beyond the man to whom it is shipped, a man of equal rank with himself.

At Portland the opium is safely stowed away and delivered in small lots to the market or sent to San Francisco. The transactions are all spot cash, each agent receiving his compensation upon rendering the service.

When a man is caught by the customs officers the opium ring usually secures his release upon $500 bail, and he promptly skips across the line to British Columbia. The ring puts up the forfeited bail and there is no informing or "peaching."

There is something awful in the thought of this great criminal combination of money and talent, bravery and viciousness that extends its ramifications through every strata of society on Puget Sound. The taint of the ring is everywhere. You know not whom to trust. The dreadful power of this combination that works in the dark, plans in secret and strikes with the swiftness of the lightning's flash is seen everywhere.

NO CONCEALMENT AT VICTORIA.

In the city of Victoria the opium ring works more openly. There is less cause for concealment because there is no sentiment unfavorable to smuggling. Of course the Chinese merchants do not have anything to conceal. They are there for the purpose of making and selling opium and they consider their business legitimate.

I am told that several of the richest merchants, who are also contractors, and furnish Chinese laborers to railroads in the United States, are now contemplating leasing a certain small steamer, which already has rather a shady reputation, for the sole purpose of landing Chinamen and opium pending the building of the ring's new steamer.

The system of espionage over customs officers and the operation of signals conducted by the opium ring is admirable. They have channels for obtaining information that are closed to our officers. If it happens that an agent of the United States customs service goes to Victoria and gets wind of an intended smuggling expedition, the opium ring is immediately aware of the fact that he has warned the Port Townsend officials and the route of the expedition is changed.

A keen commentary upon the power of the opium ring was uttered by a prominent official when he said:—

"The only way to break up the opium ring of Puget Sound is to make smuggling risky and unprofitable. The glittering profits of the business attract men whose influence and power protect the ring from discovery. Reduce the profits of smuggling and these men will be driven out of the business, leaving smuggling but the common criminal operations of a lot of low lawbreakers."

No one can accurately fix the amount of the yearly profits of the Puget Sound opium ring, but a *résumé* of the estimates which have been given to me indicate the sum to approximate nearly half a million dollars.

SMUGGLERS' COVE, SAN JUAN ISLAND.

"HIGH ROLLERS" MARRIED.

BOB GORDON, "MUSICAL MOKE," WEDS FANNIE BROACH, A SOUBRETTE.

The marriage of Miss Fannie Broach (Mrs. McMillan), a soubrette of the "High Roller" Company, to "Bob" Gordon, the "musical moke" of the same organization, has excited comment in the Eastern District of Brooklyn.

John Broach, the grandfather of the bride, was president of the Williamsburg Savings Bank. He died about a year ago and was succeeded in the bank by General A. V. Meserole. Miss Broach, who lived with her grandfather, was a recognized belle and moved in the best society of Brooklyn. Her first marriage, five years ago, to Charles McMillan, a cigar manufacturer of Broadway, was a notable event of the season, and it was a great shock to their friends when Mrs. McMillan obtained an absolute divorce two years ago.

OVERLAND PATHS FOR SMUGGLERS.

Operations of the Men Who Import Opium and Chinese Not Confined Exclusively to Waterways.

COMING ACROSS THE BORDER.

Landing to Can Salmon in British Columbia During the Summer, the Celestials Make a Break for the United States in October.

DESPERATE OUTLAWS ENGAGED.

Officials Terrorized by Murderous Roughs and in Danger of Removal by Federal Authorities if They Do Their Duty.

[FROM THE SPECIAL CORRESPONDENT OF THE HERALD.]

NEW WESTMINSTER, B. C., Oct. 6, 1891.—Congress will be pre-eminently occupied at its next session with three questions:—

1. Fraudulent and excessive pension legislation.
2. Fraudulent and unjust enumeration in Mr. Porter's census.
3. Fraudulent evasions of the revenue and open smuggling, encouraged by the high tariffs of the McKinley bill.

Of these three questions, the last is likely to present the most difficult problems, and its solution

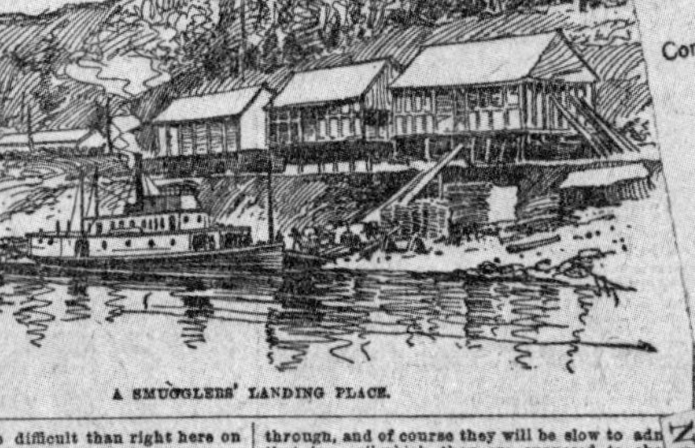

A SMUGGLERS' LANDING PLACE.

will be nowhere more difficult than right here on the northwestern border, or "jumping off place, of the United States.

A FAVORABLE SPOT.

This busy little city, with its 6,000 inhabitants, is the point of departure for the hundreds of Chinamen who make the overland trip into the State of Washington. The Puget Sound opium ring also has its agents here, and vast quantities of opium are smuggled over the trails and by the railroad into Washington, to find its way to Tacoma and Seattle and to Portland, Ore.

A large amount of prepared opium is turned out annually by the Chinese opium manufactories in this city, and heavy consignments come from Vancouver and Victoria.

The location of the city makes it a most convenient point for conducting the thriving smuggling business which exists, and there are unusual facilities for getting cargoes safely across the line. New Westminster is on the north bank of the Fraser River, fifteen miles above the point where it empties into the Strait of Georgia, the waterway that merges into Puget Sound. Steamers and sailing vessels conduct an extensive commerce with Victoria and Nanaimo, and it is only two hours by rail to Vancouver.

There is railway connection with Seattle and Tacoma, and small sloops carry contraband goods and Chinamen across Boundary Bay and land them on the Washington coast. In fact, there is every facility for smuggling from this city, and no opportunities are lost.

THE SMUGGLING SEASON.

The smuggling business is unusually good at this time for two reasons. First, the salmon fishing season is closing and the operatives are dispersing. There are twelve large salmon canneries in the vicinity of New Westminster, represent-

FRASER RIVER STEAMBOAT.

ing an invested capital of over half a million dollars. They employ five thousand men, a large proportion of whom are Chinese. These fellows have landed from China during the spring and summer, have worked hard, saved money and now are ready to make a break for the United States. Their places will be filled by new arrivals by the time the season opens again.

The second cause which contributes to the flour-

smugglers, who were on the point of killing him, but finally let him go. He immediately left the country and returned to headquarters at Port Townsend, where he asked the Collector of Customs for assignment to other duty. It was not an act of cowardice on his part, however, but simply self-preservation.

Another officer was sent, but in the meantime the Collector of Customs at Port Townsend has been removed and his place filled by another. There is a feeling that there will be wholesale removals among the officers at once, and the men on duty hereabouts are not risking their lives while they feel their tenure of office to be so uncertain. Therefore business is good in the smuggling line.

THE OUTLAWS' REFUGE.

The smugglers of the mainland, who operate between New Westminster and the small towns in Washington, are by far a more reckless, hardened and vicious class of men than those who conduct a similar business upon the waters of Puget Sound.

This is a new country. It is a haven of refuge for outlaws who have fled from the older States. Upon arriving here they naturally take to smuggling. There is good money to be made in the business and the wild, outdoor life suits them. The smugglers live in huts in the pine forests of the interior of Washington. They have their hiding places for the opium, caches they are called, and at several points in the woods are rude shanties, erected for the sheltering of Chinamen while they are making the overland trip.

It is a dangerous thing for one man to go among these fellows if he is suspected of being a revenue officer. The little station of Woolley, on the line of the railroad, is a rendezvous for a bold gang. They come into Woolley for whiskey and supplies, and occasionally a cargo of opium is shipped from there.

There are numerous trails through the woods, broad wagon roads some of them and others mere bridle paths. Every foot of the ground is familiar to the smugglers, however, and they never get lost.

HOW THE CHINESE COME.

After the Chinese get across the international boundary line and a few miles into the interior they are comparatively safe. There are several hundred Chinamen at work at various places, cutting timber and doing other work, and the new comers soon mingle with them and claim to have been in the country at work for months.

It costs a Chinaman all the way from $30 to $75 to be piloted across country from New Westminster to a safe point of destination in the State of Washington. They usually go in bunches of ten or fifteen, making a profitable venture for the smuggler. The smuggler will take along one hundred or two hundred pounds of opium to add interest to his venture. The Chinamen will make their way openly down to within a few miles of the international boundary. Then they strike for cover of the woods and under the leadership of their smuggler guide feel their way carefully along, keeping a sharp lookout for the enemy.

Three or four days may be consumed in the journey. Then the Chinamen will sudden[illegible] from the woods at a little railroa[illegible] openly board a train for the So[illegible] honest woodcutters returning from a[illegible] woods.

It is impossible to estimate exactly [illegible] of Chinamen who are crossing int[illegible] States in this section. The United S[illegible] who are sent to investigate the matte[illegible] number is small. They base their calc[illegible] on the rumors they hear of parti[illegible] through, and of course they will be slow to adm[illegible] that the evil which they are supposed to che[illegible] exists to any glaring extent. They are simp[illegible] laboring under a delusion. The parties of intrud[illegible]ing Chinamen of whom they do not hear outnum[illegible]ber by far those whom they occasionally get wind of.

MORE OFFICIALS NEEDED.

I have investigated this matter from another standpoint. There is no occasion to conceal or magnify the true situation. The bald fact remains that a constant stream of Chinamen are crossing from

TRAIL THROUGH THE WOODS.

British Columbia to the United States along the northern boundary of Washington, and the number reaches far into the hundreds in the course of a year.

I do not wish to be understood as reflecting unfavorably upon the United States officers. I have met them, and know them; they are brave men, doing good work and performing their duty as well as any one could.

BUT THERE ARE NOT ENOUGH OF THEM!

That is the situation in a nutshell. The Treasury Department has not sent enough men to protect ten miles of territory, and when you think of a belt of timber, fifty miles wide, traversed by innumerable trails and infested by a daring gang of cutthroat smugglers with three men to guard the line, you can guess how the situation stands.

The special agent of the Treasury Department, who has charge of the enforcement of the Chinese Exclusion act in this district, is stationed at Tacoma. He has some four or five men under him. I know him to be an energetic, discreet and brave officer, ambitious to perform his duty in the most creditable manner possible. Yet, he has not a sufficient force of men to aid him. He is not a man to complain of this, and he has never said it to me, but he takes what the Treasury Department gives him and does the best he can with it.

You will remember that the officers south of New Westminster have a double duty to perform. They must guard their district from invasion from the North, from British Columbia, and at the same time keep a lookout over 200 miles of coast line on Puget Sound, the bays, the inlets and creeks where the sailor smugglers land their cargoes from Victoria.

The opium ring is constantly advised of the movements of the handful of men who are detailed to protect the revenues on the mainland. It is known when these officers move from place to place and the gang in Victoria or New Westminster, as the case may be, is notified of the territory left unguarded and they immediately land an expedition thereon.

SMUGGLING ON PUGET SOUND

Chinese and Opium Still Continue to Enter the United States in Spite of Restrictive Laws.

[SPECIAL CORRESPONDENCE OF THE HERALD.]

SEATTLE, Wash., Sept. 14, 1892.—People residing in the Middle States and New England have but little conception of the extent to which the smuggling of Chinese and opium is carried on on the Pacific coast. For that matter it is doubtful if the government at Washington is possessed of anything like intelligence of the enormity of the illicit business. Some idea—rather a conservative estimate—can be had of the traffic, for such it has come to be, and one, too, of amazing proportions, by considering the amount of smuggling that is being done through the Puget Sound customs district which embraces the State of Washington. Anything like accurate information on the subject is not easily obtained.

However, the HERALD correspondent has for authority, with regard to the news given herewith, no less reliable a source than one of the deputy collectors of customs for this district, his opinions in the main being concurred in by subordinate officers—those actively engaged in the work of hunting down smugglers, reclaiming goods upon which this government has laid an enormous duty and prevent those hated natives of the Flowery Kingdom, whom Uncle Sam has denied the right of citizenship, from landing anywhere within the confines of the United States.

Naturally the government officials will, if anything, underestimate the extent to which smuggling is carried on despite their best efforts. The HERALD correspondent's informant estimates that there are on an average of two hundred and fifty contraband Chinese smuggled into the United States through the Puget Sound district monthly. Thus three thousand annually find their way into the country and to all intents and purposes enjoy every right of citizenship. L[illegible]han two years ago it is safe to sa[illegible]le that number were sm[illegible]

[illegible]LD's informant [illegible]nd pounds per [illegible]pounds in the [illegible]his is used for [illegible]r any other. [illegible]ven. [illegible] they are for [illegible] northwest [illegible] the Union. [illegible]h an extent [illegible]ist it be for [illegible]e northern [illegible]ifornia dis-[illegible]ore of the [illegible]here claim [illegible]um smug-[illegible] Columbia [illegible] through

[illegible] Chinese [illegible] Form-[illegible]o enter [illegible]f Chi-[illegible]nsend, [illegible] from [illegible]r and [illegible] rule [illegible]nited [illegible]ndled [illegible] ac-

[illegible]ttle [illegible]

[illegible] tending to a [illegible] of the law. Their dress [illegible] attire are taken into consideration. They are taught to conform as far as possible to the habits and methods of life of the Chinese residents.

HOW OPIUM IS BROUGHT.

Opium smuggling is done on a smaller scale than five and ten years ago, yet the aggregate is nearly as large. Such large quantities of the contraband drug are not handled now, but there are so many more engaged in the business in a small way that the grand total each year is nearly the same. There is seldom a batch of more than one thousand pounds taken across the line at any one time, whereas formerly it was often the case that 3,000 and 4,000 pounds were successfully brought into the country. In the first place, it will be well to consider the enormous profits to be gained from opium smuggling and it can then be better understood how tempting the business is for those who have too strong a love for money.

Opium for smoking purposes can be purchased in the city of Victoria for from $7 to $8 per pound. The duty on this grade of opium is $12 per pound. The market price, therefore, for the best grade of smoking opium in the United States is from $18 to $22. Much of it is brought over on passenger steamers plying between the cities on the Sound and British Columbia ports. There are a few sloops and small steamers of course that make a business of nothing else but smuggling Chinese and opium. The customs officers say that on most of the passenger steamers nearly every attaché of the vessel, from the captain down to the stoker, is more or less engaged in the traffic.

It is made very much of an object by the smugglers for the steamboat men to transport the drug from Victoria. The price usually paid is $1 per pound. Never a cent of this money is turned into the coffers of the companies or individuals owning the boat. It, on the contrary, all goes into the pockets of the captains and other attachés of the vessel that chance to be in the deal. It is also a fact well known to the customs officials that there are four or five seagoing vessels plying between Puget Sound cities and San Francisco, the owners of which look to the traffic of carrying contraband opium and the assistance of smugglers generally for a profit on the business of operating the steamers. The matter of carrying legitimate freight and passengers is only incidental to the other. These vessels carry all the way from 500 to 2,000 pounds at a time.

The government is mainly responsible for so much smuggling by its niggardly policy of failing to provide a reasonable number of officers [illegible] and other customs districts. In this distric[illegible] are about 1,600 miles of shore line on the Sound alone. This added to the British Columbia boundary and the State coast makes a total of nearly 3,000 miles. The Puget Sound customs district, including the Collector, deputies and customs officials generally, has just forty-five officers to guard and patrol this vast territory.

The customs officers of this district do not ex-

OPIUM SMUGGLING TO BE CHECKED.

Treasury Agents Think They Are Now in a Way to Unearth the Syndicate Which Has Been Swindling the Revenues.

PRISONER CHACE ARRAIGNED.

Commissioner Shields Refuses to Reduce His Bail—He Protests His Innocence and Explains About That Trunk.

If what the Treasury officials say is borne out there is more than one man of wealth and standing in New York who is shaking in his shoes fearing that he will be arrested, as Thomas E. Chase, of Providence, R. I., was, for opium smuggling.

Undoubtedly the opium ring is near dissolution. The HERALD pointed the way. It showed the powerful resources of the syndicate and the wholesale violation of the law by which the deadly drug was smuggled into this country and the government defrauded of hundreds of thousands of dollars every month. It was these very full charges, backed up with proofs gathered by the HERALD's special correspondent in British Columbia, which stirred the government officials to action. Much credit belongs to Chief Agent C. S. Wilbur, and he says he will not be content until he wears at his belt the scalps of all the members of the ring.

Chace is about sixty years old. He does not look like a lawbreaker, but more like a Sunday school superintendent. Until five years ago he was the partner of the dye house of which ex-Mayor Clark, of Providence, was the head. His family consisted of his wife, daughter and two sons. When Chace was arrested in City Hall Park Special Officer Wilbur thought that other arrests were being made at the same time. But in that he was mistaken.

NOVEMBER 13, 1891.

TEN SLAVES OF THE POPPY'S SPELL.

Eight Men and Two Women Who Lay at a Gotham Gate of a Hundred Sorrows.

SAW THE CHINA PUG WINK.

And Then the Police Came Like a Nightmare Into the Dreams of Florence Barnett's Flat.

SADIE TOOK ALL THE BLAME.

"When the men and women had smoked in silence for a time, when the room was thick with the fumes of opium, and the recumbent figures assumed fantastic outlines in the half light, then the carved dragons began to fight together and the beady eyes of the Joss began to glow with strange fires."

That was in Kipling's "Gate of the Hundred Sorrows." The police force thereabouts hadn't been prodded by a Lexow committee.

It was the same story in Florence Barnett's flat up in East Eighty-seventh street at one o'clock yesterday morning, except that for the Joss you must substitute a China pug dog, and for the dragons, flagons.

In this case, too, the dwellers at the gate were all very youthful—all except one, a woman. Few had the courage, or the despair, of old timers. Here, too, the women were the older devotees, though one was a girl in years. When the police came she shouldered the blame.

LAY DOWN TO PLEASANT DREAMS.

It was dark in the rooms, and in the one which figures here as the "Gate of the Hundred Sorrows" eight men and two women were grouped about a tabaret, a tray, an opium pipe and some of the drug.

Some of them lay on the floor, dreaming strange dreams as they watched the many colored fires burn in the eyes of the china pug. Some of them sat at the tabaret and watched the woman who held the pipe for the time. She was beginning to dream, too. In a few moments the pipe would be free and they could smoke themselves into another world.

There was a pillow on the floor here and there and two or three rugs, on each of which some one lay motionless. These had had their turn and the others, watching the woman hungrily, envied them.

It is a quiet house, No. 120 East Eighty-seventh street, a respectable, brown stone front of four stories. The top floor was rented a month ago to a quiet young man, who said he was Florence F. Barnett. He brought with him a mere girl, whom he said was his wife, Sadie. Both had something peculiar in their eyes.

The gas was not turned on in the rooms which the Barnetts occupied, and when the janitor mentioned it they told him they could get along with lamps for a time. The janitor wondered, but they were very quiet and it was none of his affair.

He soon found out that the Barnetts were much away from home, that they often remained away all night and came home at daybreak to sleep.

Sometimes, when they did come home at night they brought their friends with them, quiet friends who seemed to be able to ascend the stairs noiselessly from long practice. Sometimes the friends called when they knew the quiet Barnetts were at home, and glided up to the top floor in this same noiseless fashion.

Even then the Barnetts got along without any gas, and the janitor's wife, woman like, thought the lamps were used infrequently, if at all. Once or twice she detected a strange, heavy odor in the upper hallway, an odor unlike any she had ever noticed before. She had seen the china pug, but its eyes never burned for her, and so she knew nothing.

Men, and sometimes women, came late and went early. Indeed, the janitor never heard them go, is not sure now, in fact, that they ever did go. But then he is not a dreamer. Indeed, had he known about the eyes of the china pug he probably would have turned in an alarm of fire.

THE JANITOR'S DISCOVERY.

The janitor keeps bad hours too. He came home at midnight on Saturday and found three strangers waiting at his door. His wife had denied them admittance. They were young and well dressed—students, she thought. Students they were, but not of the sort she imagined. They told her they had already been up stairs to see the Barnetts and stepping out for a moment had locked themselves out. She said they must go away; that it was late, and the Barnetts were abed.

The "students" went away. But the Barnetts were not abed, nor were they alone. Other "students," eight in all, had come earlier, and those who had not already sought the rugs and pillows on the floor were waiting.

The Joss had begun to glare with fiery eyes, and the dragons to fight together in the Gate of the Hundred Sorrows.

* * * * * * *

Acting Captain Dean, at this hour, in the East Eighty-eighth street station, a few blocks away, was questioning Simkins, first name not given, who said he lived at No. 29 Willow street, Brooklyn. The Simpkins who really lives at that address denied all knowledge of the affair last night, so it was another Simkins, who was careless of his facts.

He was telling what he knew about No. 120 East Eighty-seventh street, top floor. He didn't tell about the china pug dog. They send such men to Bellevue from police stations. Simpkins had a grievance. He had gone to the Eighty-seventh street Gate once to smoke—"just for fun," he explained. When he left he did not miss his waistcoat. He noticed the loss some time afterward. If he left any more clothing there he did not tell of it.

In the waistcoat, though, he had a silver watch and a gold chain, both given to him by his mother, eighteen long years ago, when he never smoked for fun. He wished the police to recover his property without violence. He had gone after it twice himself, but he didn't smoke on these occasions, and some of the men on the rugs told him that the china pug had devoured his waistcoat, watch, chain and all at the moment the twentieth pill burned out in the pipe the night before. Simpkins, of Brooklyn, didn't believe it, although most of the smokers hailed from Brooklyn, too.

DESCENT OF THE POLICE.

The janitor at the Gate, frightened at the midnight visit, guided a squad of policemen, under Sergeant Liston, up to the top floor, soon after Simpkins had finished his story. A tall woman, who seemed still dreaming, opened the door of the Barnetts' apartments for them. They said "All right!" and brushed past her into the dining room. They struck lights and told every one to keep quiet.

The men on the rugs stirred uneasily. The eyes of the pug glowed no longer. Within ten minutes Liston had the "layout" and the prisoners in the station. Three of the men had to be assisted. They were still dreaming. The women begged for a little more of the drug.

The pedigrees given were these:—Sadie Barnett, twenty-one years old, married; Florence F. Barnett, twenty-four years old, who rented the flat; Nellie Martin, twenty-three years old and looking older, who said she was a servant;

SUNDAY VICE IN CHINATOWN.

Disreputable Resorts Where Vice and Crime Desecrate the Sabbath with the Apparent Tolerance of the Police.

SCORES OF GAMBLING DENS.

The Excise Law Is Contemptuously Ignored and Liquor Sold in Vile Chinese Restaurants.

LOW DIVES IN MOTT STREET.

Police Efforts to Make a Dry Sunday Throughout the City End in Dismal Failure.

ONLY 177 ARRESTS MADE.

Nobody Went Thirsty Who Had Money and Knew the Way to the Side Door.

Things not appointed for the Sabbath are done down in Chinatown late on Saturday nights, and even until the following Monday mornings. The Chinamen cannot be expected to distribut[e] signed confessions to the effect that on Su[n]days they and their friends purchase and drin[k] intoxicants; that they play fan-tan; that the[y] keep open house to dissolute women, and tha[t] they smoke opium in great quantities.

Neither do they issue invitations to the police to attend the orgies which they hold up in the rookerylike buildings which line the streets of the Chinese quarter. If they did, the bluecoats might be compelled to witness quarrels and fights, such as that which resulted a week ago in "Lize the Man" killing the Gorman girl, at No. ... the woman's horrible

... fur lined coat, lighted a Havana cigar and accompanied by his faithful cohort strode out into the night. At the corner of Pell and Mott they disappeared. They vanished up a staircase and a big and ugly tempered Chinaman told me, "No know you!" when I attempted to follow.

GAMBLING AT LEE KONG'S.

Down at Lee Kong's laundry, at No. 11 Pell street, the festive game of fantan was in full swing. Over the screen at the window and almost in plain view of the passers by I saw fifteen or twenty Chinamen around a table, ver[y] busy at a game of chance. The door was lock[ed]. The policeman on the beat passed without [no]ticing it. He had no time.

DENS IN MOTT AND PELL STREETS.

Here are some of the places where gam[bling] by various means was in constant progres[s] with little or no attempt at concealment:

No. 38 Mott street, fan-tan, conducted [by] Yin ("Irish"), and Li Quon Chung ("Bost[on]

No. 18 Mott street, fan-tan, managed [by] Toy and Lee Sing Dung.

No. 14 Mott street, headquarters of t[he] Lui Tong, a gambling company.

No. 11 Mott street, fan-tan and polic[y] Shue.

Nos. 6, 10, 12, 13, 15, 16, 17, 20, 22, 24, and 38 Mott street, fan-tan.

Nos. 20 and 22 Pell street, conducted by Fong, recently released from the Elmira [Re]formatory.

Nos. 21, 29 and 33 Pell street, fan-tan.

There are also disorderly houses at Nos. 6, and 66 Doyers street, and Nos. 9, 11, 12, 13, 1[5], 19 and 21 Pell street.

At No. 2 Doyers street ...

once. It is the most charitable thing that could have been said about them. They were on easy terms of familiarity with the Chinamen. Some of them hung up their shabby hats and shawls upon pegs around the room and smoked cigarettes.

They wandered back into the kitchen and talked to the cooks, or were jostled about by the waiters. Their laugh was hollow, their voices sounded at times like a chain pump on a frosty morning, and their look was life weary and sad.

Some of the creatures had come all the way from Brooklyn, for it was Sunday morning, and Chinatown always has many guests at that hour. They submitted to embraces from the Chinese guests, and said no word when they were shoved out of the way by the waiters. It was about the same scene in all.

ODORS OF OPIUM EVERYWHERE.

Towards three o'clock the red lights faded away. In the drizzling rain men and women hurried through the streets. From hundreds of windows in Chinatown streamed lights, and from hallways there came a peculiar, pungent odor.

In making inquiries for Chinamen whom I knew I was admitted to rooms where men, stretched at full length, were smoking the deadly opium, and from rooms in upper stories I caught the sound of women's laughter. The subtle odor of the drug was there, too. Into many a dark door, down into basements and up dark staircases men and women hurried, and from above came the sounds of revelry, such as were heard a week ago last night, just before Lize the Man killed the Gorman girl at a Mott street mixed ale party.

So Chinatown smoked, drank and gambled yesterday, and far into the night.

WAS NOT A DRY SUNDAY.

No Great Array of Arrests for Violations of the Excise Law.

Officially yesterday was the "driest" Sunday that New York has seen since the ante-election spasm of excise reform. As a matter of fact, verified by the experience of all such as had a nodding acquaintance with a bartender, the aridity of the day was merely theoretical.

It was a "dry" day in the official sense solely because the forty sleuths of the Central Office, reinforced by thirty extra men, were sent out at midnight on Saturday to scour the city and scoop in unwary publicans whose too intimate acquaintance with the policemen of their respective precincts rendered them secure against ordinary means of detection.

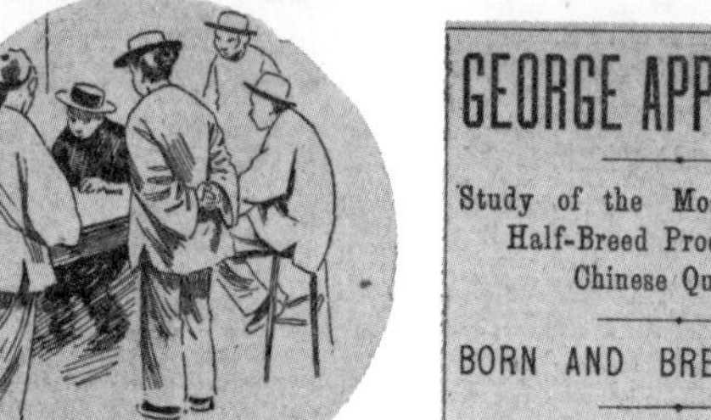

GAMBLERS

AN OPIUM DEN

As early as 1872 he was known as a "James street truck lifter"—that is to say, he was in the habit of stealing tubs of butter and other commodities from the trucks that he found backed up against the sidewalk. "Nigger" Hannon, Archie Hadden, "Johnny" Foley and "Dick" Flanagan, known in criminal circles as "Dick the Tinker," were his associates in those days, and a choice crew they were, too. Young Hadden was the son of the notorious Hadden who kept a boarding house in Water street where sailors were "shanghaied" every day in the week, and a near neighbor if his was a gentleman named Allen, who managed to acquire considerable notoriety at one time by posing as "the wickedest man in New York."

FRANK LESLIE'S ILLUSTRATED NEWSPAPER

No. 1452 — Vol. LVI.] NEW YORK—FOR THE WEEK ENDING MAY 12, 1883

GEORGE APPO'S LIFE.

Study of the Most Interesting Half-Breed Product of the Chinese Quarter.

BORN AND BRED IN VICE.

Educated to Sneak Thieving, Pocket Picking and Finally Green Goods Swindling.

VICTIM OF THE OPIUM HABIT.

Thrice He Has Attempted Suicide When Deprived of His Favorite Drug.

DOWN by the lower end of the Bowery, and just northwest of Chatham square, a few streets for the most part narrow and crooked, contain the most remarkable of all the alien colonies to be found within the limits of New York.

The student of racial traits and customs who goes down to this thickly settled region after nightfall—it is not until the gas and electric lights flare up that the life there becomes animated—can stand in the Bowery at the corner of one of these narrow streets and look right into the heart of this curious little settlement. There he will see overhanging balconies, gay with colored lamps, illuminated signs in Chinese and English, and brightly lighted

Most of us know vaguely about the colony of Celestials that clusters about the lower end of our wonderful Bowery, but there are not many who know of the hundreds of American girls who are drawn into it each year from tenement houses and cigarette and box factories to become the associates of the Mongolian. They are attracted by the color of the life that they find there, and the opium habit soon takes a hold upon them which they cannot shake off. As for the Chinamen with whom they live it must be said of them that they treat these girls more kindly and allow them more money and a wider freedom than do the roughs and thieves of their own race, whose prey they might, in the natural order of things, become.

SHOT IN POUGHKEEPSIE.

It was early in February of that year that ... went up to Poughkeepsie to meet an ancie[nt] and sandy "come on," who had left his ru[ral] home in the mountains of North Carolina, im[pelled] by some alluring essays on the advantages of using counterfeit money, mailed to him by their author, Mr. Appo, who had written them in a strain of imaginative beauty, such as can be found only in the "Arabian Nights." This "come on" wore long, white whiskers and had a large roll of good money secreted in his waistband. He met his tempter in a room in a Poughkeepsie hotel, and the latter, finding his victim loath to part with his money, became threatening in his manner and was promptly shot in the eye.

All hands were put under arrest and Appo ... removed to a hospital, where he again attempted to take his life. It was thought at first this wound would prove fatal to his reason, ... to his life, but he recovered his senses in ... or so, and was visited by a woman named ... Miller and a gentleman who represented ...f as a wealthy manufacturer from Block ..., a place which fairly teems with huge ...ies, as every summer visitor knows. Miss ... wept when she saw the stricken "crook." ...he wealthy manufacturer inquired with ...derable anxiety if "George had given any... away." Appo's nerves were in a horrible ...ition for want of opium, and he expressed ...self with much bitterness in regard to his ...ociate in the enterprise, whom he referred to ... "Dolph," and who, he declared, had sneaked ... and left him to his fate. If it had not been for the influence of the Miller woman, who relieved his sufferings with small pellets of opium which she had brought with her, it is probable that he would have betrayed the other members of his crew.

He was sentenced three months later to a year's imprisonment, and some time afterward while being drafted from Sing Sing to Dannemora in charge of Detective Jackson, of Sing Sing, he again attempted suicide. On his release he declared openly that the man who had shot him was what he called a "dummy come on," who had been hired to put him out of the way. In other words he asserted that certain of his professional associates who bore him a grudge had employed a man to impersonate a rustic gudgeon ...

MYSTERIES OF HOP SOY.

There are restaurants here, too, where one may eat hop soy with the aid of chopsticks, and drink tea from the delicate china cups which appealed so strongly to the aesthetic soul of Oscar Wilde during his visit to America. Hop soy is a sort of Celestial bouillabaisse, a mysterious stew, from which can be extracted enough vegetable and animal curiosities to stock a small museum of natural history. It is very pleasant while rummaging about in a dish of hop soy to fish up some familiar dainty like a bit of celery that can be eaten without fear of after results.

The men who go about the streets are clad for the most part in loose blouses and thick soled shoes, and wear their hair in ques, either twisted into a coil on the back of the head or hanging

IN THE CHINESE THEATRE.

straight's here that George made the acquaintance of certain nimble fingered ladies and gentlemen, who taught him the art of picking pockets, and in June, 1873, he was sent to the penitentiary for six months for practising that art himself. When he came out of prison he went into the business as a regular means of livelihood, and about two years later he was arrested for the same offence, escaped from Bellevue Hospital, and was rearrested and sentenced to a second term, for he was now looked upon by the authorities as an habitual criminal and a cunning, if not a dangerous, man. His picture had its place in the Rogue's Gallery, and his face, showing the characteristics of both his parents, was not a difficult one to remember and recognize—a circumstance which was a hindrance rather than a help to him in the profession which he had chosen to follow.

It is not strange that young Appo should have come naturally by a taste for opium smoking, a vice which now holds him enchained, and which has played an important part in his whole career of crime. As the Chinese colony grew in numbers so did the opium dens within its limits grow and flourish, but it was not till late in the seventies that the passion for the drug

A BALCONY AT NIGHT.

began to spread among the Americans and Irish who dwelt in the neighborhood.

Appo had always, by virtue of his blood on his father's side, enjoyed to a certain extent the confidence of the Chinese—a confidence which these strange, secretive people very seldom give to any one not of their own race.

While still very young he had learned to smoke and also to prepare the opium for the pipe, and it was through him that many New York roughs and "crooks" began to use the "dope" themselves and to spread the taste for it among their associates. They began to seek out the places in which smoking might be enjoyed, and in 1880, or thereabouts, there were a score of "joints" in full blast in Pell, Mott and Doyers streets and in the lower Bowery, and not one of these but had its quota of Caucasian smokers of both sexes, most of whom belonged to the criminal or dissolute classes. There were other visitors, too—actors, actresses, clubmen and others—who dropped in from time to time for the fun of the thing and because they found a peculiar charm in the heavy, pungent, soothing atmosphere, and in the outspoken frankness and freedom which distinguished the conversation of the regular habitues.

COOKING THE DOPE.

Now, at that time, the difficult art of "cooking," or preparing the opium for the pipe was known to but few except the Chinese, and the young half breed soon found that by means of his familiarity with the magical black paste and his undoubted skill in its preparation life's pathway could be made smooth and delicious with a dreamy happiness without the exercise of much industry or daring on his part.

There were a dozen ways in which he could pick up a living, if nothing more, through his connection with the "joints," and any one of these ways was safer and easier than picking pockets or purloining things from trucks and basements. He could act as guide to parties of sightseers who wanted to "do Chinatown," and he could always earn a small fee and at the same time get his turn at the pipe by cooking the opium "pills" for those smokers who were less skilful than he. Besides this, continual contact with visitors from uptown offered him rather unusual opportunities for obtaining a watch or pin now and then without having to go to Tiffany's for it.

So it happened that Appo became an habitual frequenter of the opium dens of Chinatown and a "fiend" of the most pronounced description. That is to say, he soon became so addicted to the use of the drug that he did not wish to exist without it, and it was probably on this account that when he was arrested in 1882 for the robbery of a Mexican named Del Valle, he made a desperate attempt to kill himself by drinking a vial of laudanum. On this occasion the Tombs physician endeavored to administer an emetic, but Appo kicked it out of his hands, and it became necessary to put him in a straitjacket and force the medicine down his throat.

The opium habit has always been a dominant influence in the career of this man, and it was through his indulgence in the habit that he

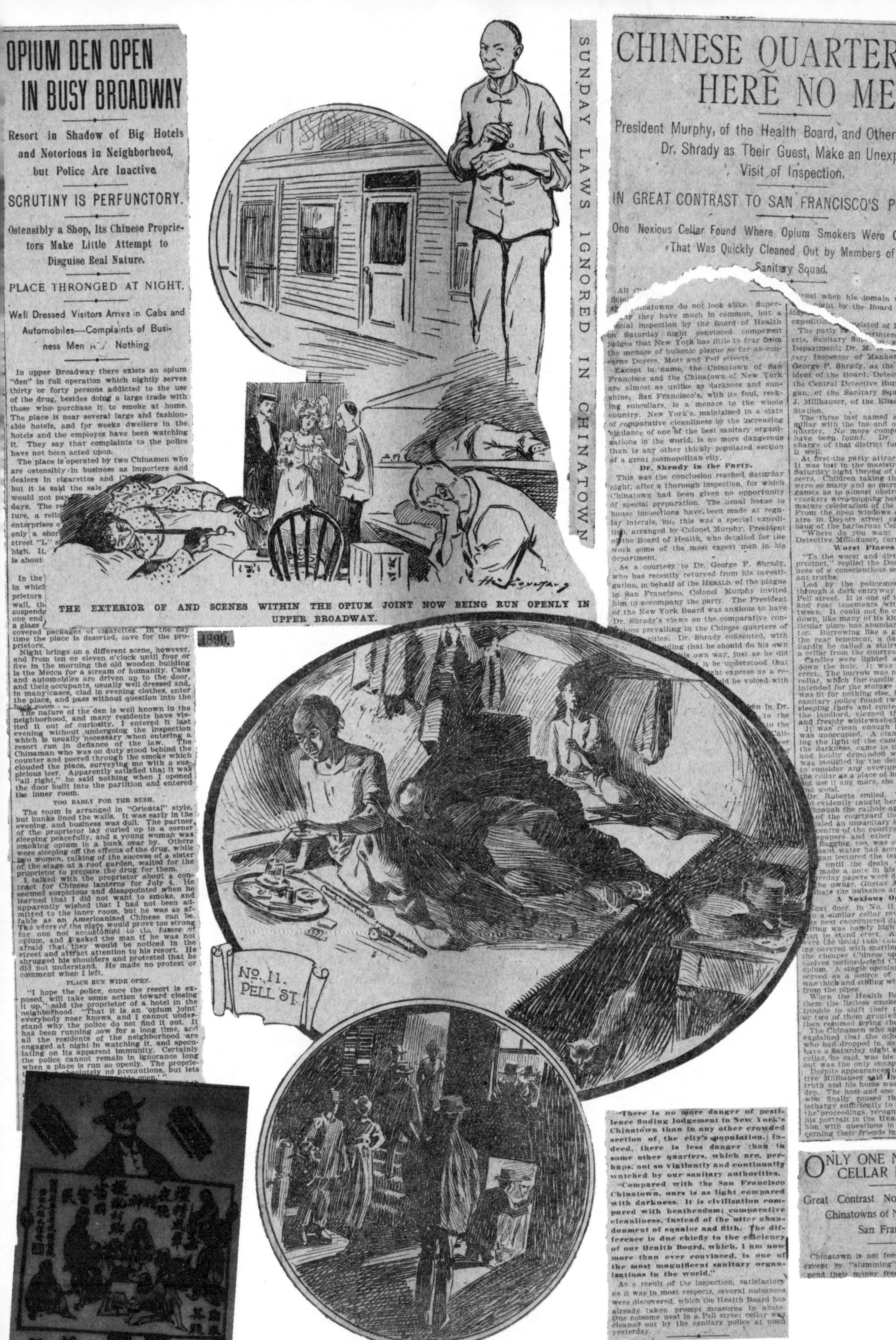

OPIUM DEN OPEN IN BUSY BROADWAY

Resort in Shadow of Big Hotels and Notorious in Neighborhood, but Police Are Inactive.

SCRUTINY IS PERFUNCTORY.

Ostensibly a Shop, Its Chinese Proprietors Make Little Attempt to Disguise Real Nature.

PLACE THRONGED AT NIGHT.

Well Dressed Visitors Arrive in Cabs and Automobiles—Complaints of Business Men [illegible] Nothing.

In upper Broadway there exists an opium "den" in full operation which nightly serves thirty or forty persons addicted to the use of the drug, besides doing a large trade with those who purchase it to smoke at home. The place is near several large and fashionable hotels, and for weeks dwellers in the hotels and the employes have been watching it. They say that complaints to the police have not been acted upon.

The place is operated by two Chinamen who are ostensibly in business as importers and dealers in cigarettes and C[illegible] but it is said the sale [illegible] would not pay [illegible] days. The re[illegible] ture, a relic [illegible] enterprises e[illegible] only a shor[illegible] street "L" s[illegible] high. It [illegible] is about [illegible]

In the [illegible] in which [illegible] prietors [illegible] wall, th[illegible] suspende[illegible] one end[illegible] a glass [illegible] covered packages of cigarettes. In the day time the place is deserted, save for the proprietors.

Night brings on a different scene, however, and from ten or eleven o'clock until four or five in the morning the old wooden building is the Mecca for a stream of humanity. Cabs and automobiles are driven up to the door, and their occupants, usually well dressed and, in many cases, clad in evening clothes, enter the place, and pass without question into the back room.

The nature of the den is well known in the neighborhood, and many residents have visited it out of curiosity. I entered it last evening without undergoing the inspection which is usually necessary when entering a resort run in defiance of the law. The Chinaman who was on duty stood behind the counter and peered through the smoke which clouded the place, surveying me with a suspicious leer. Apparently satisfied that it was "all right," he said nothing when I opened the door built into the partition and entered the inner room.

TOO EARLY FOR THE RUSH.

The room is arranged in "Oriental" style, but bunks lined the walls. It was early in the evening, and business was dull. The partner of the proprietor lay curled up in a corner sleeping peacefully, and a young woman was smoking opium in a bunk near by. Others were sleeping off the effects of the drug, while two women, talking of the success of a sister of the stage at a roof garden, waited for the proprietor to prepare the drug for them.

I talked with the proprietor about a contract for Chinese lanterns for July 4. He seemed suspicious and disappointed when he learned that I did not want to smoke, and apparently wished that I had not been admitted to the inner room, but he was as affable as an Americanized Chinese can be. The odors of the place would prove too strong for one not accustomed to the fumes of opium, and I asked the man if he was not afraid that they would be noticed in the street and attract attention to his resort. He shrugged his shoulders and protested that he did not understand. He made no protest or comment when I left.

PLACE RUN WIDE OPEN.

"I hope the police, once the resort is exposed, will take some action toward closing it up," said the proprietor of a hotel in the neighborhood. "That it is an 'opium joint' everybody near knows, and I cannot understand why the police do not find it out. It has been running now for a long time, and all the residents of the neighborhood are engaged at night in watching it, and speculating on its apparent immunity. Certainly the police cannot remain in ignorance long when a place is run so openly. The proprietor [illegible] absolutely no precautions, but lets [illegible] wide open.'"

THE EXTERIOR OF AND SCENES WITHIN THE OPIUM JOINT NOW BEING RUN OPENLY IN UPPER BROADWAY.

1899.

SUNDAY LAWS IGNORED IN CHINATOWN

CHINESE QUARTER HERE NO MENACE

President Murphy, of the Health Board, and Other Officials, with Dr. Shrady as Their Guest, Make an Unexpected Visit of Inspection.

IN GREAT CONTRAST TO SAN FRANCISCO'S PLAGUE SPOT

One Noxious Cellar Found Where Opium Smokers Were Congregated, and That Was Quickly Cleaned Out by Members of the Sanitary Squad.

All C[illegible] ficie[illegible] [Ch]inatowns do not look alike. Super[ficially] they have much in common, but a [sp]ecial inspection by the Board of Health on Saturday night convinced competent judges that New York has little to fear from the menace of bubonic plague so far as concerns Doyers, Mott and Pell streets.

Except in name, the Chinatown of San Francisco and the Chinatown of New York are almost as unlike as darkness and sunshine. San Francisco's, with its foul, reeking subcellars, is a menace to the whole country. New York's, maintained in a state of comparative cleanliness by the increasing vigilance of one of the best sanitary organizations in the world, is no more dangerous than is any other thickly populated section of a great cosmopolitan city.

Dr. Shrady in the Party.

This was the conclusion reached Saturday night, after a thorough inspection, for which Chinatown had been given no opportunity of special preparation. The usual house to house inspections have been made at regular interals, but this was a special expedition, arranged by Colonel Murphy, President of the Board of Health, who detailed for the work some of the most expert men in his department.

As a courtesy to Dr. George F. Shrady, who has recently returned from his investigation, in behalf of the HERALD, of the plague in San Francisco, Colonel Murphy invited him to accompany the party. The President of the New York Board was anxious to have Dr. Shrady's views on the comparative con[di]tions prevailing in the Chinese quarters of [the two] cities. Dr. Shrady consented, with [the under]standing that he should do his own [work in] his own way, just as he did [illegible] it be understood that [illegible]ght express as a re[illegible] [illegible]d be voiced with [illegible]

[illegible] [usual] when his domain was invaded Saturday night by the Board of Health's special expedition. [illegible]

The party c[o]nsisted of Dr. Charles F. Roberts, Sanitary Sup[e]rintendent of the Health Department; Dr. M. [illegible] Feeney, Chief Sanitary Inspector of Manhattan Borough; Dr. George F. Shrady, as the guest of the president of the Board; Detective Armstrong, of the Central Detective Bureau; John F. Gilligan, of the Sanitary Squad, and Detective J. Millhauser, of the Elizabeth Street Police Station.

The three last named are thoroughly familiar with the ins and outs of the Chinese quarter. No more competent guides could have been found. Dr. Feeney also had charge of that district for years and knows it well.

At first the party attracted little attention. It was lost in the maelstrom of Chinatown's Saturday night throng of residents and sightseers. Children taking the early evening air were so many and so merry at their sidewalk games as to almost obstruct progress. Firecrackers were popping here and there in premature celebration of the Chinese New Year. From the open windows of the Chinese theatre in Doyers street came the clash and baug of the barbarous Celestial orchestra.

"Where do you want to go first" asked Detective Millhauser, turning to Dr. Shrady.

Worst Places Sought.

"To the worst and dirtiest places in your precinct," replied the Doctor, with the boldness of a conscientious seeker after unpleasant truths.

Led by the policemen, the party filed through a dark entryway to the rear of No. 9 Pell street. It is one of the old type of front and rear tenements with a courtyard between. It could not be condemned and torn down, like many of its kind, because this particular place has abundant light and ventilaton. Burrowing like a great rat hole under the rear tenement, a dark cavern—it could hardly be called a stairway—gave access to a cellar from the courtyard.

Candles were lighted and the party crept down the hole. It was impossible to walk erect. The burrow was not high enough. The cellar, which the candle light revealed, was intended for the storage of coal and wood. It was fit for nothing else, but not long ago the sanitary police found twenty-four Chinamen sleeping there and routed them out, warned the landlord, cleaned the place thoroughly and freshly whitewashed the walls.

It was clean enough Saturday night and was unoccupied. A clamorous negress, seeing the light of the candles shining through the darkness, came to the mouth of the pit and loudly demanded who was there. She was mollified by the detectives, but refused to consider any overtures for the rental of the cellar as a place of habitation. She could [n]ot use it any more, she said, except for coal [a]nd wood.

Dr. Roberts smiled. The sanitary police [ha]d evidently taught her the lesson well. [T]hrough the rathole again and out into the [illegible] of the courtyard the sputtering candles [rev]ealed an unsanitary blemish. The sink in [the] centre of the courtyard was clogged with [new]spapers and other waste and rubbish. [The] flagging, too, was out of repair, so that [stag]nant water had accumulated. Detective [Gilli]gan lectured the tentants, poked with a [illegible] until the drain was partly opened, [and] made a note in his memorandum book. [Yes]terday papers were drawn up to be served [on t]he owner, Gustav Arfken, ordering him [to a]bate the nuisance and repair the drain.

A Noxious Opium Den.

[N]ext door, in No. 11 Pell street, descent [int]o a similar cellar revealed the most nox[iou]s nest encountered during the night. The [ce]iling was barely high enough to permit a [m]an to stand erect. Around the side walls were the usual [illegible], made of planking covered with matting, such as are seen in the cheaper Chinese opium dens. On these shelves reclined eight Chinamen, all smoking opium. A single opening at the extreme rear served as a source of ventilation. The air was thick and stifling with the pungent fumes from the pipes.

When the Health Board party surprised them the listless smokers scarcely took the trouble to shift their positions, though one or two of them grunted interrogatively, and then resumed frying the opium.

The Chinaman who appeared to be the host explained that the others were his friends, who had dropped in, as was their custom, to have a Saturday night smoke with him. The cellar, he said, was his home. A fantan layout was the only conspicuous decoration.

Despite appearances to the contrary, Detective Millhauser said the Chinaman told the truth and his home was not a regular opium den. The host and one or two of his friends, who finally roused themselves from their lethargy sufficiently to show some interest in the proceedings, recognized Dr. Shrady from his portrait in the HERALD, and began to ply him with questions in pigeon English concerning their friends in San Francisco. Sev-

"There is no more danger of pestilence finding lodgement in New York's Chinatown than in any other crowded section of the city's population. Indeed, there is less danger than in some other quarters, which are, perhaps, not so vigilantly and continually watched by our sanitary authorities.

"Compared with the San Francisco Chinatown, ours is as light compared with darkness. It is civilization compared with heathendom; comparative cleanliness, instead of the utter abandonment of squalor and filth. The difference is due chiefly to the efficiency of our Health Board, which, I am now more than ever convinced, is one of the most magnificent sanitary organizations in the world."

As a result of the inspection, satisfactory as it was in most respects, several nuisances were discovered, which the Health Board has already taken prompt measures to abate. One noisome nest in a Pell street cellar was cleaned out by the sanitary police at noon yesterday.

ONLY ONE NOISOME CELLAR DISCOVERED

Great Contrast Noted Between the Chinatowns of New York and San Francisco.

Chinatown is not fond of being inspected, except by "slumming" parties disposed to [s]pend their money freely.

INJECTING THE DRUG IN THE ARM; A COMMON METHOD
INSERTING THE NEEDLE IN THE FLESH OF THE LEG THUS SAVING THE ARM FROM SCARS

"ON HIS BACK WAS A PHOSPHORESCENT FIGURE, GRIM AND GHOSTLY."

Ideal Sketch of George B. Mabry's Wild Midnight Ride with Death.

HALLUCINATIONS OF A SLAVE TO MORPHINE DESCRIBED

Remarkable Confessions of George B. Mabry, of Georgia.

Cured of the Habit, He Now Writes of the Weird Vagaries of a Tortured Brain.

MAD RACE WITH SPECTRAL DEATH.

A latter day De Quincey is George Bee Mabry. For years a slave to morphine, the brilliant Georgian has finally conquered his mad disease. But the memoirs of his thraldom are ever with him, and he now tells the readers of the HERALD, in his own words, of the weird hallucinations which came to him with the drug. In their horrible realism and in the graphic recital of the victim the vagaries of De Quincey in his "Confessions of an Opium Eater" pale into insignificance as compared with the hallucinations of George Bee Mabry.

By George Bee Mabry.

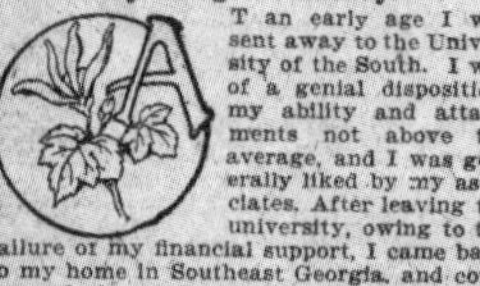

AT an early age I was sent away to the University of the South. I was of a genial disposition, my ability and attainments not above the average, and I was generally liked by my associates. After leaving the university, owing to the failure of my financial support, I came back to my home in Southeast Georgia, and commenced the study of law. I was admitted to the practice in due time, gathered a paying clientage, commenced to make a little money and settled down in earnest to the realities of life.

Four years after my admission to the Bar I was elected for a term of four years Solicitor General of the Brunswick Circuit, embracing nine counties, and served the term, working hard, and from congratulatory expressions of the grand juries and the people generally I believe I served the State faithfully. So much as an introduction.

The hallucinations or illusions of which I shall give account all occurred during a period of three years during the time I held the State's commission referred to as Solicitor General. The cause of these illusions or hallucinations was attributed by learned physicians to an excessive use of opium and morphine, to which habit I became a slave in the beginning of the last decade of years.

I have no doubt now, and I had no doubt then, of the truth of that diagnosis. My daily supply was enormous—ten grains of morphine, hypodermically administered. In justice to myself now I declare with solemn emphasis that I have been for a number of years entirely free from the habit, and that which follows in the narratives is written under the dictation of a brain unclouded by narcotic stimulant or other excitant, and I simply record the incidents as reproduced by a memory as clear and faithful as ordinary men are endowed with.

I leave the learned to explain under the laws or science of metaphysics the phenomena. I do not attribute my cure to any strength of will or constitutional ability to withstand the terrible agony that must be endured in throwing off the yoke of captivity to the opium habit, but rather to accident, which placed me where I could not obtain the drug, and therefore had to endure; and partly through the aid of a medicine, potent, I believe, to give relief if taken as directed (and therein lies the secret of the medicine's failure). My cure was effected, and I again lived, and now live, a free man.

A MAD RACE WITH DEATH.

In the fall of 1883 I was attending the Superior Court in Coffee county. Douglass, the county site, is fourteen miles away from Pierson, the little town the Judge and lawyers always stopped at en route to Douglass, which latter place we reached by buggy or horseback. As usual I rode over on Sunday evening, so as to be on hand to attend to my duties as Solicitor General Monday morning.

I arrived about dark, and, as was my custom, stopped with Joe Lichtenstein, who kept one of the taverns. After supper I retired to my room and, disrobing, I took my morphine syringe and the bottle of dissolved drug and prepared to administer to myself the injection that was necessary to keep me free of the agonies attending a deprivation of the accursed potion. I had begun to feel the need of it long before supper, but desisted until bedtime, in consequence of which I was extremely "shaky" when I attempted to push the needle beneath the skin of my left arm.

I gave a start as the point pierced rather too deeply, and that little spasm caused the syringe to fall from my hand to the floor and it was broken in pieces. I had the bottle of dissolved drug on the table by my side, and as I reached in spasmodic haste to catch the falling syringe my right arm struck against the bottle of fluid and it, too, fell with a crash to the floor and was shattered.

My God! You who never felt the pain, the mortal agony, the anguish, the wild, terrible longing for relief as felt by the opium and morphine cursed, can even remotely catch the meaning of the anguish and horror of such a situation. I quickly resolved what I must do, but in the resolution I saw the terror and pain in its accomplishment.

There was no physician nearer than Pierson, fourteen miles away. There was none of the drug or its substitutes in Douglass. I must make the ride to Pierson. I dressed as quickly as I could, went down and, calling the landlord, told him I had to go to a friend's in the neighborhood, and asked for a good saddle horse. He gave me a fine animal, which I at once mounted, and, after getting out of the light, I plied the lash and into the darkness of swamp and forest I rode.

My brain was beginning to turn cold. I felt the perspiration trickling down my spinal column. Intense pains were shooting through my nerve centres; bright flashes as of vivid streaks of lightning were playing before me. I had just entered a belt of swamp bordering a creek when I heard the swish of a lash and a large black horse, blacker than the night around me, dashed up by me. On his back was a phosphorescent figure, grim and ghastly. Plainly could I see by the pale light of his own body the deathly pallor and the

Horrors of a Wild Ride.

My solemn word for it, my horse seemed to realize the presence, for he plunged forward and flew through the darkness of the swamp. As I drew away from the spectre I heard him yell:—"At twelve o'clock to-night I will await you. You cannot live. Your doom is at hand. I am Death!"

I caught the full meaning of the words. It was a race for life. I leaned forward and urged my good horse on. He seemed himself terror stricken, for his pace was quickened, and on through the darkness and the gloom of the night he plunged.

My heart's blood rushed through the arteries in streams as cold as ice. Ever and anon I heard the sound of the black horse's footfalls, and the demoniac laugh of his ghostly rider. Once, in a paroxysm of pain I drew my pistol, until then forgotten, and pressed the cold muzzle to my temple, but a flash of vivid light streaked the air in front of me. My horse plunged wildly and the weapon was lost in the darkness of the night. "Oh, Christ, help me!" I shrieked.

I lost the sound of the black horse's tread. I heard a terrible yell, a crash as if a thunder bolt had fallen, and then, I swear, oblivion came over my senses. I was aroused by the ringing of my horse's hoofs on the iron rails of the railway. I looked around and recognized the station house and lamp of the depot in Pierson.

I was in an agony of doubt, of fear, of mortal pain. I was conscious that my horse had stopped. I listened. Far off, beyond the limits of the village, I heard the yell of the spectre. "I will be there to claim you!" was borne to my straining ears.

I struck my horse, and in a minute was before the doctor's door. Tumbling from the saddle, I staggered to the door and knocked with all my might. I heard his footsteps coming.

"For God's sake, hurry, I am dying."

He had been on a sick call and had not yet retired. He opened the door, and I fell before him. "Morphine, doctor! Give me morphine quick, or I die!"

Thoroughly aroused he lifted me, and carried me into his dining room and placed me on an easy chair. "Quick, doctor! for God's sake, quick! Death is near at hand!"

Hurriedly he emptied the drug in a glass, dissolving it in water, and drew in the accursed potion, piercing my arm. Instantly the circulation had done its work and I felt calm.

"Don't go to the door!" I shouted. "It is Death! I won the race. Hear him knocking. O Death! you've lost your sting. I have won! I have won!"

I remember no more until I was aroused by the doctor bathing my face in water. I opened my eyes and looked around. The sun was just rising. I had been placed on a couch and the doctor had been with me since my arrival. I remembered my accident, my wild ride against death, and my victory. He administered another injection and I felt well again.

My poor horse was jaded, but after a light repast I rode away to Douglass, arriving in time for court. I borrowed the doctor's little syringe, supplied myself with enough of the drug to last me, and was among the last to leave the court house at the end of the week.

The horror of that awful night, the terror of my condition and the narrowness of my escape from death will be fresh in my memory as long as life shall last. On my ride back to Douglass that morning I accompanied the mail carrier. He called my attention to a pine tree, evidently riven by lightning.

"I didn't notice that tree yesterday," he said. "It didn't storm last night. It must have been a stray bolt out of some passing cloud. Lightning plays funny pranks sometimes."

I was silent. I remembered the peal that I had heard last night. My pistol was found by a negro in the grass by the road. I never laid claim to it. I would not have owned it again for the wealth of the Indies.

ASBELL'S KNIFE LEAVES A SCAR.

I had been ill. At times I was delirious, but at no time did I forget or lose sight of the little morphine syringe and bottle of dissolved drug I had concealed beneath the

Brunswick. Dr. H. M. Branham was the physician who attended me.

After my removal I rested easier. My nerves were in a calmer state and I had freer access to my syringe and drug. I had concealed them successfully on my removal, and after my retirement in the hospital. The evening of the third day I spent in my new quarters I took an unusually large injection of the drug, and, besides, drank about two ounces of whiskey to stay the nausea that sometimes followed the use of my syringe.

I fell asleep about nine o'clock and was aroused about the middle of the night by the voices of George Asbell, now on the police force of Brunswick, and his brother, Dudley. I heard George say:—"He is on the cot by the corner. You wait here by the window and I'll go in by the side door. If he should wake or try to get away or fight you, fire through the blinds. I will go in easy, though, and try and kill him by one blow of my knife."

In an instant I was alert and planning escape. I had no weapon and felt that I was completely in their power unless I could elude them. Quickly I resolved on my line of action. There was a window in another ward adjoining the one I was in, and I determined to wait until I heard Asbell in the other room, through which he must pass before reaching me, and then I would spring through and attempt to reach the police barracks.

My brain was clear. I realized fully that the chances were desperate, and that my only safety was in my flight. I got out of bed and commenced to dress, but before I had a single piece of my clothing on I heard Asbell stumble over a chair at the door of my ward, and heard him mutter a curse and start toward me. I waited no longer, but sprang through the door of the next room, rushed to the window, hastily threw it up, and out in the dark and cold drizzling rain I leaped.

It was in the month of January. A cold spell, with rain, was upon the city, but I felt it not. Clad only in my undergarments, bareheaded and shoeless, I climbed to the top of the hospital fence, and was in the act of springing to the ground on the outside when I heard Asbell say:—"I'll kill you to-night. You let off those fellows whom I prosecuted for trying to rob me, and now, d—n you, I am going to get even with you!"

I sprang to the ground and started on a run through the woods that border the hospital. I heard the thud as he also dropped to the ground on the outside of the fence, and the race began. I became confused as to my direction, and lost my reckoning. Through bush and over logs, now dodging behind a tree, now squatting in some hollow—but it seemed of no use, Asbell was surely following. He seemed to trail me with the persistence of the bloodhound.

I was becoming weak. My heart sounded with beats like a drum. My breath was like the hissing of steam. It fairly scalded my lips as it was poured forth by my straining lungs. I felt that I was in a desperate position. Asbell was a man of fully one hundred and eighty pounds; I was scarcely one hundred and twenty. I calculated the chances of a hand to hand encounter, I unarmed and he with a murderous knife and probably pistol.

The Struggle in the Woods.

I saw Asbell about a hundred feet from me. He saw me at the same time and called to me to stop, for I had immediately turned and commenced in a wild run. I knew not where, for I was lost. But on and on I struggled, now entangled in the vines and brush of the forest, then tripping over logs, and falling now and then from sheer exhaustion. My underclothes were in tatters; my limbs were torn and bleeding; my feet were bruised and lacerated. Yet the thought of the terrible death I would suffer if overtaken by my pursuer urged me on.

Once I thought of a sermon I had heard and that had impressed me. It was on the efficacy of prayer. In the tension of my ordeal to think was to act. I stopped and listened. I heard no sound save the night bird's cry and the moaning of the trees as the winter wind touched their branches. I felt safe for at least a few minutes. Down on my knees I sent up to heaven a prayer. But again I heard approaching the steps of Asbell. My God! Could I not elude him? Off again I struggled, but I fell heavily to

Struggle with a Phantom.

I sprang up and walked rapidly to the door, my knife in hand, and just then the conductor, Lovick Du Pont, came through the door of the first class car on his way to the smoker. As he opened the door I asked him to bear witness to anything that happened. He seemed not to understand me, for calling out "All aboard!" the train moved on. He slammed the door and I had lost the opportunity of passing into the first class car with an eye witness to check Lawrence if he attacked me.

I sat down, but was in such a state of frenzy at the infamous intention of Lawrence that in a few minutes I determined to pass him if he was still at the car door, even if I had to kill him. I became an enraged being, incapable of controlling the torrent of anger and revengeful thought that completely possessed me.

At once I arose and walking rapidly to the door peered through the glass panel and saw Lawrence sitting, or rather crouched, on the steps of the coach. "Now is my time," I thought, and, opening the door with a jerk, I stepped on the platform and closed the entrance after me.

"Lawrence, you are trying to kill me, are you," I shouted. "I heard you to-night at the Screven plotting to assassinate me." My further denunciation was stopped. He sprang up and made a lunge across the rail of the two coaches at me. His aim was not true or the swinging of the train seemed to make him miss my breast, at which he seemed to strike. His knife struck the iron railing of the platform and went whizzing into the air.

Now was my time. I saw him put his hand to his hip pocket. I knew what that meant, and to know was to act. My knife was still in my hand, and sharp and bright it was. Drawing my right arm and forearm well up over my left shoulder I drove the blade into his breast. He uttered not a word and I heard not a groan, but backward over the platform his body plunged.

In an instant the horror of the situation palled me. I threw my knife out into the darkness and went into the first class car. I saw Judge Atkinson and Mr. Dart looking at me intently. Had they seen my act? I must have looked as I felt. God grant I may never feel the like again, even in delirium!

I sat down by Dart and he asked me if I was ill. I told him yes. Upon his inquiring the cause of my illness and the character, I could only answer that I believed I had taken an overdose of stimulant.

The next stop of the train they carried me into the baggage car and Conductor Du Pont stopped the train until he sent for a cup of coffee at a wayside restaurant. I drank it, and on being made as comfortable as possible, fell asleep. They aroused me at Jesup and I went into the Brunswick train. My brain was in a tempest of fear for the consequences of the murder. Would they find the body early? Would I be suspected? Would I be arrested and tried? How could I defend myself?

A thousand horrors presented themselves. A vision of the barred cell of a prison; a dream of the gallows. While in this condition I remembered I had a flask of whiskey in my valise. I went and drank enough to have ordinarily made a toper drunk. It only calmed me. I reached my home in the early morning and went at once to bed. The strain on my nerves had apparently paralyzed my sense of trouble and I slept for seventeen hours. When I awoke it was near midnight. A light was burning low. My memory was clear, all the details of the murder were with me, but I then realized it was a terrible hallucination!

HER THREE HUSBANDS.

Mrs. Edwards and Her Trio of Sometime Liege Lords Have a Merry Reunion.

Although my wish, and also fate,
To marry and to separate,
There seems no reason why
Whene'er my hubbies chance to meet
There should not be reunion sweet,
Though severed is the tie.
—"Husbands Three," not by Kipling.

Mrs. Frederick Edwards is a woman of

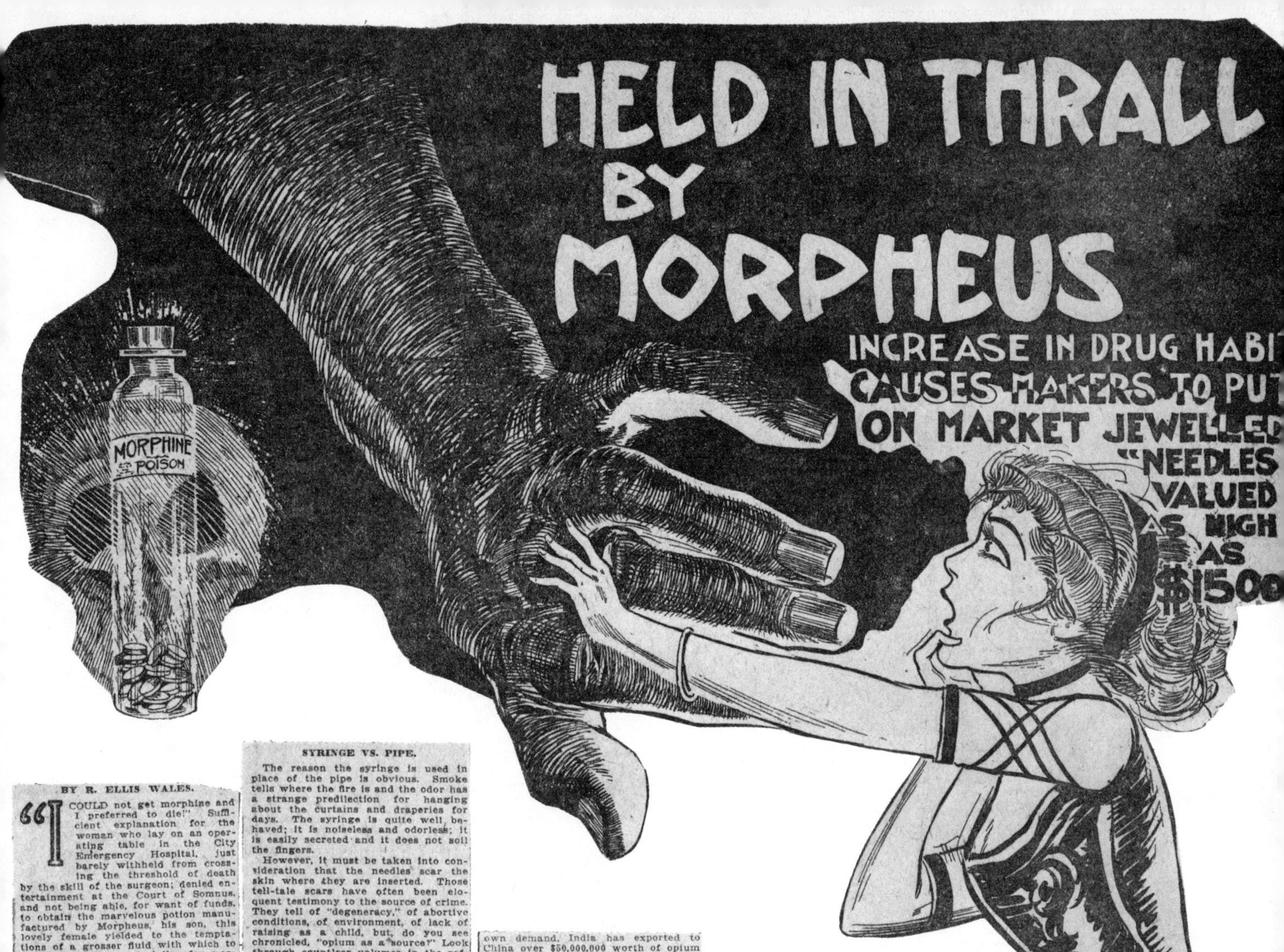
HELD IN THRALL
BY
MORPHEUS
INCREASE IN DRUG HABIT
CAUSES MAKERS TO PUT
ON MARKET JEWELLED
"NEEDLES"
VALUED
AS HIGH
AS
$1500
MORPHINE
POISON

BY R. ELLIS WALES.

"I COULD not get morphine and I preferred to die!" Sufficient explanation for the woman who lay on an operating table in the City Emergency Hospital, just barely withheld from crossing the threshold of death by the skill of the surgeon; denied entertainment at the Court of Somnus, and not being able, for want of funds, to obtain the marvelous potion manufactured by Morpheus, his son, this lovely female yielded to the temptations of a grosser fluid with which to end her existence. A dollar for morphine; 10 cents for the acid. Poverty forced her choice; she had but 10 cents, and for the lesser sum she could get everlasting oblivion.

The surgeon rescued her for what? If conscience allowed the man to control her destiny he might have shirked and accelerated the action of the fatal drug. He knew, after she revived from that heroic treatment, what Fate had in store for the woman; he knew the awful claim Morpheus had upon the luckless girl, usurping the affections of her husband, alienating the respect of her family and annihilating the faithfulness of friends. Again and again would she lie in the arms of that insidious seducer; that ravisher of the soul, the devilish imp of Somnus.

This is her story. Her husband denied her money because she spent it all for morphine. Brilliant and charming as she was to him when he reached home after a busy day in the office, made so by the secret use of the bejeweled syringe. With artificial passion she threw her warm arms about his neck and he called her his darling. He spoke of her sparkling eyes, dilated with the drug; he spoke of her vivacity, induced by drug-stimulated nerves, and he went about strong in the faith of his beautiful wife.

But one day his annihilation came. Cutting out office work, he came home a little too soon one afternoon and, seeking an article on her dresser, he found—a tiny silver case, bearing in the center of its polished lid a single brilliant emerald. He picked it up and smiled. "Just another toy for the dear; a jewel case, I suppose." Again and again he turned it over, and always that single jewel glinted luminously. He gazed into its limpid depths until it suddenly assumed the appearance of an eye and gave forth an ominous light. With the transfiguration of this gem into a Cyclopian organ came the desire to open the box, and as he did so he saw the consummation of his now-evil premonition. Shocked, he saw nestling therein a tiny syringe of solid silver, the piston-head tipped with a jewel. At its head, lying across the case, glinted the thread-like needles, and parallel with the syringe he saw the cylindrical tube containing the opiate.

HER APPEARANCE CHECKED HIM.

Crushed, but waxing wroth, he confronted his wife. Words of anger were on his lips, but her appearance checked the fiery torrent. Face drawn, eyes narrowed, mouth drawn to a pucker, colorless, her whole body, ofttimes so beautiful, quivering as with the ague, the woman stood there a panting Thing, eyes furtively glancing at the fatal casket. She did not plead for life nor forgiveness. Nay, her husband stood there paralyzed as she begged, "Oh, I don't care, now that you have discovered all; let me have it, quickly! Quickly!" and she staggered forward. The man awoke and grabbed the case.

SYRINGE VS. PIPE.

The reason the syringe is used in place of the pipe is obvious. Smoke tells where the fire is and the odor has a strange predilection for hanging about the curtains and draperies for days. The syringe is quite well behaved; it is noiseless and odorless; it is easily secreted and it does not soil the fingers.

However, it must be taken into consideration that the needles scar the skin where they are inserted. Those tell-tale scars have often been eloquent testimony to the source of crime. They tell of "degeneracy," of abortive conditions, of environment, of lack of raising as a child, but, do you see chronicled, "opium as a source?" Look through countless volumes in the reference libraries and you'll find little reference to the morphine habit. They will instruct you how to administer charity and how to make your way of reform through the seamy sections of a city, but they offer no remedy for the opium evil. The general reader thinks of opium as a mere article for smoking in Chinatown. In fact it is generally associated with the Chinese in the mind of the people. But is it not shocking that the drug is exercising its worst evil right in the midst of social institutions? If you don't believe this ask your Captain of Detectives, or some of the physicians, or nurses at the hospitals!

In searching for material for this article the writer has witnessed scenes too morbid and loathsome to be described in an article. More or less familiar with the result of this vice during his experience as a police reporter he had never penetrated the most hidden fastnesses of this lurking demon. But he has seen and can only describe it all lamely.

WANDERS IN DOLEFUL COUNTRY.

A woman who seeks the pleasant dreams induced by this treacherous drug wanders through a most doleful country and soils her pretty feet in the miasma which surrounds it. She would seek that realm of doubtful fascination so well described by Bulfinch in his "Age of Fable," where Somnus reigns with his son Morpheus, and where "clouds and shadows are exhaled from the ground, and the light glimmers faintly. The bird of dawning, with crested head, never there calls aloud to Aurora, nor watchful dog nor more sagacious goose disturbs the silence. No wild beast, nor cattle, nor branch moved with the wind, nor sound of human conversation, breaks the stillness. Silence reigns there; but from the bottom of the rock the river Lethe flows, and by its murmur invites sleep. Poppies grow abundantly before the door of the cave, and other herbs, from whose juices night collects slumbers, which she scatters over the darkened earth. There is no gate to the mansion, to creak on its hinges, nor any watchman; but in the midst a couch of black ebony, adorned with black plumes and curtains. There the God reclines, his limbs relaxed with sleep."

Such is the picture, which to the romantic eye of the woman, whose tired nerves cry out for surcease, appeals like that of an Arcady to the persecuted poet. Prosaic as it may appear, the ecstasies of this realm of dreams, sensual to a degree, must be purchased with filthy lucre. Everyday coin supplies the golden key which unlocks the vaults of the treasure, inviting the unwary and damning the soul of him who enters. The poppies nod their lovely heads, attracting by their pleasing exterior and giving their juices to become masses of pulverized joy, with their aftermath of hellish bitterness.

own demand. India has exported to China over $50,000,000 worth of opium in one year.

EXTENT OF ITS USE.

Some idea of the use to which the drug is put is shown by the recent confession in open court of a druggist in Oakland. He admitted that he had sold morphine in violation of the law, and was fined $100. Upon investigation it was discovered that he had sold at least $5 worth to one customer. When making the arrest the police gathered as evidence a batch of about forty blank prescriptions, signed by a physician; space was left blank for the amount required and the kind of drug wanted, which might be either opium, morphine, cocaine or ether. There is a crusade now on against certain druggists and others by the California State Association of Pharmacists, and through the efforts of this institution it is hoped that the evil will be restricted; at least in civilized communities.

With this expose of a legitimate druggist comes the worse fact that where opium can not be obtained ether is used. What will we have next? And can we again blame France for its introduction? From France we have g[...]
absinthe, and from France we have [...]
the knowledge of ether taking. [...]
reason for the substitution of [...]
for morphine and absinthe in Fr[...]
particularly in Paris, is that th[...]
of this colorless drug is free, n[...]
ing trammeled by edict of law.

Dispatches from the French [...]
say that some victims have [...]
seven pints daily, while a [...]
three-quarters is the usual li[...]
by general users. It is to [...]
that the seven-pint con[...]
women. The drug is ta[...]
system first by breathi[...]
with unsatiated appetite, [...]
Full 40 per cent of the [...]
who are brought into t[...]
houses of the French city are [...]
fiends.

And the worst of it, we are furnish[...]
ing ether fiends in ou[...]
What will our purists [...]
do with absinthe, opium, and [...]
rayed against them? Libertinism, the white slave traffic and the rum evil is now occupying the attention of social workers; do they realize that each one of the above named evils often finds its source in the "dope habit?" Alas, it is the foundation for countless crimes, including petty thievery, burglary and murder.

WHEN DEPRIVED OF DRUG.

People of position and means can avoid exposure and subsequent imprisonment; and are possibly immune from the temptations of crime, because they can always obtain their drug. They live their lives, sublime only in their dreams, and their punishment is meted out to them with their own conscience and physical suffering to attend them and the pauper's grave as their final destination.

APPARENTLY IN ANOTHER WORLD.

THE SENSATIONS OF A YOUNG GIRL WHILE UNDER THE INFLUENCE OF MORPHINE.

The readers of the HERALD will remember an account that appeared several weeks ago of a young girl named Emily Williams, who, while despondent, attempted to commit suicide by taking a large dose of morphine in her rooms on West Thirty-seventh street. She was discovered unconscious and removed to Bellevue Hospital, where after a whole night's work the physicians succeeded in saving her life.

I saw Miss Williams the other day, and referring to the affair she gave me an account of the sensations that she experienced.

"Of course," said she, "you know what led to the act. Well, when I had taken the morphine I at first felt very drowsy and thought after a few moments that I had gone to sleep. But I hadn't, and then began a series of sensations that I would not experience again for all the nation's wealth.

"Familiar objects about the room appeared to assume grotesque shapes and take life. I thought they moved, having arms and legs, and in queer voices chided me for what I had done. I seemed to be by some invisible power slipping further away from sounds and noises. The voices of the people in the adjacent rooms grew indistinct and finally became mere whispers. The outlines of the objects in the room grew dim and finally disappeared altogether. The room grew in size until it became a vast space like the sky, without boundaries. Clouds appeared to float by me, and a blue haze appeared to surround everything and obscure my vision.

"The lamp, which I had left burning, had taken the shape of a star, and seemed through the peculiar blue haze, to be a thousand miles away.

"I could hear nothing but the ghostly whispering of the voices, and experienced an awful sense of loneliness.

"Then the blue haze deepened in color until it became so dark that I could see nothing and the sense of floating about upon the air ceased. I tried to cry out but could'nt. On attempting to move I found that I appeared to be bound hand and foot.

"I laid in that state for what appeared to be several hours, and then I thought that my spiritual self began to diminish in size until I disappeared from wherever I was altogether.

"How long I remained unconscious I do not know, but finally I heard a roaring sound, a confused intermingling of voices and a sense of penetrating a dense darkness and emerging in a lighted place.

"I heard a faint voice remark:—'She's coming around all right,' and then life came back with a rush. I felt as though I had just come up out of deep water, and I opened my eyes. I found myself on a cot in Bellevue Hospital surrounded by nurses and physicians. You know the rest.

"I do not know whether my experiences were different from those of other people or not, but I have given you a true account of how I felt."

CRUSADE AGAINST OPIUM

High Chinese Officials Dismissed for Hitting the Pipe—A Warning to Princesses—All Opium Dens Closing and the Drug to be Wiped Out Within Ten Years—Morphine Injectors—A Look at the New Hospitals—Cutting Down the Poppy Farms.

THE LADIES OF THE PALACE ARE WARNED TO STOP SMOKING.

THE BOSTON SUNDAY GLOBE 1909.

PEKIN.

Suppose that President Taft and our national congress should send out an edict tomorrow that every man and woman in the employ of the government must give up the drinking of liquor or be dismissed from office and that no new appointment should be given to [an]yone who had contracted the liquor [ha]bit or who would not sign the [pl]edge. Let this edict relate not only to [W]ashington, but to every postoffice and [cu]stomhouse, and let its effect be so [ex]tended as to include every state of[fi]cial, even to the county clerks, sheriffs [a]nd their subordinate employes.

Let another edict provide that all [m]ust show government permits before a [gl]ass of whisky, wine or other liquor [w]ill be sold to them, and so that every [sa]loon keeper be subject to fine and im[pr]isonment if he breaks this law. Let [th]e edict summarily shut nine-tenths of [th]e saloons, and provide for the abso[lu]te destruction of all within the course [of] 10 years. Let there be laws forbid[din]g the distilling of liquors and their [im]portation; and, in short, the inaugu[rat]ion of a scheme of government re[stri]ctions which would entirely wipe out [the] manufacture, selling and drinking [of] anything intoxicating within the [spa]ce of 10 years.

[It] would be a good, big contract, would [it n]ot?

[W]ell, that is just what China is try[ing] to do as to blotting opium and the [op]ium traffic from the face of her coun[tr]y.

[Th]e Antiopium Edicts.

This crusade begins at the top. Three [ye]ars ago the great empress dowager [an]d the chief boards of the empire at [Pe]kin sent out edicts cutting down the [siz]e of the opium farms, shutting up the [op]ium dens, and requiring all dealers in [op]ium to take out licenses. The govern[me]nt commanded all farmers to reduce [the]ir opium fields by 10 percent every [ye]ar, and provided that no opium at all [sh]ould be cultivated at the end of 10 [ye]ars. It required that the merchants [de]crease their opium sales 20 percent [ev]ery year, and close out their whole [bu]siness in the space of five years. It [or]dered that all public opium dens [sh]ould be summarily closed, and that [the] retail opium shops should gradually [be] abolished. At the same time it in[au]gurated dispensaries where free [me]dicines might be had to take away [the] opium craving and encouraged the [est]ablishment of opium hospitals for [tho]se who had contracted the habit.

[I]n the same edicts it was provided [tha]t all users of opium should be regis[ter]ed; that they should be examined by [the] police, and the habitual users should [be] allowed only a given quantity of the [dru]g at certain fixed periods. These al[low]ances were to be gradually reduced [so] that at the end of five years all per[son]s under 60 years of age would be [fre]e from the habit. All users of opium [we]re required to wear badges, so that [eve]ryone would know an opium fiend [as] he walked through the streets.

[A]ll government officials, including [prin]ces, dukes, viceroys and generals [und]er 60, had six months to give up the [hab]it or to tender their resignations; officials, more or less prominent, connected with the government service in Pekin either have broken or are endeavoring to break off the use of opium. Some of these are habitual smokers, who have tried so hard to quit that they have died in the attempt. Take, for instance, Wen Hai! He was one of the highest scholars of the empire, and was connected with the grand secretariat. To hold his job he signed a declaration that he was not an opium smoker, and then stopped using the drug. He died a few months ago. Tsai Chang, another noted official, was cashiered for smoking. He is ill in consequence, and it is said will not recover. Chi Chang, the acting governor of the province of Anhwai, died the other day for the same reason, and there are many other old smokers who are said to be ill.

According to the new laws, which are more or less evaded, the smoking of opium means immediate dismissal. Government detectives or censors have been instructed to shadow the officials, and those who claim to have broken off the habit are rigidly watched. Just the other day a private secretary of one of the cabinet ministers was found to have several ounces of opium on his person, and a request for his dismissal was promptly sent forth. In one of the papers this morning I see a dispatch stating that Prince Chung, one of the imperial opium commissioners, has just denounced 20 high officials who have lied as to their use of the drug, and that he demands their dismissal. Last October two of the imperial princes were ordered to resign their posts that they might give their entire time to the eradication of their craving for the drug, and at the same time as an act of mercy, three months of extension were allowed to certain civil and military officials who had not obeyed the imperial edicts.

The crusade is being extended even to the ladies of the palace. They have been warned that they must stop smoking, and certain of these noble dames, who have been secretly selling opium to their friends, have been told that if they continue they will be imprisoned.

Among the Viceroys.

The work of stopping the evil among the clerks outside Pekin has been delegated to the viceroys and governors. There are 22 provinces in China, and the work in each of these is going on rapidly, or the reverse, according to the energy of the governor. In Szechwan, a state in the far west bordering on Tibet, one of the new district officials invited all of his subordinates to a dinner. He feasted them well, but, as they were about to leave, he closed the door, saying that he intended to keep all with him under lock and key for the next three days to learn whether they were free from the opium habit. He knew those who were not would show nervousness; and in this way he could learn how to enforce the new laws.

It is believed that many of the viceroys are still secretly smoking; and the antiopium commissioners have asked the prince regent to call a meeting at the capital of all the viceroys, governors and generals of the army who have reported that they have broken off the habit. When they appear they will be subjected to a test to show whether or not they have lied. Since this one viceroy has asked for time for some of his officials, and others have established opium hospitals and cures.

Closing the Dens.

In nearly every province of China there has been a general closing of the opium dens. In some cities a back-door business is still going on, but the public smoking has become unpopular and dangerous, and the chief opium used is now behind closed doors. In Shanghai all the dens in the native town have been shut, and fully half of those in the foreign concessions wiped out. The foreigners propose to clean out the evil and the day of the closing, the opium pipes were burnt in public and the people rejoiced. The same is true of many other cities, in not a few of which the opium dealers have since secretly resumed business.

A Mighty Crusade.

Outside the officials a mighty crusade has been going on over China to stop the use of opium among the people. Indeed, there are so many different movements that I hardly know where to begin. Every province has its antiopium societies. These meet regularly; they print and distribute antiopium literature and send out men to lecture upon the opium evil. There is one society in Canton which has distributed millions of pamphlets showing the terrible fate of the opium user. Pictures of the man before and after he has become the slave of the drug are published, and the horrors of the practice are vividly painted. Many of the societies require their members to wear a badge and sign the pledge, and many of them offer rewards for the detection of opium smokers and of the illegal selling of opium.

In some of the provinces the most rigid laws have been enacted against the users of the drug. In Kiangsu no habitual smoker under 50 can appear in court as a plaintiff. He can not institute a suit, and can have no protection from the laws as long as he continues to disobey them. In Canton there is a temple which has been given over to the antiopium crusade, antiopium pictures being pasted upon its walls. In Yunnan antiopium lectures are everywhere given, and a large number of refuges have been created to take in confirmed smokers and cure them. Hundreds of opium pipes and lamps are nailed to the walls of the government buildings and the viceroy is rapidly reducing the area of the opium farms.

At the capital of Fukien province there have been eight burnings of opium and opium fixtures, during which 1236 ounces were destroyed and the following items burned: Pipes 4433, pipe bowls 4482, lamps 3693, boxes 3497, vessels for opium cooking 500. About 9000 needles used for morphine injections were also given up and broken. In that province it is absolutely necessary to have a certificate to buy opium, and the same person can only get his supply once a month, the allowance being fixed by the opium commissioners.

Opium Cures.

I find a general belief among the Chinese that the opium habit can be cured. Everywhere pills to take away the craving are sold, and, in most of the great cities, hospitals and refuges have been established where the slaves of the drug go to break off the habit. In Foochow there are six such hospitals, and four of these report that they have already cured 3259 persons. Such institutions have been established at Pekin, Nanking, Tientsin, Wuchang, Canton and in many other places. Foreign doctors have also come in and profess to be able to cure the opium habit. One of these who is well recommended is an American, C. B. Towne. He professes to be able to cure any one of the opium habit in three days. He established hospitals at Tientsin and Shanghai. He has started one at Pao Ting Fu, where it is said that 100 patients came to him during the first month and were cured. Then the number of applications mysteriously decreased, and Mr Towne found that this came from a report to the effect that, although the cure was successful, it always killed the patient within 100 days thereafter. This story was false, but it almost broke up the hospital.

Mr Towne's institution at Tientsin was established at the expense of the viceroy, and officials who were cured received a certificate certifying that fact.

Opium vs Morphine.

the rate of about 2 cents apiece. Some men are to be found in the [street] and are ready to give one a [shot in the] arm upon asking.

In the past it was customar[y for the] members of a party to stand [in a] row and hold out their arms [with] sleeves rolled up to their shoul[ders. The] most common place for the [injection] was about the biceps, but man[y] opium fiends were tattooed fr[om their] necks to their wrists and also [other] parts of their bodies. The m[orphine] injectors make their own soluti[on and] as they use dirty water, the da[nger of] their communicating disease is [great].

The government is doing all i[t can to] abolish these morphine practi[ces. It] has stringent laws against the[m, but] they are still secretly carried [on in] most of the cities. In the mean[time I] understand that the English a[nd Ger]mans have been flooding Chin[a with] cheap hypodermic syringes sin[ce the] present crusade began, and that t[he Chi]nese imperial customs board h[as] issued regulations prohibiting the[ir im]portation, except by the foreign medical practitioners and foreign druggists. Hereafter all morphia and syringes landed without a special permit from the customs will be confiscated.

As to Raising Opium.

The greater part of the opium used in China is raised at home. That imported from India amounts to millions of dollars a year, but a far greater quantity is grown upon Chinese soil. Poppy plantations are cultivated as far north as Manchuria, and there are provinces in southern and western China where opium is one of the principal crops. The reducing of the areas of cultivation is causing a considerable loss to the farmers. The government realizes this, but, nevertheless, it insists that the laws be enforced. According to them, no ground can be planted to poppies, and the old fields must be cut down one-tenth of their original size every year.

In some provinces the viceroys have ordered the immediate stoppage of all cultivation of opium, and in others they have remitted the taxes for five or ten years upon opium lands which have been turned over to other crops. In Yunnan the soldiers have been directed to dig up the poppyfields, and the viceroy of Nankin recently issued an order that his farmers must destroy their opium seeds, and that such as had planted them should dig their fields over and put in something else.

All the opium-raising lands have been registered and the government at Pekin is keeping a close watch over the amount cultivated. The prince regent has offered medals and rewards to those who have changed their crops from the poppy to grains, and they are to be freed from national taxes for a fixed period.

In short, there is no doubt about the earnest and active efforts of the officials and of a large part of the people to do away with the opium habit. Many are resolved that it must be cut out of China at any cost, and the government is willing to submit to the enormous loss of revenue which it entails, for the good of the people.

Millions of Opium Smokers.

On the other hand, it is a question whether the opium evil is anything like so great as is generally supposed. It has been stated that more than 100,000,000 of the Chinese are opium users. Some will tell you that the whole race is drugged and that all the men, women and children use opium daily. This is untrue on its face. I doubt whether the opium habit is as prevalent among the Chinese as the whisky and beer drinking habit is among the English, Germans or Americans. In the first place, it is costly, and the bulk of the Chinese are poor. Again, the amount of opium raised in China is pretty well known, and we have accurate statistics of all that is imported. Foreigners estimate the total annual consumption at something like 40,000,000 pounds. If this were divided equally among the people it would equal only one ounce per year per head. Now the average confirmed smoker takes about three mace a day, or 90 mace in one month.

Ten mace make an ounce, and this would equal nine ounces a month, or nine pounds a year. Dividing the 40,000,000 pounds by nine gives a quotient of less than four and one-half millions, the total number of confirmed smokers required to consume all the opium raised in China. In other words, if one-tenth of the population were habitual opium smokers they would consume all the opium which China now has. If the estimate is doubled the number would be less than 10,000,000.

Dr George Morrison of the London Times, who is one of the most careful writers on things Chinese and who knows the country better than any Chinese I am acquainted with, estimates the possible consumers at less than 8,000,000.

To say that every man, woman and child in China is an opium fiend is as false on its face as it would be to allege that every man, woman and child in England and America is addicted to drunkenness.

In closing this letter I would say that it will be a long time before the hopes of the Chinese statesmen and patriots can come to fruition. The work of repression is going on rapidly, but opium is still smoked largely in secret and an enormous amount of underhand selling and smu[ggling] ... Some of the officials ... ly disol... bound i... are sec... injectin[g] ... behind t[h]... ment for ... honest, and ... a vast deal of good.

Frank G. Carpenter

(Copyright, 1909, by Frank G. Carpenter.)

CHINA'S OPIUM TRAFFIC

APRIL 2, 1911.

"LEAVE it to the Chink when it comes to smuggling hop," said the Veteran Customs Inspector, as he made himself comfortable on a bale of hemp, where he could watch the perspiring stevedores slinging tea and matting out of the big liner's maw.

"Some of the society ladies are pretty foxy getting by with silk and Irish lace, but 'for ways that are dark and tricks that are vain in getting in the poppy dope you've got to hand it to the wily Chinese.

"Before I was assigned to this job of sitting in the sun chewing tobacco and listening to the grind of the winches, I was on the searching force. I'm too fat and slow for that work now. To have the distinction of carrying a prod and a dark lantern you're got to be able to crawl into a shaft alley or grovel in a furnace, which I can't do any more. Being on the searching force ain't all smooth sailing and you can use your own judgment about the glory.

"For instance, while you're breaking your neck peeking into a ventilator the Chinks are standing by, empty-faced, giving you the ha-ha. Probably while you're ripping up things in the galley the No. 1 boys, gliding around in their soft felt slippers, are shooting the five tael tins down into the engine-room, and when you're busy sticking your prod into a boiler tube the Chinks are shifting the dope up into the music box in the social hall.

"At that the boys are doing pretty good now, but you can't blame them if they're not as busy as the Britishers over Hongkong-side, who get a bonus on the stuff they seize.

"On these transpacific liners you can expect to find the opium anywhere. When the business is as profitable as picking gold nuggets out of a creek bed you're bound to find plenty in the business, and the Chink has the game down to a science. If you had 100 secret service agents sitting in rocking-chairs around the deck and a dozen searchlights beaming over the ship the slippery yellow men would be getting the contraband off just the same; which means no discredit to the service. They're regular sleight-o'-hand performers, these Chinks. Now you see it, now you don't!

"I've seized opium hidden in the queerest places imaginable. One day I was walking through the dining-saloon and I happened to knock over one of the pots of Japanese palms they place on the tables between tiffin times. It struck the floor and burst into pieces. What do you think it contained? A dozen five-tael tins of the drug. I immediately thought of 'Ali Baba and the Forty Thieves'—although it seems 100 years since I read it—where the naughty bandits were concealed in the big pots, but instead of pouring hot oil into the flower vases I broke them open. Nearly every one was planted with dope.

"Many persons seem to be pretty sure th[at frank]furters contain poor little dogs that ... the butcher shops, but no one h... frankfurters contained opiu[m] ... there's no danger of them ... A bladder stuffed with h[op] ... hungry one day, as I was ... liner, I pulled off a sausag[e] ... nail. One bite was enoug[h] ... tained opium. We confisc[ated] ... opium sausage.

"Little did the passeng[ers] ... the big liners know that th... which jangled out the drea... over the ocean, was loade[d] ... Chinatown smoking for a ... piano smasher myself and ... thought I'd play a tune o[n] ... quite right and I opened the ... tins of the drug packed awa[y] ...

"Another time I noticed ... the siren high up on the towerin[g] ... [sever]al trips up and down the ladder w... be a paint bucket. I thought he was ... [buc]ket a little too reckless if it contained pa[int] ... [st]opped him and examined it. There was no p[aint in] the bucket, but instead a number of tins of opium. The siren yielded up several hundred tins later.

"The Chinks are always getting new ideas for concealing the contraband. You might find it in a pillow in the ladies' music-room, under a dining-hall table, in a life preserver, or in the steering gear. Yes, you've got to hand it to the Chink when it comes to smuggling hop.

"So long, here comes my relief, and I've been holding down this bale of hemp for eight hours."

40 CENTURIES OF CHINESE MEDICINE

CHINA HAS 10,000,000 OPIUM USERS

FLOTSAM AND JETSAM OF THE WATERFRONT

BRITISH ACCUSED OF KEEPING CHINA IN OPIUM THRALL

United Christian Society Says It Is Ashamed of Own Government's Action.

PROHIBITION NOW IS THEIR DEMAND

Asserts That England Is Acting Contrary to the Sovereign Rights of Old Empire.

The government has received a lengthy cablegram from the British United Christion Society for the Suppression of the Opium Traffic. It says:—

"Many thousand British Christians are deeply ashamed of Great Britain's long continued national crime toward China in declining to grant China the immediate right to prohibit the importation of Indian opium."

The society declares that this prohibition of China's sovereign right and Great Britain's insistence on a gradual reduction of the opium product is a "sin before God," and pledges its most active support to the efforts to induce Great Britain to do her duty by humanity at whatever cost.

The National Assembly has given a great impetus to the nationalization of the opium suppression movement by committing itself to the prohibition of interprovincial trade in Chinese grown opium after July next. This is supported by

JULY 26, 1908.

CHINESE WILL BOYCOTT CANADA

Retaliation for the Act Barring Opium From Dominion Territory.

Special Dispatch to the "Chronicle."

OTTAWA (Ontario), July 25.—Private advices from the Pacific Coast indicate that a very persistent boycott is at hand on the part of the most powerful body in China against the Dominion of Canada and her trade. This condition of affairs has been brought about by the recent action of the Canadian Government against the opium trade in this country. During the last days of the Parliamentary session, just closed, the Government secured the passage of an act prohibiting

EMPEROR❋OPIUM WAR❋OPER

Chinese Troops Behead Opium Growers Under Imperial Edict to Stop the Trade

A POPPY HEAD, FROM WHICH OPIUM IS PRODUCED.

LARGE STACK OF OPIUM PIPES GIVEN UP BY THEIR OWNERS AND ABOUT TO BE BURNED.

A BALL OF OPIUM ENCASED IN FIBRE, FOR EXPORT.

Government Also Shows Determination by Destroying Many Thousand Acres of Poppy Fields.

[SPECIAL CORRESPONDENCE OF THE HERALD.]

SHANGHAI, June 5, 1911.—Human heads in baskets and ears skewered on sticks testify in silent, eloquent voice that the Chinese government is bent upon extirpating opium. The unsheathed sword is being carried to the poppy fields of Central and Western China, and the blood of those who insist upon defying the imperial edict prohibiting the manufacture of opium is flowing as evidence that the government meant business when it entered into a compact with the British government in 1907 to suppress poppy cultivation.

The agreement which China made with the Indian government, which went into effect January 1, 1908, called for a reduction of the export from India by 5,100 chests a year for three years, provided that China reduced the production of native opium in the same ratio and thereafter to continue the reduction until the expiry of the trade, in 1917.

China has more than kept her bargain. Scarcely had the agreement been made than an edict went forth into the distant provinces ordering the uprooting of growing poppy and prohibiting the planting of a new crop. Many farmers, immediately under the eyes of the officials, complied with the commands of the throne at once, and by 1910, when the writer passed through Yunnan province, not a stalk of poppy was to be observed in the accessible places, where but a few years previously the land was abloom with flowers.

Many Heedless of Edict.

... the mountainous parts the fa... d and reaped and trusted for se... well known lackadaisical d... rial instructions whe... meant trouble or a... officials, and for... ed to enjoy ... t they e... things

... little respite they were once again gently reminded that an edict had been issued commanding them not to grow poppy at all.

The farmers paid no attention to the official notification. They assumed it to be but a suggestion that they should tender a larger bribe than usual, and the augmented kumsha was forwarded. To their astonishment, however, it fell upon stony ground, and that things had changed materially and extraordinarily in the land was brought home to them by a visi... force of soldiers.

At first the military depend... moral effect of their prese... about the destruction of th... regions through which they... it has to be recorded that fe... was at once destroyed. No... the troops passed from sight... than the farmers replanted the... sat down in their huts to w... mature, never thinking the sold... again return.

Have Heads Lopped O...

One day, however, the milita... sight and no more questions ... of the farmer. He was seiz... amidst the blooming flowers and... lopped off.

The news of the fate of the ... farmers quickly spread along the ... and up in the hills, and men and ... and children spent their days and ... pulling up the plants by the roots ... stroying every sign that ... that they had been ... ous business ... drug. ...

proof to the sceptics that it meant to oust the drug from the land at all costs. It made opium growing a capital offence, and into the districts about Kweichow, in the far west of Hupei province, where large areas were being used surreptitiously for poppy, went forces of soldiers to wipe the plant out for good and all. Near Taichowfu, in Chekiang, similar methods were adopted, and also in the districts ... Szechuan province, removed ... n tracks.

... Resistance.

... ers was known ... while in the ... rcely any re... ople of Chen... cided to make ... ry and assert ... use the soil as ... r they had been ... and by the end ... of one thousand ... mmand of a gen... fairly well estab... e. A pitched battle ... hills on March 1, but ... which early set in ... brought disaster to ... eir leaders, a scholar ... rofessor in a college, ... mmarily decapitated. ... shot in the fray, ... overran the

DECEMBER 2, 1908.

What Will Chinatown Do When the Opium Gives Out?

THE RACES MIGHT STIMULATE EXCITEMENT
HOOLAY
BACK TO SHUTTLECOCK
FINE GAME, FAN TAN
MEANING: THERE IS $1,000,000 WORTH OF OPIUM IN THE BONDED WAREHOUSES
AND PROBABLY A NEW BUNCH OF EDUCATIONAL CLUBS WILL BE FORMED
OPIUM SALE
OPIUM IS STRONG; DEMAND SHOWS SHARP INCREASE—MARKET REPORT

DID you notice any change in the usually calm, imperturbable manner of your Chinese cook yesterday? Did he appear more melancholy than ever, and did he nervously toy with his queue the while he gazed absently into space and allowed the biscuits to burn? Did you ask him what meant his new mental attitude toward America, and did he mumble something unintelligible that sounded to you like:

"No smokee hop some more."

That is the story in a nutshell. Poor Ah Wing's supply of opium has suddenly been cut off by order of Dr. H. W. Wiley, chief food and drug inspector of the Department of Agriculture at Washington, and when the quantity now on hand in this city is exhausted there will be no way to get more unless the smugglers are tempted to resume the old risky business of running the blockade and bringing in contraband goods.

Just now there happens to be about $1,000,000 worth of opium in bonded warehouses in San Francisco, and there is no immediate danger of a famine, but the Chinese are panic-stricken and those who can afford it are laying in stores against the time when it will be impossible to buy a single "pill" in the customary way. The price rose yesterday from a maximum of $12 to such fabulous sums as $20 and $30 a pound for the best, and the jobbers reaped a rich harvest. It is estimated that $100,000 worth was taken from warehouses and distributed throughout Chinatown yesterday and last night.

Most of the quantity still in bond will be snapped up by the rich merchants and the laundrymen; the cooks and the porters will be the first to suffer.

Last night crowds gathered about the bulletin boards to read the posters announcing the news, and there was great scurrying and shuffling of sandaled feet to provide for the rainy days coming. Those who had not the ready cash borrowed money from their friends in order to get a share of the precious drug before it was too late. Ordinarily the Chinese of average means buys a one-pound can at the time, keeping it in his house or secreting it in his room, ... be employed as cook or laundry... ...til such time as he can smoke ... ure.

... many dives in Chinatown ... nk may be rented for 15 ... the smoker bringing his ... using the pipe and ... er. As it is against ... person to retail the ... in original packages, ... selling pipefuls to ... ested.

... wing the new ... was made last ... and his Chin... averly place. ... ested in the ... ed $5 each ... smok...

pavement of most of the alleys in the Oriental quarter, and those who wooed the pipe seemed to have sweeter dreams than ever because of the fact that they had been worried almost sick over the new order from Washington, and the contrast when the drug took effect raised their spirits above the level.

The opium smokers have a real terror of abstinence. Many would die if suddenly deprived of opiates and even when faithful efforts are made to stop gradually the victim suffers untold agonies. In China the laws provide that all under forty years of age must stop smoking at once, but those over forty are given ten years in which to get rid of the habit. These laws were so framed because the Government understood what a strong hold the poppy had upon the people and it feared the consequences of too stringent regulations.

Within six months it will be impossible for the average Chinese to secure opium in San Francisco and the real suffering will begin then. Fully half of the population of Chinatown is addicted to the use of the drug, and when the supply runs out thousands will be frantic for the soothing stimulant and will be ready to commit all sorts of crimes if necessary to get it.

To what the denizens of the quarter will turn now for amusement or pastime it is hard to say. With the pipe beyond their reach and their beloved games of chance forbidden, there is little left for poor Ah Wing legally to do unless he adopts the American's way of enjoying life. It is possible that he may take up baseball, cricket, battledore and shuttlecock, cigarettes and whisky, but the things that he really cares for are lost to him with the passing of the poppy jag.

CHINESE ARRESTED IN RAIDS FINED IN COURT.

Twenty Convicted of Visiting Opium Place Fined by Judge Shortall.

Police Judge Shortall yesterday fined twenty Chinese each $5 on charges of visiting an opium den. The raid was made by Sergeant Layne and posse on the place conducted by Lee You at 114 Waverly place. ... charge against Lee You of bein... keeper of an opium place, was dis... ed by motion of the assistant dis... ttorney and You was placed on t... tness stand to testify. His testim... onvicted the visitors.

Fong C... Waverly place, arrested ... by Sergeant Layne and po... ed with keeping a fan-t... ned $50 by Police Judg... e charges against twe... rrested in the sam... ssed.

... SCAFFOLD.

... a bricklayer, living a... avenue, fell from a ... ilding at Clay and Du... noon yesterday, sus... ruises and concussion ... was removed to the ... Hospital, where his ... ted by Dr. ... Hill.

San Francisco Chr

VOL. XCVIII. SAN FRANCISCO, CAL., FRIDAY, JUNE 2, 1911.

Big Opium Consignment Found by Officers

Seized on Advance Washington Information

SMOKERS OF POPPY ARE CHEATED OF EXPECTATIONS

Government Officers Locate Many Taels of Opium in Hold of America Maru.

CHINESE ARE SUSPECTED

Secret Service at Hongkong Gives the Tip by Cable of Valuable Cache.

THE biggest single seizure of opium in recent years was made by United States customs officials on board the Japanese liner America Maru when within a half-hour after she had entered the Golden Gate they dragged from the depths of the vessel's forepeak fresh-water tank 900 five-tael tins of the drug, valued at $27,000.

While the seizure had certain bizarre effects in the hauling of the contraband from its hiding place, the discovery itself was rather matter of fact, as the Government officials had knowledge long before the steamer's arrival, through secret advices from Washington, just where the drug was concealed, and all they had to do was to go down into the dark depths of the steamer's hold and grab it.

It was shortly after the noon hour when the big turbiner went into quarantine off Meigg's wharf after her voyage from Oriental ports. While the yellow quarantine flag floated at the steamer's masthead the little Government tug Hartley was lying close by, and aboard of her was a party of anxious customs officials, eager to climb the vessel's sides and delve into her bilgy depths, where they knew that a quantity of the juice of the poppy, valued at a small-sized fortune, was stowed away.

LIKE HOUNDS IN THE LEASH.

The party of officials was headed by Special Agents L. W. Bean, J. W. Smith and W. H. Tidwell, and with them was the crack searching squad of the department—Joseph Head, C. J. Benninger, Sam Sackett and E. E. Enlow.

Like hounds held in the leash, they awaited their time, and at the given signal bounded over the steamer's side and headed for the forward hatchway. They knew just where to go. From some mysterious oracle far across the Eastern seas had come the tip that in the water tank of the America Maru would be found the contraband drug.

FASTENED TO SUPPORTING BEAM.

"And here is the rest of it," cried Enlow triumphantly, pointing to a corner of the tank, where, fastened to a supporting beam, were eight similar-sized cans. The seizure was complete as far as the advices of the officials went.

The work of removing the big tins of drug, each weighing over fifty pounds, was no easy one, and caused the finders to conjecture how the smugglers ever got them stowed away without nearly every one on the steamer being aware of their movements.

Before the America Maru reached her dock the seized cans were on the upper deck and had been inspected. They were hermetically sealed, and the contents were as dry as though they had only been stored in a warehouse. In each large tin was 100 five-tael boxes of opium. Each of the small tins had been carefully wrapped in newspaper, the wrappers being copies of a local paper of the date of last December.

The seizure caused somewhat of a sensation among the passengers and the officers and crew of the vessel. Captain Stevens and Chief Officer Satow rendered the searchers every assistance in getting the goods out of the hold.

There was a variety of expressions on the faces of the passengers when they learned that the cans of opium had been taken from the water tank from which they had been drinking daily in the voyage across, although there was some consolation in the fact that the cans were sealed and that there had been no leakage. During the last few days they had not been in the water, it having, in the course of consumption, dropped several feet below the level of the cans.

OFFICIALS HAD CORRECT TIP.

Although the customs officials had the correct tip as to the location of the opium, they are all at sea as to how it got there, who placed it there, and who is connected with what is evidently the work of a band of conspirators. Of course, the general conclusion is that the famous opium ring is once again engaged in its nefarious activities.

As sized up by the Government men, the drug was placed aboard the steamer at Hongkong. Whether it was rolled aboard in the large tins as found, sealed, or whether the cans were carried aboard empty and filled on the steamer by those engaged in the work of the smugglers cannot be said.

Suspicion falls darkly upon the Chinese waiters, pantrymen and stewards, as the officials cannot see how that amount of opium could be smuggled through their quarters and lowered into the bottommost part of the vessel without their knowledge. That a number of them, if not all, were in the secret and expected to get a "piece" out of such a magnificent winning, if it went through successfully, is the belief of the customs people and of the Japanese officers of the ship as well.

Questions asked of the Chinese yesterday, however, revealed a painful display of ignorance among them. None could remember having seen anything carried through their quarters, and to get those cans of "dope" through certainly required the services of several men, and possibly tackle.

INFORMATION A MYSTERY.

How the inside information came into possession of the Treasury Department at Washington as to the amount and storage of the drug is a mystery of the Secret Service Department of the Government. There is no doubt, though, that the tip came by cable direct from Hongkong, where it is understood a secret service man has been stationed for some time. It is also understood that the Government had information that a big opium ring has been operating for some time, and that plans had been made by its members for making several big coups after the several months of lull in endeavor to smuggle that has prevailed.

As the work of a ring, it is surmised that the smugglers have their agents in the Orient, on board the steamers and in this city. As to landing the cans of drug here, it was undoubtedly the purpose of the conspirators to drop the cans overboard and have them picked up by confederates. The cans, filled with the little square tins, held enough air, being hermetically sealed, to float.

It was stated by some of the officers of the America Maru that two cans of opium had been seized at Hongkong which were to have been brought over on the steamer.

After the seized opium had been landed at the dock, the customs officials continued their search of the steamer in hope of locating another cache of the contraband drug.

The last big seizures recently made on the Oriental steamers were several months ago when 1098 five-tael tins of opium were taken off at different times from the steamer Korea, and about the same time several hundred tins were found concealed on board the Siberia.

NOVEMBER 30, 1911.

WOMAN ARRESTED FOR DEALING IN OPIUM

Inspectors Sutherland and Charmak Make Important Arrest in Chinatown.

DRUG STORE IS CAPTURED.

Mrs. Rose Mentor, Clerks and Porter Are Taken---Chinese Smuggler Is Caught.

The crucial point in the crusade to wipe out illicit drug traffic in Chinatown was reached last night in the arrest of Mrs. Rose Mentor. Having obtained substansial evidence which, according to the Pharmacy Board, shows that she is the most important dispenser of morphine and cocaine, wholesale and retail, on the Pacific Coast, Mrs. Mentor, proprietor of the Abbie Drug Store, Dupont and Pacific street, was placed under arrest by Inspectors Fred A. Sutherland and Harry Charmak of the Pharmacy Board at 7:30 o'clock last night in her store.

Two clerks and a Chinese porter, comprising the entire staff of the drug store, were arrested with Mrs. Mentor. Mrs. Mentor is the widow of Mark L. Mentor, notorious opium smuggler and morphine dealer, who died here a year ago. With the arrest of Edward Gleason and John Edwards, the arrest of Mrs. Mentor is regarded as one of the final links of the chain which will bind up the open sale of morphine, cocaine and opium in San Francisco.

Two charges were placed against Mrs. Mentor, both alleging that she sold large quantities of morphine to Inspector Sutherland, once on November 7th and previously on October 21st. Two and a half years ago her husband was caught and convicted by inspectors of the State Board of Pharmacy, and died shortly after his release from prison.

When inspectors of the Pharmacy Board descended upon the store at 8 o'clock last evening, Mrs. Mentor had not arrived and Quong Goon, a porter, and Burritt R. Nichols, a clerk, were arrested on warrants charging them with the sale of morphine. Later Harry A. Bohlman, a clerk, entered, and he was also placed under arrest. Finally Mrs. Mentor, unsuspecting, arrived at the store and, when notified of her arrest, was overwhelmed. The inspectors of the Board accorded her the courtesy of delaying her trip to the City Prison until she could endeavor to secure bondsmen, and waited for over an hour before they removed her to the City Prison. During their wait Inspector Harry Charmak identified fifteen of the twenty-two persons who entered the drug store to make purchases, as drug fiends.

Several of the drug fiends recognized the inspectors when they opened the door of the store, and, slamming the door, made a hasty escape, fearing that they might be apprehended.

Another important arrest by Inspector Sutherland was that of Wah Shue, a Chinese. Wah was arrested in Stockton street shortly after Inspectors Sutherland and Charmak left the Abbie

JUNE 6, 19

SEARCHING FOR EVIDENCE AGAINST OPIUM SMUGGLE

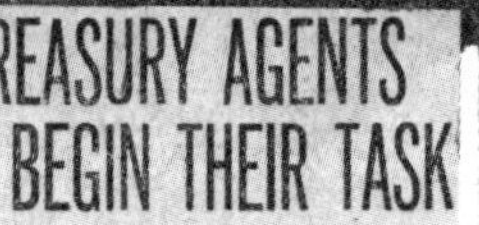

TREASURY AGENTS BEGIN THEIR TASK

They Question the Chinese Members of Crew of the America Maru.

IN THE hope of obtaining some clew to the leaders or operatives of the opium ring, whose smuggled consignment of 900 five-tael tins of the drug, valued at $27,000, was discovered by customs officials in the forepeak's fresh water tank of the Japanese liner, America Maru, June 1st, officials of the Government yesterday began a rigorous and secret examination of officers and crew of the big liner. Con

It is on the Chinese stewards, pantrymen and waiters that the Government's suspicion has fallen, as the officials cannot understand how so great an amount of opium could be smuggled through their quarters and lowered into the depths of the vessel without their knowledge; but a rigid questioning of these yesterday failed to elicit any information that might tend to confirm the suspicions. The Chinese interrogated were painfully ignorant of everything pertaining to the drug and the method used in getting it aboard.

METHOD IN THEIR ILLNESS.

"Me velle sick," was the reply to Tidwell's first question to one of the Chinese and the same sentiment seemed to envelop the others, Tidwell finally remarking that he guessed there was a method in their illness.

At the morning session, Captain A. G. Stevens and Chief Officer Satow and others of the captain's staff were questioned, but could throw no light on the smuggling, Captain Stevens declaring that he was as anxious to discover the guilty ones as the Government officials.

Captain Stevens is liable to a fine under a Federal statute, because of the contraband aboard the vessel, but he stated at the hearing yesterday that, from a view point of fairness, he could not understand why he should be held responsible any more than a hotel keeper should have to answer for whatever might transpire in his place of business.

JANUARY 24, 1908

OPIUM LAMP STARTS EXPLOSION OF GAS

THEIR senses dulled by opium and powerless to save themselves, several slaves of the pipe narrowly escaped cremation in their bunks when fire started from a gas explosion caused by the flame of an opium lamp coming in contact with a leaking pipe in an underground opium den at 753 Clay street yesterday afternoon shortly after 2 o'clock.

The smokers owe their lives to Mah Chee, the keeper of the joint, who suffered his ... his ... patr... confi... cupie...

as it had been recently raided by the police.

But down in the basement which runs under the street the vice flourished. Mah Chee was contented and dozed lazily in one corner of the den, while stretched out in bunks rising tier upon tier the slaves of the pipe were exploring blissful realms. Suddenly Mah Chee was aroused by a loud explosion. Through the blue vapors of the opium he could see a line of fire creeping along the rear wall of the room. He seized a towel and tried to beat the

SECRET PROBE AT ANGEL ISLAND

SEEK OPIUM SMUGGLERS IN SOUTH

SMUGGLING EXPOSE INVESTIGATED IN SECRET

Soldier Who Told of Operations at Fort McDowell Hurried South.

SUICIDE MAY BE LINK.

Distribution of Opium May Implicate Enlisted Men at the Presidio.

TAKING with him George Winterbottom, the soldier who, Sunday, was arrested at Angel island, to be held as a witness against a ring of smugglers who for a long time have made use of enlisted men stationed at Fort McDowell to run opium into San Francisco and the bay cities, Secret Service Detective H. Le Deux last evening unostentatiously slipped out of town and departed for Los Angeles on the Lark. A secret investigation of the alleged smuggling operations of the soldiers is under way at Angel island and the post is on the qui vive for expected arrests in connection with the affair.

That the operations of the gang which used soldiers to run the opium extended to the Presidio is the latest development, and the secret service officers now are investigating the strange attempt at suicide made by Corporal J. J. Barry near the guard

Simultaneous with the arrest of Winterbottom, men familiar with Chinatown affairs declare that opium has jumped in value almost over night in San Francisco's Chinatown.

BODY OF OPIUM FIEND BURNED

Charred Remains Found on the Upper Floor of Hall of Justice.

FOUL MURDER SUSPECTED.

Evidence Shows Effort Made to Conceal Traces of a Crime.

Some wretched outcast, one of the nameless dregs of humanity whom the police designate as "hop-heads," was murdered and cremated by his fellows last week in the tenantless fourth floor of the ruined Hall of Justice at Washington and Kearny streets. The charred stump of what was once a human body was accidentally found there yesterday by Dr. J. W. Nelson, the Board of Health inspector for Portsmouth suare. The evidence points conclusively to some shocking crime, and Detective Matthewson is now investigating the weird case.

Ever since the fire the tall building has stood, a gaunt skeleton, wrecked and useless. It takes a daring man to find his way up the shaky stairways to the upper floors, but opium and cocaine fiends care little for life. When these miserable wretches began making this rookery their habitation, the police did not molest them, for, in using this resort, they were kept off the streets.

OUTCASTS NOT MOLESTED.

The outcasts were not disturbed even when they used the charred wood of the building to build their tiny fires on the cement floors of the building and cook their scant meals. There was no danger of a conflagration, for the structure had been already purged in the greatest fire in history.

When Dr. Nelson last week, in the pursuit of his duties, noticed an unusually large fire in the fourth floor of the Hall of Justice he thought little of the occurrence. The incident had almost escaped his memory when he made a tour of inspection through the building at 2 o'clock yesterday. On reaching the third floor on the south side of the female row of what was once the city prison, he was horrified to find the blackened body of a human being. Although burned to a crisp, its head, arms and legs gone and its clothing all but totally destroyed, he decided, after a close examination, that the remains represented what had once been a man.

MURDER THE THEORY.

All the indications are that a foul murder was committed in this lonely spot. The corpse lay on its back and underneath the back a remnant of a coarse calico shirt was found, the cloth crumbling to bits when it was picked up. The smallest shred of a coat was also discovered. These remnants of garments are all that determine the sex of the victim, but the position of the body and of its clothes show that the fire burned above it. Moreover, it took a great fire to destroy all but the trunk.

If the poor wretch had fallen asleep in a drugged dream and had rolled into his own cooking fire he never could have been burned in the shocking and peculiar manner described. It took a great mountain of wood to consume as much of the corpse as is missing. The police theory is that in this ruined den some trivial quarrel over a few cents' worth of opium or cocaine precipitated a desperate hand-to-hand struggle in which the unfortunate "hophead" was murdered. Then, desiring to destroy the evidences of the crime, the rest of the band gathered a pyre of wood and tried to burn the dead man to ashes.

CONTRABAND DRUG HIDDEN ON BOARD

Customs Inspectors Find Over $30,000 Worth of Opium on Pacific Mail Liner.

THOROUGH SEARCH MADE

Wholesale Operation of the Smuggling Ring Revealed by Big Seizure Here.

MAKING a record for opium seizures at the port, Customs Inspectors Joseph Head, C. J. Benninger, P. O. Huffaker and John Toland Pa-

APRIL 6, 1911.

OPIUM SHIPPED AS DRY GOODS TO HONOLULU

Transaction Having Peculiar Features Is Now Subject of Federal Inquiry.

PERJURY MAY BE CHARGED

False Manifest Filed in the Custom-House---Drayman Is Now Scapegoat.

The seizure of 110 tins of opium, valued at $6000, by the Federal authorities at Honolulu on the arrival there of the steamship Lurline from San Francisco, has brought out a new feature of the traffic in the contraband drug. Formerly the seizures at Honolulu were of opium that was carried on steamships coming from China. This is said to be the first time that a large quantity has been shipped back from this port under concealment and been taken by the United States customs officials there from its hiding place on the ship.

Involved in this transaction is an allegation of perjury on account of a false sworn statement on the shipper's manifest, filed at the Custom-house here. This manifest was signed with the name of Scharlin Brothers, an incorporated concern, having a furnishing goods store at 937 Grant avenue, in Chinatown. Collector of the Port Stratton has referred the matter to the United States District Attorney's office for inquiry, and a prosecution for perjury may be instituted. Scharlin Brothers forwarded the opium, but claim that no member of the firm signed or swore to the incorrect manifest. This was done, they say, by the drayman who took the firm's consignment to the steamship.

DESCRIPTION OF GOODS.

Attention, consequently, has been

RECORD SEIZURE OF OPIUM MADE ON THE KOREA

PACIFIC MAIL LINER RANSACKED BY INSPECTORS

OPIUM CONCEALED IN FAKE PULLEY WHEELS
JOHN TOLAND
JOSEPH HEAD

The immense tackle block and the dummy wheels, showing how the opium was concealed, and Customs Inspectors John Toland and Joseph Head, who made the clever seizure on the Pacific Mail liner Siberia.

1911.

Seizure of Contraband Aboard Big Liner Reveals Smugglers' Clever Cache

ONE of the most important opium seizures in recent years—important because of the discovery of a cache which for ingenuity surpasses that of the opium oil cans of last year—was made yesterday morning by Customs Inspectors Joseph Head and John Tolan, when they uncovered seventy-five tins of the smuggled drug, valued

the regular sheaves piled in a dark corner.

"Say, Tolan," he asked, after soliloquizing over his stumble, "what do you think these things are doing here anyway?"

"You've got me," replied Tolan, rather perplexed.

In another corner were the two ship's blocks or pulleys, used in the

OPIUM HIDDEN IN BIT OF LEMON PEEL

Attempted Suicide of a Chinese Reveals Novel Smuggling Method

Special Dispatch to the "Chronicle."

STOCKTON, March 23.—Through the attempted suicide of a Chinese today a new method of smuggling opium was disclosed. Lee Yuen Dock, a elestial who had been in ill health, used a razor and knife in an effort to kill himself, but he only succeeded in severing his windpipe when he laid down to die. The jugular vein was narrowly missed, and friends rushed him to the Emergency Hospital, where a physician dressed the wound.

At the hospital a piece of lemon peel, the center of which had been removed and refilled with opium in considerable quantity, was found in his pocket. After he had recovered sufficiently to talk he denied knowing that there was any of the drug in the peel, which had been cleverly prepared. The officers here are of the opinion that they have discovered the cleverest scheme for smuggling opium into this country and distributing it to the various cities. The physician says several days elapsed between the time the drug was placed in the peel and the finding of it.

THE SAN FRANCISCO EXAMINER — Sporting News—Edited by W. W. Naughton — FRIDAY, SEPTEMBER 25, 1908.

AW! WHAT'S THE USE? — BY 'BUD' FISHER

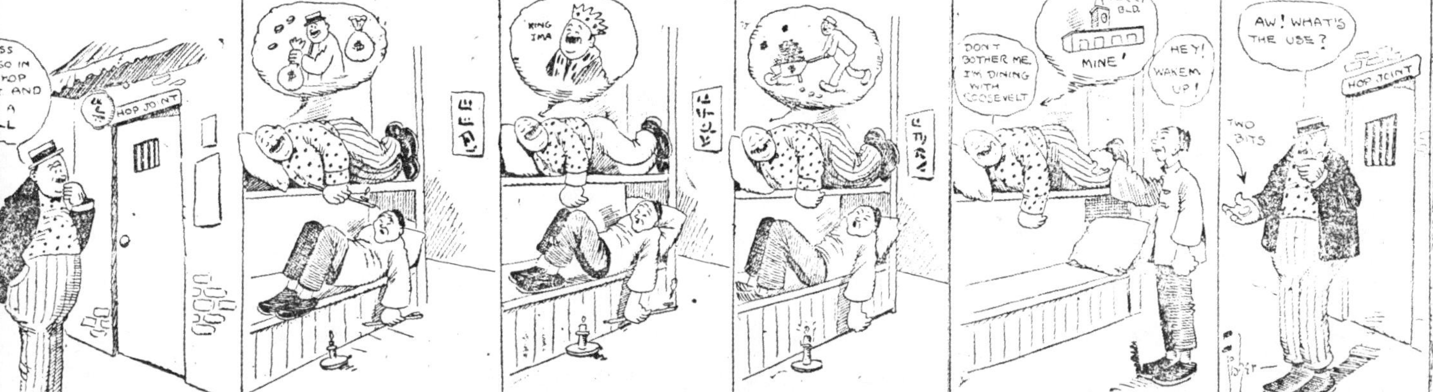

SECOND SECTION
Miscellaneous and Classified Advertisements

San Francisco Chronicle

SECOND SECTION
PAGES 13 TO 20

FOUNDED 1865 SAN FRANCISCO, CAL., TUESDAY, JULY 20, 1920 VOL. CXVII, NO

Cracked Paint Reveals $40,000 Opium Cache on Line

CUSTOMS MEN FIND NARCOTIC IN WATER TANK

Broken Surfacing Around Manhole on Nile Confounds Smuggling Attempts

SEARCHED MANY TIMES

400 5-Tael Tins Uncovered When Tank on China Mail Craft Is Drained

If the China Mail liner Nile had not been painted just prior to her departure from Hongkong for San Francisco, it is highly probable that United States Customs Inspector Ephriam E. Enlow and a squad of assistants would not have seized opium valued at $40,000 yesterday afternoon as the steamship lay moored at Pier 29.

It was the paint that spilled the beans, much to the chagrin of unidentified shippers of the narcotic.

When the Nile steamed into port last Wednesday, Inspector Enlow received a mysterious tip that somewhere aboard the steamship there was plenty of high-grade opium.

Enlow and a dozen or more assistants promptly boarded the liner and searched her from stem to stern, but not a trace of opium could they find. Although Enlow has a home at 1340 Franklin street, he began to live at Pier 29. So close a watch was kept on the Nile that no attempt was made to carry ashore the opium Enlow was so certain was aboard the steamship.

MANY SEARCHES MADE

Several times on Thursday, Friday, Saturday and Sunday, Enlow and his assistants went over the Nile from keel to topmast and back again, but still no trace of the opium was found. And then the paint betrayed the hiding place of the opium.

Enlow had noticed that the engine-room as well as the exterior of the ship presented a newly-painted texture. Seeking out one of the ship's officers yesterday afternoon, Enlow inquired:

"When was she painted last?"

"In Hongkong, just before we sailed for San Francisco," the officer replied.

A glad light brightened Enlow's face and, calling his assistants, he headed down into the engine-room. Climbing to the top of the water tank above the ship's engines, Enlow pointed out the manhole. The paint around the edge of the manhole had been cracked. Enlow deduced that the manhole cover had been removed after the ship had been painted.

OPIUM FOUND IN TANK

"No use looking in the water tank," sang out a water tender, "she's been full up with water ever since we started."

"Guess we'll take a look in the tank just the same," Enlow replied.

The manhole cover was pried off. The tank was filled with water, but Enlow was not satisfied. The tank was drained. Peering down into the tank Enlow saw nothing until he flashed his electric torch, and then his eyes rested on eight oblong boxes. The boxes were hauled out of the tank and on to the ship's deck. A hammer knocked the cover from one of the boxes. Inside lay fifty five-tael tins of opium. Each of the remaining seven boxes contained a like ...

FEDERAL MEN IN OPIUM NET

SEPTEMBER 1, 1913. MONDAY

FOUND--A RING

3 OFFICIALS HELD AS AIDS OF SMUGGLERS

Trap Laid for the Members of Narcotic Ring by Federal Men Reveals Illicit Traffic

One of the biggest opium smuggling rings on the Pacific was revealed yesterday with the indictment in Honolulu of three customs officers.

The Honolulu indictments returned by a Federal grand jury charge Frank Bilsland, Joseph Crockett and Frank Robello, customs agents, with an active part in the opium traffic.

For many months the federal authorities have tried to solve the secret of the heavy flow of opium into the port of San Francisco. They learned that the traffic in opium was being dealt in principally by what became known as the "Portuguese ring," with headquarters in Honolulu.

Opium to the value of hundreds of thousands of dollars was getting into the islands and then finding its way into San Francisco. Traps were laid and the means of operation discovered. Yesterday's indictments followed.

Federal officials assert the smugglers were getting their supply from China via transpacific boats that touch at Honolulu en route to San Francisco. If these boats were allowed to carry it through to San Francisco it might be seized here, but by landing it at Honolulu, with the alleged connivance of customs men there, the smugglers' problem ...

THE WORLD: JULY 28, 1918.

BIG OPIUM RAID IN HOTEL HOME OF TANGO PAIR

Bennetts, Self-Styled World's Greatest Dancers, Had Drugs Valued at $4,000 Wholesale, Say the Detectives.

THEATRICAL FOLK WERE SUPPLIED, IT IS BELIEVED.

Pistol, Shotgun, Rifle and Cartridges Also in Trunks—Man Denies Making Any Sales.

Acting on information that a big source of supply was open to the drug users in the theatrical profession, Detectives Judge, Johns and Waterhouse of Special Squad No. 4, under command of Lieut. Scherb, went yesterday afternoon to the King James Hotel, No. 137 West Forty-fifth Street.

They asked if Mr. and Mrs. Bennett were in. By telephone came the answer "Yes."

"Just tell them a couple of the boys are here," said a detective.

"All right; let them come up," came the reply.

The detectives went to the room indicated and rapped on the door. It was opened and they rushed in. They say they found a man with an opium layout near him and a pipe in his hand. Near him was a woman.

"Greatest Tango Dancers."

The couple, taken to the West Forty-seventh Street Police Station, said they were George Bennett, thirty-four, and his wife Mae Bennett, twenty-three. A circular they showed to the police proclaimed "the world's greatest tango dancers." Since they arrived from Europe several weeks ago the Bennetts have stayed at several high class hotels, finally going to the King James about a week ago.

This is what the detectives say they found in the couple's rooms:

Eighty-one cans of opium, each weighing about seven ounces.

One bottle of cocaine.

Four boxes and one bottle of heroin.

One loaded automatic pistol, found under a pillow.

A two-pound bag of opium ashes.

Three opium pipes and layouts.

One shotgun and one rifle with a Maxim silencer attached.

Several clips of cartridges for the rifle.

A small roulette wheel.

In a pocket of a coat, the police say, they found a pair of metal knuckles.

Had Cooking Apparatus.

Seventy-four of the cans were found in a box couch. In a wicker hamper ...

'POPPY' SMOKE AND LIQUOR A DEADLY FUSION

Mother and Three Sisters in Boston Home to Be Told of Tragic Fate of "Marie"

7 WEEKS IN MOTT STREET

Wreck of Once Beautiful Victim Shows Traces of Refinement Sacrificed to the Drug

Into a dingy tenement in the heart of Chinatown, a young woman, fresh from a night orgy of opium smoking and drinking, stumbled early yesterday morning. A few hours later she was found dead. Though the Medical Examiner's office has not yet established the cause of the death, Chinatown says:

"She tried to combine opium smoking with drinking. It always kills."

Only a short time ago this young woman, known only as "Marie" to a few intimates, lived in a bountiful home in Boston. She was the idol ...

BIG SMUGGLI... PLOT REVEAL... IN CHANCE N...

Writer to Scotch Parent of Vessels Waiting to ... Narcotics and Chines...

SEARCH IS THREAT...

Information Sent to Wa... ton by Local Officials ... Action by State Dep...

Information obtained f... letter taken from a rum r... yesterday caused Treasu...

HUGE CHINESE DOPE SHIPPING RING REVEALED

Mystic Passwords Used to Get Drug Aboard Ships Bound From Orient to This Port

Revelation of the "inside" methods of the Chinese dope smuggling ring, which keeps San Francisco flooded with narcotics through a system rooted on the other side of the Pacific ...

QUITS

AGENTS SEIZE DOPE IN TRUNK OF SECRETARY

Discovery Amazes Bolivian Vice-President; Believes Aide Dupe of Smugglers

Opium in Baggage Shortens Stay of Official Suggested as Claims Session Umpire

By JACK HYATT.

Dr. A. S. Seavreda, vice-president of the Republic of Bolivia, who has been mentioned in Washington ...

U.S. OFFICE... SMASH WA... TO GET CA...

Tins Hidden in Presiden... rison's Chain Locker; Chinese of Crew Ar...

OPIUM valued at $1,... was seized aboar... Dollar liner Pre... Harrison at Jersey City ... day.

Customs men declar... seizure one of the larges... made.

But for the keen nose of C... Inspector Edward Starace, th... 6-ounce tins of opium might ... be secreted in some underwo... in this city.

When sixteen Customs se... were about to give the Pr... Harrison a clean bill, Starace ... and sniffed again as the b... docked at Pier 9.

He thought that above the ... of bilge oil he had detected th... but pungent aroma of opium ... sixteen Government me... searched everything but the ... locker in the fore peak of the ...

"Pay out that chain!"

Partition Torn Dow...

So commanded Starace. ... fathoms of chain was paid o... created enough space for t... and seven men to attack a pa... with crowbars and saws.

After two hours of sawi... prying, the Customs men fina... tered the locker.

Thrusting about in the gloo... man felt his crowbar strike ... thing metallic. It turned ou... a package of metal opium c... ...s, concealed in a burlap... Thirty burlap bags were foun... each one had 100 eight-ounce ...

Coincident with the se... aboard the President Harriso... a disclosure that two policeme... ten others are held in bail in ... lyn in connection with an ... conspiracy to smuggle opium ... the Barber Line pier, Brookly...

The policemen arrested are ... man Dewey Hock, forty, of N... East Eighty-first street, Manh... and Patrolman Harold Butler, ... ty-five, of No. 81 Cumberland ... Brooklyn. Hock was held in $... bail, and Butler in $5,000 by ... States Judge Inch for a h... October 15.

Four Chinese, and eight ... men, including the superinte... and two watchmen of the ... Line pier are also held in bail ... case. The two policemen wer... pended following an investigat... Acting Captain Bernard McQu...

Suspected Chinese

It is charged that the two ... men permitted two Chinese ... came after their taxicab cont... several hundred cans of opium ... stopped. These Chinese were be... to be leaders of a smuggling ri...

Customs men said the Pre... Harrison is liable to a fine of ... ... today. But r... ... the skipper ... presence of the ... attach the steam... capture. The ... struck one o... main channels for surreptitio... porting of opium into this co... Customs men revealed that ... suspicions had been aroused b... large number of Chinese in the ... rison's crew. Of a roster of 18... President Harrison had 131 Chi... Moreover, the boat had just re... ...

...PIUM RAIDERS JAIL HUSBAND AND WIFE

...umes Draw Detectives to West Side Apartment, Where Drug Is Found.

...OUNG GIRL IS SEEN THERE

...oman's Striking Beauty Said to Have Wilted After Night Spent in Cell.

Charged with smoking opium, ...rs. Herman Brooks, thirty, a ...autiful woman of the statuesque ...pe, is under arrest to-day with ...r husband, Herman Brooks, ...irty-five, a salesman, as the re...lt of a raid upon their apart...ent at No. 628 West One Hundred ...d Thirty-fifth street.

The raid was made by Dr. ...arleton Simon, deputy police com...ssioner, in charge of the Narcot...s Division; Lieutenant Mooney ...d Detectives Cotter and O'Brien. ...Going to the roof of the apart...ent building, O'Brien said he de...cted opium fumes coming from ...e windows of the Brooks suite. ...hen the narcotics men entered ...th Mr. and Mrs. Brooks and a ...arried man and a young girl, also ...f the apartment, insisted they had ...t been smoking opium.

...FFICERS FIND OPIUM.

Detective Cotter said he fou... ...mplete opium ...

OPIUM IN FOOD CANS IS SEIZED

A plan to flood the United States with narcotics through the machinations of an Oriental drug ring operating out of Tokio, Japan, and Hongkong, China, was frustrated in part yesterday when customs inspectors operating under the direction of ... ...No. 351 ...second street, ... a quantity of ...roin valued at about $800.

...THERS ARE HELD.

Those arrested are Stella Wilson, ...rty-five; Louis Phillipe, his wife, ...

SMUGGLING NET LANDS ELLISON

Former Customs Guard Arrested in $50,000 Opium Plot; Raid Planned on Steamer.

Elias Ellison, former customs gua... ...

POLICE FIND $100,000 GUM OPIUM IN TRUNK

St. Louis Man Arrested as Owner of Drugs at Grand Central. Woman Companion Sought.

A trunk containing gum opium valued at $100,000, was seized at the Grand Central Terminal yesterday by detectives of the narcotic squad. M... R. Gordon, of St. Louis, was arrest... as its alleged owner.

Gordon has been under surveillan... since he registered at the Hotel Ab... deen a week ago. Several big remi...tances, in receiving which, the poli... say, he had posed as "M. H. Milla..." had been wired him from St. Louis.

Captain Henry Sherd and Detectives Thomas Law and William Cruger, working under the direction of Deputy Police Commissioner Simon, learned of the trunk at the Terminal prior to ...uesday. Its shipping label bore a ...troit address. This the detectives ...ced.

Gordon and a woman companion ...arently had planned to take the ...k to Detroit that afternoon. They ...doned the trip on learning they ... have to describe its contents. ... man appeared at the baggage ... yesterday, alone. Detectives say ...ned the trunk as his own prop... after they arrested him. Later ...ted it belonged to the woman, ...dentify he would not reveal.

U. S. Must Keep Yap Even at Cost of War"—Daniels

1915.

CHINESE DEPICT EVILS OF OPIUM

Picturesque Proclamation Under Official Seal Explains Persistent Policy.

PROHIBITION IS DEFENDED

No Consideration Given to Argument That Injustice Is Done to Those Dependent on Traffic for Livelihood.

PEKIN, May 18.—(Correspondence of the Associated Press.)—A proclamation bearing the seal of the President tells in a picturesque way the peculiar story of the opium reform in China. From the proclamation the following paragraphs are taken:

"The evil of opium is known to all ...

... portation of foreign opium and the ... sation of the cultivation of ... within a certain time limit ... persistent policy ... been pur... with regard to the prohibition of ... vation, smoking and trading in opi... and as a result of it many provi... ing all poppy plants; conseque... transportation of opium into these ... vinces has been prohibited. If ... opportunity were seized completely ... banish the opium evil, the coun... would be put on a strong footing. This is why the order was repea...

WOMAN TAKEN IN $1,000,000 OPIUM RING

Mexican Border Drug Smuggling Traffic Revealed in Arrest of Six

THREE BROTHERS IN NET

Wholesale Clothiers Accused in Scheme That Has Been Going on Two Years

Habit-forming drugs, valued at more than $1,000,000, have been smuggled across the Mexican border in the last two years, according to Federal officials, who Friday rounded up five men and a woman as members of a ring. The smuggling of drugs probably would have continued indefinitely had it not been for an accident to one of the shipments at pier 26 on April 27. On that date a box fell from an express wagon and cracked open ...

EMPLOYE OF SING FAT CO. FACES TRIAL

Son of Venerable Manager of Store Accused of Violating Two Narcotic Acts

Following an alleged confession that he was the owner of four five-tael tins of opium seized in a raid on the store of the Sing Fat Company, at California street and Grant avenue, Tong Gee, employe of the store and son of Tong Bong, store manager and for 50 years a merchant of San Francisco, was charged yesterday with violating the Harrison narcotic act and the narcotic import and export act. Brought before United States Commissioner Thomas E. Hayden, Tong Gee was yesterday released on bail of $5,000.

When Federal raiding agents found a large quantity of choice liquors and wines in the Sing Fat store, Tong Poy and Tong Kee, and his wife, Lum Shee, were arrested and charged with violating the Volstead act. Each was released on $1,000 bail yesterday.

FIVE-YEAR PROBE.

The raid on the Sing Fat store came after five years of patient labor by Federal narcotics agents to prove their suspicions that the famous store was the center of a large dope distributing traffic, it was said by Harry D. Smith, chief ...

Opium Valued at $72,496 Seized by Federal Agents In Coal Bunkers of Ship

"$200 FOR LOT."

"Receiving some money from unexpected sources, however, we were ...

... This plan was carried out ... Hong Kong, said the Chinaman, a man named Chan Kou got past the ship's guards and gave him 90 ... tael tins of opium. At Yokohama, one Lee Look gave him 116 ounces of cocaine and a quantity of morphine.

"SYSTEM" GOES WRONG.

At Honolulu the "system" went ...

'Such Stuff as Dreams Are Made Of!'

EDWARD STARACE. P. A. M'GUINNESS. E. J. FITZSIMMONS.

COUNTING SPOILS!—No uniforms show the rank of these customs inspectors, as they handle the $1,000,000 worth of opium seized aboard the President Harrison. It's rough work breaking into a ship's locker and the three show it.

Chinese in America Oppose New Empire

"Dr. Saavedra was in no way implicated in the smuggling of this opium. Nor was his secretary Ortiz anything but a dupe, an innocent tool. He is but a lad, and was given this package of opium by a man in the ...

TUNNEY KNOCKS OUT CARPENTIER IN 15 ROUNDS

Story of Fight on Sporting Page

Today

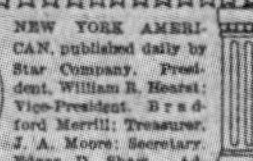

NEW YORK AMERICAN, published daily by Star Company. President, William R. Hearst; Vice-President, Bradford Merrill; Treasurer, J. A. Moore; Secretary Edgar D. Shaw. Address, 238 William St.

New York American — CHARACTER · QUALITY · AMERICA FIRST · ACCURACY · ENTERPRISE — AN AMERICAN PAPER FOR THE AMERICAN PEOPLE

FIGHT EXTRA

No. 14,982.—DAILY. Copyright, 1924, by Star Company. Registered in U. S. Patent Office. EDITORIAL PHONE, BEEKMAN 2000. FRIDAY, JULY 25, 1924—24 PAGES. BUSINESS PHONE, COLUMBUS 7000. Entered as second-class matter, Post Office New York, N. Y. THREE CENTS Within 200 Miles Radius | Elsewhere Four Cents

DRUGS AND ALIENS ON RUM ROW SHIPS

…T OBJECTS …ARCHED FOR …NTRABAND

…Article in Famous S. F. …natownn Store Thoroughly …mined by Federal Men

…Cases of Liquor and Five … of Opium Seized; Kin … Store Owner Arrested

…nbined army of Federal nar…gents, Prohibition officers …mbers of the Chinatown …squad descended yesterday …e elaborate establishment of …at & Co., the largest store …Francisco's Chinatown and …the largest Chinese import…ses in the United States, …nbed it from top to bottom …several stories in a search …traband of various sorts. …mers who were in the big …hich has been for years one …sights of San Francisco …tained while they could ex…heir business and establish …dentity after guards were …placed at the doors.

…article in the place was …d by Treasury Department …who ripped open rich man…coats and explored the …of embroidered kimonos. …vase in the establish… …ped to see if it h… …and even doll… …were pierced … …n a search for …r other narcotics.

…ARRESTED.

…result, three Chin… …Chinese woman we… …rrest, five five-tael … …ere seized and abo… …choice assorted liqu… …were confiscated in t… …ters of the huge est… …Grant avenue and C… …t.

…arrested were:

…ong, said to be one o… …al officials of the Sing… …any.

…e Gee, said to be the son of …Bong and the man whom …leral agents were seeking.

…ee, another son of Tong …

…e, a Chinese woman em…

…S COMBINE.

…id was made upon a search …authorizing Treasury De…t agents to search the en…ding. It is explained that …cotics and liquor come un…same head when the Treas… Revenue departments are …

CRACKER GAGS BIRD LOOKOUT IN OPIUM RAID

Cockatoo Tries in Vain to Warn Drug Users with Its Usual Shrill Cry of "Umpire"

BOY AIDED DETECTIVES

Four Under Arrest After Door to Flat Is Broken Down; Many Former Calls Fruitless

Sonnaugo is only a little green-plumaged cocatoo brought from Singapore by Ah Cong, a deep water Chinese seaman. Sonnaugo, which means Little Boy, … can swear …

… at No. 1… street. Raid after raid was made, but always, when the officers approached the barred door to the apartment, they heard the shrill scream, "Umpie!, Umpie!" When the door was finally crashed in there was always the unmistakable odor of opium fumes, but no trace of smokers.

Finally a detective decided that there was a connection between "umpie" and the mysterious disappearance of the opium smokers. Inquiry among the Chinese revealed that "Umpie" meant "cop." So plans were then laid to fix the little cockatoo lookout.

GIVEN CRACKERS.

Last night a small boy in the neighborhood was given a handful of American crackers and told to sneak them into Sonnaugo's cage. A few minutes later the lad returned and said that the little cockatoo was hungrily gobbling the new American parrot diet, so different from his usual Chinese nuts and sweetmeats.

4 Chinese Held After Raid by Narcotic Squad

Four Chinese, arrested when detectives of the Narcotic Squad raided the premises at No. 276 Delancey street, were held in $500 bail each for the Grand Jury by Magistrate Smith, in Essex Market Court, yesterday.

The four men are charged with possession of hypodermic needles.

CAPITAL DRUG RAID NETS 100 SUSPECTS

WASHINGTON, July 17.—In a series of sweeping raids conducted by fourteen special squads police and revenue agents early today arrested more than 100 persons and seized narcotics valued at more than $10,000.

The raids were the result of several months' investigation by reve…

$100,000 Opium Seized at Brooklyn Pier

HIDDEN POLICE SEE STEAMER UNLOAD DOPE

Capture Made After 809 Cans Are Placed in Waiting Cab; Four Chinese Questioned

Alertness of a Brooklyn policeman yesterday resulted in the seizure of 899 cans of raw opium, valued by police at $100,000.

Patrol… …tler, of the …cinct, was … Pier 36, at … Brooklyn, …xicab drew …and went …r Kendall … a door… …rs. At …ur men …of the …in the … Butler … questioning …, No. 3797 Sixty-third street, Woodhaven, Queens, the driver. Felshman told Butler two Chinese had hired him at Hester street and the Bowery, Manhattan.

Butler summoned Detectives McTiernan and McCarthy, of the Hamilton avenue precinct. Felshman was ordered to drive the cab to the station house. There the packages containing opium were seized.

CHINESE QUESTIONED.

ALLEGED OPIUM DEALER IS HELD

William Williams, alias David Matthews, who was arrested by narcotic agents on a charge of selling opium, was arraigned yesterday before United States Commissioner Boyle and held in $5,000 bail for the Federal Grand Jury.

Williams is wanted as a fugitive fro justice, having forfeited $10,000 bail two years ago on a similar charge. He was arrested Saturday in a printing shop at No. 155 West Ninety-ninth street with a man who described himself as Morris Meyer, forty-one, living at a Mills Hotel.

The Federal agents confiscated about sixty-two ounces of opium and several telegrams and letters written in code. It is said Williams supplied narcotics to a large number of addicts, many of them prominent in the theatrical and moving picture business.

Sunday Dr. Carleton Simon, Special Deputy Police Commissioner, in charge … denied M… …liams who … said he h… $500 for th…

2 PUT ON TRIAL IN OPIUM PLOT FOR $500,000

Federal Prosecutor Announces That Four, Admitting Their Guilt, Will Be Witnesses

CASES FILLED WITH ROCK

Shipment for Cuba Tampered With in Warehouse, Claim. "Volstead Fairness" Asked

The alleged $500,000 opium conspiracy case was opened in Federal Court yesterday before Judge Goddard and a jury. Assistant United States Attorney Falk is presenting … …ment's case.

… Pavlou, a former impor… …orris de Luca, president …hor Warehouse, Inc., No. …orty-seventh street, are …nts. They are jointly …h conspiracy to defraud …ment by not paying duty …d for selling 102 pounds …h there were no duty …

…her defendants in the …ecutor Falk said, had …ilty and would appear …vernment.

…ning session was occu…lecting a jury. When … Falk outlined his case …hat twenty cases of …thing 2,800 pounds, had …ted from Greece April …hey were stored in the …ion of the Anchor ware…secutor Falk declared. … of the warehouse, he was in exclusive cus… …c J. Ettinger, a custom …

…n was to have been re… … firm in Havana, … …es were schedul… … to Mexico, the pr…

TWO OPIUM SELLERS CONVICTED BY JURY

Imported Drug for Export, but Sold It Here and Sent Bricks to Cuba.

Morris De Luca, president of the Anchor Warehouse Company in East Forty-seventh street, and Thomas Pavlou, an importer, No. 144 West Thirty-fourth street, were convicted in Federal Court yesterday of selling opium.

In addition De Luca was found guilty of conspiracy to defraud the Government of revenue taxes.

Maximum sentences may be five years for Pavlou and seven years for De Luca.

The jury deliberated three and a half hours. After their verdicts De Luca and Pavlou were sent to the Tombs. Bail was denied. Judge Goddard will impose sentence Tuesday.

Both had been charged with conspiracy to defraud the Government of the duty on 2,800 pounds of opium imported to New York from Greece under representations that it would be re-exported to Havana.

The evidence showed that, instead, the opium was taken from the cases at the Anchor Warehouse and disposed of in Chinatown for $170,000. The twenty cases were refilled with bricks and shipped to Havana.

Four others indicted with De Luca and Pavlou pleaded guilty at the beginning of the trial and were used as witnesses. The four were Isaac J. Ettinger, a Government storekeeper, his son, Dr. William J. Ettinger, also known as Sardou; Nick Karaca, keeper of the Adelphia Hotel at Tenth venue and West Twenty-third street, and Steve Valiades.

3 GIRLS SEIZED IN OPIUM RAID

Charged with possessing drugs, and waiving examination, three young women were held yesterday in $500 bail in West Side Court by Magistrate Goodman for Special Sessions.

With them was arrested Moe Schwartz, twenty-eight, of No. 370 Bedford avenue, Brooklyn.

The women, with Schwartz, were arrested in a raid on an apartment at No. 136 West Seventy-second street Saturday by Sergeant Fred Wilson, of the narcotic squad, who said a complete opium smoking outfit and opium were seized.

The girls described themselves as Jean Conway, twenty-two, an actress, of the Hotel Remington, No. 129 West Forty-sixth street; Dorothy Thomas, twenty-one, actress, of the same address, and Peggy Wise, twenty-nine, a manicurist, of No. 2132 West Tenth street, Brooklyn.

Wilson said the raid followed reports that opium fumes were coming from the apartment.

DRUG FIND ENDS DIPLOMAT STAY

Continued from First Page.

Mexican. He was arrested near the Texas border. On him was a quantity of smuggled narcoics. Vasques was induced to talk and he divulged the fact that he had given Ortiz a package to deliver to 'a friend' in New York."

After Vasque's arrest, Federal agents from Washington were immediately sent to New York to see Dr. Saavedra and his party at the Hotel McAlpin, where they had a suite of rooms.

IMMUNE TO LAW.

Ortiz, Dr. Saavedra and all the members of the latter's family were traveling under diplomatic passports and therefore immune to molestation.

Two Engineers, Machinist Of Don Jose Under Arrest On Opium-Importing Count

Three men of the crew of the Philippine steamer Don Jose were arrested last night by United States customs agents charged with importing opium.

The men, who were lodged in the county jail, were Pedro DeLeon, chief engineer; Jose Clemente, third engineer, and Alberto Formentos, chief machinist.

The arrests followed the discovery of $72,496 worth of smoking opium aboard the Don Jose by customs

BLAMES OPIUM FOR HIS CRIME

When Peter La Tempa, eighteen, of No. 230 North Fifth street, Brooklyn, was arraigned yesterday before Judge Taylor in the Kings County Court on a charge of robbery, he gave as an excuse, opium smoking.

It is alleged La Tempa last November 8, with three companions, held up Peter Chiaino in his candy store at No. 136 North Sixth street, Brooklyn. They got $18.

After the robbery, Peter is said to have shot the candy store keeper.

La Tempa said that on the day before the robbery he went to a Chinese restaurant where for the first time in his life he smoked opium.

5 RICH MEN, 3 WOMEN CAUGHT IN OPIUM DEN

MURRAY HILL SUITE RAIDED BY DR. SIMON

Two of the Men Seized Were in Evening Dress; Visitors' Plea for Secrecy Granted

NAVY MAN'S EX-WIFE HELD

She Admits Ownership of Three Pipes, Claiming Narcotic Outfit Was for Her Own Use

An elaborate set of opium smoking outfits was seized early yesterday in a raid on an expensively furnished apartment in the exclusive Murray Hill section in Fortieth street, near Lexington avenue. Five wealthy men, two of them in evening dress, and three smartly gowned women, were in the apartment. The men all gave their addresses as a club near Bryant Park.

Deputy Police Commissioner Dr. Carleton Simon, in charge of the Narcotic Division at Headquarters, had direct supervision of the raid and questioned all those found in the apartment. He said no charge could be preferred against the visitors which would hold in a magistrate's court, and directed that they be released after two of the men had pleaded that their wives might divorce them and one of the women had expressed fear that her husband would divorce her if she had to go to the police station.

ADMITS OWNERSHIP.

Mrs. Marion Campbell, who said she was the divorced wife of a naval officer, was arrested charged with possessing opium. One of the men in the party gave $500 in cash to free her in Yorkville Police Court when Magistrate Simms held her for examination on Tuesday. Mrs. Campbell admitted to the Magistrate that she owned the opium and smoking utensils found in the apartment, but declared they were for her private use.

The set seized consisted of three …

…LIONAIRE …MED AS HEAD …OPIUM PLOT

…m Stein, Broadway …acter, Accused; Five …ed on Dope Charges

…five indictments for law…g dealing were handed … Federal Court yesterday. …announcement was …at the "big shot" behind …cent $1,000,000 opium …ad been discovered.

…s declared to be Abraham … Broadway character, al…der indictment on charges …al activity in narcotic …

…was indicted again with … Goodman, in whose … 636 Hudson st. Federal …und 2,060 pounds of pure …m.

…BAIL.

…an was arraigned and …75,000 was continued, de… plea of Edward A. Sil… said:

…ow $1,000,000 is a lot of … but the Government …ive all it seized for 10 … cash."

…s at liberty on the old …der light bail. He is re…to be worth millions and …eply interested in business …the Western and Eastern …

…ENTS INDICTED

…ents also were found …gents Richard Nash and … R. Keane and former … A. De Stefano, accused … to bribe Arnold Lache… …he agent who trapped …our counts were made …hem.

… Attorney Medalie said: …t to try them within a … that in another week … be free or in Atlanta

… agents intimated Stein … released on light bail …h so he could be followed …tives. This espionage, … led them ultimately to …n st. cache.

DRUG CAPTURE 'BEST IN YEARS'

Customs Men Delighted by Arrest of W. N. Dingman After 6-Months' Chase.

HELD UNDER HEAVY BAIL

Prisoner Accused of Running of Chinese and Traffic in Opium.

A trail that for six months led all along the Atlantic seaboard, reaching as far south as Miami, Fla., ended at Newark on Friday with the arrest of William M Dingman.

His capture, customs agents declared yesterday was more important to them than "a billion dollar seizure of narcotics."

Dingman, the agents said, is known also as William R. Banks. The importance of his arrest was indicated by the fact that although he was held under $10,000 bail in Newark Friday, his capture was not announced publicly by the agents until yesterday. Unable to furnish bail, he was still in the Essex County Jail yesterday, charged with transporting, smuggling and concealing narcotics.

SEIZURES OF OPIUM.

The agents reported that when Dingman was arrested he had ten pounds of opium in his possession. Subsequently, they said, they found forty cans of smoking opium and thirty pounds of gum opium in a wardrobe trunk in an uptown apartment occupied by him.

The prisoner, the agents reported, admitted that for thirty years he has been the leader of a band of smugglers who have brought hundreds of Chinese and great quantities of narcotics into the United States. He dressed fashionably and speaks Chinese fluently. He is said to be the only white member of the Gee Kong Tong of Buffalo and is a certified member of the Grand Lodge of Chinese Free Masons.

DOPE RAID JAILS GIRLS AT PARTY

Claiming to have found an opium pipe, still warm, and a small quantity of opium in a hotel room where a party was in progress, Detectives Burke, … and Hackett of the Narcotic Squad early yesterday arrested two men and two girls. Later the four were held by Magistrate Richard F. McInery in $2,500 bail each for hearing Wednesday. The charge is possession of narcotics.

The girls were Dorothy Woodward, a model, aged twenty-four, and Frances Taylor, twenty-six-year-old cabaret dancer. The men are Thomas Pulver, twenty-three, and Joseph la Rose, twenty-four. The raid was on Pulver's room in the Hotel Cumberland, Fifty-fifth street and Broadway.

OPIUM SEIZED IN RICH HOME

An expensively furnished apartment at No. 243 West Seventieth street is believed by Federal narcotic agents to be the haunt of rich opium smokers. The agents raided the apartment Friday night and arrested Jack and Gladys Curran who were held in $2,000 bail by United States Commissioner O'Neill on a charge of violating the Harrison Anti-Narcotic Act.

Two complete opium outfits and $500 worth of opium were seized. The Currans have two children, a boy of five and a girl of two and a half years, who reside with their grandparents at Providence. R. L. Curran is said to be the son of a wealthy business man of Providence. Mrs. Curran appeared in the comedy "Business Before Pleasure" several years ago under the name of Gladys Chase and later in the movies under the name of Gladys Austin.

Belief that the apartmnet was the rendezvous of wealthy devotees of the pipe was expressed by the agents after discovering a book full of names and addresses, including those …

3000 TINS OF … SEIZED IN BAGGAGE

WIFE OF CHINESE VICE-CONSUL UNDER SUSPICION.

Shipment Declared Owned by Ring Operated in Remote Region of China.

SAN FRANCISCO, Cal., July 8.—(AP)—… officials declared an audacious attempt to smuggle a fortune in opium through use of the baggage privileges extended foreign diplomats was frustrated today with seizure here by customs officials of 3000 tins of the contraband found in the luggage of Mrs. Sule Ying Kao, daughter of the Chinese minister to Cuba and the wife of the Chinese vice-consul here.

Customs inspectors said the opium was worth approximately $1,000,000.

Rare Chinese silks and laces on which no duty had been paid also were found in the luggage, which the federal officials seized aboard the liner Tenyo Maru last Friday when Mrs. Kao returned from a visit to China. The luggage was not opened, however, until authority was received today from Washington for such action. There were eight large trunks and six suitcases.

Opium Concealed in Linings.

Eleven of these pieces of baggage, the search today revealed, were lined …

INSPECTOR'S NOSE FINDS $1,000,000 DOPE ON LINER

$50,000 OPIUM FOUND ON SHIP

SAN FRANCISCO, June 22.—Opium, valued at $50,000, was found by customs inspectors beneath the boilers of the Java-Pacific freighter Modjokerto.

Attention was first attracted to the Modjokerto while she was lying at anchor in China Basin. John Kenny, a customs guard on Pier 20, saw a man rowing toward the vessel and called upon him to halt. When the oarsman refused Kenny fired five shots at him before he disappeared in the darkness.

Policeman Chris J. Buckley, in a police boat, cruised about the ship, but could find no trace of the man. Smuggling was suspected and the customs officers were notified. When the Modjokerto tied up at the How…

FINDS NO LURE IN OPIUM

1932

THRILL LACKING—Miss Winfred Howard, daughter of the Rev. Dr. Henry Howard, Fifth av. pastor, shown with an opium pipe obtained in the Orient. Miss Howard experimented with four or five pipefuls of the dope, but confesses she found no thrill in the experience.

OPIUM GIVES GIRL NO THRILL

'Opium Den' New Vienna Nightclub

1933

By Universal Service.

VIENNA, July 29.—Up a side street, past an old cemetery, down into what appears to be an abandoned cellar—and you're in Vienna's newest and, for the moment, most popular night club, "The Opium Den."

Entrance is through a dank passage, which brings you suddenly into a small, … room where people are sitting about on cushions. There are no chairs. Before each person is a foot-high table on which his coffee or drink rests. The hangings are Oriental, and over in one corner is a tiny wisp of smoke curling upward from a massive incense burner.

The only lighting comes from a slowly revolving glass ball that reflects varicolored lights as it turns. On the diminutive dance floor lithe Hindu dancers appear.

The attempt to represent an opium den without the opium is generally considered quite successful and those who seek "atmosphere" claim to find it here.

This resort and the three night clubs connected with the revue theatres are doing a fairly brisk business for Summer.

$30,000 OPIUM SEIZED IN RAID

Federal agents, who used a Chinese and marked money to trap their prisoner, arrested a tailor and confiscated what they said was $30,000 worth of raw opium in a raid yesterday at No. 241 East Fortieth street. The prisoner described himself as E. Elefteriodis.

The Government officers, Joseph … and George Coyle, of …

THE SACRAMENTO BEE, TUESDAY, DECEMBER 4, 1934

Japanese License Opium Houses In Manchukuo

Sam R. Leedom, a member of The Sacramento Bee Staff, is on a world tour. He is writing his impressions of some of the things he sees from the viewpoint of a Sacramentan abroad.—Editor's Note.

By SAM R. LEEDOM.

HARBIN (Manchukuo), — (By Mail) — In an unused doorway across the street from the Hotel Moderne a ragged human figure lay yesterday morning. It was directly opposite the writer's window and there it remained, the awkward position unchanged at noon. Passersby on the street either saw the figure not at all or after an indifferent glance passed on. A group of Chinese children played in the gutter ten feet away.

When the body was still there in mid-afternoon and there was still no change in its position, the writer became convinced he was witnessing the repose of the soundest sleeper in China or the man was dead. As a matter of fact, the man was dead and sometime late that afternoon the police got around to removing the body which was surprisingly quick action for the Harbin police. In proof of …

… is allowed to come as often as he wishes.

These opium dives are open for public inspection at any time. In an evening's round of half a dozen of them one sees literally hundreds of addicts, some smoking their long stemmed pipes, others sleeping off the effects of the narcotic and in every den there are many young girls who act as serving maids, preparing and lighting the pipes. They too, either are or soon become addicts—pitifully terrible little puff eyed creatures, all of them in their early teens.

Government Profits.

The government control of the opium trade was inaugurated for the announced … of curbing the habit. How… the real reason is that there are tremendous revenues to be realized from the tragic business. Under the present system of easy access the narcotic …

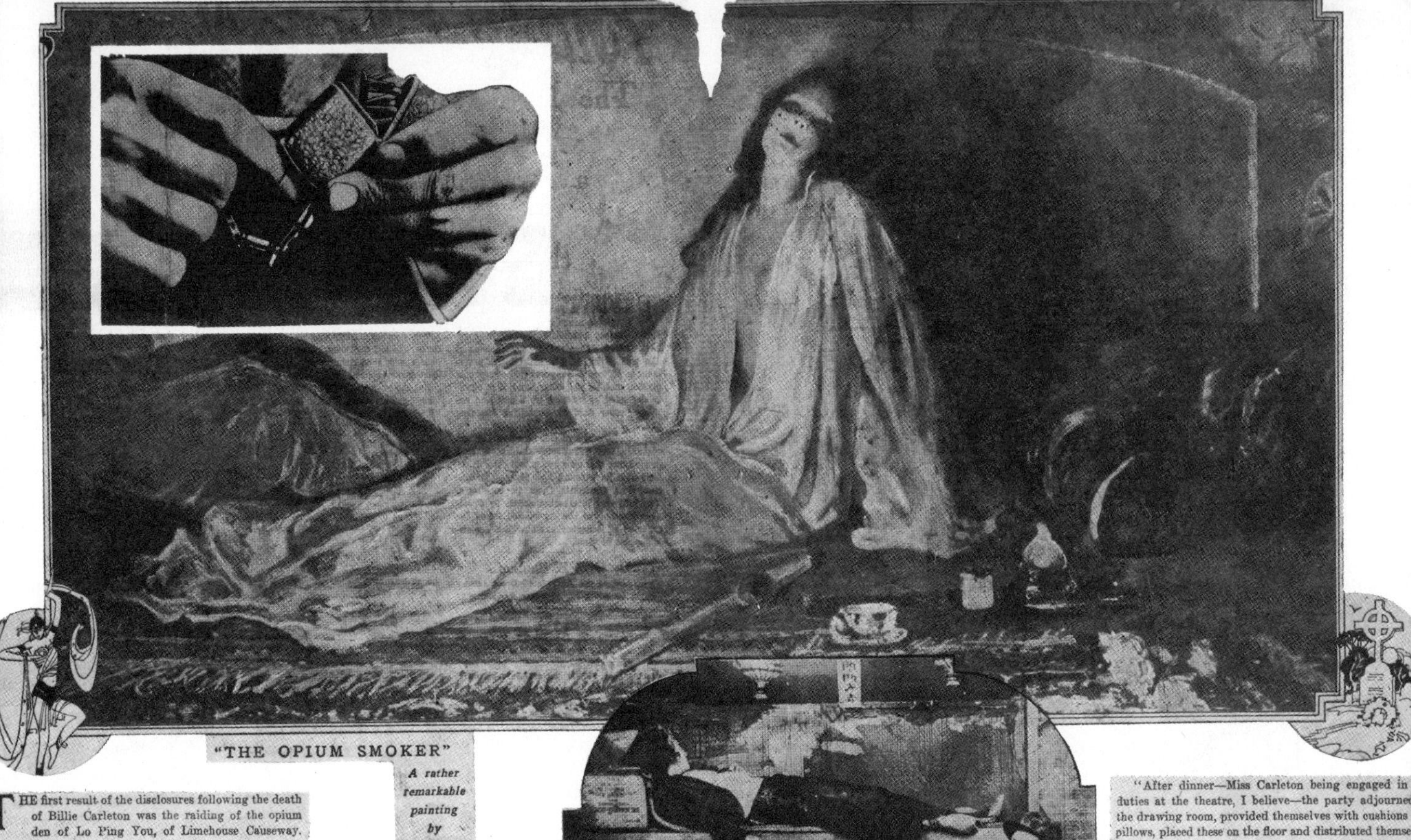

"THE OPIUM SMOKER"

A rather remarkable painting by Matignon.

THE first result of the disclosures following the death of Billie Carleton was the raiding of the opium den of Lo Ping You, of Limehouse Causeway. his was done by the London police while the coroner was ılding his inquest.

It had been brought out in the testimony before the roner that Billie Carleton had obtained cocaine and robably other drugs at an opium den kept by Lo Ping ou in London's Chinatown. It had also been discovered at this Chinaman was married to a British wife, who ad become very skilful in preparing crude opium for noking. Olive Richardson, the actress, brought in the ame of Mrs. Lo Ping You, and declared that de Veulle d told her that he was obtaining supplies of cocaine from

Both Lo Ping You, the Chinaman, aged twenty-four, nd his Scottish wife, Ada Ping You, aged twenty-eight, ho were arrested after the dramatic evidence given at ie inquest on Miss Billie Carleton, were arraigned, one the Thames Police Court and the other at the Marlborugh street Police Court, on charges connected with the pium traffic.

The Chinaman pleaded guilty to a charge of having pium in his possession without authority and with having so an opium smoking pipe and other utensils.

Mrs. Lo Ping You, who is known as "Mrs. Ping," was arged with supplying prepared opium to Miss Billie arleton and further with being in possession of opium nd of prepared opium for smoking at 16 Dover street.

eir supplies of opium, and it was there that they took er to indulge in more fantastic and brutal orgies when ie comparatively refined opium parties in West End flats ere beginning to pall.

Limehouse is perhaps the most grimly, grewsomely icked quarter in the whole world. It is far to the east the Strand, east of the Tower of London, lost in the urlieus of London's darkest east. The Causeway is the rincipal thoroughfare in this sink of iniquity, raised enturies ago above the mud flats of the Thames. Limeouse is adjacent to Whitechapel, but far more criminal nd dangerous on account of its population of Orientals ho prey on sailors.

Limehouse is the "Chinatown" of London, but it conains among its swarming thousands specimens of many aces besides the Chinese. It has become an Oriental uarter through the proximity of the vast East India ocks, where the ships bring more Chinese and other Orintals than to any other port of Europe. The ships from he East, of course, bring the opium. For many years imehouse has been the spot where opium was most easily btained and smoked and where it was distributed to the est of London. Writing nearly a hundred years ago, Thomas de Quincey, the celebrated author of "The Conessions of an English Opium Eater," spoke of Limehouse s the place whence the insidious poison came.

Limehouse made one of its numerous appearances in iterature in Oscar Wilde's book, "The Picture of Dorian Gray." It was to this locality that the chief character in hat curious work repaired for mysterious debauches, the ature of which was only vaguely suggested.

Many opium smoking dens are kept in Limehouse by Chinamen. Their chief customers are Oriental sailors and ock laborers, commonly called Lascars in London parance. With them, too, are many sailors of other nationlities, together with an assortment of criminals, dock ats and dregs of society of both sexes. Here, too, come ersons from the higher strata of society, who have exausted the pleasures of West End resorts and yearn for tranger and more brutal forms of dissipation.

The London police have in the past given little attenion to the suppression of opium smoking. The vice never ook a great hold on the respectable middle and working lasses, and the authorities thought if foreign sailors vanted to smoke opium it was their own business. There vas no carefully thought out system of laws to suppress he vice, such as the United States has had. After the war began, however, it was realized that opium smoking, ogether with all the forms of drug addiction, was a serious menace to the military efficiency of the nation. In conequence trafficking in opium and other drugs was made a seriou[s] under the Defense of the Realm Act.

Lime[house] offers plenty of dissipation besides opium smoking. Practically every sort of criminal or semiriminal entertainment can be enjoyed there at moderate prices, from a crooked prize fight down to exhibitions that

stairs ran straight to the street and above whose doorway a lamp glowed like an evil eye. At this establishment he took his pipe of 'chandu' and a brief chat with the keeper of the house, for, although not popular and very silent, he liked sometimes to be in the presence of his compatriots. Like a figure of a shadowgraph, he slid through the door and up the stairs.

"The chamber he entered was a bit of the Orient squatting at the portals of the West. It was a well-kept place, where one might play a game of fan-tan or take a shot or so of li-un, or purchase other varieties of Oriental delight. It was sunk in a purple dusk, though here and there a lantern stung the glooms. Low couches lay around the walls, and strange men decorated them, Chinese, Japs, Malays, Lascars, with one or two white girls, and sleek, noiseless attendants swam from couch to couch. Away in the far corner sprawled a lank figure in brown shirting, its nerveless fingers curled about the stem of a spent pipe. On one of the lounges a scorbutic nigger sat with a Jewess from Shadwell. Squatting on a table in the centre, beneath one of the lanterns, was a musician with a reed, blinking upon the company like a sly cat and making his melody of six repeated notes.

"The atmosphere churned. The dirt of years, tobacco of many growings, opium, betel nuts and moist flesh allied themselves in one grand assault against the nostrils."

It should be explained that this passage is part of a story about a Limehouse pugilist who was beating his child to death. The Chinese named Cheng Huan took the child to his place and cared for her. When the pugilist found this out he finished beating the child to death in order to wipe out the stain of being cared for by a Chinaman. The latter in return left a deadly snake in the pugilist's bunk, so that it stung him to death.

At another place in Mr. Burke's book we come upon this impressive picture of a Chinese drug fiend of Limehouse:

"He was a dreadful doper. Sometimes he would chew betel nut or bhang or hashish, but most it was a big jolt of yen-shi, for he got more value from that. He was a connoisseur, and used his selected yen-shi and yen-hok as an Englishman uses a cigar.

"The first slow inhalations brought him nothing, but as he continued there would come a sweet, purring warmth about the limbs. This effect was purely physical: the brain was left cold and awake, the thought uncolored. But slowly, as the draws grew deeper, the details of the

A Dirty Opium Den in New York's Chinatown, Where Men and Women of All Grades of Society Meet in Common Degradation as Slaves of the Drug.

argely through Lionel Belcher it was brought out le Veulle had held strange orgies in his Mayfair flat, ich Billie Carleton and others participated. "Unholy " the energetic coroner called them. De Veulle, his Billie Carleton and others of the set, in very neglicostume, gathered around the faint blue flame of the t oil lamp and enjoyed the evil ecstasies of the pipe. There they lay sometimes from Saturday to Monday morning, enjoying strange sensations eams of unearthly joys.

re you must stop to consider another striking figure tragedy. This was Mrs. Ada Lo Ping You, a fair- English woman and former actress, who had bethe wife of Lo Ping You, a Chinese opium resort r and hopeless victim of the habit himself.

rs. Lo Ping You was "the high priestess of the unites." She alone knew how to cook the fascinating ith perfect skill, and she made an agreeable comin sin. The opium came from her husband's place 24 Limehouse Causeway, part of the dock quarter

the ears, his eyes would close, and about the head gathered a cloud of lilac, at first opaque, but gradually lightening in consistency till it became but a shy gauze.

"Then, with all control of the faculties in suspension, out of the nebula would swim infinite delicacies of phantasy and rhyme, of the ethereal reality of a rose leaf. There would be faces half revealed and half secret, under torrents of loaded curls; faces now dusky, now strangely white; faces pure and haunting, and faces of creeping sin, floating without movement, fading and appearing. Faces sad almost to tears; then laughing, languishing faces; then cold, profound, animal faces—the faces of women, for the most part.

"The last stage of the dope dream would be a chaos of music and a frenzy of frock and limb and curl against delirious backgrounds. Always the background was the Causeway, Orientalized. The little cafe would leap and bulge to a white temple; the chimney against the sky would sprout into a pagoda, and there would be the low pulsing of tom-toms. The street would sway itself out of all proportion, and grotesque staircases would dip to it from the dim-starred night; and it would be filled with pale girls, half garbed in white and silver and gold and blue."

This is part of a story about a Limehouse girl who filled her dress with poisoned needles, so that when the Chinese drug fiend embraced her he died slowly and horribly.

"After dinner—Miss Carleton being engaged in h duties at the theatre, I believe—the party adjourned the drawing room, provided themselves with cushions a pillows, placed these on the floor and distributed themselv there in a circle.

"The men divested themselves of their clothing exce their pajamas, and the women clad themselves in chiff night dresses, and in that condition apparently prepar themselves for what I described last week, and what I scribe again, as an orgy.

"Later that evening, no doubt after her performar was over, Miss Carleton arrived, and, after disrobing h self, took her place in this circle of degenerates, I c them. In the centre of it Mrs. Ping You officiated. S had opium in the tins and the lamp and the opium needl and all accessories.

"She prepared the opium. She used the needle f the purpose of extracting small portions when it was p pared by the heating up of the small pellets used for t purpose. She placed them on a needle into the bowl the pipe which is used, one pipe being used by the wh party for inhaling the fumes of this drug. The party r mained, apparently in a comatose state, until about o'clock on the following afternoon, Sunday."

plunged into the squalor of Limehouse and steeped the selves with opium smoke in dens where criminals a Lascar sailors satisfied all their vices at low cost.

But opium rose to ruinous prices during the wa $100 for a little can of "Lai yun," or even more— then it became unobtainable. Those who have the opi habit will in its absence snatch at any drug which h something of its nerve-soothing hypnotic qualit whether it be cocaine, heroin, veronal, sulphonal or one of a number of them.

Billie Carleton's circle indulged more or less in these wretched drugs. A mysterious swarthy Egypt named Don Kimful, one who lived by magic and ot things, was of great value in finding druggists who pensed the forbidden articles. He resided at Nott Hill Gate.

Kimful, de Veulle and Belcher between them fo druggists who were willing to sell the forbidden pois

MR. CHATTERTON: And had you been smok opium?

A. No.

Q. Were you so hopelessly under the influence of drug that you did not know what happened?

A. I was able to get up and shake Miss Carleto hand. There was another little doping party at Veulle's, and there was one prior to that. I have smok opium twice in Chinatown. I have smoked opium at and Mrs. de Veulle's and at my own flat.

Q. Didn't Miss Olive Desmond give one of these d ing parties? Who was present?

A. Mr. and Mrs. de Veulle, Miss Billie Carleton, M Lo Ping You and myself. Mrs. Lo Ping is an Eng woman married to a Chinaman, and she cooked the opi I believe that Mrs. de Veulle had never taken any d before with them, and I admit that I was one of m who pressed her on that occasion to do so.

MR. CHATTERTON: A pretty gallant sort of th to do with a lady not addicted to opium.

A. It is very harmless; it is about the least harmfu them all.

Q. Miss Carleton gave a party, did she not, at Veulle's flat?

A. That is quite right. Miss Carleton, Mr. and M de Veulle, Miss Olive Richardson, Miss Rutland, M Ping and myself were present. It was last Septem The party cost $50.

Q. I put it to you that it was more like $50 a head?

A. Certainly not. Miss Carleton and I halved cost. Mr. and Mrs. de Veulle did not take any ac part, retiring to bed shortly after the opening of meeting. Then it came my turn to give a party. Th were present Miss Richardson, Miss Rutland, Mr. F and myself.

Q. Do you swear that you never gave a party at wh Miss Carleton and Mr. de Veulle were present?

A. I never recall doing that. Miss Carleton and de Veulle were not of my party because of a little frict There was sometimes friction at these parties. One ni Miss Carleton asked me to take her down to Chinato I did so. It was very late at night—I should say ab 1 or 2 in the morning—when we started. We got d there in about an hour. The taxi waited, and we retur

How the Drug Peddlers Drive Through the Streets of Paris at Night Whistling Their Calls to Draw Attention to the Slowly Moving Cabs.

Men and Women of His Social Circle in the Underworld Stretch Out and Chat and Smoke and Doze Off Into Dreams, While Dan's Skilled Attendant Cooks the Dope, Fills the Pipes and Ministers to the Guests from the Little Opening in the Centre of That Criminal Circle.

"After dinner the party adjourned to the drawing room, provided themselves with cushions and pillows, placed these on the floor and distributed themselves there in a circle. The men divested themselves of their clothing, except their pajamas, and the women clad themselves in chiffon night

Great Entrances he World of Drug Slaves

dope fiend's repertoire consists of opium, mor- :ocaine, heroin, hashish, codine, and, in England ance particularly, ether. The first door into the orld is usually opened by way of the opium pipe. so that I took my first step, and, when almost d by the drugs and mad for a cure, I made inquiries ds in the same case, they always told me the same "I just smoked a sociable pipe of opium at a party. n I got to smoking more and more—and after that orphine and the others."

second door is opened by the unscrupulous or care- sician, who gets rich or saves himself trouble by ing morphine for every ache or pain of the patient nown a number of doctors who have made excel- ngs merely through their willingness to prescribe e. Old, querulous ladies or fretful, luxurious, idle ould call in the smart doctor, lament their pains would give them, under the guise of medicine, in t name of healing, a drug that would stupefy them long. No wonder these women refuse to change ctor, and no wonder they like his medicine best. m is bad enough in all conscience, but the other e a hundred fold more ruinous to health and char- And inevitably the opium smoker turns sooner or them.

reasons for this are many. To smoke opium you ve time—an hour and a half or two hours, at least, ssary. You must also have a complicated para- a—a lamp, pipe, cooking utensils for the drug and

and Hashish Now 'ashionable" Drugs Abroad

and hashish are not so common in this country as yet. But in France, and especially in the rtre quarter, they are very common. I have exquisite drug dens there, beautiful young French urate their faces with ether, place over it a wet th and go to sleep. I have also seen at the very staurants more than one distinguished gentleman, ris for a holiday, led out of the dining room, hope- runk—so hopelessly drunk that two persons had rt him.

of course, quite familiar with the drug traffic in y of the large American cities, and from my own erience and the experiences of my friends I know horoughly the widespread use of dope in the rld of London.

ery quarter of Paris, whether it is the Champs or Montmartre, you come across people at some other whose desire it is to supply you with for- rugs. Cocaine and opium may be obtained with facility as that of going to the grocer and buying of sugar or any other commodity.

are so many hundreds of inexperienced people ce to obtain this drug that they do not take any om whom or where they buy it, with the result fall an easy prey to "fakers," who prepare antities of flour, and, wrapping them in white ll them to the drug-takers. When the fraud is d it is impossible for them to lay a charge against s, for obvious reasons. So openly are the meth- he sale of the drugs carried out that it is no won- man in the street" and the police get to know the what may be truthfully described as one of the ely practiced vices of the night life of Paris.

ast time I was in Paris I had an opportunity to some "coco," as it is called in France, by the

pensive. When opium is smoked, for instance, in an apartment it takes $12 worth of adhesive tape, first thing, to seal the doors and windows so that the fumes will not seep out and tell the neighbors what is going on behind those doors. They have to be cemented securely about each crevice, for nothing is stronger, more pungent, more easily detected, than the odor of opium.

The increasing difficulty of getting the right surroundings and the increasing expenses both tend to bring the smoker to drugs which are more easily handled and also stronger. For it must always be remembered that the drug addict steadily craves larger and larger doses. And also as the addict goes on his earning power becomes less and less with the deterioration of mind and body, so that it is not long before he or she cannot afford even the lowest opium dens. Hence, the pleasure smoker of opium soon becomes the needy, aching, insistent user of morphine or heroin. Morphine is 50 per cent stronger than opium, and heroin is 100 per cent stronger than morphine.

The procedure of an opium party is almost a ritual; almost as precisely ordered as the giving of communion in church the first Sunday of the month. First of all, the

Just How the Opium Users Arrange Their "Smoke Parties"

When the party of men and women have arrived for their opium debauch they all take places upon a large divan or couch. This is shaped twice or three times larger than a full-sized bed; it may, again, be circular. The mixing and the baking of the opium then begins. In the centre of the opium couch the little oil lamp is placed. The chef, who cooks the pill, is at the head of the couch, placed so he can manipulate the utensils over the lamp. The can of opium, resembling in a way a small tin of tomatoes, though the can is square, is within reach, and the whole outfit rests on a silver tray. There is one opium pipe—a long bamboo or ivory affair—for the whole party.

The party then reclines, except the chef. They lie, first a woman, then a man next, his head resting on her stomach. The third guest is a woman, whose head rests on the stomach of the man just preceeding her in the circle, and so it goes, till the complete circle is made. The lamp consists of a little hollow bowl, filled with olive oil; a wick runs out of this into a small burner equipped with a chimney, not unsimilar to the chimney of a lantern, though it is very much smaller.

When the lamp is lighted, as all the guests lie about waiting, the opium chef takes an instrument called the needle, long and delicate, and dips it into the can of raw opium. With it he winds the sticky mixture about, and then he lifts out enough of the dark-brown, sticky, gum-like stuff to twist into a pill about the shape of a large pea. When he has made this into an opium pill he holds it over the lamp and cooks it in the slow fire of the oil-fed wick, turning it constantly in the flame. After five minutes the needle is removed from the flame and the pill is dropped into the bowl of the pipe. Then, with all ceremony, the pipe is passed to the first user, who lowers the bowl over the lamp to keep the opium hot.

A great breath, long inhaled, peaceful, deliberate, slow, is the breath with which the opium smoker inhales his stupefying drug. This is very different from the short whiffs with which one smokes a cigarette. He smokes for five or ten minutes. Then he reclines, relaxed. He passes back the pipe, and the chef, by this time, has prepared another pill for the next smoker. After cleaning out the bowl of the opium pipe with a cloth called Sowey Poo, and an instrument called the Yenshi Gow, he again fills the bowl and passes it to the next smoker. In this way the pipe goes the rounds of the waiting circle, and as the guests give themselves up to the magic drug its effects

For opium is the luxurious and the sociable vice; and the opium pipe, often of carved ivory inlaid, sometimes modelled in silver and gold and set with precious stones, is the emblem of a drugged, luxurious comeradarie.

From opium, as I have said, the next step is morphine. Morphine is the insidious, imperative drug used alone in frantic self-defense as refuge from dread suffering. I never heard of a morphine party. To pass around a needle and jab yourself in company would be considered very low behavior by the "hop-head," or opium smoker. As opium leaves behind it a peaceful effect, so morphine leaves an effect doubly or trebly peaceful.

The drug fiend may never escape detection at the hands of another drug fiend. The opium user who becomes an addict is known to another opium user, though the two speak not the same language; though one live in a palace and the other in a teeming tenement on the eastest East Side. The opium user has, as one distinguishing characteristic, an aloofness of manner, a "don't careness" about him, aptly described by Tennyson in the poem "The Lotus Eaters."

The morphine victim may be just as aloof, but he is not so superior. He is inclined to talk more. Both the morphine user and the opium user never stand squarely on their feet and look you right in the eye. They lean; they slouch; they droop their heads; and when the observer by chance does steal a look into their eyes they notice that the morphine and the opium has contracted the pupils till they are abnormally tiny. As for physical habits, the use of these two drugs so affects the processes of elimination that great care and artificial devices, in confirmed addicts, are necessary to keep life functioning at all. And always medicines have to be used to force nature to her necessary tasks of waste removal.

The cocaine user, different from the opium and the morphine user, is alert, over enthusiastic, energetic, active, restless and excited every minute he is under his drug. He talks incessantly. He is a "leaper"—as the phrase is interpreted to mean incessant action, endless activity. He fidgets. He fumes. He never sleeps while under the influence of cocaine. He develops exalted notions. He imagines he can fight the world and beat whatever trusts or combines that ever were created. He feels more powerful than Caesar. If it happens to be a woman, she feels more coquettish than Cleopatra and more beautiful than Mary Queen of Scots, as well as more unfortunate.

The cocaine addict never is free from suspicion. And he always is sure that somebody is waiting just around the corner to assassinate him.

Hashish is a drug made from Indian hemp. It was never, in my experience, a pet vice of smart people. In Paris, particularly in the gunman and gangster sections, it is a favorite drug. There is a saying in Paris, "the hashish makes the Apache dance," and so it is. I have witnessed dances wierd, wild, exotic, by Apaches in French dens, Apaches full of hashish. Most hashish dens are in low cellars and vile habitations, in such countries as Mexico, Cuba, South America and France.

With opium, the user can cure himself without goi to a sanitarium, though, for all the other drugs a sa tarium, I should say, was the only thing. This is one w the opium habit may be cured: Take a bottle and fi it half full of liquid opium. Fill the other half wi sherry wine. Each day take from the bottle a tablespoo ful of the mixture and, as this is removed, fill it up wit pure sherry. After a while the mixture will be nothi but wine. Keeping to this daily diminishing drug, th opium slave will be uncomfortable; he will suffer, but n as when morphine is taken from him, and not unbearabl

Now, as for the amount of the dose of various drug At an opium party of, say, six guests, at least ten pi would be smoked by each guest, if each was a season smoker. The young woman smoker for her first tim is told to stop at one or two pills. It would be better fo her to do this. Ten pills would kill her. When the opiu pleasure smoker has acquired what is called the habit h has a one-a-day habit or a two-a-day habit or a three-a-da habit. This means that if he does not get his opium onc or twice or three times each day he develops what is tech nically known as a "yen."

When a victim has a "yen on" his eyes water, he yawns he aches in every nerve of his body, with an ache whic is exactly like a toothache, but it is everywhere. And ho he perspires! He suffers alternate chills and fever. Drop of sweat stand out on his forehead. The pains of child birth, severe, racking, torturing while they last, are a nothing to the pains of opium or morphine denied. An I know, for I have borne two children. Coming to mor phine, a dose of one-fourth of a grain is considered ampl for the first user. But as the user persists the dose is in creased, till ten grains are easily consumed. De Quincey the English author, who wrote the "Confessions of a Opium Eater, ate opium, and did not smoke it. Towar the end of his career he ate a dose which amounted t sixty grains daily.

This, so far as my knowledge and experience go, is the largest amount known to have been co daily by one single person. But this amount De y did no need to get all the effect possible from the drug. H merely imagined he needed that amount. If kind old nature had not arranged a means of throwing off much

EDITORIAL Sunday New York American CITY LIFE
Editorial Telephone, Beekman 2000 SUNDAY, MARCH 22, 1925 Business Telephone, Columbus 7000 E—1

DEATH AMONG THE POPPIES

This shows the story of our civilization, and it MEASURES our civilization.
Here death walks in his flower garden. In his hand are the dried seeds of sorrow, pain, blasted hope, lives destroyed.
Around him are the flowers that yield death's drug, a grinning skull in each.
Back of him, in letters appropriately made of death's heads, is written the fearsome word "OPIUM" that has meant slavery to millions of men, to almost entire populations. It is also the word that, unfortunately, means PROFIT to a few of the great nations, and therefore it must continue to mean MISERY for millions of human beings.

OPIUM and WHISKEY. Those are the words that stand for human misery, failure, shame and ruined lives.

Opium does its work in the East, where it has actually enslaved millions of men in one single nation.

Whiskey does its work among the white races of the West. It does the work so thoroughly that Jefferson, who wrote the Declaration of Independence, demanded over and over that the use of light wine and beer, practically unknown in the United States in his day, be encouraged by the Government, in order to diminish the drinking of whiskey.

Of whiskey he said, and without exaggeration: "It kills half of our men and ruins their families."

* * *

Of late opium and whiskey have taken a new lease of life, starting out afresh for more extensive killings, greater victories, millions of new victims.

Consider the dreadful hypocrisy represented in the opium traffic that curses so many.

All the solemnity and authority of the League of Nations, with a representative of the United States "observing" and "protesting," met to discuss the opium question.

The suggestion was that the opium traffic should be put down.

How could it be done? **VERY SIMPLY.**

All that is necessary is gradually to cut down, and finally to wipe out, the production of opium, except for strictly medical use and on the smallest possible scale.

The thing could be accomplished easily, for to get opium you must plant vast fields of poppies. You cannot grow opium in secret. The poppies are grown for opium only. They destroy the land, making it useless for other crops, as the essence of the poppy destroys human lives.

The thousands upon thousands of acres devoted to growing the poisonous opium-producing poppy, and **WITHDRAWN FROM THE PRODUCTION OF FOOD** that the starving people of the East need, **CANNOT** be hidden.

Those flaming fields of scarlet are spread out beneath the heavens for all the world to see. They can be measured, and the poppy poison can be figured out by the acre of poppy flowers.

* * *

You would say, "Since opium destroys human life, renders millions unfit for work and miserable, why do not the nations unite to suppress so great a curse?"

The great nations refuse to suppress the opium traffic, and the poppy cultivation necessary to opium manufacture, because **IT PAYS.**

The solemn directors of the League of Nations talked and argued and separated without doing anything, or to do anything definite, about opium. To take action would have cut down the revenues of nations powerful in the league, including the mighty empire of Great Britain and the aggressive empire of Japan. And in these days of heavy taxes following the war the great, civilized nations are not inclined to have their revenues cut down. They won't tolerate it, even when those revenues come from the deepest depths of human degradation and suffering.

* * *

For the present there is no use in protesting against the growing of poppies and the sale of the opium. That which means millions of profit every year will continue, suffering or no suffering.

It is to be hoped that by earnest appeal and warning something may be done to prevent the spread of the dreadful drug habit.

He who would try a deadly drug of whatever name—opium, morphine, cocaine—might far better put a pistol to his head and blow out his brains, so far as happiness is concerned, and apart from the question of sin.

The Bible pronounces suicide a sin. It might have pronounced the use of drugs a sin ten times greater, had that use prevailed when the Bible was written.

The suicide with pistol or knife kills only **HIMSELF.** He may inflict sorrow on others, but it passes.

The drug fiend tortures his family, ruins degrades and disgraces himself. And frequently, sinking to the lowest depths, his degradation takes the form of seeking, with malicious Satanic ingenuity, to inflict the drug curse upon others.

* * *

Poor, ignorant creatures take a drug, saying, "Just this once; I want to know how it feels"; or "I want temporary relief from mental anguish."

They would not allow themselves to be lashed with a whip, cutting their flesh to ribbons, "just once to see how it feels." But they might better stand the most dreadful lashing ever inflicted upon any slave, and have salt rubbed into the wounds afterwards, rather than try that **FIRST** dose, "Just to see how it feels."

* * *

The drug habit is formed so quickly that it is **FIXED** before the miserable victim knows it. Even as he says to himself, "I can stop when I like," he is beyond all hope of stopping.

The grip that the poison fastens upon its victims is one that the strongest will ever born in man is powerless to release.

It is the **GRIP OF DEATH** and it holds on until death.

Be warned by this picture, young and old. Drugs mean slow death for the body, quick death for the spirit. And any death, however painful, is infinitely better than the slow death and the long-drawn-out agony of the drug fiend.

* * *

As it is with opium and other drugs in the East, so, unfortunately, it is with whiskey **HERE** in the United States, and to a degree **CONSTANTLY INCREASING.**

This nation decided to rid itself of drunkenness, passed the prohibition amendment, and finds saddled upon the country now the curse of bootleg whiskey, with a brood of whiskey criminals that it has created preying upon the nation, and especially upon **THE YOUTH OF THE NATION,** and often dividing crime's profits with officials paid to prevent crime.

* * *

It is not possible to fight successfully against the opium traffic, even among the exalted personages of the League of Nations. The traffic cannot be stopped, **BECAUSE IT PAYS MILLIONS A YEAR.**

So it is, and even worse, with whiskey in America.

The accursed bootleg whiskey traffic, firmly fastened upon this country, cannot be stopped, and there is evidently no power thus far able to cope with it, for it pays not millions, but **TENS** of millions, **HUNDREDS OF MILLIONS** a year profit.

For years the criminals have carried on their business in defiance of law, aided and enriched by citizens otherwise respectable that connive at breaking the law and flout the Constitution, considering it an excellent joke.

* * *

Other nations send us their poisonous whiskey and we buy it at extravagant prices and drink it by the shipload.

And our Government looks on **HELPLESS** while other nations run our feeble blockade, their citizens fattening their purses on our "**PROHIBITION,**" a touchstone that turns everything into gold for them.

We buy millions of bottles of poisonous whiskey from abroad. And we manufacture hundreds of millions of even more poisonous stuff here at home. Tens of thousands of illegal "stills" are turning out a poison often absolutely **DEADLY.** Sometimes it kills within a few hours. It is a poison that **ALWAYS** undermines the health of those stupid enough to take it. And that poison, before many years have passed, will show the results of its work in such a graveyard crop as the nation has known only in times of plague.

* * *

Poppy growing, opium manufacturing thrive and will continue to thrive, **BECAUSE THEY PAY.**

Bootleg whiskey, fastened on this country in the name of prohibition, will apparently continue to thrive and defy the law, because **BOOTLEGGING PAYS.**

* * *

We jail small criminals, but not big ones. We imprison the little gambler, but let the gambling dives called "racetracks," with their betting rings, run wide open.

That is our brand of civilization and our brand of respect for law.

The League of Nations, that was to save the world, refuses to stop the traffic in opium, because it pays so well.

And this nation, which, through prohibition, was to make everybody sober, finds itself helpless in the face of bootleggers, big and little, foreign and domestic.

* * *

"The gentleman wants his whiskey, and does not **BELIEVE** in any law that would prevent him from getting it."

No law **DOES** prevent him. **HE GETS HIS WHISKEY AND CHAMPAGNE.**

The gentleman wishes the pleasure and excitement of gambling at the racetrack and does not approve of any law or any State Constitution that would forbid his having that pleasure. The Constitution may forbid it, but that doesn't interfere. **HE HAS HIS PLEASURE.**

The disgraceful international and nationally **APPROVED** opium trade shows that the welfare of human beings, and decency, cannot prevail against selfish financial interests of the great nations.

And our prohibition, so called—our bootleg whiskey prohibition—emphasizes the fact that the law cannot act efficiently when great fortunes can be made by flouting and despising the law.

Eventually, we must hope and believe, the people will find **SOME** way to protect themselves against the bootlegger's poison.

Isn't it time that the people set about the task?

JOIN US IN HELPING HUMANITY !!!!
HOW ABOUT JOINING ME IN HELPING HUMANITY?
AGREEMENT TO STOP OPIUM TRAFFIC
WINSOR MCCAY
J. BULL
OPIUM TRAFFIC
ENRIGHT
HUMANITY
PRISON
HOSPITAL
INTERNATIONAL OPIUM TRAFFICKER
VICTIMS
VICTIMS
LET'S TALK THIS OVER, SAM!
NO, NOT WHILE YOU PROTECT THE DOPE PRODUCERS!
OPIUM BLOC
DOPE TRAFFIC
ENFORCEMENT OF NARCOTIC LAWS
WINSOR MCCAY
DOPE TRAFFIC
CIVILIZED WORLD
Why Not Get the Big Fellow?
Copyright, 1931, by N. Y. American, Inc.
THE BIG FELLOW OF THE OPIUM RING
LITTLE DOPE PEDDLER
NARCOTIC ENFORCEMENT AGENT
REAPING HIS HARVEST---DEATH
YOUNG
OLD
RICH
POOR
INTERNATIONAL DOPE RING

WEDNESDAY, MARCH 28, 1923

"WOMAN OF MYSTERY" ARRESTED

SINGER ADOPTS FOUR STARVING

They Say—

GIRLS CHARGE AN A9DVER

Hunt for Many Missing Persons

DENTIST'S

People Who Think—THURSDAY, JUNE 19, 1924

CONFESSES "H

USE OF HEROIN LEADS YOUTHS INTO CRIMES

Sleep Producing Narcotic Once Highly Esteemed Now Is Known as Insidious Evil

By WINIFRED BLACK.

SAN FRANCISCO, Feb. 24.—When heroin first came into use in this country it was regarded as one of the greatest discoveries of the age.

A "safe narcotic."

A non-habit forming drug that would ease pain, bring sleep to the sleepless, comfort to the afflicted—easy to take and easy to let alone.

It took only a few years of use for physicians to discover that it was twice as bad as opium, twice as bad as morphine and three times as terrible a slave master as cocaine.

There is no excuse or reason whatsoever for the manufacture or the sale of heroin.

The physicians of standing have stopped using it—to any degree—and it has been discovered that one-tenth of a grain of heroin a day will make a drug slave for life out of a strong-willed man or a self-controlled woman.

Heroin is responsible for a terrific amount of crime.

Any weak-willed half-wit can take a dose of heroin and turn himself in less than sixty seconds into a bold, daring, desperate and deadly criminal.

Opium and Morphine—The will-breakers.

Cocaine and Heroin—The crime-makers.

All in the same family, don't forget that, with opium for the father and mother of them all; but cocaine and heroin the two worst of the lot.

Then Comes Marijuana

And with them comes Marijuana, and every once in a while we hear, even in this country, from the first cousin of Marijuana—Hasheesh—and every one who has ever lived in the Near East or in the far Orient knows what hasheesh will do to a poor, mild, inoffensive, drug-saturated, heart-broken, hope-broken wage toiler.

Hasheesh will turn the mildest man in the world into a blood-thirsty murderer; a man who takes hasheesh "runs amuck" with his bloody knife in one hand and his strangling cloth in the other, and he kills, kills, kills, until the hasheesh has burnt out its deady flames.

Heroin is almost as bad.

In some ways it is worse, for a man may take heroin every day and live in the house with you, and all you will ever think about him is that he is a curiously conceited, high-flown, pleased-with-himself individual.

When a man takes heroin he thinks he can do anything in the world and be perfectly safe—rob a bank, kill a man, hold up the President of the United States, murder his own mother—and be all the better man and better citizen for doing it.

But he does not say these things—outright.

He can conceal the worst of his thoughts and make you look upon him as a harmless egotist, who is rather amusing than otherwise. But be careful where you meet him, and how much money you have with you when you do meet him. He's after that money; he needs it to buy heroin, and he'll take it away from you if you are his nearest and dearest friend—even if he has to kill you to do it.

When the heroin is gone—the victim goes to pieces.

All his conceit, all his self-confidence, all his bragging is gone. He sinks down into a weeping, sobbing, shivering, begging, broken-spirited, shattered-nerved "addict," and then you begin to find out the truth.

Beware of All

Opium, morphine, cocaine, heroin, marijuana, hasheesh, codine—oh, yes, that's one of the habit makers, too; beware of it; and all the little sisters and brothers, trional, veronal, sulgonal, and toddling along behind all the others, the little well-meaning baby sister—aspirin.

How they crowd in upon us in our hurried, nervous, excited lives—the narcotics, the opiates and the near-opiates!

are we going to keep them out?

Nine-tenths of the thieves and the burglars and the holdup men are "dope fiends."

Nine-tenths and a half of all the wretched sisterhood or sorrow and shame are, first and last, "dope fiends."

And in our schools and in our homes and on our very doorsteps there is the footprints of the slave-master—"Dope."

When China began its heroic struggle to shake off the yoke of opium the old Empress Dowager listened to the advisers, who told her that it would kill at least three million people—and kill them almost outright if "dope" were to be taken suddenly away from them.

"Three million?" said the old Empress. "That is not too many. Let them die; the rest of China will begin to live."

Let us learn to look this shrouded evil full in the face—anyhow.

Perhaps, when we do that we will be able to think of some way to fight it—and win

Simon Paints Pitiful Life Led by Addict

Stimulation Soon Ceases and User Becomes Slave of Drug Habit.

By DR. CARLETON SIMON,

Internationally known criminologist and narcotic expert. Former Special Deputy Police Commissioner, City of New York, in charge of Narcotic Control.

Objects of Pity

My experience has brought me into direct contact with many thousands of addicts not only in this city but all over this country and in spite of the fact that so many have a criminal record I have always felt sorry for them. Most of them are more to be pitied

Too late the mind knows and the body feels that the habit has fastened itself deeply into the being, that here is a monster whose cravings cannot be put off or denied without cold beads of sweat breaking out all over the body, intense pains in the abdomen and in the limbs, nausea, vomiting, purging, general prostration and mental depression, amounting in many cases to complete collapse.

The drug peddler and the drug booster lure their victims by tales of imaginary pleasures and delight. This is the bait that attracts the ignorant, the curious, the weak, the seeker of new sensations of something with a "kick" in it. There are, too, many fo[...] who would "be willing to try so[...] thing once." The young man [...]

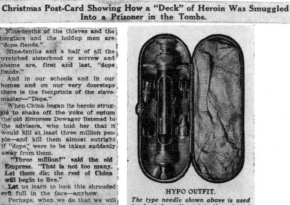

How large quantities of cocaine, morphine, heroin and opium were artfully concealed in the pages of a Bible

DRUG VICTIMS BEG FOR CURE

25 Addicts Appeal to Chief Magistrate McAdoo When Unable to Ob[tain] Supply.

ALL SENT [TO HOS]PITAL

[...]e, Is Being Peddled.

More than twenty-five drug addicts, men and women, starved out of concealment of their vice through Federal anti-narcotic legislation and seizures, have appeared before Chief City Magistrate McAdoo within the past forty-eight hours [...] to be incarcerated for [...]

[...] pathetic [...]

[...]y effective.

"[MO]ONSHINE" DRUG SOLD.

"One woman, a mental and physical wreck from the drug, told me its price had become so high even the peddlers were unable to get it. They were selling what she termed moonshine, nothing more than sugar of milk, quinine and other powders resembling heroin."

The magistrate also cited the seizure of $1,000,000 worth of drugs smuggled in from Germany [...] week as an effective check o[n] drug habit.

ALL SENT TO HOSPITAL.

He sentenced all addicts wh[o ap]plied to him to one hundred [...] in the Welfare Island hospital.

Federal agents arrested J[...] White, of Mills Hotel No. 1, [...] they recognized on the street [...] former drug peddler out on pa[...] Nathan Goldstein, No. 110 Eld[ridge] street, from whom White is sa[id to] have purchased drugs, is [...] held in $5,000 bail.

Murtagh Is Recoverin[g]

Christmas Post-Card Showing How a "Deck" of Heroin Was Smuggled Into a Prisoner in the Tombs.

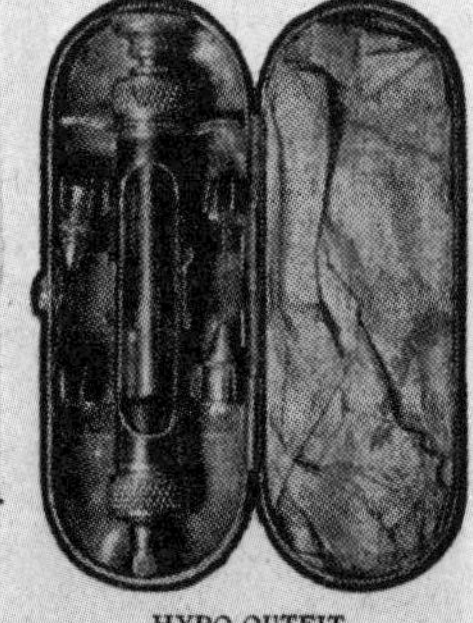

HYPO OUTFIT.

The type needle shown above is used to shoot drug direct into the veins of the arm.

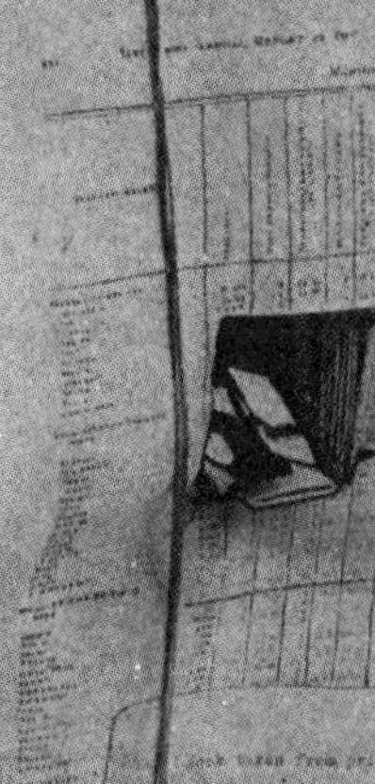

"Decks" of Heroin Concealed in a Copy of the New York Board of Health Report.

HEROIN CURSE TO HUMANITY, SAYS COPELAND

Wipe It Out and Half Addiction Problem of Country Will Be Solved, Commissioner Believes

By JOSEPH MULVANEY.

"Heroin is an unqualified curse to civilization—strike at that drug hard and half the addiction problem of this city and this country will be solved."

Dr. Royal S. Copeland, Health Commissioner of New York, advanced this definite suggestion last night to cope with the narcotic evil. Commissioner Copeland made it clear that he believes any attempt to compromise with drug legislation will be futile and he emphasized that national legislation is essential. Then he added:

"International agreements tightening up the whole drug problem are necessary, but until they can be put through the United States authorities should act toward the control of the situation in the country as best they can.

"If I were pressed for a personal judgment, I would declare that opium and morphine as well as heroin should be wiped out absolutely by their sale, possession and use being prohibited. But there are authorities in the medical world who disagree with me, and perhaps the view is extreme. But certainly there is no good purpose served in this world by heroin.

"Let morphine be used, under rigid regulation, and of course we must have the opium to get the morphine from it, but heroin is the drug of the underworld, the staple of the addiction promoter and the illicit peddler.

"It is unquestionably an evil, and the way to deal with an evil is to crush it."

S PEDDLER OF HEROIN

"FLORENCE O'NEIL," the white wife of "Black" O'Neil and the "Mystery Woman" of Harlem's black belt, as she appeared yesterday morning when arraigned in the Twelfth District Court charged with selling heroin. To her right is Detective Daniel Christ of the Narcotic Division, who made the arrest. To his right is the patrolman who was called to quell the riot that ensued when the arrest was made.

'BLACK' NEIL'S WHITE WIFE IN JAIL FOR NIGHT

Detectives Buy Narcotic at Home of Girl Who Came from the Middle West 3 Years Ago

REFINED, SHE VEILS PAST

Woman Lives in Negro Colony, in 142d Street; She Recants Admission She Is an Addict

A round-faced fresh-complexioned girl came out of the West three years ago and since then has lived at No. 237 West One Hundred and Forty-second street, the heart of the negro colony, as the white girl wife of the notorious "Black" Neil.

A pale-faced anaemic woman was arraigned in the Twelfth District Court yesterday morning charged with selling heroin. It was the girl from the West. She gave her name as Florence O'Neil.

Since she arrived in this city she has been a mystery to her negro associates. To her past she never referred.

She must have felt from the first how she had descended in the social scale and would not let her associates, least of all her family back in the West, know the degree of her descent.

KEEPS PAST VEILED.

The girl is educated and refined; her speech indicates that, and she continued the mystery of her past, even after her arrest last Saturday, when detectives of the Narcotic Division went to her home and purchased two "decks" of heroin.

She declared she was not an addict, but, taken to the Jefferson Market Court for lack of bail, the long hours of the night told on her nerve and she confe[illegible] herself an addict to procure a dose of the drug that would give her temporary relief.

Deputy Police C[illegible] Simon said that [illegible] in Des Moine[illegible] who had [illegible]

EXTRADITION STAY

Appellate Court Will Act on Charge of Attacking Cedar Grove Woman.

B.R.T. TRAINS TO USE QUEENSBORO LINES

Begin Running to Astoria and Corona April 8 with Changes at Plaza Station.

EFIES FIRM PACT

pend ague eaty ... IED ... ve ny e ... the sible 1922 l to po- uncil y to cus- Aus- offi- any fore this one in ... hat in- ent

HEROIN SALES TO YOUTHS TRAP DOPE RING CHIEF

Seven Peddlers Also Seized After Months of Work by U.S. Narcotic Bureau Agents

MINISTER STARTED HUNT

'Mike the Whip' and His Aides Accused of Selling $500,000 Worth in Only a Few Months

Discovery by a clergyman that a narcotic ring has been selling heroin to Brooklyn high school boys and girls resulted yesterday in the arrest of seven alleged dope peddlers and the ring-chieftain.

Striking simultaneously in The Bronx, Manhattan and Brooklyn, Federal agents under command of Major Joseph Manning made the arrests after months of preliminary work in whch agents bought some $25,000 worth of narcotics.

Last October a clergyman called on Major Manning. He told how he had discovered several boys and girls who were in the first stages of dope addiction. The operations of the ring, Manning said, became so widespread toward the end of October that several civic organizations also made complaints.

GIRLS FOLLOWED.

Agents of the ring followed girls suspected of being addicts. These girls went to 10-cents-a-dance halls, where they worked at night so they could continue their educations.

In these dance halls, said Manning, the drug peddlars introduced heroin to girls. The drug gave them false energy, long after muscles and nerves were tired out.

The girls, said Manning, introduced taking of heroin to young men they danced with. Thus the evil spread. It had more kick than booze.

But even though seven periodic arrests were made, the ringleader's name was kept secret.

REVEALED BY ACCIDENT.

It remained for an accident to bring the chieftain to light. Manning names Michael Partalino as the chieftain.

Kenneth D. Schneider was arrested for robbing a house in Bronxville. He was suffering for want of dope. He complained to [illegible] the drugs he had [illegible]t," and in a spirit [illegible] police that "Mike [illegible] the man who sold [illegible]hen learned that [illegible]hip" was Michael

[illegible] IN DOPE.

[illegible] Sicilian, made his [illegible]t 100th and 1st ave. [illegible] agents heroin, they [illegible]erday he was ar- [illegible]as sold. Manning [illegible]0 worth of dope in [illegible]e, two Filipinos and [illegible]ere taken i[illegible]

HEROIN TRAFFIC STIRS DEBATE AT DOPE PARLEY

England and Continentals Defend Drug Which Is Rated Beside Morphine and Opium

By WINIFRED BLACK.

GENEVA, June 4.—Is heroin a harmless and necessary drug or is it one of the most dangerous narcotics in the world, not in the least useful in the legitimate practice of medicine?

For a day and a half the League of Nations' International Narcotic Conference has been discussing the question of heroin.

Portugal, Great Britain, Germany, Belgium, France and Switzerland all believe heroin is a perfectly legitimate article to make and sell.

BRITAIN'S ODD STAND.

Britain takes a curious position, which seems to imply that one grain of heroin is a deadly danger, but whole tons are as harmless as a cup of sterilized milk.

You can't buy a quarter of a grain of heroin in England without a doctor's prescription, but British factories make and sell it by tons, in excess of any legitimate medical need.

Conservative estimates state there are in existence today fifteen tons of heroin stock. Even countries which insist it is a harmless drug admit one ton is enough to take care of all possible medicinal needs.

Delegate Vasconcellos, of Portugal, was shocked at the idea of stopping the manufacture of heroin.

CONDEMNED IN CANADA.

Colonel Sharman, of Canada, said that in his capacity as a police official it would do his heart good to know there was not a grain of heroin left in the world. As a delegate to the present conference, however, Sharman could not see his way clear to vote, in the face of certain medical objections, for the annihilation of heroin.

Britain, through Sir Malcolm Delevingne, admitted some countries appeared able to get along without heroin. He hoped that some day England would be able to follow this example, but for the present he was sorry he could not vote against heroin.

Then the question went to the Technical Committee for decision.

It is interesting to know that three expert advisers to the committee have just arrived from three great manufact[illegible] tries wh[illegible]

2 WOMEN HELD AS SMUGGLERS

The increased precautions taken by Commissioner of Correction Patterson to prevent smuggling of narcotics to prisoners in the penitentiary on Welfare Island resulted in the arrest of two women yesterday. One carried heroin, she said, the other a needle and eye-dropper.

They said they were Mrs. Charles Reynolds, forty, of 321 E. 78th st., and Mrs. Flannery, thirty, of 17 W. 66th st., who went to the penitentiary to visit Charles Reynolds and William Flannery, both serving terms for drug possession.

As the women have been frequent visitors, they were watched carefully. Keeper John Ryan, informed that they carried narcotics, told Deputy Warden Sheeha about it and the women were taken to the island hospital for search.

On the way, it was said, Mrs. Reynolds relinquished a package she said contained 2 ounces of heroin.

Search disclosed the needle and eye-dropper in Mrs. Flannery's possession.

—NOVEMBER 2, 1927

London.

As a matter of fact, millions of intelligent people in the country are recognizing that Prohibition is work-

For Prohibition	320,283
Against Prohibition	1,713,248
For wines and beer	1,933,689
Against wines and beer	285,094

Uniform State Law Is Needed to Cope with the Menace of Heroin

TOMORROW, in the Hotel Roosevelt, the World Conference on Narcotic Education, of which Richard Pearson Hobson is secretary-general, will open sessions with a double purpose:

(1) To organize an international narcotic defense association to aid in the world fight on drug addiction, the chief objective of which is to shame the nations into limiting the production of opiates to medical and scientific needs.

(2) To persuade our States to pass a uniform narcotic drug law. As tentatively drafted that law would make it a felony for one person to cause another to become a drug addict. It would also provide for the commitment of addicts after a hearing before a magistrate and enable State authority to exercise closer control over medical prescriptions of narcotics.

The worst drug yet devised is heroin derivative of morphine, and cause of most of the daredevil banditry lately so common i[illegible] our cities.

Fortunes are made by peddlers of th[illegible] super-narcotic, which outdoes all others [illegible] swift wrecking of young manhood.

Since it came into use the task of copi[illegible] with drug addiction has grown enormous[illegible] Half of our younger prison inmates are [illegible] "dope fiends," and heroin is the narc[illegible] ninety-five per cent of them prefer.

It would undoubtedly help the author[illegible] in their campaign against heroin peddlin[illegible] the scoundrelly tempters of youth could be dealt with as felons in whatever State they are located.

While education and international diplomacy are slowly preparing a better future, let us in America redouble efforts to reclaim and protect our young.

Parks—Should Be Open to the People

Libel—Is "Communist" a Fighting Word?

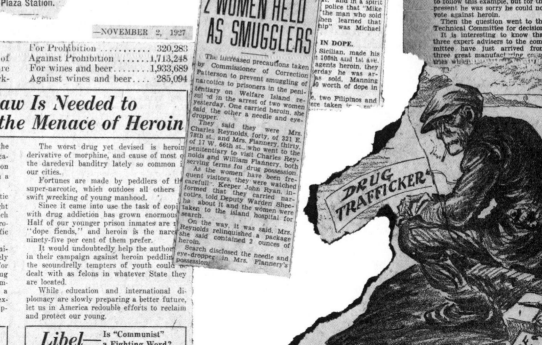

UNRAVELED a CHINESE CODE to SMASH an OPIUM RING

[M]rs. Elizabeth Friedman, United [St]ates Treasury Cryptanalyst, [S]upplied the Missing Link [to] the Canadian Mounted [Po]lice Case Against [Fi]ve Vancouver [S]mugglers.

Joined a Gang of Opium Smugglers In Order to Smash It

By ELLWOOD DOUGLASS
Of the Post-Dispatch Sunday Magazine Staff

The Inside Story of How Customs Agent Melvin L. Hanks Successfully Carried Out His Perilous and Crafty Plans Against a Notorious 'Dope' Ring.

-April 28, 1935

A "THRILLER" of the U. S. Government service—the story of a customs agent who joined a gang of opium smugglers in order to smash it—has just been obtained by the Post-Dispatch from the agent himself, Melvin L. Hanks of Seattle.

His coup and 14 hazardous months that led up to it, required not only a high order of finesse, but an unshakable nerve, for his life was almost continuously in danger. It entailed an ostensible double-cross of the United States while he planned the capture of the Orientals who considered him their fellow criminal and who had made assurance doubly sure by an oath, the gift of a cabalistic ring and ceremonious induction into the clan. It demanded his acting as their agent, protected by his badge and pistol, in the delivery of $10,000 worth of opium in Chicago and Detroit.

It culminated in the seizure of $37,000 worth of opium at the Seattle docks, the indictment of 14 men in Seattle, Chicago and Detroit, and the breaking up of a gang said to have operated without a hitch for 20 years with sales of opium estimated at $3,000,000.

While their conversation had moved ahead in mincing steps, Hanks had thought fast and furiously. Nothing could further his service to the United States quite so much as the confidence of the Chinese. With 200 miles of inland shoreline along Puget Sound, ships from the Orient had their choice of secret places to land smuggled opium. Since 1930 Hanks had sought a card which, in this devious game of fan-tan, would lure his alert and crafty opponents to land a shipment at Seattle, where it might be intercepted. Perhaps Chin Wah would provide him with that card.

But, if he carried through an arrangement with the Chinese without the knowledge of his superior officers, he simply made frame-up easy. And the smugglers had reason to wish him out of the gam[e] for, by watching inbound ships and setting Coast Guard cutters on their wake when they cruised too, too innocently up the Sound, he had troubled them deeply.

Until the customs office had obtained the assistance of the Coast Guard, steamers from the Orient had found it comparatively simple to pass up the well-guarded docks of Seattle and, somewhere on the Sound, toss the contraband overboard where a smuggler's skiff could pick it up. Coast Guard cutters, close on their wake, made the practice, if not impossible, infinitely troublesome. And Hanks was the man who spotted the steamers and sent the cutters after them.

If only he could neglect to "spot" certain steamers, it might mean something to him. At length, and at very great length, getting down to cases, it might mean $2 for every can of opium landed from these steamers—with, of course, the ultimate prospect of $10,000.

Deputy Police Commissioner Simon and Lieutenant Joseph J. Mooney Destroying Dope and Opium Pipes in the Furnace at Police Headquarters, New York.

The CHINATOWN MISSIONARY Who Became an OPIUM ADDICT

Street scene in Philadelphia's Chinatown.

Melvin L. Hanks and the cargo of opium seized when it was being smuggled ashore at Seattle.

Evil Trail Of the Opium Smoke

[S]taggering Blow to Opium Smugglers:

$500,000 Dope Seizure Here Ends 3-Month Hunt by U.S.

[MA]RCH 7, 1937

An Opium Bonanza

U. S. Agents Follow Lode To Willie Bonazi

Photograph of Part of the Three Million and a Half Dollars Worth of Contraband Drugs, Opium Pipes and Layouts Seized by the New York Police Narcotic Division in the Last Year.

Sunday
April 28, 1935—Supplement of the
ST. LOUIS POST-DISPATCH
Magazine

NEW YORK AMERICAN—"A Paper for People Who Think"—WEDNESDAY, JULY 10, 1929

Editorial Telephone, DRY Dock 8000

Oust Chinese Vice-Consul in Opium Haul

U. S.

[WA]SHINGTON [AC]CUSED OVER [RI]CH SEIZURE

[...] May Escape Prosecu[tion f]or $1,000,000 Cache [...] Husband Is Recalled

By KENNETH CLARK.

WASHINGTON, July 9.—[Ar]oused by seizure of 3,000 tins [co]ntaining opium worth $1,000,[00]0, in luggage belonging to his [wi]fe, the State Department may [de]mand recall of Ying Kao, Chi[n]ese Vice-Consul at San Fran[c]isco, it was indicated today.

Co-operating with the Customs [B]ureau, whose agents made the [h]aul, the Department asked Sec[re]tary of the Treasury Mellon for [a] complete report as a basis for [a]ction.

If investigation bears out the smuggling charge, representations will be made to Dr. C. C. Wu, Chinese Minister, to recall Kao. Dr. Wu promises to co-operate.

A Vice-Consul [...] not rate diplomatic immu[nity ...] Ambassador or [...] ever, if Kao is [...] tion of his w[...] doned. The [...] will be guided [...] District Attorney in [...] cisco.

The seizure was attributed to the ingenuity of American Customs agents, endeavoring to break up a gigantic ring.

OPIUM RUNNING MAY COST LIVES OF CONSUL, WIFE

Chinese Couple Demanded by Native Land for Trial; U. S. Action Can Prevent Deaths

By HAROLD J. T. HORAN,
Universal Service Correspondence.

WASHINGTON, July 10.—Intervention by Secretary of State Stimson appeared today the only hope for Ying Kao, Chinese Vice-Consul in San Francisco, and his vivacious wife, facing a demand that they be deported to China and possibly be put to death for having brought into this country a consignment of opium.

Mrs. Ying Kao was stopped by the customs officers on her arrival in San Francisco recently and, on orders from Assistant Secretary of the Treasury Lowman, her baggage was searched.

OPIUM DISCOVERED.

An important supply of opium was discovered by the customs officers in the baggage of the Chinese consular agent's wife. She denied all knowledge of the opium, but later is said to have admitted she had been bringing some packages for friends into the country by making use of her diplomatic [...]

[...] ington, [...] orders from the Kou[...] political order of the Chinese Nationalist Government, to request the deportation of Ying Tao and his wife in order that both be tried by Chinese law. The punishment for which they are liable is said to be death by decapitation or life imprisonment with weekly floggings.

CHINA CONSUL AND WIFE FACE DEATH IN PLOT

Oriental Law Makes Couple Equally Guilty, but U. S. May Act to Save Their Lives

Continued from First Page.

case and cabling to his government the developments.

Minister Wu tonight issued the following official statement on behalf of the Chinese legation:

"In view of the alleged smuggling of opium into the United States involving the wife of the Chinese vice consul at San Francisco, the Chinese Minister has suspended Vice Consul Ying Ko from his duties, pending a thorough investigation."

In the absence of complete evidence of the guilt of Mrs. Ying Kao, State Department officials were reticent of the procedure to be followed.

While the Chinese Consul and his wife never enjoyed diplomatic immunity since he was only in the lower [gra]des of the service, the ba[...] the Consul's wife was [...] immed[...] present, [...]

[...] said the presi[...] angles that threaten to m[...] unusually so. If Mrs. Ying Kao succeeds in proving her good faith and convinces the Treasury officials she was imposed upon by her friends back in China, she will be faced with the necessity of accepting exile from China or revealing her friends' names to the nationalist government.

Exile or Death—Which?

BOTH GUILTY!—That's the Chinese law in the case of Yink Kao, former Vice-Consul, whose wife admits bringing $600,000 worth of opium into this country belief [...] tins to contain "gifts for friends."

CONSUL'S WIFE TAKES OPIUM QUIZ CALMLY

Mrs. Ying Kao, Cross-Questioned by Customs Officials, Wonders Why All the Fuss

By WINIFRED BLACK.
Universal Service Special Correspondent.

SAN FRANCISCO, July 14.—Mrs. Ying Kao, wife of the suspended local Chinese vice consul, took out her vanity case and powdered her nose and used with much discrimination and taste—say those who saw her do it—her Oriental lip stic.

And then she went—with her little swimming gait that reminds you so much of a sleek Chinese duck—to be cross-questioned about a little matter of half a million dollars' worth of "dope" which was found in her perfectly innocent looking trunks the other day.

Mrs. Ying speaks excellent and cultivated English and she appears to think that it is really wicked of the great, horrid man in the United States Customs Service to make such a fuss about a little opium.

She didn't know what was in her trunk at all—of course she didn't. Some of her friends in China just played an irritating little joke on her.

Freedom Comes High

Associated Press Photo.

IN OPIUM NET!—Mrs. Susie Kao and Ying Kao, Chinese Vice-Consul at San Francisco, posting bonds of $10,000 each when arraigned before Federal Court, pending hearing before the United States Commissioner. Dope valued at $500,000 was seized in the baggage of Mrs. Kao, which she was endeavoring to bring into port under immunity accorded to foreign representatives.

SATURDAY, MARCH 21, 1936

OPIUM SEIZURE *Jails 'Giant' In Dope Case*

Chinese Reputedly Worth $500,000 Captured By U. S.

Harry Gee, giant Chinese, declared to be Chinatown's No. 1 racketeer and the evil genius of the city's most formidable smuggling syndicate, was arrested by Federal narcotics agents yesterday.

He was held by U. S. Commissioner Cotter in $10,000 bail, charged with possession of opium.

2 Tins of Opium

ACCUSED IN NARCOTIC SMUGGLING

[...]ERS SEIZE [CHI]NESE IN WAR [O]N SMUGGLING

DOPE IMPORTS TO BE ATTACKED BY COPELAND

San Francisco Chronic[le]

SAN FRANCISCO, CAL., MONDAY, OCTOBER 7, 1935

BEYOND CHINATOWN "FRONT"

Chronicle Photographer Sees Hop Den Raided

RAIDS IN NEWARK CHINATOWN NETS $50,000 OPIUM, 47 MEN

Glassy-Eyed Orientals Netted in Quick Foray

Notorious Chinatown — colorful, exotic, mysterious—all these adjectives are daily used to describe that teeming foreign city in San Francisco. Tourists during their sojourn here inevitably turn their steps toward the Chinese section, where bizarre Oriental goods are to be bargained for.

FIGHT GOES ON

Chinatown is far different to the State and city narcotic officials. It is the land of the taboo pin yen or opium. Night after night these men must sneak down dark alleys, crawl through transoms, or smash their way through heavy doors to catch the addicts. The unequal war against opium seems futile, for no sooner is one den raided than two others spring up in its place.

This vain struggle must continue for should vigilance be relaxed all Chinatown would immediately be smothered in the smoke of pin yen.

Early yesterday morning one of Chinatown's largest smoke joints was raided by the State and city officials. Led by State Inspector Bernard Blonder, Officers Edward [...]

treating steps. The informer has made his getaway. Inside, the agents are closing in on the den itself. Suddenly a dark form emerges from the shadows and [...]

promises have been to no avail. The addicts know nothing of what the agents speak. A search is instituted, not so much in hope of finding the dope, but more as an incentive to [...]

Five steps caught by the candid camera when narcotics officers "knocked over" a Chinatown dope den.

Top left: It's a "layout" with opium smokers. A stupefied addict blinks. His partner, with folded hands, already has "gone out."

Center: Three addicts sullenly survey a pile of ransacked finery.

Top right: Routine safety measure—Officer Ed Oliva "frisks" dope devotees for weapons.

Lower left: A woman peddler holds a $400 tin of opium and doesn't tell a thing.

Lower right: "Say A-ah!" Eyes and tongue reveal a dope addict. Officers Louis Cames and Oliva take a peek. State Inspector Bernard Blonder directed the raid.

ADDICT Hoey Yee Wong, 42, known dope addict, nervously holds cigaret while Detective Sergeant Myron Warren examines a dipper of smoked opium ashes found in his room. Addicts who cannot afford opium obtain some stimulation by resmoking opium pipe ashes, the detectives pointed out.

Arrest Chinese Opium Addicts

2 Chinese Seamen Held As Dope Smuggler[s]

JANUARY 15, 1937

CUSTOM GUARD ABRAHAM EISENBERG Examining $100,000 Seizure of Opium; Bags in Safe Are Filled with Cans of the Narcotic

International News Photo by New York American.

$150,000 Bail Set for Pair Accused Of Having $100,000 Opium

MONDAY, OCTOBER 21, 1935

Police Break U[p] Chinese Opium De[n]

Unaware of Being Stabbed, Wife Goes to Sleep; Near Death

1928

CHINESE DEFY BAN ON OPIUM BY HUGE CROP

Bumper Harvest Soon to Be Reaped; Officials Profit by "Fining" Poppy Growers

CHUNGKINK, China April 14 (AP).—In the plains and valleys of southwest China the largest opium crop since the Government's anti-opium edict of 1907 is nearing harvest. In this part of China the poppy is a Winter crop, harvested in April and May.

Openly and with the encouragement of their military overlords, the farmers have planted the poppy so extensively that in some areas food products are scarce because the fields are given over to opium growing.

PROFITS BL "FINES."

This is especially true of Kweichow, where Governor Chow Hsicheng acknowleges no master. Like his brother militarists in Szechuen and Yunan, he profits through taxes, or "fines," on land planted to the poppy and through direct taxes on consumption. A foriegner who traveled through one Kweichow district reported twenty fields poppies to one of wheat.

An American engineer recently returned from Kweichow brought an analysis of conditions which make opium the principal source of official revenue for th eprovince and virtually the only profitable commodity for export.

CARRIED BY COOLIES.

Kweichow has no roads connecting it with other parts of China. Transport is by coolies over narrow trails. One coolie carries an average load of seventy pounds, and from Kweiyang it takes him fifteen days to reach a market at Chungking on the north or twenty days to reach water transport at Liuchow, Kwangsi, to the east.

He gets about the equivalent of forty cents a day. If he carries opium his load is worth about $200 in Kweichow and double or triple that in the Chungking or Canton market. If he carries rice or other grain his load will be worth no more than $2.50 in any market, and the transport cost would eat this up before the coolie covered a third of his journey.

1931

10 ALIENS FACE BAN FOR DOPE

Ten of the Chinese seized in the wholesale narcotic raids in Newark's Chinatown early Monday were taken yesterday to Ellis Island, where they will face deportation proceedings.

Immigration officials declare these ten possessed no papers showing legal entrance into the country. Eighteen other Chinese face trial on charges of possessing narcotics, and if convicted attempts will be made to deport them.

The others, numbering 135, have been released. Many of these, according to Federal agtnts, already have left Newark.

Gold, Opium Haul Seized by British

HONG KONG, June 19 (AP) Revenue officials of this British colony reported Sunday the biggest haul of the year in the constant war against smugglers: seizure of United States $20,000 worth of gold and $125,000 worth of opium.

The gold, 22½ pounds of it, was in thin sheets wrapped about the waist of a man aboard a steamer from Macao, nearby Portuguese colony.

The opium, ownership unidentified, was found in three wooden cases in a warehouse.

CHINESE FACE DEPORTATION IN DOPE RAID

Of 151 Prisoners Taken, Ten Sent to Ellis Island; to Try 18 as Opium Den Keepers

Photo on Picture Page.

The opium den raids in Newark yesterday morning in which 151 Chinese were captured are to be followed by deportation proceedings pressed as soon as possible by the government.

Last night all but twenty-eight of the prisoners had been discharged, it was announced. Of this number ten were ordered held at Ellis Island by C. W. Pierce, head of the Chinese Immigration Department, pending deportation proceedings.

The other eighteen were held in $1,000 bail each for arraignment in Federal Court as proprietors of opium joints. They may face deportation proceedings later.

MARKED FOR DEATH.

The raids, according to Inspector Joseph A. Manning, chief narcotic agent here, were prompted by information that five men were marked for death following expulsion of thirty-five members of the On Leong Tong at its recent convention at Cleveland.

Nineteen places in Newark's Chinatown yielded before the smashing axes and crowbars of the agents. Opium, smoking pipes, yen shee, cooking lamps and other apparatus of a total value of $50,000 were seized.

The agents, however, missed the prize they hoped most to take—a wealthy Chinese, said to head an Oriental opium and smuggling ring. This man, it is said, came to Newark from Detroit a few days ago and apparently fled on receipt of advance information of the raids.

AGENT TRANSFERRED.

With the raids, it became known also, that Agent William C. Brown, who had been in charge of the Newark area, has been transferred to Detroit. This was admitted by Manning, who said Brown left last Saturday. No reason for the transfer was given.

The five men marked for death by the On Leong Tong, Manning named as Ny Fun, Mock Fang, Davey Chow and Sam Chow, all of New York, and Lee Young, now believed en route to China.

Manning said the thirty-five expelled are also members of the Tai Luk, with headquarters in Brooklyn, and On Leong leaders have become alarmed at the growing strength of this latter organization.

SIXTY IN RAID PARTY.

The raiding agents numbered sixty and most had been brought in from other cities. Eight, recruited from Chicago, arrived Sunday by plane. Others came from Washington, Boston, Syracuse, Albany, Philadelphia and Chicago.

FRIDAY, APRIL 9, 1937

DOPE CONFESSION IN COUR

SMUGGLER TRAYS A LEGED PA

Ah Nan, Chinese s penter on the Britisl Taybank, interrupte of himself and six other men yesterday on a charge of conspiracy to smuggle opium and pleaded guilty.

He told Federal Judge Moscowitz and a jury in Brooklyn that he had met three white men on a junk boat off Staten Island a week before the ship docked. Asked, through an interpreter, to point out the trio in the courtroom, he quailed and said:

Denial Shouted

"I dare not."

$30,000 OPIUM SEIZED; 6 HELD

Detective Lieutenant Joseph H. Mooney set out to avert a holdup last night. After he had got t averting successfully off his m he seized raw opium worth $30,000 to $50,000 and arrested men.

Mooney got a tip that f Chinese were going to hold up a apartment at 127 Hudson ave. Brooklyn. With Detectives Buckley, Moffett and Loures, Mooney waited outside the building until Chong Wah Hoo nineten; Chong On, twenty-two; Ah Sam, thirty-two, and another Chinese walked up.

Wah Hoo and On were arrested on Sullivan law charges and conspiracy to rob, and Sam on the conspiracy charge. The fourth man escaped.

Mooney and Moffet walked up to the apartment they had been told was to be robbed. There they found Kin Leong, fifty-two, the occupant; Zenophon Crush, thirty-seven, a Polish seaman, and Chong Choy, twenty-five.

The detectives said Crush admitted ownership of thirty pounds of raw opium found in the place, and Leong of six pounds.

An Aden Dope Merchant Weighing Out a "Tola" of Opium for One of His Customers. This "Shot" of Forgetfulness Costs the Buyer About 50 Cents.

Addicts Buy Dope from the Government

NEARLY every American tourist who touches at Aden, the chief seaport of Arabia, on one of the 'round-the-world cruise ships which occasionally calls there, expresses astonishment, even indignation, that a city under British jurisdiction should openly sell opium. Nothing like that could occur in the United States, where the Federal Government vigorously prosecutes dope peddlers, they point out. Even in war-torn China, the selling of opium is frowned upon severely, and hardened addicts are summarily executed.

Nevertheless, the British authorities argue that their policy of "open shop" opium-selling as practiced in Aden is both wise and beneficial, for if the sale, importation and possession of narcotics were entirely prohibited, as in Egypt, the result would be not to stamp out the evil but to increase the number engaged in the traffic.

"We could quote figures to prove that the prohibition experiment in the United States resulted in an unprecedented increase in crime," said one government official. "People who never had the desire to drink tried it, just to be smart, and vast criminal organizations were created almost overnight to supply liquor to those who were willing to pay for it. If prohibition were applied to narcotics here, similar evils would arise."

However, while permitting the importation and sale of drugs, Aden authorities keep a close watch on the traffic, restricting sales to an absolute minimum. Drugs may be sold only by licensed dealers. There are only a small number of these, mostly East Indians.

Only one tola, or the weight of a rupee piece, may be sold to a customer at a time. The price of a tola is two shillings, or about 50 cents. Most of this price is tax.

To the average Arab this price is prohibitive. So, more popular than opium or hashish in Aden is "khat," also called Flower of Paradise, a plant that grows in the mountains and which is said to

The "Shingle" of One of the Narcotic Stores in Aden. Its Deadly Wares Are Advertised As Openly As Food and Clothing—But the English Authorities Think This Is the Best Way of Handling the Dope Traffic.

M.BHOT
Licence T
Opium Ga
Opium R

ISLAM SHRINE TEMPLE
ARABIAN NIGHTS
ENTERTAINMENT and BALL
MUNICIPAL AUDITORIUM
CIVIC CENTER—SAN FRANCISCO, CALIFORNIA
TUESDAY EVE. JULY 30, 1935
GRAND AWARD
2 Latest Model Ford Sedans 2
Fully Equipped
THIS TICKET ADMITS ONE
537301

An Aden Dope Addict Smoking a Narcotic That He Bought Openly. The British Government Thinks This Victim Would Be Worse Off If He Had to Deal With Bootleggers of Dope.

Port of Aden, Arabia. Near the ... Operated Under the Supervis

OPIUM ORGY FATAL TO CULTURED GIRL IN

Vice and opium go hand in hand on old Ship street, in the red light district of Hongkong

China's War On Dope

CAPTURED with sixty ounces of narcotics in his possession, a Chinese dope peddler was executed at Peiping—the first man to suffer the death penalty in the North China campaign against the narcotic vices.

...actly one week later to the ...ve other dope vendors ...ummarily put to death. ...first announced, the cam...p...n contemplated the extinction of addicts.

Executing a trafficker in the habit-forming drugs, instead of killing his victims, is a good deal less drastic and has, in fact, a good deal to commend it.

There is no offense against humanity more heinous and repulsive than the dope peddler's vile trade.

For a criminal's profit, he initiates his prey into the narcotic habit, which destroys both body and soul, and causes untold misery.

The addict himself, in a vast number of cases, is made into a dangerous criminal.

Directly and indirectly, nobody can estimate how much crime and degradation the dope peddler is responsible for.

Ceremoniously putting such a murderous creature to death in the Chinese manner may be the best means of ridding the world of him.

And certainly, if the death penalty is to be inflicted, the method employed at Peiping—by shooting—seems hardly as cruel as the electric chair.

Perhaps the Chinese are—as they claim—more civilized than we are.

1937

PEDDLERS SHOT DOWN IN CHINA'S OPIUM WAR

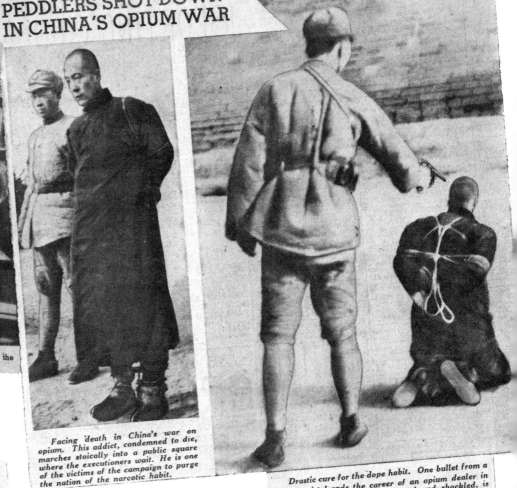

Facing death in China's war on opium. This addict, condemned to die, marches stoically into a public square where the executioners wait. He is one of the victims of the campaign to purge the nation of the narcotic habit.

Drastic cure for the dope habit. One bullet from a soldier's pistol ends the career of an opium dealer in Peiping, China. The victim, bound and shackled, is forced to kneel with his back to his executioner. He was killed in public as an example to China's many thousands of narcotic users.

Associated Press Photo.

Executing Additcs in China's Anti-Opium Crusade

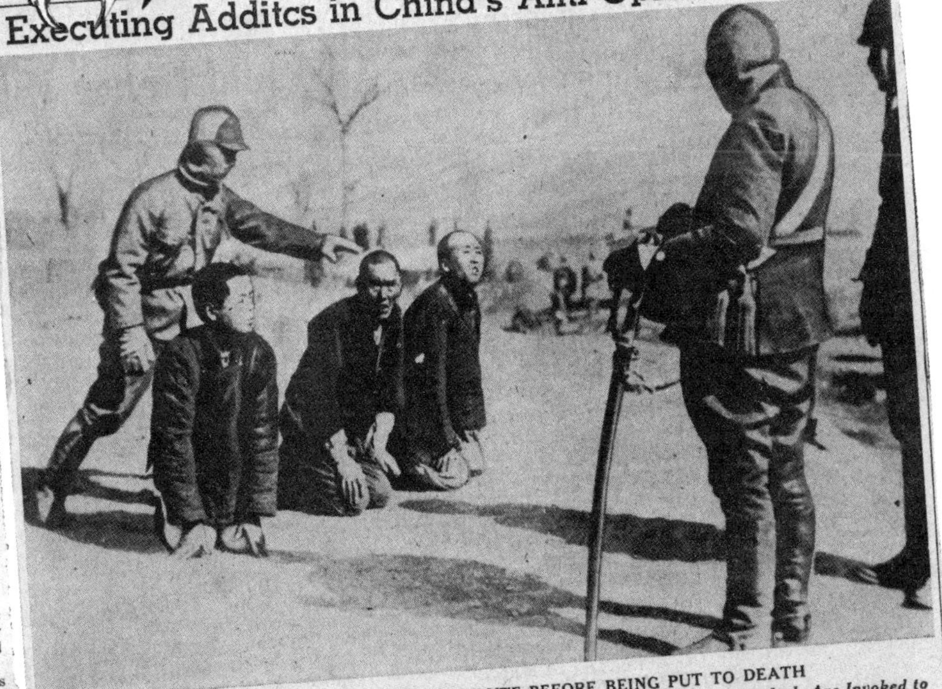

DOPE USERS ON THEIR KNEES MIN UTE BEFORE BEING PUT TO DEATH

Public Executions Like the One Shown Above Are Becom ing Common in China as Drastic Methods Are Invoked to Stamp Out the Opium Habit. Note the Expression of Ter ror on the Condemned, Proving Even the Usually Emotionless Oriental Gives Way to His Fee lings When Face to Face with Death.

...is Thoroughfare is a Dope Shop, ...ritish Government.

CHINATOWN

1937

True Story of a Dope Addict

By Guy Murchie Jr.

Foreword

WHAT IS the truth about dope? Few persons know more than the vaguest facts about the subject; even dope users themselves are often abysmally ignorant of the forces with which they are dealing.

Narcotic agents say there are many, many thousands of dope addicts in America today, and only about a third of them have any known criminal trait, which is generally petty thievery for the purpose of obtaining money to buy more dope. A few addicts (principally cocaine sniffers and marijuana smokers) have a tendency toward such crimes as murder and rape.

Federal officials agree that many, probably most, dope addicts are average respectable citizens in business and professional life, who got started on dope through curiosity, gullibility, and general ignorance.

The story of dope addiction is best told by actual cases. In preparing the article which begins on this page, the writer sought out an actual case, and supplemented it with known facts and records of dope addicts.

THIS is the true story of Josephine B——, a strip-tease dope fiend. When she was 15 years old Josephine ran away from her comfortable home in a suburb of New York city. Being adventuresome and not afraid of life in the raw, she became a chorus girl in a burlesque show. Six months later she was adept at the spicy art of strip-teasing, then in its infancy, and had married a middle-age comedian who had a leading part in her show. He was a juggler and piano player, and several times a day he would steal off by himself to take what he told her was lung medicine.

They had been married about three months when one day Josephine caught a cold. Her husband at once urged her to try some of his "lung medicine," and she trustingly complied. She found that the medicine had to be smoked. Her husband prepared it in the form of pills that looked like pieces of hard molasses, and these were heated over an oil lamp and inserted into the bowl of a bamboo pipe for smoking.

Smoke's Effect Pleases Her

On sucking the smoke from the sizzling pills through the pipe into her lungs, Josephine soon had a feeling of dizziness and a slight nausea, but there was also a soothing contentment about smoking the stuff and a pleasant sense of exhilaration. It made her feel "like lying around telling stories," and it also made her "just a little bit passionate."

The second night Josephine again joined her husband in smoking, and got to doing it regularly, even in the morning before rehearsal. And she found that many of the other show people smoked the stuff, too, and often she and her husband would lie around with the others over the evening smoke. They always would lie down while smoking, for, as her husband said, the smoke took more effect that way. It "had something to do with pressing against some nerve in your neck, which couldn't be done by sitting up."

After Josephine had been taking "lung medicine" regularly with her husband for nearly a year, one day she got into an argument with him. It was over another man in the show whom he suspected of paying too much attention to her. The result was that she stayed away from him that evening and spent the night with an older woman friend of hers, an actress named Irene. And suddenly she was taken ill, while in Irene's room, and began to ache all over. The whole world began swimming around her and she thought she was going to die, but Irene comforted her. She told her she knew she would be all right, because she knew just what was causing her trouble.

"Tell me, Irene, for heaven's sake tell me what it is," screamed Josephine.

"All right, dearie," said Irene. "It's high time you knew. It's that stuff you've been smoking. That stuff's not lung medicine. Do you know what it really is? It's opium. It's hop. Yes, dear, you got the habit, an' you got it bad. You're hooked. Bob's got you hooked."

So Josephine was a dope fiend and didn't know it. "Well," she thought, "I'm glad I know, anyway. It can't be so bad if all the other people in the show are taking the same stuff." And she lost no time in getting hold of her pipe for a smoke to relieve her writhing nerves.

After that she smoked regularly three and four times a day with the other smokers in her show. Smoking opium was cheap and easy in those days before the federal narcotic law went into effect in 1914. Opium at that time was generally delivered to wholesale drug companies by the hogshead. You could buy a good-sized can of it for $12, an amount which today would cost an addict around $200. Josephine and her husband generally got their supply from opium dealers in Chinatown, and when their show was on the road they would send to New York for it.

After 1914, however, the opium habit became increasingly difficult and expensive. Josephine's husband was dead by this time, but she herself would still smoke morning and evening with the rest of their old "hop fiend" cronies. There was quite an elaborate formality and tradition about it.

Materials Have Own Names

The various instruments for cooking and preparing the opium had their names, all Chinese, such as the yen hok (a sort of long pin for manipulating the opium pills), the yen she gou (a scraper for gouging out the yen shee, or residue left in an opium pipe after smoking), the gee rag (to make airtight the joint between the bowl and the pipestem), etc. As the smokers met in their locked room for the evening smoke they always went through the customary procedure of cooking the opium—the cooker always brewed it up in a special brass kettle and smoked the first pipeful himself "for good luck."

By this time, of course, the others were already lying about on their couches or on the floor, having removed all their clothing but underwear. This was always done as a safety measure, for opium smoke has

Opium is the first and most familiar of the many kinds of dope. Actually it is the gum or coagulated juice of a species of poppy plant, obtained by slitting the unripe seed capsules and collecting the juice as it exudes. Opium poppies were first known in the vicinity of Asia Minor, in Persia, India, and probably Egypt. In the Old Testament opium is called "rosh."

Early Greek physicians were the first to use opium in medicine, and it was publicly sold in the streets of Rome as a cure for stomach and bowel troubles. It was shipped in large round balls, black and sticky, and swallowed by the sick in pill or powdered form. Its odor was aromatic and musty, a little like licorice or molasses. Much later it was introduced into China, where it is now grown in large quantities, and its first known importation into the United States was in 1868 by a man named Clendenyn, who started the fad of opium smoking in California among gamblers and prostitutes.

Opium Useful To Doctors

Opium has from the earliest times been a useful drug to doctors through its power to reduce pain and calm the nerves. It was the most important element in the old-fashioned paregoric, or "soothing remedy," commonly given to children to help their stomach-aches and quiet them. It is still used in certain kinds of suppositories, but for the most part has been replaced in medicine by its derivatives, such as morphine, heroin, narcotine, codein, thebaine, dilaudid and others.

Opium acts as a narcotic, producing a slower pulse, slower respiration, and lessening all bodily secretions except that of the skin. Taken in larger doses, it causes unconquerable drowsiness, passing into deep sleep. Taken in quantity by one unaccustomed to its use, it is apt to result in death, the immediate cause being failure of the respiration. But if opium is administered carefully, under expert supervision, the body can stand it almost indefinitely, and in times of severe pain or intense nervous strain it is a great blessing.

The distinguishing characteristic of opium and its derivatives, as Josephine soon learned, is the fact that they are habit-forming. The cause of this is in the reaction of the central nervous system to the drug. Opium tends to slow up the speed of impulses passing through the nerves. This has the effect of dulling pain and calming the mind. But the nervous system is highly adaptable if given time, and as larger quantities of opium are consumed the nerve fibers adapt themselves to the retarding influence of the drug by developing in effect easer and easier transmission—so that sensations get through to the brain on nearly normal schedule. Thus the body becomes so adjusted to the dope that it can survive a dose big enough to kill five uninitiated men.

But the body also has become greatly dependent on continued consumption of dope. In fact, the nerve filaments have loosened up so much in transmitting impulses that if the sluggish influence of the dope is suddenly stopped they begin to transmit impulses with much greater than normal speed—speed great enough to throw the body into indescribable agony, violent illness, and (in extreme cases) to cause death.

Actor Tells Of Quitting

The case of a 34-year-old actor is a good illustration of what is in store for one who tries simply to stop taking opium, and the following confession (written a number of years ago) vividly pictures what the unfortunate Josephine was up against.

Wrote the actor: "While playing in San Francisco I was importuned by a friend to accompany him to a den in Chinatown where he was accustomed to smoke. To my sorrow, I went, found several men and women there smoking, was persuaded to try a few pipes, and from that day to this, with the exception of five months, have smoked steadily, usually twice a day.

She was a "main line shooter" in dope fiend parlance. Others, who didn't inject their veins, were just "skin shooters" and rather looked down on by the "main line" school. It took about ten minutes after each shot before Josephine was "hit" by the dope, for, as she said, her circulation was poor. Some shooters would be "hit" within a few seconds.

Here is a good place to examine the nature of morphine and of other of the dopes to which Josephine was to have access, that we may better realize exactly what she was dealing with.

Morphine is an alkaloid of opium and its most important active principle, being the narcotic part of it. Morphine was discovered in 1806 by an apothecary in Germany called Hamlin. It was the first pure alkaloid of opium to be isolated. Nearly 50 years later Alexander Wood of Edinburgh, Scotland, invented the hypodermic syringe which made morphine both a powerful agent in medical science and a horrible curse to the dope addict. By injecting morphine into a man's arm the doctor can relieve him of his severest pains and the dope peddler can start him on a most fiendish habit.

Heroin Discovered 40 Years Ago

Heroin, an even more powerful derivative of opium than morphine, was discovered also in Germany, some 40 years ago, and introduced as a nonhabit-forming narcotic. But actually it is fully as habit-forming as morphine or as dilaudid, the most recently discovered derivative of opium. Both morphine and heroin are produced generally in the form of powder or pills. Dissolved in water, they can readily be injected, though they are often eaten, or snuffed up the nose with the aid of a snuffing quill.

Heroin is preferred by some throat specialists as a remedy for coughs, dyspnea, and chest pains, but it is generally considered to have few if any advantages over codeine and other opiates. Because of this it was outlawed in the United States in 1924 and can now be sold legally only by manufacturers who have still some of their pre-1921 supply left.

After opium and its derivatives, cocaine is the best known dope. It is a shiny powder obtained from the dried leaves of coca, a shrub that grows most commonly in the mountains of Peru and Bolivia. Its effects are at first stimulating, like very strong tea or coffee, and afterward narcotic. Its principal medical use is as a local anesthetic. In surface application on mucous membrane, especially on the inside of the nose, it is particularly effective, and every one is familiar with its synthetic derivative, novocain, which is the local anesthetic so widely used by dentists in extracting teeth.

Cocaine Causes Mental Craving

The great danger in cocaine, of course, is the fact that it is habit-forming, though in a different way than is opium, for, unlike opium, cocaine does not cause bodily agony and violent sickness in its addicts who fail to take their accustomed dose. Instead it grips the addict with an intense mental craving and a nervous restlessness that few can stand for long. And as the addict continues his habit of snuffing up cocaine (or, worse still, injecting it) he increasingly develops insomnia, decaying moral and mental power, and emaciation until he dies.

Narcotic agents call cocaine the most dangerous of all dopes, because its initial stimulating effects so often distort the addict's mind, leading him to commit murder, rape, or any other horrible crime without a quaver of conscience.

The last of the common dopes is known as marijuana (Mexican for "Mary Jane") and is the dried top leaves of the hemp plant, or Cannabis indica, *which is native to India. In this country a closely related variety of hemp,* Cannabis americana, *or "loco weed," is often used instead of the Indian plant, but this is nearly as powerful and is otherwise similar in effect.*

Called hashish in India and smoked or drunk from ancient times as an anesthetic, marijuana acts somewhat as does alcohol on the system. The word "assassin" came from "hashish" because the drug so often caused natives of India to run amok and commit murder. Although it is a narcotic when taken in large doses it produces mental exaltation, intoxication, and delirium tremens of sorts. It has no indispensable usefulness in medicine today, nor is it as powerful or poisonous a drug as opium or cocaine.

Marijuana Said Easily Obtained

The great danger in marijuana however, is the fact that it is easily obtained and therefore much less expensive to buy than other forms of dope, hence the dangerous habit of smoking it is comparatively open to children and others who could not easily afford to pay for heroin or cocaine.

Wildly she picked up a piece of twine and tried to hang herself on the door—but did not know how to manage it.

Attempt to Kill Herself Fails

At last the cruel storm subsides a little as the nerves that have run wild in their sudden freedom from drug begin to adjust themselves to normality. And then what they call the "chuck habit" comes on, and the skeleton of a human being, who has not eaten for a week nor has had a normal appetite since first taking dope, suddenly becomes ravenously hungry and eats like a glutton. And a little later comes another appetite as the organs of sex, long deadened by dope, suddenly free themselves from narcotic restraint. Thus, passing from one extreme to another, the nervous system eventually mends its tortured ganglions and cells, the wasted body takes on flesh, and a human being is restored to life.

Cure Not Right Solution

No cure, of course, will ever solve the dope problem, any more than life preservers will end the sinking of ships at sea. Dope addiction must somehow be prevented from starting. Laws prohibiting the importation of any narcotics (except the small amount needed by doctors) has helped some, but the stuff is too easily concealed for effective enforcement. An intense drive to round up all dope peddlers and the big wholesalers who supply them has helped, too, but, again, it is not easy to detect a dope dealer who can conceal a month's supply in a hollow heel.

PORTLAND, OREGON
APRIL 10
NINETEEN THIRTY-EIGHT

The Northwest's Own Magazine

AN Associated Weekly PUBLICATION

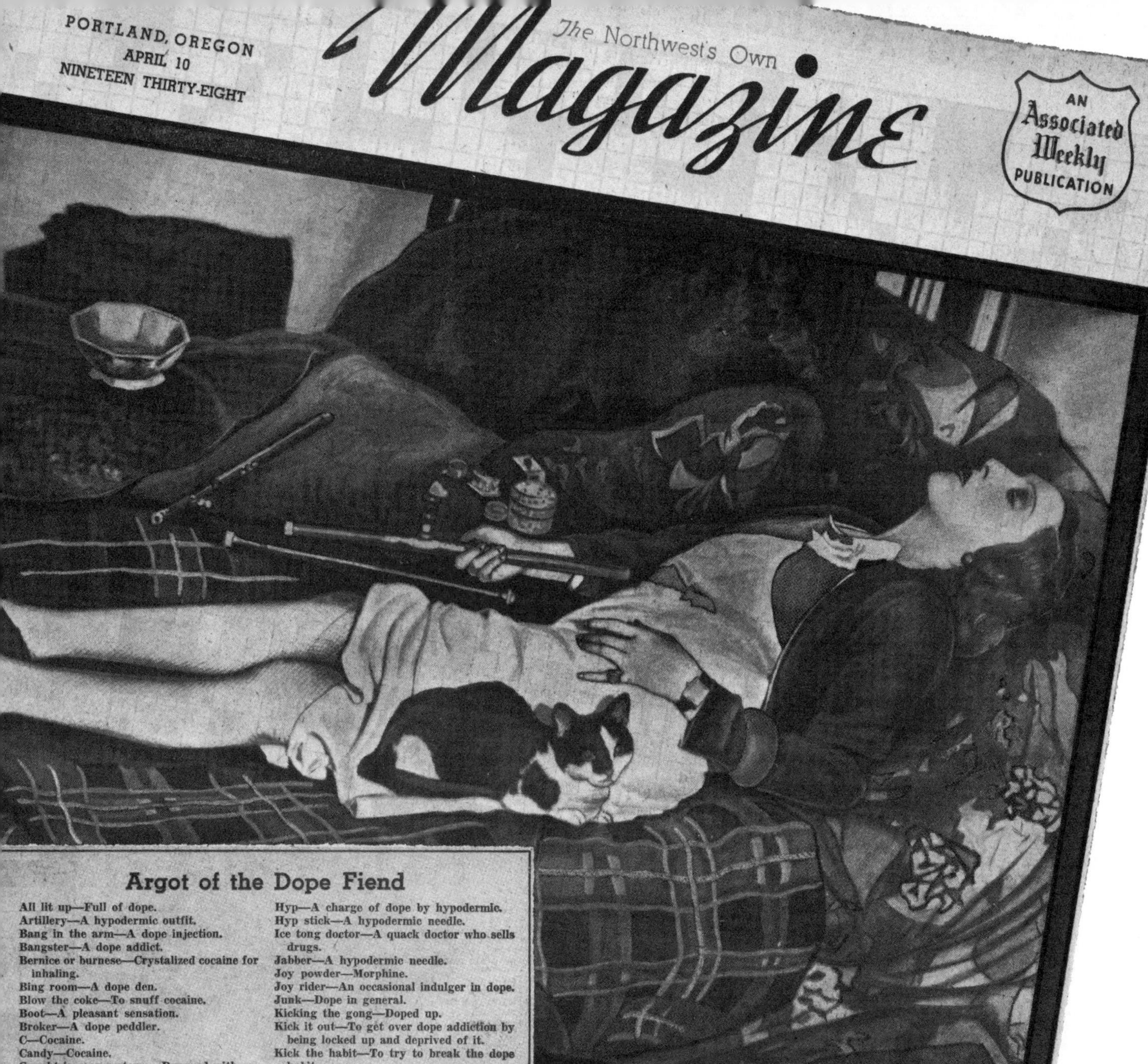

Argot of the Dope Fiend

All lit up—Full of dope.
Artillery—A hypodermic outfit.
Bang in the arm—A dope injection.
Bangster—A dope addict.
Bernice or burnese—Crystalized cocaine for inhaling.
Bing room—A dope den.
Blow the coke—To snuff cocaine.
Boot—A pleasant sensation.
Broker—A dope peddler.
C—Cocaine.
Candy—Cocaine.
Caught in a snowstorm—Drugged with cocaine.
Charge—A shot of dope.
Chef or cook—An opium cooker.
Coke—Cocaine.
Cokie or cookie—A cocaine addict.
Cook a pill—To prepare opium for smoking.
Cotton—Cloth for straining dope.
Courage pills—Heroin tablets.
Dope stick—A stick for dipping powdered dope.
Down to the cotton—Out of dope except for what's in the strainer.
Dreams—Opium.
Emergency gun—A Homemade dope injector.
Fill a blanket—To roll a cigarette.
Finger—A police informer.
From Mount Shasta—A dope addict.
Gazer—A government narcotic agent.
Gee rag—A rag to seal the joint between an opium pipe stem and bowl.
Geezed up—Doped up.
Gold dust—Cocaine.
Gong—An opium pipe.
Go on a sleigh ride—To snuff crystalized cocaine.
Gow—Dope in general.
Gun—Hypodermic needle.
H—Heroin.
Happy dust—Any powdered dope.
Have a yen on—To crave dope.
High—Well doped up.
Hit the gonger—To smoke an opium pipe.
Hokus—Dope in general.
Hop—Opium.
Hophead—An opium addict.
Hop joint—An opium den.
Hopped up—Doped up.
Hyp—A charge of dope by hypodermic.
Hyp stick—A hypodermic needle.
Ice tong doctor—A quack doctor who sells drugs.
Jabber—A hypodermic needle.
Joy powder—Morphine.
Joy rider—An occasional indulger in dope.
Junk—Dope in general.
Kicking the gong—Doped up.
Kick it out—To get over dope addiction by being locked up and deprived of it.
Kick the habit—To try to break the dope habit.
Knockout drops—Dope in general.
Load—A charge of dope.
M—Morphine.
Main line—The median vein in the arm.
Maud C—A mixture of morphine and cocaine.
Nose candy—Cocaine.
O—Opium.
Pen yen—Opium.
Pinhead—A dope addict.
Pin shot—A dope injection made with an eyedropper and a safety pin.
Pipe smoker—An opium addict.
Plant—An opium joint.
Prison junker—A prisoner who takes dope.
Reefer—Cigarette doped with marijuana.
Ride a wave—To be doped up.
Roll a pill—To prepare opium for smoking.
Shot in the arm—An injection of dope.
Smeck—Dope in general.
Sniffer—A cocaine addict.
Snow—Cocaine or any powdered dope.
Snowbird—Cocaine addict.
Speedball—A dope injection consisting of morphine mixed with cocaine.
Stem—An opium pipe.
Suck the bamboo—To smoke opium.
Toy—Horn-shaped box for keeping opium moist until smoking time.
Uncle—A federal narcotic agent.
Whiskers—A federal narcotic agent.
White stuff—Cocaine.
Wings—Cocaine.
Yen—a craving for dope.
Yen hok—An instrument for transferring an opium pill to the pipe.
Yen shee—Residue left in an opium pipe after smoking.

Table of the Common Dopes

Name of Dope	What It Is	How Generally Taken	Effects
OPIUM	Coagulated juice of the poppy plant.	Smoked or eaten.	It is quickly habit-forming. In small doses it produces mental excitement, followed by drowsiness. In large doses it weakens heart and lungs, finally resulting in death.
MORPHINE	Active constituent of opium.	By injection, or eaten or snuffed as a powder.	These two drugs are the most viciously habit-forming of all. They quickly deaden all sexual power. These victims are in such agony when deprived of the dope that they will commit murder if need be to obtain it, and can never get rid of the horrible thought of impending torture should they ever be caught short. Early death is their usual end.
HEROIN	The diacetic acid eater of morphine.	By injection, or eaten or snuffed as a powder.	
And other opiates such as narceine, laudanum (opium wine), dilaudid, etc.			
COCAINE	An alkaloid extracted from the leaves of an Andean shrub called coca.	Snuffed as a powder, eaten, or injected (usually mixed with morphine or heroin.)	This is called the most horrible of all the dopes. At first stimulating and afterward depressing, its habit results in insomnia, decay of moral and intellectual power, emaciation, progressive insanity and death.
MARIJUANA Also known (in India) as hashish, gunjah, churrus, and bhang.	Dried top leaves of the hemp plant (cannabis indicá), though in America "loco weed" leaves are often substituted.	Smoked or chewed and sometimes made into a drink.	It is habit-forming. As the victim continues his indulgence it produces intoxication, recklessness and a feeling of double consciousness, until finally the mind is weakened to the point of insanity, and, if no relief comes, death.

Also might be included as dopes such anesthetics as ether and chloroform, which grip a few indulgers with a vicious habit. Veronal or barbital, a common form of barbiturate, should be included as a habit-forming hypnotic. And there are such liquors as absinthe (made from wine and wormwood), which is narcotic in effect, and peyote or mescal (distilled from pulque), which is a spirit capable of producing hallucinations. Still another not so common variety of habit-forming dope is chloral hydrate, known as "chloral," which is powerfully hypnotic and anesthetic in effect.

Morphine, Masquerading, Evades Law

MAY 13, 1928

By ELLEN N. LA MOTTE,
Well-known Author and International Authority on Traffic in Narcotics.

GENEVA, May 12.—Like a bombshell in the Opium Committee the revelation burst this week that of the fifty or sixty tons of morphine made annually, half of it freely finds its way into restricted nations in the form of codein. Codein is a by-product of morphine, and as such is not covered by international restrictions.

These restrictions apply to the by-products of opium, but not to the by-products of the by-products. Thus codein escapes and thus it freely finds its way into countries striving to free themselves from the scourge of the poppy.

It was the German delegate to the committee who set off this explosion, and now I shall tell you how the world was given a chance to learn about codein. You have heard of

Now Germany, as I said before, is an immense maker of morphine. Twenty tons did she make in 1926. Dr. Anselmino is a chemist, rather than a politician, a quiet man with a yellow beard and silver rimmed spectacles, and a low, gentle voice. Suddenly we became aware that Anselmino was speaking—saying something important in his low, scarcely audible voice, and at once the shuffling and restlessness of the Committee stopped—all leaned forward attentively to hear what it was Anselmiro was saying.

All Wrong, He Says

Mr. Brenier's figures, he said, were all wrong as to morphine manufacture. His big block representing morphine was all wrong. It was too small—much too small. Too low, much too low. Mr. Brenier had not taken into account the amount of morphine turned into codein.

The graph simply showed the morphine that had been made into morphine and stayed as morphine. It did not show the morphine that had been used to make into codein. To show that, the block should have been twice the size.

Had any one noticed the extensive manufacture of codein, which comes from morphine, not from opium direct? All the drug factories in the world were now making codein. His own country, Germany, had made twenty tons of morphine last year, and turned fifteen of it into codeine. All other countries were doing the same. Why? Because codein does not come under the Convention, and is therefore exempt from supervision, and has no difficulty in getting from one country to another. The amount of codein made today is enormous—every factory is turning it out by the ton. Germany turns at least 70 per cent of her morphine into codein; Great Britain turns 50 per cent; Switzerland, 33 per cent.

All this because codein is exempt from control, and can move about freely. This wide manufacture of codein represents the intensive struggle of the manufacturers for the drug markets of the world. Each one in a scramble for its share of the international trade. The annual output of morphine is between 50 and 60 tons—and fully half of that codein was exempt from restrictions and could be sold anywhere.

This bombshell was dropped amidst profound silence. Not a contradiction, not a word in protest. No one challenged the German's statement. For every delegate at the table, representing countries with vast manufacturing interests, knew full well that the statement was true.

How on earth Germany came to make such a remark, no one can imagine. Is Germany going to break away from the international drug ring? Going to put her house in order? Does this statement mean a change in policy? A decision that the profits of the manufacturers are worth less than her reputation? The question is still unanswered. Why should the whole show have been given away? For what reasons?

Here now is a fine situation, a fine state of affairs! Morphine made to the tune of fifty or sixty tons a year, and half of that turned into codein! Or—is it really turned into codein? Do the manufacturers just content themselves by saying that it has been turned into codein—and let it go at that?

Signor Cavazzoni, the Italian delegat, sprang into action at once. Why, he asked, is all this morphine being turned into codein—into a derivative of opium outside all control of international agreements? We must draw our own conclusions! The time, he said, has now come for the Opium Committee to act! And for the League of Nations to act!

The poor, harrassed chairman, Dr Carrère, representing Switzerland which does a colossal trade in drugs, was hard put to it for an answer. There wasn't much he could say.

DRUG RING HAS 100,000 WAYS TO SHIP DISGUISED MORPHINE

MAY 6, 1928

Acids Convert Contraband Into Different Substance—Across International Lines Chemists Quickly Restore Original Stuff

By ELLEN N. LA MOTTE,
Well-Known Author and International Authority on the Traffic in Narcotics.

GENEVA, May 5.—Why does the international "dope" ring laugh in its sleeve at The Hague and Geneva opium treaties? Because it has thousands of ways of shipping morphine into "forbidden" countries, without violating the letter of the treaties or of the laws of the importing countries.

This amazing revelation was made in the last week before the meeting of the Opium Committee. It was made over the heads of some of the delegates who thought it best that the information be suppressed.

The method is simple; yet it works. It is magic. The manufacturers merely treat morphine with a chemical and presto! It is no longer morphine, but something else. All very well. Then it is shipped to the country in which it is to be sold, taken to a drug factory, and the chemical removed. Presto! again and you have the original morphine.

Disguised Morphine

There are countless formulae for the making of morphine-esters. An ester is a morphine that is not a morphine—while it is being shipped to a country that is trying to free itself of the clutches of the dope traffic.

A new term for me, but not so new to the opium ring. Briefly, a morphine-ester is morphine treated with an acid—benzoic acid, acetic acid—any kind of acid will apparently do. Morphine so treated at once becomes something else—an ester—and is no longer morphine. It has been by a chemical process transformed into a harmless substance, and this substance is not subject to any sort of restrictions.

Being no longer morphine but now an ester, it can be shipped from one country to another, across all the frontiers of the world, without let or hindrance. In fact, the customs authorities salute as it goes through—this harmless product. A perfectly harmless product—morphine just turned into an ester—an innocuous drug and one not falling under the control of either The Hague or the Geneva conventions. Not, like morphine, having to be recorded when it leaves one country and goes into another. Not, like morphine, having to travel round on a government license or certificate. Being, in fact, as free to travel about the world as a cake of soap—and, because it's an ester, equally harmless.

But what happens when any one of these esters is imported into a country—a country that manufactures drugs? Bang it goes into a drug factory; the acid is promptly removed; and the fortunate manufacturer is suddenly in possession of a quantity of morphine which is not recorded! He may have imported a ton of this morphine-ester and, after squeezing out the acid, he finds himself in possession of a ton, or let us say half a ton, of pure morphine.

Pretty neat! These morphine esters are now being manufactered all over Europe, but in what amounts, no one knows. It is not intended that any one shall know. This chemical change was invented so that the deadly poison morphine, could slip round the world undetected and unrecorded, and the big international drug ring has just this amount of morphine to slip into the illicit trade No records kept. No questions asked.

An ester is pure velvet. It is an opium derivative which is outside the control of both the Hague and the Geneva conventions, or opium treaties. Left out on purpose—deliberately left out. The opium ring knows its business.

How much of these esters are imported into the United States? What precautions does our Government take to exclude them? To what extent—if any—are they responsible for the drug addiction in our country?

French Opposition

Then the Japanese delegate spoke. Mr. Sato wanted it known that Japan had been the first government in the world to act in this matter. Not only does Japan forbid the manufacture of benzoyl-morphine, but of all other drugs in this class. Not only is manufacture forbidden, but it rigidly excludes all importation into Japan. Not only does this apply to all the known drugs of this type, but to any other derivatives that might come under this head. All derivatives of opium, even though left out of the convention, ought to be put in.

Sotto voce from the Dutch delegate:

"We left them out on purpose."

You can always count on the Dutch delegate to give the show away.

Mercifully for all concerned, it was 7 o'clock by this time and the meeting adjourned. Outside in the corridor, I spoke to the Japanese. I asked:

"Tell me about these drugs, these new things we have just heard of, but which are now being made by the ton. I gather that in addition to benzoyl-morphine, the one we have just heard of, there are lots of others. How many others are there?"

The reply was:

"About a hundred thousand. The chemical combinations are unlimited You can treat morphine with one acid, or with another acid—there are lots of acids—! Or you can treat it with several acids, in varying quantities—there is simply no limit to the chemical combinations you can make, each with a different formula, and yet not one of these hundred thousand combinations come under the Hague Convention."

"Then you mean," I asked, rather staggered, "that if you put benzoyl-morphine on the black list, you still have 99,999 other possibilities?"

"Oh yes," replied Mr Sato, "that is why our government has banned them all. It seemed simpler. Ours is the first government to

NEW NARCOTIC DISCOVERY TO WIN $100,000

MAY 15, 1925

Herman Metz Posts Award at Police Parley for Synthetic Morphine to Oust Opium

Former Comptroller Herman A. Metz yesterday announced a prize of $100,000 to the first chemist who produces within the next five years a synthetic morphine subject to laboratory control.

The offer is made in the hope of eradicating the narcotic drug evil and followed the statement of Dr. Carleton Simon, Deputy Police Commissioner, before the International Police Conference that the hope of controlling the evil and possibly eliminating it was in the production of a synthetic morphine that would be commercially cheaper than that produced from the poppy.

Mr. Metz stipulates in his offer that the synthetic product must be structurally the same as that produced from the juices of the poppy, and that it can be manufactured more cheaply than it can be derived from poppy growth. The formula is to be made public and not patented, and will be under

"Dope

Dope From Far East Menaces U.

By HARRY J. ANSLINGER,
United States Commissioner of Narcotics.

THE source of the world's illicit drug supply has shifted from Western Europe to the Far East, and simultaneously the Government's fight to suppress this nefarious and vicious traffic at the nation's gates has shifted from the Eastern to the Pacific Coast.

Only a short time ago, illicit drugs were pouring into the United States from Western Europe in large quantities, but this flood now has been reduced to a thin stream by the operation of the Geneva drug-control convention of 1931, the forceful representations of the American State Department to foreign countries, which heretofore had been lax or indifferent to any program of stamping out the evil, and the vigilance of our Federal Customs and Narcotic Services.

Scourged from one country to another as the international agencies seeking their extinction have been relentlessly closing in on them, the drug traffickers have now set up their clandestine factories in the Far East, principally in Japan an...

co... go to nearly any capital in Europe, call in a "broker," g... p... Y... and the order would be f... Now illicit morphine c... scarcely be obtained at any p... in Europe. The source of th... supply was chiefly Turkey, w... illegitimate manufacturer... set up factories after being dr... from France, Switzerla... and Germany, but this ha... did not last long, because th... President of Turkey st... in... shut...

There have been some indications, disclosed by the seizure of several large shipments of illicit drugs at Marseilles in the past year, that some of the traffickers were creeping back into France. This was met prompty by the French Government by establishing a Central Narcotic Bureau, not only for the purpose of eradicating the traffic in France, but to co-operate with the United States in combating the smugglers.

The drug that is coming in from the clandestine factories of the Far East is the deadliest of all—heroin. Morphine and heroin are derivatives of opium. Heroin is a derivative of morphine and about three times more powerful. It makes addicts almost immediately.

The manufacture of heroin is prohibited in the United States. ...overnment has endeavored ... persuade foreign nations t... do likewise. They have not g... to this extent, but ... agreed to permit legitimate ... manufacturers to ship the ... only to governments an... not to private individuals ... distribution.

So dang...us is this drug that the Rock...ler Foundation is spending ...t of money trying to find a ...ilar drug that does not ha... the habit... morph...

morphine and heroin altogether.

At the present time there is some illicit heroin coming into the country from Europe, but it is coming mostly from the surplus stocks manufactured a few years ago, since fallen into dishonest hands, and from clandestine factories. The problem of drug-control is no longer concerned with drugs produced by legitimate manufacturers. That is now well regulated and very little of this supply goes into illicit channels.

Five years ago the drug of addiction all over this country was morphine. Due to excess manufacture in Europe, large supplies were available and the drug at that time was selling at $12 an ounce.

Worth 6 Times Value of Gold

Today illicit morphine is about six times the value of gold. Due to its exhorbitant price and the increasing effectiveness of the Government's efforts ... the dope tr... morphine b... tically disa... the same... cocaine, w... diminishing... years, has... where there... cocaine addict...

The drug ... country toda... been definitel... the distributio... gled drug from ... through the Paci... not extended east ... Mountains, and ...latively sma...

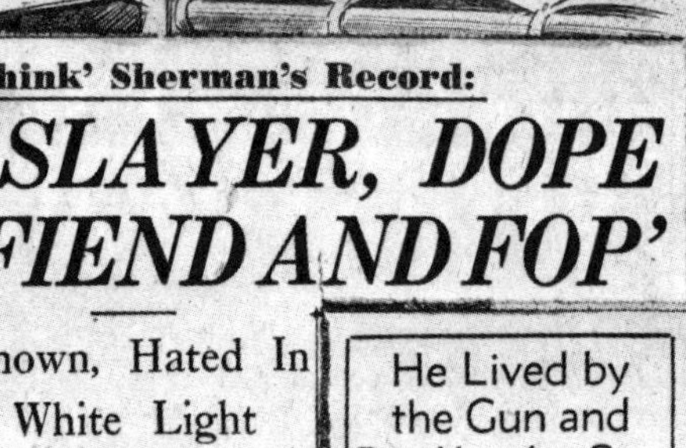

'Chink' Sherman's Record:

'SLAYER, DOPE FIEND AND FOP'

Known, Hated In White Light District

NOVEMBER 6, 1935

Charles "Chink" Sherman (born Shapiro), eyes dark-circled and staring, mouth grotesquely twisted to the left, was a foppish bad boy out of Detroit.

He was a dope addict, an opium smoker, a "sniffer," and, as one Government agent said yesterday, he was "awful bad when he was full of junk."

He was known and hated along Broadway as a chiseler and a welcher. In his death the community can be said to have suffered a considerable gain.

He was shrewd, cold and ruthless. Not a killer by instinct, but a killer if dope and circumstances combined nicely to make him one. Night clubs were his natural background and he could be seen, late at night, lounging at a corner table of one of the White Light places in all his pasty-faced elegance and with a couple of blondes.

Free Spender

It was his habit to walk into one of these spots late, share two or three bottles of champagne with his women, and pay off in new $100 bills. He was a lavish tipper. Sometimes, when he was feeling good, he tossed the waiter a $20 bill.

But "Chink" was more or less on the spot ever since he tangled with Dutch Schultz in the celebrated Club Abbey roughhouse of 1931.

He Lived by the Gun and Died by the Gun ---and the Axe

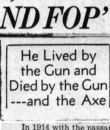

In 1914 with the passage of the Harrison Act it became a Federal offense for any physician to give morphine for any case of chronic morphine poisoning. Overnight it became a crime for the sufferer to even carry in his pocket the only medicine which can keep him from horrible agony—morphine!

How could I tell this lad the stark truth?

Here in an exclusive story for The American Weekly, as Presid... of the American Narcotic Defense Association, he tells heart-breaki... incidents in the hopeless lives of morphine addicts he has known. W... first hand knowledge he recounts fiendish plots of crime overlords ... carry on their huge money-making drug traffic.

"Don't call them 'dope fiends,'" pleads Dr. La Roe. "Morphine a...dicts are not fiends but sick people—yet the laws of our country ma... it a crime to give them the only medicine that will do any good... 'morphine!'"

It is the underworld that keeps that law on the books. What c... Americans do about it?

Four things the doctor suggests:

1. Repeal the Harrison Drug Act of 1914 which makes it a cri... for any doctor to give a dose of morphine to an addict; and a crime ... such a sufferer to carry in his pocket the only medicine that can ke... him from horrible agony.

2. Recognize chronic morphine poisoning as a disease.

3. Put every man, woman and child who is a victim of this dise... on a daily minimum ration until science has discovered a cure or a su...stitute that works.

4. Place the entire administration of these rations in the hands ... the Federal Government.

It is tragedies like those of Danny Malloy and his sweetheart Ma... the promising Fred Markham, and Julia Kaye and her innocent lit... baby that are making Dr. La Roe carry on the fight, while he a... carries on his practice and just now serves his country in the Army Medical Corps. He tells all those stories for our readers.

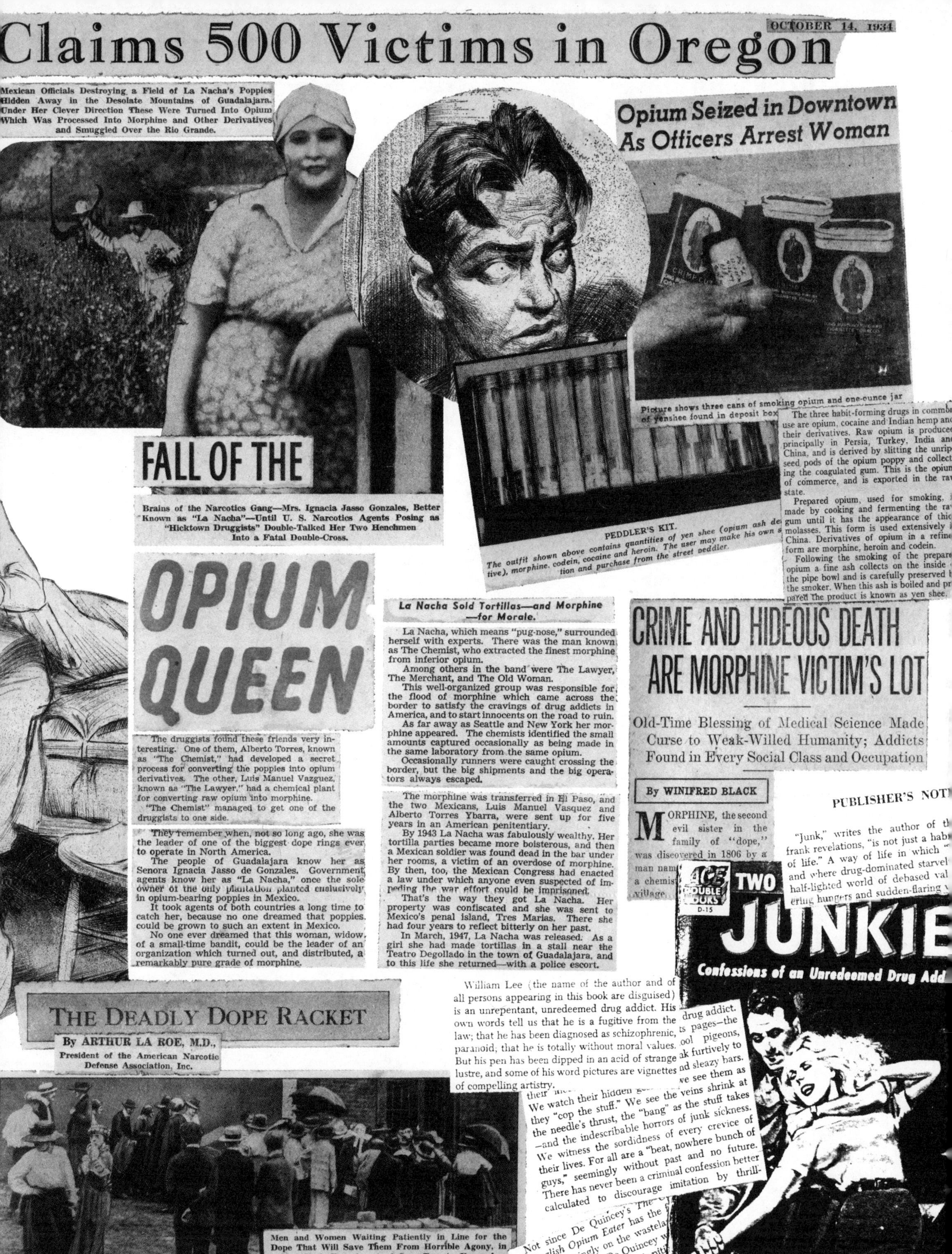

Claims 500 Victims in Oregon

OCTOBER 14, 1934

Mexican Officials Destroying a Field of La Nacha's Poppies Hidden Away in the Desolate Mountains of Guadalajara. Under Her Clever Direction These Were Turned Into Opium Which Was Processed Into Morphine and Other Derivatives and Smuggled Over the Rio Grande.

Opium Seized in Downtown As Officers Arrest Woman

Picture shows three cans of smoking opium and one-ounce jar of yenshee found in deposit box

The three habit-forming drugs in commo use are opium, cocaine and Indian hemp an their derivatives. Raw opium is produce principally in Persia, Turkey, India an China, and is derived by slitting the unrip seed pods of the opium poppy and collect ing the coagulated gum. This is the opiu of commerce, and is exported in the ra state.

Prepared opium, used for smoking, made by cooking and fermenting the ra gum until it has the appearance of thic molasses. This form is used extensively China. Derivatives of opium in a refin form are morphine, heroin and codein.

Following the smoking of the prepar opium a fine ash collects on the inside the pipe bowl and is carefully preserved the smoker. When this ash is boiled and pr pared the product is known as yen shee.

FALL OF THE

Brains of the Narcotics Gang—Mrs. Ignacia Jasso Gonzales, Better Known as "La Nacha"—Until U. S. Narcotics Agents Posing as "Hicktown Druggists" Double-Talked Her Two Henchmen Into a Fatal Double-Cross.

PEDDLER'S KIT.

The outfit shown above contains quantities of yen shee (opium ash de tive), morphine, codein, cocaine and heroin. The user may make his own s tion and purchase from the street peddler.

OPIUM QUEEN

The druggists found these friends very interesting. One of them, Alberto Torres, known as "The Chemist," had developed a secret process for converting the poppies into opium derivatives. The other, Luis Manuel Vazguez, known as "The Lawyer," had a chemical plant for converting raw opium into morphine.

"The Chemist" managed to get one of the druggists to one side.

They remember when, not so long ago, she was the leader of one of the biggest dope rings ever to operate in North America.

The people of Guadalajara know her as Senora Ignacia Jasso de Gonzales. Government agents know her as "La Nacha," once the sole owner of the only plantation planted exclusively in opium-bearing poppies in Mexico.

It took agents of both countries a long time to catch her, because no one dreamed that poppies could be grown to such an extent in Mexico.

No one ever dreamed that this woman, widow of a small-time bandit, could be the leader of an organization which turned out, and distributed, a remarkably pure grade of morphine.

La Nacha Sold Tortillas—and Morphine—for Morale.

La Nacha, which means "pug-nose," surrounded herself with experts. There was the man known as The Chemist, who extracted the finest morphine from inferior opium.

Among others in the band were The Lawyer, The Merchant, and The Old Woman.

This well-organized group was responsible for the flood of morphine which came across the border to satisfy the cravings of drug addicts in America, and to start innocents on the road to ruin.

As far away as Seattle and New York her morphine appeared. The chemists identified the small amounts captured occasionally as being made in the same laboratory from the same opium.

Occasionally runners were caught crossing the border, but the big shipments and the big operators always escaped.

The morphine was transferred in El Paso, and the two Mexicans, Luis Manuel Vasquez and Alberto Torres Ybarra, were sent up for five years in an American penitentiary.

By 1943 La Nacha was fabulously wealthy. Her tortilla parties became more boisterous, and then a Mexican soldier was found dead in the bar under her rooms, a victim of an overdose of morphine. By then, too, the Mexican Congress had enacted a law under which anyone even suspected of impeding the war effort could be imprisoned.

That's the way they got La Nacha. Her property was confiscated and she was sent to Mexico's penal island, Tres Marias. There she had four years to reflect bitterly on her past.

In March, 1947, La Nacha was released. As a girl she had made tortillas in a stall near the Teatro Degollado in the town of Guadalajara, and to this life she returned—with a police escort.

CRIME AND HIDEOUS DEATH ARE MORPHINE VICTIM'S LOT

Old-Time Blessing of Medical Science Made Curse to Weak-Willed Humanity; Addicts Found in Every Social Class and Occupation

By WINIFRED BLACK

MORPHINE, the second evil sister in the family of "dope," was discovered in 1806 by a man nam a chemis village

PUBLISHER'S NOT

"Junk," writes the author of t frank revelations, "is not just a hab of life." A way of life in which " and where drug-dominated starvel half-lighted world of debased val ering hungers and sudden-flaring

ACE DOUBLE BOOKS D-15

TWO

JUNKIE

Confessions of an Unredeemed Drug Add

WILLIAM LE

William Lee (the name of the author and of all persons appearing in this book are disguised) is an unrepentant, unredeemed drug addict. His own words tell us that he is a fugitive from the law; that he has been diagnosed as schizophrenic, paranoid; that he is totally without moral values. But his pen has been dipped in an acid of strange lustre, and some of his word pictures are vignettes of compelling artistry.

drug addict. ts pages—the ool pigeons, ak furtively to nd sleazy bars. ve see them as their

We watch their hidden g they "cop the stuff." We see the veins shrink at the needle's thrust, the "bang" as the stuff takes—and the indescribable horrors of junk sickness. We witness the sordidness of every crevice of their lives. For all are a "beat, nowhere bunch of guys," seemingly without past and no future. There has never been a criminal confession better calculated to discourage imitation by thrill-

Not since De Quincey's *The* *an English Opium Eater* has the shone so glaringly on the wastela addict. Yet, where De Quincey w of dream-phantasy, *Junkie* is piti hard-boiled. From the very ins down the addict withou nakedness.

THE DEADLY DOPE RACKET

By ARTHUR LA ROE, M.D., President of the American Narcotic Defense Association, Inc.

Men and Women Waiting Patiently in Line for the Dope That Will Save Them From Horrible Agony, in a New York Experiment of Over Twenty Years Ago Which Permitted Addicts to Get Their Drug Rations by Registering With the Municipal Bureau. They Have No Such Means of Relief Now.

's Daring "Chloroform Burglar"
WOMAN MAD
DRUNK, THE
STRANGLED B
DENTIST'S GA
Stepson, 18, Heir to Fortu
Made to Mix Cement to S
Mother's Body in Cist
"Inferiority Complex" T
Urged Killing Blamed
in Story of D
My Adventure
HOTEL DEL CORONADO
61
CORONADO, CAL.
POISON
PHYSICIAN'S FORMULA PELLETS
NUMBER 23

Exotic Drugs

Coca is a far more potent and far less harmful stimulant than alcohol, and its widespread utilization is hindered at present only by its high cost.

—Sigmund Freud, 1884

The spectrum of drugs in this chapter predicts the future more eloquently than the narcotics derived from opium. None is, in fact, a narcotic; all except nitrous oxide come from native plants used for magic medicine since time began. Watch for the emergence of the "dope fiend" image as miracle drugs pop out of the jungles into the labs and onto the streets. This, then, is a cautionary tale, and a glimpse of the world beyond.

In 1884 young Sigmund Freud bought a gram of cocaine ($1.27) and penned a classic monograph about it, *Über Coca.* His friend Carl Koller discovered its value as a local anesthetic for surgery, and suddenly the whole world, like the little Connecticut town in this chapter, was "Mad for Cocaine." Doctors prescribed it for anything from sniffles to morphine addiction; popes and paupers swigged it in wines, patent medicines, soft drinks; strangers would stop each other at corners and ask, "Can you give me a pinch?"

With widespread use came abuse. Newspapers started muckraking about the "mental decay and moral perversion of cocaine excess." Dr. Harvey W. Wiley crusaded for the labeling of drugs in medicine and soft drinks (1906); shocked consumers became aware of cocaine in their favorite brain tonics, and most manufacturers removed it. Yet when soft drinks were checked in 1909, cocaine remained in no fewer than thirty-nine of them.

The yellow-press stereotype of murderous dope fiends originated in stories such as the 1913 "Race Riot Born of a Cocaine Jag." (Then as now, race relations in Mississippi were a tinderbox; could nothing other than cocaine explain why two black kids might shoot at every white in town?) Precisely such tales led to the inclusion of cocaine in the Harrison Act a year later.

Cocaine was fashionable in Paris during World War I, and it was there that the modern-style "dope ring" first evolved, modeled (according to police) on the Standard Oil cartel, with distribution handled by street punks called Apaches. Glitter in the salons and menace on the streets—*haute monde* and *demi-monde*—the popular image of cocaine has been locked somewhere in between ever since.

Morbid fascination with Billie Carleton's death after London's 1918 Gay Victory Ball rounded out the hysteria as papers detailed the global snowball of the 1920s: tons of coke seized in San Francisco; over 3,000 people a year busted in New York (including a Zulu chief); refineries in Bucharest; smuggling on the Ganges. Police blamed sixty percent of the violent crimes in New York on cocaine.

By contrast, certain drugs were applauded by police. They found the twilight zone of scopolamine truth serum more convenient for extracting confessions than the old "third degree." Previews of brainwashing in experiments at San Quentin: "Reason is paralyzed but memory remains."

Newspaper reaction to drugs not associated with crime was much milder. Most adults had experienced nitrous oxide in the dentist's chair, and "oxygen parties" were an early fad. A *Boston Globe* 1901 cartoon depicts the transformation of Victorian gentility into vaudeville characters; George Bernard Shaw in 1933 describes himself as a cosmic dentist supplying laughing gas to the world. Amusing, not threatening.

Hallucinogens were also relatively safe as long as they remained anthropological. Crucial to this approach was the separation of quaint native customs from the dope rings of the streets. One ploy was to run features about edible versus poisonous (mind-altering) mushrooms, historical views of American Indian tobacco rites, or far-out root festivals on reservations. Another was to report scientific expeditions in search of potential medicines, like Rusby's trip to the Amazon to get *caapi (yagé)* in 1922.

Early peyote research was the prototype of modern hallucinogen research. Dr. S. Weir Mitchell's pioneering 1897 account of his mescaline visions—"Then an abrupt rush of countless points of white light swept across the field of view, as if the unseen millions of the Milky Way were to flow a sparkling river before the eye"—paved the way for the psychedelic world to come.

WHOLE TOWN MAD FOR COCAINE.

Most Prominent Residents of Manchester, Conn., Afflicted with the General Craze for the Drug.

WANT LEGISLATIVE ACTION.

Druggist Started the Habit a Year Ago by Preparing a Seductive Remedy for Asthma.

ALL MUST HAVE IT NOW.

Threaten Violence if Denied and Treat One Another to "Pinches" in Public Places.

[BY TELEGRAPH TO THE HERALD.]

HARTFORD, Conn., Dec. 27, 1896.—The cocaine habit has taken such a hold on the residents of Manchester that steps are being taken to obtain legislative restriction on the sale of the drug. The evil had its inception when a local druggist a year ago made a preparation of cocaine and menthol which could be used as a snuff. It was intended as a specific for asthma, but the prescription was passed around, and now hundreds of persons have become slaves to the stuff.

NEW YORK HERALD, JANUARY 3, 1897.

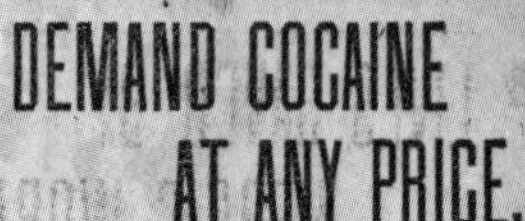

DEMAND COCAINE AT ANY PRICE.

Condition of South Manchester, Conn., a Town Whose Residents Generally Are "Fiends."

WILL HAVE DRUG OR DIE.

More Common Than the Tobacco Habit, Its Victims Are Marked by Physical Decay.

PHYSICIANS ARE HELPLESS.

Druggists Are Determined Not to Replenish Their Stocks, but Fear the Results.

[BY TELEGRAPH TO THE HERALD.]

HARTFORD, Conn., Dec. 28, 1896.—The physicians of South Manchester are astonished at the spread of the cocaine habit in that village, as told in the HERALD yesterday, but they are powerless to stay it. A stranger going to the pretty little place on an electric car will first see the conductor or motorman take out a bottle, shake a white powder in his palm and then snuff it with intense satisfaction and a long drawn sigh of relief. In the street every other man or boy is using the stuff. Strangers will stop each other at the corners and ask:—"Can you give me a pinch?" The question is readily understood and the bottle of snuff is forthcoming.

At T. L. Weldon & Co.'s drug store I learned the ingredients of the substance, which was introduced there by a Hartford doctor's prescription for catarrh. The preparation is composed of sugar of milk, magnesia, cocaine and menthol, making a volatile snuff. It is an expensive compound, a jar of it being worth $20 at wholesale.

ROUNDS OF PRESCRIPTION.

The original prescription has been copied and recopied, until there is hardly a drug store in the town where the snuff cannot be obtained. The largest dealers, perhaps, are T. L. Weldon & Co., W. B. Henry and F. E. Belcher and Co. They sell the snuff in small packages, usually in bottles, costing ten cents each.

The worst victims of the habit are the hundreds of employes of all ages of Cheney Bros.' great silk mill. It is even more common than the tobacco habit. When a man or boy gets out of the snuff he goes around until he can "raise a pinch" from some one else. If none is to be had he runs to the nearest druggist.

One clerk said to me:—"Why, they come in here at all hours of the day and say:—'Give me some of that snuff, quick; got to have it.' They act half crazy in their hurry and greed. But that isn't the worst of it. They come to my house after I am asleep and make me get up, go to the store and satisfy their cravings.

SOMETIMES APOLOGIZE.

"They sometimes apologize, but say they can't help it. They must have the snuff or die. If we won't go to the store for them, they say they will be compelled to break in and steal it. And I know they would. They have no control over themselves. They cannot sleep and they don't know what they are about much of the time."

As he spoke, a once sturdy mechanic entered and shuffling up to the counter whined out his request for an ounce of the snuff. His eyes were sunken and bloodshot, his frame was bent and his hand trembled. The victims are noticeable on the streets because of their pallor, their watery eyes and their general appearance of dejection.

The cases of the boys are specially pitiful. One of them, thirteen years old, was seized with a fit in Hayes' temperance saloon the other day as a result of indulgence in the drug, and doctors had to be summoned. A drug clerk told me that the victims became utterly regardless of expense. One workman, whom the drug clerk named, spends at least $5 a week of his hard earned wages this way. Many others, not having ready cash, run up heavy bills.

I talked with several doctors, including J. T. Dooley, W. R. Tinker, O. N. Parker, T. H. Weldon and F. H. Whiton. They say that this cocaine habit is becoming much worse than that of liquor. Once a man or boy gets the appetite, there seems to be no such thing as curing him. These doctors have studied over the matter and have prescribed in vain.

EFFECTS OF THE COCAINE.

"Nothing has any effect," said one of them. "The only thing is to shut the victim up, and as in most cases this has been impossible, we do not know just what the result of depriva- ... would be. The sensation after taking ... exhilarating—something like that ... champagne. After a time it ... feels as though he ... death, and he must ... stop at nothing to sat- ... relieve his depression. ... puling infants, young ... te giants, according to ... The spinal column be- ... cted, and then the brain ... system.

... mic only a few ... as yet what ...

... TENANT.

TOWN AROUSED AGAINST A DRUG.

Beneficial Results of the Herald's Exposure of the Cocaine Habit in Manchester, Conn.

PARENTS DID NOT KNOW IT.

Interest Aroused in Medical Circles Over an Evil That Threatened a Community.

WHAT TO DO WITH "FIENDS."

[BY TELEGRAPH TO THE HERALD.]

HARTFORD, Conn., Jan. 2, 1897.—The town of Manchester never was so deeply stirred as it has been this week by the revelations in the HERALD concerning the cocaine habit in that portion of the town known as South Manchester, really the business centre of the ... Barber. ... year under a license regime there were a few saloons, but they were kept under strict surveillance. Last November the town voted for no license, and speedily the saloon men picked up and got out of town.

THE GREATER DANGER.

But while the residents were so busy in driving out liquor, many of them were not aware that an evil more dangerous, because more subtle, was claiming its victims among them. Public sentiment is a powerful thing in such a community, but if, together with parental control, it does not prove strong enough, there will be an appeal for legislative assistance.

There are many confirmed users of cocaine snuff. What their fate will be is a question. The doctors as yet know of no specific. If the sale is stopped locally the victims, who would stop at nothing to satisfy their cravings, could go to Hartford on the trolley ... their supplies.

... around the State indicates ... fear that they may ... and the opinion ... by law ... drug.

SLAVES TO DRUGS.

Cocaine and Morphine Claim Thousands of Victims Right Here in New York.

DRUGS EASY TO GET.

How One of the Physician's Best Servants Becomes a Most Terrible Master.

IT WORKS WELL AT FIRST.

But Its After Effects Upon the Victim Are Far Worse Than Those of Alcohol.

HE little town of South Manchester is fast tending toward an unenviable distinction. If it keeps up its present gait it will soon hold the unique place of a community caught in the embrace of a continuous and almost unanimous "jag."

The HERALD has already told part of the story. A large proportion of the population go about night and day under the influence of cocaine, a drug compared with which whiskey is almost as harmless as rain water. Men and boys, even women and girls, born and bred in respectability, are slaves to an addiction as much more terrible than mania a potu as that passion is more terrible than plain, everyday hysteria.

There is nothing in all the history of ebriety that quite equals the case of this hitherto unknown Yankee village. Yet that history contains some notable cases, too. For instance, there are in the west of Ireland towns wherein pretty near the whole population are ether drunkards. It is said upon excellent authority that in these towns old women hawk the exhilarating "draughts," as they are called, about the streets; that women take eggs and garden produce to the "shebeen" to exchange for a penny's worth of fleeting bliss; that even boys and girls may be seen on their way to and from school reeling from the effects of an ether spree.

This is bad enough, in all conscience; still it is not so bad as the case of South Manchester. An ether "drunk" is a thing almost as fleeting as a snowflake on the river—a moment seen, then gone forever. It has been estimated that, whereas it requires six hours for a man to get drunk and then sober again from whiskey, the same man may run the whole gamut of exhilaration, depression, stupor and final recovery from ether in less than two hours. Four or even five "ether drunks" are not accounted by experts as a good day's work.

Moreover, ether is cheap. When De Quincey wrote of the "bliss in small packages" that came from opium eating, he had not heard of ether, which is the cheapest "spree" in all the economy of drunkenness.

Deadly Cocaine.

But what is opium or ether to the deadly cocaine! As the latter is one of the latest flowers of our blessed civilization, so it is also one of the deadliest. Cocaine is the active principle of a shrub of Peru—where the bark comes from. The shrub is coca, which is quite another matter from and must not be confronted with the harmless cocoa of commerce. The preparation sold at the drug stores is cocaine hydrochlorate, but this is generally in combination with other substances, and sold under seductive labels as a remedy for catarrh.

In this form cocaine made its entrance to South Manchester. A physician from Hartford wrote, in an evil hour, a prescription for a patient in the little town suffering from some catarrhal affection. For the matter of that, similar prescriptions may be bought in almost any drug store. I have seen them sold over counters in Broadway, sometimes with prescription, sometimes without. Not many years ago the inventor and proprietor of one of these preparations was hauled up by a medical society, and he and his dose got a great deal of unpleasant advertising in the newspapers. But the fellow "lay low" till the excitement was past, and then went on, getting rich at the awful expense of his foolish fellow creatures, as before. You can get all the cocaine you want in New York. But here's hoping that after you read this you won't want very much of it.

The stuff works like a charm at first. All the pain and distress of the mucous membranes of the throat and nose vanish like a bad dream. They give way to perfect peace, ecstasy, superlative joy, love of all mankind and womankind. The patient sees only a beatific vision. He feels that he could go right out into the middle of the street and pick roses and geraniums from the naked paving stones. The air is full of a tonic like champagne—only infinitely brighter and sweeter. The wind wafts perfumes. All nature smiles the seductive smile of a beautiful and generous woman. Life is what Mr. Cleveland said it was—a grand, sweet song.

All this at first. Then—— Well, let an eminent member of the faculty tell what comes next.

"Inebriates," says Dr. Norman Kerr, who has made a lifelong study of narcotics, "may drink excessively of alcoholic intoxicants for years without apparent mischief. But the bodily wasting, mental decay and moral perversion of cocaine excess quickly appear and as quickly increase in intensity. In some cases where the injection into the tissues has been repeated several times daily, a state of temporary insanity has been developed, characterized by attempts at suicide.

"There is a greater sense of the loss of time than from any other narcotic. Cocaine raises the temperature and is much more short lived and quick in its toxic effects than morphine. Its tendency in an excessive dose is to delirium and raving madness. There is usually at first increased mental and bodily vigor, but this quickly gives way to a feeling of intense depression, insomnia and indications of mental collapse. The complete breakdown of the mind, with palsy of the will, take place in much shorter time than in alcoholic mental breakdown."

Physiological Action.

Cocaine is most often compared to morphine, though in reality there is no fair comparison between them. "The moderate cocaine indulger," Dr. Kerr says, "has next day no unpleasant taste in the mouth, no dry tongue, no morning headache. To the beginner, the pleasurable flow of happiness

COCAINE MAY HAVE CAUSED IT.

Dr. Stickney, Charged with the Theft of a Ring, an Inmate of a Home for Habitues.

VICTIM OF A NERVOUS DISEASE.

Dr J. B. Mattison, Who Is Treating the Young Man, Appears in Court with Him.

HELD UNTIL WEDNESDAY.

Dr. Charles E. Stickney, the young physician who was arrested in a Broadway notion store on Saturday afternoon on a charge of shoplifting, was arraigned in Jefferson Market Police Court yesterday morning. Miss Louisa Alexander told Justice Hogan that she had seen the Doctor take a silver snake ring valued at ninety-eight cents and place it in his pocket. Miss Alexander is a woman detective employed in the store.

Dr. Stickney acknowledged taking the ring, but said that he had simply placed it in his pocket through absent mindedness and had walked across the store to look at something else. He denied that he had any intention of stealing the paltry jewel, and said that he was on his way back to the ring department of the store when he was arrested.

"Dr. Stickney is a victim of the morphine or cocaine habit, is he not?" I asked. Dr. Mattison parried the question.

"Whether he was or was not is not essential," he said. "He is not now, and is suffering from a nervous disorder."

"Is it not possible that the use of drugs may have led to temporary hallucination or loss of memory?" I asked.

"It is possible, though hardly likely," said Dr. Mattison. "I never knew him to do anything unexplainable before, and my theory of it is that through pure absent mindedness he started to walk out with the cheap trinket in his hand or pocket. I venture to say that had Dr. Stickney really left the store with the ring in his possession he would have returned it or its value as soon as he discovered his mistake.

DETECTIVES OVERZEALOUS.

"In times like these, when the shops are crowded and shoplifters abound, storekeepers, and especially detectives, are apt to be overzealous. It seems to me that an explanation should have sufficed and all this sad trouble avoided, and I hope when I see the storekeeper—as I shall, upon Justice Hogan's recommendation—he will understand the mistake and be fair in the matter. It has been a very unfortunate affair for Dr. Stickney, and his nerves have received such a shock as a consequence that he is now quite ill."

According to Dr. Mattison's own theories, set forth in a pamphlet read before the Columbia Medical Society, of Washington and entitled "Cocaine Inebriety," it is thought possible that Dr. Stickney may have been under some mental delusion when he took the cheap ring.

That Dr. Stickney has been a taker of drugs Dr. Mattison does not deny, and according to his pamphlet there are many instances where physicians have become addicted to the use of the seductive drug from experiments and the use of it in their surgical and medical cases.

In his paper, which is an authority and indorsed by the British medical journal *Lancet* and others, Dr. Mattison gives particular attention to the effect of cocaine on the brain and nerve centres. In his statement of symptoms Dr. Mattison says:—"At first merely over activity, then the reaction and wreck sequelling hyperstimulation; soon come the signs of tpical wretched neurasthenia." This is the disease from which Dr. Stickney is suffering.

WHAT THE DOCTORS SA

An Economical, Handy and Safe V... cinating Needle.

BENZOL IN TRICHINOS...

Means of Preventing the ...currence of Accidents from Cocaine.

(From the European Edition of the Heral... June 14.)

IGHLY to be fe... whenever a perso... vaccinated is infe... by means of the ... cet or needle if the ... erator does not ... the precaution to st... ize the instrument ... time by passing ... through a flame or ... holding it in boi... water. To reduce ... risk to a minimum ... desire was expre... in the recent discussion on vaccination in ... Academie de Medecine de Paris that in the ... ture every person should be inoculated with ... instrument used for that one person alone.

PRECAUTIONS TO BE TAKEN.

The mishaps that are attributed to cocaine have been ... vided into two categories, according to whet... they are only temporary symptoms occur... after the administration of one or two doses ... the drug, or whether they are brought on ... its continued use; in this way an acute an... chronic form can be observed. In excepti... cases the acute form may last for a relati... long time, and place the patient in a most ... agreeable and hazardous, not to say dange... position. A case of this kind was reporte... the Academie de Medecine by M. Hallop... The patient was a man who, having a tooth ... wished extracted, underwent an injection ... about eight milligrammes of hydrochlorate ... cocaine. In a few moments he was seized ... the most serious and threatening sympto... some of which lasted nearly four months, ... especially a persistent headache, accompa... by great uneasiness, insomnia, numbness of ... limbs, and by attacks of fainting, with ver... and prostration, combined with cerebral exc... ment, manifesting itself by loquaciousness ... great agitation.

M. Magitot, secretary of the commission appointed to ... amine M. Hallopeau's case, after having g... over the history of cocaine, as a local an... thetic, and mentioned the great expansion ... this substance in surgical use, endeavored, ... one of the recent meetings of the Academie ... Medecine, to free it from the opprobrium hea... upon it. In his opinion there would be li... risk of accident if the dose is proportionate ... the surface to be acted on. The dose sho... never exceed eight to ten centigrammes, sho... not be used on persons with heart disease ... with neurosis, should never be injected int... vein, the patient should always be in the ... cumbent position, the amount should be gi... gradually and the substance used should be ... solutely pure.

The precepts formulated by M. Magitot are practically ... same as those that had already been laid do... by M. Roclus in his study of the subject, ... specially in a recent clinical lecture.

PRESERVATIVE FROM TRICHINOSIS.

...ring the year 1890

ÜBER COCA.

Von

DR. SIGM. FREUD

Secundararzt im k. k. Allgemeinen Krankenhause in Wien.

Neu durchgesehener und vermehrter Separat-Abdruck aus dem „Centralblatt für die gesammte Therapie".

WIEN. 1885.

VERLAG VON MORITZ PERLES.

THE SCIENCE OF DEDUCTION.

SHERLOCK HOLMES took his bottle from the corner of the mantelpiece, and his hypodermic syringe from its neat morocco case. With his long, white, nervous fingers he adjusted the delicate needle, and rolled back his left shirt-cuff. For some little time his eyes rested thoughtfully upon the sinewy forearm and wrist, all dotted and scarred ... th in- ... he ... own ... the

'Which is it to-day,' I asked, 'morphine or cocaine?'

He raised his eyes languidly from the old black-letter volume which he had opened.

'It is cocaine,' he said, 'a seven-per-cent. solution. Would you care to try it?'

'No, indeed,' I answered brusquely. 'My constitution has not got over the Afghan campaign yet. I cannot afford to throw any extra strain upon it.'

He smiled at my vehemence. 'Perhaps you are right, Watson,' he said. 'I suppose that its influence is physically a bad one. I find it, however, so transcendently stimulating and clarifying to the mind that its secondary action is a matter of small moment.'

'But consider!' I said earnestly. 'Count the cost! Your brain may, as you say, be

HISTO...

"THE ... OI...

NEW YOR... VAIL & CO... W. ...

FELLOW OF THE ... CAL SOCIET... NEW Y... CA...

SIGN O...

A. CON...

THIR...

GEORGE N...

SOUTHAMPTON STREET ...

TOOK AN OVERDOSE.

Dr. Charles C. Joliffe Swallowed Too Much Cocaine to Ease His Pain.

RUSHED FOR AN ANTIDOTE.

Did Not Get Relief, and Then, Anxious About His Condition, Sent for an Ambulance.

WILL PROBABLY RECOVER.

He Had Once Suffered from a Broken Arm, Which Still Caused Him Trouble.

With a face of ashy paleness, a tall man, about fifty years old, walked hurriedly into F. W. Schoomaker's drug store, at Forty-second street and Park avenue, at noon yesterday, and said excitedly to the prescription clerk:—

"I have taken an overdose of cocaine! Give me an emetic or an antidote—quickly!"

He suggested one or two antidotes himself.

"I am Dr. Charles C. Joliffe and I live at No. 444 Lexington avenue," he explained.

ANTIDOTES DID NOT HELP.

An antidote was hastily administered, but had no apparent effect, and another was given.

The dose of cocaine had apparently been a strong one, however, and Dr. Joliffe finally asked that an ambulance be called, as he thought he was in a serious condition.

Policeman Glen, of the Vanderbilt avenue sub-station, was called in and sent for an ambulance from Flower Hospital, whither Dr. Joliffe had directed that he should be taken.

TOOK IT TO EASE PAIN.

Policeman Glen said Dr. Joliffe told him that some time ago he had broken his arm, but that the injury gave him great pain, and that to ease his suffering he took a large dose of cocaine in the morning. Experiencing alarming symptoms of cocaine poisoning afterward, he had gone quickly to the drug store to procure a remedy.

At No. 444 Lexington avenue, which is a boarding house, Dr. Joliffe has a room. The landlady informed me that he was a physician not practising at present, but settling up his affairs preparatory to moving away. His wife, she said, lived in Washington.

At Flower Hospital the clerk in charge refused to give any information concerning the case. Word was sent from the hospital to the boarding house later to the effect that the patient had recovered somewhat and that his condition was not considered serious.

TZINTZATZE DIED ON THE WAY.

Curious Group of Ocean Passengers, Including a Whirling Dervish, Who Continually Prayed.

DENTIST'S MAD DEED

NOVEMBER 18, 1907

Suffering from the Effects of Cocaine, Dr. Floyd Le M. Danforth Sets His House Afire.

DANCES ABOUT THE FLAMES.

They Are Extinguished by Policemen Who Find the Man Sauntering in the Street.

HIS FAMILY HAS LEFT HIM.

Inviting a Brother Practitioner to Visit Him, He Attacks Him in the Office.

Dr. Floyd Le Mott Danforth, a victim of the cocaine habit, while under the influence of the drug yesterday morning attempted to set fire to the brown stone dwelling No. 7 East 125th street, in which he has his office. After igniting his clothes he ran to the street and told a policeman what he had done. The flames were extinguished and the Doctor was arrested. Dr. Danforth is a tall, fine looking man of middle age, with a decided military carriage. He is a graduate of Cornell University and started the practice of dentistry in Ithaca, N. Y. Several years ago he moved to this city with his wife and daughter, Margaret Danforth, who is now teaching school in New Rochelle. A brother of the dentist is Dr. Loomis L. Danforth, of No. 35 East Fifty-first street, on whose advice the man who was arrested came to this city.

Dr. Danforth established a lucrative practice here and was appointed as dentist to the Juvenile Asylum at 178th street and Amsterdam avenue and the Christian Home in East Eighty-seventh street. He was then addicted to the use of cocaine and morphine, having formed the habit five years before.

HAS BEEN IN AN ASYLUM.

On two occasions before he came to this city he became so violent that the members of his family, in order to protect themselves, had to have him committed to the Middletown Asylum for the Insane. There, in each case, he soon became rational and was discharged. For a time after the last course of treatment he abstained entirely from the use of the drugs, and his business prospered. When he came to this city, however, he resumed taking the drugs, and on several occasions his wife and daughter had to leave the house until he recovered from their effects.

He was on the verge of becoming insane in September last and threatened to do himself bodily harm. Most of his patients left him, apprehensive that he would harm them while they were under his care, and all that was left to him was his institution work. His wife and daughter left him, going to New Rochelle.

FORMER SOLDIER ENDS LIFE BY THE MEANS OF COCAINE

JOHN A. CASSIDY, WHO WAS FOUND DEAD IN HIS ROOM YESTERDAY.

John A. Cassidy Becomes Tired of Wandering and Takes Poison.

BECAUSE the gas had been burning for twenty-four hours in a room in the Holland Hotel, occupied by John A. Cassidy, who had registered as Thomas R. Riley, a chambermaid notified the chief clerk of the hotel yesterday morning at 8:30 o'clock. He forced open the door and found the body of Cassidy, clad in pajamas, stretched on the floor. On a dresser were a hypodermic syringe and two vials which had contained cocaine, leaving little doubt as to the cause of death. The Coroner was notified and the body removed to the morgue.

Papers found among the dead man's effects by attaches of the Coroner's office show that as Thomas R. Riley he had enlisted as a private in the Hospital Corps of the United States Army at Manila on November 12, 1904, and was honorably discharged on November 15th last at Angel Island. The day before he became a guest at the hotel he drew $160 back pay for services in the Army.

On the other side of the note was written in pencil: "It is my desire that no disposition be made of my body until my relatives have been communicated with."

Manila. According to Clerk O'Donnell he was very irregular in his habits, usually spending the greater part of the night away from the hotel and sleeping during the day. He always appeared cheerful, and was not a drinking man. He was last seen alive at the hotel by O'Donnell on Friday evening. Cassidy stated that he was desirous of the return from a laundry of some clothing as soon as possible.

SEPTEMBER 29, 1913.

10 KILLED, 35 HURT IN RACE RIOT BORN OF A COCAINE 'JAG'

Drug Crazed Negroes Fire at Every One in Sight in Mississippi Town.

THREE WHITE MEN AMONG THE DEAD

One of Brothers Who Started Shooting Lynched, Other Dies in Battle —Guardsmen Restore Order.

[SPECIAL DESPATCH TO THE HERALD.]

HARRISTON, Miss., Sunday.—As a result of two negro boys, brothers, going on a cocaine "jag" here to-day a race riot was started in which three white men were killed and five seriously injured; seven negroes were killed, one of them being lynched, and about thirty wounded.

A serious clash between the races was prevented by the arrival on a special train of a company of national guardsmen from Natchez.

The trouble started at about two o'clock this morning and continued intermittently until ten o'clock, when Will Jones, the younger of the two boys who started the firing, was lynched just after the soldiers arrived. His brother, Walter Jones, had been shot and killed by citizens earlier in the day.

Citizens of the town who had barricaded themselves in their homes began to emerge cautiously at ten o'clock from their hiding places and by noon the town was quiet. No more trouble is feared.

The Dead.

Hammel, G. B., Sheriff of Jefferson county, white; shot while leading a posse to where the Jones brothers were hiding.

Keinstly, Frank, white, formerly a constable, shot at his home after being called to the door.

Freeman, Claude, white, of Fayette, Miss., shot at the railway station while awaiting a train.

Johanna Alken, Tom Weeks, Jesse Thompson, Teller Warren and **Thead Grayson,** negroes, killed during promiscuous shooting.

Jones, Walter and Will, twenty and eighteen years old, respectively, negroes, the last named being lynched.

The shooting was started by Walter Jones in the negro quarter, where the negro woman and Thead Grayson were shot and killed. Walter then went to the home of his mother and aroused his eighteen-year-old brother. Together they proceeded through the main street of the little town, firing at every one in sight.

Citizens, aroused from their slumber by the shots, peered out of the windows and then hastened to cover.

Shot Down in His Home.

The two boys soon after leaving their home went to the home of Frank Keinstly and when he responded to their call to come out he was shot through the head by Walter Jones. Keinstly's son, William, saw his father fall and reached for a gun, but before he could fire he received a bullet in one of his hands.

The Yazoo and Mississippi Valley Depot is near the Keinstly home and the two negroes walked in that direction. A train had arrived from Natchez just a few moments before and the conductor, E. B. Appleby, was standing at the station talking to W. C. Bond, the flagman. Without warning the two negroes fired on them and both fell. Then the negroes directed their fire at Claude Freeman who was waiting for a train to take him to his home at Fayette, Miss. He was instantly killed. The negroes then fired into the train terrorizing the passengers.

After the guardsmen arrived the negroes barricaded themselves in the depot and fired from the windows. Hammett was the first to succumb to their bullets.

The white men finally battered down the doors and dashed through the smoke. The negroes fired their last shots and then fought with fists and teeth.

One Breaks Away, Later Lynched.

Walter Jones snapped his revolver at the first white man who entered the door, but the chamber was empty. As he dashed forward to meet the white ... he fell with three wounds, dying.

COCAINE MADE HIM A BURGLAR.

Craving for Money to Buy the Drug, Penrose Attempted to Loot the House of a Newark Neighbor.

Made from His Dead Wife's Dress, and He Had Soled His Own Shoes to Leave No Clew.

With a black mask made out of a dress that belonged to his dead wife, with shoes ingeniously soled by himself so that no clew might be left for the police, and crazed with a desire to obtain money to buy cocaine, John Penrose, thirty years old, turned burglar, was discovered in the home of Alfred V. Genung, at No. 176 North Eleventh street, Newark, at three o'clock yesterday morning, and, after a daring leap for liberty from a bathroom window, was chased and captured as he crouched, still masked, under the stoop of his father's home. He surrendered to a policeman, who, revolver in hand, threatened to kill him if he resisted.

AWFUL CRAVING FOR THE DRUG.

To Chief Hopper Penrose declared that his awful craving for cocaine had led him to attempt the burglary. He has been married twice—the first time in Harrisburg, Pa., and the second time in Richmond, Va. Both wives are dead. The second died about a year ago. Then he went to Newark, and has since been working as a freight brakeman on the Delaware, Lackawanna and Western Railroad.

Penrose used cocaine in inordinate quantities, and also took a great deal of elixir of quinine. Recently the druggists who knew him had refused him credit, and limited the quantity of the drugs which they would give him even for cash. He wanted money, and, knowing Genung to be a well-to-do business man, believed he would have money in the house on Saturday night, and that it would be easy to rob the place and get enough to keep him in drugs for a long time.

He made the black mask from a piece of a dress that belonged to his dead wife, and then gathered up around the house what tools he thought would be useful to him. He got the chloroform from a druggist by saying he wanted it to use in a rubber cement. He intended to saturate a rag and place it over the faces of the members of the family into whose sleeping rooms he went. He bemoaned the fact that he did not have a few seconds more time after jumping from Genung's bathroom window.

Gold medal presented by His Holiness Pope Leo XIII to Monsieur Angelo Mariani, in recognition of benefits received from Vin Mariani.

WHY THAT SODA WATER TASTES SO GOOD

THE Bureau of Chemistry of the United States Government has issued a warning to beware of soft drinks that contain health-destroying ingredients. To prove that it is not without adequate ground, the fact may be mentioned that recent analyses of certain such beverages by Government chemists have disclosed the presence of the deadly alkaloid cocaine in no fewer than thirty-nine of them. Many of these thirty-nine are commonly sold at soda fountains all over the United States.

Cocaine and caffeine, it has been found, and other most dangerous habit-forming drugs, are freely sold to all comers, including women and children, without the slightest warning of the harmful ingredients they contain.

Nobody will seriously contend that the Government would be likely to exaggregate or sensationalize a matter of this kind. The fact is that the drug habit—unheard of a dozen years ago—is destined apparently to become a menace in this country quite as serious as opium is to-day in China. And it is being rapidly spread by the sale of some so-called soft drinks.

According to the statements of the Bureau of Chemistry, a number of the soda fountain specialties contain cocaine and caffeine. These, by reason of their powerful stimulating properties, are the favorites. They are sold not only as beverages, but as headache remedies and nerve tonics.

The alkaloid of cocaine is, beyond a doubt, one of the most dangerous of known poisons. It is a typical habit-forming drug, and indulgence in it soon wrecks both body and mind. Compared with it, opium is harmless. Because it is so new, the consequences of its use are as yet not generally understood.

Caffeine is another powerful alkaloid—a strong nerve stimulant, and is frequently utilized by physicians, on account of its efficiency as a heart excitant, to stimulate that organ in emergencies. It is the active principle of coffee; and, likewise, curiously enough, the active principle of tea. A cup of coffee, or of tea, does not contain enough of it to do any harm, but in considerable quantities—as furnished in many soft drinks—it is injurious and even dangerous.

The caffeine employed as an ingredient of many of these drinks is extracted from the dust and stems comprising the refuse of the tea-importing houses—that is to say, from what is known in the trade as "tea sweepings." It is a very cheap commercial product, and gives to the consumer of "temperance" beverages much the same sort of encouragement as that furnished by alcohol. Sometimes, however, it is derived from acid obtained from Peruvian guano. Taken regularly, it soon creates a habit, which the consumer finds very difficult to break off.

The greatest demand for soft drinks containing such poisons is in the Southern States, where almost every drug store, candy shop and fruit stand keeps them on sale. They are even sold on the trains. People of all classes—young and old, delicate women, and even little children—consume them indiscriminately. The same mischief, however, has extended in considerable degree to all parts of the country.

To go back to some of the soft drinks, however—they are often prepared under the most unsanitary and even disgusting conditions. A cellar or tumbled down outhouse, the Bureau of Chemistry avers, is commonly chosen as a suitable place in which to do the mixing, or sometimes it is a stable. The ceiling is covered with cobwebs and dirt of all sorts and the floor is littered with filth. From the boiling kettle into which the water, sugar and drug material are dumped the steam continually rises, and, condensing on the ceiling, collects the dirt in drops, which fall back into the kettle again. As for the syrups used, they are kept in big jars, which are refilled from time to time without bothering to remove the roaches and flies which accumulate in them. Inasmuch as the product is strained before bottling such details are unimportant.

The Bureau of Chemistry has a record of 1665 cases of serious poisoning and sixty-five deaths caused by "headache remedies" containing heart-depressing coal tar drugs, many of which, as already stated, are commonly sold over the soda counter. Vastly less objectionable, though absolute frauds, of course, are a majority of the brands of "bitters," "elixirs," "cordials," "nerve tonics," "exhilarators" and "dyspepsia cures"—likewise commonly dispensed at the drug store fountain—which, as ascertained by the analyses of the Treasury Department, contain from 16 per cent to 45 per cent. of alcohol.

The cocaine so frequently employed as an ingredient of soft drinks is usually introduced into the latter in the form of an infusion, or "tea." There are beverages obtainable at the soda counter which actually contain morphine.

Undeniably this is the age of drug habits, and with a view to spreading such

"Dangerous habit-forming drugs are sold freely to Women and children."

vices to the utmost possible extent the poisons are placed attractively wi... reach of the multitude, no rest... whatever being placed by the l... their sale—even to the little c...

Young children, and ... babies, indeed, seem to be ... principal victims of the "d... ing business. Many of ... "soothing syrups" a... syrups" are heavily loa... phine—the most deadly ... opium. The same thing i... of the cough and croup r... fants.

One brand of "soothing s... alyzed at the Bureau of Chemi... found to contain nine per cent of alcohol and, for each ounce, one-seventh of a grain of morphine and two-third... of a minim of chloroform. Of cour... it is the morphine that puts the bab... to sleep—whence the "soothing" p... erties of the medicine—but the chl... form helps quite a bit.

It should be remembered that c... dren are more susceptible than gro... people to the toxic effects of opiu... and its preparations—such, for exam... ple, as morphine. It seems rather har... that they should be started in as mor... phine eaters while still in the cradle. The Government Bureau of Chemistry says that great numbers of children are killed annually by such medicines, while cough, colic and other mixtures have wiped out the lives of thousands of infants.

The journal of the Americ... ciation, February 9, 1907, m... tion of the death of twin c... weeks old at New Castle, P..., ca...ed, according to Drs. Cooper an... Wa...er, of that town, by such a mix...ure. ...he parents gave the medicine in obedie...c... to the directions on the ...ottle, ... drops every two or three ...ours ... keep the infants from cry... The... were not sick. But, after be...nning to take the stuff, they lived ...r ab... one day. When Dr. Warne... the ... tending physician, saw them ...hey w... in the last stages of opium ...oison...

In the same issue of the J...urnal ... reports of the death of a child ... ten months from anot... syrup, another death of ... f... the effects of a teething syrup, ... still another from a cough sy... Many cough and other remedies wh... have killed adults are unblushingly a... vertised, says the Chemistry Bureau, ... "safe and harmless" for babies.

Some "pain-killers" and "consum... cures" contain opium or some of ... alkaloids, such as morphine. Cocaine and chloral, the latter another dangerous enslaving drug, are sold as "asthma cures" and "hay-fever cures." The remedies offered on the market for drug habits and liquor habits nearly always contain morphine or some other habit-forming drug—the consequence of taking which is that the last state of the victim is much worse than the first.

Cures for the alcohol habit are very widely sold nowadays, and they do an immense amount of harm. Many contain either an opiate or else slow emetic. If the former, the victim is made a slave to a drug far worse than alcohol. If the latter, the object of the treatment is to render the stomach so sensitive that it will instantly reject anything of an irritating nature, such as alcohol. Treatment of the kind is of no value, and is likely to injure the digestion permanently.

Many nostrums for the liquor habit, which depend for their efficacy upon nauseating the victim, are prepared in such shape that they may be introduced into food or drink without the k... ledge of the person ... takes ... Thus it is adv... may be cured ... the fact tha... most attra... ises of the... held out, a... unfortuna... to go to ... wherewit... The resu... nil, so f... good is ... the suff... paired.

ELIXIR OF LIFE

MAY POSSIBLY BE FOUND IN

PHOSPHATE OF SODA

GLYCEROPHOSPHATE OF SODA STIMULATING

COCA COLA KING NEARING DEATH

ATLANTA, Sept. 22.—Asa G. Candler, seventy-four, millionaire Coca Cola magnate and central figure in a sensational breach of promise suit two years ago, is reported near death at his home here.

Candler is suffering from kidney disease, and attending physicians fear his death, it is said. He has been unconscious several hours. He recently returned from a European trip.

Candler gained national notice when he was sued for breach of promise by Mrs. Onezema De Bouchelle, member of an aristocratic New Orleans family. He won the suit, Mrs. De B... claim...

NOVEMBER 26, 1921

3,000 ARRESTS BY DRUG POLICE IN TEN MONTHS

Dr. Carleton Simon, Chief ... Campaign, Warns Against th... New German Coal-Tar Cocai...

STILL, IT MAY HELP CRUSAD...

Lowers Prices and the Profi... Hardly Pay for Risk—End ... "Crime Wave" Talk Predicte...

Three thousand persons have bee... arrested in ten months in this city ... drug sellers and drug users by th... Narcotic Squad of the Police Depar... ment.

Dr. Carleton Simon, Special Depu... Police Commissioner in charge of dru... traffic, directed attention to this re... cord last night and warned the publ... against an increase in addiction as ... result of the new German-made sy... thetic drugs. Dr. Simon explained:

"An investigation made for me at a cost of $10,000, privately contributed, has proved that German chemists have successfully made cocaine from coal-tar, or at least a substance so closely resembling cocaine that it is at present impossible to detect the difference. This stuff has been marketed and may call for an amendment to the Federal Drug Law to cope with it properly.

CRIME WAVE IMPOSSIBLE.

"The direct importance of th... arrests ...

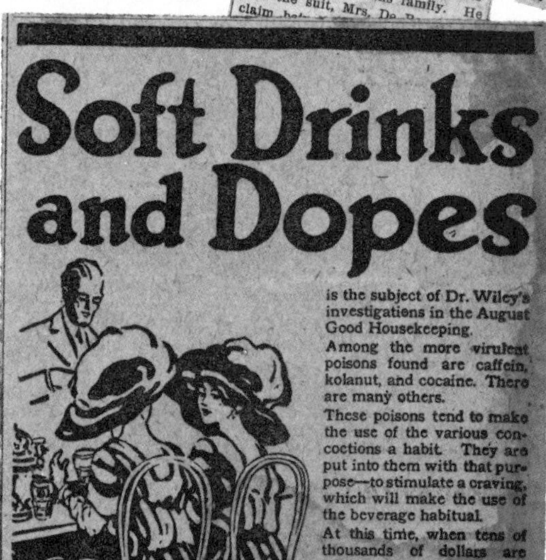

SOLUBLE HYPODERMIC TABLETS
COCAINE HYDROCHLORIDE
1-4 GR.
SHARP & DOHME
POISON

PRESCRIPTION.
This bottle contains a narcotic legally purchased by an addict. The government labels are still on the bottle.

Soft Drinks and Dopes

is the subject of Dr. Wiley's investigations in the August Good Housekeeping.

Among the more virulent poisons found are caffein, kolanut, and cocaine. There are many others.

These poisons tend to make the use of the various concoctions a habit. They are put into them with that purpose—to stimulate a craving, which will make the use of the beverage habitual.

At this time, when tens of thousands of dollars are being spent daily in the purchase of so called "soft" drinks, this article is both timely and valuable.

Parents particularly w... want to guard the childr... against this settled inroad ... the drug habit. You w... find it in the AUGUS... issue of

Good Housekeeping MAGAZINE

At All Newsstands 15 Cents the Cop...

PROGRAM

Utah-Idaho Bottlers of Carbonated Beverages

Government Chemists Find the Most Dangerous of Drugs in Many "Soft Drinks," Head-Ache "Cures" and Baby Soothing Syrups.

Testing a Bottle of Strawberry Juice in Dr. Wiley's Government Laboratory at Washington.

Der Missbrauch von Morphium und Cocaïn und seine schonende Behandlungsweise.

Für Aerzte und Laien von Dr. med. Arnold Fromme

Besitzer einer Heilanstalt für Erziehungskuren in Stellingen (Bez. Hamburg).

Zweite verbesserte und vermehrte Auflage von „Die moderne Behandlung der Morphiumkra

2 Mk. 70 Pfge.

onegen Verlag

Leipzig.

1899

End of Cocaine Seen; Harmless Drug Is Found

By WILLIAM HILLMAN
Universal Service Staff Correspondent.
BERLIN, Feb. 26.

A NEW drug, perkain, having the narcotic qualities of cocaine without its harmful effects, has been discovered by Dr. Helmut Richter, head of the Erlanger University ear, nose and throat clinic.

Physicians who have witnissed the use of perkain predict coacine will never be nessed the use of perkain sion, making its complete olition possible.

en more sensational, has been the em- f this drug with combination and pain-

"PROSIT! AFTER US A GENERATION OF COCAINE FIENDS!"
One of the many cartoons on the prohibition campaign being waged in Germany. From Simplicissimus, Munich.

Why Paris Needs to Reform!

The Wicked Extravagances that Have Caused a Campaign for the Simple Virtues in the City that Sets the Pace for the World's Frivolities.

The Artist Here Satirically Portrays the Parisienne trying to Decide Whether She Shall Wear Her Mask of Pearls or Her Mask of Gold and Rubies.

Paris, April 23.

FROM every serious element in French national life, from the Church, from the most refined circles of fashionable society and from the most thoughtful section of the press comes an insistent demand that Paris shall reform, that she shall no longer compromise the reputation of France by setting an example of wicked extravagance and shameless frivolity to the whole world.

Cardinal Amette, Archbishop of Paris, recently issued a protest against immodest fashions and cognate extravagances. Other heads of the Church made similar protests. The serious women of France have formed the League of Patriotic Frenchwomen. A committee of leading society women of this league, headed by the Duchesse de Maille, is making war against slit skirts, outrageously low corsages, colored wigs and other immodest extravagances of fashion In a manifesto the committee says:

"We appeal to all society women to protest against the fashions that are being forced on us. We ask all young and elegant women who give the tone to fashion not only to abstain from following the prevailing objectionable modes, but to fight them by setting an example worthy to be followed."

It is asserted that not only are the fashions immodest, but that the Parisian women are adorning themselves with a wealth of jewels and costly materials that must be a cause of deep-rooted demoralization. It is feared that many Parisiennes have had their little heads so turned that they will shrink from no step to keep up with their most extravagant sisters.

A striking proof of the extremes to which luxury and eccentricity are now carried in Paris is furnished by the "Gazette du Bon Ton" of Paris, a brilliantly illustrated and exquisitely printed publication, which well describes itself as devoted to the "arts, modes and frivolities." To its pages contribute such brilliant illustrators as Gose, Boutet de Monvel, George Barbier, Simone Puget and others.

Among many things we learn that the Parisienne has taken to wearing masks of pearls

A "Salome" Costume Designed for a Leading Society Woman of Paris. Her Figure Is Revealed by Her Transparent Costume, and Her Fingernails Are Dyed Red. A Very Striking Evidence of the Extreme Tastes of Parisian Society. Drawing by Puget in the "Gazette du Bon Ton," the Chief Organ of Paris Smart Society.

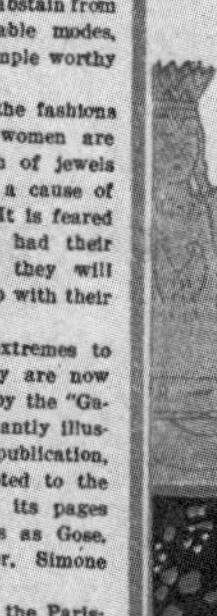

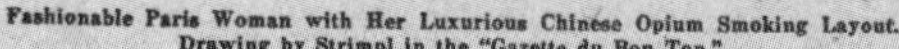

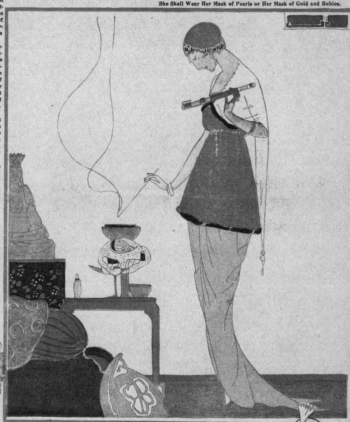

Fashionable Paris Woman with Her Luxurious Chinese Opium Smoking Layout. Drawing by Strimpl in the "Gazette du Bon Ton."

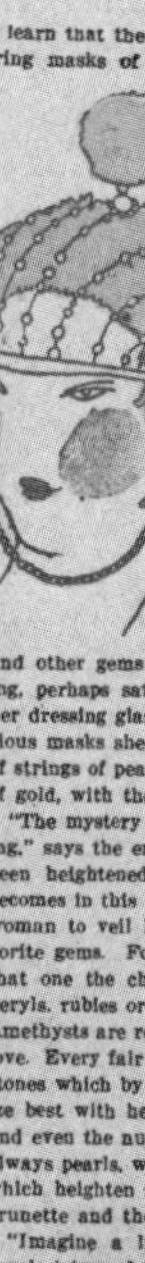

The Parisienne at the Fountain Which Pours Rare Wine. A Mere Suggestion of the Ruinous Extremes to Which Luxury and Extravagance Are Now Carried in Paris. Drawing by G. Barbier.

and other gems at her entertainments. One drawing, perhaps satirically, shows a Parisienne before her dressing glass trying to decide which of her precious masks she shall wear. On her face is a mask of strings of pearls, while in her hands she holds one of gold, with the eyeholes adorned with rubies.

"The mystery of the mask, already so very exciting," says the enthusiastic French writer, "has thus been heightened by an unheard-of seduction. It becomes in this way more personal, permitting every woman to veil her features with a web of her favorite gems. For this fair one the aquamarine, for that one the chrysoprase, for others coryndons or beryls, rubies or moonstones, sapphires or diamonds. Amethysts are reserved for those who weep for a lost love. Every fair one will choose at the jeweller's the stones which by their color and their light harmonize best with her complexion, the color of her hair and even the nuance of her glance. Then there are always pearls, which are becoming to all women and which heighten alike the charms of the blonde, the brunette and the auburn-haired.

"Imagine a little mask made of a network of pearls trimmed around the eyes with little circles of diamonds! Imagine, too, one of those big Venetian masks, such as the women of Casanova wear, woven of little diamonds, with eyeholes bordered with emeralds! Imagine a veil of gold tulle embroidered with rubies and opals, through the folds of which one may guess at the features of a beautiful face ardently desired! Imagine a torrent of sapphires and moonstones falling from a diadem or Grecian helmet in a long fringe, which the least movement causes to glisten and undulate in the light, down to the bare shoulders, illuminating the white splendors of the flesh!

"These masks of precious stones recall to our eyes the splendors of the fantastic past. They bring before us processions of the princesses and courtesans of legend and history, of the Queen of Sheba and Semiramis, of Cleopatra and Akedysseril. They take us back to the lost civilizations of India, of Persia and of Egypt. They help us, without losing our sense of the delightful present, to make those journeys into the past dear to all lovers of beauty, to dwell in 'the palaces of silk and gold in Ecbatana,' beloved by Verlaine; to the palaces of Babylon and Tyre, of Carthage and Golconda, of Damas and Ispahan, to lands of sunlight and passion."

The moralist who examines the pages of the Parisian magazine will conclude that Paris is doing its best to excel Babylon and Carthage.

One charming picture shows us the Parisienne in her "smoking costume." It leads us to believe that the fashionable Paris woman entertains herself and her friends with a pipe of opium at her "afternoons at home." In another drawing we see that a Parisienne wears stockings, largely openwork, that are visible through her diaphanous costume.

Eccentric and extravagant new fashions without number are reported. One woman maintains a special hothouse to grow a new and unique species of orchid to match her complexion. Another keeps only yellow servants for similar reasons.

From wearing colored wigs to coloring the skin was an easy and perhaps natural step. At many a Parisian dinner party you see every woman at the table with face, bust and arms colored red, green, orange, purple, blue or whatever color suits her fancy best! Wigs are usually worn to match.

Extraordinary extravagances in stockings are whispered. These delicate and perishable articles sometimes cost as much as 25,000 froncs a pair. In such cases they are, of course, specially woven for the wearer. They are made with curious openwork designs, and trimmed with precious stones.

The frantic extravagance of Paris affects the political welfare of France. The Calmette-Caillaux tragedy is regarded as an outcome of the prevailing tendency. Caillaux is said to have committed the dubious acts that excited Calmette's attacks in order to satisfy the demands of his wife and perhaps other leaders of fashion.

Earnest radicals and socialists from the country and the poor districts easily succumb to the wiles of the sirens of society. They pour the wealth entrusted to them by the people into the giddy whirl of luxury and frivolity. Hence the stern demand that Paris shall reform immediately.

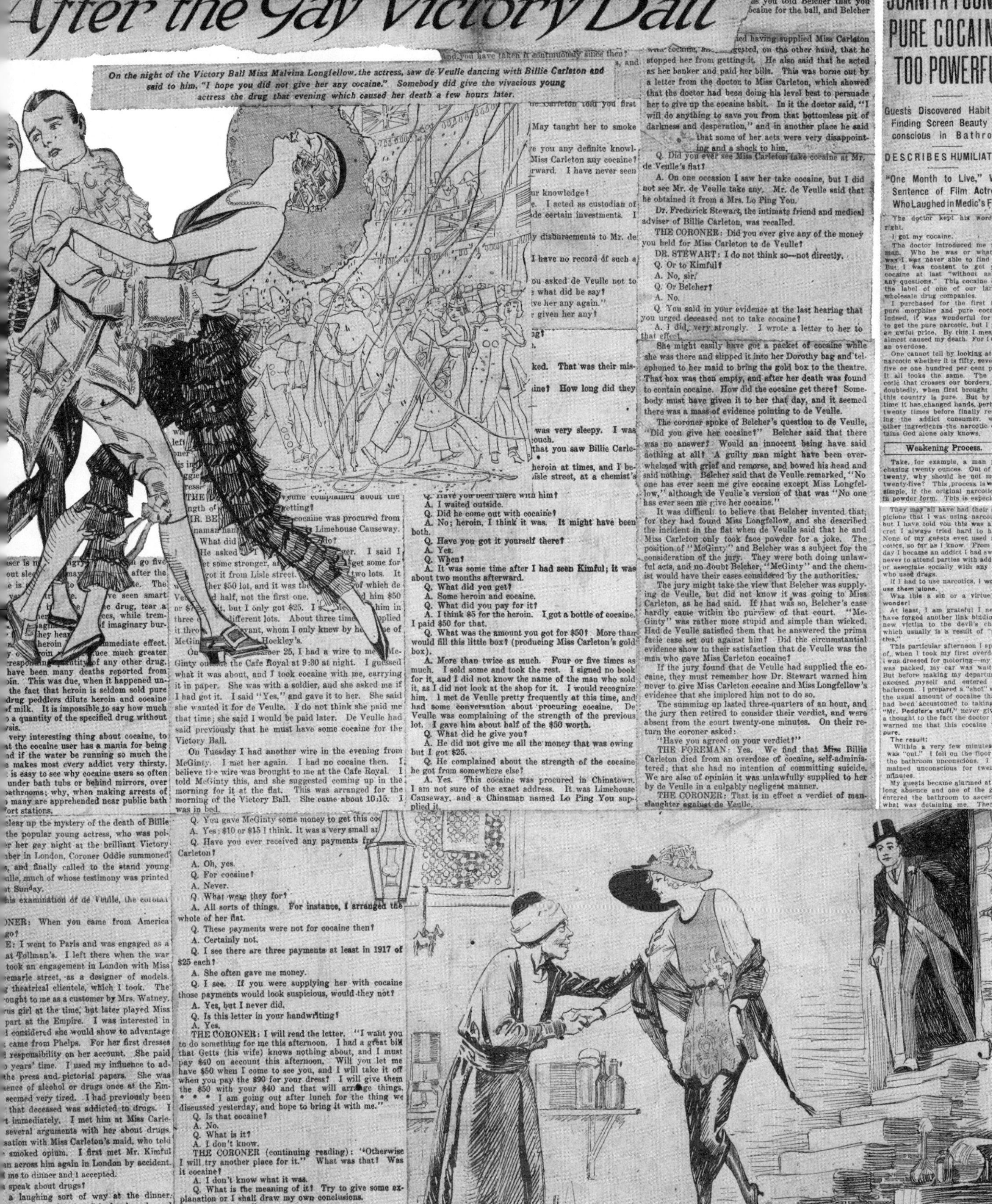

After the Gay Victory Ball

On the night of the Victory Ball Miss Malvina Longfellow, the actress, saw de Veulle dancing with Billie Carleton and said to him, "I hope you did not give her any cocaine." Somebody did give the vivacious young actress the drug that evening which caused her death a few hours later.

...you told the coroner that Miss ... cocaine for the ball?

...as you told Belcher that you ... cocaine for the ball, and Belcher

...ied having supplied Miss Carleton with cocaine, and suggested, on the other hand, that he stopped her from getting it. He also said that he acted as her banker and paid her bills. This was borne out by a letter from the doctor to Miss Carleton, which showed that the doctor had been doing his level best to persuade her to give up the cocaine habit. In it the doctor said, "I will do anything to save you from that bottomless pit of darkness and desperation," and in another place he said that some of her acts were very disappointing and a shock to him.

Q. Did you ever see Miss Carleton take cocaine at Mr. de Veulle's flat?

A. On one occasion I saw her take cocaine, but I did not see Mr. de Veulle take any. Mr. de Veulle said that he obtained it from a Mrs. Lo Ping You.

Dr. Frederick Stewart, the intimate friend and medical adviser of Billie Carleton, was recalled.

THE CORONER: Did you ever give any of the money you held for Miss Carleton to de Veulle?

DR. STEWART: I do not think so—not directly.

Q. Or to Kimful?

A. No, sir.

Q. Or Belcher?

A. No.

Q. You said in your evidence at the last hearing that you urged deceased not to take cocaine?

A. I did, very strongly. I wrote a letter to her to that effect.

...and you have taken it continuously since then?

...s, and

...Carleton told you first

...May taught her to smoke

...e you any definite knowl-... Miss Carleton any cocaine? ...rward. I have never seen

...ur knowledge? ...e. I acted as custodian of ...de certain investments. I

...y disbursements to Mr. de

...I have no record of such a

...ou asked de Veulle not to ...what did he say? ...ive her any again." ...r given her any?

...ng?

...ked. That was their mis-

...ine? How long did they

...was very sleepy. I was ...ouch. ...that you saw Billie Carle-

...heroin at times, and I be-...isle street, at a chemist's

Q. Have you been there with him?

A. I waited outside.

Q. Did he come out with cocaine?

A. No; heroin, I think it was. It might have been both.

Q. Have you got it yourself there?

A. Yes.

Q. When?

A. It was some time after I had seen Kimful; it was about two months afterward.

Q. What did you get?

A. Some heroin and cocaine.

Q. What did you pay for it?

A. I think $5 for the heroin. I got a bottle of cocaine. I paid $50 for that.

Q. What was the amount you got for $50? More than would fill this little box? (producing Miss Carleton's gold box).

A. More than twice as much. Four or five times as much. I sold some and took the rest. I signed no book for it, and I did not know the name of the man who sold it, as I did not look at the shop for it. I would recognize him. I met de Veulle pretty frequently at this time, and had some conversation about procuring cocaine. De Veulle was complaining of the strength of the previous lot. I gave him about half of the $50 worth.

Q. What did he give you?

A. He did not give me all the money that was owing but I got $25.

Q. He complained about the strength of the cocaine he got from somewhere else?

A. Yes. This cocaine was procured in Chinatown. I am not sure of the exact address. It was Limehouse Causeway, and a Chinaman named Lo Ping You supplied it.

...user is n... ...go five ...out sle... ...after the ...e is ... ...e. The ...ve seen smart ...e drug, tear a ...ces, while trem- ...f imaginary bur- ...they hear ...heroin ...mmediate effect. ...oin ...uce much greater ...responding quantity of any other drug. ...have been many deaths reported from ...oin. This was due, when it happened un- the fact that heroin is seldom sold pure ...drug peddlers dilute heroin and cocaine ...f milk. It is impossible to say how much ...a quantity of the specified drug without ...ysis.

...very interesting thing about cocaine, to ...at the cocaine user has a mania for being ...d if the water be running so much the ...e makes most every addict very thirsty. ...is easy to see why cocaine users so often under bath tubs or behind mirrors, over ...bathrooms; why, when making arrests of ...many are apprehended near public bath ...fort stations.

...clear up the mystery of the death of Billie ... the popular young actress, who was poi-...r her gay night at the brilliant Victory ...ber in London, Coroner Oddie summoned ...s, and finally called to the stand young ...ulle, much of whose testimony was printed ...t Sunday.

...his examination of de Veulle, the coroner

...NER: When you came from America ...go?

...E: I went to Paris and was engaged as a ...at Tollman's. I left there when the war ...took an engagement in London with Miss ...emarle street, as a designer of models. ...theatrical clientele, which I took. The ...ought to me as a customer by Mrs. Watney. ...rus girl at the time, but later played Miss ...part at the Empire. I was interested in ...considered she would show to advantage ...came from Phelps. For her first dresses ...responsibility on her account. She paid ...years' time. I used my influence to ad-...the press and pictorial papers. She was ...ence of alcohol or drugs once at the Em-...seemed very tired. I had previously been ...that deceased was addicted to drugs. I ...t immediately. I met him at Miss Carle-...several arguments with her about drugs. ...sation with Miss Carleton's maid, who told ...smoked opium. I first met Mr. Kimful ...an across him again in London by accident. ...me to dinner and I accepted.

...speak about drugs?

...a laughing sort of way at the dinner. ...got any cocaine, but I had a brandy and ...Miss Carleton came to stay at my flat it ...he was worried about an American officer ...tened to kill her. I was not present when ...made, but I was present when an alterca-...e between Miss Carleton and the American ...to telephone for the Provost Marshal. On ...ion the officer tried to break open the door ...get at Miss Carleton.

...TTERTON: Was it a fact that he had pro-... Carleton and that she would not accept him? ...at was the reason. The officer was sent ...ica by the military authorities. It was on ...e distress occasioned by this officer's atten-...s Carleton asked to be allowed to stay at ...member Belcher calling late one evening.

...ressed ...THE ... complained about the ...ngth of ... getting? ...MR. BE... cocaine was procured from ...naman ... Limehouse Causeway. ...What did ... do? ...He asked ... I said I ...et some stronger, a... get some for ...got it from Lisle street. ... two lots. It ...w... her $50 lot, and it was the ... of which de Ve... d half, not the first one. ... him $50 or $7... it, but I only got $25. I s... him in three ... different lots. About three time... plied it thro... vant, whom I only knew by h... e of McGin... Hockley's.

On ... ber 25, I had a wire to me ... McGinty ou... the Cafe Royal at 9:30 at night. I guessed what it was about, and I took cocaine with me, carrying it in paper. She was with a soldier, and she asked me if I had got it. I said "Yes," and gave it to her. She said she wanted it for de Veulle. I do not think she paid me that time; she said I would be paid later. De Veulle had said previously that he must have some cocaine for the Victory Ball.

On Tuesday I had another wire in the evening from McGinty. I met her again. I had no cocaine then. I believe the wire was brought to me at the Cafe Royal. I told McGinty this, and she suggested coming up in the morning for it at the flat. This was arranged for the morning of the Victory Ball. She came about 10:15. I was in bed.

Q. You gave McGinty some money to get this co...

A. Yes; $10 or $15 I think. It was a very small a...

Q. Have you ever received any payments fr... Carleton?

A. Oh, yes.

Q. For cocaine?

A. Never.

Q. What were they for?

A. All sorts of things. For instance, I arranged the whole of her flat.

Q. These payments were not for cocaine then?

A. Certainly not.

Q. I see there are three payments at least in 1917 of $25 each?

A. She often gave me money.

Q. I see. If you were supplying her with cocaine those payments would look suspicious, would they not?

A. Yes, but I never did.

Q. Is this letter in your handwriting?

A. Yes.

THE CORONER: I will read the letter. "I want you to do something for me this afternoon. I had a great bill that Getts (his wife) knows nothing about, and I must pay $40 on account this afternoon. Will you let me have $50 when I come to see you, and I will take it off when you pay the $90 for your dress? I will give them the $50 with your $40 and that will arrange things. * * * I am going out after lunch for the thing we discussed yesterday, and hope to bring it with me."

Q. Is that cocaine?

A. No.

Q. What is it?

A. I don't know.

THE CORONER (continuing reading): "Otherwise I will try another place for it." What was that? Was it cocaine?

A. I don't know what it was.

Q. What is the meaning of it? Try to give some explanation or I shall draw my own conclusions.

A. I don't recollect.

Q. Look at this paper which was found in the deceased's bag. Do you see your name there three or four times? On the top line it says, "Reggie," and in quotation marks "Pills." What do "pills" mean?

A. You see, she wanted to be wonderfully brilliant for the ball, and I was to make her a wonderful frock.

Q. Isn't it rather odd she should put the word "pills" like that? Does that suggest anything to you? Did you ever speak of cocaine as "pills"?

A. Never.

Q. You had been warned about giving Miss Carleton cocaine by Dr. Stewart?

A. Yes.

Q. And by Miss Longfellow?

A. Yes.

She might easily have got a packet of cocaine while she was there and slipped it into her Dorothy bag and telephoned to her maid to bring the gold box to the theatre. That box was then empty, and after her death was found to contain cocaine. How did the cocaine get there? Somebody must have given it to her that day, and it seemed there was a mass of evidence pointing to de Veulle.

The coroner spoke of Belcher's question to de Veulle, "Did you give her cocaine?" Belcher said that there was no answer? Would an innocent being have said nothing at all? A guilty man might have been overwhelmed with grief and remorse, and bowed his head and said nothing. Belcher said that de Veulle remarked, "No one has ever seen me give cocaine except Miss Longfellow," although de Veulle's version of that was "No one has ever seen me give her cocaine."

It was difficult to believe that Belcher invented that, for they had found Miss Longfellow, and she described the incident in the flat when de Veulle said that he and Miss Carleton only took face powder for a joke. The position of "McGinty" and Belcher was a subject for the consideration of the jury. They were both doing unlawful acts, and no doubt Belcher, "McGinty" and the chemist would have their cases considered by the authorities.

The jury might take the view that Belcher was supplying de Veulle, but did not know it was going to Miss Carleton, as he had said. If that was so, Belcher's case hardly came within the purview of that court. "McGinty" was rather more stupid and simple than wicked. Had de Veulle satisfied them that he answered the prima facie case set out against him? Did the circumstantial evidence show to their satisfaction that de Veulle was the man who gave Miss Carleton cocaine?

If the jury found that de Veulle had supplied the cocaine, they must remember how Dr. Stewart warned him never to give Miss Carleton cocaine and Miss Longfellow's evidence that she implored him not to do so.

The summing up lasted three-quarters of an hour, and the jury then retired to consider their verdict, and were absent from the court twenty-one minutes. On their return the coroner asked:

"Have you agreed on your verdict?"

THE FOREMAN: Yes. We find that Miss Billie Carleton died from an overdose of cocaine, self-administered; that she had no intention of committing suicide. We are also of opinion it was unlawfully supplied to her by de Veulle in a culpably negligent manner.

THE CORONER: That is in effect a verdict of manslaughter against de Veulle.

JUANITA FOUND PURE COCAINE TOO POWERFUL

Guests Discovered Habit on Finding Screen Beauty Unconscious in Bathroom

DESCRIBES HUMILIATION

"One Month to Live," Was Sentence of Film Actress, Who Laughed in Medic's Face

The doctor kept his word all right.

I got my cocaine.

The doctor introduced me to a man. Who he was or what he was I was never able to find out. But I was content to get pure cocaine at last "without asking any questions." This cocaine bore the label of one of our largest wholesale drug companies.

I purchased for the first time pure morphine and pure cocaine. Indeed, it was wonderful for me to get the pure narcotic, but I paid an awful price. By this I mean it almost caused my death. For I took an overdose.

One cannot tell by looking at the narcotic whether it is fifty, seventy-five or one hundred per cent pure. It all looks the same. The narcotic that crosses our borders, undoubtedly, when first brought into this country is pure. But by the time it has changed hands, perhaps twenty times before finally reaching the addict consumer, what other ingredients the narcotic contains God alone only knows.

Weakening Process.

Take, for example, a man purchasing twenty ounces. Out of the twenty, why should he not make twenty-five? This process is very simple, if the original narcotic is in powder form. This is especially

They may all have had their suspicions that I was using narcotics but I have told you this was a secret I always tried hard to hide. None of my guests ever used narcotics, so far as I know. From the day I became an addict I had sworn never to attend parties with addicts or associate socially with any one who used drugs.

If I had to use narcotics, I would use them alone.

Was this a sin or a virtue? I wonder!

At least, I am grateful I never have forged another link binding a new victim to the devil's chain, which usually is a result of "parties."

This particular afternoon I speak of, when I took my first overdose, I was dressed for motoring—my bag was packed, my car was waiting. But before making my departure I excused myself and entered the bathroom. I prepared a "shot" with the usual amount of cocaine that I had been accustomed to taking of "Mr. Peddler's stuff," never giving a thought to the fact the doctor had warned me that this cocaine was pure.

The result:

Within a very few minutes, I was "out." I fell on the floor of the bathroom unconscious. I remained unconscious for twenty minutes.

My guests became alarmed at my long absence and one of the girls entered the bathroom to ascertain what was detaining me. There I

In the early morning hours Billie Carleton and de Veulle went down to the wretched slums of London's Chinatown and sought cocaine in the evil den of Don Kimful, an Egyptian.

The World.

"Circulation Books Open to All."

"Circulation Books Open to All."

[19]15, by The Press Publishing [C]o. (The New York World).

NEW YORK, THURSDAY, SEPTEMBER 9, 1915.

PRICE { ONE CENT in Greater New York and Jersey City. TWO CENTS outside of Greater New York, Jersey City and on

CAMPING WITH 19,000 S

Weird rites performed by spiritualist[s], clairvoyants, "healers," astrologers, etc., six weeks' annual encampment at Lily [Dale]

A Double-Page Illustrated Article in the Magazin[e] NEXT SUNDAY'S WOR[LD]

GRAND DUKE GOES

GERMANY, IN NOTE

ENVOY OF AUSTRIA AFTER INTERVIEW WITH LANSING.

WILSON TO ACT ON DUMBA

"COCAINE KING" THOMAS FACES PRISON IN PARIS

Member of a Distinguished American Family Is Betrayed by a Jealous Sweetheart.

FORMED BIG "DOPE" TRUST ON STANDARD OIL MODEL.

"High Society Would Be Shaken," Police Say, if Names of Patrons Were Published.

(Special Cable Despatch to The World.)

PARIS, Sept. 8.—Henry Goddard Thomas—whom the police call "The King of Cocaine," and who is facing long imprisonment for his self-confessed attempt to monopolize the illegal sale of habit-forming drugs in France—claimed to-day to have fine American blood in his veins. To an acquaintance who visited him, Thomas declared he is the son of the late Gen. Henry G. Thomas, U. S. A., and a nephew of William Widgery Thomas, long American Minister to Sweden and Norway. He also says he is a graduate of a university in the West of the United States, but he would not name the university.

High Society Resorts.

Since Thomas's arrest and confession four days ago the Paris police have raided eighteen opium dens, whose proprietors all obtained the drug from Thomas. Six of these establishments, in fashionable quarters of the city, were sumptuously furnished and patronized by women and men of the highest social position.

"If the law permitted us to arrest the drug fiends we found in these six aristocratic dens and to reveal their names, Paris society would be shaken to its foundations," said a high police official to The World correspondent to-day.

Only foreigners were admitted to one of these resorts, and it is understood that many Americans frequented it.

Thomas's arrest was caused by the perfidy of one of his sweethearts of the underworld to whom he had supplied cocaine regularly. Jealous of him, she plotted with the police to betray him in the very act of handing her a package of the drug.

The police have obtained indubitable evidence that Thomas was scheming to obtain a monopoly of the supply of opium, cocaine and hashish and to form a huge organization in the underworld to distribute and sell the drugs throughout France.

Trust Like Standard Oil.

"Thomas's scheme was almost as big as your Standard Oil Company," a detective investigating the case said to The World correspondent.

"Thomas, who gave Dakota as his place of residence, has passed most of his time in Paris for several years. Formerly he was connected with a tourist agency here. A drug fiend himself, he was quick to perceive the increase in the use of morphia, cocaine and hashish, which is ascribed to the nervous strain caused by the war and to the Government's prohibition of the manufacture and sale of absinthe. He began to buy drugs and got them in fast increasing quantities.

At first he disposed of the drugs through women of the half-world, then through druggists and finally through agencies he established. He had a dozen such centres for the wholesale distribution of the drug in Paris alone, and the police are searching for agencies of his in Marseilles and Bordeaux.

Many druggists have been arrested charged with selling cocaine bought from Thomas or his agents, and detectives are still busy tracing other ramifications of his scheme.

His profits were large, but he had little cash when arrested, because he had spent a great sum in enlarging his organization.

Suspected of Being a Spy.

The fact that some of the drugs in his possession came from a German firm aroused the suspicion that he might be a spy, but no evidence of that has been discovered.

The family of which Thomas claims to be a member is the oldest in Portland, Me. Gen. Henry G. Thomas, who died in 1897, served with high distinction in the Civil War; he was the first regular army officer to accept the Colonelcy of colored troops. William Widgery Thomas, after being graduated at Bowdoin College, entered the American Diplomatic Service as a bearer of despatches and rose to be Minister to Norway and Sweden. Both were sons of W. W. Thomas, who once was Mayor of Portland, and grandsons of Elias Thomas, Treasurer of Maine, who married Elizabeth, daughter of William Widgery, a Judge and member of Congress. The name Goddard comes into the family on the distaff side. Thomas's grandmother was descended from Dr. John Goddard of New Hampshire, who declined a United States Senatorship.

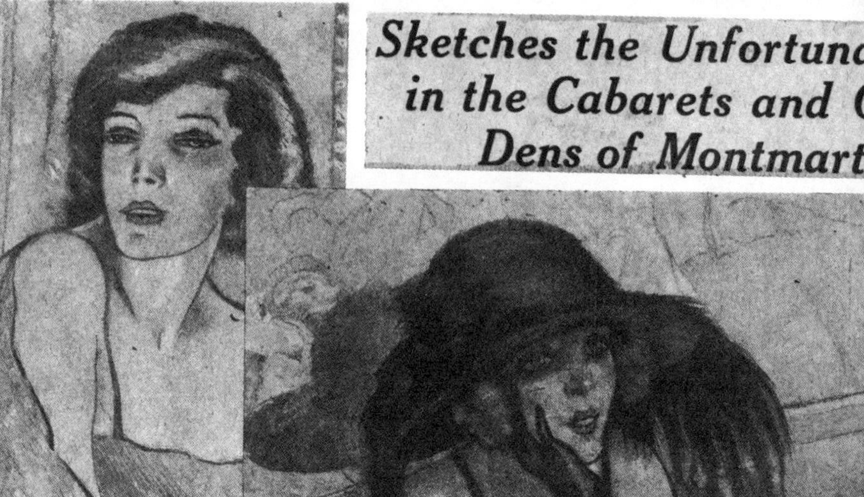

Sketches the Unfortuna[te]
in the Cabarets and [...]
Dens of Montmart[re]

Pale Jeanne No. 1—"I Must Have Some More Cocaine."

Little Pale Jeanne No. 2—Waiting for the Drug in the Cabaret.

A Slave of the Cocaine Habit Taking a Sniff of "Snow" in a Montmartre Retiring Room.

DRUG RING IN PARIS PREYS ON WOMEN VICTIMS OF WAR

Girl, Crazed by Cocaine, Falls in Street—Police Arrest Alleged Leaders Who Sold Narcotics to Those Who Had Lost Husbands and Sweethearts.

APRIL. 6, 1915.

(Special Cable Despatch to The World.)

PARIS, April 5.—A young girl, the daughter of well-to-do parents, was overcome by the effects of cocaine and fainted to-day in a street in the Latin Quarter. Two hours later, through startling disclosures she made to the police, half a dozen men and women of the Apache type were under arrest, the "cocaine ring" was shattered and a city-wide campaign was under way to rid Paris of the swarm of drug users and drug purveyors, who have increased alarmingly since the war began.

Through the evidence furnished by the drug-crazed girl, the police discovered that an organized gang exists in this city which not only deals in drugs of all kinds, but systematically seeks to teach the drug habit to thousands of men and women in order that the gang's illicit sales may increase correspondingly.

The evidence now in the hands of the police shows a startling increase in the number of drug users in the city, and especially among the women. Unnerved by the deaths of husbands, brothers and sweethearts at the front, many women of Paris have needed little urging from the drug gang's agents to induce them to become addicted to the use of cocaine and morphine to bring about forgetfulness of their sorrows.

Men who were formerly slaves to the absinthe habit, and who now find that drink impossible to obtain because of Government edict, also have taken readily to the use of drugs.

The drug habit, apparently, is not restricted to any one class, as is shown by the strong demand by the press that the police close to men and women of all stations the opportunity to obtain habit-forming drugs.

"The headquarters of the gang apparently was in a Montmartre hotel, where the girl, central figure in the disclosures, had indulged in a cocaine "spree" just prior to her collapse in the street.

In this hotel the Parisian police arrested Anna Reuillon, twenty-five years old, known in the underworld of Paris as La Grange Nana and believed to be the brains of the drug gang. They also took into custody a Frenchman, a Swiss, an Algerian and two women even younger than Nana, all of whom were well dressed and plentifully supplied with money though admitting that they lacked definite occupations.

La Grange Nana recently was tried before a court martial for causing the desertion of a drug-mad French soldier, but was acquitted owing to inconclusive evidence.

[...] that they [...] cocaine, morphine and other drugs from the manager of a big Paris pharmacy. This man, whose name the police will not disclose, is thought to control the source of all the drugs secretly being sold in this city since the war began. Paris detectives are watching him closely to obtain further evidence prior to his arrest, which is expected at any moment.

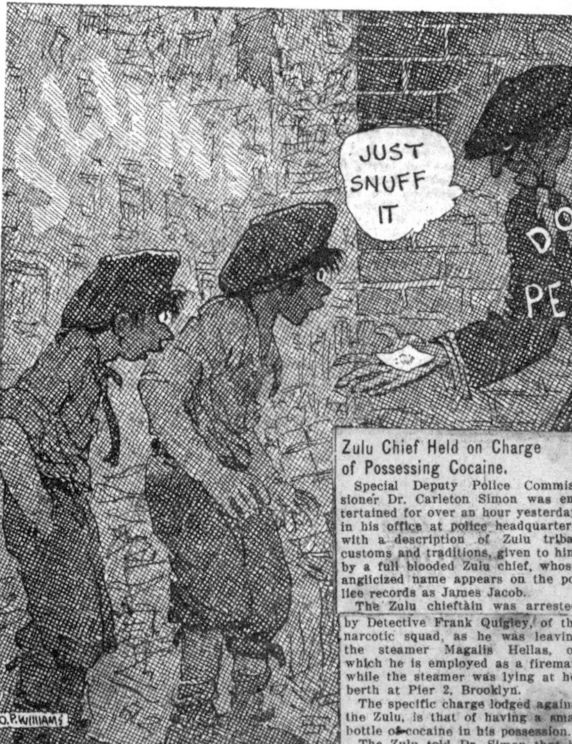

Zulu Chief Held on Charge of Possessing Cocaine.

Special Deputy Police Commissioner Dr. Carleton Simon was entertained for over an hour yesterday in his office at police headquarters with a description of Zulu tribal customs and traditions, given to him by a full blooded Zulu chief, whose anglicized name appears on the police records as James Jacob.

The Zulu chieftain was arrested by Detective Frank Quigley, of the narcotic squad, as he was leaving the steamer Magalis Hellas, on which he is employed as a fireman, while the steamer was lying at her berth at Pier 2, Brooklyn.

The specific charge lodged against the Zulu, is that of having a small bottle of cocaine in his possession.

The Zulu told Dr. Simon that he was chief of the Zulu Nasi Sillo Tribe, at Negeria, on the West Coast of Africa.

Paris Addicts

omen

Little Pale Jeanne No. 3—The Hallucination of the Cocaine.

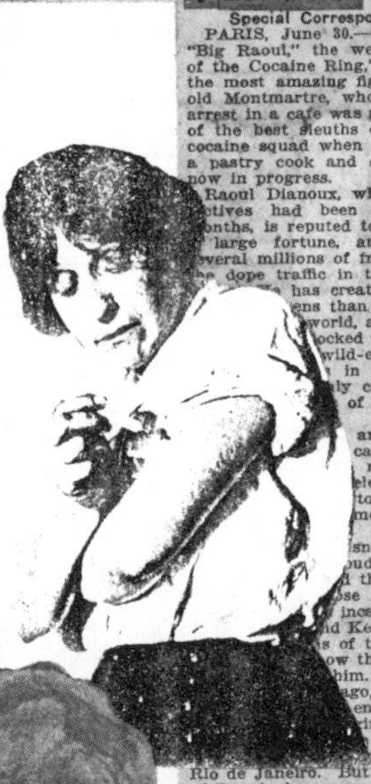

DOPE KING THREATENS VENGEANCE

Amazing Career of Man Who "Made More Artificial Heavens Than Any Dealer in the World"

JULY 1, 1923

Special Correspondence.

PARIS, June 30.—The trial of "Big Raoul," the wealthy "King of the Cocaine Ring," and one of the most amazing figures in gay old Montmartre, whose dramatic arrest in a cafe was made by two of the best sleuths of the Paris cocaine squad when disguised as a pastry cook and chauffeur, is now in progress.

Raoul Dianoux, whom the detectives had been seeking for months, is reputed to have made large fortune, amounting to several millions of francs, out of the dope traffic in the past two ... has created more ar... ens than any cocaine ... world, and now that ... locked up in La Ro... wild-eyed habitues ... in the Pigalle ... ly clamoring for ... of brain-killing

... arrest of "his ... called him, has ... many smart ... elegant boule... to drive up to ... ment in No. 10 ... to replenish ... snuff boxes.

... oudly proclaims ... threatens dire ... se who are re... incarceration.

... nd Kerbrat, two of ... s of the Paris co... ow their man, and ... him. They knew ... ago, when he is ... engaged in the ... irls, whom he ... mysterious ... Aires and Rio de Janeiro. But the methods of Raoul always were so cleverly carried out that it was impossible to catch him. Raoul and two of his men usually met in a little cafe about noontime. "I have a customer for two jade necklaces and an amber lavalliere," one of the lieutenants would say to Raoul, who would appear only slightly interested. Then, after a few indolent puffs at his cigarette:

"What are they willing to pay?" Raoul would ask. The sum mentioned would never satisfy him, however, and after some bargaining the two lieutenants would leave disappointed.

And, yet, within the week, two pretty black-haired girls (the jade necklaces) and a plump blonde (the amber lavalliere) would be on their way to South America to be employed there as "shop girls" in some large establishment. They would be well provided with funds and apparently authentic letters from their future employers.

In this manner more than three hundred good-looking girls of Paris are believed by the police to have been "exported" by Big Raoul—never to be heard from again.

In 1919 Raoul was arrested on the charge of white slavery, but it was impossible to prove the full charges against him and he escaped with a sentence of eight months' solitary confinement.

Soon after his release from prison Big Raoul started a new firm in the Rue de Bruxelles, a firm of importers this time, but without name over his door or letter-heads on his stationery.

He began to import cocaine from Germany and other sources, and soon employed an army of salesmen in Montmartre. These lieutenants were recruited among the many unemployed who were willing to sell human souls to the master in return for a few small banknotes.

The business of Big Raoul became more and more lucrative, but the detectives were not able to catch him in flagrante delicto until a few days ago, when a handsome motor-car was seen stopping in front of 10, Rue de Bruxelles.

The two sleuths, Martin and Kerbrat, had rented a room across the way, and had been watching the place for months. During all this time they had seen nothing out of the ordinary, but when the motor-car stopped a moment in front of the house under observation they noticed a strange little scene.

A woman's bejewelled hand was protruding from the car window and beckoning to a man who was standing near the entrance of No. 10, but the man did not move. He simply stared at the occupant of the car and refused to understand.

The motions of the hand became more frantic, thumping impatiently upon the frame of the open car window, but the man paid no attention to it. Instead, he shrugged his shoulders, and with his hands in his pockets, walked leisurely away. The hand disappeared, and the car quickly drove on in a direction opposite to that taken by the man.

The little scene looked suspicious to the detectives, who noted the number of the automobile, and proceeded to investigate.

Two hours later Martin nonchalantly walked up to the Place Blanche and sat down at a little table on the "terrace" of a cafe, where he was joined presently by Kerbrat. The two men embraced each other, and behaved as only two brothers would after years of separation.

The little comedy was for the benefit of Big Raoul, who was sipping his vermouth at a table right next to theirs. The detectives immediately proceeded to entertain one another with their experiences in various parts of the world, one as a pastrycook and the other as a chauffeur. They used the southern dialect for the benefit of Big Raoul, who is a native of Marseilles, and were apparently so absorbed in their reminiscenses that they paid no attention to the pretty young woman who had stepped from a handsome motor-car and taken a seat at Raoul's table.

They knew the young woman. She was Anna Woksler, lyric artiste, known as "Olga," and inscribed upon the police records as being "without permanent place of abode." Her hand was the same they had noticed tapping the car window in front of 10, Rue de Bruxelles.

Presently Martin heard her say to Raoul:

"I was at your house two hours ago, but you were not in, it seems, or your man would have given me a sign. I need some snuff for the Baronne de B——, and she will have a fit if I don't bring her some at once."

The next moment the two detectives saw a street vendor of cheap candy passing slowly in front of the terrace and calling out his wares.

"Have a box of that candy, Olga," said Big Raoul with a significant look.

The woman took the box offered to her by the street vendor, and Raoul paid the man a franc for it.

Then, suddenly, Raoul and Olga became aware of the fact that the conversation at the next table had ceased.

They looked up into the faces of the sleuths, who were bending over them, and the next thing they heard was a polite invitation to accompany "the pastry-cook and chauffeur" to the police commissary. Even the candy man had to join the party.

Big Raoul vehemently objected to having his liberty thus interfered with, but the officers were obdurate. Olga and the candy man were locked up in goal, and Raoul was prevailed upon to show the detectives his apartment in the Rue de Bruxelles.

Triumphantly, Big Raoul showed them through his apartment, opening every drawer and closet for them, but nothing was found that could incriminate him.

Again the officers thought they had failed to "nail" him, when Kerbrat happened to open a window that looked out upon the rear court of the building. And there, on the sill, was a small packet containing enough cocaine to drug all Montmartre.

"I wonder who put that there?" said Raoul Dianoux, gasping with apoplectic astonishment.

Half an hour later Big Raoul sat in his prison cell, still musing.

"I would give a hundred thousand francs to know who put that stuff on my window-sill," he said to the keeper.

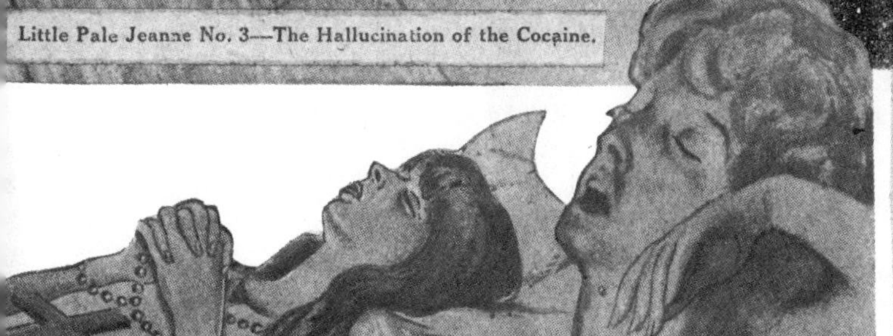

Edouard Chimot, the Distinguished French Artist.

Chimot's "afternoons"—the "Afternoon of Cocaine," the "Afternoon of Opium," the "Last Afternoon"—are three sermons in line, more potent to suppress the drug plague than a symposium of all the pulpit appeals ever uttered. His pictures without words carry conviction and tell a story that words cannot.

Psychologic, not merely intellectually high-brow, is the theme upon which Chimot embroiders his variations. Behind the masques of his "little women" he reads their very inner history and tells it to you with a burning realism combined in just proportion with an equally hectic impressionism. Call his models wantons if you will, but these frail creatures are human beings after all. Chimot does not let one forget that.

The types of Paris dope fiends—lips the color of a half-cooked liver, pale under their rouge—are no more marked than those of other like agglomerations of humanity—they are no better in moral fundamentals; certainly no worse than elsewhere, though here they may seek the lime-light unabashed, as the moth seeks the candle-flame.

"Little Pale Jeanne" is the latest celebrity en vedette in the quartier excentrique which forms the kernel of 20th century Montmartre. She takes "coco," as cocaine is called here, punctures herself with the morphine needle or hits the pipe of distilled essence of the poppy-fields of India indiscriminately, seeking thus a sovereign felicity, ... towards all the wo... she passes out bey... wills, when and w... what the French ... d'opium.

It is sad of cou... powerful enough to... hand, under-the-tab... It is either this, or t... busy with other c... fountain-head and c... source. If the Opiu...

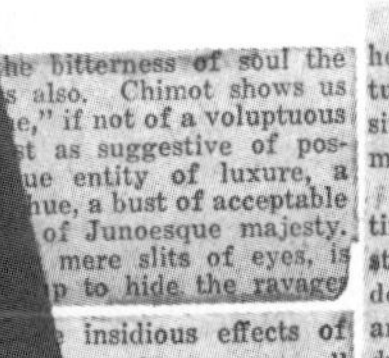

... he bitterness of soul the ... s also. Chimot shows us ... e," if not of a voluptuous ... t as suggestive of pos... ue entity of luxure, a ... hue, a bust of acceptable ... of Junoesque majesty. ... mere slits of eyes, is ... p to hide the ravage

... insidious effects of ... rs and arms are well ... unlovely, even now. ... tiny feet and dainty ... s. Clothed always ... ventionally, modish... In short she is of ... her station as typical of ... class as a shepherdess of Fragonard or a courtesan of Boucher of theirs.

Lea... actu... tion ... will h...

Chi... Montm... almost ... and the ... es and their ... excitations readily ... soon to expire—all are accentuated by the varied orchestration accompanying a sordid, tinsel gayety.

"La Petite Jeanne Pale" is a type of Montmartre's dope addict of to-day. Yes, of to-day! To-morrow she will be no more. Momentarily placidly content she is never really happy wall-flowered as she is, awaiting her "coco" by some surreptitious hand, while others dance their cares away.

Gay she may appear at times, doubtless she really is in a half-forgetfulness, though the inscrutability of her features ... Three or four years of moth-like fluttering and she ... -dead in some mean garret ... haps in the little white bed ... tal. And then follows the ... n of the medical school. ... e she has of reform. No ... ny encouragement. Some ... btless. One has heard of ... has seldom had a tangible ... thereof. In general they ... "coco" or "snow" or the ... pipe come to be constant ... r grip can seldom be re-

$100,000 IN COCAINE SEIZED ON STEAMER

Port Surveyor's Agents Also Find Large Quantity of Liquor on Two Ships.

DRUG FROM MARSEILLES

Paris possesses the largest collection of drug addicts of any great city in the world and Montmartre, the quarter of the artists, is the section where they are most easily found.

While Montmartre contains the studios of many genuine artists, hardworking men of talent, it is also the site of the most hectic night restaurants and amusement resorts of Paris. Here are the Cafe of the Rat Mort (Dead Rat), the Abbaye de Theleme, the Auberge du Coucou (Inn of the Cuckoo), the Cabaret du Lapin Agile (Cabaret of the Agile Rabbit), Cabaret Singe Bleu (Blue Monkey) and scores of others.

The resorts of Montmartre are filled with the pretty, frail little women who make the lure of Paris and with thoughtless pleasure seekers, Americans and others, from all parts of the world. It is among these women that the greatest number of addicts occurs, for the burden of their lives becomes at times so terrible that they crave anything that will give them a few moments of forgetfulness. But women of wealth, many of them Americans, have also fallen into drug addiction through visits of mere curiosity to the bohemian resorts.

The dash of morphine, first taken to help a girl through the weariness of nocturnal dissipation, soon becomes a necessity on the morning after. The allowance must be steadily increased.

She arrives at a stage when she is continually under the influence of opium instead of indulging in an occasional debauch. She acquires the pale, wax-like and unnatural color of one who uses the drug habitually. She cares little for food and at times seems hardly alive. She lives in fact only for the moment when she can feel the seductive poison pouring through her veins and carrying her into an unearthly realm of deadly delights. During the few moments when she is free from the influence of the poison she is a pitiful wreck.

When a girl has reached the stage where opium has plainly set its stamp on her body she loses her appeal for the ordinary pleasure seeker and tourist, however much he may have laughed at her early indulgences. It is surprising, however, to see the great number of women who can afford to continue in the path of the drug-taker. This is explained partly by the fact that there are many men and women of considerable means who are drug-takers and desire company in their indulgences. They are willing to supply the drug to some of the poverty-stricken addicts, just for the sake of company, even though the poor creatures have lost most of their attractiveness.

Another curious fact is that a large proportion of men criminals in Paris are drug addicts. A burglar, after making a haul in the middle of the night, will resort to some den to dream and forget his troubles under the influence of opium. These criminals are often liberal in their way and will buy opium for the poor wrecks who cannot afford it themselves.

A Parisian reformer has estimated that there are 50,000 drug addicts in the Montmartre district alone. Some of the unfortunates are artists' models. It is possible for a model to pose when under the influence of morphine, although the physical decay caused by the drug must in time unfit her for most characters.

The poor girl who has taken drugs until she has lost all her charm is exiled from the high-priced restaurants and the society of wealthy tourists and sinks into evil dens, frequented by wrecks and criminals. So she slips down the way to the morgue and the city graveyard.

Thus it happens that Montmartre offers an opportunity to study every class of woman at every stage of the deadly path of drug taking.

Morphine indulgence by women in the cafes and dance halls is really quite ordinary. Girls who are young and still in vogue often carry an imposing array of gold receptacles for drugs at their waists. When the entertainment grows tiresome a girl will recklessly jab herself in the arm with a morphine needle to create a little artificial happiness within her. Others dash a drop of morphine into their champagne or brandy.

The maddening habit of eating hasheesh, or Indian hemp, has lately become fashionable. To the woman who has eaten hasheesh every sensation changes its normal character. She thinks that her beauty is irresistible. She thinks that she charms multitudes when she opens her mouth. She thinks she is a bird and can fly over the tree tops. She takes a ride in a taxicab and thinks she is in heaven. Then comes the reaction, which is marked by a frantic desire to kill some one, accompanied by great physical exhaustion.

A peculiarly deadly drink now favored by the patrons of the gayest Montmartre resorts is a mixture of brandy and ether. This produces the maximum of intoxicating effect on the nervous system with the minimum effect on the digestive organs.

Girls who have found stimul... in this combination can sometimes f...h a lot of artificial gaiety to a party.

COCAINE, BROUGHT TO U. S. AS BLESSING, SOON A CURSE

Addict Army Here Grew Rapidly as "Glorious Discovery" of 35 Years Ago Was Bought for Base Uses and Became Ally of Crime

By WINIFRED BLACK.

SAN FRANCISCO, Feb. 23.—Cocaine came into America about thirty-five years ago.

It was hailed as a glorious discovery and for a long time no one realized the insidious and cruel danger it brought with it.

Physicians, dentists and the makers of patent medicines, too, made immediate and very practical use of it.

All at once people who were taking new "catarrh cures" found themselves victims of the cocaine habit.

And in no time at all the country was sprinkled with "coke" fiends, from Maine to California and from Chicago to New Orleans.

Force Behind Crime

What is behind the gunmen and his gun today? Nine times out of ten, cocaine.

What is behind the holdup and the brutal murders of bank cashiers and petty shopkeepers and payroll masters?

Cocaine—nine and a half times out of ten.

What steadies the nerves and quickens the pulse of the boy bandit—cocaine.

Boys under twenty, girls of sixteen and seventeen, musicians in dance halls, waiters, dentists, school teachers, entertainers, taxi drivers—these are the "snow birds" of today.

That's what they call cocaine victims in the underworld talk—"snow birds."

Take "Sleigh Rides"

When a "snow bird" is going out to a cocaine party, he says he's going for a "sleigh ride" and intimates to his associates that there will be plenty of "bells" to decorate the excursion.

Morphine and opium send you to sleep.

Cocaine wakes you up, starts your heart to pumping, makes your eyes blaze, fills your head with strange, wild schemes—turns the commonplace into the heroic.

A harmless, good-natured boy of seventeen will take two or three "sniffs" of "snow" and turn into a cold-blooded, cruel, blood-thirsty bandit, ready to hold up his own father and kill his own mother to get money enough to go out and buy some more "snow."

A little easy-going, foolish girl of sixteen will take two or three "sniffs" of "happy dust" and she thinks she's a queen of the world—such a poor, bedraggled, bedizened, silly little queen of such a terrible, degraded and degrading world.

U. S. Full of Stuff

And the country is full of the stuff.

The annual consumption in the United States of cocoa leaves today amounts to over a million pounds.

Enough cocaine comes into this country to give every man, woman and child in the United States two and a half doses.

Seventy-five per cent of the cocaine manufactured is used not to deaden pain, not for a local anaesthetic, but to drive boys and girls crazy and manufacture criminals by the wholesale.

And there is no legitimate use for cocaine anywhere in the world today.

Recent inventions provide local anesthetics for the dentists and the surgeons; cocaine has no right to exist at all.

And yet it comes in legally, a hundred and fifty thousand ounces of it, every year and nobody knows how many hundred thousand ounces come in illegally.

Cost Runs High

It takes from three dollars to thirty dollars a day to keep a "coke fiend" supplied with "snow."

That's where the thieves come.

That's why young girls suddenly begin to forge their fathers' names on checks, that's why every once in awhile some brilliant high school boy is caught stealing money in the cloak room—he has to have cocaine and he must have money to buy it.

The whole habit usually begins at a "party."

There's a new thrill in it—some boy with a big car meets a mysterious man at some dance hall some night, and the man tells him to bring his crowd to such and such a place and he'll give them a real thrill.

And the boy fills his car with fellows and girls and they go and meet the mysterious man, and the thrill turns out to be a box of "joy powders."

"Sniff the Snow"

The boys and girls "sniff the snow," the girls begin to laugh, the boys begin to sing, the party is a huge success.

And there's not a cent to pay—not a single penny.

The mysterious man loves to see boys and girls happy.

But the next time there's a "sleigh ride" the mysterious man sells the "snow" at a good big price—and after that, he has a nice new bunch of customers.

And every one of his new customers will bring him in three or four more, for one of the marked characteristics of the cocaine user is the desire to get other people to using it.

It is an endless chain—and its links reach from the lowest dives in the lowest part of the big cities, to the beautiful homes in the suburbs, yes, and out to the lonely farm and down into the kitchens, and out into the fields.

It is easy to recognize a "snow bird"—there is something about the walk, a sort of high-stepping, hysterical gait—there's something about the hair, the way it stands out from the scalp; there's something about the alternate moods of hideous depression and sudden wild elation—and a "snow bird's" face always twitches—more or less.

The dull boy who becomes suddenly brilliant, the brilliant girl who becomes suddenly dull—watch them and see if they haven't a little package of white powder somewhere among their possessions.

Up in Canada the blank forms which the government sends out to juvenile court officers requires a statement as to whether or not the child before the court is a victim to drugs.

Does that tell you anything?

Think it over and it will.

Factitious Bravado

Cocaine turns a cowardly sneak thief into a bold robber.

Cocaine makes a mild man over into a wild man, and it speeds up the whole human system till the ordinary world is nothing but a half-forgotten dream to a real cocaine addict.

He lives from dose to dose. He begins with one "sniff" and goes on and on till he often takes a dozen doses of "cocaine" in one night or one day, and when he does that he is gone.

His nose-bridge begins to fall. His stomach muscles twitch. He cannot live for a half hour in any kind of comfort with the drug out of his system.

If he tries it, he feels as if beetles were crawling under his skin. His legs and arms twitch. He jumps [illegible] sits down, twists in his

Give him one "sniff" of cocaine and watch him change!

The dull eyes brighten, the twitching mouth begins to smile, the tortured body relaxes, the pitiful broken wretch is gone, and there before you is a voluble, loud-talking, loud-laughing, boasting, bragging, self-confident creature, who will try anything, anywhere, anytime, just to show what a big fellow he really is.

He'll go out and hold up a bank. He'll murder a harmless shopkeeper in his shop. He'll kill some helpless woman on the steps of her own house, within reach of a dozen people—until the cocaine has died out. When that happens, he is a poor, broken, useless wreck again.

And that is cocaine—the "kid catcher"—for most cocaine subjects are little more than children. The modern gunman is not a "man" at all. He is a mere youth—seventeen to twenty or at the most twenty-two—that's the gun-

60 PER CENT OF ALL VIOLENT CRIMES TRACED TO COCAINE

Underworld's Pet Drug Makes Youths Into Thugs and Slayers; Stealthy Narcotic Most Noxious for Trapping Boys and Girls

By WINIFRED BLACK.

"SNOW." "Joy Powder." "Happy Dust." These are some of the names by which the Underworld calls cocaine, one of the most deadly drugs in existence.

The "dope" ring, the big distributers and the "dope" peddlars sometimes call it "the kid catcher."

They do that because cocaine is the one drug that boys and girls pick up first, and it is astonishing and horrifying to discover how many boys and girls there are in this country today who are "snow birds," as the police call them.

WINIFRED BLACK.

Do the police know cocaine? Do the police know murder? and robbery and kidnaping and all the kindred crimes? They have a name for these crimes in police circles.

"Coke stuff"—that's what they call gun plays, holdups, bold robbery, outrageous and maniacal murders.

All these things are tarred with the same unmistakable brush.

All these crimes, or nearly all of them, are committed by men who go for "sleigh rides," as they call a cocaine party in that strange, secret, whispering life we call the underworld.

The Underworld's Drug

Cocaine is as much a part of Underworld life as food and drink is a part of normal, healthy, human existence.

Cocaine begins in the Underworld and ends there—but it does not stay there all the time. There are cocaine parties that are nowhere near the slums and there are "snow birds" who move in the very best society in every city in America.

Cocaine and the automobile—these two factors have changed the whole police problem of America.

Ten years ago nobody had ever heard of an armored car in a peaceful, commercial, downtown district in a peaceful, commercial city.

Now the banks use them as a matter of course.

Are times harder? Do men need money more than they did years ago? Are the money guards and the police less efficient—not so quick, not so courageous as they used to be? Is this the reason of the armored car?

Ask the first police official you meet, and he'll laugh at you. He'll say:

"'Coke.' 'Coke' or heroin, or maybe marijuana, but it's mostly 'coke.'"

"Cocaine commits over 60 per cent of the crimes of violence in America today. The gang that's going to rob a bank, or hold up a little storekeeper, peps up on cocaine to make the killing and they make their get-away in a high-powered automobile.

"'Coke' and the motor car; they're the first aids to crime in this country today."

Ask your own chief of police about it, he'll tell you.

Ask your chief in San Francisco. Ask your chief in Chicago. Ask your chief in New York. It's the same story. Cocaine, "dope," that's the answer. Or at least the most important part of the answer to the armored car question.

Doped and Brutish!

Gerhard Kuhne, chief of the bureau of criminal identification in the City of New York, says:

"The atrocious manner in which the victims of holdup men are abused and uselessly maimed shows conclusively that the gunmen while committing these crimes are not rational.

"I doubt if they would have the courage to attempt such crimes if they were not full of drugs at the time.

"This is verified by the fact that in all crimes of violence of recent years, where the offenders are apprehended, they are found to be drug addicts, and admit they were loaded with drugs when they committed the crime.

"The notorious Whittemore gang, who have all been recently convicted, one to hang, two more to serve forty years each, and the others not yet sentenced, all use drugs.

"Drugs are the cause of from fifty to seventy-five per cent of our crimes in New York City today and throughout New York State."

It is the same story from East to West and from North to South.

Put an intelligent detective on the trail of a man who has just committed some peculiarly atrocious murder, or some amazingly bold robbery, and that detective will start his work by looking first of all for the man's "snow bird" friends and his "coke" trail.

A "snow bird" crime has fingermarks that are as plain as day to any experienced police officer and to every detective who knows his business.

Gunmen who run in "gangs" are almost without exception "coke" addicts. Morphine dulls the senses. Cocaine sharpens them.

A man with a sniff of cocaine at work in his system can hear better, see better, run faster and shoot more quickly than any other man of his equal abilities in the world.

He can talk more and talk faster and brag more than any other man of his own natural capacity, too.

Worldly the Victims

No natural boy, and no normal girl, wants to take a hypodermic of morphine. That craving comes usually only to those hardened in the ways of the world.

The "snow birds" begin to be

INDIA COCAINE CARGO SEIZED

CALCUTTA, May 25.—Cocaine smuggling on the River Ganges has received a heavy setback as the result of the seizure of a cocoaine cargo valued at $75,000 by the authorities. The cargo constituted one of the largest hauls ever made on the famous Ganges.

The raid was staged as the climax of a dramatic series of events in which the wireless played an important part.

Following a radio message from the British India Steam Navigation Company's liner Talma, a Calcutta port tug rushed at full steam on a six-mile dash to the mouth of the Ganges and arrested the occupants of a river boat which had been seen by the captain of the liner sending signals to the shore.

As the tug approached the smugglers were seen to throw rubber bags into the water. Their leader escaped by jumping overboard and swimming ashore, but seven members of the gang were taken into custody. The tug's crew fished out the rubber bags, which were full of cocoaine to the value of $75,000.

9 SEIZED IN BATTLE BY COCAINE RAIDERS

Chapter 1—The House in Gough street—A little "coke" party—The author meets Dawson Sue, the Pug and Denver May—Dawson Sue "cooks a shot" and serves her company as a society woman would tea.

Chapter 2—Secrets of the underworld—Something about the coppers on the beat—An orgy in drugs—Hallucinations of the dope fiends—"Coke bugs"—Dawson Sue tells how she broke into "the habit"—"Sniff H and a shot of "c."

Chapter 3—Walla Walla Sam tells how a woman "broke him in"—A stretch in "the big house"—The suffering of a "fiend" without his "stuff"—The silent battle—Roaming the streets for "a shot"—Why a "crook" uses "the stuff."

Chapter 4—The footfall outside—"Ditching" the "layout"—A tense moment—"The harness bull"—Money versus jail—Fine discriminations of "the law"—"The bail bond shark" as a "friend in need"—The "pinch" of a peddler—$400 and where it went—A transformation in Dawson Sue under the influence of morphine and cocaine.

Chapter 5—An hour of sleep before day-break—Alone on the stair—In a house with dope fiends—A kit of burglar tool: The Banana Kid—Taken for a cop—"Real folks"—

Chapter 6—"In the faint light of the early morning s[...] looked drawn and ill"—The Banana Kid "swipes the la[...] out"—Playing angel to the hop-heads—Out on the stree[...] to "connect"—Transfers for an alibi.

Chapter 7—The Spindle Kid—Men and women of the dope world—"A quarter of each and make it fast"—Staked out—A child of the drug dens—"The gutter hyp"—How they "buy" on the sidewalks—The sufferers.

Chapter 8—Another little coke party—Bright eyes—"When do we eat?"—The fondness of fiends for sweets—A suggestion from Dawson Sue—"Too early, too light"—A shadow from the crime world.

Chapter 9—The metallic click of the hammer and trigger of a gun—A handful of cartridges—A sinister errand—Dawson Sue "calls" Walla Walla Sam—Denver May and the story of her love—"Go out and find the Pug; I'm afraid they got him this time."

Chapter 10—Looking for a "needle" in the proverbial haystack—A voice out of the dark—An unwelcome burden—The mystery gun—Uncomfortable moments—A smile and dimpled cheeks — "You're a dear" — Meeting Harry the Rat—"M" and "c" and then "m" and "c" all over again.

Chapter 11—The picking of a pocket—A dip's pride—A message from the night—"An errand of mercy"—The "Girl in Fillmore street"—A beautiful fiend—"Where is he?"—Tear-drops from eyes of blue—"The stuff!"—The shock.

Chapter 12—A striking contrast—"Don't make things harder for me"—The story of a girl fiend—The lone "shot"—"Don't kid me"—A plea for sweets.

Chapter 13—The mart of dope in the heart of San Francisco—The dairy lunch hang-out of the gutter hyps—

THE HOP-HEA[...]

PERSONAL EXPERIENCES AMONG THE USERS OF "DOPE" IN THE SAN FRANCISCO UNDERWORL[...]

BY FRED V. WILLIAMS

TONS OF RAW COCAINE REACH U. S.

"The bindle buyers"—The old doctor and his story—Harry the Rat again—From the stage to thieving—The power of dope over a man's will—Frayed cuffs—The stampede to "connect."

Chapter 14—Down an alley—The ragged figure from out the night—Under the sidewalk with the dope fiends—Ghosts of the night—"Pin shots of 'c'"—Boy dope fiends—"The rush of blood washed the 'gun' away."

Chapter 15—The boy fiends tell how they started on dope — "Fanned" in the dark — A newspaper red with blood—"God, what a life!"—"If a guy could get reduced; if they could take him off the stuff easy"—Men become animals, wallowing in the filth and refuse of the lot.

Chapter 16—"Cocaine first numbs; then quickens!"—The effect of the drug on the human brain and body—Delusions the fiends suffer—Grim statues in the dark—The coil of the cocaine snake—Dawn—When folks begin to miss things.

Chapter 17—"The hole"—An old box with a keg and a candle—The Ace of Spades—"Go ahead. Don't mind me. Blow your head off"—A tip on some of the swell opium joints in town—The Ace of Spades asks about Penny Meade and his mob of dips in New York—"The Clinic Kid"—"I use $18 and $20 worth of 'c' and 'm' a day."

Chapter 18—The life story of a famous underworld character—A white girl and opium—When a "mob" cleaned up $750 in 20 minutes—Stalling the "dicks"—The business of opium running in a big town—The cocaine inspired confession of the Ace.

Chapter 19—Working with an opium smuggling gang—The "transfer" of 28 "tins"—Switching the suit cases at the Ferry building—Government dicks thrown off the trail—The smugglers' code—"Tailed" by the government men—A my

Chapter 20—"The office"—A woman on the job—Into the shadows of The Embarcadero—"The Mud" is safe—The "crow's nest"—The strange men in the hallway—Cocaine for courage—The cough in the dark.

Chapter 21—In the shadow of a doorway in San Francisco's Chinatown—Music from the tong house—The shelter of Portsmouth Square—A Chinese restaurant—Teapots of opium—"Lo Fun—Lo Fun—government man—government man in Chinatown."

Chapter 22—"You've got all Chinatown crazy tonight"—A cold reception from "Long Jack"—A spectre from prison—"In the depths of the old Chink's eyes lurked the tragedy of 20 lost years"—A fake "shot"—At the door of a hop joint.

Chapter 23—"In Scott street lived the Red Raven and his girl"—"The black spider"—"Poppie was 24, somewhat pretty, slender, graceful of movement and dark of eyes"—Blackie, the peddler on Fillmore, tells how dope is smuggled into the U. S. A.

Chapter 24—Some characters of the dope world—Ping Pong and his partner—The Tigress and the Darby—"Inside stuff" on the big rings that handle dope in this country—The Cocaine Louis ring—"Jails may be clogged with the unfortunate victims of 'the habit,' but jail doors open as fast as they close on 'the ring.' They have plenty of money to grease the hinges."

Chapter 24—The traffic in drugs—What it costs to manufacture the stuff and what the fiend pays for it on
e street—Immense profits—Doping dope—Twenty thou-
nd slaves to the "habit" in San Francisco—Hypos and
nokers—Costs $3 to $10 day to use "the stuff."

Chapter 25—A visit to a first class opium joint in San
rancisco—How the hop is bought, used and the kick it a
gives—The women of the hop bunks—
"yen."

Chapter 26—Silk kimonos and the patter of slippered feet—Chatter in the opium fumes—Pipe dreams that are myths—The crook and his pipe—Diamond studded bowls—Deceit and the smoker—"It is the unwritten lay of the opium joint that a man tend the pipe of his woman companion."

Chapter 27—Opium joint etiquette—The slant-eyed Chink presides over the party—Smoking just for fun—That "all in" feeling that finally heralds "the habit"—"Old Top, you're one of us now; you can't get away."

WALTER N. BRUNT
766 MISSION STREET Printer SAN FRANCISCO
1920

WITH ARTICLES ON DRUG HABITS BY DR. WM. C. HASSLER, CITY HEALTH OFFICER OF SAN FRANCISCO, AND CAPT. JOHN J. O'MEARA, CHIEF OF THE SAN FRANCISCO POLICE "DOPE" SQUADS

"Cooking up a shot" for her company.

—St. Louis Post-Dispatch—January 10, 1937

The DOCTOR WATCHED HIMSELF DIE

And Recorded His Dying Symptoms on the Wall as His Brain—Under the Influence of Narcotics—Grew Feebler.

OMAHA, Nebraska.

THROUGH the dark hours with which one day ended and the next began, Dr. Edwin Katskee carefully watched himself die. He observed how his mind and his body were affected by the thing that was killing him. He tested his reflexes, examined his thinking, noted the acuteness of his vision, the failure of the power of speech, convulsions, the loss and the regaining of ability to use his muscles. He made a strange record of these observations. On a wall of his office, above the couch on which his body was found, he scrawled the grim data, using pen, pencil and crayon. Rambling, not entirely coherent, in places illegible, Dr. Katskee's last clinical notes attempted to add to scientific knowledge of what it is like to die of cocaine poisoning.

Whether Dr. Katskee deliberately killed himself and merely took advantage of that opportunity to describe his dying sensations may never be definitely established. In official records his death is called a suicide. But members of his family insist that he was a martyr to science; that he risked and lost his life in a scientific experiment with a dangerous drug. He himself, apparently, after he saw that death was inevitable, wrote on the wall: "Not suicide—overdose." There was an illegible word before "overdose"; it might have been intended for "definitely."

On the evening before last Thanksgiving day Dr. Katskee began the death watch in which he was both the watcher and the watched. About 7 p. m. he appeared in the lobby of the hotel in which he had his office with the rubber tube of an apparatus for measuring blood pressure around an arm. Half an hour later he telephoned a drug store for a bottle of cocaine and a bottle of a preparation containing morphine; the latter, it was to be discovered, he regarded as an antidote for cocaine poisoning.

ABOUT 1 a. m. Dr. Katskee walked out of his office and had a bellboy tighten the ruber tube around his arm. He returned quietly to his office and was not seen alive again. Some time after daylight his father, uneasy over his absence, called at the office. He found his son on the couch, dead. The rubber tube was still on his arm, but the rest of the blood pressure apparatus, broken, was in an adjoining room. And on the office wall was the story, jumbled and incomplete, of his death.

The story was difficult to follow. At one place was the penciled direction: "Start here," but ahead of this in natural reading order were the words: "Cocaine poisoning — not suicide. Can't act (something illegible) use phone."

High on the wall had been written in pencil, "Can now stand up." Under this, in crayon, were these notes:

"Clinical course over about 12 minutes

"Symptons

"Convulsions followed by paralysis of tongue

"1) Speech and only tongue movable."

Beside this, written in ink, apparently as an afterthought: "Can't understand that movable tongue and no speech. Voice o. k."

"2) Staggering g a i t preceding paralysis.

"3) Paralysis. . . ." The passage ended in a series of wavy lines, apparently an attempt to write that failed altogether.

Evidently the paralysis was only temporary, for a paragraph that presumably was written later was also inscribed high on the wall: "Thoughts clear. For a better understanding of the bad reactions we see in rectal patients . . . cocaine as applied topically or injected when novocaine is ineffective. I hope the better able to tell you, Katskee."

And at another point:

"Eyes mildly dilated. Vision excellent. Partial recovery. Smoked cigarette. Called help. Convulsions decreased when brain functioned on thoughts. Deeper the thinking less the paralysis and convulsion.

"My little way of contributing to the medical and surgical archives of clinical research.

"After depression is terrible.

"Advise all inquisitive M. D.'s to lay off this stuff.

"Cocaine addiction will be a major problem in the U. S. A. in the near future. But I maintain we as M. D.'s should know more about it than the patients themselves. In general it may be compared to insulin and hypogrycenin (word almost illegible) which can be counteracted by carbohydrates.

"I guess all the loquaciousness due to the drug and not myself as I am (two illegible words, possibly 'by birth') as quiet as a person under ether." Toward the end of this sentence the letters became more and more disconnected and sprawling.

After the bellboy had been called to the office at 11:30 the following paragraph had been written:

"Pull out cork and hold open bottle to nostrils of patient.

"Help to be called if needed.

"Police—instruct them that breathing is paralyzed and we need artificial respiration and oxygen to inhale. They will do the rest. They will call the fire department. If possible keep me out of the county hospital or university hospital. Any hospital will do, the closer the better.

"Dr. Katskee."

In a message saying the best antidote for cocaine poisoning was morphine or sodium luminal, there was the remark that "I will require a large dose."

Carrying the possibility of a ghastly significance were the scrawled words: "All memory gone. Phone numbers and addresses not clear that come. They must be there originally and are driven up by this super sensation." They lend support to the theory that Dr. Katskee, carrying out alone a dangerous experiment, let it go too far; that when he wanted to stop the progress of the poisoning to which he had subjected himself, he found it was too later; he couldn't help himself and he couldn't summon help.

There were solutions of both cocaine and morphine in glasses. Eight small punctures in one of the doctor's arms were evidence of efforts to inject morphine; he had not been able to reach a vein with the hypodermic needle. Congestion of blood in and around the left eye was attributed to rupture of a blood vessel, which probably occurred in a strong convulsion as the doomed man staggered about the room, struggling to gain control of his body.

The physician who was first called after Dr. Katskee's body was found, said morphine injected in tissues would not act as quickly as an injection in a vein. Some Omaha doctors expressed doubt that morphine given either way would be effective as an antidote for cocaine. They pointed out that while morphine lulls whereas cocaine excites, both would be fatal in excessive doses. They agreed that luminal has some value as an antidote.

It is reported that Dr. Katskee's father found three notes written by his son, one addressed to him personally, one recording some of his dying sensations, and one apologizing to the hotel for writing on one of its walls.

NOTED ALIENIST ASSAILS TRUTH SERUM AS DE[T]

JUNE 29, 1923

SCOPOLAMIN AS TRUTH DRUG HELD USELESS

New York Criminologists Say Effect Is to Unbalance Mind, so "Confession" Is No Good

LIKENED TO TORTURES

Dr. Simon Finds Nothing but Superior Intelligence Is of Use Against Prisoners

Reports that California authorities attached importance to experiments with scopolamin on prisoners in the San Quentin prison excited interest in New York yesterday.

According to telegraphic reports the use of the drug had proven valuable in making prisoners tell the truth about their crimes. As a result, the report continued, the innocence of apparently guilty prisoners had been proved, and others had disclosed the commission of secret crimes.

DR. GREGORY'S OPINION.

Warden Lewis K. Lawes, of Sing Sing, said:

"I would like to get hold of some of this drug. If successful, its use would solve many of our problems."

Dr. Menas K. Gregory, director of the psycopathic ward of Bellevue Hospital, said:

"Scopolamin produces a mental unbalance which might cause differing effects upon different persons and under different conditions. It might easily lead them to distort facts."

LIKENED TO TORTURES.

Dr. Carleton Simon, Special Deputy Police Commissioner, said:

"Scopolamin produces exaltation and an excitable stage in which the mental mooring is loosened. This effect is observable in the early stages of narcosis from many drugs. It does not infallibly result in the telling of the truth. Belief in some quick, sure way of getting the truth from others has always been evidenced by the impatient and gullible.

"These have sought to get the truth by such methods as torture, plying their victims with liquor, listening to the ravings of persons under laughing gas, ether and chloroform, hypnotism and anything except superior intelligence.

EFFECT NOT INFALLIBLE.

"Of course so-called confessions induced by scopolamin could not be upheld in a court of law, even if the subject were telling the truth, because of the constitutional rule against self-incrimination."

Dr. Perry Lichtenstein, Tombs physician, said:

"Like all drugs, scopolamin is not consistent. It might just as well release a purely imaginative statement from a patient as the truth. Its use in the case of a person with a weak heart might endanger his life."

Boy Injured by Auto Gets $4,500 Damages

A settlement in the sum of $4,500 for damages suffered by Haskis Gabay, seven, of No. 131 Orchard street, ... made before trial ...

THIRD DEGREE BY DRUG USE IS DENOUNCED

JUNE 30, 1923

Scopolamin, Known for 2,000 Years, of No Value as Truth Compeller, Dr. Jelliffe Says

ACTION SAME AS LIQUOR

Makes Victim Admit Crime He Did Not Commit or That Has Never Taken Place

The use of scopolamin as a truth compelling drug was denounced yesterday by Dr. Ely Smith Jelliffe, the noted psychiatrist. Dr. Jelliffe said:

"Scopolamin and similar drugs have been known for more than 2,000 years. If such agents had the effect now claimed for them it would have been discovered long ago."

Dr. Jelliffe's attention was called to the assertion of Dr. E. M. House of Ferris, Texas, who advocated the use of scopolamin as a "humane third degree" for the purpose of eliciting the truth from suspected criminals. He observed:

"The intoxicating effects of scopolamin, which destroys the victim's caution and loosens his tongue on subjects about which he is ordinarily reticent, do not differ from the effects of other intoxicating agents. They suggest the natural inquiry: How much truth do you get out of a drunken man? How much reliance can you place on what a drunken man tells you?

TRUTH AND PHANTASY.

"When a person is intoxicated by scopolamin or any other drug, truth and phantasy are inextricably mixed in his talk. If the person is deceitful, has suppressed desires and hidden delusions these will come to the surface with everything else. The deeds he has admired, the good and bad deeds he has envied and wished he had performed, will be claimed by him. He will even seek to do things he would not do in his sober senses, just as a drunken man acts on his impulses.

"The use of scopolamin or any such agency and reliance upon what the subject under its influence says would present a very grave danger. The subject is likely to confess to crimes he never performed. These may be of two classes. The first would be a crime which actually occurred and which was performed by some one else. Under the influence of the drug the subject, who for instance had wished to kill a murder victim actually slain by some one else, would boast that he had performed the deed.

ADMIT MIND CRIMES.

"The other class of crime to which an intoxicated subject would lay claim under the scopolamin or other drug influence would be a crime which in fact had not occurred at all, but which had its existence only in the subject's imagination. It would come to the surface because he had thought about committing such a crime, had perhaps even worked out the details, but had lacked, perhaps, both the opportunity, or the recklessness to commit it.

"In fact with subjects of a criminal tendency we would find that under the influence of scopolamin ...

DOCTOR SCORNS 'ANTI-LIE' DRUG

City Alienist Says It Quiets Nervous Persons, but Does Not Provoke Truth.

OCTOBER 22, 1923

The use of scopolamin, the new and so-called "truth-provoking" drug, in the cure of insanity and the extortion of truth from criminals under its influence, was branded as "bunk" yesterday by Dr. M. Mortimer Sherman, chief alienist for New York City, for the boroughs of Brooklyn and Queens, and noted authority on mental disorders.

Dr. Sherman, who is attached to the Brooklyn State Hospital for the insane, said that in all the years of his experience he had never known of a case of insanity which had been cured by this method. He said:

"We hear of a great many ways to cure insanity. First, it was thought that some forms could be cured by an injection into the body of a pus extract found at the roots of the teeth. Then we had auto-suggestion, electro-therapeutics and chiropractic; and now someone comes along with a drug. It's all bunk, in my opinion.

ACTS AS SEDATIVE.

"In the first place, scopolamin is a sedative, and its action is such that it retards not only the mental but the physical phenomena. A normal person, under its influence, if the dose administered be of sufficient quantity to act without rendering him unconscious, becomes slow in movement, speech and thought, very much like pictures taken by the slow-motion camera, and it certainly would not be fair to judge his normalcy while he was under the influence.

"The reaction to a heavy dose of the drug is sleep—in other words, a sudden change from life to death. There are no intermediate stages. How in the world can we hope for a reaction when consciousness has been abolished?

"If we do not give a sufficient amount to produce sleep, we get a confused state of mind. The brain functions only in so far as its operation is automatic, such as the hearing. One can hear automatically without listening to what is being said.

EYE RETAINS NOTHING.

"The eye retains nothing of what it sees while the patient is under the influence of the drug, and when he becomes normal again he remembers nothing of what has transpired, even though he may have carried on a conversation with some one before. Naturally, all senses being deadened, there is no such thing in the subject as a sense of judgment. How then can we expect a normal judgment in such a person? How can we believe them? It stands to season that, all senses being retarded, if a criminal were given the drug and then questioned, such a long period of time would have elapsed between the question put to him and the time for his answer that the original intent would be lost.

"This idea of criminals telling the truth while under the influence of the drug is a myth. You cannot use a metaphysical agent to counteract a physical phenomenon, and you cannot use anything concrete to deal with an abstraction, and the mind is con...

TRUTH, THAT'S ALL
By Roy K. Moulton
Drug Turns Trick

For the past few days some scientists and policemen have been experimenting on criminals with a new truth-telling drug and the results have been great. They even got one man to tell the truth in answer to sixty questions. He never lied once.

However, I will make a bet that I can answer sixty questions without lying, if they are the right questions, even without a shot of this drug. I answer over a hundred questions without lying when I make out my income-tax blank last Spring. About the other thirty questions I answer on this occasion I am not quite so sure.

Roy K. Moulton.

The experiments with the class of three criminals were, in the language of the inventor of this truth serum, 100 per cent perfect. I will try to explain the scientific phases of this new marvel.

* * *

They give a criminal a shot of this serum in the arm and he begins telling the truth and he does not let up until he has told not only all he knows but all he has heard during his entire life.

This serum is designed for use mainly on criminals. The inventor does not claim that it will make honest men tell the truth, which I suppose would be classed in some cases as a supreme test.

It would be interesting to try this serum out on some politicians. In the New York Mayoralty campaign, now in its supreme spasms, this truth-telling serum might turn out to be a great blessing to the community.

Policemen and scientists have tried the serum on criminals but they have not given the latter a chance to try it on the policemen and scientists.

* * *

There will probably be a great demand for this drug when the inventor gets to turning it out in carload lots. Every lady will carry a hypodermic syringe ready loaded and friend husband will get a shot in the arm as soon as he steps in at the front door.

This will either increase or decrease the number of divorces, and us scientists have not decided which, as yet.

Then, again, we figure that the Government is going to make a lot of money if enough of the new serum can be procured to hand a shot to every rich income-tax payer in the country. If it will make some of those birds tell the truth, it will be known as the greatest find since the Standard Oil Co. discovered America.

* * *

When the United States Senate convenes, the clerk will rise and say: "Before the Senate comes to order, all members are requested to step into the cloak room with right arms bared and Dr. Woozis will administer the opening shot of Scopolamin. Those not constrained to tell the truth by the first shot will continue to get them every morning until they take effect."

That, of course, will be a hard test, but the scientists claim there is no end to the cleverness of this drug.

The next great test, after that of the criminals, will be made on three theatrical press agents. If the drug gets them to answer sixty questions truthfully, nothing will remain to be said or done and the drug will find a place in every home medicine chest.

SEPTEMBER 4, 1925

'Truth Drug' Shows Mrs. Willow Did Not Plot Deat[h]

DOCTOR'S TALE AMAZES COURT

Woman Under Scopolamin Influence Revealed No Preknowledge of Crime.

'OR ELSE THE DRUG FAILED'

Young Shadel Is Brought Into Room, but Not Allowed to Testify at Time.

By JOHN A. MOROSO,
Staff Correspondent of N. Y. American.

MIDDLEBURG, Pa., Oct. 14.—A sensation was sprung at the opening of the trial of Mrs Anna S. Willow for causing the murder of her husband, Harvey Willow, by her boy sweetheart, Ralph Shadel.

A witness said Mrs. Willow had received a hypodermic injection of the drug scopolamine, used to make criminals tell the truth.

Dr. E. R. Decker, her physician, was the witness. He explained that he used the drug without consulting any one. Mrs. Willow herself did not know the nature or purpose of the injection. Decker said:

"From my reading of authorities I knew that it had been successfully used in Kansas and California; that it dulls the conscious mind and releases the subconscious.

"I gave her the prescribed amount of scopolamine and sat back to hear what she would say about her share in the crime. We had been talking about the murder before I gave it to her. She became semi-conscious and began to talk."

ALL IN CONFUSION.

The District Attorney and Mrs. Willow's lawyers were thrown into confusion. No one seemed to know just what to do.

The defendant leaned forward with strained features and frightened eyes. What had she said while under the control of the drug?

Finally Albert Johnson, for the defense, asked Dr. Decker:

"Was the test successful?"

The physician replied:

"From what she said it was either a failure or she is guiltless of any knowledge that Shadel was going to kill her husband. She talked about the crime, but she did not tell me the things I expected her to tell me.

"She was in a condition when the truth would come out. The drug acted as it should have acted.

"She told of Ralph's return from the woods and said that she cried, and then he cried." The doctor quoted her as saying:

"Ralph wanted me to poison him but I would not."

OCTOBER 15, 1925

"Twilight Sleep" Used Instead of "Third Degree" to Get Truth From Prisoners

THIS CERTIFIES THAT
Clifford R. Clark
The Chas. E. Hi...
IS A MEMBER OF THE
ALLIED DRUG TRAV...
(OF CALIFORNIA)
IN GOOD STANDING FOR THE YEAR ENDING ...
SECY.-TREAS.

TOR

Drug That Makes You Tell The Truth

Truth and Nothing but in "Twilight Sleep" Zone

r. House of Texas at last finds opportunity to test his scopolamin treatment in substitution for "third degree" methods in examining persons accused or convicted of crime—American Medical Association convention astounded at results—Experiments in San Quentin Prison result in disclosing identity of a "mystery man," indicating innocence of another convicted of murder, and causing a wife-slayer suspected of killing 12 "wives" to refuse to submit to the drug—Criminologists predict that "truth serum" will empty the prisons of the estimated 5 per cent of their inmates who are innocent, save guiltless suspects from gallows or chair, and establish fact of guilt when it exists

The Unfortunate Girl Was Now Partially Under the Influence of the Ether. Clearly, Without Hesitation or Embarrassment, She Told Her Story, With Careful Description of the Two Men, and Even Recalled the Number of the License Plate of the Automobile.

By ZOE PARKER.

THE fistic third degree, employed throughout the Anglo-Saxon world, and the torture rack of the Orient, face a new challenger. Scopolamin, the "truth serum," at whose demonstration medical men and criminologists stood aghast recently at San Quentin ison in California, may empty our jails of the 5 cent innocently convicted, make perjury impose, and reveal the names of an army of unknown minals, if the claims of its discoverer, Dr. R. E. use of Ferris, Tex., continue to be verified.

Dr. House and his "truth serum" were the sension of the recent convention of the American dical Association in San Francisco. Following the sion of the American Research Anesthetist Asiation, medical men and police officials traveled San Quentin Prison, where, with the drug scoponin, producer of "twilight sleep," secrets were laid e in the lives of condemned men, the identity s established of a "mystery man" who had wanred for months without knowing his own name, l in one case the innocence of a man convicted of rder was indicated.

Scopolamin (pronounced scope-a-lay-min) is not v to medical science, being employed in "twilight ep" obstetrics, and, as explained by Dr. House, st to employ it in criminology, the drug renders conscious will impotent. Leaving memory active, permits the subject to answer questions from exience.

'With the dormant scopolamin," explains Dr. use, "the subconscious mind will respond to facts. estions propounded to a patient under such a conon invariably bring truthful answers. In more n 500 cases there is yet to be recorded a failure."

Prior to the announcement of his findings to the dical fraternity at the convention in San Fraco, Dr. House had experimented in Texas.

Possibilities bordering the miraculous are opened in the field of criminology by this discovery, acding to those who witnessed the demonstrations in Francisco, Berkeley and San Quentin Prison. ere men were laid on the operating table as in a gical case, given the "truth serum" by hypodermic

It was at his own wish that the "Walking Dead n" went under the influence of the drug. Then, the twilight zone, when the auditory nerve probes field of memory, the man answered the questions opounded by Dr. House. Promptly he replied, say; he was Pierre Burns, that he was born in Luxberg, and that he had served with the Canadian

Among the astonishing possibilities of the "truth rum," which name, by the way, Dr. House does t favor, the discoverer outlined the following in s address before the convention of physicians:

1. Persons arrested as suspects can be made to quit or convict themselves.
2. There would be no further necessity to grant munity to a known criminal, for the reason that s evidence could be obtained and corroborated witht his consent.
3. A perjurer, at the command of the Judge, could made to tell the facts, as they exist in his mind; in her words, the truth; many women, for instance, ve sworn away their honor to protect a guilty husnd.
4. In time of war, spies could be made to divulge formation before being shot.
5. Statistics reveal that only one person in 10 who e tried is convicted. The nine who escape from ck of evidence would show, under the influence of e drug, those who are guilty.
6. One-third of the arrests now made are miskes. The expense of trying this third could be ved. It is from this class that the innocent in the nitentiary are recruited.
7. Compiled statistics show that almost half of e expense of maintaining our Government goes to e control of crime. If Uncle Sam could use scopomin, in the hands of trained men, it would mean e saving of millions of dollars a year.
8. Its adoption would do more than any other known method to prevent gang robbery. Criminals soon would learn that the arrest of one would reveal the names of all.
9. It would accomplish more than any other type of "third degree" in obtaining confessions, for the reason also that many would prefer to confess than to take the medicine; the drug would serve as a positive check and a "club."
10. Statistics show that 5 per cent of the inmates of every penitentiary are innocent. If this method could be standardized, it would clean every penitentiary of its guiltless prisoners; furthermore, there would be no more innocent persons sent there.

Not only does the subject under the influence of scopolamin tell the truth, but it is impossible for him to tell a lie, according to Dr. House, for the reason that his volition in the matter is destroyed and there is nothing to be revealed except the record of memory experience in the mind. As proof of this he cites

"The principle involved in the use of scopolamin in criminal work is based upon the recognized functions of the brain and these clinical observations:

"The brain's most powerful center is hearing; it is the last center to succumb to an anesthetic, and the first center to function again after an anesthetic. I have observed (and which is strangest of all to me) that the center of hearing can, and does, make the other four centers function before those centers are influenced by their own special nerve.

"The only function the auditory nerve possesses, when stimulated by a question, is to carry the sound waves to the auditory center, and the only function the auditory center has is to invoke memory. Under the influence of scopolamin, a suspected criminal is rendered oblivious to existence; appreciation of environment is eliminated; the willpower is nonexistent.

"In such a state of unconsciousness, if the individual is engaged in conversation the moment the auditory center asserts its power, he is too helpless to protect himself by inventing replies to the questions propounded."

Scopolamin is extracted from the scopola plant and is an alkaloid long known to scientists. Chemically, it has the composition of hyoscine, an important drug used in the cure of narcotic addiction:

An interesting experiment was made in checking up the use of the "truth serum" with the mechanical "lie detector" employed in the Berkeley Police Department. Dr. John A. Larson, the only Ph. D. police officer in the world, inventor of the lie-detecting machine, was delighted with the results obtained, checking favorably both ways. The principle of the mechanical detector is that of registering the emotions through blood pressure and heart beats. A subject always reveals excessive emotional reactions when telling an untruth. This is registered on a chart by the machine.

The lie detector has been employed in "third-degree" work in the Berkeley Police Department for more than a year and some startling results have been obtained. In one instance a girl co-ed at the University of California confessed to a diamond

large penitentiary. These tests now have been made, with the startling results told below by a special correspondent of the Sunday Magazine who lives at Berkeley, Cal., where some of the successful experiments were confirmed.

The article in this magazine last November carried the first serious discussion of the use of scopolamin in this connection, in any publication other than a medical journal.)

NOVEMBER 5, 1922.

Scopolamin, drug employed in childbirth cases, puts subjects into condition where reason is paralyzed but memory remains—Texas doc

TEXAS has a doctor who wants to go to the penitentiary—any penitentiary where he may have the privilege of experimenting upon the prisoners in a scientific effort to learn whether they are innocent

questions. Divested of all scientific phraseology, his method is to give the subject of the investigation opportunity to talk in his sleep.

This does not mean natural sleep. It means a sleep, or a condition of semi-consciousness, induced by drugs. "Truth serum" is the nickname applied by the laity to the drug administered by the Texas doctor for this purpose. It is not a serum at all: it is a vegetable extract or concoction known to chemistry as scopolamin. This drug is an important part of the "twilight sleep" treatment introduced a few years ago in cases of childbirth. The use of scopolamin in criminology is suggested by Dr. House, who advances the belief that it will be found much more useful in getting facts from accused persons than the strong-arm police method known as "the third degree."

At the recent fall session of the Medical Association of the Southwest, in Hot Springs, Ark., Dr. House was reported by the Associated Press as seeking indorsement of a plan "to experiment with 1000 prisoners at the Federal Penitentiary at Leavenworth, Kan., in an effort to determine the value of 'scopolamin anesthesia' or 'twilight sleep,' as a means of securing truthful statements from criminals." Instead of the word criminals the word convicts, of course, was meant. Dr. House apparently believes, as do many other thinking men, that to be a convict does not imply necessarily that one is a criminal. In his paper at the Hot Springs meeting Dr. House expressed the belief that if the form of anesthesia mentioned were recognized and used by courts many injustices would be avoided.

"Scopolamin," says Dr. House, "will depress the cerebrum to such a degree as to destroy the power of reasoning. Events stored in the cerebrum as memory can be obtained by direct stimulation of the centers of hearing."

The theory appears to be that a person under the influence of the drug, bereft of reasoning power, is unable to protect himself, if such protection be indicated because of guilt, by thinking up a lie to cover the case; in other words, he is able to tell only the truth, which he draws from his stores of memory.

"The successful use of scopolamin in criminology," according to Dr. House, "is based on the fact that a feeble stimulus is capable of setting in operation nerve

pulses that are as potent as those produced by strong stimulants, just as a small percussion cap can set in motion the potential energy of a ton of dynamite. The stimulus of a question can only go to the hearing cells. In pursuance of their functions, the answer is automatically sent back, because the power of reason is inhibited more than the power of hearing."

"Scrivener," said Dr. House, "was given first 1-4 grain of morphine and 1-100 grain of scopolamin. In 20 minutes he was given 1-200 grain of scopolamin. In 30 minutes he was lightly anesthetized with chloroform and allowed to rest 30 minutes, when 1-400 grain of scopolamin was administered. In 20 minutes he failed to respond to the memory test. To insure safety and save giving more scopolamin, he was anesthetized with chloroform to complete unconsciousness, and engaged in conversation at the earliest possible moment."

If Mrs. Warner should be put under the influence of ether would she reveal the name of the man who forced his way into her home that morning and riddled her guest with his well-aimed bullets?

Would her tongue, under the stimulation of the anaesthetic, disclose enough about recent events in her life to make perfectly clear the motive for this murderous attack on Mr. Reid?

DR. ... special preparation of ether, well-known anaesthetic, which broke down all reserve and secrecy when administered to the patient. Under the influence of this drug Dr. Cotton said that the patient would babble his innermost thoughts and secrets and always tell the absolute truth.

...urder of "Big Jim" Colosimo, known as the king of Chicago's night life, be explained if pretty Dale Winter, his bride of less than a month, were questioned...

"Dale Winter, the cabaret queen whom Colosimo had married three weeks before, is said to be the only person who knows the name of the man who made the appointment that lured her husband to his doom.

Would she, under the influence of ether ... relations with Rueckert she might reveal some hint that would enable the police to run down his murderer?

Further experiments in the use of ether in criminal investigations will be watched with interest to see whether this drug may not prove of the greatest service to the police and the courts in clearing the innocent of suspicion and punishing the guilty.

Exactly what the police needed to know and which had baffled them because of the condition of their only witness was now made clear. The drug had made it possible for the police to find the clues which, without the aid of the drug, had eluded them. The experiment had worked precisely as Dr. Cotton...

"One breath of ether, less than an ounce of it, and five seconds of time, and the girl was ready to tell what the officers had tried for most an hour to get from her in vain. It seems to me it opens a vast field of possibilities in dealing with criminals or the victims of criminals or in handling unwilling witnesses. Etherization destroys the will to withhold facts, even though they may be derogatory to ourselves or others."

DR. S. WEIR MITCHELL

Describes the Exquisite Visions Induced by

THE MESCAL BUTTON.

Placed Himself, for Science' Sake, Under the Influence of the New Mexican Indians' Intoxicating Drug.

The following is a portion of a paper upon the drug mescal, written by Dr. S. Weir Mitchell, and read by him before the Neurological Society. The portion published is that description of the intoxicating effects of the drug, as experienced by the writer after having voluntarily placed himself under its influence for tre purpose of studying its action.

THE history of the use of mescal by the Indians of New Mexico is very well known in the United States, and especially through the valuable papers of Dr. Prentiss, of Washington, D. C. These so interested me that I asked him to favor me with some of the extract. Profiting by his kindness I made a trial of the drug on May 24, 1896, by taking it as I shall now relate.

At noon of a busy morning I took fully one and one-half drachms of an extract of which each drachm represented one mescal button. I had in a half hour a sense of great gastric discomfort and later of distention. At one P. M. I took a little over a drachm. Between two and three P. M. I noted my face as flushed; the pupils were dilated midway, the pulse eighty and strong. I had a slight sense of exhilaration, a tendency to talk, and now and then I misplaced a word. The knee jerk and station were normal. Between two and four o'clock I had outside of my house two consultations and saw several patients I observed that, with a pleasing sense of languor, there was an unusual amount of physical endurance. I went rather quietly, taking two stairs at a time and without pause, to the fourth story of a hotel and did not feel oppressed or short of breath. This is akin to the experience, as I learn, of the mescal eating Indians, and to that of many white men.

Meanwhile my stomach was more uncomfortable, and I saw the first evidence of any change in my color records. On closing my eyes (while in my carriage) I held longer than usual any bright object just seen. As to this, however, I am not as sure as I am concerning the later phenomena. About ten minutes after four P. M. I drove home, and after taking half an ounce of extract in three doses I lay on a lounge and read, becoming steadily more conscious, at first of a left frontal pain (not severe) and soon after of a dull occipital ache, felt on both sides and at or about the occipital bosses. Yawning at times, sleepy, deliciously at languid ease, I was clearly in "the land where it is always afternoon." At half-past four P. M., rising to make notes, I became aware that a transparent, violet haze was about my pen point, a tint so delicate as at times to seem doubtfully existent.

At this stage of the mescal intoxication I had a certain sense of the things about me as having a more positive existence than usual. It is not easy to define what I mean, and at the time I searched my vocabulary for phrase or word which should fitly state my feeling. It was vain.

At this time, also, I had a decisive impression that I was more competent in mind than in my everyday moods. I seemed to be sure of victoriously dealing with problems. This state of mind may be easily matched in the condition of some men when pretty far gone in alcohol intoxication. My own mood was gently flattering—a mere consciousness of power, with meanwhile absolute control of every faculty. I wrote a long letter of advice dealing with a rather doubtful diagnosis, and on reading it over was able to see that it was neither better nor worse than my average letter. Yet the sense of increased ability was so notable that, liking to test it, and with common sense disbelief in its flattery, I took up a certain paper on psychology which a week before I had laid down in despair. I grieve to say that it was less to be comprehended than ever. My ignorance would have remained bliss had I not made the experiment. I next tried to do a complicated sum, but soon discovered that my ordinary inefficiency as to figures was not really increased.

A mood is like a climate and cannot be reasoned with. I continued to have for some two hours this elated sense of superiority. I was for this while in that condition in which some people permanently abide.

The further test of writing a few lines of verse was tried. I found there was much effort needed. I lay down again about twenty minutes after five, observing that the outer space field seemed to be smoky. Just at this time, my eyes being closed, I began to see tiny points of light, like stars or fireflies, which came and went in a moment. My palms were now tingling, my face a little flushed. About twenty minutes to six the star points became many, and then I began to observe something like fragments of stained glass windows. The glass was not very brilliant, but the setting, which was irregular in form, seemed to be made of incessantly flowing sparkles of pale silver, now going here, now there, to and fro, like, as I thought, the inexplicable rush and stay and reflux of the circulation seen through a lens. These window patterns were like fragments coming into view and fading.

Hoping for still better things in the way of color, I went up stairs, lay down in a darkened room and waited. In a few minutes the silver stars were seen again, and later I found that these always preceded any other more remarkable visions.

The display which for an enchanted two hours followed was such as I find it hopeless to describe in language which shall convey to others the beauty and splendor of what I saw. I shall limit myself to a statement of a certain number of the more definite visions thus projected on the screen of consciousness.

During these two hours I was generally wide awake. I was comfortable, save as to certain gastric conditions, which were not so severe as to distract attention. Time passed with little sense for me of its passage. I was critically attentive, watchful, interested and curious, making all the time mental notes for future use.

Especially at the close of my experience I must, I think, have been for awhile in the peculiar interval between the waking state and that of sleep—the "praedormitum"—the time when we are apt to dream half controlled stories, but as to this I am not very sure. As a rule I was on guard with every power of observation and reflection in full activity.

My first vivid show of mescal color effects came quickly. I saw the stars, and then, of a sudden, here and there delicate floating films of color—usually delightful neutral purples and pinks. These came and went—now here, now there. Then an abrupt rush of countless points of white light swept across the field of view, as if the unseen millions of the Milwy Way were to flow a sparkling river before the eye. In a minute this was over and the field was dark. Then I began to see zigzag lines of very bright colors, like those seen in some megrims. I tried to fix the place and relation of these tints, but the changes were such as to baffle me. One was an arch of angled lines of red and green, but of what else I could not determine. It was in rapid, what I may call minute, motion.

The tints of intense green and red shifted and altered, and soon were seen no more. Here, again, was the wonderful loveliness of swelling clouds of more vivid colors gone before I could name them, and, sometimes rising from the lower field, and very swiftly altering in color tones from pale purples and rose to grays, with now and then a bar of level green or orange, intense as lightning and as momentary.

When I opened my eyes all was gone at once. Closing them I began after a long interval to see for the first time definite objects associated with colors. The stars sparkled and passed away. A white spear of gray stone grew up to huge height and became a tall, richly finished Gothic tower of very elaborate and definite design, with many rather worn statues standing in the doorways or on stone brackets. As I gazed every projecting angle, cornice and even the face of the stones at their joinings were by degrees covered or hung with clusters of what seemed to be huge precious stones, but uncut, some being more like masses of transparent fruit. These were green, purple, red and orange; never clear yellow and never blue. All seemed to possess an interior light, and to give the faintest idea of the perfectly satisfying intensity and purity of these gorgeous color fruits is quite beyond my power. All the colors I have ever beheld are dull as compared to these.

Colors of Marvellous Intensity.

As I looked, and it lasted long, the tower became of a fine mouse hue, and everywhere the vast pendent masses of emerald green, ruby reds and orange began to drip a slow rain of colors. All this while nothing was at rest a moment. The balls of color moved tremulously. The tints became dull, and then, at once, past belief vivid; the architectural lines were all active with shifting tints. The figures moving shook the long hanging lines of living light, and then, in an instant, all was dark.

After an endless display of less beautiful marvels I saw that which deeply impressed me. An edge of a huge cliff seemed to project over a gulf of unseen depth. My viewless enchanter set on the brink a huge bird claw of stone. Above, from the stem, or leg, hung a fragment of some stuff. This began to unroll and float out to a distance which seemed to me to represent Time as well as immensity of Space. Here were miles of rippled purples, half transparent, and of ineffable beauty. Now and then soft golden clouds floated from these folds, or a great

HERALD, SUNDAY, JANUARY 10, 1897.

himmer went over the whole of the rolling urples, and things like green birds fell rom it, fluttering down into the gulf below. Next, I saw clusters of stones hanging in nasses from the claw toes, as it seemed to ne miles of them, down far below into the nderworld of the black gulf.

This was the most distinct of my visions. ncautiously I opened my eyes, and it was one. A little later I saw interlaced and umberless hoops in the air, all spinning wiftly and all loaded with threaded jewels r with masses of color in long ropes of clusered balls. I began to wonder why I saw o opals, and some minutes after each of hese circles, which looked like a boy's hoop, ecame huge opals; if I should say fluid pals it would best describe what was, however, like nothing earthly.

I set myself later to seeing if I could conure figures, for so far I had seen nothing uman in form, nor any which seemed alive. had no luck at this, but a long while after saw what seemed a shop with apothecaries' ottles, but of such splendor—green, red, urple—as are not outside of the pharmacies f fairyland.

On the left wall was pinned by the tail a rown worm of perhaps a hundred feet long. t was slowly rotating, like a catherine wheel, nor did it seem loathly. As it turned, ong green and red tentacles fell this way nd that. On a bench near by two little warfs, made, it seemed, of leather, were lowing through long glass pipes of green int, which seemed to me to be alive, so inensely, vitally green were they. But it were vain to find in words what will decribe these colors. Either they seemed trangely solid or to possess vitality. They till linger visibly in my memory, and left he feeling that I had seen among them colors unknown to my experience.

A Vision of Wondrous Surf.

Their variety and strange juxtapositions were, indeed, fascinating for one to whom color is more than it is to most men; nor is t possible to describe the hundredth of what saw. I was at last conscious of the fact hat at moments I was almost asleep, and hen wide awake. In one of these magic moments I saw my last vision, and the strangest. I heard what appeared to be approaching rhythmical sounds, and then saw a beach, which I knew to be that of Newport. On this, with a great noise, which lasted but a moment, rolled in out of darkness wave on wave. These as they came were liquid splendors, huge and threatening, of wonderfully pure green, or red, or deep purple, once only deep orange, and with no trace of foam. These water hills of color broke on the beach with myriads of lights of the same tint as the wave. This lasted some time, and while it did so I got back to more distinct consciousness and wished the beautiful terror of these huge mounds of color would continue.

Were I to take mescal again I should dictate to a stenographer all that I saw, and in due order No one can hope to remember for later record so wild a sequence of color and of forms. But since to talk does not disturb these visions, a perfect account might easily be given.

No one has told us what visions come to the red man. I should like to know if those of the navvy would be like those of the artist, and, above all, what those born blind could relate; and, too, such as are born color blind. In fact, a valuable range of experience is here to be laid open.

I predict a perilous reign of the mescal habit when this agent becomes attainable. The temptation to call again the enchanting magic of my experience will, I am sure, be too much for some men to resist after they have once set foot in this land of fairy colors, where there seems to be so much to charm and so little to excite horror or disgust.

PREMATURE BURIALS.

Dr. Jennings, of Paris, Points Out Grewsome Possibilities and Actual Facts.

"[illegible] YOU ME[illegible] SAY HE WAS [illegible] POISONED?" SAID SHE.

"THE BIG BIBLE LAY OPEN ON THE FLOOR"

THE AUTOBIOGRAPHY OF A QUACK

AND

THE CASE OF GEORGE DEDLOW

BY

S. WEIR MITCHELL, M. D.

LL. D. HARVARD AND EDINBURGH

ILLUSTRATED BY A. J. KELLER

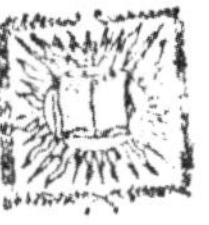

NEW YORK

THE CENTURY CO.

1900

DR. S. WEIR MITCHELL

NEW YORK HERALD, SUNDAY, JULY 29, 1894.

GAS ALWAYS ON TAP.

An Office Where Nitrous Oxide Gas Is Regularly Administered to Patients.

CALLED COMPOUND OXYGEN.

Analysis Made for the Herald Shows Two-Thirds Nitrous Oxide.

A DOCTOR'S METHODS EXPOSED.

Personal Experience of One Who Inhaled the Deleterious Compound.

EDICINE in common with many other matters in our social life has its fads, indulged in chiefly by women. So long as they are harmless they may be suffered to pass unnoticed. The latest development in the way of fads in medicine is, however, of so dangerous a character that attention must at once be called to it to put the unwary on their guard. It is extraordinary that in spite of the advance in popular knowledge of medical science that any nostrum will find its advocates, regardless of its composition.

Yet it seems almost incredible, as appears in the following account of a visit to the establishment, that numbers of ladies go there daily and openly inhale for real or imaginary ailments nitrous oxide gas, dangerous to the health, under the misleading name of compound oxygen, under the direction of an alleged physician. The habit is as pernicious as indulgence

ADMINISTERING OXYGEN TO A PATIENT.

in opium, chloral or any other intoxicant or narcotic, and should be subject to the same legal penalties.

Nitrous oxide gas, sometimes known as laughing gas, is an anaesthetic. Testimony as to its dangerous results when administered as described is given by physicians of high standing. ing.

ONE LARGE EMPORIUM.

Comparatively few people in the city are aware that there is at least one large emporium established in the central part of the town, where nitrous oxide gas is sent out promiscuously to whoever chooses to ask for it. This establishment is situated at No. 33 West Thirty-fourth street, and is known as the Heidelberg Compound Oxygen Company.

Dr. Frank Northrop is the proprietor, and he has been advertising most extensively for years. Religious papers and standard weekly and monthly magazines have inserted in their columns the carefully worded advertisements which give the information that no better remedy exists than Compound Oxygen Gas.

POPULAR FORM OF TREATMENT.

That it has become a popular form of treatment for diseases of all kinds is evidenced by the large number of prominent people who have been led to believe that they will be restored to perfect health by means of a delightful cure, which not only is free from all pain in the taking, but actually makes the world seem beautiful for the space of two hours at least.

In order to learn the exact properties of the gas, it was necessary to become a patient, go through with the entire process of taking the gas, watch carefully the effect, and then procure enough to carry away for analysis. Preparatory to doing this, however, I took the precaution of having a few inhalations of the regulation nitrous oxide or laughing gas given me, in order to be able to distinguish any similarity in taste and effect.

When I first called at No. 33 West Thirty-fourth street and asked for Dr. Northrop, I was quite uncertain as to the manner of procedure at the place, but had thought it a good plan to concoct a plausible story of long continued ill health, from nervousness, which had indeed, I asserted, nearly amounted to nervous prostration.

"MISS JOHNSON," OF ST. LOUIS.

I was Miss Johnson, of St. Louis, for the time being, and very desirous of taking up the study of medicine, which I had hitherto been prevented from doing by the illness referred to. "Now, would this oxygen gas help me?" I anxiously asked the doctor, to which he replied that there was probably no form of disease where this gas had been so beneficial as in nervous troubles of all descriptions, and he was convinced that I could and would be cured. After this statement from Dr. Northrop, not the slightest doubt remained in my mind that I could have safely chosen any disease, with equal certainty that his assurances would have been the same.

The interior of No. 33 West Thirty-fourth street, where the Heidelberg Compound Oxygen Company is established, is most luxuriously furnished. You pass through a handsome wide hall, with a touch of old English style, to a parlor filled with easy chairs, silk curtains, pretty tables and softest carpets. The rear of this room is partitioned off by heavy portieres to serve as the treatment room, or the place assigned for giving the gas.

AIR OF LANGUOROUS COMFORT.

This also possesses a delicious touch of languorous comfort in its rare articles of virtu, a handsome piano and innumerable bric-a-brac. Ranged along the wall in this room are six big armchairs, which are separated from each other by means of thick curtains.

About three feet in front of each of these luxurious resting places are tall white and gilt pedestals, on which stand elaborate mosaic urns filled with the so-called oxygen. Long rubber tubes in silk net casings run from the urns to the seated patient, and a little glass mouthpiece, connected with a check valve, is attached at the end of each piece of tubing.

When the entire establishment is in running order and each chair occupied by patients whose sole interest in life for the moment appears to be centred in the tube she or he grasps so firmly, the only possible picture suggested is that of an exceedingly fashionable opium den. Dr. Northrop is an interesting character to meet. He is a man about thirty-six years of age, medium height, well proportioned, wearing a full dark beard and dresses well.

A SUAVE MANNER.

His manner is the perfection of suavity and fatherly kindness. He is always interested in your particular case, solicitous about your family and friends, most active in his attentions to patients under the treatment, and invariably convinced that you are going to receive a thorough and complete cure for your particular ailment.

The Doctor waxes loquacious from the instant you place yourself under his care. When advising with him regarding the condition of ill health you imagine yourself to be in, he is sympathetic, full of good advice, and agrees with you in everything you say. He thinks it advisable for you to begin the gas treatment at once, and after you seat yourself in the big armchair ready for the cure, he immediately takes you under his wing, and soothingly describes how, gradually, but surely, your ailment will disappear by the aid of the gas. On the ground of taking up the study of medicine, I made several casual inquiries of Dr. Northrop concerning the compound oxygen, and its composition. With an assumption of wonder at its curative powers, I asked if any nitrous oxide was included in the ingredients.

MEDICATED OXYGEN.

"No, not a particle," answered he earnestly. "Of course I cannot tell you just what compounds are used for the cure, as it is my own formula, but it consists of medicated oxygen, prepared carefully for its curative qualities."

"Are you the head or manager of this Compound Oxygen Company?" was my next question.

"Well, to tell you the truth," he answered, "there is no company at all. It is really my own cure and I just advertised it 'company' for commercial reasons."

I then suggested that it seemed foolish to bury one's light under a bushel and that if there was any renown connected with the oxygen cure I should think he would wish it, with which idea he fully coincided and added that he often wished he had used his name in the business and that he should never be so foolish again.

It was on the occasion of my second call that I took my first instalment of the compound oxygen. At this trial the Doctor himself manipulated the tube from which I inhaled the gas. Inserting the glass mouthpiece between my lips, he gave me short whiffs of the gas, cutting the supply off after four inhalations by means of the little check valve, and continuing this treatment at intervals of perhaps five minutes for three-quarters of an hour. My sensations during that time were decidedly pleasant.

A DELIGHTFUL GLOW.

A delightful glow began stealing over me, beginning at my head and extending to the tips of my fingers and toes. I felt exhilarated and perfectly contented, had a decided inclination to talk a good deal for the first half hour, which was followed by several languorous, drowsy moments, when I would have enjoyed the luxury of a short nap.

The taste of whatever was emitted from the tube placed in my mouth was decidedly sweet, and produced a slight tingling sensation at the end of the tongue; at the same time a sort of electric thrill ran through my entire nervous system.

As these were exactly similar sensations to those I experienced on taking the gas admitted to be nitrous oxide, when my physician gave it to me, I felt convinced that Dr. Northrop had made a misstatement as to what his "compound oxygen" was composed of.

Determined, however, to give it a second trial, I called there the following morning for another treatment.

The charge for the oxygen cure, Dr. Northrop had informed me, was $40 for thirty treatments, or $1 50 for single treatments, the last arrangement being the one I selected.

RECEIVED ME CORDIALLY.

Dr. Northrop received me cordially on my arrival, and inquired very particularly as to how I had slept, eaten and the rest, and then proceeded to arrange the easy chair and the gas apparatus for my use again.

I suggested to the Doctor that as I now understood the modus operandi that I be allowed to engineer the operation myself, as I had noticed several of the other patients doing.

To this he willingly assented, and as soon as his back was turned I took three long, full inhalations of the gas, at the same time breathing back into the tube again without removing it from my mouth.

I did this for the purpose of ascertaining just what the effect would be if the gas were taken without sandwiching in a little pure air between whiffs, which had been the Doctor's method the day before. Instantly, almost, I experienced identically the same sensation that had followed the taking of nitrous oxide gas or laughing gas when having a tooth drawn. I felt assured that with one or two added inhalations I should have been made unconscious. Upon removing the tube from my mouth and then breathing in the gas at slow intervals, which I did as soon as I had recovered from the effects described, the same delicious sensations of the day before returned and life seemed again a rose garden.

UNPLEASANT AFTER RESULTS.

For about an hour the pleasurable excited state lasted, and then gradually died away, followed by a tightening of the heart, a feeling of exhaustion and a most distressing headache, from which I suffered throughout the entire afternoon.

In order to ascertain whether or not I was correct in believing that the Doctor's compound oxygen was nothing more nor less than nitrous oxide gas, I at once set about securing a quantity of it for analysis.

In order to carry out my plan I told Dr. Northrop that a friend who was confined to the house and not able to come to his office desired to test the treatment, and I asked him if he would allow me to take her some. He seemed very willing that I should do this, although he did not even ask me what her illness was, and went on to say that there were a number of patients on his books to whom bags of the "oxygen" were sent regularly every day.

When prepared for transportation the oxygen is placed in big rubber bags, covered with silk netting and provided with stop cocks—short rubber tubes with glass mouthpieces.

Three of these oxygen bags I secured in this way and then took them to an expert analytical chemist for analysis, whose certificate is as follows:—

CERTIFICATE OF ANALYSIS.

"The sample of gas received from the NEW YORK HERALD on July 12, 1894, contains:—

Nitrous oxide	66.73 per cent
Nitrogen	26.22 per cent
Oxygen	7.04 per cent

"The sample therefore consists of about two-thirds nitrous oxide and one-third air.

"E. G. LOVE, PH. D.,
"Analytical and Consulting Chemist.
"NEW YORK, July 18, 1894."

Now that my suspicions regarding the gas were confirmed I determined to ascertain what the effects of continued use of nitrous oxide gas would be and if its promiscuous use was sanctioned by physicians generally. According to high medical authorities the action of nitrous oxide can be more fully compared with the action of chloroform than with the simple exclusion of oxygen from the blood.

The conclusions regarding nitrous oxide from the laborious investigations which have been made are that it possesses special anaesthetic properties, and that it produces special effects upon the nervous system.

WHEN DILUTED WITH AIR.

When diluted with air these effects are limited to the manifestation of a peculiar exhilaration. When inhaled without dilution the gas produces first excitement, then anaesthesia, and finally asphyxia, and as it is not decomposed in the blood, consequently it cannot replace oxygen or yield oxygen for the respiration of the tissues.

Moreover, that, though nitrous oxide gas is commonly supposed to be absolutely harmless, by consulting authentic medical records it is found that there have been a number of deaths from inhaling nitrous oxide gas.

In carrying out my investigation I saw several physicians on the subject.

Dr. Allan McLane Hamilton, who was one of the first to recommend the use of nitrous oxide gas as an anaesthetic, said he believed that nitrous oxide judiciously administered was a valuable agent.

He had recently been called in consultation to see a patient who had an attack of heart failure as the result of the careless use of gas procured, he believed, from what he called "an advertising charlatan."

MOST DANGEROUS.

Dr. Hamilton considered the taking of gas in the manner just described as a most dangerous one and likely to result in the patient acquiring the habit, which is as dominating and disreputable, he declares, as is the abuse of alcohol, opium, chloral or any other poison.

Dr. Hamilton went so far as to declare that the continued use of nitrous oxide gas would, in his opinion, produce heart failure. "Why is it, then, Doctor, that so many people believe in the absolute harmlessness of nitrous oxide gas?" I asked.

"Because they neither know anything of its composition or of the proper method of its use," he answered decidedly. "It should not be administered except under the advice and direction of a physician."

Dr. C. L. Dana, another prominent neurologist, was equally emphatic in his denunciation of the promiscuous peddling of nitrous oxide gas.

"I have known of many persons, dentists particularly, who have acquired the ether or chloroform habit, and as nitrous oxyde is administered in much the same manner as are these agents the danger is equally great."

"Have you ever heard of this so-called compound oxygen, Doctor?" I inquired.

"Yes," he said. "I had a patient who disappeared from my care for a time, and who, when he returned, said he had been using compound oxygen. He was thoroughly infatuated with it, and I told him he ought not to go about taking drugs or gas in that indiscriminate fashion, adding that if he wanted to take gas he had better have it fresh from my apparatus and under my direction."

Dr. Dana further said that he had given nitrous oxide to melancholy patients, but declared that it should never be taken except under the supervision of a physician, and even then used very judiciously.

DR. GRAEME HAMMOND'S VIEWS.

When I questioned Dr. Graeme Hammond on the subject he said that he had heard of the Compound Oxygen Company in Thirty-fourth street, and, in fact, had known several persons who had taken the treatment for various ailments.

"From what I can learn," he said, "people go there and take this gas, which produces the most delightful sensations. For an hour or two they feel intensely exhilarated and their ills appear much lessened. After that the reaction comes. The gas habit becomes as dangerous as that of any other opiate."

Dr. Hammond further said that he considered nitrous oxide too powerful to be given by inexperienced persons or novices. Its effects, he declared, were exactly similar to those produced by opium. "It is undoubtedly true," added he, "that the nitrous oxide habit could be acquired without any difficulty and become a decidedly powerful one." The effect on the person taking it was the same as if liquor had been imbibed to a considerable extent, he said.

PERSONAL EXPERIENCE.

One prominent physician with whom I talked gave me his own personal experience in the use of nitrous oxide gas. He had prescribed it, he said, in melancholia, and in testing the strength before administering it he had discovered its peculiarly happy effect. Before long he found himself going over to his gas apparatus whenever he felt slightly worn out with work, and taking several inhalations to restore the lost tone to his system. When, after a while, his heart began to act strangely and other unpleasant symptoms arose, he at first attributed them to the excessive use of tobacco, but when after restricting his smoking, he determined to discontinue the use of the gas. Almost at once the improvement became noticeable, and in a short time the unpleasant symptoms had entirely disappeared.

This physician said, moreover, that he made it an inflexible rule never to administer the gas to a patient without the presence of an assistant or other witness. "Medico-legal records are full of cases where women patients when under the influence of nitrous oxide gas have imagined themselves subjected to indignities. Dentists are especially victims in this regard."

Professor Rudolph Kobert, an eminent German medical authority, in his treatise on poisons and inebriation, speaks of one reported case of excessive and chronic use of nitrous oxide, or laughing gas. It is that of a young chemist of Boston, whose daily inhalation of the gas for a long interval resulted in his falling into a state of delirium and excitement, accompanied with delusions, which lasted a month. After these passed away, however, his mind did not return to its original clearness, and he was placed in an insane asylum.

In the same treatise Professor Kobert refers to nine (9) cases of reported deaths from nitrous oxide, as well as a series of unpleasant accidents and after diseases, such as headache, hysteria, vertigo and epilepsy; these results happening from but one administration, which would seem to prove that it is not only not a harmless drug, but an exceedingly dangerous one, even if used in a moderate way.

Having been deceived as to the real character and constituents of Dr. Northrop's "compound oxygen," and as all the physicians I had talked with had agreed that no one but a physician should administer the particular gas which Dr. Northrop's turned out to be, I determined to learn, if possible, what his standing was in the medical profession.

NONE KNEW HIM.

None of the doctors I had interviewed knew him, nor was his name in the printed register which is supposed to contain the names of all physicians practising in New York city. Inquiries at the Board of Health and of Medical Director Dr. Cyrus W. Edson failed to discover the fact that "Dr. Northrop," as his patients call him, had any right to the title.

Further and complete search of the records at the County Clerk's office proved that Northrop had not registered there, the law requiring all physicians to so register having been in effect since 1880. In order to ascertain to just what an extent Northrop is making himself liable, by prescribing and administering any drug or remedy without having acquired the proper credentials, I called on Lawyer Robert C. Taylor, counsel for the State Medical Society, at his office in the Postal Telegraph Building.

AMENABLE TO THE LAW.

Mr. Taylor informed me that under the old law Northrop could have been prosecuted on a criminal charge, but that now his course comes under section 153, chapter 661, of the State Laws, which says that every person who shall practise medicine within this State without lawful registration shall be fined $50 for each violation.

At this rate, if Northrop should be prosecuted, Northrop, from the number of patients I saw during my two visits to the Heidelberg Compound Oxygen Company's parlors, would be liable to the county for a very considerable sum.

According to the law any incorporated medical society of this State or county entitled to representation in a State society may bring an action against him in the name of the county for the collection of such penalties, the expenses of the prosecution being retained out of the total of the fines imposed.

Undoubtedly many of Mr. Northrop's gas patients are attending his office regularly day after day under the impression that they are being greatly benefited, and from what is understood regarding the gas, it does undoubtedly produce a momentary cessation of pain. As long as this effect continues the patient feels better, and as the amount of gas is increased in the daily treatment the results are more lasting, until she becomes convinced she is being cured, and in this way also the nitrous oxide, or compound oxygen, habit, can be easily acquired.

BOSTON SUNDAY GLOBE—NOVEMBER 17, 190

WHEN OXYGEN PARTI

AN AMBITIOUS PLAN FOR A NITROUS OXIDE CARRIAGE. (Probably for 1800.)

BECOME THE RAGE SOCIETY WILL WAKE UP.

—The Inhalation of Oxygen Causes Great Mental Exhilaration.)

A RESOUNDING VERBAL THUNDERCLAP FROM THE TONGU

Reared as Victorian But Prefers Ways of Moderns.

Copyright, 1933, by Universal Service, Inc. Special Radio Dispatch.

ABOARD S. S. EMPRESS OF BRITAIN, April 10.—George Bernard Shaw is a Victorian—because he was reared as one. But he believes that moderns, and especially women, have the edge on Victorian relics.

The Irish dramatist and critic, whose pointed gibes at tradition have used a good deal of ink and white paper in his time, today characterized himself not only as a Victorian, but also as a "cosmic dentist" who has not only hurt but also helped the world by deadening the nerves of its bad teeth.

New Dress Significant

While Shaw and his wife were doing their last afternoon turn around the deck of the Empress of Britain today before docking ... morning in New York, ... the bewhiskered ... to be interviewed about his Victorian beliefs—and other matters.

He was asked whether the relationship between man and woman has changed, to his mind, in the last twenty years, and his answer was:

"Tremendously — but not fundamentally. Changed dress transformed the relationship.

"Really a Victorian"

"I am really a Victorian. In my time we used to load women with clothing so that ...e exhibition of a feminine ...kle was historic.

"If by accident a woman ...splayed her ankle in falling ... of a carriage, the popu... came from miles around ... the phenomena of peo... narrating for years that ... had seen a woman's ...

...eople would tell how they ... a person who saw a ...n's ankle. All made a ...ry of anatomy. Now ...hange of styles brings ... out into the open. ...e cruising I saw women ...ed for dancing, sports ... swimming. They wear ...ically nothing.

... is astounding, but the ...sformation is a good ...

...Dressmakers are Victorian-...ded because formerly it ...nt a mile of material to make a dress, and now it takes only an inch.

"The same revolution took place in feminine talk. Modern women will discuss any-

CHEMICAL EXPERIMENTALIST.

131. BREATHING INTOXICATING GAS.

thing, and they swear a good deal better than men. They bring anything into conversation openly and casually.

"When I hear women talk I have to turn my head the other way. But it's a good thing."

His Characters Prudes

Reminded that the characters in his early works talked frankly, Shaw replied:

"My characters were comparative prudes. Modern women talk subjects tabooed in the Victorian era.

"We talked subjects like the weather in my youth. And children were dressed so you could not tell between the sexes. I dressed in a shimmy, with drawers below the knees, stays, a flannel petticoat, a cotton petticoat and a long gown.

Wife Makes Sure Shaw Wears His Flannel Pajamas

THE WORLD'S OUTSTANDING FIGURE IN LITERATURE!

MRS. George Bernard Shaw is her husband's confidential adviser.

She also sees to it that her husband wears his flannel pajamas and that her own bed linen is used in their stateroom.

She sees that Shaw sticks to his vegetarian diet — porridge, butter, sugar, no coffee, no tea for breakfast.

Anyway, G. B. S. is pretty easy to keep in hand. Even at meals or cocktail parties, he touches only orange juice.

"Dress and speech have had a tremendous influence on feminine evolution. Women do anything a man can do except think like Shaw."

Wanted to Sing in Opera

Shaw posed for the newsreel photographers. Asked if he'd like to be an actor, he responded:

"No, I wanted to be an opera singer. My dramatic technique requires operatic characters making long speeches, as in the opera. English people like to hear long speeches.

"Present-day drama critics only read movie sub-titles. They go to the movies instead of to plays."

"I've shot my bolt. However, I expect to write 30 more volumes before I lay down my pen for good.

"I am a dentist pulling the teeth of the world. When I started preaching there was

Shaw, Here Today, Calls Himself 'Cosmic Dentist'; Has Pulled World's Teeth with Laughing Gas, He Says

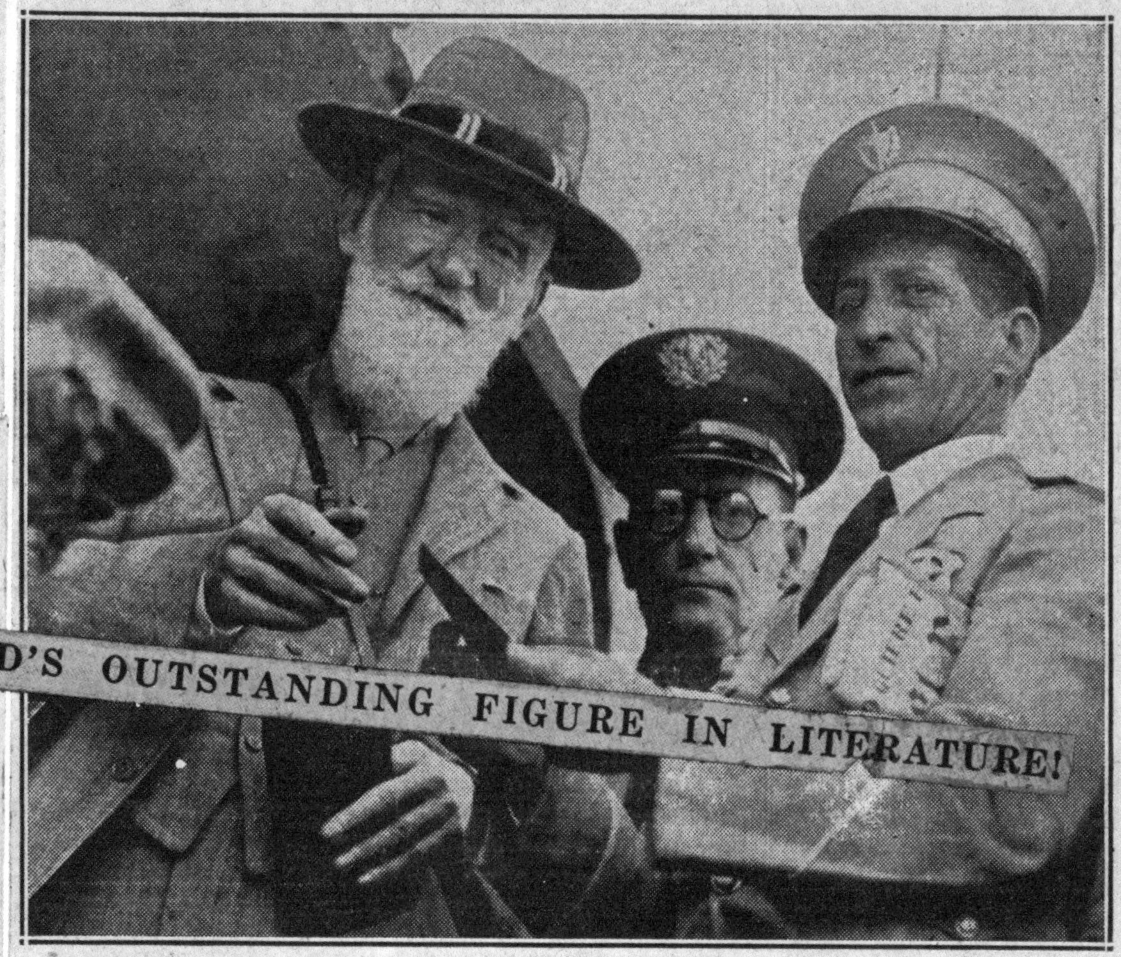

GET READY, NEW YORK—The one and only George Bernard Shaw, who will gaze upon and be gazed upon by the one and only New York today, pictured with immigration inspectors when his ship stopped at Havana. Picture from International News Photograph Service.

universal pyorrhea. Nobody likes to have his teeth pulled, but he feels much better afterward.

"I have put in my witticism for laughing gas and I think I have been useful."

"Others Boobs, Too"

Shaw tempered his barbs at America today and said:

"Americans are interesting. I've said they were boobs about politics, but so are other nationals.

'I've Shot My Bolt,' He Says, but Plans 30 More Books.

"But it's strange how you can get a rise from Americans. If I tell them they have only two legs, they bristle up, thinking I mean Europeans have three legs.

"Until recently Americans have copied Europe, but they now have the beginnings of a genuine American originality in art, literature and the drama. Young Americans come to London to get away from the U. S. A. and ask me where to study. I advise them to go back to the U. S. A. and stay there.

Shaw May Tour City Before Talk Tonight

George Bernard Shaw, perhaps Marxism's dearest friend and America's severest critic, arrives today for his first visit to that fabulous city about which he has heard and talked so much—New York.

He arrives this morning on the world-cruising liner Empress of Britain, which leaves at noon tomorrow.

Adivces from the vessel have been that he will come ashore only for one brief address at the Metropolitan Opera House and will return immediately to the liner.

But there were rumors among friends yesterday that he now plans to leave the boat in the late forenoon or early afternoon for a drive around the city. It was said he expressed an especial desire to see Central Park and the neighboring districts.

His subject in his Metropolitan address before the Academy of Political Science, it was announced yesterday by Miss Ethel Warner, director, will be "The Future of Political Science in America." The speech will be carried on a coast-to-coast National Broadcasting Company network.

TOADSTOOLS AND MUSHROOMS—WHAT ARE EDIBLE AND WHAT POISONOUS.

COMMON FIELD MUSHROOM.
AGARICUS CAMPESTRIS—EDIBLE.

OUR FRIENDS AND FOES AMONG THE FUNGI.

This Is the Season When Many Persons Are Killed by Eating Poisonous Varieties.

BY JOHN GILMER SPEED.

AT this season every year we read in our newspapers reports of illnesses and deaths from toadstool poisoning in various parts of the country. This will continue to be the case so long as people generally stick to the idea that there is only one mushroom, and that all the other fungi of the fields and forests are poisonous toadstools. It would be much better if people who are fond of these elusive growths should arrive at the correct conclusion that all of the fungi they see growing are toadstools and then learn which are the friends and which are the foes of man.

I have never seen a case of genuine—that is, fatal—toadstool poisoning, but I readily understand how those who gather mushrooms for their own consumption or for the market can make the fatal mistake of including in a basket of meadow mushrooms (Agaricus campestris) a specimen or two of the one toadstool which kills—the deadly amanita.

The Toadstool Habitat.

The meadow or field mushroom always grows in the open, preferably in an old and well established pasture which is tolerably free of weeds and of long grass. These mushrooms are white on top and pink, turning to purple and then to black in full maturity underneath. They are erratic in their growth, but where one is found in a time of favorable weather conditions the hunter is pretty sure to find others, sometimes very many others. Here is the danger. The careless, inexperienced or unobservant gatherer picks up all that come in his way. Now the amanita rarely, if ever, grows in the open. It likes a shady place.

In pretty nearly every pasture there are trees left for the shelter of the grazing cattle. Under such trees the same conditions which encouraged and induced the growth of the delicious and wholesome campestris will cause the deadly amanita to spring up. Then again, a great many pastures are fenced by hedges and bounded by woods. Under trees and in other shady places, especially at the edge of woods, is the favorite habitat of the amanita. On top it looks very like the campestris, and it is easy indeed to gather one or more by mistake. And even one will play havoc with a whole family in a large dish of a good variety. In this way I make no doubt many hundreds of people have been killed. No one would eat a dish of these deadly toadstools. They would not be grateful to the taste, but one in a dish of the campestris would not be noticed.

The Deadly Amanita.

The best protection against this deadly toadstool is to know it well. I do not know that every one would be able to recognize it from a description, but even a dull person having once observed it closely would know it ever afterward. It has decided and unmistakable characteristics. While the top of the cap of the amanita is frequently white and quite similar to that of the field mushroom, the gills on the under side are never pink, but always white. Then again, the stem always has a veil or the remains of one, while the stem grows out of a bulb or cup. This cup is called the poison cup, and some persons believe that this is the source of the poison. Such, however, is not the case, as the whole fungus is as poisonous as possible, and the cup has this appellation merely because the cup is a characteristic of all poisonous specimens.

Puffball.
LYCOPERDON CYATHIFORME—EDIBLE.

There are some edible toadstools which spring from a socket, but it is well for amateurs to avoid all those that so grow and to classify them as too dangerous even to experiment with.

This deadly toadstool cannot be detected by any of the old women's tests. They will peel, they will not blacken a silver spoon that is left in the vessel while the toadstools are cooking, they may be picked in the early morning, they have solid stems, and so on, and so on. Indeed, all of those popular notions are wrong, and those who hold to them but cling to ignorant ideas that have often been refuted. And yet, if you should go into a company of twenty-five persons ordinarily well informed, you would find that twenty at least of them believed more or less implicitly in these worthless tests.

The Toadstool Antidote.

Within the last ten years an antidote to the poison of the amanita has been discovered and fully tested. It was Captain Charles McIlvaine, of Haddonfield, N. J., who published this discovery to the world, and by so doing he has placed in the hands of physicians a tolerably sure cure of this deadly poison. Captain McIlvaine recommends the subcutaneous injection of atropine until one-twentieth of a grain be given or the patient's life saved.

This antidote has often been tried successfully, and if all physicians knew about it there would be few deaths from toadstool poisoning. The difficulty is that physicians rarely have such cases, and then, with such a case, the medical man rarely knows what to do. With untried tackle he goes fishing for something else than the amanita, and in consequence fails to save his patient.

The poison after it begins to work acts very quickly, and therefore there is no time to be lost. Especially is it dangerous for the doctor to bother about what kind of toadstool his patient has eaten. In ninety-nine cases out of a hundred he would be no wiser after knowing than he was before. The thing for him to do when the case is serious is to get his atropine and go to work with his hypodermic syringe. Here is Captain McIlvaine's recommendation for treatment:—

"The physician called upon to treat a case of toadstool poisoning need not wait to query after the variety eaten. His first endeavor should be to ascertain the exact time elapsing between the eating of the toadstools and the first feeling of discomfort. If this is within four or five hours one of the minor poisons is at work, and rapid relief must be given by the administration of an emetic, followed by one or two doses of sweet oil and whiskey in equal parts. Vinegar is effective as a substitute for sweet oil. If from eight to twelve hours have elapsed the physician may rest assured that amanitine is present, and should administer one-sixtieth of a grain of atrophine at once."

The Danger of Ignorance.

But the totally ignorant had better leave both toadstools and mushrooms alone, even though many tons of excellent food should go to waste. I do not think that ignorant people deserve such good food. Pork and beans are good enough for those who will not take the trouble or who lack the capacity to learn enough to know the difference between the good and bad fungi which grow in such plenty from the spring to the autumn of the year.

I think also that amateurs, unless very accomplished, should confine their attention to a few varieties about which an observant person will not be apt to make any mistakes. Most of these are agarics, though with them should be included the fairy ring champignons, the boleti, the morels, the oyster mushroom and the humble puff ball. Of these the Agaricus procerus and the Agaricus campestris are, to my thinking, easily the best; and at the same time most easily detected.

The "fairy ring" is delicious, and is often found in abundance on the lawns and in pastures. I believe that all boleti are good, though some of the more conservative authorities have two groups, one of which they call poisonous. I believe also that the russulae are good—that is, harmless; but in this class there is also a difference of opinion.

Mrs. Ruth McEnery Stuart, the novelist, is an accomplished amateur, and in a letter to me just written by her in Massachusetts she says that the russulae she has found this summer have been too much decayed to be used for food. This has not been my experience in New Jersey, but it is surely true that all russulae decay very quickly and they should be gathered very soon after they show above the surface. The Russula virescens is an excellent toadstool. On the top it seems to have been sprinkled with Roquefort cheese. I have gathered a peck of these in an area twenty yards square. The spring mushroom, the morel, is easily known, and it is held in well deserved esteem.

The other day I found a splendid specimen of the oyster mushroom, Agaricus ostreatus. It weighed several pounds and made a splendid dish. I happened to be staying at a summer hotel and offered it to the other guests. None partook of it; some were polite in their refusal, others acted as though they felt sorry for me, while still others seemed to be under the impression that I had designs against their life. Poor misguided ones! They missed a good supper—but maybe they also missed having a bad night, for they were all apparently genuinely afraid. Heaven knows I do not blame them. In eating toadstools it is well to be on the safe side if to get there requires total abstinence from fungus consumption.

Too Much Enthusi[asm.]

The enthusiastic mycologist ... at finding that an untested va[riety will not] kill nor yet make ill the parta[ker] ... he is apt to set it down as exce[llent] ... I have learned to take these sta[tements with] a grain of salt, for there is va[st difference] between eating and enjoying ... licious and merely escaping the st...

Some of the varieties set d[own in the] books as esculent are actually ... most recent experience was wit[h Lac]tarius piperatus, or the peppery ... toadstool. This is closely relat[ed to] Lactarius volemum and the Lacta[rius ...]osus and in form is exactly the ... grows in much greater abundance than the others, and I thought the other day when I saw thousands of them in the woods that I would put the recommendations of the experts to a test. I had a dozen or so stewed. It made an appetizing dish to look at, but the taste was most abominable, while the odor was offensive. As to this variety my curiosity is satisfied, and I shall not try the peppery milk white toadstool again.

Fairy Ring Fungus.
MARASMIUS OREADES—EDIBLE.

This was the last experience of the kind, but there had been many before, so I have concluded that though these gentlemen may have reached safe conclusions as to the harmlessness of the classified varieties, I do not believe that they are to be implicitly trusted in the matter of good and bad taste.

But one skilful mycologist is of more service in instructing a novice than all the books that have been written. The ambitious book of W. Hamilton Gibson, with its exquisitely drawn and colored illustrations, is a very baffling work. Mr. Gibson in his text confessed that he did not know many varieties. And so, in treating of only those he knew, he bewilders rather than enlightens, for we find scores that are not in his book, but resemble some of them so closely that a novice with Gibson's book under his arm is sure to be puzzled on every side.

One day in the woods and fields with a man such as Captain McIlvaine, however, is of infinite value, for such an expert can explain each specimen as it is found, and then the amateur with a good memory will not be apt to forget.

A WHOLE TRIBE WIPED OUT.

How the Brave but Misguided Timoche Indians of Chihuahua Were Exterminated.

UP to ten years ago there existed in the mountains of Northwestern Chihuahua, Mexico, a small remnant of what had been a large and brave tribe of Indians known as the Timoches. They were formerly allies of the Yaquis, but confined their fighting to encounters with the various predatory bands of Apaches which roamed through the western portion of the Sierra Madres, devastating and destroying the homes, property and lives of Mexicans and Indians alike.

In the many incursions of the Apaches the Timoches had lost a majority of their fighting men, and when by the effort of the Mexican and American forces the Apaches were finally subdued and Geronimo and the other savages who for years had been leading them were properly imprisoned, the Timoches settled down in their mountain homes to reunite the so-called families of their band and organize tribal relations.

Their habitations were mostly to the north of the town of Concepcion, now Guerrero, and not far from the line of the Chihuahua and Pacific Railroad, now building.

Timosachic was a little town, which was looked upon as a sort of centre of their stamping ground, and here they had built a church, which was served by a priest from the Cathedral at Chihuahua.

Intelligent and Religious.

The Timoches were different from any other Indians of Western Mexico, generally larger and finely formed; their complexions were light and hair fine and different in color and texture from that of the ordinary Indian. The women, too, were of good figure and face, and in intelligence in advance of the Mexicans. They were most faithful in their religious observances, and were marked for their steady conduct and good citizenship. During the year 1894 the Timoches were visited by a fanatical woman pretender, who, styling herself Santa Teresa, announced herself as having a mission from heaven, and that the mission looked to the regeneration of Mexico through her agency. And the Timoches, the simple hearted Indians, were attracted by the adventuress, who also claimed extraordinary healing powers through Divine aid.

The Indians flocked to her standard and the demonstration became of such form that the Mexican government sent an officer and a detachment of soldiers to arrest or summarily squelch Santa Teresa. The Timoches, acting under her orders, killed the soldiers, and the officer hurried back to Chihuahua to carry the news. Then a larger force was sent under the command of a colonel, and he was killed, as well as the greater part of his command.

Martial Law Declared.

Then it was found that an agent of the Timoches had arrived in Chihuahua and informed the leaders of the Church party of the success of their revolt, and, thinking this an opportune time to overthrow the liberal party and the reform laws of Juarez, the Church party greatly aided and encouraged the Timoches, until the elements of discord became so evident that martial law was declared in that city, and a heavy force of regular troops was despatched to dispose of the recalcitrant Indians. Meantime Teresa was urging the Timoches to defy the government, claiming that God was directing her, and that by His help she would cause them to conquer.

The infatuation of the poor creatures, together with the information that the Church party in the city of Chihuahua was about to revolt against the government, was such that they determined to fight to the end, and threw up entrenchments around their town and provisioned in great quantity the church which stood in the centre of the town.

Was Well Fortified.

This was also fortified with great walls of stone, at each entrance port holes were cut, to command the road upon which the soldiers were to come, the women and children of the tribe were brought hither, and upon the attack being made in overwhelming force, a most deadly battle was fought. Having fallen back upon the church, where had been stored extra arms and ammunition, the women were used in loading the guns, and for three days a most gallant defence was made and hundreds of Mexican soldiers were killed. Finally artillery arrived and a bombardment of the church began. The soldiers were stationed on every side of the church, and the destruction of life after each cannon fire was followed by the yells of dying women and children, but the Indians fought to the last, and one old woman, it is related, stood close to one of the port holes and said words of cheer to her aged husband, and in turn to her five stalwart sons, and when they all fell, she called her two grandsons, boys of twelve and fourteen years of age, to aim the Winchesters at the foe, telling them that God had honored their fathers with a glorious end.

All Killed but One.

The Mexican soldiers, embittered by the loss of their comrades, showed no quarter, nor did the brave Timoches ask it. Of the tribes of seventy-two Timoches but one man exists to-day. Two hundred and sixteen Mexicans were killed and 310 wounded, among whom were several officers. Santa Teresa escaped during the engagement. Several weeks elapsed before quiet was finally secured in Chihuahua, but to this day there are sullen looks and defiant words seen and heard when "the uprising of the Timoches" is spoken of. The church has been rebuilt and is at present well attended by the newcomers to the section.

ARTIFICIALLY GROWN PEARLS

Results of Experiments in Cedar River, Ia.

THE method of producing figures and symbols from the fresh water mussel (Dipsas plicatus) of Lake Riwa, Central China, has been in vogue many centuries. Superb examples of Buddha and flat, pearl-like discs — produced by inserting between the mantle and shell of the mollusk small tinfoil figures of Buddha or small hemispherical discs which in time become coated by the pearly nacre—are to be seen in collections such as that of the Field Columbian and other well known museums.

Experiments of a like nature, with the "rough shelled" unios, of Cedar River, Ia., have been practised by the writer the past three years with fair success. An average sized shell, or shells, from a section of the river bed known to produce brilliantly lustred shells, were allowed to remain in the sun until the valves parted. With a quickly inserted wedge in the opening the shell is immediately dipped in water to sustain life.

The operator then carefully lifts the mantle from the shell, and, with a pair of tweezers, drops in a pellet of wax, glass bead or other small article that he is desirous of having coated. Care is taken not to strain the muscles by forcing the wedge while the clam is resisting the intrusion.

After the objects are placed in that part of the mussel showing the best color, the mantle is drawn to place, the wedge removed and the shell allowed to resume its normal condition. With a sufficient number "fixed" in the above described manner, they are then placed in a pond or bayou that will not freeze its depth in winter.

At the expiration of six months, or one year at most, the unio will have thrown over these irritating foreign substances a nacreous covering that securely fastens them to the shell. Usually about two-thirds of the object thus fastened remains above the shell, though it is presumed that in time the natural growth of the shell would entirely efface this.

By careful work it is possible to remove these objects so as to have considerale pearl surface, though their commercial value is small, very small indeed in comparison to more perfect gems.—Popular Science News.

Insurance Agent—We can't insure you.

Old Man—Why not?

Insurance Agent—You are ninety-four years old.

Old Man—What of that? Statistics will tell you that fewer men die at ninety-four than at any other age.—Exchange.

Horse Mushroom.
AGARICUS ARVENSIS—EDIBLE.

SWELL GIRLS AS TAILORS.

IN a room back of one of the swellest fancy work and embroidery shops just off Fifth avenue may be seen a group of summer girls in the early mornings of any week day just now. They are there to learn how to make waistcoats, for it is now the proper thing to present "home made" embroidered waistcoats to husbands, brothers and sweethearts.

"Single breasted and buttoned straight up, but with no collar and sufficiently low cut to show the cravat and a bit of the shirt front," is the formula to be followed in cutting out the ground work canvas for the waistcoat given to me by an authority. When this is done the tailor sets a trim, taut silk binding about the edge to give it the right "set." A swell Fifth avenue tailor said:—

"The canvas worked waistcoat in subdued mixed colors is well suited to street wear in the morning, and will be popularly worn, just as any ordinary waistcoat. Devised at first for billiards, golf and the bicycle, it is so adaptable and unobtrusive as to be useful for any ordinary function.

"Those worked in the flat, cross-stitched, in a dull, dark shade, are in excellent form; also the black and dull blue combination, black and hunter's green, and quiet shades of bronze brown and terra cotta.

"The largest majority of the home worked vest patterns sent to us so far have been done in cross stitch, in either silk or worsted, the coloring being warm shades of red and profusely sprinkled with tiny pink hearts. In these we put a back and sleeves of satin to match the ground work, and they are worn chiefly for sporting purposes.

"Another style is to work dimity colored flowers in between or over the main pattern of a black brocaded waistcoat. Double breasted waistcoats, to be worn with frock coats, are acceptable in this style.

FLY AGARIC.
AMANITA MUSCARIA—POISONOUS.

GASTRONOMIC PORTO RICO.

Cocoa Water Ice Is All Right, but Beware of Mavi—Our New Colony's Cuisine.

THERE is to be an overturning of most of the old established rules of cooking and liquid concoctions in Porto Rico with the Americanizing of the island. On the other hand, there will be adoption by the Americans of certain confections which heretofore have been ... them. Generally ...

... cocoa ice ... choose to call it. It is a ... ice made from the milk of the cocoanut. This is placed in the revolving freezer can, about which is packed the Porto Rican artificial ice and salt. The process of making it is practically the same ... that used in making our ice cream ...

The Porto Rican ... ble, very inferior to the ice m... the United ... which run ... gover-

... Porto Rican is able t... are clamoring for veget... hotels, and they will ge... ican's dollar is being ... more on the island ea...

GENII OF DEATH LURK
IN THE TOADSTOOL

... these few places, instead of putting the bottled beer on ice, they put the ice in the beer after it had been poured into the glass. Americans fumed and protested at this treatment of the beer. Patrons of the hotels begged their landlords, through interpreters, to put bottles of beer on ice, to be called for as they wanted them.

The Boniface solemnly promised to do as requested, but when the patron brought his friend around to the hotel "to have a cold bottle of beer," the ice was dropped in the hot, frothing lager in the same old Porto Rican way.

The Deadly Mavi.

When the American saw that the Porto Rican would never master the beer on ice proposition, he asked for the Porto Rican substitute for beer. Then he was given the mavi. This has a sort of biting, flat taste. He did not like mavi at first, but he thought that with a third or fourth glass of it he would form a different opinion of it. He did, too—when he woke up. As a teamster friend of mine eloquently expressed it, "Three glasses are worse than a kick in the face from a mule."

Captain Lyons, of Company K, Sixteenth Pennsylvania volunteers, who was in charge of the Ponce jail the first week our soldiers occupied the city, had two victims of mavi laid out side by side in the prison courtyard, as living (or seemingly dying) examples of the effect of the Porto Rican cheap drink. To all outward appearances these men were dead. One of them was about to be taken to the deadhouse when the surgeon discovered there was still the faintest pulse possible.

One man was in this deathlike stupor for thirty-six, and the other for forty-nine hours. When Captain Lyons found what they had been drinking, he marched all his men past the cots of the apparently dead men, that they might take warning and ... small drinks. ...

WILL HUN...

Mine Said T... the A...

Deadly Agaric.
AMANITA PHALLOIDES—POISONOUS.

The Juice of the Jungle Vine That Cures FEAR

In the Heart of South American Jungle Showing the "Courage Flower" Vine, Caapi, Growing About the Tree in the Centre, and One of the Searchers for the Precious Growth Holding His Rifle Ready to Repel Savage Attack.

At Last Medical Science Feels That It Has Found in the "Courage Flower," Caapi, a Non-Habit Forming Draught to Overcome Mankind's Greatest Enemy.

Science Resorts to All Sorts of Means to Overcome Fear. Below Is a Photograph of a Patient in a Washington Emergency Hospital Having His Mind Diverted by a Radio Concert as Surgeons Operate on Him.

FEAR—A Notable Interpretation of Mankind's Curse by Sybil Thorndike, Famous English Actress.

By Dr. W. H. Ballou

GORDON McCREAGH, explorer, is back from South America, bringing with him in a little black box a thing that may free you and me, in our moments of greatest pain and terror, from our deadliest enemy—fear.

This little black box reposes in a Philadelphia laboratory. It is cherished as though it contained the Hope diamond. What it does contain is simply 10 pounds of sticks and leaves.

That is all—10 pounds of jungle roots.

Yet $50,000 was spent to get those roots; men suffered and died, paddled miles of rivers and crossed leagues of forest, fought fever and beasts and reptiles and the points of poisoned arrows, just to wrench out of the wilderness the juice which, given a man before an operation, may make him laugh at Death, or, given an expectant mother, may take her painlessly through childbirth.

The roots make Caapi. And science believes it has discovered, in Caapi, a drug which, like hashish, will banish fear; but which, unlike hashish, may be administered without any terrible, habit-forming results.

The story of what Caapi will do for mankind cannot be written until the juice distilled from the leaves is properly analyzed and tested. Then it may be a story to interest personally every human being. But the story of how Caapi was found and how it was brought back to civilization may be written now. It is one of this century's greatest romances of danger and achievement in the name of science.

A Craven Becomes a Hero

For many years the medical profession has heard of Caapi, but only vaguely. Baron Humboldt, the German explorer, heard the natives of Brazil speak of a strange potion which made the savages of the hinterland reckless in battle. Richard Spruce saw the vine with vivid red blossoms which his guide called the "courage flower." Weiss, another famous explorer, witnessed an Indian change from a craven to a Hector after tossing off a cup of liquid brewed from the vine.

Such stories from South America smacked too much of the fabulous to be taken too seriously by doctors and chemists. And yet they were interested, for one of the great needs of science was to find some means to rid man of fear.

If some way could be found to deaden the tortured mind during an operation, as parts of the body are deadened by the injection of anaesthesia, and if this could be done without the use of ether or chloroform—dangerous to the heart action—millions of lives might be saved.

Dr. H. H. Rusby, president of the College of Pharmacy of Columbia University, decided to get the sample. The Rusby Mulford Expedition was formed, financed and launched, with Caapi as its principal quest.

Difficulties of the Quest

The members of the expedition had their work cut out for them. The only country where Caapi was known to grow was in the hinterlands of Colombia, Peru, Ecuador and Brazil, and this is one of the few unexplored sections of the globe.

Three million years ago, where this tableland rises today, was the Andean Sea. When the waters receded after some great physical cataclysm, they left a range of mountain and valley on which animal and plant life flourished as it did in the world's dawn.

And, through the ages, life changed there but little. Great serpents still glide these forests. Strange mammals snort through those jungles. Beautiful ferns tower to extraordinary heights. Exotic flowers burst into blossom. It is the home of the boa constrictor, the anaconda, the tapir, the bird of paradise, the orchid—and Caapi.

Few white men have ever penetrated into this wilderness. Bands of savages have been known to block the trails and stalk the rivers. They are not seen, for the weapons they use are silent, and horribly effective—arrows tipped with a poison that has but to scratch to kill.

Every precaution was used to defeat hardship, disease and whatever enemies might be encountered. The members went heavily armed. They carried devices for sterilizing every drop of water. Their packs contained serums and antitoxins preventive of fever, tetanus, smallpox, snake venom and other perils. Three tons of canned and powdered food were included. But, despite all protections, several died. Dr. Rusby was forced to return home, dangerously ill. There were left only McCreagh, Duval Brown and G. S. McCarty.

Up the Rio Negro and the Rio Waupes they went by paddle and portage. Their luggage bearers were Colombian rubber workers. After many days these deserted, taking with them most of the food and ammunition. McCreagh, Brown and McCarty turned back in pursuit. For three days they tracked the deserters through almost impenetrable forests. At last they came up with them. There was a pitched battle. The natives were defeated. Some were killed. The rest fled. The victorious trio, undaunted by the delay, set their faces again to the unknown.

One day, paddling up the Rio Tiquie, a tributary of the Waupes, a black shadow whizzed past the head of McCreagh and struck the water with a tiny splash. It was an arrow. A dark splotch spread from its head and melted into the water. If it had struck him, McCreagh would have been killed.

The boat was stopped. The three men beat the woods until they found their man. He was jabbering with anger. But McCreagh calmed him. Instead of using force, he turned on the man a simple pocket flashlight. The fellow's eyes all but popped from his head. He fell to the ground in an attitude of worship.

The flashlight did what no amount of gunpowder could have accomplished. The tribesman, released, brought his companions. They, too, fell to the ground and worshipped. McCreagh and his two companions thereafter were held as gods. Surrounded by savages armed to the last man with poisoned spears, they were treated like princes.

The chief of the tribe took McCreagh to his village. He followed the white man about as a little boy would trail a champion prize-fight[illegible] lavished on him gifts of fried ants[illegible] steaks, salads of fish fins. He o[illegible] wives by the dozen, if he would ha[illegible] them. But McCreagh wanted only one thing—Caapi.

By signs and what little of the native tongue he had picked up, McCreagh communicated to the chief his desire to witness a fiesta. Thus, he had heard, had the tribesmen make an occasion for the drinking of the drug.

The chief assented. McCreagh watched them cut a cinnamon-colored, knotted vine, winding about the foot of a tree, into short pieces. The pieces were pounded into a powder. This was put in a pot, and to it were added leaves from the chaco tree in layers. Water poured into this mess completed the preliminaries. For an hour the pot boiled over an open fire until the brew was a deep wine color. The warriors were ready for the feast.

While women and children were banished on penalty of death, McCreagh, with startled eyes, watched the men seat themselves around the pot in a double circle, their spears upright. A cup-bearer gave each man his gulp of the Caapi. The effect was soon apparent. Man after man rose and danced with reckless abandon, boasting of what he would do to his enemy. For 10 minutes they fought with each other like wild beasts. Then, falling to the ground exhausted, they slept. Afterward they described beautiful dreams and visions.

McCreagh got all the Caapi he could carry. On their return to America, Fate seemed to be against the party. At sea a hurricane struck their ship and the specimens collected at such infinite pains were all but ruined with water. But the members did bring back for the National Zoological Gardens at Washington the largest and strangest collection of wild animals ever received by that institution. And McCreagh, in his little black box, brought back the pot of gold at the end of the rainbow—the prize find of the quest—Caapi, the drug that kills fear.

COURTESY AMERICAN MUSEUM OF NATURAL HISTORY

Another Picture of the Caapi Vine with a Chiriqui Kink-Ajou, One of the South American Jungle Beasts, Using It Monkey-wise, as a Stairway.

At Left—The Explorers' Boat on the Rio Waupes Just Before the Guides Deserted, Leaving Them Alone to the Mercies of the Forest and the Savages.

MY LADY NICOTINE

Facts About the Ways of Indian Smokers.

They Do Not Use Tobacco as White Men Do.

Smoking a Religious Rite and an Aid in Business.

Preparations That Took the Place of Tobacco.

Among Some Tribes the Pipe is Seldom Seen.

When Sir Walter Raleigh was surprised one morning by his servant who found him smoking a pipe, and, thinking that he was on fire, threw a bucket of water over him, he inaugurated that discomfort which it is said all users of the weed must undergo by way of preliminary training; yet oddly enough, in the home of tobacco, among the Indian tribes, no such preliminaries are undergone by neophytes. It is no unusual thing to see an Indian mother smoking a cigarette and occasionally allowing her child, still in arms, to take a puff or two. The average Indian commences to smoke when he is less than a year old, and he continues the practice until he dies, but he seldom smokes to excess, and he can hardly be said to smoke regularly, in the way that we do.

Raleigh little dreamed of the far-reaching consequences to follow his use of tobacco. But little over three centuries have elapsed since that day when he took an involuntary cold bath, yet we have drifted so far from that time that it might be interesting to hark back and see what the Indians, the original users of the weed, have done with it.

The Indians do not regard tobacco as we do nor do they use it in the same way. While there is a social side to their smoking the principal use of the leaf is ceremonial and religious. It has always been so with them, and even now, when the native preparations are largely replaced by the cheaper and more convenient supply at traders' stores, the old religious feeling is still there. There is something about tobacco which turns the mind of the smoker into contemplative moods, the savage mind not less than the mind of the poet. Could we procure them doubtless we could find Indian equivalents for the song of Aldrich to his pipe:

The curling wreaths like turbans seem
Of silent slaves that come and go—
Or Viziers, packed with craft and crime,
Whom I behead from time to time,
With pipe-stem, at a single blow.
And now and then a lingering cloud
Takes gracious form at my desire,
And at my side my lady stands
Unwinds her veil with snowy hands—
A shadowy shape, a breath of fire.
O, Love! if you were only here,
Beside me in this mellow light,
Though all the bitter winds should blow,
And all the ways be choked with snow,
'Twould be a true Arabian night.

There is no one thing so freely given from friend to friend as tobacco. Perhaps this arises partly from the convivial nature of the practice, perhaps from some bit of that divine equality of which the poets sing. Certain it is that back in its prehistoric home it exercised the same mellowing and softening influence that has come to be associated with it among us. The Indian will buy whatever he needs when he has money—sugar, coffee, calico or what not—but he cannot bring himself to buy tobacco; he cannot profane the "sacred soother" by buying it as he would a horse. Yet a smoke is an indispensable part of every transaction, whether it be a religious ceremony, a declaration of war, or the purchase of a yard of calico. The traders have come to recognize this, and in every store there is a little tin basin on the counter (and generally nailed to it), containing tobacco, cigarette papers and matches, which are freely used by all comers. Even the worst "beats" are sensitive to any remark about their use of this free tobacco, and any allusion to it will drive them out of the place and keep them away for days.

In its present forms tobacco has far outgrown the early preparations. Originally the leaf was merely dried and crumbled in the hands, and the native tobaccos still in use by the Indians are prepared in this simple way today. In the early part of the 17th century the Virginia tobacco was imported into England in the leaf and was rubbed small for use in a pipe, but the Spanish tobacco came in the form of tightly rolled balls, nearly the size of a man's head. This tobacco was cut into small pieces on a maple block, and the pipes, being filled, were lighted with embers from a fire of juniper wood, taken from a chafing dish with silver tongs. This paraphernalia was an indispensable part of a smoker's outfit.

Among the Indian tribes of the northwest, where the tobacco plant is not indigenous, various preparations took its place before the advent of the traders. Among these were the leaves of the sumach, which were dried for use and afterward when needed were crumbled in the hands. Much more prevalent, however, was the use of the bark of the red osier, known among frontiersmen as killikinik or kinnikinik, which name is said to have been derived from the language of the Dakota. This material is the thin semitransparent bark of inner skin of the young shoots, which are available so long as they retain their red outer skin.

In the preparation of killikinik the bark was peeled and dried for future use. Although smoked at all times, it is considered best in winter. To prepare it, the curly shavings are laid on a piece of board and with the left hand passed under the blade of a large knife which is worked up and down after the manner of a fodder cutter. In using the material at the present day two parts of the minced bark are mixed with one part of plug tobacco, similarly hashed, and only enough for the day's use is prepared at one time.

For a long time after its introduction into Europe tobacco was smoked only in pipes, as it is now among the northwestern Indians. Oddly enough, the early European pipes closely resemble the present Indian forms, being short and straight in the stem and higher and narrower in the bowl than the pipes of today. The Indians much prefer their own pipes if they can get them, but pipes of native manufacture are now seldom found in use, although numbers of fine specimens can be seen in the museums. The favorite material was catlinte or red pipestone, and, although this material is found only near the present town of Pipestone, Minn, so highly esteemed was it that it passed by barter from tribe to tribe and has been found over 1000 miles from the place where it was quarried. When first taken out this stone is soft and easily carved. Afterward it becomes hard and takes on a fine polish. Sometimes the bowls of these pipes are inlaid with tin or lead, forming elaborate and beautiful designs.

In social or in ceremonial smoking the pipe is never actually put into the mouth, but is pressed against the lips and the mouthpiece remains dry. In taking the smoke the lips are slightly parted at the corners of the mouth and the air which is sucked in mixes with the smoke and is drawn into the lungs. To be perfectly au fait this must be done with considerable noise; according to Indian etiquette such noise is necessary in order to indicate satisfaction.

In ceremonial smoking the pipe or cigarette may be handed to the right-hand neighbor to light, but in smoking it must always pass to the left, from hand to hand. This is the true ceremonial direction, "the path of the sun." During a ceremonial smoke silence is maintained, and if any conversation becomes necessary it is conducted in a whisper. At intervals puffs of smoke are directed toward the six cardinal points of the Indian system, which are the same as ours, but include in addition, the zenith, the abode of the wind gods, and the nadir, the home of the dead.

Among the southwestern tribes the pipe is seldom seen. Smoking is universal, but tobacco is used in the form of cigarettes consisting of a few grains rolled in a piece of corn husk. In former times every Indian carried some of the latter in his pouch, and when he met a white traveler his first inquiry was always for tobacco. Plug was preferred, and chipping off a few grains with his thumb nail, he carefully wrapped them in a corn husk (they never rolled a cigarette, but always wrapped it), he would light one end of it in the fire or with a match and proceed to enjoy it. Such cigarettes are hardly as thick as a match, but judging by appearance and noise, they yielded the smoker an immense amount of satisfaction and pleasure. It is an essential part of Indian etiquette to testify openly enjoyment of something given; thus in eating it is necessary to smack one's lips, belch and so on; otherwise the host will feel offended. Similarly, in smoking the smoke is sucked in with a loud noise, puff after puff, until the cigarette is consumed. But, contrary to our habit, the smoke is swallowed; apparently none of it is emitted.

The smoker, says Thackeray, has great physical advantages in conversation. Breaks never seem disagreeable when filled up with puffs of smoke. "I have no doubt," he adds, "that it is from the habit of smoking that the Turks and American Indians are such monstrous well-bred men. The pipe draws wisdom from the lips of the philosopher, and shuts up the mouth of the foolish; it generates a style of conversation contemplative, thoughtful, benevolent and unaffected."

Carlyle goes further and suggests the great advantages of introducing the practice of smoking into parliamentary assemblies. "Tobacco smoke," he says, "is the one element in which, by our European manners, men can sit silent together without embarrassment. A man may take to his pipe again the instant he has spoken his meaning, if he chances to have any. The results of which salutary practice, if introduced into constitutional parliaments, might evidently be incalculable. The essence of what little intellect and insight there is in that room—we shall or can get nothing more out of any parliament."

To the Indian, smoking is a sacred rite as well as a social indulgence. It is associated with practically all their religious observances, and something of the sacred character of the practice has been transferred to the material itself, for tobacco is often used as an offering to the dead, or sprinkled on rocks or in places considered sacred. It is also sent as a peace offering, either to individuals or to other tribes. Sent with other offerings and some proposition or question, it is equivalent to a request for an answer—an Indian R. S. V. P. When a long journey or some serious undertaking is in hand there is always much deliberation and frequent recourse to the pipe or cigarette, accompanied sometimes by retirement and prolonged fasting.—(New York Commercial Advertiser.

THE BOSTON SUNDAY GLOBE—SEPTEMBER 17, 1899.

QUEER ENGLISH LAWS.

One Forbids Britons to Eat Meat on Wednesdays Under Penalty of a Month's Imprisonment.

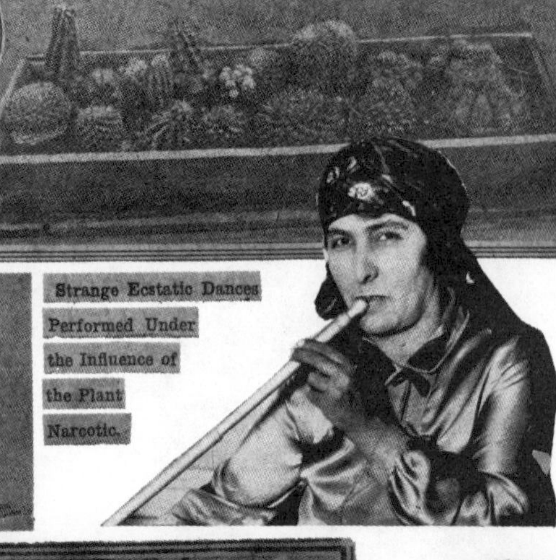

Specimens of High Cacti Collected by Irving G. Noyes

Strange Ecstatic Dances Performed Under the Influence of the Plant Narcotic.

Types of Some of the Sacred Mushrooms.

which it is known is "flesh of God."

The Mystery Man, with the Aid of a Few Cactus "Buttons," Can Foretell the Future.

The Mystery of Mexico's Sacred Mushroom

Drugs That Still Puzzle Science
Peyote-Eating Indians in the Grotesque Make-up They Don for the Ceremony of Collecting the "Devil's Root."
ROBERT MOYER
CRAZED by the drug, the youth raced through the jungle, dragging the two warriors after him.
INDIAN SQUAWS PAST AND PRESENT
Mrs. A. T. Woodward at the left and Rub Big Chief at the right have just been introduced on the White House grounds. Both are full-blooded Osage Indians, but each has a different idea about dress.
The Rock Creek Indians line walls of their "long tent" for ritual and feast at recent root festival. Ground in center is considered sacred. The ritual varies with the different tribes.
Inside the Long Tent: Root Festival Sacred Indian Rite

"Artificial Paradise" Evil Cactus Root

"A Huge Cliff Seemed to Project Over a Bottomless Gulf and on Its Brink Was Set a Great Bird Claw of Stone. Things Like Green Birds Fluttered Down From It, Clusters of Fabulous Jewels Hung in Masses From the Stone Toes, Swarms of Multi-Colored Butterflies Appeared, and Mingled With Visions of Every Delight That Paradise Could Possibly Hold."

A LITTLE vegetable god whose shrine is often a tomato can, where none but the devout may see him grow, is reuniting the remnants of a once-powerful federation of American Indians.

It is the peyote, a small spineless cactus which grows in Mexico and some distance north of the border but is now carried as far as Canada. If an Indian eats the peyote reverently, takes four puffs of tobacco, sings four tuneless Indian songs, utters four prayers and performs other ceremonies, he will have visions of the happy hunting ground, "until the sun, who is a man, looks in the door of the tepee and sees the moon, who is a woman."

Then it is all off.

The peyote is one of those deities who thrive on adversity. When the Spaniards conquered Mexico they found some of the natives eating a "diabolic root," which they condemned on religious grounds. But it was of small importance because its devotees in those days were comparatively few.

Toward the end of the last century the cult had spread to some of the remnants of the plains Indians and others north of the border, where it was vigorously opposed by missionaries as an "evil root" because the ceremonies seemed blasphemous and because the peyote was undoubtedly a drug which produced illusions in the form of visions.

The legislature of Wyoming forbade its use on the ground that it was a habit-forming narcotic drug.

A drug it certainly is, and a strange and powerful one, but opinion is divided as to whether or not it is habit-forming. Though the visions are pleasurable, like those induced by various forbidden drugs, the taking of peyote is too heroic a proceeding to be popular. The few white men who have subjected themselves to the cactus divinity, in the interest of science, report that it is not only followed by a hangover but the visions are preceded by an awful headache.

Within recent years the peyote cult has expanded with almost explosive speed among Indians even in Canada where the "dream" cactus does not grow and is forbidden to enter.

But how can a customs inspector stop a deity who enters in the pocket of an Indian slouching across the border at some wild spot where there is no customs office? In the U. S. A. it has become more or less legalized as a sacrament connected with the duly incorporated Native American Church, with its 13,500 Indians as registered members.

Its grip on the modern redskins proved a common bond to hold together the racial remnants and preserve the last shreds of their traditions. Its power to do this is based, perhaps more than anything else, on providing a race which suffers from a crushing inferiority complex with an escape from wretched reality through an occasional preview of the paradise which the Great Spirit still reserves for his faithful, humbled ones.

What does the Indian see when his spirit visits the happy hunting grounds? That is a secret which he does not care to reveal because the Great Spirit might be offended and the Road Chief, who sits in on the ceremonies and directs the spirits of the communicants on the road to the Indian heaven, would refuse to guide him the next time. The ceremony has been best described by Vincenzo Petrullo, author of "The Diabolic Root," published by the University of Pennsylvania Press.

He achieved the triumph of being permitted to take peyote at the same time as the Indians and learned all the details of the ceremonial among the Indians of Mexico and Oklahoma. He it was who learned that the Delaware Indians and others grew the cactus in tin cans, not so much for fear of detection as to prevent it from being seen by irreverent eyes.

The late Havelock Ellis, famous psychological investigator, made a scientific report on the effects of the peyote as a drug. In London, he took it in the form of a decoction of mescal "buttons," as the little dark knobs which grow in the form of a sort of crown on the cactus root are called. This must not be confused with the Mexican alcoholic drink, also called mescal.

At 2:30 P. M. he drank the first of three doses of a decoction of three buttons with the immediate result of a headache. At 3:30 he took a second dose which heightened the headache and brought on stomach discomforts and within another hour, nausea, all this before the slightest sign of visions. At 6 P. M. he still had some headache but the nausea had gone and slight color phenomena were beginning.

At 6:40 P. M. by closing his eyes he began to have visions on the "curtains of his eyelids." Not till 7:30 P. M. did anything like paradise appear and then it was more like a white man's heaven. He writes:

"Lying with closed eyes; vision a vast field of golden jewels, studded with red and green stones, and ever changing and full of delight. Air seemed flush with perfume. All discomfort vanishes.

"9:10 P. M. Break off—cannot write. Visions continue brilliantly. I have seen thick, glorious fields of jewels, spring into forms like flowers and then turn to gorgeous, butterfly forms. The visions were living arabesques.

"At 3:30 A. M. settled down to sleep with slight headache and visions took on sombre colors, like browns and blacks."

The great, if not greatest, of nerve specialists, the late Dr. S. Weir Mitchell, tried the effects of peyote on himself. Dr. Mitchell began the experiment at noon. He took 1½ drams of extract, each dram equal to one "button." An hour later he took another dram, and at four o'clock an additional one-half dose.

The results were successful and he described the vision as follows: "An edge of a huge cliff seemed to project over a gulf of unseen depth. My viewless enchanter set on the brink a huge bird claw of stone. Above, from the stem or leg hung a fragment of the same stuff. This began to unroll and float out to a distance which seemed to me to represent time as well as immensity of space. Here were miles of rippled purples, half transparent and of ineffable beauty.

"Now and then soft golden clouds floated from these folds, or a shimmer went over the whole of the rolling purples, and things like green birds fell from it, fluttering down to the gulf below. Next I saw clusters of stones hanging in masses from the claw toes, as it seemed to me miles of them, down far below into the underworld of the black gulf. This was the most distinct of the visions.

"The visions closed with the beach at Newport, the waves liquid splendors, huge and threatening, wonderfully pure green, or red and deep purple, once only deep orange, and with no haze of foam.

"The show was expensive," concludes Dr. Mitchell, referring to the before and after effects. "The experience was worth one such headache and indigestion but not worth a second."

The late Dr. William James paid the price of the trip to paradise but never got there at all. He wrote to his famous brother, Henry James:

"I had two days spoiled by a psychological experiment with mescal. Weir Mitchell sent me some to try. He himself had been in fairyland. I took one button three days ago and was violently sick for 24 hours, and had no other symptom whatever except that and the 'katzenjammer' (hangover) the following day. I will take the visions on trust."

The Indian never takes his peyote alone like that but always ceremoniously with many others, in a tepee which must be built just so, with 21 poles and an entrance to the east, through which the rising sun can look in and see the moon which is a crescent - shaped mound in the center of the tepee.

The master of ceremonies is the Road Chief who attends to the construction of the tepee, provides the tobacco and appoints the other three chiefs. One is the Fire Chief who builds and tends the fire near or within the mound. This fire must be started not with matches but from sparks of the old-fashioned stone-age flint and it must have 12 cedar faggots, in groups of four, spread in crescent form, and plenty of cedar seed.

The fuel is furnished by the Cedar Chief and the very important drum by the Drum Chief, who is the fourth dignitary. Four is a sacred number to the Indian because animals have four limbs and he has four senses. For some reason he does not consider touch as one of the senses.

"After I have placed this Father Peyote here, all this dry peyote and the peyote tea is for your use."

He then rolls a cigarette made from tobacco and sage, wrapped in a corn husk, then passes the "makings" to the Drum Chief, then the Cedar Chief and then going to the left to all the members serving last the Fire Chief who then has to take a lighted stick from "Grandfather Fire" and give a light to everyone, himself last. After all have had four puffs the Road Chief makes a long prayer, followed by everyone else who feels like praying. When this is done the peyote is passed around. The rest of the evening is occupied by songs accompanied by the Drum Chief, and prayers, everyone being entitled to four songs and four prayers.

At midnight the Road Chief sings the midnight water call, and the Fire Chief brings in the water which the Road Chief blesses. The Road Chief then takes his whistle and goes outside of the tepee. Outside, facing east, he blows one long, four short, and one long blast on the whistle. Then he prays to the east, the south, the west, and north, the Cedar Chief singing a song for the prayer in each direction.

The Road Chief then reenters the tepee and takes his seat addressing the members. About five o'clock the Road Chief sings the morning water call, and the Fire Chief says, "A messenger has arrived with water."

The real entertainment is the trip to the happy hunting grounds, as directed by the Road Chief. At dawn, when the sun looks in the tepee door and sees his woman, the moon, there, they all have to be back from the land of the spirits.

The peyote breakfast is brought in by another woman messenger. It is specially prepared and is usually hominy and dry jerked venison, or raw beef, ground fine by stone pestles and seasoned and sweetened.

Every one then eats and spends the rest of the day sleeping it off. These trips to paradise keep them contented but they do not care to go there too often for the same reason that made Dr. Mitchell decide that once was enough.

A TALE to chill the blood and frighten the brave was told by Victor Forbin, French traveler and scientist, after a stay in the interior of Colombia with a tribe of Counas Indians. Here he saw, and insisted that he was not dreaming, the drug which makes prophets.

An apparently normal youth was brought to the chief's hut where the witch doctor offered him a concoction prepared in Forbin's presence. So far as Forbin could discover, this medicine or drug was made by dipping a thin creeper, which looked like North American ivy, into a cup of boiling water. The boy drank it and then collapsed into a deep sleep.

Two robust tribesmen tied strong ropes around the youth's shoulders and none too soon. Suddenly, uttering a terrible cry, the drugged youth leaped to his feet in one bound, his face in the grip of the most horrible contortion which made him completely unrecognizable, and rushing out of the door he dragged his two guards with him. They pursued him, trying to check the speed of his mad rush without hindering his movements. Behind him followed the chief, the witch doctor and Forbin.

After a wild chase of 20 minutes, the witch doctor administered the antidote. As effects of the drug wore off, the youth kept muttering as the Indians listened very attentively. The chief explained, "he can see things a long way off." And he did. In this prophetic state, the boy said he saw the village of Ganatchipi in flames. Two weeks later, Forbin learned the village burned to the ground, although it was 200 miles from the scene of the strange experiment.

By Rene Bache

A LONG-PUZZLING mystery of ancient Mexico is now being worked out by scientific experts of the United States government, with the expectation of turning it to useful and profitable account. It relates to the "sacred mushroom" of the Aztecs, revered by them as a holy plant, and to this day eaten by some tribes of Mexican Indians in religious ceremonies.

It is a powerful narcotic, producing the most fantastic visions, and is regarded by the Indians as a key which, in the ceremonial, opens to them all the glories of another and better world.

The plant grows wild, though not plentifully, in the valley of the Rio Grande, in barren and even rocky soil. But the government experts have recently undertaken successfully to raise it under glass in pots; and the active principle, a hitherto-unknown alkaloid, has been separated from it in the form of white, needle-shaped crystals.

In all likelihood this alkaloid—called "anhalonin," after the botanical name of the plant—will prove very useful in medicine. Dr. Lyman F. Kebler, chief of the division of drugs in the chemistry bureau at Washington, is at present conducting preliminary experiments with it.

Its Virtues as a "Bracer."

For one thing, the narcotic is said to have a wonderful potency in subduing the unpleasant after-effects of over-indulgence in alcohol. It it likely, therefore, to achieve great popularity as a "bracer," when, after a while, it finds its way into the hands of the apothecary. The ease with which (as newly ascertained) the plant may be cultivated under glass would suggest that the cost of the drug derived from it ought not to be excessive.

Indeed, it has been found that a tincture made by simply chopping up the plant and allowing it to soak in dilute alcohol for a couple of weeks is a most serviceable remedy for nervousness, headache and insomnia. When chewed (the Indians say) it stops the painful coughing of consumptives.

So far as ascertained, the narcotic does not affect in any way the intellectual faculties, even after long and habitual use. Furthermore, it is remarkable in having no Nemesis. In other words, there is no depressive or other disagreeable after effect.

It was Mr. W. E. Safford, a botanist of the government plant bureau, whose original researches identified the plant with the "sacred mushroom" of the Aztecs. But it is not a mushroom at all. It is a species of cactus, somewhat resembling a radish in shape, covered with sharp prickles, and with a button-shaped top—the latter being all of it that appears above ground.

The early Spanish missionaries in Mexico, finding it employed for vision-producing purposes in the native religious ceremonials, naturally disapproved of the plant. They called it "devil's root," and pronounced the eating of it a crime not less heinous than that of eating human flesh.

Even at the present time the buying and selling of it is forbidden in Oklahoma, where the Kiowa Indians (who formerly dwelt in the Rio Grande valley) still use the plant in their religious festivities, obtaining it from traders. The missionaries complain of it, and—though none of them, nor any agency physician, has tested it or taken the trouble to witness the ceremonial—their representations have caused the federal government to inflict severe penalties for the offence of using or possessing it.

The government experts, however, have recently made a number of interesting experiments with the plant. In one of these a young chemist was the "subject." Before going to bed he swallowed three of the "buttons" (cactus tops), and then awaited results. The first sensation he felt was one of slight nausea. This soon passed, and, closing his eyes, he experienced a series of curious optical impressions. Beautiful designs, more or less geometrical, in brilliant and ever-changing colors, floated before him.

He swallowed a fourth button, and thereupon passed in review a series of delightful visions. His mind, in the mean time, remained clear and active. Stretched on his bed, he watched with u most pleasure an ever-changing panorama of infinite beauty and grandeur. To some extent he was able to control the visions. By fixing his mind on something unpleasant, he summoned into view myriads of crawling monsters and multitudes of gruesome forms with human faces. But, though horrible enough to frighten anybody under normal circumstances, these nightmare phantasms were to him merely jolly and amusing.

There was no distressing subsequent reaction. But experiments with other persons proved, rather curiously, that the sound of a monotonous drumming (such as the Indians make when they eat the plant in the ceremonial) greatly enhances the beauty and variety of the visions. It is easily understood, then, why the aboriginal cactus-eater indulges in this performance—the group thus engaged sitting all night with their blankets drawn about them, and each man ready to take his turn with drum and rattle.

The sensation they experience is said to be one of ecstatic happiness. Their hallucinations are supposed by them to be a supernatural grace, by which they are permitted to pass through the portals of Paradise and communicate with the gods. Some of the religious societies among the Mexican natives look upon the ceremonial as a kind of communion, in which the cactus is eaten as an incarnation of Deity. A popular name by not only medicinal value, for the cure of many diseases, but also to sustain the body against fatigue. One who eats it, it is claimed, feels neither hunger nor thirst, but it gives him courage to fight, and protects him from danger. Nay more, it is even said that it gives to the person under its narcotic influence the power to penetrate beyond the barrier that limits normal knowledge, to see into the future, and to predict what is soon to happen—for example, a change of weather, or an attack by an enemy.

The prickly root as well as the top contains the narcotic alkaloid, but, for some reason unexplained, the buttons have commercial preference. In the dried state they are brown in color, hard and brittle, but soften quickly in the mouth. They have a rather nauseous and bitter taste. The "button" of the growing plant forms a sort of compact tuft, and at the proper season bears a flower.

Analysis of Wild "Dream-Plant."

Incidentally to the process of "taming" the wild dream-plant here described, with a view to rendering it useful to mankind, the government experts have subjected it to a thorough analysis. Dr. Kebler obtained from it, by maceration in alcohol, a brown sirupy liquid which, on being taken to pieces by laboratory methods, yielded not only "anhalonin"—the active principle already mentioned, which took the form of brilliant white, needle-shaped crystals—but also another alkaloid, very poisonous.

The possible importance of this newly-discovered alkaloid, "anhalonin," is not to be lightly underrated. One should remember that two of the most valuable of known medicinal substances, quinine and cocaine, were made known to modern civilization through a previous acquaintance with them by Indians who had ascertained the usefulness of coca leaves and cinchona bark—the latter as a remedy for malaria.

Photograph of the Evil Cactus Root Which Sends Forth Neither Branches Nor Leaves, Seeming "To Conceal Itself in the Ground as Though Unwilling to Harm Those Who May Discover and Eat It." And Left, the Peyote "Buttons," on Top of the Root, Containing the Drug.

By EDWARD PODOLSKY, M. D., and BRUCE COLE

EDGAR ALLAN POE would find his facile imagination stretched to the doubting point. Boris Karloff might even find these things difficult to portray. We are speaking of the curious and strange diseases and drugs which bewilder and often bedevil men of medicine and science.

You may not think there's anything new in the world, but physicians and chemists and pharmacists are finding new things every day and some of the things they find are mighty distasteful, although some new drugs and combinations of drugs may prove beneficial in whipping new diseases.

MOST curious of the facts and legends of medical lore is that of the zombies, those half-living, half-dead creatures with no will or mind of their own who become the obedient slaves of anyone administering them a drug said to be brewed from cactus poisons in Central America and the Carribbean region.

Whether the drug actually exists no one seems to know for certain, but many trustworthy travelers insist they have seen zombies who do not speak, look with unseeing eyes, live apart from other plantation workers and exist on a diet which contains no meat or salt, and work years for their masters without making any demands in returns.

The "zombie" poison is put into somebody's food, and he apparently dies within a few hours. In reality, he is thrown into a profound state of catalepsy which resembles death. He is buried as dead, but if removed from his grave within 24 hours he is recalled to a pseudo-like existence. The cactus-like poison has a strange effect on the nervous system. It is numbed into mechanical activity. The mind and will are gone and all tasks are performed mechanically.

Salt is said to be the only antidote to this poison, and this is, of course, kept out of their diet.

Stringent laws against use or manufacture of this drug have been passed in some countries, which would indicate the tales of zombies were not pure fiction. Authorities insist there are no more zombies in those countries.

Chant de l'hicouri (Peyotl).

Notre autorité ainsi

Oncle hicouri

Les ancêtres l'ont fait ainsi.

s'est arrêté, regardez !

Jackie Grant, an Atlanta, Ga., boy, astounds doctors and himself with an ailment which has no name and apparently no cure because no one seems to know the how or why of it. Something inside the boy's head ticks all the time like a cheap alarm clock, and the noise is faintly audible to anyone standing beside him. Jackie says it doesn't bother him, although he is tired of people asking him what time it is.

LA PLANTE QUI FAIT
LES YEUX ÉMERVEILLÉS

LE PEYOTL

(Echinocactus Williamsii Lem.)

Préface de M. le Professeur ÉM. PERROT

ALEXANDRE ROUHIER
DOCTEUR EN PHARMACIE.

« Toute plante est lampe. »
V. Hugo : *L'Homme qui rit.*

GASTON DOIN et CIE, ÉDITEURS
8, Place de l'Odéon, Paris-6^E
1927

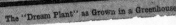

The "Dream Plant" as Grown in a Greenhouse

By a Member of the Post-Dispatch Sunday Magazine Staff

NORMAN, Oklahoma.

HE ancient culture of the Indians is vanishing at so rapid a rate that science, even with all the modern resources at its command, is engaged in what is probably a losing race to record dwindling customs, swiftly fading rituals. Changes are occurring with such rapidity that 12, 15 years may see it all obliterated.

Here in Oklahoma, where a great many Indian tribes are concentrated, partly through various historical accidents, the race is especially keen, for the experts are acutely aware of the unique value of what is passing. Prof. Forrest E. Clements, head of the department of anthropology at the University of Oklahoma, is attempting to record on motion picture film ceremonies and dances which will soon be lost.

Thus far he has had remarkable good fortune—not attributable to good fortune so much, perhaps, as to the care, persistence and tact with which he approaches the whole problem. He has recorded several ceremonial dances, particularly among the Cheyennes, which have never before been seen by white men.

Just now Prof. Clements is laying his plans to make a movie of a peyote ceremonial, the curious half-Christian, half-Indian rite, about which so many fantastic rumors and legends have been circulated. It will be difficult, he says, to get this down on a movie film, for the ceremonial takes place only at night and depends in part for its religious potency upon the atmosphere of semi-darkness within the tepee. Flood the scene with the calcium flares necessary for movie making and there is strong doubt whether you will get anything very significant, even with sophisticated peyote users.

It is evident, according to Prof. Clements, that the peyote ceremonial is gaining converts. And that does not surprise anyone, he adds, who understands the nature of this ceremonial. Essentially it is a compromise between the primitive religion of the Indians and the Christianity that the missionaries preach among them. It is opposed by the old tribal leaders, naturally, for it signifies the waning authority of the ancient Indian culture. Briefly, its history is as follows.

The peyote button, a blackish chip, tufted with soft white down, from a species of cactus that grows in Southwest Texas and in parts of Mexico, had been used for many, many years by the plains Indians, the Cheyenne, Arapahoe, Commanche and other tribes. It was chewed or swallowed largely for its supposed medicinal value, although there was associated with it some slight religious significance. Then in 1893 a member of the Winnebago tribe from Wisconsin came traveling in Oklahoma, to meet his cousins, the Cheyennes and the Arapahoes. He suffered from a serious disease, and on the advice of his hosts, took peyote.

He returned to Wisconsin and announced that he had been cured by this magic drug that was the secret of the plains Indians. His wife, who suffered from the same disease, began to take the peyote which he had brought back with him, and she, too, enjoyed a miraculous cure. These two Winnebagoes, with a third who also visited the Arapahoes and was blessed by the healing power of peyote, were chiefly responsible for the modern form of the ceremonial.

IT SPREAD with extraordinary rapidity among widely separated tribes. And Prof. Clements explains why. The time was ripe for some such compromise form that would, in a sense, reconcile the two cultures, the Indian and the Christian. In repeated instances the Federal Government had forbidden the Indians to practice their ancient ceremonials, since many of these involved trial by torture and sadistic and masochistic practices. While these torture ceremonies persisted secretly—exist today in remote, lonely secrecy—the pressure of the whites was too great. The peyote ceremony was a convenient blend of Indian and Christian gods, a more or less painless transitional form.

The missionaries fought it, some with intense conviction, because they felt that it was godless, blasphemous, and because they maintained that the influence of the peyote was harmful, physically and mentally, to users of it. The most carefully considered opinion today, in the Government and among experts, is that the actual effect of peyote, upon the body and the mind, is all but negligible. Prof. Clements holds that peyote will produce whatever effect the user believes it will produce. As the ceremony lasts all night, the participants usually sleep all the following day and white observers point to this as evidence of the debauching effect of peyote. But the result would seem to be about the same as follows an all night poker party.

It is not surprising that legends and rumors have grown up around the peyote ceremonial, for it is surrounded with a certain strangeness and a certain secrecy. It varies somewhat from tribe to tribe, but the following description is one which several white observers have confirmed:

Soon after sundown the Cheyenne ceremony begins. All preparations have been made. The participating Indians, mostly men, infrequently women, seat themselves on blankets in a semi-circle along the tepee walls.

The entrance to the tepee faces east, from where, toward the close of the ceremony, the rising sun will be peering in. The sun is a man, Indians say. He will be looking in and facing a moon inside the tepee. The moon is a woman.

The moon inside the tepee is the altar of the "Native American Church," which is the incorporated title in Oklahoma of the religion of the peyote sacrament. It is an earthen mound a few inches high, with its ends pointing toward the tepee entrance. Inside the crescent a fire is kept aglow with sticks crossing each other, forming as nearly as possible another half-moon. One of the worshipers is designated fireman, an honored post, and is seated at the north side of the entrance, where he can best attend the fire.

When everyone is seated around the half-moon, the leader, whose place is at the west end of the tepee and facing the entrance, passes corn leaves and tobacco and sage around the semi-circle, always toward the left. Each of the worshipers rolls a cigarette, using both tobacco and sage inside the corn leaf, and rubs some of the sage, as a scented ointment, on his face, hands and part of the body. A torch is taken from the fire and passed around to light the cigarettes.

IN FRONT of the leader are the articles used in the ritual, such as the drum, cane, eagle-bone whistle, gourd rattle and feather fan. The cane he ceremoniously waves over the fire or merely holds in his hand as the rites are in progress.

Each worshiper takes four puffs from his cigarette and lays it away. Four is the key number to the peyote ceremony. There are four winds, and above them is God. There are "four" senses, for an Indian does not include touch among the major senses. Every animal has four limbs. And so on; there are many explanations showing that four is an important number.

The fireman strews the fire with cedar leaves, which emit a pleasant odor. Then the leader ceremoniously places a large peyote button on the half-moon altar, and the setting is complete.

The leader offers a prayer. All prayers are to some Supreme Being, but individual Indians have different names for Him. Some pray to "Maheo," the Cheyenne word for God. Others to the Great Spirit. A few to the "Above White Man." The name of Jesus may enter into the prayers.

Here was the prayer offered by a Cheyenne Indian at a recent peyote ceremony that was held near Clinton:

"Maheo—Help the man who is responsible for this meeting (the host), and his children and give them an upright living.

"I am having a pleasant time tonight and I am thinking tonight about you. I want you to know, Oh, Maheo, that I am a poor man in this world and I pray for the people who are here, and I ask you a good life for them.

"I wish that you would help this man (the host) who is responsible for this meeting in every way you can, and keep him from bad ways. I am going to give him this body and he will eat it and he will remember you as long as he lives."

The leader eats four peyotes and passes "this body"—the cactus buttons—around so that everyone present may eat four. That is just enough to cause the average user to see the so-called visions—ribbon rainbows—and begin to sense a feeling of bliss.

Song and prayer comprise much of the all-night ceremony. The leader sings four songs while the person at his side beats upon the kettle tom-tom—an iron kettle with buckskin stretched over it, to drum-head tightness, and water inside. At the same time a gourd rattle—a dried gourd, much like those used by Cuban rumba bands, but filled with pebbles and gaudily decorated — is vigorously swung.

After the leader sings four songs, the drum is passed around to the left, and each of the worshipers sings four songs while the man at his side beats the drum.

THE songs send eerie echoes through the night. They are weird relics of an earlier day, haunting songs without words and with melody that jumps strangely from mysterious note to mysterious note. "Hi, hi, hi, hi"—and so on they go, swinging along with strange rhythm, accompanied by the piercing beats of the buckskin-covered kettle drum.

After having eaten the peyote buttons, the worshipers are inspired to compose new songs, and those new songs which make hits are again sung at future gatherings. Worshipers who do not feel inspired to sing are not obliged to do so.

At midnight the leader blows his eagle-bone whistle four times, and there is a short break in the ceremonies. The fire is extinguished and the fireman sweeps the ashes and twigs from inside the half-moon altar. A new fire is immediately built, and cedar leaves are again thrown on it. A bucket of water is brought in and passed around, each person taking four sips.

After the water is brought in those who want to may go outside and stretch themselves after the many hours of cramped sitting inside the tepee. From that point the ceremony is mainly a repetition of the first part, except that each worshiper eats as many peyote buttons as he wants to.

By the time ten, fifteen or twenty buttons have been consumed most Indians see their brightest visions. They may see gigantic mountains and beautiful streams of water right there in the tepee, or herds of purple buffaloes wearing big sombreros and shooting peyote buttons from red, white and blue trees with bow-and-arrow. There is apparently no limit to the hallucinations.

If too many buttons are eaten, however, the hallucinations become unpleasant. Gorgeous valleys may turn into giant dragons.

In the morning, when Mr. Sun peeks in the tepee and sees Miss Moon inside, the worshipers are still there and are not a bit sleepy, for the peyote keeps them awake. A short while after sunup the leader blows his whistle four times, and a young woman, who has been waiting outside for the signal, comes in with water. When she enters, the men inside, cramped from sitting in close quarters all night, stir around and stretch.

The woman then goes out and gets breakfast, usually consisting of corn, meat and fruit, which together with the water comprise four things. She brings the breakfast into the tepee, sits down, and takes four puffs from a corn-leaf cigarette. Everyone present takes four small pieces of meat, four handfuls of corn, and four pieces of fruit.

Then the ceremony comes to a close, but few of the Indians go home. Most of them eat more breakfast outside, for peyote—or the fatigue of an all-night session —makes them hungry.

AT NOON a big feast of beef is provided by the host for everybody. By the time that is finished, sleepiness begins to set in and everybody goes home and sleeps.

More women now than formerly participate in the peyote ritual. More boys and girls of school age take part. Many go to school during the week and to peyote feasts on Saturday night.

It was upon the suggestion of James Mooney, field investigator for the United States Bureau of Ethnology, that the Oklahoma Peyote Indians organized as the "Native American Church," thus helping protect themselves against anti-peyote legislation. Mooney, who died a few years ago, after he had become famous in Oklahoma, made a close study of peyote uses among the Kiowa Indians in Oklahoma.

Secretary of State J. L. Lyon of Oklahoma issued the charter for the "Native American Church" in Oklahoma City in October, 1918, to representatives of the Cheyenne, Otoe, Ponca, Comanche, Kiowa and Apache tribes, and since then other tribes have become affiliated.

The purpose of the charter, as officially stated, is: "To establish a self-respect and brotherly union among men of the native race of Indians and to foster and promote their belief in Christian religion with the practice of the peyote sacrament as commonly understood among Indians."

Sunday Magazine—St. Louis Post-Dispatch—June 3, 1934.

The Diabolic Root

A STUDY OF PEYOTISM, THE NEW INDIAN RELIGION, AMONG THE DELAWARES

By

Vincenzo Petrullo

UNIVERSITY OF PENNSYLVANIA PRESS
THE UNIVERSITY MUSEUM
Philadelphia
1934

The Little Moon Peyote Meeting of the Delawares of Oklahoma as Sketched by Vincenzo Petrullo, First White Man to Attend Their Secret Ceremonials. The Moon (7) Is a Crescent-Shaped Mound of Earth on Which Rests the Chief Peyote (6) With the Paraphernalia (5) Behind It. The Cedar Chief (1) Sits at the Left of the Road Chief (2) With the Drum Chief (3) at His Right. The Fire Chief (4) Tends the Fire (9) Sweeping the Ashes Into a Crescent (8) With the Turkey Wing (10) and Keeps Water in a Bucket (11). (Reproduced by Special Permission of the University of Pennsylvania Press.)

So Strange Were the Visions of the Peyote-Eating Indian Cults That Scientists Investigated by Eating the Plant Themselves—And, as the New University of Pennsylvania Press Book Reveals, Were Transported to Their Extraordinarily Similar "Heavens of Hypnotic Jewels and Intoxicating Color"

The Spread of the 'Peyote Ritual' Among the Oklahoma Indians

New Religion, a Cross Between the Old Barbaric Rites and Christianity, Involves the Use of a Cactus Plant Which Its Users Say Causes "Visions."

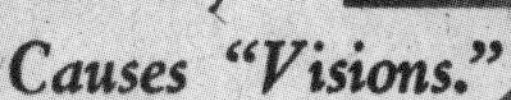

Goose, a ...inent leader ...he Cheyenne-...aho reservation near Clinton, ...ahoma—a ... of tribal lead... ...pposed to the ...d of the ...eyote cult.

An unusual photograph of a peyote ceremony—one of the few ever taken. Note the half-moon altar in the center.

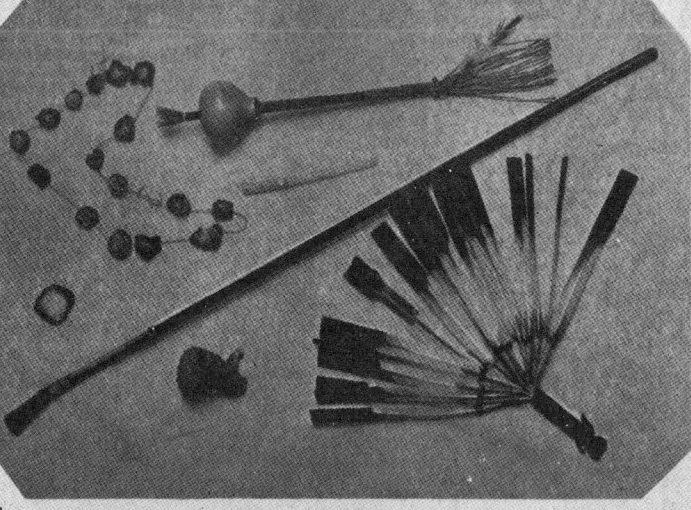

The articles employed in the peyote ritual. On a string in the upper section are sixteen peyote buttons and nearby is another — an unusually large one, also a gourd rattle and eagle-bone whistle. Below is a peyote cactus in its entirety and the feather fan. In the middle is the adorned cane which the leader uses.

Drums Used to Stimulate the Effect of Cactus Dreams.

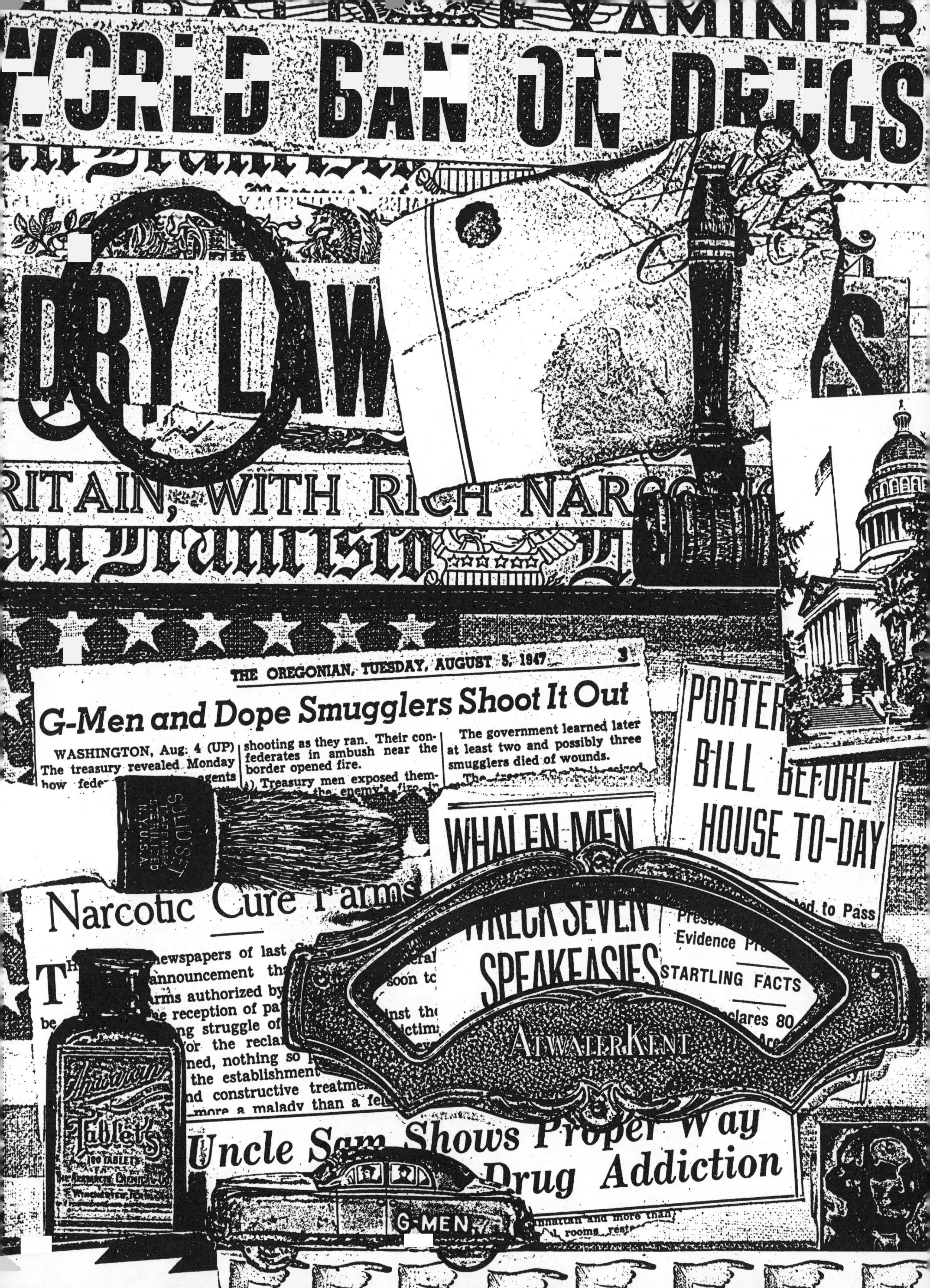
DRY LAW
RITAIN, WITH RICH NAR
THE OREGONIAN, TUESDAY, AUGUST 5, 1947
G-Men and Dope Smugglers Shoot It Out
WASHINGTON, Aug. 4 (UP) The treasury revealed Monday
shooting as they ran. Their confederates in ambush near the border opened fire.
Treasury men exposed them-
The government learned later at least two and possibly three smugglers died of wounds.
PORTER BILL BEFORE HOUSE TO-DAY
WHALEN MEN
WRECK SEVEN SPEAKEASIES
SOLID SET TRADEMARK STERILIZED N.Y. U.S.A.
Narcotic Cure Farms
newspapers of last
announcement
arms authorized by
reception of pa
struggle of
for the reclai
ned, nothing so
the establishment
nd constructive treatme
more a malady than a
Evidence
STARTLING FACTS
Tablets
100 TABLETS
ATWATERKENT
Uncle Sam Shows Proper Way
Drug Addiction
G-MEN

Narcotics Laws

All laws which can be violated
without doing any one
any injury are laughed at.
—Spinoza, c. 1660

This chapter is a quick panorama of Law written bold: generations of patchwork legislation born in racism, bred in imperialism, dying in futility; and underneath it all, the inexorable force of supply and demand. The nation's first narcotics laws were local ordinances aimed at Chinese opium smokers in San Francisco (1875) and at cocaine-using blacks in the deep South at the turn of the century. The Pure Food and Drug Act of 1906 required labeling of drugs in patent medicines, removal of cocaine from soft drinks, and prosecution of druggists who dispensed "poisons" to addicts.

Missionary zeal for "protection of native races" led to a meeting for a "World War on Opium Traffic" at Shanghai in 1909. The Hague Convention of 1912, though largely ineffective in reducing world production of narcotics, gave the United States an international treaty excuse for the Harrison Act (1914), which forbade nonmedical opiate or cocaine use entirely. Court decisions between 1915 and 1922 made it impossible for doctors to prescribe drugs to addicts—and the black market boomed. (In England, on the other hand, the Dangerous Drugs Act of 1920 was interpreted to give doctors their choice of treatment for addicts, and the black market was negligible.) America soon consumed ten times more dope than any other country. The Jones-Miller Act (1922) tried to stem the tide with bureaucracy, a Narcotics Control Board, and five-year sentences for pushers.

U.S. authorities decided that the solution was to cut off sources of supply in the opium-bloc nations, adroitly blaming England and Japan for America's drug problem. Newspapers crusaded fiercely for ten long years (1923-1933), while the League of Nations debated in Geneva. Tough treaties limiting world drug production to amounts needed for medical use were passed in 1925 and 1931 and ratified in 1933. Consequently illicit trafficking skyrocketed.

Meanwhile a very human question had arisen: what to do with thousands of addicts flocking cold turkey to crowded jails and dubious clinics? Police proposed isolation camps called addict farms. Programs in upstate New York provided a model for federal hospitals at Lexington and Fort Worth that were approved in 1929 but not operational until many years later. Drug use rose dramatically as prohibition gangsters took over distribution. An estimated one to four million addicts consumed $5 billion worth of dope in 1929.

Before 1930 federal narcotics enforcement was a subdivision of the Treasury Department's prohibition bureau. In 1928 racketeer Arnold Rothstein was murdered, and investigations laid bare his top-level dope ring allegedly supplying eighty-five percent of all narcotics in New York, Chicago, and Hollywood. Then came the real shocker: Rothstein had once put the son and son-in-law of Colonel Levi Nutt, head of the U.S. drug police, on his payroll as lawyers when the I.R.S. tried to prosecute him for tax evasion. A grand jury further charged narcotics agents with "corruption, incompetence, and wilful neglect of duty." Congressman Stephen Porter pushed for a Federal Bureau of Narcotics independent of the graft-riddled prohibition bureau. Consequently, President Hoover deposed Nutt and replaced him with an obscure booze-buster named Harry J. Anslinger as commissioner of the new bureau (1930). Thus came to power the man who would dictate U.S. drug policy for the next three decades.

Anslinger's first campaign was for Uniform State Laws against opiates, cocaine, and the "new menace" marijuana. Most states adopted these codes. Anslinger recognized the power of combined print and broadcast media, promoting the Marijuana Tax Act on radio and in the press, lashing out against physician-addicts, senators suspected of graft, and even little old ladies who grew garden poppies. Successfully silencing liberals who called for repeal of the Harrison Act because of the "untold suffering" it caused addicts, Anslinger offered instead harsh minimum mandatory penalties in the Boggs Act (1951). After retirement as commissioner in 1962, he remained influential as a delegate to the U.N. narcotics mission until his death in 1975.

Yet, world drug use continues to rise—and still zealous officials, quick as robot clockwork, call for more laws, stricter penalties, tighter control.

No. 29, Vol. V] WEDNESDAY, DECEMBER 31. [1879.

No. 1, 1879.

DIEU ET MON DROIT

VICTORIA, BY THE GRACE OF GOD, OF THE UNITED KINGDOM OF GREAT BRITAIN AND IRELAND, QUEEN, DEFENDER OF THE FAITH, &c., &c.

A REGULATION

(Made in the name and on behalf of Her Majesty under the provisions of the Western Pacific Order in Council, 1879.)

TO PROHIBIT THE SUPPLY OF INTOXICATING LIQUORS TO NATIVES OF TONGA, AND OTHERS RESIDENT IN THE FRIENDLY ISLANDS.

[L.S. ARTHUR GORDON,
H. C.

I. If any British subject, in Tonga, sells or gives, or otherwise supplies to any native Tongan, or any native of any island in the Pacific Ocean resident in Tonga, any wine, spirits, or any other intoxicating liquor, he shall, on conviction thereof before the Court of Her Majesty's High Commissioner, be liable to a penalty not exceeding ten pounds, and in default of payment shall be liable to imprisonment for a peri... month.

II. If it sha... ...or spirits have been gi... ...fide fo... ...hall, in the judgme... Cour... ...the Court to d...

SIGSBEE'S NIECE OPIUM VICTIM?

...oman in Bellevue Hospital Says the Captain Who Commanded the Maine Is Her Uncle.

HAD THE PAREGORIC HABIT.

She Had Been Taking It for a Long Time and Interference Was Necessary.

...e Sigsbee, twenty-four years ..., well dressed and seemingly a... ...sed of every comfort, was ad... ...alcoholic ward of Bellevue Hos... ...t at her own request.

...e says she is a niece of Captain ...e Maine. She has lived for two ... Mrs. Fields, who keeps boarders ...East Seventeenth street.

...here from Albany, her birthplace, ...ago. She was employed most of ... a candy store in Broadway.

... she received a prescription made ...m paregoric, while she was a stu... ...e Albany City College, and out of ...acted the paregoric habit.

...ntington diagnosed the case as ...piumism. Miss Sigsbee was escort... ...hospital by George Fox, a brother ... Fields and living in the same house. ...elds says Miss Sigsbee is a woman ...ement and culture, and verifies the ... relationship with the famous Cap... ...of the ill fated Maine. She says the ...bit has grown to such a degree that it became necessary to place the young woman in an institution.

At Bellevue Hospital the doctors say she is ...n a serious condition, but believe they can ...store her to her normal state.

WELL DRESSED WOMAN ACCUSED OF STEALING.

DRANK LAUDANUM TOGETHER.

George Blakeley Dead and Lillian Spatz Dying, and No Reason for Their Act Known.

[BY TELEGRAPH TO THE HERALD.]

BRADFORD, Pa., July 1, 1897.—George Blakeley, proprietor of a printing office and secretary of the School Board, is dead, and Miss Lillian Spatz, a waitress in the Williamson restaurant, is in a precarious condition, the result of laudanum, supposedly taken with suicidal intent.

Blakeley's office was closed until three o'clock this afternoon, when the girl staggered out of the door and asked for water. Blakeley was found lying dead in a back room. Near his body was a woman's hat, and fastened to it with a hatpin was a piece of paper, upon which was written, "Take this to Mrs. Jennie Spatz."

... probably die, has not re... ...give any account of ... ...he First, Second ...id to be about ...The County ...for settle... ...to-da...

NATIVE CLERGY ... PHILIPPIN... CHURCHES

Plan of Archbishop ... Settle the Troubl... Has Been Caused ... Presence of the F...

ROME, September 26.—T... of a pontifical bull on the ... stitution of the Philippine... It will indicate the gener... aims of Archbishop Guidi's ... nila. The Apostolic Deleg... reorganize the whole ecc... archy of the archipelago, ... new dioceses and will pro... the archbishopric of Ma... maining bishoprics, afte... convoke a synod to estab... erning ecclesiastic affair... the customs of the isla... South America.

Archbishop Guidi is ... most liberal ideas re... ment of the Philippin... letter to Governor T... glad he had been ch... with him in the pacifi... and hoped to be able... sistance.

One of the first p... bishop is the establi... seminaries to ... which are d... foreigne... ...d to ...

CHURCHMEN FIGHT THE OPIUM MEASURE

Bishop Thoburn Declares Proposed Philippine Law in Every Way Wrong.

SUGGESTS JAPAN'S METHOD

Sale of Opium Should Be Restricted, He Thinks, to Druggists Only.

MEANS BRIBE TO THE PEOPLE

Proposal to Devote Income to Education Regarded as Weakest Clause in the Bill.

HERALD BUREAU,
No. 734 FIFTEENTH STREET, N. W.,
WASHINGTON, D. C., Thursday.

Strong protests have been received by Secretary Root against the bill now pending before the Philippine Commission authorizing the government to sell the opium traffic concession to a private concessionary for a bonus of $500,000.

Bishop J. M. Thoburn, at the head of Methodist missionary interests in the Philippines, called upon Mr. Root to-day, accompanied by the Rev. Wilbur F. Crafts, of this city, to protest against this measure, which he declared could not be described in a milder term than that of a bribe offered to the public conscience of the American people.

"In every case," said Bishop Thoburn, "the concessionary will inevitably do his utmost to increase the sale of the drug, and in this effort his resources will be such as to baffle all attempts at discovery of illicit practices. The sum expected to be realized from the sale is so large that the concessionary will be obliged to use hidden arts to opium dealers in order to recompense him for the monopoly.

BRIBE TO THE PEOPLE.

"The proposal to devote the income of the sale of the opium monopoly to education is the weakest clause of the whole bill. It is a bribe to the American people. The Filipinos are the people most concerned, and we are bound to legislate ...

Bishop Thobu... Trade in ...

JULY 10, 1903.

MANNE AND CUSTOMS OF DIFFERENT COUNTRIES.

Chinese Opium-Smokers.

WE subjoin a few particulars of the Opium-Smoking Dens in China, one of which our artist has so faithfully rendered—having with admirable skill depicted the "idiot smile" on the countenances of the two debauchees, who are evidently fast merging into a state of insensibility:

The rooms where the Chinese sit and smoke opium, are surrounded by wooden couches, with places for the head to rest upon, and generally a side room is devoted to gambling. The pipe is a reed of about an inch in diameter, and the aperture in the bowl for the admission of opium is not larger than a pin's head. The drug is prepared with some kind of incense, and a very small portion is sufficient to charge it, one or two whiffs being the utmost that can be inhaled from a single pipe; and the smoke is taken into the lungs, as from the hookah in India. On a beginner one or two pipes will have an effect, but an old stager will continue smoking for hours. At the head of each couch is placed a small lamp, as fire must be applied to the drug during the process of inhaling; and, from the difficulty of filling and properly lighting the pipes, there is generally a person who waits upon the smoker to perform the office.

A few days of this fearful luxury, when taken to excess, will impart a pallid and haggard look to the features, and a few months, or even weeks, will change the strong and healthy man into little better than an idiot-skeleton. In the hours devoted to their ruin, these infatuated people may be seen, at nine o'clock in the evening, in all the different stages. Some entering half distracted, to feed the craving appetite they have been obliged to subdue during the day; others laughing and talking under the effect of the pipe; whilst the couches around are filled with their different occupants, who lie languid, while an idiot smile upon their countenances proves them too completely under the influence of the drug to regard passing events, and fast merging into the wished-for consummation. The last scene of this tragic play, is generally a room in the rear of the building, a species of *morgue*, or dead house, where lie those who have passed into the state of bliss the opium-smoker madly seeks—an emblem of the long sleep to which he is blindly hurrying.

...t it, or swallow it in the form of ...thers, like the Chinese, smoke it; while ...opean countries, where its use is far less ...n, it is mostly taken liquid, as in laudanum. ...m is procured from the unripe fruit, or heads, of the common or white poppy (*Papaver somniferum*); and the usual way of collecting it is to make incisions in the skin of these heads while they are still on the stalk, when there oozes from them a creamy juice, which becomes hardened on exposure to the air. This is afterwards scraped from the heads and made up into small cakes. ...ulture of the poppy f... this ... branch ...

after his ... excessive quantities it seems ... faculties, and to reduce its wretch... lowest state of misery, ending at last ... death. It is rarely that a man habitu... use of opium is able to break from his infatuated indulgence. In our own country, Coleridge and De Quincey, both opium-eaters, have left on record, in glowing language, their experience of the effects of this exciting but pernicious drug, and the difficulty they had to encounter in their determination to renounce it.

...As regards the ge...

OPIUM-SMOKERS.

BRITAIN GERMANY ITALY AUSTRIA

PROTECTION OF NATIVE RACES AGAINST INTOXICANTS AND OPIUM

FRANCE SPAIN PORTUGAL

UNITED STATES

CONGO FREE STATE SWEDEN & NORWAY DENMARK

by ... Wilbur F. Crafts
and
...and Margaret W. Leitch

HOLLAND SWITZERLAND

TURKEY PERSIA ZANZIBAR BELGIUM

SMELLED CREOSOTE, CRIED "OPIUM DEN!"

Anonymous Letter Wr... tles Police and Mrs... Who Is Ill in B...

"IMAGINATIVE T...

Home of Widow Invad... tives, Who Find H... from Neura...

PUNGENT ODOR ...

Comes from Small Bott... scribed by Physic... Patient's S...

Neighbors of Mrs. P... lives in the apartment... Eighty-eighth street, c... and to the police of... station yesterday by... munication which stat... was in the house.

Captain Schmittberge... John Walsh and anoth... dress. The detective... was the pungent odor... by Mrs. Coxe's phy... diffused through the... the suspicions of sev...

OPIUM CAUSED MAYER'S DOWNFALL

MRS. GIBERT WON'T STAND OPIUM AND RUM

...t, Son of the Wealthy ... a Former President ... York Club, Is ... Separation.

...T SHE IS NOT GOOD

...ced Her $5,000 Yearly ... Marriage Law Non- ...tended to Kill Her ... Not Live.

...of the late Frederick ...of the New York Club, ...r 6, 1878, in the Church ...he Rev. D. A. Merrick, S. ...ie T. Gibert. For many ...a trust estate, under his ...t to about $15,000 yearly, ...t $8,000. ...d sumptuously, residing ...city and...

OPIUM IN OVERDOSE

Analysis of Mrs. Bessie Marcou's Stomach Proves That She Was Poisoned.

HAD TAKEN 118 GRAINS.

Coroner Hoeber Says That the Woman Was a Habitual User of Morphine.

POISONOUS DOSE WAS GIVEN.

McGillagh Had Said That He "Would Sit in the Electrical Chair for Her."

The chemical analyses of part of the contents of the stomach and intestines of Mrs. Bessie Marcou, who died under suspicious circumstances September 15 at No. 162 West Thirty-fifth street, made in accordance with Coroner Hoeber's instructions by Chemist Scheele, has resulted ... most important discovery, which ... was poisoned ... the woman self. ... her than her- ... -half of the ... 118 gra... ...ous qua... ...ontents of the ... ...alyzed...

HER SYMPTOMS THOSE OF OPIUM POISONING.

More Experts Testify for the Prosecution in the Trial of Carlyle W. Harris.

LINE OF THE DEFENCE.

Lawyer Jerome Seeks to Show That the Presence of Morphine Might Have Been Due to Innocent Causes.

HARRIS SAID HE WAS SORRY.

Congratulated Himself That He Had Signed the Prescription "Medical Student"—"M. D." Might Have Got Him Into Trouble.

SEC. JOHN HAY, who by letter has aided native races crusade, p. 15.

PRES. GROVER CLEVELAND, who urged legislation to forbid exportation of rum to Africa, p. 11.

LORD SALISBURY, who as Premier forwarded letters favorable to protecting uncivilized races against rum.

PRES. THEO. ROOSEVELT, whosigned Gillett-Lodge act and joined Senate in proposing universal treaty, p. 1.

PRES. WILLIAM M'KINLEY, who endorsed Gillett-Lodge bill and proposed universal treaty, p. 1.

President William McKinley, *in Message, Dec. 3, 1900*:—We have been urgently solicited by Belgium to ratify the international convention of June, 1898, amendatory of the previous convention of 1890 in respect to the regulation of the liquor trade in Africa. Compliance was necessarily withheld, in the absence of the advice and consent of the Senate thereto. The principle involved has the cordial sympathy of this Government, which in the revisionary negotiations ...

Lodge Resolution, *Adopted by U. S. Senate, Jan. 4, 1901, also approved by President Roosevelt: Resolved,* That in the opinion of this body the time has come when the principle, twice affirmed in international treaties for Central Africa, that native races should be protected against the destructive traffic in intoxicants should be extended to all uncivilized peoples by the enactment of such laws and the making ...

President Theodore Roosevelt, *in Message, Dec. 2, 1901:* In dealing with the aboriginal races few things are more important than to preserve them from the terrific physical and moral degradation resulting from the liquor traffic. We are doing all we can to save our own Indian tribes from this evil. Whenever by international agreement this ... attained as regards races where we do not possess ...

Secretary John Hay, *U. S. State Department (in letter of Dec. 11, 1901, replying to Chairman of Native Races Deputation)*: Your suggestion that I call the attention of the nations concerned to the Resolution of the Senate, adopted Jan. 4, 1901, as likely to have influence by indicating the concurrent opinion of the two branches of the treaty making power, the Senate and the Executive, has my ... circumstance that ...

ATLANTA, GEORGIA:
DUN... DICKSON, JOB PRINTERS, 11 NORTH BROAD STREET.
1878.

OPIUM POISONING.

THE TRAFFIC IN AND THE USE OF
OPIUM
IN OUR OWN AND OTHER COUNTRIES.

OPIUM

A DOCUMENT
BY THE REPRESENTATIVE MEETING OF THE YEARLY MEETING OF FRIENDS FOR NEW ENGLAND FOR
1881–1882.

Protection of Native Races
AGAINST
Intoxicants & Opium
BASED ON TESTIMONY OF ONE HUNDRED MISSIONARIES AND TRAVELERS

...ence of opinion of every civilized and Christian ... sources of crime and misery to society equal to ... toxicating liquors, in small quantities, to be drunk ... criminately to all parties applying. The statistics ... show a greater amount of crime and misery attributable to ... the use of ardent spirits obtained at these retail liquor saloons than to any other source.—*U. S. Supreme Court, 137 U. S., 90, 91.* ... Intemperance, largely through foreign introduction, is rapidly on the ... throughout the earth, and Christianity owes it to herself and to ... of Christendom to support and encourage every effort of missions ... for saving the world from its ravages.—*Rev. Jas. ... Christian Missions and Social Progress, Vol. I., pp. 79, 80.*

...SHINGTON:
GOV... PRINTING OFFICE.
1906.

PRESIDENT OF THE UNITED STATES,

Very truly Yours
Benj Harrison

REPORT OF THE COMMITTEE APPOINTED BY TH... TO INVESTIGATE THE USE OF OPIUM AND ... AND THE RULES, ORDINANCES, AND LAW... ...ING SUCH USE AND TRAFFIC IN JAPAN, FORMOSA, SHANGHAI, HONGKONG, SAIGON, SINGAPORE, BURMA, JAVA, AND THE PHILIPPINE ISLANDS, AND INCLOSING A LETTER FROM THE SECRETARY OF WAR SUBMITTING THE REPORT FOR TRANSMISSION.

Intoxicants & Opium in All Lands and Times

STATISTICAL ABSTRACT RELATING TO BRITISH INDIA 1903–4 TO 1912–13
EXPORTS OF OPIUM

	1903–4	1904–5	1905–6	1906–7	1907–8	1908–9	1909–10	1910–11	1911–12	1912–13
	£	£	£	£	£	£	£	£	£	
China Treaty Ports	1,610,296	1,504,604	1,130,372	1,031,065			1,234,432	2,203,670	3,614,1	
Hongkong	3,576,431	4,036,436	3,775,826	3,771,409						
Straits Settlements	1,365,743	1,262,834	1,163,529	1,150,50						
Java	63,402	78,383	70,960	78,11						
Siam	93,323	58,0		30,1						
Macao	0	0								
Japan	0									
French Indo-China	212,247									
Other Countries	58,668									
Total	6,980,110									

Page 196 Table 170

Petition Patterns.

[For individual signatures. Another form below.]

... Protection of Native Races Against Intox... and Opium.

...persons authorize the use of their na... ...e sixteen great nations that in 1892 no... ...c in slaves, firearms and spirituous liqu... ...in protection of native races, to extend th... ...separate and united action so as to protect a... ...stricts that are inhabited chiefly by similar... ...y those that are under Christian government, aga...

RESIDENCE. POSITION OR OCCUPATIO...

...d certifies the genuineness of these signatures.

...cannot use the above pattern to gather the names of ...vited to at least sign his own name to the followin... ...may attach my name to petition to sixteen nations... ...ded. Protection of Native Races against Intoxicat... ...th name give residence in full and occupation)... ...er petitions suggested on this page (of those given la... ...ress and the President) to The Reform Bureau, 210 ... ...ington, D. C., U. S. A.

... Public Meeting or Churc... ... Society.]

THE IMPORTATION OF OPIUM BY THE UNITED STATES.

From U. S. Bureau of Statistics.

	Opium—crude or unmanufactured—free.		Opium—crude or unmanufactured—dutiable.		Prepared for smoking, and other containing less than 9 per cent of morphia—dutiable.	
	Lbs.	Dollars.	Lbs.	Dollars.	Lbs	Dollars.
1890..	....	....	473,095	1,183,712	34,465	269,586
1891..	389,497	981,632	77,057	220,743	74,462	567,035
1892..	587,118	1,029,203	......	....	79,466	547,528
1893..	615,957	1,186,824	......	....	62,222	446,422
1894..	716,881	1,691,914	......	....	50,102	340,771
1895..	358,455	730,669	......	....	139,765	920,006
1896..	365,514	683,347	......	....	98,745	735,134
1897..	1,072,914	2,184,727	......	....	157,061	1,132,861
1898..	14,414	32,340	100,431	233,267	100,258	652,341
1899..	....	....	513,499	1,223,951	124,214	823,203
1900..	....	....	544,928	1,123,756	142,479	1,065,965

FROM STATI... PAGE ...

French Indo-Ch...
Java........
Siam........
China-Hongkong...
Straits Settlement...
United Kingdom...
Treaty Ports, China........ 927 2,907 1,180
Macao........
Japan........
Other countries........
Total........

...,93 | 204,328
226,500 | 110,712
18,433 | 80,572
27,833 | 58,148
18,295 | 0
119,913 | 0
19,223 | 100,659
| 47,543
2,280,031 | 1,175,639

OPIUM MONOPOLY

President William McKinley, *in Message, December 3, 1900:—We have been urgently solicited by Belgium to ratify the international convention of June, 1898, amendatory of the previous convention of 1890 in respect to the regulation of the liquor trade in Africa. Compliance was necessarily withheld, in the absence of the advice and consent of the Senate thereto. The principle involved has the cordial sympathy of this Government, which in the revisionary negotiations advocated more drastic measures, and I would gladly see its extension, by international agreement, to the restriction of the liquor traffic with all uncivilized peoples, especially in the western Pacific.*

Treaty ratified December 14, 1900. (*See document, Executive*

LODGE RESOLUTION, ADOPTED BY U. S. SENATE, JANUARY 4, 1901.

Resolved, That in the opinion of this body the time has come when the principle, twice affirmed in international treaties for Central Africa, that native races should be protected against the destructive traffic in intoxicants should be extended to all uncivilized peoples by the enactment of such laws and the making of such treaties as will effectually prohibit the sale by the Signatory Powers to aboriginal tribes and uncivilized races of opium and intoxicating beverages.

NEW YORK HERALD, WEDNESDAY, MARCH 27, 1895.

EASY TO BUY POISON.

Police Captain Pickett Has Been Investigating the Sale of "Knockout Drops."

ARRESTS ARE TO FOLLOW.

Detective Wilber Found No Difficulty in Purchasing Chloral from Many Druggists.

THEY OPENLY VIOLATED THE LAW.

Legislature To Be Asked to Pass a Law Making It a Felony to Carry the Poison.

Police Captain Pickett has determined to put a stop to the sale of "knockout drops" if possible. So many men have been found unconscious with their pockets empty in the streets that the Captain has come to the conclusion that it is time to remedy the evil.

He consulted with several reputable physicians in the Tenderloin district and then detailed Detective Wilber to investigate the manner in which the drug is obtained by the "knockout" thieves and also to secure evidence against druggists who violate the law. Detective Wilber was selected because he is familiar with the drug business.

"Knockout drops" are made of a solution of chloral, and section No. 402 of the Penal Code provides that all druggists who sell any poison without recording the name and residence of the person receiving it, except upon a prescription of some practising physician, are guilty of a misdemeanor.

EASY TO PURCHASE IT.

Detective Wilber made a tour of the Tenderloin district and he had but little difficulty in purchasing the drug without a prescription and without the druggists recording his name. As a consequence Captain Pickett and the detective will visit the Jefferson Market Police Court this morning and will apply for warrants for the druggists.

The Captain visited the wholesale druggists and learned that while the reputable druggists sold but little of the drug, in many stores in the Tenderloin district the poison is sold in quantities so large as to be out of proportion to their sales of other drugs.

The root of the whole evil, says Captain Pickett, lies in the fact that there is no punishment in the Penal Code for those who are caught with the drug in their possession.

NO LAW TO PUNISH THEM.

Only a short time ago Captain O'Connor captured three suspicious characters in his district, upon each of whom was found a phial of the "knockout drops," and yet when the prisoners were arraigned in court it was found that there was no law under which they could be held for trial.

Captain Pickett will hold a consultation with Superintendent Byrnes to-day in relation to the discoveries made by his detective and will then consult with members of the County Medical Society and ask that body to co-operate with him in having a law passed which will make it a felony for any person to have the drug in his possession, unless he be a physician or a man of established reputation, who can prove conclusively that he has purchased the drug under a physician's prescription and for a lawful purpose.

DECEMBER 31, 1908.

PLAN WORLD WAR ON OPIUM TRAFFIC

Proposal by United States to Leading Nations for Suppression of the Drug.

HERALD BUREAU,
No. 1,502 H STREET, N. W.,
WASHINGTON, D. C., Wednesday.

The proposals of the United States for the suppression of the opium trade throughout the world, to be discussed at the conference at Shanghai, China, February 1, have been submitted by Secretary of State Root through United States Ambassadors and Ministers to Great Britain, France, Germany, Italy, Holland, Portugal, Persia, Russia, Siam, Japan and China. A confidential letter to diplomats, made public here to-day by the International Reform Bureau, which is one of the prime movers in bringing about the conference, thus states the position of the United States with respect to the conference:—

"Our idea is that each government's commission should proceed independently with the investigation of the opium question on behalf of its respective country, with a view, first, to limit the use of opium in the possessions of that country; second, to ascertain the best means of suppressing the opium traffic if such now exists among the nationalities of that government in the Far East and, third, to be in a position so that when the commission meets at Shanghai the representatives of the various Powers may be prepared to co-operate and to offer, jointly or severally, definite suggestions of measures which their respective governments may adopt for the gradual suppression of opium cultivation, traffic and use within their Eastern possessions, thus assisting China in her purpose of eradicating the evil from her empire."

The Reform Bureau, with the Anti-Opium Federation of London, is appealing to public men in all the nations participating in the conference to assist in creating a public sentiment against the opium traffic which shall be reflected at the Shanghai conference.

SAN FRANCISCO CHRONICLE, APRIL 3, 1908.

DRUGGISTS WHO SELL POISON TO BE ARRESTED

Charles B. Whilden, Secretary of the State Board of Pharmacy, and Miss Ethel Wigley, who has assisted in trapping many local druggists; and photograph of some of the evidence.

Prosecutions of Those Who Supply Dope Fiends With Drugs.

W. L. BOURNES, clerk, Mission Drug Company, 10 Mission street.

Edward P. Salmon, clerk, Mission Drug Company, 10 Mission street.

George E. Atwood Jr., of Gates & Atwood drug store, 203 Third street.

Paul N. Hanby, proprietor of drug store at 1766 Seventh street, West Oakland.

Fred A. Korman, clerk in Frank W. Allen's drug store, Kentucky street.

The five men named will be arrested this morning on warrants sworn out by Charles B. Whilden, secretary of the State Board of Pharmacy, charging them with having violated section 8 of the act approved March 6, 1907, regulating the sale of poisons in this State.

Section 8 reads: "The sale of morphine, codeine, heroin, opium and cocaine, their salts, compounds or preparations, is hereby prohibited, unless upon the prescription of a physician, dentist or veterinary surgeon, licensed to practice in this State, except preparations of opium containing less than two grains of opium to the fluid ounce.

BEGINNING OF CRUSADE.

The members of the State Board of Pharmacy say that the arrest of these five men is but the beginning of a crusade that is to be carried on in the bay region to stop the sale of poisons to drug fiends. Twenty-four other warrants have been prepared against drug clerks and proprietors of drug stores in the bay region, and all these men are expected to be arrested within the next few days. The evidence against the accused men is said to be complete. The deputies in the office of the State Board of Pharmacy have been three months collecting evidence against the drug clerks of this city and the Oakland region, and have piled up in the offices of the Board, enough poison to kill 6000 men. In every case, men watched the sale of the poison to a man who did not present a prescription for it, and in three cases, marked coin was passed and afterward obtained by the authorities who will prosecute the cases.

"This is but a continuation of a campaign that we are carrying on all over the State to enforce the observance of the law regulating the sale of poisons," said Secretary Charles B. Whilden of the State Board of Pharmacy yesterday afternoon, "and we intend to keep it up until no druggist in the State will dare to sell poison to a dope fiend unless a doctor's prescription is presented for it. Under the old law it was hard to obtain convictions, but now we have a law that will stick, and we shall enforce it."

FORTY-FOUR CONVICTIONS.

Up to date the State Board of Pharmacy has had forty-four persons arrested for violating this law, and has obtained convictions in every case. In Los Angeles twenty-one drug clerks were fined $100 each for violating the law; in Sacramento there were six convictions, in Fresno one, in San Diego eight, in San Bernardino three, in San Jose eight, in South San Francisco one and in Richmond one. The maximum penalty for violating the law is a fine of $500 and imprisonment for sixty days; the minimum penalty is a fine of $30 or fifteen days' imprisonment.

The authorities of the State Board of Pharmacy have been busy in this city for the past three months and announce that some of the largest drug stores in the city will be haled into court for selling poisons without a prescription.

Confirmed drug fiends, who realize their predicament and are anxious to break away from the habit, have been used by the State Board of Pharmacy to catch the druggists violating the law, and in every case these men have not urged the druggists to sell them drugs, but have simply gone in as ordinary customers and asked for the drug. That the druggists knew that they would be violating the law is shown by the fact that in most cases the clerk to whom the dope fiend applied for drugs always looked up and down the street to make sure that no one was in sight before making the sale. But Secretary Whilden of the State Board, accompanied by Deputies G. D. Pratt and G. W. Appleton, were on the lookout and saw the sales. The package of drug was then obtained and marked for identification by all participants to the transaction and will be used in the trial of the cases.

MARKED COINS USED.

In the cases of W. L. Bournes, Edward P. Salmon and George E. Atwood, marked coins were used, and afterwadr secured from the druggists, the detection being made Wednesday night. In some of the cases each man was caught selling poisonous drugs to men without prescriptions as many as six times.

Among the deputies who have been aiding in the work of detection is Miss Ethel Wigley, secretary to Charles B. Whilden. To her has fallen the work of compiling the evidence and looking up the cases of the men accused. "Miss Wigley has been of great assistance to me in this work," said Charles B. Whilden yesterday, "she has looked up the records of the accused men, and has found that in many cases they have been convicted before of violating the drug laws."

Attorney Thomas O'Connor will represent the State Board of Pharmacy in San Francisco and Attorney John W. Stetson will represent the Board in Oakland.

Acting under the provisions of the Pure Food law, which gives him the authority to debar all deleterious foods and drugs, including habit forming drugs, Secretary of Agriculture Wilson has recently issued an order keeping opium designed for smoking out of the United States.

LOS ANGELES EXPRESS, THURSDAY, MARCH 21, 1912.

IN CRUSADE AGAINST HABIT-FORMING DRUGS

DR. HARVEY W. WILEY

WILEY CLASHES WITH DRUG "DOPERS"

Former Federal Chemist in Heated Argument Before Pure Food Board

ADVOCATES REGULATION OF SALE OF NARCOTICS

Appears as Private Citizen and Nearly Comes to Blows With Opponents

(BY ASSOCIATED PRESS LEASED WIRE)

WASHINGTON, March 21.—Dr. Harvey W. Wiley, appearing as a private citizen before the pure food board in advocacy of a regulation guarding very strictly the use and sale of opium, morphine, cocaine and other habit-forming drugs, aroused the anger of drug representatives by referring to them as "dopers."

A heated argument ensued and for a moment it looked as if blows might be possed.

Dr. Wiley finally consented to withdraw the term "dopers," but said he would still insist on calling them "manufacturers of poison."

Hague peace conferences.
Call the third Hague conference without delay. Ind. 76: 429-31. D. 4, '13.
Hague conferences. Outlook. 106. 577-8. Mr 14, '14.
Hague conferences. U. S. Bur. Educ. Bul. 1913, 12: 24-7.
Influence of The Hague in ending war. Lit Digest. 47: 461-2. S. 20, '13.
Sounding the slogan of peace anew at The Hague. Cur. Opinion. 55: 233-4. O. '13.
Hague peace palace.
Meeting-place for the world's peace-makers. O. S. Straus. il. R. of Rs 48: 440-2. O. '13.
Palace of international peace. L. Fielding. il. House B. 35: 42-4. Ja. '14.
Practical workshop for international achievement. A. S. Hershey. il. Ind. 75: 662-6. S 18, '13.
Supreme court of the world. il. Ind. 75: 280-2. Jl. 31, '13.
Temple of peace ridiculed. Lit. Digest. 47: 278. Ag. 23, '13.
World's court of justice. R. of Rs. 48. 480. O. '13.
World's temple of peace. W. Caird. Liv. Age. 279: 44-7. O. 4, '13.

CHICAGO EXAMINER 1912

LONG FIGHT ENDS.

The jury's verdict brought to a close a long and unceasing fight to land Clancy and the members of the ring of which he is the head. For many months the Federal narcotic squad, of which Harry B. Smith is the chief, has been accumulating evidence against the ring, and it was Smith's agents who on various occasions purchased narcotics at the Coronado Bar and also at the apartments of Clancy.

After reciting the indictments against Clancy and codefendants, Judge M. T. Dooling, in his speech to the jury, proceeded to call the attention of the trial jury to the strict provisions of the Harrison Narcotic law, of which the defendants stood charged with violating.

The court pointed out that the Harrison Narcotic Act is a revenue act designed to control the disposition of narcotic drugs, and that all persons authorized under the act to sell, deal or dispose of such drugs must first register with the Internal Revenue Collector of his district and pay a special tax; that it shall be unlawful for any person to purchase, sell or dispense such drugs except in the original packages, and absence of appropriate tax-paid stamps shall be prima facie evidence of violation of the law.

Judge Dooling further called the attention of the jury to the fact that it shall be unlawful for any person not registered under the provisions of this Act, and who has not paid the special tax provided for by

"Circulation Books Open to

Copyright, 1915, by The Press Publishing Co. (The New York World).

June 30, 1906. [S. 88.] [Public, No. 384.]

CHAP. 3915.—An Act For pr adulterated or misbranded or poi liquors, and for regulating traffic t

Pure food act. Manufacture of adulterated, etc., food or drugs in Territories and District of Columbia unlawful. Penalty.

Be it enacted by the Senate States of America in Congre any person to manufacture Columbia any article of food within the meaning of this of the provisions of this sect for each offense shall, upon five hundred dollars or shall or both such fine and impris for each subsequent offense less than one thousand dollar or both such fine and impris

SEC. 6. That the term "drug," as used in medicines and preparations recognized in th copœia or National Formulary for internal substance or mixture of substances intende mitigation, or prevention of disease of eith The term "food," as used herein, shall inc food, drink, confectionery, or condiment b whether simple, mixed, or compound.

Drugs. In case of drugs:

False name. First. If it be an imitation another article.

False contents. Second. If the contents of have been removed, in whole

Failure to state narcotics, etc., used. been placed in such package, on the label of the quantity opium, cocaine, heroin, alpha indica, chloral hydrate, or ace of any such substances conta

Foods. In the case of food:

Imitations. First. If it be an imitation tive name of another article.

WOODROW WILSON, President; THOMAS R CLARKE, President of the Senate *pro temp* dent of the Senate *pro tempore*, December 1915; NATHAN P. BRYAN, Acting Preside 1915; CHAMP CLARK, Speaker of the Hou

CHAP. 1.—An Act To provide for the registratio revenue, and to impose a special tax upon all perso facture, compound, deal in, dispense, sell, distribut leaves, their salts, derivatives, or preparations, and fo

Be it enacted by the Senate and House of Re States of America in Congress assembled, That of March, nineteen hundred and fifteen, ev imports, manufactures, compounds, deals i utes, or gives away opium or coca leaves facture, salt, derivative, or preparation ther collector of internal revenue of the district

SEC. 6. That the provisions of this Act to apply to the sale, distribution, giving aw sion of preparations and remedies which d two grains of opium, or more than one-f phine, or more than one-eighth of a grain one grain of codeine, or any salt or derivati fluid ounce, or, if a solid or semisolid pr dupois ounce; or to liniments, ointment which are prepared for external use only, exc and other preparations which contain coc or alpha or beta eucaine or any of their sa stitute for them: *Provided*, That such re are sold, distributed, given away, dispens cines and not for the purpose of evading the of this Act. The provisions of this Act cainized coca leaves or preparations mad preparations of coca leaves which do not co

Professional use by physicians, etc. (a) To the dispensing or to a patient by a physician, under this Act in the cours *vided*, That such physician, a record of all such drugs amount dispensed or distrib of the patient to whom su except such as may be disp whom such physician, denti attend; and such record sha the date of dispensing or di tion, as provided in this Act

SEC. 12. That nothing co to impair, alter, amend, or of Congress approved June entitled "An Act for prevent tion of adulterated or misbr drugs, medicines, and liquor for other purposes," and a

Partly cloudy

Stories

How Uncle S
The Serio-Co
Right and W
The $1,079,5
Strange Stor

"Circulation Books Open to All."

In Next S

V YORK, FRIDAY, APRIL 16, 1915.

PRICE { ONE CENT in Greater New York / TWO CENTS outside of Greater

ure, sale, or transportation of foods, drugs, medicines, and purposes.

esentatives of the United it shall be unlawful for tory or the District of ulterated or misbranded, on who shall violate any of a misdemeanor, and be fined not to exceed ne year's imprisonment, retion of the court, and ereof shall be fined not ne year's imprisonment, eretion of the court.

Terms defined. "Drugs."

clude all Pharma- and any he cure, animals. used for animals,

"Food."

sale under the name of

originally put up shall ther contents shall have fail to bear a statement any alcohol, morphine, chloroform, cannabis erivative or preparation

r sale under the distinc-

ice President; JAMES P. SWANSON, Acting Presi- 31, 1914, and January 2, *pro tempore*, January 22, atives.

December 17, 1914. [H. R. 6282.] [Public, No. 223.]

of internal port, manu- um or coca

Opium and coca leaves. Producers, etc., of, and compounds, required to register. Post, p. 1912.

he United e first day produces, s, distrib- d, manu- r with the , place of

Drugs not affected by Act.

construed or posses- nore than n of mor- nore than em in one ne avoir- parations intments, its salts hetic sub- parations as medi- provisions to deco- to other

Proviso. Conditions.

Further exception.

any of the aforesaid drugs rinary surgeon registered ional practice only: *Pro-* rinary surgeon shall keep distributed, showing the and the name and address dispensed or distributed, ibuted to a patient upon surgeon shall personally period of two years from drugs, subject to inspec-

s Act shall be construed the provisions of the Act neteen hundred and six, cture, sale, or transporta- nous, or deleterious foods, lating traffic therein, and t thereof, or of the Act

this Act, to have in his posses or under his control any of aforesaid drugs, and such pos sion or control shall be prima f evidence of a violation of the ac

In his charge, Judge Dool further called the attention of jury to the charge that evide had been introduced tending show that narcotic drugs had be found in the premises known 187 Mason street and at 599 O'Fa rell street, but he cautioned t jury to be convinced beyond a rea sonable doubt that the defendant, or some of them, knew of the ex istence of such drugs in thes premises, or consented to th placing of the drugs there.

The court said that if the jury was convinced beyond a reasonable doubt that if the offense was com

AS FIFTEEN DRUG SLAVES ARE TAKEN IN FOR CURE, 20 MORE ARE SHUT OUT.

Pitiful Begging by Addicts Who Come Late, but the Metropolitan Hospital Can Take No More Just Now of Those Who Find Federal and State Laws Depriving Them of "Dope."

BELLEVUE GETS PATIENTS FOR A RIGID TREATMENT.

Federal District Attorney Announces His Determination to Enforce Law to the Utmost, a Start Coming With the Arrest of Edward W. Graupner, Accused of Selling Drugs.

Fifteen emaciated and distracted drug slaves were admitted yesterday to the Metropolitan Hospital on Blackwell's Island. All begged hard to be let in to undergo the treatment which the Charities Department officials have put in operation for their benefit.

But twenty other drug slaves who begged with equal earnestness to be allowed to enter the institution had to be kept on the waiting list.

All had been driven from cover by the operations of the new Federal Anti-Narcotic Law and by the renewed activity of the police under the Boylan law of this State.

The Federal law, known as the Harrison act, has had the effect of cutting off the New York City drug addicts from their former sources of supply in Hoboken, Jersey City and Philadelphia. Importing the stuff across the Hudson has become so risky that the traffic has almost ceased.

Twenty-five Out as Cured.

The "dope" wards of the Metropolitan Hospital have been taxed to their capacity for weeks. Twenty-five persons were discharged yesterday as cured, though of course the doctors cannot say that the patients will not be back again unless the new law completely cuts off their supply of drugs.

Bellevue, from 12.30 A. M. yesterday to 10.30 last night, admitted on their pitiful pleas nineteen drug slaves, some of whom were physical wrecks. They told pitiful tales of the suffering they had undergone after they had been cut off from their usual supplies of morphine, cocaine or heroin.

Bellevue last night had fifty-five cases of drug addiction.

There is a fixed course of treatment, lasting ten days to two weeks. It begins with drastic doses of medicine that take every trace ... out of the ...

Drug Fiends Giving Up Fight; 147 of Them in 3 Hospitals

It is estimated by the police and the Federal authorities that 500 drug fiends have been caught or have surrendered in New York City within the last two weeks.

The rush of the drug addicts is attributed to the new United States Anti-Narcotic Act, which went into effect March 1.

This law requires a record to be kept on Government blanks of every particle of opium, coca leaves and their derivatives, imported, made, prescribed and sold or given away. Every commercial handler of these drugs is taxed, and the aim of the measure is to stop all interstate unlawful trafficking.

Already this law has cut off New York's supply of contraband "dope" from New Jersey and Pennsylvania and has driven the poorer drug slaves from cover, half crazed at their deprivation.

Last night there were 147 "dope fiends" in three of the city hospitals, as follows: Metropolitan, 60; Bellevue, 55; Kings County, 32.

In public and private hospitals in Greater New York there are fully 2,000 drug addicts, the police say.

The prisoner, who was held by Commissioner Houghton in $3,500, was charged with having sold powdered opium and morphine without a prescription to Lee Chee, a Chinese. The arrest was made on the complaint of Assistant United States Attorney Harold A. Content.

"It is of the utmost importance," Mr. Content said last night, "to arrest druggists who violate this law. They are the real cause of the diffusion of drug addiction and they are the main source of supply for the 'joints' in the Tenderloin, in the negro sections and in Chinatown."

The Federal officials say Graupner is awaiting trial in a similar case brought a month ago.

There have been five prosecutions here by Federal officials since the Harrison act took effect. The first prisoner, a druggist, pleaded guilty.

Another druggist, Frank Leonard of Eighty-fourth Street and East End Avenue, on March 16, swallowed cyanide and died in the arms of the policeman who had just arrested him.

A Chinese waiter was sentenced to serve two months and pay $100 fine for having smuggled a can of opium.

The fourth case was that of a druggist who is awaiting trial.

The fifth arrest was that of Graupner.

Mr. Content said last night he believes the Harrison law will end the wide use of habit-forming drugs.

Lieut. Henry Scherb, in charge of Police Commissioner Wood's "Dope Squad," said yesterday he believed the Harrison law will solve the drug problem in New York by closing the avenues of supply, in conjunction with the Boylan law.

It was said at the office of the United States Attorney that there has been practically no opium or cocaine smuggled from abroad since the Harrison law went into effect, and that the restricting effect on interstate traffic in drugs has been marked.

Score of Suicides in Chicago; One "Cure" Is Attacked.

(Special to The World.)

CHICAGO, April 15.—There have been a score of suicides in Chicago, and the hospitals have been besieged since the Harrison law went into effect. One drug habitue—Mrs. Mary Willis, twenty, who tried to break off the habit by taking a "cure" a friend suggested—died.

Coroner's Chemist W. D. McNally reported: "A chemical examination of the brown fluid in the bottle labelled 'Dr. Weatherby's Remedy' showed 20.6668 grains of morphine sulphate per ounce."

After Hard Fight, St. Louis Is Mastering the Situation.

ST. LOUIS, April 15.—The City Hospital had more than 300 applications from drug slaves in the first week after the Harrison Act took effect and the institution was crowded until a few days ago.

At one time the drug patients had a fight with the attendants when the ... was cut down. But with ... been a n...

Price Goes Up in Frisco, but You Can Get the Stuff.

SAN FRANCISCO, April 15.—Habit-forming drugs have risen slightly in price here under the operation of the Harrison Act. But it is reported that drug slaves who "have the price" find no trouble in getting all they want.

DRUG USER FLEES WHEN REVIVED AT HARLEM HOSPITAL

"Red Mike" Doyle Sneaks Out of Yard as He Is About to Be Transferred to Prison Ward in Bellevue.

SHARP TEETH WAIT IN ANTI-DRUG LAW.

Federal Statute Makes Rigid Rules and Provides Heavy Fine and Imprisonment.

(Special to The World.)

WASHINGTON, April 15.—The Harrison Anti-Narcotic Law provides that every person or concern that imports, manufactures, sells or gives away opium or coca leaves or any form of them shall register with the Collector of Internal Revenue and shall pay a special tax of $1 a year.

It is unlawful to sell, barter, exchange or give away any of the aforesaid drugs except in pursuance of a written order of the person who is to receive them. All such orders must be on blank forms supplied by the Government. The orders must be preserved at least two years, and duplicates are to be filed at once with the Internal Revenue Collectors.

Physicians, dentists and veterinarians must record all their prescriptions. All persons who handle drugs are required to keep exact records, all of which are open to the Government.

Certain public United States and State drug officials are excepted, as are medicines containing not more to an ounce than two grains of opium, one-quarter grain of morphine, one-eighth grain of heroin, or one grain of codeine, or their salts or derivatives.

No unregistered person may have the drugs in his possession.

The maximum penalty for a violation of the act is $2,000 fine, or five years in prison, or both.

Men Crazed for Lack of Heroin Made a Vain Pilgrimage.

(Special to The World.)

BOSTON, April 15.—Since the Anti-Narcotic Law took effect, Boston's *drug slaves* have overrun the hospitals in search of relief. Word spread early in March that heroin had been stored in large quantities in a certain Vermont town and purchases could be made at high rates. The result was that "dope fiends" went to the Vermont town in scores from many points in New England, but found nobody with narcotics for sale.

Many permanent cures have been effected in hospitals here, it is ...

Chinese Physician Did an Immense Pittsburgh Trade, It Is Said.

PITTSBURGH, April 15.—Dr. Jin Fuey Moy, a Chinese physician, was arrested to-day here charged with selling and possessing opium without having registered. It was alleged he wrote 10,000 heroin prescriptions ... days.

Quakertown Thinks Its "Fiends" Have Fled to This City.

(Special to The World.)

PHILADELPHIA, April 15.—The police say the Federal law practically has cleaned Philadelphia of its "dope fiends." Many of them, it is said, have fled to New York City, where they have settled in the Tenderloin.

For a time the police were overwhelmed with requests from unfortunates for help in their suffering. It was decided to establish a clinic in a hospital for them. All such persons now coming into the hands of the police are sent to the Philadelphia Hospital or to one established at Holmesburg.

WHITMAN'S O.K. ALL THAT'S NEEDED TO END DRUG EVIL

Signing of Boylan Law Amendment, Experts Say, Will Finish Work Begun With Rush to Hospitals.

MAKES IT MISDEMEANOR TO POSSESS MORPHINE.

Federal Service Says "Remedy Is in Hands of Medical Profession."

The strange scenes through which New York City has been passing in the last few weeks in connection with the arrest or trembling surrender of hundreds of "dope fiends," young and old, marks the beginning of the end, according to the police and the District Attorney's prosecutors, of the great epidemic of drug addiction that has been sweeping over the community for several years.

The only thing needed to hasten and make doubly sure the victory over drugs, the authorities say, is Gov. Whitman's signature on the amendment to the Boylan law making it a misdemeanor to possess morphine or its derivatives without a license and making it a felony to sell any of these habit-forming drugs to a child under sixteen.

The present astonishing rush of the "dope fiends" toward the hospitals and asylums here is due to two causes:

First, to the operation the Federal or Harrison Anti-Narcotic Law, passed by Congress and signed by the President, which went into effect here and elsewhere on March 1, 1915.

Second, to the specialized activity of the police. A detail of sixteen men, known as Special Squad No. 3, under Lieut. Henry Scherb, has been created at Police Headquarters, and this body of trained men, aided by an unknown number of "stool pigeons," is raking the town for the drug-fiends. The District Attorney is co-operating and so are the Judges in General Sessions and the Justices of Special Sessions.

The United States Government is enforcing the Harrison law through the Internal Revenue Service. This law requires that every particle of morphine, opium, cocaine, heroin or other habit-forming drugs brought into the country from abroad or manufactured in this country shall be registered. No wholesaler or retailer can import or sell these drugs except on blanks furnished by the Government.

None of the narcotics, to quote from the law itself, can lawfully be "produced, imported, manufactured, compounded, sold, dispensed or given away" until all the forms and formalities of the law have been complied with. Every doctor, dentist and veterinarian must account for every drachm that comes into or goes out of his possession. An annual Federal tax of $1 is levied on all who handle the drugs.

The first effect of the Harrison law has been to cut off New York's supply of "dope" from New Jersey and Philadelphia.

No matter how strictly the Boylan law was enforced here, the drug dealers, peddlers and fiends had simply to cross the North River to get unlimited quantities. Hoboken was for years a distributing point. Some of the contraband drugs sold in Hoboken and Jersey City were smuggled in from Europe on the ships, but most of it came from Philadelphia or Newark, N. J., and was manufactured there, the police say.

Before the Federal law took effect it was a daily experience to have cocaine and morphine and heroin brought to Hoboken from Philadelphia by automobiles. A dealer could order the dope in the Quaker City in the forenoon, send an auto for it with a trusted messenger and get the goods here in the afternoon.

The second effect of the Harrison law was to boost the price of the dope beyond the reach of nine-tenths of New York's drug slaves. This is what has been driving the half crazed, despairing fiends into the open in the last few weeks. This showdown of the army of addicts has revealed the fact that three-quarters of them use heroin in preference to straight opium or cocaine.

The extent of the traffic and the length to which it has become organized is shown by the fact that within the last few days the Scherb squad caught a man who has been in the country only three months and who speaks no English, but who was doing a lively trade in Harlem, it was alleged, selling dope. He had four "decks" in his possession when seized.

Just before the Federal law was signed the New York police found a large quantity of dope that had been made in Germany and apparently smuggled through Italy on a Mediterranean steamer. At least the New York wholesale firm whose German branch houses' labels were on the goods denied the stuff had passed through the New York branch. A search of the New York branch's books is now being made.

The Federal authorities have put on extra inspectors, to stop, if possible, all drug smuggling. Opinions among local officials differ as to whether this can be done, owing to the added temptation of "famine" prices and profits; but it is agreed that in no event is the smuggling likely to be enough to restore the old conditions here.

The conviction last week of a druggist named Paul Borchard, Republican leader of the Thirteenth Assembly District, had a moral effect on the whole body of drug traffickers. Justice Kernochan sentenced him to six months and $500 fine and called him the central office of the drug traffic in the San Juan Hill district.

The desperation of alleged "dope" dealers when they are seized by the police is illustrated in the case of Frank Leonard, who, as soon as he was put under arrest, March 16, at Eighty-fourth Street and East End Avenue, took cyanide and fell dead in the patrolman's arms. The problem of suppressing the dope evil here is only partly solved by the capture of the offenders. There still remains the difficulty of clearing up the habit in the victims, who, in most cases wild-eyed, emaciated and partly crazed, are likely to die unless promptly and intelligently handled.

This was the case with Charles Hunt, twenty years old, of No. 204 East Ninety-sixth Street, who, deprived of dope for a week, surrendered to the police the other night at Second Avenue and One Hundred and Fourth Street and then died in the ambulance on the way to Bellevue.

Many of the captured or surrendered fiends have been in a critical state mentally and physically. In many cases they have to be put through a slowing up process at the hospitals, the dope being gradually reduced day by day until they can stand its entire deprivation. This is an expensive process for the city at the present high prices for drugs.

Decrease in Sales.

Sales of habit-forming drugs to children have diminished in the last month or two, according to Charles G. Bond, who, with Ernest K. Coulter, is on Judge Swann's Committee to Deal with Drug Addiction.

From April 1, 1914, to Jan. 26, 1915, by data compiled by Mr. Coulter, 3,590 men and women in Manhattan and the Bronx were committed as drug habitues to various institutions.

There has never been a dope "survey" of this city, and so estimates differ widely as to the actual number of addicts here. In Ohio the State Board of Health recently stated the number there, after a survey, at 4 per cent. of the population.

On this basis the drug fiends in New York City would number 200,000. The Federal Government not long ago, through its Public Health Service, guessed the cocaine users in the United States at 200,000 on the basis of a Tennessee survey, or about 1 in 500 of population. On this scale the share of New York City would be only 10,000.

The police fear the cocaine users more than any other class of dope fiends, because cocaine sharpens the wits and makes crooks more nervy and more crafty. Whiskey, the police say, only makes a man think he is smarter; morphine makes him duller, but cocaine actually does make him smarter for the time being, though he suffers a corresponding reaction when the effect is over. Morphine soothes; cocaine exhilarates.

It has been testified time and again in the last few years that at least 60 per cent. of the criminal classes are dope users. Of the 400,000 pounds of opium and its derivatives imported by the United States in a year not more than 20 per cent. is properly used, it is estimated by the Swann committee.

The District Attorney's prosecutions under the Boylan act are directed by his assistant, Floyd Wilmot, aided by Mr. Deane and Mr. Lockhart.

The Swann committee, organized through the efforts of Mrs. W. K. Vanderbilt sr., who aided in the campaign for the Boylan and Harrison laws, consists of:

Edward Swann, Judge of the Court of General Sessions; Dr. S. S. Goldwater, Commissioner of Health; Katharine B. Davis, Commissioner of Correction; Frank L. Polk, Corporation Counsel; Dr. John W. Brennan, in charge of Bellevue and Allied Hospitals; Dr. O. F. Lewis, Secretary Prison Association; Cornelius F. Collins, Justice of the Court of Special Sessions; H. Clarke Barber, Superintendent Society for Prevention of Crime; Theodore Rosseau, Mayor's office; Floyd H. Wilmot, District Attorney's office; Ernest K. Coulter and Charles G. Bond.

Remedy Pointed Out.

The Hygienic Laboratory, United States Public Health Service, this month has sent out a warning against drug "cures" as follows:

"After all, the remedy for the present condition lies well within the hands of the medical profession and the really reputable hospitals and institutions already organized. If the law be strictly enforced and the supply of "dope" through other than proper channels absolutely cut off, the medical practitioner has an opportunity such as he has never before had.

"Whether institutional or home treatment will prove the more practicable is a question which must be determined by actual trial in each individual case, guided by the particular conditions therein appearing. Just because these conditions do vary in each case, no rule-of-thumb method can be adopted.

"The general principles which can be applied in any case are (1) to gain, if possible, the confidence of the patient and secure his obedience to instructions; (2) to eliminate any drug which may remain in his system; (3) to repair the wreck caused by the drug through hygienic, dietetic and perhaps medicinal measures adapted to the special needs of the particular case.

"Whether in any given case the drug can at once and finally be withdrawn is a question which the attending physician alone can determine. Granted that the law is enforced, the supply is wholly within his control, and none can gainsay nor interfere with his right to administer any narcotic when and where he deems it necessary."

SATURDAY SAN FRANCISCO, SEPTEMBER 18, 1920

ISOLATION OF DRUG USERS ON ISLAND
S. F. PLANS FORCIBLE CURES FOR J

SEPTEMBER 28, 1920

OUT S. F. DRUG RING

PHARMACY BOARD ORDERS 12 NEW OPERATIVES TO ROUND UP SMALL PEDDLERS, HIGHER UPS

140 Agents, Addicts Bagged in First 5 Days of Crusade; State Senator Crowley Plans New Bill to Provide an Island Hospital

TWICE CONVICTED PEDDLER WILL FACE FELONY CHARGE
BRADY WARNS S. F. DOPE RI

...trict Attorney Orders $5,000 Bail for ... Distributors; Drive Planned on Higher U... Addicts in Jail Support P...

habit without a certain amount of will power behind it. While it is possible for him to stay completely under this masterful influence he cannot assert himself.

In an institution of isolation he would have an opportunity to regain some of his former control...

SEPTEMBER 3, 1917

DRUG CRUSADE AID TO FAKE SANITARIUMS

Reputable Physicians Are Driven from Treating Addicts by the Publicity Given to Raids

Many Deterred from Study of Disease, Which Whitney Law Was Designed to Encourage

By J. E. WATSON.

In an article published in the New York American on Sunday morning the writer quoted sections of the New York State Anti-Narcotic law of 1917 providing for the relief of drug addicts in crises such as that now facing New York City.

The question now arises as to whether or not a conspiracy exists to defeat that law and re-establish a condition that has resulted in the protection of fake sanitariums and the accumulation of vast fortunes by so-called narcotic drug addiction specialists at the expense of the addict.

Witness how such a crusade against narcotics as that now being carried on by the Federal and city authorities would bring about this result.

The average physician is a man to whom the ethics of nis profession are sacred.

Then word is passed about that "the authorities are after drug doctors," spectacular arrests are made and the same old inane talk starts about "the degradation of drug taking."

This has but one effect upon the honest physician. He dischadges his patients, discontinues his study of addiction disease and retires from practise of this interesting phase of medicine—thoroughly intimidated by threats of prosecution and consequent court proceedings.

The result is that his patients are driven to the underworld with its illicit supply of narcotics for relief or seek the advice of keepers of fake sanitariums.

True, the State law offers protection for honest physicians treating addiction patients, but the doctor does not feel that he is called ... pionee... sible ... There ... the a...

Now ... condition is exactly what is most desired by the narcotic sanitarium faker. He has spend ... in educating the public to ... that the addict can quit h... "will power"; that add... vice of the degenerate... disease condition exis... patient's mind.

Behind these dis... of humanity are ... names are byw... probity through... tingly or unw... beards have h... addict for a ... Wittingly or ... promoted mis... against addi... decades to re...

Their rake-... their names t... A per capita ... tering the fa... acted and v... built up by t... sensical addic...

Of course th... this condition ... his drug ... sources provi... titioner, the ... to their sanit... heavily for t... scribed.

Addicts Pawns of Master Shoplifter, Charge of Police

U. S. CLINIC TO SELL DRUGS TO ADDICTS

AUGUST 7, 1919

Mayor Calls Conference to Perfect Plans for "Clubhouse" Where Cures May Be Made

Collector Wardell Secures Sanction of Government for Novel Experiment in Curbing Habit

The establishment of a drug clinic in San Francisco for the exclusive use of drug addicts, to be conducted under Government supervision, will be asked at a conference to be called today by Mayor James Rolpb Jr., Federal State and municipal authorities, are invited to the gathering.

The object of the clinic will be two-fold—to sell to narcotic victims at one-eighth the present cost the drugs necessary to maintain their sanitary and health, thereby eliminating the growing illicit drug trafficing, and to establish a scientific and modern permanent cure.

HAS U. S. SANCTION.

The project here was sponsored by Justus S. Wardell, collector of internal revenues, who yesterday received official sanction from Washigton for the Government's participation in the work.

Commissioner of Revenue Roper has sent instructions to Wardell immediately to put his plan into operation here, calling into co-operation the Federal law-enforcing agencies, State and local medical societies and the police.

... and experts now concerned ... the growing use of ... the working ...

WHERE HOPE REPLACES DOPE

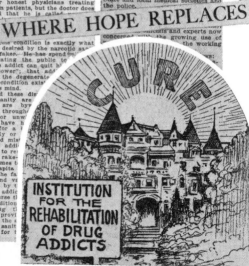

CURE

INSTITUTION FOR THE REHABILITATION OF DRUG ADDICTS

Drug Smuggler, Peddler Faces Heavy Penalty

HERE is what the courts can do with convicted drug smuggler or peddler:

The Federal law provides a maximum punishment of $2,000 fine or five years imprisonment, or both.

The State law is more indulgent, as violation does not constitute a felony until after the thi... It provides: ...

Peddler Gets Six Months; 30 Users Of Dope in Court

Nine women and a score of men, drug add... were arrested ... ared in police ...

..., one of the prisoners made an attempt to escape ... the courtroom of Police Judge ...ick. Al Williams, bailiff in ... saw her running from the ... and recaptured her. She ... into custody until today. ...edy, another woman who ... a raid on a Polk street ...ay, was so ill from her ... days that she was ... stand. She was ...

DRUG ADDICTS

MAKE FIRST NARCOTIC SALE FELONY WITH LONG PRISON TERM, URGES HEALTH CHIEF

Drastic Laws and Prompt Action Advocated by Dr. George E. Ebright to Cope With ... Increase in the 'Dope' Habit

POLICE JUDGES ADOPT POLICY OF 'LIMIT' FOR EVERY PEDDLER; ADDICTS MAY ALSO GO TO JAIL

Plans on Foot to Have Doctors Detailed to Treat Victims; Half-Way Steps Abandoned in Campaign ... Traffic in Dope

PROVES 'DOPE' ADDICTS CAN BE CURED

NARCOTIC PROBLEM SOLUTION SEEN IN THE SEGREGATION OF ADDICTS UNDER TREATMENT

Treatment of Addiction in Isolated Hospital Is Held by Experts to Be the Best Solution

Judges, Police Officials and Physicians Indorse Scheme to Shield Victims From Peddlers

Isolated Hospital Plan Approved By Drug Victims

The proposition for an isolated hospital for the cure of drug addicts, to be placed on some island, is being approved enthusiastically not only by the doctors who treat victims of the dope habit, judges who sentence them to jail for offenses committed while under the influence or to get money with which to purchase the poison, but now comes praise for the plan from the victims who are in jail.

"If we can be spared the torture of the first ten or twelve days in jail while we are deprived of our drugs...

SATURDAY CC

S DEMANDED ED ADDICTS

CO-OPERATION

'DOPE' SANITARIUM UNDER FEDERAL PROBE;

BARKER'S SANITARIUM RAIDED FOR DOPE

'Physician,' Held Prisoner in Office, Grabs Phone; Officers Knock It From His Grasp

"Doctor" Admits He Was Stage Hypnotist and Circus Magician Before Starting "Dope Cure"

Police Seize Records of Dope Hospital

CALIFORNIA
ANTI-NARCOTICS
THURSDAY
SF
OCTOBER 27TH
CONVENTION
DRUG EVIL
DEATH

JANUARY 3, 1923

'DRUG CURE' SPECIALIST TO FACE GRILL

Pharmacy Board Says Woman Purchased Morphine Without a Doctor's Prescription

Barker Arraigned, Gives Bond; Charges Frame-Up; Silent on Marked Bills; Lists Seized

By MRS. W. B. HAMILTON,
Representative Woman's Club Leader of San Francisco.

The arrest of "Dr." John Barker on charges of violating the Federal narcotic control laws has brought to light, according to the evidence gathered by the authorities, a condition of grave public concern.

Posing as a benefactor, this man, the Government officers declare, has used this subterfuge to cloak an unlawful traffic in narcotics, feeding the weak victims of narcotic drug addiction—a malefactor surely, rather than a beneficent healer of disease.

That aspect becomes such an outstanding element in this case that it calls for the stern invoking of the full power of the law.

I speak strongly for I feel strongly the utter helplessness of those that have been unfortunate enough to fall into the trap.

The story of "Dr." Barker carries a lesson which I earnestly urge every citizen, man and woman, who has the welfare of his fellow beings at heart, to read.

Aroused by the exposure of an insidious new form of the "dope" menace in the arrest, as an illicit peddler of narcotics, of "Dr." John Scott Barker, prominent Oakland drug-cure specialist and self-styled social reformer, Federal and State authorities yesterday turned a glaring searchlight upon the conduct and activities of the Barker hospital for addicts.

Social workers, who had unquestioningly accepted "Dr." Barker's self-assumed title and leadership in the anti-narcotic crusade which he recently launched in Oakland, learned with amazement of the event of Monday night, when a woman, posing as an addict, handed the "physician" a marked bill and received in return a quantity of morphine—without even the pretense of a prescription.

ARRAIGNED IN COURT.

It was announced yesterday, from Board of Pharmacy headquarters in the Flood building, that this was the second purchase of the kind which Mrs. V. P. Merrill of Marysville had made from "Dr." Barker.

The same fact was also brought out at Barker's arraignment, which took place yesterday morning before Uni 1 States Commissioner Albert Hardie in Oakland.

Barker, pale and nervous after a night in the Oakland city jail, was brought before the commissioner and informed of the charge against him—two counts of violation of the Harrison anti-narcotic law.

JANUARY 4, 1923

tance, was three to six grains of morphine a day. The record concluded:

Treated for morphinism for two weeks and partial withdrawal accomplished.

Reid later entered another sanitarium, where he is recently reported as improved in health.

MANY "TIPS."

A raid upon the Barker drug cure sanitarium, conducted by "Dr." John Scott Barker, Oakland "social reformer" and anti-narcotic crusader, now under arrest on Federal charges of illicit drug peddling, yesterday brought to light new evidence of the narcotic menace in its latest, weirdest form.

BARES PATIENT'S NAME.

Prominent in the correspondence was the name of Juanita Hansen, motion picture actress, to whom reference was made as a former patient in the Barker sanitarium at Oakland.

"Dr." Blessing came post-haste to San Francisco yesterday to interview H. B. Meader, president of the Board of Pharmacy, in regard to the raid. Blessing denied that he and Barker were partners, but said he had gone into business after consulting with Barker, and had secured the privilege of using the "Barker Cure" by paying 25 per cent of his receipts to Barker.

The significant point about both institutions, according to Board of Pharmacy officials, is that neither is headed by a qualified physician.

NOT REGISTERED.

Proof that Barker is not registered under the laws of California as physician, pharmacist or registered nurse, came as a surprise to Oakland social workers who have always accepted without question the title commonly appended to his name.

Indictment of Barker by the Federal grand jury in this city will be sought on Friday, according to the decision of a conference yesterday at State Board headquarters.

Here is her story:

I had had a series of operations, which were unsuccessful, and which were followed by intense pain. To relieve these pains, from which I thought I would die, I was given morphine by a physician. After some time, to my terror, I found that I was an addict.

I called on "Dr." Barker, and a little later went to his hospital and underwent his treatment. He assured me he would cure me completely in three days. The treatment consisted of a bitter medicine—I do not know what it was—and at the end of the three days I left his place, a physical and practically a mental wreck.

I was unable to leave the habit, and in the interval "Dr." Barker supplied me with drugs. I returned to the hospital for the cure on two other occasions, with results like the first.

"HE DISCOURAGED ME."

Finally I told "Dr." Barker that I would have to try another cure as his did no good. He discouraged me, and it was then that he offered to give me the name of an "operator" or peddler, who he said would always keep me supplied with drugs. The inference was that my case was hopeless.

He charged me, on one occasion when I was desperate, $120 for two ounces of morphine solution. On another occasion he wanted $60 an ounce, and when I told him I hadn't $60, he put the price down to $40, which was all I had with me.

Mine is but one of several similar cases of which I know.

More recently I went to another physician, and with his aid a cure of my drug addiction has been accomplished.

It was stated yesterday at the offices of the District Attorney of Alameda county that abatement proceedings would be brought against the Barker property if the Board of Pharmacy charges are sustained in court.

On the occasion of her first visit to Barker, it was stated, she was able without difficulty to make a purchase of $5 worth of morphine. The quantity given her for this sum would make an ounce of morphine worth nearly $500, it was stated.

Monday night, prior to attempting a large purchase, two precautions were taken. First, Mrs. Merrill was taken before an Oakland police inspector and thoroughly searched, to prove that she had no drugs in her possession.

Next, she was escorted to the Barker hospital by detectives, who watched as she ascended the steps. This was to establish that she received no drugs from any outside source in the meantime.

Paper money was given her, which had previously been marked and the number recorded in the office of District Attorney Ezra Decoto.

Mrs. Merrill disappeared within the house, and a few minutes later emerged with her purchase. She handed over the packet of morphine and stated it had been given to her by Barker himself.

Inspector Roy Jones then rang the doorbell. "Dr." Barker responded in person and was informed that he

RECORDS NABBED.

Several record-books, similar to the one seized at the time of Barker's arrest, were found. Like the first, these bore the record of persons treated and references to various transactions which the investigators will endeavor to trace.

Among the most notorious of these names are those of Sam Morlen and Sam Shurgin, both of whom at present are serving terms in jail for peddling narcotics.

The entries show that Morlen was tr... th... B... In... B... "d...

IN DRUG EXPOSE

Mrs. V. P. Merrill, who brought about arrest of Dr. John Scott Barker (also pictured) of Oakland for alleged violation of Harrison narcotic law.

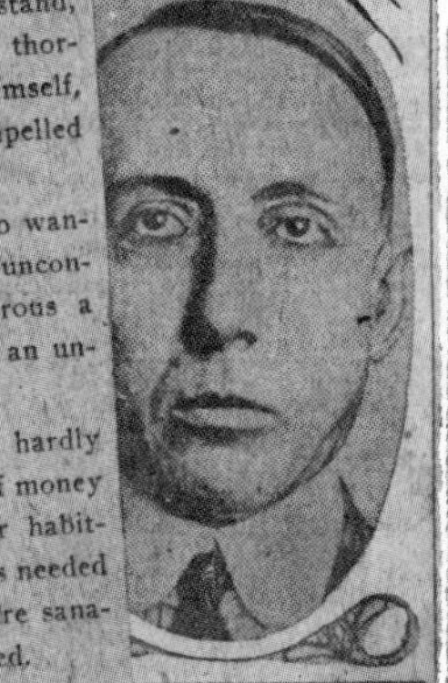

Start This Drug Probe

EVERYONE wh... the most superf... of the facts i... nows that the diffic... ational. It is intern... The dope which dr... manufactured, to be s... ry as well as in Japa... Austria and in Englan... of most of the habit-f... opium. And opium c... and Persia. Poppies a... under government sub... The way to stop this... therefore, by stopping... The culture of the... stopped.

We in America cann... fore international actio...

Congressman Porter... House Foreign Relat... has in his charge a re... gressman Kahn of thi... an international confer... evil.

It has been in his co... time. On April 25 Co... said he had assurances... man Porter that the... be reported out on t... House some time durin...

No one knows how... will last. It may be b...

State Should Cure Addicts

THE movement for establishing a State institution for isolation and cure of drug addicts in California is based upon the little-realized fact that drug addiction is really a contagious disease.

From some mysterious cause which alienists only imperfectly understand, the user of narcotics is not only thoroughly enslaved by the habit himself, but is irresistibly and viciously impelled to pass the vice on to others.

Every addict who is left free to wander through society and meet uncontaminated persons is as dangerous a menace to the general health as an unquarantined smallpox patient.

And when one learns the hardly credible facts as to the amount of money spent yearly in this nation for habit-forming narcotics, the sum that is needed for establishing a State drug-cure sanatorium seems insignificant indeed.

Dr. Carleton Simon, special deputy ... of New York city

JANUARY 6, 1923

Associate of Oakland Hospital Head Sought for Arrest; Conspiracy Charge Filed

"Dr." C. B. Blessing, owner of a Los Angeles drug cure sanitarium at which Wallace Reid was unsuccessfully treated and which advertises the "Barker Cure" for addicts, was charged today with the crime of conspiring with "Dr." John Scott Barker of Oakland to violate the Federal anti-narcotic laws.

A new line of investigation was undertaken by the State Board of Pharmacy, based on information gathered in the recent raid upon the Barker sanitarium, which, it was believed, would bring out the connection of Barker and Blessing with a State-wide ring of narcotic smugglers.

JANUARY 5, 1923

BAY DOCTORS, DRUGGISTS HIT IN DOPE QUIZ

Case Against Former Circus Hypnotist Appears Complete, Says Federal Investigator

Involving well known transbay physicians and drug concerns in the ramified activities of the Barker "dope" cure sanitarium, whose proprietor, John Scott Barker, is under arrest on Federal charges of illicit drug selling, an exhaustive re-check of medical records was undertaken yesterday, and partly completed.

Sufficient progress was made to warrant the investigating authorities in stating that disclosures were imminent along one of the following lines:

1. Either physicians friendly to "Dr." Barker recklessly signed prescriptions for narcotics, in behalf of patients in his sanitarium who were not there to receive narcotics, but a "cure" based on "twilight sleep"; or

2. Someone in the Barker sanitarium repeatedly forged the names of certain physicians to the aforesaid prescriptions; or

3. The hospital records, including Barker's list of patients and the clinical "histories" of each patient's case were falsified; or

4. Some way existed by which Barker procured narcotics

1,100 ON ADDICT LIST.

Though the names are withheld, here are some of the 1,100 persons treated by "Dr." Barker for addictio to narcotics:

A clergyman, formerly high in the councils of his church, with a parish in Berkeley.

The son of the sheriff of one of the inland counties of Central California.

A former leading woman at an Oakland theater.

A man, after whose name was marked the significant letters, "R. N.", meaning Royal Navy.

Three physicians, one of them treated no less than four times.

An orchestra leader in a large cafe patronized by society dancers.

A leading man of a theatrical company which as frequently performed in Oakland.

The manager of a large eastbay restaurant.

Three or four cases of husband and wife.

MONDAY SAN FRANCISCO, SEPTEMBER 20, 1920

DRUG RING OF NATION-WIDE SCOP

$20,000,000 IN NARCOTICS SMUGGLED INTO U. S. YEARLY, SAYS GOVERNMENT REPORT

Police Commissioner Theodore Roche Latest to Voice Necessity for Proposed Island Hospital Where the Victims May Be Isolated

Just as the seriousness of the narcotic drug situation in San Francisco, Los Angeles and other communities of California has within the past few days been unveiled to the public with unusual emphasis, just so there is being manifested on all sides the demand that proper measures be instituted at once to cope successfully with the grave problem.

The measures which are being advocated are these:

1. The immediate establishment, on an island, of a competently managed hospital for treatment and cure of drug addicts.

2. Renewed, increased and unrelenting war on the drug peddler.

3. A campaign of education whereby the public will be taught the fact that the addict to narcotic drugs is the victim of a disease, and only in a comparatively small percentage of cases a vicious person.

Physicians who have made a lifelong study of the subject, and Government agents whose function it is to deal with illicit drug traffic, are a unit in declaring that the establishment of the isolated hospital, to which addicts can be induced to go in the knowledge that the necessary treatment will be given them pending cure, will do more than any other single thing to break up the underground drug-selling ring.

NEW VICTIMS MADE.

The magnitude of the operations of this insidious combination of men who for their own profit exploit the misfortunes of the addict, and, according to official declaration, go even so far as to make new addicts for increased consumption of the drugs they sell, is vividly portrayed in a recent Government report. From the investigation related in this document the following facts have come to light:

While the value of narcotic drugs legitimately manufactured and handled in this country exceeds $20,000,000 annually, this amount is exceeded by the quantity and value of narcotics smuggled in and sold at exorbitant prices by the illicit drug peddlers. The report states, further:

"The so-called dope peddlers appear to have a National organization for procuring and disposing of their supplies. For the most part it is thought, they obtain these supplies by smuggling them from Canada and from Mexico, although smaller quantities are secured in this country from unscrupulous dealers, or by theft.

"That considerable quantities of these smuggled drugs are exported from this country for the purpose of re-entry through illicit channels is indicated by ever-increasing exports to Canada and Mexico."

Among those prominent in the community who yesterday added their voice to the expressed demand for the proposed island hospital was Police Commissioner Theodore Roche. He said:

"Public institutions have been created and utilized to success in the aid of habitual drunkards and inebriates; why not to assist the habitual drug-user?

"Considering the nature of the malady and its effect upon his mind, what could be more appropriate than an isolated hospital?

MEANS MONEY SAVED.

"Public funds expended in the prosecution and punishment of criminals who have become such through the use of drugs, money expended in maintaining prisons and reformatories, could all be saved and the value of the labor and efficiency lost could be conserved in event the great evil were obliterated.

"It must be obvious that the mere maintenance of some agency where drug-users can obtain relief and incidental treatment cannot effectively cure the evil or stem the advancing tide of increased addicts. Under these conditions the existing illicit traffic would permit additional doses to be procured and the user remain without benefit. The drug habit is a disease. The persons suffering from the disease are as varied as are the drugs from which they suffer. Each is possessed of a temperament and characteristic different from the other. We find these addicts in different stages of the disease, some early and some late. In treating them you are dealing with morbid human beings whose nervous systems are shattered. In order to bring about an effective cure it is essential that these different elements should be carefully studied and each case treated according to its peculiarity.

AID REDEMPTION.

"It is essential that an institution ... state with eyes of forbearance, and whose hearts, touched by his pitiful degradation, would prompt them unselfishly in the name of civic duty to minister to his needs and finally accomplish his redemption."

San Clemente Island Asked for Drug Addicts

LOS ANGELES, Sept. 19.—A potential Molokai has been found for the Californian drug addicts.

Addiction to narcotics is a disease which must be treated under healthful, out-of-doors conditions in an isolated sanitarium. Los Angeles has a desperately aggravated drug addict situation, as has been pointed out in "The Examiner."

Dr. Robert William Thomas, former head of the San Diego county drug clinic, announced today that he is ready to do for narcotic addicts what Father Damien did for exile lepers at Molokai.

Dr. Thomas' proposed site for a guided but self-supporting colony of dope victims in San Clemente Island. There he proposes to cure the addicts medically by the withdrawal method and psychologically by teaching them new, rigorous, healthful, economic and social habits.

San Clemente Island is 65 miles off the Pacific coast and is due south of Catalina Island.

Dr. Thomas would begin his addict colony in a small way. He would go to the island with a group of perhaps 25 addicts, volunteers, or those for whom he would have obtained suspended jail sentences on condition that they go with him to make the experiment.

He would live with the addicts on the island for one year, during which period the very word drug would be forbidden mention.

The men, provided with nets and small sailing vessels, would earn their living by fishing—in Southern California waters—as certain a mode of livelihood as exists anywhere.

At the end of a year those who wished to leave and had established good records might do so. Those who were incorrigible would be sent to prison. Those who were content to stay might be allowed to remain on the island and retain their shack there.

Agnew Superintendent Favors Hospital Plan

SAN JOSE, Sept. 19—Dr. Leonard Stocking, superintendent of the Agnew state hospital for the insane, today voiced whole-hearted approbation of the proposal to establish an isolation hospital on an island, for the care of victims of the drug habit. His statement to "The "Examiner" follows

"I have watched with peculiar interest the campaign of "The Examiner" against the drug curse and have taken an unusual interest in the various statements and suggestions made.

"Probably the greatest necessity is a place to care for the unfortunate addicts of the habit. These people must be under absolute control at all times during the period of recovery from the drug habit. The drugs can be gradually withdrawn properly in a period of four or five days after which the eliminative treatment will follow quickly and the administration of tonics and upbuilding medicines can begin.

"But the cure must be sure and every addict of the habit should be kept under absolute control for a period of several months until his or her system has fully recovered and does not cry out again for the drug. Of course, there are those who will go back to the habit just because they refuse to do otherwise. There are people who just naturally like to dissipate and for them there is no cure.

"Hence it is that I am absolutely in sympathy with the proposal to isolate the drug addicts. They are now sent to the state hospitals, which are incapable of handling them. Furthermore the drug victims are not desirable in a hospital and should be kept by themselves. That the isolation hospital should be on an island would be very satisfactory. I do feel, however, that it should be within a reasonable distance of the center of population and such an institution should be governed by a commission with absolute authority and control over it to regulate the length of time which a patient would remain within it. Such an institution is the only real solution of the drug problem, together

DRASTIC JAIL TERMS URGED IN DOPE EVIL

Chief of Federal Anti-Narcotic Squad on Coast Tells Need of More Severe Jail Penalties

OCTOBER 16, 1921

Punishment for venders of illicit narcotics that will be equal in severity to the seriousness of their crime was demanded yesterday by Harry Smith, chief of the Federal Narcotic Squad on the Pacific Coast.

Smith declared that elimination of the "dope" traffic, or at any rate its reduction to practically nil, was entirely possible through a campaign of vigorous law enforcement. In order that such a campaign should have its maximum effect, he said, the legal penalties of fine and imprisonment should be drastically increased.

The drug habit is spreading in California and on the Pacific coast, despite the vigilance of Federal and State officials charged with combatting it.

Slowly, but surely, this insidious evil is launching additional tenacles upon new groups of victims—seizing them in its grip and holding them fast.

Such is the conclusion which must be drawn from statements made in the last few days by men detailed by the Government to stem the narcotic tide that is threatening to engulf men, women—and children too, in ever-increasing numbers.

With the recent re-organization of the Federal Narcotic Squad as a unit, operating now directly under the Commissioner of Internal Revenue instead of being a dependency of the Prohibition Commissioner's office, there has been manifested the Government's realization of the extreme seriousness of the situation. And a more concrete effort is being made to combat the soul-destroying appetite for drugs which, the Federal agents declare, is being fostered more and more by the addict peddlers of morphine, cocaine and heroin.

According to the declaration of the men who are constantly on the track of the drug peddlers, the spread of "dope" and of "dope users" is alarming. The evil is getting into the army and into the navy. It is reaching out to engulf high school boys and high school girls. It is being temptingly put in the way of shop girls. Drugs are being peddled to the Indians right on their reservations. They are finding their way to roadhouses, where "cocaine jags" are said to be becoming fashionable as a supplement to enjoyment threatened by failing supplies of liquor.

The utmost vigilance seems unavailing to prevent the constant influx of narcotics, by underground routes, into the United States, the agents declare. From the Orient, from Mexico, from Canada, and from Europe by way of the eastern ports, illicit drugs are being smuggled into the Pacific States. The sources of supply, the agents declare, are practically untracable, the great difficulty lying in the fact that the illicit drugs pass through a number of hands before reaching the peddler on the street.

And it is this peddler, the officials assert, who, himself an addict in the great majority of cases, constitutes the greatest menace of all who are active in the various stages of the nefarious traffic.

It is he who constantly is creating new victims—that he may secure money not alone to provide himself with the drugs he craves, but to be enabled to live without work. And his profits are enormous.

So it is upon the peddler, the agents declare, that the efforts of the law must be concentrated. Be he an addict or be he not, he will have to be exterminated before the drug evil can be minimized.

URGES PRISON TERMS.

Federal officials who have been interviewed by "The Examiner" within the past few days point out a remedy, which, if adopted, will do much to secure the desired result. These officials are not permitted to be quoted by name—for the Internal Revenue Department imposes silence upon those whom it charges with the detection of violation of its laws. But one of them, whose life is devoted to hunting down the drug peddler, said yesterday:

The Harrison Narcotic Law, under which the drug traffickers are prosecuted, provides a maximum sentence of five years in the penitentiary and a fine of $2,000. It should be amended so as to provide a minimum penalty of a year's imprisonment in a Federal penitentiary. That would soon put an end to county-jail sentences of short duration, at which the peddler snaps his fingers.

In the second place, the law should be amended so as to provide for deportation of every alien convicted of its violation. A vast

AMERICA LEADS IN IMPORTATION OF NARCOTICS

Dr. Copeland Says U. S. Uses Ten Times as Much Opium as Citizens of Any Other Land

NOVEMBER 2, 1921

TRAFFIC IS BEYOND CONTROL

Health Officer Sees Only Remedy in Limiting Supply and Permitting Sale by Dispensaries

By DR. ROYAL S. COPELAND.

If I owned a newspaper, it seems to me I should run an editorial every day on the evil of narcotic drugs and the terrible effects of drug addiction.

Hardly a day passes but a dispatch from some city in some part of the world tells of the growth of this deadly habit.

The importation of opium into this country is about three-quarters of a million pounds annually. This means that for every man, woman and child in America there is imported more than forty gains of this dangerous drug. No other civilized country imports more than three gains per capita. We are using a dozen times as much opium as are the citizens of any other land.

"We have laws designed to control the distribution and use of habit-forming drugs," you naturally say. "Why do they not curb the evil?"

INTERNATIONAL BUSINESS.

These laws do not work, because the opium business is an international affair. It cannot be controlled by one country acting alone. There was a conference and agreement, known as "The Hague Convention," intended to regulate the opium evil. That has failed for many reasons. But by a very simple procedure the United States and Canada could end the whole devilish traffic so far as they are concerned.

Here is a plan which would surely succeed:

Let each country determine the amount of opium needed for the legitimate use of the medical profession. This would be an arbitrary estimate, of course, and the amount might not be hit upon accurately at first. However, that is unimportant, because, if necessary, the figures could be changed from time to time.

Off-hand, I should say the United States should import not to exceed seventy thousand pounds, and Canada eight or ten thousand pounds of opium.

Let each country have its quota of opium made into morphine and such other opium derivatives as are of recognized medical value. This should be done under government oversight.

DISPENSARY SYSTEM URGED.

Let opium and its derivatives be sold only in recognized establishments, as liquor is dispensed by legitimate druggists in the United States, and as it is sold by government agencies in the Province of Quebec. This would make available to the medical profession such amounts of opium as are essential to the honest practice of medicine. Some simple regulations should be made to ensure the good faith of all concerned.

Having provided for their own sick, let the United States and Canada absolutely prohibit the exportation of opium, morphine and all others of its derivatives.

This would end the smuggling into the United States of large quantities of narcotics now shipped from the United States to Canada and other countries, but secretly brought back into the United States. Such smuggled drugs, in large quantities, are now sold clandestinely on the streets of New York and other cities. Large amounts of American morphine are used in Canadian cities.

Until the importation and manufacture of these terrible poisons are regulated, and until exportation is prohibited, the evil will go its

MUCH DOPE BEING MADE IN AMERICA

Morphine, Heroin and Cocaine Manufactured in This Country From Imported Raw Products

U. S. IS REVEALED AS SUPPLY BASE FOR NARCOTICS

Loophole in the Harrison Law Permits Traffic in Drugs to Thrive on a Large Scale

EXPORTATIONS UNMOLESTED

DECEMBER 9, 1921

Great Quantities of Opium and Other Products Are Smuggled Back by an Underworld Route

By JOSEPH MULVANEY.

Through a loophole in the Federal anti-narcotic statute vast quantities of opium, morphine and heroin are distributed throughout this country and illicitly disposed of to addicts.

This condition, unforseen when the Harrison law was enacted several years ago and since permitted to stand uncorrected, is, in the opinion of almost all authorities on addiction, responsible for a substantial percentage of the evil in this country.

JUSTICE C. F. COLLINS.

The loophole in the law permits the exportation of opium and its derivatives from America without restriction or regulation. Rigid regulations govern the sale of the drug domestically, but no check or trace of exports is made.

As a result huge stores of opium, morphine and heroin are purchased regularly in the United States, shipped to Mexico, Canada or abroad unrestricted and then smuggled back to this country for sale at great profit. Some citizens of Japan and Germany are among those most active in this business, according to the police.

LOOPHOLE EXPLAINED.

Justice Cornelius F. Collins, of the Court of Special Sessions, chairman of the Judiciary Committee on Narcotics of this State, described the situation thus:

"To get opium legitimately in this country you have to be registered and entitled to purchase it, and you have to give a formal order. But anybody from a foreign country can purchase it without any restriction. So it is shipped out of this country, then smuggled back.

"Why are Detroit and Buffalo such large drug-distributing centers? Why is the situation so serious in Florida, St. Louis and Texas? Simply because smuggling is so largely indulged in there, due to the loopholed law, which practically deprives the police of an opportunity to follow it up in those cities. Could we trace those who buy from the outside, as well as those who buy from the inside of this country, we would be in a far better position to handle the situation."

Dr. Carleton Simon, Deputy Police Commissioner in charge of the Narcotic Division, said:

"Certain interests in Japan are importing from America every ounce of habit-forming drugs that they can buy here. Out of Seattle one ton of such drugs was shipped to Japan in a single month. The bulk of all drugs manufactured in Japan, and almost all bought here by Japan, are sent back here by way of an underground drug smuggling ring.

"Even though the Japanese have to pay a higher price for the American products as a result of freight and other charges, that is easily offset by the tremendous profits.

MAINLY IN SEAPORT CITIES.

"The cities most afflicted with the curse of narcotism are the seaport cities. There is hardly a ship that enters this port, perhaps not one that traverses the high seas, that does not carry hidden narcotics. There are trunks full that are shipped by boat and rail through this country and never examined.

"Recently we seized a trunk at Grand Central Station, which was filled with gum opium and destined for St. Louis. Two empty trunks returned to New York from St. Louis for reloading were also seized. From evidence collected we have learned that the ramifications of this particular ring extends all over the country."

Dr. Simon said that the narcotic division of the Police Department recently seized a trunk in South Brooklyn filled with drugs, which had been smuggled from Germany, to Switzerland, to Italy, to Spain, to South America and thence to this port.

Justice Collins and Dr. Simon are agreed that closer restriction on importation and exportation of opium is

CONGRESS PLANS WAR ON NARCOTIC EVIL;

Voices in unison
Oh, say, can you see

AY CC

REVEALED

MOVE TO BAR DOPE INFLUX FROM ORIENT

Decision Made to Close Foreign Postoffices as First Step; Japs Principal Offenders

Chairman Porter of House Committee Promises Startling Disclosures at Investigation

DECEMBER 25, 1921

WASHINGTON, Dec. 24.—(By Universal Service.)—A Congressional investigation of the international traffic in habit-forming drugs will be made immediately after the arms conference adjourns, Chairman Porter, of the House Foreign Affairs Committee, announced today.

Porter, who also is chairman of the American Advisory Committee on Pacific and Far Eastern Questions, said that information received by his committee proves conclusively that a sweeping investigation is necessary.

The advisory committee of which Porter is chairman made a thorough study of the drug traffic in its investigation of the Far Eastern problems and recommended to the arms conference that the foreign postoffices in China be abolished as the first step to end the traffic.

CONDUCTED BY JAPANESE.

The records of the committee show that the traffic has been conducted through the foreign postoffices, principally the Japanese.

"The decision to close the foreign postoffices is the biggest step yet made toward doing away altogether with the traffic in drugs," said Porter.

Representative Julius Kahn of California, author of the resolution now pending before the House foreign affairs committee, calling for an international agreement to end the drug traffic declared today that he will present "startling" facts to the House when his resolution comes up.

Chairman Porter of th... committee ...

$100,000 DRUGS SEIZED IN FIRST NEW LAW CASE

Smuggling Plot Thwarted When Cargo of Steamship China Is Seized by San Francisco Agents

FULL PROSECUTION ORDERED

Federal Customs Chief Wires His Officers to Go the Limit—Says People Are Behind the Act

1922

By Universal Service.

WASHINGTON, May 31. — The United States went into action to-day against the drug evil, employing for the first time its newest and most powerful weapon, the Jones-Miller Anti-Narcotic law.

This measure, promoted and supported by the Hearst newspapers as an effective means of destroying the international drug smuggling ring, makes it impossible for addicts to obtain morphine and cocaine.

Although only a week old, this measure has already resulted in the seizure of a vast quantity of opium intended for use in the United States, and its drastic provisions are to be used in prosecuting the offender as an example of what others may expect.

To the San Francisco customs officers belongs the distinction of making the first case under the new law and to the United States Attorney there will go the distinction of making the first prosecution.

$100,000 DOPE SEIZED.

The Steamship China, while in San Francisco, was visited by the customs officers and $100,000 worth of opium seized. This was Saturday. The papers were forwarded to Washington for instructions.

The record had not reached here to-day, but E. W. Camp, head of the customs service, dispatched rush messages to both the United States attorney and the customs officers at the Port of San Francisco directing them to prosecute under the Jones-Miller Bill. Mr. Campbell said to-day:

"It appears to be a typical crime of the sort the Jones-Miller law ... designed to prevent and ... ke at once. ... direct ...

A Case for Vigilance

THE people of San Francisco have a fight on their hands.

They must fight to keep for themselves the fruits of their gigantic expenditure of money and energy in developing the Hetch Hetchy project.

A proposal is being made to sell to ... rofit of ... ergy to ... s which ... ple and ... e to the ... ks and ... as con- ... project. ... the city ... e huge ... was put ... rvation ... of the ... West. ... hase of ... eration. ... er way ... he city ... yet un- ... source ... sell to ... d Cen- ... of San ... a have ... r their ... e ques- ... istrator ... nion of ... illegal ... Hetch ... rations. ... of le- ... nsound ... people, ... Raker ... on the ... n Fran- ... city ob- ... y upon ... licated

AMERICA IS WORLD'S BIGGEST OPIUM MART

FEBRUARY 27, 1922

17 Times as Much Brought Into This Than Any Other Country, Figures Show.

Seventeen times as much opium is brought into the United States annually than to any other country of the world, according to figures made public yesterday in the campaign against the drug evil.

The estimate was given out by Charles E. Lathrop, secretary of the Social Service Department of the Episcopal Church in the United States, who said a large portion of this opium is immediately exported to Japan, China, Mexico and Canada. Large quantities are smuggled back into the United States from Canada and Mexico, he added.

Health Commission Royal S. Cope- various national social service agencies to secure the enactment of Federal legislation to prevent the exportation of opium from the United States.

In speaking of the figures, Mr. Lathrop said:

"Much of our difficulty arises from opium shipped to Mexico and Canada, for this is easily smuggled back to this country where it may be sold without restriction. We ought to have a Federal law forbidding the exportation of drugs to any other country. The United States Public Health Service should give to the Secretary of State the estimated amount of opium to cover all our medical necessities and no greater amount should be imported. Then if Canada also would enact such a law much of our difficulty would be overcome."

To Control DrugMaking

A BIG step has bee... fight against the... United States...

The narcotics cont... the House Thursday... forced, will go a lon... cluding habit for... America.

It will end the p... which some American drug manuf... turers are engaged, of ma... from raw opium the dr... later export, of wh... in... way into China and ... is later ... gled back into this country throu... cit agencies.

It will do what it propose... control the commerce in h... drugs in the United St...

It will go a great w... off the supply of th... use drugs as an...

But it will no... cannot, for the reason that it cannot control the source of the drug supply.

All the habit forming drugs used by addicts are made from opium; all save cocaine, which is made from coca leaves. These latter come from certain South American countries. Opium is made from poppies grown in Persia and India.

In India the British government subsidizes the poppy growers by making loans, without interest, for handling their crops. The raw opium is sold at public auction monthly in Calcutta and thence makes its way into the hands of manufacturing chemists in Europe, the Orient and this country.

The world's supply of drugs made from opium will not be cut down until the culture of the opium poppy is restricted.

There is in the House Foreign Relations Committee a resolution by Con... ng upon the ad... every effort to in... nation to prevent ... transportation" o...

HEAVY SENTENCES FOR CONVICTED DRUG PEDDLERS

U.S. JUDGES

LONG TERMS FOR 2 DAZE DRUG SELLERS

OCTOBER 11, 1922

Heavy Sentences Imposed on Warning; First Convictions Under New U. S. Law.

NO LENIENCY, SAYS GARVIN

Fifteen Addicts Seized; Eight Chinese Captured in Raid on Bowery Lodging House.

Brooklyn drug pedlers were thrown into panic last night as news circulated that Federal Judge Garvin has sentenced two of their number to five-year terms in Atlanta Prison.

The convicted pair were just the ordinary, common variety of street vendor, who possibly had fifty customers each to whom they sold narcotics, but the significant feature of the case was the severe warning given by the Judge as he imposed the long terms.

... the stiff punishment ... eted out in the New ... under the Miller- ... s law, which carries ... nalty for men con- ... ssessing narcotics ... this country.

...HEARST PAPERS.

... is passed last May ... advocation by the ... merican and other ... pers.

... sentenced were Jo- ... nd Ernest Goriano. ... e worked up by Fed- ... gents working under ... Ralph H. Oyler.

... ffect of Judge Gar- ... was shown when ... another seller, who ... to stand trial, re- ... and pleaded guilty. ... a term of two and a ...

... said:

... drug sellers in the ... ict to understand ... l receive no more leniency from me once they are convicted of selling narcotics for profit. I shall give them the maximum sentence whenever possible.

REMOVE PUBLIC MENACE.

Peddler of Dope Nabbed at Very Doors of Jail

At the very doors of the Hall of Justice John Schumake, well-known peddler of "dope," was plying his trade yesterday afternoon when he was caught.

Portsmouth Square, just across Kearny street, was his market place. His customers were Roy Finley, Bud Pollard and others.

D. R. Dunbar and Inspector Mc Carthy of the State Board of Pharmacy were well acquainted with Schumake, but he had successfully evaded them until yesterday.

Feeling unduly safe within view of the walls which have imprisoned other drug peddlers and from which they have been sent to the penitentiary, Schumake peddled his wares as freely as the peanut vendor.

Dunbar and McCarthy arrested Schumake and his two customers, Finley and Pollard, while they were engaged in the sale and purchase of narcotics. They were taken to the city jail, to appear in Police Court this morning.

Lasker Acts to Stop Drug Smuggling

JULY 12, 1922

By Universal Service.

WASHINGTON, July 11.—Chairman A. D. Lasker of the Shipping Board has taken drastic action to stop the smuggling of drugs on Government-owned vessels.

He announced to-day that a special committee of investigation has been named to inquire into the situation at San Francisco. Admiral Benson and former Senator Chamberlain, members of the Shipping Board, now on the Pacific Coast, have been ordered to meet with this committee and recommend the necessary regulations, or amendments to the narcotic law.

C. S. Stanton, Editor and Publisher of the San Francisco Examiner, who has been a leader in the Hearst Newspaper Campaign for anti-narcotic legislation, has been made a member of the investigating board.

Elmer Schlesinger, general counsel for the shipping board, is directing the legal phase of the inquiry and will promptly change prevailing regulations on ships, or suggest new legislation, following the completion of the San Francisco probe.

The case is the outgrowth of a new and startling development since the recent enactment of the Jones-Miller Anti-Narcotic Law, a measure passed at the instance of the Hearst newspapers.

Customs officers searching the S. S. Empire State now the "President Wilson," at San Francisco discovered a quantity of opium concealed about the vessel.

Under the provisions of the new ...

In order to collect this fine San Francisco customs officers proceeded to deny clearance papers to the ship and suggested a libel for the amount of the fine. The case was appealed to the Treasury Department, and it was ruled that the Government could not libel a Government-operated ship. As a reason for this it was stated that it would mean that the Government is, in effect, fining itself.

Under the operating agreement with the company now in charge of the "President Wilson" the amount of the libel would have to be paid by the Government and not the company. The same rul... would prevail it was said, in ... case of smuggling liquor, aigre... or jewelry.

Mr. Schlesinger declared:

"The Shipping Board is g... to do everything within its p... to stop the bringing in of ... on Government-owned v... We are going to follow the ... mendations of the spe... mittee named to lo... Empire State case.

"We do not beli... master of a ship... circumstances, ... smuggling and ... punish him wh... rance of it, pro... cised the nec... think, however... be found to ma... vessels extraor...

"No one is more ... the matter than Mr. Lasker and I. We only wish to be fair. An ...

JONES-MILLER ANTI-NARCOTIC BILL

HARDING
SIGNED
NARCOTIC
EVIL
PROTECT YOUR LIBERTY —
YOUR RIGHTS AS

MAY 29 1922

LID CLAMPED ON DOPE IMPORTS TO U.S

DOPE PRODUCTION CURB

DECEMBER 8, 1921

OPIUM TRADE MUST STOP, SAYS SOLON

Congressman From California Introduces a Resolution in House for Ban on Traffic

Manufacture and Transportation in China Are Increased by Postal System, He Charges

WASHINGTON, Dec. 7.—(By Universal Service).—A resolution expressing the sense of the American Congress that the international traffic in habit-forming drugs be suppressed, was introduced in the House today by Representative Kahn, Republican, of California.

The resolution also requests the American delegates to the conference on limitation of armaments to arrange for an early conference of all civilized nations to take steps to prevent the manufacture or transportation of the drugs.

Since the world-wide efforts to suppress the drug traffic were halted by the war in 1914, Kahn said in explaining his resolution, it has been found that Japanese post-offices in China have been distributing centers for increasing amounts of opium, morphine, cocaine and other drugs. He said:

"Thirteen nations took up this matter in 1913. It was agreed that they ought to have the signatures of the thirty-four other civilized nations by December 1, 1921, to an agreement to suppress the drug traffic. If all the nations had not signed by them it was agreed that the time be extended.

"The nations were all working on the matter when the world war commenced in 1914, and so it was lost sight of for the time being.

"When the armistice was signed it was found that large quantities of opium and morphine were being transported into China and distributed through the Japanese post-offices there. In the year 1918 it was found this traffic amounted to 68,000 tons of opium and 12,000 tons of morphine.

Of course an effort was made to stop the importation of all habit-forming drugs into China.

"We desire that our government, England, France and the other European governments help China to redeem her population. That is the

Drug Offenders to Get 5 Years by Porter Bill

By Universal Service.

WASHINGTON, Feb. 21.

CHAIRMAN PORTER, of the House Foreign Affairs Committee, introduced a bill to-day providing for a minimum penalty of five years in prison and a fine up to $5,000 for first violations of the anti-narcotic laws and a mandatory prison sentence of fifteen years for further offenses.

Commenting on his new measure, Mr. Porter said:

"This bill should not be confused with the resolution now pending for the effective control of production, but I consider it prudent, pending negotiations over that important question, to materially stiffen the sentences in the hope that it will minimize to some extent the evil in the United States.

"Inasmuch as Congress will adjourn March 4, there is little, if any, hope of passing this measure, but I intend to re-introduce it when Congress convenes. The purpose in introducing it at this time is to give those who are interested in the suppression of this traffic the opportunity of expressing opinions as to the wisdom of the measure during the recess of the Congress."

THAW STARTS TRIP

OCTOBER 1, 1922

U. S. WILL CALL PARLEY TO HALT OPIUM TRAFFIC

Great Britain, Persia and Turkey to Be Asked to Help Suppress Shipment of Drugs Here

SITUATION IS ALARMING

State Department Admits Smuggling on Large Scale—American Consumption Greatest

By Universal Service.

WASHINGTON, Sept. 30.—The Administration is soon to call a new International conference for the regulation of traffic in opium and narcotic drugs. The nations which will be requested to participate are Great Britain, Persia and Turkey.

The wholesale smuggling of drugs into the United States, admitted in an official bulletin from the State Department yesterday, was the subject of a lengthy conference between President Harding and Representative Stephen G. Porter, chairman of the House Foreign Affairs Committee, at the White House to-day.

The principal object of the proposed conference will be to restrict the output of opium at its main source, which is in India. The official view is that if Great Britain, the chief financial beneficiary of the illegal traffic, will come into the conference, the problem will be solved.

CONGRESS TO BACK MOVE.

Following the White House conference to-day it was stated that Congress will back up the movement for some positive action, especially in view of the State Department memorandum.

Admittedly the most difficult part of the task of suppression will be to induce Great Britain to give up the rich opium revenues from India.

Chairman Porter told President Harding to-day that the traffic has reached the proportions of a national menace. It is useless, he said, to attempt to break up the traffic by the arrest and imprisonment of peddlers of drugs. The only hope of effective suppression is restriction of supply at the source. This can be done only by an agreement with the producing countries, he said, since no opium originates in the United States.

Mr. Porter recited startling figures to show the growth of opium addiction. The medicinal needs of the world per year, he said, are only ten tons, while world production, emanating mostly from the Ganges River, in India, is 1,211 tons. Turkey and Persia produce small amounts of the drug. He declared:

U. S. CONSUMPTION GREATEST.

"Perhaps the most alarming part of the whole question is the fact that consumption of opium and its derivatives in the United States vastly exceeds the consumption in any other country in the world. The ratio is nearly 7 to 1. American consumption is thirty-five grains per capita per annum. Other consumption is only five grains.

"Every year [illegible]41 tons of opium is put at auction in Calcutta and sold to the highest bidder by the opium monopoly of India. Nearly 99 per cent of this amount goes on errands of destruction."

Representative Porter said that as soon as Congress convenes he will introduce a resolution calling a conference between the United States and the opium producing countries. There will be no difficulty in passing such a resolution quickly through both houses, he said. President Harding, through the State Department, will then call the conference.

With the support of the Administration now lined up, the conference is assured. The suppression of the drug traffic throughout the world thereafter will depend upon the attitude of Great Britain, which directly controls nine-tenths of the supply.

Women in Knickers Barred from Dances

MUSKEGON, Mich., Sept. 30.—Women wearing knickers must stay

U. S. TO GUARD WORLD PORTS IN DOPE WAR

Emissary of Hughes on Way to Capitals in Move to Halt Drug Supply at Source

By WILLIAM P. FLYTHE,
Staff Correspondent of Universal Service.

WASHINGTON, Jan. 3.—A first line of defense against the drug smuggling evil is being established by the United States in the ports of the world, it was learned today.

Acting under the direction of the narcotics control board and the customs service agents are to be located at points from which drugs are shipped and either prevent their shipment or guarantee that the shipment will be seized upon arrival at an American port.

This step is made possible, officials state, under the operation of the Jones-Miller act, a measure that provides for the drug control board.

At the suggestion of Secretary of State Hughes, who is chairman of the control board, Colonel O. G. Forrer, drug expert of the internal revenue bureau, is on his way to European and Asiatic capitals to make the preliminary arrangements. He carries special credentials from Secretary Hughes, which will enable him to make a complete survey of the origin of the drug traffic, it was stated.

"Probably the most effective means in the world to check the drug evil in the United States is to prevent it ever reaching the United States," said Colonel Forrer, prior to his departure. "It is like a disease; once it reaches here it is difficult to check it.

"Unfortunately drugs may be easily concealed and frequently escape the eye of the customs officers at the American port. With agents at the ports from which the ships depart and with the co-operation of foreign officers, we should be able to check smuggling completely.

PORTS CLOSED TO NARCOTICS PENDING QUIZ

1923

Embargo Decision Ef Until Legitimate Need Country for Year Are

House Resolution Urges Ha to Call Production Halt Six Drug Growing

WASHINGTON, Federal Narcotics to-day announced it more applications cotics pending a de amount of su is advisable to country during th

By WINDER Staff Correspond Serv

WASHINGTON, long as an ounce duced, it will find

"The only way to evil is to strike a dea root."

On this theory, Stephen G. Porter, Pennsylvania, chair House Foreign Affai duced a jo

PORTER INSISTS DRUG MUST BE HIT AT SOURCE

JANUARY 4, 1923

Futility of Controlling Habit Through International Conferences Previously Shown

LEAGUE HELPED TRAFFIC

Bill to Limit Production of Raw Narcotics Is Declared the Only Practical Remedy

By Universal Service.

WASHINGTON, Feb. 10.—Hearings will begin on Tuesday before the House Foreign Affairs committee on the Porter resolution which strikes at the root of the narcotic drug evil.

The resolution would request the President of the United States to take the initiative in securing an agreement by the governments of the countries in which narcotic raw materials are grown to limit production to the minimum of medicinal needs.

Celebrated medical and scientific authorities will testify at these hearings as to the ravaging effects of narcotics on humankind, and officials of the Government and numerous organizations will disclose the extent to which the evil has cemented its grip on the people of this country.

By REP. STEPHEN G. PORTER,
Chairman of the House Committee on Foreign Affairs.
(Written Expressly for Universal Service.)

The "dope" evil has reached a point where immediate drastic action to check it is imperative.

Like a great octopus, it has stretched its tenacles into many countries of the world, and unless successfully combated, it soon will have a strangle hold on civilization itself. Humankind is at stake.

The ravages of narcotics everywhere are plainly observable. Religious, moral, civic and legal authorities all agree "dope" is the enemy that is threatening the fabric of society in this and other countries.

INCREASE ALARMING.

Official reports show the unlawful use of morphine, heroin, codeine and cocaine is increasing in America at a rate that alarms those charged with responsibility for the welfare of our people. Irreparable injury is being done to the health and morality of our

Estimates of the number of in the forty-eight States ra as 2,000,000. The low official estimate, is 1,000, on that basis, one persons in the

Congress Feels Urg for U. S. Drug Crusad

CHAP. 190.—Joint Resolution Requesting the President to urge upon the g ments of certain nations the immediate necessity of limiting the production of forming narcotic drugs and the raw materials from which they are made to the a actually required for strictly medicinal and scientific purpose

Whereas the unlawful use in the United Stat opium (the coagulated juice of Papaver son derivatives (morphia, codeine, heroin), and from coca leaves—Erythroxylum coca) and made from these plants or their by-product irreparable injury to health and morality a from continued use, is increasing and spreading

Whereas the special committee of investigation o drugs appointed by the Secretary of the Trea dated April 15, 1919, having considered the secr the unlawful sale and use of these drugs, and ties in obtaining information which would give the exact ber of addicts in the United States, says: "The committee the opinion that the total number of addicts in this co probably exceeds one million at the present time," and fu addicts was reported as t majority of addicts of all e or opium or its prepara

HO

DOCTORS WILL TELL OF PERIL THREATENING ALL AMERICA

Porter Calls for Start of Hearings on Resolution to Limit the Production of Narcotics

DR. SIMON TO BARE EVILS

Offers of Scientists' Co-operation and Praise of Campaign Pouring In from All Sides

By Universal Service.

WASHINGTON, Feb. 8.—Hearings on his resolution for the limitation of the production of narcotic raw materials to the actual amount needed for medicine and science will begin next Monday morning, Chairman Porter, of the House Foreign Affairs Committee, announced to-night.

Chairman Porter plans first to call well-known physicians to testify as to the hideously destructive effects of "dope" upon the health and morality of addicts, and the ns from continued use.

WORLD-WI NARCOTIC B HELD CERTA

Head of State Department Resolution to Restrict G of Raw Material to Chec

Negotiations Will Be Set Way With Britain and Nations to Stop Drug T

By WINDER R. HARRI
Staff Correspondent Universal Serv

WASHINGTON, Feb. 13. opening hearing on the resolution to restrict the grow narcotic raw materials to mi medicinal needs was given momentum today when Sec Hughes formally approved urged prompt passage of the ure.

This indorsement from the of the State Department with it the administration's hearted sympathy with the ment to eradicate the "dope at its source. It also signifie the Secretary, who must hand negotiations with Great B Persia, Turkey, the Nether Peru and Bolivia, has no fea the move will be unwelco them.

The first witness at the op of the hearings today was Dr. Lambert, noted alienist of York. He was on the stand the foreign affairs committe

Bryan Indorses Porter Proposa to Limit Dru

By Universal Service.

WASHINGTON, Feb. 2

THE Porter resolution limitation of growth production of habit-form drugs was unqualifiedly dorsed by William Jenni Bryan to-day.

During a visit to the Capi Mr. Bryan had a brief conf ence with Representative P ter, author of the resoluti who presented the Commo with a copy of the meas and explained its purpose. T former Secretary of State pressed his hearty approv and later said:

"I am strongly in favor the immediate passage the resolution. It seeks wipe out a great evil."

WORLD WAR ON DRUGS LAUNCHED IN CONG

PRESIDENT PLEDGES FULL AID IN DR

U. S. CARRIES NARCOTICS WAR

ORCE POWERS TO END TRAFFIC, HOUSE IS URGED

...he result of the meeting of ...n at Shanghai, China, in ... in 1912, a treaty was mad... the conference at The Hague ...een the United States of America and other powers which ...ended to suppress the illicit traffic in habit-forming na... ...ugs, and notwithstanding that upward of seven years ...ssed since its ratification, the treaty and the laws in purs... ...ereof subsequently adopted by the contracting powers ...terly failed to suppress such illicit traffic, by reason of th... ...at the treaty attempted to regulate the transportation and ... these drugs without adequate restriction upon production ...urce or root of the evil; and

Whereas in June, 1921, the opium advisory committee of the council of the League of Nations adopted a resolution urging the restriction of the cultivation of the poppy and the production of opium therefrom to "strictly medicinal and scientific" purposes, which resolution was approved by the council of the league but when said resolution was presented for final approval to the assembly of the league, which is composed of a representative from each nation which is a member thereof, it was amended by striking out the words "strictly medicinal and scientific" and substituting the word "legitimate" in lieu thereof; and

...most of the heroin addicts are comparatively young, a portion of them being boys and girls under the age of twenty. This is also true of cocaine addicts," and as this report is in harmony with the opinion of many who have carefully investigated the subject; and

Whereas the annual production of opium is approximately one thousand five hundred tons, of which approximately one hundred tons, according to the best available information, is sufficient for the world's medicinal and scientific needs, and the growth of coca leaves is likewise greatly in excess of what is required for the same needs, and thus vast quantities of each are available for the manufacture of habit-forming narcotic drugs for...

E PASSES BILL FOR WORLD DOPE BAN

EBRUARY 27, 1923

"The only way to eradicate ...e evil is to strike a death ...low at its root."

ORLD URGED TO CUT UTPUT OF NARCOTICS

...solution Calls on President ...o Ask Other Countries to Co-operate in Fight

...PECT SENATE UNANIMITY

...arding's Approval Forecast ...y Endorsement Already Given by Secretary Hughes

By Universal Service.

WASHINGTON, Feb. 26.—...e House of Representatives ...night gave its indorsement ... the fight being waged to free ... human race from the ...urge of habit-forming nar...ic drugs.

...y unanimous vote it suspended ... rules and passed the Porter ...olution calling upon the Presi... ...at to urge upon foreign govern...nts the immediate necessity of ...iting the growth and production ...opium and coca leaves and their ...rivatives to the amount actually ...uired for strictly medicinal and ...entific purposes.

DICTS SEE 'RIGHT DIE FROM DRUGS'

...is Rounds Up Eighty in ...rive and Some Bare the Hideous Traffic.

By BASIL D. WOON, ...versal Service Staff Correspondent.

...ARIS, April 15.—The familiar ...an of "personal liberty" was ...ded in the Paris courts yes...ay by a band of eighty drug ...ers and addicts in the most ...azing trial which Paris has seen ...many years.

...ll day a procession of morphine, ...m and cocaine maniacs went ... the witness box and admitted ...g quantities of drugs. They af...ned that anyone, even a ...nger, can buy in Paris almost ... kind of a stipefiant desired ... great ease.

... witnesses each made the...

HARDING'S PEN SPEEDS DRIVE AGAINST DRUGS

President Signs Congress Resolution to Join with Other Nations in Limiting Supply

HUGHES PLEDGES ACTION

Negotiations to Open at Once with Lands That Grow the Bases of Opium and Cocaine

By Universal Service.

WASHINGTON, March 2.—President Harding to-day signed the joint Congressional resolution urging that the United States take up with certain foreign governments the necessity for curtailing at the source the production of habit-forming drugs.

Secretary Hughes immediately pledged the "closest attention" of the State Department to the conduct of negotiations with the nations involved, in order that a satisfactory solution of this "most serious problem" might be reached.

TO MOVE AT ONCE.

Preparations were made immediately for the diplomatic steps which must be taken toward agreements which will limit production to the amounts "necessary for strictly medicinal and scientific purposes."

Negotiations will be conducted with two groups of nations.

The growth of the poppy for the production of opium will be taken up with Great Britain, Persia and Turkey. India, a British possession, produces considerable quantities of opium.

Reports from London already indicate a growing British appreciation of the drug menace; and the negotiations with the English Government, it is known, will receive considerable popular support on both sides of the Atlantic.

BLOW AT COCAINE.

The second group of negotiations will be conducted with the Netherlands, Peru and Bolivia, relative to the coca leaf and its derivatives, chiefly cocaine. The Island of Java, a Dutch possession, produces coca leaves.

Secretary Hughes's deep interest in the drug problem assures prompt action in carrying on both sets of negotiations.

Following the signing, President Harding sent the pen to Representative Porter, of Pennsylvania, author of the resolution.

Famous Trader Dead; Owned 2,000 Violins

Britain Strikes Heavy Blow at Traffic in Drugs

LONDON, March 1.

GREAT BRITAIN struck a blow at the "dope" traffic to-day, when the House of Commons passed on second reading the Dangerous Drugs act.

This measure imposes heavy penalty upon persons selling or illegally having in their possession narcotic drugs, while powers of search and seizure are conferred upon the police.

Home Secretary Bridgeman declared that the traffic in narcotics has reached dangerous proportions in England. He said:

"It is necessary to check the international agents of the drug sellers who are at work in England."

U.S. Aid Sought by World League in Drug Fight

By Universal Service.

WASHINGTON, March 17.

THE United States will be asked by the nations of the world to suggest the way for international drug control.

This was the report to the State Department to-day by Dr. Rupert Blue, America's representative on The Hague Narcotic Commission, after a conference with the spokesmen for the member countries.

Dr. Blue said that every nation pledged itself to a programme of control of narcotics, particularly such a plan as would keep the drugs from being dumped into America. They are anxious to stamp out the evil and will look to America for guidance.

This situation, State Department officials point out, gives this country the opportunity to have the plan already worked out for America adopted as a world-wide programme.

Embargo Lifted on Drugs When Quota Is Fixed

WASHINGTON, March 27.

A COMPLETE agreement as to the amount of narcotics needed annually in the United States for legitimate scientific and medical usage was reached this afternoon at a conference between American drug manufacturers and the Federal Narcotic Control Board. ing of the agreement on the amount of narcotics needed for medicinal use in this country the Government this afternoon lifted the embargo on the importation of habit-forming drugs.

The principal provision of the agreement is that the...

DOPE EVIL TO BE AIRED IN WORLD COURT

Ex-Surgeon General Blue Sent to Take Up Proposed Restriction of Poppy Growing

Step Is Preliminary to Formal Negotiations With Nations Classed as Drug Producing

WASHINGTON, March 7.—(By Universal Service.)—The United States today took direct action on the Porter resolution passed by Congress to suppress the international traffic in drugs and strangle the world wide dope ring.

Rupert Blue, former surgeon general of the Public Health Service, and now official medical adviser for this government overseas, was ordered to go before the opium commission at The Hague.

He is to report back at the earliest date possible with the latest available data on the growth of the raw products from which "dope" drugs are derived.

U. S. SUMMONS DRUG MAKERS TO CONFERENCE

Fight for World Control Will Open in April After Parley March 27 Decides Needs

LICENSE SYSTEM IS PLAN

Dr. Rupert Blue Reports from Hague Nations Are Ready to Follow America's Lead

By Universal Service.

WASHINGTON, March 19.—The State Department will begin its fight to break the world drug ring and check the importation of crude narcotics soon after April 1, following a conference of the Narcotic Control Board with drug manufacturers to be held here March 27.

The object of this meeting is to establish the absolute legitimate needs of opium and cocaine for medicinal practices.

This determined, the State Department will take up with foreign chancellors the problem of limiting production and importation.

WILL LIMIT CRUDE DRUGS.

The Government will start only...

U. S. IS URGED TO BREAK WITH DRUG NATIONS

Anti-Narcotic Parley Wants Relations with All Lands Encouraging Evil Severed

INDIA IS OUTDONE HERE

Commissioner Wallis of New York Reveals U. S. Per Capita Consumption Is Startling

By Universal Service.

WASHINGTON, May 4.—Frederick A. Wallis, Commissioner of Correction of the City of New York, presented a resolution at the National Anti-Narcotic Conference to-night that urges President Harding to sever diplomatic relations with any country declining to enter a world-wide agreement for the suppression of the drug evil.

Commissioner Wallis startled the members of the conference with the assertion that the per capita amount of opium consumed in the United States each year is thirty-six grains, even more than that used by the natives of India. He said:

1923

OPIUM PARLEY BREAKS UP IN ROW OVER U. S.

American Delegation Walks Out of Opium Board Meeting After Presenting Ultimatum

TAKE PLAN OR LEAVE IT

U. S. Chairman Declines to Enter Into Discussion of the Narcotic Control Proposals

GENEVA, June 1.—The entire United States delegation walked out of the meeting of the Opium Commission at the League of Nations here to-day.

The Americans refused to answer questions regarding their proposals or participate in any discussion of...

GENEVA ADOPTS U. S. OPIUM SUGGESTIONS

Resolution, Accepted with Minor Reservations, Urges Manufacture Limitation.

ALL NATIONS FAVOR ACT

Restriction of Drug to "Medicinal Necessity" Part of American Plan.

GENEVA, June 5 (By Associated Press).—The American delegation and the other members of the the Opium Advisory Committee of the League of Nations, after lengthy consultations, reached an arrangement to-night which was accepted by all parties with minor reservations.

The resolution adopted says:

"The Advisory Commission on Traffic in Opium accepts and recommends to the League the proposals of the representatives of the United States, as embodying general principles by which governments should be guided in dealing with the question of the abuse of dangerous drugs, and on which, in fact, the International Convention of 1912 was based, subject to the following reservation by the representatives of France, Germany, Great Britain, Japan, The Netherlands, Portugal and Siam.

U. S. TO PRESS GENEVA FIGHT AGAINST DRUGS

Secretary Hughes Decides to Send Porter Mission Back to Ask Practical Action

PRESIDENT IS HOPEFUL

Envoys Will Represent U. S., but Will Not Take Part in Debates of the Assembly

By Universal Service.

WASHINGTON, Aug. 17. — The United States will go back to Geneva to carry on its fight for the elimination of the deadly opium traffic from the face of the earth.

President Coolidge announced today that the same delegation which several weeks ago secured the adoption by the League of Nations Opium Advisory Commission of the American plan with a reservation had been reappointed to attend the meeting of the League Assembly, at which the resolution will come up for ratification.

LEGISLATURS WAR ON DRUG

SENATE PASSES BILL TO JAIL SELLERS

UNANIMOUS VOTE GIVEN TO DRUG MEASURE

General Approval of Plan for Imprisonment; Second Offense Under Law to Be Felony

Scheme Worked Out by Pharmacy Board for Care and Cure of Victims Also Is Included

APRIL 9, 1921

By WILLIAM H. JORDAN.
Examiner Bureau, 1011 Seventh Street

SACRAMENTO, April 8.—The campaign to put into prison every dealer in the illicit traffic in narcotics in California received a decided impetus today when the Senate, without a dissenting vote, passed Senator John J. Crowley's bill, which materially strengthens the State poison act.

Senator after Senator expressed his approval of the measure. It greatly strengthens the existing law by providing for imprisonment on every offense of those convicted of selling habit-forming drugs.

The convicted dealer, under the provisions of the bill, will be sent to the county jail on the first offense for six months to one year. For subsequent conviction a felon's cell awaits that dealer.

The bill likewise looks after the addict by giving the victim of the drug traffic an opportunity to clear his mind and body of the effects of the narcotic.

DRUG VICTIMS.

Pharmacy Board Backs 3 Drastic Bills to Correct Law Weaknesses

First Offense for Peddling of Drugs Made Felony; Hospital on Island for Addicts Urged

JANUARY 4, 1921

BY WILLIAM H. JORDAN.
EXAMINER BUREAU.
1011 Seventh Street.

SACRAMENTO, Jan. 3.—The habit-forming drug traffic is to be attacked in the State Legislature.

Three measures, calculated to correct weaknesses in existing law and aimed at suppression of the business as well as to the care of the drug addict under proper State control and supervision, are to be presented to the Legislature with the sanction and approval of the State Board of Pharmacy.

A drastic tightening up of the penal law as to the unlawful sale of drugs and provision for an island isolation hospital for treatment of addicts are the two outstanding phases of legislation which will be asked for by the officials of the State board.

PROVISIONS OF BILLS.

The bills, which are being drafted, provide:

1—Making the first offense of peddling of habit-forming drugs a felony.

2—Making it a felony to have the drug in unlawful possession and providing for the confiscation of any vehicle, particularly automobiles, illicitly used for drug peddling.

3—Establishing a hospital on a remote island where the drug addict may be treated and not so environed as to throw temptation to escape in his way while under treatment.

LEGISLATURE GETS DRASTIC NARCOTIC ACT

Bill Providing Prison Terms for Every Form of Drug Violation Filed in Dope Fight

No Quarter for Opiate Dealers Demanded by Solon-Doctor Who Drafted New Measure

JANUARY 30, 1923

By WILLIAM H. JORDAN.
EXAMINER BUREAU.

SACRAMENTO, Jan. 29.—Direct and drastic attack was made today in the State Legislature on the illicit narcotic traffic in California.

Standing flatly on the platform of no further trifling with the evil from the unlawful dealer, shutting off every avenue of escape in the courts from full punishment, Assemblyman David C. Williams introduced a measure which carries with it a thorough revision of the State poison act penalties under which prosecutions have been conducted in this State.

The outstanding feature of the remodeling is contained in its penal clauses. These are designedly severe. The author of the act declares that the time has come to punish with all the force the law can command. The bill provides:

1—State prison term of not less than two years for those convicted of unlawful selling of prohibited narcotics, including morphine, cocaine and heroin.

2—State prison term of not less than two years for all persons convicted of unlawful possession of such narcotics.

3—State prison term of not less than two years for those convicted of unlawful possession of opium and opium smoking apparatus.

4—State prison term of not less than two years for a registered pharmacist convicted of unlawfully dealing in narcotics.

Provision is also made for an indeterminate sentence to the State penitentiary of those that are convicted of successive offenses against the law.

The bill also provides, as does also the present act for the prosecution on a felony charge, with State prison term, of those using boys or girls under the age of 16 years in the traffic.

There is also continuation of the provision for the seizure of automobiles used in illicit dealing in narcotics.

For technical offenses against sections of the law covering the sale of hypodermic syringes and the like, conviction on misdemeanor counts is provided with prison sentences or fines.

Imposing of fines for violations of the penal clauses relating to sale or possession of narcotics is eliminated under the bill from the State poison act.

That elimination, the author explained today, is done deliberately after a careful study of the existing act, as well as the conditions revealed by the examination of the narcotics situation whch has been given to the subject. Assemblyman Williams takes the position that the law must not only be enforced, but that there must be no room whatsoever for the escape from deserved punishment of the violator of it.

In a statement on the bill as it was introduced, Assemblyman Williams said:

From every point of contact

HARDING'S AID IN NARCOTIC FIGHT ASKED

Los Angeles Legislator Moves That President Call World Parley to Crush Drug Traffic

San Francisco Assemblyman Implores Prompt Action by the District Attorneys' Staffs

By WILLIAM H. JORDAN.
EXAMINER BUREAU.

SACRAMENTO, Jan. 22.—Concrete form was given to the battle in the State Legislature against the illicit narcotic drug traffic today when resolutions were offered calling upon constituted authorities to fight for its suppression.

One of these resolutions "requests and urges" President Harding to call an international conference for adoption of a program of suppression among the nations of the earth and to work out a general program for crushing the traffic in all of its forms.

That was presented in the assembly as a joint resolution for action by both houses by Assemblyman Charles B. Dawson of Los Angeles county. A second series of resolutions offered by Assemblyman Louis Erb of San Francisco, directed attention to the death of "Wally" Reid and urged utmost activity of district attorneys in narcotics traffic cases.

DRUG MONSTER HAS TENTACLES IN EVERY STATE

Vendors Boast That One Customer Is Good for Six More Addicts in Time

PLAGUE EVER INCREASING

Survey Shows Federal Government Is Almost Helpless in War to End Traffic

DRUG PERIL GROWTH STIRS U. S. OFFICIALS

Mellon Is Asked for More Agents, as Convictions Increase 100 Per Cent.

By Universal Service.

WASHINGTON, Jan. 20.—Citing a startling increase in Drug law violations, the Narcotic Division of the Treasury to-day appealed to Secretary Mellon for a larger force of agents adequately to enforce the law. The report stated:

"During the fiscal year 1921-22 the number of arrests for the illegal use and sale of drugs increased 65 per cent over the figures for the previous fiscal

AMERICA LEADS REST OF WORLD IN ADDICTION TO NARCOTICS

JANUARY 21, 1923

1,000,000 to 4,000,000 Users of Dope Consumed 100,000,000 Ounces During the Year

TRAFFIC HAS U. S. HELPLESS

Like War, Evil Is Too Great to Be Faced by Anything Less Than Entire Population

By JAMES WHITTAKER.

The United States has abandoned all lines of defense against the dope traffic.

It is defenseless against an evil that has already tainted two and a half million of its population and is vigorously ready immediately to multiply that number by six.

In the last five years dope has fought a great battle for evil and, in America, has won

A six-month survey, begun last July in this city and extended since to include dope-stricken towns in every State in the Union, culminates to-day in the documental proof which permits the current issue of Hearst's International Magazine to make the cold statement:

"The United States now uses more dope than all the rest of the world combined."

The estimates of the number of dope addicts in our population range from the one million quoted by Deputy Com-

Mrs. J. J. Rooney to Lead Women in War on Drugs

THE organization of a woman's committee to fight the steady advance of the narcotic drug evil will be effected at a meeting called by Mrs. John Jerome Rooney, to be held in rooms 1 and 2 on the third floor of the Hotel McAlpin on Wednesday at noon.

The meeting will be addressed by Mrs. W. B. Bonfils (Winifred Black), who has made an exhaustive study of the narcotic drug traffic, and by either United States Senator-Elect Royal S. Copeland or Dr. Carlton Simons, head of the Narcotic Bureau of the Police Department.

Mrs. Rooney has invited fifty of New York's best known women workers, most of whom are public speakers. It is her intention to establish a speaker's bureau, from which speakers can be assigned to meetin[illegible] in Ne[illegible] eral [illegible] ment.

Mrs. Rooney [illegible]

STIFF PRISON TERMS VOTED FOR PEDDLERS

Unanimous Action in Upper House Ratifies Program Designed to End Drug Traffic

By WILLIAM H. JORDAN.

SACRAMENTO, April 9.—By unanimous vote the Senate today passed Senator Crowley's bill which is designed to "put teeth" into the State poison act for the prosecution and punishment of illicit narcotic traffickers.

The measure covers amendments which have been made by the State Board of Pharmacy, and particularly one relating to penal sections, the outcome of an intensive study of the narcotic traffic by Dr. A. E. Osborne, allenist of national repute, and Senator from Santa Clara County.

Dr. Osborne's amendment was consolidated with the Crowley bill, which as passed represents the best thought of those that have been actively prosecuting an investigation of the narcotic traffic in all of its ramifications.

The bill makes unlawful possession of prohibited narcotics punishable by imprisonment in a county jail or State penitentiary for terms not more than six years for the first offense and for ten years for subsequent offenses.

The section reads as follows:

Any person convicted for having in possession any of the narcotic drugs or their derivatives mentioned herein, shall for the first conviction be punished by imprisonment in the county jail or in the State penitentiary for not more than six years; for the second, and each subsequent offense of which said person so convicted shall be found guilty, said person shall be punished by imprisonment in the county jail or in the State penitentiary for not more than ten years.

Another section tightens up the State law relating to seizure of automobiles used in the unlawful handling of prohibited narcotics.

U. S. IS WORST DRUG ADDICT RECORD SHOWS

Mrs. Treadwell Quotes Government Reports Making America World's Biggest Use

APPEAL MADE TO HARDING

Chicago Women Voters Want International Conference for Action Against the Evi

Special Dispatch to the N. Y. American.

CHICAGO, Jan. 6.—Showing by Government reports that America is the world's greatest drug user manufacturing thousands of tons of cocaine, morphine, codeine and heroin annually, and having three-fourths of it, after being exported smuggled back into this country for illegitimate use, Mrs. Harriet Taylor Treadwell, president of the Chicago League of Women Voters to-day astounded members of her organization.

No organization in the country worked harder for the passage of the Jones-Miller measure a year ago than did this one, which was formerly the Chicago Political Equality League and which is now one of the largest organizations of women in the country.

APPEAL TO HARDING.

After hearing facts presented by their president, the women passed unanimously the resolution she presented asking President Harding for an anti-narcotic week and for an international conference whereby all civilized countries can unite to stamp out the drug evil.

Mrs. Treadwell said:

"Do you know that Government reports show that we in the

SENATE PASSES BIL

Americans Use More Drugs Than Res

F DOPE;

United States use forty times more narcotic drugs per capita than any other white nation? That we use seventeen times more per capita than the Chinese, who have always been considered the drug-drenched nation of the world?

"Three and a half tons of these drugs are enough for the legitimate practice of medicine for the whole world. This amount is based upon quantities used in hospitals, dispensaries and in private places in the large cities of the Atlantic seaboard.

STARTLING COMPARISONS.

"Yet the Government of India alone supplies 936 tons of narcotic drugs a year; China, according to English reports produces 7,000 tons and in the last fiscal year Turkey produced 470 tons and Persia 594 tons.

"Comparisons among the nations are enough to start us into immediate activity. Think of this: In Austria the consumption of narcotics per capita is one-half a grain. In Italy one grain. In Germany two. In Portugal two and a half. In France three. In Holland three and a half and in the United States thirty-six.

She told the women voters, whose interest is for fine citizenship:

"What kind of a drugged nation are we being converted into? Think of it—150,000 ounces of cocaine being imported annually. Seventy-five per cent of this for illegitimate use.

"These are figures that make the mothers of the country sit up and think. China awoke to the horrors of drug slavery some years ago, and fought two wars to keep opium and its derivatives out of China.

WORSE THAN CHINESE.

"We here in America are seventeen times worse by actual statistics than the Chinese. Not a pleasant thought, now, is it?

"It is for us who fought for the Jones-Miller bill to do everything in our power to help clear up this situation."

The "Ohs" and "Ahs" at the statements of Mrs. Treadwell showing home conditions in drug using crystallized themselves into immediate action. Copies of the resolution will be sent not only to President Harding, but to the United States Senators and Represent

SMITH TO ASK DRASTIC LAWS ON NARCOTICS

Governor Tells Committee of Physicians He Will Adopt Most Recommendations

MEDICAL BAN IS OPPOSED

MARCH 19, 1923

Executive Says Proposal to Confine Drug Addicts Is Too Costly to Undertake

Governor Smith will send a special message to the Legislature recommending drastic legislation for narcotic drug control, providing the State with machinery now lacking to cope with the evil.

The Governor, yesterday, in a letter to the Committee of Physicians appointed by him February 26, to study narcotic control and rural health problems, declared he would make the committee's recommendations the basis of his message.

The physicians report that the narcotic problem has received their most serious study and consideration. They recommend that so far as possible criminal addicts undergo institutional confinement. They also recommend increasing the penalties on illegal vending of habit-forming drugs.

STATE LAW ASKED.

Their most important recommendation suggests "that the essential provisions of the Harrison Narcotic Act be embodied in a State law similar to the narcotic amendment to the New York City Sanitary Code.

However, because evidence obtained from all sources shows that the practising physician is responsible for less than 2 per cent of all drug addiction, according to report, "the provisions for registration and reduplication of blanks should be omitted from the State legislation and the profession allowed to prescribe or administer narcotics in ordinary practise without restriction."

CONFINE ALL DRUG USERS, SIMON PLEA

98 Per Cent of Addicts Are Criminals, Says Head of Narcotic Bureau.

To eliminate the drugs in this country it will be necessary to place the criminal addict in confinement for life, as is now being done with the imbecile, was the opinion expressed yesterday by Dr. Carleton Simon, head of the narcotic division of the Police Department, to two hundred Broadway business men and their wives.

The occasion was the weekly luncheon of the Lions Uptown Club, held at the Hotel Marie Antoinette, over which S. H. Peterson presided.

Dr. Simon said that of all the addicts in the United States only 2 per cent could blame their habits on their doctor. The other 98 per cent, he said, were criminals who gained their knowledge of drugs from their connection with the underworld. He added:

"As a menace to society the criminal addict should be treated ...

SIMON WANTS STATE TO CURE DRUG ADDICTS

Urges Three-Year Restraint for Every Habitual User as Means to End Traffic

MAY 4, 1923

By Universal Service.

WASHINGTON, May 3.—Dr. Carleton Simon, Special Deputy Police Commissioner of New York, asserted before the national anti-narcotic conference here to-day that over 7,000 violators of the narcotic laws have been arrested in New York City in the last two and a half years.

Dr. Simon claimed that more than 50 per cent of the habit-forming drugs distributed in New York City was smuggled in. He said the supply exists because it is profitable and will continue to exist until some method is found to reduce the demand.

DEMAND MAKES SUPPLY.

To bring about a reduction in the demand for drugs, Dr. Simon urged enactment of State laws whereby "we could send away for a cure and custodial care and restraint for three years every addict apprehended by us." He added:

"In this way we could lean up New York City of the illicit trafficker of drugs within three years. We could remove the market for drugs within New York City. We, as police, would very much like to see international action, national action and State action to strike at the supply.

"But we do not have to wait for these great bodies to move, we can strike at the supply by attacking the demand. We can use the business laws, or the economic laws that are unfailing in their results. It is the demand that makes the supply profitable."

Dr. Simon claimed as an indication of the police work in New York that fewer "beginners" in the use of habit forming drugs are being arrested. He added, however, that there is an increase among "chronic repeaters." He scouted the idea that narcotic addiction is an offshoot of medical treatment. He said:

"It is true there are some who might be termed medical addicts, but they are a negligible factor."

REASON FOR INCREASE.

Dr. Simon attributed the rapid growth of the evil in New York City to previously existing State laws, which allowed physicians to prescribe for narcotic addicts. He said:

"In the interest of public welfare, we have always been opposed to the opening of clinics where the addict can obtain his drug to foster and encourage and keep alive the habit. In New York this experiment failed. The daily dosage was reduced on the cards and prescription, but most of the patients bought an extra amount from the street venders, who would be thick in number around the clinic, attracted and flocking there as vultures do to their food.

"The morphine which they would be able to get practically at cost did not satisfy them, and the balance of their money went to the street peddler for heroin and cocaine. Even the cards were counterfeited and a number of disreputable physicians started writing prescriptions, doing a wholesale business on the basis of twenty-five cents a visit.

HE BLAIMES SMUGGLER.

"In one instance such a physician installed an office in an empty loft and his desk was a soap box. Any system or law which will enable physicians to keep addicts under their care and permit them to walk the street while receiving treatment, only furnishes them with an opportunity to buy additional drugs, and thus supports and encourages the illicit traffic."

Dr. Simon gave it as his opinion that it would take a long time to secure effective international agreements to control the supply of habit forming drugs. Concerning the smuggling, he said:

"We hear a great deal about ...

ONE TINY TOWN WORST VICTIM OF DRUG EVIL

Fewer Than 5,000 Persons in Somerset, Ky., Yet 4,000 Prescriptions in Two Years

"DOPE" FOR ALL AILMENTS

Three Leading Physicians in Lexington Are Accused in True Bills by Grand Jury

By A. L. SLOAN.

SOMERSET, Ky., Feb. 8.—How the claws of the hideous dope traffic are gripping the backbone of the Nation—the countryside—is revealed in the return of indictments by the Federal Grand Jury sitting in the Eastern District of Kentucky, in which leading citizens are charged with wholesale violation of the government narcotic laws.

With the return of formal accusations against several doctors and druggists come disclosures of the amazing growth of drug addiction in the rural districts.

Out of the hills of the Blue Grass region, with its high American traditions, comes the revelation of the dope menace eating its way into the very heart of the United States.

Thousands of prescriptions for narcotics seized contain the names of members of prominent Kentucky families, in some instances nationally known.

EXCUSES ARE MANY.

The prescriptions call for morphine and cocaine in unusual quantities. Excuses for the doses entered on the prescriptions range from mule kicks to tuberculosis, including stomach ache, nervous dyspepsia and rheumatism.

The Grand Jury which heard testimony at Lexington, found conditions appalling in Somerset, a town of fewer than 5,000 inhabitants, and indicted two well known physicians and a druggist of that place.

The doctors are James A. Bolin and Glen E. Jasper, and the druggist is William Stigal.

Three physicians in Lexington, all members of powerful political machines, are hit in the true bills which charge the wholesale prescribing of narcotics irrespective of Government laws.

They are Dr. E. J. Brashear, county physician; Dr. R. T. McWilliams, chief physician for the Kentucky Reformatory, and Dr. Elmer Northcutt, house physician at one of the large hotels. Since investigation was begun by the Federal authorities all three have resigned their posts.

STATE OPENS LEGAL BATTLE AGAINST DOPE

Legislature Seeks to Strengthen Police Powers in Effort to Crush Dealers in Narcotics

Two-Year Prison Term Urged for Offenders as Amendment to Present Anti-Drug Law

By WILLIAM H. JORDAN.

EXAMINER BUREAU.

SACRAMENTO, Jan. 19.—The battle against the illicit narcotic drug traffic opened today in the ...

WOULD ISOLATE DRUG ADDICTS UNTIL CURED

Dr. John W. Perilli of Bellevue Regards Use of Narcotics as Among Worst Social Evils

"WORLD SEEMS ASLEEP"

Urges Life Imprisonment for Drug Vendors to Eradicate Grave Menace to Society

"Isolate the habitual drug user, as completely as the leper of Molokai; keep him segregated from society until he has been cured of the greatest evil and ill in the world to-day."

This was the plea last night of Dr. John W. Perilli, trustee of Bellevue and Allied Hospitals, as he indorsed the nation-wide outcry against the drug evil.

Society to-day, according to Dr. Perilli, is absolutely at the mercy of the drug addict. He said:

"The time has come for speedy action in the drug campaign, if we are to prevent a demoralization of society. The world has shuddered at the horrors of social evils that have filled our asylums, brought misery, want and woe to thousands of innocent persons, and carried countless thousands to untimely graves.

"Yet the world in general seems asleep when the drug question comes up. It seems willing to allow this monster of evil to roam unmolested, despite the fact that thousands are enrolled yearly as new victims.

TIME TO STRIKE NOW.

"Now is the time to strike a telling blow against narcotics. I would advocate segregation for the habitual users of drugs.

"First of all, the men, women and children—and there are thousands of little ones throughout the country who know the use of drugs—who are in the first stages should be taken on probation. Every effort to effect a cure should be made.

"If, after trying, they fall by the wayside another effort to help them shake the shackles that spell death should be made.

"Give them a helping hand a third time. But then, if they fail, send them to the new Molokai—the home of the drug addict.

"There let them stay until a cure has been effected or they have passed on.

"Keep them from society in general, for a campaign of education will teach the world that no social evil is a graver menace to-day than the use of narcotics.

"Relatives and friends of the drug addicts, instead of regarding their isolation as an injustice, should consider it a blessing. They should realize it protects the family, and also removes from the community one of its gravest menaces.

DRUG ADDICTS WIN FREEDOM

"The Farm" Up the Hudson, Dr. Simon's Experiment, Proving a Success.

MEN HELPING ONE ANOTHER

Personality Developed by Their Understanding as Interviews Reveal.

MAY 12, 1924

By JEAN HENRY.

"It's the first twenty-four hours that show whether an addict can come back or not."

That is what Barney D. told me yesterday. Barney has special knowledge of the subject, because he was a drug addict for twenty-three years and in the last four months has come to a state of mental and physical peace that anyone could envy.

After six months of the cure at Bellevue Hospital, Barney came out to "The Farm." He came voluntarily, as have all others who are there with him. He can stay as long as he pleases; he can leave to-morrow. That is the understanding.

"The Farm" is a place of mystery, spreading its broad acres along the Hudson north of Poughkeepsie, and can be found only by rarest chance. A benefactor who insists on keeping his name anonymous lent this gracious old estate with its stately colonial mansion facing the Hudson to Dr. Carleton Simon, Special Deputy Police Commissioner, to renew the spirit of men who have been addicted to drugs.

TWELVE REMAIN THERE

For the last two months the experiment has gone on. Twenty-five men have gone out to the farm. Twelve remain. Four of those who have left have fallen into the old habit, the others are still going straight.

The men who remain feel their responsibility. Upon the success of their rehabilitation rests the fate of many drug addicts. Daily they go through their self-imposed tasks, their setting-up exercises, their reading—aware that their return to normal life blazes the trail for thousands of others. They watch each other with keen, wise eyes, hoping for the first signs of a changed outlook on life. That is why Barney said to me yesterday:

"The first twenty-four hours out here show us which way a man is going to swing. It all depends upon the inner nature. Some have it in 'em, others haven't. Drugs do something to a man's morale; he is the prey of his own imagination and the prey of his bad companions."

Jerry—tall and bronzed, cowpuncher and thief extraordinary in other days—breaks in to remark:

"That's it. A lone man might flounder around without finding himself. Out here we see the improvement in each other and know we can come back if the other fellow can. We work on each other. If we find a man is no good, we hold a court of our own, give him a fair trial and ask him to return to town. We're serious.

"A man came out here not long ago. He wasn't willing to play fair; he had taken the cure, but he saw a friend before he came out and got some

Drug Addict 'Cures' to Go Under Probe

JUNE 12, 1922

A widespread and thorough-going investigation of the pathological side of narcotic drug addiction has just been urged by the American Medical Association as a supplement to the world-wide crusade against the drug evil initiated by the Hearst newspapers.

At its recent convention this powerful body adopted a resolution indorsing House Resolution No. 528, introduced by Congressman Lester B. Volk, of New York, calling upon Congress to probe the validity of claims for "cures" of addiction.

Judge Cornelius J. Collins, chairman of the narcotic committee of the New York State Association of Judges and Justices, last night hailed of the Volk resolution was in direct controvention of the claims of members of special committees of the American Medical Association, whose members have asserted that narcotic addiction carried no disease symptoms and was readily curable by police methods.

The action of the American Medical Association in indorsing the proposed Congressional investigation is reported in the current issue of the association's official journal. It negatives the findings of the Council of Health of the A. M. A., upon which Federal narcotic regulations are promised.

At a recent meeting of the American Public Health Association similar action was taken.

The Volk resolution alleges a "conspiracy" exists to promote sanitarium treatment by exploitation of addiction.

PUTTING TEETH IN NARCOTIC ACT

the World Combined

DRUG PARLEYS BILL REPORTED

House Foreign Affairs Committee Approves Appropriation for World Conferences.

HUGHES LAUDS MEASURE

Points Out U. S. for 20 Years Has Sought International Action to Curb Evil.

By Universal Service.

WASHINGTON, Feb. 21.—The House Foreign Affairs Committee to-day voted unanimously to report out favorably the bill of Chairman Porter to appropriate $40,000 for the participation of the United States in the two international narcotic conferences scheduled for this year.

The committee was supported in its action by Secretary of State Hughes. The Secretary's approval was contained in a letter to Chairman Porter, which was read to the committee. In it the Secretary stated:

"This resolution has my full and unqualified approval, and I feel sure that its prompt passage is necessary to enable this Government to continue 'ts efforts to obtain a complete international understanding in regard to the limitations which must be placed upon the production and dissemination of opium and coca leaves and their derivatives.

IN KEEPING WITH POLICY.

"The preamble to your resolution shows so fully the background of the narcotic situation that it is hardly necessary for me in this letter to state any further reasons for American participation in this work.

"I may add, however, that for nearly twenty years the United States has occupied a prominent position in urging international action in this regard and in carrying out the international obligations it has assumed for the control of the traffic.

"I trust that Congress will authorize an appropriation that will permit the Government to continue in the future as it has in the past.

"I thank you for this opportunity to express my views as to the need for further international activity in the work of suppressing the illicit traffic in nacotic drugs."

The Porter resolution sets forth that it is only by international cooperation that the suppression of forming narcotic drugs can be accomplished, and that this Government is bound by the Hague Opium Convention of 1912 equally with other governments to work toward this end.

As the result of conferences in January, May and September, 1923, between the representatives of the United States and governments represented by the League of Nations, the latter governments agreed that the United States' construction of the Hague Opium Convention represented the objects which the treaty was intended to accomplish, and that any other construction would render the treaty ineffective and of no practical value.

FAR-REACHING DECISION.

Accordingly it was decided:

"If the purpose of the Hague Opium Convention is to be achieved according to its spirit and true intent, it must be recognized that the use of opium products for other than medicinal and scientific purposes is an abuse and not legitimate.

"In order to prevent the abuse of these products it is necessary to exercise the control of the production of raw opium in such a manner there will be no surplus available for non-medicinal and non-scientific purposes."

It was further decided that two international conferences should be called in the latter part of 1924 to agree upon a plan to enforce the treaty in accordance with this construction and interpretation. It is to defray the expense of American participation in these conferences that the $40,000 appropriation is sought.

FEBRUARY 22, 1924

Publicly admitting that it was Japanese officials who were implicated in the opium scandals, Mr. Sugim...

JAPAN BOLTS PARLEY

Continued From First Page.

...d that nations often are blind to their own faults, but quick to see the defects in others. He added that no international accord was

JAPANESE BOLT OPIUM PARLEY

Conference at Geneva Virtually Collapses

TENSE SESSION IS HELD

Nipponese Resent Charges Preferred by Delegate From Great Britain.

SCANDALS ARE ADMITTED

Mikado's Officers Said to Have Been Involved in Illicit Trade.

GENEVA, Nov. 16.—(By the Associated Press.)—The international conference for the suppression of opium smoking in the far east virtually collapsed today when the Japanese delegation announced that it could not sign the proposed agreement because of the discrimination against Japan in connection with Japanese importation of opium.

Not since the Corfu dispute between Italy and Greece has the palace of the league of nations been the scene of such tense incidents as marked today's forenoon session of the opium conference, the object of which was to arrange not alone for the suppression of opium smoking in the far east, but for the curbing of excessive opium production in China.

Japanese Virtually Bolt.

In consequence of charges by the British delegate and the apparent impossibility of obtaining satisfaction concerning Japan's freedom to purchase opium abroad, the Japanese delegation virtually bolted the conference.

The morning session adjourned with all the delegates admitting that the conference had virtually collapsed, since it had achieved nothing on its programme. Nevertheless, on the earnest appeal of the presiding officer, M. Van Wettum of Holland, the delegates agreed to reassemble in the afternoon and take up points in the programme which were less contentious in nature than the questions which had produced the rupture.

This morning's clash was caused by Japan's allegation that she was being discriminated against by other powers, chiefly Great Britain, in connection with the shipment of opium and further, that when the Japanese government issued import certificates they were not always recognized by the other powers.

British Statement Resented.

The break was immediately due, however, to Japanese resentment over the statement made yesterday by Malcolm Delevingne, the British delegate, that Great Britain could not habitually recognize import certificates because of scandals over them which involved high officials in one far eastern country "whom he preferred not to name."

The British position was that despite regularly issued import papers, opium, as well as other narcotic drugs, often were diverted on the way to the country of purchase and forwarded to other destinations, where they were used for illicit purposes and illicit gain, thus bringing a stain on the name of Great Britain, which permitted the export.

The Japanese contended that when they tried to trans-ship opium at Hongkong the British

NOVEMBER 17, 1924

BRITAIN AND JAPAN BLOCK WORLD DRUG BAN

DECEMBER 30, 1924

Onus of Drug Evil Placed on Briton

By PROFESSOR ETTORE LEVI,
Member of the High Council of Italian Hygiene.
Special Cable to Universal Service.

ROME, Dec. 29.

THE production of and traffic ... imposing problem of interna...

Several hundred millions ... mined both their morals and wor... erate poisoning—that is to say, b... be avoided.

Morover, this poison tide ri... Japan, North and South America...

Public opinion is sensitive ... catastrophes such as wars, earth... the tremendous damages result... deeply touched world opinion, the latte... the insidious work of opium as a race poison, wh... rapidly becoming more destructive than any war.

The opium question being, above all, a fundamental problem of international morals, all civilized States are either directly or indirectly involved.

Primary responsibility lies with the British and Japanese governments, which profit by the opium production. But almost equally open to condemnation are all the ci... lized powers which have inexcusably acquiesce... tolerated such an insult to civilization.

They are now paying the penalty, for with all ... genuity they are unable to close their own frontiers ... insidious drug.

Nations, just as individuals, engaged in the u... traffic cannot escape the consequences of their imm... deeds. In the British Isles, as in the dominions, regulat... have proved vain to stamp out the spread of the vice, wh... chronic revolt in India is intensified by this tragic mor... weapon, which England has forged against herself.

All laws and regulations by conferences will be useless until the predominating influence of Britain in the League of Nations council is turned against the trade in and cultivation of the poppy itself.

The British people, who lead in many fields of human activity, cannot tolerate a further continuance of the condition, which is contrary to all modern ideals of morals, economics and international health.

When British public opinion is adequately enlightened it will know how to react on the Government so as to force a renouncing of the chronic poisoning of a hundred million Asiatics. That will be a great day for humanity and will save the empire from sure moral and economic danger.

I believe, however, that the mission of leading the world crusade against opium should belong to the United States. They have recently given the world a wonderful example by the eradication of another race poison—alcohol. Let the United States win the gratitude of the world by defending not only themselves, but the helpless Eastern peoples against a still more dangerous destroyer—opium.

DECEMBER 18, 1924

League's Failure on Opium Pact

THE failure of the Opium Conference is as near as confession of total depravity as any band of nations could make.

The sordidness of those powers who sat with us in pretended eagerness to smash opium and its derivitives, and free mankind from dope is the finest possible endorsement of those who kept the United States out of the League of Nations!

...less abandonment by such ...eds of millions of opium ...eir freedom would reduce ...uch powers, should be suf... the scales from the eyes of ... such League or the World ... it.

...he armistice these foreign ...red reams of idealism; they ... us to join their enchanted ... mankind, yet when we sat with them to kill the poppy curse, these evangels of world-wide altruism stripped off their ascension robes and stood revealed as colossal dope peddlers!

Japan and Great Britain said there was an irreconcilable difference between them and us. There was; we wanted to kill opium and they wanted to commercialize it!

believe in

PREPAREDNESS?

AMERICA WITHDRAWS FROM OPIUM PARLEY

DECEMBER 14, 1924

OPIUM PARLEY FAILS TO ACT

Conference Closes When British, French and Chinese Refuse to Sign Protocol.

POSTPONEMENT IS ASKED

Victory Seen in American Delegation's Fight Against Treaty of First Gathering.

By Universal Service.

GENEVA, Dec. 13.—The American delegation's fight against the treaty, adopted by the First Conference on Opium Smoking, bore fruit to-night when British and French delegates announced they could not sign, and asked indefinite postponement of the meeting called for the signing ceremony.

The meeting was adjourned pending further advice from the British and French delegations. It is generally thought by the other delegates that this development means that the First Conference has been wrecked on its own failure.

ADVICE FROM LONDON.

Delegate Delevigne said he had received word from London that the American proposals to raise the question of smoking opium at the Second Conference had been brought up in the League of Nations Council and that the Council made suggestions which the British Government desired to talk over with Austen Chamberlain, Foreign Minister, when he returned to London. Therefore it was desired that Delévigne propose adjournment for the present.

M. Bourgeois, French delegate, said he was not in a position to sign to-day. Sze, of China, announced that he would not sign because he did not know how to interpret these two statements.

Then, paraphrasing Bret Harte's reference to the Heathen Chinee, Sze said:

"For ways that ...
tricks ...

...governments ...ingless treaty and rejected the American proposal that the Second Conference take up and write a genuine convention it would place them in an untenable position in the opinion of the world and would ...

Prelate Says Opium Makes Men Beasts

...NCE ARCHBISHOP FREDERICO ...CHINI,
...ble to Spain.
... Universal Service.

...raffic in opium is the most in...ful destroyer of the mind which ...guished from the beasts. ...enumbing. It is characterized ...nse of honor. It forces man to ...thy pleasures as the beasts, to ...s divine endowment, superior. ... from man the dignity and re... intelligence, his reason and his ...grades him, should have the scorn... ...vidual and every nation without

...of returning to man those qualities ... in which he is created deserves ...tion from every honorable man and

DECEMBER 31, 1924

British Opium

ALONG the Ganges, rank on rank,
The opium poppies flame,
Six hundred miles, on either bank,
Red with a nation's shame.
Two thousand tons, in numbers round,
We hope to sell the whole,
With drugs enough, in half a pound,
To blast a human soul.

CHORUS.

WHO'LL buy our British opium,
To the highest bidder sold?
Who'll drug the British conscience
With an opiate of gold?

THERE'S millions in the opium trade,
And titles are to sell;
You'll prosper, with the devil's aid,
He pays his servants well.
With golden bribes and acres wide,
You'll have a flattering ring,
And parasites, on every side
Will hail the opium king.

CHORUS.

THEN, who'll buy British opium,
To the highest bidder sold?
Who'll buy the British consciencce
For ten million pounds in gold?

England and ...

Bishop Brent Returns, Hopeful of Opium

POPPY GROWING CUT EXPECTED

England and France, Clergyman Is Convinced, Favor Drug Reduction Now.

FIRST CONFERENCE SCORED

Geneva Meeting of Eight Producing Nations "Disgusted" Him, Says U. S. Delegate.

Ultimate success of the battle by the United States to erase the narcotic drug evil from its Asiatic sources was predicted by Bishop Charles F. Brent, of the Episcopal Church. He returned yesterday on the steamship Leviathan from the International opium conference at Geneva.

India, Bishop Brent said, despite the desperate efforts of certain interests to continue the unrestricted growth of the deadly poppy plant, eventually will be forced into line.

England and France, Bishop Brent pointed out, always leaders in the campaign to prevent curtailment of drug production, now appear to have been won over by the appeals of the United States Government. At present they are not backing India, Siam and other countries which want to continue unlimited poppy growth.

DISGUSTED AT ATTITUDE.

Bishop Brent denied that he had quit the conference at Geneva because of the attitude of the drug growing countries. He admitted, though, he was "thoroughly disgusted" with the failure of the first conference held at Geneva during November to take a definite stand opposing the continuation of the narcotic drug evil.

The Bishop left Geneva, he said, because he had planned to be back in the United States before Christmas.

Representative Stephen Porter, of Pennsylvania, chairman of the American committee attending the convention of forty nations now in session, is handling America's position admirably, Bishop Brent said.

Speaking of the efforts to write a world-wide treaty which would gradually stop the unrestricted growth of narcotic drug plants in India and other producing countries, Bishop Brent said:

"The first conference, in which the United States was not represented, collapsed, or did worse than collapse. It was composed of the eight nations in which opium smoking is temporarily allowed under the Hague Convention. These countries are Great Britain, France, India, Netherlands, China, Japan, Siam, and Portugal.

AGREEMENT A TRAVESTY.

"On December 5 this conference reached an agreement, which fortunately has not been signed, that was a travesty. It was immediately attacked by our delegation.

"Representations were made to the British and French Governments that the agreement reached by the conferees was so bad that America could not countenance it in any way as a signatory of the Hague Convention. It was stated that if it were signed, it would be a degradation of the very principle of international compacts."

These representations were made by Bishop Brent personally to Premier Herriot of the French government and officials of the English government, within the last two weeks.

When he spoke to the ... the Bishop said ...

... respect to stopping opium smoking by progressive action, but they presented instead, a disgraceful proposition which entirely side-stepped the issue.

EXPECTS GRADUAL CUT.

"However, I feel certain that that agreement, still unsigned,

'Drink 'Old Fritz' as a Nationalist,' Is Berlin Slogan

"DRINK 'Old Fritz' Cordial and show you are a

ITALY GUESSING AT MUSSOLINI

Year's Primping Cost Americans 117 Millions

WASHINGTON, Dec. 21.

THE nation spent considera-

CAPITAL FOUND SAFE IN RUSSIA

Mexico Plans ... of Submerg...

Dr. Cansaurane Expects ... Poor

SEER PRAYS AS WORLD FAILS TO END

DECEMBER 14, 1924

Bishop Brent Tells Why Opium Parley at Geneva Failed

Episcopal Prelate, Reviewing Conference for Hearst Publications, Stresses League Impotency to Deal with Evil.

Special Cable to the New York American.

GENEVA, Dec. 14.—The conference of six of the most powerful nations of the world to agree upon laws to repress free trade in opium, cocaine, and other drugs is a failure. This international conference was held under the auspices of the League of Nations. It was called to carry out a pledge given at The Hague by all nations and later adopted by the League.

It is a failure because two nations, Great Britain and Japan, do not want illicit trade in opium, cocaine and other narcotics repressed. They both obtain very large profits from that illicit trade in the Far East.

China, having more opium smokers than any other nation, being thereby the greatest sufferer from the demoralizing, debilitating effects of opium smoking, is anxious to have the opium trade suppressed. But Japan objects because Japan conducts at a profit the Chinese opium trade.

Monopoly Made Tighter Than Ever

FEBRUARY 26, 1925

Moral Failure of the League Just Witnessed at Geneva

THE Opium Conference at Geneva is over. Representative Stephen G. Porter, Bishop Brent and the White Cross International Anti-Narcotic Society have done a magnificent piece of work toward releasing humanity from a terrible curse. They fought for the production of opium on a medical and scientific basis, and the only way ever to accomplish this is to *strike at the production of opium*, especially in countries that produce it for the sole purpose of smoking and chewing. Stephen G. Porter was not able to accomplish this, so he left the conference.

He did what President Wilson should have done in 1919. By this stand, supported by President Coolidge and Congress, he has, for the first time, created understanding and sympathetic public opinion. America has put its case before the world, with Ireland, China, Japan, Egypt, India (not British India) and all the other eastern nations stanchly standing behind us, and thereby has disclosed those nations responsible for the continuance of the traffic.

Ellen La Motte, ...

... The whole ... anxious to put down opium. The Europeans are equally determined to keep it up."

Ellen La Motte's opinion had the powerful backing of M. Wilson Harris, a publicist, who wrote in The London Daily News:

"If the conference fails, it will be because Anglo-American co-operation, which would have carried everything before it at Geneva, is lacking—and it is lacking because OPIUM IS A

the United States, derives revenue from opium. *Nine-tenths* of the world's production is used for revenue. Great Britain claims the right to furnish the drug to her subjects in India and proposes waiting on China's success at suppression, *after which* Britain is willing to begin to prepare to start to get ready to inaugurate her own campaign!

After the war the British Indian Government signed a contract with the British Hong Kong Government for another five years to supply opium in large monthly quantities. This was acknowledged in the House of Commons. (Rev. C. F. Andrews.) Great Britain has now established a morphine factory in the Straits Settlement. Opium has been pouring into Syria, Siam, North Borneo, Ceylon and Assam.

Mesopotamia was awarded to Great Britain by the League of Nations. Yet her first act upon assuming control was to establish an opium monopoly there *to sell opium for the purpose of raising revenue.* Is it any wonder the Orientals want to ... from the domin...

... And he also ... the fine race of Assamese being practically destroyed under British control.

Dr. Sze, Chinese representative, predicted that, if the Powers refused to act, the Orient would be swept by a tidal wave of moral indignation which would have repercussions on the economic and political structure of the entire world. Perhaps the moral warning will not worry Britain, but the economical and political menace may be effective to a degree.

It is amazing that a man of Lord Cecil's prestige and reputation should be willing to uphold the British Government's policy ...

FEBRUARY 7, 1925

OPIUM PARLEY NEAR A CRASH AS U. S. BOLTS

Porter, Withdrawing on Coolidge's Advice, Says Purposes Cannot Be Achieved.

GLOOM PERVADES SESSION

Disappointed Powers to Continue Conferences and Yet May Sign a Convention.

GENEVA, Feb. 6 (By Associated Press).—Undermined by the loss of its main prop in consequence of the withdrawal to-day of the American delegation the International Opium Conference still stands to-night, but in a terribly weakened condition.

Nobody even attempts to conceal this view. The conference, however, will continue, and presumably many of the delegations in attendance will sign the convention.

FEAR LOSS OF PUNCH.

But despite the assurance given in the communication of Stephen G. Porter, chief American delegate, that the United States will not cease its efforts through international co-operation for suppression of illicit traffic in opium and other dangerous drugs, the fear is widespread that American withdrawal from the conference will have the effect of taking the punch out of that body's efforts to conduct anti-narcotic warfare.

The statement of Mr. Porter, that he was acting with the authority of the President of the United States, indicated clearly to the delegates that the American negotiators had made no hasty decision, but had withdrawn after mature deliberation and constant consultation with Washington.

PORTER SENDS NOTE.

Mr. Porter, who will go to Paris to-morrow and sail from Cherbourg for New York on the steamer President Harding February 12, to-night sent a note to Herluf Zahle, president of the conference, that he was leaving Geneva ... was ...

... needs.

The impossibility to attain the suppression of opium smoking in the Far East only served to increase the difficulties of getting opium production restricted.

American Withdrawal Sanctioned by Coolidge.

By Universal Service.

WASHINGTON, Feb. 6.—The American delegation's withdrawal from the opium conference at Geneva was authorized by President Coolidge, it was said to-day. The reason was that the conference could not reach an agreement that would be satisfactory to the United States.

OPIUM PARLEY STILL SEEKING AMERICAN AID

1925

Leaders at Geneva Consider Keeping U. S. on the Central Control Board.

GENEVA, Feb. 9 (By Associated Press).—Although the American delegation has withdrawn from the International Opium Conference and there seems little likelihood the United States will sign an anti-narcotic convention, conference leaders have decided in private meetings not to eliminate the United States from the list of countries which will appoint members of the Central Control Board.

This means that Great Britain, France, Italy, Japan, the United States and Germany, plus those countries having non-permanent seats on the Council of the League of Nations, will designate this board, which will supervise international traffic in narcotic drugs and opium.

The first four countries named will be the permanent members of the council. This unofficial decision must be ratified by a plenary session of the conference, however.

U. S. PRINCIPLE FAVORED.

If approved it virtually means that the Council of the League will decide whether the United States shall be invited to participate in the election, for, as the United States is not a party to the convention, some special invitation to Washington would be necessary.

It also is pointed out that an American expert could be elected to the board, because no restrictions exists as to the nationaality of members, the only condition imposed being their impartiality and disinterestedness.

Commenting on the decision to keep the United States on the appointive list, league officials said to-night it was in consonance with the determination not to make any important changes in the Opium Convention just because the Americans had departed.

Another plan of the leaders is to incorporate in the convention the American principle that cultivation of opium shall be limited to medicinal and scientific requirements, allowing, however, the various producing countries to make reservations.

COMPROMISE PROPOSED.

Viscount Cecil, of Chelwood, chief ... delegate to the con... ...orrow probably will ...e compromise for... without sacrificing ... principle, will not ... the opium-growing ...

... the convention is ... of the delegates. A plenary session will be held to-morrow and final adjournment of the conference by Friday is within the realms of possibility.

S. Alfred Sze, chief Chinese delegate, who followed the Americans in withdrawing from the conference, still is in Geneva awaiting some news from the First Opium Conference, which was restricted to Far East countries and powers having territories in the Far East.

Father and Sons Feast After Doing the Cooking

...pan Block U. S. in Fight to Curb Opium

League of Nations Adopts Plan to Cur

LEAGUE EXPERT BRANDS 'DOPE' WORLD MENACE

Dame Rachel Crowdy Says Great Profits and Ease of Smuggling Biggest Obstacles

Profits are so great and smuggling of it so easy that the illicit traffic in opium and other habit-forming drugs is one of the greatest menaces which confront the world today, declared Dame Rachel Crowdy, chief of the Opium Traffic Secretariat of the League of Nations.

Arriving here yesterday on the White Star liner Olympic on her way to Canada to attend the wedding of a niece, Dame Crowdy stressed the enormity of opium smuggling. Although she has centred her efforts on the subject for years with the leaders of other nations, the League of Nations official does not believe the traffic will ever be completely eliminated. She added:

'It brings great profit to those who engage in smuggling it. It can be surreptitiously shipped so easily.

INTEREST AN OBSTACLE.

"Then, again, while attempting to control the evil, we come face to face with heavily-invested interests, that manufacture narcotic drugs legally.

"The League, I fear, will never reach its ideal in limiting production of opium to the amount necessary to science and medicine, but we hope it can be reduced to a 'street brawl, instead of a revolution.'

"Up to the present time, the League cannot claim to have accomplished any great reduction in the improper use of opium. Our best work, however, has been in bringing the question to the surface, and interesting all nations in concentrating on the problem.

PRAISES AMERICA.

"America, I am happy to say, has been extremely energetic in its co-operation."

Two valuable systems aimed to suppress smuggling of opium have been evolved, Dame Crowdy said. One is the export and import certificate, by which importers and exporters must obtain permission from governments of both countries.

Foe of Opium!

International Newsreel Photo.
DAME RACHEL CROWDY.

DOCTORS FIGHT DOPE BARGAINS

CHICAGO, Feb. 20 (INS).—No quarter for the drug peddler; no compromise with dope.

ITALY'S LEAGUE ENVOY CALLS FOR DOPE WAR

Likens Battle to Fight Against Slavery a Century Ago; Calls for Health Crusade

By SENATOR STEFANO CAVAZZONI,

Member of the Italian delegation to the League of Nations, members of the League's Advisory Committee on Drugs, and leader in the fight sponsored by Premier Mussolini for effective international action against the drug evil.

Universal Service Special Cable.
Copyright, 1929, by Universal Service, Inc.

GENEVA, Sept. 15.—The fight that is breaking out all over the world against the abuse and illicit traffic in drugs has a great moral value. I think it can well remind us of the fight against slavery of a century ago.

Slavery sopped up the energies of the populations; morphine, heroin, cocaine—these poison the blood of the young and old of the races, be they of the Orient or Occident.

CALLS MEN TO ACTION.

The hour has arrived to call on all men of good will, strong and generous souls that never have been lacking in the United States, to participate in the holy crusade for the health of humanity.

My country, in this fight against the abuse of drugs, intends to protect the physical and moral health [of] our population. Italy is surrounded by nati[ons]... At produce [an]d manufac[ture]... It is a co[untry of] transit and exposed to the ... contraband. I have had ... most severe measur[es] ... commerce fro[m] ... coming—not ... an instrumen[t] ... transporting ... under false na[mes] ... This would ... comm[...] ... br[...] throw[...] ... [...]m ... world ... sensiti[...] ... this t[...]

ITALY MAKES NO DOPE.

Everyone knows in Italy there is no cultivation of opium poppies, or drug manufacturing. We are not moved by any personal interest in this campaign, but by the great desire and decisive will to contribute to the salvation of present civilization and fight a menace not artificially exaggerated.

The moral and physical damage is extending with great rapidity, and all honest people are as one in the endeavor to wipe from our escutcheon this shameful blot.

Every year numerous confiscations are effected. These indicate a very enormous supply, yet it is far less that the actual amount manufactured and placed in unimpeded circulation to poison the world.

One European factory alone furnished to one house, specializing in contraband, enough heroin to supply the legitimate need of the whole of Europe during an entire year.

DOPE SMUGGLERS SLY.

Each country tries to apply administrative measures of rigorous control but there are few measures the dope smugglers have not found some way of circumventing.

There is not a town in the new or old world where "Bella Donna" is not found.

It is generally in the low quarters of great cities, in night clubs, in houses of ill fame and in dance hall that commercial and organized vice flourishes; it is in these dives that individuals, and the peace and fortune of families are wrecked. It is in the midst of all this that smugglers carry on their nefarious work—with their heavily-financed organizations and their well-paid agents. There exists the art of seduction, flatter...

LEAGUE ADOPTS AMERICAN PLAN TO CURB DOPE

SEPTEMBER 20, 1929

Principle of International Action for Limitation Is Accepted After 10-Year Delay

By GEORGE W. HINMAN, JR.,
Universal Service Special Cable.

GENEVA, Sept. 19.—Without a dissenting vote the League of Nations this afternoon accepted the American doctrine of effective international action for direct limitation of the manufacture of noxious drugs.

After ten years of delay today's triumph came only after vigorous attacks from Latin-American and other victim nations had convinced the League's conservative old guard it was useless to attempt to hold out further against an aroused world public opinion.

FEATURES OF RESOLUTION.

The fifth commission finally approved the resolution as follows:

1—Formally accepting the principle of direct limitation by international action;

2—Asking the League's advisory committee on narcotics to prepare plans for such limitation;

3—Directing the advisory committee to submit the plans to the League council with a view to convening an international limitation conference at which both manufacturers and victim nations will be represented for an agreement on the rationing of production;

4—Enlarging the advisory committee so as to "insure more effective representation of non-manufacturing countries."

PROPOSALS COMBINED.

The resolution combined the British proposal for a narcotic and disarmament conference with the Italian demand that this conference include a representation [fr]om victim nations. The com[mit]tee also recognized the Italian ... league's pres... [ex]pressed into ... the pro...

The Uruguayan spokesman asserted his government has "regarded the league's negligence as immoral."

COUNTESS WARNS.

Countess Apponyi, of Hungary, vice-chairman of the commission, warned if the matter were merely referred back to the advisory body that body of experts might "again" see fit to ignore the commission's wishes.

BELGIUM BACKS U.S. PLAN TO CUT DOPE TRAFFIC

Letter Set at Naught Efforts of League Advisory Board to Bury American Project

By GEORGE W. HINMAN, JR.
Universal Service Staff Correspondent.

GENEVA, Oct. 23. — Effective action to control the drug traffic in accordance with principles of the so-called American plan has been decided upon by the Belgian Government.

Support of the plan submitted by the State Department of the United States was pledged today in a letter from the Belgian Government to the Secretary General of the League of Nations.

Belgium declares it already has taken steps to put the principles proposed by the United States into practice, and asks that "serious measures be taken in the manufacturing countries to en...

EFFECTIVE DOPE CONTROL NEAR, DIPLOMAT SAYS

League Conference Will Settle Amount of Drugs to Be Made, Member of Parliament Writes

By PROF. PHILIPS J. NOEL BAKER, M. P.

Former Member of the League of Nations Secretariat, and Delegate to the League of Nations Section From Great Britain During the Peace Conference.

Universal Service Special Cable.
Copyright, 1929, by Universal Service, Inc.

GENEVA, Switzerland, Sept. 22.—Effective international action for the direct limitation of the production of morphine, heroin, cocaine and other dangerous drugs seems now assured.

In one of the most important resolutions ever placed before the League of Nations it has been agreed further steps be taken without delay to limit the manufacture of these drugs strictly to the amounts required for medical and scientific purposes.

DIRECT LIMITATION.

The principle of direct limitation has finally been accepted and in accordance with the proposal put forward by the British Government there is to be summoned a conference of manufacturing and representative consuming countries to formulate an agreement as to the total amount of these drugs to be manufactured annually and as to the quota to be manufactured by each country.

In advocating this, the British Government sought immediate action. It was for that reason we opposed resolutions involving investigations which would only delay adoption of concrete measures.

The principle for which Great Britain stands is that everything having to do with the drug traffice and manufacture of drugs is of general interest. We therefore proposed international action by the governments to achieve immediate results.

TO SETTLE ISSUE.

Broadly [spea]king, the coming ... to settle two ... world pro... d in the ... aration of ... mong the ... results achieved by the [ex]pected conference will be preliminary and not final. The agreement reached will be introductory to a larger and wider agreement, covering the whole problem—for instance, the springing up of new factories in countries not now manufacturers of dangerous drugs.

It will fall within the competence of the league's advisory committee on opium and other dangerous drugs to study the measures of general interest which will still remain unsettled after the conclusion of the agreement rationing the output of the manufacturing countries of today.

EXPERT FINDS ALL NATIONS FIGHTING DOPE

Vice-Admiral Drury Lowe Says Public Opinion Demands Effective World Control

By VICE-ADMIRAL S. R. DRURY-LOWE, Retired.

(The author, former commander of the British Grand Fleet and a veteran of Somaliland, German East Africa and the Dardanelles, has been a student of the narcotic evil for many years and is fully qualified to discuss methods of fighting the opium traffic.)

Copyright, 1929, by Universal Service, Inc.

LONDON, Oct. 12.—Awakening public opinion in almost all civilized countries is demanding some effective form of international control over vast social evils such as the traffic in dangerous drugs.

Modern chemistry has been principally responsible for the introduction of the drug-taking habit. Morphine and heroin, the principal alkaloids of opium, and cocaine, are infinitely more powerful drugs, a few doses of which set up a craving which it is almost impossible for the victim to resist.

DANGER WIDESPREAD.

It is manufactured drugs of this sort which have become such a danger to Europe and America, as well as to the East.

The effectiveness of the international campaign against the drug traffic depends largely upon the force of public opinion. In 1927, India began to reduce her legitimate exports for non-medical purposes, so that within a few years they will be extinguished altogether except for strictly medical purposes.

These control reforms mean a sacrifice of about $5,000,000 annual revenue.

One of the countries which catered to the smuggler contended restricted poppy cultivation would mean expensive substitution of other crops. Alternative crops and gradual improvement of the primitive agriculture were arrived at, and in 1927 Persia agreed to reduce poppy growing by 10 per cent for three years, beginning this year.

CHINA A PROBLEM.

China remains a stumbling block. The new Nationalist Government, however, will certainly try to cope with this disastrous situation and will no doubt create a Government monopoly as the means of fighting it.

Publicity is one of the chief weapons in the hands of the League of Nations. Early this year four big international firms engaged in the drug traffic were placed on an international "black list."

Governments have been slow in moving, but if they are really determined and are backed by public opinion they should be able to ...

OPIUM HELD ACCOUNTABLE FOR ALL DRUG ADDICT EVILS

Concentrated Essence of Poppy Finds Its Way Into Many Places and Helps Produce Criminals; Easily Concealed by Users

FEBRUARY 23, 1927

By WINIFRED BLACK.

SAN FRANCISCO, Feb. 22.—If there were no opium in the world there would be no morphine.

Morphine is the concentrated essence of the juice of the poppy.

Opium itself comes in a lump of dark stuff that looks like a big wad of gum.

It must be cooked and made into a pill and then smoked.

Opium takes a quiet room, a heavy, cumbersome pipe, a little cooking flame, knowledge of the way to make the pill—and locked doors and airtight windows that will not let the telltale smoke escape.

Easily Carried

Morphine—You can carry morphine enough in your vest pocket to kill a good-sized village and not even make a bulge.

The trained nurse will give it to you by the doctor's orders and you will bless the doctor and nurse for it when it is given to relieve unbearable pain.

But ... the pain is over and you ... the house what ... phi[l] of ...ing, twisted logic to the whole thing.

What is a mere human life compared to the stopping for one minute of the horrible, gnawing craving that possesses an addict to the very core of his soul and body?

Morphine addicts, like opium smokers, are mild and harmless while their systems are full of morphine and opium.

Take it away from them and they are wild beasts of savage cruelty, absolutely impervious to any human pity or sympathy of any kind.

Many of the most brutal murders in America have been committed under the urge for morphine. Once get the drug and the piteous victim sinks back to harmless helplessness again.

Doctors, lawyers, nurses, school teachers, newspaper men, many of these are victims of morphine.

Children Addicts

Boys and girls under twenty, thousands of them, all over this country.

In New York State alone, according to official figures, there are ... morphine addicts, and that is ... [th]ose who are known ...

Medical Aid Needed To Solve Dope Evils

League Considers Only Economic Problem, Says Psychiatrist.

By DR. EMILE TOULOUSE,
Medical Director for Psychiatry and Mental Prophylaxy of the Department of the Seine.

[The author, because of his success in the field of treatment of sociological problems as related to the individual mentality, is thoroughly qualified to discuss the social menace created by the illicit international traffic in dangerous drugs. This is his second and final article.]

Copyright, 1929, by Universal Service, Inc.

PARIS, Oct. 23.—Since the World War, the number of narcotic addicts has increased, rather than ...

Blease Produces Opium He Bought Near U.S. Capitol

By Universal Service.

WASHINGTON, Oct. 23.

A STARTLED Senate today saw an opium pill produced on the floor, which Senator Cole L. Blease, of South Carolina, declared was purchased "within the shadow of the Capitol."

After Senator Copeland, of New York, a physician, had examined the opium and pronounced it apparently genuine, the "pill" was referred to the District of Columbia Committee, which is conducting an investiga...

Telephone, COLumbus 7000

Opium Group to Consider U. S. Dope Curb Plan

JANUARY 27, 1930

...ope Trade

...OTE TO LIMIT MANUFACTURE IS UNANIMOUS

...pokesmen of Great Powers Indorse American Principle; Co-operation of U. S. Urged

...y GEORGE W. HINMAN, JR.
Universal Service Special Cable.

GENEVA, Sept. 24.—Amid em...atic avowals of spokesmen of ...e great powers of their deter...ination to combine for conquest ... the narcotic evil, the tenth ...sembly of the League of Na...ons today unanimously ratified ...e long-delayed project for com...tting the dope menace.

Spokesmen for Italy, France ...d Great Britain voiced their ...ational resolve to put an end to ...e dope scourge through an in...rnational agreement directly ...miting the manufacture of nar...tics to legitimate medicinal and ...ientific needs.

...LEADS FOR U. S. SUPPORT.

The first speaker was Senator ...avazzoni, of Italy, who has ...rved as Premier Mussolini's ...ader in his country's fight for ...doption of adequate measures to ...mbat the menace. The plan ...dopted follows one long advo...ted by Senator Cavazzoni, em...odying principles supported by ...e United States. He said:

"Above all, we must consider the participation of the United States, which is supremely de...irable. American public opinion ...s entirely sympathetic to the ...nternational movement against ...rugs."

Deputy George Pernot, France's ...pokesman, looked forward hope...ully to a successful outcome of ...e battle, now that the principle ... direct limitation has been ac...epted.

Professor Philip J. Noel Baker, ...e British delegate-author of the ...esolution providing for the ac...eptance of the "direct limita...on" principle and the projected ...onference for the purpose of ...aching an agreement, said:

"We have seen how the social ...ife of the country is gravely ...nenaced by illicit drug traffic, ...nd we hope all countries will ...hink in terms of the lives of ...uffering people throughout the ...orld."

By KENNETH CLARK.

WASHINGTON, Sept. 24.—Vig...ous drives to suppress narcotic ...muggling will result from the ...enate's action in restoring the ...ouse anti-opium provisions to ...e Tariff bill, officials of the Cus...ms Bureau declared today.

The new provisions will enable ...e Government to assess penal...es of $2 an ounce against ship ...wners who engage or connive in ...muggling, and to hold vessels, in...uding common carriers, on which ...pium is found unmanifested.

...OPE'S OUTPUT FAR ABOVE NEED

MAY 3, 1928

By HERBERT L. PHILLIPS.
Universal Service Staff Correspondent.

...CRAMENTO, May 2.—The world's ...ug factories are producing ap...oximately 100 times the amount ... narcotic drugs required for me...inal purposes.

California's legislation for treat...ent of addicts is "a compromise" ...d can only be regarded as "an ...tering wedge" which later may be ...ended into a programme of prac...al value.

...

...ate are gathered here for their ...seventh annual ...

DOPE MENACES RACE, DECLARES FRENCH EXPERT

Supply Called Double Possible Needs; World Crusade on Great Evil Declared Need

By DR. EMILE TOULOUSE,
Medical Director for Psychiatry and Mental Prophylaxy in the Department of the Seine.
Copyright, 1929, by Universal Service, Inc.

The author, because of his success in the field of treatment of sociological problems as related to the individual mentality, is thoroughly qualified to discuss the social menace created by the illicit international traffic in dangerous drugs.

PARIS, Oct. 20.

THE League of Nations can no longer be permitted to view the illicit traffic in dangerous drugs as merely an economic problem. The problem is biological and medical; on its solution may depend the welfare of the established state in general and the preservation of a high type of mankind in particular.

Contrary to popular belief, the number of drug fiends in the world is considerable. In the United States alone, during the period of 1927-28, there were approximately 100,000 drug addicts in a population estimated at 120,000,000. And about 90 per cent of these toxicomaniacs used morphine, an alkaloid of opium.

World Effort Needed

For the defense of all mankind, the peoples of the world must make a collective, concerted effort to settle once for all this conflict between the needs of the psychic life of an addict and humanity as a whole. As industry has become powerful through expert organization, so must the war be waged on the international drug ring.

We must staff our crusading army with experts, doctors, scientists—men who realize what benefit to humanity would result from the stamping out of this monstrous evil.

One knows that for ages in all countries, man has searched for the elusive "cure-all" to appease his physical and mental pains and worries—the elixir of life. He has sought the aid of plants containing the essence of this mysterious power to mollify his thoughts and feelings.

Science Plays Part

The poppy, from the juice of which comes opium, was once, like the lowly barley, a cereal, cultivated centuries ago by the peoples of the Mediterranean. Coca leaves were chewed by natives of South America; the Indian hemp (hashish) was used for similar purposes by several tribes in Africa.

Tobacco, coffee and tea have become universal in use. And then, finally, chemistry has produced the "nervous medicines," the list of which grows longer almost daily. In this list we find opium, from the poppy's juice; and the alkaloids of opium, morphine and heroin; cocaine, chloral, and hundreds of others which take the place of the 100 per cent narcotic.

Through all this, humanity pays a heavy toll to the toxicant Minotaur.

Egypt Overrun by Dope

Same Peril Faces America

U. S. TO INSIST ON LIMITATION OF DOPE OUTPUT

Will Enter League of Nations Conference Only if Opium Manufacture Is Reduced

By KENNETH CLARK,
Universal Service Staff Correspondent.

WASHINGTON, Dec. 22.—Careful study will be given to the League of Nations' proposed narcotic Drug Limitation conference in Geneva next year before the United States accepts the invitation to participate, it was lerned today.

America's decision will be based on what action the League's opium advisory committee takes at its meeting in Geneva next month in preparing the agenda.

If the committee approves a programme whereby the manufacture of dangerous drugs can be actually reduced, the United States will be inclined to attend.

MANUFACTURE BASIC EVIL.

If, however, the committee leaves any loopholes whereby manufacturing nations can maintain their present vast oversupply of drugs, American officials believe the United States can accomplish more toward solution of international drug traffic by rejecting the invitation and exerting moral pressure to bring about a conference to limit both the manufacture or drugs and the production of opium, the source of the drugs.

The purpose of the proposed conference is to reduce drug manufacture to the world's actual medical requirements, preventing an oversupply for illicit uses.

However, fears have been aroused in America whether this goal can be attained without enlarging the scope of the conference.

U. S. RECOMMENDATION.

American officials point out, before any effective suppression of the dope traffic can be gained the nations must adopt stringent measures to curtail opium production. They insist manufacture and production are inextricably linked and must be solved together.

John K. Caldwell, State Department representative on the Federal Narcotics Board, who is going to Geneva in January as an official American observer, is being urged, therefore, to recommend that the Advisory Commit...

LEAGUE SCORNS U.S. OPIUM PLAN

FEBRUARY 1, 1929

GENEVA, July 31 (AP).—What was known as "the American plan" for controlling the opium and narcotic evil was rejected today by the opium committee of the League of Nations. The committee decided, 7 to 4, the plan was impossible of application.

China, Italy, France and Germany made up the minority. Their delegates advocated the plan be included in the programme for the next meeting to permit more exhaustive study.

Sir John Campbell, a Scotchman, who represents India, derided the plan and protested against the "tortuous manner" in which the scheme had been brought before the committee. He said that although the project was submitted to the United States Government by C. K. Crane, of Los Angeles, it had really been proposed by a former Spanish member of the Secretariat of the League. He charged the whole thing was a piece of skillfully organized propaganda.

The plan proposed that each country should state its narcotic needs in advance and announce publicly where the drugs were to be manufacured and purchased.

The plan found a defender in Sto...

ITALY LEADS IN BATTLE TO ABOLISH EVIL

Japan Aids American Drive Against Reluctance Seen in Six 'Producing' Nations

By WINIFRED BLACK.
By Universal Service.

SAN FRANCISCO, Jan. 26.—Just enough "dope" manufactured in the whole world for the legitimate use of doctors and scientists—and not one pound or one ounce or one grain more.

That is the American plan for control of the narcotic menace and today the news from Geneva looks as if the American idea may be at least considered with some show of impartial justice by the League of Nations opium advisory committee.

The sub-committee, which was appointed yesterday to consider ways and means of carrying such a plan into practical use, seems to be a good working body.

AMERICAN OBSERVER.

Switzerland, Germany, Japan, France Great Britain, India, Holland, Italy are all represented and John Kenneth Caldwell, the American, has been asked to "sit in" as an unofficial observer.

Cavazzoni, of Italy, is sure to hold that committee down to business as long as he is in it.

Italy does not raise opium and it does not manufacture any kind of narcotic drugs, and Italy is determined to keep the dope evil out of Italy—no matter where else it creeps like a slimy snake.

Japan seems to be making a good straight fight for the real control of the culture and manufacture of dope.

Germany, France, Switzerland, Great Britain, India and Holland are all in the dope traffic up to their elbows and it is very interesting to see exactly how they are going to meet the plain, practical American plan of plain practical limitation.

It seems rather a pity that China is not represented on the sub-committee—China is making a desperate effort to throw off the yoke of dope slavery which was forced upon that country by Great Britain at the expense of a hideous war.

I wonder if the Swiss delegate will bring his personal adviser to the sessions of the sub-committee—the gentleman who sat next to him during all the sessions of the last opium conference.

Very intelligent and practical person this particular gentleman. He ought to know something about the drug trade, he is the head of one of the great drug-making and drug-selling and drug-exporting firms of Switzerland.

There are just forty-one great narcotic drug factories on earth and one-quarter of one narcotic drug factory can turn out enough dope to stupefy and deprave the entire world.

BIG BUSINESS.

Big business will have representatives somewhere within easy reach of that sub-committee—be sure of that.

Whether the sub-committee will pay attention to big business when the resolutions, which will determine the next step in the fight, are drafted or not remains to be seen.

Take the little matter of the "ester."

Do you know what an ester is? I never heard of one in my life—until now. An "ester" is an innocent drug that can be exported and imported freely.

A manufacturer can import a ton of these "esters"—take it to his factory and remove the acid and there he has a basket of chips with a quantity of morphine which is not accounted for or recorded. And he can slip that morphine in and out of all sorts ...of interesting channels and ... even call up a friend on the ...phone about it.

An "ester," you see, is m...phine — just plain, every-... death - dealing, brain - steal... heart-breaking morphine wh... has been treated with an acid.

ACID MAKES "ESTER."

It's morphine—till you put it ... the acid. And after the acid ... in the durg it is not morphine ... all, its an "ester."

There are all kinds of "esters"—scores and scores of them—simp... little idea, isn't it?

Japan does not like the "esters." Japan forbids the manufactur... and importation of "esters."

At the last opium conferenc... an earnest British delegate raised the question of "esters."

He said the situation was grave and he asked that benzoyl-morphine be put on the list of drugs controlled by the conventions.

Good honest gesture, wasn't it? The only trouble that that idea is that benzoyl-morphine is just one "ester" and there are 99,000 other "esters" pouring gaily out of the factories daily like water pouring from a broken fire hydrant.

What will the new sub-committee do about the "esters"? Let's watch and see.

EXPERTS FIND WORLD NEEDS REDUCED HALF

Advisory Commission to Study Alarming Illicit Traffic in Drugs in Past Few Years

By GEORGE W. HINMAN, JR.
Universal Service Special Cable.
Copyright, 1930, by Universal Service, Inc.

GENEVA, Jan. 19.—Under the anious eyes of all those throughout the world concerned with fighting the norcotic menace, the League of Nations Advisory Commission on Opium and Other Dangerous Drugs assembles tomorrow for the most important session in its history.

The vital features of the meeting may be summarized under three heads, whereof the first two lead directly to the third. These are:

1. Startling evidence revealing the alarming extent of the illicit traffic in narcotics during the past years;

2. New scientific calculations, practically cutting in half the previous estimates relative to the world's legitimate drug requirements;

3 The preparation of a programme for the general international limitation conference to be held under the League's auspices probably next October or November, wherein all the principal producing as well as the "victim nations" are expected to participate.

OPIUM BLOC ACTS.

BRITAIN HOLDS FRIENDLY BOUT WITH NIPPON

Inaction Marks Sessions to Work Out Plans to Curb Narcotic Peril to Nations

JANUARY 31, 1930

By JAMES T. WILLIAMS, JR.
Universal Service Special Cable.
Copyright, 1930, by Universal Service, Inc.

GENEVA, Jan. 30.—No progress was made at today's meeti... the "League of Nations' Ad... Co mittee on Traffic in O... and Other Dangerous Dr...

GENEVA GROUP FAILS TO STRIKE AT DOPE ORIGINS

After 2 Weeks' Discussion Committee Plans for Parley on Manufacture Limit Only

By JAMES T. WILLIAMS, JR.
Universal Service Staff Correspondent.
Copyright, 1930, by Universal Service, Inc.

GENEVA, Switzerland, Jan. 29.—Although the thirteen session of the League of Nations advisory committee on opium and other dangerous drugs began two weeks ago, members are pecking away at half measures instead of laying foundations fore effective worldwide warfare against the terrible narcotic traffic.

Nor is there any prospect they will come to grips with the main aspects of the problem during this session. The committee is occupying itself solely with the question of limitation of manufacture, and if the Council of the League approves the committee agenda, the League will call an international conference to discuss that question.

BEGGING QUQESTION.

U. S. UNDECIDED ON FUTURE DOPE PARLEY ACTION

Non-Committal at Geneva on Joining Later Conferences; Observer Called to apital

By JAMES T. WILLIAMS, JR.,
Universal Service Special Radio.
Copyright, 1930, by Universal Service, Inc.

GENEVA, Feb. 5.—The United ...tes today refused to commit ...f regarding participation in ...y future conference the League ...f Nations may call regarding ...affic in narcotics.

This action was taken through John Kenneth Caldwell, American observer at the ...sion of ... mittee ... other ...on ex...hing-... ...nited ...nter-...com-... ...

TURKEY BALKS DOPE CONTROL, LEAGUE CHARGE

DECEMBER 19, 1930

Report Asserts Entire Output of Narcotic Factories Goes Into Illicit World Traffic

By KENNETH CLARK,
Universal Service Staff Correspondent.

GENEVA, Dec., 18.—The charge that the entire enormous output of Turkish narcotic factories goes ... firms en... dope traffic is con... ...the recent ...cotic traffic.

PEDDLERS LISTED.

It was decided to send the governments a confidential list of all persons engaged in the horrible traffic.

By Universal Service.

WASHINGTON, Feb. 5.—President Hoover was given a full report today on the efforts being made in Congress to smash the narcotic evil, by Representative Porter (Rep., Pa.), chairman of the House Foreign Affairs Committee.

SUPPRESSED REPORT SHOWS MILLION DRU

REMOVE DRUG ADDICT FIRST, PORTER URGES

MAY 20, 1925

Leader in War Against Narcotics Gives His Remedy; Would Eliminate Peddler

"Rehabilitate the drug addict. Remove the unfortunate from the streets and treat him as a sufferer from a disease, not a vice. Thus you will eventually eliminate the drug peddler and the smuggler."

This was the keynote of a speech delivered last night at a meeting of the White Cross International Anti-Narcotic Society, at the Hotel Astor, by Representative Stephen G. Porter, of Pennsylvania, head of the American delegation to the recent International Opium Conference at Geneva.

GIVES DRUG FACTS.

Representative Porter, who has aided in stemming the spread of the narcotic evil in the United States, summed up the solution of the problem in these words:

"While habit-forming drugs, except heroin, are indispensable to the medical world, large quantities of narcotics are smuggled into the United States.

"Drug peddlers reap a ready sale and huge profits despite the stringency of the narcotic laws.

"Addiction is now recognized by the medical profession as a disease and should be treated as such by scientific and humane methods instead of committing its victims to penal institutions."

Representative Porter points out that the secrecy connected with the unlawful sale and use of drugs makes it impossible to even approximate the number of addicts, but the estimates vary from 200,000 to 1,000,000.

FOUR MILLION DRUG ADDICTS, U.S. ESTIMATE

DECEMBER 25, 1925

Nation-Wide Campaign Needed to Check Startling Use of Heroin, Lineberger Believes

By WALTER F. LINEBERGER,
Representative in Congress from California.
Written Especially for Universal Service.

WASHINGTON, Dec. 24.—Co-operation by the Federal Government in a nation-wide educational campaign is needed to check the rapid increase in addiction to heroin.

The crime wave sweeping the country can be attributed largely to that cause.

Stirred by the growing ravages of the heroin evil, the House of Representatives has passed joint resolution No. 65, introduced by me, suggesting that the Federal Government join in a World Conference at Philadelphia.

MILLIONS OF ADDICTS.

Assistant U. S. Attorney General Cram estimates that 40 per cent of all prisoners convicted in Federal courts are drug addicts or peddlers of narcotic drugs. It is estimated that there are from 1,000,000 to 4,000,000 drug addicts in America.

The annual consumption per capita in Italy is 1 grain; in Germany, 2 grains; in England, 3 grain; in France, 4 grains; and in the United States, which does not grow one commercial poppy or coca leaf, the enormous amount of 8 grains per capita is consumed each year.

NARCOTIC ACT FAILS, DOCTOR MEETING TOLD

MAY 28, 1925

Louisiana's Health Officer Declares Drug Evil as Bad as Before Harrison Edict

"The Harrison narcotic act has failed. It has given enormous impetus to illegal drug traffic. There are today anywhere from 80,000 to 4,000,000 drug addicts in the United States."

Dr. Oscar Darling, State Health Commissioner of Louisiana, thus criticised anti-narcotic legislation before the American Medical Association convention at Atlantic City yesterday.

CHALLENGE TO OFFICERS.

He told a distinguished gathering of scientists and physicians that drug addiction was one of the three most serious problems which challenge the abilities of public health officers throughout the nation.

He went on:

"We have positive knowledge peddlers and smugglers are active, and that there is prescribing by unscrupulous doctors. And we know above all that the producers of opium in Oriental countries are bending every effort to maintain the export of opium."

NARCOTIC LAW HIT IN APPEAL

FEBRUARY 16, 1926

An attack on the Harrison narcotic law, on the ground that it violates the Tenth Amendment of the Constitution, was made yesterday before the United States Circuit Court of Appeals.

About 3,000 Federal prisoners, now serving sentences for violating the law, may be affected by the result of the case.

The attack was made by Raymond Wise, counsel for Frank Mortello, convicted in the United States District Court several months ago on a charge of selling narcotics.

The attorney's recourse to the Tenth Amendment, which provides that all legislative powers not delegated to Congress are reserved to the States, is said to be the first of its kind in this jurisdiction.

In a recent narcotic case before the United States Supreme Court, Justice McReynolds served notice

WORLD-WIDE BODY FORMED TO FIGHT DOPE

Senator McKinley Elected President, Copeland Vice-President at Philadelphia

1926

By WILLIAM E. LAWBY,
N. Y. American Staff Correspondent.

PHILADELPHIA, Pa., July 8.—The World Conference on Narcotic Education, in session here since last Monday, formally perfected tonight a permanent international organization to combat the spread of narcotic addiction.

More than 250 delegates, representing nations, States, cities and public institutions, subscribed unanimously to a constitution and

FEDERAL DOPE ADDICT AID BILL DRAFTED

Measure Prepared by Shortridge and Senator Young Will Be Offered Congress This Year

JULY 21, 1925

By WILLIAM H. JORDAN.

Drafts of a bill to be introduced in Congress this winter, enlisting the direct co-operation and aid of the federal government in the care and rehabilitation of narcotic addicts was prepared yesterday at a conference between Senator Samuel M. Shortridge and Senator Sanborn Young of Los Gatos.

It is the intention to bring to the problem all of the information and expert knowledge of the government department, backed by a dollar for dollar appropriation to States and municipalities, which are particularly engaged in reaching [...] a solution of that phase of the narcotic traffic.

LAW OFFICERS BACK PORTER NARCOTIC BILL

Wardens of Federal Prisons, Prosecutors and Judges All Advocate Farms for Addicts

By Universal Service.

WASHINGTON, April 25.—Wardens of the Atlanta and Leavenworth Federal Penitentiaries, district attorneys and public health officials arrived today to appear before the House Judiciary Committee tomorrow in support of the Porter Bill to establish two farms for victims of the narcotic drug evil.

Warden T. B. White, of the Leavenworth Prison, and Warden John W. Snook, of Atlanta, declared the Porter Bill would be a great factor in relieving the overcrowded Federal penitentiaries, besides aiding in the restoration of drug addicts as useful citizens.

Narcotic Study by Rockefeller Board Under Way

PHILADELPHIA, July 8.

An attempt was made at the World Conference on Narcotic Education today to bring out the stand of the Rockefeller Foundation on the programme of the conference.

Dr. E. C. Terry, of the Narcotic Division of the Bureau of Social Hygiene, was asked by Dr. Clarence J. Owens, director-general of the conference, to give "the attitude of that foundation toward this great problem."

Dr. Terry responded that the Rockefeller Foundation was engaged in research work and had reached no conclusions.

JAPANESE CUT USE OF OPIUM

NARCOTIC EVIL GROWTH LAID TO SMUGGLING

JULY 19, 1926

Official Statement of Commission Reprinted; 95 Per Cent Brought in Illegally

Dr. Clarence J. Owens, director general of the World Conference on Narcotics Education, who presided over the sessions of the conference at Philadelphia July 10-15, made the following statement last night:

"The statement made recently by Commissioner Arthur Woods as to the number of narcotic addicts in the United States should not go unchallenged. He quoted from a document that had been issued by the Treasury Department giving 110,000 as the number in the United States. This number, however, was based on the registered, legitimate importation of narcotics into the United States.

MOSTLY SMUGGLED.

"The same document, however, indicates that ninety-five per cent of the narcotics brought into the United States is smuggled into the country.

"During the conference in Philadelphia, a reference was made to the document on the floor of the conference, and Captain Richmond Pearson Hobson, who is the president of the International Narcotics Education Association and secretary-general of the World Conference on Narcotics Education, revealed the fact that the document of the Treasury Department previously published, containing a survey of the United States, gave the number of addicts in the United States as more than one million.

"This document was prepared under the direction of Congressman Henry T. Rainey and an official commission. This document was suppressed by the Treasury Department for some reason, all copies being destroyed and the type melted down, and even the filed copies were said by Captain Hobson to be destroyed.

REPORT REPUBLISHED.

"A demand was made, in the past few weeks, on the Treasury Department to republish and make available the document that had been suppressed. This has been done and one thousand copies were delivered in Philadelphia for the World Conference.

"Now, Commissioner Woods should not base his arguments on the spurious document giving 110,000, but should base his arguments on the official document just published, indicating more than 1,000,000. It is estimated that there are more than 110,000 addicts in New York

MEXICAN DRUG CONTROL TOLD

PHILADELPHIA, July 8—Basilio Bulnes, Mexican Consul in Philadelphia, an official designee to the First World Conference on Narcotic Education, in a special statement for the New York American, explains how the republic to the South controls the drug traffic within its borders.

By BASILIO BULNES.

Mexico's control of the narcotic situation within its borders is solely by legislation and rigid law enforcement.

Ports on both the Atlantic and Pacific Coasts and the boundary between the United States and Mexico are carefully inspected. Only under special permits issued for every individual case may importations of habit-forming drugs be allowed, and then only after careful consideration of an applica-

HOME-GROWN POPPY URGED AS DRUG CURB

JULY 16, 1926

Strict Federal Control Possible if Opium Is Raised Here, Tombs Physician Declares

America should produce her own opium from the homegrown red poppy, and prevent importation of any of the drug into this country by keeping the sale and manufacture entirely under control of the Federal Government.

So declared Dr. Perry M. Lichtenstein, Tombs Prison physician for the past thirteen years, in a statement issued last night. He announced he has treated tens of thousands of drug addicts.

In this manner, Dr. Lichtenstein declared, can the drug traffic, growing alarmingly, be controlled. He cited instances in which poppies had been grown in New York, Pennsylvania, Kentucky, California, Florida, Georgia, New Hampshire, Maryland and other States at various times since 1781 and told of the good quality and quantity of opium that had been made from the seeds. He asserted that England could not try to prevent the growing of poppies in India without danger of a revolt. He declared:

"Why buy opium from other countries when it can be produced here? Why cannot the drug be produced by the experts in the Department of Agriculture and only enough be grown for the medicinal needs of the country? Why cannot the United States Public Health Service be the agency for distributing the drug? A conference for the purpose of stopping smuggling of drugs into this country would then be the proper thing.

"A conference to stop addiction by obtaining the co-operation of other nations will never succeed because of political and other considerations. Cultivation of the poppy by private individuals would be prohibited. This is an entirely different problem from the liquor question, for the latter may be made from any number of substances, but opiates can only be made from the poppy. I predict that the narcotic problem will not be solved until we grow the poppy here. We can then treat it as a hospital instead of as a police problem."

$400,000,00[...] YEAR'S TOLL [...] DOPE TRAFF[...]

JULY 20, 1926

U. S. Narcotic Survey Gr[...] of 300 Reports 7,000 [...]dicts in N. Y. City Al[...]

By ARTHUR HACHTEN,
Universal Service Staff Corresponde[...]

WASHINGTON, July 19.—[...]cotic drug peddlers in the U[...] States are reaping more than $[...]000,000 annually from 91,245 [...]tims of the "dope" habit, accor[...] to a survey just completed by [...] Narcotic Law Enforcement D[...]ion of the Treasury Departmen[...] was made known today.

This nation-wide survey of [...]bitual drug users was compile[...] 300 Federal narcotic agents. [...] years ago a similar survey reve[...] 110,000 slaves to the drug evil. [...] former years the total was m[...] higher, officials said.

PANIC PRICES.

"Dope" is now at "panic" pr[...] in many sections of the coun[...] Colonel L. G. Nutt, chief of [...] narcotic forces declared. An a[...]age price of $1.50 a grain [...] morphine was taken for the $[...]000,000 estimate. Habitual narc[...] drug users consume about e[...] grains daily, he said.

At Birmingham, Ala., the pric[...] morphine per grain has jumped [...] $16, it was reported. New Y[...] "dope" bootleggers quote aro[...] $1 a grain.

NEW YORK SUPPLIES.

New York is the main source [...] supply for the bootleg "dope" t[...]fic of the entire country, accord[...] to Federal officials.

The amount of narcotic dr[...] diverted from legal to illegal ch[...]nels is negligible as compared [...] the volume smuggled in, accord[...] to Colonel Nutt.

Private investigators of drug [...]diction in the United States h[...] estimated the number as high [...] 1,000,000. Federal officials say t[...] figure is a "gross exaggeration.

New York City exceeds by [...] all other cities in the number [...] habitual "dope" users, the su[...] revealed. The Federal estim[...] placed the total addicts there [...] 7,000, with 10,000 in the en[...] State.

"There are at present two bi[...] before the State Legislature [...] which the general public sho[...] be interested. They are the hi[...]

Model Hospital Planned Here for Narcotic Addict[...]

YOU ARE A BRUTE, A THUG, A SCOUNDREL! YOU GO THERE!
CRIMINA
Sh

DDICTS IN U. S

COOLIDGE SIGNS BILL FO

DOPE-CURE FARMS

J. S. TO DEFEND NARCOTIC LAW

MARCH 20, 1927

WASHINGTON, March 19.—Government legal forces were marhalled today to meet the most hreatening attack yet made on the Harrison Anti-Narcotic Law, the hief weapon for combatting widepread illegal traffic in drugs.

Foes of the law have succeeded in njecting questions of constitutionaly sufficient to place this issue, tenatively, before the Supreme Court.

The high tribunal has set down or argument April 11 the case of Harry R. Alston, convicted in Iowa f unlawful purchase of morphine nd cocaine, which involves the contitutionality issue.

Alston carried the case to the Eighth Circuit Court of Appeals, which expressed doubt as to the uestions raised by his attorneys nd asked the Supreme Court to rule n the constitutionality.

Denial that any such ruling is necssary to the disposition of Alston's ase probably will be made by the overnment's legal experts, it was nderstood today. Should the Sureme Court rule otherwise, howver, the Department of Justice is repared to enter a strong defense f constitutionality of the statute as ell as the vital need of it to check afficking in narcotics.

A brief setting forth the Departent's contentions soon will be filed.

Alston pleaded guilty to an indictent in December, 1924. He was entenced to four years imprisonent. His attempt to show uncontitutionality of amendments to the Harrison Act, making it a crime to urchase unstamped narcotic drugs, as made in a writ of error sued ut to the Circuit Court.

LACK OF CASH HAMPERS WAR AGAINST DOPE

SEPTEMBER 6, 1928

Agents Doing Great Work, but U. S. Bureau Needs More Men and Money, Says Prosecutor

Commenting on the inadequacy of the Federal Narcotic Division's funds to cope with the problem of the major seller of drugs, and laying bare the reasons for the apparent immunity of the "higher ups" in the dope traffic, Assistant U. S. Attorney Todarelli writes in the September issue of the Grand Jurors magazine.

FINE WORK BY AGENTS.

Interesting figures for the New York area are embodied in the article. Todarelli points out:

"In the State of New York for the fiscal year July 1, 1927, to Junt 30, 1928, only thirty-three agents 'made' 773 cases, of which 754 resulted in convictions. In our own Southern District of New York 199 cases were presented by the Narcotic Bureau to the United States Attorney's office, of which only two resulted in acquittals." only two resulted in acquittals.

"The Narcotic Bureau may well point with pride to this remarkable record of achievement, handicapped as it has been by lack of personnel and lack of financial assistance. The irony of the situation

FEBRUARY 26, 1927
FOUR MILLION DOPE ADDICTS
IN AMERICA NEED RESCUING

COURT UPHOLDS ANTI-DOPE ACT

APRIL 10, 1928

WASHINGTON, April 9 (AP).—The Harrison anti-narcotic act withstood assault in the Supreme Court today and was declared in all its features a valid and constitutional attempt by Congress to raise revenue while suppressing illegal use of narcotics.

Basing Federal jurisdiction on the constitutional authority of Congress to raise revenue, the Court, in a decision by Chief Justice Taft, declared Thomas J. Casey, a Seattle lawyer, and Frank Nigro, of Kansas City; must serve the sentences imposed on them for violating the act. Justices McReynolds, Sutherland and Butler, dissented.

Discussing the charge that the act was an attempt on the part of Congress to exercise the police power reserved to the States, Chief Justice Taft declared recent amendments had made it a revenue producer. Whatever might be the right of a resident of a State to buy opium under State laws, there could be no valid contention that Congress could not place on excise tax on its sale.

Congress Urges Speeding Up of Narcotic Farms

WASHINGTON, Jan. 31.

REPORTING conditions in the Federal prisons as "disgraceful," due to overcrowding and lack of a general governing policy, a special committee of the House today recommended remedies.

Speedy establishment of two farms for narcotic addicts, as provided in the Porter law, was urged.

FOES OF DOPE OPEN WORLD CONFERENCE

First Blows Struck in Fight to Arouse All Governments Against Narcotic Menace

Special Dispatch to New York American.

PHILADELPHIA, July 5.—Slaves to narcotics outnumber by ten times the chattel slaves of ante-bellum days, declared Captain Richmond P. Hobson, general secretary of the International Narcotic Education Association, today as he called to order the first world conference on narcotic education.

Plans for the establishment of a model Narcotic Rehabilitation Hospital in New York City were announced yesterday by the New York branch of the Narcotic Rehabilitation Association of Washington. This announcement is of particular importance in connection with the national observance of Narcotic Education Week, which opened last Thursday.

At the present time there is no hospital devoted exclusively to the scientific study and care of drug addicts. A bureau of research will be connected with the hospital.

BILLS INTRODUCED.

The necessity for education and measures to prevent the growth of the drug evil, as well as the need for hospitals for the cure and treatment of drug addicts, is being stressed by the World Conference on Narcotic Education during the week.

Representative Hamilton Fish of New York has introduced two bills in the House of Representatives to aid the enforcement of the narcotic laws. One bill increases the present inadequate appropriation of $200,000. The other permits agents of the Narcotic Bureau to be sent to other countries. In making the announcement of the introduction of these two measures, the World Conference on Narcotic Education pointed out the need of their enactment because of the world-wide activities of the "drug rings."

SPONSOR UNIFORM LAW.

Legislatures of the various States, now in session, have had presented to them the Uniform Narcotic Act, which the Conference is sponsoring. Crime and drug addiction are closely related, figures given out by the Conference snow. It is estimated 60 per cent of the crimes involving moral turpitude are committed by drug addicts. The passage of the Uniform Narcotic Act is being urged as a means of minimizing the part drug addiction plays in crime.

He presented an impressive table showing that in the years from 1897 to 1908, before Governmental control, opium smokers in Formosa in-

one time five per cent of the popu-

NEW U. S. LAW WILL HELP END NARCOTIC EVIL, SAVE ADDICTS

JANUARY 20, 1929

Rep. Porter, Measure's Author, Calls It Boon to Nation; Gives W. R. Hearst Credit

All "Drug Slave" Convicts Will Be Sent to Farms First for Rehabilitation

ARTHUR HACHTEN,
By Universal Service.

WASHINGTON, Jan. 19.—President Coolidge today signed the Porter Bill, creating two Federal farms where narcotic drug addicts may be cured of their affication.

The President invited Representative Stephen G. Porter (Rep., of Penn.), chcairman of the House Foreign Affairs Committe and author of the bill, to breakfast with him at the White House to witness his signing of this measure, which has been described by health authorities, Federal judges and civic leaders as "a boon to the nation."

NARCOTIC DIVISION CREATED.

Responsibility for drafting plans and constructing buildings is placed upon the supervising architect in the Treasury Department.

Management and control of the institutions is vested in the Secretary of the Treasury, who is to create a narcotic division in the Public Health Service. This division shall have immediate control of the institutions. The law says:

"The care and treatment of the addicts shall be designed to rehabilitate them, restore them to health and train them to be self-supporting and self-reliant."

The surgeon-general is to co-operate with the several States in providing information and assistance in creating similar State institutions.

United States attorneys are required to report to superior authorities the names of all convicted persons who are drug addicts.

Inmates of the narcotic farms may be employed in manufacturing commodities only for the Federal Government and not in competition with private business.

THIRD OF CONVICTS ADDICTS.

Estimats were that close to one-third of the prisoners in the federal penitentiaries are addicted to habit-forming drugs.

A score of United States attorneys, Federal judges and wardens of prisons joined in the appeal to Congress to pass the bill, reporting they held high hope of reducing the crime wave by restoring citizens in the grip of narcotics to society as useful citizens, and thereby reducing the demand for illicit use of narcotic drugs.

Conditions in Federal prisons at present were said to be not conducive to the cure of these unfortunates; that special treatment for them was required.

The Porter narcotics reorganization bill should command the attention and support of the medical profession as a whole. It seeks to accomplish three main objects.

First—In transferring the machinery for the regulation, manu-

only better enforcement but a more enlightened understanding

PASS DOPE BILL, DOCTORS' CHIEF ASKS CONGRESS

DECEMBER 7, 1929

President Wm. G. Morgan of American Medical Assn. Urges Curb on Narcotics

Thorough Probe of Cash Dope Compromises Assured

DOPE COSTS U. S. FIVE BILLIONS

FEBRUARY 12, 1929

By KENNETH CLARK.

WASHINGTON, Feb. 11.—Drug addiction costs America the staggering total of $5,000,000,000 annually, Representative Fish, Republican, of New York, told a House judiciary subcommittee today.

He estimated the crime burden of the country at $10,000,000,000 yearly and laid at least one half to criminals "loaded with dope."

Representative Stobbs, Republican, of Massachusetts, a committee member, interposed 90 per cent of all criminals used drugs. He said:

"There are a lot of young criminals who wouldn't commit murder if they weren't full of drugs. Dope gives them courage to commit acts of violence."

Porter Reform Bill Designed to Bring Customs Bureau and Narcotics Unit Closer

By KENNETH CLARK.

WASHINGTON, May 4.—One of the primary purposes of the proposed Porter narcotics reform bill will be to promote closer and more harmonious co-operation between the Customs Bureau and the Narcotics Unit of the Treasury Department in enforcing the anti-drug laws.

DOPE LAWS JAIL 5,200 IN YEAR, RECORD TOTAL

Addicts' Crimes Increasing Rapidly; Federal Prisons Hold One-third Drug Fiends

By KENNETH CLARK.

WASHINGTON Aug. 7.—How extensively the dope evil has spread over the country was strikingly revealed today in an announcement by the Federal Narcotics Division, that 5,200 persons were convicted during the 1929 fiscal year for violating the drug laws.

This far exceeds all previous records.

The aggregate sentences imposed on the narcotic offenders totaled more than 11,000 years

agents.

REPORT FOR LEAGUE.

CASH SETTLES SEVENTH OF ALL U. S. DOPE CASES

FEBRUARY 24, 1929

Federal Figures Show Extent to Which Practice Goes in Enforcing Law for Revenue

By A. M. ROCHLEN.

Copyright, 1929, By Los Angeles Examiner.

LOS ANGELES, Feb. 23.—Private checkbooks, instead of public courts settled one out of every seven cases f national dope laws' violations taken up by Federal authorities in 1928.

throughout the land are "fined" and punished without due process of law.

This was the answer today of State officials and anti-narcotic campaign workers in the West to the recent defense by Federal narcotic enforcement officials of the cash compromise system as "justifiable and constituting in a measure, enforcement of the Harrison Act."

OFFICIAL FIGURES.

Statistics show 1,221 cash compromises, against 4,850 cases tried in court during the fiscal year of 1928.

In a report of the "Traffic in Opium and Other Danger Drugs" or the year 1928, issued by the U. S. Treasury Department, narcotic laws enforcement officials reveal an interesting cross-section of the Harrison Act's operation in the following language:

"FEDERAL INTERNAL REVENUE NARCOTIC LAWS.

"Violations, criminal (minor or technical violations excluded from this figure), reported—8,653.

"Cases tried in courts—4,850.

"Convictions—4,738.

"Acquittals—112.

"Per cent convicted—97.6.

"PENALTIES.

"Aggregate sentences imposed—8,786 years, 4 months, 28 days.

"Total fin imposed—$184,213.99.

"Cases compromised—1,221.

"Total amount accepted in cases compromised—$67,210.95."

These are the Government's own figures. Because the Narcotic Division considers every case compromised a closed secret, as provided by law, there is no opportunity to learn just why the United States collected $67,000 from persons who did not even go to court, when those who did stand trial paid only $184,213.99.

BANKRUPTCY FEARED UNDER SENATE PLAN

OCTOBER 12, 1929

Dollar Declares Companies Using Every Means to Stop Smuggling

The passage by Congress of the act making steamship owners responsible for fines imposed by the Federal Government for opium smuggling aboard their ships would result in bankruptcy for practically every steamship line plying between San Francisco and the Orient.

Such was the consensus of opinion among local shipping men yesterday in discussing the law, recently passed by the Senate, and now awaiting passage by the House of Representatives before becoming a law.

CAPTAINS NOW LIABLE

Under the law as it exists at present, when the Government makes a seizure of contraband opium on a steamer, the captain is

cedure and order the Government to collect the full amount of the fine, and would also make the own-

wners Say New Opium Law Would Wreck Lines

ARNOLD ROTHSTEIN SHO

DECEMBER 16, 1929

19 Days—of Waiting

NINETEEN days have passed since Arnold Rothstein was murdered and the police are as ignorant of the facts of the case as on the night of the killing.

GAMBLER WHISPERED NAME OF SLAYER ON DEATHBED

... proved on him and he was not tried for the crime, but it gave the police an excellent alibi for their failure. That was a break. Perhaps another escaped convict will be found to have committed the Rothstein murder.

U.S. 'Too Poor' to Buy Dope from Rothstein

ARNOLD ROTHSTEIN, slain gambler, was long known to Federal authorities as one of the important "higher ups" in the dope smuggling ring operating locally. The Federal operatives, however, never were able to get positive evidence against Rothstein, because they lacked funds which would permit them to make narcotic purchases on a scale sufficiently large to interest Rothstein.

This was revealed yesterday by Assistant United States Attorney Thomas J. Todarelli, in an address before the second annual conference of committees of the World Conference on Narcotic Education and the International Narcotic Education Association, now in session at the Waldorf-Astoria.

BIG ONES ELUDE NET.

It was impossible for the government to catch Rothstein, just as it is quite generally impossible to trap any of the other kings of the local dope traffic, Todarelli declared, simply because the narcotic bureau is not adequately financed for "big play" among the peddlers. The best they can do is to occasionally trap the "little fellows," who ordinarily sell not more than twenty or thirty ounces of contraband narcotics.

The speaker urged Congress be petitioned to appropriate enough money to enable the department to make a comprehensive drive against the dope smugglers and peddlers.

PROGRESS ON BILLS.

He declared eighty-five per cent of the nation's illicit supply of drugs comes in through the port of New York, with but thirty odd inspectors and investigators to stem the tide. He suggested a measure patterned after the Baumes Law which would stiffen the penalty for dope convictions.

Considerable headway was made during the day toward the perfection of the trio of anti-narcotic measures which will be submitted to some of the forty State legislatures during the coming Winter.

Measure No. 1 seeks to block distribution of narcotics by permitting the arresting agencies to seize any vehicle or conveyance upon which the contraband is found.

PLAN LIFE TERMS.

Measure No. 2 dwells upon the hospitalization and isolation phases of the crusade, and gives the authorities power to seize and isolate any addict without apologies to the prisoner.

Measure No. 3 stiffens existing penalties for dope sales convictions, and would impose life sentences on peddlers found guilty of making an addict out of a minor person.

SAFES REVEAL SECRET HOARD OF ROTHSTEIN

Million in Stocks Shown as Well as $500,000 Bank Account in Paris; Also Jewels

What the Federal authorities found in the safe deposit box and private safe of Arnold Rothstein, notorious gambler, who was shot, November 4, in the Park Central Hotel, was ascertained by the New York American yesterday.

Both caches were opened by the police shortly after the murder, but until this time the complete contents were not made public...

In the safe de... in the American Exch... Trust Company, ... Forty-ninth ... ticles we...

...

In ... apartment, ... the following ... covered:

1—Russian rubles, with face value of about $1,000,000; actual value about $40.

2. A bank book of a Paris bank in the name of Mrs. Caroline Rothstein, showing deposits of $500,000.

3. Bill of sale in connection with the purchase by Rothstein of an Hispano-Suiza automobile.

4. Cancelled checks, drawn by Rothstein but signed by Mrs. Caroline Rothstein.

5—Two wedding rings and pieces of odd jewelry.

6—Several letters, confiscated by the Federal authorities, which are supposed to reveal the form... of a dope ring.

DOPE RUMORS BRING U. S. INTO CITY TRUST QUIZ

APRIL 30, 1929

Federal Agents Seeking Proof of 'Frozen' Loans to Narcotic and Rum Interests

Official cognizance was taken by Federal officials yesterday of long current rumors that one of the reasons the City Trust Company failed for an estimated $1,500,000 was because of "frozen" loans made to narcotic drug dealers and bootleggers.

Assistant United States Attorney John H. Blake, who investigated narcotic matters in connection with Arnold Rothstein, announced he was investigating the reports, which have been in circulation since the bank closed its doors February 11, ten days after the death of its president, ...

... the relationships of City Magistrate Vitale, I felt it my duty to transmit the folder in the files of Arnold Rothstein marked 'Albert H. Vitale.'

"I now feel it my duty also to place before the Committee of the Bar Association the fact that in our raid made last night upon the notorious resort of Louis Faccarona, alias Louis Black, there was seized a per-...

SECRET AGENTS SEIZE NARCOTIC TRADE CHIEFS

U. S. Officers Stage Roundup of Manhattan Racketeers; Tuttle Accuses Speakeasies

Federal agents made a smashing series of narcotic raids up and down the length of Manhattan Island last night and early today in a surprise assault on three huge "dope rings" backed by the slain Arnold Rothstein.

In one telling blow, struck shortly after midnight, 135 men and women were rounded up and questioned by agents who descended upon a Harlem dance hall.

At ...:30 o'clock this morning, in ... to the persons being held ... fourteen prisoners had ... to the Federal Build... ...rteen were under ... being questioned ... Tuttle, who ... thes after ... from a ...

...nsive raid-... ...ried out by ..., headed ... whom had ...-of-town. ... to this ... raiding ... of the ... weeks, ... in the ... nda in ... howed ... for ...

...dlers, ...esal-... ...phine, ... opium in ... their investigations, ... asserted. They purchased ... in quantities ranging from ...0 to $5,000 and spent a small ... une in gathering the evidence ... at led to the most extensive series of narcotic raids this city has known.

12 MEN INDICTED.

During the course of the investigation, the Federal Grand Jury has heard evidence and has prepared secret indictments against at least twelve men. These indictments will be handed down ...orrow.

... investigators discovered ... that dope was being ... ...keasies. One ... Tuttle, ...street, ...es ar-...

... Louis ...ed by ... of the ... Dur-... said, ...hipped narcotics from New York to Hollywood; offered to supply them with narcotics worth $2,000,000 within twenty-four hours; described a dope factory somewhere in New Jersey, and boasted of "immunity" from annoyance in this city.

"HEADS OF RINGS."

Faccarano was found in a dance hall known as the Performers and Entertainers Club, No. 2221 Seventh avenue. At the ...

VITALE DINNER GUESTS LINKED TO 'DOPE' RING

Believed Full Probe Will Reveal Identity of Directors of Syndicate Dealing in Narcotics

DRIVE ON DOPE OVER YEAR OLD

The Government's drive against the drug rings actually extends back more than a year. On December 7, 1928, agents raided a Forty-second street hotel and seized opium, cocaine, heroin and morphine valued, at street prices, at $2,000,000.

Information for this and subsequent raids was obtained from papers taken in the offices of the Rothmere Realty Company, No. 45 West Fifty-seventh street, a Rothstein enterprise.

The day following the first raid two trunks containing another $2,000,000 worth of narcotics were seized in Grand Central Terminal. These were the property of Joseph Unger, who was arrested the same night—a month after Rothstein was shot—when agents flagged a Chicago-bound express at Buffalo.

From here the trail jumped to Chicago, where another seizure of drugs, valued at $1,000,000, was made and where Mrs. June Boyd was arrested.

Still acting on information from the Rothstein files, agents ten days later in Jersey City, seized packing cases labeled "brushes." They had been shipped here on the French liner Rochambeau.

... to $5,000,000 ... Joseph ... but silen... fused t... his exe... guilty ... laws ... is no... years...

BUSI...

USED TO HIDE DRUG TRAFFIC

New Yorker Got in Clutches of Gambler, Federal Men Say, and Aided Him for Years

WASHINGTON, Nov. 25.—Federal authorities are investigating well ...

Who Owed ROTHSTEIN $400,000?

Here's List of Claims Administrators Are Trying to Collect.

ARNOLD ROTHSTEIN.

Life Not Worth a White Chip, Says Damon Runyon.

ARNOLD ROTHSTEIN.

When Fate Dealt the Cards—

ACE OF DIAMONDS.
Arnold Rothstein got his first "lucky break" in a poker game with Charlie Gates, and the $40,000 he won started him on the road to fortune.

KING OF DIAMONDS.
Luck piled up his original stake into huge sums and soon Rothstein found him-... ment houses and many other real estate propositions.

QUEEN OF DIAMONDS.
Meanwhile, despite his unsavory career, Rothstein was happily married and shielded his wife from the publicity attaching to himself.

JACK OF DIAMONDS.
It seemed, indeed, as if life ... royal flush. His last big game, however, found all the chips piled in front of his opponents.

DEUCE OF SPADES.
And the last card he got was death by an enemy's bullet. Thus the game ended for the biggest gambler of them all.

ROTHSTEIN RICHES TO FOLLIES GIR

DECEMBER 29, 1929

U. S. RAIDS ROTHSTEIN 'DOPE RING

T!

TUTTLE STARTS DOPE WAR!

Officials' Names Found on List of Dope Baron

CHARLES H. TUTTLE

Ex. 1.
U. S. Dist. Court

NUMBERS FREQUENTLY CALLED

NEW AND CHANGED LOCAL NUMBERS
OUT OF TOWN NUMBERS

NAME	CITY	NUMBER
Blackie	Harlem	1682
Angelina Gemson	Fordham	1005X
St. Lukes Hospital	Cathedral	[illegible]
Al Vitale	Fordham	6435
Billy [illegible]	[illegible]	10134
Boxing Commissioner	Worth	2808
Willie-Willie	Lehigh	1281
Jake the Mork	Dry Dock	9756
[illegible] White	Harlem	7209

FEBRUARY 20, 1930

Grand Jury Finds Corruption in United States Narcotic Bureau

GRAND JURORS CALLED TODAY TO STOP FLOW OF NARCOTICS

85 Per Cent of Dope Sold in Country Brought in Through New York, Prosecutor Says

No Suspect to Be Spared in Searching Investigation, Federal Attorney Pledges

The narcotic traffic in all its ramifications and those connected with it will be subjected to an extensive investigation by the Federal Grand Jury, commencing today.

United States Attorney Tuttle, in announcing a nation-wide investigation of the traffic last night, emphasized its importance by asserting 85 per cent of all narcotics smuggled into the United States come through the Port of New York. Among witnesses called will be students of the dope traffic and representatives of welfare organizations.

Tuttle promised the inquiry w[ill] be no respector of persons wh[ere] there is suspicion of guilt. He said:

"Beginning with today our Federal Grand Jury at is morning session will make a thorough investigation of the traffic in narcotic drugs, not onl; with a view to further indictments, but also with a view to making a searching study of the traffic itself and reaching constructive results and recommendations.

NATION-WIDE PROBE.

"The inquiry will seek to get at the bottom of the whole subject, no matter where the trail may lead or who may be affected. It will seek to ascertain the extent and the sources of the extensive smuggling of narcotic drugs into this country and to fix the responsibility therefor.

"It will seek to ascertain the methods and channels of distribution within the country, and it will investigate with determination all suggestions of corruption and collusion in the

"God Have Mercy On Us!"

U. S. NARCOTIC CHIEF'S SON IN ROTHSTEIN QUIZ

Rolland Nutt Also Said to Have Been Gambler's Lawyer; Called Again in Dope Probe

The inevitable shadow of Arnold Rothstein flitted yesterday across the Federal Grand Jury's investigation of the traffic in narcotics.

When Rolland Nutt walked into the Grand Jury room as a witness, there were whispered reminders in the corridor that he once had served as an attorney for Rothstein.

ORDERED BACK TODAY.

Nutt, a Washingtonian, is the son of Colonel L. G. Nutt, chief of the Federal narcotic agents of the United States. Whatever the nature of his testimony, the son's contribution to the investigation was of sufficient import to induce the Grand Jury to order his return today.

Federal Attorney Tuttle would not say last night whether it had been brought out before the jury that Nutt had served as Rothstein's lawyer. That matter, Tuttle said, was something he had not yet determined.

There were two other witnesses at yesterday's session, which began what Tuttle promised to be an exhaustive inquiry into the narcotic traffic.

One of the other two witnesses was Gottlieb Haneke. He is an accountant associated with L. P. Mattingly, son-in-law of Colonel Nutt. The name of the third witness was not revealed, but he was described as of more than ordinary importance.

SIFT BIG N. Y. RINGS.

Though there is no limitation on the scope of the investigation, its major concern at the moment is with three articular drug rings operating in Manhattan and the Bronx on a stupendous scale.

Rothstein's possible connection with these groups as their financier is being inquired into on the basis of documents found among his records after he was murdered.

When some of his dope agents were arrested in Washington a few years ago Rothstein furnished their bail.

Tuttle plan: to place on the stand at an early date, possibly today, Miss Marion Scott, former night club hostess, arrested last week on a narcotic charge.

JANUARY 22, 1930

U. S. Jury Finds Corruption in Narcotic Bureau

Rothstein Loan to Nutt's Kin Charged.

AGENT SCORED

Need of Complete Reorganization Found.

Enforcement of narcotic laws was placed under fire yesterday. Here are the developments:

1.—New York Federal Grand Jury charges that evidence exists of corruption, incompetence and wilful neglect of duty in the Federal Bureau of Narcotics, particularly the New York office.

2.—Jury charges that L. P. Mattingly, son-in-law of Col. L. G. Nutt, deputy narcotics chief, borrowed $6,200 from Arnold Rothstein.

3.—Col. Nutt, in Washington, denies the charges and declares the bureau's record "can't be matched elsewhere."

4.—James M. Doran, prohibition commissioner, announces prompt consideration will be given Grand Jury's charges.

Senational charges that there exists evidence indicating corruption, incompetence and wilful neglect of duty in the Federal Bureau of Naicotics, particularly in its New York office, were filed yesterday with Federal Judge Bryant.

The charges were embodied in a presentment by the Federal Grand Jury for January.

It is an eleven-page document that in its milder paragraphs is a scathing criticism of the men enforcing the narcotic laws and that reaches a peak in charges that:

L. P. Mattingly, son-in-law of Colonel L. G. Nutt, Deputy Commissioner of Prohibition in charge of Narcotics, borrowed $6,200 from Arnold Rothstein and the Rothstein-Simon Company.

RELATIONS "INDISCREET."

Mattingly and Rolland H. Nutt, son of Colonel Nutt, were "indiscreet" in relations with Rothstein.

Witnesses testified the New York bureau, under orders from Colonel Nutt, "padded" reports on its years activities by including 354 police cases, an' the padded reports went to Congress with requests for appropriations.

The "usefulness" of some men in the local bureau is ended and the office should be reorganized "from top to bottom."

There is evidence indicating ccorruption in the New York bureau.

There is evidence at least one of its agents uses dope and others are open to suspicion.

Circumstances indicated collusion when eight New York agents surrounded the persons in a narcotic sale and permitted the "higher up" to escape, arresting only a small abettor.

In consideration of the seriousness of the "padding" charge, the jurors recommended that the testimony of witnesses be sent to Secretary of the Treasury Mellon "in order that the Secretary may take such summary action in the premises as he deems proper."

United States Attorney Tuttle said last night he had forwarded copies of the presentment to the Attorney-General, who, in the usual course of procedure, "can distribute them to th eappropriate offices."

As to minutes of the Grand Jury Tuttle said h: would ask Judge Bryant for permission to transmit copies of ther: to Secretary Mellon, the head of the Customs Service and others.

Tuttle said as soon as possible he would take up the narcotic investigation again before another Grand Jury.

In a preamble the jury called attention to the fact so long as foreign countries continue to manufacture narcotics in excess of medical requirements, "drug addiction in the United States will continue to be a socia lmenace."

The jurors began their investigation of the various phases the first of the year and found a situation they regarded as so serious that they voluntarily devoted three extra weeks to their task. Even though they accomplished much in this added time, they wrote:

"There are still other features of this subject which ought to be investigated."

The alleged padding of reports began last April and continued for several months in the administration of George W. Cunningham. Cunningham, however, is not named in the presentment as head of the local bureau.

ORDER SENT BY PHONE.

The purpose of the padding, it was said, was to add New York City police cases to the files of the Narcotic Bureau. William E. Blanchard, assistant deputy commissioner, and numerous other witnesses described the practice, it was said. The presentment recited:

"This practice had its origin in an order telephoned from the Washington narcotic office to the New York office. We think it significant that, although orders to the New York office customarily were in writing, this particular order was telephoned.

"The said assistant deputy commissioner testified that in telephoning the order he did not approve of it, but was acting on orders from the deputy commissioner, Colonel L. G. Nutt.

"The latter denies he gave any other order than merely to send in a list of the cases made by the Police Department of New York City.

"The fact is, however, that the aforesaid practice continued until the end of the fiscal year, with the knowledge of the Washington office and without protest.

"We feel that this practice was grossly improper. It misrepresented the true facts and created a false record as to the accomplishments of the New York office and its agents and of the narcotic service itself."

After recommending that the testimony be sent to Secretary Mellon, the presentment added:

"We respectfully venture to believe that the aforesaid practice merits severe action against all persons responsible therefor."

In the Mattingly-Nutt phase of the investigation, the presentment described in detail formal business arrangements. Mattingly, in association with one Gottlieb Hanke, has a law and accountancy business.

APPEARED IN TAX CASES.

Rolland Nutt, for fixed monthly payments, represented Mattingly & Co.'s clients before the tax unit of the Treasury Department and before the Federal Board of Tax Appeals.

The Internal Revenue Department levied an income assessment against Arnold Rothstein in January, 1926. Then, according to the presentment, Rothstein, at the instance of Mattingly, executed a power of attorney to Mattingly and Rolland Nutt to represent him. The assessment was compromised in 1927, it was said.

Rolland Nutt never met Rothstein, the jury found, and acted merely as the 'ashington representative of the Mattingly office in the matter. But the presentment continued:

"We find that from time to time and for personal purposes L. P. Mattingly borrowed from Arnold Rothstein and through Rothstein from the Rothstein-Simon Company, Inc., of which Arnold Rothstein was a member, sums aggregating approximately $6,200.

"Colonel L. G. Nutt has testified that he did not know that either his son or his son-in-law had ever represented Arnold Rothstein in any matter until this inquiry began, and that he did not know of the aforesaid assessment proceeding.

"Both Rolland Nutt and Mattingly testified that they had never represented any one in a narcotic case, although, in connection with income tarx matters only, both of them various times represented before the Treasury Department various concerns dealing in narcotic drugs.

"Even though these aforesaid acts may be thought indiscreet, we find no evidence that the enforcement of the narcotic law was effected thereby."

Where it began its discussion of the New York Narcotic Office, the presentment said that the conduct of some agents had been investigated. It continued:

"It finds evidences of gross dereliction and incompetence on the part of some of them—dereliction so pronounce: that certain of the other agents have expressed themselves as feeling that it was actuated by improper motives."

The report described how "a large sale of $500 worth of narcotics" was surrounded by eight agents as it was taking place, but that the principal seller "was allowed to escape and only the small abettor of the sale was actually arrested."

Supply as well as seller was lost when agents also failed to search the seller's quarte.s promptly, it was said. The jurors reached this conclusion:

"The whole circumstance strongly indicates collusion between some of the agents present and the said principal."

Citing other derelictions of duty, the report continued:

"We believe there are not sufficient safeguards as to prosecuting and checking the stocks of seized narcotics. The assistant deputy commissioner himself describes the present method as 'loose.'

"We are of the opinion the usefulness of certain of the men attached to the New York office is at an end and that the situation calls for a complete reorganization from top to bottom."

Admittedly, howeve:, there was not sufficient proof for a bribery indictment.

The jury made several recommendations for more effective control of narcotics. One was that Federal laws be amended to provide a graduated scale of increasing penalties for chronic offenders. A second was that sufficient funds be appropriated to enable agents to apprehend principals in the traffic.

Urging closer co-operation between all Federal departments in policing narcotics, the jury said:

"In the last two days of this investigation we have had much testimony concerning a Customs agent and have heard him testify. We think the evidence is such that, with the permission of the court, a summary of it be placed before his superiors with a view to drastic action."

The jurors expressed "deep appreciation" of the co-operation of Federal Attorney Tuttle and his assistants, John M. Blake and Alvin McK. Sylvester.

It also thanked Representative Stephen G. Porter, author of several proposed ...

U. S. DOPE JURY SEEKING NUTT SON-IN-LAW

Hoover to Order Drastic Narcotic Bureau Shakeup

"Effective March 1, 1930, Colonel Levi G. Nutt, Deputy Commissioner of Prohibition in charge of narcotics, has been transferred from that position to the position of field supervisor in the prohibition bureau, and will serve generally throughout the United States and its territorial possessions.

"Mr. Nutt's headquarters will be in Washington, D. C., but he will make frequent trips to the various field offices of the prohibition service.

COLONEL L. G. NUTT.

President Backs Mellon in Quiz of Service.

NUTT MAY GO

New York Chief Also Believed Hit in Probe.

By KENNETH CLARK.

Copyright, 1930, by Universal Service, Inc.

WASHINGTON, Feb. 22.—A drastic shakeup in the Federal Narcotics Enforcement Service is imminent, Universal Service learned today.

President Hoover and Secretary of Treasury Mellon have decided upon this course as a result of charges in the New York Federal Grand Jury of corruption and inefficiency in narcotics enforcement.

The official axe is to fall on the high officials mentioned in the Grand Jury's presentment. It is likely the first changes will be the removal of Colonel L. G. Nutt, as Deputy Commissioner of Prohibition in charge of narcotics and the replacing of George W. Cunningham as narcotic agent in charge of New York. Other changes will be made in the New York bureau.

TWO "INDISCREET."

The New York Grand Jury, under the direction of Federal Attorney Tuttle, spent weeks investigating the narcotic situation. Its report revealed the connection of Arnold Rothstein, slain Broadway gambler, with the American dope rings.

The Grand Jury went so far as to brand as "indiscreet" the action of Rolland Nutt and L. P. Mattingly, son and son-in-law respectively, of Colonel L. G. Nutt, in handling income tax affairs for Rothstein. It was disclosed that Mattingly had obtained a loan of $6,200 from Rothstein.

Since the return of the presentment, the Treasury Department has conducted a searching investigation. So grave have the charges been regarded that President Hoover has discussed the problem of reorganization with Secretary Mellon.

The details of the proposed shakeup are being worked out and probably will be announced next week.

PORTER TO PUSH BILL.

To effect a more permanent and satisfactory reorganization, Representative Porter of Pennsylvania, who testified before the New York grand jury, will press for prompt action on his bill to create an independent narcotics bureau in the Treasury Department.

This would mean the appointment of a high calibre official as commissioner of narcotics, with sweeping powers to suppress the illicit traffic.

Aroused by the grand jury's disclosures, administration leaders in the House and Senate have assured Porter of their enthusiastic support of the plan. They have expressed in unqualified terms their disapproval of the present set-up, in which the narcotics enforcement service is only a subdivision of the Prohibition Bureau.

In addition to the separation, the bill will provide adequate machinery for scientific surveys by the Public Health Service and non-governmental experts of the needs of the country for narcotic drugs.

HOOVER OUSTS NUTT AS DOPE BUREAU CHIEF

WASHINGTON, Feb. 28.—A wholesale shake-up of the Federal Narcotics Enforcement Service was announced by the Treasury Department today.

Colonel L. G. Nutt was removed as deputy commissioner of prohibition in charge of narcotics enforcement, and transferred as a field supervisor in the Prohibition Bureau.

Harry J. Anslinger, Assistant Commissioner of Prohibition, was appointed temporarily as Federal Narcotics Chief, in place of Col. Nutt.

The thorough housecleaning was exactly as announced exclusively a week ago by Universal Service.

CAUSED BY GRAND JURY

It was decided upon by President Hoover and Secretary Mellon, following the sweeping presentment of the New York Federal Grand Jury which investigated the narcotic activities of the late Arnold Rothstein. The presentment charging corruption and inefficiency in the narcotics division.

The reorganization which includes the transfer of many narcotic field officers, will take effect tomorrow. It marks the first move of a vigorous campaign by the Government to suppress the dope evil.

The new policy will be to concentrate on the gigantic dope rings which are flooding the country with enormous quantities of narcotics.

TO SPEED PORTER BILL.

Anslinger's appointment is only temporary, as the Treasury Department is to support the Porter Bill, to effect a permanent reorganization through creation of an independen Narcotics Bureau. An effort will be made to [illegible] up this bill in Congress.

Prior to becoming ass[illegible] hibition commission[illegible] was director of [illegible] the Prohibitio[illegible]

[illegible] capacity, he has been an [Am]erican delegate to international liquor and narcotics conferences held in London, Antwerp, Ottawa and Paris.

He first entered the Government employ as a consular officer, serv[ing at] The Hague, Hamburg, Germany and La Guayra, Venezuela.

Other changes include:

Transfer of Joseph A. Manning, narcotic agent in charge in Nashville, Tennessee, to New York, succeeding George W. Cunningham, now agent in charge in New York City. Cunningham goes to Nashville, his home city.

ALL MUST GO.

Transfer of the entire force of Federal Narcotic Agents in New York. They will be replaced by agents from various parts of the country.

In announcing Nutt's removal, Seymour Lowman, assistant secretary of the Treasury, declared:

"Col. Nutt has been an active and zealous officer, and the duties he is to assume March 1 are of great importance. It is felt that because of his wide experience he will render great service to law enforcement in his new position."

Anti-Narcotic Crusaders Confer

International Newsreel Photo.

PLAN WAR ON DRUGS!—While House Ways and Means Committee yesterday heard new evidence on illicit traffic in drugs, leaders in the fight against the evil conferred as shown above. Left to right are Harry J. Anslinger, Government operative; Representative Stephen G. Porter, of Pennsylvania, and Representative William I. Sirovich, of New York.

FEBRUARY 3, 1930

PORTER TO PUSH NARCOTIC BILLS

By Universal Service.

WASHINGTON, Feb. 2.—Heartened by the nation-wide indorsements of his new bills striking at the dope evil, Representative Porter, of Pennsylvania, announced today he would press for prompt action in Congress.

Canvass of Congress indicates a widespread demand for the legislation.

One measure is to create a separate narcotics bureau and the other will require all dispensers of habit-forming drugs to have Federal licenses.

Porter has received many letters stressing the necessity for such legislation from high Federal and State officials, leading hospital authorities, physicians, dentists, druggists and enforcement officers.

As it is in line with the Administration's programme transferring prohibition to the Justice Department, Porter is acting first on the independent Narcotics Bureau bill.

Chairman Hawley, of the Ways and Means Committee, announced he would send the bill to the Treasury Department tomorrow for a formal report. Treasury chiefs have intimated they have

Dope Smugglers' Methods Unmasked in Congress!

U. S. Bars Dope Exhibit in Fear Of Hijackers

By Universal Service.

WASHINGTON, March 7.

FEAR of "hi-jackers" caused the Government today to refuse a request of Representative Sirovich (D.) of New York to have $200,000 worth of seized dope sent to the House floor as part of a narcotic exhibit. An official explained:

"We are afraid hi-jackers might seize the stuff while it was being conveyed to the Capitol."

However, Sirovich had present during a speech on narcotics an exhibit of dope paraphernalia that covered several tables. Three armed narcotic agents were sent along to guard it.

NEW CONGRESS BILL PROVIDES NARCOTIC CZAR

All Legal Dealers in Drugs to Be Licensed; $5,000 Fine or Two Years for Violator

REP. PRALL REP. O'CONNELL REP. SIROVICH

International Newsreel Photo.

HOUSE HEARS LECTURE!—Backed by hundreds of exhibits, Representative William I. Sirovich, of New York, tells, on the floor of the lower House of Congress, how dope smugglers ply their trade. He is shown holding a Bible that was a drug cache. Representative David J. O'Connell, of New York, is at the Speaker's stand (top, center), and Representative Anning S. Prall, also of New York, is shown leaning on the clerk's desk.

JANUARY 24, 1930

MARCH 8, 1930

Sivorich Blames Spread Of Dope Evil on Dry Law

WASHINGTON, March 7.—Prohibition has been in a considerable measure responsible for the increase in drug addiction throughout the United States, Representative Sirovich (D.), of New York, informed the House today. He said:

"Of all substitutes for strong drink, none so quickly and so thoroughly destroys the body, stupefies the mind and stultifies the moral nature as opium and its derivatives."

BLAMES BRITAIN.

Sirovich laid at the door of the British empire the chief blame for saturating the world with dope. He pointed out that dope, produced abroad in quantities 500 times in excess of medical needs was flooding the United States and debauching 1,000,000 American addicts.

To illustrate how the fabulously profitable traffic is conducted Sirovich had arrayed on tables in front of the Speaker's desk a unique display of opium pipes, hypodermic needles and various ingenious containers and devices used to peddle and smuggle drugs. He exhibited a Bible in which great quantities of dope had been concealed between the pages to avoid detection.

MANY FEAR ALCOHOL.

In reply to a question by Representative Schafer, (R), of Wisconsin, he declared that with the advent of the Eighteenth Amendment innumerable persons who used alcohol as a stimulant turned to the more dangerous habit of drugs. A physician himself, Sirovich declared:

"Many of these persons are so afraid of industrial alcohol with all its poisons that they take drugs."

Schafer suggested the Eighteenth Amendment should be repealed and the money and agents devoted to its enforcement turned over to the narcotics force, as "dope is the real evil in this country."

Sirovich agreed that prohibition is unenforceable and that narcotics should be granted additional appropriations.

Sirovich said:

"While we are sinking battleships, we should sink the drug factories which are making the world unsafe for humanity.

TONS SMUGGLED IN.

"Three tons of opium and its derivatives are necessary to look after the medical and scientific requirements of the world. Still, almost 200 tons were smuggled into the United States during the last year, 85 per cent of which came through the harbor of New York.

"Immediately after prohibition went into effect 850,000 pounds of crude opium, enough to produce thirty-five tons of morphine, were imported into the United States. One ton is enough to supply the medical needs of North and South America."

MENACE TO WORLD.

Sirovich described how England had forced two wars upon China "to force upon a helpless people a traffic lucrative to Great Britain," and added:

"As we study the statistics of the countries of the Far East and realize that the use of habit-forming drugs is constantly increasing—in most

HOUSE LEADERS FAVOR SINGLE DRUG DIVISION

La Guardia Repeats Call for Congress Probe on Control; Porter to Introduce His Bill

By KENNETH CLARK

WASHINGTON, April 16.—The Porter Bill, to re-organize and consolidate Federal narcotic enforcement agencies under a separate bureau, was endorsed by leaders of the Seventy-first Congress today.

Representative Porter, Republican, of Pennsylvania plans to introduce the measure later in the week.

HOUSE ACTION FAILED

At the last session, the Senate unanimously adopted the resolution, but the House failed to act. A fund of $50,000 would be authorized for the work. The committee would report its recommendations to Congress next December. LaGuardia said:

"Before any comprehensive narcotic legislation can be passed, it is necessary for Congress to dissect the drug problem, to determine the extent of dope addiction, to expose the flagrant abuses arising under present laws, and, through a scientific survey, to find what remedies must be applied.

"I favor an independent Federal Narcotics Bureau, under aggressive leadership, and I think Congress should go into this subject thoroughly, in order that no mistake will be made in passing legislation."

Under the programme fostered by President Hoover, prohibition enforcement would be transferred from the Treasury to the Justice

AVOID COMPLICATIONS

"Enforcement of the Narcotics and Prohibition laws should be separated. The Harrison Anti-Drug Law is an internal revenue measure. Therefore, to avoid any complications, the Narcotics Bureau should remain under the Treasury. As an independent agency the Narcotics Bureau would be able to make a real drive against the dope traffic."

Representative Slack, Democrat, of New York also supported this view. He said:

"The records show that the Government has spent between $250,000,000 and $300,000,000 to enforce prohibition. During the same period we have spent but $8,000,000 for narcotics enforcement.

"Crime caused by drug addicts is estimated at $1,000,000,000 yearly. Yet, in fighting the horrible menace of dope, we have expended a sum thirty-seven and one-half times less than poured into the effort to enforce prohibition. Narcotics enforcement must

APRIL 17, 1929

Opium Traffic Called Menace to World.

LAWS THAT ARE NEEDED!

IF the Porter bills are passed and signed, a great step to absolute control of the narcotic menace in the United States will be achieved.

Under these proposed laws, which the Ways and Means Committee of the House of Representatives are now weighing, a Narcotic Bureau will be established, and all dispensers of narcotic drugs must be licensed. But dispensers will be licensed only after a thorough scrutiny of their qualifications and personal integrity.

Apothecaries, doctors, dentists—all must come under the provisions of this licensing act. They will dispense narcotic drugs with as great a sense of responsibility as a judge administering law. They will be registered as **SERVANTS OF THE PEOPLE**, and as such will be directly accountable to the Government, represented by the Narcotic Bureau.

The Porter bills embody the principles for which the Hearst newspapers have been striving for years, both through legislation and education.

Against the justness of these laws there can be no argument. To abolish illicit peddling the Government must begin by permitting the sale of opiates only through channels that it can rigorously control. All that flows through other channels will be **CONTRABAND**.

SEPARATE DOPE BUREAU BACKED BY FEDERAL BAR

Association Votes Support to Porter Bill, Now Before Senate; Passes Jury Reform

The Federal Bar Association, comprising lawyers practicing in the Federal courts, went unanimously on record last night as supporting creation of a separate Government narcotic bureau.

The association passed a resolution, sponsored by Federal Attorney Tuttle backing the bill of Representative Porter, which would create the bureau. The bill, which passed the House, is before the Senate Finance Committee.

Urging passage of his resolution, Tuttle asserted New York City was the centre of the country's traffic in habit-forming drugs. He added:

"Certainly the drug laws should be enforced as well as the prohibition laws. To do that, we must have a separate bureau."

U. S. Lax in Dope War; Porter Declares

By Universal Service.

WASHINGTON, March 7.—Representative Porter (R.) of Pennsylvania appeared before the House Ways and Means Committee today to plead for passage of the Porter bill, creating an independent Federal Narcotics Bureau as a means of curbing the illicit dope traffic.

The bill has the indorsement of the Treasury Department and of authorities on the dope evil throughout the nation.

Although the dope traffic has enslaved between 400,000 and 450,000 American citizens and has levied a toll of between $1,000,000,000 and $2,000,000,000 on the country, narcotic enforcement, Porter told the committee, "has been treated by the Government as a minor, instead of a major, matter—as a stepchild of prohibition."

As an example, he said, "we spend twenty to twentyfive times as much to enforce prohibition as to enforce the narcotic laws."

The new bill, eliminating the present cumbersome and impractical methods, Porter said, will provide an aggressive, concentrated administration that will arm the Government to war on "the hideous evil that destroys all whom it touches." Such a consolidation has long been needed, he added.

Aside from domestic improvements, the measure, he stated, will enable the United States to obtain the necessary co-operation from foreign nations to strike the evil at its source.

Oscar R. Ewing, of New York, attorney for the three opium manufacturers in the United States, echoed Porter's views, saying:

"The bill will make certain important administrative improvements over existing law. There is a distinct advantage in consolidating the work under a separate bureau. We want to support the bill."

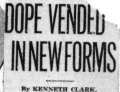

CRUSADER!—Representative Stephen G. Porter, of Pennsylvania, yesterday carried fight for his anti-narcotic measures to House Ways and Means Committee.

CONGRESS WILL RUSH DOPE BILL

By KENNETH CLARK,
Universal Service Staff Correspondent.

WASHINGTON, March 9.—Belief that the bill creating an independent Narcotics Bureau will be expedited through Congress, to effect an early strengthening and reorganization of the Federal narcotics system, was expressed today by Representative Porter (R.) of Pennsylvania.

Hearings were concluded yesterday before the House Ways and Means Committee. An executive session is to be held shortly to draft a report.

As no witnesses appeared to oppose the legislation, Porter is hopeful of a favorable report.

Porter's next attack on the dope traffic will be through the companion bill he has introduced to require all drug dispencers to have Federal licenses. The purpose is to remove addicts and convicts from the ranks of persons entitled to prescribe or sell narcotics.

The President's National Law Enforcement Commission next ...he first ...traffic. ...f Rep- ...York ...a New ...y Cap-

U. S. REDUCES DOPE IMPORTS

By KENNETH CLARK.
Universal Service Staff Correspondent.

WASHINGTON, Jan. 14—The Federal Government took steps today to dam the flood of dope inundating the country.

In line with recommendations of the Hearst newspapers, the Federal Narcotics Control Board, announced a material reduction in the amounts of opium and coca leaves which may be imported legally this year to be manufactured into narcotic drugs for medical purposes.

A comprehensive survey by the Hearst newspapers showed that the imports in the past have been in excess of the actual medical requirements. The board, which has been deliberating for three months, fully supported this finding.

During 1930, American drug manufacturers can import only 128,000 pounds of opium and 201,000 pounds of coca leaves.

The imports during the 1929 fiscal year were 144,925½ pounds of opium, and 242,834 pounds of coca leaves, giving the United States a higher per capita consumption of medical drugs than reported by any other of the big powers.

FLAYS BRITAIN

"The fact seems to be that the British Government is responsible for the large quantity of opium flooding the world today. The cultivation of the poppy is fostered by the government; manufactured into drugs in the government factory and into morphine by British firms in London and Edinburg; and sent out into the world through trade channels—illegal and otherwise.

OPIUM MONOPOLY.

"Great Britain has established an opium monopoly, which encourages poppy growing, even to the extent of lending money without interest to thosoe who are willing to cultivate the plant.

"The time for commercializing the life-blood and flesh of human beings should be relegated to the age of barbarism. The time has come when the United States should call a halt in the name of humanity to any nationss of the world who exploit the weaknesses of human beings through drug addiction.

"We must tell them to destroy at least three-fourths of all the pharmaceutical drug houses operated throughout seven nations and only allow to remain half a dozen of these institutions owned, operated and controlled internationally, and see that only that amount of opium and its derivatives are manufactured that are necessary to care for the medical and scientific needs of the world.

"Let our country, that has always stood for idealism and for progress, continue to battle against drug capitalists, who have made the world unsafe for humanity."

Sirovich estimated there are ...0,000 to 100,000 drug addicts in ...ew York City alone.

U. S. Druggists Ask Senate To Approve Porter Dope Bill

DOPE VENDED IN NEW FORMS

By KENNETH CLARK.

WASHINGTON, Feb. 21.—Narcotic peddlers are turning to new forms of dope to whet the cravings of thousands of addicts all over the nation. Marijuana is one. It is known as the "killer drug," and some of the most atrocious crimes in recent American history have been traced to its addicts. It is a form of hemp, first brought into this country from Mexico.

Marijuana, according to reports, is sold in California as a cigarette for 25 cents each. In Chicago these cigarettes are three for a dollar.

There is no Federal law to control marijuana cigarettes.

There are yet other narcotics on the peddlers' lists. "Skid chains" they are called in the underworld. These are derivatives of morphine.

WORLD DRIVE TO 'SMASH DOPE TRAFFIC'

CO-OPERATION OF CONGRESS, STATES URGED

NOVEMBER 22, 1928

Narcotics Delegates Demand Uniform Laws Based On New York's Strict Statute

CONCERTED action on the part of Congress, the forty-eight States and the larger cities of the United States in smashing the narcotic traffic is expected to result from efforts of the World Conference on Narcotic Education and the International Narcotic Education Association.

Delegates are assembled for the second annual conference at the Waldorf-Astoria.

More than 150 delegates from all parts of the world were present when the initial session was opened by Captain Richmond P. Hobson, Spanish War hero. The primary object of the two organizations, Captain Hobson explained, is the standardization and codification of Federal, State and municipal laws governing narcotic transportation and the treatment of addicts. The sessions will continue until Saturday.

Drive Launched

A determined drive will be undertaken, it was announced, to stiffen the State and municipal statutes regulating the traffic.

Hobson told the conference that 50,000 girls disappear "down the drug road" every year. Drug addiction today, he said, is the most serious of all public problems, and he pointed out there are five times as many convictions under the narcotic laws in a year as there are for prohibition offenses.

A new model anti-narcotic measure, patterned somewhat after the New York State law, will be introduced in each State Legislature which meets during the present Winter. Captain Hobson said:

"The measure makes the trafficking in narcotics a felony instead of merely a misdemeanor. Another provision of the law would penalize with life imprisonment any drug peddler who induces a minor to become an addict.

"In addition to fortifying and unifying the anti-narcotic statutes, we want to remodel the Federal law so that every alien convicted of drug selling can be automatically deported at the completion of his prison term.

Much to Be Done

"There is also much to be done in the way of bringing about a revision of school text books on the subject of narcotics. We think an educational campaign will be one of the most effective weapons, and we want to begin educating children on the evils of drugs as soon as they can read.

"After some pioneering work has been accomplished in America, it is our intention to arouse the world powers to its seriousness. There are in existence several treaties which specifically limit the amount of narcotics which may be manufactured, but little or no attention is being paid to them."

The new measure will embody some of the good features of the laws now in existence in New York and California. The hospitalization features have been taken from the California statute.

3 BILLS STRIKE AT DOPE EVIL

By WILLIAM E. LAWBY.

ALBANY, Jan. 15.—Swift mobilization of public sentiment behind a programme of anti-narcotic drug bills which he today introduced in the State Legislature is the purpose of Senator William Lathrop Love, Kings Democrat.

The measures, three in number, are sponsored by the world conference on narcotic education, which comprises notables in public life and of bar and church. They represent the conference's proposal for tightening up the laws designed to curb the evil of drug addiction. The bills were prepared by Senator Love, a physician, in co-operation with the narcotic conference recently held in New York.

The public health law is amended by the first bill to clarify the definition of drug addiction. It is made unlawful for any drug addict under any circumstances to possess narcotic drugs except under prescription of a physician for the treatment of the habit. This is designed to overcome the inevitable desire on the part of the addict to cause others to become addicted. Imprisonment until their addiction is cured, is the penalty.

While for a first violation of the foregoing prohibition, the crime shall be regarded as a misdemeanor, subsequent violations, under the Love bills, are made felonies. This provision, if enacted into law, would bring chronic offenders within the application of the Baumes habitual criminal or fourth offender law, making them liable to life imprisonment.

The second bill of the group proposes to give triple damages to anyone who is injured by reason of the illegal furnishing or administering of narcotics.

The third bill would make it an offense of assault, second degree, unlawfully to administer or cause to be administered narcotics in any form.

Man Held as Slayer Victim of Assassin

U.S. BAR SEEKS ANTI-DOPE LAW FOR ALL STATES

OCTOBER 3, 1929

But Officials Find Three Big Faults in Uniform Measure Aimed to Check Great Evil

By KENNETH CLARK.

WASHINGTON, Oct. 2.—Aroused by the growing narcotic evil, the American Bar Association, at its forthcoming annual meeting in Memphis, may approve a uniform State narcotic act and recommend its adoption by all the States.

The idea back of the project, which is supported by the American Medical Association is to protect the legitimate dealers in drug and plug up the leaks whereby dope has escaped into unscrupulous hands.

While the draft of the proposed model act follows generally the lines of the Federal narcotic laws, officials who examined it today said it revealed some serious defects and weaknesses.

MUST HIT BAD DOCTORS.

In the first place, they pointed out, there is no provision for the automatic revocation of the State Medical License of a physican who is a drug addict, or has been convicted of a narcotic offense.

They hold narcotic enforcement can never be successful until physician-addicts are driven out of the medical profession.

Second, there is no provision for the segregation of narcotic addicts or for their rehabilitation.

Third, there is no ample safeguard to restrict diversion of drugs from legal channels into the hands of dope peddlers. No adequate check is placed on prescription of drugs.

ALREADY IN U. S. LAW.

All these purposes omitted in the State act either are incorporated now in Federal Legislation, or will be offered through the Porter Narcotics reorganization bill. Congress has authorized two narcotic farms and Representative Porter is proposing to withhold registration from physician-addicts.

Federal officials feel, therefore, that any model law for the States at least should go as far as Federal legislation in attacking the dope traffic.

If the draft circulated by the committee will do this, it will receive the blessing of those governmental experts who are combating the drug menace; otherwise, they think the proposed act can accomplish little or nothing more

HOOVER BACKS U.S. IN DOPE WAR

By Universal Service.

WASHINGTON, Jan. 21.—President Hoover today sent a message to Congress recommending $35,000 be appropriated for American participation in the International Conference on Limitation of the manufacture of narcotic drugs, to be held at Geneva, Switzerland, May 27.

The President transmitted a statement by Secretary of State Stimson, declaring the United States always has taken the lead in seeking international co-operation to stamp out the illicit narcotic drug traffic and urging the appropriation. Stimson said:

"It has been the aim of this government to bring about international co-operation in dealing with this problem, and to persuade other governments to limit the amount of narcotic drugs manufactured to the amounts essential for medical and scientific purposes."

The United States has been successful in establishing arrangements with nineteen countries for exchange of information on the movement of illicit drugs, with a view to co-operation in their suppression, Stimson said.

As an example of the magnitude of the problem, he cited the seizure of 17,500 ounces of morphine from the steamship Alesia in New York on December 15.

UNIFORM STATE LAW URGED TO FIGHT DOPE EVIL

Harrison Anti-Narcotic Act Inadequate Alone, Anslinger Tells National Conference

1931.

ATLANTIC CITY, Sept. 9.—Only through adequate State enforcement can progress be made in combating the drug traffic in this country, Harry J. Anslinger, Federal Commissioner of Narcotics, declared here today at the annual meeting of the National Conference of Commissioners.

Urging the commissioners to draft a uniform State law on narcotics, Anslinger asserted that, while a few of the State measures now in effect were adequate for the purpose, the majority were in such a "chaotic condition as to render them ineffective if not useless."

Quoting figures to show that drug addicts of the world pay three billion dollars annually for "dope," the Federal Commissioner said a campaign to wipe out the traffic was not only humanitarian in its purpose, but would result in a universal economic improvement.

The Harrison anti-narcotic act, the Federal measure for coping with the illegal sale of drugs, Anslinger said was effective only as a national measure, and in dealing with the importation and smuggling of dope. He added:

"The Harrison act is one of the best of our Federal statutes. It was not meant, however, to control the drug traffic in the States. The government cannot invade State rights."

STATE DEFENSE BODIES TO FIGHT DOPE PLANNED

NOVEMBER 26, 1931

NEW NARCOTIC LAW STRIKES AT DOPE QUACKS

OCTOBER 6, 1932

Model Code Would Revoke Licenses of Doctors, Dentists, Druggists for Illegal Sales

By Universal Service.

WASHINGTON, Oct. 5.—A smashing blow was struck today against unscrupulous medical practitioners who illegally dispense narcotic drugs.

Without discussion, the national conference of commissioners on uniform State laws approved a provision in the proposed uniform State narctotic code authorizing State courts to revoke licenses of physicians, dentists, druggists and others who have been convicted of narcotic offenses.

HEART OF MODEL LAW.

This provision was the heart of the model law which has been drafted for adoption by the States.

Only recently Federal authorities asked State medical boards to revoke licenses of nearly 700 physicians who were either addicts themselves or had been convicted on narcotic charges. The request was virtually ignored.

A protective provision was inserted in the model law to permit restoration of licenses after hearings if "good cause" can be established.

N. Y. MAY ACT FIRST ON MODEL NARCOTIC LAW

OCTOBER 11, 1932

Assemblyman Dickey Announces He Will Offer Legislation at Next Session

By KENNETH CLARK,
Universal Service Correspondent.

WASHINGTON, Oct. 10.—New York State took the lead today in the nationwide drive for enactment of a uniform state narcotic law to smash the dope evil.

Assemblyman Howard W. Dickey, of Buffalo, announced he would introduce in the New York legislature the model narcotic code approved here last week by the National Conference of Commissioners on Uniform State Laws.

BAR APPROVES UNIFORM STATE NARCOTICS ACT

OCTOBER 13, 1932

Measure Placed Automatically Before Legislatures; Machine Gun Code Also Passed

UNIFORM STATE NARCOTIC ACT WINS APPROVAL

OCTOBER 21, 1932

State Legislatures Will Be Asked to Adopt Model Code In Move to Check Dope Evil

By KENNETH CLARK,
Universal Service Correspondent.

WASHINGTON, Oct. 20. — Nationwide approval of the uniform State Narcotic Drug Act was reported today by Harry J. Anslinger, Federal Narcotics Commissioner.

State legislatures meeting this Winter will be asked to adopt the model code as a major offensive against the dope evil. Drafted by the national conference of commissioners on uniform State laws, the code received the enthusiastic indorsement of the American Bar Association.

ADOPTION URGED.

Representatives of the American Medical Association and of other leading professional and industrial groups have urged its adoption by all the States.

Dr. Carleton Simon, noted physician and ex-health commissioner of New York, wrote that a uniform State act is "a subject I have always advocated."

Marihuana, prevalent in the Southwest and West, is reported by police to be widely employed by gangsters and criminals to fortify them to commit atrocious crimes. The model code would outlaw it everywhere.

In a recent article in the Hearst Sunday newspapers Harry J. Anslinger, the United States Commissioner of Narcotics, issued new warning that the fight against "dope" has not been won—it has merely shi[...]

With all our borders u[...] Anslinger pointed out, the Pac[...] danger area from this "nefariou[...]

Referring to the "twilight z[...] eral jurisdiction in which man[...] refuge, the Commissioner said:

"The Federal Government [...] pierce this zone by persuadi[...] uniform narcotic law.

"The Legislatures of four [...] Jersey, Nevada and Florida—h[...] law...but the plan is meeting [...] ance in other States."

Public opinion—the public opi[...] must break down that resistance.

The Uniform State Narcotic La[...] books of EVERY State.

VOTE FOR

HARRY E. WALSH

FOR GOVERNOR

Not a Politician. Just a Plain Traveling Man Who Has Made Good

ADDRESS
2318 W. 13TH ST.

LITTLE ROCK, ARK.

(OVER)

[...] humanitaria[...] [...]arcotic addicts, he asserted, pa[...] [...] THREE BILLION DOLLARS annually for "dope." To wipe out this enormous and nefarious traffic would resul[...] in "a universal economic improvement."

As the [...] showed further, the Harrison Act, [...]ctive NATIONALLY only. Under [...]s, there is a twilight zone which the [...]t invade. Police duty in this zone [...]RATE STATES—and without uni[...] such action remains uncertain. [...]good narcotic laws. The suggested [...]n until ALL States have such laws.

Governors Should Urge Legislatures to Pass Uniform Narcotic Law

NOVEMBER 20, 1932

Federal Machinery Limited in Combatting Drug Traffic, Declares Anslinger

Need for a uniform State narcotic law which is being urged for passage by the various States to supplement the Harrison Act in combatting the drug evil throughout the nation is discussed in the accompanying article by Commissioner Anslinger.

By H. J. ANSLINGER,

U. S. Commissioner of Narcotics.

STATES which first legislated against the use of narcotic drugs prior to the enactment of any Federal statute were impelled to do so to secure their citizens against injury to their health, morals and general welfare. The earlier laws were designed to eradicate the evils of opium-smoking and the maintenance of opium dens.

Later, some of the States enacted laws covering other narcotic drugs and providing various penalties for their violation; but so little knowledge of the traffic was possessed by the drafters of the various acts that a comparison reveals such a varied expression of ideas on a single subject as to create a situation which may only be classed as absurd.

Nevertheless, up to 1914 when the Harrison Act became effective, there was a real effort, on the part of States which had enacted such legislation, however ill-advised, to enforce the provisions of their laws to the fullest extent.

The primary purpose of the Harrison Act, of course, was to create and protect revenues for the United States. It has been so construed by the U. S. Supreme Court, with the added statement that the law has a moral purpose also.

Responsibility
Investigating Left to State Authorities.

It was contemplated that the authorities of the various States would accept and discharge the responsibility of investigating, detecting and preventing or punishing the local retail illicit traffic conducted by the ordinary peddler and the institutional care and treatment of drug addicts within their jurisdictions.

This however, did not [illegible] to be the case. Notwithstanding the limited power of the Federal Government, State officers immediately became imbued with the erroneous impression that the problem of preventing the abuse of narcotic drugs was one now exclusively cognizable by the national Government, and that the Federal law alone, enforced by Federal agencies only, should represent all the control necessary over the illicit narcotic drug traffic.

In very few States was any attempt made to accept a just part of the burden of enacting and enforcing laws to control the traffic.

This attitude on the part of the States has resulted in an anomalous situation. The public prints from day to day bring news of a number of banks that have been robbed by an organized gang; details of kidnapings and of gambling rackets; and articles concerning the operations of a lone bandit who has held up a number of stores and citizens.

What is the result? Editorials criticize the police and clamorous demands are made calling upon them to apprehend these menaces to the community well-being. The police, ever active, are stirred to greater activity. The man-hunt is on. The offenders who have unlawfully taken the property of fellow citizens must be caught, prosecuted and punished.

No one suggests that this is anything but a State problem. The person who would suggest that the Federal authorities be called upon to catch this hold-up man would be ridiculed. Yet in this same community the insidious, despicable drug peddler, carrying on his nefarious work of unlawfully taking away not only the property, but the peace of mind, the morals, the health of the citizens, and undermining the general welfare of the community—what of him? Ah, that is different.

Despite the fact that the sole right to punish such criminals, under certain circumstances, lies only within the police power of the State, and that the founders of our country never contemplated that such activities should be dealt with by the national Government, enforcement officers as well as legislators in a number of the States have decided that "Uncle Sam" is the proper person to cope with this particular menace to the community.

Illogical
Passage of Adequate Laws Prevented.

This illogical attitude has not only prevented the passage of adequate laws which would be of inestimable benefit to the State's own citizens, but has resulted, in a number of the States, in an almost complete failure to enforce the laws already on their statute books, even in those aspects of the crime with which only the State itself may deal.

The dockets of the Federal courts have become flooded with cases of a minor character which should have been handled in the State courts, but which were not thus handled either from lack of adequate laws or for reasons put forth solely because the duties and responsibilities appear burdensome, expensive or distasteful, resulting in a slowing up of the prompt and orderly process of justice in major cases.

Some of the reasons advanced by many State and municipal prosecutors for their reluctance or open refusal to prosecute such cases may be catalogued as follows:

FIRST—That sentences imposed in Federal courts are more severe than those imposed in State courts.

The sentences referred to are those given major violators. It is obvious that it does not lie within the power of State and municipal courts, where the State law has made the offense a misdemeanor, to impose sentences equal to those which are imposed in Federal courts in cases of greater magnitude and where the offense is a felony.

SECOND—That it is difficult to find a jury which will convict, because in the smaller communities the menace of narcotic drugs is not understood.

This argument is plainly fallacious. The general public is fully aware of the menace of such drugs, and in the smaller communities it is usually found that the violation of such a law is regarded as a graver criminal offense than in the urban districts.

Women's Status
State Claims No Jail for Such Prisoners.

THIRD—That the accused is a woman and the State has no suitable institution in which to care for such prisoners.

This is but an added argument for the enactment of State legislation for the treatment and care of all addicts, men and women, and the excuse flows only from the desire to place the burden of the necessary financial outlay upon the shoulders of the Federal Government.

FOURTH. That voluntary applicants for treatment strenuously object to incarceration in a State prison.

This is but an added reason for the enactment of legislation by the States for the purposes set forth above.

FIFTH. In the State of Texas, because of an attack on the validity of the State law, upon which no decision has been handed down, the police department throughout the State has disbanded the narcotic squads, leaving to the Federal Government the burden of taking all cases into the Federal courts.

Examples of what became necessary in two Texas cases are cited. Carrie B., an addict, was arrested and found to be in possession of one grain of heroin. Because of the necessity of placing a Federal charge, this woman was arraigned for the purchase and possession of this one grain of heroin. Thus it has become necessary, because of the failure of State enforcement to invoke the majesty of the law of the nation to decide what disposition shall be made of the case of this poor unfortunate.

Action Delayed
Left to Ponderous Machinery of U. S.

In the case of "Black ——," two narcotic agents and two city detectives arrested this man for the sale of two grains of morphine. Here again the ponderous machinery of the Federal courts must be resorted to, taking up the time of two Federal officers, less than 250 of whom are assigned to guard the welfare of 122,000,000 people.

The proposition cannot be too forcefully expressed that the States, having supreme police power within their own boundaries to enact and enforce all laws necessary to the peace, health, morals and general welfare of their citizens, are not hampered by the narrow limitations that restrict the Federal Government in its fight to control the illicit narcotic traffic.

Need Customers
Sales Only Means for Adding Business.

U. S. DROPS PLAN TO LINK DRY AND DOPE BUREAUS

APRIL 14, 1933

Cummings Says Geneva Treaty Requires Separate Group for Narcotic Enforcement

By WILLIAM H. DOHERTY,
Universal Service Correspondent.

WASHINGTON, April 13.—Narcotics enforcement will be continued as a separate governmental function, the Administration decided today after a study of the Geneva anti-narcotic treaty, which provides that separate bureaus shall be maintained by the signatory nations to combat the drug evil.

CUMMINGS' VIEW.

Attorney General Cummings said strong arguments had been made against the proposal to transfer the narcotics division to the prohibition bureau, and added:

"One objection is that narcotic drug enforcement activities are not only national but international in scope and character.

"After prolonged effort, an international treaty has been developed which provides each nation shall have a separate department to fight against the improper use of narcotics. To make such bureaus subordinate to prohibition would be violative of either the terms or the spirit of the treaty.

"PROBLEM IN ITSELF."

"Also, many think that narcotics should be treated separately and distinctly as a problem in itself. These objections are important and are entitled to very thoughtful consideration."

Cummings also said that the economies that might be effected in the proposed narcotics transfer would be very small. He added he favored consolidation of the prohibition and industrial alcohol bureaus, and said an executive order to this effect probably will be issued soon.

LEGITIMATE USE OF DOPE IN U. S. DROPS 25 P. C.

JULY 14, 1933

Attributed to Drive Against Diversion Into Illicit Channels and Finding of Substitutes

By KENNETH CLARK,
Universal Service Correspondent.

WASHINGTON, July 13.—America's legitimate consumption of narcotic drugs has dropped to the lowest point in history, it was revealed today by Harry J. Anslinger, commissioner of narcotics.

Anslinger shortly will issue orders permitting the importation of only 100,000 pounds of opium into the United States next year to manufacture into drugs for medical and scientific needs.

This is a decrease of approximately 25 per cent from the average of the last few years.

2 CHIEF REASONS.

Two principal reasons are responsible. First, the Federal Government is waging a relentless campaign to drive from the medical profession unscrupulous practitioners who have been diverting drugs to illicit channels. Secondly, scientists in research laboratories are developing synthetic drugs as a substitute for habit-forming narcotics.

Gangsters, racketeers and peddlers are finding it more difficult to obtain supplies.

With ratification of the Geneva anti-narcotic treaty, European factories are no longer able to supply almost unlimited amounts to American traffickers.

Japan and the Far East are now the principal sources of illicit dope. It is seeping into the United States on trans-Pacific steamers.

Peddlers are "cutting" dope they sell. Analysis of 100 samples of heroin recently seized in widely separated cities showed the stuff contained but 12 per cent pure drug.

Another step in the Government's campaign against the dope evil will be taken July 29, when the cornerstone is laid for the Central Buildings at the new narcotic farm at Lexington, Ky. Another farm is to be located at Fort Worth, Tex.

APRIL 11, 1933

THE NEW JERSEY NARCOTIC BILL

BEFORE its recent recess the State Senate of New Jersey passed the Uniform State Narcotic Law recommended to all the States by the Federal Narcotic Bureau and the Commissioners on Uniform State Laws.

With the Legislature again in session it is to be hoped that the Jersey Assembly will speedily complete this highly important legislation.

The Senate bill, as introduced by Senator Young and sponsored wholeheartedly by Senator Richards, the Republican leader, was given most careful consideration in the Senate Committee on Public Health. All the questions raised by the medical, dental and veterinary professions and by the pharmaceutical industry were fully met. Senator Leap, the committee chairman, commended the bill to his confreres as

JUNE 6, 1933

NARCOTIC BILL SIGNED—The Uniform Narcotic act, long advocated by the Hearst newspapers, was signed yesterday by Governor Harry Moore at Trenton, N. J., in the presence of a group that had campaigned for it.

1934

U. S. DOPE RAIDS SPUR DRIVE FOR DRASTIC LAWS

By WALTER FITZMAURICE,
Universal Service Correspondent.

WASHINGTON, Dec. 9.—Government's ruthless war against the dope traffic has won its greatest victory on a nationwide front.

Ask Drastic Laws.

Led by Senator McCarren (D.) of Nevada, Senators Sheppard (D.) of Texas, Clark (D.) of Missouri, Norris (R.) of Nebraska and others joined in calling for drastic legislation.

McCarren proposed the Harrison narcotic act be amended to give the Federal Government authority to revoke licenses of dope-dispensing doctors where State Medical Boards failed to act. This would be under the Federal power to enforce treaties, to which this Government is a party, regulating the traffic in dope.

Final reports tonight from 15 district headquarters throughout the country showed 765 in custody, by far the largest roundup ever achieved in the dope war.

Murderers in Net.

Among peddlers taken were forgers, counterfeiters, bank robbers and murderers, according to Deputy Commissioner Louis Ruppel. Among the dope victims held were 178 women.

Drug-crazed parents were revealed initiating their children as addicts. Peddlers, particularly in Cleveland, O., were exposed as enticing children to use dope. Anslinger said:

"We have dealt the traffic a crippling blow, but the fight is far from won. Our staff has proved itself efficient enough to cope with the dealers. The issue now is up to the courts. Dealers should be sent up for long prison terms and their victims sent to curative institutions."

Ocean divers have been utilized to smuggle Manchukuan dope into this country at Seattle, agents discovered. The dope has been dumped overboard from Japanese ships into Puget Sound, to be picked off the bottom at night after the ship has cleared port.

The scheme was revealed by a Chinese, seized in Seattle with a five tael tin of opium and a diving suit.

VICTORY IN WAR ON DOPE

JULY 31, 1935

'SITUATION IS WELL IN HAND' —DR. MOTT

"Our conference was addressed by the drug experts of the League of Nations. They know their facts. Hitherto it seemed they were stabbing in the dark. Now they can enumerate the countries where the drug traffic is under control.

'LONG FIGHT AHEAD'

"There is a long fight ahead. When the evil is stamped out in one country, it breaks out in another. Turkey was one of the worst spots two years ago. Now it is one of the best controlled. But unfortunately, the evil has broken out in Bulgaria.

"Although the United States is not a member of the League, we can be proud of the part she has played in the struggle. American missionaries have supplied invaluable information."

Dr. Mott said new drugs, 50 times more powerful than opium, are being manufactured in America, Germany and Hungary.

Also arriving on the Aquitania was Justice James Clark McReynolds, of the Supreme Court of the United States, returning from two weeks' rest in England. He said he found England gre[illegible]proved since his last visit [illegible]ars ago.

League Votes Wide Open Dope Parley to Include

GENEVA DEALS OPIUM BLOC HEAVY BLOW

JANUARY 25, 1931

Broadening of May Conference to Cover All Manufacture Follows U. S. Proposals

By KENNETH CLARK,
Universal Service Staff Correspondent.

GENEVA, Jan. 24.—The "opium bloc" of the League of Nations received a terrific blow today when the League Council voted to open wide the scope of the May conference on narcotics to encompass limitation of manufacture of all drugs.

The council's action, taken at the demand of Quinones de Leon, Spanish member of the body, was the step urged by the United States through John K. Caldwell, Washington's observer at the meetings of the Opium Advisory Committee.

U. S. DISSATISFIED.

The United States was dissatisfied with the present agenda of the May conference, which would exclude whole categories of dope from control.

The council had voted previously to study the American proposal of limitation of cultivation of the poppy, from which opium is derived.

League Issues Mandate On German-Polish Strife.

GENEVA, Jan. 24 (AP).—The Council of the League [of] Nations topped off a [...] laborious sessions [...]ing the [...]ish mi[...] [...]ement [...]f the [...] the [...] [...]ani[...] [...]ties [...]ons [...] [...] [...]r[...] man[...] Polis[...] all c[...] Fu[...] ment[...] Counc[...] Mea[...] nad been taken [...]oute the League's mandate.

№ 21367

THE REMOVAL OF THIS COUPON TERMINATES THE PRIVILEGE OF ADMISSION

FIFTEEN CENTS

21 COUNTRIES JOIN IN FIGHT ON NARCOTICS

Tuttle Tells of Criminals as Addicts; Governor Roosevelt Urges Widest Co-operation

Eloquent evidence of the extent to which dope promotes crime was given by Charles H. Tuttle, former United States attorney, at the annual meeting of the World Conference on Narcotic Education in the Commodore Hotel yesterday.

The former Federal attorney spoke after the conference had heard a message from Governor Roosevelt endorsing its campaign and urging national and international co-operation to check drug addition.

Presiding at the afternoon session, Tuttle outlined the latest findings of the Narcotic Survey Committee, of which he is a member. He said:

"Of 832 cases of drug addiction studied in hospitals, seventy-three of the patients had police records. Of 456 persons arrested by the police narcotic squa , only 107, less than one-fourth, were first offenders.

"Of the other 349 persons, 100 were narcotic sellers as well as users, and 84 had previous convictions for felonies."

DOPE RING POWERFUL.

Charles S. Whitman, former governor, stressed the need for uniform narcotic laws and efficient treatment of addicts. He asserted that the governments of the world were far behind the progress achieved by organized drug conspirators and explained:

"The international dope ring is powerfully organized on a world wide scale. It is ably financed and equipped with experienced lawyers and chemists on its staff."

Twenty-one nations were represented at the conference, including Great Britain, France, Germany, Japan, China and Sweden. All speakers emphasized the essentiality of international teamwork to reduce the plague of addiction.

UP TO HEALTH BOARDS.

Responsibility for the enforcement of the law would be charged to the Department of Health in each State. The bill also recognized the drug known as cannabis indica as a narcotic. This measure has been submitted to every State in the union.

Judge Cornelius F. Collins of General Sessions described the his-

WORLDWIDE DOPE RING ATTACKED
SOVIET ACCUSED OF PLOT TO CONTR[...]

FACTORIES FAR AHEAD OF LOCAL NEEDS

FEBRUARY 20, 1931

Threat of Monopoly Regarded as Most Serious Aspect of World Narcotic Control

Charges that the Soviet Government plans to control the world dope market and flood western Europe and America with narcotics were made during the World Conference on Narcotic Education, held at the Hotel McAlpin last week.

The charges against the Soviet Government were:

1—That factories for manufacture of narcotic drugs in that country are being expanded beyond all possible needs for local consumption.

2—That the Soviet will attempt to secure a monopoly of the world market by underselling Turkish and Persian productions.

3—That the threat of a Soviet drug monopoly is the most serious phase of the entire narcotic situation.

COLE HITS COMMUNISTS.

Indictment of this move was voiced by Senator Frederick B. Cole, of the Rhode Island State Narcotic Board, regarded as one of the outstanding experts on narcotics in the country.

Senator Cole said:

"With religion tabooed by State order, with moral standing at a discount, and with little credit or obligation in the society of nations, the Soviet Government is in an excellent position—from their point of view—for a world drive to control drug markets.

"Not only is it a great commercial chance for the Soivet, but it is also peerless opportunity to shatter the resistance and stamina of what they choose to call "capitalistic countries."

FIVE FACTORIES OPERATING.

It was pointed out that, according to figures supplied by the Soviet Government itself the "Gosmedtorgprom," or Soviet drug factory alliance, had five factories operating in the vicinity of Moscow alone, while many others were scattered throughout the Soviet Union.

While less willing to commit himself than Senator Cole, Captain Richmond P. Hobson, president of the International Narcotic Education Association, confirmed the reality of a Soviet drug danger in part.

Hobson and Dr. Kelly Fly Dope Evil on Radio.

DOPE CONTROL URGED TO END EVIL 'IN YEAR'

MARCH 1, 1931

Illicit Sale Could Be Smashed Quickly If Production Was Curbed, Says MacCormack

Illicit traffic i nmorphine, heroin and cocaine could be smashed in one year's time if the countries where such drug derivatives are manufactured reach an agreement on the control of the manufacturing.

This statement was made yesterday by Colonel D. W. MacCormack, former director of Interval Revenue for the Persian Government, in a radio address over the Columbia system. The address marked the final day of the fifth annual observance of Narcotic Education Week.

CITES EXCESS PRODUCTION.

Colonel MacCormack declared:

"There are probably not less than 10,000 tons of raw opium produced annually. Not more than 300 tons are required to meet the medicinal and scientific requirements of the world. Under the most favorable conditions, many years must elapse before the excess production can be suppressed.

"Presenting the position of the Persian government at the 1927 session of the League of Nations Assembly, I pointed out the ineffectiveness of attacking the opium problem from the angle of controlling production, and insisted the reduction proposed in producing countries should be met by an equivalent reduction in manufacturing of derivatives.

CONTROL IS PROBLEM.

DOPE 'PARLEY' DEVELOPS INTO SALES SESSION

1931

Winifred Black Tells of Siam 'Dross' Plan and How Other Nations Gave Their Approval

By WINIFRED BLACK,
Universal Service Correspondent.

SAN FRANCISCO, Nov. 22.—The news from Bangkok indicates the League of Nations opium conference is turning from a conference to suppress narcotics into a sales conference, with a lot of good old practical rules to govern it.

We thought we'd had about all the ways to produce deadly narcotics, but it seems we've only just begun.

"Dross" is the sediment left in the opium pipe after the opium is smoked.

It's stronger than the opium itself and it has always been considered so dangerous the Siamese have collected it every year and destroyed it. It has cost the Siamese Government $1,500,000 a year to collect and destroy this dross.

SIAM CHANGES MIND.

DOPE PARLEY'S ANGER STIRRED BY PORTUGAL

Delegate Bitterly Assailed o[n] Refusal to Back Penalty fo[r] Making Addicts of Young

NOVEMBER 17, 1931

By KENNETH CLARK,
Universal Service Correspondent.

BANGKOK, Siam, Nov. 16.—Portugal today reached the heigh[t] of audacity, its attitude on dop[e] getting too raw even for th[e] League of Nations' world confer[-]ence for suppression of opiu[m] smoking. When cajolery and per[-]suasion failed to budge Portugal'[s] opposition to the proposal fo[r] compulsory punishment for per[-]sons inducing minors to indulg[e] in the opium vice, the conferenc[e] bitterly assailed Delegate Joa[o] Magalhaes.

SEES NO OFFENSE.

Advancing the theory that th[e] victim and not the tempte[r] should be blamed, Magalhae[s] argued that "an invitation to [a] minor to smoke opium, even i[f] followed by disastrous results cannot be held an offense."

Sir Malcolm DeLevingne, chie[f] of the British delegation, warne[d] the conference it would be "eter[-]nally damned by public opinion" if it temporized on this question.

Several huddles were held a[t] the President's desk to find a solu[-]tion. Finally they decided to as[k] the conference to endorse the prin[-]ciple of punishing the tempter[s] of minors. Everybody would agre[e] to that since the absence of defi[-]nite commitments would leave th[e] countries free to act as the[y] pleased.

QUIET BURIAL.

A quiet burial was accorded a resolution introduced by DeLev[-]ingne providing for compulsor[y] imprisonment for organizers o[f] dope gangs even though they d[o] not participate in the actual [...]

DOPE PARLEY FAILS AGAIN

NOVEMBER 24, 1931

Universal Service Correspondent.

BANGKOK, Siam, Nov. 23.—Eric Ekstrand, director of the League of Nations' opium section, today placed the stamp of failure on the League's Conference for the suppression of opium smoking.

GENEVA PARLEY IGNORES NEED FOR DOPE CURB

Committee, Instead, Talks of Means to Give Protection to Narcotic Manufacturers

By KENNETH CLARK,
Universal Service Staff Correspondent.

GENEVA, Jan. 10.—The League of Nations' Opium Advisory Committee occupied itself today with a bland discussion of means "to protect the interests of narcotic manufacturers and opium producers," rather than the task designated to it—the regulation of narcotic manufacture and production and methods of curbing the illicit dope traffic.

Dr. Woo Kaiseng, Chinese delegate, summed up today's sessions thus:

"It reminded me of a meeting of the board of directors of some narcotic factory seeking to protect its profits."

IGNORE REGULATION.

Instead of proceeding to draft the convention for the May conference on narcotic regulation, designed primarily to put a stop to the illicit traffic, committee members stressed the necessity of protecting the interests of dope manufacturers.

M. N. Ito, Japanese delegate, wh[o] earlier criticized the British draft [...] rations [...]

PARLEY VOTES TO DESTROY ALL SEIZED DOPE

But Attempt Will Be Made to Take Force Out of Resolution by New Amendments

JULY 1, 1931

By WINIFRED BLACK.
Copyright, 1931, by Universal Service, Inc.

GENEVA, June 30.—The European drug cartel lost a battle and won a battle in the great dope war of Geneva today.

Great Britain led the fight on both occasions. Once she won and once she lost.

In the international agreement now being discussed there is a paragraph which provides for a certain per cent of drugs above the amount legally manufactured in each country. Ten per cent above the legal allowance would be right.

GHOSE ATTACKS LEAGUE ACTION ON OPIUM EVIL

NOVEMBER 30, 1931

President of India Congress, in Radio Address, Says World's Conscience 'Doped'

A moratorium has been declared on the conscience of humanity—only in this way can be explained the "criminal apathy of public opinion on the burning questions of the day," Sailendra Nath Ghose, president of the India National Congress of America, declared last night in a radio address over WGBS under the

LEAGUE 'JOKER' PERILS FIGHT ON DOPE TRAFFIC

MARCH 30, 1931

Draft Would Make Signature of All Manufacturing Countries Necessary for Effect

By KENNETH CLARK,
Universal Service Staff Correspondent.

GENEVA, March 29.—Trickery of the League of Nations in dealing with the opium question threatens to wreck the narcotics limitation conference here in May, it became apparent today.

Pursuing its policy of protecting the profits of the opium interests, the League obviously is maneuvering to place the conference, which the United States will attend, at the mercy of European drug manufacturers.

RATIFICATION OF ALL.

These manufacturers, whose factories have been pouring tons of dope into the illicit traffic, are seeking to nullify the fight of consuming countries to smash the dope ring.

The latest League trick is discovered in an article of the draft convention prepared by the Opium Advisory Committee for the May conference. The article declares provisions of the convention shall not come into force until ratified by all exporting or manufacturing countries.

SEEK FIXED DATE.

Such a procedure, anti-narcotic leaders point out, would enable any manufacturing country to block the will of the nations victimized by dope trafficking, and frustrate effective limitation of

FIGHT ON DOPE IMPERILLED BY 'TRICK' WORDS

WAR LAUNCHED AT CONFERENCE IN WASHINGTON

APRIL 24, 1931

Health Directors Act on Appeal of Dr. Cumming for International Co-operation

Universal Service Staff Correspondent
By EDWARD L. RODDAN

WASHINGTON, April 23.—The Pan-American conference of Health Directors today laid plans for a united drive to eradicate the illicit drug traffic from the Western Hemisphere.

Resolutions were introduced aimed at concerted action to eliminate dope smuggling and asking the help of producing countries in shutting off sources of supply. These resolutions will probably be adopted tomorrow.

This action is expected to have a powerful influence upon the meeting of the League of Nations [...]

Holland Dope Stocks Grow, League Says

By Universal Service.

AMSTERDAM, May 30.—Holland is accumulating here exces[-]sive stocks of coca leaves, from which the drug cocaine is made, i[t] is charged by the secretary of th[e] Central Opium Board of th[e] League of Nations, following a[n] inspection tour.

Although legitimate cocaine con[-]sumption has decreased 50 pe[r] cent, Dutch importation of coc[a] leaves from Java jumped 12 pe[r] cent in a year, the report said. The stocks total 1,500,000 pounds.

Holland is one of the group o[f] European countries which is o[n] record as opposing too drastic lim[-]itation of drug manufacture a[t] the League's narcotic conferenc[e] starting in Geneva tomorrow.

NATIONAL DOPE COMBINE ASKED

MAY 26, 193[1]

By KENNETH CLARK
Universal Service Correspondence.

GENEVA, May 25. — Nothing short of a program calling for government monopoly of narcotics will satisfy Poland at the League of Nations' narcotics conference which begins here Wednesday.

Dr. W. Chodzko, Polish delegate told Universal Service today:

"Poland is partisan to the government monopoly plan of narcotics manufacture and distribution. Suppression of the illicit traffic is a humanitarian, not a business problem.

All Varieties

...T CONFERENCE ... WORLD'S DOPE SUPPLY

1931

New Treaty Marks Important Step In World Anti-Drug War, Says Hobson

DOPE PARLEY WARNED BY U. S. EVIL MUST END

Caldwell Startles Delegates with Flat Statement Their Plans Are Unsatisfactory

By WINIFRED BLACK.
Copyright, 1931, by Universal Service, Inc.

GENEVA, May 30.—John K. Caldwell, chairman of the American delegation and vice-president of the International Narcotic Conference of the League of Nations, made a good, plain statement about dope in good, plain English today.

He told the conference America is not satisfied with any of the plans offered for a determined and effective fight against the curse of narcotic drugs.

WANTS TRAFFIC STOPPED.

Caldwell made it clear America wants the illicit traffic in drugs stopped. Not some drugs, but all habit-forming narcotic drugs. He said:

"America believes the one way to stop the flooding of the world with the poison of narcotics is to limit production of the crude materials from which narcotic drugs are made."

Up to the time of Caldwell's statement we had heard nothing but noble platitudes and high-minded generalities.

Gaston Bourgois of France took an entirely economic point of view but dressed his reference to francs and sous with a very pretty line of sentimental eloquence.

Setsuzo Sawada of Japan, opposed the quota system, but wished to be sure Japan gets her fair share of the quota if that plan carries.

JAPAN'S OPINION.

Japan is of the opinion that a government monopoly of narcotic manufacture and distribution will help commerce and industry as well as protect the health and morals of the people.

Down with morphine—maybe.
Out with cocaine—perhaps.
Away with opium—when convenient.

DOPE PARLEY NEEDS EXPERT MEDICAL ADVICE

Winifred Black Points Out Necessity of Establishing Narcotic Quota for Profession

By WINIFRED BLACK
Copyright, 1931, by Universal Service, Inc.

GENEVA, May 10.—Who is going to represent the noble and enlightened profession of medicine at the Dope Conference in Geneva?

I wish the American Medical Association would send a few good old-fashioned doctors, who hold their profession as a sacred trust. Doctors who really care what happens to their patients.

The Narcotic Committee of the League of Nations has been in existence for some years. Its reports so far have dealt interestingly with the necessary quota for each dope-raising or dope-making country.

ACTUAL NEED UNKNOWN

But nobody ever comes forward with any definite estimate of the actual amount of dope actually needed in honest medical practice; so much of a quota for this country, so little for that.

Argument, discussion, anger, bitter words. Doctor Woo Kai Seng, Chinese delegate to the last conference, rose in the midst of one of these very "practical" discussions and said that the whole proceeding reminded him of the meeting of a board of directors of a big business monopoly.

How much money is invested and who owns the stock in these investments? How much of the dope manufactured really goes into legitimate channels? Nobody seems to have the faintest idea and so far nobody has taken the trouble to "check and double check" on this mysterious business.

ONE POINT OF VIEW.

The delegate from Germany insists that codeine is not a habit-forming drug and ought

GENEVA PARLEY FAILS TO FACE DOPE PROBLEM

Manufacturing Nations Unwilling to Act on Limitation Plans, Says Winifred Black

By WINIFRED BLACK.
Universal Service Correspondence.

GENEVA, June 9.—Tomorrow and tomorrow.

This is the theme song of the dope conference. Sometimes it sounds like a cradle song, but the baby refuses to go to sleep.

And back of all the nominy-piminy is always the silky voice of trade and the clink of money.

Who is going to sell the most dope—that's what the conference seems like to me in the last analysis.

PERFECT UNITY.

Five great manufacturing nations, France, Great Britain, Switzerland, Holland and Germany, stand together like a family of brothers. They may have their quarrels at home. But when they get among strangers—that's different.

It is whispered that drug cartels are making all this delay in the hope that delegates will sign anything to get back home.

Italy, Russia, United States, Argentina, China and Japan appear to want to get something really done.

America sticks firmly to the American plan, which rests on the solid foundation of the limitation of raw material.

WOULD EXEMPT MORPHINE.

A delegate from India caused mingled laughter and indignation

BRITON BLOCKS VITAL VOTE ON DOPE TRAFFIC

Threatens to Return Home if Conference Agree[s to De]struction of Seized [Drugs]

By WINIFRED BL[ACK]
Copyright, 1931, by Universal [Service, Inc.]

GENEVA, June 29.—[Sir Mal]colm Delevingne, Brit[ish dele]gate, today tore off [the velvet] glove he has been we[aring and] showed the League of N[ations In]ternational narcotic [conference] an iron hand doubled i[nto an] aggressive, threatening [fist].

The conference, abou[t to end a] tedious discussion by [a vote] which would have me[ant some]thing, shivered and sh[ook like] what a well-known [writer] once called innocuous [desuetude].

It happened like [this: The] conference was discus[sing what] to do with narcotics se[ized in un]derground traffic.

DEFIES DELEGATES.

Some of the delegat[es wanted] to destroy these drugs. Som[e] wanted the Government to kee[p] them and make them over fo[r] the regular trade, thus reducin[g] the quantity of needed raw ma[]terial. The situation had be[en] discussed thoroughly and [the] conference was eager for a vot[e]. Delevingne didn't want the vote.

He said he never would consent to any agreement to destroy underground seizures. He denounced the conference for giving such a chance for a serious split in its ranks.

Sir Malcolmn hinted the conference would vote his way or he would go home.

VOTE IS AVOIDED.

JULY 9, 1933

Thirty-Six Nations Are Allied in Pact To Crush Evil

By CAPT. RICHMOND PEARSON HOBSON
President of the World Narcotic Defense Association.

A TREATY convention, which undertakes to limit the manufacture and regulate the distribution of narcotic ... 9, in the ... e against ... ome of a ... orld-wide ... s required ... b-divisions ... neva Convention ... s evolved. ... r only nine ... atification ... e April 15. ... January, ... ginning of ... addiction, ... cted evils. ... a rapidly ... e provided ... ic opinion ... measures ... world are ... e order of

GENEVA ANTI-NARCOTIC TREATY
Turkey France Spain
Bulgaria Poland Sweden
Italy Canada Mexico
Portugal Switzerland Persia
Cuba India
Egypt Great Britain
JOHN BULL

36 Nations Ratify
[Pu]blic Sentiment Must Now Back Up World Drive

U. S. DELEGATE BAITED ON PLEA AGAINST DOPE

He Urges Limit on Raw Material; Britain and Germany Immediately Vow Objection

By WINIFRED BLACK.
Copyright, 1931, by Universal Service, Inc.

GENEVA, June 17.—The day of miracles has not passed. We sat in the opium conference today and heard the dumb speak and saw, at last, the dead arise.

But we also saw the dumb begin to stammer and watched the dead collapse again into a new made grave.

It looked yesterday as if all hope for accomplishing any real results in this widely heralded conference was hopelessly gone.

The American delegation, which was looked to for leadership, seemed to be in a haze.

AMERICAN IN ACTION.

The American plan was presented so badly and so late that it was fairly pooh-pooed out of existence.

Today Harry J. Anslinger arose in the American delegation and made a real speech. The conference was galvanized into attention.

ANTI-WAR DRIVE ON AT GENEVA

By KENNETH CLARK.
Universal Service Staff Correspondent.

GENEVA, May 10.—In an atmosphere clouded with suspicion and mutual distrust, a League of Nations' committee will meet here tomorrow to attempt to strengthen the means of preventing war.

The committee's purpose is to enlarge the League Council's power to pursue so-called conservatory measures, even to directing troop movement against nations which threaten war.

The following countries are represented on the committee: Germany, England, Spain, France, Greece, Guatemala, Italy, Japan, Norway, Holland, Poland, Jugo-Slavia and Chile.

Linked with the project is Article 16 of the League Covenant, which authorizes the League to enforce sanctions, military and economic, against countries which refuse to do the League's bidding.

If the sponsors have their way, the Council, in the event nations mobilize for a fight, would be given the right to compel the withdrawal of military forces behind a neutral zone and keep them there while Geneva decided what to do. The Council would send commissioners to observe the situation.

ACTION URGED ON DOPE PACT

MARCH 8, 1932

WASHINGTON, March 7.—Prompt ratification of the League of Nations opium convention, signed in Geneva last July, was urged today in a report of the American delegation.

BRITAIN, REICH AND JAPAN BACK ANTI-DOPE PACT

Their Ratifications Expected This Week; Prospects for League Convention Brighten

MARCH 30, 1933

GENEVA, Mar. 29 (AP).—Prospects for adoption of the League of Nations convention for limitation of narcotic manufactring became very bright today with the announcement that Great Britain and Germany expect to send their ratifications tomorrow and that Japan's will be forwarded in a few days.

These three countries, plus the United States, which already has ratified, would give the four manufacturing nations required.

25 APPROVALS NEEDED.

The convention, concluded here in 1931, requires that 25 ratifications, including those of four manufacturing countries be deposited by April 13 or the convention will be defaulted.

A total of 25 also appears in sight, for ratifications already have

BRITAIN MAKES LEAGUE'S DOPE CONTROL SURE

Latest Ratification Brings 25 Nations in Line; Central Board to Govern Traffic

APRIL 2, 1933

GENEVA, April 1 (AP).—Adoption of the League of Nations narcotics convention drafted in 1931 was assured today with the receipt of Great Britain's ratification.

This brought the number of ratifications to the required 25.

The League of Nations' narcotics convention embodies two methods of combating the narcotic evil.

The first aims at international control of the international shipment of narcotic drugs and the materials from which they may be manufactured. The second pledges the nations ratifying the treaty to exercise internal control over production of the drugs and their materials.

CENTRAL BODY TO RULE.

To accomplish the first purpose, the convention would set up a Central Control Board, to which each nation would submit estimates of the quantity of each narcotic drug it annually required for medical and scientific purposes.

Nations failing to supply estimates would have their requirements fixed by a supervisory body, working in co-operation with the League of Nations.

The United States has led all along in the endeavor to achieve this international accord. It was the second nation to ratify this treaty by a unanimous vote of the Senate on March 23, 1932.

Tribute must be paid to the Hearst newspapers in particular for the splendid co-operation given the anti-narcotic crusaders in the long fight to curb the illicit narcotic drugs traffic.

ANTI-NARCOTIC PACT GOES INTO EFFECT JULY 10

Ratification of Treaty Complete; Expected to Halt Flow of Dope Into U. S.

By KENNETH CLARK,
Universal Service Correspondent.

WASHINGTON, April 10.—The world's most smashing blow at the dope evil was taken tonight when ratification of the Geneva Anti-Narcotics Convention was completed.

The State Department announced the international convention for limitation of narcotics manufacture had been ratified by the required number of nations and would go into effect July 10.

The manufacture of narcotics is limited to the world's actual medical and scientific needs. Strict control of distribution is imposed, and the signatories pledge unceasing war against dope traffickers.

WILL STOP FLOOD.

The treaty will stop the flow of tons of dope which have been inundating American shores from abroad. The State Department said:

"The advantage of the treaty to the United States lies in the fact it will limit the quantities of dangerous narcotics manufactured in other countries, will render much stricter the control abroad of the legitimate trade, and will afford better facilities for suppressing the illicit traffic."

Twenty-nine countries have ratified, although only 25 were needed to make the treaty effec-

AUGUST 28, 1933

LEGAL 'DOPE' OUTPUT CUT TO WORLD'S NEED

New Menace Springs Up in Outlaw Plants of Far East; Opium Demand Falls Off

By KENNETH CLARK,
Universal Service Correspondent.

WASHINGTON, Aug. 27.—A notable victory for America's aggressive international war against the dope evil was recorded today.

For the first time in history, the output of licensed narcotic factories everywhere has been restricted to the world's actual medicinal requirements, estimated at 16½ tons of morphine, heroin and cocaine.

A world survey of the dope traffic also revealed the legitimate demand for raw opium, from which narcotics are manufactured, has dropped 500 tons since 1929.

NEW MENACE RISES.

But while the legitimate trade was never under better control a new menace has arisen in connection with the illicit traffic.

Clandestine dope factories are springing up almost overnight in China and Japan. The individual output is small. The aggregate is reaching proportions alarming to enforcement officials.

Secret agents believe many of these factories are controlled by two or three large international rings with American connections.

American traffickers are now unabl to obtain supplies in Europe. Investigation is being made. So far little co-operation has been received from Japanese and Chinese officials. Japan exercises only nominal control over drug dealers.

OPERATE IN FAR EAST.

Confidential reports show notorious European traffickers are operating in the Far East. The punishment for dope violations out there is measured in weeks or months, not in years. Of the illicit factories, investigators reported

"Some chemical knowledge and a simple plant are sufficient for the extraction of morphine of a sufficient degree of purity for illicit purposes, and whenever opium is easily obtainable, the establishment of such 'factories' is a danger against which a constant watch will have to be kept.

DOCTORS URGED TO FIGHT DOPE

MAY 12, 1933

By Universal Service.

FORT WORTH, Tex., May 11.—A call to the medical profession, to purge itself of unscrupulous practitioners who misuse narcotic drugs, was sounded tonight by Dr. Walter L. Treadway, Assistant Surgeon General of the Public Health Service.

He told the Texas Medical Association that individual physicians were abusing their professional privileges to obtain dope for addicts under circumstances that "cast doubt as being for bona fide medical treatment." He said it is up to the medical societies to stop this.

Dr. Treadway has charge of building the two new Federal narcotic farms, where addict-prisoners will be sent for rehabilitation. One farm is near Lexington, Ky., and the other outside of Ft. Worth. The Hearst newspapers launched the campaign for these farms.

Dr. Treadway said drug addiction is widespread throughout the United States. He said the evil is not restricted to any class, but "it is through and on the people, like an epidemic disease."

M'ADOO URGES NEW FUND FOR NARCOTIC FIGHT

Assails Slash in Allotment to Enforcement Bureau, Poingting Out the Dangers

OCTOBER 28, 1933

By KENNETH CLARK,

Universal Service Correspondent.

WASHINGTON, Oct. 27.—Senator McAdoo (D., Cal.), today demanded a halt in the pinch-penny economy program that threatens a breakdown in Federal narcotic enforcement.

At a time when prohibition racketeers are turning to the dope traffic, and vast amounts of dope are being smuggled from Japan and China, Federal narcotic funds have been cut more than 40 per cent.

IMPOSSIBLE TASK.

The Narcotics Bureau today is operating on a budget of only $1,000,000, trying to break up an illicit traffic running into untold millions. The task is almost impossible.

McAdoo announced he would appeal immediately to Budget Director Douglas to grant an increase in narcotic funds. Failing there, he said he would carry the fight to Congress this Winter, feeling it will readily see the necessity for greater appropriations to safeguard the country from the dope menace. He said:

"Crippling the Narcotics Bureau's work is disastrous at this time. With the coming repeal, prohibition racketeers are entering the dope traffic. Some of the country's most vicious criminals are participating.

"I feel we should not only restore the $1,700,000 which Congress appropriated two years ago for enforcement, but should increase the amount."

DOPE CENTER SHIFTS.

The distribution center for illicit dope has been shifted from New York to the West Coast by the closing down of European factories. The major supply now comes from Japan and China, and Pacific Coast officials fear a serious danger.

It is feared a breakdown in enforcement, caused by the slash in funds, would result immediately in so reducing prices of dope in the illicit market that narcotics would come within the reach of thousands, thus contributing to an increase in addiction in the United States.

For the current fiscal year Congress appropriated $1,400,000 for narcotic enforcement, but $400,000 was lopped off by the administration in the economy drive. Enforcement has become virtually hogtied.

HORNER PLANS INQUIRY INTO DOPE SLAVERY

DECEMBER 7, 1934

Illinois Governor, Shocked by Piteous Woman Addicts, Will Dig at Roots of Evil

By Universal Service.

CHICAGO, Dec. 6.—Aroused by the pitiful plight of 13 women narcotic addicts held on shoplifting charges, Governor Henry Horner announced tonight he would call on the forthcoming session of the State Legislature to make a searching investigation to determine the methods by which the women were made victims of the "dope traffic." He said:

"In this day of modern enlightment it is amazing to realize that human beings are being dragged into a slavery more shocking and worse than the slave traffic of pre-civil war days.

"The loopholes have to be plugged and I am taking it upon myself to see that they are plugged!"

Driven to Crime

The 13 women addicts arrested with 200 others in raids in Indiana, Illinois and Wisconsin were held today for a hearing Jan. 2 on shoplifting charges.

The women said they were driven to shoplifting and other petty crimes by their great need for money to spend for narcotics.

The majority of the women came from good families.

U. S. EXPECTS 95 P. C. DOPE CONVICTIONS

Narcotics Chief Predicts Certain Punishment for Nearly All of 791 Just Seized

WASHINGTON, Dec. 10 (AP).—A "swell job" was Secretary Morgenthau's commendation today to the Treasury's narcotic bureau which has put 791 illicit narcotic handlers behind bars in a nation-wide sweep still funtioning at top speed.

Harry J. Anslinger, narcotics chieftian, predicted convictions of those arrested would average 95 per cent.

Helpful Move.

Morgenthau said today a decree by President Mendieta of Cuba prohibiting shipment of Cuban alcohol to ports known as smuggling bases was "the most helpful move against overseas smuggling since I came into the Treasury."

He said the Treasury was "delighted" with Mendieta's order which immediately blocked shipment of 80,000 cases of alcohol.

WASHINGTON, Dec. 9 (US).—Price of bootlegged dope soared 2,000 per cent today as terrified traffickers hid their smuggled supplies and fled to cover before the Government's relentless drive.

Among the prisoners was a reputed Dillinger gang girl—Laura Smart, seized for drug addiction in St. Paul. She was held for the Justice Department on suspicion of having harbored lieutenants of John Dillinger before the No. 1 public enemy was slain in Chicago and his cohorts scattered.

$400 to $800 an Ounce.

Deputy Narcotics Commissioner Louis Ruppel revealed frantic addicts were begging dealers for "shots" at prices averaging $400 an ounce, in contrast to a price of $20 prevalent before the drive.

Few dealers had dope available, even at this unprecedented price, Ruppel revealed. In Washington, he said, a few tins were reported changing hands at $800 an ounce.

Telegrams piled up on Commissioner Anslinger's desk revealed a loosely organized dope syndicate operating from New York to San Francisco interlocked in certain

Tons of Illicit Narcotics from Europe New Menace to U.S., Expert Reveals

Balkan Dope Flood via France Now Swells Traffic from Far Eastern Sources

DECEMBER 9, 1934

By FERDINAND TUOHY,

Noted European Commentator on Current Events.

CRUSADERS—Commissioner of Narcotics Harry Anslinger (left) and Congressman Porter, who have waged a long fight against the drug evil in the United States.

WHEN U. S. Commissioner of Narcotics Anslinger lately announced that "the general new position (in regard to dope) is of the most serious description," he had his eyes fixed on the Pacific Coast and the great increase of drug smuggling from the Far East, principally heroin.

However active the Japanese may be in shipping clandestine consignments of narcotics direct to California and places further south for subsequent transition to the United States, the Commissioner would do well not to relax his vigilance on the Atlantic seaboard.

Evidence is accumulating that the newly-installed "drug barons" of Shanghai, Dairen, Osaka, Tientsin and elsewhere in the Orient, are sending their devilish merchandise three-quarters way round the globe, via Europe, to attain the immensely profit-yielding North American market.

Recent seizures of heroin at Marseille and Antwerp have revealed this new and grave circumstance. Whereas it had been believed that drugs shipped from Europe to the United States emanated very largely, if not wholly, from secret sources and factories in Europe itself, it has now become plain that this is no longer the case.

A good deal of the clandestine supply for Americans still derives from Bulgarian and Macedonian sources, yet there is evidence that an ever larger quantity of dope, churned out cheaply in the Orient, is finding its way to European ports, and that the bulk of it is destined for re-shipment to the United States and Canada.

Dope Situation Is Out of Hand

The Opium Section of the League of Nations is fully aware of this situation and it is anticipated that the U. S. delegate, Stewart Fuller, will raise the matter at the full-dress Drugs Conference early in 1935.

The world situation in regard to high-power dope (heroin, morphine, cocaine) has for some time past been steadily growing worse until today it has gotten out of hand.

Geneva officially admits that *a hundred tons* at least of illicit dope has been put in circulation during the past five years.

If it be said that *three-quarters of a ton* of heroin, the monthly output of one clandestine factory uncovered at Radomir, near Sofia, equals 187,000,000 "shots" or a double dose a day for 3,000,000 addicts, some idea will be grasped of what is going on.

Furthermore, the estimate of twenty tons a year illicit output was made in 1933. Since then the picture has become much darker. We are aware that the most puissant animators of the traffic have settled down in the Far East adjacent to the poppy fields that supply their hidden factories with raw material.

But that is not all. In the same period, no fewer than ten countries which never manufactured drugs in the past have obtained the right to do so.

The newcomers are Belgium, Bulgaria, Hungary, Kwantung Leased Territory, Norway, Poland, Sweden, Czechoslovakia, Yugoslavia and Spain. Between them they have already erected seventeen new and entirely superfluous factories. In competent quarters the liveliest fear prevails that not all of these countries will manufacture only for their own needs, as they now claim to do.

Again, there is the extraordinary behavior of Bulgaria. Japan, France, the Shanghai "barons" and Bulgaria represent the Big Four in the widespread contemporary drug racket. Bulgaria alone is known to possess ten clandestine factories and it is certain many more are secreted in the hills next door to the Macedonian poppy fields, new acres of which are being steadily planted.

Bulgaria's importation of acid acetic anhydride, for the manufacture of heroin, has multiplied eighty-six times inside two years. The amount she imported last year was enough to make five tons of heroin, four times the legitimate needs of the entire world. Her production of raw opium has increased sixteen times within a like period.

Bulgaria is the "Japan" of Europe in this dope outrage on humanity. Her dope king is one Lazoff, who, without the faintest doubt, enjoys protection in return for a rake-off to high places.

When "pressed" by authorities, he moves along and sets up factories elsewhere. These are very easy—a disguised garage and a few portable laboratory requirements are all that are necessary. Lately he has acquired several laid-up Danube steamers and established floating laboratories.

Balkans Produce Tons of Narcotics

What is being incredibly tolerated in Bulgaria is of scarcely less importance to the United States than that which is happening under Japanese auspices in Jehol, and in the new general dope metropolis, Shanghai, since the high-power stuff distilled in the Balkans is being smuggled to America through Havre, Cherbourg, Bordeaux, Antwerp, Rotterdam, and Hamburg. In the south, Naples and Genoa are also used but in lesser degree.

It is hardly necessary to use Italy on this account as the safest route to the New World is through wide open Marseille.

The situation in Marseille, in France, generally, will monopolize the remainder of this expose, inasmuch as France must be arraigned with Bulgaria, Japan and Shanghai as the arch-sinner in the current poisoning of the world.

But with this difference:

With respect to the narcotic problem, Canada is in much the same situation as the United States, but Canada is not so lenient with drug traffickers. The sentences are heavier, and if bail is fixed it is purposely set so high that an offender cannot make it. In a recent case a smuggler's bail was set at $100,000. This same man was afterward convicted, fined $3,000, sentenced to 14 years in prison and 10 lashes. Canada still uses the lash on the drug peddler and finds it a powerful deterrent.

Naturally, it is difficult to determine whether or not drug addiction is on the increase in this country. Abroad reports are that it is increasing, particularly in Japan. It is estimated that one person out of every thousand in this country is an addict.

France is not known to be manufacturing clandestinely. Her crime takes the form of allowing her territory to be used as transiting corridor and as warehouse for hidden stocks.

The French attitude is clear-cut. It is this: "Fire away! Poison the earth, for all we care! So long as you don't poison French people!"

French newspapers admit that the country is "inundated" with illicit dope, but state that French nationals are adequately protected. The inundation is almost entirely for re-export.

It will be instructive to follow up just what happens on French soil. Vessels from the Far East and from the Aegean (Salonika chiefly) carry smuggled and camouflaged dope to Marseille.

The uncrowned king of Marseille is a one-eyed Corsican who sprang from nowhere at the height of the boom decade. He is a member of the Chamber of Deputies. But even he is obliged to watch his step when faced with a local group of gangsters who preside over the drug and white slave traffics.

Marseille Center Of Drug Traffic

This group of gangsters did not hesitate to murder and do away with the body of the British Consul, Mr. Lee, when he busied himself with the dope racket.

A percentage of the police and Surete are more than suspected of being susceptible to the pressure—and gifts—of this gang.

This great port, rotten at the core, is today the most important place in Europe insofar as the war on the dope traffic is concerned!

Clandestine consignments are put ashore in all manner of ways. The smuggled opium is mostly warehoused in the surrounding districts. It is too bulky to shift except in response to individual orders. Thereupon the necessary quantity of the raw material is sent by courier to Paris and thence to the Americas.

High-powered derivatives — morphine, heroin, cocaine—are usually forwarded direct to Paris from the ship. A courier goes to Marseille, makes his contact, and travels back with one or two valises (one grip will hold heroin worth a million francs.)

A favorite method, on arrival in Paris, is for the courier to enter a waiting car and leave the dope-filled valise when he descends at his hotel or apartment.

The car is driven to a specific garage where the valuable cargo is taken in hand.

For the most part, stocks are held in a kind of rabbit-warren clearing houses such as a group of furnished rooms in back streets. The idea of the "warren" is that a really big seizure can never be made.

Some traffickers go in for stunt hide-outs — such as the dealer who kept his stock behind a long-forgotten tombstone in Montmartre cemetery. It is from these gentry that the crews of Atlantic liners derive their "merchandise." Heroin pills are the very latest mode.

Another growing trick is to soak dope for shipment in innocently-named mixtures, and the stuff is duly "unsoaked" on the other side of the Atlantic.

The British not long ago were suspicious of several cases of an unknown concoction labelled "Lubrinole." When seized it was found to be saturated in morphine. The French exporting firm indignantly asked for the return of their merchandise, but of course, did not get it. A little later the same people were caught exporting morphine as "colorant" in a dye stuff.

The principal European drug "barons" make Paris their working headquarters because of the unexampled leniency shown them. The most hardened offenders are let out on 10,000 and 15,000 francs bail, after which ensues every form of legal postponement until the affair is allowed to peter out. The culprit has bribed his way back to freedom—and to an immediate resumption of his deadly business.

Seizures made in France are not destroyed as in other lands but are auctioned to agents of three government - controlled drug factories, the money thereby obtained going to reward the agents who discovered the smuggled dope in the first instance. The three factories, already manufacturing sufficient narcotics for France's requirements, have all this seized stuff as surplus—last year fifteen times as much morphine and eighty-eight times as much heroin was seized as was legally manufactured.

France Distributes Illicit Narcotics

The State factories transform this surplus seized stuff into codeine and put immense quantities of this dangerous, habit-forming but not forbidden drug on the world market. Codeine can be easily converted back into morphine and heroin. So, in essence, the dope France seizes goes back into the illicit traffic by a round-about route.

All this is perfectly well-known and is admitted. The chief auction centre is situated in the Boulevard des Dames at Marseille, where authorized buyers—and perhaps some others who are not—assemble monthly.

Recently one of the principal inspectors of the Surete at Lille was uncovered as the dope king of the North, with direct channels to Antwerp and Rotterdam . . . The confessed inability to insure the destruction of some heaps of crystal, when the output of whole factories can be checked to ten grams, beggars characterization. In England, no difficulty at all is en-

The Federal Government has been endeavoring to pierce this zone by persuading the States to adopt a uniform narcotic law. In the protection of the health, morals and general welfare of the people from this dreadful evil, the States certainly have an equal responsibility with the Government.

Between the point to which the operation of the Federal narcotic laws extends and the point where the operation of the State narcotic laws, most of which are archaic, begins, there exists a twilight zone which affords a safe refuge for the dope trafficker and racketeer.

Uniform Laws Must Be Passed

To conclude: If twenty tons illicit dope was being manufactured annually up to 1933, three and four times that amount is probably being churned out today, thanks to the mass-production in various quarters that has set in since. As Russell Pasha, the great authority, says:

"Europe and America are faced with the danger of a flood of cheap narcotics. Out in China they have got over the difficulty of an inferior cultivation and are now turning out raw material that satisfies."

It is urgently necessary to arraign the four prime culprits, Japan, Bulgaria, France, and Shanghai Leased Territory, at next year's conference.

Makers of Addicts

HARRY J. ANSLINGER, United States Commissioner of Narcotics, told the House Appropriations Committee this week that one physician in every hundred is a narcotic addict.

To uninformed minds the percentage may seem small.

Actually, it is a very disturbing figure—for it represents a rate of addiction among physicians which is TEN TIMES the rate for the population at large, and BOTH RATES are steadily increasing.

The disclosure ought certainly to assure that the Federal Narcotics Bureau will receive IN FULL the $1,249,000 appropriation which it seeks for 1935.

It should likewise assure prompt passage by Cong... of Senator McCarran's pending amendment to the ... Narcotics Act, which would permit the Narcotics ... to prosecute and to un-license dope-peddling ...s whom State medical boards permit to carry ...licit trade.

* * *

...RT of his proposal Senator McCarran, also ... before the House Committee, said:

...timony confirms my long-held convictio... ...cal profession provides the BROADE... hell of dope enslavement.

DRIVE TO BALK U. S. FIGHT ON DOPE CHARGED

DECEMBER 20, 1946

Federal Narcotics Head Says Certain Medical Interests Are Spreading Propaganda

By Universal Service.

WASHINGTON, Dec. 6.—A drive to strip the Federal Government of all punitive power to curb the drug evil was charged to certain medical interests today by Harry Anslinger, Federal narcotics commissioner.

Behind the campaign, he charged, is the International White Cross, self-styled Anti-Narcotics League of California. The league was founded by Dr. Edward Huntington Williams, California psychiatrist, convicted in Los Angeles November 17 of violating the Harrison Anti-Narcotics Act.

From its San Francisco office, Anslinger charged, the White Cross League has been flooding the country with propaganda urg-...tion of the Narcotics ... "persecuting" physi-...ausing "untold suffer-... addicts.

...cal Pamphlet

...typical league pamphlet in Anslinger's file states its argument thus:

"The Harrison Anti-Narcotic Act is a complete failure. Morphine prescribed by all the physicians in the United States is not a drop in the bucket compared to foreign narcotics smuggled in and distributed. Why waste money in such a sham fight against the traffic?"

The same pamphlet urges amendment of the Narcotic Law to abolish the Narcotics Bureau and permit dope victims to be treated through a clinic system under the direction of the U. S. public health service in cooperation with city, county and State health boards, "the narcotics to be given habitual users at cost."

Anslinger branded the league's plan a variation of the notorious system imposed by Japan in the Island of Formosa, where addicts are "licensed" and supplied with narcotics. He said:

"This system simply promotes consumption and spreads the evil. It would enable unscrupulous doctors to issue unlimited prescriptions for their own profit."

Anslinger cited a recent article in the Journal of the American Medical Association as proof unscrupulous physicians are a main root of the narcotic evil.

Greedy Doctors

Testimony Links Bilbo in $1000 Gift Over Dope

WASHINGTON, Dec. 20 (AP)—A story of ten $100 bills sent to Senator Theodore G. Bilbo by a man wanting his help in getting narcotics was related to senate investigators Thursday night and brought an immediate denial from the Mississippi senator.

Bilbo also branded as "lies" or "hallucinations" the charges that he profited from relations with war contractors. These charges led to the inquiry by the senate war investigating committee.

DR. HARRY J. ANSLINGER
Tells of narcotics deal

The matter of the narcotics came out piecemeal from four separate witnesses whose testimony conflicted at points. They were:

Edward Terry, Bilbo's former secretary. He said that Dr. A. J. Podesta, Vicksburg, Miss., told him he gave Bilbo $1500 for a Natchez, Miss., man who wanted a permit for daily doses of narcotics.

Dr. Harry J. Anslinger, federal commissioner of narcotics. He testified Bilbo called him to his office October 11, 1945, about a letter from Podesta with accompanying certificates that a Harry Carr of Natchez required a regular supply of drugs.

Treasury Agent Testifies

Harry Holt, special agent for the treasury. He testified that Terry had informed the treasury of the alleged payments and he (Holt) had investigated. He said that on April 30, 1946, he interviewed Podesta at Vicksburg.

Podesta told him, Holt related, that he sent the certificate to Bilbo and that Anslinger's office later approved narcotics for Carr, who was described as a sufferer from asthma and other ailments and as a long-time user of narcotics. Holt quoted Podesta as saying that still later Carr told him he wanted to "do something" for Bilbo, so the physician suggested a contribution for Bilbo's Juniper Grove Baptist church project.

Bilbo Back on Stand

Senator Homer Ferguson, the Michigan Republican who has ramrodded most of the probe, said angrily at the time: "This is not the only man who has committed perjury in this hearing."

Which was a masterpiece of understatement.

Even to cynical newsmen, the carelessness with which truth has been treated throughout the Bilbo hearings has become sickening.

War contractors, politicians and penny-ante business and professional men have glibly although unofficially admitted their lies (there is no other word) to reporters and idle spectators outside the caucus-room doors.

Moreover, they usually do it lightly—with a laugh.

Terry Folds Up

In the midst of this examination Terry, who was standing to the side of the committee room, staggered a few feet and collapsed in a chair.

The committee granted him permission to leave and he left on the arm of his attorney, Paul Dillon.

Ferguson demanded that Bilbo produce all records he has of church gifts. The Mississippi senator said the committee could have them and all his personal files if they wanted them.

"I haven't anything to hide," Bilbo declared.

At that point, the hearing was recessed indefinitely. The committee members will examine Bilbo's files in private and decide whether they will call Podesta and Carr as witnesses.

Bilbo Feeling Oats

Control of Dope Meets Obstacles

JANUARY 3, 1950

GENEVA, Jan. 3 (AP)—The permanent central opium board ...said delay of some...

NARCOTICS

Committee approves new narcotic mea... U N Bul 5:822 O 15 '48
Control of narcotic drugs; how present ... national system works. U N Bul 2:605 ... 3 '47
Crime and illicit drug traffic; seizure re... reveal methods of operations. U N B... 125-6 F 1 '49
Decisions on narcotics control. U N Bu... 247 Mr 15 '48
International control of narcotic drugs. Int Concil 441:303-73 My '48
Measures to control narcotics reviewed ... Council. U N Bul 4:178-9 Mr 1 '48
Morphine substitute made; known by t... different names: amidone, dolophine 10820. Science N L 52:98 Ag 16 '47
Narcotics control, a pattern for disarmam... U N World 1:44-5 S '47

...statistics on its opium ... pointing out "the presence of Iranian opium in the illicit traffic in many parts of the world."

The board reported that "almost complete collaboration" had been attained with the Soviet Union. In the last year, the board said, the Soviet Union has supplied most of the statistics requested except those on consumption for 1946, 1947 and 1948.

Narcotic Drugs Found on Rise

GENEVA, Jan. 13 (AP)—The United Nations permanent central opium board reported gloomily Tuesday that the number of narcotic drugs has almost doubled in the past five years. It called for a tightening of drugs control throughout the world.

The board, headed by Herbert L. May, United States, will end a five-year term next March 1 and will be succeeded by another.

The report expressed concern over an ever-wide use of synthetic narcotic drugs without any significant fall in the use of the chemical derivatives of opium.

It also pointed to the "increase in use of codeine" in the last 20 years and the impossibility of finding out how much production of coca leaf is illegal. Bolivia and Peru, the chief coca producing countries, do not provide statistics to the board.

JANUARY 14, 19...

DOPE NOT NEEDED, PHYSICIAN ASSERTS

By CHARLES N. WHEELER,
Universal Service Correspondent.

CHICAGO, Dec. 13.—Dr. Francis W. McNamara, for twenty years head physician at the Cook County jail, declared today that habit-forming narcotic drugs are not necessary in the practice of medicine.

During his practice in Cook County medical institutions approximately 180,000 patients, Dr. McNamara said, passed through his hands, and not one had been administered habit-forming opiates by him.

OCTOBER 18, 1941

Uncle Samuel Bans Poppies

If you have any of three certain kinds of poppies in your garden or awaiting next season's planting time, don't be a dope, but burn 'em right away before Uncle Sam gets you.

That was the warning here Friday of Elizabeth M. Bodger of Bodger's Seeds, Ltd., El Monte, Cal., at the closing session of the annual convention of the Tri-State Seedmen's association at the Multnomah hotel.

The reason is, she said, that foreign opium sources are bottled up by world conditions and Uncle Sam is keeping an eye on at least three varieties of domestic poppy from which the drug is extracted, and woe be unto persons, commercial or laymen, who have them in their possession.

Three Varieties Identified

The varieties are known as carnation-flowered poppy, peony-flowered poppy and cardinal-type poppy, all oozy with the forbidden opium.

Mrs. Bodger said government agents visited her company's huge plantings in California and ordered that from 35 to 40 acres of the poppies be uprooted and burned under the narcotics law.

CHECK LACKING ON NARCOTICS PRESCRIPTIONS

State Has No Power to Regulate Their Issuance; U. S. Watches Wholesale Orders

Disreputable physicians of New York City and State may prescribe narcotics, no mater htow damaging they may be, without any direct check on their activities by either State or Federal agencies.

Must Preserve Records

Druggists and physicians are required to preserve for two years each record of a narcotic prescription. In some cases, Federal agents say, physicians plead ignorance of the law, while in other cases, where improper dispensation can be proved, the physician may settle the case by payment of "compromise money."

There have been comparatively few convictions of physicians in this dictrict, Federal agents say, but convictions are common in the Middle West and South.

What State Law Says

Under State law a physician convicted of violating the narcotics law automatically loses his license, while if he is accused of being an addict proof must be established before his license can be revoked.

To keep a direct check on all physicians and druggists would require a large personnel of inspectors, Igoe explained. In New York City there are 70 wholesale establishments licensed to distribute narcotics. Each files a monthly report, showing sales, to whom made, quantity, and stock on hand. These reports are checked and analyzed by Federal agents.

DECEMBER 11, 1934

Harry P. Anslinger, head of the Federal Narcotic Bureau, is to be congratulated. He is accomplishing wonders, particularly when one considers the limited staff—250 in the entire country—and the limited means at his disposal.

Control Narcotic Traffic

MARCH 29, 1937

THE proposal by Senator McNaboe to establish a Narcotic Control Bureau in the State Health Department is one of the most important bills before the New York Legislature.

The measure provides for the expenditure of $27,500 by the bureau in its first year, which is the MINIMUM REQUIREMENT for starting a Statewide fight against one of the greatest modern evils.

Practically all efforts to cope with narcotic addiction and traffic in the State are now confined to New York City.

The problem of controlling narcotics has been increased alarmingly by the oversupply of narcotic drugs in Oriental countries. These supplies are SEEKING A MARKET, and they threaten to inundate the Western World.

America must raise effective barriers against this de-

Pass the Narcotics Bill

MAY 13, 1936

WITH a considerable number of Governor Lehman's anti-crime bills already on the statute books, it has become especially important that the Legislature, before adjourning, should pass the McNaboe Bill—Senate Bill No. 959—to establish a Division of Narcotic Control in the State Department...

The State Na...

In New York ... Health Departme...

Upstate, enfo... lack of an organi...

Illicit narcot... huana, are a sour...

More than th... public health prob...

With the pend... the State will be a... this problem.

PUBLIC LAW 255—NOV. 2, 1951

Be it enacted by the Senate and House of Representatives of the United States of America in Congress assembled, That section 2 (c) of the Narcotic Drugs Import and Export Act, as amended (U. S. C., title 21, sec. 174), is amended to read as follows:

"(c) Whoever fraudulently or knowingly imports or brings any narcotic drug into the United States or any territory under its control or jurisdiction, contrary to law, or receives, conceals, buys, sells, or in any manner facilitates the transportation, concealment, or sale of any such narcotic drug after being imported or brought in, knowing the same to have been imported contrary to law, or conspires to commit any of such acts in violation of the laws of the United States, shall be fined not more than $2,000 and imprisoned not less than two or more than five years. For a second offense, the offender shall be fined not more than $2,000 and imprisoned not less than five or more than ten years. For a third or subsequent offense, the offender shall be fined not more than $2,000 and imprisoned not less than ten or more than twenty years. Upon conviction for a second or subsequent offense, the imposition or execution of sentence shall not be suspended and proba-

Bilbo Brands All Charges 'Lies,' Blames Negro, Communist Groups

Bilbo Witnesses Swear to Tell Truth But Change Stories When Off Stand

Bilbo said Negro and Communist-dominated groups who oppose his philosophy are behind efforts to blacken his name and drive him from the senate.

"They want Bilbo destroyed and unseated because of my convictions and ideologies which are opposed to the great objectives of the all-out Negro groups and Communist groups in America," he argued.

Bilbo had appeared completely at ease as he alternately stormed at, ridiculed and belittled the allegations that he profited from relations with war contractors.

DECEMBER 20, 1946

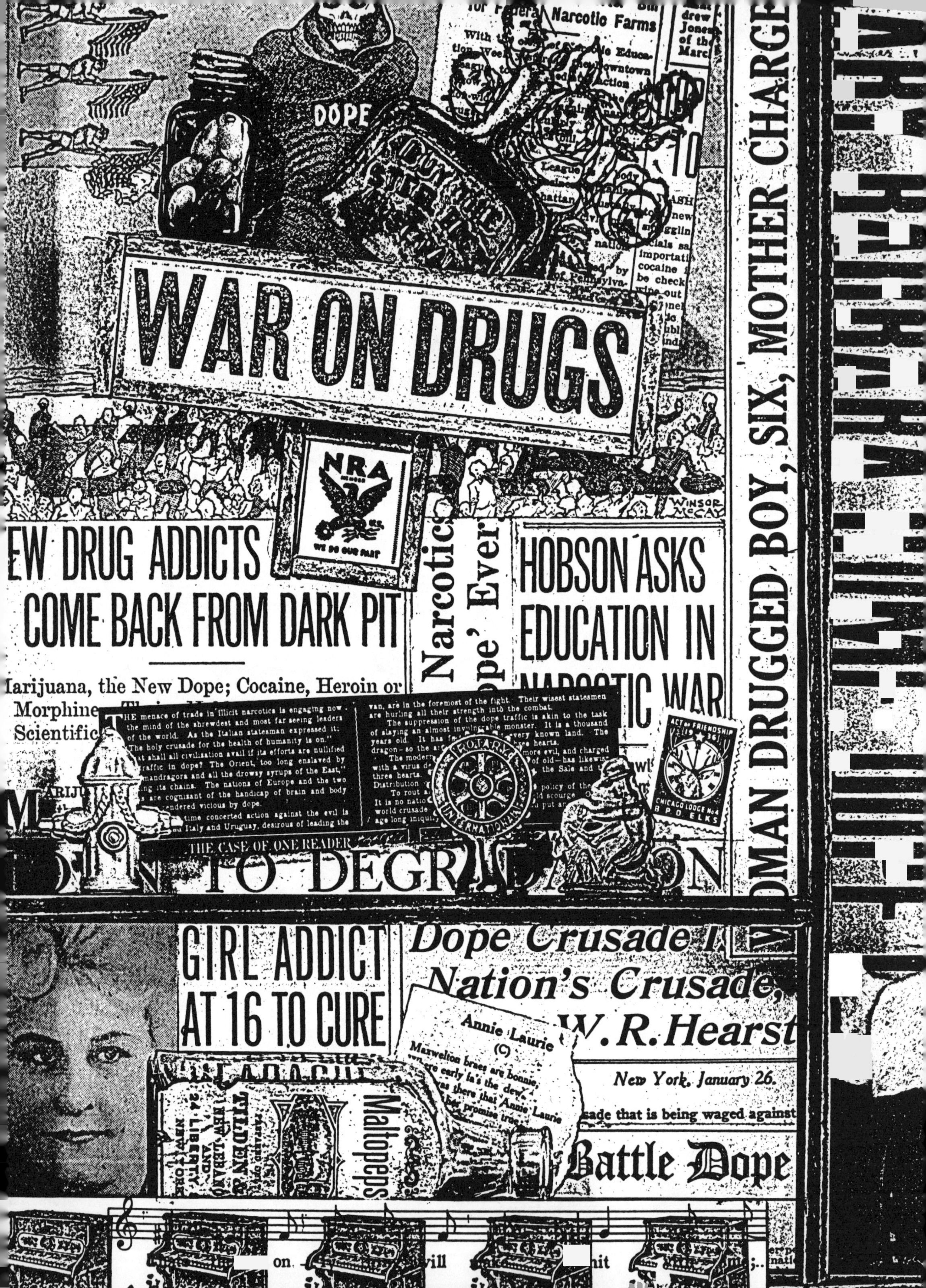
DOPE
Narcotic Farms
WAR ON DRUGS
NRA
WE DO OUR PART
EW DRUG ADDICTS
COME BACK FROM DARK PIT
Marijuana, the New Dope; Cocaine, Heroin or
Morphine
Scientific
Narcotics
pe' Ever
HOBSON ASKS
EDUCATION IN
NARCOTIC WAR
ROTARY INTERNATIONAL
ACT OF FRIENDSHIP
CHICAGO LODGE No 4
B P O ELKS
THE CASE OF ONE READER
TO DEGR
ON
OMAN DRUGGED BOY, SIX, MOTHER CHARGE
WINSOR McCAY
GIRL ADDICT
AT 16 TO CURE
Dope Crusade
Nation's Crusade
W. R. Hearst
Annie Laurie
New York, January 26.
sade that is being waged against
Battle Dope
Maltopeps
TILDEN &
NEW LEBANON
24 LIBERTY
NEW YORK

The Dope Crusades

Dope is a world scourge.
Only a world crusade—
truly a Holy Crusade—
can put an end to this age-long iniquity.
—New York American, *1929*

It's Anti-Drug Week in Hell, and all the gang is here: matrons and mayors, ranters and raiders, crapulous crusaders, dames and doomsayers; star reformers, reformed stars, dry czars and commissars; police, parents, politicians, preachers, presidents, party poopers; rabbis, Rotarians, bishops and Elks, Knights of Columbus, Salvation Army, Mooses and Masons and (special guest star) Mussolini. Soft-shoe routine by Richmond P. Hobson to the tune of Sara Graham-Mulhall's latest hit, "Opium the Demon Flower." Demonstrations of addict farming techniques by Simon and Porter. Keynotes by William Randolph Hearst and a chorus of sob sisters. Refreshments provided by W.C.T.U.; pipe display courtesy of Harry J. Anslinger.

Sentimentality, "the ostentatious parading of spurious and excessive emotion" (James Baldwin), is what the drug crusades were all about. Their purpose was to increase newspaper circulation by arousing public sentiment, leading to short-lived reform. Scorn was the key element, emblazoned in buzz words, nonstop exaggerations, opinions posing as news.

A 1921 *San Francisco Examiner* crusade introduced Hearst's antidope drives with pseudo-poetry: "Nepenthe of Kindly Death is 'Evil Town's' Surcease for Ghosts of Poppy Trail"; " 'Paradise Alley' Is Fetid Haven of San Francisco's Drug Addicts"; and so forth. Such headlines could inflate even the most inconsequential news item—in this case, a reporter's guess that 10,000 drug users lived in San Francisco—into a major event.

At the heart of every crusade was a fearsome image, a dragon to slay. Usually inhuman: demons and ogres, devils in dominoes, trees bearing skulls, reapers of souls, vultures and spiders, panthers and volves, and most of all, snakes, those age-old Vipers of Vice—all preying on society. Today these monstrous images seem ludicrous and camp; they were not intended as such.

Here the art of Winsor McCay shines brilliantly. Though he could deftly depict venomous tyrannosaurs and spiders creeping over the world, the best of his horrors—such as the graveyard ghoul labeled "Dope," leaning on a shovel and glaring at us with malevolent eyes—are preceptibly human. McCay has his film director's perspective working, as in the cartoon in which we look up at the "coming generation" whistling along the sidewalk as peddlers lurk in the bushes, or the cinemascope effect of a throng of children fleeing a "dope traffic" demon, right off the page into our laps.

The Kiddie Dope crusades of the 1920s illustrate how inflammatory stories were used to manufacture laws. "Dragging the Children Down with Dope" became a hallowed cliché, useful in relation to any drug from tobacco in the 1890s to hallucinogens today. Its dark underside was the obverse: minors being used to lure customers and distribute dope.

Taking these heart-clutchers as reality ("Dope, Making Boys Kill, Is Curse of City"), officials pressed for ever-increasing penalties. Street crime, from the youth gangs of Chinatown to juvenile delinquents in Harlem, has been a major basis of drug laws for over a century. When each new law was passed, the newspapers would indulge in orgies of self-congratulation—until it became apparent that the new rules were as ineffective as the old in stopping drugs and crime, and the crusades would begin again.

Despite a moral concern in these crusades about protecting society from dope, there is very little sense that peoples' lives were actually at stake. What the crusaders were asking was, in fact, not to slay some dragon but to put some kid in jail. Such specificity gets lost in the abstract mythology of fanged warty monsters, demon snakes, and black death.

But monsters grown too familiar induce only yawns. Eventually, repeated exaggerations (marijuana "addictive," heroin "lethal") weaken language to the point of nonsense. Disbelief overcomes hysteria, and it becomes pointless to read newspapers for news—a perilous result indeed!

Furthermore, forbidden fruit always tastes delicious. Ironically, crusades advertise the very drugs they preach against. Anti-drug publicity is drug publicity nevertheless, and when it is spun out day after day in snappy stories with eye-catching graphics, the power of the media in promoting drug use becomes quite apparent. This tragicomic flaw in the heart of sensational journalism continues to this day.

'PREPARED BY ALMIGHTY' TO MAKE THE NATION DRY

Dame Crowdy Tells Of Anti-Opium War

Restriction of traffic in opium has been one of the most important ends sought by the League of Nations since its organization, Dame Rachel Crowdy, for eleven years head of the League's Committee on Social Questions, said yesterday

She Urges Women Prohi Enforcers

Here They Are—the Czars of the Anti-Saloon League

Unite Forces in War on Drug Evil

BACK ROW, reading from left to right—Dr. Homer W. Tope (the second man with the hat is not a member, only an innocent bystander), Dr. A. H. Briggs, James A. White, and S. E. Nicholson. MIDDLE ROW—W. F. Cochran, Rev. M. P. Boynton, A. S. Thomas, W. M. Forgrave, Rev. E. S. Shumaker, C. E. Coleman, E. A. Maness. FRONT ROW—Dr. Howard H. Russell, Dr. Wayne B. Wheeler, Dr. A. J. Barton, Dr. Ernest H. Cherrington, Dr. F. Scott McBride, Bishop Thomas Nicholson.

Photograph by Underwood and Underwood.

THEIR WORD IS LAW—Members of the Executive Committee, the all-powerful self-constituted, self-perpetuating body that has the league within its grasp. This committee has had full control of the expenditure of $67,000,000 to impress its will in politics upon the legally constituted officers of the Government. It controls all the machinery of the league. While it dominates Senators and Congressmen, its long arm reaches out towards the White House and the Federal bench. This committee is virtually the whole Anti-Saloon League in itself. Two of the full nineteen membership were not present when this photograph was taken.

BIG BUSINESS IS SOLICITED BY THE LEAGUE

and for the special work for 1924 now begun, including the big convention at Washington in January for publicity and public sentiment

Duty of Liquor Foes to See Laws of Nation Are Enforced to Last Lett

Mrs. Armor, Known as "Georgia Cyclone," in Ra fire Talk, Tells Hearers of Evils of Whisky Traffic

"Opportunity, and Being Afraid to Grasp It," was the theme of the annual W. C. T. U. sermon, delivered Convention Hall of the Civic Auditorium yesterday afternoon Mary Harris Armor, affectionately known

Mrs. M. H. Armor

IN FIGHT TO FINISH, SAYS FEDERAL HEAD

Administration Determined to Enforce Laws; Will Request More Money if It Is Needed

FORCE DRUG LAW TO LIMIT, U. S. ORDERS

ENLISTED FOR NARCOTIC WAR

DOPE DEALER AND 5 'PALS' CAUGHT IN RAID

Police in Night Foray Seize Widely Known Purveyor, With $2,000 Supply and Tools of Trade

Mrs. Gifford Pinchot, who has asked President Harding to "scrap" the male prohibition force and appoint one of women. They'll dry America at once, she promises.

Army of Feminine Dry Agents Asked

Special Dispatch to The Chronicle.

WASHINGTON, D. C., Feb. 21.—"I can get 5000 women at once to enforce the prohibition laws, and they will enforce them, too. They won't be subject to the bribes that are a scandal today."

This is the proposal that Mrs. Gifford

RESCUE VICTIMS FROM TOILS OF DRUGS

S. O'Callaghan. John T. Williams. Dr. W. E. Musgrave. Judge W. P. Joh

"BIG THREE" IN S. F. DOPE WA

Col. L. G. Nutt, chief of narcotics division of federal prohibition department, left; Roy A. Haynes, federal prohibition commissioner, center, and Samuel F. Rutter, federal prohibition director in San Francisco, who will lead drive to stamp out traffic in

Present W. C. T. U. Officers Slated for R

Margaret C. Munns, Treasurer. Mrs. Ella A. Boole, Vice President. Mrs. Sara H. Hoge, Assistant Recording Secretary. Mrs. Elizabeth Preston Anderson, Recording Secretary

CRUSADER — Capt. Richmond Pearson Hobson, president of the World Narcotic Defense Association and leader in the fight against illicit drug traffic.

WOMEN CHEER PLEA FOR WAR ON DRUG EVIL

Theatre Assembly in Appeal to Harding to Proclaim an "Anti-Dope" Week in Nation

DETECTIVES AS "ADDICTS"

STEPHENS TO URGE DRASTIC DOPE PENALTY

Governor William D. Stephens' message was read to the convention by J. S. O'Callaghan, president of the State Board of Pharmacy. Governor

SACRAMENTO ORGANIZES FOR DOPE WAR

LEADERS OF NEW DRUG ASSOCIATION

GIRL DOPE VICTIM

With no opposition in view, it is confidently expected that present officers of the Women's Christian Temperance Union will be chosen for succeeding terms at the annual election today. Principal officers in the organization are shown.

All Cigarette Smokers Are Liars, Says Foe of Tobacco

By EDDIE BOYDEN

James A. Walton, state superintendent of the anti-cigarette league of California, made a speech yesterday.

James not only is state superintendent of the state anti-cigarette league of California, but he lives, breathes and has his beans in the city of Loce Ahng-hayl-ace, a burg which is situate in New Iowa.

By DR. CARLETON SIMON, Deputy Police Commissioner

(Narcotic Division.)

THE value of the narcotic drug campaign of education to which the Hearst newspapers are giving widespread publicity, is inestimable. The Society for Suppression of the Narcotic Drug Evil is performing a splendid service to humanity. Its campaign aims to stop the spread of addiction, and I wish to say that our concern is the non-criminal addict and the prospective addict; but we should waste little sympathy on the criminal addict and dope peddler.

By JOHN F. HYLAN, Mayor of the City of New York.

THE amazing revelations in the country-wide campaign against the narcotic drug evil have convinced me that no greater menace to the nation exists within its borders to-day. I have been shocked by the records of the Narcotic Division of the Police Department, which show that 6,000 arrests for narcotic drug addiction and possession of narcotics have been made here within the last two years, and that this is only a small portion of the city's addicts, most of whom continue the habit secretly and safe from police detection.

Because of the lax Federal control, it is most desirable that a campaign of education should be conducted, so that persons innocent of the evil effects of the use of narcotics should be warned in time.

Sanity League Is To Join in Fight Against Drugs

PERILLI URGES ALL TO TELL OF ADDICT FRIENDS

Trustee of Bellevue Says Vigilance Committee to Report Cases Would Aid Drug War

effective speakers at the session of the Narcotic Control Association of California, at day. Below is shown a section of the delegates to the great humanitarian conference.

Arouse Public Opinion, Urges Walker

CRUSADERS AGAINST DOPE

HOBSON FIGHTS ON—Captain Richmond P. Hobson, central figure in the lower row, is still a militant warrior against the narcotic evil. At the conference of two important committees yesterday, he was flanked by Assemblyman H. W. Dickey, at Hobson's right, and James A. Manning. In the upper row are (left to right) Captain S. Adams, L. Ackoepfgen and Major Sydney Brewster.

N. Y. American Staff Photo.

MILLION IN U. S. USE NARCOTICS, EXPERTS TOLD

California Governor Asks Citizens To Aid in Campaign to End Menace

SACRAMENTO, Feb. 23.—Declaring that the narcotic drug evil is a "constant and serious menace to the social institutions of our State," Governor Young today, in a formal statement, urged Californians ...

Here is his statement: "It is to be hoped that our citizens will co-operate to ... possible extent in the ... of this national ..."

Drug Menace to America Growing Rapidly

SMASHING BLOWS AT DRUG EVIL are delivered by our Senator-Elect, Dr. Royal S. Copeland, in Chicago speech. "Narcotics are undermining the moral and physical health of our nation," he said, pounding home his points as shown in above moviette. (International Newsreel.)

DOPE CONTROL ... AIM ... VELT

NATION CALLED BY SHORTRIDGE TO FIGHT DRUGS

California Senator Appeals to Chamber of Commerce for Wide Education Campaign

RIGID LAWS NOT ENOUGH

Press, Pulpit and Schools Are Urged to Point Out Evils; Plea Is Made to Congress

Roosevelt's Statement On Proposed Survey Of Narcotic Problem

Governor Franklin D. Roosevelt issued the following statement yesterday concerning his proposed narcotic drug survey:

ALBANY, March 9, 1930.

INFORMATION comes to me almost daily about the moral, physical and economic devastation in the wake of the narcotic drug evil. These reports are deeply disturbing. ... of educational campaigns relative to this evil and ... Government has enacted laws and ...

Smith Supports Narcotic Week

ALBANY, Feb. 19.—Governor Smith late today emphatically endorsed Narcotic Week, to be held the week beginning Wednesday, February 22. He said: "Narcotic Week should bring sharply to the minds of the people the danger to public health from the use of habit forming drugs. "The State of New York has gone as far as it ... down this evil ... people to the ... best be brought ..."

GOVERNOR SMITH.

GOV. ROOSEVELT.

Lady Astor Asks World Aid in War on Dope

By LADY ASTOR, M. P.

(Lady Astor, born an American and first woman member of British Parliament, has since her first election in 1919 been active in the campaign against the organized illicit international traffic in dangerous drugs.)

Copyright, 1929, by Universal Service.

LONDON, Oct. 15.—The problem of stopping the drug traffic and ... young people from be...

CRUSADER!—Lady Astor, who is active in the campaign to halt the illegal traffic in narcotics.

ANTI-NARCOTIC BODY CALLS SPECIAL MEET

NATION OPENS DOPE WEEK

Recent revelations in the Rothstein murder case, which have focused attention on an international narcotic ring, give particular im...

FELONY DOPE LAW URGED

MRS. EVERETT A. IRWIN, of Washington, D. C., whose series of articles warning against the use of drugs begins in to-day's New York American.

DOPE MENACE FAST GROWING, WOODS WARNS

Yale University Press Will Publish Result of His Narcotic Study Tomorrow

NEW HAVEN, April 16.—The world faces a serious dope menace, in the belief of Colonel Arthur Woods, former New York Police Commissioner and chairman of President Hoover's Commission on Employment. He will publish tomorrow through the Yale Uni...

Dope Perils Future Of Race, Says Larson

GOVERNOR L... statement: "I have be... nation of the week be...

GOVERNOR LARSON.

DR. JOHN W. PERILLI, trustee of Bellevue Hospital, who endorses the crusade against habit-forming drugs.

ence, do everything in ... against even the least beg... ous poisons."

Doheny Slayer's Use Of Veronal Reveal...

Narcotics Undermine Nature, Says Copeland

UESDAY, JULY 10, 1934

LEADERS IN BATTLE AGAINST DOPE EVIL

HEAD MOVE—Admira... Pearson Hobson, left, world foe of the narcot... ...tured with Mayor La Guardia at the World N... ...se Association banquet yesterday.

City Is Aroused Over Dope Menace

...KE PART—Charles B. T... ...er of Correction MacCo... ...hown with Commis... ...is work often deals ... aware of the evils

...ACK DRIVE—General John ... L. Bullard are two more a... ...left, and Lt. Gen. ...ders of the world ...ampaign to restrict and reg... ...arcotic trade.

DRUG VICTIM'S WIDOW WARNS CITY OF PERIL

Narcotics Easy to Get as Whiskey and as Many Using Them as Bootleg Liquor, She Says

FEARS EFFECT ON YOUNG

Immediate Steps Toward Better Enforcement of Laws to Check T... Are Urged

ANTI-POPPY DRIVE TO BEGIN TO-NIGHT

Friends of Freedom for India Hold Meeting Urging Limit on Drug Production.

TO EDUCATE CULTIVATORS

Drs. Copeland, Simon and Perilli to Speak in Fight on Source of World Menace.

© E. O. HOPPE - LONDON

Diana Manners (now Lady Diana Cooper), who was ...y responsible for the great Victory Ball and who was inexpressibly shocked by the developments of the ...llie Carleton inquest that she wrote articles for the press and made addresses to help the crusade of cleaning up the plague spots of London.

TRAFFIC IN DOPE BEATS PIRACY, LEAGUE HEARS

Portuguese Win British Members' Approval of Resolution Demanding Repression

Aids Drug Probe

CONGRESSMAN PLANS TO BAR ILLICIT DRUGS

No Nation Alone Can Suppress Traffic; Halting Flow at Source Seen as Best Idea

Representative Stephen G. Porter (R.), of Pennsylvania, came to New York yesterday and testified before the Federal Grand Jury investigating the illicit traffic in ...

Dope Evil's Spread Alarming to World, Claims Capt. Hobson

ALARMING spread of the dope evil in the Unit... vealed in the accompanying article prepared ... papers by Captain Richmond Pearson Hobs... General of the first World Conference on Narcotic Ed... has been in session in Philadelphia. Captain Hobson p... ling figures on the growing drug menace, outlines the ... conference to combat it and also charges that powerful ... aligned against the educative programme of the world ...

By CAPT. RICHMOND PEARSON HOB...

Secretary General World Conference on Narcotic ...

California Leads U. S. in War on Drugs

'HIGHLY ENCOURAGING'

ANSLINGER PRAISES RAIDERS

Sees Beginning of the End for Dope Traffic

By HARRY J. ANSLINGER, U. S. Commissioner of Narcotics,

Copyright, 1934, by Universal Service.

WASHINGTON, Dec. 8.—*We hope and believe the raids by Federal and local officers mark the definite beginning of the end of the dope traffic in the United States.*

The results have been highly encouraging. Our agents have captured some of the biggest shots ...

HARRY T. ANSLINGER.

U. S. PUSHES WAR ON PHYSICIANS WHO SELL DOPE

State Legislatures Urged to Pass Uniform Law for Suppression of Traffic

By Universal Service.

WASHINGTON, Dec. 8.—Campaigning to enlist the States in its drive to suppress dope peddling physicians, the Federal Narcotics Bureau is urging all State legislatures to adopt a uniform anti-narcotics law.

Physicians, dodging penalties of the Federal Anti-Narcotic Act, can be jailed and deprived of their license under the State Act, which permits prosecution for illegal possession of narcotics where the Federal Act does not.

To date, seventeen States have applied for drafts of the act and nine have adopted it, with resultant marked decrease in the dope traffic of those States, Harry J. Anslinger, Federal Narcotics Commissioner, declared today.

Few Lose Licenses.

Out of 938 convicted physicians cited to State medical boards by the Narcotics Bureau in two years, only 63 have lost their licenses, 9 ... were suspended, 26 admonished and 55 granted probation in the ...

DRUG ADDICT FARMS URGED IN CONGRESS

Segregation for Sufferers from Narcotics Instead of Jail Terms Asked in Bill

By STEPHEN G. PORTER, Congressman from ...

Steps Down!

DRIVE ON DRUG EVIL ON TODAY

Hang Drug Peddlers, Pastor Asks

... at Nation's Vitals

ISOLATE DRUG VICTIM, URGES DR. MUSGRAVE

In Circulation

San Francisco Examiner

Monarch of the Dailies

TUESDAY SAN FRANCISCO, AUGUST 12, 1919

10-YEAR-OLD BOY KILLED FOR STONI

DRIVEN TO DEATH BY CIGARETTES.

Willie Ross, Fifteen Years Old, Hanged Himself in His Room with His Skate Straps

HIS MIND WAS UNBALANCED.

While His Parents Were at Church the Boy Took Occasion to End His Life.

FATHER FOUND THE BODY.

[BY TELEGRAPH TO THE HERALD.]

CAMDEN, N. J., May 23, 1897.—Willie R. Ross, a fifteen-year-old boy, an inveterate cigarette smoker, suddenly became insane this morning, and, going to the third story of his home, on North Twenty-sixth street, Stockton, committed suicide by hanging himself.

The lad had been smoking many cigarettes ily for several months, and his father and other had noticed that he had been acting rangely at times for two or three weeks. His parents went to church this morning nd left him with the other children playing round the house. When they returned home ne of the daughters told her father that Willie had been acting queerly and had gone o his room soon after they left.

Mr. Ross immediately went up stairs and nd the door leading to Willie's room locked. father called "Willie," and, receiving no answer, broke in the door. There hanging to a rafter was the lifeless body of his son. He quickly cut the body down and sent for Dr. Fensinger, but it was too late—the boy had been dead about an hour.

"Willie" had taken the straps from his skates and, fastening them together, made a noose around his neck. He fastened an end of one of the straps to a rafter, and deliberately strangled himself to death. The generally accepted theory is that excessive cigarette smoking had driven him insane.

BOY LEFT A SKULL WRAPPED IN PAPER EDWARD YENNI'S HOUSE.

It Was for "Mr. Samuels," but Perhaps Somebody Was Playing a Practical Joke.

DEATH OF A BABY WHO SMOKED TOBACCO.

Diphtheria Ends the Life of Trenton's Infant Prodigy at the Age of Five Years.

HAD A PASSION FOR CIGARS.

He Acquired the Habit When Only Seven Months Old and Puffed Away at a Pipe While in His Perambulator.

[BY TELEGRAPH TO THE HERALD.]

RENTON, N. J., Nov. 10, 1890.—Winfield Scott ock Doran, the phenomenal boy smoker, lied in this city in the fifth year of his ath was not caused from the use of the er, but from an attack of virulent diph been sick only a week. ay after taking medicine he spat it her's face, which became swollen fro It is supposed, which was produced sive use of tobacco. The mother's l by it. His mother says that he sm ime he was seven months old. She nd the men used to take him upon t they were smoking their pipes a ew puffs.

the breath. But taking a lit day after day, can not be any one.

REVIEW QUE

1. What did the farmer plant i potatoes?
2. What was done with the tobac
3. What is the name of the poison
4. How much of it is needed to kil
5. What harm can the nicotine in
6. Tell the story of the visit to the
7. Why are boys made sick by the
8. Why does not smoking a cigar k
9. What is said about a little p

REVIEW QUESTI

1. How does alcohol look?
2. How does alcohol burn?
3. What will alcoh

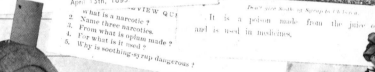

HEALTH READER,

WITH SPECIAL REFERENCE TO THE EFFECTS OF ALCOHOL, TOBACCO, ETC. UPON THE HUMAN SYSTEM

Prescribed by the Board of Education for New Brunswick in accordance with an Act of the Legislature passed April 13th, 1893.

REVIEW QU

What is a narcotic?
2. Name three narcotics.
3. From what is opium made?
4. For what is it used?
5. Why is soothing-syrup dangerous?

CHAPTER IX.

OPIUM.

ALCOHOL and tobacco are called narcotics (nar-kŏt'iks). This means that they have the power of putting the nerves to sleep. Opium (ō'pi-ŭm) is another narcotic.

Don't give Soothing Syrup to Children.

It is a poison made from the juice of poppies, and is used in medicines.

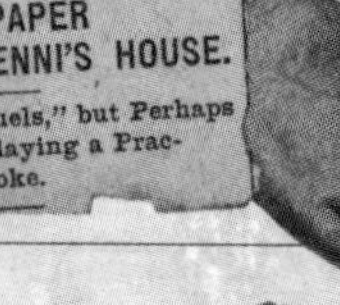

METAL HEAD

Dope Peddler's Child Who Was Used to Dispel Suspicion

Gets the 'Dope' on Santa

Continues Story of Escapades with Criminal Gang While Under Drug Influence.

Bo

SDAY

CHICKENS

Race Track Siren Was a Drug Fiend

Doris Vernon, Mystery Girl, Tells How She Escaped Twice from Husband; Rode Freight Train; Jailed.

In preceding chapters Doris told how she eloped at fourteen years with a stranger to avoid entering a convent; how her husband made her a moonshine runner in the Kentucky mountains. To-day she reveals—but let Doris continue her own story:

After escaping from that Kentucky mountain cabin, where my husband forced me to sell moonshine to the coal miners, I reached the railroad track. A freight was just pulling out. I climbed up on a coal car, and went to sleep.

Just before the sun came up I felt someone shaking my arm. It was the "shack," as they call the brakeman. He said:

"Come on, young fellow, and tell it to the Judge."

Remember, I was still in overalls. A constable took me to the Judge—we had reached a little Virginia town—and he asked me:

"What do you mean by stealing rides, kid?"

DECEIVED AGAIN.

Then I started to cry. I remember yet what he said:

"Well, I'll be hornswoggled if it ain't a gal."

Doris Vernon Tells of Drug in Her Food

A Virjinia girl who married a stranger at fourteen to avoid being sent to a convent, Doris was forced to sell moonshine in the Kentucky mountains. She escaped from her husband, and when only thirty-six cents remained, met a strange, "fatherly gentleman" in Johnson City, Tenn., who offered to aid her. As Doris says:

"How was I to know that he would make me a drug siren, the spider that drew many a sportsman into the net which his criminal band spun at the nation's race tracks?"

To-day Doris says—

That "fatherly gentleman" took me to the Glenrock Hotel in Asheville, N. C., where he introduced me to a blonde who once had been beautiful, saying:

"Louise, dear, this is little Doris Vernon. We shall take care of her until she is able to work."

Doris Vernon.

His wife kissed me. Later I came to know that was a kiss of betrayal, for two months later I awoke one morning feeling like I wanted to jump out of the window. I ran to Louise, as she insisted I should call her, and began crying:

"Something's wrong. I'm dying. I'm going crazy."

MORPHINE IN FOOD.

Louise, dressed in a faded kimona, stood in the middle of that room and laughed, saying in a brutal manner I'd never known before:

"You're lost now, and you've got to do as I say. Why, kid, you're a drug fiend, and there's nothing lower in this world. Here, sit on this couch while I—"

She went to her trunk and took out a hypodermic syringe. Coming over to me, she commanded:

"Now roll up your sleeve."

I obeyed, so nervous was I that I scarcely knew what I was doing. She gave me a "shot of morphine." As my nerves quieted, she explained with a grim smile:

"Now, you feel better, eh? Then listen: For two months Roger and I have been feeding you morphine in your food. Two days ago we stopped it. That's why your nerves began shouting this morning. You'll have to have morphine each day now as long as you live. If you do as we say, you'll get it. If not, then you can go into the gutter and die."

Dime Novels Lure Girl from Home

Police Search City for Fourteen-Year-Old Miss Who Disappeared a Week Ago.

MISS MARY CLAY

15-Year-Old Girl in Dope Dragnet

Used as Lure by Peddler, Sleuths Say

A sordid story in real life, outrivaling Dickens' famous tale of Fagan and little Oliver Twist, was revealed yesterday when police detectives under Captain John J. O'Meara trapped William Harvey, alleged drug peddler, in the McKinley Hotel, 1278 Market street, and then arrested a slim, lit... she was ... a tray o...

To the ... of Cath... taken in ... story of ... her hom... promise ... cisco...

were engaged in a search for it yesterday afternoon and last night.

Meanwhile the two Harveys are being held at the city prison, the girl having been transferred to the Juvenile Detention Home by order of Judge Sullivan on account of her youthfulness.

Operating out of District Attorney ...hew Brady's office, George Duf... ...nd J. Corridan, in the early hours ...rday morning arrested three ...ed drug peddlers, John J. Sulli... Ray Cook and Toney Sourbis, ...

1st Portland Run

The CAPITOL

IT'S VIVID! IT'S DARING!... IT'S POWERFUL! BUT IT'S TRUE!

"DOPED YOUTH"

See the TRUTH about America's newest NARCOTIC MENA...

Five Big Acts of VAUDEVILLE

Attend Matinees Avoid Night Crowds!

Rivoli

Daring Expose of Marihuana

"ASSASSIN OF YOUTH"

MARIHUANA

2nd Hit—Sally Blaine in "Numbered Woman"

Doris' Innocent Look Hid $500,000 in Dope

Virginia Girl, Once Tool of Band of Int...tional Crooks, Tells of Drug Runnin...

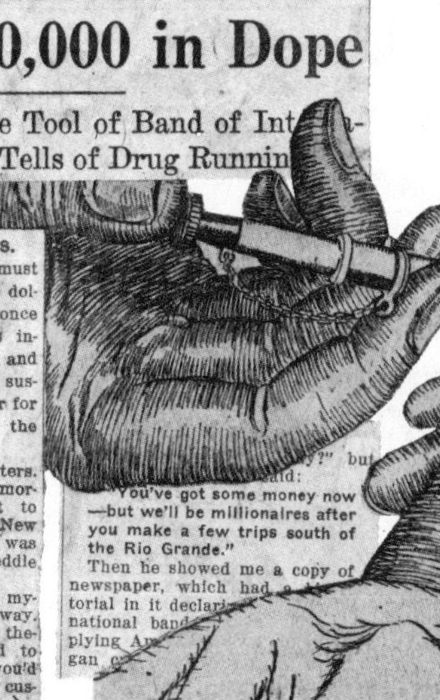

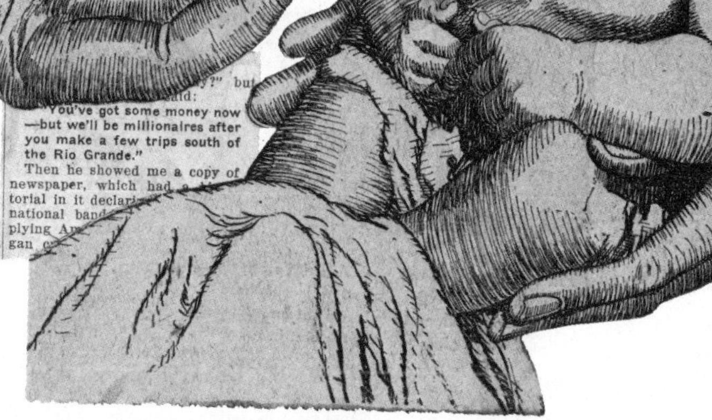

DRUG RUNNER FOR 3 YEARS.

Inthe next three years I must have brought in half a million dollars worth of drugs, and never once was I stopped by a customs inspector. I was too young and innocent looking for the mto suspect that I was the dope runner for the biggest criminal band in the United States.

Cincinnati was our headquarters. From there the dope—both morphine and heroin—was sent to New Orleans, Chicago and New York City. In those places it was made into small packages to peddle to dope fiends.

Of course I peddled a little myself, especially on Broadway. There's a certain hotel in the theatrical district where I used to hand the stuff out. Maybe you'd like to know the names of my customers.

Well, there was a ceratin famous star who just had to have a shot of morphine—but there, I've told enough. Why drag their names into the mud?

Anyway, I want to forget it all, now. I'm trying to fight back to self-respect. And maybe I'll find my share of happiness by trying to help others.

...?" but ...id:

"You've got some money now —but we'll be millionaires after you make a few trips south of the Rio Grande."

Then he showed me a copy of newspaper, which had ... torial in it declari... national band... plying Am... gan ...

...by Benson
AND THE OPIUM SMUGGLERS
HIS TRAIL WASN'T HERE TWO WEEKS AGO. LOOKS LIKE IT'S WELL TRAVELLED.
COMING FROM MEXICO, THAT MEANS ONE THING. SMUGGLERS. WE'D BETTER WATCH IT TONIGHT.
I CERTAINLY HOPE YOUR SCHEME WORKS, YOUNG FELLOW.
I'M SURE IT WILL.
IT HAD BETTER. WE WOULDN'T STAND A CHANCE AGAINST THAT SUB-MACHINE GUN.
COME OUT OF THERE SLOWLY, ONE AT A TIME.
YOUR PLAN WORKED SWELL, BOBBY.
AND DON'T TRY TO REACH FOR A GUN!
WE'VE GOT THOUSANDS OF DOLLARS WORTH OF OPIUM HERE. YOUR REWARD IS GOING TO BE A VALUABLE ONE.
YOU KNOW WHAT THAT MEANS, TEX.
YOU BET. NOW WE CAN ISSUE A LOT MORE BOBBY BENSON MONEY TO PUT IN EACH BOX OF FORCE.
FORCE
MONEY
VOID

Human Derelicts Openly Ply Pernicious Dope Trade In Streets of Sacramento

Human derelicts, ruined by death-dealing narcotics, plying their trade openly—not furtively a bit, except for the watch they keep for victims at the State capital of California—that is one of the pictures which Annie Laurie presents today.

10,000 Drug Addicts in S. F., Girl Reporter Finds; Dope Is Openly Peddled

When "The Examiner" inaugurated its "drug crusade" its initial step was to learn the facts. It had in its files court records, statistics, reports from dependable men and women of the city which detailed the extent of the curse and a sheaf of accusations against the people who were said to be dope drugs.

"The Examiner" wanted proof. It wanted to know from the inside to what extent San Francisco was in the grip of the nefarious traffic.

By HELEN TRUE

SAN FRANCISCO EXAMINER: SUNDAY, OCTOBER 9, 1921

'DOPE' SELLER DROPS DRUGS OUT WINDOW

Officers, Anticipating Action, Catch Packages as They Fall Down Lightwell Off Powell St.

Harry Davis, alleged dealer in narcotics, fell into the hands of State Board of Pharmacy detectives early yesterday.

(EDITORIAL)

San Francisco Must Destro[y] Drug Traffic, Adding Addict[s] To Toll of Wrecked Live[s]

IN its unrelenting fight on the drug traffic "The Examiner" has developed an amazing story of this greatest scourge of modern civilization, and the greatest menace to orderly, sane and balanced progress. "The Examiner" tomorrow will begin publication of this exposure, revealing hitherto unsuspected ramifications in the narcotics trade.

[FR]EEDOM MUST

'Street of Living Dead' Harbors Dope Sellers in Heart of San Francisco

L. A. Addicts Spend $7,500 a Day for Drugs

Policy of Segregation Approved in South

STARTLING USE OF NARCOTICS IS REVEALED BY TRAGEDIES

YOUNG WOMAN W[...] DRUG VICTIM

[...] Registered Drug [...] ed in Movies; Ex- [...] Olive Thomases

[F]RENCH CUT O[...] MYSTIC TEMP[LE]

TUESDAY SAN FRANCISCO, OCTOBER 25, 1921

Curb Narcotic Curse, Is Governor's Plea to Dope Convention

Governor William D. Ste[phens] [...] drug traffic [...] convention of California officials which opens Thursday at the Civic Auditorium to map a campaign [...]

Nepenthe of Kindly Death Is 'Evil Town's' Surcease For Ghosts of Poppy Trail

Into the haunts of "Evil Town" went Annie Laurie [...] horror of it all. She explored the very depths of [...] terrible illicit drug traffic has brought into some [...] country.

By ANNIE LAURIE

DOPE PEDDLER CONVICTED IN FELONY CASE

"PARADISE ALLEY" IS FETID HAVEN OF SAN FRANCISCO DRUG ADDICTS

(Continued From Page One.)

S. F. NOT WORSE THAN OTHER LARGE CITIES

These disclosures do not imply that San Francisco is the most wicked city on earth. It is not worse than any other large city, whose inhabitants are from every country in the world. In all such cities the same conditions prevail in greater or less degree.

[FR]ENCH DECLA[RE] CHIEFS OF [...]

ON WHITES I[...]

Drug Evil Invades Cities, Towns as Ruthless Ring Coolly Recruits Victims

This is the first article of a series by Annie Laurie, the famous writer, exposing the horrible menace of the drug traffic and sounding an alarm to all California to combat its insidious influence. In her article tomorrow she will journey into the "Street of the Living Dead" with its awful [...] of this unchecked traffic.

DOOLING URGES HOSPITAL TO AID ADDICTS

Big Dope Dealers Should Be Sentenced to Prison [...]

DEPTHS OF CHARNEL HOUSE HOLD DESPAIRING VICTIMS OF DOPE

(Continued From Page One.)

"DRUG PALACE" YIELDS CACHE OF NARCOTICS

S. F. PHY[...]

Cunning and Resource of Dope Peddlers Reflected by Their Attitude in Court

There is nothing very hysterical about this alarm that is being sounded by the enemies of the Drug Traffic—not when they arrest a "dope" peddler on the postoffice steps and another on the church stairs and shoot at a third on Clay street.

They will try a student at the University of California next week on a charge of peddling drugs. The education of children into the Satanic mystery of dope begins on the streets of San Francisco long before college days.

These things are not the product of a vivid imagination and a facile pen. They go down on the cold, unsentimental records of the police courts. There they stand and some day they may be read into the arraignment of those "who pass by on the other side."

GIANT SH[...] OF BRITAIN [...] GUARD PA[...]

From Bases Provided [...] ions, English Fleet [...] Watch; Follows U. [...]

Suggestion That Chan[ge] [...] tem Is Due to Desi[re] [...] the Naval Activity [...]

[...]F TO [...]DRUG [...]TION

Prisons Are Filled by Dope Victims

Vice Spreads All Over Country

Nation-Wide Campaign Held Vital

By ANNIE LAURIE

They're all coming to the convention next Thursday.

NARCO[TIC] MENA[CE]

FEDERAL C[...]

TEARS of the P[...]

THE SAN FRANCISCO EXAMINER

[DO]PE CASES TO [BE] RUSHED BY [F]EDERAL COURT

CUNNING OF DOPE PEDDLERS IS REFLECTED BY ATTITUDE IN COURT

(Continued From Page One.)

GIRL A[...] IN DOPE [...] SENT T[...]

'EVIL TOWN' IN FAIRYLAND IS PEOPLED BY GHOSTLY FIGURES ON 'POPPY TRAIL'

(Continued From Page One.)

DOPE PEDDLER JAILED IN FIGHT

Caught selling narcotics on the steps of St. Patrick's Church on Mission street, William "Goldie" Hindley and Joseph "Nig" Redman, notorious drug peddlers and addicts, were arrested yesterday by Inspectors D. R. Dunbar and J. McCarthy of the State Board of Pharmacy after a rough and tumble battle.

THE SAN FRANCISCO EXAMINER: SUNDAY, OCTO... 1921

TY FEDERATION OF CLUBS BACKS ANTI-DRUG CONVENTION

000 WOMEN EDGED TO COTIC WAR

Army of Two Millon Drug Victims in U. S.

Conference Will Plan Means to Cut Ranks

By ANNIE LAURIE

Two million of them now—not a million, as the statistics informed us less than a year ago... the streets—and every day at a stated hour the addicts and the fiends met together at the clinic. ... we are irretrievably bound up in it. The Army and Navy is affected. They wait at the gates of the very...

LEGION BATTLES GRAVE MENACE

The American Legion is to take an active part in the anti-narcotic traffic convention Thursday, October 27, at the Exposition Auditorium.

Invitations have been sent to every American Legion Post in Northern California for delegates to attend the convention.

That also has been done as to Legion posts in San Francisco through the State adjutant's office.

The narcotic problem comes with particular force into the Legion because of ...

CHINESE CLAIMS DRUG FRAUD

Following the presentation of an application for a new trial in the case of Ong Quong, convicted of selling drugs, made by Attorney Ollie Hamlin Jr., sentence in the case was deferred by Police Judge Edward J. Tyrrell in Oakland yesterday morning. Quong was found guilty by a jury late Friday evening.

Previous to bringing in its verdict the jury, through its foreman, W. E. Hoogs, asked instruction from Judge Tyrrell ...

Salvation Army Leader Will Speak on Dope

The Salvation Army, whose work reaches the lowermost depths of human degradation, into the purlieus of the victims of the narcotic traffic, is to be represented at the public convention on Thursday, ... 10 a. m. at the Exposition ... to concentrate ... upon the eradication ... Col. Andrew Craw... commander of the ... with headquarters in ...

PASTORS ENLIST IN DRUG WAR

From the pulpits of many San Francisco churches today will be made the announcement of the coming public convention to devise means effectively to fight and stamp out the drug evil, ...

OFFICIALS BACKING DOPE WAR

...ce of Invitations to Anti-...tics Convention to Be ...

S. F. Dope Convention Is First in U. S.

New York and Chicago to Follow Suit

Definite Action on Traffic Assured

By ANNIE LAURIE

How clean and fresh and brand new the world looks—after the rain. Old Tamalpais has a head-dress of clouds, as if he, too, were house cleaning—and across the bay the Berkeley campanile gleams through the purple and rose of the ...

...the country has at last awakened to the danger of this insidious evil and intends to stand behind the government in a determined fight. If that isn't good news, I don't know what is.

Silence is the worst weapon in the world against such an enemy.

The organized and cynical power of the drug ring thrives—not in the open light of day; not in the face of honest publicity, but in secret and in the dark.

$15,000 DOPE FOUND IN NEW SHIP PA...

Customs Surveyor, ... 'Examiner' Camp... System of Search...

WAR OPENED ON BOOTLEG DRUG STORES

Retail Druggists Seek Aid of U. S. to Put an End to System ... Hurts Real Business

...t Licenses Be Given ... Legitimate Trade; Close ...ation Is Promised

Government Monopoly Is Urged to Curb Growth Of "Drug Snake" in U. S.

"The Drug Snake"—the terrible narcotic evil!

What is California going to do about it?

That is the question which is put to every good citizen—every man and woman who has at heart the best for humanity in this great State.

Annie Laurie today presses home to you the problem. She has vividly told you some of the horror of it all.

She presents to you today some of the outstanding things that have been done here and by the Federal Government.

Temporizing must stop.

Bring to bear every force in the State to combat this growing, insidious vice that is crushing young womanhood and young manhood.

By ANNIE LAURIE

The Drug Snake—how are we going to kill it?

What are we going to do to take the menace and the horror of it out of our everyday lives?

The fight against the traffic in narcotics in this country ... is only just beginning ... but it is beginning ...

DRUG ORGIES CHARGED BY S. F. WOMAN

Fashionable Matrons Mentioned as Frequenters of Edifice in Geary-Richmond District

Man Who 'Buys' for Pastor Goes to L. A. as Publicity Makes Morphine Scarce Here, Charge

With the discovery of morphine bottles in the "New Era Temple," 6214 Geary street, ...

...ERMAN FOOD SUPPLY, ...LLED DOPE DEN FOR RICH

...ARTIAL ROLL IN RUHR; ... NARCOTIC RING JAILED

...ARY 4, 1925—ONE HUNDRED AND TWENTY-FOUR PAGES. DAILY 5 CENTS, SUNDAY 10 CENTS

...AN, 3 OTHERS IN DOPE NET:

...D TO KU KLUX KLAN

S. F. GRAND JURY ASKS CURB ON DOPE EVIL

Dope in San Francisco

DOPE addiction ... Francisco.

Not only are ... bers of addicts in th... most of these have be... past, but there are incr... that the use of habit-fo... growing among people i... ered conservative and re...

This, with a clear in... connection between dope... crime, is the essence of a ... just made by the narcoti... of the County Grand Jury.

The committee has do... worth while in pointing o... relationships between the ... forming drugs and criminali...

"An extremely large perc... criminals convicted not only ... peddling but of such crimes a... burglary and robbery, are foun... drug addicts.

"It is driven home forcibly as ... of investigation that TO CUT ... DRUG ADDICTION IS TO ... DOWN CRIME."

Increasing drug addiction ... means increasing criminality; it... increasing human misery for the ... themselves and for all those rela... them in any way.

To make an attack upon dope ... make an attack upon the most insi... enemy now aiming its shafts at c... ized society.

The report under consideration ... properly confines itself to recomme... tions of local and State activity ag... the menace.

But it recognizes the ultimate re... and states it. That ultimate remed... the control of the production of the ... products from which dope is fabrica...

The ultimate remedy can be app... only through international agreem... And that international agreement ... be arrived at only through the pres... of public opinion throughout the ... lized world.

It is well that the Federal author... see the situation and are preparin... act.

Clean Exteriors

Wins Beauty

PROBERS LINK CRIME SPREAD TO NARCOTICS

"Definite Increase in Use and Distribution of Drugs" in City Noted by Quiz Board

Congress Bill to Restrain Production of Opiates by World Pact Approved; Action Urged

Ending a searching three-months' inquiry into the "dope" evil as it exists in San Francisco today, the city and county grand jury last night, in a report submitted by its ...

...OZE ... F. ...RED

Depths of Charnel House Hold Somebody's Sisters In Murk of Dope Trail

The Charnel House—that's about the end of the "dope" trail. Somebody's Sister and Somebody's Wife live there. Annie Laurie has been to call on them and today tells the pitiful and sordid story of several human wrecks. One of them used to be a school teacher. "Funny, isn't it?" I call it a scream"—those are her bitter words.

You would not care even to peep into the Charnel House? But... haps you had better, to see where somebody's ... of the by-products of your day ...

HIGHTOWER IS KLANSMAN, SWART SAYS

District Attorney Gives ... tion Regarding ...

...RT AID IN S. F. DOPE

A STORY OF SAN FRANCISCO

2 SENTENCED, 6 CONVICTED IN DOPE ROUND-UP

Heavy Penalties Asked by Board of Pharmacy; Drugs Found in Possession of the Captives

Fourteen men charged with violating the State poison law, all of them rounded up by the authorities during the last two days, appeared in the ... court yesterday morning.

...special committee headed by B. H. Brainerd, secretary of the grand jury, and consisting of Charles H. ... Mish, Thomas F. Duffy, Jr., Cornelius V. Collonan and William L. Barry.

Testimony and advice of investigators, detectives and medical men were utilized by this committee, and the recommendations are ascribed to the suggestions made by these experts.

...FE OF 'DOPE ...NG' JAILED ...N SMUGGLING

...Sam Morlen, With Baby in ...ms, Arrested; Illicit Drug ...ound Hidden ...

Amazing Data Shows Spread Of 'Dope' Evil

HERE is the "drug traffic" situation in California:

There are approximately 10,000 drug users in California. Of that number between 2,000 and 2,500 live in San Francisco.

Most of the narcotics consumed in California are smuggled into the State from ...

DOPE PEDDLERS MUST GO, SAYS U. S. ATTORNEY

Williams Announces Plan Under Way for Strong Campaign Against Dealers in Narcotics

HAYNES OPENS S. F. WAR ON DOPE TRAFFIC

Forty Killed.

THE DRUG HABIT
MURDER
BLACKMAIL
VICE
BOOTLEG
CORRUPTION
RACKETS
DOPE
UNDERWORLD
GRAFT
FEDERAL AUTHORITY
DOPE
DRUG EVIL
ENRIGHT
DOPE EVIL
NARCOTIC TRAFFIC
INTERNATIONAL DOPE RING
DOPE
NARCOTIC EVIL
SOCIAL AND CIVIL LIFE OF OUR COUNTRY
HOMES
DRUG EVIL
NARCOTIC TRAFFIC
COCAINE
MORPHINE
OPIUM
COCAINE
DOPE TRAFFIC
DRUG HABIT
DOPE RING

DRUG EVIL
THE DRUG FIEND
VICE
DOPE
LOCAL ENFORCEMENT
DOPE
DOPE
NARCOTIC DRUG MENACE
DOPE
DOPE SMUGGLER
DOPE PEDDLER
DOPE TRAFFIC
SPEED

THE SAN FRANCISCO EXAMINER: FRIDAY, MAY 12, 1922

U. S. Drug Slave Nation, Says Authority

But States Start Battle Against Dope

By ANNIE LAURIE

SENATE TO ACT ON DOPE BAN

3 TRAPPED IN DOPE RING LAIR

JOS. CLANCY CONVICTED OF DOPE SELLING

Dope Ring Crumbles in San Francisco as U. S. Jury Finds Him Guilty on Eleven Counts

Clancy Conviction Victory

False Security of Dope

By ANNIE LAURIE

Stop Drug Production, Says Federal Chief

Washington Official Knows Vice Ravages

By ANNIE LAURIE

Big Business to Fight Narcotics Evil

Insurance Companies Join Dope War

By ANNIE LAURIE

Money talks, they say.

AVALANCHE OF LETTERS ASKS NARCOTIC ACT

Write to Legislature

PUBLIC DEMANDS LAW

ANNIE LAURIE TELLS OF DOPE

What of Liner's $100,000 Dope Cargo?

First Test of New Law Vital to America

By ANNIE LAURIE.

THE SAN FRANCISCO EXAMINER: THURSDAY, JU

New Narcotic Law Is Pull Proof---So Far

Dope Ring to Find Law Enforcing Certain

By ANNIE LAURIE

CITY OFFICIALS TO ATTEND OPENING OF CASTRO THE

(Continued from Page

Dope for Sale---Apply Only to Uncle Sam

Sole Solution of Terrible Narcotic Evil

The Underworld is a kind of supercity which includes all cities, a supersium of each, living always without the law and according to its own convention of life by the wits. Vice is its single recreation. Dope is the core of its vice. Crime is the bedrock of the Underworld and dope is the core of crime. The Underworld is the dope tragic. The dope peddler is ex-officio a member of the Underworld.—"Hearst's International Magazine."

By ANNIE LAURIE.

NERVE MURDERS.

PROBLEM REALIZED.

CHILD ADDICTS.

'Paradise Alley' Is Fetid Hell-Hole of Lost Souls In Grip of Deadly Drug

By ANNIE LAURIE

PORTER DOPE BILL TO GET CLEAR WAY

FATE OF BRUNEN KIN TO BE GIVEN TO JURY TO-DAY

Summing Up Is All That Remains Before Dottie and Harry Mohr Learn Verdict

DEFENSE IS CORROBORATED

Neighbor of Accused Man's Sister Says He Saw Harry at Her Home When John Was Slain

By ANNE DUNLAP,

Far East Finds Ready Dope Ma

Beginning of Immense Drug

"A drug ring is neither more nor less than an impostor's commercial organi of the Underworld. It does not matter that the importer in question happens to buyers, his retail sellers and his general staff just as any legitimate importer nee sistent and as orderly about his affairs as any other commercial operator. He c legal shadow of a doubt that his business is not what the law positively know to be implicated in casual, incriminating sales. His agents and retailers attend t them when they are caught."—Hearst's International Magazine.

By ANNIE LAURIE.

AMERICAN

SNOW FLAKES

HERALD CHICAGO EXAMINER

OFFICE: MADISON AND MARKET STS. SATURDAY, NOVEMBER 26, 1921. SPORTING NEWS, MARKETS, PICTURES AND CLASSIFIED ADS. TELEPHONE MAIN 5060

"DOPE" DEATHS INCLUDE CITY'S BEST KNOWN NAMES

NARCOTICS SOLD ON STREET, USED EVEN AT PARTIES

Winifred Black Tells of Sale of Drugs on Lake Shore Drive by Veteran.

BY WINIFRED BLACK.

Dead—of morphine—One of the most public-spirited, well-known, well-loved women of Chicago.

Dead—of morphine—The president of one of the biggest and best of the women's clubs of this city.

Dead—of heroin—A writer known and beloved in every home in Illinois, a woman of refinement and culture.

Dead—of cocaine—One of the light... wittiest women writers of...

HERALD CHICAGO EXAMINER

MADISON AND MARKET STS. FRIDAY, DECEMBER 2, 1921. FICTION, SOCIETY, STAGE AND MOVIE NEWS, PICTURES AND CLASSIFIED ADS. TELEPHONE MAIN 5060

...GS WRECK LIFE AND HOPES OF GIRL SCHOOL TEACHER

SLEEPS ..., WAKES ...RS OLD ...E EDUCATION ...LEY CALLED SUDDENLY

WINIFRED BLACK DECLARES DOPE PARLEY FARCE

Famed Writer Tells Radio Audience Britain Dominated Delegations, Had Own Way

Describing the Geneva conference for the suppression in narcotics...

TELLS U. S. TRUTH ON DOPE

TRAGEDY AT GENEVA—Winifred Black, noted writer for Hearst publications, tells over the WEAF radio what she saw and heard at the Geneva Conference on narcotics.

SEABURY SEEKS UNDERWORLD LINK TO POLICE

...r Name ...at of Son

MOTHER, VICTIM OF DOPE, LOSES HER 2 CHILDREN

...ed Black Discovers Dixie ...r Different from Olden Days

By WINIFRED BLACK.

...ORLEANS, June 23.—What's a lion peeler? I am willing to wager that you haven't the faintest idea. I did not have myself until this day of Our...

I saw a pair of blue rompers which she was making for him the other day, feather stitching them or something, and there are five or six between her and her little brother. But, believe me, what a fascinator that little girl is. All the boys are crazy about her, she is not crazy about...

At the piney woods frolic with me.

DOPE PEDDLER CALLED LOWEST OF CRIMINALS

Igoe Reveals Average Addict Spends $3 Daily, 90% of Which Is Gotten Illegally

Denunciation of the dope peddler as the vilest form of criminal was made last night by Frank L. Igoe, head of the Federal Narcotics Bureau here, in a radio address over Station WHN.

Speaking on the subject, ... Narcotics," Igoe ... average addict ... dope. This ... of the cases, ...

DANGER IN PAROLE

Weak-Kneed Judges at Fault

A CALL TO CITIZENRY

By WINIFRED BLACK.

WASHINGTON, Dec. 14.—A national police West for the training of officers in the detection of crim... the bringing of criminals to justice—and keeping them in the hands of justice no matter what political pull or what powerful influence of any sort these criminals and their friends may have.

The regulation of pardon and parole.

The strict surveillance of crooked lawyers and weak and easily influenced judges.

Keep politics out of the la... politicians out...

...tentiary on some pretext or...

No one with a human... wants to make it one sin... harder for a man who's trying to go straight.

But we must realize that ...mendous proportion of org... crime in this country is com... by ex-convicts who are on parole or who have been, by queer quirk of fate, pardoned; they had no intention whats... of going straight and only w... the pardon to give them a ch... to go crooked again.

Who'll Make Them Beh...

And now how about ... crooked lawyers and weak jud... Who's going to make them... have?

WINIFRED BLACK.

NATION WARNED ON NEW INFLUX OF CHEAP DOPE

Reduced Appropriation for Narcotic Bureau Crippling Fight on Growing Menace

By WINIFRED BLACK.

SAN FRANCISCO, Nov. 28.—Nickel Day bargains in dope. Month-end sales of misery and shame.

Murder and suicide at a price cut sale, such as was never known in the United States before.

Good news, great news for the dope users—poor, miserable unfortunates. What kind of news is it to the rest of us mortals who are trying hard to get back on our feet again and look the rest of the world in the face?

Getting back on the job again, are you, neighbor?

You and your son and your brother-in-law have found something to do after months of weary waiting that drove you close to despair. Honest hard work that will help you keep the woman and children you love in some sort of decent, civilized comfort.

Happy days, good days, splendid days, no wonder we feel like chanting hallelujah and shouting hurray and three times three, many of them.

AMERICAN PICTORIAL—A Paper for People Who Think—FRIDAY, JANUARY 12, 1923. Business Telephone, Columbus 7000

Winifred Black Says: Women Can Keep Secrets

As Private Secretaries to Great Men They Have Proved Their Trustworthiness When Confided In.

MISS FRANCES LOUISE STEVENSON, the English girl who has been Lloyd George's secretary for ten years, says that women ought to go into the government service—go in early and stay late. Miss Stevenson ought to know.

She is pretty and blue-eyed and fair...

WINIFRED BLACK

NEW YORK AMERICAN—A Paper for People Who Think—SUNDAY, FEBRUARY 26, 1928 Business Telephone, Columbus 7000

...d Pledged to Rush Porter Narcotic Bill

DYER PRAISES ACT PROVIDING 'DOPE FARMS'

60 Per Cent of All Convicts Are Addicts

Smugglers Big Problem in Narcotic War

Regulation of American Factories Helps but Little

By WINIFRED BLACK.

IS the man who poured gasoline over a woman, set her afire, and let her burn to death—a drug addict? The police declare that he is.

And what is much more important, every police authority in this part of the country declares this hideous murder is a typical drug addict crime.

Solution Depends on Getting at Source of Traffic

LABOR CHIEF ASKS SCHOOLS TO FIGHT DOPE

SEA TRADERS ASKED TO AID DOPE BATTLE

...e Flood Feared as Result ...Cut in Narcotic Control Fund

By WINIFRED BLACK.

...FRANCISCO, Nov. 1.—The ... traffic again—and worse ... ever.

most powerful and most bitterly degrading dope ever brought into existence for the destruction of human beings.

Why manufacture 537 pounds of...

...ast year under the terms of Geneva in 1931, those manufactured 537... We needn't go into...

WINIFRED BLACK, Writer, Exposes Dope Peddling Activity.

Winifred Black Starting on Tour of...

WRITER WILL STUDY TYPES, DESCRIBE THEM IN ARTICLES

...inifred Black, the noted special writer for the Hearst ...ers, is starting on a tour of the United States for the ...the types who make up the United States.

WINIFRED BLACK.

...know all about it over in Europe, and the forces that have been fighting the dope evil in this country know about it, too.

They are whispering strange things in Washington and in New York and in New Orleans, while in San Francisco the State and the Federal narcotic officers are almost in despair over the fight ahead of them.

Don't let's talk generalities; let's get down to plain open cards on the table.

Over in China they are making 12,000 tons of opium and 90 tons of morphine and heroin per annum. These are official figures, mind you.

CHINESE TRADE GROWS.

Up to the last few months Japan has done most of the handling of these enormous profits. But since Turkey and Germany and Switzerland have cut down...

PRESS, RADIO, PULPIT FIGHT...

Unseen and Insidious, Drug Habit Creeps In,

Crime Due to 'Drug Wave,' Declares Narcotic Chief

By WINIFRED VAN DUZER.

"It is not a crime wave but a narcotic wave that is rolling over the city.

"The bandits, murderers and gunmen spreading terror here practically all are users of drugs. They are not registered with the State Commission, and so are able to roam at large, venting their viciousness upon thee public.

"One hundred thousand dollars' worth of narcotics is sold every day upon New York's streets!"

Dr. Carleton Simon, Special Deputy Police Commissioner in charge of the drug traffic division, yesterday made these astonishing statements.

25 Millions in 'Dope' Smuggled Since May

...ines Levied Against Ships Where N... ...cotics Are Found Cut to Ridicul... Small Sums on A...

...DAY, DECEMBER 7, 1921

...inifred Black Tells of Drug Ring Havoc

By WINIFRED BLACK.

...HINGTON, Dec. 6.—Eighteen attractive, intelligent, well-educated American girls were ... into the police court in Seattle the other day, and every one ... half mad with cocaine.

six months there will be half a dozen victims in the town and each one of them is good for six victims more.

...By Winifred Black

My Country 'tis of Thee

Chicago's Huge, but Orderly Negro Colony Amazes Writer; and They All Seem to Be Prosperous.

"The Ghetto was as exciting as the black belt was quiet and orderly."

Gangsters Carry Machine Guns in Viol... and Any Street Serves as a Convenient Battleground.

Moose Indorse Movement for Anti-Drug Week

CLIFTON LODGE, No. 657, Loyal Order of Moose, of Passaic, having 150 members, has passed unanimously a resolution calling upon President Harding to set aside an "Anti-Narcotic Week" to awaken the public to the drug danger.

The resolution recites that despite existing laws the traffic in narcotic drugs, including morphine, cocaine and other opiates, is spreading to an alarming extent, according to official evidence and that of the Hearst papers, and calls upon the President to call an international conference to make plans for control of traffic in narcotics between the various nations of the world.

Copies of the resolution were dispatched yesterday to President Harding and to the United States Senators and Representatives from New Jersey.

Harding to Hear Elks' Appeal for Drug War Today

CHICAGO, Feb. 1.

PRESIDENT HARDING will receive to-morrow a delegation of prominent Elks, who will emphasize to him the country-wide drug menace, said a message to J. K. Sinek, exalted ruler of the Chicago lodge.

Sinek will present to the President resolutions from 800 lodges in the several States, representing more than 500,000 Elks.

Eleven thousand school teachers will be organized in an active campaign to protect Chicago school pupils, President Robertson of the School Board announced to-day.

Plans for the campaign followed the written "confession" of George Roth, eighteen, of Lane Technical High School.

The authorities pronounced Roth a fakir, but his grandmother insisted he told the truth.

RICH MAN IN ICE CAKE MAY BE DRUG VICTIM

Herman Michael, of Stapleton, Missing for Weeks, Found Frozen to Death.

SLEEPING POTIO

250,000 Masons Enter Crusade Against Drugs

By Universal Service.

WASHINGTON, Feb. 10.

ANOTHER great ... tion enrolled ... rapidly-expanding ... ing the narco...

The new ... members of ... of Veiled ... chanted R... Masonic ...

Roy Jan... Ba... of the Aryan Gro... cago, accompanied ... members of the W... Grotto, called at the ... House and presented ... tions pledging the order ... co-operation in any step ... President may decide to ... to stamp out the "dope ... menace.

Monarch Battis acted as the personal representative of Edward A. Pelouze, grand monarch of the Supreme Cou... of the order. Representa... Elliott W. Sproul, of Illi... escorted the delegation to ... White House.

President Harding had sufficiently recovered from ... cold to receive his bro... prophets. Secretary Christ... assured the delegation, ho... ever, that the movem... against the narcotic drug ... has the President's most ... thusiastic support.

Monarch Battis left for ... President, in addition to ... resolutions, a letter stro... endorsing the proposal ... strike at the menace by li... ing it at the source of pro... tion, as embodied in the ... ter resolution now pending ... fore the House Foreign Affa... Committee.

Elks Ask Harding for War on Dope

B. P. O. ELKS WAR ON DOPE—Prominent members of fraternal orders carry to President Harding resolutions from 800 lodges against narcotics. Left to right: Gus Northdurft, Patrick L. McArdle, Bruce A. Campbell, William J. Sinek, A. L. Sloan, of the Chicago American, and Louis M. Cohn.

14 PHYSICIANS ORGANIZE TO AID DRUG FIGHT

...t Men Headed by Dr. ...nd Will Be Advisors ...ression Society

Elks Head T... How Drugs Br... Up Two Famil...

By Universal Service.

WASHINGTON. Feb. ...

WILLIAM J. SINEK, Exa... Ruler of the Chicago Lodge of Elks, recited to the House Foreign Affairs Committee to-day two glaring examples of how narcotics break down character and ambition and leave poverty and misery in their wake. He said:

"A few weeks ago a young war veteran came to see me, saying he wanted to be ... He had a record of four months on the front, and had been ...ed two of the highest ...r valor. ... had started using ...e in Texas, where a ... gave him an injec...r rheumatism. He ...isappeared, leaving ...ung bride on their ...oon.

...little suburban town ...Chicago, a young ...came ill, and a doc... her morphine until ...ame an addict. The ...ran out of funds and ...ed everything to ...ey. ...tor refused to help ...ss she produced ...g of intrinsic ... Unable to comply ... demands for cash, ... she gave him ... eggs, pork, vege... ...d finally a $30 set ...ware for $5 worth ...

DOPE DEADLY, SAYS PENRHYN STANLAW

Artist Who Saw Downfall of "Wally" Reid Applauds Fight Against Evil.

Penryhn Stanlaws, artist, il...trator, originator of the fa... "Stanlaws Girls" and directo... motion pictures, yesterday ... cussed the drug traffic.

Stanlaws, who recently rea... as a director for the Famous ...ers' Lasky Corporation, is in ... York on a business trip pre... tory to going abroad. He has ... for two years in the heart of ... wood, worked side by side ... famous stars, and saw the ... downfall of "Wally" Reid.

He spoke with vehemence a... the drug traffic:

"Dope is a deadly thing to ... with. Like flirting with d... No. It is flirting with a c... treacherous death. Abou... there is no doubt. To kill ... the duty of big Americans.

"It is fortunate that "Wally" Reid was the only Famous Players actor who used drugs. I watched the effects, the deadly work of a foul enemy, play with its victim as a cat with a mouse. Only by keeping forever away from drugs can a person keep from becoming a drug addict.

"All over the country, and especially here in New York, are dens filled with struggling des... men. Nowhere in the countr... have I found anything to compa... with the metropolis.

"The whole of America nee... warning, and I believe that M... William Randolph Hearst ... doing a great service to t... country. I have seen many ... the stars of Hollywood read ... drug warnings with sincere ... thusism."

Mr. Stanlaws is regarded as ... of the greatest judges of feminine beauty ... his conn... poratio... conte... to Euro...

Detective Tells Lions Club of Illicit Traffic

The Lions Club yesterday heard strong endorsement of "The Examiner's" campaign against the illicit narcotic drug traffic, from Nick Harris, private investigator, whose business activities have given him wide experience with the criminal side of the drug habit.

Harris said the time was opportune for the organization actively to engage its attention with the narcotic problem. He cited many instances of the way that the user of narcotic drugs is led into crime. Harris dwelt specially upon the spread of the traffic.

"This is a subject which well can receive the careful study of the International Lions Clubs" said Harris. "It reaches right into our life and society in most dangerous form. We cannot strike too strongly at this traffic."

City Supervisors

The ... day ... ment ... drug ... Jame...

DRUG APPEAL ISSUED BY SALVATION ARMY

Churches Summoned to Join in Movement to End Sway of Habit.

OPPORTUNITY IS SHOWN

Co-operation with Authorities to Redeem Victims of Vice Emphasized.

...SHINGTON, Feb. 10.—The ...on Army formally called ... Federation of Churches ...st of America to-day to join ...concerted movement toward ...ation of the increasing dev...ns of the drug habit and ...demption of the million or ...addicts in the United States. ...mmissioner Thomas Estill, of ...York, head of Salvation Army ...ties in Eastern and Southern ...s, sent the invitation at the ...est of the annual congress of ...Eastern social department now ...ssion here. He said:

...kers Sought ...d in Fight ...nst Drugs

...al to public speakers ...nd their aid in the ... of education against ... of the narcotic drug ...made yesterday by ...n Jerome Rooney, ... of the executive ... of the Society for ...on of the Narcotic ...

...ooney said she de...kers—men and wo... will be free to ad...tings of various or...s in the Metropolitan ...

...tained from govern...ords regarding the ... evil in the United ... be furnished by ...ey at her office in ... 218, Metropolitan ...

ROTARIANS URGED TO JOIN DRUG FIG...

Dr. Carleton Simon Tells J...sey City Club of Need t... Eradicate Traffic.

SAYS IT INVADES SOCIE...

Organization Asks Harding ... Appoint "Anti-Dope Week" as Aid to Education.

Resolutions requesting Preside... Harding to set aside a week to ... known as "Anti-Dope Week," an... to call an international conferen... in an effort to control the narcoti... drug traffic, were adopted yeste... day at a meeting of the Rotar... Club, of Jersey City, held at the Carteret Club.

The meeting was addressed by Dr. Carleton Simon, Deputy Police Commissioner, in charge of the Narcotic Bureau. Dr. Simon emphasized the necessity for a campaign of publicity and education as the most effective weapon in combatting the narcotic evil.

DRASTIC RULES TO CURB TRADE IN NARCOTICS

Hughes, Mellon and Hoover Prepare to Make Permanent System Hearst Newspapers Urged

BOARD TO CHECK IMPORTS

Applications of Drug Manufacturers for Crude Materials to Be Rigidly Scrutinized

W.C.T.U. Reports World Action Only Drug Cure

PHILADELPHIA, Nov. 14.

THE question of narcotic drugs was discussed by Sara Graham-Mulhall, former First Deputy Commissioner of New York State Department of Narcotic Drug Control, and Dr. Joseph Chamberlain, professor at Columbia University, at the W. C. T. U. convention to-day.

Both speakers agreed that the problem was international and that world-wide unity would be necessary to preven... the illegal...

SYNAGOGUES JOIN BATTLE ON NARCOTICS

200 Congregations Promise Support of Bill to Establish U. S. Dope Addict Farms

Another national organization yesterday joined the battle against narcotic drugs.

The Committee on Co-operation of the United Synagogue of America adopted a resolution pledging its support of the Porter and Shortridge narcotics bills, pending in Congress. The United Synagogue of America is an organization of 200 synagogues and congregations throughout the coun... Of these, sixty are in the ...

To advise ... through hospitals and institutions to care for unfortunate addicts.

To present at the next meeting of the several bodies resolutions calling upon President Harding to set ... a week known as "N... Anti-Narcotic Week ... upon the nati... ... the calling o... ... ference o... ... con... evil at its ... ... the transpor... ... of unnecessa... ... cotics from o... other.

A committee ... for the respective ... nounced as follows: Colonel W. Gray ... man; Henry B. Law, ... Leroy L. Goddard, treas... The organization was ...

...RE ...EEZE

...enace;

SCOTTISH RITE MASONS LEAD WAR ON DRUGS

Complete Organization Formed to Smash Traffic in Dope to Cover the Entire Nation

Special to the New York American.

CHICAGO, Jan. 7.—Oriental consistory and co-ordinate bodies of the Ancient Accepted Scottish Rite Masonry, with 13,000 thirty-third and thirty-second degree masons, have declared war on the dope evil and formulated plans for an aggressive campaign against the traffic and use of habit-forming drugs.

A complete organization to co-operate with the government and other agencies engaged in the work of exterminating the vicious traffic has been formed, it was announced by Colonel W. Gray Beach, officer of the order and Chief of Federal Narcotic forces in seven states, with headquarters at ...cago.

Colonel Beach has been named chairman of the organization which will function in co-operation with the heads of the several Scottish Rite bodies, including Edward L. ...son, commander-in-chief of Oriental Consistory; Roy W. Hill, ...

and a definite programme formulated following a speech made by Colonel Beach, in which he pictured the ravages of the terrible dope scourge from his own experiences as a veteran narcotic officer.

"The States should enact laws with teeth in them to co-operate with the Federal Government. Above all, the course of supply for dope in this and other countries is the root of the evil and should be first attacked to alleviate the condition and stop the traffic."

Buffalo Drug Ring Broken, Says Agent After Raids.

BUFFALO, Jan. 7 (By Associated Press).—With twenty-four persons under arrest, four of them women, on charges of violating the Federal Narcotic act as a result of the raids by Federal agents this morning, Ralph H. Oyler, Federal ... New ...

LEAGUE THANKS HEARST PAPERS FOR DRUG FIGHT

International Anti-Narcotic Organization Votes Praise at Washington Conference

SERVICE TO NATION"

Preamble to the Resolution Points Blessings of Crusade; Opium Embargo Is Lifted

Special to the New York American.

WASHINGTON, March 28.—A resolution of thanks and enthusiastic appreciation to the Hearst papers was adopted at the conference of the International Anti-Narcotic League held here. An open letter sent to the New York American by the leag...

"This ...

K. C. Members Urged to Enlist in Drug Crusade

URGING all members of the Knights of Columbus to interest themselves in the present war upon the narcotic evil, Columbia, the K. of C. monthly magazine, will say in its March issue, which has just gone to press:

"Whatever may be the caus... of the seemingly wide an... certainly dangerous sprea... of the drug habit, its cu... is plainly prescribed—sym... pathetic study of the addi... and firm measures again... the unscrupulous vendo... who profit by addiction."

Negro Found Guilty As Narcotics Seller

Edward Lewis, negro, was convicted of narcotics selling by a jury in Judge Michael J. Roche's court yesterday. He will be sentenced next Monday. Lewis was prosecuted by Attorney C. W. Kelly of the State Board of Pharmacy.

Moose Regents to Study Drug Evil

A. Van der Naillen Jr., grand regent of the Loyal Order of Moose, will leave today for Washington where he will confer with James J. Davis, secretary of labor, and regent of the order, upon important questions concerning the lodge in the West.

One matter which is expected to come up for consideration is the narcotic drug question. The Moose organization with its million members has declared war upon the sale and use of habit forming drugs.

WALLIS QUITS PO... TO AID DRUG FIGHT

Door Check—American Legion
Belle Monti Country Club
February 18, 19...

LEGION AIDS DRUG CRUSADE

The American Legion yesterday announced the appointment of a legal advisory committee, composed of attorneys, members of the legion, whose services have been placed at the disposal of John T. Williams, United States attorney, and Matthew Brady, district attorney, in the fight against the illicit narcotic traffic. The committee stated:

"The committee's services as special prosecutors whenever required will be available to the federal and the city and county government. It is the intention of the local County Council of the American Legion to throw its full ... the fight against the ...

IN IN DRUG BATTLE

THE HEARST PAPERS ADVOCATE:

...reement of English-speaking people to preserve peace among themselves and
...mote the peace of the world.
...onal representation in the United...

"EXAMINER" COMMENDED BY HEALTH LEAGUE

CIVIC

Commendation of "The E...
...fic in narcotic drugs and co...
...ursued:

LA FOLLETTE THANKS HEARST

William Randolph Hearst, Madison, Wis., Sept. 6, 1922
New York City.

Wisconsin Progressives all feel a deep sense of gratitude ... the splendid fight for sound Americanism and right eco...mic politics which the Wisconsin News has made in the cam...gn just closed.

TODAY'S
...ew York American

FIRST SECTION

TALK OF THE TOWN
By Ralph Record

...policy—the necessary po... ment; so is morality, so ... courage, so is common se...

When we are goo... because we desire to be: it is because we have to be.

Experience proves the unwisdom of the opposite course.

And so, eventually, we will all be virtu... again, and sensible again.

Our hard experience will make us so.

But we have got a good deal to go through ... fore that day arrives.

Sincerely,

WILLIAM RANDOLPH HEARST.

Hearst Campaign on Drugs Aided by War Veterans

By Universal Service.
WASHINGTON, Jan. 15.

THE United Spanish War Veterans to-day approved the campaign of the Hearst newspapers for suppression of the drug evil and pledged their co-operation in 700 ...

NEW YORK AMERICAN, published daily by Star Company. President, William R. Hearst; Vice-President, Bradford Merrill; Treasurer, ...

BOOST ... GREATER CITY OF THE WORLD NEW YORK

CHARACTER QUALITY AMERICA FIRST

New York

Mr. Hearst Urges All to Fight Drugs

TO OUR EDITORS:

In referring to the crusade that is bei... the terrible evil of drugs please do not ca... Hearst crusade or the fight of the Hearst p... ...appropriate the crusade in any way. ...de of any indivi...

His untimely end came through ... Here we have a startling example of ...ening young men of this country, ... traffic in drugs.

Mrs. Bertha Westbrook Reid, mother of W... Reid, yesterday sent the following letter of ap... to William Randolph Hearst:

January 20, 1923

Mr. William Randolph Hearst,
New York American,
New York City.

Dear Mr. Hearst:

Although I do not know you and you ... know me, you will recognize me as the mot... Wallace Reid, my beloved son, one of the ... boys in the world—one of the finest young m... ever trod the face of God's earth.

... to you to expos... and fight for the correction of the drug evil, I a... appealing to one who is always willing to listen ... anything that is just and good.

Yours truly,

BERTHA WESTBROOK REID.

RAVING OF GIRL DRUG VICTIM IS TOLD IN DIARY

Closer to the Line Separating Sanity from Madness, She Collapses While Writing

THOUGHTS OF ONE DYING

Elizabeth Houde Knew Only Four Who Withheld Morphia Until All Else Failed

By JAMES WHITTAKER.

Copyright, 1923, by Universal Service.

India Backs Hearst in Fight on Drugs

PROFESSOR TRAKNATH DAS, international secretary of the Friends of Freedom for India, telegraphed yesterday from Milwaukee his commendation of the proposal of Mr. Hearst to summon an International Opium Congress at Washington as part of a world-wide war on narcotics. His telegram follows:

Milwaukee, January 26, 1923.

William Randolph Hearst,
New York American,
New York City.

India, under the British Government's present opium policy, produces more than 1,200 tons of opium annually which is drugging the Indian people through about 7,000 licensed opium shops, and indirectly the whole world.

The vast majority of the 315,000,000 of people in India, and such recognized national leaders as Gandhi, Sir Rabindranath Tagore ...

FOREIGN VETERANS JOIN NARCOTIC WAR

Commander-in-Chief Huston Lauds Action of Post in Detroit.

MAGAZINE ISSUES APPEAL

All Units of V. F. W. Asked to Backs Hearst Papers' Campaign.

Colonel Tillinghast L. Huston, commander-in-chief of the Veterans of Foreign Wars, yesterday ...

London Press Hails Hearst's Proposal for Union of Peace

By H. H. STANSBURY,
Universal Service Staff Correspondent.
LONDON, Jan. 3.

WILLIAM RANDOLPH HEARST'S proposal for a co-operative agreement by English-speaking peoples as a safeguard for world peace was given most important news display in all the London newspapers this morning.

The Times printed the Hearst statement in full, as did also the Daily Telegraph, Daily Chronicle, Morning Post, Daily Express, Westminster Gazette, Daily Mirror, Daily ... Mail.

HEAVY FIRE BY CONGRESS UNLOOSED ON POISON LIQUOR

Black's Resolution Calls for Prosecution of Dry Agents Ordering Use of Drugs

...eller Holds House Members Who Ignore Warning "Guilty of Slaughtering Thousands"

RAID ON HOTEL SAID TO EXPOSE BIG DRUG RING

Hearst Papers Win Anti-Drug Crusade

By Universal Service.

WASHINGTON, Sept. 23.—Drastic rules for the suppression of the international drug traffic were agreed upon at the State Department to-day ... to be wholly inadequate in every way, following a survey by the Government that has gone into every phase of the drug evil.

Government experts have been able to fix the amount of drugs which physicians will legitimately ...

CRUSADERS ACCLAIM HEARST LEADERSHIP

Commissioner Simon Believes ... Secretary of Commerce Hoover ...

The importation of crude opium and coca leaves, from which morphine and cocaine are made, far in excess of what is needed, is to be turned back at customs houses.

Drastic regulation of shipping to suppress smuggling is to be employed. Penalties so severe will be imposed, the officials believe, that few will take the risk ...

Mr. Hearst Thanked for Aid in Fight Against Narcotics

INTERNATIONAL
NARCOTIC EDUCATION ASSOCIATION
(Incorporated)
LOS ANGELES

Hon. William R. Hearst,
Dear Mr. Hearst:

I am enclosing extracts fro... ...ngton office on the observanc... WEEK. This does not include th... as well as ... the countr... co-operation... control, in ... during the ... cartoons, ... impossible ... results of ... country and ... readers of y...

The ser... very timely, ... addiction, is ... at an alarmi... circles it is ... Anti-Narcotic ... Act, will be ... chiefly to a l... tion on the ... laws are in a...

I wish t... appreciation ... the Internation... ...Education Ass...

HOBSON LAUDS HEARST AID IN NARCOTIC WAR

Declares Heroin Users Are Increasing at an Alarming Rate; Urges Education.

Nation-wide co-operation of State and Federal officials, newspapers, civic, social and welfare organiz... ...ons and churches in the reco... ...tic Education W...

PORTER SEES VICTORY NEAR FOR DOPE BILL

Narcotics Farm Measure to Be Favorably Reported as Result of Hearst Support

By WINIFRED BLACK.
SAN FRANCISCO, March 20.—
Good news.
Here it is:
Washington, D. C.

TO COPE WITH NARCOTIC RING

Assemblymen Burchill and Bloch Propose Joint Committees to Delve Dope Traffic

HEARST PAPERS PRAISED

Legislator Hopes People Will Be Aroused by Publicity to Danger Knocking at Doors

Dope Bill Wonderful, Hearst Wires Porter

By Universal Service.
WASHINGTON, Jan. 21.

THE passage of the new Porter law, creating two farms for treatment of narcotic drug addicts, brought many telegrams of congratulations to Representative Porter (R.), of Pennsylvania, sponsor of the measure, today. Many were from prison officials and civic workers. One made public by Representative Porter was from William Randolph Hearst, who first suggested the legislation.

Mr. Hearst wired:

"My dear Congressman Porter: You introduced a wonderfully good bill and made a wonderful fight for it. I congratulate you most heartily.

"I do not know any recent measure which will confer more benefit upon the country and you must take great satisfaction in your good work."

DRUG ISSUE PUT UP TO LEAGUE BY U. S. ENVOY

Porter Tells Delegates to Choose Between Opium Traffic and Our Friendship

"CANNOT HAVE BOTH"

Nations with Finger in Pie Debate Question and Plan an Early Answer

HEREWITH is presented the inside story of the fight being waged by the official United States delegation before the International Commission now in session at Geneva to devise means to curb world traffic in narcotics.

Stephen G. Porter, chairman of the congressional committee which framed the American narcotic law, is head of the United States delegation. He carries a very important letter from Secretary of State Hughes asking the commission to urge the League of Nations to use its influence to get England's Eastern dependencies, Japan and China, to stop subsidizing the production of plants from which morphine, cocaine and opium are obtained.

By ELLEN N. LA MOTTE.

Copyright, 1923, by Universal Service.

GENEVA, May 28.—The League of Nations is faced with a momentous decision as to whether it intends to abolish the opium trade or to uphold and protect it.

The United States of America has put this question squarely up to the League and is awaiting the answer. The answer will be given in two or three days when those nations which have a stake in the opium trade have had time to consult and come to a decision.

In plain words the question they will have to decide is:

"Which will prove more valuable in the long run—American friendship of opium revenues?"

CANNOT HAVE BOTH.

They cannot have both. The Hague opium convention was an international agreement to stop the drug traffic. The United States was a signatory to that agreement. The League of Nations included the agreement in its covenant and the opium committee of the League was entrusted with the work of putting it into effect.

The league, however, through action of its assembly, has completely distorted The Hague convention and so altered and changed it that it now serves to protect the drug traffic and to secure the opium revenues of nations and of vested interests generally.

As a signatory to The Hague convention the United States asked leave to appear before the opium committee and state its opinion of this juggling with the convention. On Friday, May 25, the American position was stated by Stephen G. Porter, head of the American delegation. Mr. Porter spoke with the full force of America behind him—both houses of Congress, the Administration and the American people.

FOUR ARE UNDECIDED.

The four countries whose minds are not made up are France, Holland, Japan and Great Britain. All have big financial interests at stake and colonial revenues to safeguard.

Great Britain has two representatives on the committee—Sir Malcolm Delevigne of the Home Office and Mr. Campbell, who represents the India office of India. Mr. Campbell came out flatfootedly in opposition, since India is the great opium-producing country which supplies the British colonies in the Far East, as well as the French colony of Indo-China, the Dutch colony of Java, etc.

He said:

"India will not give up this opium traffic, which would mean to many millions an act of sheer inhumanity."

MAY 29, 1923

Narcotic Evil in China Blamed Upon Eur

APRIL 29,

MORPHIA AND COCAINE SMUGGLED IN BY OTHERS

By ELLEN N. LA MOTTE,

(Well Known Author and International Authority on the Narcotic Evil.)

GENEVA, Switzerland, May 20.—Startling revelations of the extent of the traffic in morphine and cocaine in China, that nation much abused as the "source" of opium, have done much to stir the seven-year apathy of the Opium Committee of the League of Nations.

China, the good old football, is, it seems, more sinned against than sinning.

It may produce opium, carried away incidentally, by foreign ships, but it does not produce morphine and cocaine, the deadly sisters of degradation. They come from Europe and from Japan, and they are being dumped into China in huge quantities.

And out of it all is coming a new threat of international discord.

China has found a champion in the person of Mr. Lyell, who is English, and a newcomer to the committee.

China is a large producer of opium, practically all of which—or

sumed in that country. The opium committee likes to pretend that it is being smuggled out in large quantities. They say that nearly all the ships "coming from China" are loaded with it. But the Chinese delegate on the committee takes exception to this statement—he has a pleasant way of stating that these ships "coming from China" are coming under the flags of other countries. Only, unfortunately, when the Chinese delegate speaks, no one pays much attention to him.

When the British delegate speaks

the other side, our side—Japan, Germany and Serbia.

And there are two out-and-out opponents of opium, Italy and China.

Thus we have the pro-opium group, the anti-opium group, and those on the fence. In addition there are three assessors or experts, not representing governments and without votes. These are Mr. Brenier, who is French; Mr. Dunham (American) and Mr. Lyell, who is English. Mr. Lyell is a newcomer to the committee and is fearlessly outspoken. In him China found a champion.

Now for several years "conditions in China" has figured on the agenda. And each time, the poor Chinese delegate has been bullied and hectored, chiefly by the British delegate. The opium block excuses its masterly inactivity on the pretext that you must first clear up China. They make no allusions to the part they have played in bringing about China's downfall but they deeply regret that disturbed conditions in China make it impossible for China to enforce its laws against opium production. Therefore, they say, until China is cleared up, they can't do anything. And they jolly well see to it that China never is cleared up—because they themselves won't clear out.

Well, on a certain day, the agenda showed that "conditions in China" were coming up for discussion. This

tion in China, I wish to remark that at the present time there is no one government in China. Of course, I cannot say how many governments there are, but there are several, and they are all at war with one another. It is perhaps no exaggeration to say that there are a million men under arms, and, further, that it is very hard to find pay for them.

"A year ago, a Chinese friend of mine in Shanghai told me that the opium revenue for the Shanghai district was no less than $20,000,000 (Mexican), or £2,000,000. This friend is an honest and reliable Chinese business man, not a member of an anti-opium society. His estimate, I believe, gives a reliable idea of how enormous the total opium revenue must be, if it is this for the Shanghai district alone.

"Now, the Chinese generals, who are very hard up and have to pay their men, are more angels than you and I, and so I believe that as long as this civil war continues it is useless to expect that this revenue from opium will be given up. I wish I might think it would be. The Chinese generals may grow wings, but we can't count on that—nor on any real amelioration in China while this struggle continues. There is nothing, therefore, that this committee can do with regard to opium.

"But with morphia the situation is entirely different. Morphia is not manufactured in China, but all of it is smuggled into China from Europe and Japan. I hope you will excuse me, therefore, if I say a few words in regard to this angle of the situation.

"Twenty years ago I was stationed in the little town of Shasi, on the Yangtse, several hundred miles from the coast. There I found thtat morphia injections could be had at street corners from peddlers for a few cents. I have now no first hand information as to present conditions, but from

what I learn I believe th situation is even worse. Ch being flooded with morphia.

"But this flood will not d China, for China is indestru Despite all these poisons, floods of opium and mo China is in a state of expa The Straits Settlements, a istered by Great Britain, hav come practically a Chinese c Chinese coolies and their fa are pouring into Manchuria the Chinese farmer in the west is pushing into Mongol

"In my forty years of l China I have been struck b incalculable harm done to B interests by the conviction Chinese that England is re sible for the introduction of into China. We all know th feeling that has existed to England on that score. But the Chinese people fully rea and they are beginning to u stand—the evil that has been them by the peoples of Eu and of Japan through mor and cocaine—their ill-feeling wards these nations will be finitely more intense than ev was towards England.

"The idea is growing these countries, in order t a few of their nationals by the situation, are indiff to the poisoning of China. extremists (in China) now be that these nations and Japan deliberately poisoning China weaken and debilitate her.

"This situation, therefore, tlemen, is one with which committee is called upon to d

This speech was delivered a profound silence. The cha feebly said that the matter now open for debate, and pe some conclusions might be d from the statement just There was no discussion—no clusions— nothing. Whatever clusions the opium bloc dre kept to itself.

Manufacturers of Narcotics Wage War on Dope Evil Foes

Fight on Illicit Sale Led by Italian Delegate.

By ELLEN N. LA MOTTE,

(Well known author and international authority on the traffic in narcotics).

GENEVA, April 20.—A battle of titanic proportions is being waged by rich and greedy narcotic manufacturers on one side and humanitarians on the other before the Opium Committee of the League of Nations. Upon its outcome there will be one or two issues:

Either the illicit wholesale trade in narcotics will be banned by international accord, or it will continue as it is today with its ever-increasing horde of human derelicts.

The struggle in which the committee is gripped was precipitated by the Italian delegate, Signor Cavazzoni, backed by Premier Mussolini. He has introduced a plan before the committee which would make the smuggling and illicit sale of narcotics impossible.

His plan is simple and expeditious. For that reason the powerful manufacturers are blocking it at every step and with all the resources at their command.

MADE IN EIGHT COUNTRIES.

Narcotic drugs, such as morphine, heroin, cocaine, etc., are made in only eight countries—the United States, Great Britain, France, Holland, Germany, Switzerland, Japan and India.

Except the United States, which has strictly limited its manufacture, the rest of these countries are turning out drugs as fast as they can make them, in huge amounts.

Italy does not manufacture narcotics and Premier Mussolini and other prominent Italians are outraged over the illicit drugs being smuggled into their country. It hurts his people—ruins them, Mussolini declares, and he wants this stopped.

The position of Italy at present is that of the United States—helpless under the activities of the smugglers and peddlers. Mussolini sent Signor Cavazzoni to Geneva to see what he could do about it.

Now there are vast fortunes for hundreds, even thousands, of people in these illicit drugs. The manufacturing countries do not want their trade interfered with. On previous occasions Cavazzoni has pleaded with the Opium Committee to ration their factories and limit their output. His pleas fell on deaf ears. There was nothing doing.

TIME WAS NOT RIPE.

The delegates from the manufacturing countries announced the time was not ripe for such drastic action.

Rebuffed, but determined, Italy approached the problem from another angle and presented a plan to the committee known as the Cavazzoni Memorandum. This is a minutely detailed scheme for blocking every avenue of escape into illicit channels.

Where Supply Comes From

This table of figures on production of narcotics in various countries during 1926 was recently given out by the Opium Committee of the League of Nations at Geneva.

The table was made from a huge graph based upon reports submitted annually to the league by the various nations. The graph was finally given to the press, despite the objections of the British, British Indian and Dutch delegates, who sought to suppress it. The figures are in kilos. (1,000 kilos equal one ton.)

	Morphine.	Heroin.	Cocaine.
Great Britain	5,762	315	—
France	—	—	—
Holland	—	—	—
Germany	20,700	1,800	2,400
Switzerland	8,038	3,973	70
Japan	825	1,120	1,509
British India	1,977	—	—
United States	2,938	—	818

mittee on April 12. The United States is represented by an "observer," John Caldwell. Routine business was started but always in the background hovers the thought of that sub-committee at work.

KEEN FIGHT LOOMS.

What will happen when it reports? Will it kill the Cavazzoni plan, rip it to bits, tear out its vitals and leave but a harmless skeleton? Who knows? There is thunder in the air. Suppressed excitement. Bound to be a fight!

Annual reports were submitted by each government to the committee as to the production of raw opium, coca leaves; the amounts and kinds of drugs manufactured; also statistics of export and import. The reports are extraordinarily valuable contributions to our knowledge of the whole evil situation.

The League is the clearing house for all this information and the splendid work done in preparing this and other equally valuable documents cannot be too highly praised.

Mr. Brenier (one of the three assessors or experts attached to the committee) presented a huge graph for consideration. This enormous graph, in colors, was hung up at one end of the room and showed in striking manner what was happening all over the world.

The damning columns representing the manufacture of drugs looked about six feet high; in fact, had to be that high to accomodate the output.

At once the delegate from British India objected. He was sure it wasn't accurate. Please take it away. Then the French delegate said it was a good graph, based on figures given in the annual reports Surely no one could object to that.

In fact, went on the French delegate, he wanted that graph reproduced in small size so that each member of the committee could have one o study. Prompt objections came from the British and Dutch delegates. There was a lively scene but the French delegate won.

The next day the graph was again the cause of bickering. Should the offending documen, the annual report containing these embarrassing statistics, be given to he press or withheld? The press on the front bench whispered loudly to the effect it was no good coming to report a meeing if they could no get a look at he subject under discussion.

The British India delegate said that while all were in favor of the fullest publicity, it seemed wiser to suppress this document for the moment and not give it to the press.

DELEGATE BACK IN FRAY.

Again the French delegate jumped into the fray. This document, he said, gives the figures on which the graph was based. You all objected to showing that graph because it was obscene—obscene because it showed the naked truth.

Well, we got a vote in favor of that obscene graph, so there is no reason why we should not give out the figures which show up the nakedness—the truth, in other words—of these various countries.

So the document was given to the press.

By the figure it will be noted the "naked truth" does not apply to either France or Holland. Neither of these two countries has ever given one single figure, at any time, as to the amount of drugs they manufacture. Presumably, to use the French delegate's word, their "obscenity" is too great to be exposed.

Let us assume they manufacture as much as Germany, or even more. The total manufacture, even without these two countries is staggering. No wonder there is a drug problem.

By ELLEN N. LA MOTTE.

GENEVA, May 26.—Not content, it appears, with ha gently smothered the only sincere plan to choke the illicit traffic, the League of Nations Opium Committee now seem termined to give the world dope ring protection from th noyance of publicity.

It was Signor Cavazzoni, the fighting Italian delegate, who presented the simple and honest schemee to quell forever the world-wide industry of narcotic smuggling. And it was Cavazzoni who found himself a Don Quixote, hurling himself vainly against the windmills of the Opium Bloc. Cavazzoni's plan was buried in an avalanche of fine phrases, agile equivocations.

Now, with the eager Italian's disturbingly honest proposal out of the way for the time, the committee seems about to sterilize itself against the bearing of what so far has been its only fruit—publicity.

Much Light Shed

This, it seems, will be brought about with the ratification of the Geneva Convention of 1925. But first let me show how valuable this publicity is to those honestly engaged in fighting the world bane of opium.

I have spoken of the valuable documents issued by the league in connection with the work of the Opium Committee. These contain a gold mine of information and are equally important not only for what they contain but for what they omit.

It is important to know that two great drug-making countries, France and Holland, refuse to give any statistics. It is important to note the discrepancies betweent the imports recorded by one country to another and the exports recorded by these same countries.

It is important to know that morphine changed into codein is not recorded at all—nor the morphine turned into esters. All this information, either given or withheld, has an immensee significance. It shows the various devices and dodges by which the opium trade keeps going, yet evades the laws.

Another point of immense importance is the public meetings of the Opium Committee. When they were first held they were private. Since May, 1923, they have been open to the public; there are a few private sessions, but not many.

"Beans Are Spilled"

In these open meetings, important documents have been discussed and the discussions have brought all sorts of nastiness to light. "Beans have been spilled," unwittingly, but thoroughly. You have been able to see the line-up of the nations—

astute and clever than the and the powerful influence cf Britain dominates the Commit

But now, one fears, this va publicity may come to an en is distasteful to the "commerci terests," however valuable t world at large.

Three years ago the big Conference was held at Gene draw up a better treaty than Hague Opium Convention of which was full of holes and al drugs and opium to leak all ove place.

It was from this conference the American delegation with after fighting for three mont improve upon the Hague Co tion, not to draw up another This sieve, however, was produ the Geneva Convention of 1925, many respects it is weaker than of the Hague.

Ratification Urged

The British have been makin intensive drive to get this Ge Convention ratified—they did themselves, at once. But the countries hung back. This inter campaign makes one "smell a It was the Italian delegate smelled it first and mentioned it.

This Geneva pact carries wit a Central Board, consisting of e members. To this board is to given supervision of the opium ation.

It is to sit in secret and no vision is made for open meeti It has no power—it can me "watch the trend of the inte tional traffic in drugs" an dif one country is importing too m it can advise the Council that country may become the centre illicit trade.

On the face of it, it seems a fu body. What then, are the reas for this terrific effort to estab it? What lies behind? What is "nigger in the woodpile?"

It is the Opium Committee it that has aroused these suspicio The Committee has never permit any discussions as to the relati between itself and the Cent Board. Repeated efforts have be made to define the different fu tions of the two bodies, to find what work would be assigned to Committee, and what to the Cent Board.

Suspicion Stirred

QUAKES ROCK CORINTH AGAIN

BALKANS PLOT PROBE WIDENS

...nd Japan by Dope Expert

THE ETHICS OF OPIUM

By ELLEN N. LA MOTTE

Author of "Peking Dust," etc.

A revaluation of the whole situation with respect to opium is needed, and the League of Nations, realizing this, has issued a call for a new international conference to meet next July—quite possibly in our own national capital.

This new book of Miss La Motte's constitutes for the general reader the indicated revaluation and checking up of the world situation as regards opium.

One of the things long and bitter experience has shown is that the key to the problem and the only hopeful basis of control is a knowledge of the state of affairs in the producing countries. "The Ethics of Opium" is, in the main, a clear, thoroughly informed and well-documented exposition of the situation, first in India and other British dependencies—twelve chapters are devoted to this—and then in China and other independent nations and their colonies, which are covered by nine chapters. The first and introductory chapter treats in general of The World's Drug Problem, and there is a chapter devoted to the Hague opium convention. But, in the main, the book is a mass of evidence which tends to show that there has been no sincere effort on the part of commercially interested powers actually to prevent the traffic in opium.

Miss La Motte has given much of the adult portion of her life to the fight against opium. This is her second book on the subject.

12mo, 204 pages

Price $1.75

At all bookstores — Published by

THE CENTURY CO.

353 Fourth Avenue New York City

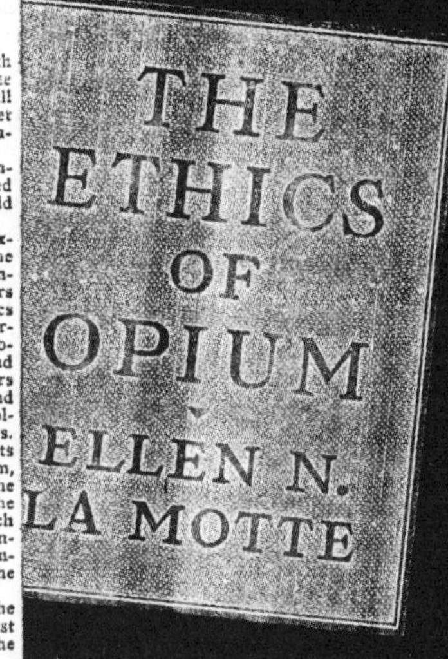

The Opium Monopoly

La Motte

$1.00

Macmil...

THE OPIUM MONOPOLY

By

ELLEN N. LA MOTTE

Author of "Backwash of War," "Peking Dust," "Civilization," etc.

IN an absolutely friendly spirit (utterly different from that of various busy societies for the inciting of hate against the British) this book points out a real evil maintained under British administration in the Far East. The evil is the opium traffic. The point of view is that of an enlightened international conscience. The purpose is to cleanse the world of a poison, and a great empire of a foul stain. The basis of the argument is the official "Blue Book" or handbook, against which exception cannot be taken.

OPIUM: THE DEMON FLOWER

By SARA GRAHAM-MULHALL

Winner of the Annual $5000.00 Distinguished Achievement Award of the Pictorial Review

SARA GRAHAM-MULHALL

Formerly First Deputy Commissioner
New York State Department Narcotic Drug Control

Author - Lecturer - Sociologist

FOUNDER
FOUNDATION FOR WORLD NARCOTIC RESEARCH AND RECLAMATION

Is the drug evil destroying American civilization!

Can We Escape its Sinister Menace? How

READ

DOPE

The Story of the Living Dead

By Winifred Black

Foreword by Fremont Older, famous editor

This startling book will ... war of silent danger, w...

$1.00 a copy at all ...

Star C...

Because she loves the best things on earth, she can write most lovingly about the worst. Because she gives her admiration to some sturdy old woman who lives in poverty in a humble house beyond reach of the railroad tracks, and is not even aware that she lives in beautiful courage, Mrs. Black can turn to pen and ink and tell the story of the lives of weaklings and what narcotics do to them. And because she loves California poppies beside California roads, she can write of the curse of the white Indian poppies that put men and women into the gutter.

I believe this book will have a wide ... ence in stimulating people to figh... evil that this splendid woman h... so brilliantly for ten years ... she has done has les...

Mr. Hearst has in himself the same fierce disgust for this devastating evil, and the same compassion for its victims, that move in every line Mrs. Black writes. I do not know when or how Mr. Hearst became interested in this particular work, but ever since he began his career as an editor and publisher he has fought the battles of the poor and the weak, and has tried to make the world less harsh toward them. He never forgets Narcotic Week, nor forgets to remind his editors when it is approaching. This unfailing memory of his is frequently very disturbing to his employees who may lack his youthful interest in common humanity. He ... whenever the occasion ... his readers ... Government ... nally, when ... more than ... accomplish

... much about ... story to tell ... ut. But be... see that the ... as the world ... ade of hers is ... de in her busy ... en she began ... ng girl, and I ... h those years. ... ough all of her

... les, and quickly brought to her a ... udience. I know of no other ... n America whose work has ... lives of so ma... women and ... is loved today in millions of ... es.

... is one of the few persons I have ... really love human beings and hu... , and are glad to be alive in the ... rough a lifetime of many sorrows she ... lost the zest for living that is the ... her remarkable success. She loves this ... d loves every part of it. She loves the ... ings men and women do, and condones ... little weaknesses; she loves their fine ... , but most of all she loves courage and ... ence and generosity and largeness of heart, these are a part of Winifred Black, of Annie ... urie as we know her in California, and they ... ake her what she is.

She loves the fog that comes down over San Francisco hills, loves the white ships on the bay, loves the blue and white lilacs on California's hills, the red berries on the mountains, the flowers in shadowed places, the gay poppies of this state out West. She has a healthy attitude tow... she has gusto for living she stands fo... and hom... for joy t... women ... of the li...

In these pages Winifred Black tells the story of narcotic addiction, and I do not know of anyone else in this world who could tell it as effectively as she does. She knows thoroughly this story of human weakness. She knows where the drugs come from and where they go; she knows what kind of people become addicts, and why they become the pathetic victims of a narcotic; she knows what they were like before, and what they are like after they lose their grip on themselves and sink into this worst form of human degradation. Anyone who reads even the first page of this book will see at once how well she knows this story and how she feels about it.

Back of Winifred Black in her soul-stirring crusade against the narcotic evil stands William Randolph Hearst. They both have *pity*—that divine quality without which our superiority to other forms of life would become an idle boast. Without it we can never have a real civilization.

Mantle of Secrecy Placed About Dope Evil by League

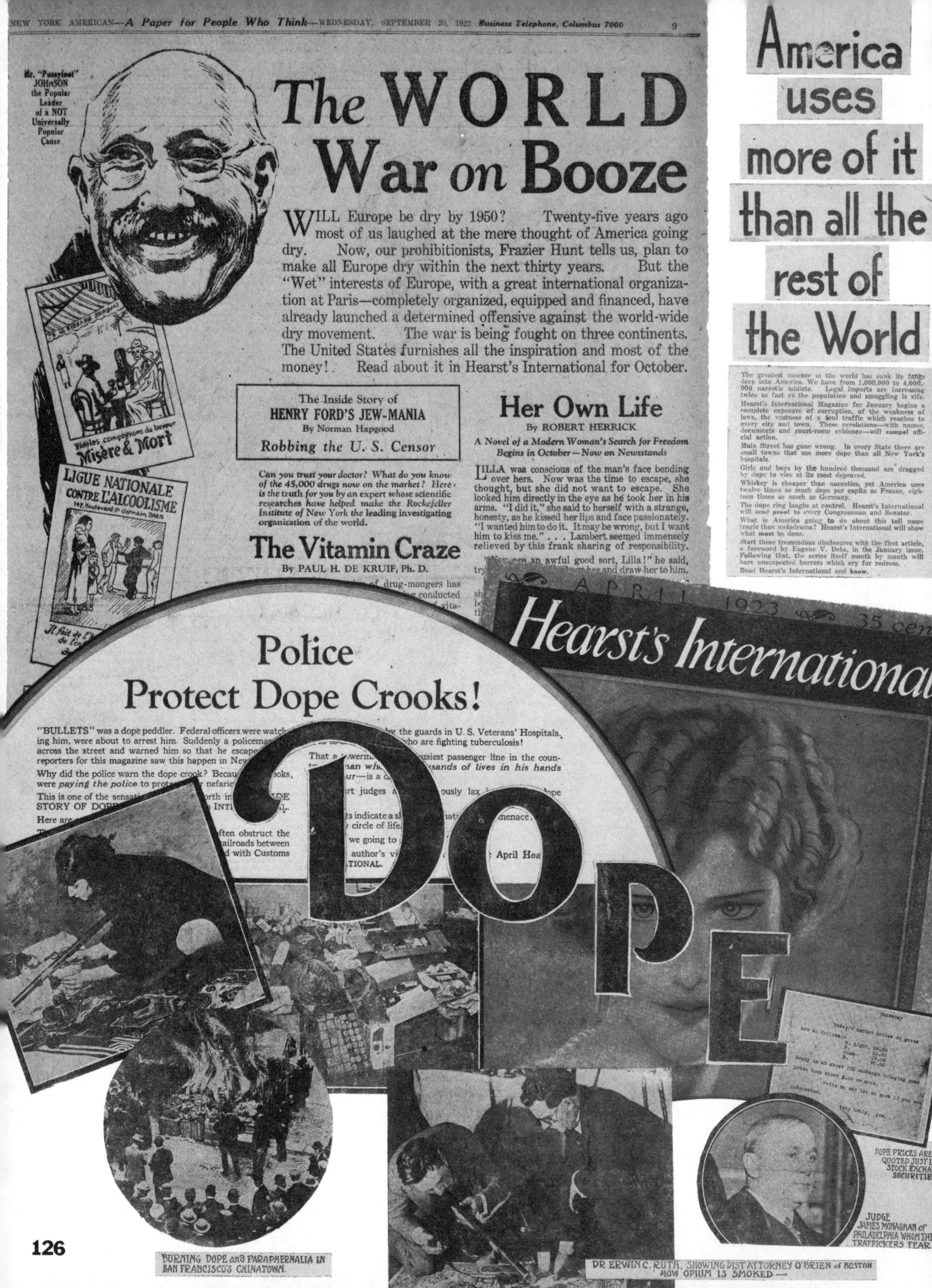

NEW YORK AMERICAN—*A Paper for People Who Think*—WEDNESDAY, SEPTEMBER 20, 1922 *Business Telephone, Columbus 7000* 9

Mr. "Pussyfoot" JOHNSON the Popular Leader of a NOT Universally Popular Cause

The WORLD War on Booze

WILL Europe be dry by 1950? Twenty-five years ago most of us laughed at the mere thought of America going dry. Now, our prohibitionists, Frazier Hunt tells us, plan to make all Europe dry within the next thirty years. But the "Wet" interests of Europe, with a great international organization at Paris—completely organized, equipped and financed, have already launched a determined offensive against the world-wide dry movement. The war is being fought on three continents. The United States furnishes all the inspiration and most of the money! Read about it in Hearst's International for October.

Fidèles compagnons du buveur
Misère & Mort
LIGUE NATIONALE CONTRE L'ALCOOLISME
147, Boulevard St Germain, PARIS

The Inside Story of
HENRY FORD'S JEW-MANIA
By Norman Hapgood

Robbing the U. S. Censor

Can you trust your doctor? What do you know of the 45,000 drugs now on the market? Here is the truth for you by an expert whose scientific researches have helped make the Rockefeller Institute of New York the leading investigating organization of the world.

The Vitamin Craze

By PAUL H. DE KRUIF, Ph. D.

of drug-mongers has ... conducted ... vita-

Her Own Life

By ROBERT HERRICK

A Novel of a Modern Woman's Search for Freedom Begins in October—Now on Newsstands

LILLA was conscious of the man's face bending over hers. Now was the time to escape, she thought, but she did not want to escape. She looked him directly in the eye as he took her in his arms. "I did it," she said to herself with a strange, honesty, as he kissed her lips and face passionately. "I wanted him to do it. It may be wrong, but I want him to kiss me." . . . Lambert seemed immensely relieved by this frank sharing of responsibility.

"... an awful good sort, Lilla!" he said, try... her and draw her to him.

America uses more of it than all the rest of the World

The greatest menace in the world has sunk its fangs deep into America. We have from 1,000,000 to 4,000,000 narcotic addicts. Legal imports are increasing twice as fast as the population and smuggling is rife.

Hearst's International Magazine for January begins a complete exposure of corruption, of the weakness of laws, the vastness of a foul traffic which reaches to every city and town. These revelations—with names, documents and court-room evidence—will **compel** official action.

Main Street has gone wrong. In every State there are small towns that use more dope than all New York's hospitals.

Girls and boys by the hundred thousand are dragged by dope to vice at its most depraved.

Whiskey is cheaper than narcotics, yet America uses twelve times as much dope per capita as France, eighteen times as much as Germany.

The dope ring laughs at control. Hearst's International will send **proof** to every Congressman and Senator.

What is America going **to** do about this toll more tragic than melodrama? Hearst's International will show what **must** be done.

Start these tremendous disclosures with the first article, a foreword by Eugene V. Debs, in the January issue. Following that, the series itself month by month will bare unsuspected horrors which cry for redress.

Read Hearst's International and **know.**

APRIL 1923 35 cen

Hearst's International

Police Protect Dope Crooks!

"BULLETS" was a dope peddler. Federal officers were watch... ing him, were about to arrest him. Suddenly a policema... across the street and warned him so that he escape... reporters for this magazine saw this happen in New...

Why did the police warn the dope crook? Becau... ooks, were *paying the police* to prote... nefaric...

This is one of the sensat... orth in ...DE STORY OF DOP... INT... AL.

Here are ...

...ften obstruct the ...ailroads between ...d with Customs

...by the guards in U. S. Veterans' Hospitals, ...who are fighting tuberculosis!

That a ...werm... usiest passenger line in the coun... *...nan wh... sands of lives in his hands ...ur*—is a ...

...rt judges a... ously lax ...ope

...ts indicate a sl... nati... menace. ...circle of life. ...we going to ... author's vi... April Hea... ATIONAL.

DOPE

Today's market prices on goods are as follows: ... Light ... Dark ... Cash ...

Dope is at about 10% ... price down about $.00 or more.

Write me and let me know if you are interested.

Very truly, Joe.

DOPE PRICES ARE QUOTED JUST L... STOCK EXCHA... SECURITIE...

JUDGE JAMES MONAGHAN of PHILADELPHIA WHOM THE TRAFFICKERS FEAR

BURNING DOPE and PARAPHERNALIA IN SAN FRANCISCO'S CHINATOWN.

DR ERWIN C. RUTH, SHOWING DIST ATTORNEY O'BRIEN of BOSTON HOW OPIUM IS SMOKED—

Rodney Thompson's Conception of "Dope."

One of Walt Louderback's Illustrations of "The Temptress."

Zaharoff, the Richest Man of Europe.

From "Ponce de Leon and the Ring-Tailed Monkey."

Dope

Do you know that you can buy DOPE on the steps of the Public Library in New York; in Grant Park, Chicago; in the corridors of the Post Office in San Francisco; from the Main Street druggist in the towns of the nation?

Do you know that Somerset, Kentucky, a typical American town of 5,000, used 116,033 grains of morphine in 18 months, while the great hospitals of New York used only one-third of that amount?

Imports are increasing twice as fast as population, and smuggling is rife.

By official Government estimate, from one to four million inhabitants of the United States are addicted to the use of narcotic drugs. America uses *eighteen times* as much opium as Germany, *twelve times* as much as France.

A half-million pounds are imported annually. Forty-five thousand pounds should satisfy the medical demand. The rest is used *illicitly*.

During the year ending June, 1922, 6,651 cases of criminal violation of the narcotic laws were reported by the Federal authorities. This does not begin to represent the *actual* violations.

"The Inside Story of Dope" begins in the February issue of Hearst's INTERNATIONAL. Sidney Howard, the author, does not resort to melodrama. He gives *staggering*, authentic truths of the most *dangerous evil* on the face of the earth as it exists in this country. He throws the light of publicity into stricken homes and degenerate revelries; into jails and houses of correction; into the wretchedness of the charity wards of public hospitals, and into the *coffers of political campaigns.*

In the February number of Hearst's INTERNATIONAL

Eve—brought up to date by *Blasco Ibanez*, the famous author of *"The Four Horsemen."* Men to her are as pawns—toys to be played with and cast away when they are broken. ... debts mean nothing to her ... ruption of her hunt ...

And even in th ... ress" pursues her ... end of *every* temp ... NATIONAL Ibane ... ful background of F ...

"——if the Governm ... longer to keep off t ... These are the words ... klan has begun a sup ... It is forcing the grea ... *nothing*. No State is ... exposure of the klan ... uments and proofs. In ... NATIONAL Mr. Hap ... trols the courts.

He is the *richest m* ... Constantinople, son of ... Once a fireman in Turk ... ford University, titled h ... every European nation— ... No fiction can surpass th ...

Once he was sent to p ... had been shot full of le ... from prison. And the co ... morning as the body of ... *escape.*"

He is said to have decl ... enough to write his story, ... *travelled 5,000 miles* and ... tries from London to Co ... document for the February ...

Can a monkey's gland ma ... prance like a youth of thirty ...

Gland worship has been ... have acquired halos of digni ...

There is something in the ... Kruif in his article "Ponce ... key" in the February Hears ... ware the *faker!*

Each of the 24 features and ... issue is of absorbing interes ... than 100 superb pictures—... this the *most talked-about* ...

Hearst's Inter...

A LIBERAL EDU...

Norman Hapgood, Edito...

35 Cents a Copy

Februa...

STARTLING CONFESSIONS of a DRUG ADDICT

Fashionable Englishwoman Reveals the Frightful Experiences She Endured in Trying to Break the Grip of the Drug on Her Tortured Mind and Body

MISS Brenda Paul, attractive daughter of a titled Englishman, recently shook off the pitiless grip of the drug habit. She had been brought up in the luxury of life among the English aristocracy and was welcome in the salons of social leaders. Yet she became a drug addict!

How and Why She Became a Slave to the Habit

The fashionable young woman now reveals the almost unbelievable miseries of a drug addict's life. In an exceptionally interesting series of articles, she tells of the fate of other slaves to the drug habit and discloses the schemes and devices of traffickers in dope. Look for the first article in this unusual series in *The American Weekly* next Sunday!

Miss Brenda Paul, daughter of Sir Aubrey Dean Paul, of L... who frankly reveals the miseries of a slave to the dope hab... the tortures she endured to escape the thraldom of th...

READ THESE ASTOUNDING REVELATIONS

Starting Next Sunday

in

THE AMERICAN WEEKLY

Greatest Circulation in the World

—America's most interesting Weekly Magazine— Distributed every Sunday with

CHARACTER · QUALITY · AMERICA FIRST · ACCURACY · ENTERPRISE

New York American

AN AMERICAN PAPER FOR THE AMERICAN PEOPLE

New York's Most Interesting Newspaper

Tune in Your Radio and Hear

Front Page Dramas

Present

PONY BO...

with

FRANK LUTH...

RADIO AND STAGE ...

A thrilling story of ... West in the days ... pony express.

Based on a st... in the AMERICAN WEE...

See Radio Pa... For List of Sta... Featuring Th... Broadcast...

COMING GENERATION
HOME
DOPE PEDDLER
NARCOTIC TRAFFIC
DOPE PEDDLER
BUY A LITTLE DOPE TODAY?
"Dragging Children Down with Dope"
Physician to Ascertain If Child Was Drugged
NARCOTICS RING SEEKS YOUTH OF THE NATION AS PREY
STUDY OF DOPE SCHOOLS' TOPIC
A round-table discussion of "What High School Children Should Know About Narcotics"
CHILD'S MIND, BLANK FOR 5 DAYS, BRINGS DRUG THEORY
Woman in Brown' Hunted All Over State as Abductor; Kidnaped Girl Near Collapse
DOPE PEDDLER
Mothers Giving Children Narcotics May Cause Formation of Drug Habit
Demure Nurse-Mai
Drugs Helpless Little Ones
PROHIBITION
CHILDREN PLIED WITH DRUGS BY DOPE PEDDLERS
U. S. Attorney Ameli Startles Brooklyn Club with Story; Calls Conditions Appalling
"The 'rats' of the underworld are preying on the school children of Brooklyn. They ply them with drugs. In some instances, they have succeeded in making
CALIFORNIA BOA
THAT CHILDREN BUY DOPE IN TEN-CENT QUANTITIES
Boys and Girls Throughout Country Led Into Slavery by Dealers in Morphine and Cocaine; Story of San Francisco Lad Related
DRUGGED IN AN AUTO, SHE AWAKES IN LOT
Girl of 16 in Court Implicates "a Lame Boy" and "a Blond Policeman."
CHILD OF 12 A TOOL IN DRUG SMUGGLING
Ninety-six Hypodermic Needles Hidden in the Clothing of a Little Girl.
land Gang Preying School Children Smashed
ARRESTED HERE
ail Order Ring Broken Jp; 100 Women and Baby Addict in Net
How "the King" Was Trapped Through His Fifteen-Year-Old Agent
One day a man entered the back room of the produce store and asked for some cocaine.
Children Taught to Steal to Get Their Daily Drug
In all cases the drug peddlers drive their victi the limit of their financial possibilities.
Poor girls stint themselves from food and clothe turn over the larger part of their weekly wages dope peddlers in their insistent cravi
PARLEY BARES USE OF DOP BY CHILDR
President's Telegram to ference Indorses Camp Against Illicit Tra
PROHIBITION MAKING OUR YOUT
LIFE'S PATH
DOPE
FANATICAL PROHIBITION
YOUTH OF THE NATION
INTEMPERANCE

YOUNG GIRLS BOUGHT DRUGS, IS CHARGE

Police Say That Cartero, Arrested with Woman, Did a Large Traffic in Brooklyn.

A Little Chinese Girl Who Was Found to Be the Distributing Agent of a Drug Gang.

Youth of Land Being

BABY A DRUG ADDICT—Far reaching narcotic scourge is shown in life of this taught craving by mother, herself an who used heroin to quiet the child.

Boy Drug Peddlers Make One Bad Error

MOTHER SAYS DRUGS MADE BOY A SLAYER

SALE OF DOPE TO BOYS BRINGS ARREST OF TWO

BOY DRUG PEDDLER HELD WITH

Detectives Hear Sale Negotiated on Street in Alleged Deal

As a result of many complaints by mothers in the Harlem that drugs were being sold offered for sale to young boys men were under arrest yesterday. Several hours later, police arrested a man who barricaded himself in a room in an east street and accused him

RING OF BOY DRUG VENDORS IS UNCOVERED

Youth Tells U. S. Court Scores of Lads, 15 to 17, Are Operating in S.F. Under Two 'Hop Kings'

Young Peddlers Organized and Assigned to Districts by Other Boys; Police Seeking Leaders

Testimony that scores of boys between the ages of 15 and 17 years peddling large quantities of opium, morphine, heroin and cocaine in San Francisco for two men known as "Butch" Lencsl and "Goldy," obeyed by the youngsters as "Kings of the Hop Ring," was given by Martin McGowan, 1512 Clay street,

GIRL, 12, TO DISTRIBUTE DOPE IN SOUTH

New Orleans Veteran Arrested; Manchurkuo Becomes Vast Factory for Narcotics

By WINIFRED BLACK,
Universal Service Correspondent.

SAN FRANCISCO, Nov. 26.—How would you like to send your little 12-year-old daughter out peddling dope?

They caught a man doing this very thing down in New Orleans the other day.

Where do you suppose she went when her father gave the packages of deadly poison and sent her out to sell misery and shame and despair, at so much a grain?

Down to the levee where the giant black men buy cocaine to make them "step lively," when the mate calls orders from the deck of a lumber schooner, down from one of the bayous loaded to the water's edge with cypress logs.

Up dark ill-smelling alleys, where the human wreckage seems to gather by some weird and evil instinct.

TO FAMOUS HOTEL.

CHILDREN USED IN NEW ORLEANS DOPE TRAFFIC

Small Army of Boys and Girls Revealed as Peddlers of Narcotics for Big Dealers

"A small army of boys and girls, many of whom are still in high school, is being used by large scale narcotic dealers in New Orleans to peddle narcotics on a commission basis, J. B. Greeson, head of the United States narcotics division here, charged Monday, announcing that police and Federal officers of New Orleans have opened up a relentless war to stamp out this practice.

BOY DRUG VENDERS TAKEN 'RED HANDED'

Four Messengers Sell Narcotics to Addicts.

WITNESSES ARE DETAINED

"Coke" Parties Given at Which Uninitiated Are Taught to Form Habit.

Four messenger boys, alleged to have made a practice of retailing narcotics, are lodged in the county jail in default of $1000 bond each, and several other individuals who are believed to have been active in distributing cocaine and morphine are in the city jail as the result of a clean up in the drug traffic made yesterday

DOPE, MAKING BOYS KILL, IS CURSE OF CITY, SAYS MAYOR

World War, Which Made Life Cheap, and Gangsters Are Other Causes for Conditions

Lauds Hearst Papers' Narcotic Drive; Insists New York Is Not as Bad as Pictured

EXCLUSIVE

By JAMES J. WALKER,
Mayor of New York City.
Copyright, 1929, by New York American, Inc.

NEW YORK'S Crime Wave?

A crop of gangling youngsters . . . youngsters who under more ideal home environment might be staunch, useful citizens . . . their spirit of bravado stirred by a handful of conscienceless gang leaders, who play the puppet kids for all the world like a master of a marionette show . . . the sly, fearful introduction of opiates to these boys . . . sanity becomes maniacal . . . a gun never manufactured for immature hands suddenly turned loose in the palsied fingers of youth . . . murder . . .

That's New York's crime wave!

Drugs!

Dope, if you will!

The most damnable curse of modern

DRINK CONSCIOUS'

Youth Death

New York American

AMERICA FIRST · CHARACTER · QUALITY · ACCURACY · ENTERPRISE

AN AMERICAN PAPER FOR THE AMERICAN PEOPLE

BROOKLYN

THURSDAY, FEBRUARY 26, 1925

PUPILS IN CLUTCHES OF DRUG EVIL

ORGANIZED GANG SELLING TO STUDENTS

County Clerk Kelly Declares Dope Traffic Shows Alarming Increase.

RESPONSIBLE FOR CRIME

Says 75 Per Cent of Convicted Criminals Are Addicts.

A sweeping investigation of reports that narcotics are being peddled to high school students in Brooklyn will be launched today by Howard W. Ameli, United States Attorney.

Ameli's first act this morning, he said last night, would be to ask the Federal narcotics division in Manhattan for full assistance in "getting to the bottom of the whole situation."

He expressed himself as shocked over a situation disclosed in complaints to him by parents that school children were being sold narcotic drugs.

On Saturday Federal narcotic agents arrested two boy students, one, William Goldstein, sixteen, of Alexander Hamilton High School, being accused of actually selling eighty grains of morphine to an agent in the Flatbush section of Brooklyn. The other boy Solomon Raichelson, seventeen, was charged with being an accessory.

SHOCKING ANGLE REVEALED.

Ameli said:

"I haven't had a full report on these boys as yet, but their arrest discloses a shocking angle in our dope investigation. Six months ago we drove out a gang of addicts who were accused of hanging around high schools. We never suspected that students themselves would be accused of use or sale of narcotics.

"The arrest of these two boys may disclose only an isolated case, or may be general. That's what I intend to find out in the morning."

Goldstein, who was employed after school hours in the Tilyork Pharmacy, No. 1075 New York avenue, Brooklyn, was accused by Federal Agent Max Roeder with having made an appointment and sold the drug to him at Snyder and Albany avenue. It was alleged that Raichelson stood on a corner nearby acting as a lookout for Goldstein.

FATHER EXPLAINS INCIDENT.

Louis Raichelson, builder, No. 191 East Thirty-ninth street, Brooklyn, father of the boy, told his side of the story last night. He said:

"Young Goldstein told me that my boy, Sol, had nothing to do with it. 'It is true,' young Goldstein told me, 'that I am guilty as far as stealing morphine from the drug store is concerned, but I did it because the detective had begged me to get it for him for five weeks. I did not know he was a detective.

"'He gave me to understand that he needed it and needed it badly, and told me to be a regular fellow and get it for him. He convinced me I was taking no chances. He offered me $50 and I finally consented. The two other boys whom he got to help also urged me to get the stuff for him. In fact, they were the [...] who introduced him to

The "two boys" referred to are Alfred Linstad, sixteen, of No. 140 East Thirty-first street, Brooklyn, and Gerald H. Faulkner, eightee[n]

That the use of drugs is responsible for more than seventy-five per cent of the crimes committed by youths of the borough, was another startling statement made by the county clerk yesterday. This figure he based on the number of drug addicts convicted of crime in borough courts.

CITES CRIMES.

The alarming number of shootings and hold-ups recently perpetrated in the borough is attributed by the county clerk to the growing use of drugs. In urging a drive to end the menace Mr. Kelly merely echoed the warning uttered a few days ago to Brooklyn parents by Mary Hamilton, first policewoman, who spoke of the menace of the closed dance-hall where young girls are hired as "hostesses."

It is the habitues of these places, it was declared, who lure the high school students, many of them young girls, into vicious habits, including indulgence in drink and drugs.

As a result, the number of abandoned baby cases has increased to such an extent that it is one of the greatest problems the police department faces at the present time.

In his denunciation of drugs and those who are placing this pernicious and insidious menace directly in the paths of thoughtless, unwary children, Mr. Kelly, speaking to the Twelve-forty-five Club yesterday said:

URGES ACTION.

"Everyone in Brooklyn is and has been alarmed for some time about the numerous hold-ups and shootings committed in the borough. I believe from my experience in the County Clerk's office that drugs are responsible for the majority of these crimes.

"I am surprised at the apathy of Brooklyn people toward the problem. Drug addiction is a menace which is growing with leaps and bounds, and I urge you business and professional men to start a drive to organize all Brooklyn bodies into an effort to drive out this menace.

"If you have any doubts on this score, come down and visit the County Court any day as my guest."

BIG REWARDS OFFERED BOYS TO STEAL DOPE

Procurors Seek Students Who Work in Drug Stores After School; Conference Called

SEEK DRUG SUPPLY.

These men he has learned, have tried to get boys working in drug stores to steal heroin and morphine on the promise of large monetary rewards.

The investigation follows the arrest last Saturday of William Goldstein, Alexander Hamilton High School student, and Solomon Raichelson, Colb, College student.

DOPED CIGARETTES.

Government informers also say that a cigarette containing hasheesh is being sold to high school boys. These cigarettes have an exhilirating effect and are sold for from twenty-five to fifty cents each.

These same informers say that such cigarettes have been purchased by the more opulent students and given to their girlfriends at high school dances and parties. These cigarettes, according to Government narcotic agents, while not essentially habit forming, have an effect that usually leads to the need for drugs to keep the user in a normal condition.

THE WORLD: THURSDAY, DECEMBER 24, 1914.

CAUGHT AS HE SOLD "DOPE" TO BOYS IN A PUBLIC SCHOOL

John Grasso Held in $3,500 Bail by Magistrate Herbert, Who Says Prisoner Ought to Be Sent Up for 20 Years.

A systematic traffic in narcotics, principally heroin and cocaine, to school children was unearthed yesterday by detectives of the Fourth Branch Bureau, under the direction of Capt. Bolan. Complaints by parents have been coming into the bureau, which is in the district of Inspector Ryan, who is now on vacation, that heroin and cocaine sellers have been dabauching the children of the public and parochial schools of the neighborhood.

Detective Caspers was detailed to find out the extent of the practice and to arrest the traffickers. Yesterday he noticed John Grasso, in front of No. 301 East One Hundred and Sixth Street, which is opposite a public school, between Lexington and Park Avenues. St. Cecilie's parochial school is also nearby.

Caspers says he saw boys from ten to sixteen years old, give Grasso small sums of money and get something in return. Caspers arrested Grasso and took him to Magistrate Herbert's court. Caspers told the Magistrate that he had found twenty-three powders or "decks" of cocaine on Grasso and money amounting to $24.80. Magistrate Herbert held Grasso in $3,500 bail for examination to-day.

Six Others Arrested.

"It is lucky for you," said the Magistrate, "that I will not have the final jurisdiction in your case. If I had and you were convicted I would send you to prison for twenty years, not a day less. Any man who will sell poison to children deserves a sentence no milder than that."

In the last two days detectives of the Fourth Branch Bureau have made six other arrests of men accused of selling narcotics to pupils of the public and parochial schools. The schools are located on Ninety-ninth Street between Second and Third Avenues, at One Hundred and Sixth Street and Lexington Avenue and on One Hundred and Sixth Street between Second and Third Avenues.

Four of the men who were arraigned before Magistrate Herbert gave their names as Henry Schuster, twenty-three, a paver, of No. 2148 Second Avenue; Edward Gluck, twenty-four, of No. 1514 Washington Avenue, Bronx; Frank Smith, twenty-six, a laborer, of No. 26 East One Hundred and Fourth Street, and William Berlin, who is known as "Willy the Wop" and, according to the police, has a reputation as an ex-burglar.

Gluck was held in $1,000 bonds and the bail of the others was fixed at $2,500 each. All were charged with selling or having the drugs in their possession. Ten "decks" of heroin and $8 in quarters, dimes and nickels were found on Shuster by Detective Caspers. Schuster, in reply to a question by Caspers as to why he was selling the drugs to children, said: "It's the easiest way to make money."

Negro Leaps From Window.

Clarence Watson, a negro, who gave his address as No. 150 East Ninety-eighth Street, tried to escape from Caspers, who had pretended that he wanted to purchase some of the drugs. Watson took the detective to a tenement at No. 2031 Second Avenue, but, suspecting Caspers was a detective, he jumped through a second floor window. He crowded seven "decks" of heroin into his mouth and dropped three "decks" on the ground. The detective forced the negro to disgorge two of the "decks," but he swallowed enough of the stuff to cause him to be taken to the Harlem Hospital. Before Watson surrendered Detective Caspers had to fire two shots over his head to stop him from jumping over fences.

Detectives Phelan and McCullagh captured "Willy the Wop" in the tenement at No. 283 East One Hundred and Fourteenth Street. Three men and four women were found in the room with Berlin. Among other articles found in the room, according to the

SUSPECTED OF BEING CHIEF OF OPIUM SMUGGLING BAND

Japanese Salesman Is Sent With a Fourth Prisoner to Join Two Others in Tombs—Students May Be Implicated—"Trust" Squealed on Rivals—Adriatic Fined $5,000.

SCHOOL CHILDREN ENSLAVED BY 'FREE SAMPLES' OF DOPE

Dozens of Tearful Pleas by Parents Led Federal Agents to Trail of Cleveland Ring; Mystery Woman Furnished Clue

CLEVELAND, Dec. 8 (AP).—A scheme to enslave high school children to narcotics was uncovered here today by Federal agents as they rounded up ten of th alleged leaders in the plot in a series of swift raids.

Not content with selling to persons already addicted, the ring was making scores of new victims, the Federal officers said, by giving the boys and girls enough "free samples" to chain them to the vice.

Most of the gang's new victims are students at Addison Junior High School, located between a respectable neighborhood and one of the city's notorious sections.

Pleas By Parents.

Although the officers were unable to say how many students were made victims of the narcotics traffic, dozens of letters from parents to Federal officers show

automobile and he was charged with its illegal possession.

Offered Samples.

Oscar L. Bell, chief of the raiders, said a woman whom he described only as "Jane," named Testa as a man who proposed to furnish narcotics to her free if she would distribute them as samples to the Addison School students. "Jane," the officers said, is the estranged wife of a prominent Cleveland business man.

One of the most vicious angles of the ring's activity, the Federal agents said, was that few of the school children who were made addicts have sufficient money allowances from their parents to buy the narcotics at current prices.

Thus, to satisfy their craving for the narcotics they have been faced with the alternative of exposing themselves or obtaining money from dubious sources.

Fearful of Death.

Recruits Addicts in Scho

DOP

U S Opens Sweeping Probe of High School Dope Sale

DAY SAN FRANCISCO, OCTOBER 20, 1921 THURSDAY CO

PEDDLER ARRESTED AT HIGH SCHOOL

pread of Drug vil Appalling, ociety Is Told

HILADELPHIA, Oct. 19. —Sarah Graham Mulhall, rmer deputy commissioner of Narcotic Control Board of w York, told the American umane Society at tonight's sion of its annual conven n that conditions resulting m drug addiction in the ited States were "appalling,"

U.S. OFFICIAL INDORSES WAR ON DRUG RING

"Examiner's" Campaign Against Traffickers Is Praised by Chief of Narcotic Bureau

STATE, U.S. OFFICIALS TO FIGHT DRUGS

Police and Civic Authorities of All Northern California to Attend Dope Conference

Who's to Blame for Dope Menace?

Officials Work With Limited Means

Convention May Find Solution

By ANNIE LAURIE

Who's to blame, if your daughter goes to a "snow" party, "just for fun" and learns the effect of cocaine?

Who's to blame, if your boy wants to "speed up" for some examina-

cod for our daily market. Strange they should be so secret about it.

Over the border of Mexico, it comes in—they've been known to smuggle twenty Chinamen across at one time there—why not a few thousand dollars' worth of a narcotic drug?

OLD OFFENDER, WAITING YOUNG VICTIMS, HELD

Notorious Criminal, With Poison in His Pocket, Is Captured at High School of Commerce

St. Patrick's Church, the Y. M. C. A.—and yesterday it was one of San Francisco's public high schools that was invaded by the malignant army of the illicit drug traffic.

On the steps of the High School ... Howe and Franklin ... it

... with ... short ... of them had suc- ... of "Nig" Howe, ... of poison was ... with an eye ... point that is ... orities.

... owe's com- ... ll go into ... and plead

...LES.

... when arrested ... dly drug— ... poison.

... after ... found $1,800 ... ine, mor-

... by E. R. Dun- ... McCarthy and William ... of the State Pharmacy

... have been looking for Howe ... past, and so have the ... es," said Dunbar. ... two weeks ago ... shifted his

... and drug selling ... stated he had "done time" for murder.

In criminal circles he is known as "The Quail," and also as "Nig" Howe. The authorities who have been fighting the huge increase of the drug traffic know him as one of the boldest and most successful drug venders in the traffic.

$200 A DAY PROFITS.

The extent of his operations is to be inferred from the fact that a bank book, found in his room, showed deposits in a local bank amounting to $160 to $200 a day for months past.

The lowest day was $160 and the highest was slightly over $200. The average was around $185 a day. Except for Sundays, no day was omitted.

The arrest was due to the close system of espionage effected by the State officials. Acting on a "tip" that their man had adopted a rendezvous at the High School of Commerce, the three agents approached the spot and saw Howe, across the street from the school, playing with a little 6-year-old girl.

He is an expert whistler, and was whistling an alluring melody to entertain the child.

As the detectives watched, Howe crossed the street and took up his position on the high school steps, evidently expecting a customer to approach. A moment later he was in custody.

When arrested, he revealed the whereabouts of his room and led the officers to the place. Lying on the bureau was a loaded revolver.

The finding of the $1,800 worth of drug in Howe's room was a matter of some ... under ... tress, ...

Dope ...

ROFESSOR, ILLER, WOOED IANY CO-EDS ITH DRUGS

ectives Find He Was Noti- ed to Stop Love Affairs or e Expelled from University

yer of Theora Hix Plans to ight for Life; 3 Alienists tudy His Actions in Jail

By JOH NB. PRATT, ..

w York American Staff Correspondent.

OLUMBUS, June 22. — While nists at the county jail tod y e watchng Dr. James E. Snook, sed Ohio State University pro or, under first degree murdenin ment for the fiendish slaying of pretty college love-mate, detec s were raking up evidence of e of his love adventures.

t alone did Snook have his illicit fling with Theora K. Hix, ming university co-ed, whom he essed he killed with hammer pocketknife, but other college , it now develops, were fleeting cts of his wandering passion.

ELY AT BARNARD.

thorities working on the cam tragedy divulged today that ra Hix, a year ago, during a orary separation from the pro or, was a student at Barnard ge, New York, but she became sick and wanted to return to mbus.

st February the lovelorn girl e Dr. Snook she wanted to be with him. Characteristic of scrupulous aversion to writing rs that might bob up to betray ove affairs, Snook sent word to ra Hix through Marion T. s, employe at the horticultural rtment of the university.

ers, a former sweetheart of the ctive co-ed, had often talked to k of the professor's love entan ent with her, so at Snook's urg Myers wrote Theora Hix to back to Columbus and she hur home, after being away from k for eight months.

THE CARPET."

ng with this, authorities re d that the complacent Snook a week before he slew Theora told Myers as he met him on niversity campus one morning:

Vell, I've been jacked up for g with that girl. They've had on the carpet. I've got to her up."

ok grinned as he added, with er:

"You can have your old flame back."

In revealing this phase of the love tragedy, authorities said Snook had been haled a month ago before an official of the university and warned he must put a stop to his love affairs with co-eds, or he would be expelled from the college. It was after this that Snook, in fear for with Theora Hix.

And it was his blunt renunciation of the girl who, for three years had been his loveliest mistress, that culminated in her brutal murder, the night of June 13, at the New York Central rifle range, on the lonely outskirts of the city.

He added:

"It is all summed up when we point to Snook as a man who would kill to slip out of trouble. It was not degeneracy with him, it was the cunning of a deliberate murder."

USED DRUGS ON GIRLS

In unravelling the love exploits of the supposedly staid university professor, the authorities informed the New York American representative that Snook had used drugs upon campus girls who figured in his amours. Posing as a sedate university faculty man, Snook is pictured as fervently wooing girl students. Not merely two or three, but many of them were Snook's transitory loves. In at least one instance an official told this correspondent Snook is alleged to have given narcotics to one young co-ed that resulted in her becoming an addict.

As this young girl, now happily out of her drug enslavement and married, relates the direful tale, Snook gave her drugs to put her within his power. She went with him. They loved desperately. But only for a little while. For Snook tired of her and picked up another "flame," as he flippantly called them.

All through Snook's life during the last five years there runs the scarlet of his vagrant, yet burning love for girls of the campus. And of his thrusting them aside soon for others.

SORDID PICTURE.

But his affair with Theora Hix ran more consistently than others of his love caprices. Snook has revealed t odetectives since his arrest that he actually did love the fair girl from the South. He would not put it in his confession, but they have dragged it out of him.

And so the whole sordid picture of Snook's past is being pieced together, while lunacy experts have the disgraced university professor under

BODY MUTILATED.

For the first time, today, the authorities divulged that Snook, aside from crushing in the skull of his sweetheart and slashing her throat with his pocket knife, had mutilated her body, evidently with the idea of making it appear her slaying was the work of a degenerate.

This Snook did, County Prosecutor John L. Chester believes, to throw suspicion from himself. His whole fiendish act had been calculated and cold-blooded.

The New York American correspondent asked:

"Do you think Snook is a degenerate?"

The prosecutor replied:

"Far from it. He was a miserable flirt, an unconscionable fiend. But I do not believe he was of the degenerate type."

The prosecutor went on to say that every act of Snook's—the sedulous efforts to keep his double-life from exposure, his coaxing his sweetheart to ride to the scene of the tragedy, his hiding the gruesome tools of murder, his schemes to throw suspicion away from himself, all were those of a man of an essentially bal-

Drug Viper Stalks Path of Boys, Girls

Peddlers Seek Innocents in Public Schools

And Now 'The Quail' Is Loose Again

He Merely Sold Dope at High School

So He Gets Bail—For It Is the Law

By ANNIE LAURIE

Admitted to bail—Rogue Riderhood, alias "Nig" Howe, alias "The Quail"—and his case will come up next week some time.

Twenty-nine years in the penitentiary he has served, at one time and another, for burglary, for robbery, for dope selling and, by his own confession, for murder.

And now he is up for trial, accused of being a dope peddler, and keeping his stand for business on the steps of the Commercial High School.

Twenty - nine years, and all

friendly as they? Who so ready to help them to forget—with a little white powder? Even if he has no money, they'll accommodate him somehow, if he goes to the big peddlers—particularly if he ha... compensation check coming ... some day.

And when it does com... gets it?

The mother who has ... everything for her bo... whose heart beat ... when he march... eyes right—to...

He himself, ... suffered so much, and com... illusion and despair?

Not at all— ... of these.

The dope p... ne ... one who gets the ... whe... or victim's comp...tion cashed.

LOOKED LIKE ...T.

High School Youths Arrested For Peddling Narcotic Drugs!

TWO schoolboys in the Flatbush section of Brooklyn are under arrest, one charged with actu- ... er pledges of the strictest

Drug Habit Clutches High School Pupils

2 SCHOOLBOYS SEIZED ON DOPE SALE CHARGES

One, 16, Accused by U. S Agent of Peddling Morphine Lad of 17 Called Lookou

MAN BELIEVED DRUG TEACHER HELD BY POLICE

Many School Children Addicts in Neighborhood Where

27,000 Teachers Join Dope Drive

Strict obedience of an order of the Board of Education to warn children against the destroying effects of narcotics and alcohol was begun yesterday by 27,000 teachers in the New York public schools.

Such teachings will be included, Harold Campbell, acting superintendent of schools, explained yesterday, in the hygiene and physiology classes.

This order from the school board, it was revealed, is in keeping with the present nation-wide agitation against dope and alcohol.

Now the Dope Evil Is At the School Doors

Keep Right After the "Ring," Capt. Layne

DOPE
DELUSION
DOPE
DOPE
NARCOTIC TRAFFIC
DOPE
DOPE
DOPE
DRUG EVIL
DOPE
DOPE FROM THE ORIENT
DRUG EVIL
ILLICIT DRUG TRAFFIC
DRUG HABIT
DOPE
ADDICT
DOPE TRAFFIC
DOPE

DOPE EVIL
WORLD WIDE DOPE RING
THE MANUFACTURE, SALE AND DISTRIBUTION OF DOPE
DOPE TRAFFIC
DOPE
$1,000,000 IN DOPE
DOPE PEDDLER
DOPE FROM EUROPE
DOPE TRAFFIC
DOPE PEDDLER
GUN MAN
DRUG EVIL
HOME
HABIT-FORMING DRUG VENDOR
PRODUCTION, MANUFACTURE AND SALE OF DOPE
DOPE TRAFFIC
DOPE
DOPE
UNDESIRABLE NIGHT CLUBS
VICE
MISERY
POVERTY
SHAME
CRIME
DISEASE
DOPE EVIL
INTERNATIONAL DOPE RING
INTERNATIONAL DOPE RING

SMUGGLING "Dope"

—Photos by Sponagel & Herrman

THE 47 VARIETIES
Inspector J. P. Thompson looking over the forty-seven different containers for opium, morphine and cocaine in the curio cabinet at the San Francisco Customs House.

THE STAFF OF LIFE ABUSED
Eighteen bottles of Scotch found concealed in loaves of bread in the bakeshop of the President Taft. The loaves were hollowed out and the ends were fixed back again with toothpicks sunk beneath the surface.

THIS TRUNK WORTH $17,000 "EMPTY"
Inspector Botkin found 115 tins of opium beneath the false bottom of this cheap piece of baggage belonging to a Chinese steerage passenger.

WEARS EXPENSIVE LINGERIE
A sudden influx of black baby dolls from the Azores caused Chief Customs Inspector R. H. Wilcox of San Francisco to investigate. Inspector J. H. Hessler discovered that they were stuffed with Spanish hand-made lace.

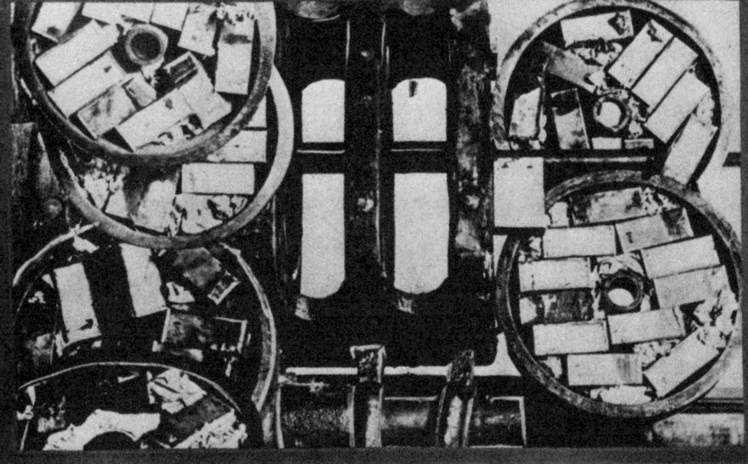

SHEAVES OF A GOLDEN HARVEST
When a customs inspector pried the side sheaves off a number of blocks in the storeroom of the steamer Siberia he found that instead of being just "ship's equipment" they were hollow and contained $11,250 worth of opium.

ANOTHER OIL SCANDAL
The opium tucked away in this oil drum is a thousand times more precious than the "flowing gold" the drum is supposed to contain.

A SILK-LINED PILLOW
An attempt to smuggle in several hundred dollars worth of silk shirts from the Orient.

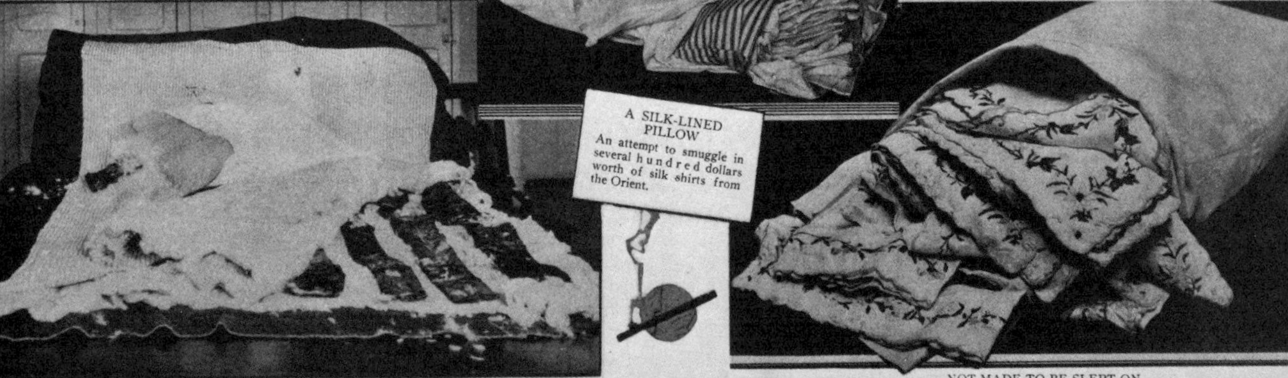

"THE STUFF THAT DREAMS ARE MADE OF"
A mattress stuffed with thousands of dollars worth of opium.

NOT MADE TO BE SLEPT ON
A poor subterfuge used in an attempt to evade duty on hand-embroidered silk handkerchiefs from the Orient.

A Million "Dope" Addicts Now *in the* United States

Experience of Veteran Narcotic Agent Leads to the Belief That the Drug Curse Has Increased Fifteen Times During the Fifteen Years of Restriction by the Federal Government.

By a Member of the Post-Dispatch Sunday Magazine Staff

DOPE peddlers, in creating a "market" for their bootleg sales of narcotics at the exorbitant price of $437 an ounce, have brought about the alarming increase in drug addiction which has occasioned widespread comment and the suggestion in some quarters that the Harrison antinarcotic law of 1914 should be repealed by Congress.

Before the law was passed, narcotics might be had with the readiness and ease of the purchase of a package of cigarettes over a drug store counter. Morphine was obtained by druggists at about $12 an ounce and sold at a modest profit. An ounce is 437 apothecary grains, six of which constitute the average daily dose for an addict. With slight variations, other narcotics were available at about the same price.

A veteran narcotic agent told the Post-Dispatch that drug addiction, referred to by Dr. Royal S. Copeland, United States Senator and former Commissioner of Health in New York City, as "the most dreadful of human afflictions and the curse of the generation," has increased 15-fold during the 15 years of restriction by the Federal Government. For obvious reasons he would not permit the use of his name.

Explaining that his figures were estimates based on his observation as an agent, since it has been impossible for the Government to collect accurate statistics, he added that the number of addicts in the United States now is probably 1,000,000, a figure comparable to the number of men golf players, or sufficient to make a city nearly the size of St. Louis and its environs.

"Furthermore," he said, "three out of four become heads before they have passed out of their teens or twenties. And another thing," he said with emphasis, "not only has the number of addicts increased, but their character has changed. The dishwasher in a restaurant, the handyman and odd-jobs hunter formerly was able to buy at a drug store enough drugs 'to keep him comfortable' notwithstanding his small earnings.

"But what has that type of addict become today, with the price of narcotics distributed by bootleggers increased from $12 to $437 an ounce? He can't buy $6 or $8 worth of dope a day and wash dishes or mow lawns. Sometimes, when we have struck the main source of supply in a city, the price goes even higher.

"The price is determined, more or less directly, by the activity of narcotic agents, for the peddler's profit must be in proportion to the risk entailed.

"THIS meek, docile, unobtrusive weakling, driven to desperation by excruciating pain resulting from his inability to obtain his 'medicine,' is found today as the bank robber and the hired killer. Or, again, we find him as a dope peddler, because of the enormous profit.

"The comparative desirability of the latter occupation has increased the number of 'shot tossers.' The result of that condition—and persons who are not addicts also have swelled the number—is the answer to the question of why there are more addicts. Three-fourths of the peddlers arrested are addicts.

"The retail bootleg field has become crowded, naturally. Competition increases. The peddler approaches a down-and-outer.

" 'What's the trouble, pard?' he may inquire sympathetically. 'Too bad. Here, let me fix you up. This'll make you feel better.'

"An acquaintance is formed and the soothing effect of a shot in the arm or a sniff of 'snow' to the ill or melancholy unfortunate is demonstrated gratis. It is but a matter of giving him a few more doses and a customer who is willing to pay, and willing to do anything to be able to pay, has been made.

"Then there are the sanatoriums. Nine out of 10 are merely dispensing stations, where those sent for cure are content to remain until they are discharged when the length of time they have remained there starts to become a suspicious circumstance.

"Lest this statement work an injustice, it should be said that it is no easy thing to cure them. I say 'cure' instead of 'break' the habit, because these persons are subject to terrible physical torment when deprived of their 'medicine.' They are not merely in the toils of a habit, they are sick. And my observation has been that only about two out of 25 discharged as cured from a reputable sanitarium do not, at some later time, start the use of narcotics again.

"To the ordinary person," the agent replied, when asked if his figures were not too high, "the situation probably is astounding. They know nothing of it and dismiss such statements with a remark of disbelief, challenging their accuracy because they have not been gathered with the methodical machinery of the Census Bureau.

"Such facts cannot be gathered accurately. There are snowbirds and hypes that give no outward appearance of their addiction. Those who mind their health and do not indulge to excess may continue a normal apearance for many years. There is no check on the amount of narcotics smuggled into the United States, and we can judge only as a result of our experience. I have worked in all parts of the country and I know what I am talking about.

"CONTRARY to popular belief, 80 per cent of habitual narcotic users have no disease or illness. The only thing the matter with them is that they have come to require the stimulation of a certain amount of drug. And persons in every stratum of society have become its slave.

"This," said the agent, shaking a three-ounce bottle of light, flaky substance, "is cocaine, which exhilarates the user, whereas morphine or heroin brings him only to a normal point of physical and mental ease."

Pouring a small quantity into the palm of his hand, he tossed it into the air and it drifted downward slowly, scintillating in the sunlight.

"That's why it is called 'snow,' and the users referred to as 'snowbirds,' " he explained. "It is also known as 'happy dust' and 'flying powder,' and may be dissolved in a small quantity of water and injected in the arm as morphine is administered. This is the more popular way, although, because it is light, it may be poured into the hand and sniffed into the nasal cavity. The action thus is slower, however."

Senator Royal S. Copeland.

Tiny white pills, wrapped in paper, then were exhibited as morphine, known to the illicit trade as "M." Another bottle, containing larger cubes, was described as morphine sulphate. Two cubes held together in the sunlight produce the colors of the rainbow as the light filters through the contiguous sides.

Opium, used by few others than Chinese, is heated over a small flame and the fumes inhaled through a pipe as the smoker lies on his side. Hence, the expression, "laying on the hip," and "blowing a cloud."

Cocaine is an extract of cocoa leaves. Morphine and heroin are products of opium.

Much of what the agent said is corroborated by United States Government Public Health reports, or even in the classics, Thomas De Quincey, English scholar, having recorded more than a century ago, in his "Confessions of an English Opium Eater," his experiences and sensations as an addict and his harrowing suffering in untwisting "almost to its final links, the accursed chain which fettered me."

The records of more than 2000 persons reported as violators of the antinarcotic laws are analyzed in the Public Health reports of a month ago by Dr. Walter L. Treadway, chief of narcotics division, United States Public Health Service.

Of those arrested, 74 per cent were addicts and 17 per cent were women. Of the addic's, 75 per cent were born in the United States, 52 per cent being of native parentage.

Addiction was established in 20 per cent of the cases before the age of 19, 34 per cent between 20 and 24 and 22 per cent between 25 and 29. Thus, 76 per cent of the addicts had started the use of drugs before they were 30 years old.

Two-thirds used morphine and one-fifth opium. Cocaine and heroin followed in order as to popularity. Virtually all administered drugs by hypodermic injection except in the case of opium smokers.

THE educational level of the narcotic users, Dr. Treadway states, corresponds with that of the general population, more than 4 per cent being college graduates, 3 per cent high school graduates and 20 per cent had attended high school for varying periods. Thirty per cent of those remaining had finished the eighth grade and about twice this number had attended school, only 11 per cent of the total being illiterate.

In response to inquiries as to the reasons for contracting the habit, half attributed it to the influence of other addicts, 23 per cent to use of drugs in medical treatment, 18 per cent to self-treatment for relief of pain, 1 per cent to curiosity and the remainder to other causes.

Seventy-six per cent use no alcoholic drinks, 18 per cent use them moderately and only six-tenths of 1 per cent are excessive users. The remainder used unknown quantities, definite answers not having been given.

"Drug addicts sometimes seek treatment for the purpose of ridding themselves of the slavery of the drug," Dr. Treadway reports, "because relatives and friends insist; because of a desire to impress those concerned with the enforcement of law that they desire to improve their ways; because the temporary isolation during treatment affords a convenient refuge from police, or because of their desire to reduce the average daily dose so that the resumption of the habit at some subsequent date would be less expensive on account of the quantity of the drug required to maintain their comfort."

HIS tables show that 957 out of 1592 had not taken any treatments; that 262 had taken one, 93 had taken two, 40 had been treated three times and that 27 had taken from four to ten "cures." Of the total, 214 were classed "unknown."

Less than 18 per cent of the addicts examined were deformed, diseased or infirm, the report concludes.

A statistical analysis of the population of Federal prisons, prepared by Sanford Bates, United States Superintendent of Prisons, shows that drug-law violators numbered only 289 in 1920, six years after passage of the Harrison act. This figure was less than 8 per cent of the total population of 3682 in the Atlanta and Leavenworth penitentiaries and the Alderson and Chillicothe reformatories.

On last April 1, however, 2449 drug-law violators were confined in these institutions, constituting 22 per cent of the population of 10,977.

De Quincey, the scholar, wit, philosopher and man of the world, in his famous autobiographical work, mentioned above, vividly pictures the fantastic dreams he experienced while under the influence of laudanum, an opium derivative to which he was addicted during the greater part of his life, and the agonizing pain attendant to his efforts to "release myself from the horrors of opium" and "from the palsying effects on the intellectual faculties."

The son of an English merchant in comfortable circumstances, De Quincey was born in 1785, and, at the age of 20, while a student at Oxford, started the use of opium, "not for the purpose of creating pleasure but of mitigating pain." He struggled four times to rid himself of the habit, and 15 years before his death, at the age of 74, at last was successful. Of interest, in view of the belief of some medical men that narcotics affect reproductive ability, is the fact that De Quincey, who married at 31, was the father of eight children.

INFORMATIVE excerpts from his best-known writing include the following, bearing, more or less directly, on the findings of Dr. Treadway: "By accident I met a college acquaintance who recommended opium. Opium! dread agent of unimaginable pleasure and pain! I had heard of it as I had of manna or ambrosia, but no further; how unmeaning a sound was it at that time! What solemn chords does it now strike upon my heart. . . . I, myself, who have never been a great wine drinker. . . . The primar[illegible] opium are always, and in [illegible] degree, to excite and st[illegible] system. . . . It does not [illegible] necessity, produce inactivit[illegible] . . . Farewell to smiles a[illegible] peace of mind, hope a[illegible] dreams and the blessed co[illegible] sleep . . . for I am now a[illegible] Iliad of woes. . . . I have [illegible] cord the pains of opium."

After addiction was [illegible] firmly, De Quincy recounts:

"I was buried a thousand [illegible] stone coffins, with mum[illegible] sphinxes. . . . I was kissed [illegible] cerous kisses by crocodiles; [illegible] confounded with all unutter[illegible] things, amongst reeds and [illegible] mud. . . . The cursed croc[illegible] came to me an object of mor[illegible] than almost all the rest. . . [illegible] that I must die if I contin[illegible] opium. . . . I determined, th[illegible] if that should be required, to [illegible] throwing it off. . . . Think of [illegible] one . . . still agitated, wr[illegible] throbbing, palpitating, shattered[illegible] The moral of the narrative [illegible] dressed to the opium eater. . [illegible] he is taught to fear and tre[illegible] enough has been effected. . [illegible] heartily wish him more energy; I[illegible] him the same success."

Few addicts, however, confess [illegible] habit with the simple candor of [illegible] Quincey. They seek to conceal the [illegible] making it impossible to determ[illegible] with any degree of accuracy, the t[illegible] number in the United States.

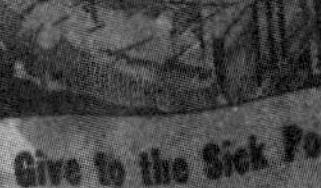

Mussolini Leads Way In Crushing Dope Evil

Italy Jails Smugglers and Peddlers for Life with No Hope of Pardon; U. S. Acting at Last.

MARCH 9, 1928

By WINIFRED BLACK.

"I HOPE that America will organize the world conference on the serious question of opium addiction, and I shall come in person to attend it in America."

WINIFRED BLACK.

That is what Mussolini says in a letter received by Mrs. Sarah Graham Mulhall, former deputy commissioner of the Department of Drug Control of New York.

Mrs. Mulhall was sent by the Federation of Women's Clubs to study the work of the Opium Commission of the League of Nations, and she is now planning to enroll eight million American women in the fight against "dope."

Italy does not grow narcotic plants.

Italy does not manufacture narcotic drugs.

Will Protect People

But Italy has no intention of being made a dumping ground for narcotics and Mussolini himself is determined to keep "dope" and "dope" sellers and "dope" smugglers and "dope" users out of his country.

He isn't going to wait until it is necessary to build refuges for the poor slaves of "dope."

He isn't going to have "dope" smuggled into his country and woe betide any human being who tries to sneak up an alley and sell cocaine or morphine or marijuana or heroin or codeine to any man, woman or child in Italy.

Any such person as that will not be sent to prison for a month or so, or a week or so, or maybe a day or so and then turned loose to spread the hideous contagion of "dope" like a leprosy in the community.

Faces Life Sentence

He will be sent to prison for life and nobody will find any pardoning board to let him out again on any pretext, any time, anywhere, anyhow.

Italy was not invited into the advisory committee in the League of Nations sub-committee on opium.

But that didn't keep Italy out of it.

Mussolini sent Signor Cavazzoni, an exceedingly agreeable but most plain spoken person, to the meeting and the signor called attention to the fact that the committee as it then stood was made up of representatives of countries which were making an excellent income either in growing narcotic plants or manufacturing narcotic drugs.

Demands Place

Cavazzoni did not say exactly that he considered the wolf rather a poor member of a committee for the protection of Little Red Riding Hood, but he didn't leave very much doubt as to what he meant when he demanded a place for his country on that Opium Commission.

If America had awakened to this "dope" evil in time, as Italy has done, we might not have to build refuges for the pitiful slaves of a devastating disease.

Two or three years ago the average American looked on "dope" as a strange vice entirely belonging to the underworld.

The everyday, clean-living, straight-thinking American never dreamed "dope" was going to come anywhere near his life or his home or anyone he loved.

America Too Late

The average American has changed his mind.

He has had to change it. He has seen "dope" creeting into his own home and into the homes of his friends. He has watched the horrifying growth of youthful crime and he has finally got it into his head that "dope" is at the bottom of a great percentage of that crime.

Out in Seattle, the White Cross Society is enlisting thousands and thousands of men and women in this war.

The Seattle Council of Churches, the Kiwanis clubs, the Rotary Club, the University Commercial Club and half a dozen other civic organizations have telegraphed to Washington asking their representative in Congress to take a stand in this matter and to begin by voting for the Porter bill when it comes up next week.

Emergency Situation

The Seattle Elks have broken their rule against political activities and have enlisted almost to a man in the war against "dope."

In New York the committee on co-operation of the United Synagogues of America has adopted a resolution pledging its support to the Porter narcotic bill.

United Synagogues of America has sixty synagogues in the immediate New York district and two hundred synagogues throughout the country.

All these bodies are working for the Porter bill. And they are also interested in the Shortridge bill in the Senate, which asks for a larger appropriation for the Federal narcotic service work.

Schools Co-operate

The New York public schools are taking up the fight and teachers from now on will be obliged to teach the effect of narcotics on the human system.

All through the Middle West the women's organizations have rallied to the cause.

The Porter bill will be one of three important steps in a great national and international plan to conquer the evil which is making such fearful inroads.

The bill, if it becomes a law, will take care of the poor wrecks of addicts who cannot take care of themselves.

It will protect the innocent from "dope" infection.

It will lock up the dope peddler and keep him locked up.

Locks Up Smuggler

It will lock up the "dope" smuggler and keep him locked up.

It will make it possible for every State to know a place where a "dope" addict can be sent for humane, kindly and scientific treatment.

And it won't cost the State one penny more than it would to send that same victim to a prison or county jail to "suffer it out" in hideous agony . . . and then go out into the world to begin the whole wretched business all over again.

The Porter bill means hope for the "dope" slave, protection for those not already infected, and a sane, practical way of handling the problem of the crowded Federal prisons.

If that bill passes, America will have taken one long step forward in the determined fight on the "dope" traffic and "dope" slavery.

Ex-Crown Prince Sells

MUSSOLINI:

'WHY I AM FOR TEMPERANCE RATHER THAN PROHIBITION'

"Efficacy of America's Dry Experiment Is Doubtful; in Italy We Have No Use for Absolute Prohibition Because Italians Are Temperate in Use of Wine," Says Duce.

By BENITO MUSSOLINI,
Premier of Italy.

By Special Cable.

MAY 25, 1930

ROME, May 24.

I AM more of a moderate "wet" than a "dry." I am against excess in the interest of national discipline. I am not unmindful of the blessing which a glass of good wine brings to a workman and his family. I recall with keen emotion the happy days of the vigorous and healthy peasants of my native village when on a Sunday they gathered about and there sipped pure wine ciously ing ... -trade- ... to suggest ... innocent pleasure ... pressed?

... other hand, my checkered career through many lands ... varied circumstances has brought me face to face with much misery that was induced by alcohol. Great is the ... injudicious excesses in the indulgence ... to be a simple pleasure should ... makers to seek an opposite ex... ... and altogether of that pleas... Italy to keep the balance ... extremes.

BENITO MUSSOLINI.

Personally, I do not use wine because it does not agree with me, but I fully appreciate the beauty of a glass of sparkling ruby or golden blond nectar which is a typical product of the Mediterranean civilization.

Moderate
Italians Temperate in Use of Wine, Says Duce

Moderation in all things is biblical wisdom. Moderation is so tersely expressed in the Oriental proverb: "One glass of wine makes a man into a lion, two into a rabbit, three into a monkey and four into a swine."

The policy we have followed in Italy, however, has been one of increasing ... striction as the broad ... alistic scheme. W... need for absol... because ... perate... ... is ... to the problem, if indeed it can be called a problem, in Italy.

And while I am decidedly more a "wet" than a "dry," I cannot see any world-wide sweep of the prohibition movement, even though there are advocates in almost every country. For all their years of intense activity they have accomplished little or practically nothing in countries where wine has been a staple article of food for centuries and where the populations of these countries have been bred in ... individual control ... of wine.

After all ... hol is ... ph... ... take ... is no ... my aim to ... the physical and ... and, even to a very decided degree, the spiritual well-being of the Italian people. What we have done has always had that aim and

'Why I'll No Longer Let Women Teach in the Schools of Italy'—Mussolin

Mussolini Joins U. S. War on Narcotic Evil

GENEVA, Jan. 31.

PREMIER MUSSOLINI, influenced by the aggressive fight of the United States against traffic in narcotic drugs, is planning a state monopoly of narcotics commerce in Italy, it was revealed here today.

Signor Cavazzoni, Italian delegate to the International Opium Commission, during debate upon the proposal of the Americans to limit the manufacture of opium, made the revelation.

the Geneva anti-opium convention, to which the United States is not a party, should be given a fair trial before other schemes are adopted.

WASHINGTON, Jan. 31 (AP).—Representative Stephen G. Porter, of

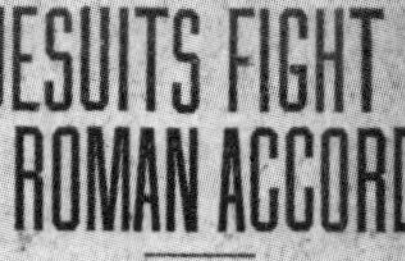

JESUITS FIGHT ROMAN ACCORD

By PRINCE PIGNATELLI.
Universal Service Special Wireless.
Copyright, 1929, by Universal Service.

ROME, Jan. 31.—New obstacles loom in the path of settlement of the Roman question. It is reported today from a reliable source that the Jesuit order is strongly opposed to the settlement plan.

The opposition seems to resolve itself into a bitter battle within the church—the Jesuits against the adherents of ... scheme, headed ... papal secr...

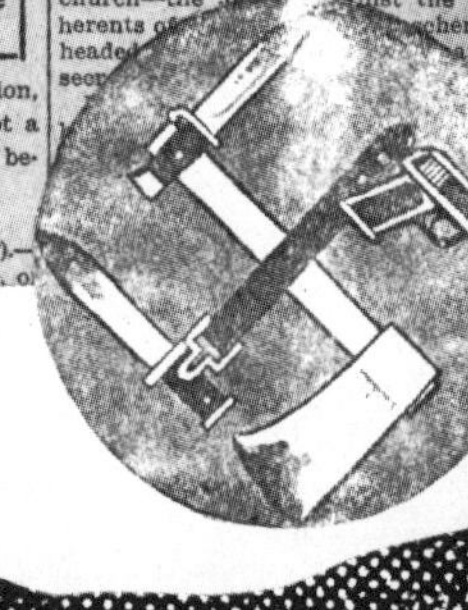

APRIL 3, 1929

Chamberlain and Mussolini Agree on All Policies

By Associated Press.

FLORENCE, Italy, April 2.

PREMIER MUSSOLINI lunched with Sir Austen Chamberlain, British Foreign Secretary, today. They

Austen Chamberlain Premier Mussolini.

discussed the general state of European politics and at the conclusion let it be known their governments were agreed on all policies.

FUNGUS YIELDS 'VITAMIN' DRUG

By HOWARD W. BLAKESLEE,
Associated Press Science Editor.

A drug "many thousand times as potent as the well-known cod liver oil" was described last night by Dr. Alfred F. Hess of Bellevue before the American Institute.

The powerful substance is ergosterol, after it has been exposed to ultra-violet light. Ergosterol is an extract o fa common fungus named ergot, which until recently attracted little attention. Today Ergot has leaped into such prominence that it is considered as perhaps a part of every animal and vegetable cell, which hakes it one of the important constituents of the human body.

But the vital factor ... Ergosterol ... Instead it ... violet light, ... tion. This ... when applied ... bul to oils, ... foods, makes ... equivalent to ... internally.

Duce Asks Doctors To Discourage Thin Figures in Women

ROME, Jan. 28 (AP).—Premier Mussolini has called on Italy's physicians to discourage women's desire for a thin figure as weakening the race.

FAMILY JAILED IN DOPE SEIZURE

An entire family, father, mother and daughter, was committed

MUSSOLINI

INSIDE STORY OF THE MANIAC DICTATOR

HITLER

DOOMED TO DIE

PRICE 50¢

SMUGGLED PHOTOS OF NAZI ATROCITIES! HITLER'S STRANGE LOVE LIFE! CRIMES OF GERMAN LEADERS!

EX LIBRIS

Adolf Hitler

DAMNING EVIDENCE—Hermann Goering, the No. 2 Nazi, would give much if the hospital certificate shown above could be destroyed. Signed by the eminent Dr. Karl A. Lundberg, it reads: "Capt. Goering suffers from morphine, and his wife, Baroness Goering, nee Frikerrinna Fock, suffers from epilepsy, and that is why their home does not seem a fit place for her son, Thomas Kantzau."

INSANE VIOLENCE—The Langbro Insane Asylum at Langbro, Sweden, was once the address of Hitler's right hand man, Goering. The asylum is shown at right. Private sanitariums refused to accept Goering as a patient because of his insane violence and uncontrollable frenzies. Hitler uses Goering's drug addiction to blackmail him when Goering threatens to get out of control.

Stockholm 16 April 1926

MORPHINE ADDICT—Hermann Goering's mind was seriously affected by the vicious habit in which he indulged. A gross ungainly creature, he has an insane vanity and a childish love of uniforms.

NAZI NO. 2 MAN AS DOPE-FIEND

GREETS FLIERS

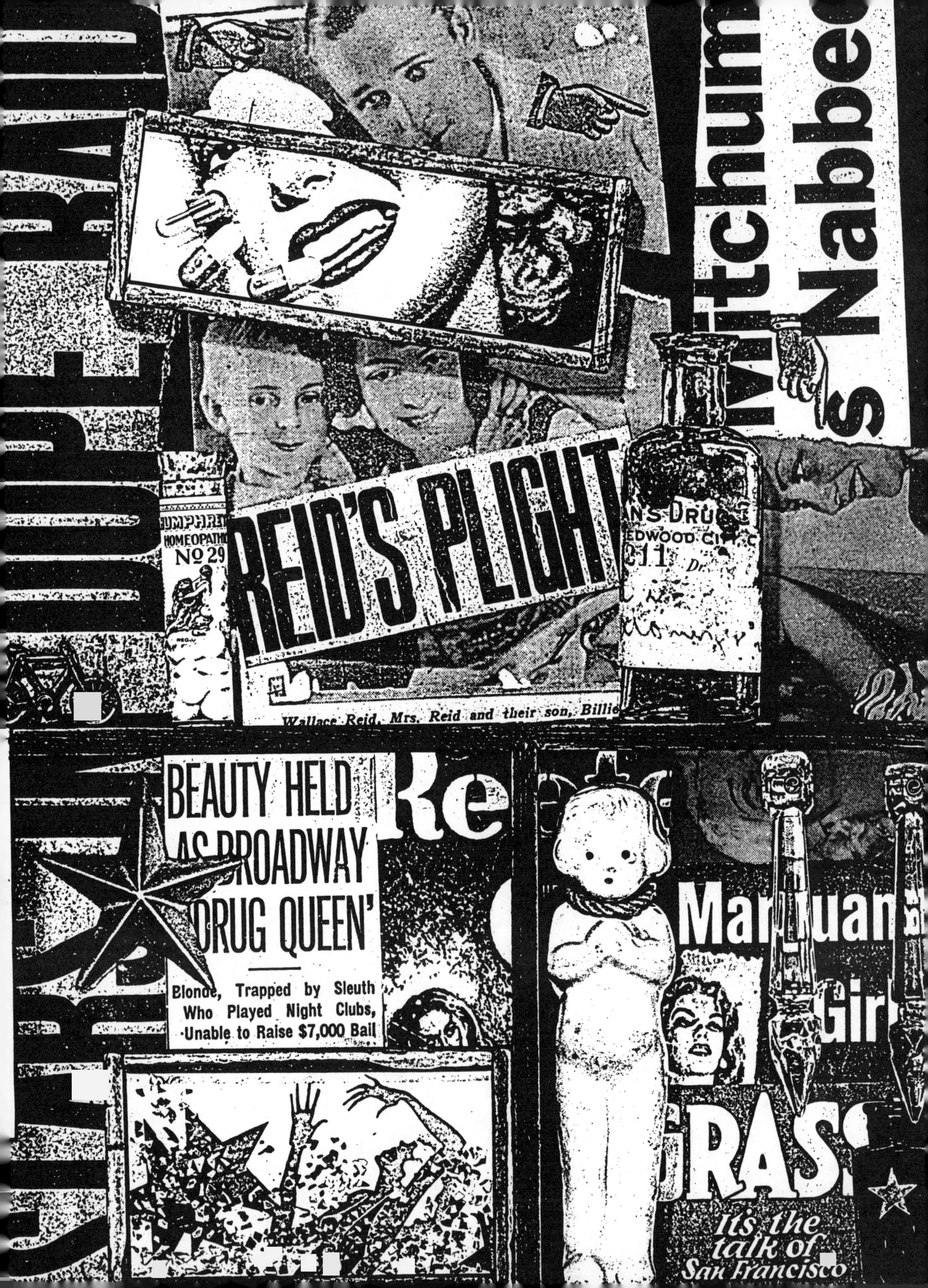

REID'S PLIGHT
Wallace Reid, Mrs. Reid and their son, Billie
BEAUTY HELD AS BROADWAY 'DRUG QUEEN'
Blonde, Trapped by Sleuth Who Played Night Clubs, Unable to Raise $7,000 Bail
Girl
It's the talk of San Francisco

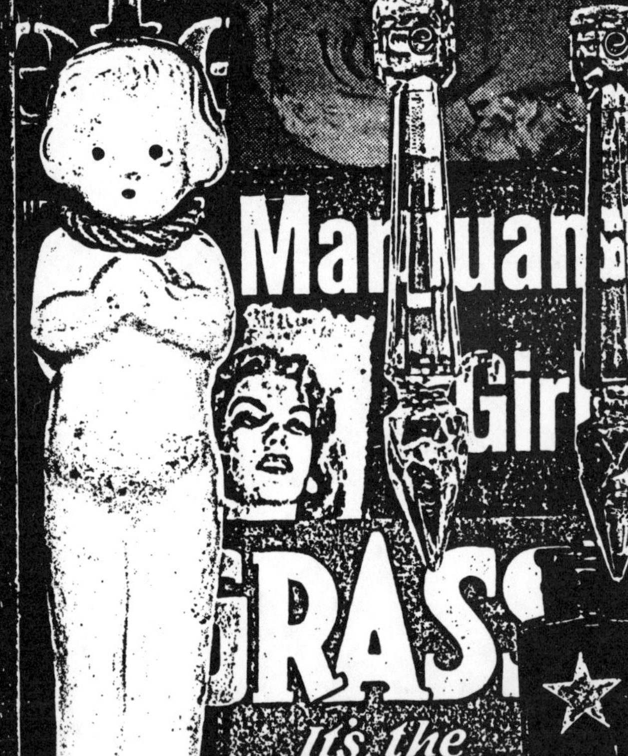

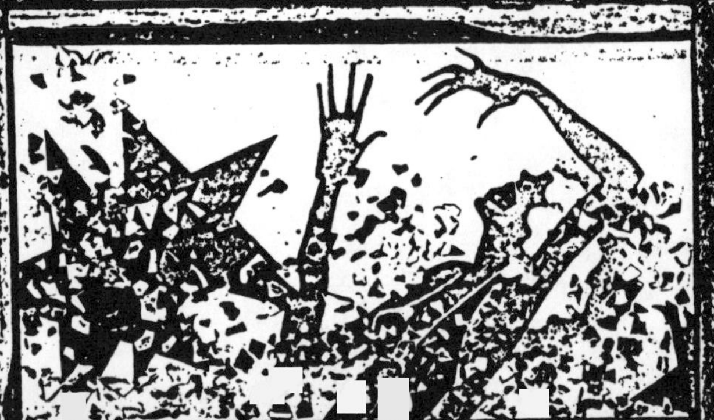

Celebrities and Drugs

We pay for our fame with tears of blood.
—Regine Flory, 1922

In 1822 Thomas De Quincey began the tradition of romantic addiction literature with his *Confessions of an English Opium Eater.* There have always been poisonings and drug-related crimes, of course, and people who have claimed their erratic behavior was due to dope. The dimension that De Quincey added was a sense of prideful self-destruction, ego-accomplishment gone astray. How the sensational press turned this tradition to its own purposes is glimpsed in this chapter. These are the roots of contemporary drug scandals, which originated as the Victorian era crumbled and a new century came of age.

Out of the heartland they came, rebelling against parents and marriages and boring lives, the starry-eyed hopefuls. They came to escape, to make something new, to create the art of themselves. Like Dixie Dixon, they were "crazy with the joy of living... a fiercely burning flame." They came wherever the flame burned bright—to the cities, to the continent, to the stage, and most of all to Hollywood during the infancy of film. Hollywood set the styles and mirrored the styles, pantomimed on silent celluloid: carrening cars, Keystone Cops, pratfalls, The Tramp, the great escape.

They became heroines tied to the tracks. They became waifs and smittens, Sheiks and Shebas, extras in epics, casting-couch converts to sin and good times. When they worked, they worked hard, up at dawn, not off the lot until dusk, or midnight, or never made it home at all. And when the morning came, and they were just too pooped or hung over or sex-drained to perform? Every lot had a friend with a bit of coke or smack in hand to ease the pains.

And the scandals rolled in. Olive Thomas, star of *The Flapper* (1920)—dead by her own hand in Paris while trying to score heroin for herself and her husband Jack Pickford. William Desmond Taylor, a top director—murdered, cried the tabloids, because he had beaten up a dealer supplying drugs to his lover. Fatty Arbuckle—accused of raping an actress, crucified in the nation's papers; though he was acquitted in court, Hollywood was put on notice that its private lives were private no more.

Will Hays, "czar of the censors," compiled a Doom Book of suspected stars. At the top of the list was Paramount's matinee idol, Wallace Reid. Locked in a padded cell, Reid confessed his addiction and died in 1923. His wife and mother *both* launched a crusade in Hearst's papers, every Bible-thumper in America joined in, and the witch-hunt was on.

The clinics where Reid had sought treatment were raided. Records revealed hundreds of famous names, among them Juanita Hansen, the original Mack Sennett girl. According to Kenneth Anger's *Hollywood Babylon,* she had been turned on by an actor known as The Count, who had also first supplied heroin to Reid, Mabel Normand, Barbara La Marr, and Alma Rubens.

Faced with a merciless drubbing in the press, Juanita had but one choice: confess and crusade. Hearst front-paged her story for weeks in 1923 and a year later was still running features about her cure. In 1928 she was scalded in her shower, and her roommate said she'd been shooting up again. In 1934 she claimed to be cured once more. In 1936 she was busted with a needle, but no drugs were found, and she faded from the scene.

Reid's and Hansen's stories set the mode that Hearst used time after time: crucify, confess, crusade. Marion Davies was often his pipeline, procuring, for example, Alma Ruben's confessions for him. Other papers copied this technique, and every gossip columnist went to school on it. It worked posthumously too, as seconal and chloral hydrate suicides piled up when hundreds of silent stars couldn't make the talkies. And of course, the confessors didn't have to be Hollywood folk; any celebrity could suffer the same way, crusading contritely in the scandal sheets—or being crusaded about. It was a pitiful climax to the American dream.

HINT OF PLOT TO EITHER POISON OR DRUG MRS. GOULD

Name of Negress Mentioned in Court in Connection with a Virginia Episode.

MORE TIPPLING TALES AND CURSING STORIES

Former Servants Testify That in Their Opinion the Plaintiff Took Too Many Drinks.

SAY SHE SWORE VERY OFTEN

Coaching Drives Are Recalled and Also Occasions on Which Mrs. Gould Is Said to Have "Reeled About."

Mrs. Katherine Clemmons Gould makes the charge that an attempt was made to drug or poison her while she was at her Blue Gap farm, in Virginia, in November, 1906. This became known late yesterday afternoon when Robert Trotter, a carpenter who had been employed at both Castle Gould and in Virginia, was being subjected to a severe cross-examination in the trial of her suit for separation from Howard Gould, before Judge Dowling in the Supreme Court.

Trotter had testified to having seen Mrs. Gould several times under the influence of intoxicants, both at Castle Gould and in Virginia, and spoke particularly of one Saturday night at the Blue Gap farm when she fell from her chair to the floor.

"Did you know in Virginia a negress named Betsy or Betty Foster?" asked Clarence J. Shearn, counsel for Mrs. Gould, and the witness said he did, and when Mr. Shearn asked another question DeLancey Nicoll, counsel for Mr. Gould, objected and the objection was sustained.

"This is a material question, as you will see by my next one," explained Mr. Shearn to the Judge, and then, turning to Trotter, he asked:—

"Did you put anything in Mrs. Gould's coffee that Saturday night?"

"I certainly did not," replied Trotter.

"Did you get Betsy or Betty Foster to put something in her coffee?"

"I certainly did not," he replied.

To Hear More of Drug.

"Didn't Mrs. Gould charge you with having attempted to poison or drug her by putting something in her coffee?"

"She certainly did not."

"Did you ever hear of this charge before?"

"Not until I read something of it in Mr. Sells' testimony in the newspapers."

Mr. Shearn did not press the matter further and would not discuss that charge after the close of the day's session, saying, however, that more would be heard of it later in the trial, which now bids fair to last another week. Judge Dowling called Mr. Nicoll and Mr. Shearn to the Bench yesterday and after a consultation it was announced that the sessions of the trial would last until fi[ve] o'clock to-day and until six o'clock [for] the remainder of the trial.

With no more display of emotio[n than] an occasional gasp or a shake of th[e head] Mrs. Gould sat yesterday and hea[rd some] of her former employes tell in d[etail of] times when they had seen her u[nder the] influence of intoxicants. One m[an testi]fied that she called one of her ch[...] one of those hyphenated app[ellations] which for all time and in all la[nds have] been considered a sufficient pro[vocation] for a fight.

Mrs. Gould looked really shocke[d when] she was charged with using this [expres]sion, but the greater part of the ti[me she] was making notes in a book and w[hisper]ing suggestions to her counsel.

One young woman who sat through [the] sessions of the trial was said to be a Hu[n]garian actress who was making a study o[f] emotions, but so far as Mrs. Gould an[d] her emotions were concerned it was [an] unprofitable day for the actress.

Servants Are Heard.

Twenty or more former servants of the Goulds, men and women, were in court waiting to be called. Some of them will testify for and some against Mrs. Gould, and many of them, like some of the witnesses yesterday, were discharged by Mrs. Gould. In all the cross-examinations Mr. Shearn brought out the names of the other persons present at the times testified [an]d some of these are known to be friendly to Mrs. Gould and will testify in rebuttal.

Robert Trotter, who gave the most damaging testimony against Mrs. Gould, made

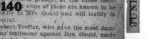

JUNE 17, 1909.

Attempt to Drug or Poison Mrs. Gould; Servants Tell of Tippling and Bad Language

MRS. HOWARD GOULD

THE NEW YORK HERALD.

NEW YORK, SATURDAY, MAY 13, 1905.—EIGHTEEN PAGES.—[COPYRIGHT, 1905, BY THE NEW YORK HERALD COMPANY.]

HERBERT CROKER DIES ON TRAIN; DRUG SUSPECTED

Son of Former Tammany Leader Placed on Car by Negro While in a Dazed Condition.

ON WAY TO RANCH IN BLISS, OKLAHOMA

Kansas Authorities Believe Young Man Was Robbed and Shipped from City.

HAD JUST LEFT RACES

Porter of Hotel Who Carried New Yorker to Train Tells of Visit to Chinese Resort.

[SPECIAL DESPATCH TO THE HERALD.]

NEWTON, Kan., Friday. — Herbert V. Croker, son of Richard Croker, former leader of Tammany Hall, was found dead this afternoon on an Atchison, Topeka and Santa Fé train between Newton and Kansas City. He had died from the effects of a drug administered at Kansas City last night, where he took the train for Bliss, Okla.

This is the second son of Richard Croker to die this year, his son Frank having been killed in an automobile accident in Florida a few months ago.

As far as can be learned Croker arrived in Kansas City early on Thursday and spent the afternoon at the Elm Ridge race track. He is known to have been in the company of several patrons of the race track before he boarded the train for the South.

The conductor noticed Croker lying in his seat in the car, apparently sleeping, and he did not make a determined effort to arouse him, until just before Newton was reached, when he found that he was dead. The body was taken off here and an inquest held to-night.

A telegram from Richard Croker, Jr., gave instructions to hold the body pending instructions, which have not yet come.

The first clew to Croker's identity was a letter found in the dead mans' pocket. This letter was addressed by Zahc Mulhall, formerly of Oklahoma, who is now holding a Wild West show in New York city, to "Joe" Miller, manager of the famous "101" Ranch at Bliss, Okla.

Inquiry by telephone elicited the information that Croker was not known at the Bliss ranch. Evidently he was on the way to the ranch for an outing.

Following a message of inquiry sent to New oY krcity, the cgoroner took charge of the body and empanelled a jury.

According to stories of passengers and the conductor on the train upon which Croker died, the young New Yorker was placed on the train at Kansas City by a negro about ten o'clock last night.

Passengers on the train took particular notice when young Croker was assisted into a chair car because he was helpless, as if from liquor or drugs. The negro assisted Croker into a seat and then gave him a purse containing a railroad ticket and $19, counting the money out to Croker. The passengers heard Croker say:—"Now I want you to send me the rest of it."

The negro asked Croker to write his address, but Croker refused, and finally the negro wrote as Croker dictated. The address was "Bliss, Okla., care 101 Ranch."

Immediately Fell Into Sleep.

Immediately after the train started Croker fell into a sleep, snoring loudly. Later he grew quieter. As the train neared Newton, the conductor, who wished to take up Croker's ticket, shook him to arouse him, and found him dead. There are no marks of violence on the young man's body, and the police do not believe he died of heart trouble, as he was of fine physical development.

Beside the letter from Zach Mulhall introducing Croker to "Joe" Miller, of the No. 101 Ranch, Croker's papers contained a letter of introduction from J. D. Carroll, of New York, to Miller; a letter signed "Carter," from New York, and an affectionate letter from a woman in West Twenty-second street, New York. The two latter letters were not made public.

It is the theory of the local authorities that Mr. Croker was drugged and robbed in Kansas City and placed on the train to get rid of him. The police of Kansas City have been notified and requested to hunt for the negro who placed Mr. Croker on the train.

Mr. Croker did not register at any hotel in Kansas City, and at the race track his expenditures and manner were not such as to attract attention. Tod Sloan, a jockey, who formerly rode for Richard Croker, and was well acquainted with Herbert's brother, was at the track all afternoon mingling freely with the horsemen and bettors, and he did not even hear that Croker was in town. It appears that Croker did not make his identity known anywhere in Kansas City.

Negro Found in Kansas City Tells of visit to Chinese Resort.

KANSAS CITY, Mo., Friday.—The negro who put Herbert V. Croker on the train last night was Charles Woodson, a porter at the Coates Hotel. Woodson says that Croker had been drinking when he arrived at the hotel about eight o'clock last night. After checking a small valise at the hotel the negro says they went together, at Croker's suggestion, to a chinese resort in Sixth street, between Wyandotte and Delaware streets, where they remained an hour. Woodson says that he then took Croker directly to the train at the Union station.

Croker's valise is still at the check stand at the hotel. He did not register at the hotel, and it is not believed that he went to any other hotel during his brief stay in Kansas City. Woodson tells a straight story, and the police do not think that he was guilty of robbing Mr. Croker or otherwise abusing his confidence.

HERBERT V. CROKER AND HIS FRIEND ZACH MULHAL[L]

MOTHER PROSTRATED BY DEATH OF SON

CROKER DRUGGED AND NOT ATTIRED IN OWN CLOTHING

Authorities Convinced the Young Man Was Robbed and Garments Changed in Kansas City.

INITIALS IN HAT ARE NOT HIS OWN

Coroner's Jury Finds New Yorker Died from Effects of Narcotic Poisoning.

EVIDENCE OF FOUL PLAY

Young Woman, Declaring She Was Herbert's Fiancee, Tells of Plan for Oklahoma Marriage.

[SPECIAL DESPATCH TO THE HERALD.]

NEWTON, Kan., Saturday.—Additional evidence has been found that convinces the local authorities that Herbert V. Croker was drugged and robbed in Kansas City, before being placed on the Sante Fe train on which he died.

The coroner's jury has rendered a verdict that the young man died of narcotic poison administered in Kansas City, and investigation has shown that the clothing he wore evidently was not his own, being of cheap material and badly soiled.

The hat Croker wore had on it initials other than his own and bore the trade mark of a Minneapolis (Minn.) firm. His own clothing evidently had been stolen and other garments given to him. No jewelry or valuables of any kind were found on his person.

The local authorities have not performed an autopsy upon the body, and will not unless instructed by the Kansas City police to do so. The relatives of the dead man do not seem to want this done, having asked that the body be embalmed at once.

The Coroner's jury to-day brought in the following verdict:—

"We find that said Herbert V. Croker came to his death on May 12, 1905, on Santa Fe train No. 17 while between Kansas City, Mo., and Newton, Kan., from the effects of narcotic poisoning, taken into his system at Kansas City, Mo., before boarding said train, by means and manner unknown to this jury."

Physicians say that from the symptoms Croker might have died from opium poisoning, though they are not sure that this was the drug used. They agree, however, with the Coroner that the man had been drugged and that this caused his death.

MAY 14, 1905.

MORE THAN OPIUM, SAYS ONE WITNESS

Although Police Believe Negro's Story Trainmen Insist There Was No Smell of Whiskey.

KANSAS CITY, Mo., Saturday.—Although the police of this city appear to be anxious to prove that the death of Herbert V. Croker was due to overindulgence in whiskey and opium, there is evidence to show that the New Yorker met with foul play while in this city.

As a result of the work of detectives here since yesterday, Charles Wilson, a negro hotel porter, who placed Croker on the southbound Santa Fé train on which he died; Ah Lee, a Chinaman, who, it is said sold Croker opium at his place in the North End, and Ah Ghee, a Chinese inmate of Lee's place, are under arrest. The stories of all three, told to the police to-day, were the same—to the effect that Croker had gone to the Chinaman's place of his own free will to smoke opium.

Lee told the police that he had given Croker five opium pills, and that the latter had smoked three of these. Ghee told the same story. Wilson declared that his only connection with the case was in piloting Croker, at the New Yorker's request, to the opium den, to several saloons and to the railway station. Chief Hayes says he believes the story told by Wilson to be true, and that he is confident that neither the negro porter nor the two Chinese are criminally responsible for Croker's death.

ANOTHER STORY TOLD.

In the building in which Ah Lee has rooms, the Twin City Club, a negro organization, also has quarters. There another story is told. F. W. Payne, a negro, the manager of the club, said that Croker had accosted him as the New Yorker passed down the stairs from the Chinaman's rooms, Croker having mistaken Payne for Wilson, the porter.

"As soon as I looked at him," said Payne to-day, "I saw that the man had something besides opium in him. He had no control of the muscles of his neck. [His] head wabbled and his color was ghas[tly]. His eyes were glassy and his lips w[ere] quivering."

A. J. Rader, conductor of the train [on] which Croker died, returned to Kan[sas] City to-day. Rader, repeated the st[ory] already told by himself and other m[em]bers of the train crew regarding Crok[er's] arrival at the train in company with [the] negro, his dropping into a deep sleep [and] the fact that attempts to arouse Cro[ker] showed him to be dead.

"There was no smell of whiskey," s[aid] Rader, "and I am convinced from his [ap]pearance that he had been drugg[ed]. Croker did not make a move after be[ing] placed in the seat at Kansas City unt[il] found him dead, seven hours later."

Although Wilson, the negro porter, w[as] frank in all his admissions to the pol[ice] and told a connected story that fits closely with all they had learned about [the] case from other sources, he was [put] through a severe examination.

COL. ZACH MULHALL (PHOTO BY GUEVIN)

Odor of Drugs in Mrs. Leslie Carter's Play

MRS LESLIE CARTER

EVELYN VAUGHN

ACTRESS SHOWS DISTINCT POWER

Unpleasant Drama Furnishes Her an Opportunity for Emotionalism.

MRS. LESLIE CARTER
—IN—
"VASTA HERNE."
CAST OF CHARACTERS:

Dudley Maury, M. D.	Charles Clary
Hartley Bellaire	E. J. Ratcliffe
Charlie Andrews	Louis Myll
Peter Mallenhope	William Shay
Hampton	George Duval
Ben Ali	Master Percy Sherman
Mrs. Mallenhope	Alice Butler
Jane McGann	Florence Malone
Minnie	Lily Cahill
Vasta Herne	Mrs. Leslie Carter

By RALPH E. RENAUD.

"VASTA HERNE," which Mrs. Leslie Carter presented at the Van Ness last night, comes pretty near proving that it is impossible to dramatize the drug habit.

Whether or not you like the play will depend on your partiality for drugstores. Within the first five minutes of the first act you are plunged into the atmosphere of laudanum and the fetid odor of the opiate permeates th rest of the drama. Perhaps Edwa Peple, who wrote it, was inspired the recent magazine attacks on pat medicines, which purported to disc ghastly tragedies in thousands of best regulated homes. But V scorns subterfuges in the way of labeled pills, hypodermic needles, the like, and takes the stuff raw, a seasoned tippler, from the b Needless to say that its power ove becomes vaster and vaster, and v and vaster. Possibly this explain title.

But it does not, as you might ex explain the action. The author s to recognize that the potentialitie drugs are symptomatic, rather t dramatic. At any rate, he tac acknowledges that the impulse wh made Vasta, in common with D Quincey, Baudelaire and other dis tinguished dope fiends, write weirdly iridescent stories is exotic, exceptional and not human or fundamental. Hence, for his real dramatic crux, he has to fall back on something more natural and elemental—the fact that his heroine has been the physical mistress as well as the mental slave of the usual gentleman called in to bear responsibilities for the pecadilloes of an emotional actress. If it weren't for that divergence there wouldn't be any play.

"Vasta Herne" is exceedingly pretentious. It professes to teach a lesson, but it is rather vague in this direction. At the end Vasta dies, quite unexpectedly, as it seemed to me. To save my life I was unable to tell whether it was because she took too much laudanum, whether she refused to take any more, or because the hero insisted on believing she had sinned not once, but many times, thus breaking a heart already weakened by narcotics. Anyway she died.

All this is not by way of saying the play has no interest. In addition to its disagreeable medical interest, which pertains to a clinic rather than a theater, it has a number of heart throbs and considerable comedy, none of which is very good. The lines, how-

FEBRUARY 1, 1910.

CANADA'S MANY BLUE LAWS BLUE AS INDIGO

JANUARY 16, 1910.

ARMAND MEGARO

MRS. MARJORIE GRAFF

Girl Victims of Poisoned Needle Numerous, Prominent Women Say

Mrs. Rogers H. Bacon and Mrs. Samuel C. Van Dusen Tell of Known Cases.

DEADLY DRUG HAS INSTANTANEOUS EFFECT

Mrs. Marjorie Graff Says She Will Push the Prosecution of Her Assailant.

That hundreds of respectable girls and young women have been the victims of white slave traffickers operating with poisoned needles in the dimness of moving picture and other theatres was the conclusion reached yesterday by the police of this city and Newark, N. J., as well as the heads of many social welfare organizations.

While one other victim of a poisoned needle was found in Newark yesterday, the case against Armand Megaro, held by the Newark authorities, who is accused of stabbing Mrs. Marjorie Graff, a Brooklyn bride, in a Newark picture house, lagged. The most important development in the case against Megaro was the abandonment of the idea by the police there that the person who stabbed Mrs. Graff used as a weapon the darning needle which was picked up in the box where Mrs. Graff was assaulted.

To Make Chemical Test of Needle.

This was done after the needle had been examined under a microscope by Dr. Harrison S. Martland, of the Newark City Hospital, and no traces of poison found on it. Later, however, the needle is to be subjected to a chemical test, as it was declared that it had been handled by so many persons that even if it had been dipped in poison so much might have been removed in the handling that poison would not be revealed in a microscopic examination.

Miss Jennie Clark, a stenographer, who had an experience similar to that of Mrs. Graff, which occurred also in Newark, confronted Megaro last night and said he was not the man who attacked her. Miss Mary Lee, another stenographer, denied with equal emphasis that she had been assaulted at all, and asserted that the mentioning of her name as a victim of the poisoned dart was the work of a practical joker.

No date has been set for the next examination of Megaro, who still is held in jail in Newark, unable to obtain the bail of $20,000 demanded.

Michael T. Long, Chief of Police of Newark, said he did not believe that the wholesale use of the poisoned darts is confined to men who are seeking to force young women into lives of shame.

"I cannot believe," he said, "that this is the work of white slave agents alone. To me it would appear also to be a skilful means of robbery, for it would be perfectly ... control of the girls ... as ...ives ... unconscious

Drug Acts Almost Instantaneously.

The detectives who have been working on the revelations made by Mr. Graff said yesterday they feel certain that the needle now in the hands of the police was not the one used by the person who attacked her. They declare they believe a hypodermic needle was used and that the point of the darning needle could not possibly have held enough poison to have affected her to the extent she is known to have been affected.

At the same time it became known that the Newark authorities, convinced more than they will admit that the attack upon Mrs. Graff was made directly by white slave agents, are endeavoring to have federal investigators take a hand in the case. Federal aid, it was definitely learned, has been promised in their investigation to the Newark detectives, as soon as they have found definite evidence upon which to base a complaint to the government officers that the crime was committed by a white slave agent.

Practically every social welfare organization in this city has enlisted in the effort to stamp out the practice revealed by the publicity following the attack upon Mrs. Graff. Reports of similar attacks have been frequent here, but the investigators have been seriously hampered by the obdurate refusal of the young women who have been attacked to make official complaints. In this position the young women usually have been upheld by relatives and friends and in practically every instance the work of the investigators has led to no results.

That the use of hyoscine, a powerful drug, may explain the almost instantaneous results which appear to have followed every assault upon women, was the official statement made yesterday for the Department of Health by Dr. Joseph A. Shear, an inspector on the staff of Dr. Ernest Lederle, Health Commissioner.

Mrs. Graff returned yesterday to the home of her parents, Dr. and Mrs. A. S. Higgins, of No. 414 Jefferson avenue, Brooklyn. There she announced her determination to see that the person who assaulted her in Newark is punished.

The poison was put into Mrs. Graff's wrist just where the wrist and hand join. The first sensation she felt was one of extreme dizziness and she could feel a sort of clumsy numbness running up her arm. She didn't know what the trouble was then, but had presence of mind to hurry to the dressing room. There a maid gave her restoratives to keep her from fainting.

In a communication to the HERALD a case almost similar to that of Mrs. Graff was detailed, but the name necessarily is withheld. The victim, a girl eighteen years old and attractive, is the daughter of wealthy parents. Two weeks ago she made an appointment to meet her aunt in a moving picture theatre in Broadway. It was unusual for the girl to go to such a place without a chaperon, but no one accompanied her in view of the fact that her aunt was to call for her with the family carriage on which rode a coachman and a footman.

Saved by Appearance of Aunt.

The girl sat in the second seat from the centre aisle in the theatre. It was an after...n performance. In the end seat a man ...ho looked at the girl frequently was seated. Across the aisle was another man, ...o whom the first spoke several times. ...uddenly the girl felt a sharp pain in her ... She paid no further attention to it, ...nking the prick was the result of a ...her maid had misplaced in dressing ... Suddenly, however, the girl raised ...and to learn the time from a watch ...was wearing on her wrist. As she ... the arm she felt another sharp ... in her leg. Immediately she got up ...started to leave the theatre. Both of ...men followed her. The girl became ..., but gasped out her name as she ...psed in front of the ticket office.

...h," said one of the men, approaching ...re the girl had fallen, 'our friend has ...me suddenly ill. I'll have to take her ...e." Just as the men prepared to lift ... girl, however, her aunt appeared and ... to her side. When the excitement ...sed by the older woman's appearance ... subsided both men had disappeared.

...rs. Rogers H. Bacon, of No. 987 Madi... avenue, a member of the House Com...tee of the Girls' Vacation Committee ... West Thirty-ninth street, gave in detail ... experience of a young married woman ... related to her by a close friend of the ...man who was the victim. The truth of ...e young woman's story has been estab...hed, but the details of the case were ...lated in confidence, and for that reason ...e names of the woman involved and her ...usband have been shielded.

Husband Appears in Time.

"This young woman," Mrs. Bacon said, lives in the suburbs of New York, and on the day she met with the experience took the only train to this city which would bring her here in time to keep an appointment with her husband, who was to take her to dinner down town and subsequently to a theatre. Arriving here, she had nearly half an hour to wait before the hour set by her husband to meet her. She went into a moving picture theatre near the place of the appointment.

"Within a brief time after she sat down in the theatre the young woman felt a sharp pain in her shoulder. Within another few moments she began to feel dizzy, so much so that she hurried from the theatre in the hope that the fresh air might revive her. She collapsed almost as soon as she reached the sidewalk, and an ambulance was called.

"The woman's husband arrived a... the ambulance surgeon discovered a wound in her shoulder, which, he declared, could have been made only by a hypodermic needle. The husband was compelled to argue forcibly with the surgeon before his assertions that the woman was his wife were believed and he was permitted to take her away in a taxicab.

"I related this experience partly in confidence at a recent meeting in the headquarters of the Vacation Committee and am surprised that the newspapers should have learned of it. I told of the case to accentuate the need for opening in our new headquarters a room where young girls may accept the attentions of young men in proper surroundings, which may not be had in boarding houses and furnished rooms."

The three other cases were revealed by Mrs. Samuel C. Van Dusen, of No. 132 East Thirty-fifth street. She learned of all of them in casual conversations and not through settlement work or interest in welfare associations. The same barrier of reticence was encountered, however, by Mrs. Van Dusen when she sought to investigate these stories, but her inquiries established their truth.

The first instance was that of a girl who came into the city from a suburb on a shopping trip with her mother. Thinking to complete the purchasing more quickly, the girl and her mother decided to go by separate routes through the stores, buy the articles wanted and meet at a stated time in the waiting room of one of the stores. The girl completed her part of the shopping an hour before the time set for meeting her mother and entered a moving picture theatre in Broadway.

Left Theatre and Fainted.

The girl twice while she was in the theatre felt a sharp prick in her shoulder, but attributed the pain to a pin. Soon after the second sensation the young woman arose and left the theatre to meet her mother. She collapsed at the entrance to the department store and attendants carried her into the retiring room, where her mother was waiting.

After she had been revived the girl remembered the incidents in the theatre. An examination by a nurse revealed two slight wounds in her shoulder, obviously made by the point of a hypodermic needle. The nurse declared positively the girl's collapse had been caused by a heavy dose of poison.

The second case revealed by Mrs. Van Dusen is that of a girl employed in a Fifth avenue shop. The girl was standing on the platform of a station of the Third avenue elevated line when a well dressed man jostled her. She felt a sharp pain in her arm at the same time, but paid no further attention to it. She entered the next train and rode to the desired station. The man rode in the same train. He left the car at the station where the young woman got off and was behind her when she became dizzy and fainted on the platform. The man told persons who gathered about the girl he was her husband and he was permitted to carry her from the platform. He had reached the bottom of the stairs and was about to call a taxicab when several girls living in the same neighborhood recognized the victim in the man's arms and declared:—

"Why, he's not her husband. Nellie is not married!" The man dropped his unconscious burden and fled.

"I Am Her Father," Said Elderly Man.

The other case told of by Mrs. Van Dusen is that of a girl employed in a store who felt a stab in her arm in a moving picture theatre near Columbus Circle. An usher aided her to the lobby when she became faint and she was semi-conscious when an elderly man, wearing a beard, appeared, said he was her father and that he wished to take her home. The girl, however, was recovering quickly from the effects of the poison and heard the man's assertion that he was her father. She denounced him and before a policeman was called the elderly person disappeared.

DECEMBER 7, 1913.

DRUG MONSTER EMBRACES SMALL AMERICAN TOWNS

MISERY AND DESPAIR GRIP COUNTRY AS "DOPE" GAINS NEW FOOTHOLD

Some Noted Victims Who Have Paid the Frightful Penalty Exacted by the Use of Drugs

"CHICAGO DOPE RING CODE"

WALLACE REID.

DIXIE DIXON

CECILIA LOFTUS

EVELYN NESBIT

MONA RIVARD

Narcotic Evil Enters Plain Little Homes Where People Live Who Have Always Been Considered the Very Backbone of the Nation.

By WINIFRED BLACK.

Main street gone wrong. Interesting idea, isn't it?

We've always thought of morphine and cocaine and heroin as belonging first in the hospitals and clinics and then in the red light district.

Ten, yes, even five years ago, we knew all about hop-heads and dope-fiends. We read about them in the newspapers, and we heard about them whenever we interested ourselves in the misery and despair of the slums and the horrors of the vice-districts.

We never even dreamed that these things would spread into the country like a pestilence.

Reach out to the schools and creep to the very door and inside the door of the plain little homes where the people live who have always been considered the very backbone of the nation.

How about this news from the home town?

Is it true down to the last syllable of it, or is it perhaps a little exaggerated?

Unbelievable Tale

Read the story of Summerset, Kentucky, a story with names, dates, facts and figures and see what you think about it.

When you're through with Summerset, and its an almost unbelievable tale, how about Peoria, Illinois?

Ever been in Peoria?

Pretty place, prosperous and happy looking.

Hard maples' lining the street, blue and white lilacs at the gates; green lawns; a nice well-built schoolhouse or so and an astonishing number of churches.

Lots of young people in Peoria—they run to big families in the small towns, you know.

Mary and Kate and Elizabeth and Jim and Tom and Billy, they all go to school together and build snow men in the yard when the air begins to be white with fluttering feathers—I'll warrant you could count at least a dozen snow men in the door-yards of Peoria the first day after the first real snow.

Old-Time Folks

Young People's Endeavor, Epworth League, Boy Scouts, Campfire Girls, Ladies Aid Societies, church oyster suppers, strawberry festivals, trips to town in the opera season, a regular matinee crowd in the theatrical season, fudge parties, sleigh rides, old friends, old neighbors—a town full of good, old-fashioned Americans—that's Peoria.

Well, they arrested and convicted just nineteen doctors and druggists in Peoria not so very long ago and every one of them was caught selling morphine and cocaine and heroin; selling these things to their neighbors and their friends and to the children of their neighbors and their friends.

Oh, yes, the Federal narcotics agents know Peoria — they've known it for a long time.

They caught a man in Chicago sending ounces of "dope" through the mail to Peoria—that was after the obliging druggists and the enterprising doctors had been caught and put out of business — temporarily anyhow.

And Peoria is just one Illinois town that is alive with "dope."

Finds Two Girls

There's Joliet and Elgin and Aurora. There's Rockford and Geneva, any good, lively "dope" peddler in Chicago can tell you right off where to go in any one of these towns and get enough dope to kill at least a dozen people.

Nashville, Tennessee. Dear old town, Nashville. You can't help falling in love with it to save your life. Hospitable doors, wide porches, magnolias in bloom by the "gallery." Nashville knows all about "dope."

Ask the wise old judge who sits in that district. Ask the shrewd family doctor who holds half the secrets of the town in his neighborly hands.

I saw two girls from Nashville up in the red-light district in Chicago a few months ago. One of them was as pretty as a pink and the other had such "a way with her" that she didn't have to be pretty, and they were both "dope" addicts.

Cousins, they were; good family, both of them had nice mothers and one of them had a proud and influential father living.

When I met them they were crouching in a black hole they called a room. I climbed three pairs of slimy stairs to get to them.

In a Bare Room

There wasn't a stick of furniture in the room, except a tumbledown chair and a hideous mattress lying on the bare floor.

They'd sold everything for "dope"—and they were not ready yet—to start earning money in the dreadful way that was the only thing left to them.

They learned to "dope" from a little seamstress who was making the wedding clothes for another cousin.

They started it just for fun, and it got them, just as "dope" always does "get them."

No one knew what was the matter with them when they began to change and alter slowly, surely, surely.

Tried to Cry

They were afraid to be found out, so they ran away to Chicago to hide. They wrote home that they were in the art institute ...

... fretting ... pounding on the pebbly beach ... clean and so kind ... I wondered if Bonnie Eloise never heard it when the night was dark and her heart and brain were full of the agony of her degradation.

I wondered if she never thought how clean and cool and quiet it would be at the bottom of the lake—poor girl.

And she and her cousin are only two of the great army of "dope" victims recruited from the clean, quiet country towns of the United States of America.

Out in Seattle a few months ago they brought fourteen girls into the police court—every one of them a "dope" addict.

Every one of them under seventeen and every one of them up to that time was the respectable daughter of a respectable farmer.

In Mining Towns

The mining towns of upper Michigan are crawling with "dope." Megaunee and Ishpeming, two twin villages, are set in a wonderland of green forests and blue lakes.

Strange stories they can tell you of these places—the Federal narcotic officers.

The California small towns are honeycombed with "dope" as a rotten pier is honeycombed by the work of the barnacles.

Salinas—did you ever slip through Salinas on a Summer evening with the breeze at your back and think what a quiet, typical, old-fashioned "cow town" it was?

Turn off the broad well-paved street to the left and you'll find "dope town," crowded with Chinese and Japanese and East Indians—and American boys and girls.

You can get all the "dope" you want, or could a few weeks ago—if you have the password and have the money.

The river towns up and down the San Joaquin—up and down the Sacramento.

Dope of Any Kind

What green little, clean little, blossomy little places they are; with their rows of weeping willows reflected in the river and the tall eucalyptus standing like the ragged sentinels of some forgotten king — roses, heliotrope, yellow acacia—why, the place is a bower—surely no evil can find comfort and protection there.

Wait a minute. Go down the steps that lead from the level road and the substantial houses that line the land side, and there you are in evil town, with all the ancient vile of the world leering and beckoning from every window and whispering and nodding from every door.

"Dope"—which do you want?—cocaine, morphine, heroin—name your poison, produce your money, and the new delight and ancient agony is yours.

I stood in Walnut Grove on the bank of the Sacramento one quiet Sunday afternoon and watched the cars drive in from the neighboring ranches.

A "Shot of Hop"

Handsome touring cars with the rich rancher's son and his friends, cheap little rattlebangs from the small new places of the delta, smart roadsters from the big houses of rich people who live in comfort and luxury in the richest farming country in the world—hired men and their friends in the trucks and delivery wagons, all come to spend Sunday in evil town.

And three-fourths of them coming to get what each of them would call a "shot of hop" or a "sniff of joy powder."

It was easy to pick out those who had been using the stuff any length of time. Tall; born to an inheritance of fresh air and lavish living that ought to breed a race of physical, mental and moral giants. How they shrink and pale and wither when they are once in the clutches of "dope."

How they stare and twitch and stammer when they are by accident without it for a while. How utterly besotted and bemused and enslaved they are, and how they look the part down to the last slavering, glaring minute.

The Chinese bring in the stuff; the Japanese bring it in—they never use it themselves—the Japanese — they are far too clever for that, but they sell it and make fortunes in it.

Comes from India

The East Indians bring it in in their turbans. The Mexicans bring in their own strange "dope" marihuana—they smoke this in cigarettes—and mother and father back there in the big, cool house, with the living porch and the sleeping porch, and the breakfast patio, and the fountains and the gardens and the orchards, wondering what in the world has come over son that he seems so strange and listless and half dead half the time and so wild and nervous and erratic the rest of the time.

It is no chooser of localities—the "dope" ring.

Sell it where you can, and if there are no customers where you are make customers — that's the plan.

Sober, staid New England—there's dope there.

The little villages in Massachusetts, in Maine and Vermont are beginning to harbor stranger castaways than those brought in by the hale old sea captains of the past generation.

Upon the lonely farms on the bleak hillsides—oh, yes, the "dope" has found refuge there, too.

Youth's Holocaust

Ask the New England narcotic officers, they'll tell you stories that will make the tales of the Salem witches seem pale figments of a distorted imagination.

The Gulf States, New Orleans, Galveston, Fort Worth, Natchez—what you can learn about the spread of the "dope" evil in any one of these places in just one little week would horrify and astound you.

And the terrifying thing about it all is that the victims are so young, six out of ten of them are under twenty-five, and eight out of ten are under twenty.

It is a holocaust of youth—the whole dreadful, terrifying business.

How long are we going to sit calmly by and watch it go on?

> **Kentucky Town Firm in Talons of Drug Habit**
>
> "No epidemic. Only a community of five thousand normal people, farmers of the Kentucky hills, who used 110,044 grains of morphine in 18 months.
>
> "Two hundred ounces of morphine sold by a Main street druggist in a town of five thousand inhabitants. In 1921, the Bellevue and allied hospitals to which all of New York's accidents and emergency cases go used only 92½ ounces for the treatment of sixty-four thousand one hundred and three patients.
>
> "And the twenty-seven principal hospitals of Philadelphia absorbed only 90 ounces of morphine.
>
> "That is about 1-3 of the amount absorbed by the men, women and children of Summerset, Kentucky.
>
> "And you can match the story of Summerset in every state in the Union."
>
> —That's what Sidney Howard says in Hearst's Magazine.

Wellshire Country Club

Denver, Colorado

SCORE CARD

Girl of Wealth and Refinement Forsakes Career for Dope "Friends"

BEAUTY BARES LIFE OF HORROR AS DRUG FIEND

Daughter of Wealthy Gold Miner Now Wages Fight to Rid Herself of Terrible Habit

LED ASTRAY BY BROKER

Has Tried to Quit Before, but Companions Proved Barrier. Send Her Drug-laden Candy

By ROBERT L. MURRAY.

Evelyne Standfield, daughter of a wealthy gold miner with offices in Boston, is in a private hospital fighting to free herself from the tentacles of the drug habit.

Known to the Boston art colony as "Tarzan" (in tribute to her wealth of blond hair) Evelyne is a victim of her own beauty. At nineteen she has experienced all the horrors of a morphine fiend, has lost faith in all mankind, and, finally has determined to accomplish her own redemption.

Tarzan has told me her story. She told it reluctantly—she harbors no ill will toward those who accomplished her physical and mental ruin. When she had concluded, one statement still rings in my ears—a statement that sums up the dope situation in America to-day.

BEAUTY

PHOTOS ©HEARST'S INTERNATIONAL MAGAZINE

THREE POSES OF EVELYNNE STANDFIELD, BOSTON ART MODEL

Easy to Get Dope

"There is no difficulty in buying dope if you have the money. In the case of a pretty girl, even money is not essential."

Tarzan has not only both money and beauty, but she is refined, cultured and talented. Two years ago, at seventeen, Tarzan was an artist of promise. She did some work as an artist's model, but not because she was forced to do this as a means of earning her livelihood.

"My mother died when I was a baby," said Tarzan. "Since then I have had everything that money could buy—except a pair of mother's arms into which I could run when in need of counsel. Father was away much on business and we children were boarded out and sent to various schools. The first seventeen years of my life were not different from the same years in any girl's life."

The Spring of 1921 found Tarzan a healthy, lovable schoolgirl. She had yet to smoke her first cigarette; to take her first drink of liquor. Life was good and men and women clean.

The First Injection

Then Tarzan went to Portland, Maine for a visit.

Tarzan met a wealthy broker in Portland, a married man, with offices on Exchange Street. He saw Tarzan and "wanted her." Being wise in the ways of women this man started a systematic campaign to accomplish his desires. First he taught Tarzan to smoke. Then he gave her the first liquor she had tasted.

"I did not get my first morphine directly from him," said Tarzan, "although he was responsible. There was a girl friend of Mr. H— whom I came to know and whose friendship my father objected to strenuously. Her brother owns a drug store in Portland and it was back of his prescription counter that I took my first injection of morphine. He used to refuse to give it to me as he said Federal agents were watching him, but we would steal it.

"When I returned to Boston in the fall of 1921, the realization of what had happened during those few months struck terror into my heart. All the ideals I had cherished had been reduced to ashes through the flames of a man's passion. How I would have welcomed a mother's arms at that time.

Realizes Her Plight

"Father happened upon a letter from Mr. H—— and upraided him. Fortunately he did not realize the full import of the letter or I fear that he would have killed him. After that Mr. H—— wrote his letters on a typewriter and worded them with care."

The Portland broker then wrote Tarzan:

"I did not call up or write because I thought your father might think it strange. I know what a careless devil you are in leaving your letters around for every one to read—instead of tearing them up as soon as you read them, as you should. Tell me all the news when you write, and perhaps in the near future we will have a chance to have a real old-fashioned talk if you want to. Be sure and address all your letters to my box."

It was not long after Tarzan returned from Portland that she realized that she had become a dope fiend.

"I shall never forget the horror of it," she said. "The ghastly realization that my system was crying for morphine, morphine, broke me in spirit and in health. For a time I tried liquor, but that did not suffice, and an incident one night in November brought matters to a crisis.

Life of Hospitals

"During a studio party one of the boys offered me a drink from a flask. Shortly after drinking it I became violently ill and was taken to Cambridge Hospital. It seems to me now as though my life since that time has been one of hospitals—how I detest them!"

Tarzan wrote Mr. H——, of Portland, about this affair, and received a letter telling her to be careful what kind of liquor she drank.

"It should teach you a lesson," he said.

"Men are funny, are they not?" said Tarzan, referring to this letter. "They crush the youth from a girl, and then preach to her about what she does with other men."

During the Winter of 1921-22 Tarzan met a number of people who were to play important roles in her drama. These included: Dick Henrion, a young Canadian with an apartment at No. 79 St. Botolph street; Dr. M——, a physician with offices in Tremont street; Rena Brown, a drug addict and procurer of girls; Florence Murray, proprietor of the "March Hare," a tearoom patronized by artists and "intellectuals," and a number of habitues of the "March Hare," including Dick de Rochemont, Bob Hartong, Dick Werper and others.

Gets Morphine Free

"Dotor M. gave me injections of morphine and also prescriptions. He did not charge me anything for the morphine given me in his office," said Tarzan. "I finallf got in the habit of going to his office every night."

"It was there I met Rena Brown. She has been a drug addict for years and also arranges parties for men—obtains good looking girls for stag dinners, etc."

There was also a man named Pat Cromatt, a drug addict, who used to obtain morphine for Tarzan. In May, 1922, Tarzan's father learned the true situation regarding his daughter and had a legal guardian appointed for her. She was sent to the Psycopathic Hospital for a time and later sent to Connecticut for a rest.

It so happened that the office of Tarzan's guardian was in the some building in which Dr. Erwin C. Ruth and Ralph Fry, narcotic agents, were filming a "dope" picture. Fry became acquainted with Tarzan and asked her to take a part in the picture. Several other girls, addicted to drugs, were in the picture. Among them was Mae Cookson.

H—— of an Agent"

While Fry was talking to Tarzan one day Pat Cromett came into the studio to see her. Fry took Cromett to the narcotic office, supposedly to search him. Cromett returned later and laughingly drew a hypodermic needle and a quantity of morphine from his pocket.

"He's a —— of a narcotic agent,' Cromett said to Tarzan.

Fry also tried to get Tarzan to help him "get the goods" on Dr. M——, but she refused. How Fry was later trapped in Portland and convicted of extorting money from doctors and druggists is related in "Dope," an astounding article now running in Hearst's International Magazine.

"Fry paid me nothing for my work in the picture," said Tarzan. "He promised to give me some morphine, but never did. He gave Mae Cookson some, but he didn't like me because I resented his insults."

Tarzan went to room for awhile with a girl named Louise Rodell, who to all outward eappearances was a companion for her. Tarzan told Louise of the suffering she endured during the withdrawal process—breaking away from morphine. Louise suggested that Tarzan try taking veronal.

Returns to Needle

"I was surprised to find that you can buy veronal in drug stores without a prescription," said Tarzan. "You could not credit the number of girls who are veronal fiends. Many of these are young society girls who start using veronal to 'rest their nerves.' I have taken more than a hundred grains of veronal in a single day before obtaining sleep, and the resultant dreams—they are hideous."

So Tarzan returned to Dr M——'s office and the morphine needle. She was at that time keeping company with Dick Henrion. Dick and Tarzan became leaders of the wild set whose headquarters was the apartment on St. Botolph.

Tarzan's guardian asked a girl friend, Shirley Barrett, to go to the St. Botolph street apartment and get her one day. Shirley was followed by her mother, and a scene ensued. Mrs. Barrett brandished a revolver and the party ended in disorder.

Following this affair, Tarzan was again sent to the Psychopathic Hospital, and from there to the Bloomingdale Sanitarium at White Plains, N. Y.

Gets Dope in Candy

"I couldn't stand it there with all those crazy women," said Tarzan. "One woman would come to me and say, 'Look! I have no stomach.' Another would say, 'Feel! I have no heart.' I began to wonder if any of my important organs were missing."

Tarzan was supplied with drugs even while she was in Bloomingdale. It was sent to her in candy by Boston "friends.". The candy selected for this purpose was Chinese candy, which has the same consistency as gum drops and is covered with poppy seeds. The gum drops were pulled apart and drugs placed inside.

A letter written by Rena Brown on October 5 informed Tarzan that Dr. M—— was sending her some candy. Another letter written by Florence Murray said that Dick de Rochemont promised to send some.

The candy sent by de Rochemont arrived at Bloomingdale after Tarzan had left and eventually fell into the hands of her father. It was inspected and found to contain veronal. A special delivery letter preceded the candy.

Expelled from School

"If there is anything you want let me know and I will get it for you, if possible," wrote de Rochemont. "When you want more candy let me know."

When Tarzan returned from Bloomingdale she did so upon a promise made to her father that she would go to some private school and abstain from the use of drugs. She might have accomplished this had it not been for the "friends" of her former days.

The school selected for Tarzan was Notre Dame Academy, located in Roxbury, Mass. Tarzan entered Notre Dame under her own name and determined to forget the old Evelyn Standfield or "Tarzan" and devote all her energies to the study of art. Her contagious laughter and lovable personality soon made her the favorite with the girls, and her natural talents attracted the attention of the teachers.

On October 25 Dr. and Mrs. Rena Brown wrote Tarzan that they would be out to see her the next day. Tarzan was allowed to go for a walk with them, and when she returned fell violently ill. An investigation followed and Tarzan was found to be under the influence of drugs. The officials of the school were horrified and requested her to leave the school at once.

Joins Drug Colony

Disheartened at the outlook, Tarzan again took to the "needle." Not only did she go to the office of Dr. M——, but became one of a number of girls who visit a combination sleeping quarters and office on Washington street run by a man known as "Jackie."

This place is a rendezvous for drug addicts, principally young girls. There is a back entrance used by the "regulars," one of whom is a young girl who left her honeymoon and husband to return to "Jackie" and morphine.

Tarzan met an American-born Chinese student, by the name of Sam Moy, one night in November. Strange as it may seem, Moy proved one of her few acquaintances who tried to get her to quit using drugs. But the yearn for drugs was too strong, and Moy only came to grief for his good intentions.

Tarzan's guardian found a hypodermic needle in her handbag one day and confiscated it. Confronted with the evidence, she admitted that she was using morphine.

Her father was called in and Tarzan was sent to her father's home in the New Hampshire Hills for a long rest.

Tarzan's home in New Hampshire is a veritable show place. The house has eleven large rooms, finished in black walnut and other expensive woods. A stream tumbles through the spacious grounds and disappears off down the valley. Thirty varieties of roses bloom in the front yard in the Summer. In the rear is a large orchard.

For two weeks Tarzan romped about the snow clad hills. She donned knickers and went skiing. "I expect to be shipped to Boston in pieces," she wrote a friend describing the falls she was taking.

But again the craving for drugs made Tarzan violently ill. She started for Boston to see her father and passed him on the way. So she called up Moy and went to his apartment for shelter.

Someone, jealous of Moy, informed the police that Tarzan was in his apartment and a raid followed. Tarzan was taken to the City Hospital but examination failed to show that she had been taking drugs.

Her father held a conference with Judge Hayden of Roxbury Court and Tarzan was placed on probation upon her promise to go to ahospital and remain there until thoroughly cured.

"Oh, how I want to get away from it all," she said. "I know that I will never use drugs again. If I cannot live without them, I will kill myself. But if I come out of the hospital cured, I will go away from Boston to some other city where the drug peddlars do not know me. For they are always looking for new customers, and hate to lose the old ones."

By Universal Service.

"Get In with Money," Girl Writes Tarzan

Evelyn received letters from her corrupting friends advising her in the technique of the vices recommended. Rena Brown advised her to equip herself with "pretty pictures" and a bit of becoming fat.

"Tarzan Dear:

"I stopped at C—— this noon and he gave me your portfolio of pictures; he didn't seem to want to. But the ones I want are the ones he took profile, with the lighted background making a silhouette—also the ones we took to the Post. So, when you write him, kid him along, Hon, 'cause he likes you and you can get what you want out of him. Tell him to also give me the smaller ones which are colored. Where are they?

"Why don't you write that friend of Dick's in New York. He said that he could get you work in New York City, and there must be lots of it there—only first please stay here and gain at least five pounds—your cheeks are too thin now, Hon. Get in with money and stick with it.

"RENA."

Love, liquor and cigarettes all may be taken in a lady-like manner, according to Miss Florence Murray, former proprietor of the "March Hare" and leader of Boston's colony of "intellectuals" on Beacon Hill.

Miss Murray wrote Evelyn a letter, giving her some advice on this subject and also the latest news of the "intellectuals." It was addressed to the Bloomingdale Sanitarium.

"Dear Evelyn:

"You must forgive me for not answering your letter before this. I am a very, very poor correspondent. Usually I can excuse myself by saying 'busy,' but this time not even that is true. I have sold the 'March Hare' to an Italian boy—Bob Capone—I don't think you know him. Business is picking up and the old place is pretty lively.

"Last Saturday a Boston University club of girls ordered dinner for forty-five, with red roses, favors and decorations, etc. An hour before the appointed dinner hour Dan Warren kicked up a fuss about girls going to a 'dope den' and the dinner was cancelled. Bob is now trying to collect from them.

"Dickie Kimball and I are going down to New Orleans on Cape Cod, to,morrow. Mrs. Johnstone, who lived at No. 118 with us in the Winter, has a place there. This Summer she has been running sort of a dramatic school and camp.

"I told Dickie de Rochement that you especially mentioned him in your letter and that you wanted him to send you some candy. He said he knew what you wanted—Chinese candy. He is going to write and send you some. I told Dickie Warner the same thing and I guess it took

"I have not seen Bob Hartong since his father came down one afternoon and took him home. Well, dear child, take your medicine philosophically and struggle along, I sympathize with you, bu feel it is best.

"I am good at preaching an now will deliver a Sunday morn ing sermon.

"You have the making of lady—in the real sense of th word—in you. For God's sake don't waste your youth and goo looks on those cheap commo boys who care for nothing bu excitement and good times.

"Cultivate poise and a sense o refinement, well-being, superiori ty. Make it worth while to kno Miss Standfield. If you care t smoke or drink, do it like a lad —with some technique. If yo have a love affair have one th is real—one that has some tional value. So endeth the chapter.

"I'd like to have a good tal with you some day—you kno the sort of talk a couple o schoolgirls have."

"Affectionately,

"FLORENCE G. MURRAY

Copyright, 1923, by Universal Service.

Told Wife He Took Poison Believe Towerman Insan

Joseph Pino, towerman at Win low Junction, N. J., yesterday w released from a charge of attempte suicide. He was arrested Thursd after telling his wife he had take poison. Physicians believe his mi is unbalanced.

Pino succeeded John Dewalt towerman at Winslow Juncti after a wreck in which sixty we killed.

Canada Receives Fift of Pure-Bred Hors

MONTREAL, March 24.—Follo ing the example set by the Kin Mrs. Stanton Snelston, of Englan has presented a first class st horse to Canada for breeding pu poses.

This animal, together with tho presented by the King, will shown at the principal fairs in Ca ada this Fall.

Pretty "Dixie" Dixon, the Well-Born, Gentle-Mannered Southern Girl, Who Was Lured Into the Clutches of a Gang of Drug Dealers and Murdered in a Taxicab in New York.

The Larger Amount of Heroin Shown in the Left-Hand Dish Would Be Perhaps the Quantity Which "Dixie" Dixon Could Have Taken of the Greatly Diluted Drug as It Is Sold by the New York Peddlers. The Small Amount Shown in the Right-Hand Dish of Pure, Unadulterated Heroin Would Equal the Larger Quantity of Diluted Heroin in the Other Dish. If "Dixie" Dixon's Murderer Handed Her the Larger Amount in Pure Heroin It Would Insure Her Death.

victims to take. What is handed out is a very diluted compound, but it looks and smells or tastes precisely like the original full-strength drug. So it is not hard to see how easily Mabel Dixon might have been murdered—if instead of her little dose of 25 per cent pure heroin she was handed on the night of her death a dose of a full 100 per cent pure heroin. "Dixie" thought she was taking her usual allowance, but she took four times the dose she thought she was taking—and it killed her!

I knew Mabel Dixon; met her among the flotsam and jetsam of the great New York Underworld. Of course, I had a very intimate acquaintance with some of the really great master minds of crime—men like William Humphreyes, Frank Thompson, the famous Gondorfs, who were my associates and partners. Hovering about the dens of these aristocrats of crime were the smaller confederates, who were used from time to time as occasion required by these masters of crime.

Tragedy of the Girl Who Would "Try Anything Once"

"Dixie" Dixon was a Southern girl, a member of the old and very well known and aristocratic Dixon family of Virginia. She was too good looking and too lively to live out her life in the quiet atmosphere of Danville, Va. Just how she happened to cut loose from the very worthy and highly respectable Dixon relatives and social circles in Virginia and find herself in New York City I do not happen to know. But she turned up here some years ago, without any money, and made her appearance on the stage. She was a brunette of exceptional beauty.

So when in the early hours of the morning some weeks ago Martin Ryan, a taxicab chauffeur, drove up to the Harlem Hospital with a very pretty but unconscious girl in his cab and a few hours later a telegram announcing the young woman's death was sent to Danville, Va., nobody there could believe that pretty "Dixie" had died of drugs and under such strange conditions.

Lured Into the Drug Habit by "Doped" Champagne

At just what point along her downward career Mabel was lured to the first indulgence in drugs, I am not i- formed. But I have been told that her glass of chan- pagne was gently drugged on several consecutive evening by the king of a dope trafficking ring, until the poor girl had learned to yearn for the peculiar brand of champagne which seemed so extra nice.

Step by step the girl was led on until she became a drug addict, and then she was made the useful tool of the smugglers.

A physician glanced at the eyeballs of the dead beaut in the upper berth, and at once knew that a drug ha killed her. And a hasty examination of the unconscio girl in the lower berth showed that only the most vigorou efforts would save her from sinking into the stupor fro which she, too, would never awaken.

The dead girl was Miss Dorothy Waddell, from a tow just outside of Boston. The young woman who wa barely rescued from death was Mrs. William Bruce, c New York. Both women were opium smugglers, who ha been making regular runs from Montreal to New Yor and passing the Customs House guards on the borde without suspicion.

Smuggling the Wicked Heroin in Hot Water Bags

Both were well dressed, attractive and of charmin manners, but, like "Dixie" Dixon, they had learned t know too much, and their usefulness to their masters wa approaching an end. Like the Dixon girl, they were give their daily dose. But it was the full-strength heroin tha time instead of the much-diluted drug, and the unaccus tomed dose killed Dorothy Waddell and very nearly ac complished the end of Mrs. Bruce.

Dorothy Waddell had already been in trouble wit the Federal authorities at the border. She had usuall been entrusted with bringing drugs. One favorite devic of Dorothy's was to lay a large hot-water bottle acros her stomach as the night train approached the America border. This hot-water bag was filled with heroin—bu what Customs guard would run his hand up under th sheets and disturb the hot-water bag, when a pair o sparkling eyes looked out at him reproachfully from th bed cover, and said sleepily:

"Oh, why did you wake me up!"

On one occasion last Fall, for some reason, her mas ters ordered Miss Waddell to bring through a consign ment of Scotch whiskey. There was something about th fat, padded, stuffed appearance of the young beauty's berth which awakened suspicion. Miss Waddell wa aroused and made to get out of the bunk in her wrappe —and there they found, warmly nestled in the berth with her, just thirty-three bottles of "Johnnie Walker."

The next morning the girl pleaded guilty before the United States Commission, and a month later, in the cour at Utica, was fined $200 for smuggling.

That was last November, and the United States officials asked the Canadian officials to please not let Miss Waddell return to Canada for another load. So when, shortly after New Year's, Doro... the border on a New Y... Immigration In...

Santa Anita Park
ARCADIA
AUTO PARK
No. 02567 32

...orothy was very indignant, a ... all her wiles and vampish methods of conquest.

But when she found that nothing was availing, changed her tone and told the Canadian inspector t he could go to the devil, and she would get even with hi Lifting her skirts well above her knees, she said defiant

"Just take a look at these. You see I have a cou of good legs and I can WALK to Montreal."

Miss Waddell stopped for nearly a week at the n Hotel Holland, at Rouses' Point, on the border.

She telephoned a good many messages to somebody Montreal, but did not succeed in making arrangeme with her masters to smuggle her past the border officia

Then one night Dorothy packed her grip and went board the Montreal-New York night express, and th she met Mrs. Bruce. The meeting probably had be arranged by telephone. Dorothy's exploits, her getti mixed up with the customs officials, made her a mark person. It would be dangerous to have this woman co nected any longer with the dope smuggling gang.

If they continued to use her there was danger th she would be trailed, and would thus lead the officers the headquarters of the leaders of the gang. But if th told Dorothy that her usefulness was at an end and th they were no longer interested in her—then almost c tainly the girl would go to the police and reveal ever thing.

As an ordinary, common-sense business precautio the dope smugglers must remove the danger. There w only one sure way to seal Dorothy Waddell's lips. H death, quick and unexpected, was the only alternativ Dorothy stepped on that train with orders to go back New York and report there for another commission fro the gang, and with the compliments of her masters w handed her dose of dope.

How Dorothy Waddell's Death Sentence Was Executed

It was an overdose—her death sentence. Doroth snuggled between the blankets in that upper berth an dropped into eternity, just as her masters planned th she should.

Photograph Taken in the New York Morgue of Dorothy Waddell, Who Was Found Dead in Her Berth in the Pullman Sleeper as the Montreal Express Pulled Into the New York Central Station—a Murdered Victim of the Drug Traffic.

You may have
A Souvenir Photo of Your Party
TAKEN AT YOUR TABLE for $1.00
ASK YOUR WAITER
We shall be pleased to mail photographs to whomever you may request.
Earl Carroll Theatre-Restaurant
SUNSET NEAR VINE . . . HOLLYWOOD

Mrs. Alma Hayne committed suicide mysteriously after participating in the gayeties of the second Victory Ball in London. She had had an extraordinary career of romance and adventure. She was born in Montreal, and grew up a girl of great attractiveness and talents. The unscrupulous adventurer "Count Gregory" persuaded her to pass herself off as the daughter of the Crown Prince Rudolph of Austria and his sweetheart, Baroness Vetsera, who both perished so mysteriously. She carried out this plot with astonishing success.

In the gay society of two continents she was known as a fascinating heart-breaker. Three times she was mar-

...times she was the central figure in ...episodes. The last time she married a rich ...ng English army officer of excellent family. This time she appeared to have found genuine happiness and settled down to a dignified position in social life. She had a beautiful home and was a friend of many titled leaders of English society.

Just when there seemed to be no cloud on her horizon, when she had come home with her husband from the most brilliant ball of the season, she poisoned herself. The police

Fannie Brice, the Well-Known "Follies" Star, Who Is the Devoted and Admiring Wife of the Notorious Criminal and ex-Convict, "Nicky" Arnstein.

"Nicky" and Fannie Just After the Elusive Mr. Arnstein Had Surrendered Himself to the District Attorney to Answer an Indictment Charging Him with Being the "Master Mind" in a $5,000,000 Liberty Bond Theft.

Captain Steane, the last husband of poor Alma Hayne, gave this ...amatic testimony of her tragic end:

"We returned from the ballroom soon after two-thirty in the morning. She went into her bedroom and soon called me. On entering the rom I found her standing in front of the fireplace. I saw her put her hand to her mouth—then she drank a glass of water from the mantelpiece. I didn't realize what had taken place until she said to me, 'Tony, kiss me for the last time!'"

By Mrs. Margaret Hill

CHAPTER XX.

(Continued from Last Sunday)

THE novelists and the playwrights have thrown a fictitious glamour around the criminal's life. And as I write to-day my final chapter in this series, let me insist with all my vigor that the life of a criminal is indeed a dog's life.

Crime does not pay as a business. The same amount of energy, resourcefulness and brains expended in honest business would produce very much greater profits.

The criminal is a hunted animal, and is a curse to himself and his family and his associates. Sooner or later he is almost certain to land in state prison and bring ruin upon his family.

Many women have quite innocently married criminals who have successfully kept from their wives and families all knowledge of the criminal careers of the husband or father. Other women, like Fannie Brice, the celebrated Follies comedienne and mimic, have married criminals, knowing perfectly well that the

ating about a year ago and succeeded in stealing some $5,000,000 worth of bonds, with the aid of bank messengers, the police began looking for a man who is registered in the police records as Jules W. Arnstein, but is better known as "Nicky" Arnstein. It was then that the public read with astonishment and no little disgust that the popular Follies star, "Miss Fannie Brice, was rather proud of the fact that she pas the wife of "Nicky," the crook, and the mother of his baby.

Whatever Nicky's role, if any, in the really gigantic conspiracy, the police accused him of directing the plot as soon as the brokers discovered what had happened. Naturally everybody began looking for Nicky. The victims offered $2,500 reward for the slightest clue to his whereabouts, and I doubt if there was ever a

Fannie herself says that she became Arnstein in 1917, three years after Nicky released from Sing Sing Prison, and two y before the Wall Street swindle was hatche

And yet, a year after this date, up po a Mrs. Carrie Arnstein and filed suit for $ 000 damages against the popular actress leging that Fannie had alienated the affect of her husband, Nicky. As the suit develo Mrs. Carrie Arnstein and her attorneys f some rather surprising statements al Fannie Brice. Said the first Mrs. Arnstei

"My husband is a notorious confide man, having been convicted in the Cour General Sessions and released from Sing S Prison just a few months ago.

"I was always under the impression he was a broker or a promoter, and his c viction was a terrible shock. Still, I loyal to him, and would be still if it were for this Brice woman. All of the time I visiting him in prison Fannie Brice was vi ing him, too. And I later learned that I known as Nicky's sister-in-law among prison officials, while Fannie was known his wife."

During his imprisonment at Sing Sing Nicky wr many warm letters to his first wife, usually enclos some poem he had written in the solitude of his c Mrs. Arnstein No. 1 included one of these poems in evidence:

I have lived and I have loved,
I have waked and I have slept,
I have sung and I have danced,
I have smiled and I have wept.

All these things were weariness,
And some of them were dreariness.

Frivolous Butterflies of Fast Life Frequently Kill Themselves While in the Depths of Drug Despair

ence Schenck. It was my accidental meeting with her three days before her death.

I was driving through the East Side one day from the ferry when I saw ahead a street commotion. A rough man was jostling a queer looking woman about, pushing her from him, across the pavement. It all was taking place in front of a little downstairs entrance to a miserable looking small cafe.

I directed my chauffeur to stop. He did, and I got out. I went up to the woman; I felt very angry with that brutal man. When I reached her the woman turned about.

To my dismay and instant concern I saw who it was. This wretched woman was Florence Schenck.

She recognized me in an instant. In the same instant I took in her sad condition. She was dressed, principally, in a worn man's suit coat and a pair of flapping men's rubbers, several sizes too large for her.

But she addressed me with all her former grace when, in her handsome house in London, she poured tea for Vanderbilt.

"You," said she, with her grand manner upon her; "you see how this man has treated me! Why, he even laid hands on me—on ME!"

"And so I will again," said he, brutally, "if you dare to come into my place begging. We won't be bothered with panhandlers like you."

"Don't you dare to touch this lady!" said I to him, severely. He drew a little back, for he felt that my limousine, my furs and my handsome gown represented wealth, and, therefore, power behind me.

It was then that Florence said a sentence which made me want to smile while a tear trickled down my face.

"You know I am still beautiful," said she, in her tragic besottedness. "You can tell—this man—that I am a LADY."

MISS BILLIE CARLETON IN THE COSTUME SHE WORE AT THE FATAL VICTORY BALL.

WHAT I have said in previous chapters about the wicked drug habit and its degrading influence in America is even more true in most of the great cities abroad.

Perhaps there is no worse drug-cursed city than London just now. I have been through everything in the great British capital, and am quite familiar with the extent of the drug horrors of London.

I know that the readers of this page have read in detail the sad story of the untimely end of pretty Billie Carleton, the English show girl, who startled all England by her mysterious death on the night of the great Victory Ball with which London celebrated the end of the Great War.

Billie Carleton, who was the star in "The Freedom of the Seas," at the Haymarket Theatre, was one of the prettiest and most popular girls in the fashionable Bohemian set of London, which included many Americans. Among her friends were Mrs. Vernon Castle, the American dancer, and Malvina Longfellow, another American artist.

The first Victory Ball, which was organized by the famous Lady Diana Manners, the Duchess of Westminster, and other titled women of equal celebrity, was the most brilliant affair of its kind ever held. Pretty Billie Carleton was one of the most admired figures in the vast throng of gay dancers.

At 4 o'clock in the morning she went home with a gay party of men and women to her charming flat in Savoy Court Mansions, one of the most exclusive establishments in London. On the way to her flat she stopped at the rooms of Mrs. Vernon Castle, in the same building, to show her the wonderful dress she had worn.

Billie Carleton put on a negligee costume, and her friends all breakfasted with her in her room. They left her apparently sleeping, but she never woke up. W... her maid was unable to awaken her the ... she called a doctor, and he found her de... ton had taken poison.

After a long investigation it wa... twenty-two-year-old girl had been a ... Reginald de Veulle, a man of titled fa... come a dressmaker's designer, was sen... eight months for supplying Billie Car... Another person convicted was Mrs. Lo... pretty English wife of a Chinese opium de... lured Billie Carleton and others to a rema... den in Limehouse Causeway.

But what I am about to relate concerns the later career of pretty Florence Schenck, when she was certainly no longer pretty Florence. It was after Vanderbilt had thrown her over and she had had her public scandal with Wilson, the Vanderbilt stable manager, that Florence Schenck sank rapidly to the depths.

It was just a year before her death that I happened to be in Paris and met a rather well-known and rich New York stock broker who had known Florence Schenck during her earlier, prettier and more prosperous days. By accident this broker heard that the woman was in Paris in distress, and, in remembrance of the old days, he took the trouble to hunt her up.

He found Florence living in an attic in the thieves quarter. As he entered the room with a French detective he was shocked to see the pale, grinning face of Florence Schenck, lying on a mat of loose straw. The girl who had worn a million dollars' worth of jewels at one time, w... sharing this wretched den with two Paris Apaches—... lowest of the night prowlers, who steal up on a man ... dozes in drunken stupor on a dark bench, snatch... watch or scarfpin and slink back into the shadows.

Photograph of Pretty Florence Schenck When She Was in Her Prime, and the Last Photograph of the Unfortunate Woman, Showing Her Face Bloated With Drugs and Dissipation.

The three bottles had apparently contained cocaine, but Freda's death, which was accompanied by agonizing pain, was not due to cocaine. Dr. Spilsbury, the coroner's physician, was unable at first to decide just what the poison was that caused death. The suggestion was made that it was cocaine mixed with a small quantity of deadly poison, probably cyanide of potassium. The poor girl, after taking part in a series of drug seances, had awakened in a state of utter moral and physical collapse, and seized upon this ingenious and deadly mixture to end ...

A coroner's inquest was held on Freda Kempton, and then came a series of revelations which have shocked the public and proved that London is perhaps more affected by the drug evil than any other city.

She returned home at 6:30 the following ... remained in bed during the whole of the ... eight o'clock she burst into the room of the house ... of the flats, crying:

"Oh, my head! My head!"

She said she was suffering from unbearable pain and then collapsed. Within a few minutes, groaning terribly but unable to give any explanation of what had happened to her, sh... died.

Poor Sarah Cowen! How "Too Much Society" Started Noted Beauty to the Drug Addict's End

recall, too, the end of Peg Whitney. Peg, like ...e Lang, the beautiful young actress who gave the ... to the Margie Lang cocktail, was a Show Girl. I ...never forget Peg's end. It came, as she said, "just ... I am getting prosperous."

...course, Peg, and even Margie, were never in my ... They were far too careless, and far too common, ...o have had the lengthy career that I have had. But ...s the pity, perhaps. Now, Peg had been the sweet... of a young man here who, in all his "virtue," threw ...side when at length he picked out a simple little ...rom New Jersey to be his wife.

..'m going to get married," he had told Peg, brutal...ough. "I've got to turn 'respectable' one of these ... Well, here's luck, old girl, and a check."

...or Peg was heartbroken, for she loved this man ...inally had decided to turn "respectable." I have ...wondered whether poor Peg ever debated in her ... how it was that a man could always turn respectable, ...ever he decided, while she was left in her disrespect...y forever. Peg, after the man left her, was what ...call in Underworld circles where I never mixed, a ...rer."

...at means that she would meet men, on the race ... at dinner, at the stage door, wherever she could, ...ake them to play at the gambling houses in whose ...y she was. Well, after the man left her, Peg took ...ugs worse than ever, till she lost her place in the ...dway show and wasn't even able to pay her hotel ... She lived at various first-class hotels, Fifth avenue ...y, till she would find a plug in her door, when the ...as due, and she couldn't pay it, and then she'd leave, ...uble, losing her clothes, of course.

...e gambling houses, moreover, for which she worked, ...ed her shamefully. She was supposed to be paid ...r cent of all the "business" she "steered" for the ... Often, I have heard folks say who knew, poor ...would "steer" fifty thousand dollars into a place ... Saturday night. That should mean five thousand ...g. But, also, I have heard, during the last of at

IT was the night of the great Victory Ball—November 27. The famous Royal Albert Hall in London was gayly decorated with the flags of the victorious Allies. England's best known men and women of title, of wealth and fashion, the diplomatic representatives of the foreign embassies, the stage favorites of London theatres were there. Lady Diana Manners led the grand march as "Britannia," the Duchess of Westminster was "England," the Countess of Drogheda was "Air." All wore fancy dress, and four thousand tickets had been sold.

The hand of fate singled out one of the youngest, prettiest, most popular women among those four thou...sand revellers to mark that night with a tragedy wh... has shaken all London. Miss Billie Carleton, the fa...nating little comedy star of "The Freedom of the ... at the Haymarket Theatre, sparkling with animati... at the ball. In the early hours of dawn her g... breakfasted in her apartments at Savoy Court ... That afternoon her lifeless body was found in ... She had been poisoned by some narcotic drug.

drugs. Dr. Stewart, whose strange relation to the dead girl is hard to understand, gave her morphine freely, but tried to keep her from cocaine.

Malvina Longfellow, Fay Compton and Mrs. Vernon Castle, all well-known stage women, figured in the testimony; and Olive Richardson, another actress, answered embarrassing questions without a blush.

Among such a galaxy of stage favorites it was to be expected that some intimately interested millionaire would be uncovered. The coroner easily found one. Mr. John Marsh, retired gentleman of means, had been a friend in need, and had often supplied Billie Carleton with money, "frequently in large amounts"—in fact, on the day of ...

Miss Sally Cowen, Who Inherited $3,000,000 from Her Distinguished Father, Who Was President of the Baltimore and Ohio Railroad, and Who Sank to the Depths of Degradation and Lost Her Property and Good Name Through the Use of Drugs.

THE body of a woman, poor and emaciated, lay in the New York Morgue last week, unclaimed for 24 hours. The clothing was drab and coarse; the skinny fingers were bare of ornament. It was the body of a drug addict, a "dope fiend," that most pitiable, wretched and despised of the unfortunates.

And this shrunken frame, with the gray-streaked hair; this sallow face, ravaged and lined with the marks of narcotics; this pathetic derelict—was Sarah Cowen, the daughter of a great railroad president, once a pampered child of wealth. Only a few years ago she was considered one of the most beautiful girls in Baltimore. She was a debutante, popular, wealthy and sought by many suitors.

Now she lay in a corner of the morgue. The deep lines in her face were composed. The bony hands were peacefully crossed. It was quiet in the morgue, and the room was darkened. An attendant, perhaps, came in noiselessly, looked about to see that all was well, and closed the door softly as he went out. Sarah Cowen had found rest.

This was the end of the journey for a girl who had tried to go the pace that society sets, and had found the pace too fast. It was the inevitable end of a woman who, instead of giving her tortured nerves the rest and sleep that nature demands, resorted to opiates to quiet them.

It is not likely that the world will ever know who first introduced Sarah Cowen to morphine. Perhaps some society matron, noticing the tired eyes, the twitching hands, the slightly hysterical note in her voice that betrayed overstrain and tension, called her into another room and cajoled her with the soothing words: "Just a tiny injection of this, my dear—it won't hurt a bit—and you'll feel like a new person. It's positively wonderful how it ... up. No danger at all, just a little stimula... again, perhaps, it came about in an entirely different way.

But, however it began, it ended in the morgue. It ended when a woman of 33 years, and looking every day of 50, was carried, dead, out of a hotel room, and taken to the public mortuary to be held until someone

SUNDAY MAGAZINE—ST. LOUIS POST-DISPATCH—AUGUST 14, 1921.

JUNE . 25, 1925–

'Love Potion' Parties New Thrill on Br

SNEEZING DRUG CHECKS OPERA

BERLIN, Feb. 25 (AP).—Sneezing powder proved the undoing of a theatre cast at Weissenfeld recently.

During a performance of the operetta, "Liebfrauenmilch," at the local civic theatre, young mischief makers threw boxes containing sneezing powder against the curtain.

The effect proved disastrous; the actors had to sneeze so violently they were unable to sing or speak a word. The show had to be interrupted.

Only after the rowdies had been ejected from the playhouse and janitresses equipped with brooms, brushes and vacuum cleaners had finished clearing stage and curtain of the disastrous powder could the performance be resumed.

SAYS DRUG CAUSED JOHNSTONE TRAGEDY

Actor's Friend Declares Absinthe Drove Him to Kill Kate Hassett.

Absinthe drove Barry Johnstone to conceive the tragedy which wrecked his life and that of Kate Hassett, in Philadelphia, according to Samuel H. Wandell, who was one of his most intimate friends for many years and who has made a careful investigation of the circumstances which led up to the shooting. It was to Mr. Wandell that Johnstone dictated the story of his association with the woman, as he lay on his deathbed in the hospital.

"The cause of this terrible tragedy by which two lives were blotted out was unquestionably the effect of absinthe," said Mr. Wandell yesterday. "Johnstone stated to me in his dying confession that Kate Hassett was a confirmed absinthe drinker, and that she had acquired the habit through her acquaintance with a lawyer in Chicago. He declared he never had drank it in his life until the time when the Modjeska company was in New Orleans, in March, 1902. It was there that Kate Hassett 'introduced' the drink to him.

"To use his own expression, 'She was at it off and on and acquired a thirst for it. I got into the habit of drinking it through her. I took a good many drinks of it, and in Philadelphia I drank absinthe at Green's, at the Walton and at a cheap place. I couldn't stop drinking it.'"

SUITOR HELD, SOUGHT DRUG TO WIN WIFE OF ANOTHER

Harrington Park (N. J.) Realty Operator Asserts Druggist Told of Its Rare Efficacy

Keeping Her Last Tryst; Victim Collapses in Cab and Dies in Hospital at Englewood

Walter During, twenty-eight, realty developer of Harrington Park, N. J., was locked up in Hackensack last night following his admission to police that he had given a "love potion" to Mrs. Ethel Wheeler, thirty-nine, who died Monday. He is charged with murder.

During met Mrs. Harrington, whose husband, Herbert, is a buyer for a New York department store, about a month ago when he sold them a home in Harrington Park, one of the developments his firm was handling.

Despite heir difference in age and the fact that Mrs. Wheeler had been twice married and was the mother of a daughter of seventeen, the two were much in each other's company. But, apparently During was not satisfied that his love was reciproa ed, according to the story polie claim he told them. He went to a friend who works in a drug store and confided in him.

COLLAPSES IN CAB.

Police charge that During admitted that this druggist friend gave him some love powder, which he was told would surely win the woman's affections.

During was jubilant when he kept the tryst Saturday night. He told police he and Mrs. Wheeler went to a roadhouse at Coatesville where they had several soft drinks and started home. While at the roadhouse During, according to police, put part of the "love potion" his druggist friend had given him in Mrs. Wheeler's drink.

After they parted and Mrs. Wheeler had started home in a cab she collapsed. The driver of the cab took her to Englewood Hospital, where she died Monday.

SWAIN'S LOVE POTION KILLS WOMAN

LOVE POTION CASE PROVED, HART ASSERTS

Prosecutor Has Two Notes Written by Dying Woman; Mother Defends During

District Attorney A. C. Hart, of Bergen County, N. J., yesterday made the flat statement that the evidence that Mrs. Ethel Wheeler, of Harrington Park, had been poisoned by Maurice During, her admirer, was complete.

Mrs. Wheeler, thirty-nine and mother of a seventeen-year-old daughter, was poisoned by a dose of cantharides put into a drink by During and which the young man gave her as a "love philter," Hart declared.

The prosecutor said that the drug clerk who had sold the drug to During had made a signed statement. He pointed also to two notes written by the woman during the agonizing moments preceding her death. Prosecutor Hart declined to give out the contents of one of the notes in detail beyond saying that in it Mrs. Wheeler said that she believed During "doped" her drink.

MOTHER BLAMES WOMAN.

In the other note the woman said:

"I have thrown up so much blood I can't talk."

Hart was shown a statement made by Mrs. Elinore During, mother of the man who is now in Hackensack jail. In this statement Mrs. During declared Mrs. Wheeler had given her son the poison; that he had called on her at an office she has in Manhattan and had become so ill that it became necessary to have his stomach pumped out by Dr. Grimes, of Beaumont, N. J.

She said:

"This woman hounded my boy. She called for him every morning in her motor car. She would honk her horn until he came out to her.

"I pleaded with her to keep away from my boy. She was ruining him. My entreaties were in vain. I never broached to Maurice the matter of his relations with this woman that he did not reply she was wholly responsible for them. He didn't buy that drug. It was Mrs. Wheeler who bought it."

PROSECUTOR REFUTES HER.

District Attorney Hart said of this statement:

"On Monday morning During telephoned the Wheeler home from Closter and asked Mrs. Wheeler to meet him that day. It was his practice to telephone her. She was not the seeker. In fact, we have evidence that on Monday she intended to break with him and that this was the purpose of her meeting him.

"It is not true, as has been said, that she supplied him with liquor. The evidence is that he carried a flask and was a heavy drinker. We found a bottle of gin in one of his coat pockets at Harrington Park this morning."

Detective Nathan Allen got a singed statement from a clerk at Menrow's drug store, in Hackensack, saying he had sold to During a half pound of powdered cantharides for $1.50 and, also, 21 cents worth of the cantharides tincture.

At the Hackensack jail, During yesterday declined to make a statement.

HUSBAND'S VERSION.

The husband of the dead woman declared it would be utterly impossible for his wife to have had any such relations with During as stated by the young man's mother. He said:

"I had no idea that she had ever met During. He was the realty man that sold us our house and I did all the talking then. My wife was a good woman. She could not have received the many phone calls mentioned, nor could she have made them without my having noticed them."

HABITUES USE DEADLY DRUG FROM WHICH WOMAN DIED

American Investigator Finds Cantharides Sold Without Regard to Law on Rialto

Women Greater Users Than Men, According to Dispensers of Dangerous Chemical

Love potions of the deadly preparation which killed Mrs. Ethel Wheeler, of Hackensack, N. J., bottles containing the sickly green tincture of cantharides, are being bootlegged in enormous quantities by Broadway druggists.

Jaded habitues of the White Light districts, seeking to lash their lethargic emotions by doses of cantharidine and other supposed aphrodisiacs are purchasing the drug free and in large quantities.

Sensational disclosures developed at the very beginning of an investigation conducted by the New York American into the death of Mrs. Wheeler, she died in agony following an over dose of love philter.

TRAFFIC UNCONTROLLED.

Among the disclosures were:

1—The love potion can be sold over the counter in this State without a doctor's prescription, but the druggist is required by law to take the name and address of the purchaser and the use to which the drug is expected to be put. This was not done when The American investigator made several purchases yesterday.

2—Love philter cocktails are served in several of the smarter up-town "speak-easies." These consist of five drops of cantharadine in a Bacardi cocktail made with rum, lime and the white of an egg.

3—"Love philter parties"—Bacchanalian orgies in which passions are inflamed by the use of varied stimulants, have been common among the searchers for the elusive new thrill.

4—Prominent neurologists are treating increasing numbers of cases of "cantharidism," a morbid condition due to the excessive use of the aphrodisiac.

The first drug store entered by the American investigator was on Broadway above Times Square. The clerk in the rear of the store was asked for some Spanish Fly.

As he wrapped up the small bottle he was asked:

"Most of that sold is used for an aprodisiac, isn't it?"

"Sure, in this district."

"Do you sell much?"

"Take a look at that bottle. It's pretty empty, isn't it?"

"Well, how much should you give a person when you use it that way?"

"Anywhere from three to five drops. Better be careful, an overdose is poison. That's fifty cents."

The investigator paid and slipped the bottle into his pocket. The clerk handed him change and grinned:

"Well, good luck. No more than five drops, remember. I didn't put a label on the bottle. Don't think you'll want one."

VIOLATE STATE LAW.

Similar sales were made in other drug stores. These were in violation of the State Pharmacy law as T. Leon Laskoff, member of the State Board of Pharmacy, later explained.

"Attempts have been made to purchase cantharadine for what we supposed to be aphrodisiacal use in my store at Lexington avenue and Eighty-third street. We have always refused a sale.

"The law on the sale of cantharadine is this: It is listed in cule B, among drugs termed medium poisons. When a druggist makes the sale of such a drug he first must be aware of the purchaser's character.

"The druggist must also satisfy himself that the drug is to be put to a legitimate use—utilization as a love potion is of course not legitimate—and then take down the purchaser's name and address.

"By satisfying these conditions, he can legally sell cantharadine without a doctor's prescription."

WHERE LAW FAILS.

But through the loop-nole offered by the requirements of Schedule B there is pouring the ingredients for love philters, sometimes deadly. The preparation is being dropped into cocktails to "jazz up" the flagging spirits of the super-sophisticated.

"A dash to a shakerful."

This was the dose suggested by a seasoned bartender in an exclusive drinking resort in the upper East Side, not far from Central Park.

He explained:

"I used to hear of it, of course, but lately some one started throwing love philter parties and we've been asked to fix up a cocktail.

"All I do is make a regular Bacardi and put the drug in. They say it works best that way. The stuff spoils the looks of Scotch."

The bartender reached to the shelf for a small bottle and poured a few drops into a half-finished Scotch high-ball.

Sex Drug Ends Tiredness, Dispels Common Worries

COLUMBUS, O., Sept. 8 (AP) The effects of a new sex drug which is helping certain types of people to succeed in their work and cutting down common worries and fatigues were reported to the American Psychological association here Thursday.

The drug, a concentrated hypodermic, is in use at the Yale Institute of Human Relations upon persons who are under-developed sexually. The experiments are co-operative, with assistance of Yale medical school scientists.

Plants Yield Extract

The hypodermic is an artificial male hormone, usually made from the extracts of plants.

... ward to take their part in social activities lost their fears and shyness, reports showed.

Emotional instabilities largely disappeared. Some persons stopped bursting into tears, as they had been accustomed to do with no apparent provocation. Others ceased to suffer unexplained fits of anger. Periods of sulkiness were relieved.

New Energy Given

Notable ph... end... all... day... phys... Ne... stopp... and l... alway... The...

... as lambs and afraid to step for-... proved.

NOVEMBER 24, 1929

By SAILENDRA NATH GHOSE.
Universal Service Special Correspondent.

CALCUTTA, Nov. 23.—The discovery of a mysterious drug which revives human life at the vanishing point was announced here today by Sir Jagadish Chandra Bose, famed Indian scientist.

The surprise announcement was made by Sir Jagadish to a gathering of leading scientists, public officials and national leaders assembled for the anniversary meeting of Bos Institute. Sir Jagadish said:

"The drug was extracted from a plant in the sub-Himalayas and its properties were discovered at the institute while I was experimenting to determine whether the hearts of plants and animals are identical in their response to stimuli."

While it may come somewhat as a surprise to the non-scientific world that plants have hearts and regular pusatory systems, Sir Jagadish explained that sap is propelled through the system by organs similar to those in worms.

Plants poisoned to the point of death were marvelously transformed to the living by injections of the new drug, which is of greater strength than the better known stimulants like digitalis and strychnine. In less than two minutes, such plants ceased to droop and appeared as fresh as if just plucked.

The scientist repeated the experiment with a frog, the heart of which was poisoned and which had stopped beating. A few drops of the drug and the heart beat revived and the frog was none the worse.

that the experiment was conducted with human beings, in collaboration with the authorities of the Calcutta Medical College.

After first proving its non-injurious effect upon human tissues the drug was applied as a heart stimulant to hospital patients of such low resistance from streptococcal infections that they were momentarily in danger of death from "heart failure."

The drug revived heart action, giving the patients renewed strength with which to combat the attacks of the infections from which they were suffering, medical authorities claimed.

The main importance of the new drug, it is believed, will be its power to cause permanent revival when the heart has failed so completely as not to be affected by digitalis and strychnine.

New Drug Counteracts Death, Famous Botanist of India Announces

dway

In Narcotic Trap

Paula Ives, Hollywood musician
d actress, who was caught with a
pply of dope in her home.

ILM BEAUTY ADMITS BEING DRUG ADDICT

dge Suspends 140-Day Jail Sentence When Paula Ives Promises She Will Take Cure

eriff's Narcotic Squad Raids Star's Home; Prisoner Noted Beauty and Versatile Musician

LOS ANGELES, Jan. 25.—Paula es, beautiful and accomplished tress and musician, who has de- hted scores of audiences both on stage and screen, today pleaded ilty in police court to having dope her possession.

Her appearance before Judge chardson came as the sequel to sensational raid on her Hollywood me by members of Sheriff Trae- r's narcotic squad, led by Deputy eriff Harvey Bell and Inspector em Peoples of the State Board of armacy.

She was taken to the county jail iday night, where she gave the me of Paulina Jones, and it did t become known until today that Paulina Jones" and Paula Ives re one.

OWS TO TAKE CURE.

After she had entered her plea guilty Judge Richardson sen- nced her to 140 days in jail, or a arantee that she would take a re for the habit. This she prom- ed to do, and a satisfactory show- g was made to the court this ould be carried out.

To arresting officers she admit- d that she had been a drug-user r four years.

Paula Ives is probably one of the st known vaudeville performers the United States. She was un- r contract for many years with e largest vaudeville circuits in e country and will be remem- red by theatergoers as a beauti- l girl with marvelous versatility the matter of playing musical struments.

From time to time between vau- ville engagements she appeared pictures, achieving considerable ccess. She also is the author of veral scenarios, and has been a ominent figure in Hollywood film rcles.

IRST RAID FAILS.

She purchased a handsome home DeLongpre avenue, where she ved for a considerable time, when e left the stage. On one occa- on her home was raided by a arcotic squad, but no incriminat- g evidence connecting her with e use of dope was found.

In the second raid the officer dis- overed a small quantity of mor- hine and it was upon this violation that she was booked.

U. S. CONSUL IS STONED BY JAPS

MONDAY SAN FRANCISCO MARCH 17, 1919—SIX PAGES

ROBBED, SLAIN IN STUDIO

MARCH 16, 1923

MODEL KILLED IN BED BY DRUG; 2 MEN SOUGHT

Dorothy King Found by Maid in West 57th St. Apartment, Diamond Rings, Gems Gone

LAST SEEN AT MIDNIGHT

Mother and Police Reticent, but Hallboy Tells of Her Return from Dinner Party

Miss Dorothy King, said to be one of the most beautiful art models in New York City, was found slain in her studio apartment on the fifth floor of No. 144 West Fifty-seventh street shortly after noon yesterday.

The startling discovery was made by Miss King's negro maid, Ella Bradford, who had called at the apartment at 12:30 o'clock after having spent the night at her home.

The maid, after opening the front door with her pass key, stepped into Miss King's bedchamber and found the body of the model lying across the body.

CHLOROFORM BESIDE BED.

An empty chloroform bottle on the floor at the foot of the bed gave mute evidence as to how the slaying had been ...

LAW SEES WAY STILL OPEN TO GERMAN OFFER

"Yes!" Premier Says Bluntly in Parliament, Asserting He Was Receptive in Paris

PEACE MOVE BELIEVED ON

Britain Insists Proposals Be Made Directly to France; Business Demands Parley

By JOHN T. BURKE,
Universal Service Staff Correspondent.

LONDON, March 15.—Colonel J. C. Wedgwood, laborite, demanded in the House of Commons to-night to know whether the Prime Minister has tried to get in touch with the German Embassy to receive the proposals from Berlin which Dr. Bergmann vainly attempted to present to Premier Poincar... ing the Premiers' confere... Paris in January.

Premier Bonar Law stat... way was open then to Germ... submit any proposals, had ... sired to do so.

A blunt "Yes" was the pr... reply to Commander Kenw... who asked whether the wa... still open.

PEACE MOVE UNDER WA...

The most important memb... Parliament agree with Lord ... Cecil, who declares a me... reach a settlement of the ... tions question is informally ... way, and that the gover... backed by Holland, Denmar... Sweden, is in a receptive mo...

The government insists, ... ever, that the proposals m... made direct by Berlin to Par...

FIRST and exclusive photograph to be published of Dolores Dixon, the nineteen-year-old complainant in a suit against "Babe" Ruth. She is asking $50,000 damages. Ruth has declared he would like to "see what this girl looks like." Both the public and the famous baseball star can see here the features of the maid who has brought suit.

LOVE STI

In the frantic search
for effective sex potions,
men have tried everything
from Spanish fly to mandrake roots,
unaware that these aphrodisiacs
are deadly killers in disguise.

Cantharides, better known as Spanish fly, is prepared from blood and crushed bodies of blister beetle,

NARCOTIC HUNT DELAYS BURIAL OF MRS. RUTH

Trace of Poison Also Sought in Autopsy; "Babe" Will Pay All Expenses of Funeral

By SAM BLAIR,
New York American Staff Correspondent.

BOSTON, Jan. 15.—Two men waited in an emotional agony today for medical and chemical specialists to complete examination of the body of Mrs. "Babe" Ruth. She died last Friday during a fire which swept the residence of Dr. Edward H. Kinder, Watertown dentist, with whom she had been living as his wife.

Meantime a new inquiry had started when the Federal Government entered the case this afternoon. United States narcotic agents went to Dr. Kinder's Back Bay office and began a search of his records to learn the names of those for whom he has prescribed drugs.

FUNERAL POSTPONED.

The funeral of Mrs. Ruth, which was to have been held today, has been postponed so that specialists for the State can search for indications of poison.

The chemists' examination will establish with certainty whether Mrs. Ruth could have fled the blaze in the Kinder house if she had not been in a stupor because of some narcotic or poison.

A report this afternoon that Mrs. Ruth had been murdered with a blow of a hatchet was discounted tonight ...officials. They said that any cut ...was undoubt-

1929

GIRL MODEL ROBBED AND SLAIN IN STUDIO

Continued from First Page.

the police last night, had remained in Miss King's apartment for forty-five minutes and then left. The other man, he added, had remained indefinitely, the boy declaring he did not see him leave at all.

Dr. Baker, of Bellevue Hospital, who accompanied Medic... ...er Norris to the ... ...e girl had been de... ...urs at the time ... ...vered her body. H... case of homicide.

...LICE ARE RETIC...

...ewspapermen we... ...n but little inform... case from police of... ...is was reticent. ... ...ver, that Miss Kin... in her night robes a...

...m other sources ... ...d that, except for ... dresser drawers, ...nd its fixtures were ... condition. The po... ...n find a handker... ...at might have bee... ...e chloroform was ... ...irl's nose and mouth

...AMOND RINGS GO...

...heory that robbery ... ...otive for the murde... ...hat when the ... ...s. Anna King, No... Hundred and First s...

arrived with her two sons at the apartment.

Mrs. King told the police that two large diamond rings owned by her daughter were missing, as well as a pair of diamond earrings and other jewelry. Mrs. King also declined to discuss the matte... newspaper repo...

'MY GOLF GIRL,' NAME SHE SAYS RUTH GAVE

The $50,000 suit of nineteen-year-old Dolores Dixon against "... Ruth developed ... tions ...

Search for Dope Halts Ruth Fun...

TWO AWAIT FUNERAL.

Delay in the burial has intensified the mental anguish of "Babe" Ruth, who waits in his hotel suite here, and of Dr. Kinder, who was released after his surrender yesterday.

Ruth, of course, will attend the funeral. He is providing the costs of burial and has expressed compassion for the dead woman.

But Kinder's presence at the funeral is problematical. He, himself, will not declare his intentions. His friends say he is anxious to attend the services and to watch beside the grave as the remains of the woman, whom he says he loved, are lowered into it.

DID NOT SUSPECT WIFE.

The baseball player was willing, however, to discuss another topic, Dr. Kinder and his relations with Mrs. Ruth. Asked if he and the dentist were old friends, Ruth said:

"I never saw or heard of him.

I did not suspect my wife was friendly with them. My wife came to Boston after we separated, and I supposed she wished to be near her family. I knew nothing about her dual life until my pal, Arthur Crowley, telephoned me Saturday afternoon."

"It just isn't true."

Nora declared she had accompanied Helen (Mrs. Ruth) to New York last December 10, where they visited Ruth. She said the home-run specialist demanded that Mrs. Ruth divorce him so that he might marry another woman.

It is a matter of grim irony that just as Nora was uttering her sentences another sister of Mrs. Ruth's and two of her brothers were meeting with the "Babe" and, with the help of attorneys, arranging a pact of peace.

Both the brothers, William J. Woodford, of New York, and Thomas Woodford, of Dorchester, had earlier confided to this reporter:

"Ruth must do all in his power to protect the reputation of our ..."

...ference—and

brought to an und... Boston.

BURGLARY POS...

District Attorn... nell, of Middlese... charge of the in... the body would... burial until th... proving death ... been exhausted...

One of the ... tioned for the ... was burglary ... supposed th... many thous... appeared fr... mediately h... But officia... were safe ...

DECEMBER 2, 1921

DRUG FIEN

FIND WOMAN ARBUCKLE WITNES

NURSE'S STORY RIDDLED, SHE IS DISCOVERED UNCONSCIOUS

Mrs. Irene Morgan Testified She Served with Canadian Company Captain Denies Ever Existed

PHYSICIANS FILE REPORT

Defense Hails It as Corroboration of 1913 Diagnosis That Virginia Rappe Was a Sufferer

SAN FRANCISCO, Dec. 1.—Mrs. Irene Morgan, defense witness in the Roscoe Arbuckle trial, was found unconscious at noon to-day in her room at the Clift Hotel.

According to the house physician she had been drugged.

Captain Theodore Rayward, of the Canadian expeditionary forces, had testified this morning in refutation of defense testimony by Mrs. Morgan, war nurse. She had testified she was connected with the Canadian forces and also that she attended Miss Virginia Rappe.

Mrs. Morgan said on the stand that she had been affiliated with the "Fifth Company in the Canadian Hospital Service at the front." Rayward testified that there was no "Fifth Company."

Mrs. Morgan said also that she served in the battle of the Marne in 1917. Rayward said the battle was in 1918.

DOCTORS FILE REPORT.

The special medical commission's report that Miss Rappe's bladder showed evidence of chronic inflammation and the presence of rupture, was submitted to-day.

The defense contended the bladder rupture, which caused Miss Rappe's death, was the climax of a chronic condition and not caused by external force applied by Arbuckle, as the p... tion alleged.

The commission was name... court and counsel for both...

REID'S ILLNESS BRINGS PULPIT ON HOLLYWOOD

Preachers Urge Civic Board to Get at Facts Underneath Reports of Scandals

DRUG RING HUNT STARTS

Authorities Seek Narcotic Chiefs, Who Are Said to Have Fled from Country

Special Dispatch to the N. Y. ...

LOS ANGELES, D...

"Let's get the truth a... wood."

That plea was hurl... Council to-day by Me... ers of Southern Ca... sult of the critical... lace Reid.

The ministeri... pointment of a c... delve in the do... oy people and... of the indust... sistent rumo...

REID SLI...

Meanwh... furore w... recent a... iliness w... ad na... impro...

Ph... at...

... normal, his ... what above ... pulse 112 as ... The dys... he has suf... to be somewhat ... not yet, by any ... danger."

... BEDSIDE.

...by Davenport Reid, ... at the actor's bedside ... day. She read to him

...aw enforcement agencies ... to unearth the "ring" ... alleged to have made ... prey.

...lication of Reid's illness and ...ause, according to local offi... probably frightened the narc... distributors out of the country. ...unty and city authorities have ...ken action.

PREACHERS MAKE PLEA.

The Methodist preachers asked the co-operation of the Ministerial Union and the Church Federation in their action. Their plea to the City Council said:

"For many months the very nation has been stirred by stories of immorality connected with certain movie studios and movie people of Los Angeles. These stories have neither been proven true nor have they been disproved. They have only been affirmed and denied.

"During the last week daily papers have carried the tragic story of Wallace Reid, a world famous star, who is now reported to be in a local sanitarium battling for his life. His wife and mother-in-law openly charge that liquor, dope and fast parties have been the cause of his downfall. It is persistently rumored that the names of some of the biggest producers and actors in Southern California are linked with his ruin.

"In all this the city has suffered irreparably. The movie industry has suffered. These conditions either obtain or they do not ob-tain. These stories ... true or false.

"Therefore we petit... Council to authorize ... commission of unbiase... women, to the end that ... may be known.

"We ask further that ... mission organize at once ... lect one of the ablest a... courageous attorneys in ... to assist in their investig...

"We urge all produce... others interested in the fat... of the movie industry to join us in this petition, and we call upon Will Hays to use his best endeavors to this end."

DECEMBER 19, 1922

Los Angeles Ministers Ask City Council to Get Truth About Film Colony

DECEMBER 13, 1922

'EVELYN NESBIT' ORDERS FOUND IN DRUG SEIZURE

Letters Signed with the Name of Harry Thaw's Former Wife Are Discovered in $50,000 Raid

SENT FROM ATLANTIC CITY

She Is Said to Be Playing There in Boardwalk Cabaret—Movie Actor in Hollywood Involved

In a Greenwich Village raid yesterday in which $50,0000 worth of drugs wre seized, detectives of Dr. Carlton Simon's Narcotic Division discovered letters from two well-known theatrical figures.

The raid is believed to have revealed one of the main sources of drug supply to addicts on the stage.

Some of the letters wre signed by a well-known motion picture actor of Hollywood, Cal.

Others were dated from Atlantic City and signed "E. Nesbit."

In one of the Atlantic City letters, the address of the correspondent was given as "Palais Royal Cafe, Kentucky avenue and Boardwalk." One was signed "Evelyn Nesbit."

It was said that Mrs. Evelyn Nesbit Thaw, former wife of Harry Thaw, has been dancing in a Boardwalk cabaret.

COFFEE BLENDER RAIDED.

The raid was made by Detectives Moog, Masson and Higgins, on the apartment of William Williams, forty-two, a coffee blender of No. 263 West Eleventh street.

The drugs seized consisted of sixty-five vials, each said to contain twenty tablets of morphine, a small vial of heroin and thirty-six hypodermic needles, some gold.

The letters signed "Evelyn Nesbit" and "E. Nesbit," written from Atlantic City, were about twenty in number.

According to Dr. Simon, one of these letters purported to speak of automobile supplies. In this letter, he said, "Spare parts for the car," in the jargon of drug addicts, refers to narcotics, and "spark plugs" to hypodermic needles.

SOME OF THE LETTERS.

Some of the letters follow:

"October 11, 1922.

"Dear Mr. W:

"Next time you want to communicate with me, you must address me care of Palais Royal Cafe, Kentucky avenue and Boardwalk. Am now located there, and also, just on general principles, when you come again to Atlantic City it is always well to bring fresh parts for the car.

"Those last 'spark plugs' seem to be of an inferior grade; even break at the least pressure. I understand some makes are much better than others. Always bring the small size outfit.

"Let me know when you are coming, as you generally arrive so late in the day that it's not possible to get to a bank. But if I know you are coming, I can prepare for you.

"Sincerely,

"E. NESBIT.

CALLS SERVICE "DANDY."

"Dear Mr. Williams:

"Have been in bed with the worst cold I ever had in my life, and all my affairs have been at a standstill, however, am sending you a cheque immediately.

"Hope the market is okay for you and that if I invest in the stocks you advise—it will be okay. When I see you—will tell you exactly how I hope to better my stocks and investments. MANY THANKS, for such DANDY PROMPT SERVICE.

"Believe me — I appreciate same and will prove my gratitude when I see you.

HELD AS DRUG PEDDLER.

After Williams had made a signed statement, he was arrigned before Magistrate Edgar Frothingham in Jefferson Market Court and charged with selling narcotics. He was held in $1,000 bail for Special Sessions.

Walter Lang, forty, of No. 203 Division street, Brooklyn, and William Braun, thirty-two, and expert accountant of No. 105 West One Hundred and Sixty-third street, were held in $300 bail each, charged with possessing narcotics.

The Hollywood police have been notified of the discovery of the letters from the motion picture actor.

HOLLYWOOD ACTRESS NABBED WITH DOPE

LUCILLE BAST, ACTRESS, DIES OF SLEEP DRU...

Body Found in Pittsburgh Hotel After She Left Relative... Complaining of Nervousne...

TRAGIC LETTER IS FOUN...

Coroner Asserts Girl Know... as Marshall on Stage Kill... Herself, but Brother Denies

PITTSBURGH, March 23.—Af... Lucille Bast, thirty-four, a Ne... York actress, was found dead ... day in her room at the Fort P... Hotel, the victim of an overdo... of sleeping powders. A search ... her room brought to light a tra... love letter.

In the letter the actress e... pressed the conviction that "so... time, somewhere, in this world, ... out of it, there must be a mome... and a place to retrieve our m... takes."

The missive, written in pencil ... the back of a letter received fro... one signing himself "Bunny," rea...

"My Dearest—Into the life o... every woman there come man... problems and many solution... but only one great thing—th... man. You are that to me. W... have travelled the road tha... springs from nowhere and wend... its way along the rocky height... to happiness, but in our case... dear, it can only be realized i... the great beyond. I love yo... always, remember that I lov... you, my most happy moment... have been with you, but I mus... do my duty. Goodbye, dearest... how I shudder at the words. M... prayers and eternal love ar... yours."

CHLOROFORM FOUND.

Conditions surrounding the dea... of Dorothy King in New York we... repeated in part at least whe... hotel employes, who broke in... Miss Bast's room, found a part... filled bottle of chloroform. Exa... ination of the body proved, ho... ever, that death had been d... solely to the sleeping potion. Se... eral letters from a friend in A... lantic City were also found amo... her effects.

The Coroner, after an autops... rendered a virdict of "suicide" a... there will be no further police i... vestigation.

Miss Bast, who lived in New Yor... at No. 331 West Forty-sixth stree... came here ten days ago to visit th... family of her brother, B. F. Bas... He said that she had been appea... ing on the stage as Lucille Ma... shall and had come to Pittsburg... in a highly nervous condition as ... consequence of her failure to r... ceive a part in a Broadway show... He scouted the suicide theory. H... said:

"I don't believe my sister in... tended to kill herself and there... is nothing to indicate murde... either. Her death may have been... due to an overdose of sleeping... powder. If there was another... man in her life, we did not know... anything about it."

HURT BY EJECTION.

According to Miss Bast's othe... relatives, she was divorced severa... years ago and assumed the stag... name of Marshall.

Evelyn Nesbit Denies Attack on Hollywood

LOS ANGELES

ANOTHER denial was added to-day to the published quotations in some Los Angeles newspapers. Evelyn Nesbit sent this telegram to the Los Angeles Examiner:

"I never said Hollywood was gateway to ruin; never lived there. Know nothing of present conditions there. Please publish truth."

A Los Angeles newspaper, not the Examiner, published what purported to be a statement by Miss Nesbit this morning.

U. S. PRESSES WAR ON DRUG SMUGGLING

Treasury, Co-operating with Haynes, Will Increase Corps of Customs Narcotic Sleuths.

By Universal Service.

WASHINGTON, Dec. 18.—The Federal Government is preparing for a vigorous attack on the drug evil in this country at ... it was reveal...

... the customs in... forces will make possible, in the opinion of Treasury officials, a more rigid enforcement of the drastic provisions of the Jones-Miller Narcotic act.

Prohibition Commissioner Haynes, in charge of narcotic enforcement,

Beautiful Singing Canary and Gilded Cage

to be awarded by

ALHAMBRA GROTTO

Kansas City Pilgrimage Fund Committee

at their MASQUERADE PARTY

in January or February, 1920

Watch for Announcement

TEN CENTS No 16018

WAS URGED TO GET EVEN WITH TAYLOR

DRUGGED

SEPTEMBER 29, 1922

ACTOR ACCUSED OF GIVING GIRLS CRAZE FOR DRUG

John Paul Jones, Arrested for Possessing Morphine, Said to Be Booster of the Habit

BRUNETTE ALSO IS HELD

Broadway Banker's Son Led to the Captures Through Search for a Young Woman

By the arrest of John Paul Jones, a well-known actor, on the charge of possessing morphine, Dr. Carleton Simon, Deputy Police Commissioner in charge of the Narcotics Division, asserted he has finally landed a "drug booster" who has caused numerous young women in Broadway's gay circles and in the Bohemian haunts of Greenwich Village to become addicts.

One of the victims of Jones, it was learned, was George Tiffany, of No. 37 East Ninety-second street. This young man, known in the underworld as both Tiffany and Harrison, was sent to Bloomingdale Asylum as a hopeless slave to narcotics.

BRUNETTE ALSO HELD.

Jones was held in $1,000 yesterday by Magistrate Smith for a hearing Monday. At the same time a brunette, who gave the admittedly fictitious name of Mrs. Stella Gordon, was held in $500. The arrest of Jones was made in her luxurious apartment in West Seventy-second street, near West End avenue.

This young woman, said Dr. Simon, is a member of a prominent family. She is seen daily on a horse in Central Park, or on the green of a fashionable golf course. Jones admitted that she had once taken drugs, but said she had shown amazing will-power and broken herself of the habit unaided.

Jones is a man of talent. He played a good role in John Drinkwater's "Abraham Lincoln." He was with Alice Brady a year ago in "Forever After." He played the principal part in "The Hand of the Potter," given two years ago by the Provincetown Players.

BANKER'S SON IN CASE.

Indirectly, the cause of the ...

HELENE FRENCH, former Follies dancer, now locked up as drug addict, once the daughter-in-law of United States Senator Bert M. Fernald. She tells how drugs dragged her down to poverty and misery.

HELENE FRENCH TELLS OF LIFE AS DRUG SLAVE

Show Girl Falls from Days of Luxury, Applauded by Thousands, to Prison Cell

HER STORY WARNS OTHERS

Thrice Wed, Once Bride of Hays Fernald, Son of Senator, Wanders the Streets

The roaring applause of the theatre crowds in the shadows at the Follies; adulation of scores of lavish admirers; parties galore; thousand-dollar gowns that were worn but once; trunks full of dainty ... —these were ...

By HELENE FRENCH.

From the highest to the lowest—that is how far I have fallen. From the most exclusive social circles to success in Broadway shows—in the "Follies" and in Shubert productions for seven years.

Then lower and lower, to the point where detectives accosted me, to the point where all my fine clothes were held in hotels, so that I was ashamed to ask for work, to the day I resorted in desperation to drugs (a habit I learned as an army officer's wife)—and to-day in the Jefferson Market Jail.

How did it happen?

Several things helped, but one man started me on the road. He is one of the wealthiest young men in New York. He is married now, ... I'll just call him "George"— ... first name. I ...

YOUNG ...

My mother died when ... young. If I could have gone to her for advice I'm sure I would be happy now. If young girls only realized how much their mothers can save them from—there would be no family quarrels.

My father was a stern old New Bedford sea captain. He was well-to-do then, and sent me to exclusive schools. It was when I was home on vacation from a university in Tennessee that I met Hays Fernald, the son of Bert M. Fernald, of West Poland, Maine. Mr. Fernald, Hays' father, was then Governor of Maine, and is now United States Senator.

Hays was charming and polished. I, being a silly little girl of fifteen, became infatuated with his man-about-town air. He was thirty-four then—more than twice my age.

We were married. It didn't last long. We had nothing in common, and after I left him to go on the stage, we were divorced.

It was then that George came into my life.

FOLLOWED HER.

I was stopping at the Tuxedo Hotel; with a girl friend. I was still young—young and unspoiled. I noticed him in a box, several nights. I was registered at the hotel as Mrs. Fernald. He followed me home one night, and got up to my room by telling the clerk he was Mr. Fernald.

I didn't want to make a scene, and thought he was drun... I had only called for ... night and had him arres...

He told me who he was ... violent love to me and ... couldn't live without ... promised me he would always treat me tenderly and take care of me. He said that for business reasons he was forced to marry the daughter of one of the wealthiest families in the world, but in a few years he would get a divorce and marry me.

And I believed him. What a fool I was. For two years he visited me. I lived in a $3 room. He didn't give me a nickel. Then, in 1917, after I was making a big success on the stage, he suddenly started giving me $300 or more a week. He told me to buy a bungalow on Long Island and use the money for that and for the furniture. I did.

THOUSANDS APPLAUD.

Life was a song then. I never wore the same gown twice. My hose and clothes were made to order for me.

Different was my luxurious apartment from the cell I share now with another girl who has gone the same way. And I have worn this same old dress for months.

I was so happy. Then I learned I was to be a mother. I was rapturously happy. I had always wanted children. I was singing all that day, waiting for George.

I was sure he would marry me. We were planning to go out to our bungalow in a few weeks.

When George came in, I threw my arms around him. I told him our secret. He flung himself away from me.

And he rushed out without kissing me goodbye. I have never seen him since. I was too proud then to beg him for help. I would now.

Then I married a young naval officer, Lieutenant Raymond S. Falls, and went to Portsmouth, Virginia, to live with his mother.

OCTOBER 11, 1923

Clears Hollywood of Unjust Stigmas

By Universal Service.

WASHINGTON, Feb. 8.

DECLARING that a Grand Jury investigation would prove that reports of general drug addiction in Hollywood have been exaggerated, Narcotic Agent Harry D. Smith to-day made his report to Chief Agent L. G. Nutt. He said:

"My statement to you that conditions in Los Angeles and particularly in Hollywood were grossly exaggerated will positively be verified and will bear investigation by a Grand Jury or any inquisitorial body.

"Everything considered, I feel safe in saying that conditions on the Pacific coast are as good ... of the count...

MAN BOOTED FROM HOME OF FILM ACTRESS INCITED TO KILL

Deputy Sheriff Gives Details of Severe Beating Given Peddler and of Hatred That Followed

NEW CHECKS ADD MYSTERY

One Made Out to Valet Sands ... Blanks with ...

Special Correspondent of the ...

LOS ANGELES, Cal., Feb. 26.—Further revelations concerning the fight between William Desmond Taylor and a drug peddler—an incident believed by many to have been directly responsible for the film director's murder—were made here to-day by Deputy Sheriff Harvey W. Bell.

The story was told to him by a drug addict now incarcerated in the county jail here for a minor offense.

On the day in question, according to the informant, Taylor went to visit a noted screen actress at her home. When he drove up to the house he noticed that the woman was at her back door, talking to a man whose appearance was that of an underworld character. Taylor apparently had seen the man before, and knowing the actress' proclivities for taking opiates, he suspected ...tly that the man was a peddler.

...N WAITED AT REAR.

Nevertheless he rang the bell, and ... actress herself answered, telling ...

"Wait a minute," Taylor said. "You're not going back to that stuff again are you? That's the same fellow who was bothering you before, isn't he?"

The actress evaded his questions and began an effort to placate the nervousness of both men.

In disgust Taylor left the house, walked around to the rear door and ... abusing the peddler.

GAVE MAN A BEATING.

Finally, in a rage because the man insisted in peddling his wares to the star, Taylor gave him a severe beating and kicked him off the back steps.

As a result of this incident, according to the addict now in jail, the entire drug ring began to laugh at the peddler and made him the butt of their jokes. Dozens of these persons, including the two sisters for whom the police are searching, urged him to reprisals, while many in the film colony who heard of the incident acted in a similar manner toward the actress.

MABEL NORMAND'S PARENTS GO TO AID

Star's Collapse Serious and She Is Secluded in Her Altadena Home.

FEBRUARY 27, 1922

NOTED WRITER ISSUES APPEAL FOR FAIR PLAY

Spent More Than a Year a... Hollywood and Declares Viciou... Element Is a Tiny Minori...

MAJORITY DEEPLY WRONG...

Earnest, Honest, Hard-Work... Army Injured by Criticism T... Only a Few Should B...

ELINOR GLYN, noted Eng... writer, has written a ... ring appeal for fair play to film industry in view of who... sale criticism since the Tay... tragedy.

Good in Filmdom Far Outweighs Bad

...try was written ... New York American by Elinor ... noted author:

By ELINOR GLYN.

America is supposedly a d...racy. It had a magnificent start, its laws being framed at a time when the world had emerged into a fair state of civilization—and yet, as Mr. Brisbane frequently points out in his masterly leading articles, the most appalling cases of injustice, which would disgrace a corrupt autocracy, seem to be continually occurring.

One of the greatest is going on now.

It is the hysterical, illogical attack upon the moving picture community, which has sprung forth as the aftermath of the tragic Taylor murder.

My sense of justice won't let me remain silent about it any longer.

I feel as I did once when I was a child, and hit a big man in the street with my little parasol because he was beating a horse carrying a heavy load.

FEBRUARY 24, 1930

Her Film Career Now Closed by Death

Two Hollywood Scandals Shadowed Life of Actress

LOS ANGELES, Feb. 23.—Shadows of two great Hollywood scandals darkened the life of Mabel Normand, capricious comedienne of the screen.

To her public she was the winsome, dark-eyed, laughing girl who capered through such well-remembered pictures as "Mickey," "Peck's Bad Girl" and "Sis Hopkins."

But her life was a slowly unfolding tragedy, quickened by her roles in the murder of William Desmond Taylor, motion picture director, and the shooting of Courtland S. Dines, Denver playboy. Dines was not fatally injured.

Miss Normand, daughter of Claude Normand, carpenter and stage manager of the Stapleton, Staten Island, Club, entered the moving pictures by way of the Keystone comedies in 1915.

She had first served as a model in New York for such artists as James Montgomery Flagg, Charles Dana Gibson, the Leyendeckers and Henry Hutt.

FIRST TRAGEDY.

The first tragedy entered her life with the murder on February 2, 1922, of William Desmond Taylor, one of the best known of the West Coast directors.

Mabel rushed to the Taylor home a few hours after the murder in a frantic effort to obtain letters she had written, in which she called Taylor "Blessed ... made public the contents of the letters.

Later it developed that Miss Normand had visited Taylor the day he was shot. Police found in Taylor's watch a picture of Miss Normand, inscribed, "My Dearest." Investigation produced nothing definite and Mabel went to Europe "to forget."

The shooting was revived in 1926 with a story told by Mary Miles Minter to the Los Angeles prosecuting attorney, Asa Keyes. Again Miss Normand's name was mentioned. Once more the investigation led nowhere.

STILL NO RESULT.

In the latest revival of the mystery, extending into this year, Superior Court Judge Doran in Los Angeles disposed of the matter by saying definitely the new investigation had developed no evidence that in any manner involved Mabel Normand or Mary Miles Minter.

The second affair to attract world-wide attention in which Miss Normand was involved was the shooting on New Year's afternoon, 1924, of Courtland S. Dines, son of Tyson Dines, wealthy Denver attorney. Dines was shot in his home, police charged, by H. A. Kelly, otherwise Horace A. Greer, Mabel's chauffeur.

Dines recovered and subsequent court investigation fo... the principals hazy as to de... Nothing more happened.

Again Miss Normand retired from the pictures. She tried after her marriage to Lew Cody, the ...

WIFE BARES WALLY REID'S FIGHT ON

DECEMBER 17, 1922

FILM STAR'S RUIN LAID TO NARCOTIC RING

Mate of Actor Denounces Persons Who Intrigued and Kept Him Supplied With Drugs

I'll Tell All, She Vows in Her Determination to Expose False Friends of Screen Hero

LOS ANGELES, Dec. 16.—"I will keep no secrets. I will tell all that I know of the drug traffic in Los Angeles and the East. I have pledged my life to the relentless fight against that frightful horror. I will be as merciless with them as they have been with 'Wally.'"

Dorothy Davenport Reid, remembered heroine of cinema thrillers, stood straight and tense and made that promise today.

A few blocks from her pretentious home, in a private sanitarium in Hollywood, her famous husband, Wallace Reid, was bravely fighting to throw off the deadly effects of prolonged addiction to narcotic drugs and whisky.

Reid, a victim of the fiendish ring that is spreading the drug habit throughout America among rich and poor alike, is a pathetic example of a man whose weakened physical condition, due to an accident, was exploited by the dealers in narcotics. The habit which he contracted is most prevalent among the poor, particularly lumberjacks and other classes of migratory labor.

"I cannot blame Wally," his wife said. "He has been different somehow, since an accident three years ago, near Eureka. His nerves were shattered.

"Wally had studied pharmacy. He thought he was strong enough to use narcotic drugs in just sufficient quantity to keep his nerves steady for his work.

FIGHT FOR RECOVERY.

"But men who pretended to be friends intrigued him into using more and more of the terrible stuff. Finally it broke him. Now he has promised to make the fight for recovery and he is going about it bravely as he goes about everything.

"He is better today. I feel in my heart he will continue to improve, day by day until all the poison has been worked out of his system. Then we will start again.

"But for the man who sold him drugs and who inveigled him into using more than he should I have no mercy. I shall fight them as long as I have strength."

Reid's breakdown several weeks ago followed a long abstinence from narcotics, his wife said.

DRUGS AND WHISKY.

"He had been trying so hard to cure himself," she explained.

"It wasn't only drugs; whisky, I believe, had even more to do with his condition.

"There had been no wild parties at our home for 18 months. In all that time Wally went from home to the studio and then back home. It was really an effort to get him to the few social functions I cared to attend."

Battle on Drugs

Wallace Reid, noted film star, who is fighting to break the shackles of narcotics slavery, and his wife, Dorothy Davenport Reid, who blames alleged friends for keeping him supplied with the dope after he had started on his ruin.

DRIVE BEGINS TO END COAST DRUG TRAFFIC

Los Angeles Police Chief Asks Council for Special Secret Service Fund.

HAYS PROMISES FILM AID

Wallace Reid Reported Better, Actor's Physician Saying He Can Take Nourishment.

By International News Service.

LOS ANGELES, Dec. 19.—Planning a drive against narcotic peddlers, Chief of Police Oaks requested the Police Commission today to recommend to City Council an appropriation of $10,000 for a special secret service fund to investigate the alleged drug ring.

Simultaneously, Will Hays, head of the motion picture industry, now in Los Angeles, issued a statement that the film industry will cooperate in every possible way to check narcotic trafficking.

REID REPORTED BETTER.

Wallace Reid, still unaware that the story of the cause of his illness has been made public, was reported "a little better to-day after a fairly good night," by his attending physicians.

Reid is said to be able to take a little nourishment and to rise from his pillow for a few minutes without fainting.

Mrs. Wallace Reid told to-day of her plans to make her husband's Christmas as cheerful as possible. She said:

"I'll trim a little Christmas tree and set it on the table near his bed."

CALLED HIM "LITTLE BOY."

With a reminiscent light in her eyes she continued:

"Wally has always been just a

DECEMBER 20, 1922

PRESIDENT OF POLAND SLAIN BY ASSASSIN

U. S. SOLUTION ASSURED FOR REPARATIONS

Keen ... To U.S. ... Germ... By Fr...

Dope Kill...

Today

Idea.
...67.
Not Wicked.
...an Trotzky.
...r Brisbane

VOL. CXV...

Reid Fights Dope, Influenza, Pneumonia

Temperature 103, Heart Weak, Dr. Reports

"He May Die at Any Time," Doctor Reports, Citing Low Vitality of Patient.

(Continued from Page O...

eased person—not to be cen... shunned. Rather let us sanely and sympathetically ... to help him, try to restore hi... health.

Hays was giving the case ... "dope stricken" idol of the ... sheet more thought than he ... expression to, but what he di... fit to say, was made with ass... sincerity.

REFUSES BURDEN.

The head of Los Angeles' g... est industry said that it woul... presumptuous of him to inte... himself into a war here upon ... traffickers in narcotics.

Hays continued:

You have federal, State, cou... ty and local authorities to ... that the narcotic laws are obey... Would it not be appearing to ca... a reflection upon their efficien... were we to take it upon ourselv... to try to execute the law?

But I am here always to c... operate, like any good citizen, ... seeing that vice is suppresse... and vicious agencies and persor... kept within bounds.

I cannot fail to overlook th... facts if anything is being done t... undermine the morale and moral... of the people in the industry ... represent. But, logically, I cannot take it upon myself with propriety to try to usurp the functions of the constituted authorities.

DENIES POLICE DUTIES.

Would the head of any great industry personally act as policeman if the people of that industry were being demoralized by or subjected to influences demoralizing to their well being and efficiency?

Shall I act as a narcotic law enforcement officer?

He further continued:

I have had no evidence directly placed before me regarding the activities of narcotic agents in the community. If I have such it will be considered, as I have indicated, as an incident in the inspiring program for a better Hollywood in every way—a better Hollywood, better pictures, better people. We are in a way to realize all these, I firmly believe.

Hays took objection to statements published here yesterday crediting him with belligerent intentions toward dope agencies as a sequel of the Reid case. The further statement that he had formulated a program on inquiry into narcotic conditions here was denied.

"Hays has no 'projected inquiry' into the Reid case, it was stated on his behalf. The statement was made that, beyond his brief and sympathetic statement relative to Reid's condition, Hays had no comment to make regarding the case.

Wallace Reid, movie hero, now struggling in the coils of the dope habit in a Los Angeles sanitarium is not worrying Federal and local narcotic officials a hundredth part so much as is the real and widespread menace of the drug traffic as revealed in the arrest of William Williams with whom Reid is said to have done business as a "customer."

MONDAY, DECEMBER 18, 1922

DEADLY DRUG EXACTED ALL REID OWNED

Wealth, Health, Talent, Then Life Itself Were Handed Over by Star to Fetish Morphine

'FRIENDS' LED HIM ASTRAY

Contracted Habit in New York, When, Suffering from Insomnia, He Took Narcotics

Wealth, health, talent, ... self—

Wallace Reid yesterday paid the fourth installment, life, exacted by morphine, the most treacherous and deadly of masters. Wealth gone, health broken, talent threatened, Wallace Reid tried gamely to rebuild and cancel his debt. But morphine, aided by whiskey,

BEFORE AND AFTER

The idol of millions of movie fans, Wallace Reid, as he appeared before he fell a victim to the drug habit.

"Friends" induced him ... use narcotics after an illne... Conscious of ruin ahead, R... began his come-back fight.

At the summit of a golden career, Wallace Reid, idol of millions of movie fans, saw only happiness ahead with his beautiful family.

Wally was injured in an... dent. "Friends" caused h... take up drugs. He realize... road to ruin and disgrac... just ahead.

Tragic Case ... Start...

STAR'S ASHES STAY IN LAND HE ADMIRED

...idow Hopes His Death Will Aid Others in Battle to Free Themselves of Drug Habi...

...OS ANGELES, Jan. 21.—Wally ...'s ashes will remain in the ...hland amid the palms, and ...ge groves and flowers, which ...ved so well.

...s widow, Mrs. Dorothy Daven... Reid, has so decided.

... urn containing the famous ...n star's ashes may be placed ...iche in beautiful Forest Lawn ...tery, Mrs. Reid said today, al... ...h she intimated that she might ...e to keep them nearer her— ...ps in her own home.

...emorial to Wally Reid's mem... planned by his widow. Al... her plans are not fully ... out, Mrs. Reid said the ...al would be along lines the ...mself would have approved ... will be a testimonial to his ...attle for life.

...S HEARST PAPERS.

...n speaking of her late husband's fight for a return to normal living Mrs. Reid said:

I want to express by heartfelt thanks to William Randolph

WAGING GRIM BATTLE

Wallace Reid, favorite of the films, who has been in the shadow of death six days, and his wife, Dorothy Reid Davenport, who bared to the world her husband's addiction to dope with the vow that she will expose the "false friends" who gave Wally the drugs.

Source of Reid's Dope Supply Probed

NEW YORK, Dec. 17.—(By Universal Service.)—The plight of

Doctor Who Had Reid as Patient Held in Drug Sale

OAKLAND, Cal., Jan. 1.

DR. JOHN S. BARKER, proprietor of a sanitarium for the cure of drug addicts, where Wallace Reid, it is said, was once a patient, was arrested to-day by agents of the State Board of Pharmacy, c... with selling drugs."

Associates of Dr. Barker told how he had said he was to receive $25,000 from Reid if the actor was cured of the habit.

Wallace Reid at Height of Career

AN AMERICAN PAPER FOR THE AMERICAN PEOPLE — AMERICA FIRST

Francisco Examiner

Monarch of the Dailies

REG. U.S. PAT. OFF

The Weather. San Francisco bay region: Friday generally cloudy and unsettled; moderate northerly winds. Mount Tamalpais: Friday generally cloudy and unsettled.

Complete weather report on page 20.

SAN FRANCISCO, FRIDAY, JANUARY 19, 1923—THIRTY PAGES. CC DAILY 5 CENTS, SUNDAY 10 CENTS: DAILY AND SUNDAY PER MONTH, $1.15

"...ALLY" FELL VICTIM TO DRUGS

JANUARY 19, 1923

...e wistful look which ...ged to one of worry when ...ncountered the opposition ... drug-weakened body.

The smile returned again for a while when Wally thought he had won his fight. Again life seemed sweet.

But drugs do not permit "come-backs" and Death claimed Wally yesterday in Los Angeles.

... the sake of his wife and ...ren the famous star steeled ...will to throw the deadly ...e of drugs out of his life.

For a time life seemed sweet again. He thought that he had mastered the dread enemy and was happy at the thought.

Now struggling between life and death in a Los Angeles sanitarium, Wally is making a brave fight, and his admirers hope he will win.

DECEMBER 18, 1922

...ally Reid ...nt for Drug Ring

HALF MILLION LOSS BY SCHOOL BLAZE

...housands Honor Movie Idol Dope Killed

MOURNERS—Thousands crowded little Los Angeles church and filled streets in immediate vicinity (as shown above), at last rites for Wallace Reid, noted film actor who died in fight against drug habit. (International Newsreel.)

FILMDOM MOURNS STAR

Wallace Reid, who succumbed to ravages of narcotic drugs yesterday in Hollywood. Above, as he appeared at height of career; below, left, opening pile of mail from admirers; right, in character makeup.

SEAPLANE CRASH KILLS OFFICER

1,000 DRUG ADDICTS IN DOCTOR'S BOOK

Society Women on List of Barker, Pretended Crusader, Now a Prisoner on Coast.

OAKLAND, Cal., Jan. 2.—A book containing the names of more than 1,000 persons, including society women, as well as scores of known drug addicts, was found to-day and identified as the property of Dr. ... Barker, formerly Wally

WALLY MARTYR, SAYS MOTHER

(Copyright, 1923, by Universal Service.)

NEW YORK, Jan. 18.—"My boy died a martyr to principle. He made up his mind he would conquer drugs or die in the attempt. He is dead, but he is a victor in death."

Mrs. Bertha Westbrook Reid of this city, widowed mother of Wally Reid the moving picture star, who died today in Los Angeles after a futile struggle with the after effects of drug poisoning, tonight thus characterized his passing.

"I pray that his death will accomplish a great purpose and I feel that it will. It will probably accomplish more than volumes of sermons, of warnings, or crusades against this horrible drug evil.

"I think his brave struggle to fight off the effects of the habit was a wonderful thing."

SCREEN IDOL SUCCUMBS TO DRUG CURSE

Death Snaps Final 'Fadeout' as Romantic Hero Courageously Fights to Shake Off Habit

Had Been Reported on Road to Recovery; Faithful Wife at His Bedside When End Comes

By LOUIS WEADOCK,
Staff Correspondent of Universal Service.

LOS ANGELES, Jan. 18.—"Wally" Reid has played his last scene.

After a long, hard fight against odds greater than those that he overcame in the moving pictures in which he starred for eight years, he died in a Hollywood sanitarium this afternoon, his hand in the hand of his wife.

The doctor's certificate says he died from congestion of the lungs, but everybody who knew him knows that the drug habit killed "Wally" Reid. Nobody knows it better than does the young and beautiful wife whose loyal and unselfish devotion to him he tried his best to reward by putting into his struggle to free himself from that habit every bit of his strength and courage.

His strength failed, but his courage was with him to the last.

"Dot, we'll be at it yet," was one of the last things he said.

Dot was his pet name for his wife—Dorothy Davenport Reid, mother of his six-year-old boy Bill, and herself an accomplished actress who gave up her own career in moving pictures, where she had been a high-salaried leading woman, that she might devote herself entirely to him and to their home.

During the forty-eight hours preceding his death she did not leave his room in the Banksia Place Sanitarium. During the last six weeks she had been out of his sight only for a few minutes at a time, because whenever he awoke from his troubled spells of sleep his first words always were "Hello, Dot," and his first gesture was to reach out for her hand.

Until a very few days ago she and Dr. G. S. Herbert, who was his attending physician, were so confident that Wally had won his fight that they agreed to the proposal of Jesse L. Lasky, by whom he was employed, that he begin work in a picture, shooting of which was to begin July 1.

RAVAGED BY DRUGS.

But although he had not touched narcotic drugs for weeks the ravages which their use had made upon his remarkable constitution were so great that when a relapse came early today he had no stamina left with which to pull him through.

Wally was only thirty-one years old and had the body of a trained athlete. In that body burned an intrepid spirit that far surpassed the heroic qualities with which the characters he played were endowed. Yet he had begun too late to fight. By the time he gave himself into the care of the physicians so much damage had been done to his body that not even his dauntless soul could win the battle alone.

There is a certain grim irony in the fact that his death came just

(Continued on Page 3, Co[l. 3])

WALLY REID DRUG WRECK; WIFE VOWS REVENGE

SHE DECLARES WAR TO THE END AS MOVIE STAR FIGHTS FOR LIFE

So-called "Friends" Lured Actor Into Use of Narcotics Following Accident Three Years Ago

HIS STRUGGLE TRAGIC ONE

But Loyal Woman Feels Poison Will Be Driven Out, "and Then We Will Start Again"

Special Dispatch to the N. Y. American.

LOS ANGELES, Dec. 16.—"I will keep no secrets. I will tell all that I know of the drug traffic in Los Angeles and the East. I have pledged my life to the relentless fight against that frightful horror. I will be as merciless with them as they have been with Wally."

Dorothy Davenport Reid, wife of the matinee idol of the films, stood straight and tense and made that promise to-day.

A few blocks from her pretentious home, in a private sanitarium in Hollywood, her famous husband, Wallace Reid, star of countless screen successes, is bravely fighting to throw off the deadly effects of prolonged addiction to narcotic drugs and whiskey. She continued:

"I cannot blame Wally. He has been different, somehow, since an accident three years ago near San Francisco. His nerves were shattered.

"FRIENDS LED HIM ON."

"Wally had studied pharmacy. He thought he was strong enough to use narcotic drugs in just sufficient quantities to keep his nerves steady for his work.

"But men who ... friends misguide ... more and more ... stuff. Finally it ... He has promised ...

AMERICAN PICTORIAL—*A Paper for People Who Think*—FRIDAY, JANUARY 5, 1923 Business Telephone, Columbus 7000 3

Wally Reid Stone Blind for a Week as He Fights Drugs; He's 'Not Bad,' Just a 'Boy Who Made a Mistake,' Says Wife

After Suffering from "Kleig Eyes," a Movie Malady, He Has Stretch of Hard Luck and Finally Becomes a Total Physical Wreck.

[The Pictorial to-day continues the story of the fall of Wallace Reid, film star, as a prey to dope peddlers. The narrative, written by his wife, was begun in the main section of the New York American.]

By MRS. DOROTHY DAVENPORT REID.

Wife of Wallace Reid, Internationally Known Film Star.

(Copyright, 1923, by the Los Angeles Examiner. All Reproduction Rights Reserved.)

I CAME home one night to find the servants fluttering all over the place, and the yellow boy who opened the door was almost white.

"Mistah Reid velly slick man, velly slick," he chattered.

I found Wally unconscious on his bed. One of the boys was working over him. Wally had fainted on the drawing-room floor, and the servants, fearing he was dead, had carried him laboriously upstairs to bed.

When he recovered he had no recollection of the events of the early evening, and as he lay helpless there he grinned gamely at me and said:

"We're winning, mamma; we're winning. We'll lick it yet."

Wally always had wanted a baby girl. Playing in Long Beach one night a tiny curly-haired youngster strayed into my dressing room. Her clothes were a sight. Her hands were black with the grime of the theatre alley, her playground. But her face, beneath her tightly curled hair, was sweet and wistful. I found the old grandfather who cared for her and the next night I took her home—Betty, who is now our own.

"WEEK OF DARKNESS."

I wish you could have seen ... For an hour ... floor with the youngster, and ...

The rest of the story may be briefly told. By the first of September Wally was again abstaining from drugs. It wasn't easy, as I have tried to make you see. It was a terrible struggle against physical agony.

Then in September his "week of darkness" came. For several days he had worked "under the lights," as the studios say. It had been inside work and he had gone through his paces hour after hour with the giant Kleigs smashing their dead-white radiance into his eyes.

One morning I heard him pattering around the bedroom and into the dressing room. Suddenly he gasped—a quick, horrible indrawing of the breath. His voice came in a childish wail:

"Mamma, mamma! Come here. Where is the door?"

WALLY GOES BLIND.

In the space of a heartbeat he had gone blind. The studios call it "Kleig eyes." It is a blackness which follows over-exposure to the glare of the Kleigs. I helped him back into bed that morning, and later he was dressed. He was totally helpless. Oculists could not help him. For one week he was in the dark, seeing nothing, groping his way about the house, his eyes shielded by smoked glasses.

Drawn into that terrible blankness Wally was alone with his thoughts. The agony of his abstinence from drugs abated not one whit. He was like a child, dependent upon me for everything.

"Mamma," he would call, "please don't leave me; don't leave me alone in the dark." I stayed with him constantly. I think he must have gone through hell that week.

Valiantly, with his vision still "fuzzy," he went back to work and finished the picture, seeing very little of the things around him. A room was a blur. He had to be directed at each turn: "Right, Wally; feel that chair?" or "Left, through that door there!" Finally the picture was finished.

A few days' rest at home did not improve his condition. He decided to go into the higher mountains for a week. He intended to shoot and play tennis; he could do neither. He re... But ... heard him say: ...

Fighting a Man's Battle—Wife Sorry for Him, but Not a Bit Ashamed, for Wally Is Not Vicious and Is More to Be Pitied.

"No matter what comes now, mamma, thank God, I've bucked the drugs."

ENTERS SANITARIUM.

His condition worried me. I decided to put him in a sanitarium for two weeks. Apparently he improved. He wanted to "go somewhere," and we went on an eight-day motor trip, making easy jumps. His condition grew worse. We tried every known remedy without effect.

When we returned he decided he wanted a touch of the desert. We went to Palm Springs, an oasis on the edge of the great Mojave wilderness of sand.

He seemed to rest there and enjoy himself. After a week he became discontented and talked constantly about home. So we came back.

In an effort to get him to exercise I engaged a professional boxer and athletic trainer, who came to the house and lived with Wally. But even that failed.

The trainer rigged up a bicycle arrangement and forced Wally to exercise, much against his will. Still the dysentery persisted and Wally grew weaker. Toward the last the trainer carried him in his arms up and down the steps and through the gardens at the house.

MAKING SECOND FIGHT.

I suppose I grew panicky. At any rate I took him to a hospital and the best specialists obtainable poked him and probed him and pierced him with needles in an effort to diagnose his illness. They failed.

The nerve-racking days in the hospital sapped what little strength he had left, so now he is back in the sanitarium making his second magnificent fight with death.

... have ... not ashamed of anything he has ...

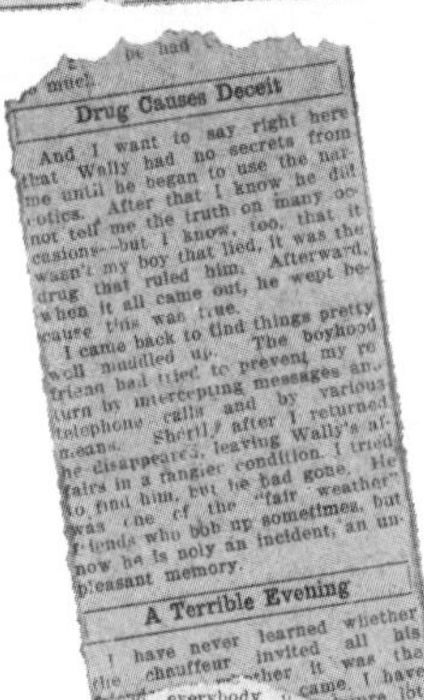

... he had ... much.

Drug Causes Deceit

And I want to say right here that Wally had no secrets from me until he began to use the narcotics. After that I know he did not tell me the truth on many occasions—but I know, too, that it wasn't my boy that lied, it was the drug that ruled him. Afterward, when it all came out, he wept because this was true.

I came back to find things pretty well muddled up. The boyhood friend had tried to prevent my return by intercepting messages and telephone calls and by various means. Shortly after I returned he disappeared, leaving Wally's affairs in a tangier condition. I tried to find him, but he had gone. He was one of the "fair weather" friends who bob up sometimes, but now he is only an incident, an unpleasant memory.

A Terrible Evening

I have never learned whether the chauffeur invited all his ... whether it was the ... everybody ... came. I have ... motives. It was a nightmare ... distrust. And all this time he ... tinued to work.

"Keep Off the Stuff!"

Yet, during the worst of this terrible time, he harped ... friends and acquaintance ... drug evil. "Keep off ... have heard him ... again. He h... himself, had ... that he was ... seemed to ha... might fall in...

He preach... Bill, our boy ... sermons—I an... didn't underst... old personality ... with Bill. Tim... heard him say ...

... or to him, ... He came back ... dentist's on the last day so weak he could hardly walk. Yet the next day he resumed work.

THE SECOND LAPSE.

There was no necessity for it, I suppose. The studio always has been patient with him, and very kind. He was simply so loyal he would work if he could walk. And he did. ... San Diego on location and about that time ... went into vaudeville for a few months.

At that time he had conquered the habit. He was taking nothing at all. He was tortured day and night ... agonies of abstinence, but he was winning his ... The agony of the dental operation must have been responsible for ...

in Perils of Drug Addiction

JANUARY 5.

Conquering of Drug Evil Described — Wallace Reid Doing Come-Back

Mrs. Wallace Reid (Dorothy Davenport) brings to a climax today the fifth and final chapter, begun yesterday, in the story of the tragic career of her actor husband. She has described the early circumstances that drove him to the use of drugs, of their ruinous influence and of his suffering and his struggles to conquer the habit. In conclusion she told of his triumph and despite a temporary relapse, of complete mastery of himself and today of his present battle to come back.

By MRS. DOROTHY D. REID, Wife of Wallace Reid, Internationally Known Film Star.

(Copyright, 1923, by the Los Angeles Examiner. All Reproduction Rights Reserved.)

IN the space of a heartbeat he had gone blind. The stud...

"go somewhere" and we went on ... day motor trip, making ... condition grew ...

REID'S WIDOW URGED TO SPEED DRUG FILM

Letters and Telegrams Pour in Commending Memorial to Screen Actor.

POLICE HEADS WIRE PRAISE

Hope for Men and Women of Future Seen in Promised Crusade.

MRS. "WALLY" REID, widow of the motion picture actor, who has dedicated her life to combating the drug menace.

MRS. REID TELLS PLANS TO FIGHT NARCOTIC EVIL

Widow of Movie Actor Says Treating Addicts as Criminals Aggravates Trouble

"It seems unfair to brand a person tortured by a craving for narcotics a dope fiend. The victims of drugs are not criminals and should not live fugitive lives like hunted things, with the stamp dope fiend attached to them wherever they go. They are sick and need sympathetic understanding of their condition more than anything else, and

Mrs. Reid Will See Drug Film Premiere

MRS. WALLACE REID is coming from California to attend the first local presentation of her anti-drug film, "Human Wreckage," which opens at the Lyric Theatre Wednesday evening, June 27.

AMUSEMENTS

Wally Reid's Mother Begs Mr. Hearst to War on Drug Menace

DEATH OF REID NOT IN VAIN, IS MOTHER'S PLEA

"My Dream Boy Is Asleep," She Says, but His Fight Offers Hope and Help for Others

EVIL MUST BE CRUSHED

Publicity, Such as the Hearst Newspapers Are Giving, Will Conquer Vice, She Declares

By Gene Fowler.

(Copyright, 1923, by the N. Y. American.)

The woman who knew Wallace Reid best pointed the way yesterday to the rescue of young men and women from the curse of the drug habit. Mrs. Bertha Reid, bowed with grief but holding her emotions in leash, stood for many silent minutes before the last photograph that "Wally" sent her—a picture inscribed to "Mother Bertha" from "Cottontop." Then she said:

"My dream boy is asleep. I do not feel that he has sacrificed his life in vain. For, if he won a victory in death rather than lose to the other side, there is hope and help for others.

"In his death there was a martyr ... could be alive today ... do in a few ... many ... years ... was ... man...

TWO pictures of "Wally" Reid idol of a million film fans. To the right he inscribed the lastpicture to his mother: "Mother Bertha—hurry back, dearest. Wally Cottontop." At left, an art study of "Wally" in the role of a crusader in mail armor.

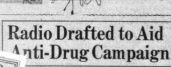

was borne out by his mother, who added:

"Wally was not afraid of death. ... was to falter and ... clean in ...

Radio Drafted to Aid Anti-Drug Campaign

...dio was employed last ... the great campaign of edu... which aims to eradicate the drug evil.

...casting from the Bamberg... on in Newark, Dr. Carlton ... deputy police commissioner ...rge of the Narcotic Bureau, ... the alarming increase in ...ion. He spoke particularly ...dicts, of whom he said there have been many within the ... of his voice.

... Simon mentioned the death ... Wallace Reid, the motion picture star, a victim of the drug habit. He said in part:

"It was with a feeling of deep regret that I read of the passing of a brilliant mind into the great beyond in the death of Wallace Reid. It is a matter of great misfortune that this mind was cut ...

vampire who with lulling wing robs its victim in fearless tranquility.

"The vampire robs his victim only of his healthy, vital blood. Narcotics do more. They not only rob the addict of his vitality, but also of his mentality.

"They do so by enslaving upon the mind and the body a habit, the bonds of which man can only break when they are lightly forged. Often then it is too late. It also produces a weakened resistancy of that mental self-assertiveness which we term the will. How strong the habit has become is only demonstrated by an attempt to break it.

SLAVERY IS COMPLETE.

"The black slave of fifty years ago was held as serf in some in...

SING SING DECLARED MARKET FOR DRUGS

Narcotics More Easily Obtained Than on Broadway, Says Physician.

That narcotic drugs are obtainable in Sing Sing Prison more easily than on Broadway, was the assertion made to Supreme Court Justice John Ford yesterday by Dr. Harold Gilbert, of No. 1215 Grand Concourse, the Bronx.

Dr. Gilbert had been testifying in a suit for annulment in which the wife alleged her husband was a drug addict prior to and since her marriage, when Dr. Gilbert, turning to Justice Ford, remarked:

"Three out of ten persons residing between Twentieth and Fiftieth streets, are drug adicts. This is chiefly because the drug peddlers are scattered so thickly through this section of the city.

"Another deplorable thing in the battle against the drug evil is that it is so easily obtained in prisons. I can take you to Sing Sing and purchase drugs more easily than on Broadway."

MRS. BERTHA WESTBROOK REID, mother of the famous star, posed for this exclusive photo by New York American photographer yesterday. She is shown studying a picture of her dead boy.

(Copyright, 1923, by the New York American.)

JANUARY 20 1923

WALLY'S DEATH SPURS CRUSADE AGAINST DRUG...

Women's Clubs to Join Movement to Eliminate Traffic in "Dope" from Hollywood

MESSAGES TELL OF GR...

Funeral of Film Actor to Be Held This Afternoon ... Elk's Lodge Reading Rit...

LOS ANGELES, Jan. 19.—... deep feeling aroused in all sect... of this State over the prema... death of Wallace Reid, young ... actor, from narcotic drugs, pr...ises to result in a widesp... movement to suppress the ... traffic in Hollywood.

Women's clubs and other so... organizations are expected to ... in the crusade.

The film studio world that k... Reid as a friend and compa... and the film-loving public that ... lighted in Reid's effervescent ...trayal of youth in hero scene ... joined to-day in sorrowing over ... passing. Messages of sympa... poured into the De Longpre ...nue Reid home, where Doro... Davenport, his wife, was in vir... collapse from grief and the st... of the months-long vigil she ... kept with Wally. The messa... came from stars and fans ali... many from Europe.

LAEMMLE REGRETS LOSS.

Carl Laemmle, president of ...versal, with which Wally wo... in the early days, telegraphed:

"Motion pictures are suffer... a great loss."

Theodore Roberts, who had ...peared as Wally's irascible fa... in countless pictures, said:

"This is one of the sadd... things I have ever known. I ha... known Wally since he was t... years old, then a little blo... haired baby just learning to pr...tle and walk. Among a host ... friends I have on the other si... Wally is one of the closest ... best thought of."

Mary Pickford said:

"My heart goes out in sy...pathy to the wife and mother ... Wallace Reid. His death is ... great tragedy, because I know ... would have lived down every m...take he made. He was a cha...ing boy with a great genius."

The funeral will be held to...row afternoon in the First ...

COURT TELLS JURY TO WAR ON 'DOPE'

Simon Says Drug Victims Tempt ...

THREE GIRLS, 3 MEN HELD IN DRUG RAIDS

JUANITA HANSEN, PICTURE ACTRESS—$1,000 a week motion picture [...]ing woman before she first took narcotic drugs. Greater success was just [...]. She had her own big bank account [and] lived in self earned luxury.

JUANITA HANSEN, DRUG VICTIM—To-day a penniless victim of drugs, forced by circumstances to leave lodging after lodging. Now making a bitter struggle to get a new chance in life. She says she is cured.

Photo © by New York American

[...] The doctor I had brought with me from New York talked with the doctor in charge of the sanitarium for perhaps an hour. He then came upstairs to see me. I had brought the doctor with me from New York because I had confidence in him. He had agreed to stay with me at least three or four days, until I really was well on the way to my hoped-for cure.

Cure Cost $2,500.

This hope was blasted. After his talk with the doctor down stairs, he came up to tell me that he had decided to go back to New York, that Dr. X would have sole charge. When I asked why, he answered:

"I feel Dr. X is as capable as I in handling your case."

To my mind, neither of them knew very much about narcotic cases. Yet the "cure" was to cost $2,500.

I remained three weeks in this sanitarium. The first week I [...] all the time. The sec[...]

I went to one of the finest doctors on Fifth avenue. Oh, yes, he would be very glad to help me. Of course I would have to have his nurse, and the fee would be a thousand dollars.

Quits Doctors

After calling on that doctor a few times, I discovered how little he knew. Most doctors know very little of narcotics. This is an age of specialists in the medical profession as elsewhere. I don't think that doctors ought to be permitted, unless they have a special license from the State, to treat narcotic cases.

The only doctor that I have ever met who really seemed to cure addiction is in Oakland, California, and he is not a doctor of [...]

Quarterly. I had my Bible and my textbook. He had told me to read my lesson and talked to me kindly. I was not afraid.

Torture of Denial

I got through the first day all right. I slept quite well the first night. However, the second day is written in my memory book so strongly I shall never forget the torture, the agony, the horrible nerve strain.

Again it seemed to me I had just reached the end of things.

When would this thing stop? Why should I live? I wanted to die. I shouted. I screamed. The treatment was not human.

I wanted to arouse the world. [...] to get [...] dealer the price had been $80 a[n] ounce. And this was only a litt[le] over $50.

Dope at Last.

I handed the young man $10, tell[ing] him to get me [...]

[...] of me [...] would [...] he re[...] He [...] gone [...]

Changed Her Poison

Then I went to San Franc[isco] [...] remained only one day. Jus[t] enough to look up Mr. P[...] procure an ounce of morphine [...] find the name of anothe[r] [...] Springs. During my jou[rney] [...] had formed another plan [...] proceeded to carry out.

I destroyed every identi[fication] mark on my clothing a[nd] [...]gage and set out for anot[her] [...] Springs near Chico, Cal.

I took another name. A[...] let alone.

Now to carry out the r[est of my] plan!

I had morphine, and [...] two weeks I was taking [...] a day. But I was slee[ping] every night, eating thre[e meals a] day, exercising, taking [...] And the hot baths helped me [...] gain a great deal in weight.

right there on the street, for the asking, my first "bindle" of heroin. The devil had set his trap, and I played into his hands.

Begins to Sniff

Having located the man, who [a]fterwards, I learned, was a ped[...]dler, from whom I could purchase the white powder, and having ob[tained] his telephone number and address, my double work, whic[h] consumed sixteen hours a day, wa[s] no longer an impossible task.

I found that with a little sniff [...] this heroin in the morning, I wa[s] able [...]

I have often wondered if it [was] weakness or cowardice, whethe[r] sin or virtue to want to work, w[...] work. That is all I wanted to [...] There was no thought of pleas[ure]. There was hardly time to sleep.

Becomes Addict

It was probably a month la[ter] that I realized and discovered [...] myself that this was surely ha[bit] forming.

What a terrible awakening!

You will never know wha[t a] shock this was to me. I discov[ered] [...]

been an addict. The police [...] was taking drugs at the time I [was] arrested. I deny it.

Do not feel I am vindictive o[ver] my arrest. Remember, I wish o[nly] to help, and my motive is only [to] do good.

Prevention Better Than Cure

First let us begin at the beginning of things, page one of my life book. Now turn over a few chapters to the chapter marked "To-day." I am pronounced cured of narcotic addiction. I now weigh 125 pounds, which is my normal [...]

Cocaine has a tendency t[o keep] one awake, in fact, it does [keep] one awake. It is impossib[le to] sleep while under its influ[ence]. Therefore, at night, when [the] time for me to retire, I had t[o in]crease the amount of morphin[e to] offset the cocaine I had take[n during the] day.

In Dealer's Web

Cocaine itself is the most [de]structive of all narcotics. [...] because it is so [...]

Takes the Needle

About this time, when I was m[aking] a purchase one day from [the] "dealer," I met a young woman w[ho] told me about a fur. So I went [to] her apartment to look at it. [Of] course, having met her at the de[aler]'s, I knew that she was one of t[he] fraternity. I purchased the [...] coat.

Then in the course of the ensu[ing] conversation she asked me wha[t I] had been taking. I told her hero[in] and that I sniffed it through [the] nostrils. Then she told me ab[out] some NEW PLAYTHINGS that [be]longed to the devil.

She told me there was only [one] way to take narcotics, and that [was] hypodermically. She [...]

This never worried me. Inst[inct]ively I felt that I ought not t[o] figure my arms with the need[le] therefore took the shot in m[y] [...]

An Ounce at $80.

Now to the dealer, to s[ee about] morphine! I bought an [ounce] which cost me $80. That [...] lasted me about a mont[h] my supply was getting lo[w] [...] the peddler again, to fin[d] my chagrin, that he ha[d been ar]rested. I did not know [...] peddler in the city of [...] at this time. But I mus[t] [...] The quantity that [...] the first ounce last[ed] [...]

I told him I wanted morphine.

$80 an Ounce

He quoted me a price of $80 an ounce which was quite agreeable.

This "reasonable price," however, didn't last long when he discovered his new customer was Juanita Hansen, the picture star. A few weeks later, when I went back to get the second ounce, I heard the self-same tale I had heard from peddlers before. His new shipment had not arrived and he had promised the only ounce he had left to someone else for $95. I knew no other place to buy, so I bid $100 and got it.

One day while visiting the girl from California, who at that time had a gorgeous apartment, I told her how hard I was working. I told her I had increased the amount of morphine, but it seemed to have lost its charm.

In the morning I was so tired it required all my strength to dress myself for the studio, and it was with great effort that I managed to get through my strenuous work.

Turns to Cocaine

Did she know anything that could help me? Oh, yes! She would give me something then and there. It was COCAINE.

[...] effect was very pleasant. [...]

It seems to be a common belief that when taking narcotics you have visions or dreams. That is absurd. It is merely a pleasant sensation. You feel at peace with the world.

Drugs Easily Obtained

Little did I dream that this was the first step, a false step, which would cause me years of heartaches and mental anguish. Neither at this party nor at any of the numerous parties that followed was I ever warned that this was habit-forming. I was only told to beware of an overdose, as it might [k]ill me.

"Cure" Destroyed, Narcotics Recapture Girl in Five-Day Trip to Coast

[TH]URSDAY, MARCH 29, 1923

[JU]ANITA HANSEN TELLS OF FIGHT WITH DRUG EVIL

[Fil]m Actress in Own Story [T]ells How She Fell from Stardom [t]o State of Abject Poverty

TRYING TO COME BACK

[Sa]ys She Is Cured of Habit [a]nd Would Have Others [P]rofit by Her Downfall

Dragged into the gutter by [na]rcotic drugs!

Here is one of the most [dr]amatic of all the drug ruina[tion] stories yet told. It is the [sto]ry of a girl, told by herself. [It] is the story of Juanita Han[sen], who was but yesterday a [mo]tion picture star with a con[tra]ct that paid her $1,000 a [we]ek and an interest in her pic[tur]es.

She was on the high road to [tre]mendous success. To-day, [wh]en she might be making a [sal]ary at least equivalent to [th]at of the President of the [Un]ited States, she is a penniless [vi]ctim of the narcotic drug evil.

She is making a fight to get [a] chance to "come back." She [wi]ll tell you in this series of [ar]ticles how easy the downfall [w]as and how bitterly she has [pa]id for her weakness.

Says She Is Cured

Miss Hansen says she has at last [be]en pronounced cured. The New [Yo]rk American is not in a position [to] state if she is really cured or [not]. She herself says only death [ca]n prove that point. For the pur[pos]es of her revelations, it is not [ma]terial whether there has been a [cu]re or not.

This drug victim, the one-time [pi]cture star, is highly intelligent. [Sh]e is illustrative of the fact that [n]arcotic drugs respect no persons [in] their ruinous spread throughout [th]e land.

Miss Hansen, having fallen from [on]e of the high rungs of the ladder [of] success down to the bottom, has [th]ought deeply and seriously about [th]e drug evil, and she has acquired [a] philosophy about it that will do a [lo]t of good to the public in general.

She thinks, for instance, that [ig]norance of the power of such [dr]ugs is one reason so many per[so]ns innocently are blighted by [th]eir spell. She says that if at [th]e start she had some knowledge [ab]out narcotics she probably would [n]ever have taken her first fatal [s]niff."

"Teach the young all about drugs and warn them," she cautions.

Once Under Arrest

Juanita Hansen reached the point where she was arrested for having drugs in her possession. The police say she was guilty. She maintains she was innocent of this particular charge. The magistrate released her saying he did not like the way the evidence was gotten. But this, too, is immaterial.

The point is that here is the story of narcotic drugs from the lips of a victim who has paid a tremendous price. She has written a series of fifteen articles exclusively for The New York American.

In these articles she tells even how she went alone, armed with a gun, into dangerous parts of the city to get her narcotics during the period wherein she admits she was so much a slave that she took "all the narcotics a human being could take and still live."

When you have read this amazing story, with its thrilling incidents, its amazing frankness and its surprising philosophy, you will want to take a hand in stamping out the Great Drug Evil.

Here is Miss Hansen's own story:

By JUANITA HANSEN.

Copyright, 1923, by the N. Y. American.

For two and a half years I was addicted to the use of narcotic drugs. Recently I took treatment at Oakland Sanitarium prescribed by Dr. John Barker. I was discharged as cured.

I am free from the habit that held me a slave, and I thank God for my liberation from the terror of life-long addiction to which I seemed to be doomed.

There is no question about my cure. What may happen in the future I cannot foretell, but I believe I possess the power of will necessary to combat any desire to return to that most dreadful condition of slavery.

I feel that my terrible experience qualifies me to speak with authority on the subject of drug addiction, and the purpose of these articles, which I have undertaken to write for the readers of the New York American, is to sound a solemn warning to the youth of the nation, to light the road ahead and reveal the many pitfalls; to point the way to a cure for other addicts, and to give them courage to attempt to break the shackles of habit; and most of all, to urge the Government to bestir itself to reach out its powerful arms and gather in the smugglers and peddlers of narcotic drugs, and kill this evil at its source.

These articles will address also that great body of God-fearing and home-loving families who are ignorant of the dangers that beset them; whose children may, innocently as I, myself, become enmeshed in the toils of this chain, Dope.

Government records show that the number of addicts has increased enormously in the last two years. The chain that binds, holds and destroys so many human beings is growing alarmingly.

JUANITA HANSEN HUNTED DRUGS WITH A PISTOL

Film Actress In Desperation Invaded East Side Haunts on Mission in Taxicabs

HAD REVOLVER IN GLOVE

Determined to Get Narcotics and Also to Escape Harm, She Took Life in Her Hand

ACTRESS TELLS OF PURCHASING HER FIRST DOPE

Long Siege of Illness and Then Hour After Hour of Hard Work Complete Ruin

AT LAST AN AWAKENING

Met Heroin Peddler by Chance and Innocence and Devil Connived to Bring Downfall

Once started, her downfall was rapid! Juanita Hansen, the thousand dollar a week motion picture girl who landed in a cell charged with drug addiction, continues the revelations of her life as a drug addict.

To-day, in her second story, she tells how she was deceived into believing narcotic drugs the secret of great physical and mental strength. Heroin was tightening its clutches on her until she was actually unable to work without it.

She lays it all to her ignorance of the great danger of narcotic drugs. Had she known, had she been told, she says, the thing which she considered her salvation could never have proved to be her destroyer.

How she made her first actual purchase from a peddler is told herein.

Following is Juanita Hansen's own sto[ry], rapidly developing into a compelling drama of real life:

ARTICLE NO. 2.

By JUANITA HANSEN.

Copyrighted by N. Y. American.

I had played with the devil's toys. I told you of this in my article of yesterday. The devil himself had set out to do his work.

Six months had elapsed, probably, since I had seen any of the people who were present at the parties of the previous year. I had no desire, or perhaps I should say craving, for any of this white powder called heroin, until—

I was one of the first to be stricken with the flu in California. This was in the month of October, 1918. In January the following year I had the first attack of sleeping sickness, the after effects of the flu. This was the first case to go on record.

PHYSICIAN GAVE JUANITA ONLY MONTH TO LIVE

Actress Tells How She Defied Death Sentence of Doctor and Finished Her Picture

GREW WEAKER EACH DAY

Relates How She Finaly Got Through Work and of Going Up-State to Begin Cure

GIRL TAUGHT FILM ACTRESS TO USE NEEDLE

Found First Shot Wonderful, Writes Miss Juanita Hansen, but It Only Hastened Pain

WARNS OF ALL DOCTORS

Declares Few of Them Know How to Treat Dope Addicts; Tells of Visit to New York

In this, her third article, Juanita Hansen, the former motion picture girl, who, under the scourge of narcotic drugs dropped from a thousand dollar a week life of luxury into a New York police station cell, tells how she developed from a "sniffer" of cocaine into a "needle" addict.

Miss Hansen, who says that over $6?,000 of hard-earned motion picture salary went through her fingers like water, gives the details of how her first hypodermic "shot" seemed to give her a great sense of satisfaction, while in reality it was sending her further on the path to ruin.

In this article, she takes up the subject of "dope" doctors and says that in general they do no good.

Following is Miss Hansen's own story:

THIRD INSTALMENT.

Copyright 1923, by New York American.

By JUANITA HANSEN.

The length of time it takes to become an addict is a subject greatly discussed to-day. DeQuincy, author of "Confession of An Opium Eater," says "In less than one hundred and twenty days no habit of opium-eating could be formed."

DeQuincy, like myself, had at one time been bound to the chain of narcotics, and his cure was considered a miracle. He referred only to opium.

I cannot say that I agree that it takes four months to form other narcotic habits. Of course I think that conditions alter every case.

In two and a half months I became an addict. It would have been easy to break this habit had I not been under contract, and could have been free from work, for just a few days, for treatment. However, to-day I could acquire the habit anew in less than a week.

Warns All Addicts

CLUBMAN KIN OF CRIMINALS IN DOPE WORLD

Juanita Hansen Tells of Finding All Sorts and Conditions in Home of a Drug Peddler

HEARD ROBBERIES PLOTTED

Man Who Supplied Actress Attempted to Blackmail Her When She Ceased Her Buying

JUANITA USED BLUFF TO ROUT A BLACKMAILER

Drug Peddler Made Threat of Exposure by Telephone, but Actress Defied Demands

WARNED HIM OF PRISON

Tells of Appeal to Doctor and His Promise to Supply Her with Needed Cocaine

How a narcotic drug peddler turned blackmailer and attempted to wring money from her by demands delivered by telephone is told by Juanita Hansen, film actress, in this eighth section of her candid tale of her slavery to cocaine and morphine.

Though quaking with fear, she "called his bluff" and warned him she would put him in prison—where he eventually went.

Miss Hansen tells, also, of her appeals to physicians for help to shake off the deadly coils of the drug monster that held her in slavery.

ARTICLE NO. 8.

By JUANITA HANSEN.

Copyright by New York American.

BLACKMAIL!

Now, I was to find out the full meaning of the word blackmail. Experience was my bitter teacher.

A few days after my precipitate break with the grasping peddler—my only dope "connection" in New York—Uncle Sam's mail brought a letter to my apartment. I did not recognize the scrawling handwriting.

I opened it. As I remember, it read (and I am rendering it grammatical):

"I cannot understand why you have not been to see me. I am holding that candy for you? See (C) what I mean?" (Note—"C," of course, stood for cocaine.)

The note continued:

"I expect to hear from you."

This curious communication was signed "T."

Then a Veiled Hint.

JUANITA TELLS OF COWARDICE FACING MOTHER

Met at Station by Loving Parent, Strives Unsuccessfully to Hide Addiction

HELPED BACK TO HEALTH

Medicine Ignored, She Fights with Will and Faith as Her Only Weapons, and Wins Out

Soon after her fight for a cure, Juanita Hansen, the film actress, was tempted and again became a slave to narcotic drugs, as she tells in this twelfth chapter of her story.

Fortified with cocaine, she went home to California to face her mother she strove to hide her se[...]

FILM ACTRESS ENMESHED BY DRUG SPIDER

Juanita Hansen Reveals How Peddler, Preying on Craving, Got $150 an Oz. for Cocaine

IT LASTED HER A WEEK

This Narcotic Worst of A[ll] "Devil's Playthings," Making Sleep Impossible, She Says

HARD WORK PUT MISS HANSEN IN HANDS OF DRUG

After Yielding to Urge in Winnipeg, Actress Quickly Lost Ground She Had Won

"PEDDLER IN EVERY TOWN"

No Trouble Experienced in Buying Dope in Any of 25 Cities She Visited on Tour

Only a brief period of sunshine, happiness and freedom from the slavery of narcotics was vouchsafed to Juanita Hansen after her seeming cure in California.

In this twelfth instalment of her absorbing tale of the struggles of a drug addict, the film actress tells how she was tempted and again fell. This time it was sheer weariness from a steady grind of hard work in vaudeville that drove her into the spider's web. Once more she searched for drug peddlers and found them in twenty-five cities.

ARTICLE NO. 12.

By JUANITA HANSEN.

Copyright 1923 by N. Y. American

To play in the sunshine!

I was free!

I felt so well fortified, so strong. I thought I had thwarted the Devil. But I was mistaken. My antagonist was still stronger than I. He set about to resume his work. He caught me asleep one day. He caught me off my guard. How he worked his fiendish will I will narrate presently.

In the meanwhile, I was happy. I played and laughed and enjoyed the sunshine, free from narcotics. My one loyal playmate in these happy hours was a little pinto pony, "Freckles."

Dear Freckles! Long, intimate rides over the mountain roads about Los Angeles. Our daily routine in the quest of permanent health: eight miles on the Melrose dirt road, along the ridge of Hollywood Mountain, twenty-five miles a day, Freckles and I.

We were free of the "Devil's Toys." We were free! Free! Freckles was my one and only playmate and he believed in me.

Hard Work in Varieties.

JUANITA WINS LONG STRUGGLE AGAINST DRUGS

Specialist Tells Film Actress That Her Own Strong Will Power Effected the Cure

MOTHER IS OVERJOYED

Parent Read Happy Truth in Her Daughter's Eye on Surprise Visit to Los Angeles

FILM ACTRESS HAS PLAN FOR DRUG CONTROL

Juanita Hansen, Who Won Long Fight Against Dope Habit, Seeks U. S. Aid for Addicted

URGES SYMPATHETIC LAW

Asserts New York Narcotic Commissioner Hurt Her by Ill Advised Summary Action

In this, the last article of her series, Miss Juanita Hansen tells of her final cure from the drug habit. And being cured, after years of slavery to drugs, she suggests a programme for the benefit of other unfortunates who are still in the thrall of drugs and who are yet to be there. She declares that the United States Government should take over the cure of drug cases, conscript specialists, cure the addicts and then limit the source of supply.

ARTICLE NO. 15.

By JUANITA HANSEN.

Copyright, 1923, by the N. Y. American.

Cured!

Seven months had passed. All desire for narcotics had left me. Why shouldn't I believe that I was cured?

I was being rewarded at last. My contracts, as I told you in a previous article, were nearly arranged. How happy I was. My struggle of two years was over!

And then—

Fate, perhaps, played her part. Again the world turned upside down. For a narcotic commissioner in New York didn't believe I was cured. Why?

It is my one desire to encourage all narcotic addicts, urge them to give up this curse. For such it is. And to assure them there is a reward. I expect the assistance though of all narcotic boards. They must help me—not destroy the work I am trying to do.

My arrest nearly broke my heart. It almost crushed everything I believed was good. Would it not have been a little more human, a little more Samaritan-like, to have come to me, and quietly asked:

Law Did Not Help Me.

"I am not quite sure of you, Miss Hansen. I have read of your 'cure.' But I w[...] sure. Will you com[e to my of]fice for an examination before a medical board?"

THURSDAY, APRIL 12, 1923

JUANITA HANSEN, NOTED BEAUTY, DRUG PRISONER

YOUNG ACTRESS SEIZED IN RAID IN APARTMENT

Accused of Possession of Narcotics, She Denies Charge and Friend Indorses Story

ONCE VICTIM OF HABIT

Pretty Blonde Has Conquered Weakness and Arrest Now Is an Injustice, Is Her Plea

Juanita Hansen, nationally known film actress, was charged yesterday in West Side Court with possession of morphine. She was released in $300 bail for a hearing to-morrow.

Miss [illegible]nsen passed Wednesday nigh[illegible] Thirtieth street police [illegible] her arrest by Detecti[illegible] and O'Brien of Speci[illegible] Commissioner Carleton [illegible]on.

She was [illegible]stody in the apartment [illegible]ett, an actress, of No. 29[illegible] first street.

The detectives told [illegible] found a small box whi[illegible]lieved to contain morphi[illegible] morphine needle.

ACTRESS DENIES CHARGE.

Miss Hansen, a beautiful blonde of twenty-six, indignantly denied all knowledge of the paraphernalia seized. Her companion, also a striking type, was equally insistent in denying any knowledge of the materials.

Both declared that Miss Hansen is not an addict. Miss Barnett said:

"Juanita has been stopping with me as my guest. The detectives who came to the apartment recently helped me re-

SOCIETY DOPE PARTY BARED IN SEIZURE

Drug Seller, on Way to Supply Guests of Broker's Wife on [illegible] Hill, Nabbed at Door

[illegible]man, cultured and re[illegible] the best social circle[illegible]ess at a society "dope[illegible]er suite at the fashion[illegible] Court apartments on [illegible]was revealed yesterday [illegible] arrest of Fred Robinso[illegible]tic peddler.

[illegible]inson was o[illegible] the

IN MESHES OF DOPE NET

JANUARY 12, 1923

Juanita Hansen, moving picture actress of Hollywood, whom police are holding following a narcotics raid on a New York apartment [illegible]erday. [illegible] questi[illegible] as to the activities of "Dr." Scott Barker's sanitarium by local authorities.

SCANTILY CLA[D] GIRL HELD A[S] DOPE PEDDLE[R]

Juanita Hansen, Garbed [in] Oriental Sleeping Robes, Nabbed in Gotham Apartme[nt]

Arrested in a dope raid which Ne[w] York police conducted in that c[ity] last Wednesday night, Juanita Ha[n]sen, motion picture actress of Ho[l]lywood, spent the night in a Gotha[m] jail on a charge of illegally posses[s]ing narcotics.

She was booked under the na[me] of "Jane Hausen."

The film actress was located in [a] West Eighty-first street apartme[nt] garbed in an Oriental sleeping ro[be] following a search of se eral wee[ks]. When arraigned yester lay Mi[ss] Hansen, according to telegraphic a[d]vices, protested that she was t[he] victim of a police frame-up and d[e]clared that the arrest and ensui[ng] publicity would ruin her career.

She was committed to prison [in] default of bail but later when t[he] amount was reduced to $300, whi[ch] was furnished by a surety compan[y] she was released and her hearing s[et] for Saturday.

NAME ON LIST.

The actress' name became identi[fied] with the drug traffic so[me] weeks ago when Wallace Reid's a[d]diction and illness became known [to] the public. Her name was found [on] a drug peddler's list along with th[at] of Reid's who is now struggling [to] break from the coils of the habit [in] a Los Angeles sanitarium.

Louis Zeh, secretary of the Cali[for]nia State Board of Pharmac[y], when informed yesterday of her a[r]rest said that members of the boa[rd] had been of the opinion that Juani[ta] Hansen was in New York for th[e] purpose of obtaining narcotics a[nd] smuggling them to her Hollywo[od] friends. "Our agents have be[en] watching Miss Hansen's movemen[ts] for a long time," Zeh said, "she h[as] been under suspicion for years."

TO BE QUESTIONED.

The name of Miss Hansen wa[s] also found on the books of "Dr." Charles B. Blessing who conducte[d] the Barker Sanitarium in Los An[geles] and who now faces charg[es] with "Dr." John Scott Barker [of O]akland—founder of the "Barke[r] [cure] for drug addiction—for viola[tion of] [th]e Federal narcotic act.

[illegible] from New York [illegible] [after]noon quoting Dr. H. [illegible] San Francisco and pre[illegible] California State Pha[rmacy] [illegible]s the authority, d[e]cla[illegible]ita Hansen is to [be] questi[oned by poli]ce regarding th[e] activiti[es of Dr. J]ohn Scott Bark[er] of his O[akland sani]tarium, with [a] view of [illegible]idence th[at] could be use[d illegible] of Bark[er] before the fe[illegible]re.

According to [illegible] Mi[ss] Hansen may be a[illegible]on light upon alleged "[illegible] parties that are rep[illegible] been held at the Barker [illegible] upon which the Board of [Phar]mac[y] agents have for some mon[ths] be[en] endeavoring to collect authentic in[formation].

ANOTHER FILM STAR REVEALED AS DRUG ADDICT

Juanita Hansen Cured, According to Records, Seized in Oakland Sanitarium

REID THERE TWO WEEKS

Names of 100 Victims of Narcotics in California Reported in Lists Taken by Police

Special to New York American.

LOS ANGELES, Cal., Jan 3.—Another star of the films has fought the battle that faces the narcotic addict.

She is Juanita Hansen.

According to her family she has won the fight.

Seizure of records at the Barker sanitarium, 145 North Gates street, to-day revealed that Miss Hansen had been a patient last Summer at an establishment in Oakland, and had taken treatment for the use of narcotics. Dr. John Scott Barker, proprietor of the Oakland sanitarium, was arrested Monday charged with violation of the Harrison narcotic act, and is in jail in San Francisco.

ADDICTS' NAMES FOUND.

The local sanitarium is operated by Dr. Charles Blessing, who asserts that Dr. Barker has nothing to do with the Los Angeles Hospital. Dr. Blessing said he calls his place the Barker sanitarium because he uses the Barker system. Correspondence between the two men is said to indicate a close business association.

Two large cabinet drawers containing the records of the local sanitarium were seized by police, and it is said the names of more than one hundred narcotic addicts in southern and northern California were found. Among the patients was Wallace Reid, who was admitted to the sanitarium October 19 and remained two weeks.

CURED, SAYS FATHER.

According to the police, the establishment was recommended to Reid by Miss Hansen after her return from Oakland, where it is said she was cured of her habit.

Stephen Craig, her stepfather, at his residence, No. 1167 North Berendo street, last night said:

"Juanita is in New York now, although I know very little about the matter, it is true that she was a user of narcotics and took a cure in Oakland. She is in the best of health now. I had a telegram from her yesterday. She told me she weighs 145 pounds and is getting along splendidly. She said she has had a flattering offer to go back into the films and intends to sign a contract in the near future. It was when Juanita became very ill last summer that we first learned she had become addicted to morphine and we were very happy when she succeeded in conquering this insidious habit."

CURED OF DRUGS

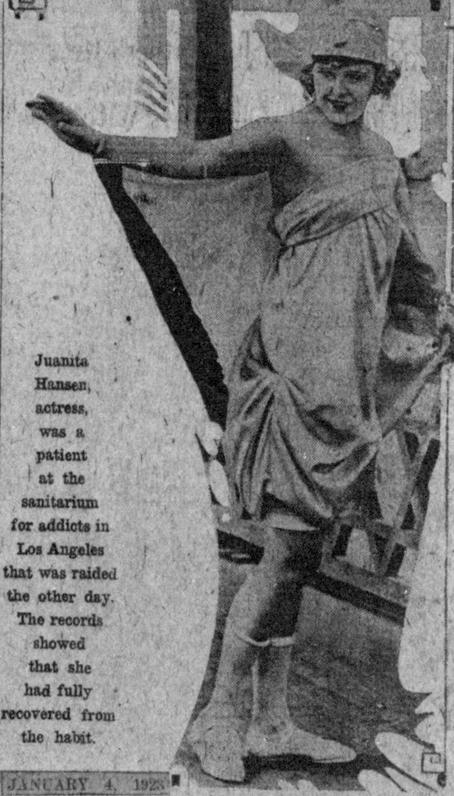

Juanita Hansen, actress, was a patient at the sanitarium for addicts in Los Angeles that was raided the other day. The records showed that she had fully recovered from the habit.

JANUARY 4, 1923

U. S. TO BLOCK DRUG SHIPMENTS ABROAD

World's Ports Will Be Scene of American Agents' Fight to Halt Smuggling.

By Universal Service.

WASHINGTON, Jan. 3.—A first line of defense against the drug smuggling evil is being established by the United States in the ports of the world, it was learned to-day.

Acting under the direction of the Narcotics Control Board and the Customs Service, agents are to be located at points from which drugs are shipped and either prevent their shipment or guarantee that the shipments will be seized upon arrival at an American port.

This step is made possibe, officials say, under the operation of the Jones-Miller act, a measure that provides for the Drug Control Board andwhich was passed at the instance of the Hearst newspapers.

4,533 Violators of Anti-Drug Law Get 4,352 Years

By Universal Service.

WASHINGTON, Jan. 3.

DRUG addicts and peddlers convicted in 1922 must pay for their folly with 4,352 years of penal servitude, the Internal Revenue Bureau announced to-day.

During the year, 4,533 persons were sentenced for violations of the Anti-Narcotic act, the sentences ranging as high as ten years and as low as a few months.

The shorter sentences are for addicts who have been confined while they undergo treatment for a cure.

TYPHOID GRIPS 20 IN QUEENS VILLAGE

Million Moose Pledge Aid on Dope Crusade

CHICAGO, Jan. 11.—Approved by Secretary of Labor Davis, national chief, the Loyal Order of Moose Lodge, with about 1,000,000 members, has pledged itself to aid in a nation-wide campaign against smuggling and illegal traffic of drugs, it was announced today.

LOIS WEBER'S [illegible] BARED

7 NABBED IN NARCOTIC RAID

Four women and three men were arrested yesterday in a raid on a rooming house at 1307 Octavia street, which has been used as headquarters for narcotic addicts according to the police.

Mrs. Louise Barker, proprietress of the house, was held in jail for sentence today. Police Judge Daniel S. O'Brien said he would send her to prison for ninety days for violating the State poison act.

Patrolmen W. Maguire and Con Brosman, who made the arrests, claim that Mrs. Barker has been peddling narcotics while dressed in masculine attire.

Her husband, known as Charles Aubrey, alias Nichols, was arrested last week as a suspected dope peddler and will appear for his preliminary hearing in police court this morning.

Tony Ryne, a[illegible] alleged peddler, was tak[illegible]ter-

Film Star Jailed On 'Dope' Charge

NEW YORK, Jan. 11.—Arrested in a West Eighty-first-street apartment, where detectives found her garbed in an Oriental sleeping robe, Juanita Hansen, motion picture star, spent last night in a police cell on a charge of illegally possessing narcotics, it was disclosed today.

Miss Hansen when arraigned today protested she was a victim of a police "frameup." She declared the arrest would "ruin my career." The court held her in $500 bail for examination Saturday.

Detectives had been looking for Miss Hansen for several weeks since her name was found on a drug peddler's list along with that of Wallace Reid, movie star, who is

JANUARY 12, 1923

now recovering in California from illness that followed a breakdown caused by his fight to break the drug habit.

Miss Hansen was committed to prison in default of bail, but later the amount was reduced to $300, which was furnished by a surety company, and she was released.

Juanita Hansen has been reputed to be a narcotic addict in San Francisco and the bay region for several months. It is said that on several occasions she entered sanatoriums here and came out apparently cured, only to take up the habit again in a few weeks. Her name was listed on the books of the Barker sanatorium in Oakland, which recently was raided.

Louis Zeh, secretary of the California State Board of Pharmacy, said yesterday his officers had been watching Miss Hansen for some time, knowing she was a user of narcotics.

Actress Passes Night in Prison

Juanita Hanson, taken in police net and charged with being in possession of narcotics.

Juanita Hansen Tells of Victory Over Narcotic Habit

JUANITA HANSEN, motion picture actress, photographed in court yesterday, just before a charge of having narcotics in her possession, was dismissed by Magistrate McQuade.

JUANITA HANSEN FREED IN COURT OF DRUG CHARGE

Magistrate Abruptly Closes Case Against Actress, Not Even Hearing Her Defense

HER ARREST DESCRIBED

Detective Says He Surprised Her with Cocaine and That She Pleaded for Release

Charges of illegal possession of narcotics against Miss Juanita Hansen, motion picture actress, were dismissed in the West Side Court yesterday by Magistrate McQuade.

Miss Hansen was arrested on January 11 in the apartment of Mrs. Ruth Barnett by Detectives Cotter and O'Brien, of the Police Narcotic Squad. The detectives alleged they found her in possession of a hypodermic needle and cocaine.

Dismissal of the charges was abrupt and without the introduction of any defense.

SPEEDILY DISMISSED.

Immediately following the completion of the prosecution by Assistant District Attorney Auleta, counsel for Miss Hansen, Joseph A. Rosenback, said:

"I move, your Honor, that the charges be dismissed because of the manner in which the arrest was made and because the sanctity"——

The Magistrate said:

"Both charges dismissed."

Detective Cotter was the first witness called. He said:

"On the night of January 11, about 12:10, I went to the apartment of Mrs. Barnett, at No. 29 West Eighty-first street. I went to the bathroom and while there heard a spoon drop.

DESCRIBES ARREST.

"The door leading to the adjoining sleeping apartment was slightly ajar. I saw Miss Hansen in there with a hypodermic needle in her hand. I rushed into the room and grabbed her right wrist. With her left hand, she attempted to destroy a pill box containing white powder, which was standing on a dresser.

"This powder has since been analyzed by a city chemist as cocaine.

"The spoon was still hot and on the end of the hypodermic needle, were a few small drops of the solution which had been cooked in the spoon."

Mr. Rosenback then cross-examined the detective. Cotter said he had been to the apartment of Mrs. Barnett several times before and that she supplied information to the police. He denied she was a "stool pigeon."

HANSEN GIRL'S RELEASE STIRS DRUG SCANDAL

JANUARY 18, 1923

MARCH 9, 1924

THE GIRL WHO CAME BACK

These two photographs of Juanita Hansen show the change that was brought about in her victory over the drug habit. The picture at the right shows her as she appeared before taking the cure.

FORMER STAR NOW AIDS IN FIGHTING EVIL

Actress Arrives Here to Give Story of Her Successful Battle Against Use of Drugs

Erstwhile Motion Picture Star, Once Physical Wreck, Gets Back Health; Takes 3 Cures

Juanita Hansen, the "girl who came back," is in San Francisco to tell her story of her fight and victory over the drug habit—to warn the ignorant—to give the authorities the benefit of her experience and observation in handling "cures"—a subject which she has studied in every great city in the United States.

During her week's stay here she will lecture on the drug evil at Pantages Theatre, and visit the prisons and hospitals and courts of San Francisco.

"They never come back," is an old saying regarding drug addicts.

"It is also the least true," says the former stunt actress of the movies, "and I am a living proof of that, for I have come back and I shall stay back and what I can do others can also."

So the Hollywood beauty, plump and pink cheeked and without any trace of the terrible addiction that once carried her to the edge of that pit of oblivion which is the drug-user's ultimate end, will tell San Francisco her story. It will be her last public appearance in the fight against dope. The year which she has given to the battle against narcotic addiction in America is up and she will return to Hollywood to resume her life in the motion picture colony.

Juanita Hansen fell from a motion picture idol—the golden haired blue-eyed girl whose fearlessness and youth brought her $1,000 a week salary—to a pitiful 95-pound wreck unable to work, to eat, to think, unless she had dope.

IN SANITARIUM.

When full realization of her plig... was upon her she put herself ... ium to take a cu...

JANUARY 24, 1923

PLEDGE TO FREE ACTRESS IS LAID TO AN OFFICIAL

She Is Quoted as Saying She Was Told Charges Against Her Would Be Dropped

POLICE BLOTTER "FIXED"

Name "Juanita" Reported Altered to "Jane" at West Sixty-eighth Street Station

A scandal is developing as a result of the release of Juanita Hansen, film actress, who was accused of illegal possession of morphine.

There are two phases to this development.

One is that a certain important public official, according to Miss Hansen, met her between the time of her arrest and the day of her trial in West Side Court, and said to her:

"Don't worry, honey. It'll be all right. Right or wrong, you'll be free."

The second phase is that the police blotter of the West Sixty-eighth street station was doctored on the night of Miss Hansen's arrest, January 10. The girl originally gave her name to the desk lieutenant as "Juanita Hansen," then it was changed to "Jane Hansen," to disguise the identity of the prisoner.

ALMOST ESCAPED NOTICE.

She was known, naturally, to her friends and film followers as Juanita Hansen. As "Jane Hansen," she could pass unnoticed and that is what almost happened.

The story as related to the New York American brings in the name of Anne Luther, film actress, as hostess in her apartment at the meeting between Miss Hansen and the important public official. This meeting is reported to have taken place on Monday, January 15, two days before the trial of Miss Hansen.

Miss Hansen and Miss Luther have been chums for years. They were both named by Evelyn Nesbit in her divorce suit against Jack Clifford, dancer.

Miss Hanson was arrested on the night of January 10 by Detectives Cotter and O'Brien, of Deputy Commissioner Simon's Narcotic Division, in the apartment of Mrs. Ruth Barnett, No. 29 West Eighty-first street. She spent the night in West Thirtieth Street police station and was released in $300 bail the next morning by Magistrate McQuade, before whom she appeared for trial on Wednesday, January 17.

The detectives told the court they found in the prisoner's possession a small box containing morphine and a morphine needle.

ABRUPTLY DISMISSED.

Detective Cotter was testifying when Magistrate McQuade interrupted:

"Charges dismissed."

The defense of Miss Hansen was not made. She did not have to take the stand. When leaving court she declared that Mrs. Barnett, formerly an actress, was a "stool pigeon for the police."

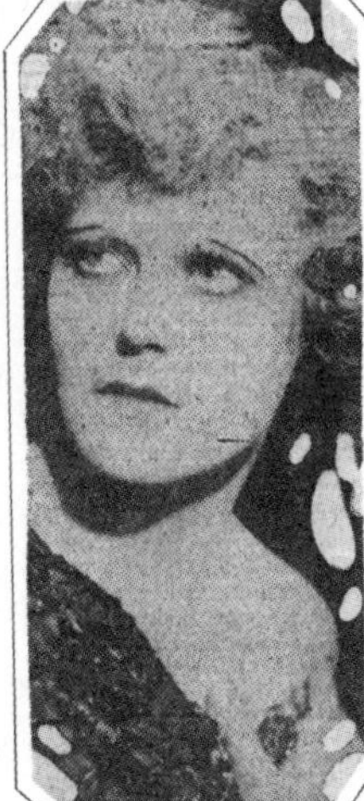

NOVEMBER 16, 1929

'SHOWER BATH VICTIM' USED DOPE, SAYS GIRL

Mystery Witness Testifies She Shared Rooms; Doctor Holds Morphine Would Dull Senses

Jaunita Hansen's shower bath suit suffered a breath-taking jolt yesterday in White Plains Supreme Court.

A mysterious Linda A. Marshall not only said she shared the apartment which Miss Hansen claims she was scalded, but averred the screen star used drugs.

Miss Hansen wants $100,000 from the hostelry. She said she steuued under a shower in June of last year—turned on the "cold" faucet and was showered with scalding water and steam.

SAYS SHE USED COCAINE.

Prefacing her testimony with a stubborn refusal to reveal anything about herself, and admitting he rname fictitious, Miss Marshall said:

"Just before she stepped into the shower, I saw her jab a needle into her leg. She took cocaine to stop a headache. Later, I was awakened by her screams."

The witness said she ran to th shower and found her companio crouched behind the curtain. H water was running, but there w no steam. Under cross-examin tion, she admitted she did know whether it was cocaine u in the injection, but said M Hansen mentioned the drug name.

GETS PAY FOR TIME.

Further questioning elicited information defense repres tives paid Miss Marshall $1 cash, and guaranteed he weekly until the suit is s Because of this, she said sh celled a theatrical engagen California.

Dr. Perry Lichtenstein next witness. He said a who took a dose of m might be seriously scal would not notice the h perature of the water. could be scalded, he said realizing what had happ too late.

ACTRESS RAPS NARCOTIC CHARGE

LOS ANGELES, Dec. 25.—(AP)—Liberated from jail on Christmas Eve, Juanita Hansen, queen of movie serials twenty years ago, today protested her arrest on suspicion of violating the state narcotic act.

Released On Bail

Friends in the federal theater project, where the blonde actress earned $94 a month, supplied the $1,000 bail which brought her freedom after she was jailed yesterday.

It was not soon enough, however, for the 39-year-old woman, who has won and lost two fortunes, to take her place in a trilogy of Christmas dramas, opened here last night with a federal work-relief cast.

Miss Hansen was taken into custody by Detective-Lieutenant F. H. Duede and two state narcotic inspectors when, Duede said, a narcotic administration kit was found in her possession.

Meant For Friends

Indignantly, the actress insisted she had no narcotics, but merely was on her way to see a sick friend with a hypodermic syringe and needle with which to administer a coal tar product her physician had recommended.

"I haven't taken narcotics for three years," she said. "I can't understand why they have done this to me. A doctor could prove in two minutes that I haven't taken narcotics for years."

Twice, the ex-film star said, she has rid herself of the narcotic habit and she is an ardent campaigner against the narcotic traffic. In January, 1934, at an Oakland sanitarium, she said, she was cured finally and completely.

Earned $1,000,000

From 1914 to 1922, the Nordic beauty is estimated to have earned more than $1,000,000 in movie serials and feature-length pictures. Seven years ago, she turned on a shower in a New York hotel room and was burned severely by scalding water and steam. She sued for $250,000 and eventually ... judgment of $10...

THE SACRAMENTO BEE, FRIDAY, DECEMBER 25, 1936

MADE IN USA AMERICA

Magazine Section

The Sunday Oregonian.

Magazine Section

NO. 22

VOL. XLI

PORTLAND, OREGON, SUNDAY MORNING, MAY 28, 1922

The Sensational Sequel to the Drugging of Dixie Dixon

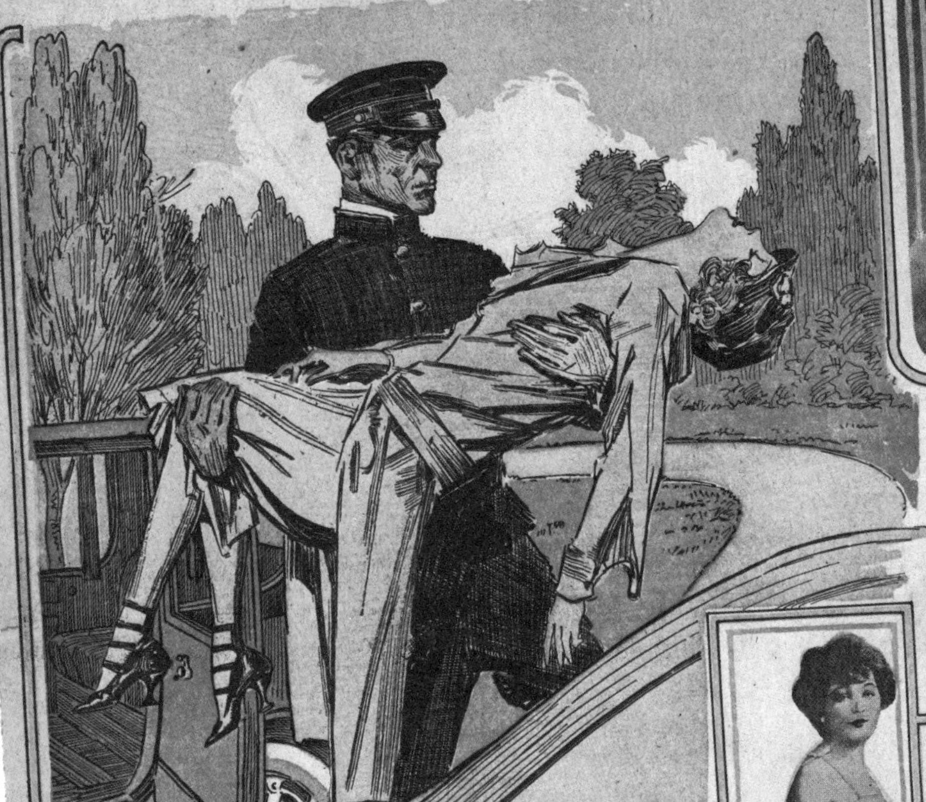

"Dixie Dixon," Mabel Dixon Terrell, Virginia Belle, Whose Death From a Drug, the Police Say, Was Brought About by a Gang of International Dope Vendors Who Feared She Would Tell the Authorities What She Knew of Them.

She Was Only a Fluffy Little Chorus Girl, But the Probe Started by the Parents, Who Wouldn't Believe She'd Killed Herself, Has Revealed the Suspicious Death of One Other Girl, and Has Led to the Seizure of Vast Hoards of Dope.

A CHARMING, spirited southern girl rebelled against the restrictions of her home time, married almost immediately upon graduation from a finishing school and went to live in Chicago. "I just overflowed," she said, when explaining to a friend why she left the place of her birth. Within a short time she was again swept from her moorings by the high tide of her emotions. She moved on to New York—where life offered more of a challenge.

Not so long ago a chauffeur carried into the Harlem hospital the inert body of this girl dying of drug poisoning.

Such was the beginning and the end of Dixie Dixon, a "Virginia thoroughbred, a creature gone crazy with the joy of living.

"Who drugged Dixie Dixon," and "why?" are still unanswered questions. Her parents, Mr. and Mrs. J. M. Terrell of Danville, Va., say their daughter was drugged to death. They are supported in this belief by the opinions of both American and Canadian investigators, who declared, almost immediately after her death, that Dixie Dixon was murdered by a clique of international drug smugglers, now being shadowed under the direction of Dr. Carleton Simon, chief of the narcotic squad, New York city.

Scarcely had they voiced these opinions when Dorothy Wardell, who, like Dixie Dixon, had gone on the stage, died from causes exactly similar. The body was discovered when the Montreal express steamed into the Grand Central that morning. Mrs. Winifred Bruce, Miss Wardell's companion, was apparently in a dying condition and was sent to Bellevue hospital. An examination of their effects revealed that the two women had been engaged in smuggling drugs and liquor from Canada.

Dorothy Wardell and Dixie Dixon were friends. And, while the police do not say that Miss Dixon was in league with the dope smugglers, they had what they considered indisputable evidence that Miss Dixon, like the Wardell girl, knew the smugglers' secrets.

And so the sensational sequel of Dixie Dixon's drugging has not been limited to her own tragic death nor even to the death of Miss Wardell. Hundreds of other persons, both men and women, are women, are threatened with the same fate. The Canadian secret service has intercepted letters showing that the smugglers are using Dixie Dixon's death as a warning to whatever persons may have an incriminating knowledge of their operations. Not only that, but a threat heard in a railroad station north of the line was:

"Dixie Dixon is out of the way and never will talk again."

These words were whispered into the ears of a young and pretty girl by a man whom the police suspected of being implicated in drug running. The girl started and, drawing away from the man, made a break for a train that was drawing out.

Vast Extent of Operations.

These drug operations are represented as being of such a vast nature that even the police can only make rough estimates of the extent and personnel of the ring. Already drugs appraised at $3,000,000 have been confiscated by Dr. Simon. Outside of the agents themselves there are hundreds of young girls, who inadvertently or through design, have been mixed up with this traffic, it is known.

Occasionally one of these girls talks to the wrong person. Some idea of what happens to the girl then may be gained by referring to the case of Dixie Dixon.

The real story of her death may never be known. The police can only supply such information as was contained in the testimony of Martin J. Ryan, a chauffeur, who carried the dying girl to Harlem hospital.

According to his story, he met Dixie Dixon the night of her death when she was searching vainly for something with a "kick in it." Ryan did not say that he was a close companion to the girl. He knew, of course, she had had her days of grandeur, but she didn't appear to be particularly depressed over her lost estate.

He made the rounds of the downtown

Ryan was alarmed, but he thought he would wake her up by driving around a bit, which he did. When she didn't recover, he took her to the Harlem hospital and carried her inside in his arms. She died without recovering consciousness. An autopsy was performed by Dr. Benjamin Schwartz of the medical examiner's office of New York, and her death was attributed to heroin poisoning

a time. When she called us up after these intervals of silence it was, as a rule, for financial help.

"Of course, it was a dreadful thing to do, but last September when she had run up a big bill at one of the best hotels in New York and didn't have the money to pay for it, we thought it would be a lesson to her if we allowed the hotel people to have her arrested. She was in the Tombs

Dixie Dixon as She Appeared on the Stage.

Dr. Carleton Simon, Head of New York Narcotic Squad, Who Is Seeking Dixie's Slayers.

Opposed to the theory that Dixie Dixon was the victim of a drug smugglers' plot, is the belief held by Mrs. Kitty Jennings of the Bronx, New York, that she committed suicide. Mrs. Jennings knew her well and was able to rescue her from many serious predicaments. She said:

"Dixie Dixon was the most irresponsible girl I ever knew. She was charming, fascinating and beautiful. She was the true Irish type, with dark blue eyes, long curling eyelashes and rave...

She always ha...

for nearly nine days. Even that didn't tease her. So we engaged Robert Conn... to defend her. The judge let her off with a suspended sentence after sending... her husband—R. M. Bliss, who, thou... separated from her, was sending her regular allowance—and advising him to take her home. The next thing we heard about Dixie was her death...

"I don't...

cabarets...

o'c...

to...

S...

her...

stop...

whic...

were...

cut o...

Dixie...

She...

off, a...

ance.

"It's the w..." she said, "but I'll try it."

Soon afterward she lost consciousness.

...doesn't attempt it with others around. Once she tried to throw herself out of the window and I caught her just in time.

"She would disappear for months at

...who ... burning ... no satisfaction in ... pleasant respectability of a small ... so she married and went to Chicago ... the discipline of marriage was onerous. She rebelled again and ... but a separation was avoided by

(Concluded on Page 2.)

NIGHT LETTER

Form 2280

THE WESTERN UNION TELEGRAPH COMPANY

INCORPORATED

25,000 OFFICES IN AMERICA CABLE SERVICE TO ALL THE WORLD

ROBERT C. CLOWRY, PRESIDENT BELVIDERE BROOKS, GENERAL

RECEIVER'S No. 961

TIME FILED 12:02

CHECK

Tragic Drug Doom of Beautiful Regine Flory

How the Pet of Paris Forfeited Fame, Fortune and Life to Her Craving for Narcotics.

A Photograph of the Lovely Mlle. Regine Flory Taken at the Height of Her Sensational Career as a Dancer Shortly Before She Committed Suicide in the Office of a London Producer.

At Left: the Entrance of the Famous "Follies Bergere" in Paris, Where Beautiful Regine Flory for Many Seasons Was the Favorite.

LONDON.

THE mystery behind the tragic suicide of Regine Flory has just been solved, through her own personal diary, which was confided, for publication, to her manager, Max Viterbo.

For more than twelve years the beautiful actress had been secretly a "drug slave," addicted to morphine, cocaine and opium. She had tried sanitariums, specialists, even long periods of voluntary imprisonment—but could never break the chains that bound her—and finally sought relief in death.

A few weeks ago, at the height of the brilliant career which had brought fame, riches and a long series of triumphs in every European capital, she flew from Paris to London, to consult with Sir Alfred Butt, director of the Drury Lane Theatre, about a possible British engagement. She called at his office by appointment, at ten o'clock in the evening, gorgeously dressed and covered with jewels.

After a short talk with him, as he turned from her for a moment, Mlle. Flory drew an automatic pistol from her handbag and shot herself. As she lay dying, the first wild rumor was that she had done it because Sir Alfred had refused her an immediate engagement at the Drury Lane. But that became manifestly absurd when it developed that she had just received an offer of $1,500 a week to play "Maritza" in New York and that she could also return to the Folies Bergere in Paris any time she liked.

The next suggestion was that she had been disappointed in love, and it was recalled that two years ago she had thrown herself into the Seine, from the Pont Alma, because of an unrequited passion for a young actor of the Comedie Francaise.

Then her own manager, M. Viterbo, revealed the tragic truth—the story of the mental torture and physical suffering which she endured for years trying to break herself of the drug habit, and which she could finally endure no longer.

Viterbo revealed the facts reluctantly, and out of a praiseworthy loyalty to his star's memory. He felt that she did not die solely because of her desperate, unsuccessful struggle against narcotics, but because she had "loved and suffered too much."

"Her heart," he said, "which she brought to rest by a bullet, wore itself out by dint of intensive living, and by her desire for undivided affection, absorbed in the pursuit of fugitive visions. Her mind had always retained the impress of the great Porto-Riche, who was her master and her friend. For several years, she made the most praiseworthy struggle against the implacable enemy (drugs) which ravages present-day society. Again and again she went to Switzerland in a courageous endeavor to fight the evil besetting her. She endured the most poignant suffering in combating her merciless enemy. Her organism could not for a single day do without the drug which doctors are compelled sometimes to use in order to preserve their patients."

As proof of the long, bitter fight she had made, and as a warning to others who may be caught in the same toils, M. Viterbo has made public some of her letters from Switzerland, and a part of her diary.

From one sanatarium, in which she had permitted herself to be locked up in the desperate hope of being cured, she wrote:

"Heavens! How full of wretchedness I am! What awful tortures of mind and body I suffer here, far from the Paris which I love and detest. Two months are like two centuries. Will I be able to live through this dreadful solitude? I feel myself abandoned and alone—lost, quite lost."

Later she wrote:

"I am in the most terrible period of my treatment. What one is capable of suffering can hardly be believed. Sometimes I feel like putting an end to it all. I took an hour to write these few lines, so wretched is my physical condition. I am writing in my bed, on my knees. It does not look like my old bed of which I was so fond—(a gorgeous, gilded and canopied affair in Paris, painted with Cupids, like that of a queen). Over me now are heavy blankets and around me wretched pillows. No flowers, no furs, no perfumes, no laces, no love. I feel myself small, and, oh, so terribly depressed and lonely!"

A few weeks later, having suffered the tortures of the damned and gone through the "cure" to its bitter end, she hoped pathetically that she might be freed of the curse at last, and in a moment of buoyancy, wrote:

"The doctor has promised that in a week's time I shall have motor drives and horseback rides. I have grown very much thinner, but I am putting on flesh again and look less like a skeleton. Sunday a week they are going to let me have luncheon at Montreux. I look forward to it as a moment of wild enjoyment. And then I shall see Paris again! I wonder what . . . is doing. Does he still wear those flaming ties which are an offense to my eyes, and a head like a wolf's with hair that refuses to be combed."

Alas, a few weeks later she did return to Paris. She was welcomed, acclaimed, and soon again was dancing nightly on the stage of the Folies Bergere, slenderer, but still beautiful and as full of bubbling vitality as ever. But with the renewal of the hectic life came the craving for drugs. She became nervous, listless, unhappy, and finally succumbed, beginning to take small doses of cocaine again.

Viterbo tells of how horrified and hopeless her friends were when they realized what was happening, and of how Madame D. ——, her faithful companion and friend, formed a well-intentioned plot to help her. The chemist from whom it was learned she obtained her drugs was bribed to give her doses of reduced strength. But Mlle. Flory discovered the plot. She began disappearing for a day at a time, to visit doctors and stores of evil repute, and would come back satisfied, her eyes unnaturally brilliant, gay and elated, but a little bit ashamed at having deceived those who had gone to so much trouble to help her. From time to time she would announce her sudden intention of going on a short journey, would break her theatrical engagements, disappear for a week or ten days, and come back a wreck.

Her friends exercised such a surveillance over her in Paris, that sometimes, it was believed, she would fly to London and visit the Chinese dens of Soho and Limehouse.

"It isn't that I enjoy the effect of the drugs any longer," she wrote, "but life without them has become a greater horror than I can endure."

Of these horrors behind the scenes, with which only her trusted and intimate friends were familiar, the general public knew nothing. When Flory reappeared, as she did again and again, at the Moulin Rouge or the Folies Bergere, she seemed, at least behind the footlights, to be her brilliant, beautiful old self.

She had hosts of admirers, was showered with gifts, was the toast of Paris. It was during one of these periods that she gave the celebrated interview, in which she hinted at her own tragic secret:

"Glory, fame, beauty, happiness! What nonsense! When I think that women like me are the objects of jealousy and desire, and that we are feted and flattered and envied, I wonder what woman in the humblest walks of life would change places if she knew the real truth—the whole truth—of what lies behind our masks.

"Old gentlemen, college boys, snobs, millionaires, crowned heads all seek our favors. Ruling sovereigns ask to be presented to us, and give us jewels. If poor Gaby Deslys were still in this world, you might ask her about that. Statesmen, heroes, are at our feet. We live in luxury. And yet no one knows the Calvary of our life. All of us—most of us at least—are wretched women who drag our glory along like a ball of iron chained to our feet, and we pay for our fame with tears of blood."

The final tragedy of her career is described by Sir Alfred Butt, in whose office it occurred. The business appointment had been fixed for ten o'clock in the evening. A curious rumor that Mlle. Flory intended committing suicide had preceded her to London and reached Sir Alfred's ears. He and other friends had taken steps to have her watched—but when she arrived, apparently gay and happy, registered at the Savoy, entertained a number of friends for luncheon and afterward at tea, he felt that the whole thing must have been an absurd joke.

"When she called at my office," said Sir Alfred," her manner was so calm and natural that I dismissed any fear of tragedy.

"When I told her that I could offer her an immediate engagement, she told me that the Shuberts had offered her $1,500 a week for a New York appearance to be followed by an American tour, and I advised her to take it. I told her I thought the 'Maritza' part would suit her admirably. There was a lull in the conversation, and my attention wandered. She seemed perfectly calm, and I had forgotten all about the warnings of a possible tragedy. She seemed simply a brilliant, beautiful, calm woman, at the height of her career, with other triumphs beckoning, who had come to consult me on a business matter.

"I must have bent over my desk, or looked aside for a moment. Suddenly I heard a terrific explosion, and saw Mlle. Flory sag forward in the chair, as a smoking automatic pistol dropped from her hand. When a doorman and others rushed into my office, we found that she had shot herself through the heart."

...t: Mlle. Regine ...as She Appeared ...ondon Magazine ... Time When She ...ecame Popular ...s Night-Life.

DANCE OF THE PIPE.

A Series of Silhouette Impressions of Mlle. Flory, Who, According to a Close Friend, "Paid Daily Tribute to the Opium Pipe and Other Drugs" Until She Was Its Slave.

At Right: Another Photograph of Mlle. Flory Taken Some Years Ago Before She Became a Drug Slave, Showing Her in an Ironic Pose with an Imitation Opium Pipe.

Newspaper Feature Service, 1926.

Beatrice Pearsall's Life as Wage-Earner Ended at Wally Reid's Big "Snow Party"

MISS PEARSALL STARTED DOWN AT DOPE PARTY

FEBRUARY 25, 1923

Young Woman Tells of Wild Drug Orgy That Terminated Career as a "Good Girl"

STAGED BY WALLY REID

Now in a Sanitarium, Where She Tells New York American the Full Story of Her Life

By JAMES WHITAKER.
Copyright Universal Service.

Reminiscent as she sits curled at the foot of her bed in the detention room of Glenwood Park Sanitarium, Greensboro, N. C., Beatrice Patterson Pearsall, deteriorated since the day she attended Wallie Reid's $25,000 dope party, tells the Hearst International Magazine representative the story of her life. She says:

"I wonder whether I reached my heights when I joined Wallie Reid's 'snow party' guests or earlier, when I was quite a good little girl, superintending my uncle's house or studying in the girl's finishing school."

The house which Beatrice ruled is in Lisbon, N. D., where her uncle, Dr. Thomas C. Patterson...

Nightgown Parties

Beatrice tells of nightgown parties after school bedtime, when the girls crept single file over balconies and fire-escapes to the roof, there to indulge in such rudimentary vices as cigarette smoking and secret gossip.

Again Beatrice returns to Lisbon, this time the elegant product of one of the best Eastern refineries of maidenhood. A bit too elegant for Lisbon she was, and she tells of being "cut" by the jealous local...

End of Wages

The $25,000 drug party given by Wallie Reid marks the end of Beatrice as an earner of honest wages.

Skip all the sordid details of the manner in which La Rose met Beatrice in the "Studio," a Greenwich Village resort, and went successfully to work to train her to his purposes. We can turn to a written record of the result of that training and let it hint of what it consisted.

Beatrice, decked out in fine...

Between the Lines

The remarkable thing about this remarkable letter is the history of its writing. Note the three illegible... Each represents an...

Drug Goes, Too

Everywhere a dope fiend goes, the drug goes too. In safety, Uncle Patterson thought, on the Florida grape-fruit farm, the two girls soon established intimate relations with some high-living members of a golf club just outside Jacksonville and found their heroin through them. Beatrice continues:

"My uncle thought I came back to New York last year cured of my Greenwich Village follies. I came back with a worse dope habit than ever. Ask anyone what kind of girl 'Buddie' Pearsall was and, unless you find someone too timid to acknowledge any knowledge of me, the answer will be: 'Oh, that hop-head!'

"I was a 'hop-head' all right—and it took every cent I could make doing small bits for a film company and playing the organ in some of the big Broadway motion picture palaces to pay my dope peddlers."

It was the collision of two hard facts which pushed Beatrice into the arms of her last dope peddler, fug... criminal John J. La Rose of ...wich Village.

Her drug need increased. Her earning capacity diminished.

DRUG CLA... MOVIE GIRL 4 MEN HELD

"Dorothy Ross" Implicates Them for Supplying Narcotic Through the Mail.

'I a Drug Addict? No!'

DOPE-CRAZED TORCH SLAYER WRITES AGAIN

Imogene Wilson, as Mary Nolan of the films.

LOS ANGELES, July 31.—Mary Nolan, beautiful young film star, formerly Imogene Wilson, of the Ziegfeld Follies, declared tonight she was the victim of a plot engineered by persons who sought to blast her reputation by circulating reports she was a narcotic addict.

The reports were widely published. The basis for them was the fact that United States Commissioner David B. Head, on the strength of affidavits laid before him, issued search warrants yesterday permitting officers to examine three of her apartments.

One of these is in a Hollywood hotel, another at a beach club at Santa Monica, and the third her dressing bungalow on the studio lot where she is employed.

NOW IN HOSPITAL

Miss Nolan is in St. Vincent's Hospital, suffering from a severe case of sunburn. She said tonight as a nurse dressed her inflamed back:

"I, a drug addict? I never heard of such a thing! Such a report is utterly without foundation—it is ridiculous—it is preposterous for words.

"Yes, I know. They have been calling me up repeatedly—at my hotel and at the studio. But I can scarcely believe those two women could say such terrible things about me."

FELL ASLEEP IN BOAT.

Miss Nolan unquestionably ha a severe case of sunburn. He back is badly scorched and so ar her legs. She fell asleep in a boa on Lake Arrowhead last week end, she said, and is a victim t over-exposure.

The records of St. Vincent' Hospital show "sunburn" and tha only is what she is being treate for. She is under care of Dr Leland Hawkins. A private is in attendance on her.

So far as narcotic addiction i concerned, Miss Nolan was exonerated tonight by V. H. De Spain Federal narcotic investigator.

He visited the hospital with the three search warrants in his pocket. None of the apartments had been examined.

NO NEEDLE MARKS.

The affidavit of one of the two nurses had said Miss Nolan's arms were "full of punctures from hypodermic needls." De Spain examined her arms carefully. He said:

"I failed to find a single mark of a needle. I am firmly convinced Miss Nolan is not an addict."

Joyce Hawley Tries to Die But Drugs Fail Bathtub Girl

MORE NOTORIETY—Joyce Hawley, the wine bath girl, whose escapade stirred all America, is in print again in a more tragic way. Seeking to forget her woes, she nearly killed herself with a drug overdose in Chicago.

Special to the N. Y. American.

CHICAGO, July 25.—Joyce Hawley, "Lady of the Bath," sought peace and quiet today—probably for the first time in her brief and blazingly public career—and almost died.

The girl who stepped from a tub of wine into the first page of every newspaper in the country took thirty-five grains of a powerful sleeping potion in her room at a loop hotel some time before dawn.

But instead of peace, and sleep, the overdose brought hysteria. For two hours women attendants of the hotel held her while she writhed on the bed, clad in pink silk pajamas.

A hypodermic injection quieted her sufficiently to make possible removal to the County Hospital, where the drug was pumped out and she was reported on the road to recovery. Before removal she cried:

"I was tired of it all. I wanted to sleep."

A week ago she lost her place at the Lincoln Tavern as a cabaret entertainer, when Mayor Dilg, of Morton Grove, ordered the management to stop her show because of "unwholesome notoriety."

The Lincoln Tavern job ... cepted after several idle wee... it lasted just six nights. ... seventh night she was arrest... fined $50 for speeding past ... lights.

MARCH 18, 1925

Drug Dazed

WEARING ONLY a night gown, covered by a fur coat, Mary Haynes, vaudeville actress, was found huddled in the doorway at Lexington avenue and Twenty-sixth street yesterday morning. She was dazed from laudanum, taken to relieve earache. A passing taxi driver took her to Bellevue Hospital.

JULY 26, 1926

Affidavit on Opium Parties Offered at Showgirl's Trial

FACING DOPE CHARGE—Mrs. Phyllis Emerson, former showgirl, charged with possessing narcotics, admits having smoked opium in 1932, but asserts the supply which Government agents say was found in her handbag in December ... placed there by them.

DOPE RAID JAILS 10-C.-A-DANCE GIRL AND 4 MEN

Arrests Made After Clergyman Charges Hostesses from High Schools Sold Heroin

$79,000 Paid Starr Faithfull by Politician in Six Years to Se

MONEY GIVEN FOR 'INJURIES,' SAYS LAWYER

Starr's Party Friend Sought in Dope Smuggling

LONDON, June 15.—One of the persons who attended the party at which Starr Faithfull was a guest on the liner Franconia when it sailed from New York on May 29, is now being traced by special investigators in Brussels in connection with

STARR'S DIARY POINTS MOTIVE FOR MURDER

S

Cor
Gi

Starr Faithfull Was Drugged at Time of Drowning

JUNE 16, 1931

Reveal Boston Politician Paid $79,000 to Starr.

TWO MEN HUNTED

Identified as Companions of Victim on Last Day.

Dramatic and important developments crowded swiftly into the Starr Faithfull death mystery yesterday. They were:

1—The official report of Dr. Alexander O. Gettler, city toxicologist, showed the exotic Starr went to her death drugged into insensibility. Gettler reported to District Attorney Edwards of Nassau County, that the stomach and brain of Miss Faithfull contained enough veronal to have rendered her unconscious, but not enough to have killed her.

2—The New York American, learned exclusively the names of two men police are seeking as those who were with Starr Faithfull on Friday, June 5, the day she dissappeared. They are Bruce Winston and Jack Greenaway, the latter an actor. A

NEW CLUES—A new portrait of Starr Faithfull, investigation of whose death has produced more important clues. She was paid $79,000 by a prominent politician and was helplessly drugged at the time of death.

Photo Copyrighted by Boston Daily Record and Supplied by Int'l Newsreel.

THER TELLS VN STORY OF TARR TRAGEDY

Taxi Of

Murray chauffeur, New York complete a known actio His narra

The Beautiful Movie Star, Alma Rubens, Who Spent the Last Years of Her Life in a Hopeless Fight Against Her Addiction to Dope.

Not All the Talent and Beauty of the French Movie Star, Edith Mera, Could Compensate for the Tragedies Drug Craving Brought Her, the Last of These Horrible Disease and Death.

'DOPE' SHOOTING TRAGEDY

ACTOR, DEPRIVED OF 'SHOT,' KILLS HIS WIFE

THEN SHOOTS HIMSELF

Crazed by being deprived of the drugs which had made him a narcotic addict, Harry Glaser, 57, onetime vaudeville headliner, shot and killed his common-law wife, Mona Clark, in a dingy $14 a month flat at 88 Amsterdam ave., yesterday.

He then turned the gun on himself and shot himself through the lungs and head. His condition was declared critical. He was removed to Bellevue Hospital's prison ward, charged with homicide and possesion of narcotic equipment.

Police found a "needle" outfit in the untidy rooms, where unwashed dishes were stacked. Cunningly hidden in a toy gun were three vials which police declared had contained heroin.

EMPLOYED AS DOORMAN

37 W. 72nd st., had been driven mad by the excruciating pains suffered by dope users when they find themselves without their "shot." The dead woman, police reported, had been earning a few dollars each week as a maid in a hotel at 224 W. 49th st. She was a drug addict, police said.

Inspector McDermott, in charge of the investigation, said the former vaudevillian who had recently been employed as a doorman at

HARRY GLASER
In Vaudeville Days
International News Photo by New York American.

EARNINGS WENT FOR 'DOPE'

Although the couple managed to earn sufficient money between them to live decently, their earnings went for the purchase of "dope," police said. Both had been arrested as drug users. They had evidently spent their last money over the week-end in appeasing their craving for dope and finding themselves without further funds, quarreled and the shooting followed.

ACTOR RUINED BY USE OF DOPE

One-time associate of b Broadway stars, now unshave seedy, a man who said h Arthur Paguette, vaudevill dian and night-club ent was in West Side Court y charged with possessing a

Detectives Herbert and said they arrested Paguett lumbus avenue and Seven street Saturday with a pac heroin in his pockets.

Paguette, his face covered wi stubbly beard and his once fashionable clothing soiled, gave his ago as thirty-six and his address as No. ty-third street. oke as he said: de as high as $7 ave been in sho Dressler, Marie ska Suratt.

"The last show I appeared was 'The Red Rose.' Recent have been singing and danc night clubs.

They are going to send m now. But I know I'll come ht. I want to go back business."

guilty of held ns.

HEART-BROKEN!—Frieda Ben Moshe, twenty-five, a singer, recently of Cairo, Egypt, is shown here apparently still in good health after she had cried, "I am about to die!" She came here hoping to captivate audiences and

Two Photographs of Mabel Normand. Above Shows What Despair Wrote on Her Features Before She Died. The Lower Photograph Shows How Gay, Reckless and Fun-Loving Mabel Was Before Fate Filled Her Life With Unhappiness and Suffering.

The Beautiful Artists' Model, Laura Dayer, Found Oblivion in an Overdose of the Drugs That Had Made Her Life Unbearable.

Julia Bruns, Once "America's Most Beautiful Girl," Who Won Success on the Stage, But Before She Died Dope Ruined Her Career and Reduced Her to Poverty Like This.

Mary Duncan Rescued From Drug Kidnaping

Actress Hurt in Leap from Auto When She Smells Chloroform.

APRIL 17, 1929.

SANTA MONICA, Cal., April 16.—Mary Duncan, well known screen and stage star was seriously injured in a leap from a fast moving auto here today after a stranger had tried to chloroform and kidnap her.

Miss Duncan, suffering from severe cuts and bruises in a hospi tal here, told police she had accepted the stranger's offer of a ride her own car had given out of fuel. Bet.reen Beverley Hills and Sawtelle, sh e said, the man began acting queerly and she detected the scent of chloroform.

When she tried to get out of the car the man seized her, she said, and in the struggle part of her clothing was torn off. She finally managed to jump through a window of the moving machine to the pavement. Workmen near the scene took the actress to a hotel and she was later removed to a hospital.

Late tonight Miss Duncan's physician said she was too seriously injured to talk to anyone.

MARY DUNCAN

Sleeping Potion Blamed fo

OVERDOSE LED TO COLLAPSE, SAYS CHEMIST

Inquiry Seeks to Determine Quantity of Drug Taken by Star; Funeral Rites Today

Jeanne Eagels, tempestuous actress, died from an overdose of a sleep-producing drug, it was revealed yesterday by a chemist's analysis.

Dr. Alexander O. Gettler, city toxicologist, and his assistant Dr. Harry Schwartz, discovered a quantity of chloral hydrate in her body. This drug is the "knockout drops," long storied in melodrama of saloon days.

Miss Eagels' death was discussed yesterday by her physician, Dr. Edward E. Cowles, whose assistant, Dr. Alfred Pellegrini, had prepared to treat her just before she died. Dr. Cowles said:

"It is unnecessary for me to state whether I personally prescribed chloral hydrate for Miss Eagels. Chloral hydrate is ordinarily given to those addicted to liquor. I can only state that at all times Miss Eagels received proper medication. She could, however, have gotten the chloral hydrate without a prescription."

NO SUICIDE INTENT.

Dr. Gettler's finding was that only traces of alcohol existed in Miss Eagels' body, while the chloral hydrate was found in her brain as well as her stomach.

There was no suspicion on the part of any medical authority, however, that Miss Eagels had taken the chloral with suicidal intent.

Miss Eagels seemed to sleep peacefully in death yesterday. Her mortal form was covered with pink velvet, which streamed at the Campbell funeral establishment, Broadway and Sixty-first street.

Across the street, at Loew's Lincoln Square Theatre her latest talking film was playing while her real voice which once captivated the stage was stilled in death.

FUNERAL TODAY.

The funeral rites will be held at 11 o'clock this morning at the Campbell chapel. Her body will be placed this evening on a train for Kansas City. There will converge her mother, Mrs. Julia Sullivan Eagels; her brothers, Paul and George; her sisters, M s W. K. Ackerly, of Needles, Cal., and Miss Helen Eagels, who is in this city.

There were many floral offerings yesterday, and notables of the stage were included in the throng passing by her bier.

Speaking of the actress, David Belasco said:

"Jeanne Eagels was a woman of tremendous ability. Success came to her too late, and this tardiness embittered her. She had been through much and couldn't forget it."

Sam Harris, producer of "Rain," said:

"She was a great woman and a great actress. She was to appear in a new play for me before Christmas.

Heiress "Doped"

SLEUTHS SEEK LEGAL GROUNDS TO ANNUL UNION

Multimillionaire Father Silent on Ranch, Where Girl Is Reported to Be Hidden

Private detectives, acting on behalf of a relative of Dolores Elizabeth Ford, beautiful Smith College girl, whose mother denies a published report that the heiress is married to a colored cabaret employe, are investigating the possibility that the girl might have been drugged into a mixed marriage.

Information revealed to the New York American by Tom Garrett, soft-spoken Southern hypnotist and friend of the heiress, led detectives on this trail. Garrett told The American that Dolores Elizabeth Ford, while under hypnotic influence, told him she had been married to Eugene Newton, a colored man, but said she had been "doped" or "drugged" at the time of the marriage.

FATHER SILENT.

William Ford, multimillionaire glass manufacturer, father of Dolores Elizabeth Ford, declined to answer a long distance telephone call yesterday at his ranch, Darby, Mont. The New York American also telegraphed to him for a statement, but received no response.

The daughter is reported to be in seclusion with her father at the Montana ranch.

BRIDAL SECRET TO RELATIVES

CINCINNATI, July 19.—If William Ford, multi-millionaire manufacturer, is planning any action following the published reports of the marriage of his lovely daughter Dolores to Gene Newton, colored employee in a Harlem night club, his intentions are being kept secret here.

Ford, whose wealth is rated at nearly twenty millions, is reported by relatives here to have sought seclusion on his cattle ranch at Darby, Montana, taking his daughter with him.

In his absence, none of those closest to him here would admit possessing any information whatever about the reported marriage to the New York colored man.

Only Mrs. Allen M. Ford, wife of William Ford's brother, who now carries on alone the family interest in the general agency for the Aetna Life Insurance Company which was inherited from their father, had anything to say.

COLORED MAN'S BRIDE INSISTS SHE WAS DOPED

7-20

Didn't Do It Willingly, Girl Tells Friends; Insists She Left Husband Right After Ceremony

Lulled into psyshic sleep by the man she was infatuated with, Dolores Elizabeth Ford, heiress beauty of twenty-three, first blurted out the astounding news of her reported marriage, it was learned by the New York American yesterday.

Blurted it out, and said she "wouldn't have done it if she hadn't been doped."

Tom Garrett, dark and handsome hypnotist, revealed this yesterday in a conversation in his apartment at No. 231 West Seventieth street. It was Garrett who induced the hypnotic state in a seance last March in Miss Ford's apartment in the Hotel Ansonia. As the beautiful and eccentric girl succumbed to the mood he induced upon her while his long fingers caressed her face, he commanded:

"Tell me, Dolores, what is it that is troubling you so?"

ADMITS MARRIAGE.

She writhed as if in great pain, then answered:

"I don't want to tell. It's about my marriage."

"Why, Dolores, don't be silly. Is he a Chinaman?"

Garrett laughed at this, but Dolores, still in the trance, shuddered and is quoted as replying:

"No—colored. Listen to me. I have to tell you. It was a frame-up. I'd had a lot to drink. I was doped—didn't know what I was doing. Those are the facts. I went to a party, I met this man. Next morning I found I was married. I left him at once and I swear I never lived with him."

All this so shocked Garrett, he said yesterday, that he hastily began bringing Miss Ford out of her artificial slumber. But she cried to him:

"I'm wild, but I'm not that wild, Tom. I've never had anything to do with him since. I'm telling the truth. None of my marriages was real. The first, annulled. The second, divorced. This one, O, I can't face it."

Garrett says he told her calmly:

"Dolores, your statements don't hold water. You had to get a license to marry. Why not get an annullment?"

GAVE HIM MONEY.

"I'd die if my parents found out. No, I see Gene Newton occasionally and give him money. I don't get any license. If I signed anything I was doped."

At the same seance was a third party, Louis de Matti, nineteen-year-old subject of Garrett's hypnotic demonstrations. De Matti was later to experience Miss Ford's friendship also, and it was from a trip she took with de Matti last month in a "flight from herself" that her father, William Ford, multi-millionaire Toledo manufacturer, brought her back recently.

According to Charles Ascot, friend of both Miss Ford and Garrett, the madcap girl first met the hypnotist in early March at the Dame Fortune Tea Room, No. 62 West Fiftieth street, run by Mme. Blanche Terry.

Ascot was rehearsing the "Vernon Sisters" for a musical act. One of the sisters, whose real name is Mary MacDowell, is Miss Ford's best friend and was living

JULY 20, 1929.

HYPNOTIST!

Tim Garrett, hypnotist a student of criminology, ga the Ford heiress treatme to quiet her nerves, it said.

had managed to meet the hy notist, and was going around w him.

Garrett is of an old Virgi family. He has been engaged the practice of hypnosis for ei teen of his thirty-three years. was attached to the Medical search Board of the U. S. Ar during the war and treated sh shocked cases, amnesia, and ne ous disorders with hypnosis, curing results that brought considerable note.

LEFT WITH DE 5MATTI.

Later, Garrett said, she switc her affections from him to Matti. When she left with Matti, Garrett said he was prised to receive a visit from gene Newton, who said he was heiress' husband.

From the lips of the thirty-n year-old colored man, short statue and aggressive in man Garrett heard a different stor the marriage.

He admitted yesterday that Ford had been much in his c pany after meeting her, and s

"She is a beautiful, brillia girl and I enjoyed her socie She was artistic, moody a tempermental. One eveni we walked far up near Harle and suddenly she began to shi and want to turn back. S seemed to to be afraid somec would recognize her. She w preoccupied, distrait. I told I could solve her mood if I hy notized her, and when I t her back to the hotel she p mitted me to hypnotize her."

Newton revealed Dolores as a girl seeking constantly new thrills, new subjects to cupy her over-active mind. an allowance of $250 a mo plus large quarterly divide from stock, she sometimes ha much as a thousand dollar month to spend. Her del many nights was to visit Ha cabarets, he said, in his comp and throw fifty-dollar bills the dance floor for the en tainers.

DRANK LITTLE.

She did not smoke or drin

RUTH TO MARRY THIS MORNING

— Another murder came Mrs. Hattie. appeared and es Kirk, a sus- bandoned her go, on the day er Jeanne was has been in- gamy.

ine. He got most of

n't a complete fool. 25,000 worth of dia- didn't know I had doesn w it now. er will, told this story, her ed with diamonds, beau- n platinum. The gems sing. She was known to

"DOPE"—Chicago detective shown with parts of an extensive opium layout that was found in the apartment of the Kirks, after the couple had been arrested in connection with the murder of Betty Chambers, Chicago butterfly."

FEBRUARY 5, 1928

GIRL BANDIT'S THREAT

'White Diamond' Brain

Death of Jeanne Eagels

n Mixed Marriage?

ONE!—Dolores Eliza-
th Ford, who has set a
ntinent by the ears
rough the story she was
arried to a colored man, is
New York no longer. Re-
orts have her on her mil-
onaire father's Montana
nch.

D HEARD OF BRIDAL.

ut Miss McDowell did admit
he New York American, from
home in Ohio, that she for
nths "heard about the mar-
ge of Dolores to the colored
n."

Mrs. Ascott, a booking agent
musicians and singers and
end of Mme. Reiner, conduc-
of the Bauer Conservatory
d wife of Fritz Reiner, of the
ncinnati Orchestra, was also
estioned.

**"I married a colored man.
sten to me. I have to tell you.
was a frameup when I mar-
ed Gene Newton. I had a lot
drink. I was doped . . . didn't
now what I was doing."**

OCTOBER 12, 1929

Out of Depths!

GOING TO SEA!—Winning her battle against drug addiction, Alma Rubens, famous film actress,

ALMA RUBENS CURED OF DOPE

LOS ANGELES, Oct. 11 (INS).—Alma Rubens, film star, will be released as cured of drug addiction within ten days.

Relatives today said they had so learned from officials of the State Narcotic Hospital at Patton.

Miss Rubens is to be taken on a two months' sea voyage by her mother, Mrs. Theresa Rubens. The actress' recovery was reported complete, as a result of gains she made in the last three weeks.

JANUARY 22, 1931

Film Star's Vitality Also Sapped by Narcotics.

Alma Rubens Dies of Pneumonia; Weakened by Worry Over Arrest

HOLLYWOOD, Jan. 21.—Alma Rubens, great star of the silent film, "Humoresque," died today.

Weakened by worry over her arrest January 5 last, on a charge of smuggling narcotics into San Diego from Mexico, she was a victim of double pneumonia.

Dr. Charles Pfleuger, her personal physician, refused to disclose where Miss Rubens died, but another authority said the end came in the house of a friend. At her bedside were her mother, Mrs. Theresa Rubens, and her sister, Mrs. Hazel Large.

FOUGHT DOPE HABIT.

Alma Rubens, who was thirty-one, had won one grand fight—a seven-month battle against morphine.

This morning the three physicians in attendance at her final illness announced they were optimistic she would rally, although she had been unconscious three days. But the inroads of narcotics had sapped too much of the actress' vitality.

She was at the threshold of a talkie career in January, last year. The dusky-haired enchantress of the silver screen was about to embark on a new career before the microphone when she suddenly went to pieces.

Miss Rubens attacked a woman in front of her movie studio. Later she attempted to use a paper knife on her physician; she chased him through Hollyw[illegible] streets, shrieking.

Miss Rubens [illegible]aken to a sanitarium. It was [illegible]n, in February, 1929, that s[illegible] revealed to the world she was a drug addict. She was sorrowful, but she was game. It was the old story. At the time, she said:

"I had a terrible pain; I was ill. So I went to a doctor. He cured my pain with a medicine . . . so I thought. Later, when I got pains, I took tat medicine. And when I learned it was a drug, I became frightened.

"I went to another doctor, and tlod him about it, of my fears. He laughed; said I would be all right. I kept on and on."

Miss Rubens suffered those months of fighting. She went mad with anguish, with craving, and was strapped up time and again. But the young woman, who pulled herself up from a chorus to stardom by her own bootstraps, kept up the fight.

WELCOMED BACK.

On October 11, 1928, she was discharged as cured. The world applauded, and in the following February she was welcomed by producers and managers in New York. Her husband, Ricardo Cortez, handsome man of the films, the man who signed the order placing her in a sanitarium, was back with her.

Alma Rubens seemed her old self as she and Cortez took up an apartment. She was booked in vaudeville in New York. She was a success, as such comebacks go.

But there was a fly in the ointment. Cortez gave out interviews that he had helped his wife up the ladder out of the muck of narcotics. Miss Rubens became infuriated, and publicly said she was to divorce Ricardo, for her fight had been made alone. She had aid, but from women friends, she said then.

Police were called by Miss Palmer. And Federal agents. They searched her apartment, then took her wardrobe apart, opening seams of her dresses and evening gowns.

They found 100 grains of morphine in one seam, they said, and again Alma Rubens was a prisoner. She was put under $5,000 bail.

But death was a release for her—from narcotics and a criminal charge.

IN HAPPIER DAYS—Taken during her last visit to New York, this photo shows Alma Rubens, who died yesterday, as she appeared during her glamorous days as one of the country's leading cinema actresses. She died a victim of pneumonia.

TAPE MURDER VICTIM FOUND DEAD UNDER PILE OF CUSHIONS

Body Clad in Silk Pajamas; Torn Notes in Waste Basket Indicate Quarrel with Her Common-Law Husband; Former Chum and Mate Held, but Vehemently Deny any Knowledge of Crime;

Special Correspondence of N. Y. American.

CHICAGO, Feb. 4.

"Revenge is the sweetest thing I know of."

These few words, prefaced only by the salutation, "Dear Gordy," are believed to have been the death warrant of Betty Chambers, beautiful twenty-year-old "brains" of a bandit gang that levied $3,000,000 toll on banks and jewelry merchants.

Notes in Waste Basket

A few lines were found on a torn sheet of note paper in a waste basket, along with other torn sheets, when police searched the apartment of Betty Chambers shortly after her "tape murder." The girl's body, clad in purple silk pajamas, was found under a pile of silken cushions on the floor.

The base of her skull had been crushed, her neck was tightly wound in an electric light cord and nine yards of adhesive tape were fastened across her nose and mouth. Her slayers had triply insured death.

The torn notes in the waste basket were addressed to J. Gordon Chambers, said to have been her common law husband, with whom she had quarreled, and whom she had chased from the hotel in which they were living at the point of a blazing pistol.

Other fragments of letters, all addressed to "Gordy," indicated that she had pleaded with him for a reconciliation, that she had accused him of neglecting her for another woman and that she had decided to end it all by suicide.

Police declare, also, that she had threatened to reveal the activities of the bandit gang of which they were both members, had theatened to betry the members into the hands of the authorities.

ROAD OF DOPE LEADS BEAUTY DOWN TO CELL

Babe Reynolds, Ex-Assemblyman's Daughter, Once Broadway Butterfly, Held in Court

Ten years ago, Babe Reynolds, young, beautiful, was one of the most popular girls on Broadway.

Yesterday she was arrested and held in $1,500 bail for trial in Special Sessions Court.

DRUGS DID IT.

[illegible] found an expensive fur coat belonging to Betty and a torn and discarded photograph of the murdered girl. Also was found an extensive opium layout, and Doris, when first arrested, was so befuddled by the fumes of opium that she could not talk coherently.

Roy Miller, chauffeur for Betty Chambers, also taken into custody, declared that Chambers had purchased the tape which had been wound around the girl's mouth and nose.

The two Kirks and Miller were charged by the police with murder, although the evidence against them so far is purely circumstantial. Chambers and another man named Miller, "Joe" or "Eaglebeak," as he was familiarly known, are believed to hold the key to the mystery of the bandit woman's death.

F REVENGE BRINGS DEATH

f Gang in $3,000,000 Raids

What Drugs Did

FROM THE HEIGHTS, wealthy, a Wellesley graduate and socially prominent, Mrs. Doris Clements Wilson (above), has fallen to arrest in Chicago as a shoplifter—her fortune dissipated and health wrecked. "Dope," police say.

SCULPTOR REVEALED AS CONFIRMED D

DOCUMENTS AT HOSPITAL SHOW HABIT

JANUARY 12, 1926

William O. Partridge, in State Institution, Better, Wife Declares in Statement

William Ordway Partridge, one of the foremost in the ranks of American sculptors, was revealed last night by records in Bellevue Hospital as a "user of several drugs."

Again he is in the State Hospital for the Insane at Central Islip, L. I., where he was taken Sunday night protesting to police that he was being "railroaded." He is denied to even his closest friends. No one came forward yesterday to effect his release.

Although physicians at the hospital refused to detail the nature of his case, records in the psychopathic ward at Bellevue Hospital show that he suffered his first mental collapse more than two years ago.

LIBERATED TWICE.

According to the files of Dr. Menas S. Gregory, in charge of the ward, Patridge first was admitted to Bellevue April 11, 1923, and suffered from the "excessive and continuous use of several drugs." His age was given as sixty-one.

April 18, 1923, Supreme Court Justice O'Malley signed an order committing him to the Central Islip Hospital for treatment for psychosis.

He was paroled later and released, but committed again October 12, 1925. Six days ago he again was freed.

Central Islip authorities refused to divulge who had telephoned the hospital for the famous sculptor's reincarceration Sunday night.

The original papers committing Partridge to the asylum gave his wife's name as complainant.

Mrs. Partridge said her husband was a victim of persistent insomnia from which he had been suffering for several years. She added:

"His temporary condition is due to persistent insomnia. He is getting better and we have every reason to believe he will be entirely well within two months."

She added that her husband's utterances that he was being "railroaded" should be taken as those of a sick man.

The nationally famous sculptor's incarceration this time was effected only under his most violent protest.

GENIUS NOT REMUNERATIVE.

Police stopped his cab. His guard, James J. Powers, produced commitment papers and he was allowed to return the sculptor to the hospital.

'DOPE' SENDS NOTED BEAUTY TO CITY JAIL

Mrs. May Landgren, Aristocrat, Who Wedded 3 Millionaires, "Gets 5 Months"

Wealth, social position, fame as a beauty were Mrs. May Landgren's only a year or two ago. Yesterday, her life wrecked by narcotics, she stood before three Judges in Special Sessions to hear herself sentenced to five months in a New York workhouse.

Thirty-four years old, when life that once had held every possible prospect of happiness should have been reaching fullest bloom, she was tried and found guilty of obtaining drugs by fraud and deceit.

A PITIFUL PICTURE.

Daughter of the old Van Alen ...

Prominent Persons' Names in O

BULLETS RAIN ON POLICEMEN AS AXES SMASH A BARRED DOOR

Fusillade Comes from Scared Inmates of House in Mott Street, Who Have Fear of a Hold-up

2 LEAP FROM FIRE ESCAPES

Men and Women Whose Names Were in an Address Book Are to Be Summoned and Questioned

Two spectacular raids on opium dens in East Side tenements were staged yesterday by Federal agents and detectives of the police Narcotic Division.

On one of the prisoners taken the authorities found an address book containing the names of many prominent men and women, who, it was said, might be customers of the opium resort. They refused to disclose the names, but said the persons would be interrogated by the Federal Attorney to-day, with a view to determining whether they frequented the place.

TWO JUMP TO FLEE.

Thrills in plenty were supplied in the first raid, made at No. 126 Mott street, when two of the inmates, a man and a woman, jumped from the second floor fire-escape to the sidewalk to escape.

Occupants of the upper floors, alarmed when the detectives started to batter down a heavily-barricaded door, opened fire on the raiders, presumably in the belief that they were staging a holdup.

Eight prisoners were taken in the raids and six opium pipes and several thousand dollars in drugs were seized. Dr. Carleton Simon, special deputy police commissioner, in charge of the Narcotic Division, knew nothing of the contemplated raids and was indignant when he learned that four of his detectives had been enlisted by Ralph Oyler, Federal narcotic chief, to assist.

FEBRUARY 20, 1922

FEDERAL AGENTS YESTERDAY raided apartments in Mulberry and Mott streets, capturing several men and women and seizing drugs. At 124 Mott street, Ethel Kelly leaped from a fire escape, using an umbrella as a parachute. It collapsed and she was badly hurt. Volleys of shots were blazed at the raiders, who returned the fire.

BRILLIANT LIFE RUINED BY DOPE

Graduate of Heidelberg and the University of Upsala, Sweden, former professor at Dallousie University and recently teacher of architecture at Cooper Union, John Sigge Rundgren confessed yesterday in Essex Market Court that he had become an almost hopeless drug addict. He said:

"I want to take the cure and rid myself of the habit. Then I will be able to look the world in the face. Life has been a hell on earth for me the last six years."

What this hell meant to a drug user was still further revealed when he told of spending more than $300 of his $375 monthly salary with a drug peddler.

Rundgren told the court that while living in Halifax, Nova Scotia, the seat of Dalhousie University, he had been given a white powder while under treatment for a stomach disorder, ...

Admits Being Drug Fiend

CHINATOWN RAID FURNISHED TIP FOR HIS ARREST

His Name Found in Book of Addresses of Patrons of Underworld Resort Police Broke Up

When Funds Were Cut Off He Left Theatrical District; Guard Hired to Protect Him on Trips

More details of the amazing career of George Tiffany, scion of the proud Tiffany family who was incarcerated in the Bloomingdale Hospital for the Insane on Monday, a hopeless drug addict, were revealed yesterday.

It is a tale of New York high life, of a young man of culture and refinement waging an unequal battle against the drug that had enslaved him. It reveals this close relative of the proud Tiffanys as a habitue of the underworld, a pitiful victim of the drug venders who could not overcome a mad desire for narcotics.

And through the whole story runs a sad tale of a shattered romance of a woman from a lower strata of society who loved this son of wealth deeply, not for his money, but for himself. This woman fought bravely with him against the deadly drug, but the tide of battle always flowed against her, and now she is alone, her hopes gone and left only memories of the one great love of her life.

GIRL TELLS OF DRUG "SCHOOL"—Giving her name as Catherine McDonald, twenty-four, of No. 841 Fulton street, Brooklyn, but later admitting both name and address fictitious, this girl, wrecked by drug habit, told police yesterday she had been introduced to narcotics by diamond-bedecked woman at a public dance and then introduced to drug salesman.

Girl Leaps 2 Stories with Umbrella Parachute in Drug Raid

MYSTERY GIRL SEIZED IN RAID HAS RICH MAN FOR A GUARDIAN

AUGUST 26, 1922

Chicago Woman of Unknown Parentage and Origin Receives Money for Unknown Reason

MARRIED ARMY OFFICER

Cannot Tell How Drug Habit Started—Husband Says Millionaire Gave Her Money

CHICAGO, August 25.—A pretty young woman, claiming to be an English heiress with a millionaire Chicagoan as her guardian, was taken into custody by Government narcotic agents to-day in a raid on a store frequented by negroes.

The woman, a striking brunette with bobbed hair, questioned by Agent William J. Spillard, aid to Chief Beach, of the Federal dope staff, provided the officials with the most baffling mystery they have been confronted with in their dope investigations.

Her name is Mabel Howard Rockwell Schaeffer. Her husband, Michael B. Schaeffer, is an officer of the United States Army.

Her guardian, she told her questioners, is Oscar C. Bunte, millionaire president of the Protectu Company.

IGNORANT OF HER ORIGIN.

So mysterious was her story that Colonel L. G. Nutt, national chief of narcotic agents, who is at present in Chicago, was called in to hear the statement of the woman.

The mystery arose when the girl repeatedly stated that she was en...

Drug Victims.

A SENSATION was created the other day in Paris by the wholesale conviction and sentencing of fashionable drug victims.

More than twenty customers of Comte de Delporto were charged with distributing illicit drugs to fashionable circles of Paris society and were sentenced by the court to jail terms and fines.

Those sentenced included Comte Henri de Beaurepaire, husband of Mrs. Ferris S. Thompson, widow of the American multimillionaire.

Many fashionable addresses, such as the rue Henri Martin and Avenue Montaigne appeared on the list of those convicted, who were given terms of from three to four months in jail, suspended sentences, and fines of from two to five thousand francs each.

Comte de Delporto, who, it was claimed, was furnishing drugs to society people, escape... ...ears in jail in... ...year suspen... ...in the countr...

EIGHT TITLED HEADS IN PARIS DOPE RING

JUNE 29, 1924

Leader Said to Be a Count and Now Seeking Refuge in America.

HEIRESS SQUANDERS STRANGE LEGACY ON DRUGS:

G ADDICT

Mrs. Gould's Story of Having Been 'Doped

m Den List

Louis Camp Seeks to Balk Possibility of Dope in Bout

EVER WATCHFUL—Mrs. Wilma Gould using her lorgnette on defense witnesses during trial of her $500,000 suit against her husband's family.

PRINCESS WINS LENIENCY ON DOPE CHARGE

JULY 10, 1934

Tragic Story Wins Sympathy; Lost Estates in Russian Revolution, Deserted by Husband

Shabbily dressed, sobbing at her plight, Princess Concordia di Melikoff, member of the Czarist nobility who now lives on a relief roll, received a suspended sentence yesterday on a narcotics charge.

She was arrested last month by a policeman who said she smashed a vial of heroin when he took her in custody in the San Juan Hill district of the West Side.

A few days ago she pleaded guilty to a charge of possessing dope, but the tragic story of her life, as it was revealed in a probation report, threw a different light on the case and won the sympathy of Special Sessions judges.

PROBATION REPORT.

In the report it was disclosed that the 42-year-old royalist who fell from riches to rags was posing as a narcotic addict when she was arrested. Only by taking such a pose, she said, could she get

Big Ring Reported Broken:

Strip Dancer Held In Narcotic Raid

Her 'Audience' Is the Court in Uncle Sam's Own Drama

4 Men Arrested, $25,000 Stock and Gun Taken

MARCH 25, 1937

A red-headed strip-tease dancer and four men were held yesterday after police and Federal agents announced they had smashed a big narcotic ring and seized $25,000 worth of opium, morphine and heroin.

The dancer, Mrs. Angelina Rivoti, who graced the stage of the People's Theatre on the Bowery as Agnes Murray, kept raiders waiting for 53 minutes in her Brooklyn apartment while she changed from negligee to street clothes. (Rapid calculators figured this 52 minutes longer than the time she takes to change from dress to undress in her act).

In the apartment, suspected of having been used as a supply base for several Eastern States, the agents found 16 pounds of gum opium, 71 five-tael tins of morphine tablets, a complete opium smoking outfit, 36 empty opium containers and a .38 calibre revolver.

Aisle 10 Row D No. 4 RINGSIDE $3.00 Retain Check. No Money Refunded. HOLLYWOOD LEGION STADIUM FRIDAY, APR. 8, 1938

Joe Will Cut Loose Today In Drill

SEPTEMBER 21, 1935

By LEWIS BURTON,
N. Y. American Staff Writer.

POMPTON LAKES, N.J., Sept. 20.—It is the unanimous verdict of the Joe Louis entourage that Mad Max Baer personally is dope enough. Opposed to further dopery on Tuesday night, Messrs. John Roxborough and Julian Black, the eminent mangers of the Brown Meat Chopper, will request the New York State Athletic Commission on the afternoon of the big brawl to prevent such goings-on in Baer's corner.

"We feel compened to do this because of rumors we've heard in connection with other Baer fights," said the soft-spoken Roxborough. "We will ask that they do something to prevent use of strychnine, hypodermic needle or any artificial stimulant. Even though it's only hearsay, we want to make sure that it is a fair contest."

The unnatural stimulants, in the profound judicial opinions of Messrs. Roxborough and Black, do not include sherry, whiskey or similar elixirs.

LIQUOR GETS O. K.

"He can go and get himself drunk, for all we care," they agreed magnanimously.

The doping rumors are traced directly to Mad Max and one of his late seconds, Mike Cantwell. In post-Braddock speechmaking, Cantwell made vague allusions to hopping influences and Baer more than once has introduced strychnine into conversation.

COFFEE WOULD HAVE NULLIFIED DRUG, HE SAYS

MARCH 6, 1935

Detective Describes Raid on 'Prince' Mike's Apartment; Tells Also of Petting Parties

By JAMES STREET.

Her husband's clan and kin seek to prrove Mrs. Edward Gould suffered with indigestion and not knockout drops the night she wastrapped in a bedroom skit with the shy and counterfeit "Prince" Mike Romanoff.

The foundation for the prosiac contention was set by Dr. Harry Lichtenstein yesterday. He's an authority on narcotics and scoffed at Mrs. Gould's plea that her senses were stunned by a mixture of chloryl hydrate and caffein. He said the caffein would have neutralized the dope.

THE author of "The Legend of Aleister Crowley" cites several amusing incidents to indicate how complete is the belief in Crowley's wickedness.

"The publishers of his autobiography, now in the press, have had some fun," he writes. "Weird customers have walked into their offices, uttering cryptic warnings and have vanished, leavin... One of them ... fingers wher... Crowley.' His ... all the time ... said: 'That ... can read tho... are thinking ... weird visitor ... merely wit... crossed, nio... ber, remem... Hamlet's fat...

"Wickedest Man in the World"

HE HAS been accused of every crime in the catalogue, from cannibalism to high treason. The principal papers to attack him, the Sunday Express of London and John Bull, have not hesitated to impute to him every unnatural and perverted vice, all the sinister and unmentionable sins. They have pictured him as a fiend incarnate, practicing the black mass and other orgiastic rituals. They have strongly hinted that he plotted the murder of a friend in order to place the man's wife in his power. There has been absolutely no limit to which they have not gone.

And Crowley never replied in any way whatsoever.

"It has taken 100,000,000 years to produce Aleister Crowley. The world has indeed labored and has at last brought forth a man ... Crowley has twisted a subtle cord, on which he has suspended the universe, and swinging it round has sent the whole fickle world conception of these excogitating spiders into those realms which lie behind Time and beyond Space."

"From time to time," Stephensen says, "he 'mysteriously' disappeared; to reappear eventually in his old haunts, looking years younger, refreshed in body and mind, even more sardonic, witty, vituperative and 'wicked.'"

Crowley took an active part in the controversy over Epstein's monument to Oscar Wilde in Paris. When the police refused to permit it to be unveiled, Crowley unveiled it by a stratagem "in the interests of art." The legend grew.

—December 14, 1930.

Crowley was born in 1875 of a family of religious fanatics, members of the repressive Puritan sect, the Plymouth Brethren. His mother usually designated him by the mystic name of "The Beast 666," which always has perversely pleased Crowley. As a boy and in adolescence his chief hobbies were poetry, chemistry, mathematics and chess, and the sport he liked best was rock climbing, at which he early attained great skill. He was sent down to Cambridge at 20, the possessor of a fortune of $200,000, which he had inherited on the death of his parents. In 1898, his third year in the university, he published five volumes of verse, "Aceldama," "White Stains," "The Tale of Archais," "Songs of the Spirit" and "Jephthah." Within 10 years he was to publish more than 30 volumes, most of them privately, and all of them beautiful examples of the printer's and engraver's crafts. "His poetry was 'outrageous' in the manner of Swinburne, Baudelaire and the Yellow Book. One of his earliest works was a poetic reply to Kraft-Ebing."

THE DIARY OF A DRUG FIEND

BY

ALEISTER CROWLEY

RIVAL DRUGS GROOM GOING ... VEDDING

...nds in Hospital ... at Church While ... Vaits at Altar

Followed by Cere... Desp... Neve...

SHOPLIFTER URGED BY DRUG CRAVING

Woman Addicted to Habit 30 Years Admits Stealing Two Dresses to Buy Narcotics.

9 OTHERS ROBBED STORES

...to Workhouse for ...s for Stealing ...alued at $3.

...rs a drug addict ...

BEAUTY KILLED BY DRUG HABIT

Mrs. William Witty, Know... Stage as Hazel King, D... in Squalor.

MATE IN SOUTH AM...

Became Ill in Taxi an... to Bootblack's Disma... ter Street Hom...

The beauty of Hazel ... chorus girl, formerly in ... Garden revue, won ... heart of William Witty ... nent importer and exp... friends thought that sh... tle down to a quiet d... But in the absence ... band in South America ... back to the ...

NOTED BEAUTY'S SUICIDE CAUSED BY NARCOTICS

Winifred Black Tells How Dope Ruined Life of Countess Apponyi, Wealthy Viennese

By WINIFRED BLACK.
Universal Service Special Correspondent.
Copyright, 1931, by Universal Service, Inc.

GENEVA, May 13.—The beautiful Countess Dina Apponyi, wife of a great ocean steamship line director, killed herself the other

Dope 'Bargain' Ruined Career, Says Doctor

FEBRUARY 9, 1930

Dope Paved Way to Crime Career, Woman Says.

LIFE PITIFUL

Compares Doom with That of Baby Slayer.

In response to numerous requests, the New York American herewith re-publishes, for all its readers, the poignant story of Mrs. Ruth St. Claire, written after she was sentenced to life imprisonment for shoplifting;

By RUTH ST. CLAIRE.

I'm just another victim of narcotic drugs. Morphine—taken, at first, to kill pain—has doomed me to a hopeless, drab existence behind gray prison walls.

I took two baby dresses from a store to give to a friend for Christmas—and am sentenced to life imprisonment.

Mrs. Gladys Parks took the lives of two innocent babies—she gets off with twenty-... years.

I entered the court room sick in mind and body—distraught—... dazed—never thinking when I pleaded guilty that the Baumes law would be invoked against me. Fifteen minutes was all it took them to dispose of my case, sending me up for life!

I expected to go to prison. ...ned the thought, I'm a ... of the narcotic ... thought that if I ... away some place where I ... get the morphine ... would be hope of regeneration for me.

BILLIE HOLIDAY
Chosen As The Greatest Female Singer
1949
Singer Held In Dope Raid
Billie Holiday Free on Bail
LADY SINGS THE BLUES
BILLIE HOLIDAY WITH WILLIAM DUFTY
"One of the most candid self-portraits ever painted on a typewriter." —NEW YORK HERALD TRIBUNE
BILLIE HOLIDAY SEIZED IN RAID
Singer Taken on Dope Charge; Manager Also Held
FREE ON BAIL
SERVED TIME
TELLS OF RAID
BLAMES ANOTHER
PAID HIGH PRICE

HOLLYWOOD

DORE SCHARY — A COMMIE RED FELLOW TRAVELER

The Mayer regime at MGM continued peacefully until a few years ago when **Dore Schary was let go by RKO** and picked up by MGM. The New York office of MGM placed producer Schary as production head with powers second only to L.B. **That is when the trouble began!** Schary and Mayer, as time passed on, couldn't see "eye-to-eye" on matters, and they often split wide open on important issues.

BERKELEY'S RED CONFUSION

Students For Democratic Action, a not-too-old Communist Red headed by Red Sympathizers and Red Fellow Travelers, is the organization making a determined effort to cause more confusion in and around the University of California with their Red propaganda. **The Students For Democratic Action** members have been passing large red and pink capsules with Commie propaganda enclosed. Students receive the capsules through the mails, in library books, in the seats of parked cars and find them on the lawns and steps of the University of California. As I've often related, the University of California, horrible as it may read, harbors more Crummie Commies, Red Sympathizers and Red Fellow Travelers, than any other University in America.

MARION DAVIES NEPHEW "STOOGE" IN HEARST BRIBE

The citizenry is well aware that Hollywood has been "slopping" around in "affairs" and DOPE which is both vile and disgraceful. That being recognized, people now wish to know when the housecleaning is going to start. When will the many guilty persons be brought to the front and punished? They are also asking, will studio executives also be disciplined and brought to trial for permitting such promiscuous activities?

Sex Offenders

Sex offenders, perverts and vice gangs are not new to California. Suddenly, out of the blue, John Q. Public hears about sex crimes on the radio, reads it in newspapers and magazines and finds it the topic of conversation on buses and streetcars and over the dinner table.

For certain, DOPE addicts, sex perverts and other unnecessary nuisances will soon be faced with startling revelations being prepared against them. This is no game of cowboys and Indians. This game is played for "keeps." Responsible studio big-wigs don't seem to care if Hollywood becomes a heavy "grey" zone of crime through narcotics, etc., etc. **But fortunately, that is why federal law enforcement agencies were born . . . born to handle even those who believe they are**

DREAMS, INC., BOMBSHELL

GARLAND — PARSONS DREAMS, INC.

STUDIOS PROTECT "DREAMS, INC."

JUDY GARLAND VICTIM OF HOLLYWOOD TURMOIL

FLYNN — DOPE — WALK

POLITICAL CORRUPTION

VICE FACTS

DOPE EXPOSES

DO NOT UNDERRATE THE LATTER STATEMENT. I TOLD YOU ONCE THERE WOULD BE DOPE ARRESTS, AND THERE WERE.

Judy Garland is only one of several thousand boys and girls over a period of years, who have been hurt, kicked around, misled through parties and vice, victims of violence in and out of studios, forced to attend vile parties or else, broken into the "Reefer Smoking Habit" and threatened with beating, if they refuse to be a "PEDDLER" of "DOPE" or "VICE."

Milton Mezz Mezzrow

To all the junkies and lushheads in two-bit scratchpads, and the flophouse grads in morgue iceboxes.

(R.I.P.)

To the sweettalkers, the gumbeaters, the highjivers, out of the gallion for good and never going to take low again.

(You got to make it, daddy.)

To Bessie Smith, Jimmy Noone, King Oliver, Louis Armstrong, Zutty Singleton, Johnny Dodds, Sidney Bechet and Tommy Ladnier.

(Grab a taste of millennium, gate.)

To all hipsters, hustlers and fly cats tipping along The Stroll.

(Keep scuffling.)

To all the cons in all the houses of many slammers, wrastling with chinches.

(Short time, boys.)

It's a funny thing about marihuana—when you first begin smoking it you see things in a wonderful soothing, easygoing new light. All of a sudden the world is stripped of its dirty gray shrouds and becomes one big bellyful of giggles, a spherical laugh, bathed in brilliant, sparkling colors that hit you like a heatwave. Nothing you cold any more; there's a humorous tickle and great meaning in the least little thing, the twitch of somebody's little finger or the click of a beer glass. All your pores open like funnels, your nerve ends stretch their mouths wide, hungry and thirsty for new sights and sounds and sensations; and every sensation, when it comes, is the most exciting one you've ever had. You can't get enough of anything—you want to gobble up the whole goddamned universe just for an appetizer. Them first kicks are a killer, Jim.

Really the Blues

REWARD
TRUE CRIME CASES

MILTON "MEZZ" MEZZROW

MEZZ MEZZROW... the colorful Chicago clarinetist jams with **Pops Foster, Tommy Ladnier**

HOLLYWOOD DOPE ADDICTS

VICE SQUAD

Gene Krupa, drum beating high priest of jitterbugs, who gave marijuana to 20 yr. old John Pateakos, paid with jail term.

MOVIE STARLET LILA LEEDS JOYFUL ON RELEASE FROM PRISON

Former Dead End Kid, Huntz Hall, arrested with friend on a narcotic charge, mugs for cameraman.

She is the real Hollywood dope addict—the furtive, unknown little victim of a giant octopus that lives off human flesh and blood.

Hollywood is a "natural" for the dope pusher.

The movie capital of the world is a never-never land of high pressure, frustration, brief and unhinging flings at fame, pitiful disappointments, rib-crushing competition. In that soil the weedbeds of marijuana can flourish, the fevered dreams of stronger drugs can provide

Did Injustice Triumph?

Did it all start with Robert Mitchum? Did this star set a bad example to Hollywood teenagers?

WHISPER

THE STORIES BEHIND THE HEADLINES

EXPOSED: HOLLYWOOD

HUSH

WHAT YOU DON'T KNOW ABOUT

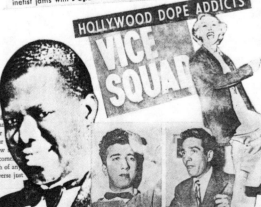

Slaves of the Devil's Capsules

Aimee Semple McPherson—the Evangelist Habitually Took Sleeping Pills, and the Bottle, Left, Lay Near Her Bed When She Was Found Dying—Probably From an Overdose Accidentally Taken When the Drug Had Dulled Her Mind.

Bobby Soxers and Downy-Cheeked Boys Take the Pills with Various Drinks, Say They Get a "Jolt," Call Their Sprees "Goof-Ball Parties."

Those "Harmless" Little Sleeping Pills, So Easy to Obtain, Are Gaining Victims by the Millions, Kill 10 to 20 a Day, and Have Become the Nation's Fastest Rising Menace

A Criminal Trade Must Always Find New Customers—If It Cannot, It Creates Them. The Rich Field Now for Barbiturate Racketeers Is Among the High Schoolers.

LADY is worried. She tries to sleep. She … about for a little while that seems … and then she opens a brown glass … pours out one or two brilliant red, … blue or green capsules. She swal… and shortly thereafter the evil … capsule takes her over, body and …

Th… pills to put her to sleep. … these sleeping pills, how… effect is to destroy the … she has already taken a … forgets she has taken …

… next morning—and … the rate of 10 to 20 … autopsy and an in… …ing she said during … lady is a suicide and not entitled to be buried in holy ground.

The drug thus widely used is a barbiturate, a sedative. Properly employed under expert supervision, it is a valuable agent in the practice of medicine. Indiscriminately thrown open to public use, it is a threat. Fifty thousand drugstores over the length and breadth of the nation are dispensing the various forms of this subtle drug under restrictions so loose that they count for little in the protection of the ignorant public.

Even more sensational, because of the circumstances, was the death from poisoning of the Mexican motion picture star, Lupe Velez, a few months later. It was officially determined to be suicide. Lupe had for years been taking sleeping pills to pacify her high-strung nerves. Mercurial, intense, living always on the heights or in the depths of emotional stress, she was the type to which drug relief is most dangerous.

Late in November 1944, she had announced her engagement to the handsome Austrian-born actor, Harald Ramond, the "only man who is able to control Lupe, so naturally I am going to marry him." There was reason for her to marry, since she was an expectant mother.

SHE was found, dead in bed, in her luxurious Beverly Hills home. Several seconal capsules were scattered upon the satin coverlet. On the bed table was a vial bearing a Mexican label. She had written this note:

> Harald:
> May God forgive you and forgive me, too, but I prefer to take my life away and our baby's before I bring him in shame or kill him. How could you, Harald, fake such great love for me and our baby when all the time you didn't want us? I see no other way for me, so goodbye and good luck to you.
> Love,
> Lupe.

Unquestionably the convenience of these potentially deadly drugs may be an incentive to suicide. Nobody would think of leaving a loaded pistol or a bottle of carbolic acid handy

November 25, 1945

proved by the U. S. Department of Commerce figures, showing an increase in five years from 4½ million to 2½ billion grains. In other words, the total of doses taken every year has jumped to a grand total of five billion, allowing half a grain to a dose. At last reports it was a $20,000,000 industry. Experts on the subject believe that the next figures will nearly double this. Uncle Sam is on an unparalleled barbiturate binge.

Among some drug manufacturers, the incentive to push sales mountainously high is great, since the profit is large. Any company can perfect a new barbiturate by having its chemists slightly alter the molecular structure of a previously made barbiturate.

The new product then may be patented under a trade name, and the sale price of the product can be fixed by the maker.

Since the makers decide on their own prices, the limit is what the trade will bear; steadily rising sales are reflected in steadily rising returns.

SLEEPING pills—barbit… headlines last year wh… Sister Aimee Semple M… Four-Square Gospel and… Los Angeles revivals, wa… …tel room. Tw… …ently …

"America's Opium," an experienced public health official terms the little "harmless" sleeping pills, the use of which in this country is reaching such ominous proportions.

"A national menace," adds a law enforcement officer.

They are a menace because it is so easy to buy them legally; almost as easy, illegally. Now glance at some of the results.

A car goes zigzagging from side to side of a Los Angeles thoroughfare. A woman with glazed and staring eyes sits beside the wheel. The car hits the curb and luckily stops before anyone is injured. "Drunk," say the police. But there is no liquor on the woman's breath. In her pocket is found a vial containing 96 sleeping tablets. That is the answer to her wild, half-conscious ride.

A Massachusetts woman buys 200 of these pills, murders her lover, and goes to jail after ineffectually poisoning herself.

A laboratory scientist in a mountain town "dopes up" on a form of the drug, robs his best friend, and terrorizes the streets with a loaded revolver.

A car full of high school boys and girls go out on a "Geronimo jag" (barbiturates taken with liquor) in a borrowed car, and, when the party is over, the car is a wreck, and the boys are crazed and fighting.

A once prosperous real estate man is admitted to a Chicago hospital, both legs rotted to the bone with ulcerous sores. He has been taking his drug in the form of self-administered

Juvenile courts in our cities note an increasing record of barbiturate drugs use among the boys and girls brought before them. Out of 200 delinquents questioned in one court, 7 per cent confessed to indulgence in "goof balls."

A motion picture headliner of ten years ago is a nervous wreck in a sanitarium, having formed a habit from taking "sleepers" for the very nervousness which they served only to fix upon her. Nearly five per cent of all suicides, excluding self-destruction by gas, are attributed to these easily procured poisons. A popular movie actress finds the bedside pills too convenient a form of escape to resist and, in a fit of lovesick melancholia, takes a fatal dose.

A distinguished woman religious leader swallows her self-prescribed allowance, forgets it in the daze which it produces, repeats, and dies.

A young man, his imagination overstimulated by a mixture of drug and alcohol, confesses to a serious crime of which he is innocent.

THE draft-evading pills were traced to a surprising number of pharmacies, not only in the San Francisco region but throughout the state. Nearly 50 druggists were indicted. The promising traffic was ruined before it got a good start. Few, if any, of the $10 investors got their money's worth.

The American Medical Association lists the following evils from the promiscuous use of the barbiturates:

Habit formation.
Toxic (poisonous) cumulative action.
Successful as well as unsuccessful suicide attempts.
Substitution for alcohol.
Causative factor in motor accidents.
Recognized factor in criminal attacks.

Long ago stringent laws put an end to the wholesale creation of dope fiends through the unbridled use of opium, morphine and cocaine. Any person in unauthorized possession of these drugs is not only liable to jail but is more than likely to go there, thanks to the viligance of enforcement officers, Federal, state and local. But these same officers are impotent to combat effectively the new barbiturate drugs under the present slack laws or no laws.

Not until the sleeping pills are listed and controlled as narcotics will the pernicious trade be checked.

FOR many years stringent laws have controlled such perilous and habit-forming drugs as morphine, heroin, cocaine, hasheesh, and the like. The public is well instructed in the risks which their … involves. Traffic among addicts has been …ly cut down. Some victims have now turned …e less enslaving and destructive but still …rous barbiturates.

…gislation is urgently needed, classing these …s with the narcotics and limiting their sale. …thout such safeguards the public will lack …ry protection, and the record of barbiturate …des, crime and delinquency will continue to

…orge P. Larrick of the Federal Food and … Inspection Division strongly favors Federal …or barbiturates similar to the Narcotics Act …lling this, that the sleeping pills be placed … the supervision of the Narcotics Bureau.

…need a law," he says, "that makes every transaction in the distribution of barbiturates a matter of record. We ought to be able to determine at a glance what retail store has been getting excessive supplies."

Expert opinion upon control of the barbiturates may be summed up in the following general suggestions.

1. Federal action identifying these drugs as dangerous narcotics and placing them under the Narcotics Act. This would favorably influence state legislation, since the states tend to follow Federal lead in such matters.
2. No retail sale except upon a physician's prescription.
3. Prohibition of the refilling of a prescription except upon express permission of the prescribing physician.
4. Make every transaction in the transfer of a barbiturate drug, from manufacturer to consumer, a matter of record. Thus an accredited official could determine readily what stores were doing an abnormal business.
5. As is now the case with the … other habit-forming drugs, declare … private possession of any barbiturate … the authority of a physician.

… upon full and honest labelling of … containing the drug; sta… …unt …ll or capsule, names of … …nd. … directions for use, warning that the … are dangerous and potentially habit-forming, and notice that it is not renewable.

For Lupe Velez, Desperate and Remorseful, Sleeping Pills Were the Way Out of a World Grown Suddenly Too Complex. Those She Swallowed Took Her Life; Those She Scattered on the Satin Coverlet of Her Bed Told the Story.

…e Grand Jury Called Charles E. Bedaux, …ed-Up Engineer and Intimate of the Duke … Windsor. But He Never Answered—…leeping Pills Stilled His Voice Forever.

Bela Lugosi, well-known Dracula of screen fame, signed himself into hospital for treatment after being on drugs for years.

Judy Garland is hugged by Marlene Dietrich backstage at Palace, after suicide attempt.

GOOF BALLS OVER HOLLYWOOD

The stars' switch to barbiturates is understandable. Goof balls are easy to get. There is scarcely a doctor in Hollywood who does not recognize his patient's genuine need for some sedative amidst that bedlam. And the barbiturates are just as effective in banishing worry and excitement as the narcotics, wi… damaging aftermath and mo… portant, there's no stigma a… messy conflict with the law.

Blonde Anne Sterling lies on a stretcher in a Hollywood hospital where her stomach was pumped in the belief she had taken an overdose of goof balls.

French glamour girl Corinne Calvet reached for sleeping pills in the wake of her stormy divorce from actor John Bromfield.

When Abigail Adams, 37-year-old actress, was found dead, police listed case as suicide.

The limp form of actress Susan Hayward is carried from a car at a … hospital by detectives who had to batter their way into her house.

…E GOOF-BALL BINGE

…USH

…OU KNOW—September 25¢

The climate is wonderf… in Los Angeles. But dope, sex and sin are the shame of Hollywood and Souther… California.—Is the mov… industry to blame for th… serious vice conditions?

Is Benzedrine harmful?

The great constipation racket

DETECTIVE WORLD

INSIDE detective

HEADQUARTERS DETECTIVE

Though the industry is trying to keep it under wraps, the situation is acute. Goof balls are all over Hollywood! The blunt fact is that the movie capital is in the grips of a barbiturate craze and dozens of its best known stars and starlets are either sleeping pill addicts or are on the verge of addiction.

The shock in the wake of Judy Garland's impetuous action did not stop the alarming cycle. After Judy, such talented and popular stars as Mary Astor, Anne Sterling, Diana Barrymore, Corinne Calvet, Abigail Adams and, last but not least, Susan Hayward, were felled by sleeping pills.

When Sleeping Pills Lie Handy at the Bedside, Death Lurks There, Too. The Care-Driven Civilian Swallows a Couple—and Then, in a Daze, Takes Too Many More; the

BARE LEGS
SHOCK CHIEF
"The exposure of the bare legs of girls that goes with the wearing of California bathing suits is indecent. The California one-piece knit bathing suit is all right, but stockings should be worn with it."
This was the assertion of Chief of Police R. C. Miller of Atlantic
BLUE RIBBON GARAGE
Phone 1107
1916 19th St.
No. 100
CLAIM CHECK
CLAIM CHECK No.
24432
JAZZ GIRL
Queen of the Underwo
Who Worked in Partn

The Jazz Age

Opium? No! Cocaine? No! The Great American Brain-Killer is Dance Music. . .
—Portland Oregonian, *1932*

It was F. Scott Fitzgerald, an alcoholic, who named it the Jazz Age—appropriately enough, for jazz and booze fueled the whole giddy era. Newspapers became almost mythic, recording the stuff of dreams and nightmares: "Ruddy cheeked collegiates down from New Haven on the loose with gin bottles protruding from dinner jackets danced with those abandoned women with eyes suspiciously bright from cocaine."

Insanity and drugs were the key metaphors. Left over from the Gay Nineties were artists gone mad from absinthe or opium, stuck in asylums, still painting and writing. Their plight was recognized (Utrillo, for instance, was awarded the Legion of Honor while "making superb masterpieces in a sanatorium for inebriates"), which led to a whole modern genre of schizophrenic art and prison writing.

In 1931 biochemists at Cornell declared that insanity was related to brain proteins and could be cured with drugs—an interesting hint of present research on endorphins, the opiate-like protein molecules manufactured naturally in the brain. But even this could not explain "Ouijamania, the Strangest Craze of All," with ghastly spirits driving policemen naked into the streets and commanding youngsters to kill their parents.

The temperance movement had spawned an intemperate era, a world-shaking generation gap. Winsor McCay captured it brilliantly in a two-panel cartoon. In one frame a little girl calls hesitantly from the door of an old-fashioned saloon, "Father, Dear Father, Come Home with Me Now." On the other side, twenty years later, old dad yanks the flapper out of a swanky speakeasy: "Daughter, Dear Daughter. . ." But many a young man and woman discovered that "you can't go home again."

To prohibition moralists having fun was sin: dancing, drinking, playing cards, and most of all jazz itself—"The Opiate That Inflames the Mind and Incites to Riotous Orgies of Delirious Syncopation." For the first time an entire generation found itself outlawed—by the Volstead Act—and learned to laugh at the laws, "buying that thing called fun" in speakeasies. Going to jail? "I just love prison! Such gobs of human interest!" gushed Tex Guinan, "queen of the whoopee makers."

"You are all a lost generation," said Gertrude Stein of the expatriates who fled to Paris in droves. A new high-flying, devil-may-care internationalism: "Wild Orgies by American Girls in Grip of Paris." Economic effects: "The price of 'dope' in Paris is now so high that only Americans can afford its indulgence." Not quite: the capitals of Europe—London, Paris, and Berlin—dazzled in postwar decadence, with cocaine on bistro tabletops, ether sucked from silk hankies, elegant opium dens the rage, and "hashish making the Apache dance" in Montmartre.

Fads and flappers conquered the world: bobbed hair, short skirts, the charleston and the tango, sultry vamp stares, cigarettes, knickerbockers, one-piece bathing suits, midnight auto rides, petting—men and women breaking loose from outmoded drudge roles, living fifty years ahead of their time. Magnificent women! Isadora Duncan, Josephine Baker, Billie Carleton—Alice B. Toklas whipping up a batch of hashish fudge on rainy days. And hints of hippies, too, in San Francisco: "Nature Girl" never wore shoes or any flapper's adornments, dressed in a simple shift and Indian headdress, kept animals, studied dance.

Up the river from New Orleans with jazz came the reefer. A black-and-white cultural mix, hymned in the first truly American music. Old oompah blues was replaced by soaring improvisation: Louis Armstrong and Earl "Fatha" Hines playing "Muggles" (1929). Teapads in Harlem and Al Jolson on the silver screen. "The increase in use of drugs is alarming." "Whether you're crazy or sane depends on where you live." "Ex-Follies Beauty, Who Wed Negro, Has Nervous Breakdown."

Radio, rum, dope, and jazz took the blame, Few indeed were the reporters who saw, as Louis Reid did in 1932, that "this dance music which echoes through the homes of America. . . is the most definite contribution to American civilization which radio broadcasting is making today." By 1934 the Jazz Age had vanished, crushed by the Depression—"campus youth today is sane, sober, and purposeful"—but nobody could foresee the age of rock 'n' roll.

NEW YORK HERALD, SUNDAY, FEBRUARY 7, 1897.

INSANITY AND ART.

A French Asylum Has Made Experiments Which Promise Wonderful Results.

MOST REMEDIAL OF WORK.

Even Lunatics Who Have Never Before Touched a Brush Show Unsuspected Talent.

FORGET THEIR MANIAS.

HE French degenerates in art are looked after at government expense. Not the fancied degenerates against whom Nordau has been waging a degenerate war, not the heroes of intellect upon whom the little German professor has been raining his ineffectual blows, but the unknown artists whose brains have physiologically and pathologically given way under the strain of existence, so that their owners had to be cooped up in madhouses, sanitariums and hospitals.

The recent passage of a small appropriation by the city of Paris for the purchase of artistic appliances devoted to the use of the crazy artists of the Asylum of Ville-Evrard has drawn public attention to a curious feature in the life of the great metropolis.

Of course the funny man saw his opportunity at once. He suggested that now he understood how certain paintings in the Salon had come into existence. He rang the changes upon this extremely obvious jest.

The social philosopher has seen his opportunity as well as the funny man. He has made a study of the crazy art department and has found it full of hopeful lessons in morbid mentality.

WORK AND MADNESS.

Every one knows that work is considered by alienists to be a powerful aid in curing the mental invalid. Every hour employed by a lunatic in some regular toil is an hour conquered from dreams and divagations. During all the time the patient is absorbed in his work he loses sight of his special mania. When work becomes a habit to him his equilibrium is more and more likely to be completely restored. The curative power of work is even more valuable than that of sleep. It is not surprising, therefore, that the experience at Ville-Evrard has proved most satisfactory to the medical faculty. Over sixty-three per cent of the entire number of lunatics have been interested in artistic work. A few were artists before their entrance. The majority were not. Some of them had never attempted to draw in their lives, yet in the short space of a few months they turned out fairly good work.

Now sixty-three per cent is practically the entire number of lunatics that were sane enough not to need the gentle restraint of a padded cell or a straitjacket.

HINT FOR SING SING.

Is there not here a hint for the workless New York prisons? If lunatics can be turned into artists at short notice, why not convicts?

A great revolution has been worked in the Paris asylum. Formerly all were indiscriminately set to work at some mechanical occupation, which disgusted and wearied many. One day an epileptic who had been a theatrical scene painter, said in the hearing of Dr. Marandon de Montyèle, head physician of the men's department:—

"Ah, if I only had my pencils and brushes again! I feel that my hand is losing its cunning through enforced idleness, and when I am well again I will be unable to find work."

"But what could you do with your pencils and brushes?" asked the Doctor, who had himself often thought over the danger which the other had suggested. "Here we haven't any theatrical decorations to paint."

"Well, I'd paint frescoes on the walls of our corridors, or, if need be, I'd paint little pictures on canvas that might be used here and there for decorative purposes. After all, even if my work were no good to others, it would be good to me. It would keep me in practice."

This conversation introduced a new idea into Dr. Montyèle's mind. It germinated into other forms. He decided ... only ... would be beneficial ... that ... would ... the ... which ... persecuting-persecuted have forgotten their imaginary enemies, a hopeless

former life suddenly remembered his former pursuit.

Nor is this all. Seeing their comrades at work, other lunatics who had never known the love of art, who had never been trained in artistic work, caught the fever. Interested at first only in their neighbors' work, they eventually developed an individual interest in art. They tried their own hands at the same work. Some of them have made astonishing progress.

A patient suffering from the manie des grandeurs, who had never felt the slightest artistic instinct stirring within him, learned at the end of three months of hard work to evolve landscapes from his inner consciousness which had real feeling and a sense of atmosphere. He was a little tailor. Disgusted with life, he had frequently attempted suicide, and it was not until he took up the pencil that his mania showed possibilities of eventual recuperation.

Then there is the epileptic patient who suggested the idea. He is making astonishing progress. His asylum work is infinitely superior in originality and perfection of detail to anything he ever did in his saner days.

CURIOUS CASES.

There is an engraver of brass who executes without a model chandeliers, vases and cups of more than ordinary beauty. The official report says of him:—"Outside of his trade, of which he preserves a perfect memory, he is incapable of the slightest consecutive occupation. At one time he was afflicted with the mania of persecution and of greatness. To-day he cannot connect two ideas, nor has he left sufficient intellectual vigor for delirium. His profession alone survives amid the wreck of his mentality."

Compare this case with that of a miller who has become in the asylum a sculptor in wood. He had no previous training. It is not a case of survival from the past. It is a new and hitherto unsuspected talent that has been developed in his insanity. Unfortunately, this poor devil thinks himself enveloped by spiritual influences, and believes that he has no liberty of thought or action. Only the other day, as he was carving a stag, he placed the piece of wood under his chin. When some fellow patient remarked on this he explained that an uncontrollable power had forced him to this eccentricity.

Then there is an alcoholic patient who had once been a painter on porcelain. Nine years ago he became a drunkard. He fell lower and lower, until his intellect was almost destroyed. For many years he was unable to do any work. At the asylum, however, he again took up his brush. With the resumption of his old work he made rapid steps toward recovery. He has already painted more than two hundred plates, which adorn the walls of the refectory, and which have a positive commercial value.

The complete success of this experiment should stimulate Americans to introduce it here.

CRAZY ARTISTS AT WORK.

JONAH AND THE WHALE.

Biblical Scholars Agree That the Story Was Merely a Myth.

TO THE EDITOR OF THE HERALD:—

One would imagine from the commotion raised by certain ministers over Dr. Lyman Abbott's sermon on "Jonah and the Whale" that the subject had never been discussed nor the veracity of the story questioned by a preacher until now. There is the same old cry:—"It is in the Bible, which is the word of God. Therefore it must be true."

Unfortunately for these clerical critics the Bible is not a single book, but a collection of books, many of them (like Jonah) being by utterly unkn... authors, and others, or portions of othe... last twelve verses of the Gosp... and the so-called S... edly spurio... inent Biblic...

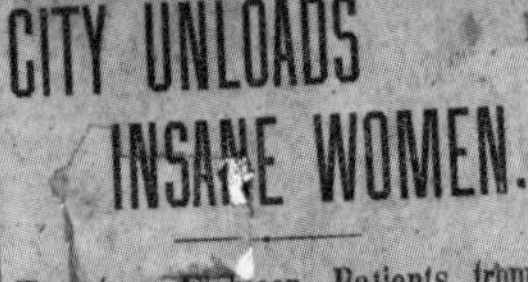

Transfers Eighteen Patients from Bellevue Hospital to Ward's Island Despite State Officials' Objection.

MACDONALD'S EDICT DEFIED.

In Their Old Clothing the Demented Women Were Left on the Island's Pier.

BELLEVUE'S GATES ARE CLOSED.

Guarded Against the Return of the Patients in Violation of the Court's Order.

Amazing Case of the Raving Maniac Spending His Last Days Painting Superb Masterpieces in a Sanatorium

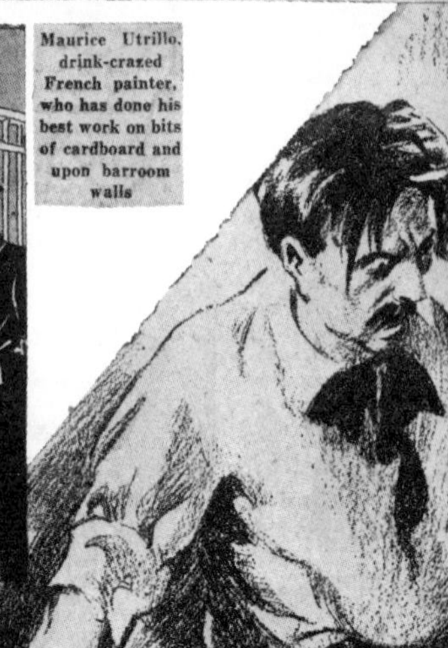

Maurice Utrillo, drink-crazed French painter, who has done his best work on bits of cardboard and upon barroom walls

Insane from Absin...

By R. S.

Paris.

A RAVING-MAD painter, who is spending his last days making superb masterpieces in a sanatorium for inebriates, was presented with the Legion of Honor recently, the French Government's supreme tribute to one of the greatest artistic geniuses France has ever produced.

He is Maurice Utrillo, the derelict and disreputable Bohemian who has immortalized Montmartre with his palette and brush, but wrecked his life doing it. Standing on the edge of a madman's grave today, at the age of 45, it is said that he has not drawn a sober breath for almost thirty years, except during the nine times he has been interned in insane asylums and drink-cure establishments. He does not have the slightest realization that he is the greatest French painter of his generation; that the pictures he sold for a single drink a few years ago are now priced at thousands of dollars, and that he will go down through the centuries in legend as another Francois Villon. And Utrillo does not care about any of these things. All he has ever cared about is alcohol. He himself has often confessed that he never painted for the love of painting, but only to satisfy his insane appetite.

AND so, from the age of 15 or 16, Maurice Utrillo became known as "The Drunken Painter" of Montmartre. He carried his palette, his paint tubes and his brushes about with him in his ragged clothes and dashed off most of his work on pieces of cardboard, barroom walls and even in the washrooms. As he never had money, a barkeeper would demand a painting of some sort for a bottle of wine and he would work like a demon for several hours in order to have his drink. And then, craving more liquor, he would agree to do another scene, so that most of his work was done when he was intoxicated. In fact, he was never sober and so he was the butt of all sorts of coarse jokes. It was sport to invite "Monsieur Maurice" to have a drink and then drop cigarette ashes in his glass when he was not looking. If he burst out into one of his insane fits of anger out he went! He could sleep in the gutter or be dragged off to the police station for the night, just as he cho...

Perhaps this early barroom painting was crude, but there was a strange realism about it that gripped even his riffraff associates. These works are valued much more highly today than his later and more polite productions. Any one of them will bring a thousand dollars, and from there up to five or ten thousand.

For years the police looked on Utrillo as a vicious derelict, and many a night they smashed his head open with their clubs when he fought them. The time finally came when he was an honored guest in any station on Montmartre hill, regardless of his condition, and every policeman was begging for a little painting. And, though dead drunk, he would sit up all night in a station dashing off little things for the uniformed bulls!

4 MAY 12, 1901. NEW YORK HERALD

REFINED WOMEN IN INSANE PAVILION

MRS. EDITH HEATHMERE

MISS LALLIAN HEATHMERE

believe persons were scheming aga... and trying to get her money, and ... sometimes sent for me for tr... I found her in a very excited ... She was a woman of a ner... vous temperament, of a hi... melancholy or despo... she was rather of a ... disposition, and th... and her daughte... ing instance... filial devot...

Dr. A... third ... Heath... year... rega... pris...

THE OPIUM-SMOKER

TONE-POEM

75 cents

MEMORY

A MINIATURE

50 cents

Poems from the Lyrics of Arthur Symons

Insanity Is On Steady Increase

ARTHUR SYMONS TELLS HOW HE WENT MAD

The Celebrated English Author's Own Story—Recently Disclosed for the First Time—of the Most Harrowing Experience in His Life.

The tragedy of Utrillo's life is reflected in his pictures, most of which were done when he was in a semi-crazed condition. Until recent years he wandered about Montmartre, painting and drinking, but finally his reason gave way and he was placed in a sanatorium

MEMORY

As a perfume doth remain
In the folds where it hath lain,
So the thought of you, remaining
Deeply folded in my brain,
Will not leave me; all things leave me:
You remain.

ARTHUR SYMONS

THE most pathetic side of Utrillo's life is the ceaseless effort he made to save himself from this awful appetite. Time and again he went to the home of some friend, or some private sanatorium, and literally begged on his knees to be taken in and saved from himself. In some cases he signed contracts with the directors of these sanatoria to paint so many pictures for his keep. As usual, he would paint from memory.

But after one or two days this sober, drinkless existence would become unbearable, and he would wreck the place to escape from it.

One of these friends was a former policeman named Gay, who had opened a bar and then became so interested in seeing Utrillo paint that he himself became a painter of some merit. Gay locked him in a back bedroom, at Utrillo's own request, a hundred times or more, but the next day he would be bribing little boys, peeping in his window, to go and buy him a bottle of wine at some other bar. When he couldn't get wine he drank all of Madame Gay's perfume for the alcohol in it.

"He was a part of all that dreaming, poverty-stricken, eccentric youth that somehow flourished in the old, decayed village on the hilltop of Montmartre before the war. In a generation of hard-drinking Bohemians, half artist, half vagabond, half anarchist, half apache, the lean, unhappy figure of Utrillo was the most desperately poor, the most abominably a b a n d o n e d, the butt of his enemies and the despair of his friends. The Utrillos of that period are the most r e m a r k a b le documents of the profound, unthinking misery of a human soul. All the bleak loneliness of the decaying quarter of the Bohemians, the bar

He writes the account long afterward, of course, long after the phantoms of his brain had receded and he had won his way back to the light of sanity. The book is really a series of impressions. The author, perhaps because it was impossible to do so, does not attempt to give a chronological account of his mental collapse. The narrative is occasionally broken by sketches—grateful tributes—of those who aided him financially and in other ways during this difficult period of his life.

An early photograph of Symons.

Symons, although he has never had a wide public, is one of the most distinguished literary survivors of the last generation. He has written a number of books—verse, plays, literary criticism, travel. He knew Rossetti, Oscar Wilde, William Morris, all the literary titans of the 'nineties. His reputation goes back to the beginning of the nineteenth century, considerably before he lost his mind.

ARTHUR SYMONS has a strange story to tell. He describes how he went mad. As nearly as he is able, he recalls his reactions as the shadows of madness were obscuring his mind. The terrible agony, the torture he endured as he tried without avail to cling to sanity.

Published the other day under the title, "Confessions," it is an extraordinary human document. Other authors have written about mad people, Edgar Allan Poe for one. Other authors have written during periods of insanity, have written wildly and fantastically. Gerard de Nerval, French novelist, was such a one. De Quincey wrote while under the influence of opium. But Symons tries to trace the very course of madness as it ravaged his remarkable mind.

be a Criminal and Lunatic or a Vagrant, unjustly hurled into hell. There was a small grated window high up on one of the walls; there was the 'Judas' (so ironical and so cruel a name used for so cruel a purpose)—the slit-hole of hell through which the horrible gaolers are obliged to look—middle of the door; there was bed—a bed of tor- With an ef-

"Then the unforeseen happened," he continues. "Two Bersaglieri (military policemen) were strolling along. They saw me; in an instant they seated themselves beside me. I was questioned and cross-questioned. Then they promised to take me back to the Hotel Europa. I walked between them. At a certain tavern we stopped. We went in; I imagined they were going to give me a drink. On the contrary, to my horror, I was thrust into a dark room without one ray of light. I stumbled about, in vain. Then they let me out, and I walked between them—an endless journey, it seemed to me. They took me to the hotel, where, of course, I asked for my room. There was no answer. Then ensued a long conversation between these two men and the hall-porter, who brought some under-manager who was made to sign some documents—I was unaware of their contents.

"THEN, escorted between these two terrifying beings, I found myself face to face with the Ducal Castle. They knocked. I was thrust in, and, with no examination whatsoever, I was seized by two gaolers—something about me having been said to them—pushed down interminable stairs to a dark corridor. The iron-barred door of a dungeon was flung open. They fastened and locked manacles on my they flung me on

"AFTER they had let me breathe some air, that abnormal nervous strength which I have always possessed in an extraordinary degree, raised all the madness that was burning me like hell's fire; and I fought with these three gaolers—in the wild idea of escape—with a ferocity which at least equaled theirs. I know not how long that struggle went on. I caught one of them by the throat and nearly strangled him; I hit another in the pit of the stomach so furiously that he fell backward on the floor.

"Then—in Balzac's phrase—began my Gehenna. My feet were of course naked; these gaolers had iron-shod boots, and two of them attacked my naked feet with such venomous violence, with such inhuman ferocity, that the blood was drained out of them by reiterated kicks, so that the blood which covered my feet and which covered that part of the floor on which I lay is beyond any calculation. In an instant I was manacled and flung back into my den. I probably took an hour to crawl back to my bed, after which I certainly swooned. I cannot imagine how I was able to sleep that night; probably from sheer exhaustion."

Another day of torture and agony began. But suddenly came a miracle he had never expected, the order for his release from the dungeon. It was by a rare stroke of luck that it came, the fact that Italy's ambassador to England at that time, the Marchese di San Giuliano, had expressed great admiration for Symons' work a year or two before and had invited him to dinner. Informed of Symons' disappearance in Ferrara, the ambassador in cipher

"JAZZ JUST LIKE DEADLY DRUG"

"Give Us Again the Dreamy Music of Blue Skies and Moonbeams," Cries Composer of Old-Time Popular Melodies, as He Compares Modern Jazz to the Opiate That Inflames the Mind and Incites to Riotous Orgies of Delirious Syncopation

THE effects of jazz music are so pernicious that jazz ought to be stamped out just as the use of opiates is, Pietro Mascagni, the Italian composer, recently told a gathering of Rome correspondents.

Harry von Tilzer

"I believe that jazz in all of its different forms and development should be stopped," the composer of "Cavalleria Rusticana" was quoted as saying. "The Governments of the world should stop it in the same way that they are stopping opium-smoking and the use of cocaine.

"For this so-called music is to the spirit what opium and cocaine are to the body."

Then, right on top of this jeremiad, comes word from London that Ben Bernie's Band has been refused a labor permit to land in England. The authorities did not go so far as to say that they considered the members of the jazz orchestra as undesirable purveyors of drugging music—their only explanation was a printed form from the

as cocaine. It loosens all the inhibitions. That's why nice girls get up on the dance floor and perform all sorts of gyrations which surprise themselves."

Mr. von Tilzer is conspicuously different from the popular conception of a Tin Pan Alley musician. No cigarette drooped from the corner of his mouth, his immaculately kept hands bore no trace of nicotine. Tall and of athletic build, he was quietly dressed in light English tweeds. His hair is silver-gray; his eyes twinkle with fun and grow dark with earnestness alternately.

"What about stopping it as Mascagni suggests?"

The question was put tentatively. It was rather audacious to imply that a man should advise the cutting off of his own very lucrative source of income.

"Oh, it will die of its own accord," he said easily. "As a matter of fact, it isn't the 'jazz' songs that make the most money. Not one single great hit has been a jazz song.

"First, though, let me explain the meaning of the word jazz. Do you know ... I was a boy that word was ... was used only in the very ... dance halls and resorts, and ... to certain gyrations and ... used by the performers. ... ever forget my horror when ... it applied to music. You ... music. My mother wanted me ... thorough musical education, ... in a hurry to make money.

"In this atmosphere the essence of true love was distilled. Hesitating, and with reverence, the boy would turn to the girl and murmur:

" 'Darling * * * Will you marry me?'

"Nowadays, the sheiks and the shebas are blind to any such beauty.

"The orchestra strikes up some blaring, bleating, crashing, smashing perversion of one of the old classics, or the latest 'jazz" tune, and the boy turns to the girl and suggests, casually:

" 'Say, kid, slip us a kiss, huh?'

"She answers, 'Aw ri'. Say let's hoof this one; it's the toad's pajamas.'

"THROUGH the amazing mazes of the erratic gyrations they misname dancing, they drag along, drugged by the music.

"Now, Mascagni probably never witnessed one of these scenes," Mr. von Tilzer smiled, "yet, he must have visualized them.

"If he has heard any of our so-called jazz orchestras they must have been of the best. Whiteman, for instance, plays melodies in syncopated time, and the effect is very soft and beautiful to our ears. It may be, however, that in Germany and Italy, where the love of music is inborn, these sounded barbaric.

"In England they are very fond of jazz music. The Prince of Wales was frank in confessing that he was a 'jazz' addict; he prefers the music of a jazz band to any other for dancing. Parisians also have welcomed syncopated music. Their temperaments are different, and they are not actually 'brought up' on c... ...as are the Italians and the ...

"Wha... dignant, ... classics ...

"What about the possibilities of the Governments of the world stopping it in the same way that they are stopping opium-smoking and the use of cocaine?"

Such a possibility seemed remote—but so have other possibilities (not to mention prohibition).

And Mr. von Tilzer considered it quite seriously before answering.

At last: "I don't believe there is any way to prohibit a craze or custom in our country," he said. "If any one tried to seriously introduce jazz into Germany or Italy, or if any of their composers started to write jazz music, I believe it would be prohibited there because great music is so much a part of their national life.

"When people get tired of jazz here it will pass away and not before. And," he continued after a pause, "I believe they are beginning to get tired of it.

"In looking back over the thirty-four years that I have been in the game, I have found that there is an evolution in songs which lasts for about seven years. I can mark out five definite styles of songs in that time. In that, we are different from other nations.

"While I cannot say that jazz orchestras are definitely on the wane, I know that jazz songs are.

"There is a certain psychological reason for the popularity of a song. For the last few years it has been the freak—not the jazz—song which has made an outstanding hit.

"And the first sign of the passing of the jazz song came with the banana songs: 'Yes, we have no bananas!'

"The words were senseless, but it cer... ...they were sense...

"I AM discussing these 'freak' songs which were not jazz, just in order to demonstrate to you that you cannot 'stop' any style of music or song which the public, for its own mysterious reasons, adopts.

"Here was a song which flaunts a man who is a criminal in their faces. It makes a hero of him. It was a song that should have been obnoxious to all who love law—and good music.

"Performers objected to singing it—yet the audiences demanded it. It became a regular bone of contention between the theatre house managers, agents and singers. The commercial houses did not want to exploit it.

"All were absolutely powerless against the demand.

"It is easy enough to say: 'The public be damned!' But any one who has ever come up against a real American public demand finds that he himself is shoved to one side."

"The reason for the popularity, then, was what?"

OBVIOUSLY the ragtime composer had dragged in "The Prisoner Song" to point a moral and to explain an obscure point.

"Because this is the age of prohibition," he remarked. Then, with a quick smile, he amended: "I'm not referring just to the Eighteenth Amendment. I really mean that this is an age of protest against all prohibitions. Even persons who heartily approved of Prohibition with a capital P indorsed 'The Prisoner's Song,' but were not aware why they did.

"We are living in a peculiar age. So ...con... ...spect ... That ... the ... law- ... con- ... quite ... in- ...s. ... no one knows.

"Compare this 'Prisoner's Song' with another 'Prisoner's' Song of many years ago. This ballad I refer to was written about a man in jail whose conscience was touched by a little bird which sang outside his window one day. The song doesn't glorify the man in any way—it tells the story of how he longs for freedom, but realizes too late that his imprisonment was justified by his crime. Its keynote is remorse.

"That song would not be popular today—yet it might be next year. There's no telling!

"We are now due for a new type of song. Somebody will strike it and lead off. That one will gather all the cream."

PAVLOWA COMPARES JAZZ TO WRESTLING

Sports, Not Dancing, Best for Fat Man, She Says on Arrival from Europe.

Anna Pavlowa, here on the Homeric yesterday, in close-fitting gray charmeuse, said she has five new ballets for an American-Canadian tour. One is Russian, two Hindu and one each Chinese and Japanese.

She looked as lithe and slender as ever. She attributed her good health and figure to constant exercise. She was asked:

"Would you advise fat men to dance and grow thin?"

She replied:

"Not esthetic dancing; that is for women, save when men dancers are required as partners for the stage. The proper exercise for men is sports. Women should dance. It is good for them. Not wild dances, which you call jazz, but nice dancing."

"But something must be done for the increasing number of fat men of America. What would you suggest?"

"I'd say that they should not eat so much candy and sweets and should drink more liquor. I would like to see every man in America have his daily glass of beer. Beer is good for men. Every good man should have his beer."

She seemed bored when asked what she thought about jazz, saying:

"It will die out. It is too much like wrestling and boxing."

Mrs. George Whelan, wife of the president of the United Cigar Stores Company, also was on the Homeric.

Let's Have a Plain Talk on Dance Halls And a Redlight Girl—And Another Kind

DANCING IN S. F. DANCE HALLS SUNDAY AFTERNOON FORBIDDEN

(Continued From Page One)

been withdrawn?" asked Roche.

Very Rev. A. F. McMahon, O. P. Provincial of the Dominican Friars, from whose order came the first protest, answered by saying in part:

"Tonight I appear before you in regard to the matter of the Winter Garden, situated in that same section of the city that has been before your Honorable Board since the 13th of December. I am not here to make an argument, nor am I here even to make a request. The question of the Winter Garden has been argued in your presence, and you have decided two weeks ago if the petition calling upon you to close it be still in force, it must be closed tonight.

"In consequence of that decision, and by the will or wish of others, and by the force of circumstances, the duty has become mine to make a statement that the protest is still in force."

THREATS VOICED.

When Roche ordered the place closed, Attorney Edward Cunha, for the management, threatened legal action to annul the action of the police board. He cited a charter amendment of January, 1919, giving the board jurisdiction over certain lines of business, but omitting dance halls. He asked for a respite of one week in which to obtain an opinion of the City Attorney, but Roche concluded the matter by saying that he could secure an injunction if the legal status of the case warranted it.

Alfred P. Maas then came up for judgment.

"Last week I approved of this application, but on learning certain things concerning the conduct of this man toward certain females connected with his institution I am now opposed to the granting of the permit to him."

Maas replied that it was "no use to go up against a cop," and left the place without putting up any defense.

Then the following recommendations submitted by the committee from the San Francisco Center were adopted as regulations by the commission. Fourteen of them read:

1—That all halls holding regular permits for dancing be held responsible for the character of the dances given in the hall. Permits to be revoked if order is not maintained.

2—The proprietors shall give the Police Department notice at least seven days in advance of any proposed rentals for commercial dances.

3—No license shall be issued unless person receiving license is actually operating under such permit.

4—Permits shall not be granted to irresponsible groups or individuals for dances to be given in unlicensed halls.

5—All commercial halls or dances must be supervised.

6—Supervisors should be placed in halls on a basis proportionate to the number of patrons.

7—Managers should be of good character and competent or be removed.

8—Dancing academies having social nights should have supervisors when the number of patrons corresponds to the open commercial halls and in all cases should have supervisors if the character of the management requires it.

9—All public dance halls must be brightly lighted all the time they are in use and no so-called moonlight dances shall be allowed.

10—That all halls be closed at 12:30 a. m. every night.

11—That no return checks be issued or no patron, man or woman having left the hall be allowed to return the same evening.

12—There must be no undue familiarity, exaggerated, suggestive or freak dancing between partners.

13—The ordinance covering the granting of permits for masquerades should be amended to transfer the power to grant such permits from the Board of Supervisors to the Board of Police Commissioners.

14—The ordinance covering the entrance of minors under 18 years of age without proper guardian should be changed to read: It shall be unlawful for any person to falsely represent his or her age to any person maintaining or operating any public dance hall or conducting or giving any commercial or social dance for the purpose of securing admission to any public dance.

A nickel dance being conducted by Warrick D. Miller on the Great Highway and near the Cliff House was ordered closed.

And, of course, the orchestra was playing the latest fox-trots from New York instead of waltzes and two-steps. Otherwise it was the Beach I had known.

THE STUDENTS DANCED.

About half the students danced and the other half sat in the dark under the trees. Many of them had come in cars, but more on the steamer. It was most informal. Two of the girls were in knickerbockers, but the flapper told me that they were not, strictly speaking, co-eds.

They were ex-coeds—girls who were no longer atteending the university, but who were hanging around town amusing themselves. She regarded the knickerbockers as rather bad form, but excused them on the ground that the two had evidently been canoeing and had "just dropped in."

We danced two dances, so that I could see how students danced. They danced as people dance nowadays all over the United States—in a fashion that would have been regarded as indecent ten years ago and is now taken for granted. They danced as if they enjoyed it. But they also wandered off to benches under the trees as if they enjoyed that, too.

In passing through the doorway we stepped aside for a hilarious foursome. They sounded as if they had been drinking.

The Unfortunate Miss Marie Ehlers in the Very Attitude and in One of the Costumes of the Dance Which, She Avers, Gave Her Permanent Jazz Joints.

How a Pennsylvania Millionaire Is Spending a Fortune to Prove the Futurists and Cubists *NOT* Insane and Teach Us to Admire Their Strange Works as He Does

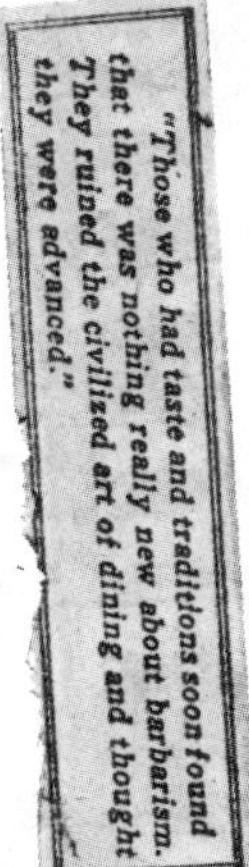

The wild beats of jazz, syncopated to the pulsations of the heart, exact as terrible a penalty from the nerves as does a drug, thinks one composer of old-fashioned melodies

iate lulls the nerves and brain into a heaven of security from which the emerges a slave to the insidious poison he must have just as the jazz devotee have the wild strains of jarring notes

The nerves of even dumb animals are not immune to the strains of jazz, and the monarch of the desert is expressing his disapproval of the entertainment by deep, throaty growls

Our Tango Madness The Death Agonies of the Dance?

Among the Cultured Youth of America, Who Seem Crazed by Quest of Jazz and Pleasure

'THE JAZZ SINGER' HAS ITS PREMIERE

FOUNDED 1865—VOL. CXVI. NO. 49 S SAN FRANCISCO, CAL., THURSDAY, MARCH 4, 1920—TWENTY-TWO PAGES

OUIJA BOARD SEANCE DRIVES T
WOODCOCK HIDING HERE ELUD
DRY SQUAD ROUTS SMUGGLE

RESIDENTS OF CONTRA COSTA FOUND CRAZED

Five Children Found With Hair Shaved Off to Rid House of Evil

POLICE BREAK IN DOORS

Money Burned by Mad Persons Who Are Half Starved When Taken Away

Breaking into a house at El Cerrito, just across the county line from Berkeley in Contra Costa county, police officers yesterday took into custody seven persons who had become insane from playing with ouija boards.

Those arrested and taken to the insane ward of the county hospital at Martinez were:

Adeline Bottini, 15 years old.
Mrs. Sangine Bottini, mother of Adeline.
Mrs. Edward Moro.
Mrs. Josie Saldavini.
Charles Saldavini.
Harry Serrario.
Louis Serrario.

The arrest of the four women and three men forms one of the most unusual stories in the history of spiritualism and occultism ever bared by the authorities in California.

Girl Blamed for Having Introduced Ouija Board

According to the authorities, Adeline Bottini, fifteen-year-old daughter of Mrs. Bottini, is the direct cause of the derangement of the seven persons because she installed the ouija boards in the house and induced unknown power, forced the inmates to hover over the mysterious boards day and night. On two occasions twenty-four-hour sittings were held.

Five children, the youngest of whom is 2 years old, were found in the house. The hair on the children had been shaved to the scalp and burned "to drive evil spirits away," the authorities learned.

On Monday $700 in currency was burned by the occupants of the house in El Cerrito in an effort to cleanse the atmosphere of "evil spirits."

All of the occupants were in poor physical shape and were suffering from lack of nourishment. The children found in the house were in a starving condition when rescued.

Admittance Refused To Police Officials

Neighbors complained to Town Marshal A. H. McKinnon yesterday of the strange doings in the house. Complaints were made that children had been lured into the house and kept prisoner.

McKinnon attempted to gain admission and when the people refused to open the door, help was asked of the Richmond police. Inspectors D. V. Shirly and Daniel Cox went to McKinnon's aid. In the meantime McKinnon called Father J. J. Hennessy, pastor of St. Joseph's Church in Berkeley. Father Hennessy persuaded the people to allow him to enter the house but admission was refused to the police officers.

After Father Hennessy returned to the street, it was decided to break in. Shirly and Cox battered down the rear door while McKinnon broke down the front door.

Four Boards Found in Residence by Policemen

Mrs. Moro, whose husband, Daniel Moro, a blacksmith, died three months ago, screamed a warning not to enter.

"My husband is here and he will kill you," she cried to the officers. Mrs. Moro's daughter, Jennie Moro, was killed two weeks ago on the streets of Richmond by an automo-

THIS NEWSPAPER IS ONE HUNDRE

"TIN PAN ALLEY" the home of jazz, is the setting for the clever new novelette by Gordon Seagrove, to be published complete in TOMORROW'S CHRONICLE

FOUNDED 1865—VOL. CXVI. NO. 51 S SAN FRANCISCO, CAL., SATURDAY, MARCH 6, 1920—T

OUIJA BOARD DRIVES TWO
MRS. WOODCOCK'S INDICT
ANGLO-FRENCH 1915 LO

S. F. POLICEMAN HELD AS CRAZED; FEARED ARREST

Martinez Man Also Seized as He Voices Belief He Is to Be Poisoned

HIGH SCHOOL OPENS QUIZ

Students Reported to Hold Seances With Board; El Cerrito Astir

The uncanny spell of the ouija board, which in a few days transformed the minds of three mothers and a high school girl of 15 years, residents of El Cerrito, from a state of normality to that of madness, yesterday claimed two more victims, one a San Francisco policeman.

They are:

Policeman E. H. Deane, attached to the Potrero Station of this city.
C. F. Forre, now being held at the County Hospital at Martinez.

Clad in plain clothes and with a revolver in his pocket, Policeman Deane was arrested in Berkeley early yesterday morning as he was wandering aimlessly along the street.

Ouiji Board Told Him He Was to Be Arrested

According to Policeman Richard Dowling, who made the arrest, Deane was acting in a strange manner.

Dowling reported at the police station that Deane had said that the ouija board had told him he was to be arrested.

"I have been consulting the board and it has given me all kinds of valuable information," Deane is reported to have stated.

Dean escaped later yesterday afternoon from the Anderson Sanatorium, clothed only in a blanket. He knocked down two guards and made his way to East Eighteenth street and Fourteenth avenue, where he stopped an autoist and compelled the driver to take him to Twelfth street and Broadway, in the heart of the Oakland business district.

Dean, in his blanket attire, jumped off the running board of the automobile and dashed madly up Broadway. At Thirteenth street he lost his blanket and dashed into the Central National Bank building in a nude condition.

Policemen from the Central Sta-

First In News In Advertising In Circulation

SATURDAY SAN FRANC

OUIJA BOARD DRIVES PO

MYSTIC WORD SENDS MAN TO SEEK ENEMY

Patrolman Elmer H. Dean of S. F. Creates Sensation in Oakland While Under Spell

Says "Ouija" Told Him to Find Foe; First Caught in Berkeley; Escapes From Hospital

Policeman Elmer H. Dean of the Potrero station, San Francisco, was taken from the crowded streets of Oakland yesterday scantily dressed and in an apparently unbalanced state of mind because a ouija board, he said, had sent him to Berkeley in search of some mysterious enemy.

The policeman had previously been picked up at Berkeley and sent to the Anderson sanitarium, Oakland, for observation. He escaped from the attendants and made his appearance on the street, climbing to the running board of an automobile and directing the driver to take him to Berkeley.

STARTED TO UNDRESS.

As the automobile proceeded, commanded by Dean with his revolver, he began to undress. Attracted by the crowds at Fourteenth and Broadway, he jumped out and then apparently discovering an embarrassing lack of clothing, took refuge in the Central National Bank building.

Dr. C. H. Walsworth, in whose offices he took shelter, summoned the police, and Patrolman W. R. Jones, arriving with a blanket, wrapped Dean up and took him to the hospital.

Dean failed to report at the Potrero station yesterday morning, and when Policeman John B. Charleston called at the Marymount Hotel in O'Farrell

Ouija Said to Hasten Insanity
Contributing Cause of Lunacy
Mental Experts Discuss Effects

Varied reasons as to the effect on the human mind of the ouija board which has durring the week caused six persons to become demented, are given by medical authorities. Physicians and mental experts assert that the result of constant consultation with the ouija board is caused by a number of conditions, all the way from superstition to weak mentality, depending entirely on the character of the individual concerned.

While it is given as a generally accepted opinion among physicians that the ouija board within itself could hardly produce insanity it does help it along, if the mind is concentrated sufficiently. This result, it is claimed,

have a strong will power, are likely to go insane."

San Francisco Lunacy Commissioner—We have had many commitments to State Asylums during the past few months on account of the ouija board. These persons who have been adjudged insane by the commission might have shown insanity by other means, but the ouija board at present occupies a prime place in demonstrating insanity. It is a fact that since the war the people generally have gone into spiritualistic things and certain individuals have become demented on this account.

There are other fads that have

NO WEDD BELLS, AV MARY PICK

Will Never Marry Agai... clares, but Will D... of Life to Motion

Mother Apologizes f... Temper in Attempt... Cameras, Reporters

4 OUIJA BOARD VICTIMS HELD TO BE INSANE

3 Women and Girl Committed to Asylum for Weird Demonstrations

STICK TO QUEER TALES

Men Arrested and Freed Assert Grief Led to Delving Into Occult

(Continued from Page 1, Column 6)

Victims of the

Mrs. Josie Soldavini Mrs. Mari

Y 5 CENTS, SUNDAY 10 CENTS: DAILY AND SUNDAY PER MONTH, 60 CENTS

NSANE. ARREST. ON SHIP

OUIJA TOLD ME TO KILL

FRANCISCO, CAL., SUNDAY, MARCH 7, 1920

Taboo at Parther

Ouija Board Denounced by Prominent

Tragic Instances at El Cerrito Bring Storm

Ardent Devotion to "Spirit" Gossip H

Question of Abolishing "Seances" Is Discussed by Experts

Is the ouija board a menace that should be abolished entirely, or is it productive of dire mental results only when the operator is of such peculiar mental make-up as to make for easy subjection to the mysteries that appear to result from seeking enlightenment from this thing of wood made by man?

Such are the questions being given consideration by psychological savants as the result of the wave of insanity that has swept the little Contra Costa county town of El Cerrito into a sphere of national prominence, all as the result of the ouija board. Opinions differ as to the extent that sanity is endangered by too close devotion to this toy, but there ... of opinion when it ... deration of the effect ... persons of certain ...

... nion concerning ... chologists go

Misinterpretation Biggest Menace to Board Devote

PROMINENT San Francisco authorities on psychiatry and ... ailments are virtually unanimous in condemning overind... in ouija-board crazes and other so-called "spiritualistic m... which they term merely forms of emotional excitement.

One of the most serious dangers, it is pointed out, is the ... to construe the "messages" received, which, the experts say, ... results in a misinterpretation.

A rabid believer in the ouija, it is pointed out, accep... thing this mysterious influence advises, without regard to ... may mean possible harm to himself or to others.

The ouija board is explained by one authority on the ... it is a tapping of the subconscious, a mental disassociation ... in the subject writing things that are really in his mind, ... may be unconscious of their presence.

To minimize the danger it is suggested that a campai... tion be conducted rather than any attempt to forbid th... boards.

... the more they have become prone to twist everything that happens into some mysterious message from past ... Ouija boards, being sim...

... others. The ouija bo... technical means of ... own uncontrolled th... ting otherwise unse...

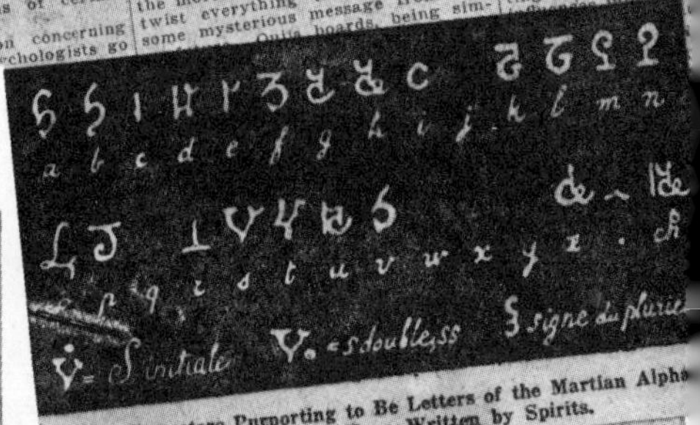

Strange Characters Purporting to Be Letters of the Martian Alphabet and Said to Have Been Written by Spirits.

The Ouija Board's "Competitor" Is a Device Copper Bronze Plating That Is Claimed to Act as a Battery for the Writing Forces and Gives Them a Definite Flow.

PER CENT AMERICA

FAIR — WEATH... SAN FRANCISCO, OA... AND VICINITY: Saturday fair weather; ... northwest winds. G. H. WILLSON, Foreca... Complete Weather Report on P...

WO PAGES — DAILY 5 CENTS, SUNDAY 10 CENTS: DAILY AND ... PER MONTH, ...

MORE INSANE. ENT EXPECTED. N WILL BE PAID

Pages 22

ARCH 6, 1920 — SATURDAY — CC

CEMAN TO STREET NAKED

BOARDS READY TO SET SPRING VALLEY VALUE

Railroad Commissioners, City Officials, Water Co. Representatives Get Together Monday

Conferees Have Data; Statistics Produced in Court Hearings Will Help in Price Fixing

Girl Hiker on Her Way to New York

Tired of Movie Acting, Seeks Big Town

Youthful Pedestrian Is Very, Very Brave; Will Earn Her Way by Entertaining.

BY CARMEN BALLEN.

"Hollywood to New York—on foot." If Miss Eve Montaldo were an automobile she'd be flying a pennant with the above inscription. Brt she's only a girl, a mere slip of a twenty-year-old girl, with big grey eyes and a roguish smile, so she has written her courageous intention on the fly leaf of her diary instead.

"If I'm kidnaped on the road, notify the Studio Club, Hollywood, Cal.," continues the diary in broad warning strokes of the pen, and then there appears the unabashed declaration: "I'm broke—but happy."

OUT FOR A STROLL

Miss Eve Montaldo, who would like girl companion to accompany her on hike 'cross continent.

INCREASE IN USE OF DRUGS IS ALARMING

Probation Officer Reports on Spread of Evil Since Prohibition Went Into Effect

Nicholl Urges Hospital in Which Drug Addicts Can Be Treated and Cured of the Habit

Ouija Board Burned; Victims In Asylums

MARTINEZ, March 5.—There is one less ouija board in the world today. Carlo Soldavini is particularly elated about that fact.

The board, which was responsible for the hallucinations of Sol... wife, her mother and sister an... teen-year-old niece, commi... asylums at Martinez on ... was destroyed by Soldavini ... day, after the insanity co... had discharged him, with ... Vico Ferraro, also member ... family.

Faith in the board's contr... three women and the girl ... portions of their clothing, ... rancy and household furnit... the authorities interfered. ... returned from the examin... davini carried out the wo... poned rites by building a ... backyard and ...

Ouija Board Drives Seven Persons In Contra Costa Ma...

(Continued from Page 1, Column 1)

house the occupants told them the ouija boards had demanded the sac... rifice of belongings and that evi... spirits must be driven from the house.

Adeline Bottini ... On Tuesday ...

... Board

Adeline Bottini

SAN FRANCISCO CHRONICLE, MONDAY, MARCH 7, 1921

Ouija Board Legislator on Job at Sacramento

Mysterious Yes-No Switch in Vote on King Tax Bill

Suffrage Flip-Flop on Vital Issue Stirs Comment

By EDDIE BOYDEN

Staff Correspondent of The Chronicle

HRONICLE BUREAU, Sacramento, March 6.— ... work-...

... nents of the bill arose and filled the air with paeans of triumphs, hats and waste baskets.

One of the waste baskets descended upon the dome of Joe Burns, the ... San Franciscan who voted ... King thing, and Joe for a ... baseball catch-...

"If I vote against this bill, my political future is ruined," Robert mourned to Jack Badaracco, Assemblyman from San Francisco.

"Rats!" scoffed the statesman from the Golden Gate.

Now there's an answer for you!

Hanley Booth, diminutive attorney for railroads and other things, ... around Friday night, seeking ... what the statesmen ... King bill the ...

RESCUERS TELL OF SINKING OF U.S. DESTROYE...

Particulars of Colli... Woolsey and Fr... Arrive in S...

Special Dispatch to The C... SAN DIEGO, Marc... first detailed story ... the United State... stroyer Woolse... coast of P...

HA... the ... on ... The ... or ar... down ... found.

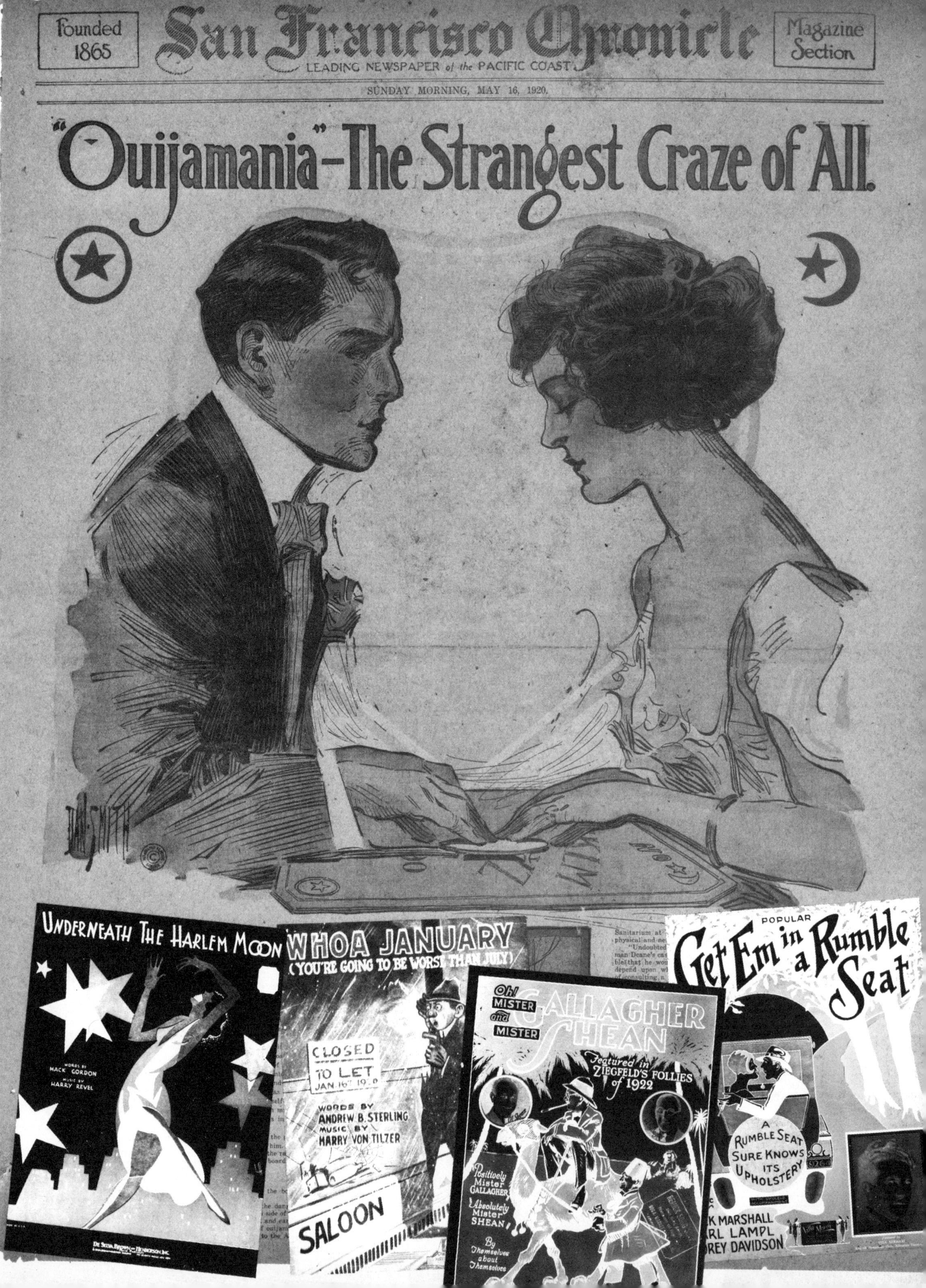

Founded 1865
San Francisco Chronicle
LEADING NEWSPAPER of the PACIFIC COAST
Magazine Section
SUNDAY MORNING, MAY 16, 1920.

"Ouijamania"–The Strangest Craze of All.

DAN SMITH

WHOA JANUARY
(YOU'RE GOING TO BE WORSE THAN JULY)
CLOSED
TO LET
JAN. 16th 1920
WORDS BY
ANDREW B. STERLING
MUSIC BY
HARRY VON TILZER
SALOON

WHAT IS ALL THIS TODO ABOUT PETTING?
WHEN EVER THERE IS A SWELL JAZZ BAND AND THE DANCE TUNES ARE HOT-
THE ONLY EXCITMENT SHE GETS
IF YOU KNEW SUSIE LIKE I KNOW SUSIE
ROLL 'EM GIRLS
(ROLL YOUR OWN)
TAKE ME TO THE LAND OF JAZZ
WORDS BY BERT KALMAR & EDGAR LESLIE
MUSIC BY PETE WENDLING
Bootleggers, Road-house Proprietors, Jazz Musicians, Makers of Exotic and Extravagant Clothing—to Them, in This Age Which Has Discovered the Com- Value of Youth,
CHING A LING'S JAZZ BAZAAR
"How am I to know you're on da level?"
Columbia
Electrical Process
Paul Whiteman AND HIS Orchestra
RUNNIN' WILD
An Ebony Jazz Tune
ELUDES NARCOTIC RING
THE SHEIK OF ARABY
HARRY B. SMITH
FRANCIS WHEELER
TED SNYDER
COLLEGIAT
COTTON CLUB
"The Aristocrat of Harlem" presents DAN HEALY'S New Revue
2 Distinctly Different 2 SHOWS NIGHTLY
CAST OF FIFTY!
Beautiful Girls
Music and Lyrics by JIMMIE McHUGH and DOROTHY FIELDS (Authors of "Blackbirds")
Dance to the Tunes of DUKE ELLINGTON'S
EVERY DAY WILL BE SUNDAY WHEN THE TOWN GOES DRY
TRY OUR SATURDAY SPECIAL BILLY SUNDAE
AIN'T WE GOT FU
DOPE
GOOD BYE HUNTER, SO LONG SCOTCH FAREWELL HAIG AND HAIG
FIVE FOOT TWO, EYES of BLUE HAS ANYBODY SEEN MY GIRL
Mrs. Warena Nelson, formerly an employe of Billy Sunday, who says she has won her uphill fight against a craving for dope.
All Imaginary—More's the Pity
Herald Times
The Weather
HOOVER DEMANDS PROHIBITION REP
NATIONAL REFER IMPERATIVE IN CONGRESS IS W
NATION'S LEADERS HAIL HOOVER MOVE AS TURNING POINT
DEMOCRATS FUME AS NATION LAUDS HOOVER MESSAGE
ATTERBURY VISIONS MATERIAL FREIGHT TRAFFIC INCREASES
MELLON STRONGLY SUPPORTS HOOVER
I SCREAM - YOU SCREAM - WE ALL SCREAM FOR ICE CREAM
YOUTH to the JAZZ GODS

Fads 'n Flap

WILD ORGIES BY AMERICAN GIRLS IN GRIP OF PARIS

Cocaine and Other Drugs Wrecking Lives by Thousands, Craze Having Begun in War Period

CURIOSITY RUIN OF WOMEN

They Want to Try Every Sensation, and Moral Sense Quickly Vanishes, Says Student of Life

By C. F. BERTELLI,

Special Correspondent of the New York American.

PARIS, Sept. 16.—The courageous stand of Senator La Mazelle in the French Upper House in July against the dance halls of the type that have been characterized as giving reproductions of the Graeco-Roman orgies was without avail.

The managers of those places refused to ruin the season at the very moment of "the American invasion." The American reformers who are here will never succeed in stamping out vice in Europe unless they first carry out a vigorous campaign in America.

Professor Martin, a leading drug specialist of France, told me to-day that the price of "dope" in Paris is now so high that only Americans can afford its indulgence. He said:

"The drug habit is immensely popular with the rich Americans, especially the women, who, once they arrive in Paris, cut up in wild fashion.

MEN ARE TO BLAME.

"The blame for this deplorable state of things is entirely with the husbands and fathers, who allow their wives and daughters to visit Europe alone. No French father would dream of letting his own women go on an American trip without escort."

Leo Tectonius, of New York, enjoys a good viewpoint of the inner workings of rings within rings in the Parisian and practically expatriated American group that maintains the entertainment for the foreign visitors. He is a pianist. He told me:

"Cocaine and similar drugs have been and are wrecking the lives of innumerable American men and women in Paris. During the war American officers were lured to the houses of the so-called society women who indulged in this vice. There they tried the insidious 'dope.' They liked it and came back for more. They tried it again and again until finally they succumbed completely to its allure.

WRECKED IN TWO WEEKS.

"I know one man—a boy of a fine family—who within a fortnight became such a wreck that he had to be relieved of duty with the A. E. F. I know of one prominent American girl who lost not only her health, but all moral sense.

"The American women are inquisitive. They have wild imaginations. When they come to France their senses become aroused. They want to try every sensation. Frequently they fall victim to their curiosity, as they lack the stamina to resist the terrible temptations."

The psychology of the pleasure seekers was explained by Claude Farrere, prominent psychologist, author of "Les Civilises," meaning "The Refined Ones." He said:

"The Parisians do not indulge in drugs to the extent that the Americans do here. Cocaine is the favorite of the Americans. They generally carry the deadly white powder in costly jewel boxes. Morphia is the oldest drug, but this season it has been discarded in favor of the more deadly heroin.

MORE DARING THAN AT HOME.

"Most of the persons now adept in the use of the sensation-giving drugs were ignorant of their very names when they stepped off the steamers. Paris is not more immoral than New York, but the Americans do here what they would not dream of doing at home.

"They do not consider that opium smoking is a danger. They think it is as harmless as tobacco. There are opium dens in Paris, the same as in San Francisco, only those here are more sumptuous.

"It is no wonder that the voluptuous surroundings that can be found here make short work of the moral sense of innocent American girls and women, fresh from clean American surroundings.

"When once such a life is tasted the sense of proportion disappears. The girls and women are likely to risk anything and lose everything to quench their thirst for novel sensations.

"Opium smoking has decreased this season, owing to the rise in price from $15 to $1,000 a pound. A single pipe to-day costs $20."

What seems to be outstandingly the worst crime of all of the Americans who find themselves in an atmosphere of restraint is the practice of bringing their wives or the young women in their care to the special establishments of a semi-private nature, where vice is without limit.

AMERICAN WOMEN A GOLD MINE.

I have before me the statements of

JANUARY 28 1923

Bill to Ban Fags of Milady Nets Capitol Puzzle

EXAMINER BUREAU

SACRAMENTO, March 14.—Some reformer is after milady who smokes cigarettes. But who is the reformer?

Yesterday a bill appeared at the Senate desk. It purported to be

Rum Girl Causes 81 Indictments

GARY, Ind., Jan. 17.—The bootlegging queen! This is the title of Miss Agnes Szabo, pretty eighteen-year-old girl of Gary, Ind. She has been acclaimed as the source of information through which a Federal Grand Jury in Indianapolis has been able to return eighty-one indict

MODERN DRESS IS DENOUNCED BY THE W.C.T.U.

State Convention at Ri Commends Educators manding Reform in

RICHMOND, Oct. 24.—T dresses worn by modern young women are "unbecom "attract undesirable attenti wearers," is the gist of a adopted by the Women's Temperance Union of Cal the close of its fortieth annual convention in the First Christian Church

FORMING FLAPPER MURALS

—By Edwin J. Clapp

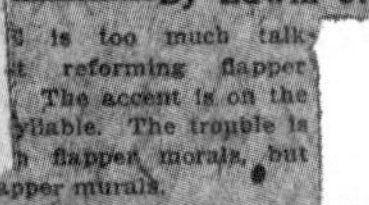

is too much talk t reforming flapper The accent is on the yllable. The trouble is flapper morals, but flapper murals.

This Titian style in young faces is an unexplainable exception to the rule that women dress and act to please me Hence short skirts, jazz, stares, knickerbockers, ette smoking, one-piec ing suits, midnigh auto rides, petting all the promiscuou passes lightly fr hand at the soir

Harding Agrees Women Are Good Dry Enforcers

By Universal Service.

WASHINGTON, Feb. 27.

PRESIDENT HARDING agrees with Mrs. Gifford Pinchot, wife of the Pennsylvania Governor, that women are adaptable to prohibition enforcement.

It was stated to-day many women are in the service of the Prohibition Bureau, and that they are efficient in running down violators.

The White House announced that the President would call anc enc forc

Feminine Legislator Attacks Prohibition

Mrs. Urbanski Fears for Younger People.

Saloons better than prohibition, finds Mrs. Marian F. Urbanski

Mrs. Summers to id War Veterans.

Dope Raiders Jail 'Tattooed Lady,' Mate

Gladys Harris, twenty-five, known as "Madame Delmar, tattooed lady," with side shows and the Ringling Brothers' Circus, yesterday was held in $500 bail with her husband, Stanley, also twenty-five, in Tombs Court on a charge of possessing n

The couple were ar 157 Park Row, wher

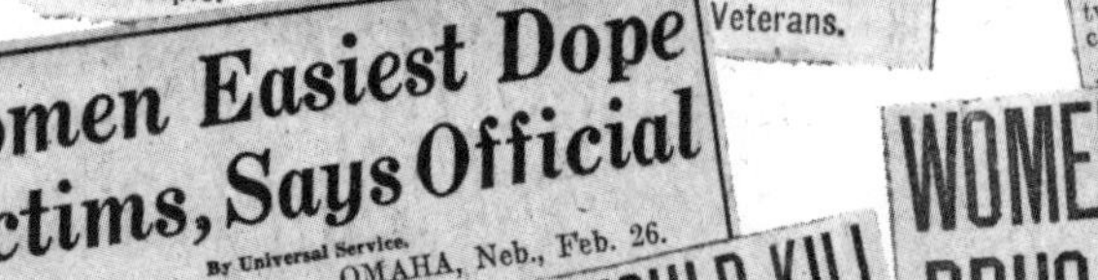

Women Easiest Dope Victims, Says Official

By Universal Service.

OMAHA, Neb., Feb. 26.

W OM su

atest drug

like, acc divisiona sota, Ne Dr Nebras Club Camp

they

WOMEN A LURE TO TEACH HABIT FOR DRUG RING

GIRL WOULD KILL FOR DRUGS, SHE TELLS DR. SIMON

Pitiful Addict Begs for Coca Declares Police Have R Underw

WOMEN MADE DRUG VICTIMS IN 'PARLORS'

Millinery and Beauty Shops Figure in Latest Drive by Narcotic Squad.

Several millinery shops and

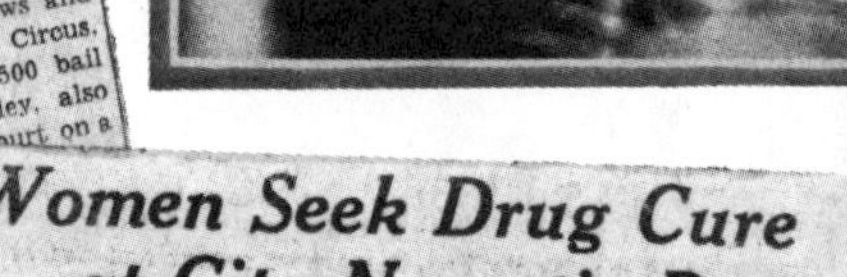

Women Seek Drug Cure at City Narcotic Bureau

Four in Hour, from Grandmother to Flapper Pass Dr. Sim ny.

By NAT J

A strange cross vealed to the rcotic Division partment, of w charge.

a single hour, little from ch constitute th the dope-fighting en addicts passe in his office. grandmother a

f a rich comple bout thirty-thre This woman ha out of pure love ate, that he wa she became a nd deserted he ble to get dope imon a year ag

ES.

merged a free returned. She ddict. A few was arrested

GIRLS ENSLAVED IN PLOT OF U. S. NARCOTIC HEADS

One Dead, Five Debauched,

1923

San Francisco "Nature Girl" Has Never Worn Shoes or Any Flappers' Adornments

Cynthia Scott Proves There's Joy in the Primitive

San Francisco boasts a real "Nature Girl."

She's Cynthia Scott, 20 years old, who, though she has never lived outside of a city, has never worn shoes and stockings or a set of corsets. Paint, powder and other embellishments of the flapper she scorns, and says they don't mean anything in a woman's charm.

Incidentally, she is a friend of animals, and her pets, cats and mice, live together amicably under her influence. It's all because of her love of nature she says. Miss Scott usually dresses in a simple one-piece dress and Indian headdress. She has achieved some note as a classical dancer.

Conquered

Flapper Has Vanished Into Her Own Home

Emancipation and business, political and profess... opportunity ... her major ... average ... ful business...

Invincible Vamp

"Darling, you asked me if you looked fat in that suit—I believe ... you look fat. ... to telephone ... And I wish ...

Unmarried Vamp

A vamp shorn of flattery, received and given, is no vamp at all.

Compliments and personalities are the big wings upon which she flutters from flower to flower; ...

Genuine Vamp

... the genuine vamp, ... married, or ... grass or sod," the ... has rightly, a diffe...

"FLAPPERS ARE AWFUL!"—That's the verdict of Anne (left) and Eleanor Gould, 13 and 14, daughters of Jay Gould.

FLIRTING CURABLE, but Vamping Soon BECOMES CHRONIC

A FLIRT is benign, and a vamp is malignant. Flirting is curable; vamping has an insidious fashion of becoming chronic.

The vamp has a single weapon. The weapon is flattery. A vamp shorn of flattery, received and given, is no vamp at all.

The unmarried vamp is a negligible element. She is merely a more or less desperate type of flirt. She may say daring things, but every one knows that she neither understands them nor means them.

KATHLEEN NORRIS

The genuine vamp is always married, or widowed, "grass or sod."

She is usually a woman without ambition, without a nursery, a profession, or responsibilities of any kind.

She is frequently a woman devoid of intelligence, all except a certain sex instinct that makes her shrewdly proud of her surface conquests, and childishly sure that all women would make them if they could.

Fortunately, for our homes, children, domestic peace and national safety, most women are not vamps. It is a cheap game, at best, ruled by petty laws of vanity and self-deceiving; too easily begun, it is awkward business to end satisfactorily. And when it is played out there is a dismal time of awakening.

'Vanished Flapper W... Just an Old-Fashion... After All'—Fanni...

By FANNIE HURST

... WOMAN ...'DOPED' HER

...r Party Host, ... After She ...apses.

...AN DRUG SELLER ...APSES IN COURT

...Chorus Girl, Who Hid ...in Camera, Gets Penitentiary Sentence

In describing the antics of the flappers, Mrs. Asquith says of a sight she witnessed in Buffalo: "One of the young men threw a girl over his shoulder, with her legs straight out, while the other photographed them."

Catholic Daughters to Discuss Flapperism

RADIO, RUM, JAZZ BLAMED FOR

Rabbi Lays 'Jazz Age' Excesses to Parents

DON'T DESPAIR!—In spite of the wave of suicides among "young intellectuals" and the materialism and pleasure-seeking of modern times, Rabbi Rudolph Grossman of Rodeph Sholem congregation forecasts a notable return to spiritual values. N. Y. American Staff Photo.

BIG INCREASE SINCE ADVENT, SAYS EXPERT

Dr. Isham Harris, Head of Brooklyn State Hospital, Tells Lions Club They Affect Mind.

Radio, jazz and liquor promote insanity, Dr. Isham Harris, superintendent of the Brooklyn State Hospital for the Insane, asserted yesterday.

In an address before the Mid-Town Lions' Club at the Hotel Commodore Dr Harris linked wireless, syncopation and hooch into an ultra-modern trinity that weakens the brains of young and old.

The three mediums of entertainment are responsible, he charged, for the increase of commitment to insane asylums in the last few years.

MORE ASYLUMS NEEDED

Dr. Harris pleaded for a campaign to build more hospitals for the insane to accommodate the increasing demand and explained:

"The static and late hours attendant on radio listening-in cause mental abnormality. Because of the irritating effect of radio on mental cases, it has been eliminated from all hospitals for the insane. Even phonographs are rarely used.

"But music provided by stringed orchestral instruments with therapeutic value, is being used with beneficial effect in certain mental cases."

Dr. Harris said that of the 45,000 persons under care for insanity in the State, 30,000 were in the metropolitan area.

JUMP TO 5 PER CENT.

He pointed out that commitments have increased from less than 2 per cent to more than 5 per cent in Brooklyn in the last two years. He added:

"The use of dangerous liquor is largely responsible, but first, dances and other flapper and cake-eater affairs have a tendency to create abnormal mental conditions in boys and girls. This is because of the exaggerated conditions these dances and events promote."

The club members pledged Dr. Harris their support in the movement to adequate care for the State's public charges.

In the madness bred of excitement some modern girls lose their poise and embark on the greatest adventure of all when life has lost its thrill or seems a dreary, gray waste

Will Art Lead Jazz-Mad World B Relig

WHY are so many of our young people committing suicide?

That is the challenging question which rises from the 1923 figures for the Nation's death addicts, just estimated by Dr. Harry Marsh Warren, president and founder of the Save-a-Life League, of New York City, which has for its aim the prevention of suicide.

More than 12,000 in this country found their burdens too difficult to bear and brought an end to their existence during the year 1923. One big insurance official has admitted that his company alone paid out $1,300,000 insurance on the lives of those who, because of fears and discouragements, wearied of the struggle and sought suicides' graves.

Laymen Interpret Large Showing of Sacred Themes at Pittsburgh Exhibition as Challenge to World Agnosticism and Bolshevist Sacrilege

ANITY

Too Much JAZZ in the CHURCH

Bodies or Souls—Which? Is the Issue Today, According to Bishop Freeman, Noted Washington Ecclesiastic, as He Contends the Church Places "Too Great Emphasis on Pastimes and Recreations and Not Enough on the Religion of Christ".

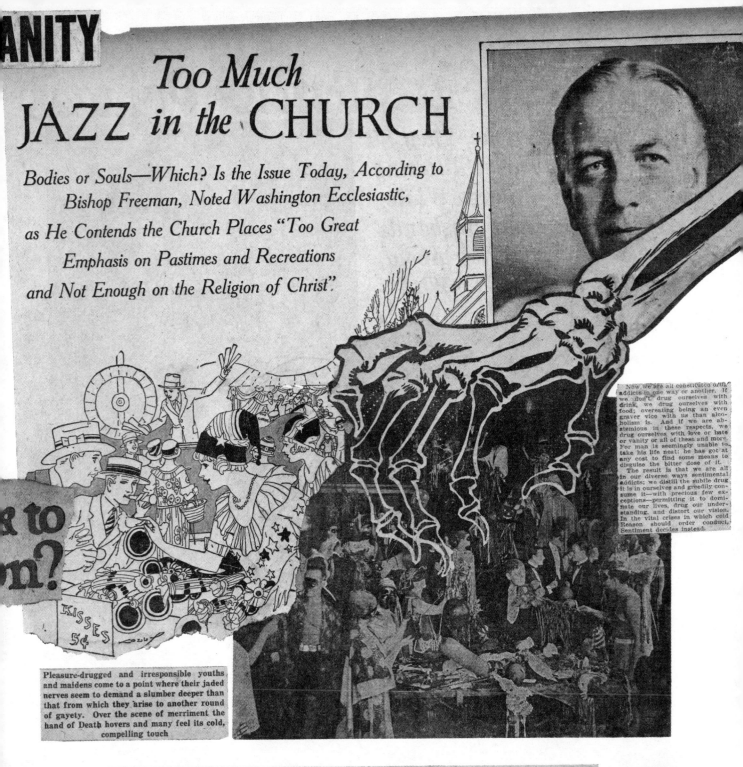

Now we are all constituted drug addicts in one way or another. If we don't drug ourselves with drink, we drug ourselves with food; overeating being an even graver vice with us than alcoholism is. And if we are abstemious in these respects, we drug ourselves with love or hate or vanity or all of these and more. For man is seemingly unable to take his life neat: he has got at any cost to find some means to disguise the bitter dose of it.

The result is that we are all in our diverse ways sentimental addicts; we distill the subtle drug it is in ourselves and greedily consume it—with precious few exceptions—permitting it to dominate our lives, drug our understanding, and distort our vision. In the vital crises in which cold Reason should order conduct, Sentiment decides instead.

k to

n?

Pleasure-drugged and irresponsible youths and maidens come to a point where their jaded nerves seem to demand a slumber deeper than that from which they arise to another round of gayety. Over the scene of merriment the hand of Death hovers and many feel its cold, compelling touch

Big Business Banishes
the Flapper

Her Dress and Deportment Are Now Toned Down as Banks and Corporations Adopt Regulations Dooming the "Vampy" Types on the Left in Favor of the Demure Ones on the Right.

FOUNDED 1865 SAN FRANCISCO, CAL., MONDAY, MARCH 23, 1925 VOL. C

JAZZ CARRIES SON OF WEALTH TO PR

Philip Valentine Tells Own Story of Wild Life That Ended Behind Bars

Son of Late President of Wells Fargo Learns His Lesson About Speed and Liquor; Tale Abounds in Thrills and Also Has a Moral

"FROM JAZZ TO JUTE"

By PHILIP C. VALENTINE

CHAPTER I

A strange chill stiffened my body. I reached out in the dark for the silken coverlet. Instead my hands encountered coarse, rasping wool. The deadly silence was broken by the clang of steel. I shook myself in an effort to cast off this hideous dream. Was I back in the war trenches of France?

As the lulling bliss of sleep released my quivering nerves I jerked into a sitting position and an uncontrolled shriek from between my lips split the air.

Shivering from the shock of my own cry I sat crouched over as I listened to shuffling footsteps along the stone floor of the corridor. A face appeared at the hole in the iron door. Then the rattle of keys and the door opened.

"What's the matter in here?" a gruff voice demanded. "Gone crazy?"

I mumbled something which seemed to satisfy him and he went away, but I sat staring into the blackness. I felt as if I were lost in the murky waters of some nauseous sea.

It was my first night in San Quentin. I lived my whole life over again in those black hours until the second-handed rays of light, reflected from the cold stone walls, struck against my still staring eyes.

Careening madly down the blazing road of pleasure in an eight-cylinder racing car, lured on by exotic perfumes and the smiles of richly clad women, I was jolted into consciousness one

INTRODUCTION

THRUST from a life of velvety luxury into sackcloth behind the bars at San Quentin was the experience of Philip C. Valentine, the 23-year-old son of the late John J. Valentine, president of the Wells Fargo Express Company. He has written of his twelve months there, most of which was spent laboring in the jute mill, where he learned to weave 100 yards of sackcloth, for The Chronicle.

Covered with lint from the sackcloth he forgot about the silken haberdashery which he once thought was so much a part of his life and he began to think of the big things in life which test men's souls. He began to blush at the thought of his wasted years when the mad hunt for thrills led him into the gayly lighted by-ways where the saxaphone wails and moonshine liquor dulls men's brains.

"I was a jazz-mad boy with too much money for my own good and too much ego in my cosmos," he writes. "Prison opened my eyes—taught me to divine many things which were formerly enigmas to me."

It is a remarkable document, written in a remarkable age when hundreds of "jazz-mad" boys are running wild with expensive cars in which alcohol does not mix with gasoline and death rides at the wheel.

Mothers and fathers should read it. They should pause and ask themselves this question: What if it were our son?

Young Valentine went to San Quentin, convicted of driving an automobile while intoxicated. He served one year behind the bars and another as a convict on parole.

We have read many stories about prison life, but they always are told by men who come from the walks of life where hardships are not unknown. Here is a story told by a fledgling just out of a nest of silken down. Accustomed to eat caviar he was forced to cultivate an appetie for the lowly bean.

Work was unknown in his life, filled with dusk-to-dawn jazz parties, but in the prison he spent ten months at work so soul-wearying that he looked upon his transfer to washing the soiled linen of the convicts as a pass to a seventh heaven.

Read the daily installments written by this son of the rich who found his salvation behind the bars. It is not the ordinary story of prison life. It is the graphic picture of the tempering of the steel which turned a softling into a man.

Wretched Treatment and Needless Shootings Are Laid to Prison Guards

'Taking of Human Life Seems Rather High Price,' Youth Declares; Airplane Raid By Photographers Provides Big Thrill

SYNOPSIS OF PRECEDING CHAPTERS

... hideous form—hanging—came into the life ... was an inmate of San Quentin, and ... conviction that capital

'Love Letters' Flourish to Splash of Soap Suds and Hot Water, Youth States

Philip Valentine Describes Correspondence Between Men and Woman Convicts in San Quentin; Finds Friends in Homicides

SYNOPSIS OF PRECEDING CHAPTERS

An eight-cylinder automobile kept ... son of a wealthy father ...

Law Snatches Youth From Career of Gayety, Hurling Him Behind Bars of Jail

Philip C. Valentine Describes First Trip to San Quentin After Being Sentenced; Heads of Prison Give Him Place in Jute Mill

SYNOPSIS

Catapulted from a life of silken luxury—jazz-mad nights days filled with the eternal hunt for more thrills—into the jute at San Quentin, Philip C. Valentine of Oakland, pampered son wealthy father, the late John J. Valentine, president of Wells F Express Company, writes for The Chronicle of his reactions the days leading up to the crash which ended in his prison tence on a charge of driving an automobile while intoxicated

He spent one year behind the bars and another in the sh of the gray stone walls while on parole. On his first night i penitentiary he awakens, expecting to find himself back in snug feather bed. An involuntary shriek from him when he izes his plight brings the guard. Through the long, black of the night he goes over and over again the drink-crazed n and days preceding the accident in which a young girl lost of her legs.

The judge who fined him for speeding and then gave h "shot" of moonshine to take away the taste comes back to mind. Then the tip from the friendly judge as to where fu libations may be obtained. The visit to the "rocking horse" wh manufacturer and the purchase of a demijohn in tribute to excellent workmanship. All this runs through the mind of youth as he sits in the chill cell looking back on his life.

Lowly Bean Main Unit of Meals, Valentine Learns On Entering San Quentin

Jazz-Loving Youth Who Hurtled Into Prison In Eight-Cylinder Car Details Primitive Ways of Convicts and Hints at Bribery

SYNOPSIS OF PRECEDING CHAPTERS

Stripped of fine linen and deprived of the luxuries attendant on a son of wealth, Philip C. Valentine dons the coarse, baggy trousers of the convict and begins his course in textile weaving under the somewhat primitive methods employed in the San Quentin jute mill.

On his first night in prison he reviews his past life and the events leading up to his arrest on the charge of driving an automobile while intoxicated. He remembers the judge who fined him for speeding and then gave him a drink of moonshine, with further information as to where a supply could be obtain...

He recalls the madness induced ... he bought from a ...

Valentine Given Loom at San Quentin and Learns Secrets of Convict '400'

Former Son of Wealth, Catapulted Into Jail Behind Wheel of Big Car, Is Admitted to Fraternity of Uniformed Brotherhood

SYNONPSIS OF PRECEDING CHAPTERS

Head waiters at exclusive hotels and cafes knew him as the life of the party and wherever he went he found service de luxe, then one day Philip C. Valentine, wealthy son of a wealthy father, John J. Valentine, late president of the Wells Fargo Express Company, found himself sitting down to his first dinner as a convict in San Quentin. ...

Valentine Thrust in Low Underground Dungeon as Penalty for Jute Strike

Youth, Who Disliked Work in San Quentin's Mill, Is Thrown Into 'Hell Hole' and Fed on Dry Bread With Water for Hours

SYNOPSIS OF PRECEDING CHAPTERS

Getting "Conwise" was a difficult thing for gay, joy-lovin Philip C. Valentine, who had danced along the brilliantly lighte paths of rich young men, with nothing on his mind but the pu suit of pleasure.

After his moonshine-mad drive from Monterey county, whi ... in San Jose, the law had stepped in and subs ...

Gilded Youth Who Served Time Relates Psychology Of Prison 'Black Friday'

Hush Falls Over San Quentin as Man Goes Up Thirteen Steps to Gallows; Son of Late Millionaire Raps Death Practice

SYNOPSIS OF PRECEDING CHAPTERS

"I was simply a jazz-mad boy with too much money for my own good and too much ego in my cosmos," writes Philip C. Valentine, son of the late president of the Wells F... John J. Valentine, as he tells ...

HALF OF SAN QUENTIN CRIMINALS ADDICT

PATH TO PENITENTIARY PAVED BY LIVES OF MEN DEBAUCHED AT EARLY AGE BY NARCOTICS

Prison Physician Warns That Importation 180 Sale of Devitiating Drugs Must Stop Or America's Youth Will Wallow in Vice

Sing Sing to Stay Completely Dry, Lawes Declares

Sing Sing will remain "bone dry" after repeal.

This was announced ...

PENITENTIARY HELPLESS TO KEEP OUT DOPE

Where Jute Takes Place of Jazz

37

N

Valentine Watches Growth Of Firing Plan and Sees 'Cons' Thrust in Dungeon

San Quentin Clique Le
Maddening Work Ho
Scheme Goes Awry;
o Destroy
ectacular
it Comes

an Quentin Inmates U
Devious Schemes to
Taste of Sugar in

ilip Valentine, Becoming Har
Prison Life, Describes Electric W

Tensest Prison Mom
Are When Convicts
Is Before Parole

Motorist Describes His Sensati
That Decided His Freedo
Lesson Never to Endanger

JAZZ!

TO DOPE

DETAILS FIRST DAY BEHIND BARS

VALENTINE RAPS CONDITIONS AT SAN QUENTIN

PRISON JUTE MILL WORK PROVES MADDENING

RRIVAL OF PRISON "QUEEN" CAUSES THRILL

Y DETAILS DAY OF HORROR IN PRISON "HOLE"

RO

FOUND BEHIND PRISON'S WALLS

GRIM PRISON WALLS HOLD JAZZ-MAD BOY

PLOT TO BURN PRISON JUTE MILL DESCRIBED

VALENTINE FREE, WARNS ALL WRONGDOERS

SHE IS VERY FOND OF HER CHILDREN! I CAN'T GET RID OF A SINGLE ONE OF THOSE PUPS AS LONG AS SHE IS ALIVE!
PROHIBITION
BOOTLEGGERS
HI-JACKERS
BANDITS
GUN MEN
KIDNAPERS
DOPE PEDDLERS
DRUG ADDICTS
BLACK MAILERS
RACKETEERS
POISON DISTILLERS
GANGSTERS
F. OPPER
EAST SIDE, WEST SIDE,
ALL AROUND THE TOWN
DEATH
GANGSTERISM
WINSOR McCAY
Phone Slugs Cast Gambler in Jail
'I Expected More,' Replies to Six Months' Term
GANGSTER ROMANCE AND TUNEFUL SONGS IN WINCHELL STORY
By REGINA CREWE,
Dapper Don Put Under Watch in Prison Dope Plot
Haggard Call Mummy Exhi a "Desecratio
200 COLLEGE FACE PROBE NAZI ACTIVI
Dickstein Orders Inquiry Every Institution Which Germans as Stude
Wife Paroled
Husband Fails to File Stabbing Charge
Bullet in Heart Beats in Rhythm With Each Throb
KANSAS CITY, Mo., March 9.
Squaw Tells How She Ended Life Of 'White Witch
DR. GUTHRIE BARS ISADORA DUNCAN
Sergeant York Gets Big Ovatio In Senate Vis
POET GONE, ISADORA DONE WITH WEDLOCK
Outburst Wrecks Hotel Suite and Dancer Sends Serge to Moscow.
HOWARD CARTER TOO MUST DIE, IS THREAT OF HIGH EGYPTIAN
Demise of All Disturbers of a Pharaoh's Tomb Foretold o "Official Seal as Warning
Man Who Put Candy in Wife's Coffin Fined
By O. D. TOLISCHUS,
Flappers Look! Gade Announces List of 'Dont's'
BELGIAN QUEEN ENTERS INNER PHARAOH TOMB
Official Opening Reveals Gold, Gems and Art Objects Far Beyond All Expectati
SOME OTHE TWIL
Thug Masked As Santa Claus Holds Up Bank
'Blues' by Kate Smith With Spitalny Band
KING'S MU DISCOVERE PHARAOH TO
Sarcophagus of Tutankh Found Surrounded by Chariots and Costly Vases
Capone's Home Raided; 6 Held, Liquor Seized
VICE AND INNOCENCE DANCE SIDE BY SID
SALT LAKE CLUB, 231 Main Street.
Mr Brigham Smith
FATHER DEAR FATHER COME HOME WITH ME NOW.
SPEAKEASY
DAUGHTER, DEAR DAUGHTER COME HOME WITH ME NOW.
QUIBBLES OF 1930
STAGE INDECENCIES POISON
SULPHURIC ACID POISON
BOOTLEG WHISKY POISON

DOPE
AND PUT HIM ON THE SPOT
BOOT LEGGER
HIJACKER
GANGSTERS
NARCOTICS
HIJACKERS RAID CAPITOL EMBASSY
DRY AGENTS BURN THREE HOMES 250 ACRES
IS THERE A SOUL; DOES IMMORTALITY EXIST - IS THERE ANYTHING MORE IMPORTANT THAN MYSELF?
"MARS UNHEARD FROM," SAYS MARCONI,
Babe's Bat Now Nightstick
SLAYER STAYS IN COMA AS HE
"THE PSYCHIC DOPE PERIL"
By SIR ARTHUR CONAN DOYLE
Ruth Proud Wearer of Badge as Member of City's Police Reserves.
George Herman Ruth, prominent clubman, turned to his natural bent yesterday and joined the police force.
A born club swinger, Babe can handle a baseball bat or a night stick
"Living Dead" Man Gives No Sign of Life When Made Ready to Atone for His Crime
CASE BAFFLES DOCTORS
'I Want to Be Loved by You,' Helen Kane Testifies in Song
By JAMES H. STREET.
Helen Kane chided counsel in song yesterday.
A few of her boisterous and blase boop-boop-a-doops bounced between bar and bench in Justice McGoldrick's court while barristers blared and beamed.
She is seeking $250,000 from Betty Boop's backers on contention that they cashed her boops in an animated cartoon. And here is some of the testimony:
"Did you ever hear the song Poo-poo-pa-poop?"
"Nope."
"Boop doop a doop?"
"Nope."
"Boop-boop-a-doop Blues?"
"Nope."
"Boop-boop a doop a do?"
"NOPE."
"What boop songs have you heard?"
"Just Don't Take My Boop-boop-a-doop Away."
"What did you sing in an engagement at the Palace Theatre?"
"Aw, Don't Be Like That."
Giggles rippled through the courtroom. His Honor tried hard not to smile.
"What else?"
"I Want to Be Loved by You."
Even the lawyers laughed.
"Anything else?"
FEAR PARIS APACHES SLEW NEW YORKERS
Sunday Schools Run With Jazz, Savant Claims
ST. VALENTINE DAY MASSACRE SUSPECT TAKEN
Burke, Indicted in Chicago Murder of Seven Gang Captured in
WANTED IN OTHER KILL
KISS-O-METER
WILD TUMULT ROCKS GARDEN DURING ATTACK ON KU KLUXERS
rom Bands of Brass to Bands of Indians
ROYAL BONES TAKEN FROM HUGE MOUND
Skeletons of Supposed Indian Princes Removed by Archaeologists; Work Halted
Hurry, Mae West! 'Pleasure Man's' Trial to Go On
Great Increase in Drug Addicts at Sing Sing
JACKSONVILLE, Fla., Nov. 1.
AN alarming increase in the number of drug addicts being admitted to Sing Sing was disclosed by Dr. Amos O. Squire,
"VICE MENACES U.S.
IS IT THE MAN WHO INVENTED PERPETUAL MOTION FOR AUTOMOBILES OR THE MAN WHO INVENTED THE ELIXIR OF PERPETUAL YOUTH WHO LIVES THERE?
NO, THOSE TWO MEN LIVE BACK IN THE HOLLOW. THE MAN WHO LIVES HERE NEVER INVENTED ANYTHING. HIS GREAT-GRANDFATHER WAS A REVENUE AGENT IN EARLY PROHIBITION DAYS.
BOOTLEG
LIQUOR
PROHIBITION

Freed on Rum Case Contempt Charge

GIVE THIS LITTLE GIRL A BIG HAND!

"I Just Love Prison!—Such Gobs of Human Interest," Says "Tex" Guinan.

FEBRUARY 18, 1927.

HERE are some of the wise-cracks and nifties with which Texas Guinan punctuated her remarks during her brief stay in jail yesterday and in the interview she gave newspaper men following her release:

"I just love prison life. Some day I'm going to knock off from work and spend a few days in a nice jail, where one finds human interest hanging around thicker than snake-eyes at a clam-bake."

"I'm getting delightfully thin now—I'll look grand in stripes."

"Somebody remarked that I drew $4,000 a week and said that was more than President Coolidge gets. That's true, but the trouble with the President is that he can't Charleston."

"Give some of these babies enough rope and they'll go out and do a Will Rogers."

"I don't have to sell liquor to draw a crowd. Last year I busted the house record at the Hipodrome, and nobody had to sell liquor to pack 'em in."

"Somebody at the club asked me for liquor the other night. I told 'em to go out and eat some ground glass—the effect would be the same."

"I guess this Longcope kid who is said to have started this raid wanted something hectic for his diary—or maybe his hope chest."

"He wanted to know if I was angry at him for getting me jailed. I should be exasperated at being shunted onto the front page with Harold Webster and Aimee McPherson."

"Longcope has a date at my club tonight. Wait till he sees the size of his check."

"The cops didn't take off their hats when they eased into my club, so I had to request the orchestra to start up 'The Star Spangled Banner'."

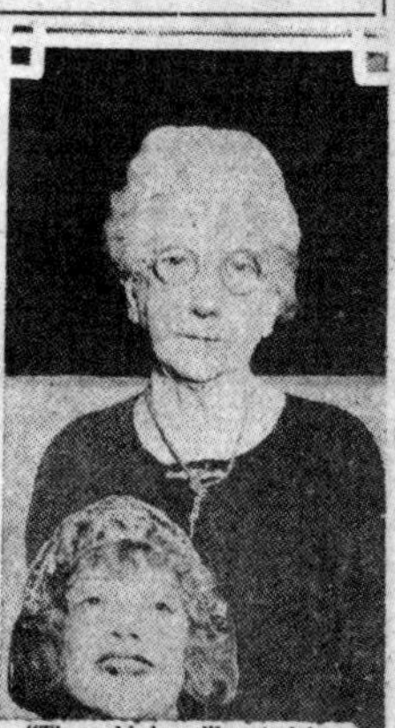

"These birds will yet drive me out of the clubs and force me to get a tent and do a Billy Sunday. I could pack 'em in just like Billy does"

"Somebody asked me what time it was early today. I told him I didn't have my watch—I'd just come back from Chicago."

"The matron at the station took a slant at my ermine coat and asked me what I was in for. I told her I'd just shot a man because he didn't return my laundry promptly."

"I've never sold liquor at any of my clubs. I get the first $4,000 every week, win, lose or draw, so the management can sell Chinese Testaments for all I care. I always get mine without any 'sales.'"

"I love these cop fellows. When I die I want six of them for pallbearers.

"The worst thing I ever do is to make folks stay up all night. And I don't have to force them to do that."

"If they don't put springs in the Black Maria I'll never patronize that line again."

"Say, sergeant, what do I sign for—a room and a bath?"

GIVE THE BOY A BIG HAND!— To prove "everything's gonna be all right" Texas Guinan posed with James Walter Longcope, Federal agent who engineered raid on her club.

AGENT ADMITS HE DRANK U. S. LIQUOR IN CLUB

MARCH 31, 1927

Counsel Elicits Statement That He Brought Government Whiskey to Make "Hit"

Federal Judge Thacher refused yesterday to give that little girl, Texas Guinan, a great big handcuff.

After hearing collegiate prohibition agents testify how they had taken Government liquor to the now padlocked 300 Club to give the impression they were "drinking" men, Judge Thacher dismissed contempt proceedings against Miss Guinan and Hyman Edson.

All in all, it was a good-natured, well-mannered hearing, with Texas on her best behavior. She had left her "wise cracks" outside. At any

TEX GUINAN'S CLUB FACING U. S. PADLOCK

Hostess Ignores Raid Arrest by Reopening Cabaret After Release Upon $1,000 Bail

Broadway, from End to End, Feels Weight of Law as Clubs Close.

Padlocks went clickety-clack all up and down Broadway and far into the Bronx yesterday. Federal Judge Bondy did the figurative snapping on some of the best known palaces of merriment in the white light district and out of it. Federal agents did the actual work.

The Club Dover, the Club Paillard, Helen Morgan's club from which H...

Hostess Receives Ovation as Raided Cabaret Reopens Gayer Than Ever.

Business as usual at the 300 club.

At 1:30 o'clock this morning Texas Guinan, its famed hostess, stepped from a taxicab to the boom of flashlights and cheers of the cab drivers that always line Fifty-fourth street.

Behind her from the cab came two sheepish prohibition agents, members of the squad of twelve who Wednesday night swept down upon her club and carried her off to ten hours in jail. Texas seized an arm of each, and creid:

"Come on in, boys, I don't feel right without you."

The three were stopped at the door by a swarm of entertainers. They braved the chill air in costumes designed only for warm night club interiors to fling their arms about the returned prisoner.

There was a small crowd in the club when she entered. The agents were tractable. She led them to the centre of the floor, asked the orchestra to play "The Star Spangled Banner," so the boys would remove their hts, and started the evening's merriment. Every man in the place was decked with a white carnation, symbol of the W. C. T. U., before Texas and her escort arrived.

It was all in fun for Texas, who said:

"I've had a million dollars' worth of publicity, and I'm happy. They can't enjoin me from entertaining the public!"

So Texas quoth and launched herself into a renewed rendition of the "Prisoner's Song." That was what she had sung when the minions of the Government had led her off the night before.

But, as they say in the games of childhood, "heavy hangs over her head." She's out, yet again she isn't out. For the Government, this very day, is planning to bestow upon Texas a choice little souvenir of last night's doings in the form of a padlock.

HAS PADLOCK POWER.

Just like Texas says, the Government can't enjoin her from entertaining the public, but the Government can keep her from performing in any place that isn't absolutely as dry as the Sahara.

Aye, mates, there's the rub. Texas herself may not be padlocked, that is personally she won't be, but the little club where she holds forth—known in legal parlance as "the premises"—is quite likely to be forcibly closed, that is if the Government has its way today. And what would Texas be minus her "premises."

Nevertheless, Uncle Sam is going to try it, and, even if nothing can stifle Texas' infectious spirits, he has three cards to play. One of these is the padlock proceedings. That was an old affair, and was hurriedly dug out of the mothballs yesterday when some one discovered that a deputy marshal had for some unknown reason failed to serve Texas personally with a temporary injunction, forbidding all persons connected with the "300 Club" even to sniff at a bottle containing liquor.

Really, that deputy marshal has put the Government in a hole. For, how can Texas violate an injunction which she didn't even know (legally) existed? So the Government is going to try to get around that by showing the injunction was a matter of common knowledge.

Then there is the little matter of the pint which the Government avers was sold, with Texas in the offing, and not saying nay, on the fateful night. That has to be disposed of. Of course, Texas can and will say she didn't know the pint existed, much less know that someone had sold it for a ten spot (which would be "small money" on Broadway.)

Anyhow, this is what happened, according to the Government's charges. A certain dapper young Government agent, meticulously garbed in dinner clothes, accompanied by an extremely demure young lady called at Texas' place. They were admitted. They were polished dancers and whenever the band struck up a tune they were out on the floor mingling with the rest.

WITHHOLD NAMES.

The Government refuses to divulge the enterprising young agent's name. He can be known only as "Mr. X." His female companion, let us say, was "Miss Y." Enter a third character who will have to be called Mr. Z. He is said to be a well known Broadwayite, and had he known what was impending probably would have cut off his right wrist before bringing the fair Texas to grief. But Mr. Z was a bit in his cups, as the saying goes. Of course,

HELEN MORGAN—HER CLUB

LON H. TYSON, being first duly sworn on oath deposes and says: I am an agent and employe of the United States, appointed and acting under the authority of the Treasury Department and am duly authorized to enforce the National Prohibition Act.

On June 13, 1928, at about 2 a. m. Agents John J. Mitchell, R. E. Herrick, my wife and I visited the Frivolity Club at Fifty-second street and Broadway, where the head waiter, known to us as "Albert" inquired whether we had been to the Helen Morgan Club. We replied that we had but that we had been unable to buy any liquor. He then said: **"I will fix you up. I will give you a card to Louis, the head waiter."**

HELEN MORGAN

At a previous visit to the Helen Morgan Club, on June 12, 1928, this man "Louis" had been introduced to Agent Mitchell, Mrs. Tyson and myself, as "Louis Zalud, who is the head waiter here," and Louis acknowledged the introduction. Albert then gave Agent Mitchell a card with the following notation in pencil on the back: "Louis Zalud, introducing Mr. Mitchell. O. K. Alfred," saying at the time that if we had any trouble we should call him.

On June 14, 1928, at about 11:30 a. m., Agent Mitchell, Mrs. Tyson and I entered the Helen Morgan Club, on the second floor of the premises described below. Entrance is through an open door on the sidewalk on the east side of building and up a stairway to second floor. At the head of stairs is a check room at the no... east corner of the building, ... the front of the building is oc... pied as a reception room, w... ladies' rest room and telepho... booths. In the northwest corn... is a small office.

Room for 200 Guests

Near the head of the stairs is an open doorway leading into the cabaret, which is a large room, with an orchestra on the left wall, a dance floor in the centre and tables and wall seats on the east and west walls. The cabaret has a ca...

Sorry, Texas; We Always Give A Girl a Break

Western Union Telegram.

81 NewYork Ny 237P Aug 1 1928

Editor N Y American

Dear sir I regret exceedingly that your paper usually so well informed printed the story about a bar at Saloon Royal where I work having been padlocked I feel that you will in justice to myself gladly correct the erroneous statement as I have never in my life worked in a night club associated with a bar and there is no bar at the club Royal where I am employed as hostess nor has there been a padlock sincerely

Texas Guinan

322P

AUGUST 2, 1928.

SILVER SLIPPER

LON H TYSON, being first duly sworn on oath ... says: ...

Representative Fiorello H. La Guardia offered a gleam of hope for the somewhat dismayed night club army. He said that the prohibition agents, in declaring they bought champagne, rye, gin and other liquors in night clubs at prices ranging from 50 cents a drink up to $25 a quart, had killed their own case. The Federal Government, he explained, cannot legally advance money for such purposes.

From Washington, however, came a speedy answer to the Congressman's point. The prohibition office there announced that the agents had not been advanced any Federal funds for their investigation, but had paid for the suppers, wine and liquors they are alleged to have bought out of their own bankrolls. The law allows them to collect from the Government on vouchers cove... their expenses.

TEXAS GUINAN—HER CLUB

PROHIBITION AGENT JOSEPH L. WHITE'S affidavit against Salon Royal, also known as Texas Guinan's Club:

That I am an agent and employe of the United States, under the Treasury Department, and am duly authorized to enforce the National Prohibition Act.

That I have visited the premises known as Salon Royal, also known as Texas Guinan's Club, which is located in the rear of the first floor of the Acropolis Hotel, No. 310 West Fifty-eighth street in New York City.

On divers occasions since February 2, 1928, I have had conversations with several individuals who seemed to have a proprietary interest in the conducting of the business therein, namely a woman known as Texas Guinan, John Johnnidis, Nicholae Prounis and Ernest Johnnidis.

TEXAS GUINAN.

On the 2nd day of February, 1928, at about 1:45 a. m., accompanied by my wife and Rudolph Malinoff, a night club entertainer whom I had met at the Chesterfield Hotel, I entered the Salon Royal and we were seated at a table in the cabaret by an assistant head waiter, whom Mr. Malinoff introduced as Ernest.

I ordered from Ernest one quart of champagne and in a few minutes a waiter brought to our table a quart of champagne in a bottle which he placed on our table and filled our glasses for a first round of drinks.

Orders Whiskey, Too

This champagne was only partly consumed, the balance remaining on the table. A short time after this champagne was served, I ordered half a pint of whisky and some ginger ale.

On this occasion, I observed Texas Guinan acting as mistress of ceremonies, seating and mingling with guests, singing songs ... entertainers. She ... in full charge.

... time she would ... ile and engage me

Miss Morgan Orders

"Later in the evening he brought Miss Helen Morgan to our table ...

Club for Dallas

During out visit Miss Morgan ca... to our table and engaged us ...

Agents Buy Drinks

The waiter then went to the kitchen and shortly returned ... the drinks, the ...

Check, $92.60

Part of the whiskey and champagne was consumed in the presence of Louis, the head waiter ...

Good Beer Joint

In an affidavit by Agent S. David Beazell, it is alleged that ... Helen Morgan's "M," ... stroll with the ...

Refers to Campbell

"She said the case was compromised by Murray and that they had some sort of agreement with Campbell, evidently referring to Major Campbell, Federal prohibition administrator, "where he

Ordered Champagne

"Mitchell in my presence told "Leo" that Moe Levy, of the Furnace Club, was going to join us, and Mitchell then handed "Leo" the card which Moe Levy handed ... on June 1, 1928, at the Fur... ... "Leo" to ca...

Mixed Drinks

We mixed the whiskey ... ginger ale and consumed a p... tion thereof. We then asked t... waiter to serve the champagn...

Handed Pint Flask

"Al" left the table and in a f... minutes another waiter came ... the table and brought ginger ...

Rye Replaces Scotch

This I smelled and tasted ... found it to be Scotch whiskey, ... I immediately told the waiter ... would rather have rye whisk... The waiter took the flask a... and returned with another ... pint flask of whiskey, whic... tasted and found to be rye ... ... for the check and ...

Dry Agent Swears He Bought Liquor in Texas Guinan's Club

La Guinan sang an im... ditty referring to her trial a... hibition in general. Some verses ran:

I was carried down to co... cused of selling liquor.
I got a hand upon the stan... made the lawyers snick...
Judge Thomas said, "Tex, ... sell booze?" I said, ... please don't be silly;
I swear to you my cellar ... filled with chocolate ... vanilla."

Now Mrs. Mabel Willebrand ... lives down in Washingt...
If she don't stop her kiddin... spoiling everybody's fu...
I, for one, will stand right ... and make a little bet ...

Helen Morgan's Employes Sold Drinks with Her at Table, Dry Agent Swears

NSIDE STORY OF NIGHT CLUB RAID

U. S. VS. "TEX"

On a Matter of "Interest"

"FROM about 4 a. m. to 5:45 a. m. the conversation with Johnnidis covered many topics, the most important of which was concerning the proprietorship of the European Club and the Salon Royal. He also advised that Texas Guinan not only received a large salary, BUT ALSO A PERCENTAGE, he having learned that by having her AS A PARTNER she took more interest in her work. John also advised that Texas hired the girls."—From U. S. Agent Erskilla's affidavit.

"NINETY DOLLARS for a cover charge! Well, I know that is absolutely ridiculous. Why, all the world knows that it's only $4 on week nights and $5 on Saturdays—but, of course, I'M ONLY A HOTESS . . . As for a bar, I wouldn't work in a place that had a bar . . . This Mrs. Willebrandt, who arranged all this, is a very remarkable woman—but Mrs. Bessie Guinan didn't bring up a damn fool either. —From Texas Guinan herself, in person.

Good Morning, Judge

WISE CRACKERS—Helen Morgan and Texas Guinan as they faced U. S. Commissioner Cotter in court yesterday. Note Texas' trick veil.

MISS GUINAN HELD PARTNER IN NIGHT CLUB

AUGUST 3, 1928

Affidavit Claims Johnnidis Told Government Men She Got Salary and Percentage

Texas Guinan actually is a partner in the night club which bears her name at No. 310 West Fifty-eighth street, according to an affidavit of Prohibition Agent Jacob Erskilla made public yesterday.

Hitherto Tex's chief defense when chided by Uncle Sam was that she was "only one of the hired hands."

But in his affidavit Agent Erskilla puts a different construction on the case from a statement he swears he obtained from John Johnnidis.

It was about 4 a. m. on the morning of last March 24 that Johnnidis waxed confidential, according to Erskilla. The latter thus portrays the scene:

"On this occa[sion] ... and myself ha[d] ... with John Johnn[idis] ... John earlier in ... European Club ... promised to buy ... Salon Royal.

ORDERED WH[ISKEY]

"John insiste[d] ... his guests and ... the right of the ... dered from the ... half pint of w[hiskey] ... afterward deliv[ered]

TEXAS HIRED [GIRLS]

"John also ... hired the girls ... them, stating ... had been with ... years. John a[lso] ... answer to a q[uestion] ... the rent, that ... ing and had ... years . . .

"On March 3[...] ing the cabaret ... we John Johnn[idis] ... Prounis, who ... table near the ... sisted that we ... cap' . . .

PROMPTLY SE[RVED]

"Whiskey so ... always procure[d] ... delay. And on ... said date have ... when ordering ... none was to be ... notwithstan[ding] ... ce n... I w... order ... ch liqu[or] ... I had ... eral occa[sions] ... well know ... an dits e... egular liqu[or] ... by those w... to be served ... I should co... would be take[n] ... "When I did ... ily purchase[d] ... de ired, and pa[id] ... ise readily ... ance the su... din came a...

JURY FREES TEX;

'Give Little Girl a Big Hand-ful!' And Here's How Tex's Club Did It'

TEX GUINAN was just one of the hired hands in the Salon Royale, but the poor little girl got a big handful of salary from the suckers she greeted so cheerily. Fifty per cent of the paofit made from Tex's patrons was stuffed into her bejeweled fist each week—an average of more than $2,000, or more than $100,000 a year.

Tex's contract, stipulating her emoluments, was introduced in evidence at her trial yesterday.

It carefully called her an "employe," and the club, the "employer," gave her a choice of taking 50 per cent of the net profits of the club or 50 per cent of the couvert charges, while she was guaranteed at least $1,000 a week.

While she chose half the net profits, Miss Guinan actually drew only $1,000 a week, it was testifi[ed] ... [th]e allowed the rest to remain in the club's ...

OH, WHAT I'LL TELL IN COURT, SAYS TEXAS

Hostess Under Indictment Declares Liquor and $90 Cover Charges Ridiculous

"I wouldn't call him a rat, o[r] anything; but, I bet at that, tha[t] this fellow White lives on gree[n] cheese!"

And that, ladies and gentleme[n], summarizes the opinion of one pr[o]hibitio nagent in particular, and all prohibition agents, in gener[al], cherished by Texas Guinan.

We find Miss Guinan at breakfast. It is a little before midnight—but that is just breakfast time to her.

She is seated in the Guinan mehage, undergoing the ministrations of a hairdresser between talk and mouthfuls. Two of her "gang"—Justine Johnson and Ruby King—are very visibly present.

CHARGE RIDICULOUS.

Miss Guinan, who has been asked to comment on the affidavit of one Joseph L. White, minion of Volstead, as it appeare din the New York American, begins:

"Ninety dollars for a cover charge! Well, I know that that is absolutely ridiculous. Why, all the world knows that it's only $4 on week nights and $5 on Saturdays—but, of course, I'm only a hostess."

Another twist, another curl, another bite, then——

"Sure, I remember 'em. This

HALF OF CLUB PROFITS HERS, TEXAS

COURTROOM MADE MERRY [BY] CRACKS

CROWD CHEERS AS JURY FREES CLUB HOSTESS

CROWD MAKES WHOOPEE!

The crowd leaped to its collec[tive] feet. Whoopee! Not so Tex. ... slid gratefully ... the ... bean ... a lo... Sn... and ...

JUDGE DEFINES ISSUE.

Judge Thomas's charge [to the] jury, impressively render[ed, the] judge standing, defined cle[arly the] points at issue. First, he sa[id, they] must decide whether the [Salon] Royale was a common nuisa[nce. If] so, did Tex help maintai[n] such? She would not have [to be] proprietor or owner to ...

HELEN MORGAN NEXT.

Interest now centres on the ... of Helen Morgan, which pr...

Another Trial Felt Futile A[fter] Guinan Acquittal; T[ex] Stages "Coming Out" Pa[rty]

Prosecution of Helen Morga[n on] a charge of maintaining a nuis[ance] appeared improbable yesterda[y as] a result of the acquittal of T[exas] Guinan. But no one coul[d be] found here with authority to ...

NERVOUS? NO, SAYS HOSTESS, TRIAL WAS FUN

APRIL 12, 1929

Has Kind Words for Almost Everybody in Her Own Story of Trial in Federal Court

By TEXAS GUINAN.

LIVE and let live. I think that is the most appropriate thing to say following my acquittal.

This is our America, and let's enjoy it. At heart we are all children. We never lose the spirit of fun. It's just that the average person lets it warp. What a mistake.

Light up your life with a smile. See how much better you feel. Make your home a night club. Make your family your audience and playmates.

Trial Lots of Fun

Tex's Night Clubs Did It!

Tex Has the Jury Twelve Up

By Arthur "Bugs" Baer

SOME new undiluted Webster definitions, gathered up with a mop at the trial of Tex Guinan:

The Government charge against Tex Guinan collapsed like a peacock's tail in a rainstorm. Tex clowned her way through all the judicial paper hoops and looked around for more.

When the jury came back with its Scotch recipe of Not Proven, Tex giggled hysterically. The entire trial had been a terrific strain on her lipstick

The Guinan was not afraid of going to jail. Right before the verdict was squandered upon her she leaned over and said:

"I would like to go to the jailhouse for about six months. I have a few freckles I would like to get rid of."

Anyway, Tex is not guilty, and the old bellringer in the tower of Independence Hall can reach for his flask again.

Every man on the jury team stated that he or she had never been in a night club.

So it looks as if Tex has twelve new customers.

APRIL 13, 1929

NIGHT QUEENS 'WISE CRACK' DRY RAIDERS

JULY 1, 1928

Texas Guinan, Helen Morgan Held in Bail by Commissioner For 'Maintaining a Nuisance'

It took U. S. prohibition authorities two hours to make up their minds what to do with two Broadway bright lights, Texas Guinan and Helen Morgan, yesterday.

Eventually, they ended up by charging them with "maintaining a nuisance." Miss Guinan greeted the charge by exclaiming:

"I'll leave it to the world, who's a nuisance. Me and Helen, or the guys who pulled the raid."

She patted Miss Morgan on the shoulder, as she looked about the dusty courtroom of Unted States Commissioner Garrett W. Cotter.

The two heavy sugar hostesses of New York's night life were led a merry chase while awaiting arraignment. They were made to report at prohibition headquarters, No. 1 Park avenue. There they were kept waiting to see Maurice Campbell, Prohibition Administrator. Then they were sent to the Federal Building, where they were searched from floor to floor.

Miss Morgan and Miss Guinan finally faced United States Commissioner Cotter. Miss Morgan pleaded not guilty and signed her bond. When Miss Guinan came forward, she took off a white kid glove and [sig]ned.

Cotter then asked in an unjudicial voice:

"How are you this morning, Miss Guinan."

She responded:

"It ain't morning no more. How are you and how's your little baby?"

"Fine."

"How much fine?"

Cotter laughed and Texas walked out of the room, free as was Miss Morgan under $1,000 bail.

Members of the staff of the United States Attorney's office were as much disgusted as the lawyers for Miss Morgan and Miss Guinan over the case. One of Mr. Tuttle's assistants said:

"We had nothing to do with these raids. They were planned in Washington. We do not plan to make any others. We are here to prosecute, not to plan raids. In the ordinary course of business, we will probably move to padlock these places, if the evidence warrants it."

Attorney Adler said:

"This is a fine joke on justice. I was an assistant United States Attorney under Mr. Bruckner. I know there are mail fraud cases, one of them involving a four-million dollar swindle, which [are] crying for trial and th[ey waste] time on a matter of thi[s kind."]

WASHINGTON, June ... Mrs. Mabel Walker Wil[lebrandt, As]sistant Attorney-Gener[al in charge] of Prohibition Cases, ... that the series of dry ... in the closing of n... New York night cl[ubs] ... morning was cau[sed by an] order from her.

Since early W... brandt said, her ... operating with ... in preparing ... extent the N... made on the ... ment.

IDENTIFICATION CARD 1930 APRIL to JUNE, Inc.

The GAS with a PUNCH

Texas Guinan Fights Conspiracy Charge

Prohibition Spider and Trapped Broadway Flies!

JULY 31, 1928

"Suckers," gaze on these gems! The effulgent lady, of course, is Texas Guinan. Agleam, asparkle, ablaze, she's the acknowledged queen of the whoopee makers. She's the queen of transmutation. She transmutes your dollars into her diamonds—your pains [into her] [plea]sure! YOU, "SUCKER."

IN LAW'S WEB!—Mrs. Mabel W. Willebrandt (at top centre) has certainly set Broadway buzzing. As Assistant Attorney General in charge of prohibition cases she selected two shining lights of the Great White Way when she caused the indictment of Texas Guinan (left) and Helen Morgan, noted night club hostesses.

SPEED!
SANITARIUM

...e Section

The Sunday Oregonian

NO.

PORTLAND, OREGON, SUNDAY MORNING, JUNE 12, 1932

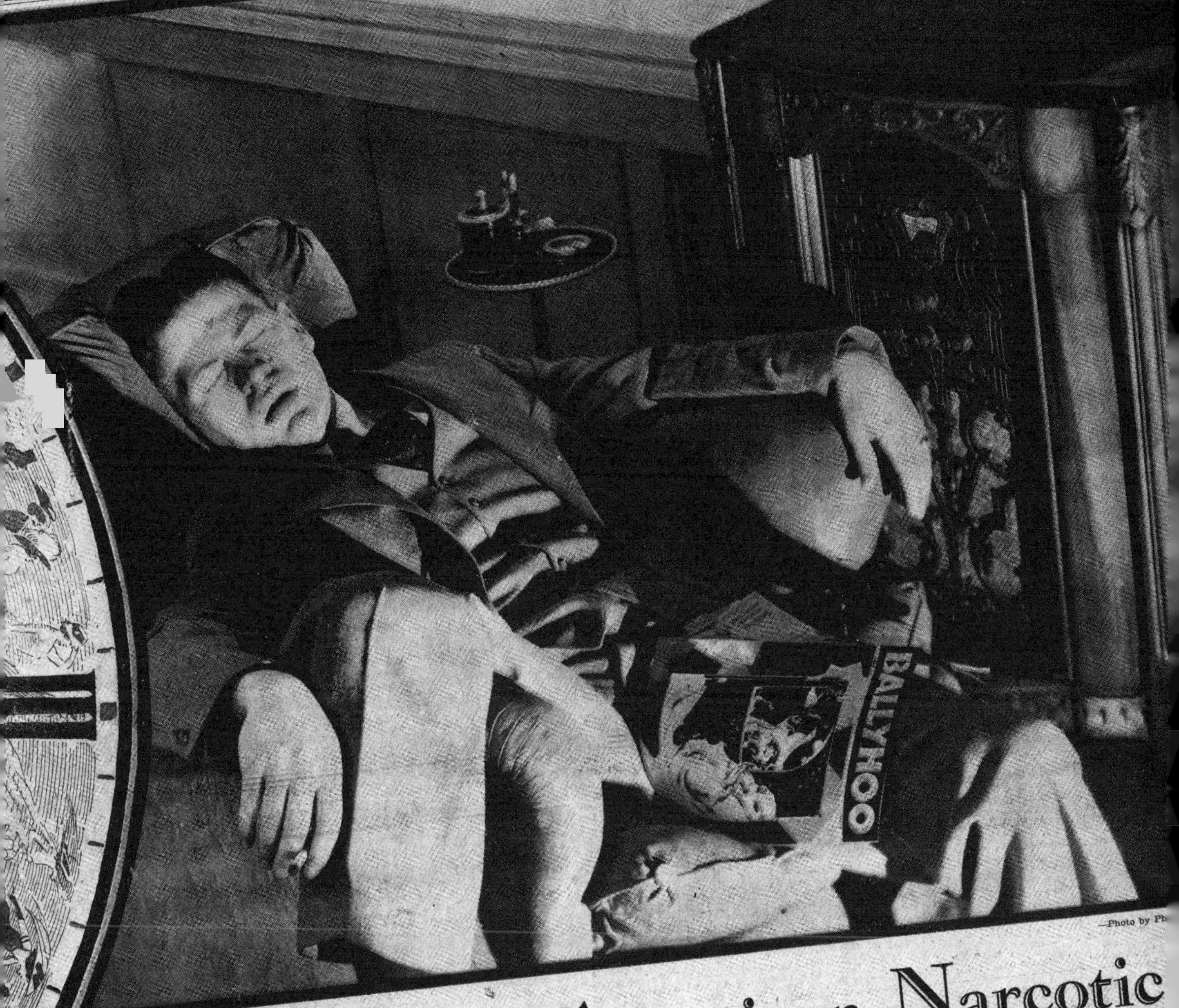

—Photo by Ph...

The Great American Narcotic

The Great American Brain-Killer Is Dance Music, That Once-Refreshing Poppy N... Is Taking the...

Opium? No! Cocaine? No! The Great American Brain-Killer Is Dance Music, That Once-Refreshing Poppy N... and Become a Concentrated Producer of Overpowering Ennui—Dance Music, on the Radio, Is Taking the...

A Dissertation on Radio ...

YOU'RE wrong! That dopey-looking dumbbell in the picture is not asleep. Indeed he is not! If you insist upon thinking he is, then that spoils this story and there's no use wasting time telling you anything more. The man's awake, but he's awake only as an oriental is after smoking $6 (Mex) worth of opium. In other words, he's doped. He's under the influence of dance music. Dance music! that once refreshing poppy now, dried up and become a concentrated producer of overpowering ennui. You've guessed it now. What we're going to say is that radio dance music, now a meaningless, monotonous noise, now used by listeners only to numb the brain, is on the skids. Its date is almost out.

* * *

...ing but a noise. ... mission singers are seldom singers. They are saxophone and banjo players who gather in twos and threes before the mike and meander in hoarse, whispery voices up and down the scale with utter disregard of harmony and even pitch. Intermission "artists" are the crows in the flower garden of the muse.

* * *

Listening to dance music, you become as immobile as a scarecrow and just as insensible to what is going on around you; you don't mind the crows a bit. Maybe you thrilled when you first heard Don Novis, able-bodied and mature, sing like a boy soprano, the lily fellow! Maybe Phil Harris with his tum-te-tums which later developed into what he called a comic baritone amused you. Maybe the Three Cheers sounded better at first than most threesomes. But now ... don't really heed. ...

... place, the musicians are seldom schooled in their art or capable of producing any music other than dance stuff. Dance orchestras are recruited from high school bands. They are saxophone tooters not too familiar with the limitations of their instruments who tootled their way through school for the fun of it and joined orchestras after graduation because the money was good and there wasn't any other job handy. And saxophone players, it may be said, are the backbone, crooked and fragile though it may be, of a dance orchestra. Not being serious students of music, or serious students of anything else, for that matter, they skim through their music at rehearsals until they can play the notes with fair degree of accuracy, but never do they practice tone. Their tones are like noises made by blowing through a hose. The saxophone is the worst-voiced and most slovenly instrument of any in the dance maze of ov... sousaphone ... suitable on... with a str... beaten wi... honked in... When yo... the playe... player w... sical ins... fiddle fro... out; violas ditto. Ba... strung with wire that should be used ... binding packing cases, are heard, but banjos are the lunatic members of the stringed instrument family, and is there anything more depraved than playing a banjo—unless it's whistling and tapping the foot while reading a newspaper?

* * *

You don't hear drums in dance music over the radio either. Drums are as necessary to an orchestra as ballast is to a dirig... ...you ever detect is a noise ... Drums ...

...pest of the ... de up of un... of the leaders ... band is about ... ll them apart. ... have to admit ... l to guide you ... tening to. You ... re are the symphony ... ng. And White... he very few real ... used to play in ... ony. All his men ... the San Francisco ... are almost his equals in ability. Their arrangements are skillfully written by real musicians, who know the players personally and their instruments and the limitations of each. Then there are the soft and slow melody-mongers who feature sentimental vocal choruses in quantities. And, of course, the hot hotchas of the Cab Calloway variety. You will be able to tell something by the apparent size of the orchestra. You will ... ll ten-piece group like Joe San... But not al...

Lucky St... interestin... over the ... millions ... fling. B... competi... now Lu... for a ... gossip.

Dan... the pic... out of ... geles, ... to sat... can't ...

Jin... until ... ploy... no t... the ... min... ner ... spl... Gri... ju...

JAZZ HAS INVADED COLLEGE LIFE, DEA

Zane Grey's Great Story,

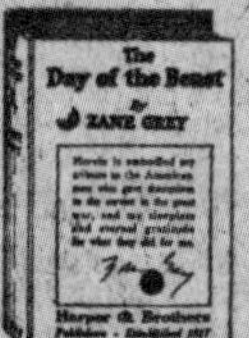

The Day of the Beast

A STORY OF OUR OWN TIME

Bobbed-haired "flappers," who paint and "pet," tote flasks, park their corsets at the jazz parties, and mix promiscuously with men at "undercover" clubs, are pitilessly revealed in this famous book by Zane Grey about an overseas veteran who "cleans up" his home town. The purpose of the book is best expressed in Zane Greys' dedication: "Herein is embodied my tribute to the American men who gave themselves to the service in the great war, and my sleepless '
for what they did for me."

OTHER BOOKS BY ZAN

To the Last Man · The Man of the Forest
The Mysterious Rider · Riders of the Purple Sage · The Desert of Wheat

HARPER & BROTHERS Established 1817 NEW YORK

WHY SENTIMENT IS THE WORLD

STATE TEACHERS ARE V

CO-EDS GRILLED ON CHARGES AGAINST FLAPPER

JAZZ DANCING SOON TO PASS, SAYS COOLIDGE

Vice-President's Philosophizes After Keynote Political Address

HOME LIFE IMPROVING

Home Brewing and Risque Dressing Called Only a Passing Whim

Special by Leased Wire to The Chronicle

CHICAGO, Jan. 11.—Calvon S. Coolidge, Vice President of the United States, who came to Chicago today to address the Hamilton Club, consented to talk to newspaper men. He gave out a few samples of his famous homely philosophy.

"Home brewing, jazz dancing and risque dresses are merely a passing whim of fashion," he declared. "Home life in America today is on a higher plane than it ever was. Just because there are more homes than ever and, therefore, more unsuccessful families than ever, it is foolish to believe that the majority of homes are deteriorating in their influence. People should emphasize more the good things of life, not the bad.

WORKING FOR NORMALCY

"In Washington today we are trying to hasten the return of normal and good business conditions as much as we can by legislation. By the revenue bills and legislation to assist railroads we are trying to help business."

During his visit here the Vice President visited the Chicago College Club, the guest of Mrs. S. W. Parker Jr., president of the regional committee of Simmons College, Boston.

Coolidge in his speech at the Hamilton Club took Alexander Hamilton as his subject.

SPEECH 1922 KEYNOTE

That speech was accepted politically as the keynote of the congressional campaign of 1922.

It was a note of warning, in effect, to the agricultural interests carried through a carefully worded statement that the farmers cannot expect "good times" until the republican majority in Congress develops a tariff law, based upon the Hamilton theory of protection, that will permit the manufacturers to resume business "as usual" and on a pre-war basis.

HOOVER SEES END OF JAZZ IN RADIO

DECEMBER 22, 1924

Better Programmes Held Big Need at Present.

TEST OF SERVICE IS FACE

Best in Music and Information Now Wanted.

INDUSTRY IS GROWING

Nation Won't Stand for Licensing or Taxing Listeners, Says Secretary of Commerce.

BY ARTHUR SEARS HENNING.
By Chicago Tribune Leased Wire.

WASHINGTON, D. C., Dec. 21.—"The radio industry can't live on an endless diet of jazz," Secretary of Commerce Hoover said today in the course of an interview on the future of wireless communication which he is supervising to the extent that national supervision exists at this time.

Improvement of the broadcast programmes Mr. Hoover deems more important right now than further regulation until it becomes possible to say what form of regulation is needed. The British licensing system, to cite one regulatory suggestion, would never be tolerated in this country, the secretary thinks.

"This country would never stand for licensing or taxing radio listeners," Mr. Hoover emphasized. "That idea only works when one company has a monopoly and all the revenue so derived goes into one pool, and we don't like monopoly. And then how are you going to keep the unlicensed folks from listening in? Are you going to have a police force snooping around for illicit aerials and searching people's homes?

Tax Held Reasonable.

"People go into theaters and pay admission and that solves the problem right there for the stage or concert hall, but it is obvious that there is no such way of getting the radio audience to pay for what it gets. So you've got to approach that some other way—leaving out the license tax scheme. I've heard only one very reasonable suggestion. That is to fix a certain tax, say 2 per cent—for instance—on the sale of radio equipment. One company reports sales running over $22,000,000 in 1923, and that will be a good deal higher for this year. You could provide enough that way to pay for daily programmes of the best skill and talent throughout the year.

"It would perhaps be possible to work it by setting up a general committee which would be charged with the duty of arranging these programmes, paying for the service of artists out of this fund. But, of course, as soon as you do that you are likely to get into conflict over what sort of programmes to put out. One thing is certain—the radio industry can't live on an endless diet of jazz.

Radio's Im

... as long ... material put out is really worth while. That is the most vital thing of all."

As Mr. Hoover expresses it, radio must render "fundamental service," and by that he means it must go beyond the ability of local broadcasting directors in obtaining talent for entertainment purposes and must furnish with fixed regularity, day by day, material of national interest and importance in music, religion and public affairs.

"Material available locally is not enough to insure continuing interest," he continued. "It must be subordinate to the transmission of nationally and internationally important material of all kinds. The local broadcasting station must, in other words, make available to the audience the greatest music, entertainment and enlightenment which the nation and the world affords.

Organization Is Essential.

"This means organization of a system of national broadcasting, the interconnection of stations, rebroadcasting by one method or another. That this is possible has already been proved. The next step is to make it a daily reality, and that step is the one I hope to see taken at the earliest moment possible. Great problems are involved here, but they can be and will be met and overcome. I think, with the same amazing rapidity that has marked the magical growth of the radio."

Mr. Hoover suggested at the third annual radio conference a month ago that organization might be accomplished on a basis similar to that of the press associations, under guidance and direction of a central agency which would furnish each day the events and material of outstanding interest and importance, furnishing it by interconnection to the various local broadcastig agencies as a regular service, free of partisan influence of any kind. Such material could then be put out locally at specified hours to supplement local programmes.

"Then we would have the industry as a genuine public service institution," Mr. Hoover added. "It would mean permanent, increasing public interest, a solid foundation for the future growth of the industry. If I were to venture any prediction I should say that this is the next step."

GIANT STILL EXPLODES

SUNDAY, APRIL 22, 1923

By LUCIAN CARY.

NEARLY every freshman who enters one of the coeducational colleges hopes to "make" a fraternity. Unless he has some reason to believe that he will be elected to membership he hopes with a depth of feeling that is difficult for one who has never known his situation to imagine. It matters. It matters terrifically.

The members of a fraternity—usually a chapter of an organization represented in many other colleges—own their own house. Fraternity houses are almost always attractive and frequently expensive. They sometimes cost as much a hundred thousand dollars.

The freshman who joins a fraternity is automatically possessed of thirty or forty friends among his own sort. He is invited, though usually only at the end of his freshman year, to live in the chapter house—which is a lot pleasanter than a hall bedroom.

He finds ready-made for him an active social life. He goes, as a matter of course, to all the social functions of his own fraternity. He is introduced to girls. If he wants to go to the Prom, he is ... party or-

... sororities, which are ... parallel organizations of college women, though it may be doubted if the co-ed is quite as dependent for her social opportunities on the sorority as the college man is dependent for his on the fraternity.

But it isn't these practical advantages that make the question of whether he will be chosen or not of such vital importance to the freshman. It isn't nearly so important to join as it is to be asked.

For to be asked is to be judged socially desirable, and not to be asked is to be judged socially ... desirable. ...

... average of ... members, a total of three hundred, then seven hundred freshmen are bound to lose.

The proportion of fraternity men to "barbs," varies in different colleges. In one of the smaller Eastern colleges for men some ninety per cent of the men in college are members of fraternities. But that percentage has no parallel in the co-educational colleges. There are commonly three times as many "barbs" as fraternity men and three times as many non-sorority girls as sorority girls.

SEEK CONGENIAL SOULS.

The standards of choice among fraternities and sororities are often impugned. And these standards are exceedingly conventional and permit only the smallest variations from a type.

A fraternity naturally chooses members that are congenial—its whole object is to form an organization of congenial souls. If Ibsen, the greatest of all modern dramatists, had been an American instead of a Norwegian and had attended an American coeducational college, he would not have been regarded as good material for a fraternity man.

He would have failed to meet any of the three fundamental requirements. For he came of a poor, obscure family; he was crusty, and he was queer. I doubt if the American college fraternity would have looked with favor on very many of the world's poets and artists and inventors if they had had the opportunity of looking them over in their youth.

SOME REFUSE TO JOIN.

There are a few boys and a few girls who refuse to join fraternities and sororities. There are a good many more who are overlooked through some social accident until it is too late. And there are still more who are barred by nothing in the world but poverty.

But however fair or unfair, just or unjust, the choices of fraternities and sororities, their members do actually constitute the socially elect. They lead. They are the glasses of fashion and the moulds of form and the arbiters of student opinion. The others, however large their majority in numbers, follow as best they can.

A questionnaire addressed ... the students of my own colleg... and answered by thirty-five hu... dred of them produced these fi... ures:

Go to dances—Sorority d... 96%; do not, 4%. Non-Sorori... do, 66 2-3%; do not, 33 1-3%.

Go to mixers—Sorority d... 14%; do not, 86%. Non-Soro... ity do, 33 1-3%; do not, 66 2-3%...

Date during the week—Sororit... do, 62%; do not go, 38%. Non... Sorority do, 30%; do not, 70%...

"MIXERS" OPEN TO ALL.

Perhaps the most significa... difference recorded is the la... paragraph. Sixty-two per cent ... Sorority girls, nearly two-third... have dates during the week ... distinct from the week-end. Thi... ty per cent, less than one-thir... of non-sorority girls have date... during the week.

But the other figures are si... nificant also. Only fourteen pe... cent of sorority girls go to stu... dent mixers, which are open to a... alike. But ninety-six per cent ... sorority girls, more than nine ou... of ten, go to dances. There is on... important fact that these figure... do not show.

The sorority girls who danc... go to far more dances than th... non-sorority girls who dance... The sorority questionnaire, as ... remarked in my previous article ... developed the fact that the ave... ... girl goe...

The figures ... of the men in college came ... like this:

Go to dances—Fraternity do... 86%; do not, 14%. Non-Fratern... ity do, 64%; do not, 36. Go t... mixers — Fraternity do, 22%... do not, 78%. Non-Fraternity d... 40%; do not, 60%. Date durin... the week—Fraternity do, 51%... do not, 49%. Non-Fraternity do... 39%; do not, 61%.

A glance at these figures show... that the girls in college ... more active ...

... in the college year and nobody knows how many more during the vacations, is obviously the flapper type. Flappe... isn't a precise term. And a goo... many sororities would resent th... implication that they were largel... composed of flappers.

One might guess in advance that their record in the class-room would be pretty poor—much poorer than that of the non-sorority girl, the girl who doesn't go to so many dances, but devotes herself seriously to the serious affairs of life. If so, one would guess wrong.

The registrar assures me, and has figures to show, that the sorority girl's marks average higher than those of the non-sorority girl.

IS THE FLAPPER BAD?

Such a fact makes one wonder. It makes one wonder if the craze for dancing hasn't hitherto unsuspected justifications. It makes one wonder if dancing isn't perhaps good for girls. It makes one wonder if the maligned flapper is as inferior to the old-fashioned girl as has been so commonly supposed.

Is the flapper bad? And if she is bad just how bad is she?

I pointed out in my previous article that the dress and manners of the college girl of the period are the dress and manners of the girl of the period outside college. The co-ed nowadays bobs her hair, smokes cigarettes (if she happens to want to), samples moonshine liquor, and regularly evades the elaborate rules designed to prevent her from running into danger.

But how far does she go? That is really the question which lurks behind most discussions of the flapper. I suspect that every attack on the flapper has originated in the mind of a person who thought, or feared, that the flapper was "fundamentally immoral."

The question was asked of two hundred sorority girls. The precise form of the question was this:

Do you believe that student morals have been affected by modern dress, dancing, manners, and if so, how?

One hundred and ten girls, slightly more than half, answered "No," with a few reservations.

F WOMEN ADMITS

xty-six answered "Yes, and for e worse." Twenty-four refused pass judgment.

PROVE OF THEMSELVES.

In one sense all this answer eans is that slightly more than alf of the flappers approve of emselves. They were asked ow far modern dress and dancng and manners had affected morals and they answered that these things hadn't affected morals. But in the larger sense ress and manners are morals. or two years now the older generation had been inveighing gainst the dress and manners f the younger generation as immoral.

One-third believe that these hings have caused an increase n sexual immorality.

I managed to ask the question n one form or another, if not xplicity, implicity, of students nd professors and deans and ownspeople and physicians. But he only definite answers I got I hould have to rule out as susect.

My informants dealt in impresions, whether consciously or ot. I shall, perforce, do the ame.

The dean of women of one of he great co-educational colleges gave me a very sharp glance ineed when I asked if it were rue that college girls were inreasingly wicked. Then she anased thoughtfully. Then she

know who is going to protect her.

"Certainly we can't. But," he concluded, "I do know that there are very few scandals—very few."

After making inquiries of some scores of students and professors and deans representing half a dozen colleges and student bodies aggregating more than a hundred thousand young men and young women I can come no nearer to answering the question he raised than he did.

IMMORALITY EXAGGERATED.

I don't know. I don't believe anybody knows. But my impression is that the immorality of the younger generation has been greatly exaggerated. My impression is that there has been very little change in the last twenty years in fundamental morality.

The flapper may wear shocking clothes; she may swear; she may smoke; she may sometimes drink; she may defy every rule of conduct laid down by parents and faculties and police. But she isn't "immoral."

Of course petting is a different matter. The girl of the period pets and is petted; or as she would be more likely to say, she is a necker. She means by petting, or necking, what her mother meant by spooning.

Is she more ready to pet than her mother was to spoon? I am not sure that the answer is "Of course."

The flapper is very frank about it. Of two hundred sorority girls ... were asked if they thought ...

"MOST DANGEROUS DRUG"

o be?" "Yes," I said firmly. "I do." "Ah," she said. "And do you ot know," she continued, "that he college is not completely isoated from the world outside? re you not aware that the ollege is not a small ... ool, uncon...

... canceing was dangerous ... cause of promiscuous loving."

SHE PERMITS KISSIN...

RNED OF JAZZ ERA

... the mothers of the girls of the period allowed themselves an equal liberty at the same age. They would certainly deny it. And how are you going to prove what they deny? Nevertheless one might be permitted to suspect that the biggest difference between the flapper and her mother is a difference of frankness.

I pointed out in my previous article that the flapper type was remoulding the co-educational college. Whereas formerly all the activities of the co-educational college were controlled by men, and co-eds were but an unregarded incident of the life of the college, campus activities are now more and more in the hands of co-eds.

I asked why it was that the flapper had succeeded in making herself an important factor in the college when her predecessor, the serious-minded girl who expected to teach in the high school, had failed.

I think we have already found a part of the answer. The flapper is not fundamentally immoral—if she were she would not have succeeded. That much is negative.

GOES AFTER THE MAN.

But there is a great deal on the positive side. The flapper has no mind to stay at home and wait for the man who never comes. She frankly goes out to look for him. That is what modern dress, and modern dancing, and modern manners really mean. The girl of the period is incomparably franker, incomparably bolder than her predecessor.

... affected by. verything?" "I do," I said boldly.

AZZ INVADES COLLEGE.

"Then," she said, "you have our answer. Jazz has invaded he common life. Jazz has therere invaded the college. But ickedness—no—there is no ickedness in college."

Many of those I questioned sed fewer words but most of hem said the same thing.

I got the frankest and the mplest answer to the question rom a man of whom I did not sk it. He was, surprisingly nough, a dean of men, whose aily task it is to deal with stuent social activities.

He had been telling me about he craze for dancing. He had ffered me some figures on the ost of dancing in college, figures hat showed a total expenditure mong fraternities and sororities fifty thousand dollars for ances in one half year.

He passed from dancing to the se of motor cars. A good many udents owned cars, nowadays, e said, and every car accommoated from two to twenty stuents—according to the pressure f the moment.

He passed from student cars to udent drinking.

"Is it true," I asked, "that raternities no longer enforce the ule against liquor in their hapter houses; that they acually drink at dances, and that he girls sometimes drink?"

NROLLMENT INCREASES.

"I am sorry to say," he said, that it is true."

He added that there wasn't nything like as much drinking mong men as there had been efore prohibition went into efect. What there was was much ss controlled than formerly and ld now actually include, as it rmerly had not, the co-ed.

"You see," he explained, "the ollege has increased enorously. In your day—you say ou entered in 1902?—there were ardly more than two thousand udents. Now there are seventye hundred. And the propor-

Explanation of the younger generation, especially the flapper, the most startling thing that has happened to these United States since the war, and an understanding of the revolt against the ideas and ideals of the older generation, are sought in this series of articles.

The author is seeking to ascertain the viewpoint of the girl of to-day by seeking her out

R-R-R-RIPPING—Joyous homecoming of Paul Whiteman, jazz king, shown with Mayor Walker in City Hall greeting, was made genuinely ripping as Paul tore his trousers in climb over Civic Virtue fence to toss coins to kids in pool.

JUNE 26, 1926

U. S. SEIZES 16 IN DRUG STORE RUM CLEANUP

Conspiracy Warrants Issued for 12 Distillery Agents and 36 Pharmacy Owners

100,000 Gallons of Whiskey Sold Illegally by "Ring," Charges District-Attorney

Warrants for the arrest of thirty-six drug store proprietors and twelve distillery agents, all charged with conspiracy to violate the Federal Prohibition law, were issued yesterday by U. S. Commissioner Cotter.

Eleven druggists and five of the agents were taken into custody early last night by Federal marshals ... on bail.

Jazz Compared to 'Bolshevism' in Berlin Paper

BERLIN, June 25.

AMERICAN jazz music has come in for one of its severest castigations at the hands of the Deutsche Zeitung, the Hitlerite organ here.

Pouring forth a column of invective against American jazz artists, whom they characterize as "bolshevists of music," the Zeitung said:

Paul Whiteman.

"Berliners are made to believe that magnificent works of musical geniuses like Mozart and Beethoven and Wagner are good enough to serve as the material for these acrobats.

"The Americanization of our industries must not be followed by the Americanization of our Kultur."

THE JAZZ MAJORITY

IT seems a little late in the day to upbraid jazz, but Henry Hadley, conductor of the Philharmonic, does it with severity. He told the Columbia Institute of Arts and Letters that those who like jazz are probably cases for the pathological ward. And to wind up, he said that jazz does not reflect a human mood and is "just the beating of tom-toms in the African jungle."

This is probably true, but is dreadfully uncomplimentary to the African drum-men. Their art is very complex; they have kept it up for thousands of years. It must be human to them, even if their drums are made, as is probable, of human skin. They go in for counterpoint, delicate rhythms and seven-part time. Even if it is not superior to jazz, it can't be much worse.

Hadley is one of the cultivated minority. He should reflect that, after all, only a small portion of the globe—one ten-thousandth of it—has produced the kind of music cultivated Occidentals like. Whether the millions of radio crooners, Siamese and Thibetan gongsters, Swiss bellringers, Scotch bagpipers, African and Asiatic musickers, and people who like the sound they make, ought to be clapped into the madhouse is the great perhaps.

NOVEMBER 28, 1932

The Loud Speaker

By LOUIS REID

ONE of the most subtle and potent influences of radio, and one seldom mentioned above a whisper in the studios, is the refinement of jazz as it is now played throughout the Republic.

Forming one-third of all the programmes of the broadcasters, jazz is definitely becoming high-hat. It is stripping itself of its sports clothes of blues, of weird effects with saxophones, clarinets, horns and traps which once characterized it. It is emphasizing melody rather than noise, and to make sure that noise does not raise again its ugly head, it is discarding horns and substituting pipe organs and accordions, it is bringing violins and 'cellos to the position once held by the drums.

* * *

JAZZ today represents all dance music, whether the music is written in fox trot tempo or in the measures of the waltz. And this dance music which echoes through the homes of America, it seems to me, is the most definite contribution to American civilization which radio broadcasting is making today. Still the hushing continues. Still the broadcasters seek to decry its force and its popularity. The word "jazz" remains anathema.

* * *

PART of the blame lies with the broadcasters. They have been too eager to join with those poseurs who see in jazz some desecration of musical taste; who are either too prejudiced or too reactionary to recognize its originality, its de-...

IT is time jazz was brought out into the open. It is time the pretense and the sham were shaken off. Its rhythms have conquered the world. It has intrigued the fancy of such composers as Stravinsky, Schoenberg, Ravel, our own Carpenter and Taylor. It has penetrated the saintly portals of the Metropolitan. It has stormed its way into Carnegie Hall. It is known wherever men congregate to forget the woes of war and the terror of taxes. Symphonic conductors no longer scorn it. You may remember Walter Damrosch, who, ever alert to the spirit of the times, said:

"Various composers have been walking around jazz like a cat around a plate of hot soup, waiting for it to cool off, so that they could enjoy it without burning their tongues, hitherto accustomed only to the more tepid liquid distilled by cooks of the classical school."

A meaningful mouthful if ever there was one!

* * *

LISTENERS are not so squeamish. They recognize jazz for what it is—a rhythmic form of popular dance music. They call it jazz and they demand it regularly and often in every part of America. With their demands go a plea for melody. Blues and "hot" effects may be appropriate in the night club, but for home diversion they quickly pall, when they do not inspire a genuine homicidal impulse.

* * *

OUTSIDE of the Negro bands which continue to serve up jazz in its aboriginal ...

of poise, that would indicate that jazz is now all dressed up and is going some place.

LISTEN to any of the popular bands on the microphones—Vallee, Lopez, Whiteman, Rolfe, Reisman, Cummings, Bernie, Lombardo, Ingraham, Fiorito in Chicago—and you will note that there is nothing of the old-time barbaric jazz in their technique. All of them have sensed that a high-hat is as becoming to jazz as it is to the purely classical.

And it is radio that has chiefly made it becoming. It was radio that took dance music out of the dance hall and the night club and placed it in the home. It was radio and its fierce competition that inspired the maestros to seek out even more industriously the great compositions of the masters for new arrangements. It was radio that showed them that if the great masters themselves can borrow tunes from each other—even Beethoven was not immune—they, too, should get busy and borrow tunes from the masters.

* * *

WHEN jazz sprang from the levees of New Orleans two decades ago and crept to the barbary coast of San Francisco, and thence on to the honky tonks of Chicago, it was a wild and primitive musical conception. It expressed the restless and barbaric rhythms of the jungle tribes of Africa, among whom undoubtedly it originated. Smart and imaginative showmen—Bert Kelly in Chicago, and Art Hickman in San Francisco—seized upon it, transformed it to a more adaptable pattern, and created a vogue which swept America like a plague.

* * *

OTHER orchestra leaders heard the call, notably Lopez and Whiteman, and soon the nation was dancing as no nation

since the Rome of Nero has danced. Broadway tunesmiths—Berlin, Gershwin, Donaldson, Kern, Confrey—worked day and night, but they could not hope to meet the demand for material. The maestros were compelled to go to new, or rather, old wells. They turned to Chopin, to Lizst, to Verdi and Massenet and Gounod. People heard beautiful music that they otherwise would not have heard, though, of course, it was presented in the quickening rhythm of the fox trot.

* * *

AND then came radio with its nod of approval. Today, as a result, jazz is more strongly intrenched than ever. It is as much a part of the American scene as the flivver and the ice cream soda. It is the chief medium of expression of our song-writers and dance directors. It is responsible in Gershwin's "Rhapsody in Blue" for one of the great modern masterpieces of musical invention. It has brought an end to the syrupy banality of the old Ballad type of music and substituted in its place a vigorous, original, indelibly American expression of gaiety and emotion.

It has produced some of the most inspiriting melodies ever conceived for a happy people—such things as "Singin' in the Rain," "I'm Just Wild About Harry," one of the greatest of all jazz tunes; "Old Man River," "I can't Help from Lovin' Dat Man," "I Can't Give You Anything but Love," "My Heart Stood Still" and "Tea for Two."

* * *

IF it were not for jazz, my revelers, we might still be singing—we couldn't dance to them—"Silver Threads Among the Gold," "Just Break the News to Mother," "The End of a Perfect Day," and "The Curse of an Aching Heart." Isn't it time, really, to give jazz a little hand?

One Girl Graduate, Now Married, Would Not Allow Her Young Sister to Attend This College for Fear She Would Have Too Good a Time, Regardless of the Rules.

her that I was trying to find out what she was like—that I shall

They—well, to be quite frand, you could smell it. "Where," I asked the flapper,

make up some credits. Somebody staged a party in the country for a movie star"—she named one of

"It meant I didn't get any credit for the work I did in Summer school—that's all." "But tell me seriously," I asked, ...

Ex-Follies Beauty, Who Wed Negro, Has Nerv

ENDS UNION WHEN DOCTOR CITES PERIL

Admits Alcohol and Blasted Love Affair Affected Mind and Led to Mixed Marriage

Helen Lee Worthing Nelson, ex-Follies beauty, has obtained a legal separation from her husband, Dr. Eugene Nelson, "colored" physician of Los Angeles, she revealed yesterday from her bed in the Neurological Institute, 706 W. 158th st.

The move was upon the advice of her physician in Los Angeles, Mrs. Nelson said, and there will be no reconciliation.

At the same time she had only kind words for the man for whom she forsook her friends and turned her back on Hollywood society three years ago.

She said:

"Dr. Nelson has always been very kind to me. I feel very grateful to him for his consideration in the past three years. He is perhaps the kindest man I have ever known. But I was not normal during much of our married life together. I feel normal now for the first time in years."

DENIES SHE IS ADDICT.

Mrs. Nelson is in the sanitarium recovering from a nervous breakdown which was brough on, she admits, by too much alcohol and by an emotional instability which goes back to a love affair she had in New York before going to Hollywood.

She denied emphatically that she was a drug addict, as had been reported, and stated that any drugs she had ever taken had been prescribed for her by doctors.

The Los Angeles specialist, whose name Mrs. Nelson withheld, told her that her marriage to the "colored" doctor was contracted through lack of judgment when she was mentally depressed.

She said that she never knew before her marriage that Dr. Nelson had Negro blood in his veins and that Dr. Nelson had never admitted it to her. She was informed, she said, by a girl "friend" over the telephone. She added:

"We—Dr. Nelson and I—never discussed that matter."

NELSON REPUDIATES BREACH

Mrs. Nelson gave out the letter from the unnamed specialist only after reports from Los Angeles came stating that Dr. Nelson denied and seperation from his wife. The letter, under date of November 26, was addressed to Mrs. Nelson's father, Richard Worthing, of Brookline, Mass., and read:

DOCTOR WRITES FATHER.

"Dear Mr. Worthing:

"Mrs. Nelson consulted me for the first time about the tenth of this month. Since that time, I have gone over her case very carefully and have gotten all the information I could from her husband and herself. I am very glad to send you my view of her condition.

"In my opinion, Mrs. Nelson has been for years in a very emotionally unstable condition.

"I believe this condition existed during her New York life and for some years before her present marriage. I believe the unfortunate outcome of her love affair in New York brought the matter to a head.

"At that time she had taken large quantities of alcohol and drugs and was extremely depressed and obsessed, and I consider her mental condition at that time accounted for her lack of judgment in contracting her present marriage.

"She has never completely returned to normal during this marriage for reasons I am sure you can appreciate as well as I.

"It seems to me that her present condition is a perfectly intolerable one and that she cannot hope to become normal while she is living under these conditions. At present she has a markedly nervous condition, with extremely severe and persistent insomnia.

"I advised Mrs. Nelson that I felt she could not regain her health unless she got out of her present environment.

"I therefore advised her going to New York to be under the care of an expert specialist in nerves whom I can recommend highly. This plan is partly arranged and Mrs. Nelson hopes to leave Los Angeles the first of the coming week.

CONDITION HELD IMPROVED.

"I am confident that if she sticks to her treament in New York she will redeem her health and normality."

Mrs. Nelson did not disclose the identity of the specialist who thus analyzed her case.

The specialist in New York to whom she was sent evidently is Dr. Thomas K. Davis, of 552 E. 87th st., for she is now in his care.

Dr. Davis was unwilling to discuss the case, but attendants at the hospital said that Mrs. Nelson had rested comfortably since her arrival there and that her condition now was "fine."

The "Follies" girl married Nelson at Tia Juana in 1927. A year ago they separated, but there was a reconciliation at the end of five days.

In 1922, when artists were describing her as "the most beautiful girl in America," and when she was appearing in the "Follies," she attempted suicide by swallowing bichloride of mercury tablets. Her father then blamed the girl's troubles on a man named "Jack."

Beauty Battles 'Mental Depression'

STAGE TO SANITARIUM—Former Follies beauty, Helen Lee Worthing, is revealed as in a New York sanitarium, battling what coast doctor describes as "emotionally unstable condition." This photo of the beauty and her negro husband, Dr. Eugene C. Nelson, was made in the "Love Garden" of their Los Angeles home, following a reconciliation after a separation of five days last December.

DRUGS GIVEN NOW AS CURE FOR INSANITY

Prof. Kappers, Eminent Dutch Anatomist, Also Describes Use of Malaria Bacteria

(Copyright, 1928, by N. Y. American, Inc.)

Professor C. U. Ariens Kappers, director of the Central Institute of Brain Research at Amsterdam, has discussed in a private lecture with American scientists at the Medical Center the newest means of treating insanity and epilepsy by means of certain curious drugs.

PROF. C. U. A. KAPPERS Describes New Cures for Mental Ills.

He also related how cases of general paralysis have been treated in Europe by means of inducing high fever in patients. One way told his stirred professional hea who numbered some of the gre names in American medicine, wa innoculate with malaria. The ter disease was treated later minor disorder.

Dr. Kappers, invited to Ame by Columbia University's de ment of Neurology, is a famous atomist and also one of the wo greatest authorities on the ner system.

Lately he had the distinctio opening the new lecture an theatre of the College of Physic and Surgeons of Columbia at Medical Centre, and afterward livered other private lectures. tribute from American educa honorary degree of doctor of sc was conferred upon him by Ya

Through scientific friends the of his professional message bec available yesterday.

DRUGS CURE INSANITY.

After telling of a deeper stud microscopical changes in the b and in the organs of endocrine cretion by neurological experts showed how insanity is being tre by means of improved forms narcotic drugs. One of these is sleep-inducing somniphene, use cases of agitated melancholia. told how Drs. Stuurman, I zy Kraus in a North Holland pr vi hospital, using only somniph gave a patient sixty to eighty d internally as an initial dose. was followed twice daily by in muscular injections for o we Dr. Kappers added:

"In this way they succeeded keeping the most agitate patie sleeping all his time, awaken only at each new injection, wh moments were used to prov them with food. Results were v favorable, especially with youn patients.

2 Plead Not Guilty To Murder Charge

WHETHER YOU'RE CRAZY

or S D P ND on W

Telephone, COLumbus 7000 3

Breakdown

Borderland Of Insanity Is Reached By Doctor Through Freezing Body

By HOWARD W. BLAKESLEE
Associated Press Science Editor

NEW HAVEN (Conn.), Oct. 6.—(AP)—By chilling his body to the early stages of freezing, Sir Joseph Barcroft, one of the world's foremost physiologists, told a Yale audience to-day he took a personal excursion into the borderland of insanity.

He was able to pass beyond the "censorship," the mind's self-imposed standards for safety. He said cold felt deliciously warm. Conventional ideas of modesty disappeared.

In still another borderland excursion, made by inhaling carbon dioxide, he passed into a sort of "land of errors," a condition in which mistakes seemed absolutely correct.

Sir Joseph's knowledge of mind and nerves contributed notable service in the World War treatment of shell shock. He is professor of physiology, University of Cambridge.

Tries Chilling Twice

Dr. Barcroft tried chilling twice, naked in a freezing room.

"In each, he said, "there was a moment when my whole mental outlook altered. As I lay naked in the cold room I had been shivering and my limbs had been flexed in a sort of effort to huddle up, and I had been very conscious of the cold.

"Then a moment came when I stretched out my legs; the sense of coldness passed away."

Censorship Goes

The nerve censorship had let down. He explained how the nerves in fighting cold draw the blood supply away from the surface. When the censorship let go, the warm blood rushed to the chilled exterior.

"Up to the point," he said, "at which shivering ceased, Nature fought the situation; my instinct

SO USED IN EPILEPSY.

'It may be mentioned that som-
phene by injection has also been
plied sometimes n combating
epileptic state.

'As prescribed, combined with a
tless diet, attacks were reduced
one-fourth and less of their for-
r frequency. But the German
minal,' called gardenal by the
ench, has been largely substi-
ed. Dr. Irving Sand, in Eng-
d, who applied it in eighty-eight
leptic cases, saw their convul-
ns reduced to 2 per cent of for-
r frequency."

'For the treatment of general
alysis there is a method nowa-
s, introduced by Wagner von
regg, which in many cases gives
ellent results. This treatment
based on the observation that
e excited patients considerably
prove in consequence of high
er. In 1786 Reuss observed the
ntally diseased being cured after
ing smallpox, usually accom-
nied with high fevers.

EX-DOPE KING JAILED, INSANE

...liam G. Patterson, at one time head of the largest narcotic ring on the Pacific Coast, was yesterday taken to the Detention Home for observation as to his sanity.

Summoned to his home, 584 Twelfth av., by neighbors who became frightened at his actions, police found Patterson wandering about the basement, armed with a revolver. They knocked the weapon from his hands and took him into custody.

Patterson and his wife, Anna E. Patterson, termed "king and queen of the opium ring," have been convicted and fined in San Francisco ...and time again on dope ...escaped

APRIL 29, 1931

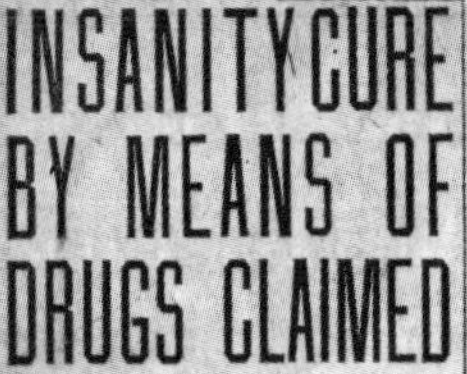

INSANITY CURE BY MEANS OF DRUGS CLAIMED

Revolutionary Theory on Treating All Mental Illness Advanced by Two Cornell Men

By GOBIND BEHARI LAL,
Science Editor New York American.

WASHINGTON, April 28.—A new method of diagnosing and treating insanity was announced by Drs. Wilder D. Bancroft and G. Holmes Richter Cornell University biochemists, at the National Academy of Science meeting today.

Bancroft and Richter have made a chemical attack on the problem, revolutionizing the whole question of mental diseases.

According to their theory, there are two main forms of insanity, due to two opposite kinds of changes in brain proteins, and accordingly there are two sorts of treatments, the opposite of each other.

THE OPPOSITE TYPE.

Treatment consists in use of certain common drugs.

Bancroft and Richter made this statement:

"There are two kinds of insanity. In one the proteins, or colloids, of the brain are too much peptized. This is the dispersion type of insanity. Patients fall into what doctors call catatonic stupor.

"The other variety of insanity results from over-coagulation of brain proteins. Maniac depression is a symptom of such a condition.

"Dispersion type of insanity can be cured or temporarily relieved by the use of drugs that promote coagulation. Such drugs are cocaine, amyl, and still better caffeine, found in small amounts in coffee.

"The coagulation form of insanity should be treated by using drugs that peptize or disperse brain colloids. Such drugs are thiocyanates and bromides.

SANE MAN CRAZED.

"A woman was in a catatonic stupor for ten years. She was treated with a mixture of carbon dioxide and oxygen gases. She recovered her normal mind. Carbon dioxide is a coagulating substance.

"On the other hand a perfectly normal person was unwittingly turned insane in a recent treatment for high blood pressure. He was given for three months sodium thiocyanate, a peptizing drug. He developed hallucinations and other signs of insanity. He was cured when the cause of the mischief was pointed out.

"Doctors can distinguish between one form or other of insanity by testing the effect of opposite kinds of drugs upon patients.

"An important cause of both forms of insanity is irritation by narcotic and anesthetic drugs, poisons within the body and alcohol.

"Many of us become temporarily insane. Certain dreams are probably produced by transient crazy states. If people knew whether they are the type that can drink alcohol or coffee safely, they might avoid such abnormal states and tendencies."

INSANITY CURE SEEN IN TESTS

By Universal Service.

BERKELEY, Cal., July 27.—Temporary restoration of sanity to patients suffering from catatonic dementia-praecox, a severe type of insanity, has been achieved by University of California scientists.

Announcement was made today of a series of amazing experiments which may open a new doorway in the treatment of mental disorders. The inhalation of carbon-dioxide gas which "super-charges" the patient's blood with oxygen and in some way, not yet explained, lifts the cloud from the brain, is the basis for the test.

Would Treat Drug Addicts Like Insane

It is not commonly realized that drug addiction is a contagious disease. Nor is the difference between the drug habit and other forms of contagious disease commonly recognized.

Smallpox cases, for instance, do not try to infect others, but drug users do. It is part of the curse of drug-taking that it is not only viciously habit-forming, but it almost irresistibly urges the victim to pass the vice along to others.

Dr. Carleton Simon, special deputy police commissioner of New York City, lately addressed the Eastern Homeopathic Medical Association on this vital subject. Dr. Simon said that more than a thousand million dollars a year is spent on narcotics. Also he declared that the problem of narcotism could be solved if only a small fraction of this vast sum were spent on hospitals, camps and colonies for the cure and after-treatment of dr... addicts.

Normal
Adjusted to demands of your group, — living and working in pattern or your society with fairly clear idea of what you want to do and why.
Neurotic
Racked by indecision — plagued by compulsions to repeat acts—often deeply unhappy—in conflicts between unconscious desires and fear of consequences.
Psychotic
You have found the "way out" sought by neurotics by sacrificing your hold on reality—by giving up the struggle. Escape takes strange forms.
Turn off that d— alarm. Even if it is Monday, I'm going to snooze another hour.
I can't sleep—but I don't see any point of getting up. If I do get up, should I go to the office or paint the kitchen? Nothing is worth doing anyway!
Don't be ridiculous! The sun can't be up. I blew it out.
Occasionally normal people have an urge to play hooky.
Apathy, indecision, sadness may mean neurotic depression.
Schizophrenia gives illusion of desired power without effort.
Mary! I have a horrible feeling that I didn't put my cigarette out. Will you take a look?
CIGARETTE IS OUT
I want to make sure no one left a cigarette burning.
CIGARETTE IS OUT
But this is the fourth time you've looked.
CIGARETTE IS OUT
Don't you know you must never smoke. "They" will burn you up if you do.
Normal folk occasionally feel anxious about possible error.
Man in drawing may be suffering from a neurotic compulsion.
A paranoiac suffers from a persecution complex, as above.
If that fool hadn't cut ahead of me, I would have won that race.
Naturally I won that race. If I weren't a good skier nobody could get me on skis. I would have given it up the way I gave up swimming two years ago.
See all my ski medals. I won them yesterday.
A normal person's whole happiness doesn't depend on victory.
He may be suffering neurotic inferiority, if he has to win.
Old age sometimes causes memory lapse—senile psychosis.
I'm so nervous about taking on this new job that my heart is thumping. Hope I make out all right!
Hello, Boss? This is Jim. Listen. About that new job you talked to me about? Could you get someone to fill in for a month or two? My old heart is acting up again.
I, Napoleon, order you men to take up your arms.
Normal people sometimes faint facing new responsibilities.
If heart is all right, he may be suffering neurotic hysteria.
Paresis (as above) is one of the end results of syphilis.
At last I've finished writing my book. I sure hope it was worth neglecting the children for.
Well, the book is finished, but I am finished too. I'll never have any more ideas. What on earth shall I fill my time with now?
I am going to write a hundred books today. They're all so terribly important.
Even if idea is successful, normal folk may have doubts.
Neurotic anxiety can lead to substituting new worry for old.
A manic-depressive is so elated he can hardly eat or sleep.
I'm swiping a souvenir teaspoon. The restaurant won't miss it.
Oh, look at all the teaspoons this store has. When the salesman isn't looking, I'll drop a couple into my bag.
Take that tray away! I'll never put spoon to mouth again. Oh, I have done such horrible things. I ought to be dead!
It's normal now and then to enjoy getting something free.
A repeat stealer may be an aggressive neurotic person.
A manic-depressive tries to adjust drive by self-loathing.
Boy, have I ever got a hangover! Ouch! My head. Oh dear, oh dear.
I would have died if I hadn't found that bottle.
Look out! There are snakes all over that wall!
Normal people drink too much occasionally, some a bit daily.
Person requiring lot to drink may be a neurotic alcoholic.
Cure for alcoholism includes removal of unconscious cause.
I'm scared stiff of having this baby. What if it isn't normal? What if I should die?
When we bought the house, this was a baby's room. I've changed it into a library and bar. I don't ever want to have a baby!
I can't rest. I don't deserve to.
Normal pregnant women have occasional fears, nightmares.
Some women avoid motherhood due to neurotic infantilism.
Change-of-life psychosis can be suffered by men and women.

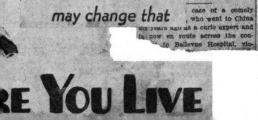

U. S. GIRL GOES INSANE IN CHINA

...Was Curio Expert
...ork Firm and Is
...e to Bellevue.

...OP IN SHANGHAI

...ble Gems to Na-
...d at Seattle; Her
...aits Her Here.

...case of a comely ..., who went to China six years ago as a curio expert and is now en route across the con... to Bellevue Hospital, vio...

Being loony is all a matter of what the neighbors think of you, but science may change that

...RE YOU LIVE

SECOND SECTION
Business and Trade, Domestic and Foreign; Stocks and Bonds. Ship News—Travel Ads.

Editorial Telephone, Beekman 2000

New York American

CHARACTER · LIBERTY · AMERICA FIRST! · ENTERPRISE · ACCURACY
AN AMERICAN PAPER FOR THE AMERICAN PEOPLE

MONDAY, MAY 23, 1927

IN THIS SECTION
Society, Drama, Music, Films. Classified Advertising. Auction Advertising.

Business Telephone, Columbus 7000

13

BUYING That Thing Called FUN!

by O. O. McINTYRE

THOSE $30 QUARTS OF CIDER 'WENT BIG' FOR MANY A NIGHT

Pleasure's Bill Showed $1.50 Sandwiches, $25 Couverts and Hoboken "French Dolls" at $5, but They Paid, Paid and Paid

I HAVE just returned from a six weeks' stay in Paris to find another Broadway. The change has come as swiftly and mercilessly as an apoplectic seizure. Post-ar madness spent itself with the suddenness of a jumper lking at the hurdle and leaving its rider in a confused and impled heap along the way.

I am, of course, referring to the Broadway of the tinseled tter. The Broadway that is recruited from among those ted under the standing head, "Buyers in Town," the Broad-y of the waisted young men with the vaselined hair, the tonic Casanovas and the perennial Helens seeking their htly Troys. In short, the night life.

It has all exploded with a mighty bang—the detonation ving only the bleached bones of the wastrels and gleaners. ere once bulged a vulgar stuffiness there is now only a stly array of white-topped, empty tables. The last despair-note of the swan song has reverberated through the moist yon. Broadway after dark is a graveyard. Kale and ewell! O, tempora, O, MORONS!

If Paul Couldn't, No One Could

Even the valiant and deservedly popular Paul Whiteman d not breast the tide. And if he could not turn it, no one l. He puts up the shutters on his jazz palace tomorrow t to tour the tanks and await a more auspicious day. in his generation is Paul. He saw the approaching cle and made his bow. He was too astute to join the ful of malingerers and t the sheriff.

e collapse of the night has been a heavy purse not only to the former s law hotel bellhops n affluent in the boot-ng bonanza but to the respectable members of uild. Scores are back they started—on the way curbs, rolling their cigarettes and waiting e "breaks."

Tarzans Lose Out

of the Tarzans of the ho insolently snatch our ust return to the earlier re refined profession of imbing. And hundreds of eautiful girls whose lips pursed in eternally plain-ckers have become little Annies in Broadway's ng storm.

have no place now to take nnie Bates, of the spoke Bates family in Big Bend, or that delightful inter-re crying him out of a on his expansive Adam's the way home in the taxi ust go back to crying the five and tens.

he Gigolo Union, Local as completely disbanded e no havens for their urotic ladies with acce ibags and misunderstand nds. The sleek libertine a new racket. Their d has curled up like a leaf in the Summer sun though it is going to be Winter, to say nothing of the Fall.

r old Broadway, after things with a split lead many moons, still finds It is still, as we say ounger accounting set, d."

Two Patrons

mirrored mosque, where ths ago an imperious ter with that aloof of his craft diffidently patrons from the press ken entrance ropes. I hts ago saw exactly among the sixty odd les. A sad-eyed young one of those portable anos, singing of the faithless lover. It was ysterical caterwauling ul in a tomb.

is not so good," I said tre de hotel. There calm in his face—and ab in his heart—as he I am just sitting up pee."

her formerly hilarious ted the same night cking at the coverlets nk into the gray precedes rigor mortis. um had become the

king up the night is not difficult to merely cracked under cover charge pyra-the barrage of pro-rtinence.

vers who sought to

-ITS THE COVER CHARGE, SIR."

JESSE JAMES' GRAND-DAUGHTER

CRAVATH

WISE PAUL—He saw the "handwriting on the wall," did the deservedly popular Mr. Whiteman. He could not turn the retreating tide that was bound to leave night clubs high and dry. Up will go Paul's shutters—he's closing the old jazz palace until better times.

SHE'S STILL A WINNER!—Texas Guinan, to whom Mr. McIntyre evidently refers as "the single exception" in the fall of night club prosperity, is still "getting a hand." Texas just seems to keep the patrons coming—But how long? That's another thought.

Queen of Wisecrackers!

OF all the New York night club hostesses, "Texas" Guinan is the most widely known. From the prairies of the Middle West to the Rockies and back again, she's the "wise-cracking" queen of them all.

Her domain is the land of jazz, the bon mot, glorified beauty. Vainly the United States Government has tried to put a padlock on her, but always, with cheerful bravado, she manages to wiggle out of the net.

Who has not heard her great slogan:

"Give the little girl a big hand!"

Many a doughty dollar has been risked for Texas' smile, the highest accolade the night clubs know. Listen to some of her wisecracks:

"Give some of these tables enough rope and they'll outdo Will Rogers."

"The worst thing I ever do is to make folks stay up all night—and I don't have to force them to do that."

"These birds will yet drive me out of the clubs. If I'm forced to a tent to do a Billy Sunday, I'll pack 'em in."

"I've never sold liquor at any of my clubs; I get the first $4,000, win, lose or draw."

ODD ROLE!—Roger Wolfe Kahn, son of the millionaire banker, Otto H. Kahn, has intrigued New York in his role of night-club owner. New York wonders if he can make a go of the game.

chase the blue hours on the Broadway polished floors simply tired of paying $1.50 for a sandwich sliced off by a safety razor and $2 for a six-cent bottle of table water. Many years ago Diamond Jim Brady, the beloved Broadway porcine playboy, caught the idea when he remarked, "Being a sucker is a lot of fun if you can afford it."

In Diamond Jim's Day

Diamond Jim, barricaded behind his diamonds, could afford it. The great majority couldn't, and so instead of greeting dawn with a hiccup they began to find pleasure in such simple joys as the radio, carpet slippers and a book and such.

If you do not believe that Broadway is staying home these evenings, make a tour of Lobsteria. I can name a dozen places—but I won't shoot, the poor devils are dying—that were packed to suffocation six months ago and which today are not netting enough profits to buy resin for the bull fiddler.

The outlanders who flock to town are finding other ways to amuse themselves. Not a night club, with one exception from Greenwich Village to the upper reaches of Harlem, is making expenses. I have this from an unquestioned authority. The single exception is a lady who has gobbled up enough space lately and needs no free puff here.

I have no desire to gloat over a cadaver, but if ever a phase of New York life deserved the ether cone it was the night club. With singularly few exceptions it catered to the worst passions of men and women. It was merely a glorified bagnio attempting to hide behind heavy brocades, dim lights and an exquisite insolence.

Countless murders, hold-ups and blackmail have been hatched in its satined depths. It drew the worst of the beetle-browed gorillas from the lower East Side to sit in Tuxedoed elegance at the ringside tables. It drew such a distinguished clientele as Harry K. Thaw, Richard Reese Whittemore, Judd Gray, Ruth Snyder and lesser cut purses and pick thanks.

Flood of Criminals

It spawned a flood of criminals from the lowest depths of the underworld and brazenly permitted them to sit cheek by jowl with adventuring young flappers playing hookey from select boarding schools. And now the rout has been complete.

Those that have not been padlocked cannot make their rent. Three night club proprietors who several years ago were rolling up the Hudson in their platinum lined limousines to country estates are now cadging along the street that lifted them to the heights and ironically catapaulted them to oblivion.

It is no secret that on the top wave of prosperity the night clubs that flourished along the Main Stem or the side streets running off either hip were able to pay all their overhead through their hat checking concessions. That is an illuminating highlight on the era of gilded graft.

Those Appoloesque figures who stood caparisoned in gold braid at the entrances to open taxi doors often paid as high as fifty dollars a week for the privilege of holding the job.

Cider wine with flossy labels costing eighteen cents a quart was gravely brought to tables in frosted silver pails and as gravely served in delicately flanged champagne glasses for thirty dollars a quart—corkage extra—and a $5 charge per chair for the privilege of sitting at the table to drink it.

Amazonion hostesses were employed to back-slap the come-ons, call them by name and intimate that without them they would lock the doors and call it a night.

Boobery Responds

And the boobery responded with the alacrity of the yokels to the "midnight session" of the cooch show on the circus lot. Men with silvered hair who would shock their boards of directors sat at ringside tables tickled pink at the idea of being familiarly greeted with "Hello sucker!"

The aristocratic ladies streamed in black face type in the Social Register rubbed elbows with the crepe de Chine divorcees with those Park Avenue apartments and day and night chauffeurs. Debutantes actually drank at tables with scar-faced, pock marked denizens of the deep.

Ruddy cheeked collegiates down from New Haven on the loose with gin bottles protruding from dinner jackets danced with those abandoned women with eyes suspiciously bright from cocaine.

Anyone who has sat on the side lines studying night life in New York knows this is not an exaggerated picture. The sordidness of the old time honky tonk loomed up as a pretty contrast. It is only fair to say that there were a number of decent, law abiding night clubs but just as fairly may it be said that they could be tolled off on the fingers of one hand.

In the beginning the night club was a fairly decent place—always sporty but a patron had no fear that in case he displayed a healthy bank roll he would be dosed with a noxious Mickey Finn and be found feet up in the adjoining alley way at dawn "rolled for his wad."

Careful Waiters

Head waiters were careful in their selections. There was modulated dance music and as an innovation immaculately and correctly groomed professional dancers floated out like puff balls to swirl gracefully about in a waltz.

There were no cavorting women

NOW EMPTY TABLES PROVE THE SPENDERS ARE THROUGH

Owners of Mirrored Mosques Stare in Wonder as Broadway's Super Graft Fades and "Boobery" Awakens to Sane Recreation

wearing about enough clothes to dust off a flute prancing about the tables between courses. A flash of silken ankle expressed the sum total of nudity.

Everybody went home at a reasonable hour and men did not go to their offices the next morning with headaches made for a horse. Many of the entertainers of that day went to stardom on the screen and on the stage. A host could take out a small party and have enough left out of a twenty dollar bill at the end of the evening to tip his cabman.

Then the gypping began. Nothing was left undone in the fine art of trimming the sucker. A twenty cent packet of cigarettes balooned to fifty cents and if you didn't give the vendor a quarter tip you got a nasty look.

Impertinent wash room attendants who brushed imaginary dust from your coat lapels demanded their tribute and if refused bestowed their guttery epithets. Annoying and scantily draped girls loitered about your table until you paid five dollars for a thiryt cent "French doll"—made in Hoboken.

The modest one dollar couvert was bloated as high as twenty-five dollars. Although the average in the so-called first-class places was about five dollars. For this one was privileged to mill about on a postage stamp dance floor in a fetid atmosphere of sour wine and stale smoke that would gag a self-respecting buzzard.

Golden Flow

And still the suckers came. They would stand wilting at the entrance for hours, eagerly waiting to ease the itch of the headwaiter's palm with a golden note to be admitted. It was morbid. It was pathological. Ordinarily sane men and women would permit themselves to be packed and jammed in these clubs night after night. Here they guzzled poisoned hooch, talked big, looked silly and would swear at the moment they were seeing life.

Gullible old dotards who should have been in bed at 10 o'clock limped out on gouty feet to have lisping young Loreleis whose conversational brilliancy was encompassed in "Ain't you the egg!" hold their palsied hands under the table.

It was a mad world, my masters. Every block in midtown had its two and three clubs. They sprouted in crevices. They mushroomed in dank cellars. They ranged from abandoned garages decorated with ten dollars worth of chintz to those ramparted behind marble facades with lacquered chairs, swimming goldfish disporting under glass-topped tables and a millionaire's son wielding the baton on a dias of bronze.

Broadway had found a super graft and rolled in clover. The assured and enameled ladies who used coyly to drop their handkerchiefs in Peacock Alleys as a prelude to a polite badger game discovered a rendezvous perfectly fitted to their calling.

Satiated Don Juans reveled in the new setting for their amours with potential Bertha M. Clay heroines. Blackmailers awakened to the fact that no longer did they have to scavenge among the below stairs gossip for juicy morsels they could exchange for cash. They merely put on a dinner suit and cupped their ear at any adjoining table in a supper Straying wives and loose hus welcomed a new paradise.

Called Night Life

This was that strange, ab existence classified as New night life, which drew ever of society to its doors. something even a blase proof metropolis had ne before and will likely again.

The recoil was like delicate watch spring. pened so suddenly Broadway is breath were sporadic spells ness but it would p Here and there Unc adorn the front w while the proprietor tive thumb at his n up around the co

Then one eveni weeks ago, restl began to look at wonder what ha boys and girls Gloomy waiter their posts like sentinels in a cemetary.

That night, it is officially recorded, and that it was not a coincidence is probable, there were sixteen persons in one of the most exclusive and most popular clubs

250. The proprietor telephoned his colleagues. Their plight was similar. They blamed it on the unwholesome publicity of the Snyder murder trial and looked hopefully toward the tomorrow. But from that night on the tomorrow never came.

All Tricks Used

Every trick of the trade was employed. Even the most popular of the supper club hostesses confessed in an awful black moment that she saw the end approaching although she was still making a little above expenses. Some of the more hopeful clung cheerfully to the idea that the Summer slump had set in earlier than usual. But it was worse than that.

Not all of them have closed. A number are hanging on by the eyebrows but they know the truth. And that truth unvarnished may be epitomized in a single line:

THE PUBLIC IS THROUGH!

It took them many months to complete the gorge and become glutted. The revulsion was as though every banqueter at the feast had at the precise moment come upon a cut worm in the salad and with a voluptious disgust had in a body rushed from the table.

It would be foolish to predict that night life in Manhattan is forever dead. In reality it is only sleeping.

Broadway at night will always be a playground. It is a definite part of the national consciousness—an overworked nation in pleasant relaxation. But gyppery is dead—dead beyond recall.

The simplest poltroon, one week removed from the south end of a north bound plow, will, in my opinion, never again pay $1.50 for a ten cent sandwich. Broadway could not continue to fool the world and in the argot of Broadway "No guy wants to be a sucker all his life."

There will be new night clubs. There will be gaudy night clubs. But their success will depend entirely upon the volume of business. Vaudeville, in an eminently more respectable fashion of course, faced a similar problem. It played to empty houses all over the land at $1.50 admission fee. Then a gentleman down in Texas decided to give the same performance continuously for twenty-five cents for any seat in the house—first come, first served. And vaudeville was saved to the outland.

House Cleaning

Broadway night clubs will, I predict, clean house and soon be operating under the same general idea. And if it doesn't, the loss will not perhaps be so colossal after all. Many will be able to struggle along without them. Even our popular young Mayor.

Those who predicted that Broadway could never be dried up are corrugating their brows. The speak-easies are plentiful, I grant you, and there is always a drink around the corner. But drop into a night club, if any, this evening or tomorrow night and ask for a drink. You may get it, but the chances are that you will not. The Big Collapse has chilled the street to its marrow.

It is afraid of its shadow. Even that gay little jazz parlor in the Fifties which appropriated Wilson Mizner's wheeze and hung a ard in its hallway reading smoking in the ele- othing more

dat- such rlie's mid- d by dis- y can about ion as a night

THE ... "In the Fo... ps of Abraham Lincoln" will be found on Page 10

SUNDAY MAGAZINE

San Francisco Chronicle

SUNDAY, DECEMBER 2, 1934

PART ONE

STUDENTS' POETRY REVEALS *that the* COLLEGE JAZZ AGE *is* GONE

Henry Goddard Leach, famous editor, after examining the verse submitted in a national contest, finds that campus youth today is sane, sober and purposeful

By Helen Welshimer

COLLEGE boys and girls are no longer hysterical about anything. Especially love! They take life calmly. The moon upon the ivy-mantled tower may rest as soft as snow, but a student with a chemistry quiz at nine the next morning will let the moon rest and get some sleep.

Love, the emotion that launched a fleet from Sparta and kept Caesar's men away from Rome a goodly number of years, plays as dominant part in the life of American youth today as it did during the lace paper Valentine era. But it isn't allowed to get out of bounds.

Henry Goddard Leach, editor of the Forum and Century, whose desire to learn youth's reaction to life, love and the New Deal, led him to conduct a national poetry contest in his magazine, announces that college poetry is now revealing the somber side of life.

"The gin-drinking, jazz-crazy, sex-feverish iconoclast who had Communist tendencies and who laughed at the older generation is gone," Leach says.

"Youth today, especially college youth, is sane and sober. It does not attack the social system, if the outcries of the young poets are any indication. Repeal apparently has had a sobering effect on youth. The jazz age is definitely gone.

"The proverbial satirical attitude of college students has disappeared. It has given way to a sane, sober but genuinely cheerful mood. Today the student wishes to co-operate. His thoughts are both creative and co-operative.

"However, the mawkish sentimentality that preceded the period of criticism has not come back. These students write about sex in a clear-eyed, objective manner. They possess a finely poised understanding of life and love.

"THE generation which seems to have founded its moral code on Freud has vanished. Freud has been dethroned by the nation's youth. Companionship and sympathetic understanding are the two goals which the new poets are seeking.

"They write about love and romance without either frustration or ignorance. It is a love of mind rather than of the senses. But the present generation of college boys and girls doesn't accept the facts of life as second-hand material. They want to make discoveries for themselves.

"These undergraduates of 1934 who have outlived both sentimentality and cynicism still write about willow trees and the lovers' moon over the meadows, but their moon has no mushy tears in its eyes."

For instance, here is a modern acceptance of love in which a co-ed puts the emotion in its place. Love, to her, rates second to the experiment she is making in a chemistry laboratory.

An Ohio co-ed gives the practical view.

"Let's try sulphuric, Bill.
Why must you day-dream now? At ...
should ...

... are alive again,' ... refrain. 'Let us sing of living.' "

A boy from Lafayette College expresses this theme in some verses called "Advice to Poets."

The dead are apart; concern yourself with life;
Sing among the quick, but resign the dead
To the public mysteries of Hippocrates and
decay.

There is no treasuring of lovers, though, in over-sweet sentimentality, caresses and withered roses. There is a sense of humor, slightly sardonic, perhaps, in the college mind.

Charlotte Radsliff, third prize-winner in the national college poetry contest.

Carol Ely Harper of Linfield College, in McMinnville, Oregon, puts it across in some lines on "Kisses." Now any co-ed knows that any campus has a fairly good kissing average. According to the poem, co-eds no longer attach as much significance to osculation as they do to an exam.

The first kiss that heated up my mouth to
love
Entrenched itself upon me with a long
storm blast.
But the last sophisticated taste of man's de-
sire upon my lips
Trembled only while I idly watched a but-
terfly that passed!

Girls maintain a more idealistic conception of love than boys have, Leach says. But even at that, the girls make a practical approach to it.

"At least 20 per cent of the co-ed verse is about home, babies and the emotions of motherhood," Leach asserts. "There are few suggestions of illicit love affairs. From wild drinking parties which were said to characterize the 'jazz decade' the students' thoughts are turning toward home and the more serious aspects of life."

Geographically, it is the student body in the south that is moved by lyricism and melody. The south, which has always had a reputation for slightly glamorous romance than the steel districts and corn belt of the middlewest, apparently lives up to its reputation. And the middlewest and west are undeniably more practical. So is New England.

The poetry survey revealed that Oregon and New England youth lead when it comes to reading illusion into scientific observation.

JAZZ love, which once swept down the highway, burning up the miles with a gasoline and gin odor, keeping pace to the beat of drums and whirl of confetti, is out.

A Pennsylvania boy says:

Do we love the less
That our love is quiet?
That we find heart-peace
Though we miss heart riot?

Elizabeth Gallagher, who won first prize in Mr. Leach's contest.

And a Smith College girl taking a different tack, replies:

Fling your hair
And swing
Touch that gnarled limb
Up—up higher
Birds fly like this high-
er . . .

Emily Dickinson, the first woman poet of America, who wore white dresses and walked in a garden, would be a little startled by the frankness, though, with which her successors talk about love. Probably the economic set-up, which has given women the right to meet men on more equal basis in the business world, is responsible for the directness of their admission of love.

Clara Jane Hopson, of The Principia College, St. Louis, Mo., has a poem called "Indecision," which is representative of this new freedom of poetry. Woman's poetry, that is!

Who are you to try to hold me?
You are only a boy
Twenty-one.
I've always dreamed of a man
Commanding and brave.
You are gentle—so gentle.
You say you are not keeping me?

You are.
I want to love a great man.
No—do not play for me now.
It is too lovely.
You speak to me through music
And bind me.
So lovely—no I want to be free.
Your eyes are so black and deep,
So very faithful.
Do not look at me—I don't want to love
you.
Oh—please don't go.
Come back.

Just as willing to admit her feeling is Carol Ely Harper, in "Desert Night."

As the powerful wind pushes the cliffs
And polishes down the canyons,
Tears from sage and greasewood
Their sharp and bitter odor,
Flings sand in fiendish figures—
I thrill! I am mad! I am here!
Take me—wild—drunk with delight!

Illusion, Leach believes, plays only about one-fourth part in love. Three-fourths of the emotion faces reality. Love is presented in the importance in which it belongs in its peculiar setting. If it doesn't amount to much it is relinquished when its moon wanes or sets.

Especially when a man talks. There is one entry, typical of others, in which the boy calls love by various names, some happy, some not, and then concludes with the entirely unoriginal line: "To hell with love."

THE fear which was voiced by many that youth would carry the shadow of the economic depression into later years seems to be ungrounded.

"The final surprise is that these college poets have already forgotten the depression," Leach explains. "One single poem, from Idaho, is about the search for a job, and that boy sounds so sturdy and gay that I am sure he will find a job without turning a hair as soon as he gets out of college.

"These boys and girls do not write consciously about politics or the New Deal, but a new security and sense of co-operation as well as initiative are implicit in their juvenile philosophy. They do not ask anything out of life that they are not ready to put into it. They welcome instead of dread the future. A senior in Miami University phrases it for the group when he says:

What shore is this, that rising through the spray
Rears its cold peaks in splendor here for me?
Like some faint figure out of dreams I stand,
Viewing this shadowy port my heart has won.
Oh you, who crowd the harbor, look on me—
More than a tattered sail put out to sea.

There has been a definite change in the trend of student thinking, according to the editor who has made a wide survey of campus thought. Leach, who is prominent as a lecturer to college audiences, and was class poet of Princeton in 1903, asserts that he has observed both in his personal contacts and through the submitted poetry, that American youth is forming its own conclusions. It is a little more fearless than it used to be.

"In my day college students asked of a new idea not 'Is it good?' but 'What do others think of it?' " he says. "I believe that youth today is turning the tide to a new era of co-operation and genuine personal courage and initiative.

"There is hope for America in such youth emerging lean and weather-beaten from the depression. These modern boys and girls do not complain, they do not berate society. Instead of cursing fate they are purposeful, ready either to adapt themselves to a friendlier social order or to reshape their environment masterfully to suit their own ideas."

THE contest, which attracted nearly 3000 manuscripts, representing 42 states and 205 colleges, has been accepted as generally indicative of the trend of student thought. Oddly enough, there are no entries from Princeton.

Dr. Robert G. Albion of the Princeton faculty, offers some interesting material in another survey which tends to show that at Princeton, anyway, Shakespeare, Byron and Browning are losing their popularity. Economics, politics, history and the social sciences are supplanting literature. Apparently where this is true, the tendency to write poetry decreases. The desire to put love into rhythm seems to die out, if not disappear entirely.

Dr. Albion's survey consisted of more than 30,000 choices of major fields of study at Harvard, Yale, Princeton, Wellesley, Vassar, and Smith. English stood first everywhere—except Princeton.

Women, even college girls, economically independent as they may claim they are or want to be, still shun the practical subjects. They write more than twice as many poems about love and its gestures as their masculine contemporaries do.

CHICAG
THAT TODD'LING TOWN
Herald Times
NOTICE
HOOVER DEMAND PRO ION REPEA
DR. HUNT'S NEW CORN CURE
REFEREND
IN CRIS
WARN
GOLD MEDALS
AWARDED THE HIGHEST
ST LOUIS MO EXPOSITION 1904
LIEGE BELGIUM 1905
GHENT BELGIUM 1913
BOTTLED AT THE DISTILLERY
LOS ANGELES
DRYS WARN COU
HOME HOOTCH? DEVIL
'Shotgun En ement' Deat
RATS GROW FASTER BY SNIFF!NG ALCOHOL
"Wet" Rodents Develop
Rapidly and Reproduce
Frequently, Doctor Finds.
MENTALITY DRYS' HIGH
Carnegie In xpert on Evolution Gi sults of Five Years eriments.
29 Peak for Killings
(Copyright, 1931, by the Washington Herald.)
INGTON, Jan. 31.—The record
n enforcement killi
1920
1921 38
1922 44
1923 33
1924 42
1925 49
1926 37
1927 56
1928 41
1929 59
1930 65
WE WANT BEER 1933
1360 LIVES
DRY ENFORCEMENT HAS COS
Follow Every Appearance on —Mrs.

Prohibition

The conflict between man and alcohol is as old as civilization, more destructive than any other form of warfare, and as fierce today as at any time since the beginning.

—Senator Henry William Blair, 1888

In the nineteenth century temperance usually meant moderation rather than prohibition. Liquor taxes led to archetypal feuds between moonshiners and "rev'nooers." The big debate at New York temperance rallies was whether or not saloons could open on Sundays. Moderates proposed Sunday beer bars, saying "soft drinks are far more unhealthful than good and light beer"—not such a ridiculous claim when soda pop contained mostly sugar, water, and cocaine.

But as suffragettes and religious reformers gained strength, a real battle over booze shaped up between rural Protestant teetotalers (who dominated the state legislatures) and urban melting-pot Catholics. From 1895 to 1920 the Anti-Saloon League, a classic single-issue pressure group cutting across all political party lines, pushed prohibition through thirty-three state legislatures. In 1917 Congress sent the states a resolution for the Eighteenth Constitutional Amendment prohibiting the importation, manufacture, sale, and transportation (but not possession or use) of intoxicating liquor nationwide. The Volstead Act was ratified in 1919, went into effect a year later, and the Noble Experiment began.

Prohibition made the Roaring Twenties roar. Dry-law enforcement was a superhuman task without enough money to fund the mammoth police force required. As early as 1923, as bootleg kings waxed fat and rum-runners beseiged every port, cries for repeal were heard. Even the most fastidious reformers had to admit that prohibition had created and not prevented organized crime. Star orators debated as gangland turmoil surged across America. Drinking became a matter of national pride, called "striking a blow for liberty."

A pivotal event came during Christmas 1926, when twenty-three New York party-goers died from poison that the feds had put in alcohol to prevent its being made into bathtub gin. A survey of eighteen states revealed thousands of deaths each year from poisoned booze. Popular sentiment shifted to "Temperance, Not Prohibition."

Particularly despised were overzealous agents (dubbed Fanatic Dry Killers by the press) who broke into homes and businesses in search of contraband, shooting first and asking questions later. Many were threatened with lynching by irate flask-toting mobs. Statistics: 1,550 people killed by dry agents in a decade. Hypocrisy: senators and celebrities flaunted the laws in famous speakeasies, while the poor turned to cheaper highs in secret "tea-pads." Newspapers attacked the dwindling dry forces for attempting to dictate U.S. policy.

Dry candidate Herbert Hoover defeated repeal candidate Al Smith in the 1928 elections, but a year later the Wickersham Commission told Hoover that prohibition couldn't be enforced, the court tangle was hopeless. Hearst offered $25,000 for a temperance program, and by 1930 the days of prohibition were numbered. Besides, the Depression argued loudly for the return of liquor tax revenue to public coffers. In 1930 a federal judge ruled the Volstead Act unconstitutional, but it took three more years for the legal machinery to bring it to a halt. Repeal finally came when the Twenty-first Amendment was ratified on December 5, 1933. The streets ran with booze for weeks, and the national insanity was over at last.

Except where drugs were concerned. Even as alcohol prohibition collapsed around their ears, reformers called for tougher drug laws. The analogy between liquor and drug prohibition was rarely recognized, because booze was not considered dope. In our time, with marijuana one of the nation's leading industries, the analogies are obvious: police busting into private lives, organized distribution networks nationwide, innocent people jailed and killed, millions of citizens protesting hypocritical laws. In this regard it is worthy of note that *decriminalization* of marijuana possession and use while its sale and distribution remain illegal, is precisely the legal situation called *prohibition* during the Jazz Age. The lessons of prohibition are doomed to be repeated until we learn them by heart. And the solution may well be temperance, not prohibition.

PROHIBITION'S ARMY IN ITS TABERNACLE. 1891.

Auspicious Opening and Dedication of the New Resort for Cold Water Folks at Port Richmond.

ALCOHOL'S LEGIONS ROUTED

Dr. Deems Addresses a Great Crowd of Faithful Partisans—Elaborate Plans Laid for the New Park.

THREE thousand prohibitionists went down to Staten Island yesterday and celebrated Independence Day by dedicating with music and enthusiasm and rattling assaults upon the rum power the new national prohibition temple that has just been built there.

It was the first time anybody except the builders and a few friends of the project had seen the institution; there was even a close race between time and the carpenters to get it ready to be seen, for the hammers of forty or fifty carpenters were ringing on it only a few hours before Dr. Deems got up to speak in it. But when the three thousand came they were more than pleased with it and all its surroundings.

That was natural enough. There was scarcely any place on Staten Island that didn't look pretty yesterday and none that looked prettier than Prohibition Park. From the hill where its 160 acres lie you can see about half the island, some of its waters and miles of green forests and fields. The air up there was soft and sweet yesterday and there was a wholesome sort of country quiet about it that was very refreshing. Perhaps it won't be so refreshing when they get that summer resort town built as they have mapped it out.

THE PLAN.

The park is about two miles or so back of Port Richmond. The two miles are mostly up into the air, and you cover them now in slow crawling hacks at a modest expenditure of ten cents. It is more expeditious to walk, but not so comfortable. When you get to the top there is on one side of the road a handsome summer hotel, not quite completed, and the temple

SCENE AT THE CELEBRATION.

or auditorium on the other. So far this is about all there is, except a few booths and wayside tents, where the dusty traveller is graciously permitted to quench his thrist in harmless sarsaparilla and feeble lemonade. But after a while there will be more hotels and cottages, and the grounds will be questionably adorned with picnic paraphernalia. Prohibitionists from New York are expected then to go down there in large numbers and take summer residences and make the place a second Ocean Grove, without the ocean and the unsympathetic visitors.

If they are looking for a nice dry spot they needn't look any further. You can't get a drink within a mile and a quarter of the park in any direction. They can possess their souls in comfort with the knowledge of successful prohibition in at least one place on this continent and draw intellectual and partisan pabulum in unlimited quantities from the auditorium and be happy generally.

The auditorium is a big, wooden structure, with an odd but rather pleasing shape, a curved roof, plenty of fresh air, a sawdust floor and seats 4,400 people.

FIGHTING FOR THE REPEAL OF PROHIBITION LAWS.

Democrats in Iowa Have Made This the Issue and Have Some Chance of Success.

STATUTES ARE NOT ENFORCED.

Whiskey Selling Seems Not to Have Decreased Under the Sumptuary Enactments.

[BY TELEGRAPH TO THE HERALD.]

HERALD BUREAU,
CORNER FIFTEENTH AND G STREETS, N. W.,
WASHINGTON, Sept. 21, 1891.

The part that prohibition is expected to play in the Iowa campaign and election this fall has raised the old question, "Does prohibition prohibit?" The sentiment in that State is believed to be decidedly against the law, and it is claimed that the prohibitory statutes are a dead letter.

The records of the office of the Commissioner of Internal Revenue contain plenty of evidence to show that so far as liquor selling goes there are as many persons engaged in the business now as there were before the present law was enacted. The report for this year has not been completed, but Commissioner Mason told me to-day that there would be but little difference between the figures this year and those of 1890, so far as special licenses to liquor dealers in Iowa are concerned.

In 1890 there were issued by the government 3,975 special tax certificates to retail liquor dealers in that State and 35 to wholesale dealers. Twenty-two brewers paid government tax, 225 retail dealers of malt liquors and 65 wholesale dealers in malt liquors. This is a rather startling showing when compared with those of former years.

In 1885 there were issued in Iowa 3,549 special tax certificates to retail liquor dealers, 52 to wholesale dealers, 100 to brewers, 229 to retail dealers in malt liquors and 60 to wholesale dealers in malt liquors. Ten years ago there were 3,965 retail, 58 wholesale, 139 brewers' and 478 malt liquor dealers' special licenses granted.

LOST NO REVENUE IN IOWA.

This comparison shows that the United States, at least, has lost little or no revenue by the passage of State prohibitory laws. Every person who wishes to sell liquors knows that he has to pay a special tax to the government for the privilege. He has great respect for the government and pays the $25 or $100 for license, knowing that if he does not the government detectives will find him out and he will be punished.

The same respect or fear does not exist with regard to State law. The fact that there were ten more government licenses granted last year to retail dealers than there were in 1890 is proof positive that prohibition is not enforced.

The claim of the democrats that the public sentiment is against prohibition is well founded. There are practically no prosecutions. It would be an easy thing for the local or State authorities to secure evidence against illicit liquor selling. In each revenue collector's office there is posted, according to law, an alphabetical list of all persons who have taken out a government license.

This is for the guidance of authorities or other persons who suspect that the local or State laws are being broken.

THE LIST IGNORED.

This list seems to be ignored in Iowa; the State law has become a dead letter, and its repeal by the democrats is likely to soon follow. The United States statutes declare distinctly that the special tax paid to the government is not authority to carry on liquor selling contrary to State regulations.

Commissioner Mason has emphasized this fact by having printed across the face of all certificates issued this year the proviso of the federal law that prevents the paying of a government tax being taken as an excuse for breaking local laws. This, however, does not seem to prevent the sale of liquors in prohibition States.

The condition of affairs in Kansas does not show so persistent and open a disregard for prohibition. Ex-Representative Perkins, of that State, to-day said:—

"Prohibition is enforced over the greater portion of Kansas. In Topeka, the capital, I do not believe there is a place of any kind where a drink of liquor is sold. There are, however, districts like that of Wichita, where the prohibition law is wholly disregarded. There the general sentiment is against the law, and there is no one to enforce it."

THE TROUBLE WITH IOWA.

"Who sees to it that it is enforced in other parts of the State?"

"The local authorities, who are representatives of the people. I think the trouble in Iowa is that the general sentiment is against prohibition, and where that is the case the law is bound to be a failure. The United States government does its part in showing where liquor licenses are granted, but no one sees fit to take advantage of the evidence thus furnished. In Kansas the 1,550 special licenses granted last year were, I think, issued altogether to druggists, who are compelled to keep liquors for medicinal purposes."

Kansas does show some falling off. In 1880 the persons who paid the special government tax numbered 1,821, against 1,550 last year. Maine, another prohibition State, has not as good a record. In 1880 there were issued 757 government licenses, while last year the number was 868. The bulk of evidence goes to show that the republican party has used prohibition as a popular fad, and has been able in the States named to hoodwink the people in times past. It is now seen that prohibitory laws are farcical and that they cannot be successfully enforced.

NEW YORK HERALD, SUNDAY, MAY 29, 1892.—FORTY PAGES.

IS THIS THE CHURCH SALOON SCHEME?

IMPROVE THE SALOON, DON'T ABOLISH IT.

Dr. Rainsford Explains His Views Upon the Subject and Advocates a Most Radical Scheme for Reform.

SUBSTITUTE BEER GARDENS.

Men Will Drink, He Says, and Beer Is Less Harmful Than "Soft Drinks"—He Believes His Idea Is Practical and Would Prove Vastly Beneficial.

EXCISE LAWS MUST BE AMENDED.

THE saloon has come to stay. We cannot abolish it. Nor is it clear that we should seek to abolish it if we could.

Men will drink. It is at least doubtful whether for all men a diet in which alcohol plays no part whatever is the best possible diet.

All good men should beware of manufacturing evil—that is to say, declaring something to be evil which is not in its essence evil, falling into the mistake that some excellent people do when they assert that to drink even moderately is a sin. This being so, there needs a recognition by the moral element in the community of the fact that the saloon keeper is not necessarily a social pariah. The unwritten law which declares him to be in all cases and of necessity the enemy of the community is an unfair law. This much, at least, is true on the one side. Now for the other.

In all civilized countries the need of restraining the drink traffic is recognized. Here I need not enlarge, for the evils of such a traffic unrestrained every intelligent man can readily con-

WHISKEY STILLS IN BIG CITIES.

Revenue Agents Estimate the Loss to Uncle Sam by Moonshine Distilleries at $4,000,000 a Year.

NORTH AND SOUTH AT IT.

The Romantic Stories of Desperadoes Are Still Confined to the Mountains, However.

"BOB" SIMMS AND HIS SON.

DECEMBER 30, 19

KENTUCKY GOING "DRY"; NEW

Bluegrass Counties Vote to Make Their Colonels All Abstainers.

MAY BUY BEER IN PLUGS

Neighbor in Cincinnati Goes to Rescue with a Pocket Device That Needs Only Pail of Water.

NEW WHISKEY NOT LIKE OLD

Complaint Made That Fault Is All with Haste in Production and Methods of Blending.

TILLMAN DENIES RESPONSIBILITY.

In a Message to the Herald He Declares He is Not to Blame for the Rioting and Bloodshed.

Knew It Would Lead to Trouble in the State if It Was Put on the Statute Book.

COUNTIES IN REBELLION.

The Governor Calls the Citizens of Darlington and Florence Insurgents and Orders Them to Dispurse.

HIS ORDERS DISOBEYED.

Governor Tillman Defends Himself in a Message to the Herald.

[BY TELEGRAPH TO THE HERALD.]

TO THE EDITOR OF THE HERALD:—

That I am in any way responsible for the present condition of things in this State is utterly false and absolutely without foundation in fact.

I did not make the Dispensary law. On the contrary I protested against its enactment and predicted, from my knowledge of the people of the State, that it would lead to violence and bloodshed.

I have not tried to enforce its monstrous provisions. On the contrary, I have urged that its constitutionality be determined by the courts, and that the people yield a read[y] obedience to the law once the law has bee[n] determined.

I did not appoint desperate or irrespo[n]sible men to enforce the law and arm the[m] with rifles with instructions to shoot an[y] one who might resist by look or word th[e] infamous work of the whiskey spies.

I did not pardon, before reading the ev[i]dence in the case, the first of the spies w[ho] was convicted, although his offence wa[s] searching premises without a warrant an[d] striking a woman, the mistress of th[e] premises.

I have never declared that I would he[...]

Governor Tillman Issues a Proclamation t[o] Citizens of Two Counties.

[BY TELEGRAPH TO THE HERALD.]

COLUMBIA, S. C., March 31, 1894.—Excitement here over the dispensary riots in Darlington and Florence counties is steadily increasing, and the situation looks graver tha[n] ever.

Business has been practically suspended a[t] the capital. Citizens are massed around th[e] bulletin boards and there is plenty of hot tal[k] by many of the most staid men in the State. Men are here from numerous other towns, an[d] they all express a determination to see tha[t] the men of Darlington do not suffer.

The latest information from the scene of th[e] trouble is to the effect that two of the consta[ble]s are in jail in Darlington. The others ar[e] in the swamp at Muldrow's Mill, with th[e] angry citizens right upon them. They seem to be doomed to die.

Governor Tillman received a despatch sayin[g] that a Sumter man had been arrested in Darlington, and unless the Governor wired tha[t] he was not a spy he would be lynched. Th[...]

a mob to lynch a man for any offence wha[t]ever.

BENJAMIN TILLMAN, Governor.

WHERE THE DISPENSARY WAR RAGES.

Governor Tillman Declared the Counties of Darlington and Florence in Rebellion.

FEBRUARY 8, 1897.

WIDOW FINDS STILL.

Mrs. Pender's Sunday Morn… Discovery in Her William… burg Apartment House…

DISTILLERS AS TE…

Daniel Ashmer Was Maki… in a Large Kettle an… Spirits Boiled…

RAN INTO NEXT…

Suspicion Was A… Investigated… denc…

FOUND A "STILL" IN A BASEMENT.

Roundsman Masterson Saw a Fire There, and the Discovery Followed.

ITS OWNERS HAD DISAPPE…

Nobody Knows Much Abo… and an Air of Mystery S… Their Moveme…

ONLY THERE A…

RUSSIAN STILL USED BY POLES IN NEW YORK.

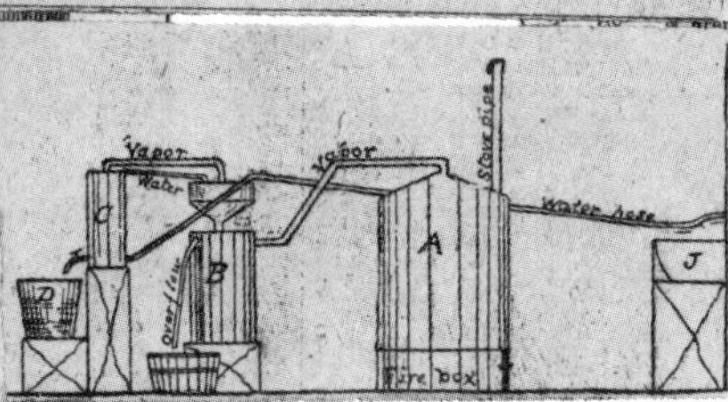

Vapor — Water — Vapor — Stove pipe — Water hose — A — B — C — D — J — Overflow — Fire box

SINCE the increase the whiskey tax … $1 10 a gallon moonshine stills have been springing up like weeds in all parts of the country. They have flourished for years in the mountains of the South, but they are now beginning to sprout up in the big cities of the North. Within the past few weeks a number of illicit stills have been discovered in New York and Philadelphia. The business is being carried on by Poles in attics and cellars. They are making whiskey from black strap molasses, for which they pay in bulk about…

NO MORE CHEAP BEER IN CHICAGO.

Thirty Million Dollar Trust To B… Organized by Englishmen and… Prices To Be Advanced.

PLANS OF THE SYNDIC…

Every Brewery in the City Pu… and Only Enough Capacit… to Supply Demand…

FIVE DOLLARS A BA…

[BY TELEGRAPH TO T…
CHICAGO, Ill., June 1, 1895… a fierce beer war. In fact… but the chances are it so… trust, representing a ca…

GERMANS ASK FOR SUNDAY BEER.

Movement Started to Modify the Existing Excise Law in Several Important Particulars.

FOR OPEN SUNDAY SALOONS.

Amendment Drafted Permitting the Sale of Liquor in a Quiet Way Afternoon and Evening.

ALL NIGHT LICENSES, TOO.

Tax on Restaurants May Be Reduced from $800 to $250 a Year.

German-American citizens of this city have begun a movement for open saloons on Sunday afternoons, and for other modifications of the present Excise law by the next Legislature. Moral grounds, not "personal liberty," are urged as a reason for the amendments.

NOT A VICE, BUT A DISEASE.

Dr. Keeley, the Expert on the Cure of Drunkenness, Is Making a Tour of the World to Study the Ways of the Drunkard.

NOVEMBER 27, 1894.

WITH MOONSHINERS

Thrilling Experiences of Revenue Officers in the Mountain Wilds of Kentucky.

WHO THE MOONSHINERS ARE.

Effective Work of Marion O. Cockrell and His Brave Deputy Marshal, Drake.

HOW A STILL IS RAIDED.

Desperate and Bloody Efforts of the Mountaineers to Rescue Prisoners.

[BY TELEGRAPH TO THE HERALD.]
LEXINGTON, Ky., March 2, 1895.

THE crusade against Kentucky moonshiners has been pushed with remarkable vigor since Major Thomas H. Shelby, who died last Tuesday, was made Collector of Internal Revenue for the Seventh district.

The work of destroying illicit distilleries is left to deputy collectors of the various districts. Major Shelby appointed for this arduous and hazardous duty a…

NOT ALWAYS SUCCESSFUL.

But all the raids made on the Kentucky moonshiners have not been so fortunate as this. Several years ago Deputy Marshals Erastus Wireman and Tom Hollefields went up on Ooton Creek, in Knott county, to capture an illicit still, and only one of them came back alive. They broke up the still and captured three moonshiners. They started toward Hindman, the county seat. Unlike Cockrell and Drake, they never took the precaution to travel at night, and before they had gone far they found themselves surrounded by five desperate looking fellows, armed with Winchesters, and whose names were afterward learned to be Isaac Sloan, Sam Sloan, Sam Adams, Randall Adams and Bill Madden. Before the officers could realize the danger of the situation the desperadoes opened fire. The first volley did not strike either one of them, and drawing their pistols they took a lively hand in the shooting.

Your average mountain man does not like to fight unless he has a great advantage over his adversary, and when Bill Madden fell to the ground, shot through the head by Hollefields, the other four ran to cover. Hollefields then saw Isaac Sloan take deliberate aim at Wireman and fire. The bullet struck the officer in the left shoulder and partially turned him around, and before he could recover another volley was fired from the brush and the brave officer sank to the earth, bleeding from two wounds in the region of the heart. But Hollefields had not been idle, for he fired the last shot in his second revolver directly at the head of Isaac Sloan. The desperadoes picked up Sloan, who had fallen face downward, and carried him off, with a bullet in his head.

While the battle was going on the three captured moonshiners made good their escape on the horses they were riding. At the beginning of the fight Wireman and Hollefields had dismounted, so when the surviving officer was left alone with his dead comrade there seemed to be no way for him to get back to civilization. Putting the body of Wireman on a large rock, under a tree, Hollefields left it and went in search of the horses. He only succeeded in finding one of them, and he led it back and strapped his dead comrade on the saddle. He…

…and although I have destroyed seventeen illicit distilleries, and thousands of gallons of mash, I have never yet been able to find a still without a pilot. Oh, yes, I have been told by many government agents that they found stills, but from my knowledge of the business I think they simply found somebody who found the stills for them.

"What do I mean? Why, every moonshiner who runs a distillery necessarily has enemies. Your average mountain man is an improvident fellow. He raises a little patch of corn, fattens a few hogs to make his bacon and to feed, probably, one horse. The balance of his corn he carries to some neighboring mill and has it ground into meal, the miller tolling it as deep as his conscience will allow. Then he takes his meal to the nearest still—they don't call them distilleries—and trades it for whiskey, the moonshiner giving him a quart of the liquor for every bushel of meal. Now, when your mountain man runs out of corn to grind into meal to swap for whiskey, his appetite for the stuff does not…

…that every moonshiner was a desperado of the most pronounced type.

"Nothing could be more erroneous," continued Colonel Cockrell, "than such an idea. Why, sir, I have talked with moonshiners by the score, and they cannot understand how the government can rightfully prevent them from grinding their corn into meal and making that meal into whiskey, any more than it can prevent them from making it into hoecakes. You must remember that Eastern Kentucky is one hundred years behind the age in which we live, except in the matter of firearms. The people who inhabit this district are descendants of the old pioneers and adventurers who came out to Kentucky during the latter part of the last century. The same cabins they occupied then are satisfactory residences for them now, and they are virtually the same primitive people. They have intermarried, until, according to the well known laws of breeding in our domestic animals, they have accentuated all the badness possessed by their daring ancestors, and the lack of restraint has caused them to feel that they are a law unto themselves. The spirit of revenge burns as strongly in their breasts as it does in the hearts of the Corsicans. They have never read that passage in the Bible where it says, 'If thy brother smite thee on one cheek, turn the other.' They believe in the doctrine of an eye for an eye and a tooth for a tooth. If any one does them an injury it must be wiped out in blood. With such a people as this to deal with, you can readily understand how difficult it is for the agents of the government to break up illicit distilling.

"This is only one of the difficulties that lie in our way. The conformation of the country is such that it is often impossible to travel, even on horseback. The distilleries are located in the most out of the way places that can be found.

…K'S DRINK BILL $1,000,000 A DAY

Quality of Liquor Sold in Metropolis Is Called the Worst Ever Put Out.

DISPUTE ON FOOD VALUE

King Edward's Physician Condemns Alcohol as Poison and Dr. Wiley Warmly Defends Its Use.

MUCH CHAMPAGNE IMPORTED

Only Best Quality Wanted in America, Although Other Countries Lead in Quantity Consumed.

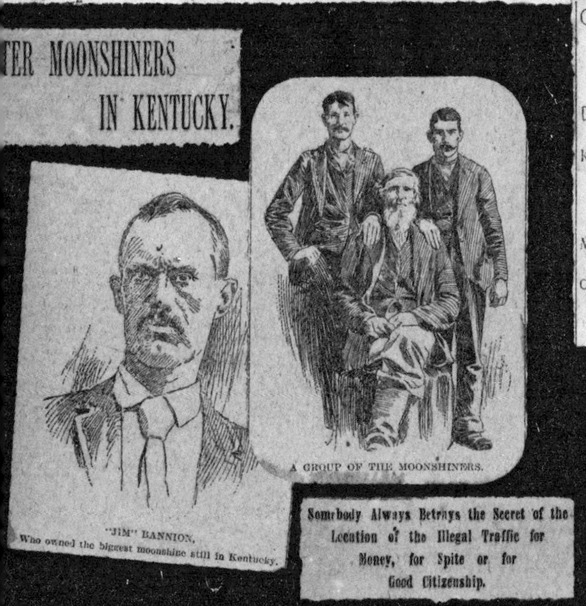

…TER MOONSHINERS IN KENTUCKY.

"JIM" BANNION, Who owned the biggest moonshine still in Kentucky.

A GROUP OF THE MOONSHINERS.

Somebody Always Betrays the Secret of the Location of the Illegal Traffic for Money, for Spite or for Good Citizenship.

The Hazardous but Fascinating Occupation of Destroying Illicit Distilleries in the Mountains.

MARSHALS PERIL THEIR LIVES.

Lawbreakers Ready to Shoot from Ambush, but Generally Cowards in Open Fight.

HOW THE STILLS ARE FOUND

[BY TELEGRAPH TO THE HERALD.]

LOUISVILLE, March 30, 1891.—The day of the Kentucky moonshiner is long past its noon. So says Revenue Agent W. J. Wilmore, whose province it is to look after all violators of revenue laws in this State and Tennessee.

I was talking with him in his dingy office in the Custom House to-day about this matter, and he gave me many interesting particulars of the adventurous work he and his deputies are called upon to do. Not that Mr. Wilmore is much given to raiding "shiners." This work is usually done by deputies in his office or in the office of the revenue collectors, but once in a while he is called to lead a dangerous expedition. No child's play this. The men who go into the home of the moonshiner with the intention of taking him captive and destroying his property take their lives in their hands. Deaths in the line of this hazardous duty are rare, but fights are frequent, and narrow escapes from wounds are many. Sometimes, too, the moonshiner hunts his hunters, and then blood is nearly always spilled.

A RAIDER'S EXPERIENCE.

F. H. Hawkins is Agent Wilmore's chief raiding deputy for Kentucky. He and A. J. Caddell spend all their time in conducting raids in the moonshine country. Neither one has ever been wounded, but they have had horses shot down under them, have been ambushed often, fired upon hundreds of times from a safe distance and have had many hand-to-hand conflicts with desperate revenue outlaws. Mr. Hawkins has been a raider for only a little over a year. In that time he has destroyed o… hundred stills and captured more "shiners"…

…climb along the edges of precipices hundreds of feet high. Later they had to ford the Cumberland River that frosty night.

Two deputies—Hollis and Daniels—ventured across and came near being drowned, having to swim their horses. Captain Hawkins and the others stayed on the other side until the river fell. Hollis and Daniels got back home several days ahead, but Daniels had an attack of pneumonia which came near resulting fatally.

SMALL PROFITS IN MOONSHINING.

In spite of the dangers of his trade the moonshiner seldom makes more than a bare living. In the first place, he is usually poverty stricken. It takes but little to start him in business. A capital of $100 to $150 is all that is necessary. Still this generally taxes his slender resources to the utmost. He must first go or send to some city and get his still and worm. These have to be made by coppersmiths, and such mechanics are not found in villages. The manufacture of these is required to be registered by law, but the moonshiner is not the only violator of the regulations of the Internal…

Revenue Department. This is shown by the fact that during the past six or seven years over seven thousand stills have been destroyed by revenue raiders, and yet during that time the twenty dollar tax assessed on the manufacturer for each still made has been paid on only 2,000. There are two reasons for this. One is the temptation to evade the tax of $20. The other is that when the tax is paid the still is registered, and can thus be easily traced by the government. The moonshiner would never buy a registered still for this last reason. He has the still and worm secretly made and shipped to his mountain home in the guise of a music box, organ… case of dry goods. An ox team, possibly hi…

A HARD AND HAZARDOUS OCCUPATION.

"Yes, the life is a dangerous one, but it has its fascinations. It is not dangerous because you have fair, stand up fights, but because of the treachery one has to encounter. Not one 'shiner in fifty will face you and fight, but they will all bushwhack. It's a common thing to be shot at as we are riding along on the roads or bridle paths. It's a wonder more officers do not get killed. Then the life is full of hardships. People are afraid to help out raiders or even give them anything to eat. The outlaws may burn their houses or kill their stock if they do. Many and many a time I have gone for twenty-four hours without anything to eat. As for sleeping out in the open air, we are often glad to get the chance. Horses are hard to get when going on a raid and it is harder to get provender for them. Corn in the mountains is always scarce and high, and mighty little hay and fodder are to be found. Sometimes you ride for many hours in a country where the only inhabitants are too poor to keep horses or mules. How in the world they manage to live I can't say."

HUNTING MOONSHINERS IN THE MOUNTAINS.

A typical moonshine raid was made by Deputy Hawkins a short time ago through Bell, Harlan and Letcher counties. The party consisted of Captain Hawkins, Deputy Agent Caddell, two deputy collectors, one deputy marshal and four "posse men." The expedition started from Pineville, ostensibly…

…little like genuine Kentucky hand made "sour mash" bourbon, carefully stilled and mellowed by age until not a trace of fusel oil remains, with a beady sparkle that rests upon the thick amber surface, as it is possible to imagine. Yet the mountaineer prefers his white whiskey to the choicest product of the finest distillery in the "Corncracker" State. Such is taste after all—merely a matter of usage and cultivation.

MARKETING THE MOUNTAIN DEW.

The moonshiner never ventures to keep more than a small stock of spirits on hand. The risk is too great. At any time a neighbor may inform upon him or an enemy revenge an insult by bringing the raiders to capture and destroy. When a few gallons have been run off the raw spirit, rank with fusel oil, is peddled out and drunk up before a fresh supply is distilled. Disposing of the product is one of the riskiest parts of the business. Sometimes this work is intrusted to the women and girls of the moonshiner's family. A little cabin is built near a town and the well known "blind tiger" is operated. More frequently the … peddles the stuff around in villages after … Picnics, revival meetings, political speakings and all sorts of gatherings are bonanzas for the trade. The liquor seller conceals himself in bushes or … spot and starts out runners, who…

MADE IN USA

THE BULLETIN: SAN FRANCISCO, SUNDAY MORNING, SEPTEMBER 27, 1903. THIRD SECTI

...THE... CRAVING FOR DRINK

Is the result of alcoholic poisoning from over-indulgence in alcoholic liquors. The poisoning is caused by the action of the alcohol upon the tissue cells, which creates in them a demand for alcohol. The craving is there whether it is satisfied or not and will constantly or periodically assert itself until the poisoned system is restored to its normal condition.

LIQUOR

Say Forbidding Sale of Will Lead to Mor Depravity.

TWO STATES EXA

Notwithstanding Temperanc Business of Distillers and ers Has Increased.

HOMEMADE FIREWATE

SAN FRANCISCO CHRONICLE, FRIDAY, MAY 24, 1907.

DRY THROATS SUFFER FROM BEER FAMINE

Mourn for Precious Gurgle of Amber-Colored Beverage.

GEE, that guy must be a Nevada millionaire; he's opening a bottle of beer"—heard on Fillmore street in 1908.

In less that a week there will be no more beer in San Francisco. The wise owners of cafes have seized the few remaining kegs and have stored them way down deep in their cellars. Small portions are doled out to favored partons but all the while the proprietor watches with a mournful countenance, the precious fluid gurgle down the dust-lined throats.

Telegrams for relief have been sent broadcast to every town and hamlet that has a brewery from Milwaukee to

RESOURCES OF STATE BANKS

HINZE WITNESS FOR THE UNION

By James B. Morrow.

WASHINGTON.

THE greatest attack ever made on property, except, perhaps, the proclamation which gave freedom to several million slaves, was begun in Columbus, O. during the second week of the present month. While the attack was publicly announced then, all of its plans had been worked out a long time in advance.

Organized temperance leaders, shrewd, fighting men, many of whom are lawyers, coming together from all parts of the Nation, declared their purpose to close every distillery, brewery and saloon in the United States. This can be done, they thought, during the next decade; some even believed that only five years will be required to make this, using their own phrase, "a saloon-

Cities Drink More Than Ever.

"The only answer to make to the figures of the Government is that liquor drinking is growing at the large centers of population and diminishing in small cities, villages and the rural sections. I would also call your attention to the undeniable fact that there is more poverty in the large centers of population than anywhere else."

"And some of the dry places," I said, "are voting back the saloon."

"Now and then, yes. But you must not overlook the thousands of 'dry' places which refuse again to be 'wet.' Good people work at their own business and trades. They drive the saloons out and then fail to remember that eternal vigilance is the price of keeping them out. They get busy about their own affairs and the beer and whisky ele-

He Is Not a Muckraker.

"Our methods in politics are op do not wear rubber heels. We carry bull's-eye lanterns. We steal up to a man and stab him back. We fight face to face in t light, but we fight to win.

"Another thing: The legislative of the country are composed who want to do right. I hav working at State capitals and in ington for more than 20 years. no muckraker, because there if any muck to rake. Bad men office. Such men are everywher

"But on the whole, our law are inherently sound at times to political let alone, they would a moral wrong. Pra favorable sentiment the liquor business persons who own di and saloons.

1913.

WAR AGAINST THE DISTILLERS

About Temperance in This Country — Half a Million Dollars Being Collected to Stamp Out a Great Evil.

WINE GROWERS TO FIGHT PROHIBITION MOVEMENT

GROUP OF MEMBERS OF THE GRAPE GROWERS' ASSOCIATION OF CALIFORNIA AT ITS FIRST MEETING YESTERDAY AFTERNOON.

Will Try to Show Benefits of Wine Drinking by Sending Lecturers Out.

1908.

FOR the purpose of defending the wine industry of California against the prevalent enthusiasm for extreme prohibition, over 100 grapegrowers from different parts of the State met yesterday afternoon at the California building, in Union square, and organized the Grape-Growers' Association of California.

Andrea Sbarboro was made president of the association, and a tax of 25 cents an acre was levied to meet the expenses of a campaign of education to offset the wave of prohibition sentiment which is sweeping over the

the daily ration in the Navy. B. F. Lamborn th there was a lamentable la cafes in California where take their wives and babies and procure a glass of wine—"saloons where any woman could go," he described them. J. F. de Louziers advised those present to "take the war into the

EVILS O

...N FIGHT PROHIBITION WITH "PERSONAL LIBERTY" SLOGAN

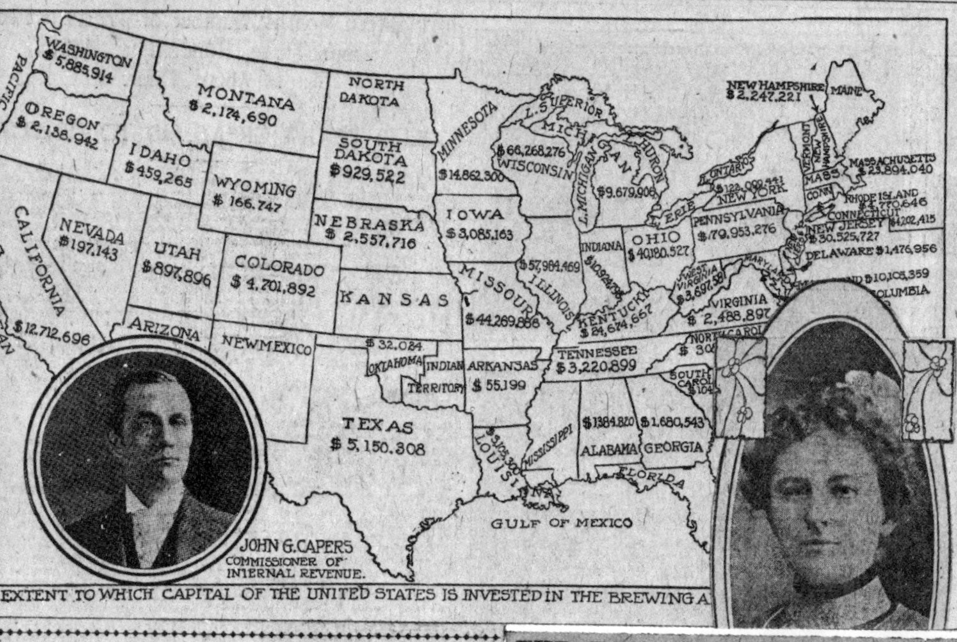

JOHN G. CAPERS
COMMISSIONER OF INTERNAL REVENUE.

EXTENT TO WHICH CAPITAL OF THE UNITED STATES IS INVESTED IN THE BREWING A...

...hose in the Trade Cite the Large Amounts Tha... Are Paid to the Government and the Great Capital Invested.

THERE IS SHOWN AN INCREASE OVER 190...

Why the Negro Scares Him.

He Admits Fraud and Force.

A List of His Enemies.

Says He Agrees With Lincoln.

Money Engaged in Nation's Liquor Trade.

Amount invested in brewing and distilling business in the United States	$612,571,558.00
Internal revenue receipts from taxes paid on liquor business last fiscal year	207,124,099.00
Increase in revenue receipts over previous year	16,444,651.00
Other revenue from liquor business paid to United States, city and State governments, yearly	60,875,465.00
	Barrels.
Last yearly production of malt liquors in United States,	54,651,637

THE BOSTON SUNDAY GLOBE—NOVEMBER 30, 1913.

WILL PULVERIZE THE RUM POWER

Senator James K. Vardaman Says He Is Going to Make It Unlawful to Sell or Give Away Liquor in District of Columbia—Negroes and Intemperance the Two Great Evils of Country.

STORY OF THE NEW SENATOR'S LIFE IS MOST EXCITING

...ng argument against prohibition ...is that if a man cannot purchase ...ts he will, after exhausting every ...source, make them himself. As ...this one has but to discuss the ...with the officers charged with the ...ent of the Internal Revenue laws. ...ficials are familiar with hundreds ...ds by which the small land holder ...rohibition States of the South may ...distil a liquid which will appease ...t for liquor, although in so doing ...very likely take his reason. And ...is one of the strongest arguments ...who oppose prohibition.

...ased on the theory that to prevent ...of liquor absolutely is an impossi... ...t is then held that since it is im... to prevent the use of intoxicants ...better to permit its legalized use ...tate and city restrictions than to ...to prevent it, and as a result send ...who will have it anyway into the ...get it. There he will drink any... ...om wood alcohol to hard cider in ...to satisfy his craving.

...IDER FALLACY.

...asion of the law by the use of the ...ill finds its semi-counterpart in ...gland in the hard cider, for which ...on is famous. Any man with an ...chard and a nearby cider mill, or ...a hand press of his own, may ...himself with an intoxicant, the ...ffect of which should not be under... ...d. Cider, which is estimated to ...from six to ten per cent of alcohol, ...ut of the Maine prohibitory law, ...er, with about three and one-half ...of alcohol, is placed among the ...hich the law frowns upon.

...ct that politics and prohibition are ...n mixed with each other is an ob... ...which seems to hold against this ...w. It is not likely that the rural ...on of Maine would have voted so ...for a law which would have pre... ...farmer from putting down a bar... ...vo of apple juice in the fall. This ...on to the farmer is generally ...ut for by those who frame pro... ...laws. The laws of the olden time ...this exemption to beer. There are ...stances where keepers of hotels ...ng houses were required to brew ...the entertainment of their guests, ...dden under severe penalties to sell ...spirits.

...ractice of prohibiting the sale of ...o the Indians in early days rarely ...wine and never malt liquors, and ...ncient Massachusetts statute it is ...n as being uncharitable to deprive ...savage creatures of any comfort ...od allowed." Many Colonial laws ...that it was the object in drawing ...encourage brewing and thereby ...inebriety. The first excise system ...ealed in 1802 and reintroduced dur... ...second war with Great Britain to ...repealed in 1817. With the aboli... ...the federal excise system at this ...l distillation sprang up with great ...Following it came that which is ...s the "era of free rum," resulting ...

of this condition, it is believed, will be the result of the continued progress of the temperance movement now sweeping over the country. During the first half of the century this intemperance prevailed to an unprecedented extent and public sentiment became aroused. The result was a wave of reform which crystallized in three movements, for absolute prohibition, working a reform by the substitution of milder drinks and a change in the habits of the people, and restrictive regulation of the traffic in liquors. Up to 1855 prohibitory laws had been passed by seventeen States. Most of these, however, remained on the statute books but a limited time. Soon the regulation of the traffic through low license laws became more vigorous and restrictive.

The introduction of our internal revenue system was, however, necessary to make them effective for the prevention of intemperance. This came during the first year of the civil war. The effect of the law was to check rural distillation, and it is claimed that in this law was found the eradication of one of the principal causes of drunkenness. During this period, which was from the introduction of the law to 1887, our consumption of spirits per capita decreased from 2.13 to 1.14 gallons and our position as an intemperate nation was reversed from the top to the bottom of the list. The introduction of high license came in 1880, when the Slocum law was passed by the State of Nebraska. It fixed a fee of $500 for towns of under 10,000 people and $1,000 where the population exceeded that number. It was at this time asserted that to diminish the number of saloons by a high license was to diminish the drinking. This is controverted by the opponents of prohibition, who hold that a high license fee tends to drive out only the saloon keeper who deals in beer almost exclusively, and that the effect of the system must be the reverse from a temperance point of view.

The New York law introducing high license applied to all saloons in the same city without regard to the kind or quantity of drinks sold became effective in 1897 and reduced the number of saloons from 33,437 to 26,847. In 1904 the New York license fee was again increased, from $800 to $1,200, and the resulting decrease was 1,315 during the first year thereafter. In each instance fully 85 per cent of the decrease was among the smaller beer saloons which had been the reputable and orderly resorts of workingmen in the tenement districts. The production of beer during the first year of the high license system decreased more than five hundred thousand barrels. Not for five years did the production make this up.

It is apparent that little thought has been given to the results which would follow the adoption of the views of prohibitionists in all the States of the Union. There is, however, something in this phase of the temperance question for business men and taxpayers to consider, something which the women and children who make up a good part of the temperance "army" are probably unable to appreciate, but which will ...

PERSONAL LIBERTY PHASE.

The question of personal liberty is one of the very strong arguments against the form of prohibitory law in use in several States. This law permits the man of means to provide himself with an unlimited assortment of liquors, but takes from the workingman the same privilege because his circumstances are not so good. Under the licensed saloon system five cents will purchase a glass of beer for the poor man and the more prosperous employer may, if he likes, pay $5 for his bottle of champagne. Under prohibition the workingman is deprived of his beer, but champagne is always at the disposal of those who can pay its price. In this way the poor man has his drink taken away from him, while the wealthy man can by a little forethought provide himself through his greater capital with as many liquors as he cares to pay for by the use of the express facilities and his own cellar. No man who cares for a drink need go without it in any prohibition State in the Union if he but provides for his thirst in advance and has the money to pay for what he orders.

Experience also shows that a prohibitory law does not necessarily control the sale of liquor. In Vermont, where a local option law has taken the place of prohibition of fifty years' standing, citizens became disgusted with the extent of the liquor traffic under prohibition and finally threw it overboard. It was found that those who desired liquor could readily purchase it and have it shipped to them from across the border, or, easier still, obtain it as desired in a club or cafe. Open bars flourished within a half block of the police office, and the police judge of the city of Burlington might from his office window mark the unsteady steps of those who wandered out from three active bars. Clubs served liquors with freedom. There were occasional raids at which liquor would be seized and later ordered destroyed, but in some instances a bar raided in the morning would be as flourishing as ever by afternoon, and fines were paid by bartenders with money furnished under an agreement with the proprietor of the saloon. Under the provision of the law providing for disclosure on the part of a man arrested and convicted of intoxication perjury flourished.

Under a law licensing the saloon liquor is served only to competent persons, and its sale to a minor or a drunkard forbidden. Liquor is not sold to minors, drunkards or incompetent persons. The keeper is required to close his place of business at a specified hour of the night and is limited as to Sunday sales. Under prohibition liquor is sold just the same, and of the poorest quality, by stealth, indiscriminately.

It is also pointed out that in the State of Maine, long the "horrible example" of the workings of prohibition, the arrests for drunkenness and drunken disturbances during 1907 have increased at the rate of 122 per month over 1906. It is declared that ...

[SPECIAL DESPATCH TO THE HERALD.]

WILMINGTON, Del., Saturday.

"WET" or "Dry?" This laconic greeting has become the common form of salutation throughout Delaware. Nothing has ever before stirred the residents of Delaware as the local option campaign now being waged has aroused them. Nothing else is heard. It is the sole topic of conversation in saloon, church, home and public meeting places. The election is to be held on November 5, and then will be decided whether local option is to prevail in all three counties and in Wilmington.

An interesting feature of the campaign is the prominent part the women and children of the city and State are taking in the fight. In fact, the women are doing the biggest part of the work, and if local option is declared, it will be due to their efforts more than to those of the men. The women are doing most of the campaigning. They are acting as detectives to spot illegal registration, and will do the same at the polls on election day to prevent illegal voting. They are organizing the children of the city, and they are making many of the speeches in favor of prohibition.

Women have gone to the registration places and as each voter approached the window they have buttonholed him, questioned him as to his residence, to learn if he is registering legally.

ACTED AS BOOMERANG.

The fact that liquor men in speeches have attacked some of the women campaigners has lost the liquor cause more votes than any mass meeting they can hold will bring them, and it has turned much sentiment toward the cause of no license.

Women at these registration places have been received sometimes with kindness and courtesy, sometimes with coldness and inattention, and on one or two occasions with decided incivility. No disorder has been attempted on the registration days, and it is not thought there will be any on election day.

November 5 will be a busy day for the women. They will be at the polls to canvass voters. They have taught the children in the schools several anti-license campaign songs and they have decorated them with the buttons gotten out by the committee, on which is the picture of a child and the words, "Vote No for My Sake." The women petitioned the Board of Education to give the children in the schools a holiday on election day.

This was refused by the School Commissioners. They then asked for permission to teach the children the campaign songs. This, too, was refused. However, the children have learned the songs and they will be at the polls on election day. They will sing their no license songs and hope to ... many men to the cause of prohibition ...

By James B. Morrow.

WASHINGTON.

A POLICY latent with sensation and war has been brought to Washington by James Kimble Vardaman, the new Senator from Mississippi. It is being impatiently held back until the Underwood tariff bill becomes a law.

"I am the best friend the negroes have in the United States, opinions to the contrary notwithstanding, but I deliberately say they are not competent for self-government, let alone for participating in the government of whites.

"Haiti is proof of my statement; so is Africa, where the natives are ruled by the same club, live in the same huts, and worship the same voodoo as was the case with their ancestors 10 centuries ago. I want the negro, however, to enjoy life, liberty and the fruits of his toil, and to be protected against mobs which seek to do him harm.

How He Stopped a Mob.

"I have prevented more lynchings ...

"Jim Crow" cars, if another item of the policy goes into the statute books, are to be attached to all passenger trains on every interstate railroad, North and South—on the Pennsylvania, on the New York Central, and on the lines to the Pacific Coast.

Thirdly, the negro, no matter whether he lives in Boston or Tallahassee, is to be "eliminated" from politics. He is not to vote anywhere or for any purpose; he is not to hold office, either as a justice of the peace, a constable, a letter carrier, or a policeman; he is not to sit on juries; he is not to enter uninvited public places frequented by whites. Marriages between the races is to be declared a penitentiary offense.

Such is the policy in the rough. The details of segregation are yet to be worked out. It can be said, however, that the white man who eats with a negro will become a social outcast. The Caucasian and the African are to stand ...

"So much for Washington. The country as a whole, I believe, is ready to repeal the fifteenth and to modify the fourteenth amendments to the Constitution of the United States. If the pusillanimous politicians are not ready, the people sooner or later will insist that they be given an opportunity to vote on the proposition."

"But," I asked, "will not the disfranchisement of the negroes by the repeal ...

"Once the negro were disposed of as citizen, the solid South would disintegrate. We should have two parties, at least, in place of one. As it is, all the white men stand together. We canno... openly discuss the great questions of the age.

"We do not agree on the tariff, but we put away our opinions on that issue and on other issues, and all of us vote the same ticket at the polls. Such un... natural cohesiveness is neither good for us nor for the rest of the country.

"But, why do we so tenaciously stick together, some one in Massachusetts may ask. I answer that there are 55,000 more negro men in Mississippi than there are white men; that the negro population in my State is 1,100,000, and that the white population is but 770,000 ...

than has the Governor of any State in this country. I understand negro character. My playmates were colored boys. Negro youths worked with me at home in the fields.

"Dinner was sent out to us in baskets. I ate mine under one tree; they ate theirs under another tree close by. I brought a negro to Washington the other day and got him a place in the Government. Lynchings have been stopped by me in person. I have gone on horseback, in buggies, and on trains for that purpose.

... meeting in Jackson. An assault had been committed upon a young seamstress who was on her way home through the principal residence street of the city. We searched every negro house in Jackson that night, making several arrests, but doing no violence to anybody.

"People in the North, when looking for a negro criminal, usually make war on the whole race. They kill and burn indiscriminately, as was done in Springfield, O; Springfield, Ill, and Coatesville, Penn. When we in the South are hunting for a mad dog, let me say figuratively, we don't shoot all the good and healthy dogs in the community.

"What is the tariff to us in the face of such a black flood? What do we care about gold, silver, or paper money, if our cities, our counties, and even our Commonwealth are in danger of negro government?

"Would Massachusetts like to see a negro Governor in the State House at Boston? Would the people of New York accept the laws of a negro legislature in Albany? Would the inhabitants of Ohio feel well pleased were negroes t... ...court? ...farmers ...ania b... ...ssessed ... and their publi...

...COHOLISM IN ENGLAND TO BE CHECKED BY LAW

...OMEN AND CHILDREN LEAD DELAWARE ANTI-LIQUOR FIGHT

U. S. Weather Forecast
CHICAGO AND VICINITY—Generally fair Saturday and Sunday; not much change in temperature; gentle westerly winds.

CHICAGO HERALD AND EXAMINER
A CHICAGO NEWSPAPER — FOR CHICAGO PEOPLE

SATURDAY, SEPTEMBER 7, 1918.

PRICE TWO CENTS. In Chicago and Suburbs. Elsewhere 3c.

35TH YEAR—NO. 104. Registered U. S. Patent Office.

U. S. PROHIBITS B

ALL BREWING TO END DEC. 1 BY ORDER OF PRESIDENT

Heads of Fuel, Railroad and Food Administrations Urge Drastic Step.

SENATE VOTES THE DRY BILL

Attempt to Delay Country-Wide Prohibition Till 1920 Fails in the Upper House.

WASHINGTON, Sept. 6.—Manufacture of beer in the United States will be prohibited after Dec. 1 next as a war measure.

This announcement was made tonight by the food administration, which said the decision had been reached at conferences between President Wilson and representatives of the fuel, food and railroad administrations and the war industries board.

LABOR SHORTAGE FACTOR.

Factors which influenced the decision to prohibit the manufacture of beer after Dec. 1, the food administration announcement said, were "the further necessity of war industries for the whole fuel productive capacity of the country, the considerable drought which has materially affected the supply of feeding stuff for next year, the strain upon transportation to handle necessary industries and the shortage of labor caused by enlargement of the army program."

Warning also was issued to manufacturers of all beverages and mineral waters that for the same reasons there will be "further great curtailment in fuel for the manufacture of glass containers, of tin plate for caps, of transportation and of food products in such beverages."

END COMES 6 MONTHS' EARLIER.

Under national prohibition legislation, passed by the Senate to-day and sent to the House, which enacted similar legislation last May, manufacture of beer and wine would be prohibited after next May 1. To-day's order will move up five months the time for discontinuance of the manufacture of beer, although the breweries may be allowed to resume operations between that date and the effective operation of the "dry" legislation, if finally enacted, since to-day's order was "until further orders."

SENATE PASSES $12,000,000 BILL.

The $12,000,000 emergency agricultural bill, with its rider for national prohibition until the American armies are demobilized after the war, was passed by the Senate without a roll call.

Before final passage of the measure, the Senate voted, 45 to 6, to retain the prohibition rider. A final effort to postpone the effective date of the "dry" legislation to Dec. 30, 1919, was defeated.

BEER SUPPLY ON HAND WILL LAST BUT 2 MONTHS

Wis., Sept. 6.—

TWO WILSONS IN BOMB NET

...years, persistently, this...

F

At last the... and the natio... The Supre... cided that wh... HAVE prohi... panies and ou... State's proh... prohibition...

...y shipping whiskey in...

The C... cided to... ton prob... ...ed States has even decided... ...in at home. Washing... ..."dry" city.

What... for twent... ...pers have been saying... WHISKEY IS A POISON, SH... ...TED BY GOVERNMENT A... BY GOVERNMENT... AS A POI... ...ALE REGULATED AS... ARE THE... ...ON, AND THE TRAFFIC STOP...

Fortuna... ...come when results are in sight, and i... ...o hope that this country, which symp... ...hed China's fight against the curse of... ...be able to tell China that we have suc... ...g OUR curse of whiskey.

Rememb... ...whiskey evil the chief sinner is THE... ...ATES GOVERNMENT, THAT SHA... ...E WHISKEY PROFITS AND HAS... THOUSANDS OF MILLIONS OF S... ...TS.

It is not... ...ard in the gutter of the United State... ...d for his whiskey dri... ...stupefied with... ...vice. ...reach at the... THEY... ...OLUTE...

...alone, for...

If ... the sake of yo... ...a slight...

Wh... liking... liking? lock hi... late. ...ging that... want to... expostu... ...all the...

But... drugs, i... Leav... Be al... And... whiskey... manufac... ...yhow." ...l make... ...hiskey...

A Heavy Hand and a Heavy Curse Lie Upon Thousands of Unhappy Human Beings.

By the Weight of the Whiskey Bottle, Not Only Whiskey Drinkers but Their Families, the Mothers and Children, Are Pounded, Hammered and Beaten Down Into Misery.

Blame Not the Whiskey Drinker, but Rather the Government That Sells the License to Deal in Poison and Takes ... of Millions of Revenue from

WILSON

REFUSES TO REMOVE JULY FIRST BAN

Will Lift the Lid When Demobilization Is Complete.

By Associated Press.

WASHINGTON, June 28.—President Wilson has decided he cannot legally lift the war-time prohibition ban before the country goes dry at midnight Monday, but he expects to do so as soon thereafter as his power has been made clear by the completion of demobilization.

In a cablegram made public tonight at the White House, the President said he was convinced after consultation with his legal advisers that he had no authority to act at this time.

Promises to Act Later.

"When demobilization is terminated," he continued, "my power to act without congressional action will be exercised." (Secretary of War Baker on June 14 stated that in his opinion demobilization would not be completed before the latter part of September.)

The message expressed no opinion as to the authority of the President, when he raises the ban, to make his action applicable only to beer and wine.

Secretary Tumulty gave out the following statement:

"The secretary to the President, at the White House tonight, made public the following cable from the President with reference to war time prohibition:

"'I am convinced that the Attorney General is right in advising me that I have no legal power at this time in the matter of the ban on liquor.

POWER TO ACT RESTRICTED.

"'Under the act of November, 1918, my power to take action is restricted. The act provides that after June 30, 1919, "until the conclusion of the present war and thereafter until the termination of demobilization, the date of which shall be determined and proclaimed by the President, it shall be unlawful, etc."

"'This law does not specify that the ban shall be lifted with the signing of peace, but with the ter-

GERI

Police to Enforce Dry Law

Chicago took President Wilson's statement that he would not lift the war-time liquor ban calmly last night.

There were greater crowds than usual at the bars and cafes, but there was no excitement, no debauch. Prohibition, though the principal topic of conversation, brought no orgy.

Most of the saloons closed promptly at midnight, as on many past Saturday nights.

"Why," saloonkeepers asked, "should we make trouble and get in bad with the police just for a few dollars? Those who disobey the law tonight may have more trouble than they can stand when the search and seizure law goes into effect."

"BONE DRY" AFTER TUESDAY.

E. J. Davis, manager of the Chicago chapter of the Anti-Saloon League said the league would make every effort to produce a bonedry Chicago from Tuesday on.

"The law," he said, "is very definite. Why wait a day or a week? We shall do everything in our power to stop the sale of liquor immediately. We think President Wilson has acted very wisely.

"As I understand it, the enforcement is up to the local authorities. The federal agents will not come in unless called by the police.

WILL MAKE A SURVEY.

"We shall help in any way possible. We shall not investigate on any extensive scale at first, but we shall make a general survey and report to the police.

"We want every saloon and liquor selling agency to be put out of business.

"The search and seizure act is in effect Tuesday. On that basis, if we find a saloon open, we shall report it and shall expect a search and seizure by the police."

POLICE TO AID ENFORCEMENT.

In the absence of Chief of Police Garrity, First Deputy Alcock said last night police would co-operate with the internal revenue department of the federal government to enforce the law. This was determined at a conference between Chief Garrity and Julius F. Smietanka, internal revenue collector, several days ago.

The plan is to arrest every man selling liquor, in saloon or cafe, as owner of a blind pig, and turn him

CHICAGO HERALD AND EXAMINER
A CHICAGO NEWSPAPER — FOR CHICAGO PEOPLE
FINAL
THURSDAY, JANUARY 16, 1919.
PRICE TWO CENTS
In Chicago and Suburbs. Elsewhere 3c.

The Soldier's Friend Helps Soldiers and Sailors Get Positions.

See Page 16.

UR FLAG

U. S. DRY TODAY

DOOMS LIQUOR

SH DRIVE
7 MILES

SUNDAY, JUNE 29, 1919.

ANS SIGN; DEFIANT

ONLY 1 STATE MORE NEEDED; 35 IN LINE

Missouri Speeds to Be 36th; 5 O. K. Amendment Yesterday

Only the vote of one state is needed to read nationwide prohibition into the constitution of the United States. That vote is expected before another day has passed.

Up to midnight the legislatures of thirty-five states—one less than the necessary three-fourths—had ratified the constitutional amendment. A race for the distinction of registering the final vote lies today between Nebraska, Missouri and Minnesota. The probabilities favor Missouri.

FIVE STATES ACT YESTERDAY.

The states which completed ratification Wednesday were:

IOWA, COLORADO,
UTAH, OREGON.
NEW HAMPSHIRE.

The complete list of states which have ratified the constitutional amendment is:

Alabama	Michigan	No. Dakota
Colorado	New Hampshire	Oregon
Idaho	Oklahoma	Tennessee
Kansas	Texas	W. Virginia
Maine	Washington	California
Mississippi	Arizona	Georgia
Ohio	Florida	Illinois
So. Dakota	Iowa	Maryland
Virginia	Louisiana	Montana
Arkansas	Massachusetts	N. Carolina
Delaware		S. Carolina
Indiana		Utah
Kentucky		

Western states whose legislatures are in session but which have not yet ratified the amendment are New Mexico, Wyoming, Minnesota, Nebraska and Missour.. The amendment will be submitted to all of them and to Nevada, where the legislature meets next Monday.

13 YET TO VOTE.

These thirteen states have not yet voted on the amendment. They are:

Minnesota	Connecticut
Missouri	Pennsylvania
Nebraska	Rhode Island
Nevada	Vermont
New Jersey	Wisconsin.
New Mexico	Wyoming
New York	

Of the thirty-five states that have taken action, fourteen have certified their action to the federal state department. They are:

Virginia	Montana
Kentucky	Delaware
North Dakota	Massachusetts
South Carolina	Arizona
Maryland	Georgia
South Dakota	Louisiana
Texas	Michigan

Certification of the vote, however, is purely a formality.

CONGRESS ACTION NEEDED.

The amendment, under its provisions, becomes effective one year from the date of its final ratification. Additional legislation by Congress is necessary to make it operative and ground work for this already has been laid.

This legislation will prescribe penalties for violations a[...]ermine how and by what agencies the law shall be enforced.

If ratification is

UTHOR OUT F SYMPATHY VITH DRY LAW

icans Delighted to Discuss ohibition "Over the Nuts d Wine," Visitor Declares

An American Critic

BY G. K. CHESTERTON.

NT to America with some notion not discussing prohibition, but on found that well-to-do Amer- were only too delighted to dis- over the nuts and wine. They even dispense with the nuts. n for the poor, drink is not al- prohibited; it is only poisoned. ition never prohibits. It never history, even in Moslem his- and it never will. By way of a test, consider what part of Moslem culture has passed permanently into our own modern culture. You will find the one poem that has pierced is a poem by a Moslem in praise of wine. The crown of all the victories of the Crescent is that nobody reads the Koran and everybody reads the Rubaiyat.

But many eminent and thoughtful Americans are eager to discuss in theory whether prohibition would be good if it could exist or in so far as it can exist. And one of them, Mr. Barry, challenged me in a friendly and even flattering fashion in an American church magazine which unfortunately I have not by me at the moment. But from his tone I venture to think we should have a great deal in common; nevertheless, I have no apology to offer for the point of view which he attacks. It is, in substance, the fact that I have never based my case against prohibition on the case for fermented liquor, but on the case for freedom. And though unfortunately, I can only criticise his interesting article from memory, I hope it will not be unfair to note in it an example of a certain view which I have more than once encountered.

PROVE HIS CASE.

Now, I notice that those who criticize my plea for liberty, especially as a plea against prohibition, in- variably fall into a certain trap. all respect for them, I confess it amusing to watch them tu into it one after another, like a of sheep into a ditch. In their ness to prove their case they always begin by proving mine. When I say, "You are clearly attacking liberty itself, for liberty of diet is the most private sort of liberty," they never do answer, for some reason or other. "Of course, there are private liberties which we should defend, but for such and such reasons we thin ception." They invaria "After all, what is libe liberty? Who has re Man is a member must obey those p which, etc., etc.,

In other words a complete conf attacking all lib that they do de possibility of of their answ scope of the they admit pression m number of they say is anything

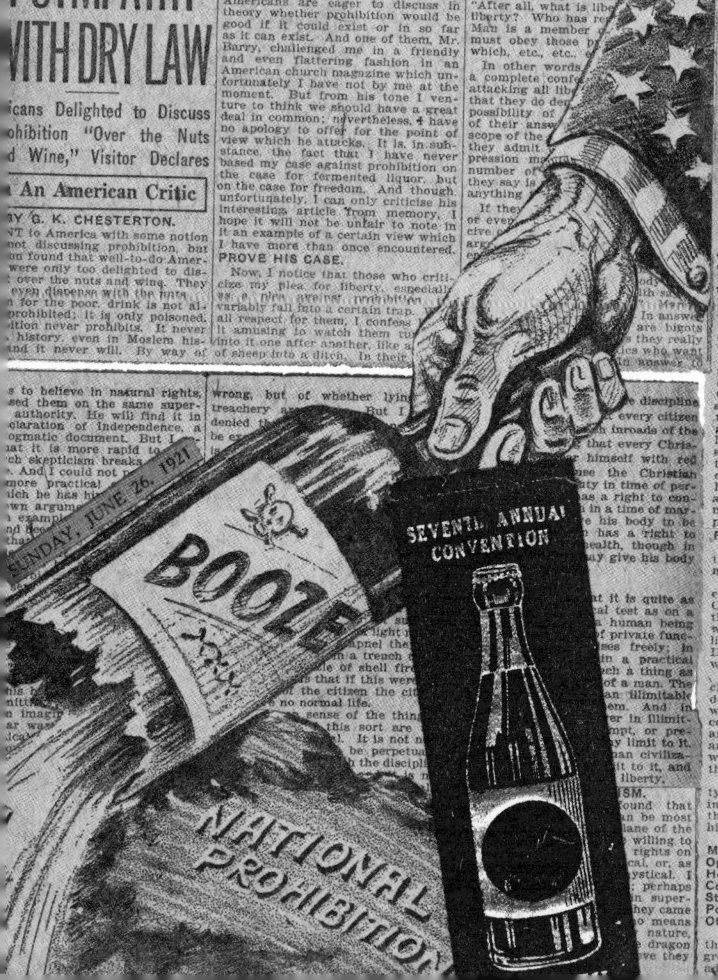

If they or even cive arg

s to believe in natural rights, sed them on the same super- authority. He will find it in claration of Independence, a ogmatic document. But I at it is more rapid to ch skepticism breaks

wrong, but of whether lyin treachery But I denied

'CUB' REPORTER'S STORIES USED IN WET CAMPAIGN

Vanderbilt Newspaper Reports Show Increase in Use of All Liquors Under Dry Laws, and British Columbia Drops Prohibition Statute

OCTOBER 2, 1921

By CORNELIUS VANDERBILT Jr.

Last summer while traveling in the West for a metropolitan newspaper, I was told to keep my eyes open for any new phases concerning the failure of prohibition.

It was therefore with a great deal of interest that I learned from a city official that Vancouver, British Columbia, had been having a hard time to enforce its dry laws. This same man added that he believed drugs had claimed a majority of the former habitues of the bar, but he would not substitute the statement for publication.

Mayor Gale of Vancouver was absent during my investigation in that city, but R. S. Jones, one of the City Councilors, who knew about as much about the city as many of its executives, showed me where to secure a great deal of my material. The police department, through Chief Inspector Dethердale, gave me proportionate figures dealing with the Oriental side of the question, and the health department, through its very able adviser, Dr. F. T. Underhill, gave me a signed report on the effect of prohibition within their observation.

FACTS SET DOWN.

I remembered what Dr. Underhill, the chief medical officer, had told me:

"To my mind prohibition has started a very dangerous disease in Canada. It is without doubt true that every man, no matter who he is, when he cannot get his stimulant, is liable to resort to other means. Drugs are the quickest and surest way of getting that stimulation.

"While the trade is being well checked in Vancouver, I have no doubt that there are other places where it is being carried on to a considerable degree. At present we are fortunate in having a very good and clean Oriental population, and we have very little trouble with them."

He had thereupon handed me a typewritten pamphlet, which stated in bold faced letters the increase in the numbers of drug users since prohibition went into effect:

Drugs—	1917.	1920.
Morphine	105	272
Opium	98	204
Heroin	134	416
Cocaine	92	308
Strychnine	0	69
Poison in food	10	16
Other identification	11	118

In this connection it was evident that heroin had perhaps shown the greatest increase. Dr. Underhill had added that although heroin was but

This Is Text Of Dry Act Before States

FOLLOWING is the prohibition amendment to the Federal Constitution submitted by Congress to the States for ratification:

Section 1. After one year from the ratification of this article, the manufacture, sale or transportation of intoxicating liquors within, the importation thereof into, or the exportation thereof from the United States and all territories subject to the jurisdiction thereof, for beverage purposes are hereby prohibited.

Section 2. The Congress and the several States shall have concurrent power to enforce this article by appropriate legislation.

Section 3. This article shall be inoperative unless it shall have been ratified as an amendment to the Constitution by the Legislatures of the several States, as provided in the Constitution, within seven years from the date of the submission hereof to the States by Congress.

KILL LEADERS!

SUNDAY, JUNE 26, 1921

BOOZE

SEVENTH ANNUAL CONVENTION

NATIONAL PROHIBITION

FOUNDED 1865 CC SAN FRANCISCO, CAL., SATURDAY, AUGUST 20, 1921

Prohibition Here to Stay, W.C.T.U. I

WOMEN ARE SHOWN QUICK-CHANGE GOWN

VICE AND CRIME

THE SALOON

POVERTY

WOMEN GET THE BALLOT

MRS MARTHA F. BUNKER A PIONEER IN THE TEMPERANCE WORK, ALL THE WAY FROM MAINE

WIFE BEATEN, BABY INJURED, IN DRY RAID

Women Searched in Their Pullman Bunks, a Coffin Broken Open and a Corpse Inspected Trunks and Hand Bags Rifled and Persons Who Resist Shot by the Prohibition Agents

"When officers, disregarding the fact that women have disrobed and retired for the night, flash their lights into the Pullman berth and under the cover, ostensibly in search of liquor.

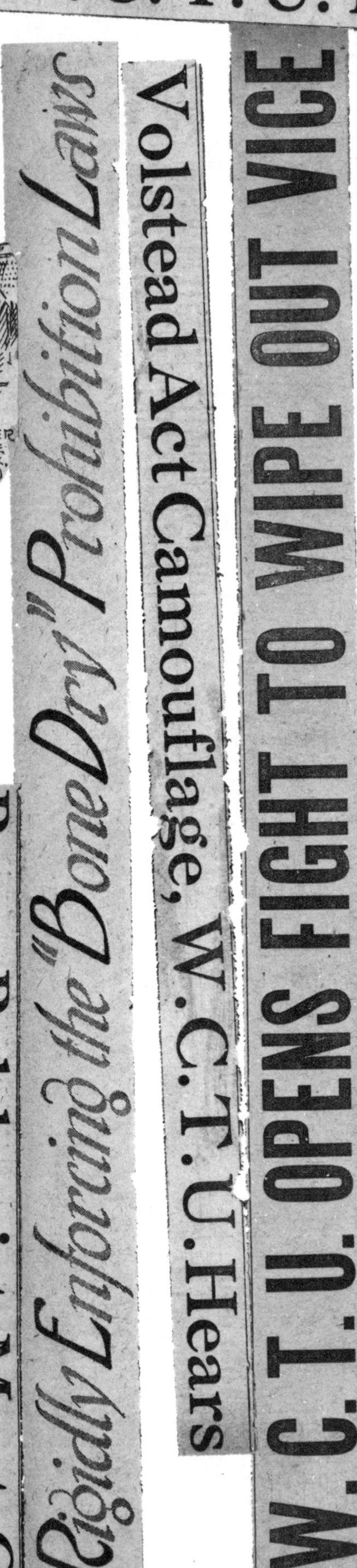

Beer Bolshevist Must Go

Rigidly Enforcing the "Bone Dry" Prohibition Laws

Volstead Act Camouflage, W. C. T. U. Hears

W. C. T. U. OPENS FIGHT TO WIPE OUT VICE

4 N THE SAN FRANCISCO EXAMINER: SUNDAY, JUNE 19, 1921

DRY LAW ENFORCEMENT DIFFICULT TASK

legates Told

EIGHTEENTH AMENDMENT.

"I'll tell you what I think about it myself, but I don't want to be quoted on the subject."

This was the attorney general's answer to my question as to his attitude toward the Eighteenth Amend-

In the first place, I myself am as much in the dark as everybody else is. Of course, prohibition is the law of the land, and it must be enforced. It must be, and it will be enforced. How long it will take to install the machinery and how long it will take that machinery to function effectively, I don't know. Now confusion is twice confounded.

DRY WORLD AIM OF PUSSYFOOT

Prohibition Crusader, Eyes Weaker and Ears Failing, Returns from 7,000-Mile Trip.

BRITISH STOLE HIS WATCH

Sultan of Zanzibar One of His Converts; Reports England Is Not So Wet.

"I'm not going to die till the whole world's dry."

This prediction or defi was flung out by William E. Johnson, who likes the sobriquet of "Pussyfoot," as he returned to New York yesterday from a 7,000-mile expedition against Demon Rum.

He had been away since June and his battle-lines were laid in as far away places as South Africa, Egypt, Arabia and Zanzibar. He came home on the steamer George Washington a day and a half late due to gales.

EYE GROWING WEAK.

His prediction followed his announcement that his one eye was becoming weaker and that he feared he was becoming deaf. He lost his right eye in an assault by British students several years ago. Supporting his prophesy, he asserted:

"Prohibition is making progress in England and South Africa and the Sultan of Zanzibar is an ardent dry. In South Africa students intervened to save me from attack while I was making several speeches.

"The situation in England is satisfactory. The Laborites favor local option, and they defeated the Conservatives."

While he talked he waved a black cigar. Asked if he favored the movement to prohibit tobacco smoking, he replied that he would not mind a ban on cigarettes, but hoped cigars would not be barred.

DEFENDS PHILADELPHIA.

New York and Chicago were more in need of a clean-up that Philadelphia, he asserted when asked for his views of Brigadier-General Butler's crusade in the Quaker City.

While he was passing through England, Johnson's watch was stolen.

Devious ways of Liquor Thieves

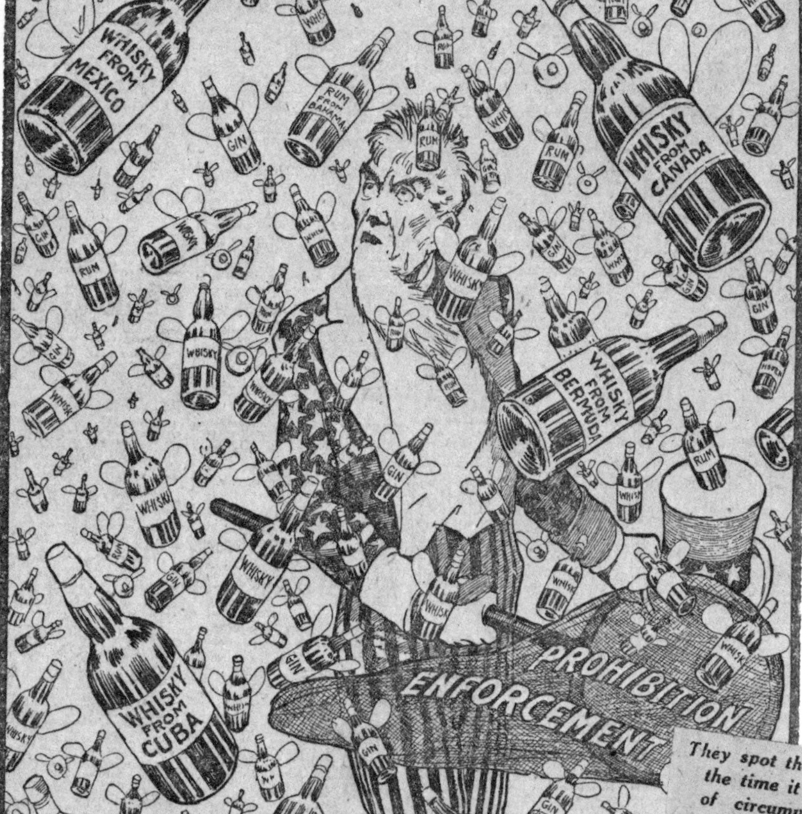

'Pussyfoot' Returns on 'Dry' Mission

They spot the rich man's reserve from the time it is stocked—Have ways of circumventing electric alarms and other safety devices — Sometimes they sell it and then steal it back — Many thefts encompassed by bribing servants—Covered vans cart away the loot, for which there is always a ready market :: ::

ALMOST pap... the ... cons... into ... of fin... somebody has r... Europe to find his liquor vaults at his ... home sadly the worse for intrusion. A warehouse has been entered in the night and many barrels of choice red liquor are somewhere, but not there.

The melancholy part about it all is that there seems to be no satisfactory defense. If a man has his wife's jewels insured he is reasonably protected. If the gems are stolen he can buy others as good with the proceeds of his policies. But if a man's vintages go no insurance will do him much good or greatly solace his palate. Fine wines cannot be replaced today, even if one is willing to go to the bootleggers, violate the law and pay the extortionate prices. Again, insurance on drinkables is high-priced, not easy to get and never issued in sufficient amount to cover the replacement value of stocks in hand.

Yet the companies which do issue insurance policies on liquors have their side of the story to tell. They have paid losses of $3,000,000 within the single year of 1921, they assert, and they estimate that this figure ... one-half and probably only one-third of ...

...ustry furnish another ... of criminals as a class ... lawbreakers and the ...rohibition liquor steal- ... stuff that dreams are ...h to be worth carting ...round the corner and ... case and fine rye for ...hief? But when doubt- ...$100 to $150 a dozen and ...that's a different matter. ...ion has been created by ...as happened when silks went skyrocketing ... war.

Large cities and their outlying country places have been the special victims of one set of booze burglars. There has been some talk, because of the similarity in technique displayed by these fellows, of a master mind and a centralized traffic in stolen liquors, but there is no real foundation for this theory. Jewel robbers always operate in very much the same manner, but no one supposes that they are all working under one guiding intelligence. Yet there is a certain loose centralization to the booze burglar business. It was not created by them, but existed ready made, another of the children of prohibition. Bootlegged liquor is distributed today, more or less exclusively, through certain definite channels. The independent bootlegger has to go to these people and make an arrangement with them or he is soon out of business and probably

-ST. LOUIS POST-DISPATCH—JUNE 4, 1922.

JANUARY 10, 1924

HIS "DRY" SMILE WORKING—"Pussyfoot" Johnson, arch foe of the "cup that cheers" returns to New York to tell us again how he is not "going to die until the world is dry." He has been campaigning abroad where the cup still cheers.

(International Newsreel)

MARTIN SHEEHY, detective, attacked in dry raid, exhibits meat cleaver that figured when patrons objected.

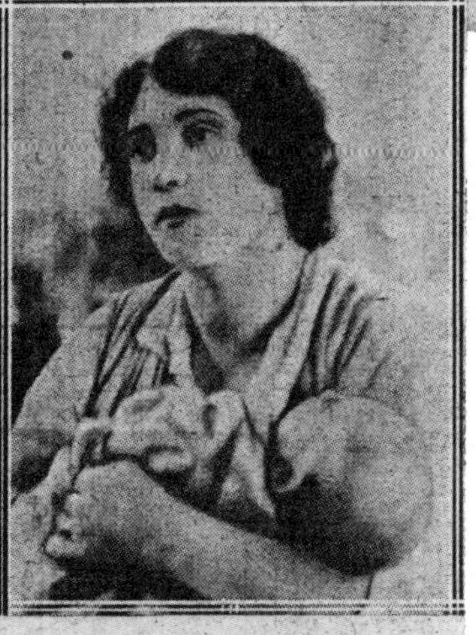

PATRONS MOB THE RAIDERS—Two detectives were injured when Mrs. Silvey Posturo (above), No. 456 East 9th street, objected to dry raid on her restaurant and customers aided her. She is held. More than-fifty joined in attack on officers.

POLICEMAN WRINGS PANTS, SAVES RUM RAID EVIDENCE

The trousers of Sergeant of Police Charles Great yesterday yielded evidence that may send Louis ... to prison for violation of ... dashed the vessel from the officer's hand.

The liquid descended in the lap of Sergeant Great. The pantaloons were doffed, and after a determined ... the hands of police ...

Bars Against the Law Anyhow, Since Volstead

LOS ANGELES, May 17.—The Lincoln Heights jail, now under construction here, will be far removed from the old types of jails with heavy bars and dark, ill-ven-

Grocery and Candy Shops Raided by Dry Agents

Prohibition agents in Brooklyn yesterday made several arrests in grocery and candy stores for alleged violations of the liquor laws.

Over a room behind a grocery store was the sign "Blind Tigers

EMBASSY LIQUOR ATTRACTS HOST OF "HOOCH-HUNTERS"

Mrs. Poindexter Shows How Diplomatic Affairs Grow in Popularity Since Dry Law's Advent

By ELIZABETH GALE POINDEXTER.

Wife of Senator Poindexter, now Ambassador to Peru.

THe diplomatic set in Washington includes some of the most interesting people it

Rudyard Kipling's Epic of the Irish Guards reaches soul-stirring climax in description of Somme battle, in Next Sunday's Chronicle

San Francisco Chronicle

LEADING NEWSPAPER OF THE PACIFIC COAST

REG. U.S. PAT. OFF.

WEATHER

Thursday fair; cloudy in morning; moderate west winds. Mount Tamalpais—Fair; moderate northwest winds. E. A. BEALS, Forecaster. Complete Weather Report on Page

FOUNDED 1865—VOL. CXXII. NO. 164 CCC SAN FRANCISCO, CAL., THURSDAY, JUNE 28, 1923—TWENTY-EIGHT PAGES DAILY 5 CENTS, SUNDAY 10 CENTS

'WET' LINERS FACING SEIZURE

ARREST RISKED BY CAPTAINS OF FOREIGN SHIPS

Washington Government Decides to Seize Vessels Carrying Liquor

HUGHES TOLD OF ACTION

Companies to Be Notified and Permitted Time to Comply With Order

FOUNDED 1865—VOL. CXXIII. NO. 98 CC SAN FRANCISCO, CAL., SUNDAY, OCTOBER 21, 1923—NINETY-TWO PAGES DAILY 5 CENTS, S

KAHR KIDNAPS BERLIN TRO

GOVERNORS VOTE LIQUOR

COOLIDGE PLAN IS APPROVED BY STATE LEADERS

Co-ordination of All Officials in Prohibition Drive Proposed

VOL. CXVIII. NO. 115. CCC SAN FRANCISCO, WEDNESDAY, APRIL 25, 1923—THIRTY-TWO PAGES

Two McDonough Brothers Held as BOOTLEG

CALL BAIL BROKERS 'MASTER MINDS' OF CITY'S LIQUOR RING

FOUNDED 1865—VOL. CXXII. NO. 47 CC SAN FRANCISCO, CAL.,

RUM RUNNING FLE

LIQUOR LADEN SHIPS APPEAR OFF HIGHLANDS

Said to Be Vanguard of Larger Fleet Due to Arrive Soon

SPEED BOATS READY

Scouts Tell Rum Runners Dry Agents Are Not Overactive

FOUNDED 1865—VOL. CXXIII. NO. 134

SEA FIGH

CUTTERS FIRE ON AND SEIZE BRITISH SHIP

Blood Flows When U. S. Men Board Runner Off Jersey; Find Leader

$90,000 FOUND ABOARD

Schooner's Flight Seaward Halted by 3-Inch Guns; Crew Is Defiant

FOUNDED 1865—VOL. CXXII, N

WASHIN PRISO

U.S. FORCE TOO SMALL TO FILL RUM WAR GAP

Yellowley Sent to Empire State to Report Situation to Mellon and Blair

LAW MACHINERY HALTS

More Than 1000 Accused Bootleggers Awaiting Trial Expected to Go Free

L. H

WHISKY

FOUNDED 1865—VOL. CXXV. NO. 152 CC SAN FRANCISCO, CAL., SUNDAY, DECEMBER 14, 1924 DAILY 5 CENTS, SUNDAY 10 CENTS

U. S. AGENTS SEIZE BIG S. F. BREWER

FOUNDED 1865—VOL. CXXII. NO. 159 CCC SAN FRANCISCO, CAL., SATURDAY, JUNE 23, 1923—TWENTY-EIGHT PAGES DAILY 5 CENTS, SUNDAY 10 CENTS

OLICE GUILTY IN RUM TRIA

UM SEIZURE VEXES BR

MPS "DRY" LID ON 'SHI

CZAR REVE

CISC

San Francisco Chronicle

LEADING NEWSPAPER of the PACIFIC COAST

REG. U.S. PAT. OFF.

...2, 1923—TWENTY-SIX PAGES DAILY 5 CENTS, SU...

...EAL S...

...XII, NO. 149 CCC SAN FRANCISCO, CAL., WEDNESDAY, JUNE 13, 1923—TWENTY-EIGHT PAGES DAILY 5 CENTS, SUNDAY...

...NG OPPOSES RUM...

...XII, NO. 106 CCCC SAN FRANCISCO, CAL., TUESDAY, MAY 1, 1923—TWENTY-EIGHT PAGES DAILY 5 CENTS, SUNDAY 10 CENTS: DAILY AND SUNDAY PER MONTH

...ASES FINE WHISKY SEIZED HERE

...TRIAL

FOUNDED 1865—VOL. CXXIII, NO. 4 CCC SAN FRANCISCO, CAL., THURSDAY, JULY 19, 1923 TWENTY-FOUR PAGES DAILY 5 CENTS, SU...

BIG SHAKE-UP IN DRY FO...

...S: DAILY AND SUNDAY PER MONTH, $1.15

...S.

...AR

...5 CENTS, SUNDAY 10 CENTS: DAILY AND SUNDAY PER MONTH, $1.15

...KINGS

...RCH 3, 1923—TWENTY-SIX PAGES DAILY 5 CENTS, SUNDAY 10 CENTS: DAILY AND SUNDAY PER MONTH, $1.15

...BESIEGES NEW YORK

SAN FRANCISCO, MONDAY, NOVEMBER 26, 1923— DAILY 5 CENTS, SUNDAY 10 CENTS: DAILY AND SUNDAY PER MONTH, $1.15

...NETS "LIQUOR KING"

CC SAN FRANCISCO, CAL., SUNDAY, JUNE 3, 1923—ONE HUNDRED PAGES DAILY 5 CENTS, SUNDAY 10 CENTS: DAILY AND SUNDAY PER MONTH, $1.15

...ON STUNNED BY N. Y. DRY REPEAL.

...GATES CLOSE ON 'TIGER' WOMAN

—VOL. CXXIV, NO. 91. SAN FRANCISCO, CAL., TUESDAY, APRIL 15, 1924 DAILY 5 CENTS, SUNDAY 10 CENTS: DAILY AND SUNDAY PER MONTH, $1.15

...HOTS FLY IN RUM RAID

...BE
...TE
...NTS

FOUNDED 1865—VOL. CXXIX, NO. 10 CCC SAN FRANCISCO, CAL., SUNDAY, JULY 25, 1926 DAILY 5 CENTS, SUNDAY 10 CENTS DAILY...

OUSTED DRY CZAR'S LIQUORS SEIZE...

Accused Chief of Reform Forces Trailed by U. S. Secret Agents After Boasting of His Drinking; Admits Wild Party Charges

Ned M. Green, Federal prohibition administrator here for the past ten months, who freely confesses charges against him upon which the Federal Grand Jury will act tomorrow, yesterday was suspended from office by acting Secretary of the Treasury Winston.

COOLIDGE URGES WOMEN VOTE

6 A. M. EDITION

San Francisco Chron

LEADING NEWSPAPER OF THE PACIFIC COAST

Ou

REG.U.S.PA

SAN FRANCISCO, CAL., SATURDAY, FEBRUARY 16, 1924

FOUNDED 1865—VOL. CXXIV. NO. 32

'DRY' SHOOTS U. S. SE

FRANK GREENE ACCIDENTALLY HIT IN CHASE

Vermont Solon Innocent Victim of Battle Between Dry Raider and Bootleggers

ON PENNSYLVANIA AVE.

Legislator Sinks Into Arms of Wife Seriously Wounded; Rum Vender Escapes

Special by Leased Wire to The Chronicle.

WASHINGTON, Feb. 15.—United States Senator Frank L. Greene of Vermont was shot and seriously wounded while walking on Pennsylvania avenue near the Capitol tonight by a prohibition agent in pursuit of bootleggers.

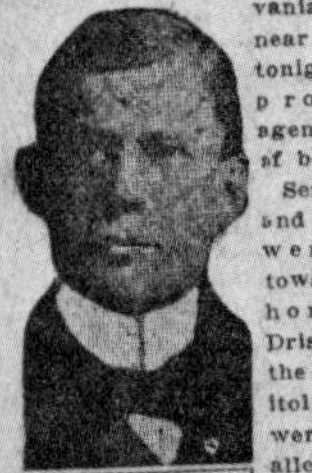

SENATOR FRANK L. GREENE

Senator Greene and his wife were walking towards their home at the Driscoll Hotel at the foot of Capitol Hill. As they were passing an alley running into Pennsylvania avenue near John Marshall place they heard shooting. The Senator sought to locate the trouble. As he stepped towards the alley the shooting continued and one bullet struck him in the forehead above the left eye. He sank into the arms of his wife just as an automobile filled with bootleggers dashed out of the alley into the avenue.

Senator Brought Down By Dry Agent's Shot

The automobile was pursued by Otis E. Fischer, prohibition agent, attached to the Prohibition Commissioner's office here. He had been pursuing the bootleggers and had fired the shots, one of which had struck the Senator. When Fischer saw that he had injured an innocent bystander he went to his aid, the fugitive bootleggers escaping.

Senator Greene did not lose consciousness and asked that he be hastened to a hospital. Fischer, with the aid of Policemen Dowd and Moore, who had been with him in the alley, called an ambulance and the Senator, accompanied by his wife, was taken to the Emergency Hospital.

Wound Not Expected To Prove Fatal

Physicians after a hurried examination of the Senator's wound were apprehensive that the bullet had lodged in the skull near the top of the head, but it was decided ... inas... pear...

Se... ous ... that ... cide... befo... doct... wou...

Th... Pro... policemen to trap a bootlegger who

SAN FRANCISCO, CAL., MONDAY, JULY 25, 1921—E

FOUNDED 1865—VOL. CXIX, NO. 10 CC

MOB TRIES TO HANG

GILROY CROWD CALLS FOR ROPE FOR RAID PARTY

Exnicios and Aids Relate Perilous Experience While Making Seizures

LYNCH 'EM,' PEOPLE YELL

Reinforcements Arrive Just in Time to Defeat Plan of Ardent Enthusiasts

Two Federal prohibition enforcement agents working under John Exnicios, Federal prohibition supervising agent, at Gilroy Saturday narrowly escaped being lynched by an angry mob of men and boys, according to Exnicios, who returned to San Francisco yesterday. The prompt arrival of reinforcements alone prevented the crowd from attempting to carry out its threat, according to the agent.

During a series of raids in Gilroy, two of Exnicios' men were standing by their automobile, in which was liquor to be used as evidence at the trials, in front of the Swiss Hotel. A man approached the machine and began searching it. He was ordered to keep away. He said he was a newspaper reporter and wanted to "know what was going on." This remark was cheered. Soon the cheers turned into jeers, and some one shouted, "Get a rope." Then cries of "Hang 'em," "Run them out of town," and "We'll show the prohibition agents how we treat them in Gilroy," were taken up. The officers warned the crowd to stand back and prepared to defend themselves.

Raiders Rush to Aid Of Besieged Comrades

People gathered from all directions and the officers say that at one time there were 200 in the crowd. Hearing the tumult, other prohibition agents, who were conducting a raid in an adjoining block, ceased their search and hastened to the aid of their comrades. The crowd then quieted down and the officers entered their machines and drove away amid jeers.

The prohibition men visited Salinas, Milliken Corners, Watsonville, Santa Cruz and Gilroy during the last three days. They made twenty raids.

undertaken by himself and men.

Agents Knocked About A Lot, Says Exnicios

The prohibition men, according to Exnicios, all show the effects of rough handling. He says that whenever a place is entered it almost invariably ends in a fight, because the proprietors and their help are determined to destroy any evidence on hand, while the prohibition officers are equally determined to capture all liquor possible to use as evidence. As soon as the identity of the agents is learned, the fracas starts, says Exnicios.

"How can we do our duty and make a successful raid unless we use force, when every effort is being

Gilroy Mob for Lynching Agents On Liquor Raid

(Continued from Page 1, Column 1)

made to cripple us or even kill us," asked the supervising agent yesterday. "We would never resort to force unless compelled to do so.

"The character of the people we are dealing with forestalls gentle methods or diplomacy. They are foreigners as a rule, and they are not in sympathy with the law and they will stop at nothing in order to destroy the evidence. If the evidence is destroyed it means a saving of $500 and perhaps a term in jail, so they use desperate means and take desperate chances. That Girloy episode is only a preliminary to some of the main bouts.

"We don't want to be rough, but when opposed we must naturally use every effort to carry out orders and enforce the law. The public knows what resisting an officer means. If we treat 'em rough it is only because we are defending ourselves. This is no excuse, it's merely a statement of facts," concluded Exnicios.

The prohibition agents are loud in praise of the police and the courts in Santa Cruz, where the authorities not only assisted the federal men in making arrests, but the judge immediately fined the guilty $500 each. During the raid on the place of Kari Cissi in Santa Cruz, the officers took 950 gallons of wine. The man admitted, according to Exnicios, that he had sold 1150 gallons at $1.50 per gallon.

From the establishment of Joe Lacatella in Santa Cruz, 250 gallons of wine were taken. Exnicios said the man has several thousand gallons of wine at his ranch home, but that the officers had no authority to confiscate it.

According to Exnicios, the following places were raided:

SALINAS—D. Mollinari, Nick Galicki, Abbot Stokes, Mike Baddich, Martin Bebek.

MILLIKEN CORNERS—Henry Buelna.

WATSONVILLE—J. P. Knusen, Jas. Trigonys, Louis Kirk, Paul Jacobsen.

SANTA CRUZ—Karl Kaiser, C. F. Piminiel, Carl Cessi, Joe Lacetella.

GILROY—Romeo Pagnnucci, G. Grafattari, G. Marsaglia, Dominico Mat-

No. 16,790. ★★ Copyright, 1929, by New York American, Inc. Registered in U.S. Patent Office. SUNDAY

DRY KILLERS LA

Capone Linked

RAID FAILED TO FIND RUM PROBE OF TWO DEATHS SHOW

Fourth Agent Surrenders to Murder Charge in South After Shooting on Farm

Legion Post Appeals to Hoover Not to Thwart Prosecution; Protests Hiring of Raiders

TECUMSEH, Okla., July 6.—While four men were held today on charges of murder after a raid by dry enforcement officers in which two farmers were shot to death, an investigation revealed no search warrant for the raid had been obtained.

DRYS MI

DRUG-LIQUOR CARGO SEIZED VALUED UP TO HALF MILLION

25 of Crew Held After Battle in Early Morning on Greek Steamship at Brooklyn Pier

ONE OF WOUNDED MAY DIE

Police Fire on Revenue Officers Waiting for Trap to Be Sprung; Cause of Agent's Act Unknown

MADE IN USA

DRY RAID ON SHIP; RAIDER KILLS SELF

UNSETTLED WEATHER

y Frees Mother and Infant Jailed on Beer Charge

CENTS, SUNDAY 10 CENTS: DAILY AND SUNDAY PER MONTH, $1.15

ATOR

Dry Agents Killed 140; 16 in Last 15 Months

WASHINGTON, April 5 (AP).—Enforcement of national prohibition was said today by Assistant Secretary Lowman of the Treasury to ... cost the lives of 135 persons ... law went on the statute ...

said it showed a decrease in the number of violent arrests by prohibition agents. This he attributed to an order issued more than a year ago that prohibition agents must use weapons only in self-defense or to prevent a felony. They were cautioned, howeve... must not endanger th... com...

Agents Learn A. B. C. of Law

SEPTEMBER 3, 1930

...S!—Left to right above ...es, law instructor; Col. ...odcock, director of Pro... ...y M. Dengler, Superin... ...s delivering their first ...students enrolled in the nation's "Dry College" in Washington. The students are taught the rights of individuals under the Fourth and Fifth Amendments to the Constitution with Supreme Court interpretations as the guiding feature.

DAILY 5 CENTS, SUNDAY 10 CENTS: DAILY AND SUNDAY PER MONTH, $1.15

PAGES

DRY AGENTS

ORK, JULY 7, 1929 SUNDAY Entered as second class matter, Post Office, New York, N. Y. PRICE TEN CENTS

ED SEARCH WARRANT

with Marlow Slaying

SED $10,000 U. S. FUNDS

'SUPER AGENTS' BEGIN U. S. DRY SCHOOL WORK

"Get Commercial Violator" Is Woodcock's First Message to 34 in Opening Class

By ARTHUR HATCHEN,
Universal Service Staff Correspondent.

WASHINGTON, Sept. 2.—With the order, "Get the commercial violator," Colonel Amos W. W. Woodcock, Federal Prohibition Director, today opened a school for dry agents.

He was addressing thirty-four "super-agents" called here for thirty days of intensive training in enforcement methods. They, in turn, will instruct the other 1,400 agents in the field.

The school opened in a typical schoolroom setting of blackboards, desks, pencils and erasers.

Stirred by many complaints of reckless methods of prohibition agents, Colonel Woodcock established the "University of Prohibition Enforcement," unique in the Government's ten-year attempt to ... America.

...R LINES.

...g the agents, Colonel ...aid:

...cannot win this cam... enforce prohibition by ... the technical and ...alities of the agents, it ...e done.

... is no need of test or ...ne cases. We have ...law marked out to keep ... the next year.

...e reach the objective of ... the big commercial vio... without too many casual...e may have further ob...s.

...UGH ONES.

...e old days of the prohibi... agent, who was rough, ... and disorderly in his ... is gone. I won't have that ... of man in the service.

... would like every agent to ...ell dressed, especially when ... appears in court. Soap, ...er, razors and shoe ... within the reach of every ...nt."

...he thirty-four agents will re...e $3,800 a year while carrying ... the educational campaign,

'ATS A WAY I STOP UM FRUM TOTIN' LICKER AN' DRINKIN AGIN THU LAW!

YOU SUSPECTED HE HAD LIQUOR, OF COURSE?

IT'S TOO BAD NO LIQUOR WAS FOUND.

DRY ENFORCEMENT

PROHIBITION

IN THE MINDS of some Prohibition Enforcers, every automobile that travels the highway after sundown, simply must contain a lawbreaker—a nullifier of the Constitution—a rum-runner or a bootlegger.

They have HOT SUSPICIONS that these automobiles

of shooting first, and ascertaining if they hav... shoot, second.

Then they face COLD FACTS and find t... CITIZENS have been slain.

U.S. DRYS TO USE MACHINE GUNS

WASHINGTON, July 30—(INS) The liquor patrol along the Canadian border has been strengthened, to meet the transfer of smuggling operations from Florida as a result of the Mediterranean fruit fly quarantine, assistant secretary of the treasury Lowman announced today.

Ten additional fast boats armed with machine guns and one-pounders were ordered placed at the disposal of Commander Martin W. Rassmussen, of the Buffalo division of the coast guard.

The intensive inspection activities of agricultural agents in Florida, it was said, has made it virtually impossible to bring liquor into Florida from the Bahamas and send it north by automobile.

Motorists are stopped ... out the Flor...

Text of Smith's
Milwaukee Speec
on Prohibitio
CRIME
DOPE
BOOTLEG WHISKY
DISREGARD FOR LAW SAPPI
NATION'S MORALS, HE SA
PROHIBITION AND HYPOCRISY
Dry Democrats Split on Indors
Here's What Wickersham Boar
Concludes and Recomme
Board Lists Points to Be Observed in Any Revision
Opposes Repeal of 18th Amendment or Return of Saloon.
Cost of Enforcing Law Has Increased $1,000,000 Yearly
Speakeasy Must Go, but the Saloon Must Nev
HERE ARE THREE DANDY FRIENDS OF MINE AND WE'RE STARVING!
I'M GLAD YOU CALLED
ONE'S NAME IS SMITH THE OTHER'S NAME IS JOHNSON!
WE MUST TELL YOU OR WE'LL BE FELONS CAPTAIN
SNEAK
SNITCH
CONGRESSMEN
PROHIBITION ARE
DRY AGENT
SUSPECTED DRY VIOLATOR
Attacking 'Ol' Demon Rum!'
Dry Congressma
Chief of Detec
Urges Act
Urges Sale o
COOLIDGE SEES NO IMMEDIATE PROS
OF REPEALING EIGHTEENTH AME
SHOTGUN ENFORCEMENT
DRY LAW
PROHIBITION
INTOLERANCE
FANATICISM
UNPOPULARITY
HYPOCRISY
Dry Law Term Failure on 10 Anniversary.
BITTER DEBATE
Ditching of Hoover Dry Proposal Cheered.
By ARTHUR HACHTEN.
THE NOBLE EXPERIMENT MUST BE ENFORCED. IT IS THE LAW OF THE LAND!
DRY LAW
HOOVER ASKS
No. 17,318.—DAILY.
U. S. JU
Urges Home Making of Cider and Light Wines
ENFORCEMENT! WHERE ARE YOU, ENFORCEMENT?
HERE I AM. EH.. WHERE ARE YOU?
WHISKY
PROHIBITION
GUNFIRE ORGY IN BOY'S KILLING BY DRY RAIDERS
Testimony Shows More Than Eighty Shots Were Fired at Student by Sheriff's Posse
SAY, SMITHY, I'M BRINGING THREE GOOD PALS UP WITH ME AND YOU'VE GOT TO FEED US.. YEP!
JONES KNOWS A LOT OF GOOD PEOPLE
THIS COCKTAIL IS REAL ISN'T IT?
HAVE YOU MUCH OF THIS
I BOUGHT A CASE OF IT YESTERDAY
LINK TO HUGE LIQUOR PLANT IS CHARGED
PRO
3 U. S. Judges i

rohibition
as Failed, Standard
earer Asserts
HOUSEHOLD OF
BOOTLEG BOOZE
RUMRUNNING
DRY LAW ENFORCEMENT
WHISKY
sailed by Congressmen
Straddling' Prohibition Issue
Highlights of Wickersham Report
Hoover Submits Find-
nteenth Amendment, Volstead Act Plank
bald Roosevelt Tells Why She Favors Repeal of Prohibition
GHTS OF
HELD BY
EMBERS
Wickersham Read Law as He Walked To Work in Youth
PITTSBURGH, Jan. 20 (AP).—George W. Wickersham, chairman of President Hoover's Law Enforcement Commission, has worked hard. He doesn't like
HOOVER URGES CONGRESS TO KEEP DRY LAW
turn!
2 Pints Cost Culprit $500 Fine in U.S. Court
GUNMAN
ZEALOT
SPEAKEASY PROPRIETOR
HIJACKER
SHOTGUN ENFORCER
GYP JOINT HOSTESS
FANATIC
BOOTLEGGER
HYPOCRITE
BIGOT
ANTI-SALOON LEAGUE
cused of Drinking Beer in Speakeasy
New Jersey Jailed on Liquor Charge
epeal 18th Amendment
uor by National Corp
A COP ANYWHERE!
THE NEAREST POLICE STATION IS, FELLAHS!
I KNOW WHERE THERE'S ONE!
DON'T MIND HOW MUCH MONEY IT NEEDS
FANATICAL DRY
FEDERAL ENFORCEMENT
$30,000,000
MENT
Chicago's School Tragedy Traced to Gin and Auto
AILING, SAYS HOOVER BOARD
ICT DRY ENFORCEMENT
DECEMBER 17, 1930—28 PAGES
TWO CENTS In Greater New York
THREE CENTS Within 200 Miles
E DECREES
IBITION INVALID
ANTI-SALOON LEAGUE
Decision Halts Arrests By U.S. Drys in Jersey Until Appeal Is Filed
sey Refuse to Hold Dry Law Invalid

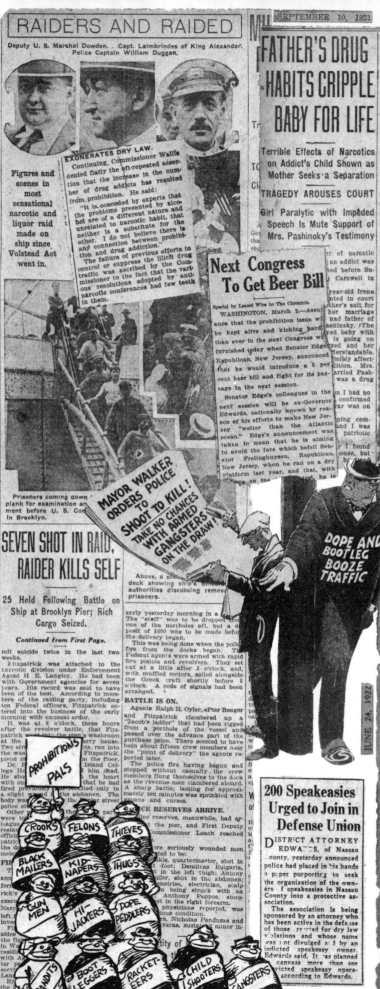

RAIDERS AND RAIDED

Deputy U. S. Marshal Dowden. . Capt. Laimbrindes of King Alexander. Police Captain William Duggan.

Figures and scenes in most sensational narcotic and liquor raid made on ship since Volstead Act went in.

EXONERATES DRY LAW.

Continuing, Commissioner Wallis denied flatly the oft-repeated assertion that the increase in the number of drug addicts has resulted from prohibition. He said:

"It is conceded by experts that the problems presented by alcohol are of a different nature and unrelated to narcotic habit, that neither is a substitute for the other. I do not believe there is any connection between prohibition and drug addiction."

The failure of previous efforts to control or suppress the illicit drug traffic was ascribed by the Commissioner to the fact that the various resolutions adopted by anti-narcotic conferences had few teeth in them.

Prisoners coming down plank for examination and ment before U. S. Com in Brooklyn.

SEPTEMBER 10, 1921

FATHER'S DRUG HABITS CRIPPLE BABY FOR LIFE

Terrible Effects of Narcotics on Addict's Child Shown as Mother Seeks a Separation

TRAGEDY AROUSES COURT

Girl Paralytic with Impeded Speech Is Mute Support of Mrs. Pashinoky's Testimony

...t of narcotic ... an addict was ... before Su... Carswell in ... year-old Irene ... nted in court ... other's suit for ... her marriage ... nad father of ... ashinsky. The ... yed baby with ... is going on ... and her ... derstandable. ... isibly affect... dition. Mrs. ... arried Pash... was a drug ... n I had no ... confirmed ... ar was on ... ping com... and I was ... patriotic ... r I found ... ouse, but ...

Next Congress To Get Beer Bill

Special by Leased Wire to The Chronicle.

WASHINGTON, March 2.—Assurance that the prohibition issue will be kept alive and kicking harder than ever in the next Congress was furnished today when Senator Edge, Republican, New Jersey, announced that he would introduce a 2 per cent beer bill and fight for its passage in the next session.

Senator Edge's colleagues in the next session will be ex-Governor Edwards, nationally known by reason of his efforts to make New Jersey "wetter than the Atlantic ocean." Edge's announcement was taken to mean that he is aiming to avoid the fate which befell Senator Frelinghuysen, Republican, New Jersey, when he ran on a dry platform last year, and that, with ...

SEVEN SHOT IN RAID, RAIDER KILLS SELF

25 Held Following Battle on Ship at Brooklyn Pier; Rich Cargo Seized.

Continued from First Page.

mit suicide twice in the last two weeks.

Fitzpatrick was attached to the narcotic division under Enforcement Agent H E. Langley. He had been with Government agencies for seven years. His record was said to have been of the best. According to members of the raiding party, including ten Federal officers, Fitzpatrick entered into the business of the early morning with unusual ardor.

It was at 8 o'clock, three hours after the revolver battle, that Fitzpatrick ... the men's washroom at the ... erry house. Two str... ots, ran into the was... Fitzpatrick, pistol in ... on the floor. Dr. ... Island College Ho... him dead. He sho... the heart with on... that he had fired previously ... only in a slight wound in the abdomen. The body was ... the ... street police st...

Above, a sce... deck showing ship's ... authorities discussing remov... prisoners.

early yesterday morning in a ... The "staff" was to be dropped from one of the portholes aft, but a deposit of $600 was to be made before the delivery began.

This was being done when the police fire from the docks began. The Federal agents were armed with rapid fire pistols and revolvers. They set out at a little after 3 o'clock, and, with muffled motors, sailed alongside the Greek craft shortly before 5 o'clock. A code of signals had been arranged.

BATTLE IS ON.

Agents Ralph H. Oyler, ePter Reager and Fitzpatrick clambered up a "Jacob's ladder" that had been rigged from a porthole of the vessel and passed over the advance part of the purchase price. There seemed to have been about fifteen crew members near the "point of delivery" the agents reported later.

The police fire having begun and stopped without casualty the crew members flung themselves to the deck as the revenue men clambered aboard. A sharp battle, lasting for approximately ten minutes was sprinkled with groans and curses.

...CE RESERVES ARRIVE.

...lice reserves, meanwhile, had ar... the pier, and First Deputy Commissioner Leach reached ...

...ore seriously wounded men ...ted to be:

...akis, quartermaster, shot in ... foot; Demitras Bulgaria, ... in the left thigh; Antony ...oiler, shot in the abdomen; ...enstrise, electrician, scalp ... being struck with an ... Anthony Peppos, store... shot in the right forearm. ... physicians reported, was ...ious condition. ...rs, Nicholas Panduzas and ...varas, sustained minor in...

... barrels, 4 gallons and 84 bottles of home brew and 173 gallons and 27 bot...

200 Speakeasies Urged to Join in Defense Union

DISTRICT ATTORNEY EDWARDS, of Nassau County, yesterday announced police had placed in his hands a paper purporting to seek the organization of the owners of speakeasies in Nassau County into a protective association.

The association is being sponsored by an attorney who has been active in the defense of those arrested for dry law violations and whose name was not divulged and by an indicted speakeasy owner, Edwards said. It was planned to canvass more than 300 convicted speakeasy operators, according to Edwards.

Dry Laxity Aids Drug Peddlers, Bryan Asserts

WASHINGTON, Feb. 21.

PUBLIC OFFICIALS who can be controlled by the wets can likewise be controlled by drug peddlers, William Jennings Bryan declared to-day in giving his wholehearted indorsement to the anti-narcotic campaign. Mr. Bryan said:

"I am in favor of the strictest and most rigid provisions possible against narcotics. But why encourage the bootleggers who are engaged in the same business?

"The wets cannot encourage violation of the Prohibition laws without encouraging the violation of other laws.

"If the people elect officials who can be controlled by bootleggers, these officials also will be open to the influence of drug peddlers.

"Law is law, and all laws must stand or fall together. Every argument against enforcement of the Prohibition law is an argument for violation of all laws. Every argument against Prohibition tends to weaken the enforcement of all laws."

$200,000 DOPE SMUGGLED IN BY RUM RING

...licit Narcotic Drugs Escape Dry Raiders in Gun Battle ...ith Bootleggers at Monterey

...t narcotics valued at $200,-... were successfully brought into ... country by the smugglers at ...terey, who were caught by Federal agents transporting 1,000 cases ... whisky which were seized by the ...ernment after a gun fight Tues...

A man and his wife are being sought by Federal agents as the heads of the illicit drug ring to whom the narcotics were consigned.

Positive information in the hands of the authorities prove that the couple, whose names are being withheld, are leaders of one of the largest illicit drug rings in the United States and they are extensive distributors throughout the country, according to the government agents.

JUNE 24, 1922

Federal Prohibition Director S. F. Rutter said that in an effort to raid a place in San Francisco yesterday books were seized which showed a large traffic in narcotics by the persons suspected of handling the contraband.

"One item showed disposal of narcotics at $1,936 to a purchaser. That is one which stood out as I remember the entry," said Rutter.

"We believe now that the narcotics were on the first automobile which the Federal agents permitted to go through. It is the custom of smugglers to send out a 'scout' car in cases of this kind. If the first car gets through the others will follow. My men saw the first car but did not stop it so that the bigger haul could be made, not thinking that they would take the risk to have the drugs in this machine."

Owners of Autos in Dry Raid All "Leave Town"

Efforts of Federal officers to serve warrants of arrest on six owners of automobiles seized in the big Monterey county booze raid of last Tuesday morning proved unavailing yesterday.

Everybody had moved.

At three hotels the "patrons" had "checked out" and at the homes of all the others they were "away on vacation" or had "left town."

Despite this, however, S. F. Rutter, Federal prohibition director, last night stated utmost endeavor will be made to locate all of them.

The owners of the automobiles, seized during the raid and now stored at a garage in Oakland, according to Rutter's records, are:

Leslie M. Moore, Menlo Park; J. ... Ferris, Grand Hotel, San Francisco; Ed O'Connor, 1230 Forty-seventh avenue, San Francisco; Mrs. C. H. Zucker, 1991 Vallejo street; C. N. Zucker, 1290 Sutter street and an address on Twenty-third avenue; S. Terry, 854 Stanford avenue, Oakland.

W. J. Allen of 621 Eighteenth avenue, San Francisco, was arrested when he called on Rutter to claim his machine, which was also ...

WALLIS SHOWS FEWER DRUNKS, MORE ADDICTS

Chief of Correction Bureau Prepares Statistics on Habits of Men and Women Prisoners

PROHIBITION NOT INVOLVED

Crime Decrease Noted, but Increase in Users of Narcotic Drugs Is Startling

Startling comparisons of statistics, showing decrease of the liquor habit since the enactment of Prohibition, are presented in a report just made public by Frederick A. Wallis, Commissioner of Corrections.

The report also shows an alarming increase in narcotic drug addiction. This increase, Mr. Wallis points out, has no relation to Prohibition.

DECREASE IN CRIME.

With the decrease in the use of liquor, there has been a big falling off in crime, amounting from 1917 to 1920, to more than 50 per cent, as shown by the following table:

PRISON POPULATION.

	Males.	Females.	Totals.
1917	87,064	14,567	101,631
1918	72,012	13,655	85,667
1919	73,437	10,051	83,488
1920	67,097	7,210	74,307
1921	42,372	4,461	46,833

LIQUOR DECREASE.

The falling off in the liquor habit among prisoners also has amounted to fifty per cent, as shown by these studies of habits of prison population:

Moderate Liquor Users.

	MALES.	FEMALES.
1917	34,347	4,317
1918	31,688	3,656
1919	30,783	2,750
1920	25,630	1,487
1921	10,633	697

Liquors Used Freely.

	MALES.	FEMALES.
1917	3,713	936
1918	1,621	458
1919	935	326
1920	483	154
1921	15	2

Liquors Not Used.

	MALES.	FEMALES.
1917	10,727	3,104
1918	8,599	3,582
1919	7,622	3,126
1920	10,674	2,401
1921	31,721	3,762

DRUG ADDICTION.

Discussing drug addiction, Commissioner Wallis says in his report:

"We think that drug addiction **is on the increase, not on account of prohibition of intoxicating beverages, but principally because there is disrespect for regulation and failure to close up opportunities for supplying these habit forming drugs.** It was only coincident that enforcement of prohibition and enforcement of the Harrison Federal narcotic law happened to occur at about the same period. The relationship, one with the other, is indeed remote."

The table showing the increase in addiction among prison population follows:

Narcotic Drug Addicts.

	MALES.	FEMALES.	TOTALS.
1917	109	3	112
1918	288	48	336
1919	416	71	487
1920	2,425	440	2,865
1921	1,984	158	2,135

Ex-Addict Nurse Drug Nemesis

BOSTON, Feb. 13.—With her experience as a trained nurse and a former drug addict as an asset, Miss Lysbeth Houde is unearthing evidence in her investigation of drug procurers, beauty parlors and the lairs where drug vendors ply their deadly trade. Miss Houde said that the narcotic vendors consider youth as their most alluring bait and go to desperate extremes to enmesh boys and girls in their toils. Once they have initiated them into the use of the drugs they insist on enormous prices for their adulterated narcotics.

Lysbeth Houde.

...PPOSE FATTY'S FILMS.

(... International News Service.)

...RTINS FERRY, O., Feb. 13.— ... Martins Ferry Women's Club ...

DR. ALEXANDER LAM... BERT, eminent Ne... York alienist, who was th... principal witness yesterd... before a United States Sena... committee in Washington ... the evils of the narcotic dr... traffic.

FEBRUARY 14, 1923

GOVERNOR SEEKIN... NARCOTIC CONTR...

Special to the New York America...

ALBANY, Feb. 13.—Gover... Smith acted to-day to meet ... narcotic drug traffic in New Y... State. He sent a letter to ... mann M. Biggs, State Health C... missioner, asking him to sug... some remedy for "this rap... increasing menace."

Governor Smith said:

"I have put the situat... straight up to Commissio... Biggs in my letter. I have cal... his attention to the fact t... since Governor Miller forced t... repeal of the narcotic drug ... and the abolition of the St... narcotic control commission, t... terrible traffic has multiplied a... drugs are much more easily ... tained by addicts.

"My mind is open on the qu... tion of what would be the b... solution. It is probable I sh... have a conference with Dr. Bi... at an early date."

Recreation of the narcotic ... trol commission is planned, acc... ing to reports.

HUGHES

Continued from First Page.

cited by Dr. Lambert to subs... tiate the assertion in the resolu... that 1,5000 tons of opium are ... duced annually, while not m... than 75 tons are needed for me... nal and scientific purposes.

The same documents emphas... the British Government's monop... of the opium traffic in India ... the great revenue derived f... dumping this agent of destruct... and death on the remainder of ... world.

JAPANESE IN TRAFFIC.

The witness also testified t... the Japanese recently establis... on the Island of Formosa a p... for the extraction of morphine f... opium.

Dr. Lambert, in response t... question, said his long experie... in the treatment and observa... of addicts had convinced him t... prohibition has not increased ... use of habit-forming drugs. Ch... man Porter asked:

"What is the effect of addicti... on health?"

The witness answered:

"At first it is taken in sm... doses for a while, and stimula... the sense of personality. Th... it induces sleepiness and inhib... action, causes dreaming and ca... lessness of one's environme... and ultimate results in failure ... eliminate from the body decom... sition products, dodging of ... sponsibility and a desire to ...

JUNE 21, 1929

DOPE IGNORED BY DRY KILLERS, WALKER SAYS

Mayor Tells Prison Keepers Narcotic Traffic Escapes During Volstead Slaughter

Apathy of citizens toward the existing menace of narcotic traffic, while the forces of government are taking little or no acttion against Federal agents for the murder of innocent people on behalf of the Volstead law was denounced last night by Mayor James J. Walker.

He was making the presentation address to the graduating prison keepers of the Department of Justice at New Palm Garden, No. 306 West Fifty-second street.

Mayor Walker got his inspiration from a demonstration of a prison keeper searching a prisoner, during which quantities of narcotics were found cleverly concealed

DOPE vs. VOLSTEADISM.

He recalled the incident as he faced the audience and said:

"That took me back to my legislative days. It reminded m of the time when the splendidly functioning Narcotic Commission was abolished and, at the same time, the paving stones of Volsteadism were permitted to be written into the statutes.

"To me, the peddling of dope is a far greater crime than the selling of liquor, and yet the dope traffic is permitted to go almost unpunished while innocent citizens are being slaughtered for the cause of Volsteadism. Why should such conditions exist?

"When in history has a Federal agent ever shot down a dope peddler?"

In commending the work of the Police Department under Commissioner Whalen, who had preceded him upon the platform, Mayor Walker declared that never in history was crime in New York City under such perfect control.

PRAISES NEW SYSTEM.

Commissioner Whalen commended the re... seven weeks' training ... new prison keepers, ... Commissioner of ... the duties of the ... under the new sys... eration, which has

FRANCES REEV...

TWO AG... and his ... mother, ...

Tuttle Launches Attack on Dope

GOLIATH sets forth in this year of 1930 to slay rum.

David will tackle dope.

Bishop Cannon says $200,000,000 will not be too much to spend on the shield and spear of Goliath.

United States Attorney Tuttle proposes to advance on the national $400,000,000 "dope racket" with a sling-shot in his one Federal Grand Jury and a few smooth pebbles—some trifling thousands of dollars.

It will baffle future historians to understand how the greatest nation of its day seethed and fumed over enforcement of a law which its citizens refused to accept and ignored the ravages of the hideous monster, "DOPE," outlawed by civilization.

Universal applause should greet the declaration of District Attorney Tuttle. Let the Federal District of New York assume national ...ligations. Washington is too busy pursuing ...e phantom ogre of prohibition enforcement.

Tuttle's declaration of war on narcotic ...rugs is a significan... ...ment. He says flatly there were more ... peddler convic... in the Federal peni... last June th... ...lons of any other o... as designated b... ...f Congress.

...he illicit ... ...rugs is increa...

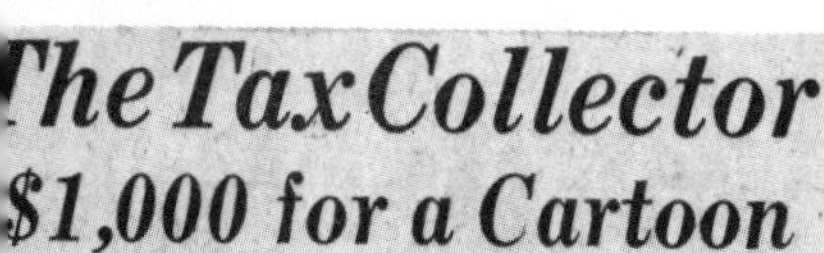

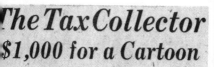

The Tax Collector $1,000 for a Cartoon

Artists of the nation, both professional and amateur, ...re invited last night to compete for a $1,000 prize, ...fered by the Hearst newspapers for the best cartoon ...nception of that figure that makes every ...nerican's life miserable—"The Tax Collector."

1935

...nouncement of the co... was made by Jos... V. Connolly, president of King Features Synd... at a dinner given in the Waldorf-Astoria by the Banshees, a new organization of New York practitioners of the lively arts.

The dinner celebrated the silver jubilee of George McManus's comic strip, "Bringing Up Father," and Connolly commented:

"I hope the prize will stimulate every cartoonist to compete in the creation of a caricature that will represent a figure as UNPOPULAR as "Jiggs" is popular. That figure is The Tax Collector."

Competitors, Connolly said, should submit drawings to King Features Syndicate, 235 E. 45th st., before Dec. 15. The award will be announced before Jan. 1.

Connolly stressed it is the intention to find a character who will become a symbol as typical of The Tax Collector as the Nast figures of Uncle Sam and the Democratic Donkey, the Rollin Kirby Prohibitionist and the Homer Davenport figure of the Corpulent Trust. He explained:

"Let me illustrate the kind of figure I mean by reminding you of certain caricatures that have played such important roles in American life during recent years.

"Most of you will recall the powerful pen of Homer Davenport that drew the obnoxious figure of the Corporation Trusts—a figure that lived until trusts were busted.

"And certainly everyone will recall the last cartoon figure that so brilliantly depicted all the fanaticism of prohibition. That cartoon was drawn by Rollin Kirby of the New York World.

"When the 18th Amendment was finally repealed, our friend and fellow Banshee, Al Smith, wrote Kirby that his creation and the use of it had as much to do with the defeat of the dry law as any agency in the land.

"Today the national bugaboo is not trusts and it is not prohibition. It is—taxes.

"The Hearst newspapers, therefore, offer a prize of $1,000 for the creation of a cartoon figure that will best typify and express a Tax Collector, Grabber or Tax-Eater."

'Dry' in Cartoon

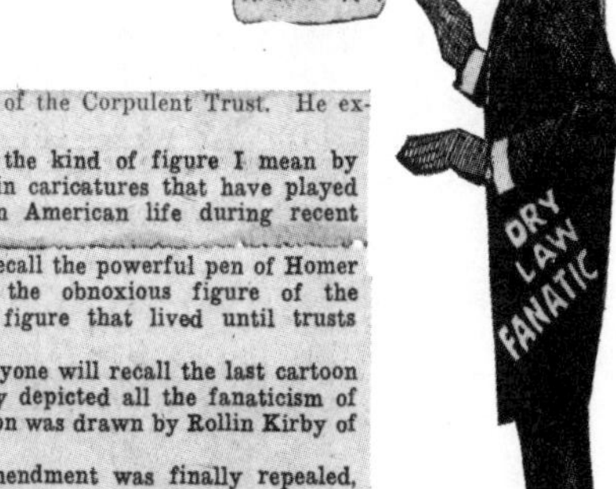

WHY PROHIBITION WAS CAST OUT

Prime Minister Tells Why Prohibition Failed

By IVAR LYKKE,
Prime Minister of Norway.
Written Specially for the Hearst Newspapers.

OSLO, November, 1926.

THE Norwegian people are a fundamen.ally sober people. They rejected prohibition of strong drinks not because they reject the idea of temperance, but because the majority of them had come to believe that the cause of temperance will be served the better without prohibition.

In this they were guided by wholly practical considerations.

If I were to sum up the main reasons which I believe induced the majority of our electorate to vote against prohibition I would say that these were:

FIRST — The conviction that prohibition did not decrease but rather increased drinking; and

SECOND—The realization that to this negative result of prohibition were added many positive evils which seriously affected our national life.

It proved impossible to enforce prohibition if we stayed within such reasonable expenditures that the country could bear them. Illegal distillation and smuggling grew despite everything that the Government could do. The mere fact that strong drink was prohibited made it appear more attractive to many, and especially to our youth. Those who should not have had any drink obtained it just the same, and those who could have had it without harm, but did not in order to obey the law, chafed under the irksome and wholly futile restriction of their personal liberty.

FINALLY—The whole prohibition question had baneful influence on our whole public life.

IVAR LYKKE.

The wholesale violations of the prohibition law created dis- ... This undermined public morality and

COST NORWAY OVER $100,000,00

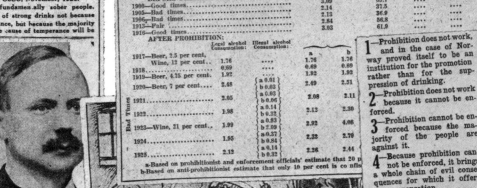

BEFORE PROHIBITION:

	Alcohol consumption per capita liters 100 p. c.:	Arrests for drunkenness in towns per 1,000:	Arrests for all prohibition violations in towns per 1,000:	Homebrewing:	Buying and Selling:	Smuggling:	Total Confiscated liquor, liters:
1900—Good times	3.09	63.7	....	....	....	....	....
1905—Bad times	2.14	37.5	....	....	....	....	....
1906—Bad times	2.13	36.9	....	....	....	....	....
1913—Fair	2.84	56.8	....	....	....	....	....
1916—Good times	3.03	61.9	....	....	....	....	....

AFTER PROHIBITION: (Bad Times: 1921–1924)

	Legal alcohol Consumption:	Illegal alcohol Consumption:	a	b	Buying and Selling:	Smuggling:	Total Confiscated liquor, liters:
1917—Beer, 2.5 per cent,					537	40	....
Wine, 12 per cent.	1.76	....	1.76	1.76	1,063	40	233
1918	0.69	....	0.69	0.69	1,495	186	1,581
1919—Beer, 4.75 per cent.	1.92	....	1.92	1.92	1,637	924	9,099
1920—Beer, 7 per cent.	2.48	a 0.01 / b 0.03	2.49	2.51	1,933	915	17,444
1921	2.05	a 0.03 / b 0.06	2.08	2.11	3,817	No st	94,149
1922	1.98	a 0.14 / b 0.32	2.12	2.30	4,659	1,596	634,183
1923—Wine, 21 per cent.	1.99	a 0.93 / b 2.09	2.92	4.08	4,454	1,600	257,931
1924	1.95	a 0.37 / b 0.84	2.32	2.79	3,953	1,078	95,387
1925	2.12	a 0.14 / b 0.32	2.26	2.44			

a-Based on prohibitionist and enforcement officials' estimate that 20 p...
b-Based on anti-prohibitionist estimate that only 10 per cent is co nfis...

1—Prohibition does not work, and in the case of Norway proved itself to be an institution for the promotion rather than for the suppression of drinking.

2—Prohibition does not work because it cannot be enforced.

3—Prohibition cannot be enforced because the majority of the people are against it.

4—Because prohibition cannot be enforced, it brings a whole chain of evil consequences for which it offers no compensation.

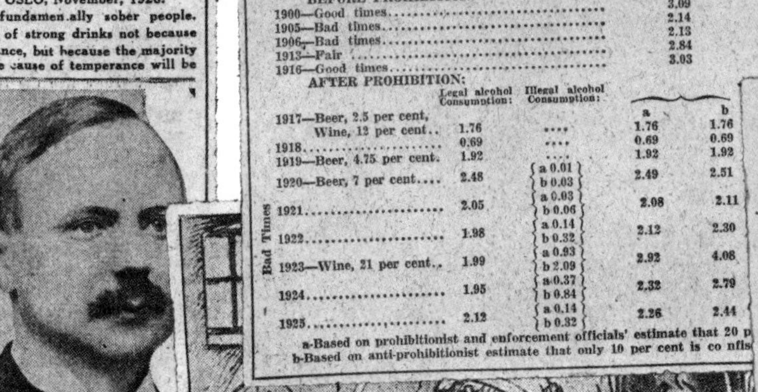

"THE POTATO CROP—PROHIBITIONISTS ARE REAPING A RICH HARVEST."

Vote a Good Thing, Amundsen's View

By ROALD AMUNDSEN,
Famous Polar Explorer.

IT is a good thing to see that people admit they did wrong when they voted for prohibition the last time.

It shows that they are people with common sense.

We all have reason to be satisfied with the results of the referendum.

IN TEN YEARS' TRIAL PEOPLE FOUND IT LED TO WORSE CONDITIONS

PROHIBITION DRIVE STIRS GERMANY

SHALL Germany go the way of America?

Shall the peaceful German "Buerger" be robbed his beer and the German worker of his "Schnapps?"

Shall "Muenchener" become a memory and century- Rhine and Mosel vineyards be turned into potato patches

These and similar questions, sounding more like ind nant protests, are agitating the German press, and the spec of a dry Germany is beginning to haunt the dreams of G man citizens.

For prohibition is becoming a serious issue in Germa and the scoffers scoff no more.

While America was straw-voting overwhelmingly agai prohibition, the German prohibitionists were holding a p vate election of their own in an effort to raise ten milli votes, and with these club the Government and the Reic stag into passing a local option bill as a first step towar making Germany dry. The voting lasted a month, fro March 14 to April 15.

Campaign Is On

An elaborate machinery was set up for the purpose. Homes were swamped with circulars about the disastrous effects of alcohol. Speakers harangued crowds to the same effect.

The prohibitionist press was full of "dry propaganda." And canvassers were visiting every household and every office to gather signatures for local option.

Three factors have converted prohibition from a fad of a few into a national issue:

1—Woman suffrage—because the women are almost solidly for prohibition and it is beginning to be felt here that prohibition must always be regarded as a possibility in countries with woman suffrage.

2—America—because America's startling economic rise, attributed largely to prohibition, the envy of Germany and t main argument of the Germ prohibitionists.

3—The Dawes plan—becau most liquor taxes are pawne as security for the Dawes pa ments, and, since every drin puts that much money into th coffers of the "enemy," abstinenc from drink can be represente as a patriotic duty. That, if ther weren't any liquor taxes, som other taxes would have to serv as pawn does not as a rule effec the first impact of the argument

The Usual Arguments

BERLIN, May, 1926.

MAY 1, 1927

"HOW SWEDEN IS PROMOTING TEMPERANCE"

Under Bratt System Privilege of Buying Intoxicants Is Limited Officially and Denied If Abused—Huge Booze Profits Eliminated

"System Is Unique"

1. The Swedes themselves and foreign observers agree that in its totality this system could not be applied to any other country except Sweden; for it requires a degree of docility and submission to control, an instinctive respect for law, and an impeccable honesty among officials, which are as unique in Sweden as the system itself.

2. The success of the system is still to be proved. It has reduced drunkeness and crime, but smuggling, rum running, home brewing and bootlegging are attendant evils, but nothing like as prevalent as in the United States.

The Swedish system does not undertake to suppress drinking entirely, by force, but seeks to educate the people to voluntary moderation—genuine temperance.

What can be said for the system now is this: It has not made conditions worst than they were before, like prohibition. It has, on the contrary, given to its friends, at least, a basis for the claim that it has improved conditions and has given them the hope that time will accelerate this improvement.

The Swedish system is the creation of one man, Dr. Ivan Bratt, who today, as head and administrator of the whole system, is the "Alcohol Czar" of Sweden, in whose hands lies the responsibility for the sobriety of the nation, and who ultimately apportions to every man, woman and youth in Sweden his or her share of alcohol.

There is no limit to the beer and light wine—including champagne—that you may purchase with your meals. Stronger wines, however—port, sherry, Madeira—are limited to a quarter of a bottle per person, and brandy, whiskey, cognac and similar intoxicants to 7½ centiliters for lunch, 12 to 3 p. m., and 15 centiliters for dinner, any time after 3 p. m. Fifteen centiliters are equivalent to a bottle of whiskey divided among five persons.

The limits are per head, male. Women get just half what the men get.

"No woman has ever protested against this rule, and it prevents men from ordering full portions for the women and then drinking it themselves," Dr. Bratt explains.

results regarding alcohol consumption may be summarized as follows:

Before the Bratt System:	P.C.
1895—economic depression	111
1900—economic boom	130
1913—normal prosperity, beginning of the Bratt System	100
After the Bratt System:	
1918—food shortage, U-boat blockade	25
1920—return to normal condition	84
1922deflation depression	84
1925—returning prosperity	68

'Government, by Putting Poison in Alcohol, Imposes Death Sentence for Misdemeanor'

MAJOR GREEN ANALYZES NEW PROHIBITION CRISIS

"Is Government Committing Murder?" He Asks, and Points Out That Industrial Alcohol Has Been "Poisoned" by European Nations for 50 Years.

By MAJOR WALTON A. GREEN,
ate Chief Prohibition Investigator Under General Andrews.
WASHINGTON, January, 1927.

HERE are the main facts of the denatured alcohol situation as it exists today:

—The Government is putting poisons —principally wood alcohol—into per cent of the pure alcohol made in merica.

—A large proportion of the synthetic liquor sold today is made by bootggers who re-distill their poisonous ixtures to recover the alcohol.

—Many people have died or gone blind by drinking alcohol concocons from which the poison has not een wholly removed.

On these facts—boldly enough stated o satisfy even the extreme wets—a drive is now on to induce he Government to change its policy.

"Terroristic Punishment of Individuals"

Their arguments are somewhat as follows:

—That the Government has no right to put poison into an industrial commodity when a substantial amount of that ommodity is diverted to the bootleg market in such a condition s to poison illicit consumers.

—That the Government's failure to control the diversion of industrial alcohol does not give it the right to poison the roduct.

—That the Government's duty under the Volstead act does not carry with it the right to poison the liquor, which is runk in spite of the law. That this indirect attempt to enorce by terroristic punishment of the individual is an unlawful ssault upon the person; that it is a haphazard, secret and ruel sort of punishment not provided by, or contemplated in, he Volstead act or any other law, and therefore unconstituional and barbarous.

—That in any case, and irrespective of legality or propriety you cannot stop the drinking of the many by poisoning the ew.

"Basic Arguments of the Wets"

These are the basic arguments on which the wets have built their attack and on which they have rung a good many clever changes.

Last Summer, for instance, the Atlantic Monthly carried a prohibition article containing this paragraph:

"At the beginning of the nineteenth century English landowners still placed spring-guns on their private premises to repel or kill trespassers. The courts finally held the landowner in damages, even without a statute. For a century no one with the aid of the law laid traps to kill another, and then the right denied to the landowners was assumed by the Government of the United States. Ten poisoning plants are operated today by the Federal authorities in the city of New York alone for the purpose of poisoning grain alcohol. In 1925 more than 500 of the inhabitants were killed in this way, besides those blinded and otherwise crippled."

"Ten poisoning plants—operated by the Federal authorities" forsooth! Rather hectic language for the usually strained Atlantic. But let it rest for the moment. I it merely as a well written sample of the hundreds of torials in the same vein which have appeared all ov country.

But the high water mark of emotional appeal wa n the poster got out by the "Association Opposed to ibition Amendment." This was a pretty little thing mother and children gathered at a bedside on wh hrouded figure. It carried the headings:

"IS PROHIBITION MURDERING OUR CITIZEN RESULTS—DEATH AND BLINDNESS! THOU SHALT NOT KILL!"

'How Widespread Bribery Is Making Bootlegging Thrive in United States'

By Maj. Walton A. Green

Former Chief U. S. Prohibition Investigator under General Andrews

THERE is no single element of prohibition enforcement which has provoked so much loose talk—founded on so little precise knowledge—as the subject of bribery and corruption.

In the first place, there is both more—and less—bribery than most observers are aware of. More bribery, in the sense that every bottle, every drink, practically every drop of liquor that is consumed today has paid a corrupting toll somewhere along the line. Less bribery, in the sense that the size of the sums paid to individual officials has been grossly exaggerated.

WALTON A. GREEN.

Why is this? To begin with, prohibition lives and has its enforcement being in an atmosphere of corruption. The press, the politicians, the Treasury Department itself are clearing houses for gossip of blackmail and bribery. This man is "wrong," that man may "go wrong," t'other man is "shaking" So and So for ten grand a month, which is the parlance of the sporting world for $10,000 a month.

Nine out of ten of the rumors are untrue. And in the tenth case, the amount involved is probably only a tenth of the sum named.

There is a second reason. It is human nature to aggrandize one's own price in the bribery market. There's many an official who wouldn't take a two-cent stamp corruptly, but who dearly loves to "be approached." It flatters his importance by setting a concrete money price on his job. It truckles to his vanity and self-esteem to go around and say he has turned down thousands and thousands of dollars.

He may not even be tempted, but he likes to play with fire just to prove to himself what an honest Salamander he is. There's nothing unlawful in hearing a hint of a thousand a month and then going out and magnifying it to a definite offer of a hundred thousand!

The official who is new to the job is peculiarly susceptible to this form of flattery. I've heard of subordinates playing up to their new chiefs by this method.

Promptly-Paid Bribery

"Colonel," says the crafty assistant, or secretary, or whatever he may be, "You've got a real he-man's job here. Responsibility—that's what. Why say, Colonel, the Finnigan mob alone would slip you fifty grand a month for just a little forgetting when it comes to withdrawals!"

"Tut, tut, and then tut," says the Colonel. But within a week the worthy soldier is telling his friends how he turned down a hundred one-thousand dollar bills laid upon his desk and then drove the dogs from his office at the point of his good old army pistol.

There is still another reason why bribes are exaggerated. More often than not the bribers don't come through or they come through with only a small part of what they promised. I have read a good many confessions, or talked with men—especially in the Coast Guard—who were taking bribes.

Almost invariably the story is the same. They were promised hundreds, sometimes thousands. But if they let the shipment through on credit—if they failed to collect-on-delivery of each and every case or sack—then the thousands were likely to dwindle to hundreds, and the hundreds to tens.

What I have written holds true of the general run of bribery the country over. I have known of brilliant exceptions, notably among the larger international rings. Some of these mobs have been well organized, owning huge fleets of contact boats, and meeting their bribery obligations—especially to their chartered Coast Guard crews—with reasonable business-like promptness.

The Bill Dwyer gang (requiescat in Atlanta) had a fairly commendable record in this respect. Their pay-off man made his regular weekly rounds with his bribe roll and kept all hands paid up. That is one reason the Dwyer outfit survived as long as it did. The Government men they bribed were inclined to stay bought for a little longer than the usual span of underworld loyalty.

Bribes Exaggerated

The underworld, too, exaggerates the sums involved in bribery. A certain notorious and buffoonish pair of shakedown prohibition agents—the Gold Dust Twins of a sizable city—were reputed to collect three thousand a week for protection from a chain of speakeasies.

It turned out to be nearer three thousand a year. And yet—and here is the point I wish to make—though the net takings of this particular pair were widely exaggerated, there were 500

Continued on Page 6

Liquor, Despite Law

Liquor has come back to stay. Unwholesome liquor—unstandardized, raw, dirty and sometimes poisonous. Liquor which ... and never a beverage. What shall we ... continue to tolerate these con... de facto alliance of ... professional

Definition of Content

... brings us back to modification at the hands ... States, once the inhibitive machinery of Feder... is removed. Permit each State to decide for ... hat alcoholic content constitutes an ... thin the meaning of ...

State Modification

...fication must be under State auspices. Those ... at our Federal Government can follow the ... Canadians, ignore the fact that our Constitu... ible to a degree. We can brea... extra- ...—but we can't bent it. The Cana... provincial ... has no such limitations. ...

Popular Production

... han that, our contraband ... pply is da... dependent upon organi... fessional ... rime against Volstead—... be—has ... he people, who have ... to imitate ... ome scale ... manufac... rural ... mou...

Faked Credentials

And the victims have to stand for it, just as they have to stand for the impostors who prey upon them—ma... ernment ... tials whic... legger, o... frightene... another. ... Societ... crimina... in gene... ful and ...

Speakeasy Victims

In short ... hibition b... extent of ... believable...

The Shakedown Boys

Right here, and to illustrate the ...ral cloudiness in which the prohibition situation has enveloped all ...ses, let me say that there are ... types of blackmail. One is ...gnized as legitimate and the ... is frowned ...

Tall Bribe Stories

If a clever crook wants to show a stupid crook that ' has influ... ence with an official all he has to do is to manoeuvre so that he can be seen in company with h... cial. The second ... dlatel...

From the Bottom Up

No. I take little stock in the stories of big sums to the higher-ups. I've seen too much of the relative ease and cheapness of buying up the little fellows wholesale. ... the little fellows who can ... turn the trick. ... ten ways is ...

Little Crooks Wholesale

I was in a position of some authority and power myself. And I have always felt vaguely hurt and unhappy because no one really tried to bribe me all the time I was there. I came to regard it as a slight upon the power of my office—perhaps a personal reflection. Certainly, I am no more ... looking than the average

DRY ACT AIDS LAWLESSNESS

"My experience with children is that they like to be with older folks; are quick, alert and particularly ... listening to what ... and do. What

impressions are registering on the minds of my sons and daughters when they see thoroughly reputable and successful men and women drinking, talking about their bootleggers, the good "stuff" they get, expressing contempt for the Volstead law, etc. At home we can and do teach temperance in all things; none of our children drink intoxicants, but what ideas are forming in their young and fertile brains with respect to law and order?

XXX AGED IN THE WOOD

'Why the 18th Amendment Will Never Be Repealed'

EXPERT SHOWS THAT MORE THAN 13 STATES ARE READY TO OVERTHROW ANY ACTION

In History of Constitution, What Goes In Never Comes Out; but, Like 15th Amendment, Prohibition Will Be Silently Repealed by Those States That Do Not Want It

By CHARLES WILLIS THOMPSON

THOUGH Senator Borah and Dr. Butler have got the country talking about prohibition more audibly than before their success in that respect is counterbalanced by their failure to get it talking about the thing they talked about. That was not the abstract question of prohibition, but the question whether the Republican Convention of 1928 should declare in favor of repealing the Eighteenth Amendment.

The convention will not so declare. It will recognize that there are several arguments against repealing the amendment, one of which is that it can't be done. It will remain in the Constitution for several reasons, one of which is that it can't be got out. The other reasons may be left for other writers to discuss. The amendment is there to stay. Whether that is desirable or not is not the question. This article is concerned only with the practical aspects of the subject.

Does this mean that we shall always have prohibition? It does not. We have not got prohibition now, and we shall have less and less of it as time goes on. Again, this article is not concerned with whether this is desirable or not; it is concerned only with facts.

What Rainbow-Chasers Think

The reason why the amendment cannot be repealed is not that it would take two-thirds of the Senate and two-thirds of the House to propose a repealer, though that is the fact. It is a good enough reason for me, because it is not conceivable that two-thirds of both houses will ever propose such a thing; but as there are rainbow-chasers who think everything is possible and even likely, it is as well to proceed to the unanswerable reason. That reason is that, after the inconceivable two-thirds majority has been obtained in both Senate House, the repealing amendment will have to be accepte three-fourths of the States.

There are forty-eight States, so thirty-six would ha ratify the amendment. Any thirteen States can kill it. ing out Kentucky and Tennessee for the sake of magnar there are ten Southern States which could not, by the stretch of fancy, be imagined as consenting to rep amendment. The two Carolinas, Alabama, Florida, V Georgia, Mississippi, Louisiana, Arkansas and Texas.

In the North the most intoxicated optimist coul agine Vermont, Maine (the original prohibition Sta sas, Iowa or Nebraska as consenting to repeal.

"Getting Liquor in Maine"

It is of no use to say that you can get liq States; you could get liquor in Maine all through six years that have passed since she put prohi statute books. Those States would never cons for the simple reason that any public man wh the repealer through would go back to private go back by the votes of citizens who themselve on the sly, but he would go back.

Of course, this limited list does not be the real number of States whose ears are c ject. It does not include California, origin which has discovered that the Eighteenth biggest thing for the Golden State since turned up at Sutter's mill in 1848.

It does not include Ohio, originally w exorably voting down every proposal to asier for the thirsty.

It does not include Indiana. the Eighteenth Amendm howls from India eal enforcem

In fact, it many as three ote for the efy the blud Anti-Saloon L Methodist Board nce and Morals, rogeny. For it wo he people who w he decision; it wou egislatures, and ures consist of pol ach one of whom has istrict a watchful and

Prohibition Special

Signs of the Times

Saloon

Crime

BEER WINE WINE

Whiskey

LIGHT WINES AND BEERS BUT NO SALOONS

COMMON SENSE

BREAK DOWN PROHIBITION

G.P. WILLIAMS

142,965 Votes For Light Wine And Beer Show U.S. Sentiment

WILL SAVINGS, INSURANCE, SOCIAL SECURITY & PENSIONS be paid off in EVER-SHRINKING DONKEY DOLLARS OR BY HONEST, FULL-VALUE DOLLARS UNDER A REPUBLICAN ADMINISTRATION

DONKEY DOLLAR

WESTERN UNION TELEGRAM

Underwood HENRY FORD

Alcohol Injures Body, Ability, and Wages affirms HENRY FORD, one of the greatest captains of industry the world has ever known.

ANY thinking person knows that Prohibition is a good thing. The on[ly q]uestion is one of enforcement. The present law is the kind [w]hich accomplishes the purposes for which it was enac[ted if pr]operly enforced. When I say I am for Prohibi[tion, of co]urse, I am for the Volstead Act too. That is

...enforce this law, and can not in any other ...army and navy? Prohibition is a part of ...uch ought to have the benefit of every ...y.

...possibly assimilate more than a very ...y one day, and it gets that amount ...distillery. More than that amount ...ability to work, and ...mention the...

Vol. 53 No. 21 MAY 25, 1926

WESTERN UNION TELEGRAM

BILLY SUNDAY

ECCLESIASTICAL "WETS"

The opponents of Prohibition may be classified under four heads:

1. Those whose "god is their belly," whose appetite for booze renders void any appreciation of the physical, moral, and economic effects of alcohol.

2. The brewers, distillers, saloon keepers, bartenders, *et cetera*, whose love for "filthy lucre" transcends all other interests; who are happy fattening off the carcasses of their fellows.

3. Those who are generally "against" laws and regulations of nearly every sort; who believe that the country should be "wide open," and every man a law unto himself.

4. Those who by church connection are affiliated with a denomination whose traditional policy has always favored "the bowl."

B.

[Und]erwood

Two of the leaders of the Anti-Saloon League, F. Scott McBride and Wayne B. Wheeler.

ENEMIES of LIQUOR

Left: Hon. Louis C. Cramton of Michigan, one of the most able "dry" leaders in Congress. He has been mentioned as the probable successor to Andrew Volstead in the House. Both Houses of Congress are overwhelmingly "dry" at present, and there is no chance whatsoever that their attitude will undergo a change.

Below: Gen. S. D. Butler of the Marine Corps (right), who haled Col. Alexander Williams (left) before an Army Court Martial on charges of intoxication. Williams was convicted. This act took great moral courage on Butler's part. He is to be congratulated on his adherence to law and order.

Right: During the recent debate on Prohibition before a Congressional Committee, delegates of the Women's Law Enforcement League stormed the Capitol with petitions. Here are but a fraction of the women who pleaded with the Committee not to modify the Volstead Act, but instead to put more teeth in the law. The women of the land, save for a handful of wanton flappers and booze ad-

I LOVE MY BILLY SUNDAY BUT OH YOU SATURDAY NIGHT

Left: A group of five hundred women from the Women's Law Enforcement League who called on President Calvin Coolidge in connection with the Senate Prohibition hearing. They were given a cordial reception, too, for the President is "all fours" for Prohibition. He is against booze both because of family tradition and because of individual conviction. He knows that the drinking of alcohol is a foe to the health, the prosperity, and the morals of the nation. The "wets" will have to get Mr. Coolidge out of the White House before they will get the President's signature to booze bills.

Shall We ENFORCE *or* REPEAL?

A keen analysis of the factors involved in the Prohibition question

International Photo

A narcotic layout as seized from an addict by Federal agents. Because drug addicts ...many shall we repeal the anti-

Rising Resentment Against EVILS of Prohibition Should Arouse Moral Elements to Action

JULY 31, 1927

ADVOCATE GES U. S. TO GHTEN LAW'

mits There Is Not Com- Prohibition; Sees Rem- in Strict Enforcement

g but draw salaries, and oon they are forgotten.

's what will happen to pro- . People will violate the law, won't arrest, juries won't and it will be a dead letter. always will drink and the law make much difference.

ourse it's nullification. Why low about nullification of the h amendment? How about ation of the tax laws and of e laws?

s are not higher than the There's nothing mysterious- ed about them. The people lves can repeal any law with- help of legislatures by ignor-

"DON'T OBEY LAW."

eighteenthe amendment is just erless to prevent drinking as eenth was to give negroes full se equality.

'll get rid of prohibition if we bey it.

en the Volstead act was in October, 1919, over the veto President, only a minority of ters had voted dry. A ma- had voted wet. In the past rs this wet majority has been ing astonishingly. It is con- that 66 per cent of the popu- now is wet.

strength of the prohibition ent was in the rural districts. the product of an isolated life arrow surroundings. In the t came as a direct and deadly o personal freedom.

ny who never cared for in- ting drinks resented the inva- f personal rights by fanatics ad forced their own views on communities by means of al statutes. They began to because they felt they had imposed on.

L COST MILLIONS.

ery effort has been made to en- prohibition. Between drinks, lane have protested their al- ce to the law. Taxpayers spent tens of millions of dol- n a vain effort to break down pirit of the people and make subservient to obnoxious sta- But the people remain stead- n defiance of the law."

his initial assault on Darrow's sophy, Wheeler said:

. Darrow openly advocates few wets really believe— ly, that prohibition of the bev- liquor traffic is detrimental to ublic welfare.

very moderate drinker runs the of becoming an excessive er, a risk that far outweighs leasure that comes from flirting a dangerous habit.

e beverage liquor traffic has had the standing in decent ty which Mr. Darrow has un- essfully tried to give it for years. est friends always have been getic about it. It was King ol—a name well chosen, be- he was the enemy to all—that cracy stands for.

EELER PAINTS RUM EVILS.

ooze undermined the national h through a century, until 13.8 ons out of each 1,000 died year- Over 300,000 of these deaths needless. When booze was shed, with its plague-laden th, the death-rate dropped and

Wet and Dry Champions

CLARENCE DARROW. WAYNE B. WHEELER.

natural resources, with potential national wealth unequalled by any other nation, the increasing army of paupers and dependents created by booze became an intolerable burden on America.

"Booze entere dinto the factories and the shops. Production slowed down. Accidents multiplied. Billions of dollars were needlessly added to the costs of manufacture, decreasing the purchasing power of the people. It paid labor the smallest percentage of its earnings of any industry. It fomented strikes and lost them. It was the agent provocateur of the labor movement.

"CORRUPTED POLITICS."

"Insurance companies looked askance on those who made booze a comrade. Welfare societies and philanthropists denounced it as the creator of poverty. Few human beings were without complaint against it for wrongs done their families, their friends or their business.

"In politics, booze was the centre of corruption. Brewers and liquor dealers sought to dominate the Government, to dictate legislation and the control of the judiciary. The freedom of the p... was fought by booze. The ba... was stuffed by its minions.

Wheeler 'Brains' of Drys; Darrow Liberal Lawyer

CLARENCE DARROW, champion of the wets in last night's debate, is an outstanding American lawyer.

He came into particular prominence as defense counsel in the Leopold-Loeb case in Chicago, and later as chief of defense for John Thomas Scopes in the Dayton, Tenn., "evolution trial" in which his opponent was William Jennings Bryan. He also figured in many other important cases.

Wayne B. Wheeler, defending the dry cause, is general counsel for the Anti-Saloon League of America. He began temperance work as a college student in Ohio. From field secretary he became superintendent of the Ohio Anti-Saloon League, and eventually was made general counsel of the national organization.

He has prosecuted more than 2,000 cases of prohibition violation and directed the legislative campaigns of the league. For years he has been the admitted spokesman of the organization.

strong for national prohibition it never would have been ratified by the legislatures of 46 out of 48 states. Fewer than 200 state senators in thirteen States could have prevented ratification, yet our opponents talk about minorities putting it over. If so, then a majority ...

BONE DRY

HELP END Prohibition

JOIN The Crusaders

100 EAST 42 ST. NEW YORK

415 MERRITT BLDG. LOS ANGELES

College Paper Describes Dry Law as 'Standing Joke'

ANSTON, Ill., Feb. 21.—The Daily Northwestern, student publication of Northwestern University, n editorial today attacked prohibition, terming it a "standing ..."

nominationally, Northwestern is thodist Episcopal seat of learn- The student paper's condem- on of conditions under prohibition now called a "dismal failure," first expression it has ever lished on the subject.

editorial says:

"The youth of the present day is sing an attitude of the greatest tempt for government, while amendment breathes a dare to most law-abiding citizen.

"When the sovereignty of a government becomes an ob- of ridicule, the institution it- begins to totter. Life is no ger sacred, and a seething hell earth results.

"Our law-makers drink while y make laws, and some of the ults are obvious. The revenue nts confiscate booze, and drink on the spot * * * even our iges drink up the evidence, ile policemen sit in saloons when y should be on their beats.

"As far as imbibing goes, people drinking about as much as r. The only difference is that y drink poison, for which they ruinous prices.

"Graft has been perfected until assumes a well-nigh legitimate pect.

"There are hundreds of men ooked enough to sell their honor standard prices.

"We can trace all this to the ccess of a group of hysterical omen who lobbied a law, through few weak, pussyfooting men. It is easier to get liquor in ashington than in any other ...

was killed in Ontario, beer stock went up like a rocket.

QUOTES SUPREME COURT.

"The New York City Health De- ...

1926

74.8 % WET

THREE TO ONE: In the 1926 referendum in New York State there were 1,763,070 votes against the Volstead Act and 598,484 votes in favor of it. That is, New York State voted three to one against Prohibition in its present form.

Thinkers Debate What to Do with Prohibition

18th Amendment Must Go—du Pont

'Millions in Taxes Turned Over to Bootleggers'

General Motors Head Praises Ford Car as Aid to Workers; Finds Dry Law Failure.

ONE of the great figures in American economics is Pierre Samuel duPont, chairman of the board of directors of E. I. duPont de Nemours Company. He is likewise chairman of the board of the General Motors Company.

In the ever shifting world of commerce, where new leaders occasionally arise over night and impinge themselves on the national scene, duPont is unique—in that he springs from old American stock.

With such a heritage, one noteworthy for its patriotic zeal and enterprise, he is in a particular way qualified to envision the changing America which is just around the corner.

At the request of this newspaper, he consented to give out the views he holds upon problems that confront this nation today.

Favors State Rights

DuPont is stanchly in favor of State rights and State duties in the face of what many regard as the steady encroachment of the Federal Government.

For example, he would blot out the debated Eighteenth Amendment, and in that matter go back to the Constitution as drafted by the founders of the Republic. In that stand, he speaks as the student of political economy, as well as the "Big Business" executive.

Where he might be expected to decry the genius of Henry Ford (since the Ford Company and General Motors are business rivals), duPont made this astonishing statement:

"If I should be asked which had done more for the welfare of the workingman, Ford or prohibition, I would choose Ford."

DuPont's reference to Ford was made spontaneously in the course of his frank discussion of the prohibition question. He had received the New York American representatives in his New York office in the General Motors Building. In reply to a question concerning his views on prohibition, he said:

"The question of prohibition is one of the most important things the country has before it. In my opinion, there is only one way to settle it—the Eighteenth Amendment must come out of the Constitution must come out of the Constitution. How that is to be done is more than I can see at present."

Du Pont was then asked:

"Do you regard it as economic question or one of personal liberty?"

He replied:

"Fundamentally, the problem is more than a question of personal liberty. The amendment simply has no place in the Consttiution. It is opposed to our whole theory of government. If we can have this Eighteenth Amendment, we can have a similar twentieth and thirtieth. Then we might as well be dead, because we will

PIERRE S. DU PONT, Chairman of the Board General Motors Corporation.

Any Change in Volstead Law By Congress Should Be Made In Behalf of True Temperance

laws even before the Eighteenth Amendment was adopted. But Mr. Hearst added that it was clearly within the power of Congress to repeal the Volstead law and substitute another law defining what drinks were intoxicating. Mr. Hearst's letter concluded

The Hearst newspapers approach the discussion of prohibition as a temperance organization. For forty years before the adoption of the Eighteenth Amendment the Hearst newspapers led the fight in this country against whiskey and hard liquors, against the saloon and against all causes and phases of intemperance.

Prohibition has had over six years' trial. It has aroused a great deal of dissatisfaction among perfectly honest, decent, "God-fearing" people. If that dissatisfaction increases, there is no question that the Volstead act will be amended.

If it is amended, it should be amended in the interest of temperance, by the representatives of people who believe in temperance, and whose only opposition to prohibition as at present practised is that it does not encourage temperance.

WILLIAM RANDOLPH HEARST.

If it is amended, it should be amended in the interest of temperance by the representatives of people who believe in temperance, and whose only opposition to prohibition as at present practiced is that it does not encourage temperance.

W. R. Hearst

In an autograph letter to the editors of all his papers five years ago, Mr. Hearst pointed out that the repeal of the Eighteenth Amendment was probably impossible because three-fourths of the Congress districts in the whole country were dry under local option or prohibitory.

Prohibition Poll Favors Volstead Modification

Is Whiskey Medicine or Not?

By DAMON RUNYON.

INDIANAPOLIS, July 30.—Neighbor, would you use liquor to save the life of a loved one?

I mean even if the use thereof was a violation of the law?

The answer probably is, you bet your boots you would. I know it is mine.

Th question really seems fatuous, yet it started a lot of jawing this way and that here in Indiana not long ago when it came out that Governor Ed Jackson, the man who had the horse, and Attorney General Arthur L. Gilliom had both used liquor under the circumstances I mention, and thus, apparently, violated the state law.

In Indiana, such is the stringency of the state dry law, which is a sort of legal right cross behind the left ... Volstead Act, that the ...

"You were then in precisely the same situation as my wife and I were in just a year earlier, when whiskey was prescribed in the cases of three of our children who lay at death's door for many weeks, while suffering from ty-

from one day to the ... friend, the Rev. E. S. ... D.D., State Superintend- ... Indiana Anti-Saloon ... a man never needs a ... his life, which proves ... that the Reverend did ... drinking.

...ns Played Safe

... an old story now, this ... overnor and the attor- ...

PRESIDENT HADLEY OF YALE SAID: "When the people, as a body, are of an orderly and law abiding disposition, and the methods of government are defective, it is often more important to focus public opinion on these defects and correct them, than to try to persuade the nation to accept laws which do not have public opinion behind them."

CALVIN COOLIDGE SAID: "In a republic the law reflects rather than makes the standard of conduct. The attempt to dragoon the body when the need is to convince the soul, will end only in revolt."

SENATOR BORAH: "The issue is one which cannot be met by modification of the Volstead Act. It is perfectly clear that that which is demanded can be secured only in one of two ways, either by repeal of the Eighteenth Amendment or its complete and shameless violation, its utter nullification. That is the issue."

Prohibition Ballot

1—Are you in favor of the existing prohibition law? ....YES ☐ NO ☐

2—Are you in favor of modification of the Volstead act to permit the manufacture and sale of beer and light wines?...YES NO

NOVEMBER 5, 1926.

STATE DRY LAW REMAINS

LIQUOR POISONING MUST GO ON!--

BAUMES LAW VALID, SUPREME CO

U.S. BEGINS DOUBLING POISON

CZAR OF DRYS TELLS MELLON LAW DICTATES DRUGGED RUM

JANUARY 1, 1927.

Use of Denaturants in Alcohol "Must Continue Until Safe Substitute Is Found"

"Deliberate Murder," Is Cry of Congressmen as Manhattan Toll of Death Grows to 41

Developments in the poison rum scandal yesterday:

1—Wayne B. Wheeler, head of the Anti-Saloon League, served an ultimatum on Secretary of the Treasury Mellon that poisoning of alcohol must continue.

2—Dr. Douglas Symmers, director of laboratories of Bellevue and Allied Hospitals, asserted 4 per cent wood alcohol contained in Mellon's new formula sufficient to induce total blindness after three drinks.

3—Total deaths from poisoned alcohol in Manhattan since Christmas jumped to forty-one.

4—Three more Governors of States denounced use of poison in alcohol by Federal Government.

5—Many Congress Representatives characterized poisoning of alcohol as attempt at deliberate murder.

6—Methodist Board of Temperance, Prohibition and Public Morals predicted 1927 drier than 1926 and declares liquor influx checked.

By M. L. RAMSAY,
Universal Service Staff Correspondent.

WASHINGTON, Dec. 31.—Wayne B. Wheeler, general counsel and chief lobbyist of the Anti-Saloon League, today served a virtual ultimatum on Secretary Mellon that poisoning of alcohol must continue.

NEW FORMULA SENT OUT TO DISTILLERS BY GOVERNMENT

Only Mellon's Choice of Proposed Non-Deadly Compound Will Alter Drastic Order

Nation Awaits Senate Session Tomorrow When Edwards Is to Fight for Wide Inquiry

High spots in the poison rum scandal yesterday:

1—Mellon's modification of poison alcohol order has not gone into effect. Double dose of wood alcohol, amounting to 4 per cent, will be injected in year's supply of 50,000,000 gallons.

2—Government officials estimate 25 per cent of the 69,000,000 gallons of poison alcohol output of 1926 is available and one-fourth of this will find its way into the hands of bootleggers.

3—Seventeen of the twenty-four Congress Representatives from New York City and Long Island denounce use of poison denaturant in alcohol. Others not heard from.

4—Poison booze claims one more victim in Manhattan, bringing death total since Christmas to forty-two. Doctors predict many others in next twenty-four hours.

5—Wayne B. Wheeler, head of Anti-Saloon League, declares new poison formula less dangerous than old.

6—Congressman Emanuel Celler, Brooklyn, will introduce bill giving physicians right to prescribe all alcoholic liquor they consider necessary for medicinal purposes.

DRUGS IN DRINK DESTROY SIGHT

Effects of the noxious chemicals placed in alcohol were revealed yesterday by Dr. Herman Wortmann, of Munsch and Protzman, chemical specialists. Regarding the effects of diethylpthalate, pyridine and other denaturants, he said:

"It is the cumulative effect that is harm... turants. ... they are ... but befo... paralysis ... often blis...

"It is ... tain the e... kill. How... denaturan... minute ... called bo...

If You Drink It, Here's Good Way to Fight Death

DECEMBER 28, 1926

"WHAT to do until the doctor comes," has taken on a new significance in these prohibition days of liquor containing ...

Congress Anger High at Liquor Drug Plan

La Guardia Calls It Deliberat...

POISON LIQUOR DEATHS JUMP TO 23 IN CITY

...y Hooch Toll More Than ...bles Itself, with 73 Suf...rs Still in Bellevue

...uring the Christmas season, ...g the year's total in Hamilton ... to forty-four. Albany reported ...eaths during the holiday sea... ...d a total of nearly 100 for the ... One is dead and three believed ...dying at San Antonio, Tex. ...the New York City liquor vic... one of whom was a woman, ...were examined yesterday in ...vue morgue who died in the ...ious twelve hours, and two new ...hs were reported for Kings ...ntyl and one for Queens. ...rohibition directors and adminis...tors will be directed to make a ...rching inquiry into the source of ... poisoned liquor here and else...ere, it was reported from Washington last night. This order goes ...gton last night. ...

SEIZED LIQUO... FOUND DEAD...

...proximately 99 per cent ... liquor seized by prohi... ...s in Greater New York d... ...ast month was found, ...is, to contain denature...

...52 per cent of this was f... ...ain completely denatured ...hich contains wood alc... ...ich is poisonous when ta... ...ink. The total amount ...onfiscated during this ...98 gallons.

Figures were given out ... Major Chester P. M... prohibition administra... ...e wished again, in view ...er of deaths resulting fr... ...rinking, to warn peo... ...nbibing "genuine st... ...he boat." He added: ...tgers often get the d... ...lcohol from those wh... ...on permits authorizin... ...e it for commercial pu... It is not meant to b... ...mpletely denatured a... ...sold on such permits." ...charge made by Chi... ...miner Norris that th... ...s really responsible f... hooch, Mills said: ...evidently spoke with ...ideration of what he... ...nment doesn't sell or ...ed alcohol to ...

CHEMIST TESTS FOR POISON FAIL

...alth Commissioner Harris broad... ...mphatic warning yesterday to ...ork drinkers to place no trust ...ical analyses of holiday ...

LETHAL ADULTERATION NOT NEEDED, LAWMAKER STATES

N. Y. Congre... Will ... Death ... ments

Dr. William I. Sirovich intends to continue his fight to stop the Government from poisoning citizens of the United States.

The representative in Congress from the Island of Manhattan, in an interview with the New York American, announced he will move to delete all appropriations for poisonous denaturants of alcohol.

At his offices, No. 539 East Sixth street, the Congressman declared:

"My philosophy may be summarized as follows: If drinking is only a misdemeanor I do not believe it should be punished by blindness or death."

Dr. Sirovich revealed that thousands of dollars have been appropriated by Congress for poisonous denaturants. Instead of these den... turants he would have harml... ones used. Such denaturants as ... recommends would make "boot... liquor unpalatable and unpotable, ... stated. Representative Sirovich ... tinued:

Total Abstainer

Alcoholic Cows Find U.S.A. Has Gone Arid!

The REAL DOPE

SEVERE INJURY May follow drinking of these small POISONS even in these small quantities

FORMALDEHYDE	1%
PYRIDINE	1%
DIETHYLPHTHLATE	1%
WOOD ALCOHOL	½ of 1%
BICHLORIDE	$\frac{1}{10}$ % 1%

PRESCRIPTION LIBERTY URGED

By Universal Service.

WASHINGTON, Jan. 1.—An amendment to the Volstead law giving physicians freedom to prescribe all the alcoholic liquor they believe nec...essary for medical purpose... for in a bill ... Celler... introd... announ...

"It ... vinous ... medical ... to quan... should ...

SCIENCE USED IN DRIVE UPON BOOTLEGGERS

New Compound Non-Poisonous, but 'a Little' Wood Alcohol Will Continue as Weapon

I'M SURPRISED TO SEE YOU IN THIS BUSINESS—JOHN!
ENGLAND
OPIUM
POISON LIQUOR

BRITISH POT; AMERICAN KETTLE

SEVENTY WERE POISONED BY EATING ICE CREAM.

ATE ICE CREAM AND FELL DEAD.

WHEELER RULES ALCOHOL

...56; Columbu... ace June 1), 3; ... burg, Pa., 6; Detro... ngeles, 30; Minneapolis, ... 23, and Pittsburgh, 130.

...LER'S WORDS "FALSE".

STILL TO USE POISON.

Wood alcohol, which is poisonous, will continue to be used in small ... with these non-poisonous ... the periodic at... on this and ...ficials declared. ...hol intended for ... be denatured, ...reventing its use ...

... W, SAD EBB.

...n't know how other Senators ...is murderous activity on ...of the Treasury Depart... ...my thought is that ...

TELLS OF DRUGS.

Dr. Norris said that in its effort to make alcohol unfit to drink the Government doctored it with such poisons as pyridine, diethylphthalate, formaline and bichloride. It was these poisons, Dr. Norris contended, ... bootlegger was unable to ...

...CORD BEATEN.

...new deaths, bringing the ... 23, overtop by five ...

WHERE GUILT BELONGS.

In a statement accompanying his bill, Celler declared:

"The guilt for the slaughter of thousands of ... should be on ... member of ... heed the ... rom poison ... roughout

POISON.

... liquor is poison, Dr. Nor-... because the bootlegger is ... the poison from ... puts ...

LAW'S END PREDICTED.

"Mr. Wheeler must know the law, but in consonance with every policy practiced by the Anti-Saloon League, he persists in propagandizing the country with false statements and misleading information in his dying effort to bolster up support for a law which has already been condemned and which I now predict will not be on the statute books of this count... two years hence."

Referring to Uncle Sam ... of the Mortician's ...

OVERWHELMIN
VOTE AGAIN
THE EVILS
PROHIBITION

Government Will Use Noxious Oil to Spoil Whiskey

4,000,000 Gallons of Poison Liquor on Market

JANUARY 3 1927

DEATH IN BOTTLES!

XXX
BOOTLEG
BOOZE
POISON

'Mr. Hearst Exposes the Anti-Saloon League'
An Editorial from Yesterday's New York Evening Post

Poisoning a Vile Way to Temperance

JULY 12 1927

DRY LEAGUE CLUTCHES AT U.S. JUDIC...

Dictatorship by Anti-Saloon League Should Go the Way of the KLAN

CONGRESS OPENS WAR TODAY ON POISON RUM

5 of 9 Drinks, Scotch Label, Hold Pyridine

Startling Result of Analyses by Reputable Chemist for N. Y. American.

Seventeen samples, taken from Manhattan's flowing fountains of booze, have just been analyzed for

WAYNE B. WHEELER

BOTH HOUSES TO GET BILLS ENDING DRUGS IN ALCOHOL

Hearst Papers' Suggestion Results in Resolutions by Britten and Senator Edwards

City Medical Chief Believes Publicity Given Poisoning Has Saved Many Lives Here

High spots in the poison booze scandal yesterday were:

1—Measures will be introduced in House and Senate at instance of New York American and other Hearst newspapers ordering the Secretary of the Treasury to stop the use of poison denaturants.

2—Publicity of poison in local liquor supply credited with low mortality list for New Year's celebration. Two new deaths were reported.

3—Seventeen samples of liquor bought in New York City and analyzed for the New York American showed all of synthetic origin. Five of nine samples of Scotch contained pyridine, another wood alcohol and another diethylphthalate—"government poison."

4—Recapitulation of death toll in eighteen States shows 2,903 were killed by poison booze in 1926.

What Do the Churches Think Now of Wayne B. Wheeler?

The Anti-Saloon League of America
Legal Department
Wayne B. Wheeler
General Counsel and Legislative Superintendent
30 Bliss Bldg., Washington, D. C.

EDWARD B. DUNFORD
ASSISTANT

TELEPHO...
OFFICE
...

March the 15th, 1927.

Dear Superintendent:

The Civil Service Commission is making up the list of QUALIFICATIONS FOR PROHIBITION AGENTS and other officers. I do not think they have included as yet the qualification that the agent or officer MUST BE IN SYMPATHY WITH THE LAW HE IS TO ENFORCE.

... in many parts of the country.

PLEASE ATTEND TO THIS AT ONCE as it will affect the attitude of more than 2,000 agents for years to come.

Yours cordially,

W B Wheeler

WBW:le

Prohibition's Death T

U.S. INFLICTS DEATH PE

Innocent Citizens Shot Do

DRY LAW ENFORCEMENT

FANATICISM

1360 VICTIMS

WITH APOLOGIES WINSOR McCAY

ARKANSAS—35

ARKANSAS COUNTY (DeWitt, county seat)

Cecil LaCotts, alleged moonshiner, killed by John H. Hopper, prohibition agent and Roy Sis...

HEMPSTEAD COUNTY (Washington, county seat)

W. H. Goff, deputy sheriff, killed by Oscar Robison, service station operator, November 5, ...

...1928.

L. E. Storey, alleged bootlegger, killed by Marion C. Burns, prohibition agent and State officers, names unknown, December 21, 1924.

Total Craighead County—2.

CRITTENDEN COUNTY (Marion county seat)

Lee Prudman, negro, alleged moonshiner, killed by Charles F. Cooley and R. N. Wilson, prohibition agents, about January 9, 1928.

MISSISSIPPI COUNTY (Blytheville, county seat)

Joe W. Carter, alleged moonshiner, killed by party of prohibition agents, including S. M. Gurley, Theo E. Burnes, Ben L. Goode, and Austin G. Sutterfield, February 7, 1925.

Total Mississippi County—1.

MONROE COUNTY (Clarendon, county seat)

Eugene R. Thompson, farmer, killed by county officers, names ...

ARIZONA—9

... COUNTY (Tombstone, county seat)

... Osborn, killed by William ...ett, Deputy Sheriff, January ... 1922.

... Parker, border immigration ...an, killed by persons unknown, alleged rum runners, July ...

Total Pima County—1.

SANTA CRUZ COUNTY (Nogales, county seat)

Claude Butler, soldier, killed by P. B. Doolittle, Customs Inspector, March 31, 1928.

Damion Marquez, laborer, killed by Carson Morrow, Border Patrol ...

COLORADO—23

BOULDER COUNTY (Boulder, county seat)

Person unknown, occupation unknown, killed by State range...

...person unknown, May 10, 1929, reported by Denver City Club.

Total Jefferson County—1.

LAS ANIMAS COUNTY (Trinidad, county seat)

James Moore, special officer, killed by Mrs. Mary Gembrin or Oresto Flor, alleged bootleggers, March 19, 1922.

Total Las Animas County—1.

...4, 1927.

Total Teller County—2.

WELD COUNTY (Creeley, county seat).

Innocruza Riggerto, occupation unknown, killed by Federal or county officers, names unknown, June 23, 1921.

Total Weld County—1.

TOTAL COLORADO—23.

CONNECTICUT—3

GEORGIA

I. S. Hughes, deputy sheriff, killed by persons unknown, alleged moonshiners, April 1, 1925.

Carl Stewart, alleged bootlegger, ...

1928.

Perle S. Thomas, traveling salesman, killed by Prohibition Agents Brownlee, Gourley and others, ...

MANATEE COUNTY (Bradenton, county seat).

Negro, name unknown, a... bootlegger, killed by J. E. ...doin, deputy sheriff, April 15, ...

Total Manatee County—1.

ORANGE COUNTY (Orla... county seat).

Harry Givens, alleged bootl... killed by Lloyd J. Gay, prohi... agent, September 4, 1922.

Total Orange County—1.

PASCO COUNTY— (Dade ... county seat)

Preston Overstreet, killed ...

BARROW COUNTY (Win... county seat)

Jesse Morgan, filling s... proprietor, killed by Ike Hal... liceman, October 16, 1928.

Total Barrow County—1.

BIBB COUNTY (Macon county seat)

James Courson, high school boy, killed in collision with prohibition agent's car, September 15, 1929.

Tommie Thompson, policeman, killed by negro, name unknown, alleged bootlegger, 1922.

Harry Green, deputy sheriff, killed by John Howell, alleged bootlegger, May 16, 1925.

Total Bibb County—3.

BURKE COUNTY (Waynesboro, county seat)

A. P. Peake, alleged rum runner, killed by sheriff's posse, names unknown, September 14, 1921.

agent, killed by J. W. Buchanan, farmer, December 9, 1926.

Walter C. Mobray, prohibition ...

P. C. Calhoun, occupation unknown, killed by A. D. Mikell, policeman, 1924.

Person unknown, killed by A. D. Mikell, policeman, date of slaying unknown.

Total Chatham County—2.

COLUMBIA COUNTY (Appling, county seat)

Walter R. Tolbert, prohibition agent, killed by Burley Adams, farmer, February 22, 1928.

'Shotgun' T...

Prohibition enforcement fatalities, a... by the Washington Herald's nation-wide ...

ALABAMA	75	IOWA	
ARIZONA	9	KANSAS	
ARKANSAS	35	KENTUCKY	
CALIFORNIA	29	LOUISIANA	
COLORADO	23	MAINE	
CONNECTICUT	3	MARYLAND	
DELAWARE	1	MASSACHUS...	
DIST. COLUMBIA	7	MICHIGAN	
FLORIDA	47	MINNESOTA	
GEORGIA	105	MISSISSIPPI	
IDAHO	8	MISSOURI	
ILLINOIS	39	MONTANA	
INDIANA	23		

OREGON—17

Non-Combata...

Let the bootlegger take ... which includes twenty women ... years of age. The exemptio... ...ted as in civilized warfare...

Killers Escape Punishment

Instances in which anyone pays a penalty for prohibition ... rare.

...learned that two deputy sheriffs were ... was supposed to be trans... ...ad to warn him and ... started on one of the ... concludes his report of ... intention was to shoot ...d."

... shooting by officers ... cent bystanders have ...

Indisputable Evidence in List

The names, the dates, and the places of prohibition killings are submitted as the indisputable evidence. The list is by no means complete. The Washington Herald ... included only the authenticated ...

Killing ...

...rnment should ... should not tak... ...spicion. ...olesale killing ...s a part of ...

1,360 Sent t...

...ates DOES im...

...0 MEN, WOM... THEIR GRAV... ...FORCE PROHI...

...s bad as that. ... children killed were no... ...n shot down. ... women certainly should ... the men, of whom man... been killed.

Government Imitating Crime

IT DOES IMITATE THEM.

It sends men out on the highways ... guilty of killing, merely on ... about their business ...

Official... somebody i... yachts may ...

There is ... put into the ... Government ... their lawful b...

WOMEN, CHILDREN AND MANY INNOCENT MEN SHOT DOWN MERELY ON RUM SUSPICION

DRY LAW ENFORCEMENT

1360 VICTIMS

ALTAR OF PROHIBITION

Dry Law Kil... Listed by S...

Below is a tabulat... of nation-wide dry k... due to shotgun enforc... since the Prohibition went into effect.

CALIFORNIA—29

...EDA COUNTY (Oakland, county seat)

...ge Hamilton Wentworth, ...ition agent, killed by Bur... ...urchill Morris, alleged bootlegger, November 24, 1926.

...ill Churchill Morris, alleged ...ger, killed by George Hamilton Wentworth, prohibition agent, November 23, 1926.

Total Alameda County—2.

...ner, killed by E. J. Ellis, U. S. Coast Guard, October 6, 1928.

E. P. Ingmire, oil company official, killed in collision with car of raiding party headed by Prohibition Agent George H. Hudson, April 7, 1927.

A. H. Hendricks, occupation unknown, killed by customs officer, name unknown, January 8, 192...

Sam Faulkner, negro youth, killed by M. B. Sheffield, negro policeman, April 24, 1927.

James W. Doran, negro chau...

RICHMOND COUNTY (Rockingham, county seat)

W. D. Smith, constable, killed ...

...uty, names unknown, about 1924.

Total Wilson County—2.

TOTAL NORTH CAROLINA—36.

NO. DAKOTA—1

BOTTINEAU COUNTY (Bottineau, county seat)

Alleged rum runner, name unknown, killed by sheriff, name unknown, 1924, reported by coroner.

Total Bottineau County—1.

TOTAL NORTH DAKOTA—1.

OHIO—49

ASHLAND COUNTY (Ashland, ...

officer, killed in automobile wreck ...

OKLAHOMA—32

ALFALFA COUNTY (Cherokee, county seat)

Clark Richards, farmer, killed by Earl Gould, deputy sheriff, or R. W. Kimmell, under sheriff, January 22, 1928.

Total Alfalfa County—1.

CADDO COUNTY (Anadarko, county seat)

——— Hensley, farmer, killed by Grover Beatty, deputy sheriff, 1922.

Total Caddo County—1.

CARTER COUNTY (Ardmore, ...

killed by Charles ... farmer, October 28, 1920.

Stanton E. Weiss, pr... agent, killed by Charles ...dler, farmer, October 28, 1920.

Charles Chandler, farmer, killed by Claude Tyler, deputy sheriff, October 28, 1920.

Eddie Cook, farmer, killed by deputy sheriff, name unknown, date of slaying unknown, reported by coroner.

Total Logan County—4.

LOVE COUNTY (Marietta county seat)

...er, killed by ... June 6, 1921.

...er, killed himself after killing Sheriff C. M. Kendall and Rev. Roy Healy June 20, 1922.

Tital Linn County—3.

MARION COUNTY (Salem, county seat)

John Kambouris, farmer, killed ...

... agent, June ...

C. H. Neal, pol... from hemorrhage ... counter with George ... November 28, 1921.

Lee La Due, oc... known, killed by off... known, September ... ported by coroner.

Total Yamhill C...

TOTAL ORE...

PEN'S'LV'NIA-24

ALLEGHENY COUNTY (Pittsburgh, county seat)

Henry Davenport, constable, killed by persons unknown, occupation unknown, December 12, 1926.

Total Allegheny County—1.

BEAVER COUNTY ...

...shiner, killed by ... alias John A. D... former for prohib... cember 22, 1923.

Total Lehigh ...

PHILADELPHIA ...adelphia, ...

CEMETERY

1360 VICTIMS OF SHOT GUN PROHIBITION

WELL DONE THOU GOOD AND FAITHFUL SERVANT.

FANATICAL DRY LAW ENFORCER

INTOLERANT DRY

WINSOR McCAY

...known, killed by James F. Du... county prohibition officer, Mar... 11, 1927.

Total San Bernardino County—...

SAN LUIS OBISPO COUNTY (San Luis Obispo, county seat)

Jose Villegas, alleged bootlegger, killed by Robert L. Knig... prohibition agent, July 14, 192...

Total San Luis Obispo County—1.

SHASTA COUNTY (Redding ...

Total Butler County—8.

CUYAHOGA COUNTY (Cleveland, county seat)

Clifford M. Munz, salesman, killed by Leonard Weeden, police sergeant, October 3, 1921.

Carl Metta, deputy marshal, killed by Sebastano Russo, alleged bootlegger, February 19, 1923.

Joe Maloponty, laborer, killed by John Jones and Horace Jenkins, policemen, October 11, 1923.

Matteo Veltry, prohibition agent, killed by persons unknown, alleged bootleggers, March 1, 1921.

John McCoy, deputy constable, killed by Frank Risler, mill worker, May, 1926.

John Snyder, policeman, killed by Vincenzo Comparro, mill worker, January, 1923.

Vincenzo Comparo, mill worker, executed for death of John Snyder, policeman, 1923.

...town marshal, May 14, 1927.

Total Grant County—1.

GREER COUNTY (Mangum, county seat)

"Bud" Riley, alleged bootlegger, killed by Delford David Dougherty, prohibition agent, and Claude Hines, policeman, March 28, 1921.

Total Greer County—1.

HUGHES COUNTY (Holdenville, county seat)

POTTAWATOMIE COUNTY (Tecumseh county seat)

James C. Harris, farmer, killed by Jeff B. Harris, member of raiding party headed by W. W. Thomason, prohibition agent, July 4, 1929.

Oscar Lowery, farmer, killed by Jeff B. Harris, member of raiding party headed by W. W. Thomason, prohibition agent, July 4, 1929.

Total Pottawatomie County—2.

...W. La Flower, lumber... ...y Neil Merrill, dep... April 23, 1927.

...n County—1.

...ANGELES COUNTY (Los Angeles, county seat)

...F. Brinnegar, policeman, ...y W. F. Beard, alleged ...ger, September 29, 1926.

...Beard, alleged bootlegger, ...John F. Brinnegar, po...

INDIANA COUNTY ...

Felix Verone, miner, killed by J. A. Craft, deputy sheriff, April 30, 1927.

Total Indiana County—1.

LANCASTER COUNTY (Lancaster, county seat)

Walter Deker, alleged ... killed himself aft... Special Officer Knapp, ...

Total Wayne County—2.

YORK COUNTY (York, county ...

DRY LAW ENFORCEMENT

1550 VIC...

DRY ZEALOT

FANATIC

1550

...ver 34,500 in Ten Years

...Y TO ENFORCE DRY LAW

...n Ruthless Warfare

TEXAS—114

Lon Walker, farmer, ...

...alker, alleged boot... by deputy sheriffs, ...

BEXAR COUNTY (San Antonio, county seat)

Frank ... Clark, border patrol inspector, killed by Eualilio Aguil... and —— Salvador, alleged bootleggers, December 13, 1924.

John W. Parrott, customs officer, killed by persons unknown, occupation unknown, January 7, 1927.

Stephen S. Dawson, customs officer, killed by persons unknown, occupation unknown, Ferbruary 28, 1928.

Harold G. Halstead, occupation unknown, killed by customs officer, name unknown, Mach 29, 1920.

Jesus Castaneda, occupation unknown, killed by customs officer, name unknown, April 30, 1924.

Mrs. C. ...ndavase, occupation unknown, killed by customs officer, name unknown, September 11, 1924.

Cruz Penales, occupation unknown, killed by customs officer, name unknown, March 30, 1927.

Natividad Rodriquez, occupation unknown, killed by customs officer, name unknown, June 5, 1929.

Thomas Morris, customs inspector, killed by alleged rum runner, name unknown, December 23, 1928.

Two alleged rum smugglers, names unknown, killed by U. S. border patrolmen, names unknown, July 23, 1929.

Ivan E. Scotten, border patrolman, killed by alleged rum smugglers, names unknown, July 20, 1929.

Charles A. Wood, U. S. narcotic agent, killed by alleged rum smugglers, names unknown, March 22, ...

...ion in U. S.

...otal of 1,360 in the United States, were ...among the individual States as follows:

...	23	SOUTH CAROLINA	33
...	3	SOUTH DAKOTA	6
...PSHIRE	0	TENNESSEE	72
...EY	20	TEXAS	114
...CO	11	UTAH	3
...	50	VERMONT	3
...ROLINA	36	VIRGINIA	73
...KOTA	1	WASHINGTON	23
...	49	WEST VIRGINIA	49
...	32	WISCONSIN	12
...	17	WYOMING	12
...ANIA	24		
...AND	2	TOTAL	1,360

...in County—3.

...OUNTY (Loudon, ...

Persons unknown, occupation unknown, killed by customs officer, name unknown, April 29, ...

John Lott, farmer, killed by prohibition agent, name unknown, 1926.

Total Covington County —1.

DE SOTA COUNTY (Hernando, county seat)

...

Geronimo Garcia, alleged rum smuggler, killed by U. S. customs inspectors and State rangers under command of W. L. Wright, captain, December 18, 1922.

Silvando Gracios, alleged rum smuggler, killed by U. S. customs inspectors and State rangers under command of W. L. Wright, captain, December 18, 1922.

Total Jim Hogg County—6.

KNOX COUNTY (Benjamin, county seat)

...Brightman, occupation un... by D. D. Collins, ... December 24, ...

WEBB COUNTY (Laredo, county seat)

Person unknown, alleged rum smuggler, killed by U. S. Customs officers, names unknown, about 1925, reported by sheriff.

C. Sata, laborer, killed by persons unknown, date of slaying unknown, reported by sheriff.

Robert Rumsey, U. S. Customs inspector, killed by five Mexicans, names unknown, alleged rum smugglers, August 19, 1922.

Crescencio Oliveda, occupation unknown, killed by U. S. Customs inspectors, names unknown, April 1, 1920.

Vincente Aguilai, occupation un...

...

...Painter, alleged moonshiner, killed by Federal and county officers, names unknown, September, 1926.

John King Grant, alleged moonshiner, killed by officers, names unknown, July, 1924.

Total Rains County—2.

ROBERTSON COUNTY (Frank-...

VIRGINIA—73

ALLEGHANY COUNTY (Covington, county seat)

Ten persons, names unknown, killed, no details, reported by coroner.

Total Alleghany County—10.

HENRICO COUNTY (Richmond, county seat)

Charles Gaines, laborer, killed in automobile wreck fleeing from officers, names unknown, October 21, 1925.

...

Total Campbell County—1.

DICKINSON COUNTY (Clintwood, county seat)

Arlett Kiser, alleged moonshiner, killed by John W. Smith, prohibition agent, February 22, 1922.

Total Dickinson County—1.

DINWIDDIE COUNTY (Dinwiddie, county seat)

Will Stafford, no details, recorded in Congressional Record.

Total Dinwiddie County—1.

ELIZABETH CITY COUNTY (Hampton, county seat)

William White, negro, laborer, ...

(Christiansburg, county seat)

Andrew Robinson, negro, laborer, killed by Robert Graham, State prohibitio officer, August 4, 1926.

Charles Burks, negro, laborer, killed by Charles Nixon, sheriff, August 20, 1928.

Total Montgomery County—2.

NORFOLK COUNTY (Portsmouth, county seat)

Howard H. Fisher, prohibition agent, killed by James Chambers, occupation unknown, July 22, 1922.

Gary D. Freeman, prohibition agent, killed by James Chambers, occupation unknown, July 22, 1922.

...

CHELEN COUNTY (Wenatchee, county seat)

Ludwig P. Johnson, prohibition agent, killed in gun battle with Pete Wheeler, sheriff, and Ralph Hand, deputy sheriff, July 25, 1929.

Total Chelen County—1.

CLARK COUNTY (Vancouver, ...

...

John Lisk, alias John Lusk, alleged moonshiner, killed by Andrew F. Sadler, prohibition agent, June 10, 1925.

Tom Wilson, alleged pilot for rum runners, killed by Walter A. Reinders, deputy sheriff, September 21, 1929.

Horatio W. Thompson, alleged rum runner, killed by Seaman Martecela, United States Coast Guard, December 5, 1922.

Frank Martin, ... killed by Leo Sow... Fitzgerald, deputy ... 9, 1924.

Total King Count...

OKANOGAN COU... ...ogan, county ...

Benton Werner, ... runner, killed by ... sheriff, November 2... Paul Antoine, In... ...ed by B. T. McC... ...e 22, 1929.

Total Okanogan ...

PIERCE COUNT... county s...

William Harvey T... ...ition agent, kill... ...rbonne, policem...

...

Total Skamania ...

SPOKANE COUN... county s...

Frank Franchi, b... by James Adams, p... June 9, 1928.

Total Spokane C...

WHATCOM COUN... ...ham, county ...

J. P. Chatfield, ... killed by Alfred A... pation unknown, J...

Total Whatcom C...

TOTAL WASH... STATE—...

WEST VIRGINA—49

BOONE COUNTY (Madison, ...

...

...UNDING DEATH TOLL ...PROHIBITION REVEALED ...Y WASHINGTON HERALD

...wspaper Survey Throughout Nation ... Ghastly Record of Killings ... Due to Attempts to Enforce ...th Amendment Since 1920

...w York American publishes the first of a series of ...marizing the results of a nation-wide survey made ...on Herald, a Hearst newspaper, into prohibition ...ties during nearly ten years of national prohibition, ...has revealed many startling facts hitherto unpub... ...conducted by Cole E. Morgan, for many years a ...erald staff and an accredited Washington corre... ...earst newspapers. Five and one-half months have ...is exhaustive research that has undertaken to go ...and city in the United States. The second ...e astounding revelations will appear in next ...

...opyright, 1929, by Washington Herald.

WASHINGTON, Nov. 30.

...NDRED AND SIXTY men, women and chil... ...graves!

...t the toll of a foreign massacre, but a record ...pts to force the Eighteenth Amendment on ...ited States.

...riod of almost ten years since national pro... ...y on January 16, 1920.

...ot include ... resulting ...eking en... ...l citizens ...vers—the ... the dry ... perhaps ...aths in ...dry law ...t which ... out.

Records Open To Inspection

WASHINGTON, Nov. 30.

THE official reports and other records on which the Washington Herald bases the assertion that the prohibition enforcement death toll exceeds 1,300 are open to the inspection of any interested official, organization or person who may wish to verify the accuracy of any statement made in this series of articles.

Transcripts of these records will be filed with Congress and the President's Law Enforcement Commission.

...n!

...e been ... the ...ose in ... prohi... ...rectly

Raiders Cause Sick Girl's Death

...hteen-year-old girl in West Virginia was critically ...oid fever when Federal and State officers came in. ...bent on finding liquor and did not hesitate to search ...mattress and pillows of the sickbed. The girl ...elapse and died.

...pectant mothers are included on the list of victims. ...child and the other died with a bullet wound in ...

...it a prohibition agent is under indictment for ... It is charged that he ran down with his patrol ...and daughter who were out in a pleasure launch ...drowned without an attempt being made to ...

...r-old boy was "accidentally" shot by police ...Vegas, Nevada. They explained they were ...tires of an automobile driven by the boy's ...

...women were killed in an explosion following ...made this very frank state...

Bootlegger and Hijacker

...otlegger kills those that interfere with his bootleg... ...hijacker, when he holds up the bootlegger on the ...his illegal merchandise, kills the bootlegger if ...

...teer kills at random those ... ...e that interfere ...

Stray Bullets Add to Toll

...g in going over the cases in detail to find how ...tims have been killed "accidentally"—that is, ...

A New Death Penalty

...hat bootlegging is a crime. It does not say ...hall be DEATH.

...nment of the United States in its attempt at ...prohibition law, inflicts death, not merely ...otlegging, but as a penalty for BEING SUS... ...TLEGGING.

...s of crime developed in this era of bootleg... ...r and whiskey racketeering, use murder as ...

...April 26, 1926.

...McKinley County—2.

...ERO COUNTY (Alamagordo, county seat)

...avid M. Orr, alleged rum ...ner, killed by Howard S. ...acham, prohibition agent, De...mber 15, 1924.

Total Otero County—1.

TOTAL NEW MEXICO—11.

...2364, November 29, 1928.

Total Niagara County—5

ONEIDA COUNTY (Utica, county seat)

Charles Kammerlohr, sheriff, killed by Isidore Comisky and Nathan Denmark, alleged rum runners, July 8, 1921.

Total Oneida County—1.

ONONDAGA COUNTY (Syracuse, county seat)

Bruno Nisico, alleged bootlegger, killed by James M. Stapleton, prohibition agent, October 31, 1921.

...officers.

...cupation unknown, October 9, 1926.

Ernest Lavrey, iron foundry worker, killed by H. H. Whitham and E. F. Watrous, customs inspectors, November 14, 1929.

Total St. Lawrence County—3.

SUFFOLK COUNTY (Riverhead, county seat)

Three unidentified men, no details, recorded in Congressional ...

...posse, name unknown, 1928.

Total Perry County—4.

PIKE COUNTY (Pikesville, county seat).

Lewis Casebolt, deputy sheriff, killed by —— Adams, alleged moonshiner, October, 1926.

—— Adams, alleged moonshiner, killed by deputy sheriff's posse, names unknown, October, 1926.

Frank Phillips, deputy sheriff, killed by Sylvan and Roland Branham, miners, April, 1927.

Roy May, alleged bootlegger, killed by Mat Sanders, deputy ...

...

Ralph Macrese, owner of soft drink establishment, killed by James R. Murtagh and Loren R. Collins, prohibition agents, June 24, 1924.

Robert Killian, occupation unknown, killed by Patrick M. Needham, prohibition agent, May 9, 1925.

Wallace J. Burns, laborer, drowned while fleeing from two ...

MAINE—1

...ND—12

NEW YORK—50

ALBANY COUNTY (Albany, county seat)

Irving Washburn, prohibition agent, killed by Joseph Zuillo, occupation unknown, July 13, 1928.

Total Albany County—1.

CHAUTAUQUA County (Mayville, county seat)

Connelly Hill, alleged rum runner, drowned while fleeing from State troopers, names unknown, May 23, 1927.

James Simpson, alleged rum runner, drowned while fleeing from State troopers, name unknown, May 23, 1927.

Total Chautauqua County—2.

CLINTON COUNTY (Plattsburg, county seat)

John L. Brissette, occupation unknown, ...

Daniel J. Maloney, policeman, ...

...

Owen Boyle, printer, killed by Francis P. Dugan, policeman, October 6, 1925.

Albert Duffy, police lieutenant, burned to death by explosion of still alleged to have been owned by Carmine Pizza, his wife, Julia, and Alexander and John Bruno ...

...special police officer, killed by C. W. Stewart and his son, Elmer Stewart, alleged moonshiners, July 29, 1924.

Sam Lilly, prohibition agent, killed by C. W. Stewart and Elmer Stewart, alleged moonshiners, July 29, 1924.

...county seat)

—— Willoughby, negro, farmer, killed by Sheriff Miles and deputies, names unknown, 1921.

Negro, name unknown, killed by prohibition agents, names unknown, 1926, reported by sheriff.

...by B. B. Upchurch, deputy sheriff, July 7, 1927.

Total Wayne County—1.

WHITLEY COUNTY (Williamsburg, county seat)

George Clark, alleged rum runner, killed by Roy W. Easley, pro...

...smugglers, ... 1927.

...e County—21.

...MICHIGAN—44.

...Carthage. ...

...ion agent, ...n, farmer, ...

...—1.

...Greenwood. ...

...s unknown, ...ficers, 1928, reported by chief of police.

Total LeFlore County—2.

MADISON COUNTY (Canton, county seat)

...

...eak for Killings

...1931, by the Washington Herald.)

...ON, Feb. 1.—The record of the years ...orcement killings shows 1929 to have ...ording to the compilation of 1,550 cas... ...he Washington Herald for the eleven ...o 1930, inclusive. The figures provide ...teresting study. They follow:

Civ.	Tot.
40	60
75	113
67	111
66	99
106	148
97	146
79	116
97	153
87	128
110	169
62	127
170	18[illegible]
1,056	1,550

...a Count—2.

...INNESOTA—1...

...sheriff, May ...

...oun County—1...

Death Toll of 'Shot Gun' Enforcement Mounts to 1,550 for Volstead Era

FEBRUARY 1, 1931

190 Sacrificed on Dry Altar Since December, 1929; Killings Nation-Wide, and Not Confined to Any One Area, Survey Shows

By COLE E. MORGAN.

(Copyright, 1931, by the Washington Herald)

WASHINGTON, Jan. 31.—Prohibition's shotgun enforcement death toll is mounting daily!

During the past year of 1930, deaths to the number of 190 have been added to the rapidly increasing list of human lives ...violence in the vain attempt to dry up this coun... ...month!

...

MASSACHUSETTS—4...

MIDDLESEX COUNTY (Cambridge, county seat)

John M. Mulcahy, prohibition ...

...by Eddie Boga... agent, June 12, 19...

...ARFORD COUN... county ...

...awrence Wenge... Prohibition ... Ford and Stev... 1924.

John Bungore, ... by Joseph ... prohibition agent, ...

Total Harford Co...

...NCE GEORG... Upper Marlboro, ...

...Total Prince Geo...

...MARY'S COU... town, count...

...Total St. Mary's ...

...SHINGTON C... ...erstown, cou...

...unter R. Stott ...t, killed by Re... painter and u... 26, 1927.

...otal Washingto...

TOTAL MARY...

The Voice of the People Making Itself Heard in Mighty Beer-For-Taxation Parade

MAY 15, 1932

Tennis Queen Wants Bootlegger To Drown in Flood of Legal Beer

DECEMBER 31, 1931

Player Doesn't Drink, But Finds Dry Law Not a Success.

Copyright, 1931, by International News Service.

SAN FRANCISCO, Dec. 30 (INS).—"The bootlegger ought to be drowned in national beer."

Thus Helen Wills Moody, tennis queen, summed up her views on prohibition today as she unpacked from a two months' journey to the Orient with her husband, Frederick Moody, San Francisco broker. She said:

"I don't touch anything myself, you know. But I don't think it is fair for the bootlegger to get all the money he does when so many others are in want. He pays no taxes, either. And look at the graft and corruption.

"It seems to me the whole thing is all wrong. Prohibition is wonderful. But it seemingly can't be made a success, so why not try to remedy it?

"People who drink beer are a happy people, aren't they?"

Mrs. Moody said prohibition was one of the things she "thought about while she was on the boat." She also wrote what she called "A New Year's Realization," proving herself author and philosopher in less than 200 words. She explained:

"I was just toying away and struck upon the idea of a New Year's realization instead of the proverbial New Year's resolution."

Here is what "little poker face" wrote:

Helen Wills Moody's New Year's Realization

TELLS DRY VIEWS—Helen Wills Moody, who thinks prohibition "wonderful," but realizes it is a failure, would have "national beer."

MILLION SPECTATORS CHEER 100,000 BEER-TAX MARCHERS

Continued from First Page.

the afternoon, got under way at 6:25 p. m.

Mayor Walker reached 79th st., the starting point, fifteen minutes before the colorful procession started, anw was greeted by prolonged cheering and shouts of:

"Seabury should see this!"

"Jimmy for President!"

A squad of mounted policemen was in the van. They were followed by parade officials, and the Department of Sanitation band.

mobile and from there watched the marchers.

After reviewing the marchers for half an hour, the Mayor left to go to his home to change his clothes before atending the dinner of the Anvil Chorus, an association of Brooklyn newspapermen, in the Hotel Astor.

At 8:30 o'clock, just as it was growing dark, the Mayor returned to 45th st. and Fifth ave. to watch for a few moments more the seemingly endless array of marchers.

BIG DAY FOR WALKER.

Protesting the 18th Blunder

By Arthur ('Bugs') Baer

The only reason we didn't march in New York's beer for taxation parade today was there was no room for our number ten dancing slippers.

One hundred thousand citizens packed Fifth ave. from curb to curb in a thundering protest against the eighteenth blunder of the constitution.

Has the worm turned? Brother, that ain't no worm. One hundred thousand people is a boa constrictor.

In addition to the ankle excursionists there were floats, trucks, blimps, airplanes, horses, motorcycles and anything that a man could cover ground on.

It was the voice of the people whether you have cotton in your ears or not.

And strangely enough, it was one of those warm May days when a glass of beer would have come in handier than snow shoes in the Alps.

when they got to the given point they were looking around for a philanthropist to donate 'em another point.

There was only one dry spy in the malt procession. They spotted him easily. He was walking on his heels instead of his toes.

You have got to hand New Yorkers credit. They are good paraders. They train for it looking for seats in the subway.

It was an inspiring sight. Plenty of music. The only time the olympic cavalcade stalled was when the Army band played the Navy's music. The boys stopped marching to go into a clog waltz.

The official music was "How Dry I Am." Next in popularity was the Wetting March from Beethoven's Hofbrau.

After this demonstration, no wets will have to write to their Congressman. The smart old Congressman will start writing

THE HIGH COMMAND—Mayor Walker, Mrs. William Randolph Hearst, marshal of the women's divisions, and Grand Marshal Daniel conferring just before the City's biggest parade began.

Associated Press Photos.

A FIGHTING ISSUE—That's what yesterday's beer-f taxation parade involved, so what more natural than t Gene Tunney should participate. He is shown (right) w a friend in a horse-drawn carriage. Picture from Inte tional News Photograph Service.

DECEMBER 22, 1932

3.2 P. C. Beer Bill Passes House, 230 to 165; Senate Will Act After Holidays, with Victory Predicted

PLANS TEMPORARY CONTROL.

The main problems the President and the experts will study include:

1—Temporary regulations to remain in force until Congress enacts permanent legislation.

2—Recommendations for hard liquor taxes. Experts generally agree the Internal Revenue levy will be between \$2 and \$3 a gallon. This is expected to raise \$400,000,000 the first year and eventually \$1,000,000,000 annually and balance the Federal budget.

3—Continuance of the liquor embargo and the enactment of tariffs to protect the domestic producers of grain and manufacturers of liquor.

4—An effective method of preventing smuggling from Canada, Mexico and Cuba.

5—An enforcement policy to protect dry States from a flood of liquor from wet States.

Prohibition Is Undermining Moral Character of Nation

TWENTY-FIVE HUNDRED Episcopal ministers, answering a questionnaire sent out by the National Episcopal Church Temperance Society, signified their dissatisfaction with the working of the ...

ing in such a way as to imperil the foundations of the Republic. The moral character of the nation is being undermined.

Anyone whose eyes are open can see this undermining process. He can see nation-wide disregard of the fundamental law of the land, imbedded in the Constitution, because ... of the people believe ... ment has no right ... their personal habi...

W. R. Hearst Urges U. S. Liquor Control To Abolish 'Dry' Evil

LOS ANGELES, Nov. 2.—Advocating "a temperance plan to supplant prohibition," Mr. William Randolph Hearst was the guest speaker this evening on the nationally famous Collier's Radio Hour. Speaking from KFI the Earle C. ... this city Mr. Hearst ...

Passage of Beer Bill To Bring State Drive On All Speakeasies

MARCH 27, 1933

Closing Will Be Sought to Prevent Illegal Competition.

TO FIGHT FOR BARS

Date for Sale Indefinite as Licenses Must First Be Issued.

Beer No Longer Contraband Here, Medalie Rules

Although the Federal ban against alcoholic beer will not be lifted until April 7, beer is no longer considered contraband in New York by the Government's prosecuting officials.

Following the statement Satur-

How Beer Bill Affects States

WASHINGTON, Mar. 14 (US).—Beer can be sold in 23 States 15 days after the beer bill is passed by the Senate and signed by the President.

Its sale can be legalized in 14 additional States by legislative action repealing or amending existing State dry laws.

In 11 States it will require amendment of the State constitutions.

The States without prohibitory laws, where the sale can start without delay, are:

Arizona, California, Colorado, Connecticut, Delaware, Illinois, Indiana, Louisiana, Maryland, Massachusetts, Michigan, Minnesota, Missouri, Montana, Nevada, New Mexico, New Jersey, New York, Oregon, Pennsylvania, Rhode Island, Washington and Wisconsin.

The States dry by State statute are:

Alabama, Arkansas, Georgia, Iowa, Mississippi, New Hampshire, North Carolina, North Dakota, Ohio, South Carolina, Tennessee, Texas, Vermont and Virginia.

The constitutionally dry States are:

Florida, Idaho, Kansas, Kentucky, Maine, Nebraska, Oklahoma, South Dakota, Utah, West Virginia and Wyoming.

NOVEMBER 9, 1933

As State Leader; Roosevelt Plan. New Liquor Laws as Repeal Wi

President to Draft Regulations Pending Action by Congress.

TO CUT INCOME TAX

La Guardia to Make Charter Revision One of First Tasks

Tammany Head Bl Chairman for Rou City Election.

WAR FOR CONT

MARCH 15, 1933

House Passes Beer Bill; Vote Is 316 to 97; U.S. Arrests J.W. Harriman in Bank Loss; Markets Open Today; 1,000 Banks Resume

APRIL 8, 1933

Rush for Beer Exhausts First Day's Supply; U.S. Will Fight Bootlegging

1,500,000 Barrels Day's Estimate of Delivery in Nation.

$7,500,000 TAXES

Brewers Fear National Shortage Within Ten Days.

Lehman's Beer Compromise Plan Fails at Parley

By WILLIAM E. LAWBY, N. Y. American Staff Correspondent.

ALBANY, April 7.—Governor Lehman and the Republican legislative leaders tonight disagreed in his latest move to ...

Breweries Here Have Plenty; Can't Deliver Fast Enough.

15,000 LICENSED

City Takes in $175,000; Health Dept. to Raid

PRACTICING FOR REPEAL ERA

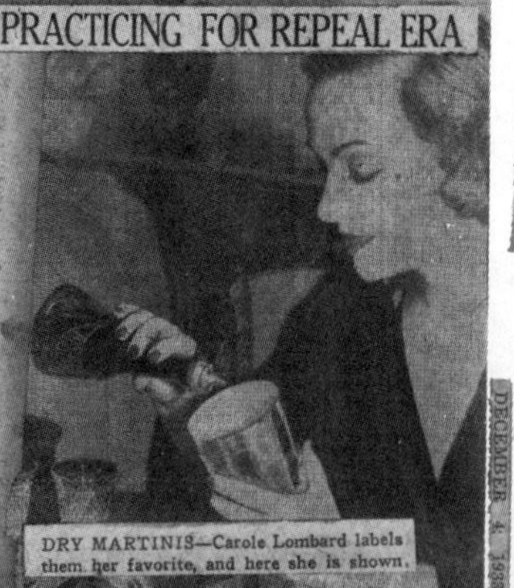

DRY MARTINIS—Carole Lombard labels them her favorite, and here she is shown,

Drug Stores Entitled to Sell Liquor for 'Off Premise' Use

66. No retail licensee for off premises consumption shall make or cause to be made ... tration fee of $10 ...

Liquor Sold to Be Take Must Be Kept in Origin

59. No retail licensee for off consumption shall keep ... licensed premises ... brand of li... permitted ...

Retail Places Close to Churches And Schools Not Permissible

72. No retail license for on premises consumption shall be granted for any premises which ... same street ...

73. No retail licen... premises consumption ... granted except where ... ises, in the judgment of ... are being condu...

Retailers Can Be Licens For 'Off Premise' Consu

RETAIL LICENSE FOR OFF PREMISES CONSUMPTION.

A license may be issued to retail for off premises consumption for: ...

45. Only ... granted t... partnershi... ety or joi... liquors a... off premi...

Wholesalers Must Supply List Of Household Purchasers

23. No wholesaler shall be engaged in any other business on the premises to be licensed.

24. ... gran...

nership, corporati... joint stock compan... and/or wines at w...

25. No wholesale...

Dealers Restricted to Use Of Own or Registered Tru

... No wholesaler shall deliver ... and/or wines, except ... and operated ... or hired and ... wholesaler from ... sportation com... State ...

persons without ... gether with a sc... the names of th... whom such liqu... purchased, their ... ness and the am... involved in such ...

Distiller's License Will Permit Manufacture of Wines Also

4. A Distiller's License may be issued for:

(a) Manufacturing LIQUORS, which shall also include the privilege of selling, at wholesale, liquors ...

any liquors and/or wine... case may be, to any per... is not duly licensed ... State Board to sell li... wines at wholesale ...

Rules Keep Manufactur Separate from Wholesa

...istiller shall be inter... ...tly or indirectly, in any ...here liquors, wines, or ...anufactured ...

licensee, a... sign, print... otherwise.

DECEMBER 4, 1933

Distillers Must List Brands Of All Products for Board

13. Each distiller shall file with the State Board, at Albany, within ten (10) days after the granting of a license, a verified list of the various brands of liquors or wines manufactured by such distiller. No new brands shall be manufactured or offered for sale by such distiller until he shall have filed ...

14 ... mon... Boar... the ... calen... upon ... the S... tain ...

LIQUOR STORES NOT PERMITTE TO ENGAGE IN OTHER BUSINES

Something More than Beer is back
Beer is back! In those three simple words a great American industry goes back to work. Hands long idle find new jobs. Faces empty of hope brighten to a new promise. Thousands upon thousands find honorable livelihood. A vast American market—a new frontier of industry reopens,—bringing sorely needed business to farmers, transportation and to hundreds of other industries. And with it, a new fountain head of tax revenue arises to add its dol- ly to a nation in need.
Beer is back! But is that all? No! To cheer, to quicken American life with hospitality of old, the friendly glass of good-fellowship is back. Sociability and good living return to their own, once more to mingle with memories and sentiments of yesterday. America looks forward —and feels better.... *Beer is back!* Yes! But much more than that. Beer at its *best* is back—the brew that everybody knew best—the king of bottled beers that outsold any other bottled beer on earth.
BUDWEISER IS BACK
Anheuser-Busch • St. Louis
HISTORIC REMINDERS
1917
December 18TH - Eighteenth amendment submitted to states by Congress.
1919
June 30TH - War Time Prohibition Law to conserve grain becomes effective.
October 28TH - Volstead act to enforce eighteenth amendment passed over veto of President Wilson.
1920
January 17TH - Eighteenth amendment goes into effect.
1929
March 2ND - Jones Law making more drastic penalties for violations of Volstead act approved by President Coolidge.
1931
January 20TH - President Hoover sends Congress Wickersham report, majority of commission advocating revision.
1932
June 30TH - Democratic National Convention adopts outright repeal platform. Franklin D. Roosevelt supporting it in his acceptance speech.
November 8TH - People of twelve states vote in favor of repeal.
1933
February 20TH - House adopts Senate prohibition repeal amendment, putting question up to states.
March 22ND - President Roosevelt signs 3.2 beer bill.
November 7TH - Ratification of twenty-first amendment assured.
Nation Is in Revolt at So Much Snooping and Spying
What Farce, What Spectacles, What Tragedy in Prohibition!
Drinking by School Children Shows Futility of Prohibition
AMERICA WELCOMES
Budweiser
KING OF BOTTLED BEER
1876
1933
Text of Amendment Creating Prohibition
ARTICLE XVIII
Liquor Prohibition Amendment
This amendment was proposed to the Legislatures of the several states by the Sixty-fifth Congress, December 18, 1917. On January 29, 1919, the United States Secretary of State proclaimed its adoption by 36 States and declared it in effect on January 16, 1920.
The total votes in the Senates of the various States was 1310 for; 237 against—84.6 per cent dry. In the lower houses of the States the vote was 3,782 for; 1,035 against—78.5 dry.
The amendment ultimately was adopted by all the States except Connecticut and Rhode Island.
1—After one year from the ratification of this article the manufacture, sale or transportation of intoxicating liquors within, the importation thereof into, or the exportation thereof from the United States and all territory subject to the jurisdiction thereof for beverage purposes is hereby prohibited.
2—The Congress and the several States shall have concurrent power to enforce this article by appropriate
Ratified Amendment Repealing Prohibition
The proposed 21st Amendment to the Constitution, as adopted by Congress and now ratified, reads:
Resolved, by the Senate and House of Representatives of the United States of America in Congress assembled (two-thirds of each House concurring therein).
That the following article is hereby proposed as an amendment to the Constitution of the United States, which shall be valid to all intents and purposes as part of the Constitution when ratified by conventions in three-fourths of the several States:
Section I.—The Eighteenth Article of Amendment to the Constitution of the United States is hereby repealed.
Section 2—The transportation or importation into any State, territory or possession of the United States for delivery or use therein of intoxicating liquors, in violation of the laws thereof, is hereby prohibited.
Section 3—This article shall be

GUNS SILENCE DIAMO
ILLINGER KILLED
IN CHICAGO TRAP
COME ON, SILVER!
Down in Street
Men.
13
CAPONE
BROOKLYN
It's Smart
To Use ICE
B I N G O
65
50
44

Crime and Corruption

After all, who knew more about the business than us?
—Lucky Luciano, 1929

For historical perspective this chapter flashes back to druggings and muggings of the 1890s, but it quickly zooms in on a more modern game called Cops 'n' Dopers. Prohibition taught us to love our folk-hero gangsters and molls, and the Depression made us envy them. Dry laws spawned a mobster mash: Babyface Nelson, Scarface Al Capone, Machine Gun Kelly, Legs Diamond, Dutch Schultz, Lucky Luciano, Arnold Rothstein, John Dillinger, Pretty Boy Floyd, Bonnie and Clyde.

Reality got blurry; it was hard to tell if the apes with submachine guns were racketeers or dry agents, stick-up artists or narks on the take. Every speakeasy floozy had a cop or politician in her pocket, and crime controlled the streets—at least according to the tabloids.

Who were the good guys and who were the bad? Officials harassed from all sides, con men fleecing the swells, or queens of the underworld selling them dope? The senator who claimed that $2,000 worth of drugs in his possession was planted by the Ku Klux Klan; the director of the play *Peter Pan* who charged police brutality when busted for his habit; or small fry like "Slippery Eel" Miller, who scraped together $75 worth of coke for detectives after promising them much more, and got three years in jail for his pains?

Then as now, police inflated dope prices and seizures. Reporters rarely saw actual amounts and relied almost wholly on police estimates, but editors were just as pleased to run pictures of stash piled high on the table. Then as now, dealers feared being ripped off almost as much as getting caught. Addicts lucky enough to escape execution on the streets eventually ended up in prison, where dope has always been available—for a price.

The Fanatic Dry Killers of prohibition had their counterpart in Killer Narks, who drew less public loathing because they operated mostly in ghettos far from the fashionable speaks. No statistics as there were for dry killings, only anonymous droplets of blood awash in a sea of crime: here a cop kills a vendor, there a drug runner dies, here a "boy shot as police chase dope peddler," there an innocent women beaten by narks.

Graft was by no means limited to busters of booze: Dope was covered as well, often by the same hands. California: State agents confess being ringleaders of a dope racket, taking protection money and then selling prisoners back the dope seized. New York: Drug traffic grips Albany, drug bosses run Buffalo, "dope peddlers are doing a greater business in New York than the bootleggers." Chicago: "Federal narcotics agents in every big city in the United States are involved in a gigantic 'dope' traffic."

A bureaucratic shuffle, a new team sent in, and soon more agents caught, more money involved, more dope on the streets than ever before. It would be pretty to think it all ended when drug enforcement was taken out of the prohibition bureau in 1930, wouldn't it? 1931: Federal narks suppress evidence incriminating fellow agents. . . And what happened to all those squads of dry agents after repeal?

The beat goes on. The game will stay the same as long as any kind of dry laws remain.

DIED AFTER BEING DRUGGED AND ROBBED.

Letter Carrier John S. Dooley Did Not Regain Consciousness, and What Happened to Him Is a Mystery.

FOUND IN A TOUGH LOCALITY.

He Was Lying at Canal and Washington Streets, and the Police Have so Far Been Unable to Find Out Where He Had Been.

IDENTIFIED BY HIS FATHER.

Money and Watch Gone and the Mark of a Blow on the Back of the Neck—He Was Steady and Industrious.

John S. Dooley, a letter carrier, of No. 9 Dominick street, who for four years has been attached to station A, at Crosby and Houston streets, died yesterday afternoon at St. Vincent's Hospital while in a state of opium coma. It is believed that he was drugged and robbed.

The case is a mysterious one, and the police of the Prince street station, under the direction of Ward Detective Savercool, are doing their utmost to clear it up.

Policeman John J. Baker, of the Prince street station, discovered Dooley's unconscious form shortly before two A. M. yesterday lying on the walk at Canal and Washington streets, almost directly in front of the Clinton, or, as it is locally known, the Spring Street Market. Baker had passed over the spot where the body lay not more than twenty minutes before. He attempted to rouse the man, but failed.

He was lying on his back. His mouth was open and his eyes were fixed. His coat and waistcoat were gone, his trousers pockets were turned inside out, and by his side lay an old black derby hat, badly battered. He was five feet eight inches in height, had fair hair and mustache and weighed about 160 pounds. His face was very red and there was a bruise at the back of the neck, whether from a blow or a fall the policeman could not determine.

A TOUGH LOCALITY.

The locality where the body lay is known as a resort for small but tough gangs of loungers after dark, and it occurred at once to the policeman that the man might have been the victim of violence. He lost no time in summoning an ambulance. Dr. Weeks, of St. Vincent's Hospital, reponded, and took the senseless man there. There was nothing by which the man could be identified.

Every effort made to restore the man to consciousness failed. The surgeons speedily came to the conclusion that he had been rendered unconscious by some drug, presumably opium, and before noon gave him up. Their patient died at five minutes of three o'clock yesterday afternoon without having recovered consciousness.

The death was at once reported to the Prince street police station, and in the meantime the police had not been idle. A rumor became current through the precinct early in the day that a man had been drugged and robbed somewhere and then laid in front of Clinton Market. The police could not verify this story and at seven o'clock last evening found themselves about where they had begun.

It was at this hour that James F. Dooley, a venerable gold beater, of No. 9 Dominick street, called at the hospital and positively identified the body as that of his son, John S. Dooley, twenty-eight years old, a letter carrier, unmarried, who until Wednesday night had lived with him. The elder Dooley is a quiet, unassuming man. He had three sons. A daughter died last January. He informed the house surgeon, with tears in his eyes, that his son was missing, and that from descriptions of the man found in front of Clinton Market which he had read in the papers he felt sure that the person was John.

THE FATHER'S GRIEF.

When told that this person was dead Mr. Dooley's feelings entirely overcame him, and he broke down and wept. He finally recovered sufficiently to identify the body. Then he made a statement to the police.

He said that his son was a steady going, industrious and sober young man, who was appointed a letter carrier and attached to station A during the last year of Cleveland's administration. Prior to this he was a gold beater in the employ of his father. The latter has for years worked for the Valleau Manufacturing Company, at No. 506 Broome street. Mr. Dooley said that he felt sure his son had no evil associates and no bad habits. He made it a custom to tell his private affairs to his father and mother. On Tuesday the young man received his month's pay of $85 just before making his last rounds, which include the territory about Clinton Market.

The next day he complained of a headache and was too ill to work, so he remained at home until three o'clock in the afternoon, when he put on a new suit of brown clothing and a new brown derby hat and declared his intention of taking a trip to Coney Island.

He had previously given his father $51 and he is known to have had $34 and a silver watch with him when he left the house. Since that time his movements until his nearly lifeless and plundered body was found have not been traced.

What became of his coat and waistcoat is a mystery. He carried his money and watch in the latter and both disappeared with the waistcoat. The broken hearted father after examining the body expressed his belief that his son had been foully dealth with.

NOT HIS HAT.

The black derby hat, he declared, was not his son's.

This gives color to a suspicion that young Dooley was decoyed to a room, and given a drugged "knock out" drink of some sort, as the police express it; that his body was robbed and then placed in the street.

An autopsy will be made on the body to-day at the direction of the Coroner to ascertain the exac cause of death and to determine whether the mark on the back of the neck—which may have been made by a club—had anything to do with killing him.

It is possible that Dooley did not go to Coney Island at all and that he spent Wednesday night in some opium joint. At station A Dooley's acquaintances spoke well of him.

ARRESTED FOR MURDER.

JAMES M'GREADY CHARGED WITH KILLING THE WOMAN WITH WHOM HE HAD LIVED.

HER STRANGE DEATH.

With Her Last Breath Mrs. Hastings Declared She Had Been Drugged and Assaulted.

HAD A BROKEN UMBRELLA.

Returning Home at Midnight Ill and Excited She Suddenly Succumbed to Heart Disease.

A MAN'S RING IN HER POCKET.

Mystery as to Where She Spent the Time Since She Left Home in the Afternoon.

Mabel H. Hastings, the wife of William Hastings, a clerk in the City Tax Office, left her home at two o'clock Thursday afternoon for an afternoon's shopping. She did not return until after midnight, when she was found by her husband in the hallway of the apartment house at No. 487 Columbus avenue, where they lived, sick and excited. She declared, over and over again, that she had been assaulted and drugged. A few hours later she died.

Mrs. Hastings is said to be twenty-eight years old, though she looked much older. Her husband is sixty-four years old and married her, a widow, seven years ago. She was somewhat addicted to drink, and, it is thought, had been indulging on Thursday night, her husband being at home, sick.

The investigation of Dr. O'Hare, a physician of the Coroner's office, showed that death was due to a complication of diseases, with valvular affection of the heart as the primary cause. There was no medical evidence of the assault which the woman asserted almost with her dying breath. A gold finger ring, evidently the property of a man, was found in her pocket. Mr. Hastings knew nothing of the ring.

SOME FAMILY HISTORY.

Mrs. Hastings was originally Miss Mabel

MRS. MABEL HASTINGS.

Hovey, of Harrisburg, Pa. She came to New York fifteen years ago, and for a few years was nurse in a family living in Madison avenue. Little is known of her life at this time. She married and became a widow. She was Mrs. Mabel Harvey when she met William Hastings, in the most casual sort of way, as an acquaintance introduced in the street. They were married seven years ago, he then being an old man. They spent their honeymoon at the Bryant Park Hotel, and after that lived in flats—first in West Ninety-sixth street and later in Columbus avenue, in the house in which she died.

They were known in the Columbus avenue house as a curious couple. It was evident that the elderly husband thought far more of his wife than she did of him. They had no children, and lived quietly in a handsomely furnished flat. The monotony of their life was varied only by the occasional visits of a few friends and the noisy companionship of four pug dogs, of which Mrs. Hastings was inordinately fond.

But there were occasional excitements in the household. Both husband and wife drank more or less, and now and then one or the other exceeded the bounds of temperance. Mrs. Hastings also developed a lively temper, and occasionally exercised it loudly on her husband, with total disregard to possible listeners. She had no masculine visitors, so far as can be learned, but occasionally broke away from home for part of a day in company with a woman friend, sometimes returning the worse for liquor. It was not known where the two went on these occasions.

SAID SHE HAD BEEN ATTACKED.

William Hastings has been ill for several days and did not go to his desk in the Tax Office. His wife, who suffered from a difficulty in breathing which she ascribed to asthma, nursed him until Thursday afternoon, when she went down town on a shopping tour, saying she would return before six o'clock. But six o'clock came and Mrs. Hastings did not return. Mr. Hastings ate his dinner alone, but he did not begin to worry then.

He did begin to worry as the clock hands got around toward midnight, and was on the point of sending a neighbor to notify the police when the door bell rang. A few moments later he heard his wife calling from below,

"Willie, Willie, Willie!" she cried. "Come down and help me! I can't get up stairs!"

Mr. Hastings hurried down stairs and found her hanging over the railing in the lower hall.

"What is the matter?" he cried.

"Oh!" she gasped. "I have been attacked on the street. I defended myself as best I could and beat them off. See, my umbrella is broken."

She held up her umbrella, the handle of which was broken off. She held the handle in her other hand, which also closely clasped her pocketbook.

"Who attacked you?" cried her husband, supporting her.

"I can't tell you now," she moaned. "I'll tell you later."

"But I want to know," persisted Mr. Hastings.

"Oh, I can't tell you now," she said faintly. "Wait till I get better. Help me up stairs. I can't get my breath."

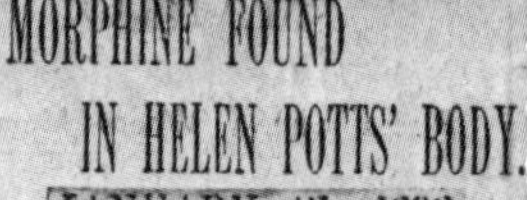

MORPHINE FOUND IN HELEN POTTS' BODY.

JANUARY 21, 1892.

Professor Witthaus Testifies That His Analysis Disclosed the Presence of One One-Hundredth of a Grain.

THE POISON USUALLY IS ABSORBED.

To Find It After Death Is an Exceedingly Rare Occurrence, so Quickly Does the Narcotic Disappear.

HARRIS LISTENED ANXIOUSLY.

His Haggard Face Became Whiter as He Heard the Witness Tell of the Results of the Examination.

"How much morphine did you find in the body of Helen Potts?"

"One one-hundreth of a grain."

To a layman that means nothing. Explained by experts, who know poisons as thoroughly as we know our own faces, it means everything. Morphine is a vegetable poison that the human body absorbs with marvellous quickness.

"I will prove," said Prosecutor Wellman to me later, "that ten grains of morphine taken as an experiment killed a strong man, a physician who had a certain antidote, but delayed taking it for twenty minutes. An autopsy was made as soon as possible and less than a grain of morphine could be found in his body. In the case of Helen Potts we shall prove that the dose of morphine that killed her must have exceeded four grains. Otherwise how could one one-hundredth of a grain have been discovered, when her death had been postponed thirteen hours by heroic remedies and the autopsy not held for fifty-five days afterward? The only wonder is that all of the morphine she took was not absorbed."

Dr. Rudolph A. W... ...sor of chemistry ...d the University ...ks on chemistry, ...tion yesterday, ...rial before Re... his schoolgirl ...ssor Witthaus a large note... he sealed jars ... the vital organs of Helen Potts from Mount Prospect Cemetery at Asbury Park and locked them in an empty room, where they were undisturbed.

MORPHINE, HE SWEARS, KILLED HELEN POTTS.

Q. What did you examine first? A. The stomach. The mucous membrane was somewhat reddened in appearance. I first began to examine the tissue and its contents separately, but presently combined them.

MORPHINE IN THE STOMACH CONTENTS.

Professor Witthaus then described minutely how the tissue and its contents had been macerated until they were dissolved in water. Then he added:—

"I injected part of the solution of the stomach and its contents into the lymph pouch of a small frog at five minutes past three o'clock. It was a lively, healthy frog. At the end of half an hour it lay flat, its front legs collapsed. When touched it jumped, but stumbled and fell when it landed. At ten minutes to four o'clock it jumped very little. It was very sluggish indeed. At half-past five o'clock the frog had recovered from the injection."

Q. How much morphine—if there was morphine in the solution—did you inject into the frog? A. It is hard to say.

Q. One one thousandth of a grain? A. Perhaps so. I can only guess at that.

Professor Witthaus told of twelve acid tests he had applied to the stomach solution. Each one of them gave a reaction that pointed out the presence of morphine. The intestines and their contents were reduced to a solution. This, by proper separation, was divided into two residues, one of which was tested with various acids for sulphate of quinine. There was no trace of quinine. The other

SOME OF THE EXPERTS.

residue was tested, drop by drop, with sulphuric and other acids, sixteen tests in all. Every reaction upon the acid tests showed the presence of morphine beyond a doubt, Professor Witthaus said. The remainder of the residue was dissolved in water. Some of this solution was injected into a frog, while into another frog was injected a dose of 3-1,000 of a grain of morphine dissolved in water.

THE FROG EXPERIMENT.

The frog into whom fluid from the corpse had been injected showed severer symptoms of opium poisoning than the frog who was dosed with morphine.

Q. As a result of your analysis did it appear that the stomach of Miss Potts and its contents contained morphine? A. They did.

Q. Did the intestines contain morphine? A. They did.

Q. Did you find any trace of quinine? A. None.

Q. How much morphine did you find? A. One one-hundredth of a grain.

Q. Is quinine as stable as morphine—does it remain in the stomach and intestines as long as morphine? A. It does.

Q. If the subject had taken twenty-five times as much quinine as morphine would you expect to find an appreciable quantity of quinine when traces of morphine remained? A. I certainly would.

Q. If five grains of morphine had been taken and the patient had been kept alive thirteen hours by artificial respiration and other means, and if the body had been embalmed and buried fifty-five days before the autopsy would you expect to find more than mere traces of morphine?

"KNOCKOUT" DROPS IN THEIR SOUP.

Thomas Watson Suspected of Attempting to Drug the Guests in a Boarding House.

ACCUSED OF PETIT LARCENY.

Took a Dollar from a Fellow Boarder on Pretence of Getting Employment for Him.

HIS STORY OF HARD LUCK.

Some of the guests in the boarding house at No. 127 East 111th street think that they recently had a narrow escape at the hands of a fellow boarder, who is charged with having flavored their soup with "knockout" drops, so that he might the more easily rob the house. Their peril was revealed yesterday when the boarder in question, one Thomas Watson, was ... the charge of ...

... and asked him for $2.30, with which he said that he would purchase for him some tools that he would need.

Huhn had only $1, but he handed that to Watson, who immediately turned and ran down the street. Realizing that he had been swindled, Huhn ran after him, shouting "Stop thief!" Detectives Donnelly and Moody, who happened to be passing, joined the chase and soon overhauled the fugitive, who surrendered without resistance.

On being searched at the station house the bottle supposed to contain "knockout drops" was found in Watson's pocket. He declared that it contained liniment for rheumatism. He frankly confessed that he had robbed Huhn and the other two men, and said:—

HE WAS HUNGRY.

"I was hungry and had no place to sleep until I went to the boarding house. I was willing to work, but could find no one to employ me, and so I grew desperate. I had to get money by some means, and I tried and failed. I don't care now what happens to me."

Huhn told the police that he was sure that Watson had attempted to drug his fellow boarders and rob the house. He said that three or four days before several of the boarders had become unaccountably drowsy after partaking of their soup, and had been unable to finish their dinner, and that afterward Watson had been seen prowling about the house.

This was denied by Watson, who admitted that he would have robbed the house had the opportunity offered, but denied positively that he had ever had any drugs in his possession.

When arraigned in the Centre Street Police Court he pleaded guilty and was held for trial. The contents of the bottle will be analyzed. Charles Keller, the proprietor of the boarding house, denied that any of his boarders had been drugged, but admitted that Watson had acted suspiciously.

KILLED HIS BROTHER-IN-LAW.

John Hunter Shoots Angelo Aborn at Crystal Lake, Conn.

[BY TELEGRAPH TO THE HERALD.]

DRUGGISTS EASILY EVADE PROSECUTION.

Not Punished for Employing Unlicensed Clerks if They Settle with the Board of Pharmacy.

DR. F. G. MERRILL'S EXPERIENCE.

Inspector Glidden's Offer to Drop a Case Against Him on the Payment of $100.

LAWYER PRENTICE IS IMPLICATED.

Dr. Cyrus Edson Admits That Legal Proceedings Are Seldom Taken Against Offending Pharmacists.

YEAR'S SENTENCE FOR ONE CENT

John Rafferty Convicted of Grand Larceny or Stealing "by Force and Arms."

TAKEN FROM A MAN'S POCKET

Judge Has Mercy on the Prisoner and Sends Him to Elmira Reformatory.

'TWAS HIS FIRST OFFENCE.

John Rafferty, alias John Williams, twenty-one years of age, who has no other home than a Bowery lodging house, was sentenced yesterday to one year in the Elmira Reformatory for stealing one cent by Judge McMahon, in the Court of General Sessions.

The complaining witness against Rafferty was Charles B. Daly, a clerk, of No. 216 Church street. He testified that he attended an auction in Maiden lane on March 23, and ...

HYSTERICAL WOMAN TELLS OF DRUGGING

Mrs. Russell S. Fowler Startled Police with a Wild Tale of Her Abduction.

FORCED INTO CARRIAGE

Revolver Taken by Man and Drugged Whiskey Given to Her by Woman with Him.

HUSBAND D NIES THE STORY

He Says It Is All a Delusion and That She Has Suffered from Nervous Trouble for Some Time.

Well dressed and handsome, a woman rushed into the Classon avenue police station, in Brooklyn, early Friday evening, startling the sergeant with her abrupt entrance and evident excitement. He knew her to be the wife of a physician of high standing. Hurrying up to the railing and leaning far over it she asked.—

"Are you in command here? If so, I have been robbed. Robbed of my revolver and drugged. The whiskey, with enough chlora... in it to kill half the girls in Paterson, was forced down my throat. It's a wonder I am alive to tell you about it."

The sergeant could not decide, from her excited utterances, whether or not she had actually escaped from some peril. He called her by name and asked if he should telegraph for her husband, Dr. Russell S. Fowler, son of Dr. George R. Fowler, long connected with the Seney Hospital. She lives only a block away, at No. 388 Lafayette avenue.

TOLD A WILD STORY.

She said, upon telling him her story first, that she had been visiting her mother, the widow of J. Frank White, at No. 120 East Forty-sixth street, in this borough, and at about four o'clock in the afternoon started for Brooklyn. She took an elevated road tran at Fifty-third street. She was so much

CHLOROFORMED HIM TO DEAT...

Four Surgeons Being S... for an "Accident" Which Killed Jacob Kline.

BEFORE THE OPERATION BEG...

One Defendant Admits the A...thetic Was Spilled, but Declares the Others Did It.

JURY MADE UP OF DOCTO...

Coroner Levy Said to Have ...gested This After a Lay Jury Failed to Exonerate.

KNOCKOUT DROPS FOR A MINISTER.

The Rev. E. W. Neil's Servant, Higbee, a Former Convict, Plotted to Drug and Rob Him.

FATAL DOSE WAS INDICATED.

Drug Furnished by William F. Clark, a Convict, Now in the Tombs for Forgery.

RICH PRIZES FOR THIEVES.

They Were to Take Costly Sacramenta Service and Presents from Wealthy Parishioners

A plot to drug with knockout drops the Rev. Edward Wallace Neil, of the Church of St. Edward the Martyr, 109th street and Fifth avenue, has been foiled by the arrest of his colored butler, William Higbee. Although Higbee is a former convict he had been employed in the minister's family for more than a year.

It was the intention of the plotters to rob the clergyman's house of his silverware and jewelry and the church of the sacramental service and vestments.

Fortunately Higbee was recognized by detectives of Acting Captain George W. McClusky's staff before he put his plan of robbery into execution. His accomplice is a notorious forger, William F. Clark, who is in the Tombs prison for passing worthless checks. The plot is revealed in letters that passed between Higbee and Clark.

Higbee and Clark met first in Sing Sing prison and formed a close friendship. Since Higbee has been acting as the Rev. Mr. Neil's butler he and Clark have been prowling abroad at night robbing houses. They had planned to rob other houses than Mr. Neil's, as their letters show.

A very genteel, mild looking, well mannered, well dressed man is Higbee. He is twenty-seven years old and is unmarried.

Clark is a "swell" rogue and has received reserved notice in former Inspector Byrnes' book, "Prominent Criminals of America." At one time he cut quite a figure in society outside of this city and posed as Lieutenant Colt, of the Twenty-second regiment. He is

WILLIAM HIGBEE.

Former Convict and Servant of the Rev. E. W. Neil, Whom He Had Planned to Drug and Rob.

thirty-eight years old.

It was by mere chance that Detectives Evanhoe and Kelly chanced upon Higbee in his new calling of butler. They were shadowing some thieves in the upper part of the city last Wednesday night and happened to pass the residence of the Rev. Mr. Neil, at No. 14 East 109th street. As they went by Detective Evanhoe caught sight of Higbee going into the clergyman's home.

"Why that is Convict Higbee going in there," said Evanhoe to Kelly. "I wonder what that crook wants in there?"

"That is the house of the Rev. Mr. Neil," said Kelly. "It may be that Convict Higbee has repented and become religious."

The detectives had seen Higbee ring the bell, and came to the conclusion that he had some semblance of right to go into the clergyman's house. Feeling that a convict could have no good motive in going to a minister's house, the detectives reported the matter, as soon as possible, to Acting Captain McClusky.

"Go right up there and find out all about Higbee's visit," said McClusky to the detectives. "It may be that he is employed by Mr. Neil as a servant. If he is, arrest him on suspicion and seize his effects."

The detectives retured that night at half-past ten to Mr. Neil's house and had a talk with him. They described Higbee to him and asked him why he had visited him. The minister informed them that Higbee was his butler. He was astounded to learn that Higbee had been a convict. He told the detectives that he had hired him at an employment agency a little more than a year ago.

On being called into the parlor and confronted by the detectives Higbee acknowledged that he had been a convict. The detectives arrested him and seized his belongings.

They found in his room three trunks packed full of goods, all of which he said belonged to him.

HIGBEE INDUCED TO TELL.

Higbee was taken to Police Headquarters. His trunks were also removed to the Detective Bureau. In one of them was found a leather valise, in which were letters from Clark to him, and some of his own to Clark. There were also two prescriptions for knockout drops and a bottle of the deadly stuff containing more than enough to kill a man.

The letters of Clark to Higbee show that they had planned to give the Rev. Mr. Neil knockout drops and rob him. Higbee acknowledged that he had given plans of the house to Clark before the latter's recent arrest. It was their intention, he said, to steal the gold and silver sacramental service of the church, all the jewelry they could get and the Rev. Mr. Neil's valuable vestments.

Elbridge T. Gerry is first vestryman of the Church of St. Edward the Martyr. Among

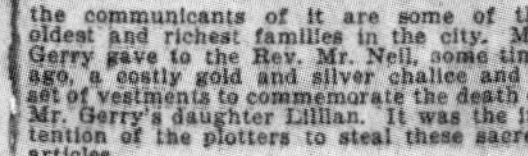

the communicants of it are some of the oldest and richest families in the city. Mr. Gerry gave to the Rev. Mr. Neil, some time ago, a costly gold and silver chalice and a set of vestments to commemorate the death of Mr. Gerry's daughter Lillian. It was the intention of the plotters to steal these sacred articles.

At first Higbee was sullen and refused to say much about his connection with Clark. He was told that he might as well make a clean breast of everything as he would surely get five years for having knockout drops in his possession. On conviction of this offence the law gives the Judge no discretionary power to give the culprit less than a five year term. Higbee finally grew a little more communicative.

Soon after being hired by the Rev. Mr. Neil, he said, he met Clark, whom he had known in Sing Sing. Clark was out on Riverside Drive, near Grant's tomb, taking a spin on his wheel. Clark proposed that they do some work together. He consented and they plied their trade of night prowlers to good effect and fortune. Higbee declined to tell where they had committed robberies.

Being a servant in a minister's family, Higbee had opportunities of associating with the servants of the wealthy. In this way he learned the houses that contained valuables and also how they could be most easily entered.

Clark is a man of good education. He has had a criminal career extending over a dozen years. His manners are those of a well bred man of the world. He is a fine looking man, and is suave and pleasant. He is the son of a well known plumber, R. Clark, of Fourth avenue, near Thirtieth street.

Since starting on his downward career he has passed under the names of Lieutenant William F. Cole, Maltby and Woodruff. It was while masquerading as Lieutenant Cole, in 1888, that he victimized about twenty-five New Yorkers with forged checks.

Among them was Louis de Bebain, then of the French line of steamers. Clark passed a check for $500 on him and was arrested. More than twenty complainants appeared against him, who had cashed checks for sums ranging from $500 to $1,000. He was convicted of forgery. Family influence was brought to bear and he was sent to the Elmira Reformatory, instead of to Sing Sing.

During 1890 he was released, and shortly afterward was again arrested for forgery. He deposited a worthless check for $1,500 in the Second National Bank, and drew against it for nearly all of it. For this crime he got ten years.

It was while serving it that he met Higbee in Sing Sing Prison. Higbee, under the name of Arthur Adams, was arrested in 1892 on a charge of robbery in the first degree. In company with John Sarginty he robbed and beat a man at East Houston street and the Bowery. Judge Cowing gave them each a five years' sentence. Higbee and Clark were released about a year ago.

Higbee was remanded in the Essex Market Police Court yesterday. He will be taken there for examination to-day.

Papers have been prepared against Clark, and he will probably be indicted within a day or two.

"The cold blooded plot to kill me is what surprises me," said the Rev. Mr. Neil to me. "There was no need of a poison to accomplish the robbery. I frequently went out on my bicycle, leaving the house in Higbee's charge. He could readily have carried off the valuables then. The detectives had plans of my rooms which they took from Higbee, and I was dumfounded when they pointed out to me the desk where my gold watch, a present from my parishioners upon the celebration of my tenth anniversary, was locked up. They also told me where my chalice and vestments were. This convinced me of William's guilt. He came to me highly recommended and I am pained at the evidence of his duplicity."

...ACOB ASTOR MAY SUE

It is probable ... sue the owners ... steamer which r... launch Corcyra ... Wednesday. In ... in the HERALD y... witnessed the si... quested to call a... street, which is t...

When I called ... young man who ... affair told me tha... vertisement did n... suit would be br... nothing to be said...

He Denies That Joan of Arc Was His "Soul Mate," but Admits That His Aunt's Oracle Possessed Materializing Power Before She Used Morphine.

SPIRITS THAT SMELL OF ONIONS.

WAS A VICTIM OF "KNOCKOUT" DROPS.

William H. Clark Took a Glass of Beer with Joseph Davie and Became Uncouscious.

ROBBED WHILE IN THE STUPOR

County Medical Society Will Aid Captain Pickett in His Crusade Against Careless Druggists.

DRUGGING IS INCREASING.

Joseph Davie, twenty-two years old, of No. 62 East Houston street, was held for examination by Justice Voorhis in the Tombs Police Court yesterday morning. He was arrested by Detective Sloan, of the Mulberry street station, on Friday night, in a saloon at No. 385 Broome street, on suspicion of having administered "knockout drops" to William H. Clark, an insurance agent, of No. 338 East 124th street.

Clark told Justice Voorhis that he entered the saloon to get a drink early Thursday evening, and was invited by Davie and another man to accept their hospitality. He joined them and ordered a glass of beer.

"I thought," said Clark, "that the beer tasted very bitter, and said so to Davie, but he laughed and told me that East side beer always tasted that way. I became unconscious shortly after, and when I awoke was some distance from the saloon and minus my overcoat, coat, hat, watch and $3 in money. I found my way to the station house, feeling very ill, and secured the services of Detective Sloan, who arrested Davie."

Davie denied that Clark had visited the saloon, but the detective has a witness who saw him enter who will appear in court this morning. Davie acknowledged that he had served a term of imprisonment for grand larceny and had been in Blackwell's Island workhouse.

FIRST DRUGGED, THEN ROBBED.

Mrs. Ray Aldridge's Remarkable Story of Her Experience in a West Twenty-Second Street House.

CHARLES SPENCER ACCUSED.

Says He Took Her Into His Room and Gave Her a Glass of Drugged Ice Water.

AWOKE TO FIND $140 GONE.

Spencer Is Well Known About the City and Has a Good Reputation as a Business Man.

Mrs. Ray Aldridge, who is said to be a musical sketch artist, told a remarkable story in the Jefferson Market Police Court yesterday morning, when she appeared as complainant against Charles Spencer, who has been the manager of several road houses and has been engaged in business for several years with James Patterson, a saloon keeper, of Seventh avenue and Twenty-second street.

Mrs. Aldridge reported at the West Twentieth street station on Friday morning that she had been drugged and robbed of $140 by Spencer in his room at No. 209 West Twenty-second street on Thursday evening. Detective Devine, who listened to her story, is well acquainted with Spencer, and he called at his house and, not finding him, left word for him to call at the station house when he returned.

Spencer walked into the West Twentieth street station on Saturday afternoon and was told that he was wanted for la... complaint of Mrs. Aldr... astounded, but ... mornin... Mag... in $5... son.

Mrs. ... came ... phia, ...

... drinking the w... unconscious and knew nothi... the following morning, when I awoke to find myself alone in the room and all my money except $18 gone. I then went to the West Twentieth street station, where I reported the robbery to the police."

Mrs. Aldridge said that she might have taken a glass of beer on her trip about the streets, but that she was sober when she visited the house.

MYSTIFIED THE MAGISTRATE.

Detective Devine told the Magistrate that he had known Spencer for twenty years, and that he had held many positions of trust. Spencer was closely questioned, and his explanation of the robbery mystified the Magistrate more than the woman's story had done. He said that he occupied a room on the first floor of the house. He had answered the bell on the night in question, and had admitted the young woman, who had asked for Mrs. Bennett.

"Mrs. Bennett, the landlady, was out," he said, "and I told her to go to a room up stairs and await her return. Shortly afterward I heard somebody crying in the hall and found the woman sitting on the stairs. I asked her what the trouble was, and she replied, 'Oh, Billie, why have you treated me so?' Seeing that she was hysterical, I took her into my room, tied a wet towel about her head and told her she could lie down on my bed, as I was going out. Then I left her, and upon returning on Friday evening learned for the first time of the charge she made against me. I never saw the woman before, and did not know that she had any money. I have ...

MRS. HAINS SAYS SHE WAS DRUGGED

In Affidavits Wife of Slayer of W. Annis Denies Accusations Against Her.

REPUDIATES HER CONFESS...

Divorce Case in Court, but Adjo... Is Taken for Purpose of Pro... ing More Documents.

Chloroformed These Families, Two.

The operations and results of the burglars' work at the houses of Dr. Rave and Mr. Maleck were almost identical. Chloroform had been freely used in both instances, and some of the persons were ill for several hours from the effects of the drug. While the Brauns were engaged in their excited search similar scenes were being enacted at the other two houses. The burglars had been just as thorough in their work. Care had been taken to drug the sleeping persons into insensibility, and then the thieves had leisurely proceeded to turn the place inside out in search of treasure.

The loss of money was not so heavy in these places as at Mr. Braun's, but in jewelry, silverware and other articles the thieves gathered up rich plunder. Several very valuable musical instruments, such as violins, mandolins and guitars, had been taken.

The news of the robbery at Mr. Braun's house was soon made public, and created great excitement, and when the other two families added their experience the town was shaken. So cleverly and quietly did the burglars conduct their raid, however, that not the slightest trace of them since they left has been discovered. It is said that the police of Brooklyn and New York will be communicated with, so that pawnshops may be watched for the stolen goods.

USED PISTOL AND DRUG ON WOMAN

Armed Robber Forced His Way Into Mrs. Richter's Rooms, with a Demand for Money.

HE ASKED FOR FOOD FIRST.

She Fell Senseless When He Seized Her and Thrust a Revolver Against Her Head.

THEN CHLOROFORMED HER.

Found Unconscious by Her Friend, Who Entered the Apartments an Hour Later.

A robber entered a woman's house and, thrusting a pistol in her face, administered chloroform to her after she had swooned from fright, and then stole a purse from her person and ransacked the rooms for booty.

Mrs. Nicholas Richter and Mrs. Herrmann Lederer, who occupy adjoining apartments on the top floor of a four story apartment house in Herrman avenue, Guttenburg, are close friends as well as neighbors, and yesterday they had luncheon together in the rooms of the former. Mrs. Lederer remained with her hostess until early in the afternoon, then, having some marketing to do, left the house, telling Mrs. Richter she would drop in again after she had done her errands.

Mrs. Lederer had hardly closed the door when there was a knock at it. Mrs. Richter, thinking her guest had returned for something, went to admit her.

Instead of the person she had expected to see she found a shabbily dressed, powerfully built man. He asked for something to eat. Mrs. Richter told him to wait a moment and she would get him some food, and, giving the door a push, intending to close it, she turned to go to the luncheon table to get something for the tramp.

HER SECOND VISITOR.

She had scarcely taken a step when the man sprang into the room, seized her by the shoulder, swung her around so that she faced him, and thrust a revolver against her forehead.

"I want your money," commanded the robber "all you've got in the house." The terrified woman swooned from fright.

Mrs. Lederer, returning to the house in an hour, went at once to her friend's rooms and, finding the door open, entered. Mrs. Richter lay on the floor unconscious, as she had fallen when the thief menaced her. The atmosphere was heavy with chloroform. Mrs. Lederer at once set about reviving the woman, but it was some time before her senses returned and she recollected what had occurred.

HAD BEEN CHLOROFORMED.

Then she was violently ill, presumably from chloroform. After she had swooned the thief, determined to silence her while he searched the house, had applied the drug to the woman. He had taken a purse containing $14 from her person and explored the rooms for more plunder, but, finding nothing else to his liking, had departed with only the cash.

The robber must have been hiding in the hallway when Mrs. Lederer passed out, but she did not see him. Mrs. Richter describes him as about thirty years old, of muscular physique, and with a light mustache. Such a person had hung about several saloons in the neighborhood during the morning.

WOMAN WITH PISTOL COUNTED TWO AND BURGLAR VANISHED.

BURGLARS DRUG THREE FAMILIES.

Midnight Thieves at Hicksville, L. I. Use Chloroform and Obtain Valuable Plunder.

STUPEFIED BY THE DRUG.

Occupants of Three Houses Were Rendered Insensible, and Every Room Was Then Ransacked.

LOSS IS MORE THAN $1,000.

Burglars Carried Off Money, Watches, Jewelry and Bric-a-Brac, in Fact Everything Portable and Valuable.

[BY TELEGRAPH TO THE HERALD.]

HICKSVILLE, L. I., June 22, 1897.—Burglars made a sensational and successful raid upon this place last night. The homes of William Braun, Dr. Edward Rave, and John Maleck were entered, all the occupants chloroformed and money, jewelry and portable articles carried away. The total value of the plunder is more than $1,000.

Hicksville has received a distinct shock. This is the first visitation of housebreakers in the history of the village. Long immunit...

GEARY WAS DRUGGED.

Given "Knockout Drops," Robbed and Left Unconscious in a Doorway.

PROMPT ACTION SAVED HIM.

Policeman Thought Him Intoxicated, but Would Take No Chances and Summoned an Ambulance.

APPLIED A STOMACH PUMP.

Remembers Nothing, but Thinks He Must Have Entered a Saloon and There Was Poisoned

Thomas Geary, of No. 338 West Fifteenth street, was drugged, robbed and left unconscious in a doorway early yesterday morning. That he is still living is due to the alertness of a policeman, who, although he thought the man was intoxicated, preferred to take no chances, and sent for an ambulance.

Geary was found about three o'clock yesterday morning ... the Macdouga... doorway of H. ... Canal street. ... head was su... prodded the m... him to get u... amined the ma... he was breat... ambulance, a... Hospital, ans... man and decl... chloral poiso... have died if ... for half an ... him to the h... and other re... was out of d...

Several ca... pockets told ... salesman fo... 23 Spring s... his pockets ... knife, and ... ment of a b...

Detective... and discov... o'clock a w... ing a third ... the place w... thought th... friend hom... them. T... were carr... he was fou... where in t...

Geary r... yesterday ... Charles, ... He could ... situation, ... been robb... hat, whic... was left ...

Geary ... up town ... with his ... brother ... street, a... and Hudson ...

He left them at eleven o'clock, and after that his mind was a blank. He had not drunk anything during the evening, but thinks that after leaving his friends he went into a saloon to get a drink and that the drug was administered to him there. He was still dazed and very weak yesterday afternoon.

FOUGHT FOR LIFE DRUG STOLE SEN...

"I Held Rogers, While Wife Chlorotorme... Him," Says Levi Perham.

"THEN DRAGGED THE BODY TO THE RIVE...

Accomplice in Vermont T... gedy Describes How Victi... Was Lured to Death.

UNSUSPICIOUS TO THE LA...

Head Was Pillowed in Wif... Lap, Perham Says, When Drug Was Used.

DRANK POISON AND THEN BEER.

Samuel Nidds Swallowed Acid in the Street, Walked Eight Blocks to

MURDERED BY DEADLY DRUG SENT IN MAIL

Quick Poison, Offered in Harmless Guise as Christmas Gift to Harry Cornish, Caused Mrs. Adams' Death.

BAFFLING CRIME IS LAID TO WOMAN.

Intimated That the Person Suspected of the Crime Is Out of This State's Jurisdiction.

DEATH IN BOTTLE OF BROMO SELTZER.

Sent with a Silver Medicine Tray

PRIL 20, 1913.

BLAME OPIUM RING AGENTS FOR CRIMES

Police Say Three Bands of Smugglers Hire Men to Slay Competitors.

KILL TO HOLD UP PRICE

Detectives Now on Trail of Two Sailors Who Are Expected to Tell Secrets of Trust.

Twoscore detectives under George S. Dougherty, Second Deputy Police Commissioner, aided by customs inspectors, are to-day following clews which they hope will lead to the arrest of three bands of smugglers of opium who do not stop at murder to hold a monopoly of their unlawful trade.

Aided by letters found in the trunk of Edward Hobson, an assistant steward on the Ancona, of the Panama line, who was decoyed to the tenement house No. 424 East 116th street last Tuesday night and there shot to death by "gun men" in the employ of opium smugglers who resented his underselling them in their business, Deputy Commissioner Dougherty has obtained information which indicates that scores of sailors plying between this country and South and Central American ports are engaged in the wholesale traffic of opium.

Investigation by detectives under Acting Captain Stainkamp, who is in charge of the detectives in the East 104th street police station, has revealed the fact that the business of selling opium and cocaine to victims of these drugs is monopolized by three bands, composed of about one hundred persons. They are organized and have a standard rate of sale for the drugs.

Women, as well as men, the detectives have learned, are dealers in the poisons, and it also has been learned that much of the stuff is sold in the Tenderloin and East Harlem. The trust also has agents in all the large cities of the country.

Detectives say, it is common gossip in the underworld that many murders which the police have been unable to fathom are committed by these bands. In every instance, it is said, the victim met his death because he sold directly to consumers of the drugs at a price lower than that demanded by the organized smugglers.

Drugs Sold to Agents.

Men of foreign birth, unfamiliar with this city, usually are the actual smugglers of opium. As a rule they are only too willing to sell their wares to the representatives of the trust in this city, who distribute the drug to the different agents in this and other cities.

In addition to these agents, it is asserted, the trust has established a chain of opium dens throughout the country in which opium, cocaine and heroin are sold. Although the police and health authorities of this city have closed many such places, it is now said their activities have not been as successful as the officials were led to believe.

Some idea of the extent to which the traffic in opium has been conducted in this city can be obtained from the fact that when the police searched the body of young Hobson they found in the lining of his clothing nine cans of opium, each valued at $50. On Leo Hobson, sixteen years old, a brother of the slain boy, who was with him at the time of the killing, and who was shot by the hired assassins of the Opium Trust, three more cans of the drug were found.

In a furnished room in lower Tenth avenue which Hobson had occupied detectives found eleven more cans of opium, which, with the cans confiscated by the police after the murder, were estimated to be worth $1,125.

Inasmuch as the Ancona started for Panama the day before the shooting it is believed by the police that Hobson, not being satisfied with the price offered him for the drug by representatives of the Opium Trust, decided to sell his wares direct to consumers.

That Hobson's movements were known to the leaders of the bands composing the trust is evidenced by the fact that when entering a restaurant in Third avenue, near East Fourteenth street, an hour before he was murdered he was approached by a man, who held a whispered conversation with him.

Trapped by Opium Trust.

It is now believed the man told where he could dispose of his contraband wares. For a few minutes afterward, Lee told Deputy Commissioner Dougherty, his brother telephoned to a man in Harlem who invited him to meet him at Third avenue and East 116th street.

The police say the man who met the Hobson boys at that place was one of several agents in the Harlem district. This man, although he was known to the dead boy, declared in the presence of Leo he did not want to buy the opium but that he knew a man who did. Accepting the man's offer to bring him to the prospective buyer, Edward Hobson walked into a trap set by his assassins, and the secret of his dealings with the opium smu... with him.

... was first reported, ...ed that the mur... ...ard

First In News / In Advertising / In Circulation

San Francisco ... Monarch of the ...

THURSDAY — SAN FRANCISCO, NOVEMBER 6, 1...

S. F. DETECTIVE IS ARRESTE...

POLICEMAN IS HELD AS ONE OF DRUG RING

Sergeant Thomas Furman Booked by Federal Operatives for Part in Narcotic Deals

Suspected Officer Is Accused of Taking $250 Bribe; Fireman on Steamer Also Is Held

Detective Sergeant Thomas Furman of the neutrality squad of the police department, was arrested yesterday by Revenue Inspector A. A. Elliott and charged with concealing and dealing with opium and other narcotics.

Furman was arrested with Peter Pedro, a fireman aboard the steamer Colusa, and Peter Pardo, said to be a dealer in drugs.

BRIBERY CHARGED.

The accused officer was arraigned before United States Commissioner Francis Krull and after the testimony had been taken Assistant United States Attorney Wilford Tulley announced that an additional charge of accepting a $250 bribe will probably be lodged against the detective today.

Furman is accused by Pedro of having obtained opium from him on October 29 last. Pedro said he found the drug on the steamer Colusa. He said he arranged a meeting with Furman at Fifth and Harrison streets and was to drive with Furman to the latter's rendezvous at Courtland avenue and San Bruno road to deliver to the officer a quantity of drugs.

SURPRISED AT ARREST.

"You can't arrest me," Furman is said to have told Elliott. Elliott took both Furman and Pedro to the office of E. C. Yellowley, agent in charge of the revenue service, where Furman put up $1,500 bail and was released.

Furman, according to Pedro, then told him that if he was given $250 the case against Pedro would be squared. Pedro said he paid the money. On the witness stand in Krull's court Furman admitted accepting the coin, but stated that is was merely a ruse to ingratiate himself with Pedro in order to gain possession of thirty tins of opium which Pedro is alleged to have had.

Pedro, under oath, said he had thirty tins of the drug. Furman said he turned the $250 over to Captain John J. O'Meara. The latter corroborated Furman's statement in Krull's court yesterday. Capt. Bernard Judge of the property clerk's office, said yesterday the money was deposited with him by O'Meara on Oct. 31 the day folowing the date Pedro said the money was paid.

OPIUM FOUND.

Elliott testified that when he encountered Furman and Pedro at Fifth and Harrison sts., he asked the officer if he had any drugs in the car. When Furman answered in the negative Elliott says he pulled up the cushion in the front of the car and found a tin of opium. He said Furman refused to account satisfactorily for the drug being in the machine.

Detectives Thomas Furman said yesterday:

Elliott knew exactly what I was about. So did my superiors in the police department. To begin with I was trying to catch members of a ring of opium smugglers.

CLAIMS WAS ON DUTY.

October 29 I had landed one of them. Two Federal officers did not recognize me. We all went to police headquarters, where it was explained to Lieutenant Goff in charge there. Elliott and Gough agreed that I should go ahead with the work. Elliott even agreed to accept a check for $1,500. This was a worthless check supposed to be given for the release of the two smugglers we were trying to land. The smugglers did not know even then that I was a policemen. As a ruse I had been placed in handcuffs.

I told them I must have some security for the check. They agreed

Faces Drug Charge

Detective Sergeant ...onas Furman of the San Francisco Police Department Neutrality Squad, who was arrested yesterday by Federal operatives and accused of dealing in opium and also of accepting a bribe of $250.

PROF FIGHTS TO HO...

Dr. Ho... to B...

Prof. ... tional d... of Calif... missed, ... instatem... next Tu... will be ... report ... had it ... at least ... final act...

Howe... regents ... faculty h... Sabbatic...

WAS IN...

Howe... leave of... obtained... tional b... He had ... division ... his leav... permane... son.

The re... demand ... has been... will be ... that he ... on the f... arily app... tion on ... and that ... to look ...

CLAIMS ...

Instead... remained... the rege... ment. H... mended ... and there... posed by... is no re... on the b... if there ... have bee...

The ide... legal act... ment is ... pointmen... tirely ... "If what... the city i... yesterday... recommen... ship at t...

Accused Detectives

Detective Sergeant George Richards (above), and Detective Thomas Reagan, charged by drug peddler with aiding conspiracy to rob him

SLEUTHS AIDED IN DOPE THEFT.

CRITICS' 'HU... BRANDS A... 'FIND' A FA...

And Thaddeus Welch P... Monterey Woman Her '... piece' Was Not Done ...

Mrs. M... $800... of ...

"Art ... Thus sp...

Conce... also a w... life is too... accepted... by the s... the reas... a recent... artistic ...

The st... leged m... famous ... good en... tradition... with M... ground, ... ward-bo... It was ... merit, e... interpret... mood, t... Mrs. M. ... Mrs. H... from a ...

Mrs. ... warded ... terey, in... that She... days of ...

SECOND SECTION

Miscellaneous and Classified Advertisements

FOUNDED 1865 — V

Exposure ...

SLEUTHS AIDED IN DOPE THEFT, SAYS PEDDLER

Police and Federal Officials Probe Charges of Confessed Smuggler Against 2 S. F. Officers

Detective Sergeant George Richards and Detective Thomas Regan Named; Make Denials

Police and federal investigation of the reported existence of a ring of San Francisco police officers that extorts tribute from drug peddlers yesterday brought to light the names of Detective Sergeant George Richards and Detective Thomas Reagan as alleged members of the ring.

Both officers, according to Captain of Detectives Matheson and government agents under W. H. Tidwell, special agent for the Treasury Department, are accused by Nels Christiansen, alleged drug peddler, of entering a conspiracy by which he was robbed of several thousand dollars' worth of morphine.

The accused detectives were questioned by Tidwell yesterday and denied ever "holding up" Christiansen, although they admitted arresting him last week.

SHOWED HIM MORPHINE.

Christiansen's story accusing the officers as told Captain Matheson and Government officials yesterday was:

I recently left a steamer which arrived here from the Orient with 125 ounces of morphine in my possession. I sold about 50 ounces when a friend of mine introduced me to Peter Dallas, owner of a Greek poolroom near the Hall of Justice.

Dallas and I then kept an appointment at the St. Francis Hotel last Friday night, but when I mentioned the subject of selling him the 125 ounces of dope at $25.50 an ounce, he said he didn't have the money with him and that he wanted to see if the "stuff" was all right.

In his machine we went to a room where I showed him the morphine. He appeared satisfied and asked me to bring the dope while we went where he had $3,190 in cash.

RUNS FROM SLEUTHS.

While we were riding along, Dallas suddenly drew up to the curb near the Tenth st. lumber yards. The machine stopped and two detectives, who were standing on the corner, started toward us.

I saw them coming and started to run. Richards kept after me and caught me, and when we got back to where Regan was standing. Dallas had been allowed to depart with the morphine and his automobile.

I then remembered that Dallas was flashing his spotlight as we

TRAFFIC ROOTED IN OFFICIALDOM, FOREMAN HINTS

Grand Jury Head Expresses Opinion That Business Circles Are Involved

EVIDENCE FORTHCOMING

Many Indictments Will Be Justified, Is Assertion of Harrelson

An illicit narcotic traffic and graft organization, having its roots in the ranks of law officers sworn to abolish the traffic and its tentacles high in the business life of the city, exists in San Francisco. This is the opinion of William H. Harrelson, foreman of the San Francisco Grand Jury, as admitted by him yesterday.

"And I wish to add," Harrelson said, "that no matter where the roots lie, nor how high the branches extend, there is a determination on the part of the Grand Jury to make a thorough investigation and exposure of the traffic. What the result will be I can not say. We are going to try to stamp out the traffic, and just as fast as the District Attorney has the evidence in shape to present to us, we are going to hear it.

TO HOLD SPECIAL MEETING

"To this end," Harrelson continued, "we shall have a special meeting of the Grand Jury tomorrow night at 7 o'clock to consider the evidence the District Attorney has to present at that time. Two hours of the session will be devoted to this purpose, the remaining hours, it is planned, to be given to other investigations now under way. We will not receive evidence concerning the Police Court graft at this meeting.

"From the evidence which Assistant District Attorney Isadore Golden has already laid before us," he added, "we are certain of the existence of an organized plot on the part of certain law officers, operating through wide ramifications with many interests within and without the city, to maintain and to increase the supply of narcotics which find their way to sales in illicit channels. I am of the opinion that no indictments will be returned by the Grand Jury tomorrow night, but it will not be long before the evidence in hand will be in shape to justify the submission of the question of indictment to the Grand Jury for vote.

EVIDENCE AMPLE

"Of course, as to the outcome of the vote I cannot say. I know there will be ample evidence presented, and that shortly, to justify not one or two, but many indictments. These will not affect officers only, either. The dope graft I believe is even more far-reaching than the Police Court graft."

From present indications, Harrelson said, "the Grand Jury will meet three times during this week to hear evidence touching the narcotic graft investigation."

In the meantime plans for continuation of the preliminary hearing of Sam Morlen, charged with violating the State poison act, before Judge Henry M. Owens tomorrow are being completed. It was Morlen's arrest by John de Vries and Emile Coret, operatives for the State Board of Pharmacy, on the charge of peddling narcotics that led to the accusation against the two officers and the Grand Jury investigation.

DRUGS ARE TRACED

The charges were made by Sa...

niner

Pages 13 to 22

THURSDAY CC

ON OPIUM CHARGE

Drug Addicts Escape Bellevue in Taxicab.

The honking of a mysterious t… cab as it entered the grounds… Bellevue Hospital at two o'… yesterday morning is believed t… been a signal for the escape o… prisoners.

Dressed mainly in pajam… slippers, they used a rope … sheets and a bathrobe to … down thirty feet from a … window of the prison w… feat landed them on the … front of the mai… Thence they m… appearance, of w… likeli… planation is that they got … the taxicab.

…dicts, charged … the narcotic law, … the hospital as pris… l. John Huntin had … ward since August … his home address … street, Covington … were … ast B… o. … atter on No…

…USE.

…nce at the … by rea… y to th… fro…

…call had been received at the Pri… George Hotel.

As the gate opened and the ta… cab rolled in, the chauffeur gave … or three blasts of his horn. W… he repeated his story at the rec… tion office, he was informed t… was no Dr. Robinson in … and no call had been t… a taxicab. After so… drove away, and … gatekeeper without … citing … ion.

ROPE FOUND DANGLING.

The supposition is that the esca… prisoners had concealed the… in the cab while the chauffe… king to the custodian of … office. An orderly of … ward missed them. In searc… ng … them, he found a scre… broke… from one of the bathro…

DRUG TRAFFICKER

SECOND SECTION

PAGES 11 TO 18

San Francisco Chronicle

VOL. CXVI, NO. 158

SAN FRANCISCO, CAL., MONDAY, JUNE 21, 1920

Higher-Ups in Narcotic Graft Pending

U.S. AUGMENTS FORCE TO RAP NARCOTIC EVIL

Every Outside Agent in Treasury Dept. to Be Used in Vigorous Campaign to Halt Smuggling

WASHINGTON, May 7. — (By Universal Service.)—Every outside agent in the employ of the Treasury Department is to be used in a vigorous campaign for the suppression of the drug evil, it was learned today. This includes customs officers at all of the ports of entry, special agents, prohibition agents and the regular force of narcotic experts in the various States.

This step is taken, it was said, because the regular force of narcotic agents, operating under L. G. Nutt of the internal revenue bureau, is too small to handle the situation without the active aid of other Treasury Department officers.

The campaign is to be especially directed at what the narcotic division believes a plot to smuggle opiates into this country on a gigantic scale, due to the restrictions which have been placed upon obtaining drugs for illicit purposes within the United States, or from the product manufactured in the United States.

Within the last month treasury officials have succeeded in closing scores of clinics where addicts got their daily supply of morphine, opium, cocaine or heroin. They also have made it extremely difficult for the druggist or the physician to prescribe opiates except in case of absolute necessity as provided under the Harrison anti-narcotic act.

But special agents of the treasury department who were sent out to make an investigation at foreign ports reported that huge quantities were being held by unscrupulous persons and were being sold to smugglers.

It was learned that there was a large stock in Japan, in Mexico and in Cuba and quite a sizable quantity along the Canadian border. Colonel Nutt visited Cuba and arranged with the authorities there to prevent exportation, and has since completed negotiations with the Canadian authorities to exercise special surveillance along the border. The Mexican authorities have offered every possible assistance and are guarding all avenues to the border.

United States customs officers have been directed to make a most minute inspection of all luggage, because of the ease with which drugs may be concealed. And prohibition officers, in addition to searching for more bulky packages of whisky, have been directed to complete their work by searching for drugs, which may be more easily concealed.

"We have to stop this drug evil and stop it quickly," said Colonel Nutt. "It is taking a terrific toll among the young men and women of the nation. Officials are beginning to fully realize that it is one of the gravest, if not the most dangerous, menaces we have. It is possible to regulate the manufacture, but it will require every facility we can muster to prevent smuggling, and we must be backed by the most drastic legislation.

The sad part about the use of … is that after a person takes … first few … the case …

JUNE 20, 1922 Bus…

DRUG RING AGENT GETS PRISON TERM

"Slippery Eel" Given Six Months to Three Years for the Sale of Narcotics.

ASSOCIATE ALSO SENTENCED

Arrested While on Way to Deliver $2,500 Cocaine to Detective.

Charles H. Miller, a hunchback, known as the "Slippery Eel" and as Eastern agent of an international narcotic ring, yesterday was sentenced to the penitentiary for from six months to three years on conviction of illegal possession and sale of narcotics. Miller pleaded guilty to the offense.

At the same time Thomas A. Dawson, an associate of Miller's, was sentenced to a similar term on conviction. Sentences were imposed by Justices Salmon, Healy and Hermann in Special Sessions.

CONTRACTED FOR COCAINE.

The "Slippery Eeel" and Dawson were arrested June 13 by Dr. Carleton Simon, Deputy Police Commissioner, and several of his detectives attached to the Police Department Narcotic Division. Miller was arrested in West Forty-sixth street as he was on his way to keep an appointment with Detective Moffat to deliver $2,500 worth of cocaine, for which Moffat had contracted.

CONFESSION LEADS TO ARREST.

Dawson, who claimed to be the "connecting rod" between Miller and buyers of narcotics was arrested directly after in his room at No. 33 Moore street, where Miller also lived. The night of the arrest Miller was able to deliver but $75 worth of narcotics.

The linking of Miller to the international narcotic ring was through the confession of Paul Larsen, one of the seven arrested on May 22nd in a Broadway restaurant by members of the Narcotic Division when $50,000 worth of cocaine was seized.

Larsen said th… the eastern … was … vent … regu… nar… ea…

WE WORK
A 896
FOR TIPS
CUSTOMER'S CLAIM CHECK
HAWAIIAN GARDENS
We are not responsible for loss by Fire, Theft, or other Causes to Vehicles, Accessories or Contents left with us.

S ARRESTED IN NARCOTIC RAID

"DOLLAR A SHOT."

"Dope for a dollar a shot" w… the trade slogan of the drug ring … the prison, Clark told the magistrate. Drug orgies were often held in his cell, he continued. The "stuff" was brought to the cell, he said, by a "trusty" attached to the prison hospital.

Clark directly charged Morgan with being the means by which drugs were brought into the prison and distributed. Bennie Bernstein, a former cellmate, he said, supervised disposal of the drugs inside the cell, while Hugh Fisher, another convict, sold the drugs at retail. Fisher, Contardi, the "trusty," Bernstein and Morgan have been held in $5,000 bail.

Detectives recently received an open letter from Charles J. Kralle, a paroled prisoner, who stated that during his confinement it would have been easy to obtain $5,000 worth of dope in the prison on short notice.

"The head 'runner' on the second floor (tier) has made a fortune since February," Kralle wrote.

Convicted drug peddlers were the guiding minds of the traffic inside the prison, he continued, many of them, in the capacity of "trusties," finding it easy to do so. Guards, Kralle charges, had become implicated to such an extent that some of the leading convict drug ring members defied their supposed jailers with impunity.

…URDAY, FEBRUARY 5, 1921

PORT HEADS CLASH ON DRUG SMUGGLING

Newton Holds Rush "Largely Responsible" for Conditions Permitting Illicit Imports.

A clash between Collector Newton and Surveyor Rush developed yesterday as a result of the investigation of graft among inspectors assigned to incoming vessels.

Mr. Rush declared that only two inspectors have been dismissed and only ten are under suspicion. He charged rivalry and ill-feeling among the forces of the Customs service here. He said the names of suspected inspectors were frequently given to the Deputy Collector assigned to baggage duty on the piers.

NEWTON REGRETS "EVASION."

Mr. Rush denied having jurisdiction over the outside forces.

Collector Newton declined to discuss the typewritten statement in which the surveyor's charges are made until he had a chance to read it. He said:

"I think it regrettable that he should seek to condone or defend the conditions on the piers for which his administration is largely responsible."

Collector Newton declared that smuggling of drugs through the port is more extensive than ever.

INDICTMENTS DUE.

Additional evidence is being prepared against several inspectors for the Federal Grand Jury. Immediate indictments will be sought by the Department of Justice.

The "real offenders," who reaped millions, will be prosecuted, it was said. Evidence against several drug smugglers has been turned over to

DRUG ADDICT CITES POLICE FOR CRUELTY

Charles H. Weston, Former Stage Director for Maude Adams and Other Stars, Clubbed and Kicked

Says He Was Deluged with Water from a Hose, Had His Jaw Dislocated and Was Denied Food

Charges of police brutality against drug addicts were made yesterday by Charles H. Weston. He appealed for protection against the police espionage system and powerful drug sellers who, he alleges, are persecuting him.

Mr. Weston, who admits that he is a drug addict, is well known among theatrical people, having been for seven years director for Maude Adams and other stars. He also staged "Peter Pan" in England, Australia and America. Before the war he was owner of a large motion picture studio in Great Britain. He lives at No. 874 Undercliff avenue, Edgewater, N. J. Mr. Weston is now under the care of a physician, who is curing him of the drug habit.

Two years ago Mr. Weston fell out of an aeroplane in England while filming a picture. He suffered a compound fracture of the leg. He says that to ease the pain he was supplied with morphine for several months, without his knowing what was being administered. As a result, he contracted the drug habit.

REBISTERED AS ADDICT.

Early in the war his motion picture studio was commandeered by the British Government, and he came to this country. Knowing of the Harrison and Whitney statutes in regard to the use of drugs, he immediately registered with the Department of Internal Revenue.

On Tuesday, October 23, he was arrested on a charge of drug-selling and lodged in the Thirtieth street police station. He was put through a third degree, and he says that when he begged for morphine a hose was turned on him. The police refused to allow him to communicate with his wife or physician. The following day he was taken to Police Headquarters. There, he alleges, he was finger-printed, photographed and beaten until he collapsed. As the result of a kick he suffered a dislocated jaw. It is illegal to fingerprint any one until after conviction.

DENIED HEARING, HE SAYS.

He was taken on Wednesday to the Jefferson Market Court. When he asked to be heard in his own behalf, Weston says that the Magistrate would not listen to him. He was remanded till Friday. No one was allowed to see him, and he was not permitted to send a letter. No food was given to him, and when he begged for a physician he was clubbed into silence, Weston alleges. According to him, one of the keepers said:

"Be quiet. We have a little graveyard here, and we bury people of your type every morning at 2:30. If you are good we will not bother you."

In desperation for medical assistance Weston says that he …

SEEK TO SMASH DOPE INDUSTRY AT STATE 'PEN'

Amazing Revelations of Ring and Its Activities Launch an Official Investigation

"SNOW PARTIES" STAGED

Trusted Convicts Were Link in Chain and Jailers Defied; Four Accused Are Held

By PAUL H. EGOLF,
International News Service Staff Correspondent.

PHILADELPHIA, July 18. — Smashing the dope rings in county prison and State penitentiary is the task now occupying the attention of this city's officials.

The penitentiary, by a drastic change in rule, the transfer of convicts who sold dope and the isolation of addicts, now has a clean bill of health, but conditions in the grim pile of imitation Egyptian architecture known as Moyamensing Prison are only being revealed.

Previous Grand Jury investigations of Moyamensing Prison have been perfunctory, the reason being that, according to a former convict, everything was especially brought up to standard in anticipation of the visit of the investigators.

VICTIMS IN FEAR.

In the Philadelphia magistrates' courts tales of wild "snow parties" in the cells, of a highly organized system of "msater-mind" dope peddlers and their "runners," all wearin gthe prison garb, are being unfolded by their victims, who cower in fear of possible retaliation awaiting them when they are taken back to their quarters.

The death of Nathan Kessler, a convicted highwayman, in his cell from an overdose of narcotic drugs concentrated attention on how such conditions could arise within the walls of a supposedly well-disciplined penal institution.

The first report of the affair, issued by the prison authorities, was briefly to the effect that Kessler had died from drugs smuggled to him by a woman on visiting day.

Coroner William R. Knight, however, who supervised the examination of Kessler's body, decided that conditions surrounding Kessler's death warranted searching investigation, and accordingly two detectives, experts from the municipal narcotic squad, were detailed to gather evidence.

Their efforts resulted in a revelation of a highly organized "system" of the dope-runners, both inside and outside the prison, and the arrest of suspects under conditions leaving little doubt as to their complicity in the wholesale cons… with which they are charged.

Charles F. Morgan, a prison guard, who resigned the day Kessler died, was held in $5,000 bail. Shortly afterward Dr. Herbert I. Burke, veterinarian, was placed un…

How to Keep Well—
Read Dr. Copeland's
Expert Advice To-day

Ship Report

ANCIENT CYRENE ART TREASURES
Old Greek city of North Africa gives up from its ruins ancient art treasures of surpassing value.
NEXT SUNDAY'S EXAMINER

MARCH 10, 1931

MYSTERY GAS OVERCOMES 25

Dr. Einstein Still Hears Reception—On a Phonograph

Professor Albert Einstein, halfway across the Atlantic to Germany, heard again on Sunday his reception by Mayor Walker at City Hall.

DECREE

American

Copyright, 1922, by Star Company. Registered U. S. Patent Office. Business 'Phone, Columbus 7000 WEDNESDAY

$100,000 DRUGS IN FIS

ACCIDENT DISCLOSES $100,000 IN SMUGGLED DRUGS when fish keg broke open on Joralemon street pier, Brooklyn, late yesterday. Federal agents to unusual activity by disclosures following Wallace Reid's collapse, are showing seizure. They are on trail of consignee. (N. Y. American)

PUZZLE—FIND THE LETTER CARRIER.

74 ARE JAILED IN SAN JOSE 'DOPE' RAID

Police Judge Imposes 6-Months Sentences in New Effort to Find Remedy for Drug Evil

DOPE RAID—A narcotic squad detective examines opium layout and guns seized in raids on two Brooklyn apartments early yesterday.

CHIEF INJURED IN BRONX DRUG RAID, one of Federal Narcotic Agent Oyler's subordinates is shown checking $100,000 worth of contraband captured at shop in Crescent avenue, near 183d street. Chief Oyler was badly cut about face and arms in breaking

$3,500,000 WORTH OF DRUGS DESTROYED—Great quantities of opium, morphine, heroin, cocaine and drug equipment, including opium pipes and hypodermic needles, confiscated by the police in the last eighteen months, were dumped into the sewer or burned yesterday under personal supervision of Dr. Carleton Simon, Special Deputy Commissioner in charge of the narcotic division.

$1,000,000!—While ... drug ring ... investigated

ILLICIT DRUG TRAFFIC GOT A JOLT when ... seized this shipment of narcotics, concealed in ... Actual value $19,290, peddlers asked ... Error in shipping proved smugglers' undoing.

Dope by the Trunkful!

SEIZED!—Deputy Surveyor of Customs Alex McKeon standing guard over two trunks containing $500,000 worth of narcotics, seized by U. S. agents on the French Line pier. (Story on Page 1).
N. Y. American Staff Photo.

DRUG HAUL—Detectives Joseph Mooney (package in hand), and Milton Muffet, of the Narcotic Squad with part of $50,000 in drugs seized in East Side raid late Monday night. (N. Y. Am.)

SEIZE DOPE IN TWO RAIDS—Detective Joseph Bremmer with part of huge drug haul, estimated at $200,000, made in Brooklyn early yesterday in two raids staged by Special Deputy Police Commissioner Simon. (New York American)

RAID NETS $500,000 IN DRUGS—Arch smugglers' cache of narcotics, smuggled from Germany in medicinal salts shipment and bales of rope, was seized by Federal agents on ships docking yesterday. Photo above shows a drum of morphine, one of a number seized. (N. Y. Am.)

See News of World in Motion Pictures in All L

CALLED IN "WORST"
Rosalind Pomeroy-Bernard (above), is a principal in conflicting State laws ... divorce and subsequent

CAB FARES ... 5 CENTS A ...
New Yellow Co. Rate Said to Be Su... Reduction to ...

WEDNESDAY, JUNE 12, 1901

DAY, SEPTEMBER 18, 1922 Business Telephone, Columbus 7000

LIGHTWEIGHT TANGLE

SAYS "BUGS" Baer:

Y FIND TAIT MAN TO SMOTH

SEATTLE POST-INTELLIGENCER, FRIDAY, MAY 10, 19

ER TURNED IN ON ENTOMBED MINERS

ditorial

922. Editorial 'Phone, Beekman 2000 Part II of N. Y.

S SEIZED ON PIE

NARCOTICS SEIZED ON SHIP

DRUGS SEIZED —Posing as addicts, detectives captured this suitcase containing $250,000 worth of narcotics in a Hester street tenement near Police Headquarters yesterday. Two women were arrested (N.Y.Am.)

$150,000 Drugs T

ARRESTED WITH ... DOPE HAUL

DOPE CHARGE CONVICTIONS 512 IN YEAR

$ 20,000

SMUGGLED DRUG HAUL— Valued at $5,000, these 1,380 vials of liquid morphine were found by detectives in room of Frederick Tripz, a German, at No. 25 South street yesterday. (N.Y.Am.)

PART OF DRUG TAKEN IN RAIDS—In several raids yesterday morning in Mulberry and Hester streets by Deputy Police Commissioner Simons and eight of his men drugs of the value of $150,000 were seized, with opium pipes and paraphernalia of drug addicts. Here is a part of

DR. CARLETO... of Police Hea... worth of drugs tak... These raids totaled t...

DOPE ... LICE FIRE

of Narcotic Squad, Great Drug Stores ng Past Year.

ED IN FROM EUROPE

Thousand Addicts Ar- d Here in 12 Months; Per Cent Convicted.

Customs Officials Study Narcotics Cache

Pipe Dreams Go Up in Smoke!

This big cache of opiu... Shown, left to right, ... of searching squad; Mi... A. John Kessel. Opium ...

SOME OF "DOPE" SEIZED in raid on China town drug dens, in which eight persons were ... rested, a man and woman risked their lives ... ing to escape and several shots were fi... Federal agents. The three men pictured ... left were among those held by the poli... will be given a hearing Thursday.

THE haul of the narcotic division of police headquarters ... the basement of police headquarters yesterday, cocaine ... tablets, phials, labels. Originally the drugs came from Eu... smugglers for the peddlers of the big cities.

U. S. DRUG CACHE — Room at Internal Revenue Department, Washington, showing part of hundreds of thousands of dollars' worth of narcotics, seized by Federal agents and now awaiting destruction. (International Newsreel)

NARCOTICS!—More than $100,000 worth of drugs and opium layouts seized during the last three months being destroyed at Police Headquarters yesterday.

Photo shows Lieutenant Joseph Mooney feeding flames, while Captain Henry Scherb and Detective Joseph Loures lend a hand.

TRAFFIC MO... Division N...

PINEX for Coughs

CLOSED CAR SHOW Grand Central Palace Sat. Sept. 23-30

RUSS REDS SEIZE SHIP IN B

3 CENTS
San Francisco's First Great Daily; Founded 1856
CALL AND POST, VOL. 107, NO. 138
SAN FRANCISCO CALL, VOL. 127, NO. 138
THE SAN FRANCISCO CALL
AN INDEPENDENT AND POST NEWSPAPER
TWENTY-TWO PAGES—SAN FRANCISCO, TUESDAY, JUNE 15, 1920
FIVE FINAL
Hotel Newsstands, Trains, Boats, 5c | In San Francisco, The Call, 3 cents. In Alameda County, The Call and Oakland

DEMPSEY ACQUITTED IN 7 MINUT

SLEUTHS TRAPPED IN DRUG RING GRAFT

HAMPION IS INDICATED F SLACKER CHARGES

n Harrison (Jack) Dempld's heavyweight champion, uitted today on the charge g the draft after the jury d seven minutes.
overnment will announce at 10 o'clock its intenarding the remaining injointly charging Dempsey anager, Jack Kearns, with to have the fighter om military duty during It is not expected that will be tried, in the light sudden termination of onal trial.
appiest kid on earth," said as men and women in the owded about him and ofongratulations. "I'm in a than I have ever been," with sparkling eyes and retched, almost, from ear
came serious. "I am on new life," he said. "The wiped clean. I'm out of am looking to a new fu-

ILTY" VERDICT

M. T. Dooling finished at 10:25 and the jury 42 the written verdict Judge Dooling, who bewarned the spectators stration.
he then announced, and ater Dempsey was the romptu reception.
ding of the case was a des waived arguments privilege the defense e prosecution in preview of the case.
ons to the jury Judge that prostitution was ccupation and that In stating that his loyed, had not coms questionnaire. This ued during the trial. that the defendant benefit of the doubt members of his famestionnaire had been pon him for support.

S REVIEWED

rted his instructions aft regulations durding that Class 4A, as placed, was not on from duty, but ees had been ex-

age, Column One

Federal Agents to Jail Jack Johnson Within 24 Hours

By W. BOYD GATEWOOD
Staff Correspondent International News Service

TIJUANA, Mexico, June 15.—Jack Johnson, former heavyweight champion of the world, who for eight years has been a fugitive from justice on a conviction of "white slavery," will be in the custody of the Department of Justice of the United States late today or early tomorrow, according to announcement emanating from the executive offices of Lower California.

Johnson has been given twenty-four hours in which to leave Mexico, the last place of refuge on the face of the earth for him.

CAUGHT IN ROUNDUP

Caught in the countrywide "drive" against undesirables, which is now sweeping hundreds of "men without a country" out of Mexico, Johnson is being deported as an "undesirable alien." American federal officers are waiting at the international line. There is no place he can go except to jail.

Such is the force of a statement made today by Superior Judge Luis Cacho of the Tijuana court, before whom charges of lawlessness and "offensive arrogance" have been filed against Johnson.

TWO SINISTER CHARGES

Some of the charges are these:

Johnson has a white valet, a poor American boy, said to have been shell shocked and gassed in the Argonne. He is Jack Johnson's slave, to do the black man's every bidding, the victim of a weakened mental force from his war experiences.

There are two sinister charges on file against Johnson by two girls. One charges a brutal attempted attack on Vincenia Espinoza, 20 year old maid, formerly in the employ of the black man's white wife, but who was forced to take haven in another house to escape Johnson's alleged abuse.

The other charge is one of a similar nature brought by an Americanized Mexican girl, by whose beauty Johnson was drawn. Then there is the common story of two white girls accosted by the negro, but protected when their friends intervened.

CHARGES ACTUALLY FILED

These charges are actually filed with the Mexican judge. Yet Johnson has not been placed under arrest. The Mexican courts move with the manana spirit here and Judge Cacho explains that these complaints are part of a chain of evidence now being gathered by the Mexican authorities as a basis for procedure to deport the prizefighter as an undesirable alien.

Part of this other evidence concerns the mysterious shooting of Jack Johnson's nephew, Gus Rhodes, a young negro whom Johnson has taken around with him all over the world. Rhodes was shot when Johnson, his white wife and others of a party were en route from Mexico City to Mexicali.

MYSTERIOUS SHOOTING

His right arm was shattered by a revolver ball. Johnson told one story immediately on his arrival in Mexicali with the wounded nephew, and another later on.

The first was that Rhodes had shot himself. But the wound was in the right arm. The next was that Johnson had shot him—accidentally.

The Mexican authorities are working on the last story, eliminating the accidental angle.

The motive for this family shooting was a domestic one, the Mexicans claim.

Continued on Next Page, Column Five

RUSS REDS SEIZE SHIP IN S. F. BAY

The Russian steamer Rogdoy was forcibly seized from possession of the old Russian government by eight Morse patrolmen, said to have been employed by the Soviet government of Russia, early today and was still held this afternoon against all invaders.

The capture of the vessel, which occurred in the China Basin, where the ship was under guard of watchmen employed by Captain M. Gordeney, representing the Russian government, was made at daylight. Threats to shoot were made by the boarders, according to John Cooney, 6335 Commercial street, who with Edward Kolb, was employed as a watchman on the vessel.

According to Cooney, the ship's third officer, who had been instructed to resist any attempt to take the craft, hid in his stateroom during the seizure.

The Rogdoy is claimed, both by the Soviets and the old Russian government and was given into legal custody of the latter recently when a libel, filed by the Bolshevik faction, by which they endeavored to gain control, was dismissed in the federal court.

Foulds, Once S. P. Attorney, Mourned

Veteran railroad men today mourned the death of J. E. Foulds, for many years connected with the Southern Pacific's legal department and at one time law partner of the late Carroll Cook. Foulds died Sunday at Berkeley, his home for twenty-five years.

Born in England in 1848, he came to California in 1871, started as a stenographer, studied law and joined the railroad's forces, which he served with but one break till his retirement in 1911.

The funeral was [illegible]

CAL. LIMITED TRAIN IS WRECKED; 2 DEAD

By Associated Press.

LA JUNTA, Colo., June 15.—At least two persons were killed today when the California Limited train, eastbound, on the Santa Fe Railroad, was wrecked at Rene, Colo. At Santa Fe Hospital here it was announced that forty injured had been given treatment. Most of those hurt, it was said, will recover.

At Santa Fe offices a statement was given out saying only two persons were killed. The dead:

A. O. Swanson, Chicago, combination barber and baggageman.

Dr. W. F. Harper, Mount Vernon, N. Y.

Rene is twelve miles south of La Junta and details of the accident reaching here are meager.

A broken crank on the engine caused the wreck, according to information reaching here. Four coaches left the track.

CALIFORNIANS HURT

The train was being pulled by two engines. The accident, according to official information, was caused by the breaking on the second engine of a side rod, which dug into the track, overturning the engine, dining car and three Pullman coaches.

The injured included:

H. J. Green, San Diego, Cal., arm and head bruises.

Mrs. Eliza H. Douglas, Los Angeles, bruises.

Miss Bertha M. Myers, Alhambra, Cal., bruises.

Frank J. Bride, negro cook, Chicago, scalded.

W. L. Anderson, negro waiter, Chicago, bruised.

Adolph Scheidler, chief cook, Chicago, bruised and scalded.

Otto Palmer, negro waiter, Chicago, bruises.

Mrs. A. C. Stubles, St. Louis, bruised.

J. W. Reeves, negro waiter, Chicago, bruised left side.

D. R. Mitchell, negro waiter, Chicago, right side bruised.

David Penn, negro waiter, Chicago, bruises.

Frank W. Freedland, Angola, N. Y., left leg hurt.

At Santa Fe headquarters here today it was stated that the California Limited is a through train, Los Angeles to Chicago. It is comparable to train No. 2, leaving this city and routed through to Chicago, and is composed throughout of Pullman sleepers and a dining car. There are no tourist or day coaches carried in the train.

It was stated that if the train was wrecked today at La Junta it would have been a train leaving Los Angeles Monday morning. There is no San Francisco connection [illegible]

Peddler of Drugs Tells Graft Story

Here are excerpts from the stenographer's transcript of Samuel Morlen's examination by District Attorney Matthew Brady and his assistant, Isadore M. Golden, in which Morlen's sensational confession of graft was made.

Questions were asked alternately by Brady and Golden. The answers are by Morlen. Details in Morlen's answers are left blank in places in order not to hinder the work of the investigators.

Q.—You have been in the business of peddling narcotics?
A.—Yes, sir.
Q.—And have you ever given De Vries any money?
A.—Yes, sir.
Q.—More than once?
A.—Yes, sir.
Q.—For what purpose?
A.—For protection.
Q.—What do you mean by protection?
A.—To let me sell narcotics and he would not arrest me.
Q.—And about how much money in all have you given him?
A.—Fifty dollars a month, sir.
Q.—Regularly?
A.—Yes, sir.
Q.—This was the regular tribute that you paid him every month?
A.—Yes, sir.
Q.—Has Mr. De Vries ever taken any other quantities of narcotics from you or from your possession before this transaction of May 16?
A.—He did not take from my possession—he took from somebody else at —— and it was mine. He came up to —— street. I had some stuff there and a year and a half ago, about that, 300 ounces. He arrested a fellow by the name of —— and he only turned in —— pieces.
Q.—And how many did he take?
A.— —— (Almost four times as much as was turned in).
Q.—How many pieces did he take up there on Ellis street on May 16?
A.—346 pieces.
Q.—How many did he turn in?
A.—That I don't know.
(Record shows that De Vries turned in approximately 125 pieces.)
Q.—What is the value of the stuff per piece?
A.—At retail or wholesale?
Q.—Give me the wholesale value per piece?
A.—Forty dollars.
Q.—Give me the retail value per piece.
A.—Oh, at retail it is accordingly—$50, $55 or $60—that is, accordingly.
Q.—Did you ever buy any narcotics from De Vries?
A.—Yes.
Q.—How much—about?
A.—About five or six different times I bought from him.

Mexico General Held In Carranza Slaying

By Associated Press.

MEXICO CITY, June 14.—General Francisco Murguia, who, with Generals Urquizo, Mariel, Montes and Barragan, is imprisoned in connection with events that occurred prior to the death of former President Carranza, has complained to the First Circuit Federal court that he was being tried by the military authorities while federal official charge of the [illegible]

NARCOTIC TRAFFIC IS BARED IN CONFESSIO

Sensational confessions implicating Inspectors John DeVries a Emile G. Coret of the State Board of Pharmacy, as ringleaders i gigantic system of trafficking in narcotics—a system that is declar to have netted them thousands of dollars in profits—are in possessi of the district attorney's office today and are to be presented to t grand jury for action.

How the traffic in narcotic drugs flourished among those prey ing upon unfortunate addicts, how protection was paid for by pec dlers to the two inspectors, and how DeVries and Coret often sol back to the prisoners the drugs they seized in raids upon the cache of drug sellers, is bared in the confessions which have been obtained.

The whole story, in its startling details, forms one of the most amazing and sensational exposes of graft and corruption laid before the county authorities in years.

Prosecution of DeVries, Coret and a woman said to have operated with them will come as a result of the disclosures culminating weeks of investigation, it was stated today by District Attorney Matthew Brady.

Foremost among the confessions obtained in the amazing expose is that of Samuel Morlen, awaiting trial as a wholesale distributer of narcotics. He has cited specific instances of negotiations with the two state inspectors. He has charged that he paid DeVries $50 a month regularly for protection.

Coret has been bared as negotiator in an amazing deal with Morlen whereby the latter says Coret offered to sell back to Morlen his own contraband drugs for $4000.

Results of an exhaustive investigation by The C[illegible]

NEWS DOWN TO THE LAST MINUTE

FREE POLITICAL PRISONERS, A. F. OF L. PLEA
(By Associated Press)

MONTREAL, June 15.—The American Federation of Labor in annual convention today called upon President Wilson and Attorney General aPlmer of the United States to secure "amnesty for all political prisoners." In a resolution the convention declared that the "further prosecution and imprisonment in the United States of political offenders is contrary to the democratic idealism and the traditions of freedom to which our country is committed."

SENSATIONAL CHARGES AGAINST PALMER

WASHINGTON, June 15.—Atorney General Palmer probably will be recalled before the Senate committee investivating primary election funds and expenses as a result of sensational charges disclosed today when a delegation from the Boston Bar Association visited the Department of Justice to protest his appointment of Daniel J. Gallagher to be United States district attorney for the Boston district. The charge being openly made that [illegible]

SAN FRANCISCO, SATURDAY, OCTOBER 23, 1920—TWENTY PAGES

DE VRIES GUILTY OF PERJURY O

ABE RUTH 'BEANED' IN GAME

CENTS

Francisco's First Daily; Founded 1856

THE SAN FRANCISCO CALL AND POST — AN INDEPENDENT NEWSPAPER

FIVE P.M. FINAL HOME

TWENTY-SIX PAGES—SAN FRANCISCO, SATURDAY, JUNE 19, 1920

Riccardi Stands Pat at Graft Trial

HIGHER UPS ACT IN 'DOPE' GRAFT

GIRL BEAUTY TO SUICIDE

MYSTERIOUS INFLUENCES FELT, SAYS GOLDEN

"Already the district attorney's office is beginning to feel mysterious and powerful influences because the underworld drug traffic trail leads to higher places."

This sensational statement was made today by Judge Isadore M. Golden, assistant district attorney, who has been conducting the investigation into the charges of graft, corruption and perjury made against John De Vries and Emile G. Coret, inspectors of the State Board of Pharmacy.

"It ill becomes the State Board of Pharmacy to take the position that nothing has been proved against the inspectors," Judge Golden said.

The fire of the district attorney's office was drawn by the attitude of the board in its efforts to shield its accused inspectors and to dash cold water on the investigation.

ISSUE PUT TO BOARD

The day was further enlivened by some direct questions asked the members of the pharmacy board by The Call.

4 Pupils Graduate In "Perfect Class" For Eight Years

Special Dispatch to The Call.

OROVILLE, June 19.—The local school department claims the four best school pupils in the state, the quartet haying graduated with perfect records, which were given in every one of their eight years in the elementary school. These pupils are Glenda Carpenter, Esther Mardou, Mildred Pyke and Alice Dunton.

Mexico New Regime Indicates Upholding Soil Nationalization

By Associated Press.

WASHINGTON, June 19.—Editoral comment in Mexico City newspepers and interviews with prominent officials of the present government of Mexico, as shown in dispatches received here today indicate there is a strong possibility that the new regime will support and endorse the famous article 27 of the constitution of 1917, against the operation of which the United States, Great Britain and France repeatedly have protested.

Excelsior, a leading newspeper of Mexico City, announced that "we found almost unanimity of opinion to uphold in all its parts the nationalization of the subsoil, which is regarded as indispensible to the development of industry."

ALOMIA INTERIOR SECRETARY

By Associated Press.

MEXICO CITY, June 18.—Salvad... Martinez Alomia was appointed se... tary of the interior today, his nom... tion completing the provisional cab... Alomia was formerly Mex... diplomatic representative in Guatem... The Mexican railway was turned... to its owners by the government... This property is British con... Queen Mary being the principal... holder.

Bandits Crack Bank Safe; Loot, $...

BARING DRUG RING SCANDAL

Samuel Morlen, drug trafficker, making the confession that opened up the expose charging Inspectors De Vries and Coret of the State Board of Pharmacy as ringleaders in the opium traffic. Left to right, District Attorney Matthew Brady, Assistant District Attorney Isidor Golden, Samuel Morlen, and Harry McKenzie, attorney for Morlen, who was instrumental in inducing his client to confess.—Photo by "INTERNATIONAL."

Drug Ring Confession

Continued From Page One

sisted by Harry McKenzie, attorney for Morelen.

SORDID TRUTH

Determined to assist the authorities and The Call in baring the whole sordid truth of the trafficking in drugs of bribery and protection, McKenzie persuaded his client to "come clean," to confess all that he knew of the underground system whereby drug trafficking was allowed to flourish before the eyes of the state inspectors paid to suppress the illicit business.

Morlen's confession has been augmented by sensational details of statements made by others who, like himself, have profited by the sale of drugs to those who have fallen slaves to the baneful influence of narcotics.

Just before Morelen gave the authorities his startling confession, word of his intention to "come through" evidently swept through the mysterious underground channels used by those in the drug traffic as avenues of communication.

ATTEMPT ON LIFE

The result was a mysterious attempt upon Morlen's life, a murderous plot, which came near silencing his tongue and keeping his knowledge of existing graft and crookedness forever from the authorites.

From out of the maze of charges and disclosures incriminating Inspectors De Vries and Coret, District Attorney Brady and his assistant, Golden, today prepared their summary of these outstanding charges, which ultimately will go before the grand jury and, according to Brady, will be used as the basis of criminal prosecution against the two accused inspectors:

That of $10,000 in narcotics seized by DeVries and Coret in a raid on May 10 on Morelen's rendezvous, only 10 per cent of the seized goods was turned over to the police property clerk and the balance, worth fully $9000, was kept by the inspectors and resold to drug peddlers.

That this system of holding out the major portions of drug seizures and appropriating to themselves the rich profits from selling to peddlers the drugs...

sponsible for shipping the drugs in interstate commerce.

Involved in one of the most sensational episodes bared in Morlen's confession is the mysterious part played by De Vries and a woman following a night raid on May 10 upon a place at 1935 Ellis street, used by Morlen as a cache for his rich stores of drugs.

STORY OF RAID

This raid, according to Morlen, was carried on in spite of the $50 a month which Morlen declares he paid to De Vries for protection and immunity from arrest while plying his trade as wholesale vender of narcotics to the peddlers selling in smaller quantities to addicts.

Half an hour after he had given his keys to De Vries, Morlen says he met De Vries at the Ellis street house. There, he says, he saw De Vries and a woman descending the stairs carrying two suit cases and a large sack.

The luggage, he declares, he placed in a waiting taxicab. The lights of the machine were turned out and the taxi speeded out Ellis street and into Divisadero.

A few moments later, according to Morelen in his confession, De Vries returned in the taxicab without the woman.

"Come on, Sam, let's go upstairs and straighten things out," said De Vries to Morlen, according to the latter.

ENTERED HOUSE

Morlen accompanied the state inspector into the house. Inspector Coret was there. Introductions followed.

"He's all right," De Vries said to Morlen, referring to Coret. "You will be able to do business with the man."

Coret then asked De Vries to state the value of the drugs that we left in the house, Morlen says.

"Do you want to go to jail or do you want to straighten things out?" Coret asked Morlen, according to the latter.

Morlen replied, "It is up to you."

Then, relating Coret's further conversation, Morlen says in his confession:

He askedme for $4000. I told him, "I can't see it to give you...

HERE'S STENOGRAPHIC CONFESSION REPORT

The folowing is taken from District Attorney Brady's stenographic report of Samuel Morlen's statements concerning the raid on the Morlen drug cache at 1935 Ellis street.

Morlen had just recounted the circumstances of his meeting with Inspector DeVries of the State Board of Pharmacy when DeVries obtained Morlen's keys to the Ellis street cache and directed Morlen to meet him later at that address. What followed is related by Morlen to the district attorney's office stenographer:

Then I saw a taxi coming up at 1935 Ellis street and a lady and Mr. DeVries came down with a couple of suit cases and a big sack. They went and put it into the taxicab and turned out the light and turned into Divisadero street. That same taxi came back with DeVries himself without the woman. I waited and then DeVries came out again and I hollered at him and he came over to me.

He came over to me and he said, "Come on, Sam, let's go upstairs and straighten things out." We went upstairs at 1935 Ellis street. We entered into the room and he introduced me to Mr. Coret. And he told me "He's all right. You will be able to do business with the man."

And Mr. Coret asked me if this stock belongs "to you." I said yes. He said to me, "What is this stuff worth?" I said, "What stuff do you mean?" And he said, "This here." And I said, "All of it? Do you mean the stock that is here or the stock that is gone?" He said, "The stock that is here."

I said, "The stock that is here don't amount to very much."

He asked me, "What will it be?" And I said, "What do you mean?"

He said to me: "Do you want to go to jail or do you want to straighten things out?"

I told him, "It is up to you."

He asked me for $4000. I told him:

"I can't see it to give you up $4000 for that amount. I will give you the $4000 providing you bring the other stuff back—what was here before." He laughed at me. I said, "No laughing about it." I told him, "You had better produce all the stuff and if you don't I will go and tell on you." He laughed at me and he said, "My word is as good as yours, maybe better."

Well, he arrested me.

of wealth direct the movements of the whole rotten system.

GOLDEN STATEMENT

Golden was equally emphatic in pointing out the enormity of the disclosures and their importance. He said:

Drug peddlers have come here and told their stories voluntarily. Their evidence coincides save for minor details. This is one of the most amazing tales of graft and law defiance I have...

S. F. SUPERVISORS ASK PAY RAISE

Barking Canine Brings Rescuers ... Man

Gasoline Shortage Investigated By Full U. S. Force

Virtually the entire local investigating force of the Department of Justice, under E. M. Blanford, today continued the investigation into the so-called shortage of gasoline and increase of prices.

The inquiry was started on orders from Attorney General A. Mitchell Palmer, transmitted to Mrs. Annette Adams, United States attorney.

The step was taken following the presentation of charges by the California Automobile Trade Association that the shortage was fictitious and designed to increase prices.

S. F. Piano Man Died By Drowning, Verdict

A coroner's jury at Daly City today returned a verdict of "death by drowning probably accidental" in the case of George W. Fraser, 1435 Willard street, San Francisco, member of the firm of Fraser & McConnell, ...

Suicide's Will "Cuts Off" Wife He ...

PETE'S BA... BOND BRI...

THE LAST ...

KNOCKED UNCO...

Senator Owen to Address Barristers

SEIZURE THREAT MA...

Statutory Charge In Divorce

COUNTS

Store will c...

Pretty Girl Agent Traps "Dope" King in Tampa

CANOS CAUGHT IN WEB OF LOVE SPUN BY SELF

Checked in Alleged Plot to Kill Hearst's International Agent Posing as an Addict

IMPORTING METHOD BARED

Narcotics Brought In by Alleged Fishermen, Dispatched by Plane, Spies Assassinated

By CHARLES MAC ARTHUR.
Copyright Universal Service.

The city of Tampa, on the west coast of Florida, has been called the dope metropolis of the South.

Morphine, heroin, opium and cocaine may be bought for less money in Tampa than in any other American city, indicating that the supplies of smuggled dope are unlimited and openly arrived at.

The location of Tampa favors this condition. It is the principal city on a coast that is indented with thousands of tiny harbors and strewn with sandy keys, made to the smugglers' order. Blackbeard and Gasparilla came flying into the mazes of this same coast centuries ago before the guns of the French and English men-of-war and found the hiding places that are being used to-day by the Cuban fishing boats, running from the revenue cutters that patrol the Gulf.

Work for Syndicate

These Cuban fishermen work for a syndicate having headquarters in Tampa. It is a most efficient syndicate, having unlimited capital and foxy executives. As illustrative of Sidney Howard's statement in the current issue of Hearst's International Magazine that "dope is the core of crime," it might be mentioned that these executives are the "best minds" of America's criminal class.

They were so slick that four Federal agents, successively appearing in their midst in the guise of New York dope dealers, could not purchase a grain of evidence with a suitcase full of money.

The syndicate preferred to play it safe, and courteously declined to sell, although there was no indication that they suspected the ruse. As one member of the band expressed it, they never trusted a stranger and never took a chance, and were therefore never caught.

The author of this confident remark, Thomas Canos, is at present kicking himself all over Tampa for the reason that he took a chance, trusted a stranger and was caught cold, all in an hour's time.

Trapped by Girl

The stranger who roped the cocksure Canos was a twenty-year-old girl just out of college and seemingly sent to Tampa by Providence for the especial needs of Mr. Canos.

The Government men had been trying to catch Canos for two weeks and had given it up when they heard of Miss Nellie Asher. She was a visitor in Tampa who had chanced to overhear two dope smugglers discussing their plans. She carried her information to Chief of Police F. M. Williams, who presented her to the Government agents as Our Nell.

It developed in the conversation that Our Nell was a cousin to J. L. Asher, the versatile prohibition agent who recently raided the city of Washington all by himself in a dozen different disguises. Inspired by Cousin Jake, Nell asked to be turned loose in Tampa. It was then Tuesday. She promised to have Mr. Canos by Thursday, dead or alive.

Others Failed

It looked as if Nell were biting off considerably more than she could chew. Mr. Canos's friends were many and powerful, and sudden death had visited others who had [illegible]oo inquisitive about the West Coast dope traffic. There was the case of the unidentified

AFTER mere men had failed in their efforts to trap Thomas Canos, suspected of being the head of a drug syndicate which flooded the country with deadly narcotics via the Florida Keys, Nellie Asher, landed the much sought Canos with her entrancing smile.

NELLIE ASHER

man, said to have been a Government agent, whose body was found behind a billboard in Ybor City, a suburb of Tampa. Another agent had been murdered in a cypress glade farther to the north a little time before, and there were many cases of assault. But Nell was undeterred.

In a week she ran into more adventure than may be found in a serial movie "thriller," barely escaping with her life, but she certainly showed a squad of veteran Government men how a good job ought to be done.

Instead of one conspirator she arrested two and obtained evidence on which the arrest of four others was based. In five days she accomplished alone what four Federal men had been trying to do for a month; and her only weapon was a smile.

On the first day of her search for Canos Nell went to Tarpon Springs, a fishing and resort town, twenty-eight miles from Tampa.

A Hundred Bayous

Tarpon Springs is the port through which dope reaches Tampa. It is a quaint little city built over a hundred bayous that reach into it from the sea. More than half of its 4,000 population is composed of Greek sponge fishers, whose picturesque boats fill the bay and give the town its sobriquet of "The Venice of the South."

The information on which Nell went to Tarpon Springs was that these sponge boats were the carriers of unlimited quantities of dope.

Not all of the boats are employed in this service, of course, but enough to reckon as a fleet. The practice is to slip out to sea, meet a Cuban fisherman somewhere beyond the three-mile limit, and transfer his cargo [illegible] dope, which is effectively hidd[illegible]ath a load of fresh sponges [illegible]ped from the ocean floor.

It is almost im[illegible] to apprehend the smuggl[illegible]he Government men are [illegible] numbers to cope w[illegible] smugglers are [illegible] that at [illegible] Gulf coast th[illegible] dope r[illegible] by si[illegible] ment [illegible]

At [illegible] thw[illegible] we[illegible] the[illegible] lighthouse [illegible] Springs. burning fo[illegible] its usual [illegible] miles ahead [illegible]

Sent[illegible]he

Nell's info[illegible]as that Canos' part i[illegible]piracy was to superintend [illegible]er of dope from the fishe[illegible] the sponge boats, whence [illegible] hustled to Tampa by a you[illegible] called Leo Day, and there [illegible]hed by airplane to the [illegible]te's retail salesmen in the [illegible]uth-Eastern States. Formerly [illegible]anos' duties were discharged by [illegible]euben Jones, town marshal of [illegible]pon Springs and known to the criminal element of Florida simply and affectionately as "Rube."

Rube Jones was an efficient director, but he thought his superiors were hogging the profits.

He decided to go into business for himself and notified the syndicate that he and his sponge fishers were out of its employ.

The next day "Rube" and his friend Bert Scott went hunting quail with their wives. The women were left to make the fire while "Rube" and Scott scared up the game. When they failed to return search was started and the town marshal and his friend were found, face downward, in a cypress swamp, plugged full of lead. Presently Canos assumed charge of the situation at Tarpon Springs.

Nell had the good fortune to meet him on the bus that runs from Tampa to the Coast and before the journey was over, Canos had made several proposals, none of them honorable. Since Nell had represented that she was wickedly inclined it was necessary for her to invent a story that would cool the dope smuggler's ardor without offending him. So she told him that she had come to Tampa on business that would interfere with the development of their romance.

Vampire Yarn

Pressed for details, she told Canos that her business in Tampa was to separate a fool from his money. She gave him an interesting story of having met a young Chicago millionaire who had recently been cured of the dope habit and who had come to Tampa to convalesce. The "millionaire" was an investigator for Hearst's International Magazine.

Nell had hoped that Canos, to further the romance, would present her with an incriminating package of dope. She assured him that her millionaire friend would give anything for just one shot and intimated that her gratitude to Canos might know no bounds. But he had other plans.

He insisted on taking the supposed millionaire into the country on the pretense of getting dope and killing him without delay, promising afterward to take Nell to California on the $5000 the millionaire was supposed to carry on his person.

Nell demurred, saying that when Canos got the money he would cease to care for her; but Canos swore passionately that he would care for her the more, as she was the ideal of his dreams. He insisted on meeting the millionaire and doing the deed that very night.

Meeting Arranged

Nell could not stop him without betraying her intentions. So she returned with him to Tampa and the meeting was arranged in a dark corner of the city park.

The investigator, whom Nell had warned over the telephone, came to the rendezvous with a roll of stage money wrapped in real $100 bills and asked for dope. Ca[illegible] gibly of ten ounces [illegible] the house of a friend [illegible] tigator insisted on a [illegible] was at this point that [illegible] ciated the philosophy [illegible] far kept him out of j[illegible] pered to Nell that he [illegible] not trust a stranger [illegible] she were [illegible] vellous [illegible] millionai[illegible] Providen[illegible] meeting w[illegible] [illegible] money [illegible] y and so quickly [illegible] But Nell squeezed [illegible] old him it would be [illegible] al mistake to arou[illegible] re's suspi[illegible] ple. Ca[illegible] small sam[illegible] murde[illegible] sed love and obstin[illegible] hair at her [illegible]

[illegible] Trap

A[illegible] n, not without hea[illegible] it was all foolish[illegible] should lose by it. [illegible] alk it over with [illegible] tates in the syn[illegible] desperately [illegible] time for that; [illegible] by a school [illegible] into the tr[illegible] he had so far [illegible]

As Canos b[illegible] the investig[illegible] ten grains [illegible]rphine and begged him to purchase ten additional ounces of the drug, two government men rose from behind the park bench and folded him in their arms.

Canos let out one squeal of surprise and disillusion as he turned to look for Our Nell. She was malignant enough to tell him that the penitentiary would not influence her love for him in the least, and that they would make that California trip when he got out.

To-morrow the story of how Nell trapped the second leader of the smugglers' gang.

Arrest Restaurant Man for Liquor Violation

Constant Scheppler, proprietor of a restaurant at No. 415 Fairview avenue, Ridgewood, Queens, was yesterday arrested by Otterich and Marx of the Twelfth inspection district, Ridgewood, for alleged violation of the prohibition act.

CC

Details of Big

DRY MEN TRAP 3 POLICEMEN IN BIG RAID

Dragnet Out Following Arrest of Officers by U. S. Agents

HIGHERUPS ARE SOUGHT

Prohibition Chief Plans Cleanup of Powerful Rum Ring

(Continued From Page 1, Column 1)

declared late yesterday that other policemen still to be apprehended had within recent weeks compelled his agents under threats of arrest to disclose their raiding programs, and that as a result offender suspects had received tips and escaped.

The smuggling craft from which the contraband liquor was being unloaded escaped, but the Federal officers fired at the crew and asked San Francisco hospitals to watch for wounded men, as they found blood on the dock at the point where the rum runners cut their lines and made for deep water. The rum-running boat was not identi[illegible] It was a small, two-[illegible] fixed at [illegible] three po[illegible] prisoners [illegible]th smug[illegible] ssessing [illegible]ky. Dur[illegible] al Prohi[illegible]r appeared [illegible]mmissioner [illegible]e amplified [illegible]y, and bonds [illegible]000. [illegible]y appeared as [illegible]used policemen [illegible] States District [illegible]Silva represent[illegible] the defendants. [illegible] the re[illegible] oth attor[illegible]ed their clients [illegible] make no[illegible]s, and it was [illegible]eclared at [illegible] last night [illegible] at no state[illegible] been made. [illegible] statement [illegible] Duffy was [illegible]ublished in [illegible] Hender[illegible] n" was named [illegible]rains" of [illegible]e smuggling p[illegible] was add[illegible] that he escape[illegible]ey Silva [illegible]er stated that [illegible] denied [illegible]king any statement [illegible] Prohibition Agent [illegible] Harvill [illegible]ected the raid wit[illegible]e as[illegible]istants, and described [illegible] suc[illegible]cess in every particul[illegible]sent the captured trucks, [illegible] the liquor, chiefly whisk[illegible] warehouses at Second and Brannon streets. He admitted that the agents had been watching for this consignment to arrive for three nights.

INNOCENT PLEAS DENIED

Refuting the claims of Lieutenant Brasfield that the police had arrested the smugglers, Harvill declared that Brasfield recognized him, pleaded to be let off and declared that the publicity of such an arrest would ruin him. Harvill further charged that Brasfield declared he had bought the three cases of liquor found in the automobile belonging to Patrolman Willever, and admitted buying five cases the previous night.

The civilian prisoners declined to make statements for publication, and their counsel, Attorney Silva, said: "I have advised these men not to talk and I have no statement to make for them."

Attorney Hennessy, after conferring with Brasfield, Willever and Barion authorized a statement in their behalf, relating the story [illegible] said had been told to him by Br[illegible]field and corroborated by the oth[illegible] In that statement Brasfield clai[illegible] that his suspicions were arou[illegible] when he was patroling his dist[illegible] about 10:30 o'clock, by a grou[illegible] motor trucks proceeding southw[illegible] toward a district where he had [illegible]tected and arrested some liq[illegible] smugglers several months befor[illegible]

STORY OF POLICE

He said that later he encounte[illegible] Patrolman Willever in the lat[illegible] automobile and they picked [illegible] Barion and started to investig[illegible] They found six trucks loaded w[illegible] whisky and placed seven men u[illegible] arrest, he said.

"Then we heard several shots [illegible] were commanded to throw up [illegible] hands," the statement contin[illegible] "To our shouts that we were po[illegible] officers the reply came from [illegible] darkness: 'Never mind; stick [illegible] up,' and then four men appe[illegible] with pointed revolvers, decla[illegible] they were Federal men, and [illegible] hands went up. They took our [illegible]volvers, although we protested [illegible] we had just arrested the prison[illegible] and they refused to listen to [illegible] protests."

Assistant United States Dis[illegible] Attorney Geis, who took charg[illegible] the case, indicated last night [illegible] the evidence will be ready for [illegible]entation to the Federal Grand [illegible] on Tuesday. The prisoners ar[illegible] have a hearing Thursday morn[illegible] February 8.

RIGID QUIZ ASKED

When informed that three po[illegible] men had been arrested in con[illegible]

Police

GOLDEN GATE

...siness Telephone, Columbus 7000 5

Smuggler Haven

POLICEMEN'S PROTECTIVE ASSOCIATION

BALL

For the BENEFIT FUND

AUDITORIUM

MONDAY EVENING

APRIL 18

1927

PATROLMAN

4701

SAN FRANCISCO CHRONICLE, SATURDAY, FEBRUARY 3, 1923 3

...sky Raid in Which Police Officers Are Implicated

...rrested in Rum Smuggling Raid

POLICE FLATLY DENY CHARGES OF DRY AGENTS

Accused Officers Issue Statements Regarding Liquor Raid

Lieutenant of Police D. H. Brasfield and Policemen William Barion and Mark Willever, brought before Chief of Police O'Brien yesterday, made detailed statements relative to their connection with the South San Francisco raid. These statements were later supplemented by written statements submitted to Chief O'Brien, which follow in full:

Lieutenant D. H. Brasfield—About 10 p. m. February 1, I noticed three trucks turning from Third street into Sixteenth street and driving down to the wharf of the Loop Lumber Company. Officer Mark Willever and Officer Walter Heagney were riding in Willever's automobile. I met them a few minutes later and told them what I had seen. I was under the impression that something was being smuggled.

Heagney took the street car and went home. Willever and I waited for a few minutes, then drove down on the dock. We met three trucks coming out. We followed them to South City, where they turned and went to a wharf near the Western Meat Company.

RETURN TO WHARF

We drove back to South City and then to San Francisco. At Seventeenth and Mission streets we met Officer William Barion of the Mission station. I asked him to get into the machine, which he did. I then told him of my suspicion that something was being smuggled, and we then drove once more to South City. When we arrived at the wharf near the Western Meat Company, we placed seven men under arrest. They were loading whisky into trucks.

At that time a machine drove up, four men jumping out. They fired several shots, and cried out that they were Federal officers. We told them who we were. They ordered us to throw up our hands, which we did. They took our revolvers, then placed us under arrest.

Policeman William Barion—At 12:15 a. m., this date, while waiting for a street car at Seventeenth and Mission streets, Lieutenant Brasfield and Officer Willever drove up and told me to get in, informing me they had followed two automobiles to South City, where they thought they were smuggling whisky. We just had reached the wharf and placed the men under arrest when I heard several shots and some one say:

"We are Federal officers. Throw up your hands!"

Which we did. They searched us, taking our revolvers and placing us under arrest.

* * * *

Policeman Mark Willever—At 10 p. m. last night while on my way home with Officer Heagney we met Lieutenant Brasfield at Eighteenth and Third streets, who informed us that three auto trucks had gone to the Sixteenth-street dock, and he suspected them of smuggling whisky. Officer Heagney left us, stating that he was going home on account of his wife being sick. I went with Lieutenant Brasfield in my automobile to the Sixteenth-street driveway.

On arriving there we saw three trucks coming out. We followed to South City, where they drove down toward the Western Meat Company. We waited around South City looking for officers. Not seeing any we drove back to San Francisco to Seventeenth and Mission streets, where we met Officer Barion, who had an appointment with Lieutenant Brasfield.

OFFICERS DISARMED

We then drove back to South City and drove down the road to the Western Meat Company, and just past the same we saw trucks at a small wharf. We drove down to them and had placed seven men under arrest when another automobile drove up, four men jumped out, fired several shots, shouting they were Federal men.

We answered them, stating we were police officers. The men ordered us to throw up our hands, which we did with the rest. The Federal officers searched us, taking our revolvers and placing us under arrest.

Brief Sketches of Policemen Held On Dry Charges

HERE are brief sketches of the three policemen who were arrested yesterday morning by Federal prohibition agents:

Lieutenant D. H. Brasfield

Born in Santa Rosa in 1875.
Joined Police Department December 31, 1908.
Promoted to corporal July 13, 1913.
Made a sergeant August 24, 1914.
Promoted to lieutenant June 30, 1919.
Attached to Park, Harbor, Richmond, Central and Potrero stations.
No charge ever filed against him.

Patrolman William Barion

Born in San Francisco in 1883.
Joined Police Department November 9, 1911.
Attached to Mission station.
No charge ever filed against him.

Patrolman Mark M. Willever

Born in Santa Cruz in 1876.
Joined Police Department May 9, 1907.
Fined $50 by Police Commission on February 18, 1909, for neglect of duty.

BATH HAD 1600 BATHERS

It is said that ancient Rome consumed no less than 40,000,000 gallons of water a day, and a most noticeable feature of the modern city is the prodigal effervescence of its water, gushing from fountains of every conceivable size and design.

CHIEF OF RAID GIVES VERSION OF BIG SEIZURE

Agents Envelop Smugglers From All Sides and Close In

"We had a tip that some liquor had been landed the night before," said Agent Y. L. Harvill, in charge of the raid, "so with two other agents and a driver I drove down to South San Francisco to a point along the railroad and street car tracks, between the Western Meat Company's wharf and the W. P. Fuller & Co. dock. There is a little wharf in between these big ones.

"Shortly after 1 o'clock a touring car drove up and passed on down the road to the little wharf. It went up and down several times and appeared to be scouting about. We made no pretense of hiding, our car being in full view of every passer-by. Soon automobile trucks approached from all direction—from north, south and west. There were six in all. They drove down toward the water, and a little while afterward, at 2 o'clock, we folowed them.

AGENTS MANEUVER

"We were doubtful at first whether or not there was anything wrong, thinking perhaps the trucks belonged to the Western Meat Company. When we got near the bay we saw what appeared to be a fishing boat at the little dock. The alleged smugglers were scattered about. We deployed and armed, approached them from the north, west and south. We shouted to the gang to put up their hands, and put 'em up high. All complied immediately, those who were away from the main crowd running back and lining up with the rest.

"Lieutenant of Police D. H. Brasfield recognized me and begged me to let him off, saying the affair, if it became public, would ruin him. He declared he had bought only three cases of whisky, which were in his automobile. One of the other policemen declared he had been on the force eighteen years, had a family and would be ruined.

PLEAS OF MERCY

"Each of the three policemen had a regulation police revolver, which we confiscated, and they also had a riot shotgun. They begged hard to be released. Brasfield made a strong appeal to me to let him go. He said he had a family and a good reputation. I replied that he should have thought of those things before he got into such a mess. He admitted he had bought five cases the night before.

"Brasfield we handcuffed with his own handcuffs he carried with him. Then we took the entire ten men to the station. The liquor was transferred into the prohibition warehouse at Second and Brannan streets. Most of it was good whisky, although there was a little Chinese wine in the lot in jugs packed in straw."

License Plates of Trucks Fictitious

Of the six trucks seized in the prohibition raid at South San Francisco, police and Federal agents were not able to find any of the owners. Five of the licenses gave fictitious addresses and the sixth named the Palm Market at 498 Clement street as the owner. Henry Blumenthal, proprietor of the market, declared he had no knowledge of the raid and denied the seized car was his.

The number plates show registry under the following names:

W. A. McGee, Hotel Atlanta, Seventh and Mission streets.

F. W. Millisack, former saloon owner at 61 Third street.

H. Schroeder, 621 Eighteenth avenue.

Palm Market, 498 Clement street.

J. J. Curran, 940 Webster street, Palo Alto.

F. K. Mills, 546 Chetwood street, Oakland.

New York Dry Men Plan Big Cleanup

NEW YORK, Feb. 2.—Prohibition authorities are preparing to launch a huge drive in New York city on "dry" law violators. It was announced tonight by E. C. Yellowley, acting prohibition director, upon his return from a conference with his superiors at Washington.

Only Small Part Of Liquor Landed

Raid Nets Small Portion of Contraband Booze

That only a small portion of the liquor which came into San Francisco recently was captured by prohibition agents at South San Francisco early yesterday morning, is the opinion of C. H. Wheeler, chief Federal prohibition agent.

"Our men had a tip some days ago that a big lot of liquor was nightly being landed," he said, "and almost the entire force had been watching landing places for the last four nights. It was only Thursday night that the long cold vigils were awarded with success when 400 cases of liquor were seized and ten men arrested at South San Francisco.

"I don't know whether the men arrested were the leaders of the gang or only employes, but I think most of them were simply working for others. I have had no opportunity to question the men who were captured. After they were arrested, I requested that their bail be set at $5000 each as I considered the matter important, but I learned that during the night they were all released on $1000 bail each and scattered, so I have not seen any of them since the seizure.

...ion with the seizure of a large ...uantity of smuggled whisky, Theo...ore J. Roche, president of the Po...ce Commission, gave out this state...ment:

"While I have not been apprised ...f all the facts in the matter, I ...ave instructed Police Chief O'Brien ...o institute a rigid investigation in ...o far as the police are concerned.

"The Police Department is charged ...ith enforcement of the Wright ...ct. If members of the department ...ave been derelict in their duty, I ...ant to know it. I have instructed ...he proper officials to spare neither ...ime nor effort to get at the bot...om of the accusations against ...ieutenant Brasfield and Patrolmen ...arion and Willever They are en...itled to a fair and impartial in...estigation as much as the Federal ...rohibition agents."

...'Brien to Sift Charges Made by U.S. Dry Agents

...onsultation With Prohi...ition Officers in View; ...olice Orders Disobeyed

After a conference with Captain ... Detectives Duncan Matheson

last night, Chief O'Brien announced that today he would have a conference with the United States District Attorney and prohibition enforcement officials to ascertain to what extent Government witnesses can testify before the Police Commission against the members of the San Francisco Police Department, who are alleged to be connected with liquor smugglers.

O'Brien said that even if the prohibition officials could not testify against the officers before the Police Commission, he had sufficient evidence to convict them of having left the city and county without permission.

Commenting on the part played by police officers in the raid, Chief of Police O'Brien said:

"Regardless of whether or not the policemen are in league with the liquor smugglers, this appears to be certain—they violated strict police regulations when they took it upon themselves to leave the city and county of San Francisco without the permission of headquarters or their commanding officers. My office is open all day. The officer in charge of the detective bureau represents me here all night. These men should have notified headquarters before going on a mission outside of the city limits. I have ordered charges filed against them before the Police Commission. Their commanding officers have stripped them of their stars and suspended them."

RUTTER SAYS POLICE ACTED AS LOOKOUTS

Charges Officers With Being Scouts for Whisky Smugglers

"We have known for some time that certain members of the San Francisco Police Department have been aiding bootleggers to land whisky at South San Francisco," Samuel F. Rutter, Federal Prohibition Director of California, said yesterday when apprised of the spectacular arrest of a lieutenant, two patrolmen and several civilians early yesterday morning.

RAID TIMED

"We not only had advance information that a ship was to unload whisky at South San Francisco, but we timed the appearance of our agents so that we could capture the smugglers redhanded. From what my agents have reported to me, I am convinced that the timing was perfect. For some time we have had knowledge that certain policemen have acted as scouts in automobiles and have kept a keen eye peeled for appearance of prohibition agents.

"I was told today by the agents who captured the policemen and civilians that Lieutenant Brasfield freely admitted that he was on hand to buy some of the whisky, but denied that he was there to aid the smugglers. Be that as it may, I am convinced that in the past there are certain members of the Police Department who aided materially in clearing the way for the booze runners.

POLICE INTERFERENCE

"Several times in the last three or four months our agents have been stopped in South San Francisco by policemen and threatened with arrest unless they disclosed their identity. As soon as my agents made themselves known, the word was passed in some mysterious manner, and all smuggling and bootlegging stopped until the agents left.

"But with the arrest of these policemen, we intend to go to the bottom of this business. These policemen and all others are charged with co-operating with us, but some of them seemed to have failed."

A Photograph of the Old Style Sing Sing Prison Uniform and Convicts Marching in Lock Step.

Interesting Photograph of the Enormous Liquor Which Has Overcrowded the War and Overflowed Out Onto the Docks Wharves at Nassau, in the Baham

A Sheriff in Delaware Administering the Whip at the Public Whipping Post.

Unusual Photograph of a Crooks' Party in a Well-Known Thieves' Cafe. Most of the Men in the Picture Have Police Records as High-Class Crooks, and Seldom Permit Themselves to Be Photographed Outside of the Rogues' Galleries. The Famous "Skush" Thomas Is the Third Man from the Left, Seated.

Eddie Guerin, the International Criminal, Whose Picturesque Career Has Seldom Been Equalled in the History of Crime.

Fac-Simile of a United States Department of Justice Warrant Which the Blackmailers Filled Out and Served on Mr. West, and Some of the Bogus Federal Secret Service and Detective Badges Which the Rascals Used to Frighten Their Victims

Homer T. French, One of the Shrewdest Confidence Operators Known to the Police.

Receptacle Provided on Jewelry Thief's Leg by a False "Calf" of Stiff Leather, Which Is Covered by Her Stockings.

Richard Golden, Who Played the Part of United States Secret Service Agent

The American Bar in Paris Where Humphreyes Planned His Scheme to Entrap the Grand Duke Boris.

"We drove up to the entrance of the Royal Palm with an endless collection of hand luggage, and half a dozen negro porters trailed along behind us loaded down with leather bags and smart cases. It was all very important as a stage setting for our future operations among the wealthy men and women at that millionaires' Winter playground.

Queen of the Underworld

eral Pershing, or impose on a popular hero like Babe Ruth without the slightest compunctions, superstitions or prickings of conscience.

To illustrate a proof of this, I will to-day tell how a party of crooks followed to Havana no less a popular hero than Babe Ruth and trimmed him to the amount of just $130,000.

The great majority of the 110,000,000 American would no more think of harming Babe Ruth than they would of deliberately injuri... In fact,

A half-dozen crooks put their heads together and decided that Babe Ruth was making a lot of money from his big salary as the foremost baseball star, and must also be gathering in considerably more money in the way of bonuses for his home runs and commissions from the sale of Babe Ruth bats, caps, suspenders and other Babe Ruth articles which are on the market and are very popular.

A little inquiry into Mr. Ruth ... his simple habits

... famous Bambino.

So ... as Babe Ruth strolled into an American bar ... and called for a cool drink of cocoanut juice ... track acquaintance edged up to the bar, shoo... with him and introduced him to "Mr. Winslow ... oil operator, who owns most of the big oil gu... the Tulsa, Oklahoma, oil fields."

... out that Mr. Winslow, "the New York mil... was a great baseball fan. Indeed, he was quite ... hero worshiper, and he made it clear that one ... ents of his life was right then an...

As the baseball season came to an end at Havana, Mr. Winslow revealed the fact that among his other interests he owned a few race horses and made a bet now and then, just for the fun of it.

So, a day or two after the ball season closed, Winslow and Jackson casually suggested that perhaps Mr. Ruth, if he had no engagement that afternoon, might like to go out to the races. Mr. Ruth was then through his baseball engagement and entitled to rest, recreation and amusement during the remaining weeks before his training should begin for the forthcoming season.

Yes, he would really like to see the track and would be glad to go along.

Of course ...

And so the game went on until Ruth had visited the track several afternoons and had seen about $100,000 in real money actually paid to Winslow and about the same sum collected as the winnings of his friend Jackson.

In all this time there was no suggestion made to Mr. Ruth that he should also try a bet. The racing men seemed to avoid the subject. They were always ready to talk about baseball, or things back in New York, or ... They bet their money and ...

... track.

Mr. Ruth smiled to himself at the nonchalance of this millionaire. And a few minutes later, when he saw the bookmaker count out and pay over $30,000 in real money to his oil magnate friend, Mr. Ruth said:

"I would not mind making a bet myself—just as a flyer."

"Well," said Mr. Winslow, with a faraway look across the track, "if you really want to bet a little I could tell you on what horse I am putting my bet to-morrow."

Mr. Ruth was pleased at this friendly offer. He had ... oil friend ... figure out the winning horse ...

1 — ...AL ISLAND: ...ilitary hospital. ...onvent. ...hapel. ...arade ground. ...maphore. ...astern fort. ...ockyard. ...al house.

2 — DEVIL'S ISLAND: A—Guerin's hut. B—Guard house. C—Telephone.

3 — ST. JOSEPH'S ISLAND: A—Stone hut refractory prisoners. B—Tanyard.

"Babe" Ruth Was Swindled Out of $130,000 by Crooks in Havana

"I have made it a rule to send along a woman with the corpse until the caffin has safely passed the border. We have got the nicest, quietest, most demure little lady, who dresses up in widow's weeds. She can pour out a flood of tears that would deceive the sharpest detective's eyes in the world. We send this girl along with the coffin,

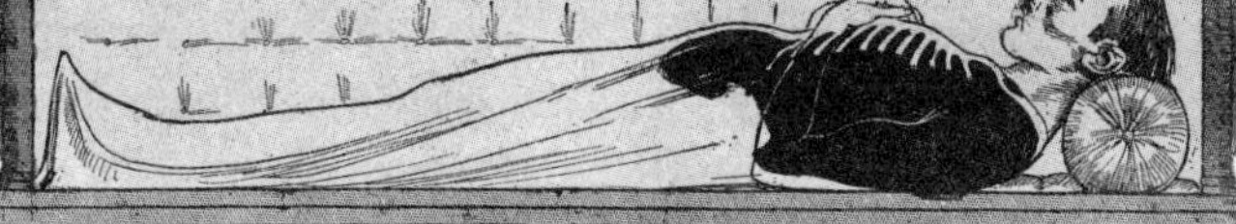

Drug Smugglers Engage an Undertaker to Cut a Hollow Cavity Where the Lungs and Internal Organs Are and Stuff the Portion Shown Above in Black With Dope, and the Remains Are Then Shipped Across the Border in a Casket.

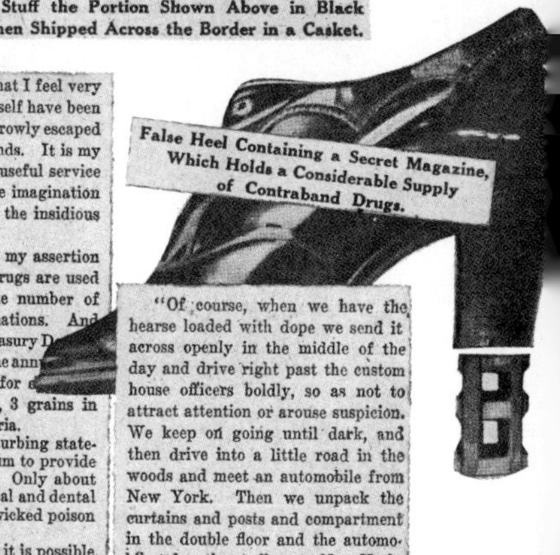

False Heel Containing a Secret Magazine, Which Holds a Considerable Supply of Contraband Drugs.

I HAVE already said in previous pages that I feel very strongly on the subject of drugs. I myself have been a victim of the drug habit, and have narrowly escaped the fate which overtook so many of my friends. It is my hope that I will be able to accomplish some useful service in the course of these articles in stirring the imagination of the American public, who do not realize the insidious and growing menace of drugs.

Perhaps some surprise will be caused by my assertion that sixty times as much opium and other drugs are used in the United States, in proportion to the number of people, as are used in some other civilized nations. And yet an investigation by the United States Treasury De... ment has revealed the astonishing fact that the ann... sumption of drugs here averages 36 grains for e... son, while it is only 2 grains in Germany, 3 grains in France, 1 grain in Italy and ½ grain in Austria.

So there is official authority for the disturbing statement that we use in this country enough opium to provide 2½ doses for every man, woman and child! Only about one-quarter of this is used in legitimate medical and dental practice; therefore three-quarters of all this wicked poison is used by dope fiends.

The readers of this page may wonder how it is possible to bring into this country such an enormous supply when government officers are supposed to be on watch to stop the forbidden traffic.

As I have pointed out in earlier articles, the profit in smuggling the dope is enormous. People of resourcefulness and ingenuity are engaged in the business, and they spend their entire time and thought in devising ways to get the prohibited drugs into the country.

I have already spoken of the steady stream of narcotics which flows into New York from Montreal. Chorus girls of the travelling road companies bring in a great deal, and there are regular professional drug smugglers—pretty girls like Dorothy Waddell and Dixie Dixon—who finally outlived their usefulness and were sent to their graves to seal their lips.

But there are many, many other ways in which the contraband drugs cross the border. It would require all the space in this article if I undertook to detail all the schemes and devices for bringing in drugs which drug smugglers have told me of. But I will give one instance here and then pass on to another phase of the subject.

I know a man who is the head of a dope smuggling ring in Canada. Only a few weeks ago he called to see me, and, with perfect freedom and confidence, told me "how business was getting along." I will call him "George." I discussed with George the death of Dorothy Waddell and Dixie Dixon and a few others, and he shook his head and said that he had long since stopped hiring girls to bring dope across the border.

"They are too dangerous," said George. "They get to taking more and more of the stuff, and they mix up with men, and the first thing you know they become garrulous and begin to tell things. No, it is too risky to use girls or theatrical shows."

How Drugs Are Smuggled Over the Border in Hearses

"You got a better scheme?" I inquired.

"Oh, yes, Margaret, it is much more certain, and we can handle it in bigger amounts," George replied, and then continued: "We are bringing the stuff across now in hearses. Nobody bothers a hearse, especially if it does not travel across the border at the same place too often.

"I have got some hearses which were specially built for stowing away the dope. The big, heavy black curtains are all made double, with hundreds of little compartments, which we pack full of packages of drugs. The posts, or pillars, that hold up the top of the coach are hollowed out and the holes are made just the right size to take the small cans of opium. There are eight of these hollow posts, and we can stow away a good big bunch of opium in these eight posts in each hearse.

"The floor of the hearse has a double floor. I have got the cutest little way of getting into this double floor compartment you ever saw. You would never find it in your life. We can carry quite a load of the stuff in that compartment between the two floors of the hearse.

"Of course, when we have the hearse loaded with dope we send it across openly in the middle of the day and drive right past the custom house officers boldly, so as not to attract attention or arouse suspicion. We keep on going until dark, and then drive into a little road in the woods and meet an automobile from New York. Then we unpack the curtains and posts and compartment in the double floor and the automobile takes the stuff on to New York.

"Sometimes I get an order for a shipment of dope to a distant city—maybe Washingt... or St. Louis. In this case we ship the stuff in the shell ... a corpse"——

"The shell of a corpse," I interrupted. "This is a ne... one on me."

"Yes, that is what we call it—the shell of a corpse," George replied. "I thought you had heard of that. Qui... a lot of us are doing it that way with long distance shi... ments."

"I don't understand," I said.

"Well, we get hold of a dead body from the morgue ... some undertaking establishment, and we have the unde... taker cut a hollow cavity where the lungs and interna... organs are. The head and chest and arms are not di... turbed, nor the lower part of the body, of course. But ... under the ribs all the way down to the hips, when hollowe... out, makes quite a big cavity. The corpse is very tho... oughly embalmed, and we pack the cavity full of drug... Then the corpse is dressed with clothes, which includ... collar, shirt, coat, etc."

The Tearful "Widow" Who Never Leaves the Coffin Alone

"Haven't they ever got on to this trick?" I inquired.

"No, we are very careful. I have made it a rule t... send along a woman with the corpse until the coffin ha... safely passed the border. We have got the nicest, quiet... est, most demure little lady who dresses up in widow'... weeds. She can pour out a flood of tears that would de... ceive the sharpest detective's eyes in the world. We sen... this girl along with the coffin, and if it is transferred ou... of the baggage car to the platform anywhere she jus... trots out and sits down on the edge of the baggage truc... or somewhere near, so that nobody comes around to loo... it over, and nobody bothers her because she looks to b... such a pitiful little widow in such sorrow in her bereave... ment."

"So that is what you mean by shipping drugs in 'th... shell of a corpse?'" I remarked. "Well, there are novel... ties in the Underworld since I abandoned activities whic... are new to me."

This, then, is one of the latest devices for bringin... wholesale quantities of the forbidden drugs into the coun... try. I reasoned with George before he left me and aske... him how he could bear to be the instrument of destructio... of so many young and innocent people, as he was undoubt... edly responsible for ruining.

"Oh, they are all doing it," said George in a noncha... lant manner as he lighted another cigar... drugs wil... always come in and there will always ... who wil... find ways of beating the law. Others are doing it, and i... I quit it would not end the business. I have got a wif... and family to look after and I might as well be makin... the profit as others."

The Hotel Plaza, in Havana, Where Mr. and Mrs. Ruth Were Stopping and Where the Gang of Crooks Also Took Rooms, to Be Near Them.

The Great American Popular Hero, Mr. "Babe" Ruth, King of the Baseball Diamond, Who Was Followed to Havana by a Gang of Crooks and Swindled Out of $130,000 at the Havana Race Track.

MARCH 21, 1923

DRUG TRAFFIC GRIPS ALBANY AND VICINITY

Reign of Triumvirate Charged Against Hypocrites Who Condone Segregated District

DOPE USERS PROTECTED

Vice Leaders, "In Right" with Administration, Warned in Advance of Federal Raids

By JAMES WHITTAKER.

If there is "comedy relief" in the tragedy of dope it is presented in the State Capitol of New York, where on the same recent day, Federal Narcotic agents hauled fourteen drug peddlers out of a notorious district of the town and the honorable legislators, two blocks away, feverishly debated a moral measure to close New York bootblack-parlors on Sundays.

With the single purpose of bankrupting the dope industry of Albany, Federal agents entered and raided the vice district on March 7. But, before their nights work was done the Government men had come into conflict with protected vice of the sturdiest kind, with the protecting police and with so many other indications of the American type of rotten borough that the court arraignments of the next day may be considered not so much an accusation against the fourteen sick felons who reeled before the bench as an indictment of the town's 100,000 odd population of healthy hypocrites who patronize, protect or condone the vice district.

DOPE, LEGISLATORS AND POLICE are close and friendly neighbors in the New York State capital. While narcotic agents raided Albany vice dens in shadow of Capitol dome Assemblymen fought over measure to close bootblack stands on Sundays and police "protected" the Albany levee.

"POUGHKEEPSIE JOE" LEWIS, CAUGHT in "DOPE" RAID and A PRODUCT, at 56 of PROTECTED VICE at ALBANY

"LODGINGS FOR MEN" (Extreme right of this picture of Notorious Division St.) ARE ALSO KNOWN to the POLICE AS HEADQUARTERS for DRUGS.

Drug Trio Reigns.

Indeed, with proof of statements of police-political protection of dope in the sensational expose of Buffalo contained in the current issue of Hearst's International Magazine as its goal, Universal Service is prepared to show that the whole of the politically powerful region linked by the eastern division of the New York Central Railway is ruled by the Triumvirate—Morphine, Heroin and Cocaine.

In Albany the symptom of this power is the vice district. Evangelist everywhere of dope, the public woman has nowhere so firmly entrenched the white powder in the position of political Boss as in Albany.

The raid plotted for weeks by agents of the New York Federal Narcotic squad turned out to be simply a house to house canvass of a certain section.

Each house yielded its master, dope peddler and police fixer. Before morning the bright blocks of Division and Hamilton streets had gone into mourning.

Unwanted Crooks.

Of the score of men caught in the Federal net, half were violators of laws other than the Harrison anti-narcotic statute. The Federal forces discovered that violation of the drug laws could not be proved against several of his catches and these he offered to the police as their share in the victory of the night.

The offer so dismayed the officers that one of them, McDermott by name, promptly decamped and left to his scared brothers of the force the solution of the problem of releasing their batch of unwanted criminals.

Their wits failing them, the police could find no better trick in the case of felon Harry Mangus, impartially procurer, dope peddler and lottery booster than to hold the door of the detention room open and whisper, in thunderous official sotto voice, advice to be gone.

On Mr. Mangus's protected person was found—alas for Albany's civic virtue!—no incriminating packet of morphine, but his pockets were full of lottery slips and what was left of the cash of a day's street gambling when he had paid off his winners and the collector from police headquarters.

Tipped by Police.

On each of the raids conducted by the Federal squad a police detachment was present. The ostensible duty of the police was to help. Their real duty, however, was patently to protect the Albany vice leaders who, sentimentally or on a cash basis, were "in right" with the administration.

When, four times in succession, Oyler's men forced their way into known hiding places of dope and its owners only to find both inexplicably absent, the knowledge that they had been preceded by a warning messenger spread among the Federal agents and an ominous silence wedged and spread between the Federal and local law enforcers.

Not until they transferred their attention to Troy, linked to Albany by six miles of trolley, the current issue of Hearst's International Magazine reveals organization and a close cousinship of vice conditions did the Federal agents obtain absolute proof of the fact that the police of the twin towns, far from aiding the Government, had rushed to the support of local crime and were shielding their favored felons heroically, as if this were by a clause in their oath of office.

Town Debauched.

Data on the age of the segregated district in Albany is not available. Whether it has continued calm[...]t since, and bridge the [...]n the loose '80s and the constitutionally amended present or whether it is a revival of recent date is a mystery unrevealed by the tight-lipped Albanians.

MARCH 22, 1923

DRUG BOSSES RUN BUFFALO CITY OFFICIALS

High and Low in Pay of Gang Chief, Whose Slightest Order Brings Quick Results

MASK TORN FROM COMBINE

Even Judges and Congressmen Caught Covering Up and Aiding Dope Vendors

By JAMES WHITTAKER.

Buffalo is the city bossed by dope. From the highest civic official to the lowest police official all are puppets and dope pulls the strings.

Investigators for Hearst's International Magazine saw a United States Congressman obediently caper for Boss Dope, saw an awed police force genuflect before Boss Dope, and will name the day and the place of the grand triumphant rout at which Boss Dope, benignantly, but with the bit of sternness his rank forgives, receive worship from the assembled Magistrates of Buffalo City.

JUDGE, PROSECUTOR AND TWO DOPE DENS

JUDGE HAZEL — COLONEL WILD BILL DONOVAN

THE ACE IN THE HOLE, A SOFT DRINK PARLOR

Boss Peddler on Trial

As we go to print, John C. White, at one time the boss dope peddler of the Buffalo tenderloin, goes to trial in the Federal court of Judge John R. Hazel. He was arrested in September, 1920, by the chief of the New York division of the Federal Narcotic service. He is prosecuted by Col. "Wild Bill" Donovan, Congressional medalist of the war and a district attorney who applies war-time tactics to his peace-time job.

These three men have fought the dope combine in Buffalo until it is groggy. If you wish to dramatize the events which are now in decorous progress in Judge Hazel's court-room, consider this the last round of the fight between champion John C. White and challenger Donovan, the former dizzy but still tricky, and watch for a foul. For dope is a foul fighter.

It has fouled the law, it has fouled a whole police force and it has fouled two successive city administrations.

Administration corruption was the subject when, at a recent conference on the subject of dope between Col. Donovan and Buffalo City officials, the former dismissed the latter with the ultimatum:

"If you don't clean your police force by yourselves, by God I'll do it for you."

Whereupon Donovan called in Federal agents and did clean up the police force for them.

It was the arrest of peddler White which originally pointed the [...]d of such cleaning.

$750,000 Cash in Safe

On September 23, 1920, information was received by the New York Federal Narcotic Bureau that a large quantity of morphine, heroin and cocaine was hidden in the house at No. 564 Michigan street, Buffalo.

The chief agent assigned men to obtain the necessary proof of this fact, which they did by making purchases of the forbidden drugs from John C. White, the owner. Shortly thereafter the place was raided, a complete opium layout was found on White's bed, a quantity of the other forms of narcotic drugs was seized, as was also a small safe found in the living room, which White refused to open.

Up to this moment nothing about John C. White or his dope had impressed upon the Federal men the fact that they had accomplished more than their usual routine arrest of a petty felon, engaged in the perilous venture of winning his daily bread by misdeed.

Mr. White began to expand ten minutes later when a taxi, containing the chief agent, Mr. White and Mr. White's safe, unloaded its cargo at the police station.

The safe was forced and disgorged $15,000 worth of diamonds and $750,000 in cash. The chief agent understood that he had caught something.

Holding his catch, he was to discover immediately, was quite another matter.

In an adjoining detention room Mr. White confidently awaited further events. The chief of police, called by the Federal agent chief on the telephone and requested to extend Mr. White the courtesies of his jail, was all sincere co-operation until he heard the name of the prisoner. Then he refused to take any share in the responsibility of locking up the master of the Buffalo Tenderloin.

White Mayor's Friend

The prisoner was presented to the city jailer, who pleaded:

"I'll do anything you ask, but please don't ask me to turn a key on John G. White."

The Federal agent chief chose the simplest method of relieving Buffalo's quailing police of the duty of jailing Buffalo's worst felon. He pulled the jailer's keys from his [...]lt, found one to fit a cell lock, [t]umbled John G. White into confinement, and locking securely behind him, satisfied himself that Mr. White would stay where he was put [...] jail experiences—[...] himself out by tossing the keys down an open drain pipe in another cell.

Then, turning to leave this inhospitable jail, he collided with more trouble in the person of an attache of the office of the Hon. Louis P. Fuhrmann, then Mayor of Buffalo. The Federal chief agent's visitor had come apace and could barely pant his message. It was that "Johnny White is our friend, and we've got to get him out of this jail before anybody finds out that he's been arrested."

There are two things which a Government agent can do in the position in which the chief agent now found himself. He can safely wink and make powerful friends or he can stand pat and make a service record—and enemies.

The chief agent couldn't remember where he had put the key to White's cell.

New Graft Concession

It was with the situation thus nicely defined that, after a Washington conference with "Wild Bill" Donovan, the chief agent in January of this year, again challenged Buffalo by taking Agents Stanley, Kenny, William E. Daly and Joseph Murphy into the tenderloin district and, remaining to see that they "put over" the thespian feat of getting themselves welcomed as desperate gun-men from New York's lower West Side, left them to a fortnight of intensive investigation of not one, but all the dope-selling dives and personages in this territory.

With the agents was Reporter William Ryan of Hearst's International Magazine, glorying in a Bowery accent and make-up and the sobriquet "Black Jack Bill," from Sing Sing.

Of all the adventure of that fortnight we must take but the incidents which contribute to our tale of Buffalo's corruption. Even of these we can find space for only the most striking.

Agent Kenny and Reporter Ryan have become familiars in the place of business operated by Gabrael Riccio, Italian ward boss of No. 169 South Division street. Somehow Mr. Riccio—better known as "The Big Wop"—has taken a liking to these two thieves from Manhattan and, one night, he takes them aside to "talk business."

"I just got the street-car pocket-picking concession," is Mr. Riccio's first word and his explanation of so curious a statement is that the Buffalo police detachment whose special duty it is to guard the strap-hanger's purse let out the picking privilege on their beat in return for a percentage.

The two, according to the plan are to travel in pairs on the street cars. One will pick pockets and pass the fruit of his toil to the other; then the original picker will submit to demonstrative arrest by the police, who will find no proof ofof crime on his person. Every one will be pleased; the public to know that its police officers are ardent, though unlucky, in their arrests, the two concessionaires with their weekly stipend from Mr. Riccio, and the police and Mr. Riccio with their split of whatever the day's bushel of pocketbooks may yield.

Later, by some incalculable twist of a suspicious drug-peddler's mind, Kenny and Ryan are reported in Tenderloinia to be just what they are—investigators. They are sitting in the back room of a "speak-easy," named the Maple Leaf, when the plan is set in motion by which they are to be forced to reveal any secret they may contain. The underworld calls in the police on this matter and Kenny notices Officer Jordan, of the vice squad, and a waiter in the pose of two conspirators.

THE STELLA RESTAURANT

MARCH 22, 1923

DRUG PEDDLERS IN ALBANY, TROY AIDED BY POLICE

Collusion Between Officers and Narcotic Ring Found by Federal Investigators

ALIEN VENDOR 'TIPPED OFF'

"Hush Money" Paid to Detectives; Addicts "Kicked Out of Sleep and Sent to Polls"

By JAMES WHITTAKER.

In Albany the recent Federal clean-up of the drug peddling league, as told yesterday, indicated affiliations between the vice district and the police.

In Troy, six miles from the New York State capital, these affiliations were proved.

A detective, member of the Troy police chief's personal staff, was caught in the act of assisting drug suspects to slip through the cordon of Federal agents thrown around the vice district.

In the words of the Federal chief agent, the incident we are about to relate is "characteristic of the majority of towns in up-State New York," and so links the police and the felon in larceny that "we (the Federal Government men) have two opponents wherever we go—the drug-peddler and the cop.

GROUP of prisoners and three Federal officers (in center) who figured in raids on drug peddlers in up-State raids when the narcotic dealers did not receive a "tip-off" in time to evade capture. Some of the drugs seized are shown. Below is Detective Thomas Dolan, of Troy.

PRISONERS IN POLICE HEADQUARTERS

Photo by Knickerbocker Press.

DETECTIVE THOMAS DOLAN

Alien a Big Peddler.

Before the Troy drug raid of March 7 last it had been ascertained by Federal Agents James J. Biggins and William E. Daley that the most dangerous of the Troy drug peddlers was one Anneillo Traddeo, an alien of eighteen months' residence in the country, already under one indictment for violation of the Harrison Anti-Narcotic Act. Biggins and Daley, disguised as drug-addicted down-and-outs and therefore eligble to a share in the gossiped secrets of the dope fraternity, had also learned that Mr. Traddeo followed the usual practice of the more successful drug peddlers of keeping himself at one address and his drugs at another.

It was thus the programme to seize Mr. Traddeo's person in the little pool-room at Hill and Washington streets and Mr. Traddeo's criminal supplies in the nearby apartment he was known to frequent.

Nicely adjusted to time and terrain, the plan was destined to be successful in all elements but the one incalculable one of police complicity in the crime industry of Troy.

Raid Tipped Off.

When, prior to the raid, the police offer of a detail of four detectives from the police chief's staff to assist the Federal men was accepted by the latter, it was impossible to read behind the blank expression of Detective Thomas A. Dolan's over-fed face the unprofessional purpose which kept him devotedly in the front rank of raiders throughout the evening and especially as the law-enforcers rushed the two entrances to the poolroom in which Traddeo was found.

Inside, when the faces of raiders and raided were counted, it was undistrustfully remarked that Dolan had disappeared.

Dolan was met emerging from the apartment known to be the hiding place of Traddeo's morphine stock as the Federal men went in. Still the Federal chief was not ready to suspect that a colleague of the local law-enforcement body had so openly conspired to defeat justice.

That Dolan had so conspired, however, became cumulatively evident during the process of search. When, hidden under some old clothing in a closet, an empty cocaine tin and a batch of the oblong papers which are used in the preparation of cocaine decks for street sale were found, it was easily deduced that the drugs which must be brought to light near such damaging exhibits had been recently and swiftly removed.

Dolan a "Collector."

A moment later Dolan and the proprietor were caught exchanging confidential signals and the Federal agents resolved to force a "showdown." A great demonstration of intended violence reduced the owner of the apartment to a state of squealing terror and he emitted a shriek for help from "my friend, Mr. Dolan."

"My friend, Mr. Dolan," hesitating between his graft and his repute, was lost. The Federal chief wheeled on him and charged him directly with having "tipped off" the owners of the removed dope and warned him that any further move he might make to protect felons from the law would be promptly followed by his arrest under Federal charges.

Later one of Detectives Dolan's squad came to the Federal chief and admitted that Dolan had the reputation of being a "collector," which word means those members of a crooked police force who are deputized to bring in the contributions from the criminals who purchase larceny license from the police.

That such license can be bought from the police of Albany and Troy is patent without such minute proof as we have troubled ourselves to adduce in the case of Detective Dolan.

The existence in both towns of organized and openly established red light districts, to which Agents Biggins and Daley, during the period of their incognito, were frequently and painstakingly directed by policemen on post, is sufficient evidence of collusion between the underworld and the police force. Nibbled away by the morphine needle this herd has fallen under and out of the underworld.

There is but one use for this refuse. The protection system of Troy has had the genius to find it. Periodically it is kicked and coaxed until it is sufficiently ambulant to vote.

Whatever the name of the candidate opposite which William street alley puts its cross he stands for:

| X | More Morphine. |

U. S. AGENT TRAPPED IN MAINE DRUG CONSPIRAC

PRINCIPALS, SCENE AND FACSIMILE RECORDS IN PORTLAND, ME., DRUG SCANDAL

MRS E. B. MARDEN.

NEAL INSTITUTE, PORTLAND MAINE

U.S. DISTRICT ATTORNEY FREDERICK R DYER

LETTER ADDRESSED TO ANNA LOCKE

PAGE FROM REGISTER of WEST END HOTEL PORTLAND ME SHOWING SIGNATURES OF MR & MRS E.C. RUTH

MRS. BERTHA BANCROFT CHAR

MAE COOKSON, who was the "Mrs. Ruth" of Dr. Ruth's Portland adventure.

Ralph A. Fry Convicted of Taking Bribes from Users of Morphine and Other "Dope" as the Price of Silence.

By JAMES WHITTAKER

BOSTON, Jan. 27.—The bad new vice which brought the Boston narcotic agents, Dr. Erwin C. Ruth and Ralph A. Fry, to the good old town of Portland, Me., was dope. It should have brought them on an errand of justice, tempered with such mercy as justice will admit. It brought them away from the girls and schemes of their Boston movie ventures on an errand of blackmail and conspiracy, tempered with such boozing as their capacities would permit.

The remarkable prevalence of drug addiction, not only in Longacre Square, New York, but in the smalle towns of the backwoods, is pointed out in the February Hearst's International Magazine in the telling series, "Dope."

Last August Fry found a stage set for his record extortion drive.

In Portland, port of his first call he found in the local branch of the nationally known Neal Institute a sweet haven for his plot.

Take the neorotic chill of Dr. Caligari's cabinet and the poison fog which hangs over the house of Usher and summon whatever else you can of true or fancied terrors and you suggest the nature of the evil which is nursed by Frederic Tozer behind the dirty double windows of the Portland sanatarium.

Without cheer, without hope, almost without life, he sits guard over his store of morphine bottles, dreading alternately the moment when his nerves will summon him to rise and let the bottled hell into his veins and the event of their confiscation by the hated authorities. And if, for a moment, he should raise his eyes, he can study the unnatural slumber and quick heartbeat of the beloved sick woman on the bed and let his science count the minutes which will pass before she, too, must whimper for her drug.

Three Successive Roles.

Successively employe, sweetheart and patient of Dr. Tozer, Miss Rilla Chapman was the weak sister of the Portland drug-addict set through whom Fry struck for blackmail.

For two years Dr. Tozer managed to hide his drug-eaten fiance from the prying world. Then she was discovered by Mrs. Hilda L. Ives, widow of a prominent Portland attorney and chief of the Portland Child Welfare League.

Mrs. Ives had a dear friend, graduate of Dartmouth, member of that school's famous football team and a practising surgeon. The young man had been badly injured in a football game. During hospital treatment of the injury, he became addicted to the morphine which was administered to alleviate his sufferings. He confessed this addiction to Mrs. Ives. She sent him to the local Neal Institute, trusting the favorable reputation which the Neal Institutes have built up by national advertising.

From the young surgeon's experiences in Dr. Tozer's asylum she drew her first suspicions of the honesty of the Portland institute. Dr. Tozer not only failed to cure the surgeon, but administered freely to his addiction and often took morphine himself in the patient's presence.

The young surgeon left Dr. Tozer's dope dispensary a complete wreck. A few months later he applied for an assignment to join a scientific mission in the Arctic. Now he has placed a thousand miles of icefield between himself and his personal devil. You must know what the drug craving is to appreciate that this is magnificent pluck. Our money is on Mrs. Ives's young friend.

Mrs. Ives felt a personal responsibility for his disastrous experience. She determined that it would not be the experience of others.

She formed an alliance with Mrs. Jane Prevost, registrar of the only nurses' exchange in Portland. It was from Mrs. Prevost that Dr. Tozer obtained nurses for the patients who came to his establishment for treatment. After Mrs Ives's appeal to Mrs. Prevost was made, every nurse assigned to the Neal Institute was an amateur detective.

Affidavits Unquotable.

In the files of this office are the affidavits made by these women Sometimes they are unquotable accounts of filth. These professional people cannot mince words when they talk of the struggle with disease to which they have dedicated their lives.

We venture hesitatingly to quote Mrs. Prevost's indignant summing up of the contents of each nurse's report:

"Baths all over the house showed neglect of lang standing. The refuse stood too long before being emptied. The dish towels and table linen were impossible to use.

"Dr. Tozer's tereatment of one woman patient showed a manner that was repulsive and disgusting. He gave her hypodermic injections against her wish, did not sterilize the skin area before inserting the needle, but spit on his finger and rubbed over the spot."

This manner of giving Miss Rilla Chapman her shots of dope is alluded to by each of the nine nurses sent by Mrs. Prevost to "keep their eyes and ears open" and report conditions to Mrs. Ives. It seems that all nine of them had the same experience: They could stick the dirty dishes in the kitchen sink, the grey linen of the beds and the soup-stained newspapers on the dining table, but when it came to witnessing Dr. Tozer's careless substitution of saliva for alcohol in the operation of administering Miss Chapman's "white medicine," they successively packed their bags and slammed the front door.

Adds one of the nine, in language more of righteous indignation than of legal document:

"And to think that the woman whom he treated in this manner was the woman he loved."

Relations between this odd pair were a study in sentimental abnormality. Miss Chapman was the daughter of respectable Toledo parents who were able to afford a Summer excursion in 1916 to Portland's famous Casco Bay cottage district. Rilla fell in love with the charming old town, got employment in the telephone exchange at the end of the Summer and was left behind when the family returned to Toledo

Alternating Love and Hate.

When she became Dr. Tozer's secretary she was neither engaged to him nor addicted to morphine. The hearts of these two cannot be read. There is only the record of their gestures. Dr. Tozer seems to live in fear of Rilla. From the bed in which she spends her life she harries and bullies him. Then there are intervals in which he is tender, she responsive. They end too soon with a return of her drug mania. One of the nurses records:

"When Dr. Tozer gave Miss Chapman a hypodermic she would scream:

"'I hate you, I hate you!'

"And then she would bite him."

Expect the illogical, the insane in the conduct of two dope fiends. The power of love is not a match for the power of drug.

When Mrs. Ives's record of Dr. Tozer's malpractice was complete she went with it to the nearest authorities empowered to act and was rebuffed. The county authorities sidestepped. It was known that many prominent men of Portland and other New England communities came to the Neal Institute to hide their alcoholic sins. It would not advance the political fortunes of the local officials to stage a raid of the place and unluckily find a bank president or a wool mill magnate soused in the back parlor. The officials were polite, but evasive.

Mrs. Ives heard that a Federal narcotic agent named Fry was in the West End Hotel and she went to him with her story. Fry had never before played in such gorgeous luck. He had come to blackmail and here was the stuff of blackmail ready to hand.

If anything, Mr. Fry was more polite to Mrs. Ives than the county officials had been. She departed satisfied and left her affidavits in Fry's honest hands.

Fry a Fast Worker.

Within a week Dr. Tozer was his tool and blackmail gold was flowing into Fry's pockets from a dozen rich sources. Mr. Fry was simple and direct and forceful, as was Napoleon.

He could have Dr. Tozer jailed for dispensing morphine illegally but, if Dr. Tozer greased his palm, Dr. Tozer would not go to jail. Dr. Tozer resisted. Very well, there was his sweetheart, Rilla Chapman. Let miserable Dr. Tozer relate his thing about Fry and Rilla:

"Regarding threats, the worst thing he did was about Miss Chapman. She had been sick all Winter. She made my place her home for five years. He said I was giving her more morphine than is allowed by the Medical Association. He said he would take her away. Miss Chapman is the woman I mean to marry. He said I would have to pay $200. He would then leave me alone regarding my records and Miss Chapman also."

Dr. Tozer greased.

Fry soon discovered a grave defect in Tozer. He could not grease often enough. After the first $200 Tozer was through. But Tozer knew every addict in the district, knew the names of reputable doctors and druggists who either used or peddled morphine. When it becomes known that a doctor is a drug fiend his practice deserts; he is a horrible example on Main street, a skeleton in his own closet.

After Dr. Tozer paid Fry once in cash he was forced to pay him a dozen times in treacheries. Fry spent a night with Tozer over whiskey bottles in the unclean den he called his office. When he came out of the house he had this list of prominent men, addicted to drugs or otherwise involved in criminal violation of the narcotic laws:

Dr. Walter Baker, practicing in Hollis and Buxton, Me.

Dr. Walter W. Dyson, of Portland, Me.

Dr. Leland H. Miller, of Fairfield, Me.

Dr. F. L. Radman, of Corinna, Me.

Druggist T. Richard Pye, of Westbrook, Me.

History of Each Case.

One by one we shall record the blackmailing of each.

Dr. Baker—Baker became criminal when, in March, 1921, he ordered from the Direct Sales Company of Buffalo, N. Y., an enormous quantity of morphine, alleging that he wished to stock up enough to carry him over a threatened railroad strike. Fry drew from Tozer the precious information that Baker was himself a drug addict. Tozer meekly accompanied Fry on his blackmail visit to Baker's Hollis office. The conversation between the three men is recorded. One passage is exceptionally cruel:

Fry—How would you like your addiction spread all over the front pages of the papers?

Baker—It will ruin my practice. It will make me a pauper.

Fry—How would you like to be prosecuted?

Baker—It will break my mother's heart.

Baker mortgaged his home and settled for $1,000.

Dr. Dyson—Dyson derived some profit from a minister of the Gospel, whose name has been kept out of these records by reason of the fact that his word is faith for one of the largest and best congregations in Portland. He needs seven grains of morphine in his right arm before he can deliver the Lord's prayer. Dyson turned $200 over to Tozer, who turned it over to Fry. There is no record of

pret... Drug... in ... bed ... paid $200. ...man—Redman ... Fry used his Mason... insignia to snare Redman, ... Mason. "Sorry I have to d... he dephored, "because I'm a ... myself, but the higher-up... Washington are on to you a... want money." The last half of Fry's remark is probably untrue; the first half, it is said, has drawn the attention of dignitaries of the Masonic order, who intend to take some occult action on his case. Redman went to his son, a professor in Amherst College. Young Redman knew exactly how to handle Fry. He called his bluff easily and Dr. Redman is now in an institution in the West progressing nicely toward cure of his twenty-year-old drug habit.

Money made Fry exceedingly happy. Side by side with the record of his Portland crimes is the record of his Portland rejoicings. Dr. Ruth, his superior officer came up from Boston with pretty Mae Cookson and registered her as his wife into a room in the West End Hotel. There was some pretense that Miss Cookson was acting the role of beautiful girl detective.

A bit of bootlegging here gets into the record. Trouble for every one concerned in the Fry expedition to Portland was not far off United States District Attorney Frederick Dyer, of Portland, met Mrs. Ives and agents of this news service and learned the facts. An honest and vigorous official had finally been found and Fry was near his finish.

STRUCTION
DOPE
INDIGNATIO
DOPE EVIL
DOPE PEDDLER
DOPE DEALER
DOPE MANUFACTURER
WINSOR McCAY
RACKETEER
SMUGGLER
COUNTERFEITER
DOPE PEDDLER
NO MONEY- NO DOPE -GO AND GET IT!
JEWELRY AND DIAMONDS
DOPE PEDDLER
DOPE
WEALTHY HEAD OF DRUG RING GETS 4 YEARS
FOUR OTHERS S
$20,000,000 DOPE RING MEN TO BE INDICTED
ARREST BA
SYSTEMA
DOPE' THE
COUNTRY-WIDE DRUG ROUND-UP EXPECTED
Letters Seized by Raiders Here Disclose Coast to Coast Nar-
DOPE RING USES MAIL, U. S. FINDS
AGENTS SNARE 4 AS 'BIG SHOT' DOPE TRADER
7 UNDER BAIL, GIRL FREED IN DRUG ROUNDUP
GANG ARSENAL SEIZURE LAYS DOPE RING BARE
Clues Gleaned in Henry St. Raid Lead to Capture of 3; May Solve Ride Deaths
11 ARE TAKEN IN DRUG RAIDS
STEWARDESS IS CAP
DOPE ADDICT WITH BANK ON JOUR
NARCOTIC BA
DRUGS OF ARMY FOUND IN A RAID IN WASHINGTON
CONCERN HAD NO LICENSE
SQUAD OF 100 COMBS BIG SHIP FOR RUM, DOPE
Rochambeau's Cargo Checked by Force 25 Times as Big as Usual to Foil Smugglers
DRUG RING KING OF EAST SEIZED BY SIMON'S MEN
NARCOTICS JAIL STRANGE PAIR
JUDGE TO JA DOPE
Opium Raider
CHICAGO HAS 25,000 ADICTS
NAMED DOPE TRAFFIC HEAD
Dope Sold in N. Y. County Penitentiary, Says Addict
RIVALS SLAY DRUG KING AS PRICE OF VENGEANCE
LAW ENFORCEMENT
BANDIT
RACKETEER
DOPE PEDDLER
CROOKED POLITICIAN
KIDNAPER
EXTORTIONIST
EFFICIENT STATE CONSTABULARY
FEDERAL SCOTLAND YARD
CRIME
DOPE
THE LAW
DOPE RING
DOPE PEDDLER
POVERTY
DISGRACE

FEDERAL LAW ENFORCEMENT AGENCIES
DOPE
POVERTY
CRIME
DISEASE
DEATH
DOPE TRAFFICKER
9 ARRESTED BY U. S. DRUG RAIDERS ON BROADWAY
DRUG TRAFFIC'S MASTER MIND BELIEVED TAKEN
Mrs. Anna E. Patterson Arrested at Big Down Town Hotel by U. S. Officers
NARCOTIC RING CHIEF HUNTED FOR SENTENCE
604 Years in Jail for 346 Guilty on Drug Charges
WASHINGTON, April 28.
DRUG RING SMASHED
DITS TAKEN
'SHOT OF DOPE' CLEARS UP OLD SLAYING HERE
Drug Addict in Jersey Jail Confesses Killing a Man in Eighth Avenue Saloon
POLICE SEIZE 48 IN RENEWAL OF DRUG RAIDS
100 Detectives, Sent Out to Round Up Vendors of Narcotics, Seize $10,000 Worth of Contraband
EX-CONVICTS IN THE NET
Boy Alleged to Have Offered Bribe
DOPE SELLERS AIDED BY HUGE ORGANIZATION
TEN CAPTUDED AS 100 AGENTS BREAK THROUGH TWELVE DOORS
$130,000 BAIL DEMANDED OF 5 DOPE SUSPECTS
2 Chinese and Others Taken in Brooklyn Raid Built Up Huge Business, U. S. Men Say
Seize Alleged Head of Great Drug Ring
eize Beaut
DRUG AGENTS RAID BOOTERY
Narcotic Menace Is Still Acute
U. S. PULLS IN ITS DOPE NET
"Drug King"=So Called, Is Convicted Now
Will He Take Higher Up With Him to Prison?
CROOK
BURGLAR
NIGHT CLUB HOSTESS
RACKETEER
BOOT LEGGER
BRIBE GIVER
HI-JACKER
THUG
DOPE PEDDLER
PURSE SNATCHER
PROCURESS
GUNMAN
BLACKJACK EXPERT
BRIBE TAKER
BANDIT
CRIME WAVE
SENTIMENTAL JUROR
BOOTLEG BACKER
DOPE PEDLER
STUPID JUROR
LEGAL ALLY OF CRIMINAL
PARENT, WHO NEGLECTS MORAL TRAINING
LEGISLATOR-AUTHOR OF CRIMINAL CODE
SHAME
DOPE
DOPE
DOPE
DOPE
DOPE

The Sunday Chronicle
CONSISTS OF TEN SECTIONS TODAY
(COUNT THEM)
1—Rotagravure Pictorial 6—Society
2—Magazine 7—City Life
3—Comics 8—Main News
4—Automobile 9—Classified, Financial
5—Screen and Drama 10—Sports

San Francisco Chronic
LEADING NEWSPAPER OF THE PACIFIC COA

FOUNDED 1865—VOL. CXXII, NO. 83 CC SAN FRANCISCO, CAL., SUNDAY, APRIL 8, 1923—

NARCOTIC

POLICEMAN KILLS NARCOTIC V
YOUNGEST S. F. SLAYER EVER TR

WILD RACE FOR FREEDOM ENDS WITH SHOOTING

Suspect Fatally Wounded After Spectacular Dash Through Crowds

COMPANIONS ESCAPE

Bystander Arrested for Attempt to Incite Attack on Patrolmen

A mid-day battle between police and narcotic addicts and alleged peddlers, staged at Howard and Third streets, just as San Francisco's business district was closing for yesterday's half holiday, resulted in the death of one man, the escape of two prisoners, and subsequent capture of a fourth alleged addict.

The dead prisoner is described by the police as William Crahan, 32 years old, who was arrested with two other alleged addicts at Third and Howard streets shortly after 1 o'clock, while locked up on a vagrancy charge at the Southern Police Station is Morris Field, alleged to be both peddler and addict.

Suspects Watched by Trio of Policemen

For some time, Policeman Frank Kennedy, appointed to the force on March 1 last, and Policeman Ben Sullivan and Oliver Cox of the Southern station had been watching the three alleged peddlers as they plied their trade. Kennedy was being "schooled" by Cox, and after observing the trio, it was decided to make them prisoners.

"You're all under arrest," announced Kennedy as the police closed in on the trio.

"What's the idea," demanded one of the prisoners. "What you got on us?"

"Just vagrants and trying to sell narcotics," replied Kennedy as the three officers and trio of prisoners walked toward the police signal station at the corner of the street intersection. Then as the officer telephoned for the patrol wagon, Crahan without warning made a dash for freedom.

Prisoner Dashes Through Crowds in Dash for Liberty

Down Third street raced the prisoner with Sullivan in hot pursuit, shouting above the din of traffic to the fleeing man to halt.

As the escaping prisoner rushed down the street, pedestrians cleared the way, for it was seen that Kennedy had pulled out his service revolver.

"Halt or I'll fire!" shouted the policeman, but the prisoner only increased his speed running first to the left and then to the right of the street, dodging here and there between wagons and around groups of frightened spectators, as they hurried or doorways and places of concealment.

"Halt!" commanded the officer

Bullet Rebounds From Pavement, Strikes Suspect

Crahan lunged forward, half falling then recovering himself. Then he crumpled upon the pavement in pain. Investigation showed that the bullet, discharged, according to Kennedy, toward the street surface had rebounded and entered the prisoner's leg.

From all directions, scores of frightened spectators rushed toward the spot where Crahan was lying upon the street. With them came Policemen Sullivan and Cox leading their two prisoners and in the excitement the pair escaped. There was no chase. They just vanished in the crowd which surrounded the wounded man.

It was then that Freid, another alleged drug addict, appeared on the scene and attempted to incite the crowd against the policeman who had shot Crahan. Instead of inciting the crowd, Freid found himself under arrest.

Crahan was taken to Harbor Hospital, where he admitted that he was a drug addict. He died on the operating table from loss of blood.

Crahan lived at the Atlantic Hotel, Seventh and Mission streets.

San Francisco Ex
AN AMERICAN PAPER FOR THE AMERICAN PEOPLE
AMERICA FIRST
Monarch of the Dai

VOL. CXXIII. NO. 43 ✶ CC SAN FRANCISCO, WEDNESDAY, AUGUST 12, 1925—THIRTY

HUGE DOPE RING OF U.

NATION-WIDE CORRUPTION IS ADMITTED AS 4 ARE SEIZED

Chicago Chief Said to Have Confessed Stealing Hundreds of Thousands in Narcotics

Hoard of Jewels Found in Homes of Three Aides; 50 Others Arrested in Clean-up

CHICAGO, Aug. 11.—(I. N. S.)—Federal narcotic agents in every big city in the United States are involved in a gigantic "dope" traffic, revealed through the arrest of Colonel Will Gray Beach, division chief of the Chicago district, and three of his aides, federal intelligence officers admitted today. Wholesale arrests are expected.

C. L. Converse, special intelligence officer, said today that Beach had confessed stealing hundreds of thousands of dollars' worth of drugs from the government. He also revealed that Beach had threatened to kill himself and every precaution was being taken to prevent any attempt at self-injury.

Federal officials said that thousands of dollars' worth of drugs, property of the government, were found in private warehouses in boxes and containers under Beach's own name so that they would be of easy accessibility.

Beach also admitted, Converse said, that not only had he seized the

MANY DOPE AGENTS FACE U. S. ARREST

Wholesale Roundup Is Expected to Follow Apprehension of Chicago Chief, Three Aides

drug evil, but had seized drugs obtained by department agents in raids.

According to reports from official sources, confessions were obtained shortly before last midnight that exposed the inside workings and technique of the most gigantic narcotic smuggling and distribution system ever conceived.

Fifty prisoners were in custody and contraband drugs and stolen property valued at $50,000 were recovered in a series of raids which spread terror through Chicago's Chinatown during the night, officials say.

Chief of the prisoners arraigned with Beach were his three most active agents—Dennis J. O'Brien, Alonzo D. Baxter, former Philadelphia minister, and Harry Deitrich, formerly of Philadelphia.

JEWELS FOUND.

Arrests of Beach and his three agents were on criminal warrants issued by Federal Judge Adam Cliffe late yesterday.

At the same time he signed these warrants Judge Cliffe issued warrants authorizing search of the homes or living quarters of the four. Agents Patrick Roche and C. L. Converse of the special intelligence corps made the raid upon the rooms of Colonel Beach. There, according to information given out by the federal men in charge, were found quantities of jewels, including many diamonds and other valuable merchandise. And, it is declared, part of this collection already has been identified as having been stolen by drug addicts.

The home of O'Brien also yielded a considerable hoard of valuables that appear recently to have been "traded in" by "dope fiends" who thus bought a share in narcotics seized by the government agents.

BROOKLYN SENATOR IN ODD DRUG PLOT—John A. Hastings (shown with Mrs. Hastings) yesterday found $2,000 in drugs among his possessions in Albany disappeared, and turned up again, with theory that it was "planted" as a result of recent "Ku Klux Klan threats."

—Senator Sees Plot in Dop

Bank President Kills Himself at Wife's Grave

GRIFFIN, Ga., April 26.

SITTING at the grave of his wife, Roswell Hill Drake, president of the City National Bank, shot himself to death to-day. Participants in the Memorial Day exercises witnesse dthe suicide.

Drake left a note in which he said the banak did not owe a dollar of borrowed money or rediscount and was in as good condition as ever in its history.

DRUG 'PLANT' CHARGE LIE, WIRES FRANCIS

Hastings Called "Insane" by Head of Firm He Accused.

Philip Francis, who was accused by Senator John A. Hastings of planting $3,000 worth of heroin in the Senator's name in the checkroom of the Ten Eyck Hotel at Albany, has wired from Kansas

...rom him.

Am leaving here to-day to arrive in New York Saturday morning, when I will give to newspaper

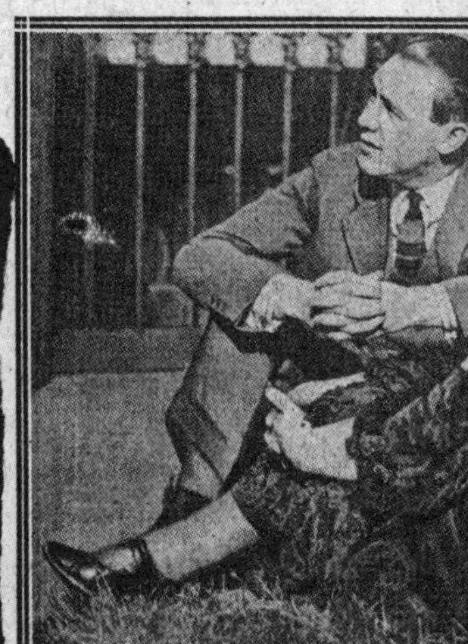

MARCH 28, 1923

HASTINGS SEES PLOT OF KLAN IN DRUGS

POLICE ACCUSE

NOTES CERTAIN THREATS

FAIR WEATHER
Sunday generally fair; moderate westerly winds.
Mount Tamalpais—Generally fair; westerly winds.

RUSADER HELD IN DOPE PLOT

DER.
D FREED

DAILY 5 CENTS, SUNDAY

. AGENTS

JANUARY 2, 1923

'SOCIOLOGIST' ARRESTED AS DRUG SELLER

Oakland Sanitarium Declared Rendezvous for Dispensing Opiates to Wealthy Addicts

"Dr." John Barker Took Marked $100 Bill in Payment for Morphine, Officers Declare

"Dr." John Scott Barker of Oakland, self-styled crusader against the narcotic evil, was arrested yesterday, and records of his alleged illicit sale of opiates to drug addicts under the guise of a "cure" were seized by State Board of Pharmacy detectives, who have been for some weeks watching the Barker Sanitarium at 431 Twenty-eighth street.

Suspicion that "Dr." Barker was mulcting drug-users, rich and poor, was borne out, according to the State officials, when the "physician" was trapped at the sanitarium with $100 in marked money on his person.

This money, consisting of bills the serial numbers of which had been previously registered with the District Attorney of Alameda county, was given to Barker ...

MAY 31, 1925

DRUG RUNNER DIES IN BATTLE

COLEBROOK, N. H., May 30 (AP).—A battle was fought between Federal officers and a band of alleged narcotics smugglers last night at Canaan, Vt., on the international boundry line.

A Canadian named Bilodean was fatally wounded.

The officers arrested a companion of Bilodeau named Pierce, who is being held at Canaan. Octave Nadeau, of Canaan, was arrested later at Stewartstown and is being held charged with possessing narcotics.

Reports ...

10 CENTS

BARED

$500,000 DOPE SEIZED IN RAID

$500,000 were ... on No. ... Federal ...

John Weiler ... bail each. They were held in $25,000 bail each. They were charged with attempting to import drugs into the United States in violation of the Harrison Act.

Federal agents said that the drugs were in five cases unloaded from the White Star liner Arabic. They were marked "bowling balls and pins for transshipment to China." One of them was opened by customs agents and the drugs found. They kept watch and when the cases were called for they were trailed to the Walker street address. The agents charge they found five similar cases packed with bowling pins and balls ready for shipment to the Orient.

JULY 13, 1926

DWYER PAID HIM $40,000 SAYS WET AIDE

Former Supercargo for 'Czar' Testifies that Uniformed Men Helped to Unload Vessels

Declares Liquor Trust Used Dozen Swift Power Boats, 4 Schooners and Steamer

By FREDERICK EDWARDS.

Uniformed patrolmen of New York City and Weehawken gave adequate protection to William V. Dwyer's rum shipments, Augustus C. Smith, former Dwyer supercargo, testified yesterday on the witness stand in the Federal court.

Sometimes, at Weehawken the police were so enthusiastically in favor of the project that they helped Dwyer's men unload their cargoes, Smith said, testifying that in two years he had made $40,000 as one of Dwyer's lieutenants, successfully running about 200 cargoes of liquor, for which he received $200 a trip.

He was caught, his evidence showed, three times. Once he escaped, abandoning his ship. Once, after Customs House guards had captured him in New York harbor, his hearing was transferred to Hoboken and mysteriously forgotten; and the third time, which marked the finish of his employment by Dwyer, he was fined.

A LARGE RUM FLEET.

A dozen swift power boats, four schooners and one 500-ton steamer, were used by the Dwyer rum trust to bring succor to New York's

JUNE 22, 1926

BOY SHOT AS POLICE CHASE DOPE PEDDLER

Detectives and Federal Agent Seize Man Who Escapes; Suspect Caught After Battle

A twelve-year-old boy was shot and the East Side was thrown into an uproar last night when police and Federal agents gave chase to a fleeing narcotic peddler.

Police again picked up a trail some four hours later and during a second exciting chase up Broadway a half dozen shots were fired. Finally Patrolman Joseph Reins knocked a fleeing man unconscious with a right swing to the jaw.

BULLET STRIKES BOY.

The excitement began when Detective Bernard Seidel and Federal Narcotic Agent Max Roder, disguised in rough clothing, seized a well-dressed young man at Elizabeth and Prince streets as a narcotic peddler.

Escaping by slipping from his coat, the suspect ran through the crowded street. Both Seidel and Roder drew their revolvers and ...red. One of the bullets struck ...eter Renda, twelve, who was play...g near his home at No. 202 Eliza...th street. The boy was taken to ... Vincent's Hospital with a bullet ... his thigh.

During the heighth of the chase ...ectives Seidel was halted by ...rolman Thomas McNamara, re...ver in hand. Not recognizing the ...ective, McNamara ordered him ...rop his pistol. The detective ...ed with alacrity and then ...ed his badge. By that time the ...ect had been lost in the crowd.

...SE FOR SUSPECT.

...ortly after midnight Patrol... David Katz, walking on Broad... near Fourteenth street, stopped ...h who answered the descrip...ent out by Seidel of the es... narcotic dispenser.

... youth bolted at Katz's ap...ce of interest and jumped on ...hbound street car. Com...ring an automobile, Katz ... and fired six shots.

...ng from the street car at ...third street, the youth was ...th one blow by Patrolman ...who had been standing on ...er. He was unconscious

...t the Mercer street station ...his name as Anthony Cau...ty-six, of No. 29 Pine ...e denied that he had any ...e sale of narcotics, and ...only because he was excited.

Ukrainian Leader Slain by Assassin

WARSAW, Poland, June 21 (AP)—Radziwill Oskilko, Ukrainian leader, was assassinated today at

RAID REVEALS DRUG TRAFFIC BY U. S. MAILS

$5,000 in Narcotics Seized in Hotel Room with a Mailing List Containing 500 Names

National trafficking in drugs through the mail was brought to ... yesterday morning when ...

POLICE WINKING AT DRUG SALES, SAYS CUVILLIER

Flays Department's Failure to Detect Vendors and Hits at Enright and "Corruption"

ACCUSES TWO POLICEMEN

2 Sisters of One Supply Addicts in Eastern Brooklyn, Second Gives Dope to Wife, He Charges

Assemblyman Louis A. Cuvillier, who recently demanded the removal of Police Commissioner Enright, said yesterday:

"The dope peddlers are doing a greater business in New York than the bootleggers, I am informed, and are collecting enormous sums of money. I often wonder, since the abolition of the State Narcotic Commission, how the dope peddlers can do such a thriving business without the police detecting the source of supply."

SPECIFIC CHARGES.

Cuvillier made this statement in a letter to District Attorney Dodd, of Brooklyn, in which he links up indirectly two Brooklyn policemen with the traffic i drugs. He declared that two sisters of one of these policemen are drug vendors among women addicts in the eastern district of Brooklyn. ...

OF AIDING RUM

"It is understood that Governor Miller repealed the State Narcotic Commission, because when we had that beneficient law on the statute book, these fortu-

VOL. CXXII. NO. 135. CC SAN FRANCISCO, FRIDAY, MAY 15, 192
FLOYD HALL IS CAPTURE
KILLER SURRENDERS, SMILING, IN ROOMING HOUSE AT CAPITAL
SACRAMENTO, July 15.—(3 a. m.)—Floyd Hall and Joe Tanko, the two escaped San Quentin murderers who have stuck together throughout five weeks of
'It Means—the Noose'
JAZZ GIRL ADMITS SHE NEVER HAS BEEN SPANKED
PRISONER COLLAPSES FOR FIFTH TIME AT TR
LYNCHERS THREATEN 'JAZZ GIRL'
Capone Goes to Trial Tomorrow on Federal Income Tax Evasion
'Machine Gun' Kelly Caught in Memphis
YOUNG SLAYER GIGGLES OVER OLD PHOTOS
GEORGE KELLY.
DIAGRAMMED DIAGNOSIS
FEATURES OF "JAZZMANIA KILLERS"
WANTED
LESTER M. GILLIS,
$5,000.00
"Get Best Lawyers in City":
LUCIANO BIDS FOR LEGAL AID
CHULTZ IN A CEL FOR REST OF TRIAL
BLOW TO BEER BARON
DENOUNCED BY CONBOY
MALONE, N. Y., July 23.—Taking defendant and courtroom by surprise, Federal Judge Frederick H. Bryant opened Dutch Schultz's second trial for iocme tax evasion today by committing him to jail for the dura-
Picture is the very latest photograph of Dutch Schultz.
HOLD-UPS THEFT SHOOTING MURDER ROBBERY CRIME
Al Capone Plans to Sever All Ties with Chicago Mobsters; Expects to Enter Legitimate Business When Freed from Prison
SAYS HE ASKED FOR ARSENIC
DOPE EVIL
CHICAGO REPORTER MURDERED BY GANGSTER
A Chilly-Looking Blonde with Frosty Eyes and Marble Chin'

FIRST PICTURES OF DILLINGER KILLING, PAGES 7 AND 8

Greatest Exclusive Circulation
The Wichita Evening Eagle has the GREATEST number of "Exclusive" Evening readers in Wichita.
"You Will Find" The Eagle "In the Home"

The Wichita Eagle

Why Pay For Waste Circulation?
Average Net 35,396

VOLUME XCVIII — Price: In the City, 3c; Outside City, 5c — WICHITA, KANSAS, TUESDAY MORNING, JULY 24, 1934 — TWELVE PAGES — NUMBER 27

DILLINGER JUST 'PUNK' UNTIL HE LEFT PRISON

Parole to Help Father on Indiana Farm Started Him On His Spectacular Career

Psychologists and behaviorists, had they had a chance to examine John Dillinger, might have been able to explain him to at least their own satisfaction. But it would have been an explanation wholly unsatisfactory to the public, and the truth about him probably lies somewhere between.

SLAIN PUBLIC ENEMY NO. 1

Rothstein, Dying, Keeps Secret with Sealed Lips

Continued from First Page.

ro, who conducted the questioning, that he "sat in" with Rothstein in a poker game last September in which Rothstein lost $360,000. Rothstein had "paid" the bulk of the loss ...

to the Park Central Hotel, at Seventh avenue and Fifty-seventh street, Sunday night at 11 o'clock by a telephone call from a man whom Rothstein regarded as an intimate. He was seated with friends at a table in Lindy's Restaurant, at ...

that "Rothstein has at least a chance for his life."

GAMBLERS HANG AROUND.

A number of men, known to be "small time" gamblers, haunted the vicinity of the hospital all ...

UNDERWORLD ... PUTTING FATAL FINGER ON DILLINGER

Unofficial Reports Tell of "Girl in Red" Who Betrayed Brutal Killer to Officers in Trade for Her Mate's Release and $15,000 Reward Money

ARREST OF DOCTOR WHO AIDED THUG NEAR

EXTRA

Who Think—FRIDAY, JUNE 19, 1931

FIFTH AVE. DOMICILE OF 'DUTCH' SCHULTZ, CAPTIVE RACKETEER

CAPONE PACKS UP; PREPARES TO LEAVE JAIL

... of Chicago Racketeers Expects to Return to His Throne Some Time Monday

PHILADELPHIA, March 15.—"Scarface" Al Capone is going to Chicago, whose underworld he ruled—and perhaps still ... when he is released from Eastern Penitentiary, probably Monday morning.

Officials' Pose with Dillinger 'Disgraceful,' Says Cummings

SLUMBER ROOM—Here's one ... Detective required by the hard-working modern racketeer. Detective Julius Salke is shown looking over the Schultz sleeping room, which, even to the bed, seems quite a bit "dolled up."

NOT SO BARREN—... ment, forsaken now, ... lord of the ... so far, to pro... day. A dete...

KILLED, TWO WOUNDED, IN NORTH BEACH BATTLE

SAN FRANCISCO, CAL., FRIDAY, DECEMBER 1, 19..

"Scarface Al" Lays Feud to Foes

Peace Efforts Rejected, He Says

By PATRICIA DOUGHERTY
Universal Service Staff Correspondent

(Copyright, 1926, by "Herald and Examiner." Reproduction in whole or in part strictly prohibited.)

CHICAGO, Oct. 13.—While Chi...

CHICAGO WARS ON GANGSTERS

By FRED VANDEVENDER,
Staff Correspondent Universal Service.

CHICAGO, Oct. 13.—Authorities here tonight concentrated their ...

DECEMBER 10, 1934—34 PAGES

ACTRESS HID DUTCH SCHULTZ

Bootleg Feudists Killed

"BABY FACE" NELSON IS ON FEDERAL HUNT-...

Reward of $5,000 Offered for Dillinger "Crazy Killer," also Known as Lester ... "Pretty Boy" Floyd also to Be Run Down

By RICHARD RENDELL
(Associated Press Staff Writer)

WASHINGTON, July 23.—(AP)—A slender little woman, dressed in summery pink, today called on J. Edgar Hoover, investigative head of the department of justice, to extend congratulations on the death of John Dillinger, and a few minutes after she left, Hoover, black eyes snapping, named Lester M. Gillis as the man now most wanted by the department.

The caller was Mrs. W. Carter Baum, widow of a special agent killed in the Wisconsin woods last April when Dillinger and his mobsmen blazed their way to freedom after being trapped at a country inn.

Gillis, named by the government ...

John 'Legs' Diamond Indicted

Face Inquiry on Charge of Harboring the Fugitive

LONG CHASE REVEALED

His Lawyers May Post Bond of $75,000 in Albany Today to Release Federal Prisoner

Two prominent attorneys and Broadway actress are under investigation by the Federal Grand Jury for allegedly harboring Dutch Schultz during the nearly two years he was a fugitive, it was learned last night.

Information involving the lawyers and the actress, said to be "beautiful and well-known," has been turned over to U. S. Attorney Conboy by the police.

SATURDAY, JULY 20, 1929 — Business Telephone, COLumbus 7000

...as Hotsy Totsy Killer

... and Chicago Open ... War on Rackets

Dead Crooks Are Good Crooks

Four East Side gunmen who fired the shots heard 'round the underworld when they put Herman Rosenthal, gambler, out of the way, paid the penalty with their lives, along with the police lieutenant who hired them.

EVIL LUCK IS LOT OF ... WOMEN IN JOHN DILLINGER ...

CHICAGO, July 23.—(AP)—Women have figured prominently in the life ... Dillinger, slain outlaw, and ...

Massacre a Monument To Dry Law--Patterson

RICHARD C. PATTERSON, JR., Commissioner of Correction, New York City, declared yesterday:

"The murder of seven men in the latest war between rival liquor gangs in Chicago this week is perhaps the most sickening testimonial to date of the ghastly failure of prohibition as it now operates in the United States.

"It is an ominous reminder that the lawlessness and organized crime that have grown out of the attempt of well meaning people to enforce total abstinence in Amer...

Dago Frank. — Whitey Lewis — Lefty Louie. — Lieutenant Charles Becker. — Gyp the Blood.

MOTH GIRL ...

Jazz, the Beat of ...

Luciano Free of Smuggling Charge in ...

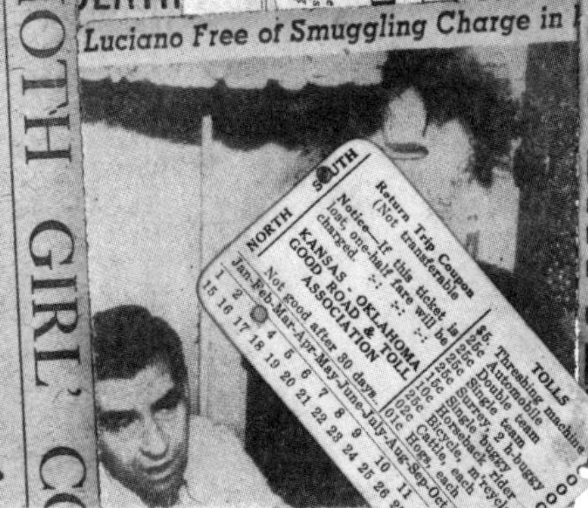

POLICE LINKED TO CHICAGO MASSACRE

Scarface Al's Brother Freed On Gun Charge

By International News Service.

CHICAGO, July 19.—RALPH "BOTTLES" CAPONE, brother of the notorious "Scarface Al" Ca...

WOMAN OF 60, GIRL, 20, HELD IN BOOTLEGGING

Clyde Barrow Slain With Gungirl After Being Lured to Trap

Breaking Up the Smuggling of Narcotics at th

Drugs Tossed Over the Wall in Loaded Golf Balls, Weighted Sticks and Hollow Pebbles; a Mother's Kiss Conveys Dose to Prisoner Addict.

FORESTALLING THE TRICKS OF THE WILY SMUGGLE

Habitual User of Morphine at End of Sentence Has His Say About Addicts and Prohibition; Says Joints Exist for Fashionable Users.

SEPTEMBER 12, 1926

DRUGS SEIZED EN ROUTE TO SAN QUENTIN

AUGUST 31, 1921

Opium Worth Thousands Is Halted in Stockton; Was Sent to Convict's Wife, Is Belief

A bold endeavor to smuggle several thousand dollars' worth of opium into San Quentin prison was frustrated yesterday when inspectors for the State Board of Pharmacy seized an automobile loaded with the drug, and arrested the driver, William Beaudikofer, owner of a Stockton garage.

A prior attempt on the part of the drug ring to invade the State penitentiary was stopped in sensational fashion a few days ago. Yesterday's seizure, which took place in Stockton, was declared to Louis Zeh, secretary of the State Board of Pharmacy, to center around the same individuals as the first attempt.

Capture of the automobile used by the drug ring in transporting the narcotic is regarded by Zeh as of peculiar importance. By the provisions of the new state poison act, passed by the efforts of "The Examiner" after a bitter fight at the last legislative session, the automobile now becomes the property of the State of California. It is the third car seized from the drug traffickers within a week.

The arrest was made by Inspectors Roy Jones and Harry Charnak of the State Board.

Beaudikofer, after his capture, confessed to the inspectors that the drug was to have been delivered to Mrs. Jack Wilson, wife of Jack Wilson, a convict in San Quentin.

VISITS HUSBAND.

It had been learned by the inspectors that last Sunday Mrs. Wilson visited her husband in the penitentiary, and asked him whether there was anything he wanted. Wilson replied in careful phrases which the prison guards interpreted as a request for opium.

Warden Demands Machine Guns at Sing Sing Prison

MACHINE guns for Sing Sing prison were demanded yesterday by Warden Lewis E. Lawes, following the New Jersey mail robbery, in which the bandits used modern artillery.

The warden proposes to mount the guns on the walls of the prison and to keep a supply of portable weapons for the guards.

Sing Sing, he said yesterday, has more long-term prisoners now than ever before, and many of them are of a desperate type.

MYSTERY GIRL SMOKER JAILED

Associate of bootleggers and drug peddlers, a pretty girl, who d[...] herself as Helen Davis, twenty-two, of No. 673 Broadway, was arraigned in Special Sessions yesterday.

She refused to disclose her real

DOPE ADDICTS GREAT DANGER IN U. S. JAILS

House Committee Finds Startling Conditions and Urges Passage of Porter's Bill

By Universal Service.

WASHINGTON, May 14.—Deplorable conditions in the Federal conditions caused by overcrowding and mixing of narcotic drug addicts with other prisoners, speak in "thunder tones to the minds and consciences of those who have the legislative power to remedy and relieve this terrible condition."

The House Judiciary Committee so declared in its report today, urging passage of the Porter Bill, establishing two farms where narcotic drug addicts may be sent for special treatment under supervision of the United States Public Health Service.

Representative Graham, of Pennsylvania, chairman of the Judiciary Committee, wrote the report, endorsing the bill backed by the Hearst newspapers.

PRISONS

The repo[...]

"The c[...] pressed by [...] dence covering the present conditions existing in the penitentiaries at Atlanta, Ga.; Leavenworth, Kans., and McNeil Island, Wash.

"These penitentiaries are seriously overcrowded, the total cell capacity being 3,778; whereas on April 1, 1928, there were 7,598 men crowded within these walls.

"Three prisoners are in many cases quartered in cells which were built for one, and six and eight prisoners are crowded in cells designed to hold four. Men are obliged to sleep in dark and poorly ventilated basements.

PACKED LIKE ANIMALS.

"This picture of overcrowding is a sad one to contemplate. To pack men as though they were animals is a brutal manner of treatment, even for convicts. Something must be done to relieve this inhuman situation.

"We are told that since 1915 the number of convictions in the federal courts has multiplied fourfold. No doubt the attempted enforcement of prohibition has largely contributed to this result.

"When one contemplates this deplorable state in these prisons of the nation, and is told there are 1,559 drug addicts in these three federal prisons, the necessity for adopting the bill which we report needs no argument."

INFORMER ON DRUGS BEATEN BY PRISONERS

NOVEMBER 26, 1924

Accused 'Stool Pigeon' in Narcotics Expose Rescued in Jail Attack

Charles Edward Burleigh, former convict and former army officer, who on Monday charged that narcotics are being smuggled into San Quentin, was attacked and beaten by prisoners yesterday in the United States Marshal's cell in the Federal building, and was saved only by the strenuous efforts of deputies, who fought to rescue him.

Among the prisoners who were hammering Burleigh when his rescuers dashed into the cell were several men charged with peddling narcotics.

Burleigh was sentenced to five years' imprisonment Monday when he appeared before Federal Judge Partridge on a charge of fraudulently cashing a war veteran's check. After sentence was passed he pleaded that he be sent to some prison other than San Quentin, where, he said, narcotics were smuggled into convicts.

He was sentenced to McNeil's Island.

VICTIM OF TAUNTS

While waiting for a prison van to [...] him to the County Jail, Bur[...]

"You're a double-crosser," one of them, a convicted drug peddler, shouted. He made a run for Burleigh, calling his mates to help him.

Before Burleigh's screams for help summoned the deputy sheriffs nearby he had been knocked down and beaten severely by the infuriated prisoners. His rescuers had to pull him from the bottom of a heap, and throw his attackers off.

PRISONERS SEARCHED

Deputies then began searching the prisoners. In the pocket of one, Milo Eggers, charged with stealing whisky in British Columbia, a knife and fork were found. Eggers admitted having stolen the implements from a waiter's tray shortly before Burleigh was attacked.

Another of the prisoners, George Watkins, charged with peddling narcotics, had concealed a small supply of narcotics in his clothing, the deputies found.

Given first aid treatment after the attack, Burleigh was removed to a separate cell and then transferred to the county jail. His statements of narcotic smuggling into San Quentin are being investigated by prison authorities.

Man Fails to Attend

By NADIA LAVROVA

LAST Labor Day we stood inside the Ingleside county jail and, through a barred window, watched the "hypos" play a stiff ball game with the "winos" in the sunny, white-walled yard.

There are 153 inmates in the county jail today. Out of this number 77, or one-half, are narcotic addicts—"hypos" in the racy slang of the jail. The other half is comprised of men who would normally prefer a drink of whisky to any other kind of "shot," and who have been nicknamed "winos" in consequence.

"I want to show you what we are up against when we match wits with the hop-heads," he said, leading the way back to his office. There he unlocked a drawer of his desk and took out a miscellaneous assortment of tobacco cans, rubber fingers, powders done up in white paper, punctured golf balls, weighted sticks and other curious objects whose purpose was by no means evident at the first glance.

O'Neill lifted a middle-sized brown pebble from his treasure store. Only it was not a pebble. Breaking off one corner, he revealed that the stone was really a cleverly colored plaster-of-Paris cast—hollow and filled with the stuff that provides artificial paradises.

"This was found on the top of our rock-pile early one morning as the 'cons' were filing but to work," he commented drily. "A confederate threw it over the wall [...]

[...] stick about six inches long. Cleverly weighted with lead on one side, it carried a generous supply of morphine done up in lead paper and tied with a string on the other.

The next exhibit was the classical post-card, so old a "gag" by this time that none but a rank novice would attempt it today. A plain postcard is carefully divided into two layers, filled with the potent white powder, pasted together again and, upon being covered with a few meaningless

He Started Early

Girl reporter: Mr. O'Neill here tells me that you have used morphine continuously for thirty-seven years. If you care to discuss the matter—how did you begin using it and why did you keep up the habit?

Drug addict; cheerfully: I cannot tell you at what age I started taking dope. However, I remember that by the time I was seventeen I was a confirmed taster of morphine. You see, I was subject to spells of headache in my youth. There stood the jar on the kitchen shelf. Before I was conscious of what I was doing I would take a little of the white powder on the blade of a knife and wash it down with a sip of milk or water. It seemed just a simple thing to do as it is for many people to take an aspirin tablet when their heads feel dull. And the morphine relieved me every time. This was before the passing of the Harrison Narcotic Act, you must understand, when anyone could buy as much morphine as the drugstore held.

Girl reporter: And so you acquired the habit—?

Drug addict: As a matter of fact I never became a dope-fiend—

Jailer: Except that you get filled up with hop any time you get a chance.

Drug addict, coldly: I repeat that I have never been, nor ever will be a "dope-fiend." I always [...]

[...] tion that is given by the booze-hounds, these addicts of the greater evil—

Girl reporter, astonished: You mean, alcohol, the lesser evil?

Drug addict: I mean alcohol, the greater evil. Have you ever seen a man from the "slave markets" of Howard street lying in an empty lot, his face black and blue and the stench of alcoholic substitutes about him—

Canned Heat

Jailer: Canned heat. That's our latest problem.

Drug addict: Exactly. Canned heat. Well, if you have seen these piteous relics of humanity brought out here, their heads lolling, and booked on a charge of drunkenness, you will never compare them to us, who take our pleasure like gentlemen. Why some of them are such confirmed boozers that nothing less than prohibition could drive them to take drugs—?

Girl Reporter: What do you mean exactly?

Jailer: He means, Miss, that since prohibition made liquor too expensive, many a wine bum has taken to using hop.

This is not a sanitarium, but a jail. And yet we do cure addicts and we do break them of the habit, for the time they are with us. Look in this album. Here was a man who weighed 140 pounds when admitted. After he had finished his fifty days he was broken of the habit and weighed 170 pounds. Here was a man weighing 130 pounds, he made eighty-five days—weighed 182 pounds when he came out. We got him back next month—and he weighed 140. Here is another man—stayed with us twenty-five days—gained twenty-one pounds.

The relatives of the addict ge[...] erally disown him—do not wa[...] to have anything to do with h[...] —his last resort is after all w[...] State.

We had three addicts here locked up for six months. Th[...] were pronounced quite cured and they were quite cured—gain[...] in weight—looked well. We [...] them out one day towards evenin[...] Next morning they—or rath[...] their bodies—turned up at t[...] morgue. Coming out they h[...] gone straight to the peddler's, a[...] an over-dose of narcotic—a do[...] that they would have been ab[...] to stand in the old days wh[...] their organisms had developed [...] resistance to the poison. As [...] was, they took it and died. T[...] whole things seems very futile b[...] what would you do?

Drug Addict: There is alwa[...] that ticklish matter of mone[...] When I started taking morphi[...] it was $[...] an ounce. Today it [...] $40 an o[...]ce—that is, if you ca[...] manage to buy an ounce at [...] time. Now I am a poor man an[...] cannot afford to do it. I buy [...] couple of grains at a time, pay[...] ing around $1.50 for the dos[...] something that costs the chem[...] ists exactly 7 cents to manufa[...] ture. By going out and buyin[...] dope whenever I get some loo[...] change I violate the law perha[...] half a dozen times a week. No[...] a man who can afford to buy h[...] year's supply at once pays one [...] third less than I do—and it [...] almost impossible to catch hi[...] breaking the Poison Act. Hav[...] you any idea how many of th[...]

[...] there are places in San Francisc[...] which are nothing else but fash[...] ionable dope clubs.

Jailer: Yep, that's so. Sil[...] cushions, Oriental hanging[...] opium pipes and the rest of th[...] setting.

Drug Addict: There, you se[...] It's the poor devils that are th[...] peddler's joy, and that give th[...] detectives something to do.

Jailer: You all end by bein[...] sore at the detectives. They onl[...] do their duty by saving you from[...] yourselves.

Drug Addict: You think so[...] All right, I will state my case. M[...] face has been photographed an[...] re-photographed ever since m[...] first conviction—which was [...] charge of buying dope for my ow[...] use—I have never been charge[...] with any other crime, as M[...] O'Neill knows. But my finger[...] prints are available to any de[...] tective of the force. Any one o[...] them knows me by sight an[...] greets me like an old friend.

Jailer: Sure, and we're a[...] glad when we have you with us.

Drug Addict: I know, I know[...] Mike, the detective who arreste[...] me exactly twenty-nine days ago[...] saw me walking down Mission[...] street at half past eight in th[...] morning. 'Hey, not so fast,' h[...] said. 'I know you're a hop-head[...] all right. Where are you going.'

"Now I was going to my plac[...] of employment, a tonsorial par[...] lor on a street off Mission. S[...] to his question where I wa[...] going I answered in all truthful[...] ness: 'To work.'

"Tell that to the judge," h[...] said and took me to the city jail.

Back to Work

Now I was on my way to work[...] Moreover, the most minute search[...] did not disclose a particle of dop[...] on my person. No needle [...]

200 CONVICTS IN 2 U. S. PRISONS B

CONVICTS FACE DOPE INQUIRY

PRISON NO CURE OF DRUG HABIT, SAYS WARDEN

Sing Sing Head Declares But One Prisoner in a Hundred Fails to Go Back to Addiction

FINDS NUMBER INCREASES

Declares His Study Proves That Capital Punishment Is No Deterrent to Murder

Major Lewis E. Lawes, warden of Sing Sing, in an address yesterday declared that drug addicts let out of State prisons go back to the use of drugs and that nothing is being done to cure them. He asserted:

"I know of one hundred different instances where prisoners

DRY RAID IN SING SING NETS 3 AND A STILL

Sing Sing attaches announced yesterday that a copper still has been found, three prisoners locked up accused of drinking and an attendant compelled to take the pledge in a big prohibition drive

Principal Keeper Thomas McInerney.

Prison attendants maintain that a plentiful supply of liquor, made from fermented prune juice and potatoes, was found and that two criminals were caught operating the still.

Warden Lewis E. Lawes, although admitting the "arrests" of three prisoners accused of drinking, denies any "hootch" was found. However, he admitted that there was a "still" hunt for a still" and that a mysterious copper apparatus was found inside the walls and confisounty Jail

After Convict's Revelations:

Governor Says Smuggling Of Dope At Prison Fought

Prisoner Reveals His Scars

ADDICTS SWINDLED EVEN WHEN IN JAIL

MAY 13, 1923

Drugs Smuggled In and Sold to Them at High Prices, Grossly Adulterated.

Incidents which show how drug addicts are preyed upon while in prison are disclosed in a report by Principal Keeper Joseph S. Hoff, of the New Jersey State Prison at Trenton, made public to-day.

Keeper Hoff tells of one case in which a visitor to the prison smuggled in a small quantity of morphine adulterated with sugar of milk. Its presence was detected when prisoners tried to distribute it and the drug was confiscated.

The idea that money could be made in that way spread and several attempts were made to sell to prisoners substitutes for drugs, such as sugar of milk and baking powder, done up in the form in which morphine is usually distributed.

One prisoner admitted that he had bought a quantity of roach powder, used it and "had not felt the same since."

The Trenton prison has among its 1,300 inmates forty-two sentenced for selling habit-forming drugs. Eighteen drug addicts were admitted in the last six months, an increase of thirteen over the previous full year.

Keeper Hoff reported that the drug addicts are receiving up-to-date treatment by compulsory abstinence or reduced doses. He says:

"Those who have been cured while in the prison are profuse in their gratitude for the time they have been compelled to serve, which has done for them what their weakened will power could not accomplish without discipline."

Salvation Army Gets $150,000 in First Week

U.S. GRAND JURY TO PROBE DOPE TRAFFIC IN 'PEN'

MAY 15, 1928

Fifteen Witnesses Called to Inquiry Today; State Continues Fatal Stabbing Quiz

The Government today will begin a grand jury investigation into traffic in narcotics among prisoners in the penitentiary on Welfare Island. The investigation follows the riot last Saturday in which one inmate, George Holshoe, was stabbed to death.

U. S. Attorney Medalie issued this statement:

"There appears to be an organized system of distribution of narcotics on the island. The examination of several former inmates indicates that this organization has a monopoly of this business and that certain inmates have regular runners and sources of supply."

SUBPOENAS ISSUED.

Fifteen subpoenas were issued for witnesses. Among prospective witnesses are Warden McCann, Deputy Warden Sheehan, Medical Director Norman and a number of former and present inmates.

Investigation of dope smuggling on the island was continued by Assistant U. S. Attorneys Rosenblum, Palmeiri and Williams.

Meanwhile the State also was continuing its inquiry into Holshoe's death preparatory to a Grand Jury investigation tomorrow as a homicide case against Joey Rao, Harlem racketeer, Frank Mazzia and Patsy Como.

TWENTY TAKEN TO TOMBS.

Assistant District Attorneys Carney and Price questioned about forty prisoners yesterday and said that twenty of these will be transferred to the Tombs today and will be taken before the Grand Jury.

Washington Prison Guards, Medics Named in Dope Ring

SEATTLE, April 26 (INS)—Cracking of a dope ring selling to inmates at Washington state penitentiary, involving several prison guards and Seattle doctors, was revealed Tuesday by Richard Everest, executive assistant to Governor Arthur B. Langlie.

Everest said a parole violator who is being held in King county jail had confessed shipping cocaine and benzedrine to be distributed by the guards involved among the inmates, who paid $1.50 for the drugs.

Everest said the office had known "for quite a while" that Seattle doctors had been mailing the small packages to the post office at Walla Walla, where they were picked up by the guards involved in the ring.

The name of the man who confessed is being withheld for his own safety, Everest said, because he must return to the prison.

Names of the guards arrested were not announced. Everest said they were apprehended by police when they picked up test packages addressed to them by Everest.

The only thing the governor's office does not know, Everest said, was how the drug was smuggled into the penitentiary.

Names of the Seattle doctors will be withheld until the charges have been filed.

2 JAILED HERE IN WIDE PRISON NARCOTIC PLOT

DECEMBER 28, 1932

Letter Sent Harlem Policy 'King' in Atlanta Bares Big Smuggling Conspiracy

Charges of a widespread plot to smuggle narcotics, letters and money into prisoners in Atlanta Penitentiary came to light here yesterday following the arraignment of Margaret E. Hancock, of 128 W. 117th st., and Harold Frank, of 90 Lenox ave.

Miss Hancock, according to Assistant Federal Attorney Maoriello, is charged with having sent money to Jose Enrique Miro, Harlem policy racketeer, who was sent to Atlanta in April for income tax evasion. The charges against Frank were not made public.

She was arrested several days ago and held in $2,500 bond for hearing Jan. 3. Frank was arraigned yesterday and held in $5,000 bail for hearing on the same date.

Maoriello said that Federal authorities in Atlanta had requested the arrest of a number of persons in various parts of the country. It is charged that a large quantity of drugs was smuggled into the prison in small packages, with the connivance of some attaches of the prison. Maorielli said a Georgia indictment has been returned, naming many defendants.

Unborn Snipes Baby Offered Many Homes

COLUMBIA, S. C., Dec. 27.—Several offers have been received to adopt the unborn child of Mrs. Beatrice Ferguson Snipes, expectant mother sentenced to die in the electric chair, it was revealed

ED AS DOPE ADDICTS

NEW YORK, JULY 1, 1928

HIDDEN DOPE BRINGS POLICE SHAK

Nunc est Cough Up

"IT ALL DEPENDS ON YOU"
"IS THAT THE SMALLEST YOU HAVE?"
NO TAINTED MONEY UNDER $10,000 WILL BE ACCEPTED!
"THANK YOU. YOU CANT BREAK THE BOX!"
DEM
GOP

1928

CUSTOMS AXE CRUSHES HUGE LIQUOR RING

Warren Orders Police Inquiry Following Federal Shakeup; Narcotics Also Involved

One of the most gigantic rum smuggling rings in the local history of prohibition came to light yesterday, following the suspension of eighteen United States customs guards, assigned to steamship piers.

Narcotics, as well as liquor, have been brought ashore in considerable quantities by smugglers with the aid of bribed guards, Philip Elting, Collector of the Port, disclosed last night.

Many more customs guards are believed to be slated for suspension and a general clean-up of the Marine police service has been ordered. Also, it was reported last night that one of the biggest and best known trans-Atlantic liners putting into this port will shortly be seized by the Federal Government.

Details of the ring's operations, now in the hands of the authorities, disclose an amazing conspiracy to defeat the Volstead act. Involved is a small army of steamship employes, working on liners down to the lowliest of freighters; also wholesale charges of bribery of pier guards, and the virtual transformation of New York harbor into the nation's greatest port of entry for bootleg contraband.

BEGAN YEAR AGO.

The conspiracy is said to have found its origin little more than a year ago in the sale of one quart of liquor in the financial district. From this has grown a de luxe bootleg business estimated at $500,000 per week. Declining to cheapen its clientele by dealing with speak-easy proprietors, the syndicate is said to cater strictly to financiers of Wall Street and lower Broadway, and to their home cellars.

The man who sold the original quart is the head of the rum coterie, and from a sole capital of that one bottle, he is reported to have built up a fortune aggregating more than $1,000,000.

He and his "get-rich-quick" story are well known along the harbor front. The liquor, it is said, had been sold to him by a boat employe, and he sold it without the usual "doctoring," whereby the regular bootlegger makes three quarts of "h[illegible] out of one of real stuff.

SWAMPED WITH ORDERS.

BLACK ATTACKS DRUG OFFICIALS AS AIDING RING

Congressman Wants House Investigation, Saying Agents Never Molested Rothstein

Charges that Federal narcotic officials made no attempt to suppress the known drug smuggling of Arnold Rothstein and his gang were made yesterday by Representative Loring M. Black, of Brooklyn.

He said he would ask a Congressional investigation of the Federal narcotic enforcement service, declaring a "high official of the Treasury Department" has already balked a Federal Grand Jury inquiry into "widespread incompetency and corruption."

Federal officers in New York would make no comment on the charge. Both Federal Attorney Medalie and Joseph A. Manning, agent in charge of narcotic enforcement in the New York district, said any reply would have to come from the head of the Narcotics Bureau in Washington.

DRIVE AT CRIME.

Representative Black said he would ask the investigation in the hope of checking the sale of drugs and curbing the "murderous crime waves" that are increased by drug addicts. He said:

"Dope is the chief patron of crime as we have it today. Without dope we would not have so many super-daring crimes."

Declaring inconsequential addicts and peddlers are arrested while the ring-leaders in dope rings are unmolested, he went on:

"The case in point is the late notorious Arnold Rothstein. Long before Rothstein was murdered, with resultant disclosures of his interest in the drug traffic, European officials were aware that he was a ring-leader in such smuggling.

"This information was passed on to American officials, but I can find no evidence of any concerted effort to suppress this Rothstein and the members of his drug gang.

"Why is it that one of the greatest drug smugglers now alive in this country, who is known to the enforcement service far and wide, has never been checked?"

Representative Black asserted that, to cover their own inefficiency, agents exaggerate values of drugs they do seize, making a $50,000 seizure bulk as $2,000,000 worth.

He said he felt sure the Democrats in control of the House would authorize an investigation.

1929

'Moral Nuisance' Spots Hunted by Anti-Crime Bureau

Agents of the police crime bureau, seeking to trace criminality to an early source, are looking for "moral nuisance" spots in the city shown to be prolific breeders of delinquents. Henrietta Additon, sixth deputy police commissioner, in charge of the crime prevention bureau, made this statement yesterday.

HENRIETTA ADDITON, Head of Police Crime Prevention Bureau.

She spoke to members of the Periscope Club of the American Women's Association at a luncheon at 353 W. 57th st. She said:

"The evolution of the youthful delinquent into the gangster is not an accident. It is a logical development, mostly, of the neighborhood from which

EVANSTON, Ill., Feb. 23.

CURIOSITY (purely scientific) killed a cat, and the humane society has become wroth.

A member of the Monocoan Fraternity at Northwestern University obtained the cat from the Humane Society's shelter.

What has become, the society inquired today, of that and the several other cats obtained by fraternity members from the shelter and never since seen alive?

The society is pushing an investigation and there is talk of arrests.

POLICE SLAY DOPE SUSPECT

DETROIT, Feb. -- (By International News Service).—Robert (Narcotic Bob) Evans, twenty-one, a suspected dope peddler, was shot and killed by police here today. Joseph Costello, thirty-five, an alleged Chicago gangster, was perhaps fatally wounded when the two suspects elected to "shoot it out" with two patrolmen in a reputed "blind pig."

Patrolman Watson was wounded.

The patrolman saw four suspicious looking men standing in front of the alleged liquor establishment. No weapons were found on the four, who told the patrolmen that two men who had just entered the building had revolvers.

The officers no sooner stepped inside the door than the pair began shooting at them from behind a stove.

WARREN'S AXE FALLS ON 4 AFTER AIDES RAID LOCKERS

First Grade Detectives on Narcotic Squad Sent to Pavement-Pounding Posts

Liquor and Drugs Found Cached May Cause Removal of Acting Captain Sherb

Commissioner Warren's axe fell upon the narcotic squad yesterday afternoon following a raid on the squad's lockers by Deputy Chief Inspector Valentine and his aides.

Four first grade detectives were demoted to the ranks as uniformed patrolmen with a salary slash of $1,000 a year each and ordered removed to various outlying precincts for duty.

The investigation will be continued under Valentine's direction, it was announced, and many more of the detectives are expected to be transferred next week. It was held certain at headquarters that Acting Captain Henry Sherb will be removed as head of the squad.

The demoted men are Herbert Moot ordered removed to the Clinton Street Station; Charles Graham, to the Morrisania; Irving Higgins, to the Bushwick Avenue, and Samuel Masson, to Wakefield Boulevard. The men have been drawing salaries of $3,500 yearly. They will now receive $2,500.

NO SIMON APPOINTMENT.

Rumors came to Valentine Friday that liquor and narcotics were concealed in the squad's lockers in the basement of headquarters.

Commissioner Warren last night denied rumors that former Deputy Commissioner Carleton Simon might be reappointed to head the narcotic squad. No civilian, he declared, would be asked to take so important a position in the police department.

Another event motivating the shakeup, it was learned, was the $1,000,000 narcotic raid in Brooklyn, in July, 1927, in which 7,901 ounces of heroin and a quantity of morphine were seized. This raid, it was pointed out, was not made by the narcotic squad, but under the direction of Valentine.

Yesterday the detectives under Acting Captain Henry Sherb were called into headquarters. Then, without being told why, they were marched to the basement and ordered to open their lockers, one by one, for inspection.

KEPT FOR EVIDENCE.

Police officials refused to state whether or not liquor or narcotics were found, but word of the finding of the needles leaked out. Then men in whose lockers they were found, it was said, explained they had kept the articles in their lockers to facilitate cases in which they were to be used as evidence.

... struggle for control of the company since Mr. Guth's appointment to the executive staff five months ago.

Guth, in opposing Miller's management in court proceedings, had stated in letters to stockholders that a large group of the stockholders planned the removal of Miller. Yesterday's action, according to Mr. Miller, was the organization's answer to Guth's campaign against him. Guth is president of Mavis Candies, Inc., of Baltimore, control of which has been acquired by Loft, Inc.

In a letter to stockholders yesterday Miller announced the action taken and declared that under his management the organization had "shown a definite upward trend" in volume of business.

U. S. Should Speedily Recognize China's New Government

THE UNITED STATES should speedily recognize the new government of China. It is a republican government, with ideals based largely on the Government of our own country.

It controls the whole of China, which for the first time since the emperor was deposed is under a single government.

It represents the Chinese people, their ideas and their aspirations.

ALL WI OWN MA

GUILTY AGENTS IN DOPE GRAFT FACE U.S. DRIVE

Treasury Replies to Juryman Who Criticized Transfers of 3 Men from New York

By KENNETH CLARK,
Universal Service Staff Correspondent.

WASHINGTON, Mar. 15—Immediate summary action will be taken against narcotic agents against whom there is evidence of graft or corruption.

That is the gist of a reply the Treasury Department prepared today to a letter from Parker Sloane, chairman of a committee of seven of the New York Grand Jury, which returned a presentment alleging corruption and inefficiency in the Federal narcotics force. The jury recommended "a complete reorganization from top to bottom."

Already the Treasury has started a drastic shakeup, including the removal of Colonel L. G. Nutt, as Federal narcotics chief, and the transfer of many agents in New York and other cities.

CALLED "REPRISALS."

Sloane's letter criticized the methods adopted by the Treasury in cleaning house, particularly the transfer of agents Oyler, Connelly and Kelly from New York, as being in the nature of reprisals because they had assisted in the inquiry.

The Treasury says the transfers are not punishments, as the agents have been sent to important centres. Honolulu, wher Oyler has been ordered, is regarded as a "pivotal point" in the trans-shipment and introduction of dope into the Pacific Coast.

It was learned today that the Treasury has sent a letter to Oyler demanding reimbursement for alleged overpayment by the Government on his expense accounts. Since March, 1929, Oyler, agent in Chicago, has been paid $679 50 on expenses incurred in New York.

Jacob Bloom, indicted by the New York Grand Jury as an alleged leader of an international dope ring, who was arrested in Southampton, England, yesterday, as he alighted from the Berengaria, will be returned to New York on the first available steamer, probably the French liner Paris, the Treasury was advised today.

MARCH 16, 1930

DOPE GRAFTING LATEST CHARGE AGAINST POLICE

Fifty Members of Narcotics Division to Be Examined in Seabury Investigation

The Seabury investigation, it was revealed yesterday, is preparing to examine more than fifty members of the police narcotic division, all of them veterans of at least ten years' service. The bank accounts of all will also be sought.

The names of substantial citizens seized under circumstances reminiscent of the methods of the vice squad and forced to pay for the privilege of being sent away to private institutions for drug-addiction treatments are known to the investigators.

The "racket," it was explained, consisted not only in extortion from fear-stricken dope users who dreaded exposure, but in the collection of fees from favored "institutions" where the police drug sleuths "steered" their victims.

FALSE NAMES USED.

Inquiry was disclosed that some New Yorkers prominent in business circles, men who might be ruined by revelation of their narcotic habits, were permitted to be arraigned under names the police knew to be false.

The power of the police "drug ring" was declared to exceed by far that of the vice squads. As an example, the impotence of a widely known political leader to protect his friends from this "organization" was cited.

WHEN "PULL" FAILED.

This political stalwart, who has been mentioned publicly in the Seabury inquiry as having intervened for friends in vice cases when apparently the friends were "framed," had to pay for the "private treatment" of at least one drug addict, and evidently was able to win only the slightest concessions from the narcotics division detectives.

The investigators hastened to make plain that the integrity of all members of the division is not challenged and that many have been found to be scrupulously honest, with virtually no savings to show for years of effort.

...DAY, FEBRUARY 20, 1930

BROOKLYN DRY AS RAIDS LOOM

Brooklyn's borough hall section was reported as dry yesterday following numerous prohibition raids in the neighborhood in the last few days. Speakeasies closed voluntarily it was said.

While the thirsty became more so, Prohibition Administrator Campbell, Federal Attorney Ameli, of Brooklyn, William C. Nolan, chief of dry agents in Brooklyn and Long Island, and several others met in Ameli's office.

They refused to reveal the purpose of the conference, but it is believed they planned further activities under the internal revenue law, which permits raids without warrants on places failing to pay a tax on liquor sold. Long Island roadhouses are expected to suffer.

Speakeasy proprietors told customers they would shut up shop until the raiding squall blew over. Federal officials, however, asserted it was no squall, but a permanent dry wave.

Germans Told to Fix

NEW YORK AMERICAN—A Paper for People Who Think

U. S. Agents Hid Dope Evidence Against Accused Mates,

17

THURSDAY, FEBRUARY 19, 1931

57 L. I. COPS SUBPOENAED IN RUM PROBE

NOVEMBER 24, 1931

'MASTER MIND' OF RING ALSO WAS ASSISTED

$50,000 Wasted in Elaborate Wire-Tapping Plan Meant to Entrap Suspect Here

Information that Federal narcotic agents suppressed evidence incriminating fellow agents and ex-agents with a man long considered the "Master Mind" of New York's illicit drug traffic reached the Federal Grand Jury yesterday.

Other startling reports were given the panel, which, as made known yesterday by the New York American, is renewing an investigation of local drug enforcement, principally to determine why its charges a year ago against certain agents were ignored in Washington. Investigation yesterday developed:

That narcotic agents wasted almost $50,000 in an elaborate wire-tapping enterprise designed to trap the "Master Mind."

. . . That this enterprise extended from New York to San Francisco, the agents setting up elaborate apartments furnished at the government's expense and maintaining these places with their girl friends on the payroll as "stool pigeons," paying them $5 a day and expenses.

That after making only a "minor case," the most important part of the evidence was permitted to be lost as a result of action taken by high officials in Washington.

WAITED LONG TO INDICT.

This particular case developed more than two years ago. Federal agents then arrested Abe Stein, his wife, Dotty, and Al Spitzer. They were released on bail, and were not indicted until a month ago.

Their case was called in Federal Court yesterday and was set down for trial Monday. In connection with it these facts were learned by a New York American reporter:

Two apartments were furnished here by the agents. One man was sent to San Francisco, where he tapped the telephones of the person in that city thought to be an agent of the "Master Mind" in New York.

But instead of fastening evidence on this dope leader, the girl stool pigeons heard information coming to him warning him that the agents were on his trail and advising of various moves being made.

Two upright narcotic agents were also on the trail of the arch drug distributor. They found one of his shipments in a railroad terminal in Jersey City, consigned to an overlord of the underworld in Chicago.

REMOVED OPIUM.

This trunk contained $50,000 worth of opium. The agents removed all except a few packages, then weighted the trunk with rocks in order no to arouse suspicion through light weight.

They then telephoned to narcotic headquarters in Washington for permission to follow the trunk to Chicago, there to arrest the consignee, but were told "not to bother," that Chicago agents would attend to that.

When the trunk reached Chicago, however, it was permitted to reach its receiver, one of the most notorious drug dealers in that city, without molestation.

The prosecution here of the Steins and Spitzer is dependent to a large extent on evidence concerning the trunk.

OFFICIAL SAYS POLICE LINKED TO SMUGGLING

Long Beach Patrolmen Lived in Luxury, Took 2 Vacations Yearly, Supervisor Asserts

Bank accounts of fifty-seven members of the Long Beach police force and their wives were subpoenaed yesterday in an effort to unearth evidence of police connivance with rum-runners.

District Attorney Edwards at Mineola plunged into a miniature reproduction of the Seabury investigation in New York, following reports that many Long Beach policemen appeared suddenly affluent and lived in luxury, though paid small salaries.

AFFLUENCE CHARGED.

Vice Witness, ...ly of Pneumonia

After All, What's a Job?

DOPE PEDDLER

2 U. S. NARCOTIC AGENTS HELD ON BRIBE CHARGE

Former Operative Also Arrested; Trio Accused of Paying Officer to Aid Fugitive

NOT LINKED TO DOPE HAUL

Goodman, Seized in Raid, Under $75,000 Bond to Prevent His Murder by Racketeers

Two Federal narcotic agents and a former agent were arrested yesterday on a charge of plotting to bribe Arnold C. Lauchenauer, a fellow agent.

Federal Attorney Medalie would not admit there was any connection between the arrest of the three and that of Abraham Goodman, who was captured Thursday with $1,000,000 worth of opium.

Goodman, arraigned before United States Commissioner O'Neill, was held in $75,000 bail to prevent his flight or possible murder by dope racketeers.

CHIEF MAKES CHARGES.

The accused agents are Richard Nash, of 186 E. 109th st., and Charles R. Keane, of Jackson Heights. The former agent is Philip A. De Stefano.

Major J. A. Manning, chief of the narcotic squad, charged that the three gave Lauchenauer $1,000 in bills in a restaurant at 442 Pearl st.

Medalie asserted the money came from Peter Ellinois, a fugitive, who was indicted after Lauchenauer, posing as an illicit drug buyer, entertained a party of racketeers at a midtown restaurant, which was raided by Federal detectives.

In return for the money, it was charged, Lauchenauer was to fail to identify Ellinois if he surrendered or was captured. Medalie asserted this was not the first time Nash had been mentioned in connection with money.

DEALERS TIPPED.

Attaches of Medalie's office said that for many months narcotic dealers have been warned from inside sources of impending raids. Tips have been sent out also where telephone wires have been tapped for evidence.

Nash was held in $10,000 bail; Keane in $2,500 and De Stefano in $12,500.

Goodman admitted the $75,000 bond fixed would serve to keep him in jail. He has stuck doggedly to his story that the 2,060 pounds of opium found in his Hudson st. office was left there for storage by an unknown truckman.

N. Y. Crime Board Puts Racket Toll Over 12 Billions

By N. Y. American Staff Correspondent.

ALBANY, April 3.—The New ...

U. S. Grand Jury Will Reopen Dope Bureau Graft Probe

Its Recommendations, Made Year Ago, Ignored, Is Charge.

ASKED CLEAN-UP

Treasury Chiefs to Be Summoned, Medalie Is Informed.

The Federal Grand Jury, which a year ago drew up a presentment condemning corruption and inefficiency in the New York Federal Narcotic Bureau, has notified United States Attorney Medalie of its intention to take advantage of its legal power and reopen the whole inquiry.

Notification was sent to Medalie Friday, it was learned yesterday. It is understood the Grand Jury will summon Harry J. Anslinger, appointed chief of the narcotic division by President Hoover, and James M. Doran, of the Treasury Department, formerly in charge of prohibition and drugs, and may also call a Cabinet officer—Secretary of the Treasury Mellon.

WILL PROBE INACTION.

It is the intention of the Grand Jury to determine why recommendations it made for improving conditions in the local narcotic unit were never followed out. It also seeks to find out why certain agents it recommended for dismissal or transfer were never dismissed or transferred.

Medalie has notified the Attorney-General's office of the Grand Jury's intention to proceed alone.

This, however, is no reflection on Medalie or his assistants, in whom the Grand Jury a year ago expressed full confidence, but a desire to avoid embarrassing the new prosecutor by asking him to investigate another New York Federal department.

VISITED MELLON.

News of the projected investigation leaked out yesterday as it became known also that the Seabury investigation has started an inquiry into the operations of members of the police narcotics bureau. The investigators have been informed that unscrupulous members of that squad, like those in the vice squad, extorted money from addicts and connived in "fixing" cases they established.

GA... I... MER SHOT, T... WN OFF HIGH R...

Three Youths Arreste... One Confesses, Police Tells of Night-Time Am...

GUN RENTED FOR 75 CENTS

Suspect Declared He Killed When Victim 'Squealed' on Dice Game, Detectives Aver

MILLION-DOLLAR INCOMES SHOW GAIN FOR 1929

Two Speeders Hit By Accidental Shot

Two men were accidentally shot yesterday as their speeding automobile was halted by Patrolman Harold Krauss after a long chase along White Plains ave.

Revolver in hand, the officer jumped from a taxi he had commandeered when the car had disregarded his command to halt. In some manner the weapon was discharged.

The bullet struck Alfred Johnson, 3933 Harper ave., in the back, glanced off and struck Frank Pheiffer, 3941 Bell ave., in the hand. After medical attention Johnson was given a summons for reckless driving.

U. S. Grand Jury to Reopen Dope Bureau Graft Probe

Continued from First Page

recommendations they made. It is understood Mellon assured them that salutary action would be taken.

Closing its long inquiry, in which it worked three weeks overtime, and indicted many, the January, 1930, Grand Jury sent its presentment to Washington.

The presentment revealed that the New York Narcotic Bureau "padded" its reports to Washington, with the full knowledge of Washington officials, by copying records of 354 police narcotic cases in 1929 with which it had nothing to do. The presentment charged there was "evidence of gross dereliction and incompetence on the part of some" of the New York narcotic agents and a suggestion of "improper motives" on the part of others.

One agent, it said, is a user of drugs, yet kept his job, and the Grand Jury held "there has not been diligence in taking steps to ascertain the truth concerning agents who have come under suspicion as users of drugs." It also said stocks of seized narcotics were "loosely" handled.

The Treasury Department took some action, removed Colonel L. G. Nutt as Federal narcotics chief and transferred Agents Oyler, Connelly and Kelly from New York. Parker Sloane, chairman of a committee of seven of the 1930 Grand Jury, promptly protested in a letter to Washington officials that these transfers appeared in the nature of reprisals upon men who had given assistance to the Grand Jury. The Treasury Department denied the transfers were in the nature of punishment.

The Treasury Department also promised summary action against agents against whom there was evidence of graft or corruption. It so happens that some members of the present Grand Jury also were members of the January, 1930, morning Grand Jury, and these have now interested the other grand jurors in what they view as official failure to act.

It became known that on Friday, the 13th, the Grand Jury unanimously adopted a resolution deciding the investigation should be undertaken and the foreman so notified Medalie.

Doran and Anslinger were witnesses before the 1930 body. Doran was then Prohibition Commissioner and Anslinger, now chief, was deputy in charge of the narcotic bureau. L. P. Mattingly and Rolland L. Nutt, respectively the son-in-law and son of Colonel L. G. Nutt, then chief of the narcotics division, also were called.

The Grand Jury found that Nutt, representing Mattingly's accountancy and law firm, had appeared for Arnold Rothstein in tax matters, and that Mattingly had borrowed $6,200 from Rothstein, but that drugs were not involved and that the transaction, at worst, was an "indiscretion."

MARCH 16, 1931

ELEVENTH ANNUAL BALL

GIVEN BY THE

PENINSULA POLICE OFFICERS' ASSOCIATION

Benefit of the Widows and Orphans Fund

5234

BAY MEADOWS CLUB HOUSE

SAN MATEO

SATURDAY EVE. September 30, 1939

UNION MUSIC BY JOHNNY DEBL'S ORCHESTRA

ADMISSION: Couples $1.00 • Extra Lady 50c • Government Tax Exempt

DRUG DEALER MADE $6,500 PROFIT ON LIQUOR HE NEVER SAW
DRUGS WORTH MILLION SEIZED
MILLIONAIRE SEIZED AS DOPE PEDDLER
Hijackers Seize 11-Ton Truckload Of Drug Supplies
$100,000 DOPE SEIZED IN RAID; 3 ARRESTED
DRUGS VALUED AT $100,000 FOUND; 6 HELD
GREATEST DOPE RAID IN HISTORY
Vast Stores of Morphine, Cocaine and Opium Hidden in Hollow Brush Handles.
TWO HELD AS SMUGGLERS
SIMON IN RAIDS GETS $200,000 IN NARCOTICS
Houses in Columbia Street and Boerum Place, Brooklyn, Entered.
$500,000 IN DRUGS IS SEIZED AT HOTEL
Five Men Arrested in Raid Forty Detectives Led by Dr. Simon.
$100,000 DRUGS SEIZED IN RAID
$250,000 DRUGS SEIZED IN RAID
GREED
DOPE
EASY MONEY
DRUG ADDICT
DOPE PEDDLER
ing Fat Raid Thrills Night Crowds in Chinatown
Put World Spotlight On Dope Profiteers
Bible a Drug-Smuggling Cache
Million in Drugs Goes Up in Smoke on Simon's Order
IF while strolling for the fresh air yesterday you felt "dopey," lay the blame on Special Deputy Police Commissioner Carlton Simon, in charge of the narcotic squad.
From the huge chimney at Police Headquarters yesterday Dr. Simon sent in smoke drugs that would sell at $1,000,000, including heroin, cocaine and morphine. The narcotics, which weighed 500 pounds, had been confiscated during
NOT EVEN BIBLE IS SACRED to dope peddler as witness by this photo taken in Federal Narcotic Division
paign for a New Shot the Horrible Dope Evil
DOPE SALE PUT ON CASH BASIS
Drug Addicts Spend $61,000,000
"Frame" Cripple as Dope Peddler
ART DEALER SENTENCED AS DOPE VENDER
Hanging Urged for Dope Venders
Eureka in Grip of Narcotics
Drugs Brought in From Canada
SCRIBBLED LINE OPENS CELL TO 'DOPE' PEDDLER
ONE MILLION VICTIMS U. S. ESTIMATES
FOUR PEDDLERS SENT TO JAIL
'Dope' Dealers To Prison
Dope Peddler to Prison
35 PEDDLERS JAILED IN 40 DAY OFFENSIVE
COURT WARS ON DOPE PEDDLERS
Narcotic Squad Raids Shop of Sing Fat, Chinese Merchant
Imagine! Placing Drug Peddling Officially on a Cash Basis!
"The saddest part of the drug horror is the cold-blooded, conscienceless way in which drug peddlers and professional criminals set about to teach young women the drug habit and cajole them along until they are thoroughly enmeshed in drug slavery. When the drug has taken firm hold upon the girl she will give that which she has guarded sacredly since she left her mother's knees if it is the price necessary to pay for the drug which she craves. When the designing scoundrel has accomplished his first victory, the descent of his victim into crime and other necessary degradation is rapid."

DOPE SATURATES SMALL CITIES
SEATTLE, PEORIA, NASHVILLE DEBAUCHED AS DRUG EVIL THREATENS NATION'S RUIN
NARCOTIC GANG TOOK VICTIM TO HARLEM CELLAR
South Dakota Banker Escaped Slaying in Dive to Which Bellboy Guides His Party
$13,000 RAID MADE IN NARCOTICS DENS
Federals and Police Join in Six Arrests.
INQUIRY LASTS MONTHS
$250,000 DRUG SEIZURE FOILS DOPE RING PLOT
$5,000 IN DRUGS AT BIG HOTEL
AND THERE THE DOPE WAS!
Here's Dope Amount Used In One Town
PEDDLER
DOPE
HABIT
VICTIM
DOPE PEDDLER
18 SEIZED, $10,000 DRUGS TAKEN IN RAID
Net Drawn by Federal Agents Tightens Around Opium Den in Newark.
EAST SIDE RAID $25,000 DRUG S
DOPE FORTUNE UNCOVERED IN BANK'S VAULT
California "Daylight" Robbers Revealed as Dealers in Contraband
Clever secret panel tapped by Lieut. S. H. Sackett bares wealth of smuggled dope hidden aboard the China Mail steamer Nanking.
NARCOTICS LEFT AT WALDO
DOPE PEDDLERS LEADS TO HIGHER
Deport the Alien Re
Rescind Recognition Of Soviet Russia!
Dope Raid Prisoners Mostly Non-Citizens.
Deportable Aliens
DRUG PEDDLER SWEARS HE
CEMETERY
TICKET SELLER
HOOVER GETS DOPE DEPORTATION BILL
PENITENTIARY
HOSPITAL
AROUSED PUBLIC OPINION
U.S. SEARCHES FOR $300,000 DOPE CACHE
$500,000 DRUG HA MADE IN MID-OC
SEIZED DOPE WORTH MILLION
ONE PORT SHIPS 15 TONS OF DOPE TO N. Y. YEARLY
U. S. Raids Sm
Biggest Dope R
22 Aliens Arre
NARCOTIC RING ARRESTS BRIN ALIEN INQUIR
Expel from U. S. All Dope Sellers
$5,000 Opium Cache Found on Java Ship
DOPE RACKETEERS
ILLEGAL NARCOTICS FROM THE ORIENT
ALIEN CROOK
FOREIGN SPY
ALIEN AGITATOR
FOR DEPORTATION
DOPE
ALIEN SMUGGLERS

WELFARE ISLE NARCOTIC RAID TRAPS THREE

1931

Quantity of Heroin Seized on Two Suspects; Further Arrests Are Predicted Soon

Trapping of three prisoners in the penitentiary on Welfare Island with enough heroin to put the entire prison poulation of 1,554 in daze was revealed yesterday.

Filing with Warden Joseph McCann of warrants against the three men brought the seizure to light. Commisioner of Correction Patterson later predicted more arrests and seizures will follow.

Under-cover agents have been at work on the island since June, when a City Hospita. butcher on the island was discovered to be an affluent drug peddler, and convicted.

These informants told McCann that the source of the penitentiary's drug supply was a m n named "Pancakes."

SUSPECTS TRAPPED.

Raymond Rodruguez, thirty-two, a Porto Rican, not a citizen, formerly of 114 E. 98th st., known among prisoners as "Pancakes," was seized.

Patterson declared Rodruguez carried sufficient heroin on his person to make about 250 "decks," or 1,000 "shots," which were sold to inmates at $1 a "shot." The drug was carried wrapped in cigarette papers, each containing one "shot."

The search led to Samuel Berman, forty-two, a Russian, formerly of 24 W. 119th st., and he was found also to have about 1,000 "shots" of heroin on his person.

WELFARE ISLAND'S DRUG SOURCE FOUND

Woman, Arrested in Raid on Manhattan Avenue House, Held in $1,000 Bail.

DECEMBER 13, 1929

In the arrest of Mrs. Mary Pyne, twenty-three, of No. 169 Manhattan avenue early yesterday, Narcotic Squad detectives said they had found the source of supply of narcotics smuggled to drug addicts on Welfare Island. Mrs. Pyne was held in $1,000 bail for examination for possessing heroin which the detectives said they found in her home.

Seven Chinese, arrested in the raid on the Hip Sing Tong headquarters at No. 15 Pell street when a miniature arsenl was discovered, were held for examination yesterday for possessing narcotics and violating the Sullivan laaw. Six other Chinese were held for Special Sessions for possessing opium.

Welfare Island Raid Bares Dope Ring, Graft and Vice; Warden Shorn of Power

JANUARY 25, 1934

EXPERT FOUND JAIL IN CONTROL OF GANGSTERS

Harry M. Shulman, who completed a two-year clinical survey of conditions at Welfare Island on Jan. 1, declared last night he had made oral reports regarding dope sfuggling, food stealing and other rackets at the prison to Deputy Commissioner of Corrections Joseph F. Fishman, and he knew, he said, that Fishman had passed on the information to his superiors.

Shulman, a graduate of the University of Chicago, was a research worker for five years for the New York State Crime Commission, and served as research director most of that time. He also assisted Prof. Raymond Moley in research connected with the Seabury investigation.

QUIZZED PRISONERS.

On January 1, 1932, he said in an interview, he was asked to conduct the Welfare Island survey for the New York Foundation, which furnished the necessary funds, at the instance of Fishman. The work, he explained, consisted mostly of interviewing prisoners and observing prison conditions six days a week, and he was constantly on the job until Fishman was removed by the Fusion administration. Shulman's story follows:

"I found that the Welfare Island prison was practically controlled by a gang of prisoners, and also by certain Tammany district leaders, the chief of whom was Jimmy Hines. The administrative control of the prison was not in the hands of Department of Correction at all, but was vested in the district leaders, who were in constant telephonic communication with Warden Joseph A. McCann and certain prisoners.

"WARDEN WOULD JUMP."

"Whenever Warden McCann received a telephone call from a district leader he would hasten to a private booth and when told Hines wanted him he would jump as if shot and literally run to the telephone.

Phone calls from district leaders always came in through a booth and never through the prison switchboard. In the case of prisoners, however, district leaders and others used the switchboard because they could get connections easier that way. Special telephones were installed in a great many cells and in the hospital ward, so that prisoners could talk directly to people anywhere outside.

RECALLS STABBING.

"Also, as the result of my talks with prison officials and prisoners, I am convinced that a reinvestigation of the stabbing on Oct. 22, 1933, of George Holshoe, a convict, would result in jail sentences for many persons now at liberty. Holshoe, you will recall, was stabbed to death in the warden's office, but the warden later said he knew practically nothing about it.

"I spoke to the warden a time or two about this stabbing and he told me it was a case of 'one man's life against perhaps a dozen others.' The warden remarked:

"This fellow got too big for the place."

"Joe Rao, former Harlem policy king and Dutch Schultz gangster, apparently was leader of the gang which actually ran the prison. He was treated like a distinguished visitor. At one time, as a matter of fact, I saw the warden spend half an hour on a busy day getting lemons so that Rao could have some lemonade.

"Rao directed all the rackets in the prison, including the drug, food, clothing and privilege rackets. He ruled wherever there was a chance for graft. Money was taken from prisoners' clothes as they arrived at the prison; the clothes were apportioned out; drugs were stolen from the doctor and taken from visitors; all the choice foods were stolen and sold to prisoners.

Bottles Hurled at Commissioner as He Seizes Inmates' Luxuries

DEPUTY ARRESTED

Pigeons Bring in Dope; Hospital Full of Faking Patients

(Photos on Page 6 and Picture Page)

Incredibly horrifying disclosures of conditions in Welfare Island prison—dominated by knife-wielding terrorists and gangsters lolling in luxury, a host of dope addicts served regularly by 300 carrier-pigeon smugglers—were disclosed to Corrections Commissioner MacCormick when he raided the place yesterday. He stripped Warden McCann of authority and jailed Deputy Warden Daniel F. Sheehan.

The 1,658 men crowded into cells howled, jeered, hissed and turned the place into a bedlam, hurling missiles that narrowly missed injuring Commissioner MacCormick when he and his aides made a "surprise" raid on the prison at 8:30 a. m. yesterday. At one moment the barrage of milk bottles and other things thrown at the Commissioner and his aides was so formidable that he could not force his way through a prison corridor.

HIGHLIGHTS OF RAID.

Highlights of the sensational raid of the prison are:

1—The Commissioner's charge that four convicts, Joie Rao, former associate of Dutch Schultz in the Harlem policy racket, Bosco Mazzio, Eddie Cleary and Peter Kenny, ruled the prison, granting lavish favors to some prisoners and decreeing punishments and hardships for others.

2—The discovery of two dove cotes of homing pigeons, one containing 100 and the other 200 pigeons. The allegation was made that capsules of narcotics were attached to the legs of these pigeons and that they flew regularly to and from the island with supplies from a notorious dope dealer. Quantities of heroin and other narcotics were found secreted in the prison.

3—The prison hospitals allegedly were operated as a "racket," sick prisoners being kept in their cells while sham patients, for a fee, were allowed to live in the hospital quarters in luxury. Eighty-two fake patients were removed from the hospital and returned to their cells after doctors examined all inmates. One patient, ill in prison for two years with sleeping sickness, was ordered removed.

WEAPONS FOUND.

4—Discovery of dozens of knives, with blades ranging from four to eight inches, so that many prisoners at all times were ready to lead a bloody break from the prison.

5—Charges that motor boat smugglers plied a regular trade to and from the prison, bringing luxuries to those prisoners able to pay for them.

6—Further allegations that many men were thinly clad, that blankets were scarce and

MAYOR ELATED OVER JAIL RAID

Mayor La Guardia appeared delighted yesterday when informed of the action of his appointee, Corrections Commissioner MacCormick, in making a surprise raid on Welfare Island.

MacCormick has been in office but 15 days. The Mayor indicated that the Welfare Island coup was just a sample of what may be expected in the way of "surprise" attacks on unsatisfactory conditions in other departments of the city government.

The Mayor said:

"This is typical of the conditions we inherited from the previous administration. It is typical of what we intend doing in every department. Yesterday it was markets, today it is corrections. Tomorrow"——

The Mayor paused a moment, then continued:

"The raid I'm interested in right now is the raid on the city Treasury that's been going on for years!"

Spain Court Urged To Free Americans

Federal and State authorities pledged their support yesterday to Commissioner of Corrections MacCormick in his drive to rid the Welfare Island penitentiary of gang domination and traffic in narcotics.

Following a conference with Frank L. Igoe, supervising Federal narcotic agent, U. S. Attorney Conboy declared the Government would investigate the dope traffic and added:

"Deputy Corrections Commissioner Marcus was, until recently, an assistant U. S. attorney. We will offer any assistance that may properly be rendered to him and he knows he is free to call on us."

DODGE DISPLEASED.

Openly displeased because Wednesday morning's surprise raid on the prison was carried out without Commissioner MacCormick conferring with him, District Attorney Dodge, nevertheless, declared he will make a drastic investigation.

Dodge said he will seek to learn if any officials were criminally negligent in the management of the prison. If they were, he said, swift prosecution will follow. Dodge added:

"I shall push my investigation to the limit and I don't care who it hits."

LEFT IN THE DARK.

But up to now, Dodge said, he has had no official information regarding the raid. He declared:

"The only information we have received has been through the newspapers. If crime is to be cleared up, the authorities should co-operate with me."

While the investigations were getting under way, Commissioner MacCormick continued his search of the prison's many wings for more narcotics and contraband. Meanwhile, Warden McCann—shorn of power, but still at the island—staunchly defended Joie Rao and Edward Cleary, gangster bosses of the prisoners.

Prosecutor Peeved Because Raid Was Secret.

Continued from First Page.

order than a deputy warden. He was affable, tractable and sensible. Whenever trouble seemed imminent among prisoners, I summoned Rao and everything was soon smoothed out."

Cleary, former Sing Sing felon, was valuable, too, said the warden. But Cleary was "yellow," he added, although useful in preventing the "Italian mob" and the "Irish mob" of prison inmates from clashing in warfare on the island.

GANGS SEGREGATED.

The gangs of both these leaders were segregated yesterday in cells in the west wing.

Deputy Commissioner Marcus began his own inquiry yesterday. He scorned Rao and Cleary, confining his questioning to prisoners from whom he expected to get, as he expressed it, "all the information I will want."

As he went from tier to tier in

JOIE RAO. BOSCO MAZZIO. EDDIE CLEARY.

PUNISHED WITH LUXURIES—Here are three favored prisoners of Welfare Island, who enjoyed all the comforts their money could buy while they were supposed to be atoning for crimes against society.

CLEANING UP WELFARE ISLAND PRISON

A PRISON AGAIN—A scene in Welfare Island penitentiary yesterday showing prisoners herded behind the bars of a large cell while Commissioner of Corrections Austin MacCormick continues his probe of the appalling conditions uncovered by his raid of the day before. Picture from International News Photograph Service.

e cell blocks, questioning here, arching there, Marcus was eased to hear the prisoners eer him. They were cheering ecause domination by a favored w had been broken.

AD 14 "CAPTAINS."

Marcus learned, for instance, at fourteen "captains" worked ıder Rao and Cleary. These aptains" cleared the smuggled ırcotics to the actual salesmen, no operated in the cell house. ne next job, he said, is to learn ow these "captains" got the nar- tics from the outside.

There are 105 keepers at the ison. Marcus said:

"Most of the keepers were ıonest, but powerless to break ıp something they knew was ad business."

OOD FOOD FOR ALL.

MacCormick's chief concern yes- rday was in establishing a sem- ance of peace among the 1,600- id prisoners. His ifrst move was insure plenty of good, hot food all prisoners. The Wednesday id disclosed that 200 influential ıngsters ate of the best while the hers had cold food, improperly epared and of insufficient quan- ty.

There was little food for the 400 prisoners, MacCormick ex- ained, because dope addicts raid- the prison kitchen and traded eaks and other foodstuffs to Rao ıd Cleary for narcotics.

MacCormick obtained the serv- es of William Monroe, civilian ok at the U. S. House of Deten- on, to manage the Welfare Island tchen. He arranged to install eam tables and abandoned the d system of feeding prisoners.

AFETERIA SYSTEM.

Instead of prisoners marching to a mess hall where their food ad become chilled in tin plates long, plank tables, the prison- s, hereafter, will help themselves piping hot victuals, cafeteria yle.

One group of prisoners, in whose outh wing cells were found wom- n's wearing apparel, is to be egregated to the hospital ward here Rao lived a life of ease. hey will have their meals out- de the regular mess hall, Mac- ormick ruled.

To ease the situation further, IacCormick removed the ban gainst visitors yesterday. But he old the visitors:

"Make no attempts to pass anything to the prisoners. If ou do, you'll never be permitted here again."

Then he thundered:

"Do I make myself clear?"

The 50-odd visitors, men and omen, shouted in chorus:

"Yes."

And the visiting was on.

While MacCormick was continu- g the searches, taking out time place fourteen more of Rao's enchmen in solitary confine- ment, Dr. Louis Berg, visting physician to the island, was re- vealing that the dope and graft conditions had prevailed there for some time.

He declared that among the coddled prisoners was the late Maurice Connolly, former Queens Borough President. Connolly, im- prisoned as a result of the Queens sewer scandal, lived in luxury in the hospital. He was there as a patient with heart disease. Dr. Berg said:

"He didn't have any more heart disease than I have."

And even while a prisoner, Con- nolly personally checked the De- partment of Hospitals budget to find "soft spots" for his friends, Dr. Berg said. He added that Con- nolly did not blush when he ad- mitted what he was doing.

KNOWN 3 YEARS AGO.

As far back as three years ago, Dr. Berg said, conditions at the island prison were disclosed in a book he wrote. He said the situ- ation was called to the attention of the then Commissioner of Cor- rections Patterson. Dr. Berg said Patterson denied the charges "in toto," without an inquiry. He added:

"All Commissioner Patterson was interested in was giving lectures."

Dr. Berg said he found diseased prisoners mingling among insane prisoners. These groups are now segregated. One insane prisoner is likely to be sent to an insane asylum on Dr. Berg's recommen- dation.

Dr. Berg said there are insuffi- cient physicians handling the large and swiftly changing prison population at the island. He pointed out that there are only three prison physicians, and him- self as a visiting physician, to do the work.

Reports that one of the men in the west wing attempted to hang himself, because he was deprived of dope, were discounted by Deputy Commissioner Marcus, who said the man "pretended suicide." He was found with a shirt knotted around his neck. There were no marks on his throat, Marcus said, indicating the knot had not been pulled tight.

MacCormick, tired after a night spent on the island and a second day of search and investigation, left last evening for his home. He gave out this statement.

JANUARY 26, 1934

U. S. Joins War on Dope Ring in Welfare Island Prison; Dodge Promises Investigation 'No Matter Who It Hits'

U. S. Joins Dope Ring War In Welfare Island Prison; Dodge Ready to Prosecute

'I Don't Care Who Is Hit by Probe,' Says District Attorney

CLEANUP GOES ON

Conditions Long Known but Ignored, Charges Prison Doctor

JANUARY 27, 1934

49 Isolated to Avert Riot On Welfare Isle; Kelly Club Raided in Market Probe

Addicts Become Violent as Dope Is Cut Off; Refuse to Work

FENCES ERECTED

Dodge, Demanding Evidence, Protests to MacCormick

Correction Commissioner MacCormick prepared yester- day to combat a rebellion among Welfare Island convicts, whose dope, graft and special privileges have been cut off. Engineers were ordered to erect wire fences in front of the ad- ministration building.

Last night, 49 of the toughest prisoners, including Joie Rao and Edward Cleary, were transferred in groups of ten, under heavy guard, from the prison's West wing to the isolated South wing. Commissioner MacCormick per- sonally supervised the transfer and explained:

"It was a precautionary meas- ure. If they try a rescue raid now, they'll find the going pretty tough."

Continuing the segregation of the 1,600 convicts into small groups, MacCormick isolated in- sane and dope addict prisoners in the hospital. Describing the ten- sion on the island as "terrific," the Commissioner said the crisis will come today or tomorrow— but that he is prepared.

WEEK-END DANGEROUS.

He emphasized that the week- end, when prisoners are not al- lowed to receive visitors and labor slackens generally, is tradi- tionally troublesome. Discipline usually is relaxed and the con- victs are accustomed to gather in groups.

The strict control under which the prison has passed in the last few days has tended to stimulate the usual week-end restlessness. However, MacCormick appeared confident of the outcome, saying:

"By Monday morning the crisis will be passed if the whole island does not blow to pieces."

PRISON SCANDAL LONG IGNORED, SAYS OFFICIAL

MacCormick Tells Classmates He Found Thousands of Reports When He Took Office

The deplorable conditions on Welfare Island were related in "literally thousands" of reports he found on his desk when he took office as Commissioner of Corrections, Austin H. MacCor- mick told his former classmates of Bowdoin College in their an- nual alumni dinner in the Bilt- more last night.

Wives of keepers, discharged prisoners and civic associations had sent in these reports to au- thorities, and he found them "just lying there," MacCormick said. After his raid of Wednesday, the task now is "is bring to trial those responsible," the Commissioner said.

He revealed he had made a "dead-pan" visit to the island a week ago, "pretending to see nothing." Then he carefully planned his raid with military strategy. He explained:

"The only way to do it was by surprise, otherwise they would have been tipped off. I have seen prisons in 48 States—and I never dreamed that one could be so thoroughly bad all through as Welfare Island."

INSANE RAN WILD.

"Up to the present, 13 insane prisoners have had the run of the island, wandering at will. Diseased and abnormal patients have enjoyed the same freedom. The insane will be transferred to special institutions. The others will remain in Correction hospital."

District Attorney Dodge, openly indignant at the raid, made with- out his knowledge, declared yes- terday not a scrap of legal evi- dence to prove any crime had been discovered. The prosecutor made the statement after conference with Deputy Corrections Commis- sioner David Marcus.

Dodge declared A. J. Smith, sec- retary of the grand jury, urged him to make an investigation of dope dealing in the prison. The prosecutor said Smith told him he had urged Marcus earlier to do the same thing without result.

Since Mayor La Guardia took office, the Department of Correction has been assembling evidence on conditions at the penitentiary on Welfare Island. For years the penitentiary has been dominated by two or more mobs of gangsters, with connec- tions inside and outside the in- stitution. They lived in the hospital wards, ate special foods, controlled a heavy traffic in narcotics and enforced their rule with violence, even with murder. Sick prisoners and others of the common herd lived in century-old cells.

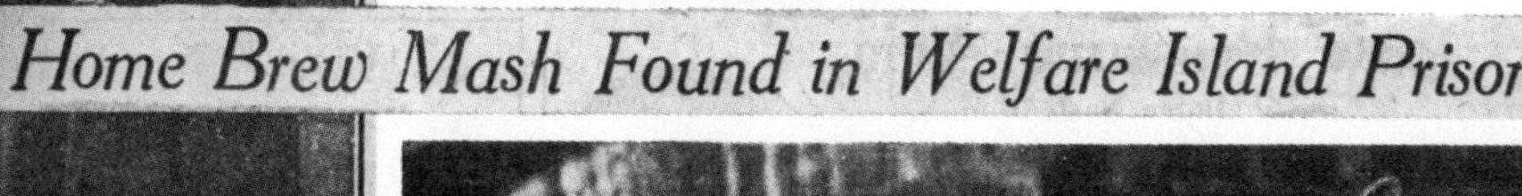

Home Brew Mash Found in Welfare Island Prison

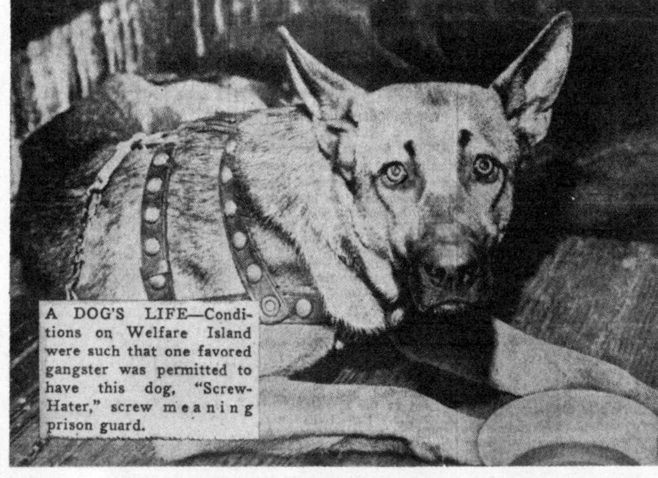

A DOG'S LIFE—Conditions on Welfare Island were such that one favored gangster was permitted to have this dog, "Screw-Hater," screw meaning prison guard.

Innocent Woman Beaten by State Narcotic Agents

FEBRUARY 7, 1935

Katherine Mitchell Sobs Out Story of Brutality by Officers

Collapse Near as She Promises to File Suit

Accosted on her way home from church by two State narcotic agents, manhandled by them and then taken to the Hall Justice where she was booked as a vagrant, Miss Katherine Mitchell, 45, 505 Twenty-ninth street, was in a state of complete collapse at her home yesterday as the result of a "slight mistake" in identity.

The story of Miss Mitchell's treatment at the hands of the narcotic agents Tuesday night was brought to light yesterday morning when she appeared in the chambers of Municipal Judge Golden, together with her brother, Lieutenant Edward Mitchell of the Fire Department, and her cousin, Police Lieutenant Michael Mitchell, to answer to the charges brought against her. Charges that were immediately dismissed.

Hysterical at the memory of what happened, Miss Mitchell is still at a loss to explain why she was singled out for the attack.

SOBS OUT STORY

"I went to St. Boniface's Church Tuesday night," she sobbed. "I was to have met a friend there, but she didn't appear, so after waiting some time, I decided to take a little walk and look in the Market street windows.

"At Market and Ellis street two men got out of a car in which there were two women.

"They came to me and seized me roughly. I could onl ythink of kidnaping. I fought as best I could.

MARCH 16, 1935

Alcohol Field Day

The alcohol raiders had a fi... day. They seized ... of liquor, more th... lons of mash and ... In Atlanta alone, ... seized.

Reports from ma... indicated the comp... of the roundup.

Cleveland gave ... counterfeiters and ... three. In San Anto... 153 arrests and 16...

Arrests in Jersey

Igoe's men also mad... in Newark, two in Un... J.; one in Schenect... Binghampton, one in ... in Troy and one in Cl...

Igoe said after the ... his men reported the ... of contraband morp... pound, indicating a ... York market.

Dope Ring Smashed

In Washington, na... smashed a dope ring ... tributing lines in Cle... Detroit. Eight alleg... salers of dope were arr... four other prisoners we... on selling charges, inclu... arrested in the shadow ... Capitol.

In numbers, the largest narcotic round-up covered Louisiana, Mississippi and Alabama, where 6... were arrested and dope value... at $20,000 was seized. ...

Roundup Begins Here

The Washington men began their roundup in Manhattan, where they arr...ed 10 men and one woman. ...hese in custody, they d... the plant, took one m... seized printing ...

Cocaine to Cruisers

Elsewhere the contraband ran through a varied list, from cocaine to cabin cruisers. It included 851 stills, capable of pouring out 500,000 gallons of liquor a day; automobiles, silks, tape... and opium pipes.

Amazi... ma...

...up was ...e. The came ...n of ...here

MAY 21, 1937

NARCOTIC OFFICIAL JAILED

Gi... Decoy Helps t... Smash Nevada Combine

Probability of wholesa... narcotic raids and arres... loomed here today followin... a crippling blow struck at a... alleged nationwide ring o... erating in Reno.

District Supervisor Joseph ... Manning of the federal narcot... bureau here, left for Reno aft... conferring with special office... from Washington, D. C.

Search for the source of suppl... turned to San Francisco after a... attractive girl detective and fed... eral agents smashed what wa... believed to be the head of th... group with the arrest of Ch... Ha..., 57, chief federal narcot... ics agent in Reno, and eigh... others.

LINKED TO S. F.

Manning was reported in pos... session of new leads that link th... source of supply with a San Fran... cisco section of the ring.

State narcotic agents here sai... Reno was a central point of dis... tribution for narcotics brought i... from the east and from man... west coast cities, including Sa... Francisco.

Smashing of the Reno grou... followed the investigations ... Joyce McAllister, Santa Barbar... girl, working with the San Fran... cisco federal narcotic bureau an... Hunter Nugent, supervisor for th... Treasury Department, narcoti... division.

NARCOTICS CHARGES

T... eight arrested in Ren... with Hansen were formal... charged with violating the na... cotics laws today and thousan... of dollars worth of dope seized ... a series of raids, was tagged f... evidence.

Hansen, the narcotic agent ... the Nevada district, is charge... with conspiring with A. V. Mc... Avoy, Woo Sing, wealthy Ch... nese, and six other Chinese.

The raids came after Miss Mc... Allister is reported to have pu... chased narcotics outside Wo... Sing's Public Club on Lake stree...

The girl gave a pre-arrange... signal which sent waiting off... cers swarming into the club.

$1000 IN PURCHASES

Before the raids nearly $10... worth of narcotics had been pu... chased by agents and operativ...

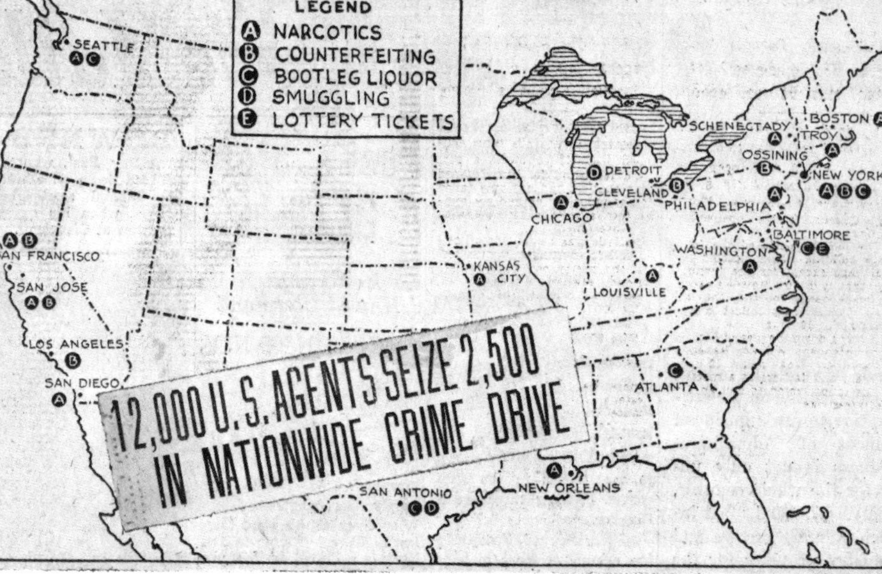

Jail Employe Linked To $500,000 Dope Ring

PROFIT IN PRISON

WELFARE ISLAND

JUNE 27, 1935

An employe of the City Workhouse on Welfare Island is being sought as the key man of a ring that smuggles $500,000 worth of narcotics into the prison annually, Warden Schleth revealed yesterday.

Schleth made this statement after John Wallace, 32, was convicted in Special Sessions of possessing narcotics while in the workhouse. Wallace, already an inmate of the prison on a conviction for using narcotics, will be sentenced on the new conviction

CHICAGO HUNTS BUSINESS MEN IN DOPE RINGS

Evidence Links Traffic ... Several in High Positio... Twelve Reported Indic...

CHICAGO, Dec. 11 (US... Twelve men were reported ... dicted here today by the ... eral Grand Jury after ... named as among the leade... the million-dollar-a-year ... traffic.

Evidence that the illeg... cotic traffic is headed ... group of men holding h... sitions in the business w... been uncovered. Miss Mar... assistant Federal distri... ney, announced, sayin... major syndicates furn... three business men.

Called "Straw Boss...

Three of those indic... Bennie Bean, Jack D... Jack Roamer, were ... Federal attorneys to b... boss leaders of the thre... operating here in the ... phine, heroin, cocaine ...

WASHINGTON, D... The catch in the Federa... against narcotics was reported by ... the Treasury today at "well over ... 800 persons."

Officials, confident of nearly 100 per cent convictions, asserted police courts were supporting the ... effort ...

NARCOTIC SMUGGLERS GET 94 YEARS

DECEMBER 19, 1936

INTERNATIONAL RING DEALT SEVERE BLOW

Narcotics smuggling was dealt a vital blow yesterday when Federal Judge Hulbert imposed sentences totaling 94 years and $66,500 in fines upon seven alleged members of the Morris Schatz international gang of opium runners.

Government agents admitted, however, that they believed the real ringleaders of the group had escaped, and the Court told the prisoners that he would reconsid... er the heavy penalti... upon them if ... the "real ma... illicit traffic."

Asst. U. S. A... charge of the ... Judge Hulbert ... smuggled into ... than 215 pounds ... pounds of heroin ... York, Manhattan ... and Normandie, ... the murder of a s... burg who gave in... Government conc... tivities.

Gang All Aliens

200 AT UTICA FLEE GUNFIRE OF U. S. AGENTS

NOVEMBER 4, 1930

Sleuths, Posing as Ohio Racketeers, Gain Gang Secrets, $17,500 Dope Also Taken

Government agents, posing as Ohio racketeers, were the key men in a State wide drive against a narcotic ring that yesterday had netted twenty-two persons, two of them women. In addition drugs valued at $17,500 were seized.

The drug warfare, carried out ... was unusual, it ... that all the ... were ... ather ... prac... ngth... ces of

Mayor LaGuardia's law enforcement chiefs girded themselves yesterday to "crack down" on the higher-ups controlling an organized vice, crime and narcotic ring in the city.

That the powerf... ated by racketee... cians, is maintain... alized vice which ... ant today ...

MURDER IS CAUSED BY DOPE

...S LONG TERM

1937

...ille—gay, spangled, ex...

...edle—moments of artificiality, stretches of morbid ...n.

...no dope. Twenty years ...uff until it was as neces... air or water. Horrible ... Desperation. Murder. ... Glaser, 59, was sentenced ... by Judge Freschi to ... to 20 years in Sing Sing ... g his common-law wife, ..., another dope fiend. His ...ning so brightly, came to ... hopeless end.

...rove both out of vaude... they managed to keep ...ser's last job was watch... apartment house door. ...d at 88 Amsterdam ave. ...ovember they could get ... heroin. For five days ... woman ...

... brain. ...ppened ...

He shot his woman—killed her. Then he fired a bullet into his ...

OLD AGE AIDE LINKED TO DOPE

TOWNSENDITE IS ALSO ALLEGED BOOTLEGGER

PROMOTER'S 'PAST' PROBED

MAY 24, 1936

WASHINGTON, June 2 (US).—A plot to control the Townsend organization was charged today to E. J. Margett, missing California director for old age pensions, who was described as a former "whisky runner."

House committee investigators produced a score of affidavits linking the Townsend organizer with California and Washington narcotic and liquor rings in the days befo... he promoted pensions.

SAID TO BE IN HIDING

CRIME RISE Linked with Use OF DOPE

America's army of narcotic addicts "furnishes one of the major social problems of the day," Rep. Hamilton Fish declared in a radio address yesterday.

There is a close relation between the increase in certain crimes and the increasing traffic in dope, Mr. Fish said, adding:

"It has been estimated that 80 per cent of addicts become criminals and that about 32 per cent of the ... in Federal ...

Addict, 23 Narcotic

JANUARY 22, 1937

'Shot' He Gave CCC Boy Nearly Fatal; Aunt Involved

Twitching and fretting in his cell in the Hudson County Jail in Jersey City is Raymon... ...

Recent Arrest of Club Owner Bared as Federal Aide Prepares to Press Drug Charges

Three financiers of a city drug smuggling ring are expected to be indicted today as result of testimony given to a grand jury by Jacob Bloom, arrested as he stepped from the liner Ile de France with drugs valued at $300,000 in his suitcase.

As this became known yesterday ti also was diclosed Federal agents have secretly arrested a Broadway night club man re... the ... on... ar... six

Six Chinese Arrested On Opium Charges

Six Chinese found smoking opium in an apartment at 7 Mul...

State - Wide Dope Ring Raid

"Oh, the menace can ... all that."

APRIL 3, 1929

Narcotics Agent Threatened With Death After Coast Ring

A HARD BLOW
At the Dope Traffic

-DECEMBER 10, 1934

From all over America Saturday and yesterday came news of smashing blows against narcotic sellers. Below are scenes from other sections of the nation as more than 750 prisoners were rounded up by Federal agents in one huge drive. The campaign was directed from Washington by Louis Ruppel, Assistant Narcotics Commissioner, and Harry J. Anslinger, head of the Federal Narcotics Bureau, also shown below as they received reports of the countrywide raids. A panic-stricken woman broke her leg when she jumped from a hotel raided in Baltimore. Pictures by International News Photograph Service.

BALTIMORE CASUALTY

MARCH 2, 195

SEIZED IN DETROIT RAIDS

CHINESE PRISONERS AT CHICAGO

ANSLINGER   LOUIS RUPPEL

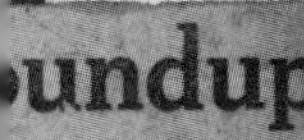

undup

REPUTED 'BOSS' OF DOPE SALE IN HARLEM SEIZED

His Peddlers Betray 'The Gigolo,' Only 21, to Federal Men; Guns, Narcotics in His Home

A dapper youth of 21, known as "The Gigolo" and long sought as the "Little Boss" of the dope racket in Harlem, was seized by Federal agents yesterday after three of his Negro sidewalk salesmen had betrayed him.

He identified himself as Nicholas Farlono, of 25-15 Welbera ave., Long Island City. In his apartment at 203 E. 97th st., Manhattan, the agents reported finding $300 in heroin, two fully loaded .38 calibre revolvers with ... "dum dum" bullets, and

Woman in Trunk Traced To Harlem Narcotics Party

2 RACING MEN JAILED BY U. S. IN DOPE PROBE

1937

Both Indicted Here, Captured In Southwest; Complaints Relate to Dealing in Drugs

Two indictments and warrants issued in Federal Court yesterday caused the arrest of Raymond Pollard, a horse owner, and J. J. Nelson, a starter, on conspiracy charges, out of town.

Drugging of horses is not mentioned in the indictments but the Grand Jury has been investigating evidence of widespread operations ... tracks throughout ...

Big Drug Shipments

The grand jury has been probing the source, destination and purpose of large consignments of heroin sent to racing communities from this city. Pollard was arrested in San Antonio, Texas, and Nelson at Little Rock, Ark. He was said to be carrying drugs. The pair will be brought here for trial.

Stutzman declared the investigation of Corrigan and the horsemen has been in progress for eight months. Assistant Federal Attorneys J. F. Dailey and J. P. Martin presented the evidence that brought the indictments.

Girl, 18, Causes Sister's Arrest As Dope User

Sickened by Fumes in Apartment, She Calls for Police Raid

DECEMBER 22, 1935

Sickened by opium fumes in the apartment where she was living, an 18-year-old girl made her way to Central Police Station and caused her older sister to be arrested in a narcotic raid.

Rena Philips, 18, here from her home at Clinton, Iowa, just two weeks, sobbed out a pitiful story of how her married sister, Mrs. Helen Parker, was using the drug, Lieutenant Alexander McDaniels told Municipal Judge Lazarus at a court hearing later.

THROWN FROM WINDOW

The lieutenant raided the apartment, at 520 Taylor street, and while attempting to unlock the dor he saw Mrs. Parker "throw something from the window," he declared.

In an alley way under the window the officer found an opium pipe and a lamp. Mrs. Parker was charged with violation of the narcotic laws and vagrancy and held on $250 bail as the court continued her case until December 27. She has a record.

Rena was booked as a vagrant at the Juvenile Detention Home to insure her being held as a material witness. Before leaving Iowa another sister warned her "to tell police" if Mrs. Parker was using dope, Lieutenant McDaniels revealed.

When she first arrived at her sister's apartment she found her smoking the narcotic with her husband and a Chinese, Rena asserted.

Narcotics Squad Raids 'Dope Den,' Nabs 7

Big-Time Peddler, 5 Women Arrested In Northwest Hotel

FEBRUARY 7, 1950

More Pictures on Page 10

The police narcotics squad cleaned out a "dope den" in a northwest Portland hotel early Wednesday, jailing a big-time Chinese peddler and six suspected helpers.

The early morning raid came after a three-week round-the-clock watch of the Alexandra Court hotel at 125 N. W. 20th place. Capt. Howard Ru... vice squad chief, "boast... raid would put a ... crimp" in local dope ...

Biggest prize in the ... Eddie Lee, 42-year-ol... ex-convict, who was ... his room with 23 b... heroin still clutched in...

The raiders describe... the "dealer," with a pa... year term for narcotic... Neil island federal pen... and a known "procurer ... titutes."

As one officer grabbed ... arm, he is said to have p...

"Take me on a state ...

A second federal ... for narcotics would ... mandatory 5-to-10-yea... term.

Lee Admitted User

Lee was also a "use..." Captain Russell said, admitting to the habit of "sniffing" eight grains a day with a fifth of whisky on top of it. Whisky and dope are a rare combination. The two don't ordinarily mix, the vice chief said.

Also arrested was a 28-year-old Vancouver night club drummer, Wayne (Buzz) Bridgford, and five women all of them with police records for dope or prostitution.

Four of the women were caught fleeing the hotel when the alarm of "a raid" broke the early morning stillness. The narcotics squad moved in at 3:35 a. m. with a search warrant. All seven were booked into jail by 7 a. m.

Narcotics Raid Nets Girls

Pair Seized Here On Dope Charge

EDDIE LEE
Caught with heroin in hand

WAYNE BRIDGFORD
Vancouver drummer arrested

Officers Grab Dope Agents

U. N. Staff Works With Peru, U. S.

AUGUST 21, 1949

NEW YORK, Aug. 20 (AP)—A vast illicit drug ring—so powerful it sparked an abortive revolution in Peru and involved United Nations action—was exposed Saturday following the arrest of the alleged ringleader.

Authorities called the arrest the first high point in an international crackdown on a huge smuggling syndicate which has plied a $500,000-a-month cocaine trade between the United States and Peru.

American, Peruvian and U. N. authorities joined in a two-year drive to smash the ring, said to have used narcotics

Oct. 15, 1946

State Narcotic Agent in Northern Cal. Area Dismissed

Marshall Burnett, northern California narcotics enforcement supervisor, has been fired on charges of "incompetency, inefficiency, discourteous treatment of the public and other (state) employes, and other acts incompatible with and inimical to the public service."

Charges, on file today with the State Personnel Board, were contained in a letter from F. J. O'Fer... tried to set up a "caste" system among his subordinates.

CHARGES SERVED

Burnett, who lives at 310 Gonsalez street here, was served yesterday with a copy of the charges, including a report by Inspector George Maloney that Burnett said he "has suffered so under the caste and disciplinary system of the Coast Guard" that he intended to run his office in similar ... Guardsman, having served as a chief petty officer in the intelligence division, and left the service to resume his state duties last year.

He was not immediately available to answer O'Ferrall's accusations, based on alleged complaints from fifteen inspectors in the state narcotics office here.

'CONSTANT THREATS'

Charges against Burnett complained that he tried to run his ... uous threats of poor performance reports, suspensions, demotions and dismissal."

This policy, the accusations went on, adversely affected morale among employes working under the accused officer.

Burnett was acc...f havin... "stated on a number of occasion... that he could not mix sociall... with the inspectors because h... was above the 'common herd' and that they were only 'an...

-GREEN
GRASS SEED
VOGUE
CIGARETTE PAPERS
FINEST QUALITY
100 LEAVES
eaucoup
IG-ZAG
SALOME
IDEAL
CIGARETTES
GOLD
DEVUELVASE AL APARTADO 697
RETURN TO P.O. BOX 697
MONTERREY, MEXICO.

Marijuana

You say you swam to China,
Want to sell me South Carolina,
I believe you know the Reefer Man.
—*"Reefer Man," 1931*

Use of hashish was fairly common among nineteenth-century adventurers and intellectuals. Newspapers treated it anthropologically—the 1895 "Orgies of the Hemp Eaters" is typical—or pseudo-scientifically, as in the "Hasheesh Antics" article two years later. Interest in marijuana medicine led the government as early as 1904 to plant the weed along the Potomac (in the area now occupied by the Pentagon) for possible commercial production—an idea quickly scuttled during the Pure Food and Drug furor of 1906, when even cigarette makers had to deny that their products were "doped."

Advertising of cigarettes sparked youthful smoking during the 1910s and 1920s, despite the outraged roars of parents and clergy who tried to get tobacco banned from public places. This, in turn, set the stage for youthful experimentation with marijuana. It appeared about this same time among Mexican farmworkers in the Southwest and blacks in New Orleans. Marijuana's easy availability in cigarette form was one of its most threatening aspects.

Though marijuana had some new features, notably its association with the hoary "Assassins" legend that Anslinger adopted as a central theme, the process of making it illegal was so familiar as to be almost a reflex. Long before Anslinger, newspapers simply plugged marijuana into already-existing crusade themes like Kiddie Dope and incitement to violent crime. For instance, compare Winifred Black's 1928 article, "60% of All Violent Crimes Traced to Cocaine" in the *Exotic Drugs* chapter with the 1937 "U.S. Ban Sought on Marihuana" article in this chapter. Other ready-made themes included insanity, instant metamorphosis ("makes fiends of boys in 30 days"), and Jazz Age moralizing against dance music, in which jazz musicians were blamed for the spread of reefer smoking no matter who else did it.

Beneath the surface was deep-rooted racism against blacks who dared turn white kids on to dope, and against Mexicans who competed with whites for menial jobs and ran border-town sin spots. Shades of Operation Intercept! In 1925 the United States considered building a wall along the Mexican border to keep out criminals (read: "wetbacks") and "dry up these pest holes of festering vice." Fearful images of knives glinting in the darkness, wanton women luring gringos with dope: "Mexican hashish. . . the sex cigaret. . . gathers addicts with alarming swiftness."

And from Mexican hot spots, we plunge into the nightmare world of. . . the University of Kansas in 1934, where two or three hundred students were "addicted" to marijuana, "known also as peyote." So much for scientific knowledge of the drug. (Anthropologists and Indian leaders did, however, save peyote from being banned in 1937 so long as it was restricted to Native American Church members).

Movies helped create violent pot images too, with top-notch variety shows like *Murder at the Vanities* (1934)—in which Gertrude Michael is splattered with blood as she finishes singing "Sweet Marijuana"—and Z-grade exploitation flicks like *Tell Your Children,* later called *Doped Youth* and recently revived as *Reefer Madness.*

As with the Harrison Act in 1914, it was thought to be unconstitutional to prohibit essentially intrastate activity like drug use directly, so the Marijuana Tax Act of 1937 was ostensibly a tax bill requiring producers and sellers to register and pay a fee. In fact, the act allowed backyard marijuana cultivation upon payment of $25; since nobody bothered to pay it and state laws forbade its cultivation anyway, police gleefully uprooted little dope gardens from Brooklyn to Sacramento all through the thirties.

Pot penetrated the hinterlands, as hemp was planted for fiber in the Midwest during World War II; and not a few servicemen sampled the drug in Asia, North Africa, and France at that time. When Robert Mitchum was busted in 1948 he said, "I'm ruined. . . this is the bitter end." It is a tribute to Mitchum's mature strength, as well as a sign of slowly changing times, that he didn't do a standard contrition crusade but instead wisecracked with his jailers, served his fifty days, and came back to popular acclaim in the family classic *The Red Pony.*

NEW YORK HERALD, SUNDAY, APRIL 28, 1895.

A SCENE IN ONE OF THE RECENTLY OPENED TURKISH SMOKING PARLORS.

NEW YORK'S NEW SMOKING FAD.

Picturesque Groups and Fighting Talk in the Rooms of the Men from Bagdad.

MANY DAINTY SMOKERS SEEN

A Fashionable Crush Early, and Later Young Men Who Talk Defiance.

GAMBLERS ALSO NUMEROUS.

Turks Have a King of Clubs of Their Own Now and Breathe Slaughter.

HE Turk and the infidel have fun and trouble almost nightly now in a so-called Oriental smoking room in Broadway, near Thirtieth street. They also have the police,

As a matter of fact, it is only the Turk who calls the resort an Oriental smoking room. The "sporty" infidel, of both sexes, refers to the place as "that new pipe joint." The police are called frequently to the place when midnight is past, and the infidel bids the Turk defiance, calls him names, shocks some of the women present by using bad language, and evinces a ...sire to fight his way into the street without ...ing for his coffee and his narghileh.

...eral dark skinned men, who say they are ... hailing from Bagdad, but who are some... ...enians, have given New York a ne... ...ipation, and New York has tak... ...kindly.

In ... "hitting" the narghileh, or hubble-bubble, has become a fad, and from early afternoon until two o'clock in the morning—even if it be Sunday morning—one may find the Turks' ...pholstered chairs and lounges crowded ... and women, whose dress ranges from correct to "flashy," and whose conversation is sometimes polite and conventional and sometimes both loud and offensive.

The men from Bagdad do not sell liquor, and their Turkish tobacco, smoked in pipes of extraordinary length, is no more intoxicating than their black coffee and Persian tea. It is their boast that persons with jags or jimmies visible to the naked eye cannot enter. They talk peace, they and their turbaned servants, until some one else talks fight. They hang upon their walls a notice warning all that they must be orderly and decorous in conduct and speech.

JAGS IN DISGUISE.

They are men of grave demeanor, these men from Bagdad. They ask nothing from the infidel but civility and money. And yet—well, there are places nearby where men and women may drink and welcome, and these men and women have lately fallen into the habit of "topping off in the Turks'" with a smoke and some coffee, and the results have not always been happy. There have been calls for big policemen from the Broadway squad not infrequently, and the men from Bagdad, unmindful of the wealth of curved weapons on their walls, now hire and arm a burly guardian of their own. He carries a big club and makes it his business to discourage or accommodate those persons who decline to pay and say they want to fight. Of late this private policeman has been very busy "calling bluffs," for it is a mixed and strange company that he has to control, and if he were not good natured he would have committed murder long ago.

I watched the men from Bagdad one Saturday night from an hour when the place was empty until the crowd had come and gone, from the first narghileh until the fight at the finish. It was not uninteresting.

First, the rooms themselves. A man and a maid in the Broadway window are busy rolling Turkish cigarettes before a curious throng outside. Behind them is a cigar case and small room, the walls of which are hung with Turkish and Persian weapons, daggers, curved swords in beaded sheaths, hanging lamps of queer workmanship, tables inlaid with pearl, water pipes with great bowls and rubber tubes for stems, and long pipes of cane.

UNDER THE SMOKE CLOUD.

Here one may sit down and smoke a cigar, but there is little novelty in that, so it is that the chairs are usually empty. Through a curtained door one enters a small room with a high and oddly upholstered ceiling, like an inverted lounge, a ceiling usually dimly visible through a cloud of blue and pungent smoke. The walls are the same—hung with weapons and curios from the East. Around the room are lounges and many chairs, all of unique workmanship and yielding luxuriousness. From a room still further back come the clatter of dishes and the sound of strange tongues. There the Turks are awaiting the crush. It is early. Their patrons are at dinner or the theatre.

A single attendant in Turkish trousers, short beaded jacket and fez confronts you and points ...ently to a sign on the wall, thus asking you ... choose between a narghileh, which is a big water pipe; a chibouk, which has a small bowl and a great stem of cane, and cigars, cigarettes, black coffee and Persian tea. Smoking is optional, but it is expected that you will drink either tea or coffee. The men from Bagdad must live.

Look into the smoke befogged room at midnight and note the change. The bouncer is at the door. The lounges and chairs are filled with men and women. Water bubbles everywhere. Dainty fingers hold pipe stems and cigarettes. Every one seems to be ogling and blowing smoke at every one else. There are women in theatre gowns who have thrown aside their cloaks, and men in evening dress, all smoking and drinking. It is already late, and the quieter patrons, whom simple curiosity drew, are going, giving place to the element often termed "sporty."

THREE QUEER CLASSES.

The crowd at midnight may be divided into three classes. There is an objectionable class made up of young fellows who are just learning to get drunk, "scrappy" youths, whose aim seems to be to swagger and use fighting talk without cause—and without fighting. They stare, and women with well behaved escorts pretend not to hear what they are saying. They will make trouble later on. It is the general opinion that they need birching.

Another class is composed of fashionably attired men and women who are anxious to see and be seen, to try this new thing from the Orient, to visit a lounging room where men and women are equal and rosy cheeked girls smoke anything from a dainty cigarette to a huge narghileh without exciting comment.

The third class is not easily fixed. It includes men of weary manner, who scrutinize the smokers and go away; gamblers, men on whose hands time hangs heavily, men who are looking for something exciting, men who have little money to spend and much to get, who would prefer a drug more powerful than the Turkish tobacco, which is the strongest served to casual patrons.

I visited the Turks with a man who has seen the old Tenderloin and the new, and who knows both.

"Any familiar faces?" I asked.

"Few," he said. "few of the Tenderloiners proper. The women are of another class. It's pretty quiet here till closing hour. And— Ah! the girl over the way doesn't like that divan."

She was tall and pretty, and she ... mouthpiece of a water pip... pouted:—

"Say, Grace"—to her com... sit on the floor. This cushi...

"Smoke up," says Grace.

"Abdul," cries the man w... "get some fire here and s... German?"

"No," says he in the odd cl...

The fire was brought, and ... men with money talked about ... esting with much laughter, su... wise.

There were about twenty you... room at this hour, all smoking ... enjoyment. The hour was late ... not novices. The younger fell... not sitting with women, were ... Three ordered nothing and talke...

An attendant stopped before th... at the sign over their heads, o... suggestive prices.

"Coffee?"

"No."

"Narghileh?"

"No."

"What?"

"Nothing."

"You can't sit here unless you ... thing."

"Oh, I guess so."

"I'll have you put out."

"Try it. I've spent money enoug... give me a seat when I want it. Wh... something I'll order it or"—with an o... know why."

The bouncer fondles a club in his slee... coals die in the bowls here and there ... smokers wait expectantly. The troubl... like the fire, and the young "sports" ... umphantly at the rest of the company.

"Now," says the leader, "we've bluf... Ginny. What'll you have?" Three pipe... for the time, peace.

A man in the corner, one of an after t... group, holds a woman's hand fondly, and ... far enough forward to get the benefit of a ... of smoke, which she blows in his eyes as ... buke.

"Right!" says her companion. "This isn't a scene from 'Romeo and Juliet.' It's a 'dope' joint. Smoke up, everybody!" And they smoke up.

It is one o'clock now, and the latest arrivals had apparently disguised their condition until they got inside. The biggest of them and the loudest knocked the fez from the head of the imitation Bedouin at the door, and returned it to him with a grave bow.

"Turko," he began, "your head's wobbly. Y'ought to let up on booze or the pipe, or you'll be flitting to paradise and the houris and those other things. When I talk you may gamble on it."

POLICE AT THE FINISH.

"The Bedouin chief grinned and nodded at the coffee and tobacco sign. The newcomers ordered pipes and coffee. When the checks were brought they threw them on the floor, cursed the attendants and glared defiance at the rest of the company. The attendants were patient, but the talk was growing more boisterous, and a little later one of the newcomers kicked over a little pearl inlaid coffee table. A Turk picked it up minus a leg. He picked up a check for coffee, took it away, added $1 to the price, to pay for repairs, and then presented the check for payment. Then the fighting talk began.

"I didn't order this coffee, to begin with," said one of the men, "and I didn't break your d——d old table. I'll pay for nothing. You're all feet. Get out of the way or I'll swat you."

The Turk persisted and stood still, holding out the check and the broken table.

"You broke it," he said, "and you can't get out until you pay for it."

The other ... rowded about the angry ... bandoned. There ... The men still re... ...gested that they ... is money, any- ... Turk in ques... ...only been here ... like a native. ... fighting, and ... d in a patrol... who wouldn't ... station, and ... the smoking ... they com- ... "It's the ... ...oor by this ... The Turks ... and the ... The Bed... ...one went ... arrested ... e. ... flourish, ... slaugh-

DRIVEN TO DEATH BY CIGARETTES

Crazed by Incessant Smokin... Young Smith Poured Poison Down His Own Throat.

UNCONSCIOUS WHEN FOUND

Health and Mind Shattered by the Habit Which He Was Powerless to Renounce.

HIGH SPIRITS BEFORE SUICID...

Crazed by cigarettes, Frederick C. Smith twenty-two years old, who lived on the to... floor of the flat house No. 68 West 100t... street, committed suicide last night.

He lived with his father, Arnold Smith; hi... mother, two brothers and three sisters. Hi... father, who is an upholsterer, had taugh... Frederick the trade and expected to star... him in business for himself next spring.

Before he began to smoke cigarettes, tw... years ago, he was robust and had red cheek... and bright eyes. The habit grew upon hi... until he smoked incessantly, and his eyes be... came dull, his cheeks pallid, his form wasted... Acute nervousness and insomnia followe... and the youth's health was shattered.

His parents realized the harm cigarette... were working upon the boy and begged hi... to abandon their use. He promised to do s... but had not the will to fulfill his promise.

COULD NOT MODERATE THE HABIT.

He abstained from smoking for one whol... day and the effect was to increase his nerv... ousness and to make him delirious. Th... family physician urged the moderate use o... tobacco, believing the habit could be broke... by degrees, but young Smith, weakened a... he was, had not the resolution to follow thi... course. Instead he smoked more than eve... and in the sleepless nights lay on his be... absorbing cigarette after cigarette until day... light came. Then he would fall into a doz... lasting only a couple of hours. This had con... tinued for several weeks.

Frederick, who had not been employed fo... some time, received word yesterday from ... former employer to report for work to-day... His father thought occupation would kee... the youth from smoking so much and lif... him from the morbid state into which h... had fallen. Young Smith also seemed please... at the prospect of returning to work.

DEATH FOLLOWED CHEERFULNESS.

He was apparently in better spirits las... evening than he had been for some time, an... laughed and joked with his family. Hi... mother congratulated him on the improve... ment in his condition.

He went out after supper, saying he woul... be back in a few minutes. He went to a dru... store in Columbus avenue and bought ... quantity of carbolic acid, with which he re... turned to the house. His mother asked hi... what he had in the bottle. He smiled an... said he had only a little medicine.

Young Smith went into the parlor an... closed the door. Alone he swallowed th... poison to the last drop.

His father heard him groan a few minute... later, and ran into the room. The boy wa... on the floor unconscious. His mouth an... throat were badly burned by the acid. Hi... father rushed to the West 100th street polic... station and had an ambulance called fro... Manhattan Hospital. Dr. Levison responde... When he reached the house the young ma... was dead.

THE CLERGY AND THE WE...

What Some of the Eminent ... Think as to the Propriety ... Clergymen Smoking.

A WIDE DIVERSITY OF OP...

Views of Dr. McCosh, Robert ... Dr. Storrs, Edward Beecher, ... Phelps, Morgan Dix, Newma... Bishop Cole, Heber Newt... Many More Eminent Pulpit Li... A Curious Collection of All ... of Opinion on What Has Long... a Subject of Random Discus...

It has always been an interesting questi... minds of many whether clergymen, from ... example, should indulge in smoking. It is a ... belief that the cigar in the mouth of the mi... an injurious example to the young. Up to t... the voice of the clergy has, save in one or t... tering opinions, not been heard. The opi... this subject of some of the most famous p... of America and Europe, as written or sp... themselves, are given below.

DR. FURNESS, AT EIGHTY-EIGHT, STILL S...

I have been a smoker from my youth up. ... not prevented me from reaching my eighty... year without any of the usual infirmities of ... save a certain stiffness in stooping to pick u... It is said that smoking leads to drinking. ... it is a mistake. It takes the place of dr... Were smoking abolished I believe there wo... ten drunkards where there is now only one. ... no faith in doing things for example's sake. ... must be done for their own sake; then only ... example good and influential.

PHILADELPHIA. WILLIAM HENRY FUR...

CIGARETTE.

Nearly Caused a Panic in a Boarding House.

Bridget Saw the New Boarder Smoking One Day.

Told Story to Occupant of Fourth Floor Back.

Gossip Magnified Lodger Into an Opium Fiend.

Landlady Investigated, But Found No Cause For Alarm.

The new boarder in the fourth floor front concluded that she would smoke a cigarette. Not that she cared at all for cigarettes. On the contrary, she disliked them. The smoke got in her eyes and made tears come, it got down her throat and strangled her, besides which the odor permeated her clothing and stayed there. She was merely smoking this cigarette to see what would happen. This was what happened:

Bridget, the chambermaid, coming into the room to make the bed, promptly discerned the pernicious odor of that little cigarette. Then, spying stealthily around she found the end of the cigarette reposing upon a corner of the mantelpiece. That was enough. She went about straightening the room in an ominous silence. When her work was done she went into the fourth floor back.

"There do be curious things a-goin' on in the next room to this, ma'am," she said to the woman who sat by the window embroidering. "Curious things! Faith, an' that's phwat I'm afther tellin' of ye."

"What in the world do you mean, Bridget?" asked the woman, sticking her needle straight into her thumb instead of into her embroidery. "What is it that's goin' on?"

Bridget mournfully shook her head. "They don't be afther behaivin' so in the ould counthry, ma'am," she said.

The woman dropped her embroidery.

"Bedad, it's the new boarder, ma'am," Bridget went on in a hoarse whisper. "It's she that's afther shmokin' a cigarbot in her room, an' that's phwat's the matter. Faith, an' ain't it enough ma'am? A laadie a-shmokin' of a cigarbot in her room!"

The woman pushed Bridget aside and sped out of the room. She made her way to the third floor front.

"Well, what is the matter?" asked the third floor front, who was busily engaged in washing out her handkerchiefs and pasting them up against the window pane to dry.

"If you only knew!"

"Tell me, then, quick. Has there been a row in the house and I not in it? If there has it's the first."

"Right you are, but it isn't a row this time. What do you suppose is happening in this very house this very minute? The new boarder is smoking cigars a foot long in her room upstairs—a foot long, those stogies. That is what you call them, isn't it? Yes. Stogies."

"What!" screamed the third floor front.

"It's the gospel truth. Bridget told me."

The handkerchiefs all fell off the window pane to the floor. The third floor front, leaving them there, ran to the woman and grasped her by the arm.

"Come," she exclaimed, "let's go and tell the third floor back. If she finds out there is anything going on in this house that she don't know about she will drop dead. We don't want a funeral."

Together they hastened to the third floor back. The occupant of the room was combing her back hair preparatory to doing it up in a psyche knot.

"What do you think is happening?" they cried with one voice.

The third floor back took her hairpins out of her mouth and looked around.

"I can't imagine," said she. "What?"

"Something awful," they declared, both talking together. "The new boarder in the fourth floor front is smoking a pipe. Think of a young girl like that smoking a pipe in a house like this. Isn't it a sin and a shame? Isn't it disgraceful?"

"Are you sure?" demanded the third floor back.

"Of course," they asserted. "Bridget told it to the fourth floor back. It's the solemn truth. We give you our word of honor."

The third floor back scattered her hairpins recklessly over her dressing table. "We'll go and tell it to the second floor front," said she. "I'd just like to know what she thinks of it. A shame and a disgrace! Well, I should think so. The girl ought to be fired out of the house this very minute. That's what she should be!"

She led the procession, her hair streaming down her back to the second floor front.

"The new boarder upstairs is smoking a pipe," they said. "Not only that, but she's got cigarettes and cigars and cheroots all over the room everywhere, on the tables and bookcases and whatnots. The mantelpiece is full of them. Even the walls are festooned with tobacco leaves brought from wherever she comes from and hung up instead of pictures."

When they had paused for breath the second floor front got in a word edgeways.

"That girl always did have a queer look to me," she said, pressing her lips together. "I spotted her the minute I laid eyes on her, the very minute she put her foot in this house. I said then: 'We'll hear from her yet.' They were my very words. 'We'll hear from her yet.' And now it has come, sooner than even I expected. I know what I am going to do."

"What?" gasped the others.

"I am going to the landlady and have her put out. That's what I am going to do. Smoking pipes in a decent house in a decent neighborhood! I never heard of such a thing in my life. Never! What are we all coming to? That's what I would like to know. Come along. We'll put a stop to this at once."

They hastened downstairs. On their way they encountered the occupant of the back parlor, who appeared to be surprised to see them all together and in such evident excitement so early in the morning.

"Would you believe it," said the second floor back, "the new boarder upstairs is sitting in her room right this minute smoking a pipe with cigars and tobacco and everything smokable under the sun around her! The room is so thick with tobacco smoke that you could cut it with a knife. Think of a young girl like that smoking. It wouldn't surprise me one single bit if she was an opium fiend, not one single bit!"

"That's just it," they reiterated in an awed whisper. "She is an opium fiend!"

The back parlor at last found sufficient strength to lift up her hands in holy horror.

"An opium fiend in this house!" she groaned. "Well, she'll not stay in it long. We will have her put out. She goes, bag and baggage, or we go. The landlady may pay her money and take her choice."

The landlady was quietly hem[illegible] napkins when they marched in on [illegible]

"Now, look here," said the [illegible] floor front, shaking a tremblin[illegible] finger in her face. "We are al[illegible] to pack our trunks and leave th[illegible] in double quick time unless you [illegible] new boarder on the fourth floo[illegible]

"Why, what has she done?" [illegible] the landlady in dismay. [illegible] boarder is a boarder and [illegible] a week is so much a week, if [illegible]

"She is up in her room [illegible] explained the second floor b[illegible] sitting cross-legged in the middle [illegible] room, dressed in Turkish trousers, [illegible] the pipe. She's got one of those nargilehs, or whatever you call them, one of those big, long bottle things with a tube to it that would reach across the room, drawing away at it for dear life."

"My land!" exclaimed the landlady, turning white. "Is that true? Are you certain of it?"

"Certain of it! Of course we are. Bridget saw her. And it don't surprise me, not one bit. Didn't I know the minute I laid my eyes on that girl that she was an opium fiend? Well, I reckon! You can't fool me. I've seen too many of them. There's always something about their eyes that gives them away, and their complexions! Goodness! Anybody to look at that girl's complexion would know that she actually lived on it. The fumes of opium are all over the house right now. We could hardly come through the halls, they made us so dizzy. If you should go into that room of hers the fumes would knock you down. It is a disgrace to the neighborhood to have such a girl around. Tell her to go, or we go, all of us in a body. We'll get out before noon. That's what we will do."

"Of course, if it's so," sighed the landlady, "she must go. I'll tell her to pack her trunk and get out at once."

She laid aside her work and went upstairs, followed by the others, who paused on the third floor and stood in an expectant group while she knocked at the new boarder's door.

"Come in," said the new boarder.

The landlady went in and looked around. There was not the ghost of a nargileh, not a single opium fume threatened her, and if the girl had been dressed in Turkish trousers she had the ability of a lightning change artist to costume herself while you wait, for she sat quietly in a rocking chair by the window clothed in a pink dressing sack and a black skirt. She arose and politely requested the landlady to be seated. The landlady took a chair and sat down. She beamed upon the new boarder.

"It is a nice morning, isn't it?"

"It is," replied the new boarder.

"How do you like your room?" asked the landlady.

"Very much," said the girl, "very much indeed."

"That rug in front of the dressing table looks just the least bit frayed," said the landlady, peering at it over her glasses. "I must get you a new one."

"Thank you," said the new boarder.

"And I'll send you up a little new rocking chair. I see the bottom of that one is coming apart from the chair."

"I'll be much obliged," said the new boarder.

Adding a few unimportant remarks, the landlady arose to go.

"Won't you stay a while longer?" asked the new boarder.

"No, thank you," said she. "I just came in to see how you were getting along. That was all. Good morning."

"Good morning," said the new boarder, and when the door had closed upon her she listened a moment to the excited explanation going on in whispers outside, then, walking to the window, stood there drumming on the windowpane and smiling all to herself.

She hadn't been born the day before. She knew exactly what had happened. —(New York Sun.

THE BOSTON SUNDAY GLOBE—FEBRUARY 19, 1899.

JULY 7, 1906.—

Southern Cigarette Men Deny Gaston's 'Dope' Tale

Dash of Rum, It Is Said, Is Added Sometimes to the Glycerine That Is Used to Keep the Tobacco from Getting Brittle.

PRODUCT IS CLEANLY MADE, THEY DECLARE

Tobacco men who came to New York yesterday for the Sixth annual convention of the Tobacco Association were exasperated to think that London should have given credence to the assertion of Edward Page Gaston that American cigarettes were "doped" and were the worst thing America sent to England.

Sarcely any cigarettes are exported to England at all, it was declared. Material for cigarettes is purchased here by agents of English companies and shipped in leaf to be rolled into cigarettes in English factories, under the restrictions of British law.

Some fundamental popular errors regarding variation in tobacco flavors were pointed out by one of the largest manufacturers of American cigarettes—who, however, exports none—W. M. Carter, of Wells, Whitehead & Co., of Wilson, N. C., who said:—

"There is only a small tract of country in the world which can produce what is known as Virginia. Part of it lies in Virginia and part in North Carolina. Different sections of this tract yield tobacco slightly different in strength and flavor from other sections.

"Now, we are all the time experimenting with blends. We send out thousands of samples each year to dealers asking them for a test—to see if any particular blend strikes the popular taste as better than what had been furnished before. We merely mix new proportions of the yields of different sections in an effort to turn out a cigarette that is stronger or more delicate, or more aromatic than the sorts we or some rival had been making.

"It is all in the mixture. Whoever effects from the product of different soils a mixture that takes the general fancy and supplants the product of a certain soil, why, he of course presently finds his trade increased. Some persons will say, 'Oh, that's not Virginia. This man has "doped" Virginia.' As a matter of fact, he has simply made a flavor by chancing upon a combination that suits more purchasers than the simple tobacco grown in one district.

AS TO THE FLAVORS.

"One year differs from another in the quality and quantity of its yield. You know a cigar manufacturer may make a hit with a cigar made from a leaf from a certain plantation. As soon as he does he buys up as much of that year's yield of that plantation as he can, sometimes a quantity sufficient to last him a long time, because he knows that the year afterward the fragrance will not necessarily be the same. Many a celebrated cigar has lost favor, not because the maker did not put in as good material as at first, but for the reason that he could never afterward renew his supply of the crop which made it famous.

"The more natural we can keep tobacco the better our trade. Cigarettes are such a short smoke that to put in foreign substances would be detected, and as soon as a smoker detects anything except pure tobacco he leaves off purchasing that cigarette or that cigar. We do use a thin solution of water and glycerine in winter. Glycerine attracts moisture from the air, and makes the tobacco easier to manipulate. If you make your own cigarettes you need something besides a dry and powdery tobacco. This treatment is perfectly harmless and is only to keep the tobacco pliable.

"We use a dash of rum in the solution—the best rum obtainable—for there is an idea that it makes the tobacco itself smoother and imparts a scent. But the rum scent soon evaporates, and it is harmless. Some companies use a little of the flavor of the vanilla bean just because vanilla is a generally popular, and, of course, in no sense deleterious, flavor for different confections. But I believe in the blends of different tobaccos to achieve an attractive cigarette.

"Nothing, I know, is put into Virginia cigarettes made in this country that is in the least injurious. Our factories are inspected weekly throughout by government officers. Very few American cigarettes are exported to England. Leaf is exported, and it is made into cigarettes in English factories under English supervision. If the English 'dope' them in the process of manufacture, why we know nothing about it."

"VIRGINIA" IS PURE.

John C. Hagan, of Richmond, secretary of the Tobacco Association, said:—"Certainly Virginia cigarettes are absolutely pure. We hang up the tobacco in the leaf for five or six months to let the air take out its rankness. Sometimes we have to wait a long time then in order to handle it, for the weather must be damp or the tobacco is brittle. If handled in dry weather the solution of water and glycerine is used upon it, merely to keep it from turning to powder during manipulation.

"All trust cigarettes are made by machines. There is no opportunity for any contaminating touch. These machines are on the principle of wool carding machines. Neither tobacco nor rice paper wrapper touches anything except steel.

"English companies have offices and buyers all through the South. They ship the tobacco in the leaf, to be made into cigarettes in England. Much of the leaf is stripped—that is, it has the stems taken out—and a great deal is shipped stems and all. It is the stem that contains the rankness; in the best cigarettes and cigars there is no part of this stem. When shavings of the stems are added it makes a low priced tobacco.

"Solutions of sugar, molasses, liquorice, vanilla and rum are sometimes used in treatment, separately; but we have always looked upon these as modifying the harm in tobacco itself—never as making it more harmful, and seldom as contributing any attractiveness. Tobacco is a product of nature, and anybody who tampers with it is going to lose his trade. It's the aroma of tobacco that is desired, and any manufacturer would have to quit who did not operate on that principle."

There was considerable discussion of the incident before the House of Lords committees, but the only indignation was that the House of Lords Committee should have been so imposed upon.

"That cigarettes are 'doped'," remarked the President of the Association, E. N. Carrington, "is a mere curious superstition."

As for the use of cigar ends—nobody believed it possible. Some small makers of cheap goods in a poor east side neighborhood, might use them, but it was doubtful, for Virginia leaf would cost little more. It was never to be observed anywhere in this country, members said, that anybody went about collecting cigar ends or "butts" as in Paris and London. And anyway, this second hand tobacco would go into cheap, small cigars if it went into anything, and would never be profitable for export.

These officers were elected:—President, E. N. Carrington; Vice Presidents, W. D. Collins, of Louisville; W. L. Petty, of Rockymount, N. C.; C. W. Bohman, of Lexington, Ky.

drugged and manfactured under filthy conditions.

Mr. Williams said, speaking for the trade in general, that the allegation that American cigarettes contain drugs is absolutely unfounded, and that, in so far as the Allen & Ginter branch of the American Tobacco Company is concerned, there is no truth in the statements that the conditions surrounding the manufacture of white paper "smokes" are not clean.

The weed is carefully sorted and handled and the house in which the cigarettes are made is kept in the best of condition. Special care is taken to keep both tobacco and house clean. Scrap tobacco, that portion of the loose leaf which becomes scattered about the floors, is carefully swept out of the way and is not used to compose any article. Special precaution is taken to see that there is a minimum of stem in the tobacco that goes into the cigarettes.

Mr. Williams is under the impression that other manufacturers of cigarettes are as careful of the conditions surrounding the product as is the case [illegible]

Without reservation [illegible] declared that the statem[illegible] drugs go into the manufacture o[illegible] cigarettes is absolutely untrue. The Allen & Ginter branch of the American Tobacco Company is the only plant in this city for the manufacture of cigarettes.

FESTIVITES MARK CASTRO'S RETURN

ECEMBER 8, 1889.—OCTUPLE SHEET.

DR. TALMAGE ONCE A SMOKER.

seems to me that this question of the use of acco by clergymen is one that every minister uld decide for himself. I do not, therefore, ak for others, but express only my own individual opinion when I say that I believe tobacco to ruinous to one's physical health, whether he be gyman or layman. It is not a rapid poison. The e for tobacco may be endured for generations, sooner or later I believe it acts disastrously in e way, either to the mind or to the body. Nor his a statement of glittering generalities. I know ereof I speak.

or many years I smoked cigars, but I do not do now. I would not now think of smoking a cigar more than I would drink a vial of laudanum. I e to give up the habit in this way:—I was liv- in Syracuse, N. Y., but had just been called to adelphia. An elder in the Philadelphia church which I accepted a call offered, as one of the ucements to my coming, that he would give me the cigars I wanted the rest of my life free of rge. He was a wholesale tobacconist and would e kept his promise. At that time cigars were er in price than they are now, and the offer nt the saving of a great deal of money to I was then smoking up to my full capacity— is, I used as many cigars as health would nit. I thought to myself what would happen if ould get them free! The thought so appalled that I made a resolution then and there to stop king and never touch tobacco again in any ner or form. And from that day to this I never e. Now, I would not take up smoking again for the surplus in the Treasury.

s I said before, every clergyman must settle the stion for himself according to his own conence and belief. But as for myself smoking is erly out of the question. It is my opinion that y clergymen who have on their tombstone ed in the Lord" might have for more appropri- epitaph "Killed by Tobacco."

ROOKLYN. T. DE WITT TALMAGE.

ROBERT COLLYER ENJOYS HIS CIGAR.

uld clergymen smoke? Well, they should if want to. The question of clergymen smoking ds mainly upon the cigars they use, in my on. If I want to smoke I do smoke, and it is y's business except perhaps my physician's. do not think that the use of tobacco has ever ny health physically, and I much enjoy a good However, I think that the question of clergy- smoking is a very foolish one. A great e with modern society is that we are ed in and around by too many barriers. uestion of clergymen using cigars is not one an concern the Church at large, or society at If a clergyman wants to smoke it is nobody's ess so long as he can afford it, provided it not hurt his constitution—and he smokes good . I enjoy good cigars and intend to smoke as often as I please. However, if the use of so affected my health of course I would drop instantly.

ROBERT COLLYER.

YORK.

[illegible]BER NEWTON IS PREJUDICED.

I fear [illegible]t my judgment concerning the use of tobacco by clergymen is not a disinterested one. I am one of that by no means inconsiderable number of unfortunate, if not guilty, beings who cannot smoke themselves and cannot endure the smoke of others, and are always in a fix between their courtesy to smokers and their regard for their own wretched nerves. To me, thus prejudiced, perhaps, the case is a clear one. The sedentary habits of the parson and the frequent overweight upon his nervous energies make the seductions of this habit peculiarly subtle, and at the same time render its evil effects physically peculiarly serious. Moreover, to a prejudiced eye like my own, it seems a very offensive habit for a "man of the spirit." I can scarcely fancy myself seeking spiritual consolation from lips whence issues the odious fumes of nicotine. The smoking habit seems so clear a luxury, and withal a more or less poisonous one, that the physical offensiveness of the smoker's presence is re-enforced by certain moral offensiveness. I find smokers, as a rule, utterly inconsiderate of the discomforts that their luxury inflicts on others—a by no means clerical frame of mind. But I confess to being prejudiced, and since some of the sweetest and best ministers I know are habitual smokers, I can only respect my own judgment.

NEW YORK. R. HEBER NEWTON.

FROM AN EDITOR-CLERGYMAN.

If any one should smoke, why deny the privilege and pleasure to a man of the cloth? If no one ought to smoke, then I imagine the clergyman should be included.

I have noticed that nearly everybody who doesn't smoke thinks it sinful, a vile habit and a waste of silver dollars, while the man who does smoke believes that it warms his heart, clears his head and helps to make life worth living.

For myself, I am my own double, a clergyman and a journalist. As a journalist I take unspeakable comfort in a good cigar. There is poetry in its lifting clouds and I watch them with a placid sense that I am enjoying a very innocent pleasure. Moreover, my clerical conscience does not rebel, but accepts the situation with serene approval.

I should say, then, that a clergyman may smoke if he wishes to. If he does not wish to he may credit himself with resisting one of the softest blandishments of this cold world, and denying his tired nerves one of the most precious narcotics that ever threw its magic spell over ill temper and substituted good nature for chronic irascibility.

You may rob others of their cigars if you have the requisite strength—and hardness of heart—but you can't get mine unless you weigh a good deal more than I do.

Yours, with a puff, GEORGE H. HEPWORTH.

NEW YORK.

SMOKING MINISTERS BAD EXAMPLES.

More than one important religious denomination, notably the Methodist, now regularly makes inquiry of candidates for the ministry as to their habits concerning the use of tobacco. A large number of conferences refuse to accept habitual smokers as preachers. I believe there should be a reform in this matter of smoking among young men, but nothing prevents it so much as the practice of a few distinguished preachers, whose habits in other respects are exemplary, but who in regard to smoking set a bad example to the young.

BOSTON. JOSEPH COOK.

HE RECOLLECTS HIS FIRST SMOKE.

I began to smoke at eight years of age and left off the same day. The cane cut from the hedge made me sick, and all my experience since has made me more sick of what I regard a dirty, costly, tyrannical and unhealthy habit. Excuse may be made for some elderly or afflicted smokers, but the practice should be specially avoided by ministers. There are in every church some who will be pained by such an example, some who may be injured by following it. Smokers are liable to become slaves to the habit, so that its indulgence gets to be a necessity of life. They are uncomfortable without it; they become reckless of the comfort of others; they must smoke in the street, in the car, in the house, in the bedroom. It often leads to drinking, wastes time and costs money which is needed for better objects.

NEWMAN HALL.

LONDON.

FROM VENERABLE DR. M'COSH.

Smoking will be put down when young ladies declare that they will not look with favor on a young man who smokes, and when congregations declare that they will not take a minister who smokes.

PRINCETON, N. J. JAMES McCOSH.

EQUAL RIGHTS FOR CLERGYMEN.

I see not why clergymen should not smoke if men of any sort or other professions do. I have never been a smoker myself, but it seems to me to be the same question mentally and physically for all persons alike, and the example of a smoking clergyman, if hurtful, is equally so by men of other sets.

BOSTON. C. A. BARTOL.

FROM THE CANON OF WESTMINSTER.

I have never been a smoker, never having felt the smallest need to adopt the practice or the smallest attractions toward it. Whether smoking is injurious to the health of full grown men or not I am unable to say, but many who begin by smoking in moderation go on to smoke in excess, and there they injure their health very seriously. It seems to me that when man has so many natural wants it is not desirable to add to them another want, which can only be regarded as artificial.

LONDON. FREDERIC W. FARRAR.

THOMAS BEECHER SAYS "DON'T."

Tobacco? Yes, it has done me damage; it has brought me benefit. Slight excess, I think, of damage. If consulted I should reply "Don't." If asked "Why not?" should answer "Why?" To use anything without a good reason is at best an experiment, and experiments are risky. Abstain until nature calls for help. Then take advice or experiment cautiously—very cautiously. A good servant may prove a most cruel master. Tobacco has its uses, no doubt. He is a rare man who learns to use it usefully.

THOMAS K. BEECHER.

ELMIRA, N. Y.

FROM THE ELDER BEECHER.

My deepest feeling is excited by the great extent to which ministers of the Gospel are involved in the sin of using tobacco.

It not only injures them physically but morally.

Against unanswerable evidence of its widespread evils, physical, intellectual and moral, they subject themselves to a habit of ruinous self-indulgence, and do all that example can do to induce others to do the same. Then of what avail is it for them to preach to men to deny ungodliness and every worldly lust?

While ministers of the Gospel oppose one with vivid eloquence, they advocate the other by example, and are a rampart to defend it against all assaults.

EDWARD BEECHER.

BROOKLYN.

BISHOP POTTER'S SUGGESTION.

I do not think that clergymen are under any obligation to smoke. Whether they ought not to smoke is a question concerning which I would suggest that you obtain the views of the Rev. Mr. Spurgeon.

HENRY C. POTTER.

NEW YORK.

A VOICE FROM ANDOVER.

Some concessions must in fairness be made to the smoking habit. It is not a sin in any man whose own conscience does not so instruct him. It should not be made a test of character, even in our private judgments of men. As a man thinketh so is he. It is not a proper subject of ecclesiastical prohibition. The distinction is not a wise one which forbids it to clergymen more imperatively than to laymen. That is not a healthy type of religious faith which lays the clergy under prohibitions which are not thought necessary in regulating the conduct of other men.

Yet there are few, if any, usages, morally innocent in themselves, of which so many things can be said to their discredit as may be said of the use of tobacco as an indulgence.

The habit is against nature. Tobacco is neither food nor drink. So far as I know, it is not medicine except to a sick sheep. No natural appetite of the human body craves it. Of the whole animal creation but one species naturally takes to it—and that is a worm. Intellectual culture is not fostered by it. Nor does it quicken or gratify spiritual aspirations.

General Stonewall Jackson once said to his daughter that since he had reached adult years he had never taken a mouthful of food at any hour of day or night without asking the blessing of God upon it. The General was a native of a tobacco growing State and probably a smoker. But it may be reasonably questioned whether he ever sought the divine blessing upon his daily cigar. What smoker ever did? Yet why not? [illegible] smoking clergymen answer the question?

An immense and increasing num[illegible]ristian believers condemn the habit as [illegible]sympathetic with the imitation of Chris[illegible]rift of the noblest and purest civilization[illegible]ply adverse to a usage which so distinctl[illegible]inates mind to matter, soul to body. AUS[illegible]LPS.

ANDOVER THEOLOGICAL SEMINARY.

ORGIES OF THE HEMP EATERS.

Hashish Dreamers' Festival in Northwestern Syria Occurs at the Time of the Full Moon.

WOMEN JOIN THE CEREMONY.

Scenes at the Sacred Dance That Surpass the Wildest Ecstasy of Any Opium Dream.

THE DRUG AND ITS EFFECTS.

STANDING in the outskirts of the little town of Latakieh, in Northwestern Syria, famous everywhere for the excellent tobacco which takes its name from the otherwise obscure and insignificant place—and turning his back on the ramshackle houses the flea invested caravansary, the malodorous bazaar and garbage strewn streets, where the scavenger dogs lie stretched out noonday sun—the traveller sees in the distance, beyond a wide stretch of green slope and alternate level, a low range of hills, on which a soft purple haze seems always to linger. These hills lie between the Lebanon, where the fierce Druses dwell in their highland fastnesses, and the Nahr-el-kebir, "The Mighty River." They are known nowadays as the Nosairie Mountains, the home of the so-called Nosairiyeh tribesmen, the modern "Assassins," or "Hemp Eaters," as they should be designated from their ceremonial use of hemp, in Arabic "hashish."

AT THE TIME OF THE FULL MOON.

The festival or gathering of the hemp eaters is celebrated monthly, at the time of the full moon, the moon being then supposed to exert a specific influence upon human beings. The sectaries meet under a sacred oak tree growing upon a hill, about equidistant from Latakieh and the valley of the Orontes, and close to a tiny village inhabited by some twenty families of the tribe.

There is an enormous drum, some three feet in diameter, standing at the entrance to the village, a couple of hundred yards off, and as soon as it begins to darken and the westering sun appears to have fairly sunk in the waters of the Mediterranean, which is clearly visible from the elevated hilltop on which the Nosarriyeh are gathered, a deafening boom comes from the instrument and rolls over the mountain tops like the rumble of thunder, rousing the tribesmen to activity, and in a moment they are on the alert. Lamps are quickly lit and suspended to the branches of the sacred oak among the dangling rags and buttons and feathers and metal scraps that decorate it. A square heap of wood is built up in front of the tree about a dozen yards from it. A sheep is brought forward by one of the men, and the rest of the tribesmen then gather around, the lamps throwing a dim light on their picturesque figures and grim countenances. The Sheikh puts his hand gently on the head of the bleating animal, it is thrown down, its throat cut, after the fashion of the Moslems, and in little more time than it takes to write the words the fleece is off, the carcass is divided and placed on the wood heap, to which fire is applied and kept up till all flesh as well as timber is utterly consumed. Now the Nosarriyeh seat themselves in a circle upon the earth, the Sheikh in the centre, with an attendant on either hand, one holding a large earthenware bowl containing a liquid, the other a bundle of stems to which leaves are attached—the leaves of the sacred hemp plant. The chief takes the stems in his left and the bowl in his right hand and slowly walks around the circle, stopping in front of each man present, who takes from him, first the greenery, at which he sniffs gently, then the bowl, the contents of which he sips. The vessel contains a sweetened infusion of hemp, strong and subtle in its action.

WHAT THE DECOCTION IS LIKE.

The taste of the decoction is sweet, nauseously so, not unlike some preparations of chloroform, and its first effects are anything but pleasant, for it produces a distinct tendency to vomit, not unlike a strong dose of ipecacuahna. As soon as all have in succession partaken of the drink, which is termed "homa,", big horns are produced containing spirits, for the Nosarriyeh are great dram drinkers. The horns of liquor are passed about and in a few moments the effects are apparent, following upon the hemp. The eyes brighten, the pulse quickens, the blood seems to bound more actively in the veins, and a restlessness takes possession of the whole body. At this moment the booming of a giant drum is heard again, giving the signal for the sacred dance which is the next item in the ceremonial of the evening. From each of the dozen parties or so into which the clansmen are divided one steps out, and the dozen individuals so designated form up against a gentle declivity in rear of them. Two of the tribe with a "reba," one stringed fiddle, and a tambourine, seat themselves and start a peculiar air in a minor key, which all those around take up, clapping their hands the while rhythmically, and to this rhythm the dancers, joining hands as they stand, begin to move gently to and fro.

The moonlight is full on them, showing up their white nether garments, but leaving the dusky faces and dark upper garments in a semi-shadow. First the dancers move slowly, a few steps to the right, then a few to the left, raising the legs sedately. The music quickens, and they quicken the pace accordingly. Further to the right and further to the left they go each time, till the movement becomes a positive allegro. Faster goes the music, faster the dancers, until with a finale furioso the men stop, panting and out of breath, at the signal of the Sheikh. He claps his hands and twelve others step out, and the figure begins as before. When these are exhausted a fresh set take their place, and this is continued until each of the clansmen has taken part in the dance. In conclusion all join hands and go seven times round the sacred oak in the direction left to right.

A CRAZY FESTIVAL.

The solemn supper is now ready, and is served by the wives of the tribesmen, who have been busy preparing it in huge earthernware dishes placed upon the ground in the middle of each group. And the moonlight meal in the shade of the sacred oak is none the less striking by reason of its being dished up by women who wear in their sashbands a sharp yataghan, of which the handle shows clearly, and a brace of pistols in the girdle. The plates are peculiar. First there is fried liver, eaten to the accompaniment of fiery arrack—the favorite spirit of the hemp eaters. Then comes "leben"—a species of sour cooked cream, with more "arak;" afterward the "kibabs" of mutton, in slices on little wooded sticks, like the familiar ware of the cat's meat man; eggs filled with a force meat of rice, tomato, mutton and onions and "pillau." Each person has a wooden spoon to eat with, and the etiquette of the table requires one to eat much and eat quickly, and to drink as much as one eats. The appetites of the Nosairiyeh are proverbial in Syria, the usual allowance of meat being a sheep for two. I can vouch for their tippling powers. Scores of them finish their pint horn of arrack in a couple of draughts, taking a couple of quarts in the course of their supper. The meal is really a match against time, and, with such good trencher men as the hemp eaters, is quickly finished.

The real business of the evening now begins. The hemp, powdered and mixed with sirup, is brought round in bowls, together with the decoction of the leaves well sweetened. Each of the tribesmen secures a vessel of arrack—for it quickens and heightens the action of the drug—and disposes himself in the most comfortable attitude he can think of. Then, taking a good spoonful of the hemp, and washing it down with an equally good drink from the liquor receptacle, he lies or leans back to allow it to operate. I take a reasonable allowance of the compound (it tastes very much like raw tea leaves flavored with sugar water), and then lie back to note the action on my own person, and watch, so far as I can, its effects upon the modern assassins whose systems are seasoned and more accustomed to the drug. Five, ten minutes pass, and there is no sensation; the men around me, with closed eyes, look like waxwork figures. Another ten minutes, and the pulse begins to beat rapidly, the heart commences to thump against the sides of the chest, the blood seems to rush to the head, and then there is a sensation of fulness, as if the skull would be burst asunder at the base. There is a roaring in the ears, and strange lights, blurred and indistinct pass before the eyes. In a moment and quite suddenly all this passes off, leaving a feeling of delicious languor, and an idea that one is rising from the ground and floating in space. Little things assume an enormous size, and things near seem far off.

EFFECTS OF THE DRUG.

The oak tree close by appears to be a mil[e] off, and the cup of drink looks a yard across the size of a big barrel. One's hands and fee[t] feel heavy and cumbersome, and then fee[l] as if they were dropping off, leaving one fre[e] to soar away from the earth skyward, wher[e] the clouds seem to open to receive one, an[d] one long perspective of light shines befor[e] the eyes. The feeling is one of estactic restful ness, contented unconsciousness, suggestin[g] the "ninirvana" of the Buddhist. This mark[s] always the end of the first stage of hemp eat ing. The aphrodisiac effects, the visions of fai[r] faces and beauteous forms, the voluptuou[s] dreams and languishing fancies which th[e] Easterns experience—these are the results o[f] larger and oft repeated doses of the drug.

Already the larger quantities of the com pound, repeated many times in the meantim[e] and stimulated by frequent draughts o[f] arrack, are beginning to show their result[s] upon the hitherto immobile figures of th[e] Nosiariyeh round the sacred oak. Again an[d] again they seize the spoon and convey it t[o] their mouths, until the hemp craze is full[y] upon them. One or two stir uneasily; the[n] another screams for "Ali, Ali!" (thei[r] founder Ali), who is identical, they say, wit[h] Allah. A half a dozen respond lustily, "A[...] hu Allah!" then empty the arrack cups besid[e] them. A few move about with outstretche[d] arms as though they were in the clouds try ing to clutch the houris, whose imaginar[y] forms they see, and, disappointed, sink back after a fresh supply of the drug has bee[n] swallowed. From the extremity beyon[d] where the women are located, come th[e] sound of singing and of laughter and th[e] rhythmic patter of feet upon the groun[d]. The ladies have been indulging on their ow[n] account, and the noise they make rouses th[e] men from their dreams. Three or four jum[p] up from the floor at a single bound, an[d] seized by the dance mania, begin caperin[g] away as for very life. They jig here an[d] there, they twine and twist, and writhe an[d] wriggle and distort themselves, awakenin[g]

FESTIVAL OF T[...]

BEGINING THE DANCE OF THE HEMP-EATERS

blows off his matchlock as he capers merrily round, while his neighbor stretches out his fingers for the arrack.

END OF THE HASHISH DEBAUCH.

In the distance we hear the sound of the women's voices as they scream and sing and dance in a noisy whirl under the influence also of the intoxicating hemp. Again and yet again the tribesmen quaff from the hashish bowl, and the riot grows wilder and madder than before. It becomes a veritable saturnalia. Flushed and inflamed, they fly from side to side, tear to and fro, whirl round on the heels, skipping in the air and jumping feet high above the ground, to the banging of the great drum in the village; the shouting of those unable to move, the screeching of the "Reba," or fiddle, which still plays on, and the crackling of the guns as they go off. Scimetars are drawn, yataghans flourished, half a dozen engage in mimic combat, slashing and cutting at each other with an all to earnest resolve to draw blood—a result speedily obtained—while yet another batch dance round and round on their heels spinning like tops in play. Faster and furious grows the corybantic rout, and in their mad excitement the men tear the garments from their bodies, throw away their weapons, fling the turbans from their heads and, naked to the waist, with disheveiled hair and eyes ablaze and extended arms, they continue their mad antics, until foaming at the mouth and bleeding from the nostrils, they sink to the earth and lie huddled in heaps, hopelessly and helplessly intoxicated with the hemp.

NEW YORK HERALD, FRIDAY, MARCH 15, 1895.

DEBESH — HEMP-EATERS TOWN IN THE MOUNTAINS

WEED'S DESIRE TO GET EVEN.

Governor Hill's Capture [illegible] the Senatorship

THE END OF THE DANCE

MP EATERS AND THE WILD DELIRIUM OF THE DANCE.

Growing Hemp in the Philippines

HASHEESH ANTICS.

Details of an Experiment Made in Chicago with Six Medical Students.

IT WAS A WILD ORGY.

Dr. Gatchell Administered the Drug and Attendants Cared for the Victims.

THEIR STRANGE IMAGININGS.

Each of the Six Was Affected Differently, All Very Peculiarly.

[BY TELEGRAPH TO THE HERALD.]

CHICAGO, Ill., Feb. 6, 1897.

MANY persons have doubtless smoked hasheesh, but not, as a rule, under scientific auspices. However, six young medical students of Chicago have had this experience under the eye of an expert, and for four hours quit the earth and roamed around the world. When they came out from under the influence of the drug they were so exhausted they could not sit up, but recovery was rapid and in a few hours they were all right again. The antics indulged in by the patients were ludicrous in the highest degree, but not one of them was aware of what he had been doing.

Strangely enough, the most phlegmatic of the six was the first to succumb to the narcotic, while the nervous and excitable one of the party was the last to yield. The experiment was termed a "hasheesh séance," and Dr. Charles Gatchell, editor of the Medical Era, who has experimented with the drug for many years and written a novel, "Haschisch," the hero of which was addicted to the use of the drug, presided and saw that the patients received proper treatment and were not allowed to harm themselves or others.

When everything was in readiness each smoker was given a small dose of the black extract to swallow, ten grains being the average first dose. Then each man was told to go ahead and smoke, which he proceeded to do. As the stuff did not burn readily many matches were required to keep the pipes going.

Each smoker was affected in a different manner. The young man whose phlegmatic temperament led his companions to believe he would not easily succumb, was the first to betray symptoms of inebriety. Although the room was still as death and nothing of a humorous nature had occurred, the stolid youth suddenly began to laugh as though something had pleased him immensely. His was not a maudlin laugh, however, but free and hearty, and he soon became uncontrolable. He was immoderate and boisterous in his hilarity, and in a few moments another patient became infected. Both laughed until their sides were sore. Exhaustion began to set in, but the mirth was still fast and furious. Finally they rolled off their bunks upon the floor and laughed until they could laugh no more, rolling around and frothing at the mouth.

One by one the students went down, the nervous man being the last. He had struggled manfully, but was finally forced to give up. The most peaceable man in his college when in his normal condition, he imagined himself John L. Sullivan, and wanted to fight every man in the room.

As the men became influenced by the drug they slid from their bunks to the floor, and a general scrimmage ensued, during which one of them received a slight scratch on the finger, at sight of which one of his companions became greatly alarmed. He insisted that the scratch was a deep cut, and said the flow of blood was something frightful. He had a pocket surgical case with him and in a short time had threaded a needle with a ligature and wanted to take a few stitches in the wound. Dr. Gatchell said this was characteristic of the effects of the drug. Everything was magnified in the eyes of the patient. Short distances looked like miles, and minutes like hours. If a man were standing near a patient the latter would consider him half a mile away. This was later illustrated when one patient beckoned to another and asked that he come nearer, so he could speak with him, although the other was within touching distance at the time.

One young man saw horses running around a race track and was making big bets on his favorite. Ordinarily he was not a betting man and never went to the races. With wild eyes and quickened breath he watched the horses go around, and then shouted out:—

"I've won the bet! My horse came in ahead!"

He is one of the quietest men in his class at college.

Another patient was under the impression he had become seized with a dangerous illness, and at once the others rushed at him and insisted upon performing sundry surgical operations upon him. Some of them rushed to the door and shouted for all the doctors in the neighborhood.

One young man, whose face betokened a strong and well balanced mentality, imagined himself a girl, and insisted that the others waltz with him. He was very restless, and spent half the time removing and putting on his coat and vest and collar and necktie. After an hour or so he lay down and closed his eyes, and imagined he saw the pictures of a cinematographe. He also talked indistinctly of green fields, brooks, blue waves, with red and yellow spangles, and things of that sort.

One of the young fellows who had been laughing so heartily got the idea that he was Jean de Reszke, and insisted upon singing an operatic duet with another young man, who he thought was his brother, Edouard. A college mate said he had never known the patient to attend an opera and had never known him to speak of the de Reszkes. The one who imagined himself Jean induced the other patient to sing the duet with him, and when they had finished they bowed to an imaginary audience, smiling as though they had received applause, and stooped down and picked up imaginary flowers thrown at them by admirers.

A patient who announced himself as Sandow picked up a small piece of wood and declared it was a 100-pound dumbbell. He raised it to his shoulders with difficulty, and when he had put it down again offered to bet any man in the room he couldn't duplicate the feat.

"It's worth $100 to any man who can do it," he said.

At one time all the men were rolling on the floor in paroxysms of laughter, and when they arose every one wanted to fight, and it was with difficulty a general row was prevented. One curious thing about the performance was that none of the patients noticed those who were not under the influence of the drug. They did not appear to see them at all and never addressed questions to them. With each other, however, they were quite talkative.

It was about eleven o'clock when the influence of the narcotic began to abate, at which time the condition of the patients was pitiable. They could not stand, but threw themselves on the floor or bunks, and panted as though they had been through a severe struggle. Big beads of perspiration stood upon their foreheads, and their faces were pale as ashes. Dr. Gatchell said the experience would not hurt them, but said it would not be a very good idea for them to repeat it. On the next day the patients appeared as well as ever, but not a man could tell what he had done or said while the hasheesh was working upon him.

Justice Hall Rats All 'Hopped" Up

Doped Rodents Give Cat Bad Night

Gil Chase, custodian of confiscated booze, dope, bicycles, jewelry, wooden legs, false teeth and the like at the Hall of Justice, has had considerable trouble with rats lately.

Someone told him that rats are fond of marihuana weed, which is a powerful narcotic.

Saturday policemen conficated a sack of the weed. Chase thought he saw an opportunity to get rid of the rats.

There is a cat named "Nigger" that holds forth in the basement of police headquarters. Nigger is death on rats.

Chase dragged the sack of marihuana out into the middle of the floor Saturday night, posted Nigger inside and went home.

Monday morning he came down to see what happened. Nigger was waiting for him inside the door with eyes ready to pop out of his head.

There were overturned cans and capsized boxes. A half dozen glass eyes, from an upset satin lined case, were glaring up at Chase from the floor. It was plain that something in the nature of a party had been going on.

There were two or three dead rats to show that Nigger tried his best to keep order.

But there was one particularly offensive rodent that staggered out directly in front of Chase and defied him. Chase gave him a kick that settled him.

Chase also discovered that fully one third of the marihuana weed had been eaten by the rats.

Nigger seemed mighty glad over the arrival of Chase.

Paper for 100 smokes

Ready Gummed

Convenient Packagé

Extra Thin

Releases 1 at a Time

Extra Strong'

White or Straw

Tasteless

Absolutely Pure

THE BOSTON SUNDAY GLOBE—JANUARY 10, 1904.

UNCLE SAM'S POISON FARM.

Government Conducts a Novel Industry on the Potomac Flats—Plants Which Yield the Most Powerful and Valuable Drugs Known to Science—Will Start Opium Growing, Too, in Texas.

INDIAN HEMP—THE HASHEESH PLANT.

BRANCH OF COCA PLANT BEARING FRUIT—SOURCE OF COCAINE, THE LOCAL ANESTHETIC.

FLOWER AND SEED OF THE OPIUM POPPY.

THE PLANT THAT YIELDS QUININE.

Uncle Sam has started in to grow poisons. He has set up a hasheesh factory, on a small scale, and is about to try the commercial production and manufacture of opium. Deadly nightshade, monkshood, henbane, foxglove, jimson weed and wormwood are among the plants which are being cultivated in an experiment garden patch, about two acres in extent, on the Potomac flats, close by the city of Washington.

The plants selected for culture in this government garden are those that yield the deadliest of known poisons, which are at the same time the most powerful and valuable drugs employed by medical science. We import something like $8,000,000 yearly of such drugs (including raw materials from which they are extracted), and it is believed that most of this money might be saved by producing the toxic weeds for ourselves. Up to the present time no attention has been paid to this kind of gardening in the United States, but the department of agriculture is making a study of it in the manner described, and proposes next year to devote extensive areas to the purpose, with a view to ascertaining the commercial possibilities of the industry.

Opium, Morphine, Hasheesh.

During the coming season, a tract of some size in Texas will be planted with the opium poppy, and the juice obtained from the seed-vessels will be prepared in the ordinary way and manufactured into refined opium of first-class quality, for sale in the market. We import an immense quantity of this drug annually, and there is no reason why we should be obliged to depend upon foreign sources for supply, inasmuch as the poppy can be grown successfully through a wide range of latitude in our own country. The only difficulty lies in

SAME, FROM WHICH A MEDICINAL DRUG IS OBTAINED.

DIGITALIS—A PULSE REDUCER.

LATTICE SHED FOR GROWING DRUG PLANTS UNDER PARTIAL SHADE.

the fact that our farmers know nothing about this or any other kind of drug-plant production. Opium is one of the most complex of vegetable substances, containing more than 20 distinct active principles, of which the best known and most valuable is morphine. The government experts intend to extract morphine from the Texas opium, experimentally.

The most striking feature of the poison garden on the Potomac flats is a patch of indian hemp, from which the famous drug called "hasheesh" is obtained. Its delicate stalks of waving green tower to a hight of 10 feet, with many branches, and at the top delicate tassels of tiny flowers. It is from the seed-vessels that is derived the substance which yields the tonix agent so celebrated in history and romance. This substance is bright green in color, and, when swallowed, produces the most extraordinary visions and hallucinations. Most people have read of that remarkable secret society in the Orient, organized for wholesale and systematic murder, whose members called themselves Hashhashin—whence our word "assassin"—and stimulated themselves for their deeds of atrocity by doses of this drug.

Deadly Nightshade and Henbane.

The government work with drug plants is being conducted by Botanist-in-Chief F. V. Coville, and the garden described is laid out in plats of belladonna, digitalis, aconite, arnica, valerian, henbane, stramonium, seneca snakeroot, golden seal, and other species. Belladonna is the deadly nightshade; digitalis is foxglove; stramonium is jimson weed, and aconite is monkshood. Golden seal is a wild plant, native to our forests, and is rapidly disappearing—on which account, especially in view of a growing foreign demand for it, no time should be lost in bringing it under cultivation.

Henbane is found wild in the northeast part of the United States. Its active principle, derived from the leaves, is a sleep-producer. Monkshood is a bushy plant, bearing violet or yellow flowers, which is abundant in the mountain forests of France and Germany. It is cultivated in gardens, and all parts of it are poisonous. In medicine its peculiar alkaloid is employed as a nerve soother.

Foxglove is likewise grown in gardens as an ornamental plant, its single stalk being adorned by a [illegible] of lovely

thought to have originated in the o[illegible] and in this country was first observed in the old settlement of Jamestown, V[illegible] whence its name. It is found nearly everywhere on roadsides and commons. The active principle is derived for medicinal purposes from the seeds.

Large quantities of crude drugs are brought to this country from the hottest and dryest regions of the earth, as, for example, colocynth, senna, gum arabic and gum tragacanth. In the United States we have vast areas of arid and torrid territory which are seeking agricultural use, in California, Arizona and New Mexico, and the government proposes to ascertain how far it would be practicable to employ them in the production of these valuable plants. In the north and north central states several important drug plants, such as digitalis, sage, summer savory, henbane and valerian, grow well. It is the idea of the department of agriculture to find

flowers. Its active principle, digitalis, is obtained from the dried leaves, quantities of which are put up for market by the Shakers of New Lebanon, O. The effect of it in reducing an over-rapid pulse is wonderful.

Poison All Through It.

As for jimson weed, which is another narcotic and a deadly poison, it is

out how to grow profitably the already established drug plants and to try to domesticate the wild ones, such as golden seal and ginseng.

No Limit to the Production.

Of licorice root and its products we import $2,000,000 worth annually, though there is no good reason why we should not produce all we want of it in th[illegible] country. We can grow wormwood, [illegible] which furnishes a valuable heart [illegible] lant, though it is best known [illegible] source of the drink most destructi[illegible] the nervous system, called abs[illegible] Goldenrod, so familiar as a wild f[illegible] of the autumn, supplies a useful [illegible] Valerian contains an alkaloid w[illegible] gently stimulates the nervous sys[illegible] and heart, for which reason it is given for hysteria. As for the colocynth plant it is much like a watermelon, with hairy stem that trails on the ground. It is a native of Turkey, and the fruit is gathered when it turns yellow, peeled and dried in the sun, the pulp thus prepared furnishing the commercial product, which is a cathartic. The Shakers have crossed the colocynth with the watermelon, the hybrid having the same properties as the former.

The department of agriculture is growing under glass cinchona trees, from the bark of which quinine is obtained. It is thought that in some parts of Uncle Sam's domain this valuable plant may be raised commercially. From Peru also have been imported specimens of the famous coca, whose leaves yield the precious alkaloid cocaine, valued chiefly as a local anæsthetic. Crosses are being made between different varieties of the coca, under glass, with a view to the production of a hybrid exceptionally rich in alkaloid.

It is proposed to separate from each kind of drug plant its active principle in considerable quantities, in order to make the investigation complete as possible. The curing of the fresh material has to be very carefully done, else the drugs will not be first-class. All of the knowledge obtained will eventually be put into the shape of a bulletin, which will be distributed among farmers for their instruction in a branch of gardening that, in the opinion of the department of agriculture, is likely to yield large profits.

NEW YORK HERALD, SUNDAY, JUNE 15, 1913.

Non-Smokers Now Trying to Banish Lady Nicotine from All Public Cars

CIGARS
TOBACCO
CIGARETTES
SOME PEOPLE ARE SO SENSITIVE THAT A WOODEN INDIAN UPSETS THEM.
DEAD CIGARS ARE BAD; SMOULDERING ROPE IS WORSE
J. NORMAN LYND

Public Service Commission to Investigate Complaints—Sixty-Five Copies of Orders for Hearing To Be Held Wednesday Are Served on Common Carriers in This City.

When an Englishman, opening his cigarette case on one of the rear seats of a Broadway car yesterday afternoon, said to his friend seated beside him, "Will you smoke with me?" and the American answered, "Yes, if the verb is transitive," neither knew to what extent they might soon be deprived of the pleasure of inhaling the fumes of the soothing weed in transit here. It all depends on the Public Service Commission and its decision next Wednesday

The Englishman might still be pondering over his friend's subtle answer by the time the Public Service Commission has completed its investigation to determine whether or not smoking and the carrying of lighted cigars, cigarettes or pipes on common carriers in New York shall be permitted in future. For many months leaders of the Non-Smokers' Protective League of America have camped on the trail of the much harassed Commissioners with pleas for a hearing in behalf of the total abstainers who scoff at the shrine of the Lady Nicotine.

Sixty-five copies of the order for the hearing in the matter by the Public Service Commission were served yesterday upon sixty-five common carriers in this city. Just to prove that these carriers are not as common as one might at first suppose, several of the recipients were the New York Central Railroad, the Pennsylvania Railroad, the New York, New Haven and Hartford Railroad, the Interborough Rapid Transit, the New York Railways, the Hudson and Manhattan Railroad, the Third Avenue Railroad, the New York, Westchester and Boston Railway, and the Long Island Railroad. It is the avowed intention of the intrepid chiefs of the Non-Smokers' Protective League to prohibit (save in restricted places aboard trains of more than one compartment) all indulgence in tobacco.

But wait. Not quite that. No matter how great the ban that may be placed on the humble stogie or the fragrant perfecto, irrespective of the possible taboo for the pipe or the gilded tipped cigarette, and even though the bare mention of "the makings" may be deemed a sufficient cause to summon the police, that good old fashioned indoor sport, the dainty munching of the quid, may be permitted. There has been no stipulation to the contrary, at any rate, and the Senator from the Middle West who comes to New York may ride aboard the cars without unduly discommoding himself or depriving himself of one of his greatest pleasures in life.

In response to oft repeated requests from the league members, the railroads have tried to stop smoking aboard the rolling stock of their respective lines, with more or less success. But the restrictions at present imposed on the devotees of the weed are not stringent enough for the league. The four rear seats even on the open cars are too great an accommodation to smokers, say the leaguers. There should be no smoking at all. Ugh! It is disgusting. Here we have men of education, culture, ability and brains spending real money on tobacco, burning it up and disseminating the fumes broadcast on the clear wholesome air of the fair city! So say the leaguers.

It is interesting to note that criticism of those who are operating to deprive them of their smoke aboard the cars does not come from the smokers. Martin O'Hanlon, a conductor on a Broadway car, expressed himself feelingly yesterday regarding the present condition of affairs. "What with the young fellows crowding into the far sides of the seats and smoking to their hearts' content and some of these old gents that wouldn't ask you where Amsterdam avenue is without dropping the last syllable of the word insisting all the rest of the time that every one aboard the car is a pagan and a thief who even reads a tobacco sign, the conductor's life is not a happy one these days.

"I've seen some who would not get off at a street corner where there was a tobacco store and some seem to suffer pangs of inward distress every time they pass a wooden Indian. Yet these fellows never raise much noise against the hogs who make travelling uncomfortable for women in the cars. The smokers in the back seats don't disturb any one except each other by smoking different brands of tobacco. For my part, I never smoke," and he adroitly discarded a piece of eating tobacco beneath the wheels of a passing automobile. "I'd get fired if I did," he said.

In answer to the league crusaders who sought his assistance in their fight, Mr.

... Avenue Railroad Company, said:—"Having regard to the state of public opinion in respect to these matters, the practice of the other railroads with whom we are competing and the silence of the Public Service Commission in respect to the whole business, I regret that I do not see any way to suppress smoking as you desire." Mr. Theodore P. Shonts, president of the Interborough and the New York Railways, expressed himself similarly.

That the smoking regulation by the railroads which permits indulgence in the smouldering weed on the four rear seats of cars is not quite clear was remarked on by Magistrate House in the Jefferson Market Court yesterday. Fred Steifel, of No. 1,931 Madison avenue, one time a star of the Princeton gridiron, was smoking a cigar on what he deemed the fourth seat from the rear of a car on which he was travelling. Trouble arose concerning the exact number of the seat, and Steifel left the car, causing the arrest of the conductor and motorman. Both were discharged.

SPECIAL NOTICES. SPECIAL NOTICES.

Lady Nicotine Is Not Hunter College Girl

Columbia University denies that smoking among women students is common there. Authorities at ... university have been aroused by ... action of the State Normal Board ... Nebraska, which has adopted a resolution not to grant leaves of absence to its teachers to attend Columbia, Chicago or Northwestern universities, because of the prevalence of cigarette smoking among women.

That such smoking is not a problem in New York's educational circles is the opinion of Miss Annie E Hickenbottom, dean of Hunter College.

Members of the Board of Education were inclined to disregard the question yesterday. The consensus was that the Nebraska School Board has acted in a ridiculous way.

STUDENTS WELL BEHAVED.

Dr. Charles T. McFarlane, controller of Teachers College, Columbia University, made this statement:

"It is to be regretted that an official body would take an action which required them to mention an institution like ours, on the basis of newspaper reports, the accuracy of which they were in no position to determine without inquiry at Columbia.

"The student body here, both men and women, is as orderly, as well-behaved and well conducted as any similar student body in the world.

"Miss Margaret Kilpatrick is president of the students' government board in Whittier Hall. Some time ago, because of disregarding a rule against smoking in Whittier Hall, two students were suspended. Their case was brought up on appeal before the students' government board and they were readmitted.

WAS MISQUOTED.

"Shortly after, a young woman without a hat, seeming to be student, came to Miss Kilpatrick's room and talked with her about the smoking at Whittier Hall. Miss Kilpatrick does not recall exactly what she said but she did not say the things which are credited to her. She did not say that we all smoke because she herself does not smoke and never has.

"No large proportion smoke, for smoking in the building is prohibited by a rule which is ... enforced. It is possible th... girls do smoke when they ... home o... ... not smoke ... wev... ... control or au... ha... ...

"Habitual" ... from Teachin...

BOSTON, Fe... State Commis... Massachusetts, ...

"I would consider it ... exclude all graduates of ... lar college from taking a ... a State normal school ... teaching, simply becau... students attending the c... question smoke.

"I believe it would be ... thing to exclude a girl fro... school because she was an... smoker.

"There are no rules in t... schools of Massachusetts ... smoking by girl students ... case that might arise w... to be dealt with accordi... facts in that particular c...

"I believe that if a ... where a girl attending ... setts normal school was ... an habitual smoker she woul... eliminated. I believe she w... eliminated on the ... did not have the ri... tude."

Ban Upon Teachers Is Unfair, Says Educator in Washington.

WASHINGTON, Feb. 21.—Mrs. Howard L. Hodgkins, acting president of the Board of Education, to-day characterized as unfair th... ruling of the State Normal Board ... Nebraska. She said:

"While I do not believe or e... dorse women smoking, I think ... ruling of the Nebraska board ... fair. Because some girls atten... ing these northwestern unive... ties smoke is no indication t... all of them smoke. I hardly th... the Board of Education here ... take up the question."

Harry A. English, chairman o... teachers' examining board, said ... his board does not go into the ... tion of whether teachers smok... it is an unwritten law that sm... by pupils or teachers abou... school buildings is about the ... offense imaginable.

PELLETIER REMOVED BY COURT DECISION

HUGE DISTILLERY FOUND IN A STABLE

Women Turning Cigar Shop Into General Store

FEMININE influence is turning the old-fashioned tobacco shop into an up-to-date version of the old "general store."

A. C. Allen, vice-president of the United Cigar Stores Co., announced yesterday his firm's stores would be made into "convenient shops" for the public.

When only men entered the stores only tobacco was sold. Now a woman enters a cigar store and goes ut with a pack of cigarettes—and also an alarm clock, a box of candy, face powder and a pair of sho... de... "g...

Women Cigar Smokers Vex Cigarette Fans

By Associated Press.

LONDON, March 10.

WOMEN'S clubs in London are up against cigar smoking.

Cigarettes were assumed to be the limit of women's smoking when several clubs established a rule that their drawing rooms might be used as smoking rooms. But many women are now smoking cigars, and cigarette smokers seem to have as much prejudice against cigars in the mouths of members of their own sex as many Victorian ladies have against cigarettes.

CIGARS FOR WOMEN

—By Winifred Black—

THE women of Wallesey in Cheshire, England, have formed a club to popularize cigar smoking among women.

Great news, isn't it, girls?

Every woman who joins the club has to sign a pledge to smoke cigars in public.

And lots are to be cast every little while to decide who shall do the public smoking. Old women and middle-aged women are joining. Young girls are joining.

I do hope nobody will pay the least attention to them—don't you?

NOW, if I really want to smoke a cigar or a corncob pipe or a clay pipe or a water bubble pipe, I would smoke it either in public or in private. But I would certainly not join any club in order to get the right. If I had a fad for eating raw lobsters or baked dog—I'd eat 'em in my own home at my own table—if I had money enough handy to pay the doctor's bill.

If I wanted to put on overalls and go to a wedding, I'd put 'em on and go, and those who love me could blush and those who hated me could laugh at me.

I WOULDN'T thank any woman for asking me to join any sort of an organization to help her make a fool of herself. No, there's nothing wicked in a cigar—a woman might be a saint and smoke a cigar, if she did it because she happened to like it. But what fun is there in it, anyhow?

I thought women who are always talking about suffrage and sex equality wanted the right to be themselves, not to be a weak imitation of a man.

If we are going to copy men why don't we copy their common sense and their lack of self-consciousness?

ASK a man to join a club for the purpose of encouraging other men to knit or embroider sofa pillows and see what he would say to you.

There seems to be a few men in the world who like to look like women and act like women, but somehow they don't feel obliged to get up clubs about it, do they?

Oh, sisters! What is there so marvelous about men that we should want to imitate them? Do let's be women as long as we have to be women.

Isn't It So?

Handling Women Smokers

By ROY K. MOULTON

'TIS a moot question. In fact, it is more than moot.

It is the mootist or mooterst or the most mootiferous question of the time.

What to do with the women smokers?

Social experts have gone at this question more than once during the past few years and have fought it to a finish, to retire defeated from the field. Great writers have tackled it pro and con, and have succeeded in leading it nowhere.

IT is a question which does not seem to respond to treatment. You can't even humor it along in the direction you wish it to take.

What to do with the women smokers?

Ah, there's more in the question than meets the human eye, or ear, or nose.

ABOUT a year ago a well-known railr... pro-vided with a s... women. It was... sex experts th... would not go... compartments...

... attitude and took the smo... car for women off.

ABOUT that time th... managers began mak... feeble effort to establish s... ing rooms for ladies i... basements of their the... Some actually were estab... and are said to be ope... business still.

But the ladies did not ... to these special room... smoke.

They smoked in the ... bules and lobbies of the ... ters and on the stairway... ing to the smoking roo... not in the smoking room...

THE secret of this wa... it is no fun for any ... to drag at a cigaret ... somebody is watching h...

Women ordinarily a... lone smokers. If they ... make it look smart and ... cipated to somebody els... waste the effort?

BOY A VICTIM OF CIGARETTES.

Charles White Committed to Bellevue for Examination as to His Mental Condition.

AT HIS MOTHER'S REQUEST.

She Took Him to Court and Magistrate Mott Turned Him Over to the Physicians.

HAD NO CONTROL OVER HIM.

Imprisoned in the pavilion for the insane in Bellevue Hospital, Charles White awaits the examination of experts to determine his mental condition. The experts have been called upon to decide whether he is a degenerate, a "cigarette fiend" or simply incorrigible.

In her modest home, at No. 2,020 Webster avenue, surrounded by her four other children, Mrs. Rose White, his mother, anxiously awaits the decision. She is inconsolable over her boy's condition and refuses to be comforted.

White is seventeen years old, and has been an inveterate cigarette smoker. He became addicted to the habit more than a year ago. At first he was content with two cigarettes a day, but as smoking them became a habit he increased the number until he consumed two packages a day. He smoked them unknown to his mother for a time, but as she had no control over him, he began smoking in the house.

TOOK HER SON TO COURT.

His mother remonstrated with him in vain. Finally the cigarettes seemed to affect his mind, and yesterday morning Mrs. White took him to the Morrisania Police Court before Magistrate Mott. The boy was sullen and ugly. His appearance gave the impression that he was not in full possession of his mental faculties.

"I have brought my boy here to have him committed to be examined as to his sanity," said Mrs. White, her voice choking with emotion. "He calls me vile names, and when he flies into fits of uncontrollable rage I am in fear of my life."

"That ain't so, Judge. I'm all right," the boy replied. Mrs. White did not wish to have him sent to an institution of correction, so the Magistrate had an ambulance summoned from the Harlem Hospital, to get the doctor's opinion respecting the boy's mental condition.

Dr. Schoonover responded. After making an examination, he concluded that White was a degenerate and took him to Bellevue. Mrs. White, a frail, pale faced little woman, gave expression to her grief as he was led away. She sobbed as though her heart was breaking.

DUTIFUL TILL HIS FATHER DIED.

"Charlie can never come into my house again," she told me at her home last night. "He has disgraced and insulted me beyond pardon. He was all right until my husband died, two years ago. Then he began to go wrong. He took to smoking cigarettes and abusing me, knowing that I would not ... him.

"His language to me was ... had to send him away, for ... moralize my four other boys, ... them to follow his example.

"Charlie worked until Octobe... in Broadway, and left for no ... lieve his mind is giving way. ... spoke to him about going to ... into a passion and called me v... simply could not stand it longe... now on the verge of nervous pro...

Something brand new in ... terprise. A widenwake ... novel idea. The SUNDAY HER... tell you all about it.

GEORGE GOULD SENDS R...

Tells Mr. Orr That the Manhattan ... pany Will Decide Upon Propo... Improvement Next Tuesday.

George J. Gould, president of the Man... tan Railway Company, yesterday replie... the letter from Alexander E. Orr, presid... of the Rapid Transit Commission, saying t... the Executive Committee of the railroad next Tuesday would take up the matter of extending its lines and improving its service and that they would at once confer with the Commissioners on the subject.

Both Mr. Gould and Mr. Orr declined to make public the contents of ...

Smoke Rings
By EARLE ENNIS

Wives—look to your laurels. Or at least to your willows. Very shortly [...] of the most dangerous young women in C[...] are to be posed on the [...] model ho[...] officially ce[...] educated in [...] smarter th[...] summer re[...] Every o[...]

on a thin dress, dab perfume on her ear flaps, and snare her man in a hammock. Only this time, it is all going to be much more deadly. A marriageable male might stand of a girl in a hammock. But when [...] trained housewife, certified [...] biscuits and bot[...] standing [...]

A Girl Where There's Smoke
—By Arthur ('Bugs') Baer—

I DONT MIND YOU TAKING MY CIGARETTES BUT DARLING, LET ME HAVE MY CIGARS
MISS JONES, IF YOU DONT BRING YOUR OWN CIGARETTES NEXT TIME-ILL HAVE TO SUSPEND YOU!

WELL, anyhow, a great transcontinental railroad is going to take another whack at it and try to solve the question of what to do with the women smokers.

On its crack trains there is now a ladies' lounging and smoking room where they can smoke and lounge and lounge and smoke with their own sex until they get to wherever they are going.

SUPER-MILD SPUDS

MARCONI AIDS RADIO THROUGH MICRO-WAVE

[...] at [...] mid- [...] three [...]oratory [...] station [...]distant. [...]lready [...]essfully [...]o-wave [...]electra [...]

[...]at sending [...] must 'see' [...] there must [...]struct wave [...]extent, this [...]micro-waves. [...]earth enters [...] there is no [...]t be used by [...]

[...]nted out that [...]could be used [...] mountainous [...]e of high masts

PRINCESS, 109, LIGHTS SMOKE

Dr. Charlotte de Goliere Davenport, born a Tartar Princess in Russia in 1824, approaches 110th birthday by lighting cigarette on arrival in Washington. Never ill, she studied music under Liszt. Of her three husbands, one died in duel, second was killed at Sebastopol. Mother of eighteen children, she recalled traveling with Mrs. Phoebe Hearst fifty years ago.

March 5, 1934

DON'T SMOKE PAINT

H. G. P. Briar Root Pipes Smoke sweet from the first fill. No paint or varnish, pores open to absorb moisture; no breaking in. All shapes and sizes. Self coloring. Mail orders filled. Repairs promptly done.

41 BARCLAY ST., cor. Church St., N. Y.

BARCLAY PIPE SHOP

Malaria, It's the now.

'Veteran' Smoker

[...]ER COMFORT—Little Jimmy Parmenter, 22 months old, sits [...] comfort of baby rocker and enjoys smoking big fat cigar in [...]ville, Fla. And he isn't kidding—he's been smoking since he was [...]nths old, according to his mother, Mrs. K. L. Parmenter, who [...] does most of his stogie smoking in drive-in theaters.

Ten years later it proscribed smoking on the campus. Getting closer. And just this semester the sign reads "No smoking in college buildings."

Next year it will be "Don't blow smoke through your nose when reciting Shakespeare."

After that this placard will be hung on the lady dean's office wall: "We don't care where you smoke provided you bring your own."

THAT lonesome smoking car for women was a complete fizzle. It remained as vacant as a chorus girl's stare, even aft[...] been glorified.

We will detour collegiate a few minutes to see how the co-eds are doing with their gin and their tobacco.

Up at Scrammons' reform school for subdebs they once had a rule prohibiting smoking within a mile of the college campus.

JULY 5, 1925

Cigars in Vogue with Some New York Girls
Meanwhile Cigarettes Gain New Devotees

By FITZ.

"CIGARS and cigarettes!" Often it is "Popcorn, peanuts, cigars and cigarettes!" You've often heard the cry.

• • •

But one day last week at the Polo Grounds a flapper screamed in response to it. She actually s-c-r-e-a-m-e-d. And when the boy came over double-quick, this particular-bobbed-hair damsel selected a perfecto. She slipped it into her handbag and sighed relief when no questions were asked.

• • •

The cigar was in the handbag and it was secure there.

• • •

Why should a flapper buy a cigar?

Here's why: She intended to smoke it and perhaps she did.

• • •

Any "smoke" store proprietor will tell you that the girls are graduating from "lady fingers" and other paper-wrapped tobacco delicacies.

They'll stand sponsor for the fact that the girls have adopted the cigar. The tobacco-wrapped cigarette is no substitute. They insist on the real thing.

• • •

The hand-made cigar industry has not felt the demand of the feminine "thirst." They're still catering solely to the man element.

But the manufactured cigar, in the milder grades, is enjoying a big "run" with the girls that no longer get a thrill from inhaling the ordinary cigarette.

We haven't seen a flapper walking down Fifth Avenue with a cigar stuck in her mouth, but we have been present in cabarets where the girls were feasting on all-tobaccos.

• • •

"The bigger they come, the harder they fall," is an old axiom. It applies to the cigars—not to the girls. Because advices are that the girls find the fat-rolled smokes

After Dinner Cigar Lands Woman In S. F. Prison Cell; Scorns Cigarette

Judge Lazarus to Determine If Women May Puff 'Seegars' After Arrest of Mary McKensey

When and where is it permissible for a woman to smoke?

Does the propriety of her act depend upon what she smokes?

Mary McKensey, late of the Blue Ridge mountains, is in the city prison on a charge of vagrancy because she smoked.

"What has this woman done?" demanded Judge S. J. Lazarus of the Women's Department of the Police Court of the arresting officer.

"She smokes cigars and a pipe, your Honor," the officer replied.

The judge looked nonplused.

"But not cigarettes"—she emphasized her disgust with a contemptuous wave of the hand. "Not by a long shot! I draw the line there."

Mary sniffed at a long cigar, wrapped in tinfoil with the relish of an epicure.

"Smokin' don't hurt no one," she confided in prison yesterday with a soft drawl of the Southern hills—"providin' you smoke the right thing. Cigarettes is fool killers. Tobacco don't hurt men—that is, see-gars nor a corncob pipe don't. Never did hurt no one as far back as I can remember.

"But some men folks have queer ideas in these here parts"—she looked significantly at a policeman.

What's the difference between Mary and her "seegar" which she lighted after dinner the other night and thousands of her sisters who daintily puff away at the "pills" Mary despises?

All first-class hotels permit women to smoke in the public dining-rooms and lobbies. Some have even provided smoking rooms. Fashionable women's clubs long ago provided smoking rooms.

Was the arresting officer a bit old fashioned?

The question is up to Judge Lazarus now: When and where is it permissible for a woman to smoke? He will decide today when Mary McKensey comes to court.

People Who Think—SUNDAY, MARCH 18, 1923

Last night, when the Miglios put Archie to bed, it was in the hope he would stay put.

$1,000 Is His if He Shuns Lady Nicotine

BAY CITY, Mich., May 19.—If he doesn't smoke until he is thirty, Herschell Whittaker, of Flint, will receive $1,000 from the estate of his aunt, Dr. Mary Williams.

Man Who Never Smoked Suffers Nicotine Poison

ALTHOUGH he had never smoked in his life, George Meyer, No. 407 Lenox Road, Brooklyn, was removed from his home yesterday to Kings County Hospital suffering from nicotine poisoning.

Meyer is 6 feet tall and weighs 190 pounds. He is employed as a florist. He sprayed some plants yesterday morning with a preparation known as "nocofume." As there was no nicotine in Meyer's system, he was overcome by the fumes.

He said yesterday:

"I'm big and I can eat anything. But I never could smoke even one little cigarette."

when I first saw him. Where I go after this, Boris, as I've named him, will go also."

SHOTS END JOY [...] IN STOLEN MAC[...]

Two Arrested in New [...] After Pistol Duel [...] Bridgeport Police

In a stolen coupe, Edw[...] Mitchell and Walter Ledde[...] of Middleton, Conn., were a[...] at the point of a pistol [...] Rochelle yesterday.

The arrest followed a wi[...] from Middletown, Conn., In[...] they nearly ran down two c[...]bles, escaped from five poli[...] in New Ha[...]ter an exc[...] of revolver shots, engaged revolver duel with policem[...] Bridgeport and had fled[...]

Magazine Section **The Sunday Oregonian.** Magazine Section

VOL. XLI PORTLAND, OREGON, SUNDAY MORNING, MARCH 26, 1922 NO. 13

Pipes for the Ladies says London

How a Physician's Chance Recommendation Started the Latest Fad of Smoking From a Porcelain Bowl With a Delicately Jeweled Amber Stem

Peggy O'Neill in Her Smoking Suit. She Doesn't Smoke Much but She Dotes on This Costume

At the Wedding of Capt. Martin and Barbara Judd at Stoke Pogis, England, the Bride Rushed Outside for a Smoke Immediately After the Ceremony

WHEN a London physician suggested that a pipe would be better for women smokers than cigarettes, he meant exactly what he said. But he hardly expected to be taken seriously for the reason that he couldn't visualize a modish woman with a paunchy, brackish pipe in her mouth. In that, he reckoned without the ingenuity of that class of merchants who are catering eternally to the whims of London's fashionables.

The physician's words, which were issued as a sort of warning against the excessive use of cigarettes on account of what had happened to a prominent 60-cigarettes-a-day smoker, resulted in a general curtailment of cigarette smoking among women. In the place of the cigarette, appears a new vogue of pipe smoking.

Now that the pipe has been placed in her mouth, Milady is wondering why she didn't think of it before. For the effect is altogether chic. Needless to say these ladies' pipes differ as much from the sturdy, inelegant paunchy male variety as a Dresden tea-cup will differ from a pewter mug. A common factor of elegance and pertness is observed in all the ladies' pipes seen in the Piccadilly hotels, tea rooms and other gathering places, but they show great variety of design. "They are distinctly insouciant," says a commentator in the Graphic. "They challenge the eye as does a modish gown. They are sharp and provocative—much smarter, I should say, than a cigarette."

The prevalent type of pipe is made up of a long, slender stem inset with jewels and a small bowl made usually of wood or porcelain, overlaid with strips of platinum, silver or gold. All sorts of colors and all sorts of jewels are used for variety's sake. But the bowl is kept small and the stem is kept slender. A number of these pipes have been sent to America, where, it is expected, they will catch on as rapidly as they have in London.

The 60-a-day smoker who was so instrumental in starting the London nicotine scare was none other than Sir William Orpen, the internationally famous portrait painter. Sir William, by his own confession, had been smoking ever since he started painting when 11 years old.

He was a moderate smoker at first, but gradually increased his daily total until he consumed no less than 60. He was what is known as a "chain smoker." That is, he would light a fresh cigarette from the stub of the one just finished. And the harder he worked the harder he smoked.

Then came a period of unusually heavy work. The famous painter was at his easel night and day. When a lull finally came, he collapsed. Doctors who were called in for a diagnosis declared he was suffering from one of the worst cases of tobacco heart they ever saw. He was put through a course of special treatment and finally restored to health. But he's off cigarettes "for life."

"It's true that I was a heavy smoker," said Sir William, in talking the matter over, "but I think this break would not have occurred had I not been overworked and tired out. I'm through, however."

Although none of London's social leaders smoked 60 cigarettes a day or anywhere near that number, so far as is known, they feared Sir William's fate. This fear became vivid when physicians began to speak of the excessive use of cigarettes as a "cumulative habit." It was cumulative, they pointed out, in Sir William's case. He had started smoking moderately, to satisfy his tobacco taste. This developed into a nervous habit. He added gradually to his daily total until his breakdown came. Such might be the case of any smoker who allowed herself to get beyond a moderate number. Sir William added his doleful word of warning against a woman's ever trying to reach a 60-a-day total. When asked if he had ever known any ladies who smoked as hard as himself, Sir William replied: "I have known several. But, alas! they're all dead."

If Sir William's example had not been a sufficient shock to the hard smokers of London's west end, warnings that have lately been sounded by prominent physicians would have certainly given them pause.

Tobacco Hearts Among Women.

An examining medical officer of the North British & Mercantile Insurance company declared that a surprisingly large number of women had been refused insurance because of "tobacco hearts." The proportion of women with this malady was greater than that of men, he said, when one took into account the fact that nine out of ten men smoke as against five out of ten women.

So firm a hold had the cigarette habit obtained on English women, that insurance companies made one of their chief questions to female applicants: "What is your daily habit as regards tobacco?"

This insurance official and other physicians, said, however, that the habit of smoking cigarettes to excess was not pronounced except among the women of the leisure and the highly-paid professional classes. Wage-earners were fairly free from the habit.

Women of the upper class have smoked cigarettes continuously and in every conceivable place ever since the war. Smoking is in order for women in the underground railways, on trains, in the theaters, in the smart cafes and hotel restaurants. It was a high mark of sociability. No party was complete without a mild cigarette orgy.

Lady Astor and her charming sister, Mrs. Paul Phipps, both of American birth, were among the heavy smokers who found it necessary to curtail their daily ration. But there is at least one professional woman in London who has never smoked very much and who thinks that cigarettes have been a baneful influence on her sex. This is Miss Peggy O'Neill, and her views on the subject are considered unusual.

"The best thing about the smoking habit I know is the smoking costume it allows," said Miss O'Neill. Her own costume is a smart affair composed of a red velvet coat trimmed with skunk fur and Turkish trousers of green silk embroidered in silver.

"I bought it," she said, "because so many of my friends have such stunning smoking suits. But the fact of the matter is, I seldom smoke. In the first place I do not care much for smoking. Secondly, I have sense enough to know that my voice could not stand a cigarette siege. You can always tell the voice of a cigarette fiend. It's peculiarly husky.

"Then I often find cigarettes annoying even when others are smoking them. They hurt my eyes. I hate to have a man smoking beside me in a theater and I have worked out a dodge to get rid of him. I tried this the first time when I was at a matinee. A man beside me was puffing at a cigarette that was particularly vile. I slipped out, tipped an attendant and told him my plan. Presently the attendant came back, tapped the smoker on the shoulder and asked him to step out as he wished to speak to him. 'If you don't look out,' he told the smoker, 'you'll have that woman fainting in your lap. She can't stand tobacco. We've had to carry her out of this theater twice.' The smoker threw his cigarette away."

In warning against excessive use of tobacco, London physicians were one in saying that it was easier to roll up an injurious habit with cigarettes than with any other form of smoking. One of them jokingly suggested that a pipe would be much less harmful. Two weeks later a d[illegible] was seen in the Ritz smoking a [illegible]eled pipe. Thus was the [illegible] smoking fad started.

Immigration Law Separ[illegible] Family at Spokane.

SPOKANE, Wash., March 25.—(Special.)—Mrs. Marie Romilly a[illegible] three youngest children are [illegible] the father and two older child[illegible] Canada, all because of the com[illegible]tions of the American and Ca[illegible] immigrtion laws.

Worse, Mrs. Romilly couldn't [illegible] Canada to visit her husband and children and her husband cou[illegible] come to the United States to s[illegible] wife and the children who were [illegible] And all this was true becaus[illegible] milly sought charity from th[illegible] and county.

The breaking up of the R[illegible] family was one of the unusual [illegible] in the annals of the immig[illegible] service. The father was depor[illegible] an undesirable because he [illegible] charity, under the usual rule t[illegible] alien who is a charge on the [illegible] can always be deported.

The Romillys were married i[illegible]ada in 1911, Romilly being a [illegible]dian. The wife is said to hav[illegible] married twice before, the firs[illegible] to an American, who died, a[illegible] second time to an Englishman. [illegible] the matter of deporting the [illegible] came up, a year ago, the Ca[illegible] authorities refused to adm[illegible] woman, claiming she was Brit[illegible] not Canadian. For that reas[illegible] was forced to stay in America, [illegible] from her husband and the two [illegible]ters who, having been born i[illegible]ada, were deported with the [illegible]

Quite recently, however, th[illegible] girls have been returned to [illegible] mother by the immigration a[illegible]ties.

Sunday, November 5, 1922

San Francisco CHRONICLE

Magazine Section

OF COURSE!!

MAN ABOUT TOWN?

FAME

FOREIGN NOBLEMAN?

The GRAND TENOR?

PIPE—DREAMS

ROLF PIELKE

U. S. and Mexic

Wickedest Spot in America—

Lucette, the French Girl, Who Paid $30 to a Mexican Bootblack to Marry Her and Thus Save Her from Being Deported.

Scene Along the Main Street in Mexicali, Showing the Dives Which Have Been Closed.

"Things were wide open at the notoriou 'Owl,' the largest drinking and gambling hal in the world.

"Suddenly, without warning, a Mexica official strode into the room, and to the startle amazement and indigntaion of the assemble gamblers, dope peddlers, rum sellers, gunme painted women and assorted thieves announce that the days of license and debauchery we over and that every crooked man and woma must get out of town."

Contraband narcotics are snea in across the Mexican border hundred different ways, and co has even been shot over by "can

Pathetic Herd of Dope Addicts Rounded Up in Mexicali and Driven Across the Border Into California, Where They Were Seized and Most of Them Locked Up in the Imperial County Jail. On the Left Hand Stands Chief of Police Hardwick of Calexico, California.

Photograph of the "Cribs" in Mexicali, Where the Social Outcasts Had Their Little Rooms, and Which Have Now Been Dismantled and the Furniture Removed.

Without warning, the dives have been closed and thousands of vicious men and women have been driven out of Mexico.

One afternoon recently, while things were wide open at the notorious "Owl," in Mexicali, the largest drinking and gambling hall in the world, the miracle took place.

Suddenly, without warning, a Mexican official strode into the room, and to the startled amazement and indignation of the assembled gamblers, dope peddlers, rum sellers, social outcasts and variegated thieves, announced that the days of license and debauchery were over, and that every crooked man and woman must get out of town.

Abelardo Rodriguez, the Governor and head of the territorial government of Lower California, Mexico, had issued the decree. The outcasts gathered in knots; some sneered, some swore and others laughed in defiance. But the Governor was in earnest, and shortly afterward there began on a wholesale scale a modern real-life version of Bret Harte's famous fiction story, "The Outcasts of Poker Flat," where two notorious women, a gambler and a horse thief were cast out of town in the roaring, wide-open days of the old Western mining camps.

Just as in ...'s story, the order of ejec-

ings is composed en... which look out upon ... rooms have glass doo... eager vampires sit, m... the men who stroll th... them over. As soon ... through one of these ... down the shade.

The rooms of these ... "cribs," and each girl's ... is nailed up near her do...

Not always do they ... webs, waiting for custo... Many are always circul... and dance halls, seeking ... and incidentally gettin... drinks that may be bou... the six hundred were ... women of other nationa... Americans. Also there w... ican women in the vice a... deported. Howev...

...at they ...s were ... ediately ... apers of ... at first ... delight ... mericans ... ast these ... hich they ... at were ... cy would be triumphant, even in Mexico. In their gratitude they deluged the Governor with letters of praise and gratitude. His Excellency Governor Abelardo Rodriguez smiled grimly at these letter... There was more in this than these good people suspected.

Next day the enthusiasts pause... in their letter writing. An un... pleasant thought had arisen. The ... newspapers, after thinking i... over, pointed out that these "Bats of Hell," as the police called them, would all fly north into California. The sudden invasion of six hundred abandoned women, many of them diseased in mind and body, in addition to a small army of equally disgusting male wrecks and criminals of every known brand, turned Southern California's joy to terror.

But why should they all pick ...

These outcasts did not look the part. They were dressed in the quietest of traveling clothes, wore no jewelry, paint nor powder, and were sober and demure. Each little group was carefully organized to look like a family. Some of the women without their paint and powder showed the inroads disease and dissipation had made upon them, but a gray wig made them appear like elderly invalid ladies travelling for their health. As a "daughter" this "invalid" would be accompanied by one of the fresher and younger of the women outcasts, and her "husband" would be one of the "solicitors."

"In the case of the male "dope-fiends" whose unhealthy appearance forced them to play the role of invalid, they would have a reasonably healthy looking "wife" and "daughter." Not one of these fugitives stopped in the southern part of California. The majority headed for the mining camps of Nevada, the only remaining spots in the United States where ... could find anything like the congenial condi... ...y had known in Mexico. A few trickled ... Chicago and New York, one or two went ...ba and one is believed to have ... boarding house in Los

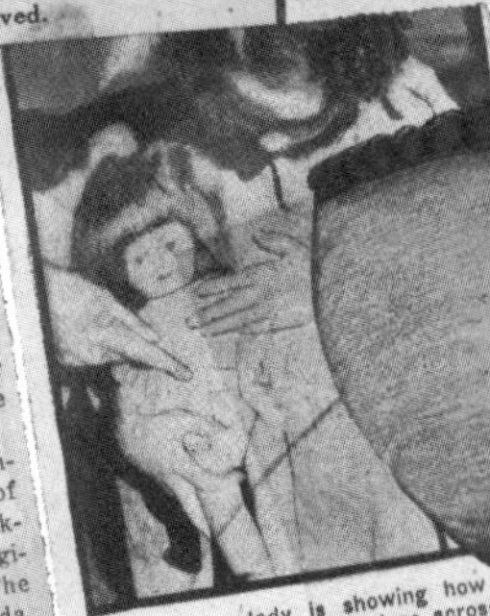

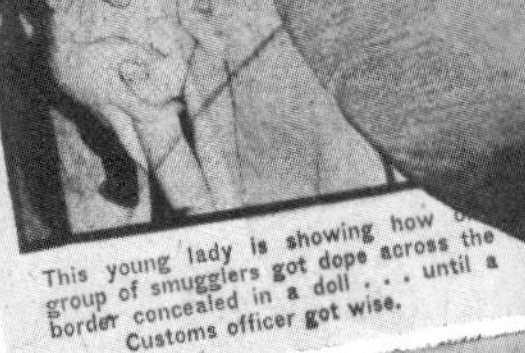
This young lady is showing how a group of smugglers got dope across the border concealed in a doll . . . until a Customs officer got wise.

Like the Famous "Outcasts of Poker Flat," the Mexican Governor Suddenly Padlocks the Notorious Resorts Along the Border and Drives Out the Motley Horde of the Underworld Scum

...profession, ... of them the only one ... looked down upon in Mexico ... tirely legitimate. It is licensed ... which collects a dollar a day from eac...

The blow fell hardest on the border to... cali, Tia Juana and Ensenada, but principally ... cali, which is half in Mexico and half in Californ... The American half, which is called Calexico, is as carefully policed and free from commercial vice as perhaps any town in the United States, and yet within a pistol shot across the line have always been the brothels where every form of vice known to man was running full blast.

The vice area in Mexicali, being controlled and regulated by the territorial and city governments, is segregated in one large block, the fronts of which are saloons and dance halls. The rear of the build-

ernor, a... country."

The girls left their newly ... gathered in anxious groups. ... dope peddlers, the crooked ... other fringes of commercializ... worried. Even the unemotio...

not legally possible ... such women as were American citizens, because, no matter how low she may have fallen, Uncle Sam has to take back one of his own daughters or sons either when another country dumps him or her back on American soil.

However, the vagrancy laws are rather vague, and can be stretched to cover emergencies, so that these wretched specimens could at least be arrested, treated ...r diseases and held until some solution of the ...n could be devised.

...rse than that was the fact that a long stretch ...er never was and perhaps never will be made ...gainst the smuggling of human beings. Even ...y during the war, with all her armed patrols ...ctrified wire fences, could not keep people ...eaking in and out.

...women of the Mexican underworld were well ...at all the police of Southern California were ...ed to stop them, but went right ahead with ... Uncle Sam's gates. Five

...an provided for herself ... type different from the ...t life because it is the ... lazy creature to make a ... under the name of Blanche ...x years in the red light dis-

...d been betrayed in a scandal ... the East which made it impos-...e. After one or two unhappy ad-... other men she found herself penniless ...ican border and took up life in the ...he did it with a clear, steadfast purpose ...t of men as much money as possible until ...d saved $30,000. Then she would go back to the United States and be independent of treacherous men and sneering women.

Through those six years she had conserved her health as far as possible and never touched drugs or liquor. She got her commissions on drinks just the same, for the waiters knew that when she called for Scotch they were to charge for it, but to give her a whiskey glass filled with flat ginger ale, which she swallowed at a gulp. Men who tried to out-drink Blanche found that it could not be done.

Twice a week she crossed the border and deposited her savings, and once a year she took a vacation alone at one of the California bathing beaches, where men found her as unapproachable as a statue. She was methodical, careful, cynical, and when the Governor's bombshell burst she had accumulated $26,000. This was $4,000 short of her goal, but she took it philosophically.

Blanche slipped over the American border alone, and now she is said to be running a boarding house in Los Angeles with most strict and uncompromising rules.

Lucette, known as "the little French dumbell," beat the game in another way. She is in Tijuana now, right under the nose of the Governor, and not ...either. Lucette had been in the "cribs" ... but with the usual help-... bothered to

bride, who must now live on her rather ... ings.

Governor Rodriguez is an honest ... tious official and his edict was a ... measure. Thus far the Americans saw things ... true light, b... they went on to assume ... idea was to ... vice they ... American... not to ref... to put an e... proportions.

In Mexic... abolish a r... upon as n... made as i... and smel... States. ... them.

W... cial s... was ... reac... was ... offici... ridin... owni...

In... Gover... would... propri... street, ... could t... was sile... wearison... might no... Rodriguez... graft syste... from the vic... main support. If he co... whole system might go to p...

This was his reason for c... and deporting such women as h... succeeded probably beyond the Govern... In addition to the dollar a day lice...

Outwitting the Crafty International Smugglers

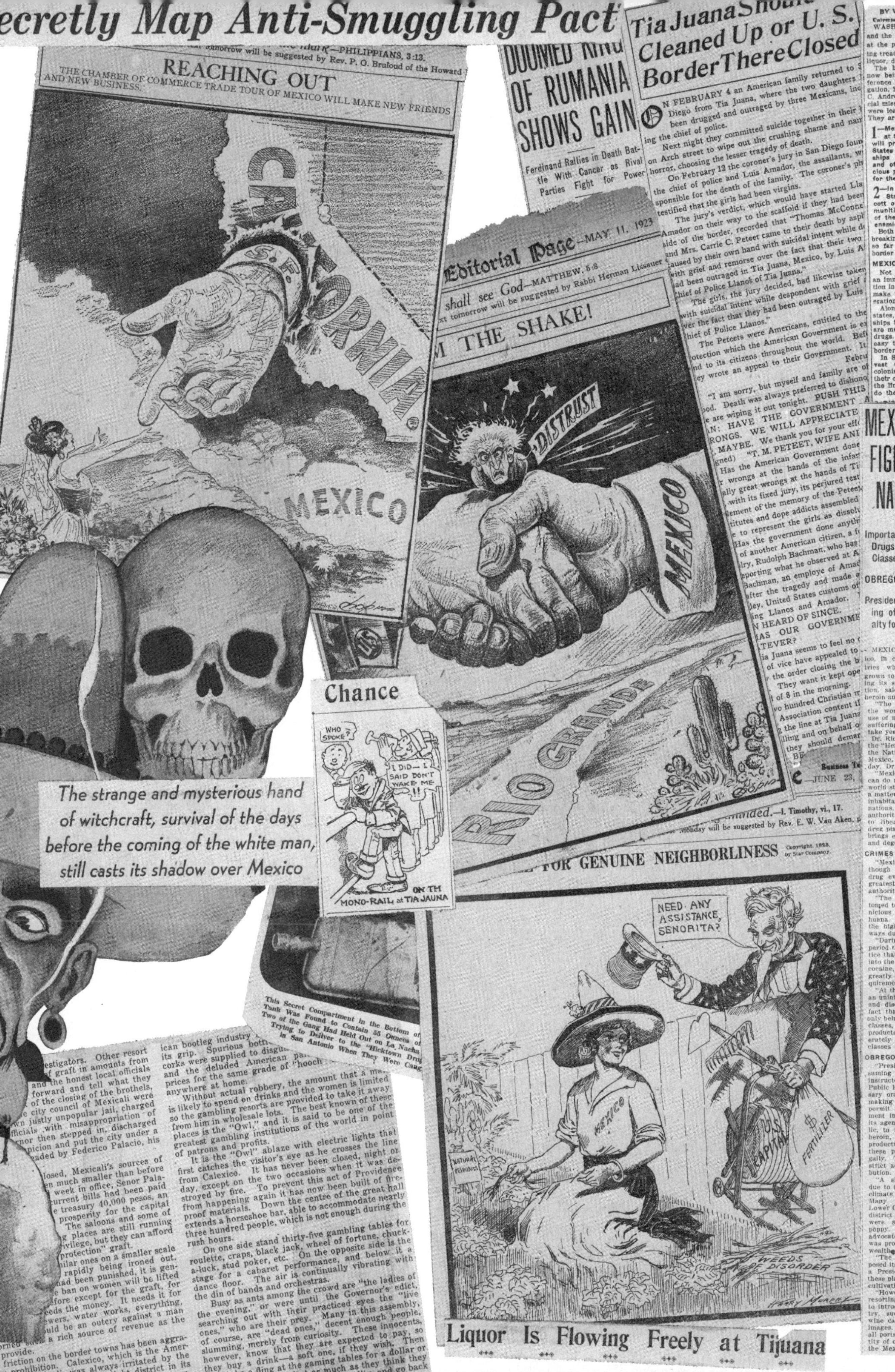

Secretly Map Anti-Smuggling Pact

BY WILLIAM P. FLYTHE.
Universal Service Staff Correspondent.

WASHINGTON, June 26.—Mexico and the United States tonight were at the point of effecting a sweeping treaty against the smuggling of liquor, drugs and dangerous aliens.

The high points of the treaty now being prepared in secret conference between an American delegation, headed by General Lincoln C. Andrews, dry czar, and an official mission of prominent Mexicans were learned by Universal service. They are:

1—Mexico agrees that her agents at the border and at all ports will promptly advise the United States of the clearance of any ships with contraband cargoes and of the movement of suspicious persons or freights headed for the border.

2—In exchange, the United States will continue the boycott on shipments of arms and munitions and will advise Mexico of the activities of Government enemies within the United States.

Both countries are concerned in breaking a gigantic drug ring which so far has been able to run the border blockade almost at will.

MEXICO RING'S BASE.

Not only has this ring built up an immense amount of drug addiction in Mexico, but has managed to make that country its base for operations in the United States.

Along the coast of the border states, where patrols are unknown, ships from the Orient and Europe are met by small craft and unload drugs. It is then comparatively easy to get them across the border.

In Sonora and Sinaloa there are vast Chinese colonies where the colonists grow poppies and make their own opium, which gets across the line in much the same way as do the Orientals.

Tia Juana Should Be Cleaned Up or U. S. Border There Closed

ON FEBRUARY 4 an American family returned to San Diego from Tia Juana, where the two daughters had been drugged and outraged by three Mexicans, including the chief of police.

Next night they committed suicide together in their home on Arch street to wipe out the crushing shame and horror, choosing the lesser tragedy of death.

On February 12 the coroner's jury in San Diego found the chief of police and Luis Amador, the assailants, responsible for the death of the family. The coroner's physician testified that the girls had been virgins.

The jury's verdict, which would have started Llanos and Amador on their way to the scaffold if they had been on this side of the border, recorded that "Thomas McConnell Peteet and Mrs. Carrie C. Peteet came to their death by asphyxiation caused by their own hand with suicidal intent while despondent with grief and remorse over the fact that their two daughters had been outraged in Tia Juana, Mexico, by Luis Amador and Chief of Police Llanos of Tia Juana."

The girls, the jury decided, had likewise taken their lives with suicidal intent while despondent with grief over the fact that they had been outraged by Luis Amador and Chief of Police Llanos.

The Peteets were Americans, entitled to the protection which the American Government is expected to extend to its citizens throughout the world. Before they died they wrote an appeal to their Government. It read:

"I am sorry, but myself and family are of good blood. Death was always preferred to dishonor. We are wiping it out tonight. PUSH THIS CLEAN; HAVE THE GOVERNMENT RIGHT OUR WRONGS. WE WILL APPRECIATE IT. MAYBE. We thank you for your efforts. (Signed) "T. M. PETEET, WIFE AND..."

Has the American Government done... wrongs at the hands of the infamous... equally great wrongs at the hands of Tia Juana, with its fixed jury, its perjured testimony, defilement of the memory of the Peteets... prostitutes and dope addicts assembled... to represent the girls as dissolute...

Has the government done anything... of another American citizen, a f... Rudolph Bachman, who has... reporting what he observed at A... Bachman, an employe of Amador... after the tragedy and made a... United States customs of... Llanos and Amador. ...N HEARD OF SINCE. ...AS OUR GOVERNMENT ...TEVER?

Tia Juana seems to feel no c... of vice have appealed to... the order closing the b... They want it kept open... of 8 in the morning. ...two hundred Christian m... Association content th... the line at Tia Juana... and on behalf of... they should deman...

DOOMED KING OF RUMANIA SHOWS GAIN

Ferdinand Rallies in Death Battle With Cancer as Rival Parties Fight for Power

...the mark.—PHILIPPIANS, 3:13.

...tomorrow will be suggested by Rev. P. O. Bruloud of the Howard...

REACHING OUT

THE CHAMBER OF COMMERCE TRADE TOUR OF MEXICO WILL MAKE NEW FRIENDS AND NEW BUSINESS.

Editorial Page—MAY 11, 1923

...shall see God—MATTHEW, 5:8

...xt tomorrow will be suggested by Rabbi Herman Lissauer

...M THE SHAKE!

Business Te...

...—JUNE 23, ...

...minded.—I. Timothy, vi., 17.

...Monday will be suggested by Rev. E. W. Van Aken, p...

...FOR GENUINE NEIGHBORLINESS

Copyright, 1923, by Star Company.

Chance

The strange and mysterious hand of witchcraft, survival of the days before the coming of the white man, still casts its shadow over Mexico

This Secret Compartment in the Bottom of Tank Was Found to Contain 55 Ounces of Two of the Gang Had Held Out on La Nacha Trying to Deliver to the "Hicktown Drug... in San Antonio When They Were Caug...

MEXICO WAGES FIGHT AGAINST NARCOTIC EVIL

Importation, Sale and Use of Drugs by Both High and Low Classes Alarms Official

OBREGON HEADS BATTLE

Presidential Order Bans Growing of Poppy—Severe Penalty for Illegal Use of Product

By Universal Service.

MEXICO CITY, Feb. 21.—Mexico, in common with other countries where the drug evil has grown to large proportions, is having its struggle with the importation, sale and use of morphine, heroin and cocaine.

"The wave of vice invading the world from the increasing use of narcotic drugs is bringing suffering to humanity which will take years to eradicate."

Dr. Ricardo Catureglio, head of the "Heroic Drug Department" of the National Board of Health of Mexico, made this statement today. Dr. Catureglio continues:

"Mexico as a civilized country can do no less than to enter the world struggle against the evil as a matter of protection to her own inhabitants. Governments of all nations, through their sanitary authorities, are actively working to liberate mankind from the drug plague, the spread of which brings early death to individuals and degeneration to the race.

CRIMES DUE TO DRUGS.

"Mexico has an interesting though serious fight, with the drug evil, and it is to-day the greatest concern of the health authorities in our country.

"The lower classes are accustomed to secretly consume a pernicious weed known as marihuana. The crimes committed in the higher social strata are always due to this toxic.

"During Mexico's revolutionary period the authorities did not notice that Europe was introducing into the country large supplies of cocaine, morphine and opium greatly exceeding the medical requirements.

"At the dawn of internal peace an uninterrupted series of crimes and disease brought home the fact that these drugs were not only being consumed by the lower classes, but that the European products were being also immoderately consumed by the upper classes of society.

OBREGON SAW EVIL.

"President Obregon, upon assuming the Presidency, promptly instructed the Department of Public Health to issue the necessary orders to check this evil making it necessary to obtain a permit from the Health Department in the Federal district or its agents throughout the republic, to import opium, morphine, heroin, cocaine and their by-products, with severe penalties if these products were used illegally. The order provided for strict accounting of drug distribution.

"A singular situation arose due to the similarity of soil and climate in Mexico to that of Asia. Many Chinese, especially in Lower California, in the southern district about the port of Mulege were successfully raising the poppy. The agricultural district advocated its cultivation, as it was proving a source of national wealth.

"The Health Department opposed its cultivation and obtained a Presidential order to destroy these plantations and prohibit the cultivation of the poppy.

"However, dealers in drugs are resorting to a thousand artifices to introduce them into the country, such as double bottomed wine casks and religious images. They ... in all ports. Recently, a large quantity of opium was confiscated on the Mexico-Guatemala frontier.

Liquor Is Flowing Freely at Tijuana

...vestigators. Other resort ...of graft in amounts from ...and the honest local officials ...forward and tell what they ...of the closing of the brothels, ...e city council of Mexicali were ...wn justly unpopular jail, charged ...fficials with misappropriation of ...rnor then stepped in, discharged ...and put the city under a ...eaded by Federico Palacio, his

...losed, Mexicali's sources of ...en much smaller than before ...week in office, Senor Palacio ...current bills had been paid ...e treasury 40,000 pesos, an ...prosperity for the capital ...The saloons and some of ...g places are still running ...ivilege, but they can afford ..."protection" graft.

...ilar ones on a smaller scale ...rapidly being ironed out. ...ad been punished, it is gen... ...e ban on women will be lifted ...fore except for the graft, for ...eeds the money. It needs it for ...ewers, water works, everything, ...uld be an outcry against a man ...a rich source of revenue as the

...scorned ...en provide. ...the friction on the border towns has been aggravated by prohibition. Calexico, which is the Amer... ...by prohibition. ...Mexicali, was always irritated by the ...and light district in its ...

...ican bootleg industry ... its grip. Spurious bottl... corks were supplied to disgu... and the deluded American pa... prices for the same grade of "hooch" ... anywhere at home.

Without actual robbery, the amount that a man is likely to spend on drinks and the women is limited so the gambling resorts are provided to take it away from him in wholesale lots. The best known of these places is the "Owl," and it is said to be one of the greatest gambling institutions of the world in point of patrons and profits.

It is the "Owl" ablaze with electric lights that first catches the visitor's eye as he crosses the line from Calexico. It has never been closed, night or day, except on the two occasions when it was destroyed by fire. To prevent this act of Providence from happening again it has now been built of fireproof materials. Down the centre of the great hall extends a horseshoe bar, able to accommodate nearly three hundred people, which is not enough during the rush hours.

On one side stand thirty-five gambling tables for roulette, craps, black jack, wheel of fortune, chuck-a-luck, stud poker, etc. On the opposite side is the stage for a cabaret performance, and below it a dance floor. The air is continually vibrating with the din of bands and orchestras.

Busy as ants among the crowd are "the ladies of the evening," or were until the Governor's edict, searching out with their practiced eyes the "live ones," who are their prey. Many in this assembly, of course, are "dead ones," decent enough people, slumming, merely from curiosity. These innocents, however, know that they are expected to pay, so they buy a drink—a soft one, if they wish. Then they take a fling at the gaming tables for a dollar or ... lost as much as they think they ...itality, and go back

Evils of the Mexican Border Hot Spots

The visitor, bent on sordid escape from his everyday life, can find relief in questionable dives of the Mexican border towns, where he can indulge in fantastic "pleasure" to be had from smoking marihuana, the sex cigaret, carousing with wanton women.

2000 Miles of Trouble

Senorita Mariana Baron, above, young, dark-eyed and vivacious, is an example of the new type of Mexican entertainer whom clean-minded tourists from America like to see and who marks a new era of wholesome amusement across the border.

Whoopee-minded visitors with money to spend, resorts featuring seductive black-eyed senoritas (or blonds from Chicago), "dope" if you want it—and a complacent policy of "anything goes"

"Hashish o

UNDAY OREGONIAN, PORTLAND, FEBRUARY 23, 1936

BY JACK HOWELL

MARIHUANA—a dread name, with terrifying implications has appeared on the American ene to give officials of the ited States bureau of narcotics more difficult problem than the eacherous opium of the orient! orphine, cocaine or heroin.

For to this unusual plant, so se officials say, may be traced any of the most horrible crimes recent history.

Once almost totally unknown in United States, marihuana has come so common that it has en dubbed a "roadside weed."

t is a hearty plant and seemgly adapts itself to most any mate. Its very prevalence is plant's strongest forte. Its y accessibility offers the great- problem in combating it.

nt Has ny Names

This commonplace plant is own by various names—mariana, hay, greefo, muggles, reef- Mex hashish, and loco weed. is a variety of hemp such as cultivated for commercial pures in Kentucky and Wisconsin. Hindus call a drug made from ery close relative of this plant ang. Arabia "bhang" is own as hashish, from which the rd "assassin" is derived.

Medical men and other scientists e disagreed upon the properties of this weed. Some have refused to classify it as a narcotic.

But law officers have long been of the opinion that the weed is one of the greatest menaces in the country today. Particularly officers in the southwest and in the west, where marihuana smoking was introduced from Mexico long before it spread to the rest of the country.

Officers Recognize Addicts' Menace

Ed Brown, veteran two-gun sheriff of the lonely Black Forest country in Colorado, once said, "I'd rather face a whole saloon full of drunken bad hombres all crying for my scalp than one lone marihuana smoker on the prod.

"A fellow might smoke that stuff for years and get a wonderful kick out of it with the world looking rosy every time, then go off on a killing spree the next time he went the route."

Nor does Joseph A. Manning district superyisor of the bureau of narcotics' office at Denver, hold any brief with those who are inclined to minimize the menace of marihuana.

"There's been a lot said about how dangerous a narcotic addict is when he has his 'stuff,'" Manning said, "but usually a morphine addict or a 'coke head' is a pretty well-satisfied individual when he takes his stuff. I've found that addicts are dangerous only when driven desperate by lack of the drug.

Makes Men Into Killers

"But even then they're children compared to a marihuana smoker. You can't tell when that stuff is liable to make a killer out of a man.

"The alarming thing about this weed is the way it has spread over the country so fast within just a few years," Manning continued, "I saw it creep along the railroads west of the Missouri river when they brought in Mexican section hands, while I was stationed at Omaha, Neb. About the same time Mexican sugar beet hands introduced it into every section in the west where sugar beets are grown."

Only by persistent effort has the Portland police department practically eliminated the growing and use of marihuana here, according to Lieutenant Pat Maloney, chief of the vice squad.

In the past year there have been only one or two arrests for possession of the drug here, Maloney says. Before its use was stamped out the weedlike plant was frequently discovered growing in backyards of Portland Mexicans.

Records Prove Evil Effects

Despite the fact that many are inclined to minimize the harmfulness of marihuana, the records offer ample evidence that the weed has a disastrous effect upon some of its users.

Recently residents of Denver, Colo., were shocked when Vance Henderson, 27, shot down and killed his aunt, Mrs. Elona Wells, 44, mother of four children. Henderson was allegedly under the influence of marihuana. Out of funds and unable to find a job, he was living with his aunt.

Mrs. Wells was washing dishes one Saturday evening when Henderson entered the house. His eyes were glazed and fixed in a corpse-like stare, his face set in a menacing scowl.

He strode to the refrigerator in the kitchen and pulled out a platter of venison. He stared at it angrily for a moment, then, snarling, dashed it to the floor. When his aunt berated him, he dashed upstairs.

Addict Shoots Own Relative

In another moment he swept back into the kitchen brandishing a revolver. Pointing it at his aunt, he pulled the trigger. Mrs. Wells died a few days later.

Police caught Henderson staggering down a street a block from the Wells home. Questioned about the shooting, he pulled his hair and screamed, "I'm crazy! You're all crazy! There was no shooting in that house! What if I did kill her?"

He was placed in a solitary cell where he continued to scream like a madman. Investigation revealed that Henderson had bought several marihuana cigarettes from a Mexican peddler that evening and had smoked them.

The next day, after recovering from the disastrous effects of the weed, Henderson again was told of the shooting. He refused to believe that he ever had a gun in his possession the night before.

Mexicans Roll Dice of Death

To stretch one's credulity to the breaking point, there's the story of the dice of death game held in a back-street dive in Juarez, Mexico, just across the river from El Paso. Four unidentified Mexicans, imbibing heavily of "sotol" (a cheap, vicious Mexican alcoholic drink) and smoking marihuana in the dive, cast about for a new thrill.

They decided upon a dice game, one wherein the loser would have to pay for a round of "sotol" and kill the first person to enter the place!

There was the sinister click of the dice upon the glass-stained table top. Then a shadow darkened the entrance of the dive, and a ragged peon slouched into the place. Before the stranger was aware of the danger, the loser in the weird game sprang across the room and plunged a knife into the newcomer's heart.

There is another story of sudden death one sun-splashed afternoon in the patio of a small crossroads cantina down in the desert, a half-day's ride south of Nogales, Mexico. The proprietor of the establishment had become enamored of a flashing-eyed, raven-haired senorita in a Nogales dance hall, and had brought her back to his place.

One afternoon they retired to the shade of the patio to smoke a marihuana cigarette each. As the servants related afterward, the couple seemed at peace with the world, lost in a reverie of pleasant dreams, apparently.

A scrawny black and dun-colored rooster, minus all his tail feathers, strolled across the patio. The comical appearance of the fowl sent the girl into a spasm of wild laughter. (The drug had made her see humor in the most trifling things.)

But not her companion. He

SAN FRANCISCO CHRONICLE

SUNDAY MORNING, SEPTEMBER 15, 1935.

UNDOUBTEDLY one of the prettiest girls on the Mexican frontier today is Senorita Mariana Baron. She is perhaps 18. Her hair is ck and curly; one "spit curl" always nes temptingly down on her cheek. The eyes dark and the lips are crimson, and the eat sombrero that Mariana wears is a gorous thing of braided felt and velvet and welry and gold.

Mariana is a good girl. The police are not aterested in her, officially; and the United tates Border Patrol officers behold her only with lugubrious sighs.

But—the entrancing little Spanish senorita. whose dances have made her the "toast of the border" and whose smile nowadays is the brightest thing along the Rio Grande, is a symbol of something more important.

She symbolizes the romantic fascination that the Latin land holds for Americans, for tourists who are out just for a sight-seeing good time, and for others whose intentions are more shady. Even a photograph of Mariana conjures in men's minds the click of castanets and musical twanging of guitars.

Unfortunately, the "pleasure resorts" of the Mexican border towns are not nearly so lovely and wholesome as Mariana's beauty suggests. She typifies what clean-minded tourists hope to see. What the officers of the law must cope with there too often is a very different thing.

ONE sleek-mannered devil from Mexico City, some years ago, went to New York and hired more than 20 pretty American girls to go to the Mexican border for jobs as "secretaries." Some he was to send on to Mexico City itself, where he reputedly had connections.

He had the connections, but they were as low down in the social and business scale as a human can sink. Quite frankly, he wanted the girls for his string of houses of ill fame.

He did not reveal this fact to them, naturally, when they were hired. He spoke only of foreign travel and good pay, of ... and bizarre pleasures in a romantic ...

He might have been guilty ... white slave coup in modern ... the smart Yankee girls ha... picious. A dullard henchman ... met these two girls at the ... Mexico City. When he tri... women often are bossed ... bucked.

The independent "gringo gals" bucked so definitely that they did their salacious escort bodily harm, got the local police into the mixup and wrecked the whole nasty plan.

HOWEVER, if that's the sort of thing one likes in the way of entertainment, one can cross the river at El Paso, Tex., for instance, and go unmolested to a red-light district, at night or in broad daylight. Juarez, city of 50,000 persons just across the Rio Grande, treats man's baser nature in more or less practical manner.

Out one mile from town is a special village, inhabited only by highly questionable girls and women and their equally questionable men. There a man can buy any conceivable sordid entertainment he may want.

If he wants to, he can indulge in the fantastic "pleasure" to be had from smoking marihuana, the sex cigaret (although these may be bought from smugglers in America, too).

If he prefers, he can dawdle in more leisurely manner with an opium pipe. for the clandestine Chinese arts have found profitable outlets here.

If he isn't careful, he is very likely in any case to lose his pocketbook, his health, his self-respect, and his very soul!

To a varying extent, that is a fair summary of vice conditions in all the Mexican towns near the border, and it unfortunately is from such unfair exhibits that Americans often judge the whole of Mexico.

"Judging Mexico from the border dives," says one officer for Uncle Sam, who operates here, "is like judgi... American city when ... first happe... its dump heaps ... stockya... s not put for...

... truth ... can be checked

THE hot spots of the Mexican border are not pointed to with pride by anybody. They exist as they may any other place—because there is a demand for them. This frontier region is still "wild," still collects its heavy quota of wanted men, of fugitives, of pitiable humans who can find no satisfaction in gentler, milder modes of living.

As places to see—and not to patronize—these "dives" do add to the interest of the better type tourists. Incidentally, more American tourists are crossing the international line into Mexico this year than ever before. New roads, new train services, new airlines and new advertising, all are catering to the American

Photo by Thomas D. McAvoy.

A red light section of Juarez in a special village a mile out of town, where highly questionable girls and women ply a sordid trade with visitors from the United States.

... in the American way. ... yond the hope of any-offi... in human flesh ... United States ... erican cities ... e line are

cludes that the dark-eyed senorita with a rose in her hair is likely to be more desirable than the blond he has been keeping in Chicago, whereas the blond is usually the more artistic of the two, carnally speaking.

"But the belief exists, and the border officers are always being called upon to get some influential traveler out of a jam. There is nothing we can do, usually, to help him."

ONE manufacturer from Houston, Tex. traveled to a border town for the avowed purpose of having a good time.

He had it! But when he limped into the El Paso police station asking for aid, he was minus his wallet, his watch, his automobile, his coat and even his shoes. The senoritas, he admitted, were not what they were cracked up to be.

Reversing the demand for Mexican girls, on the part of immoral Americans, is a constant demand for fair-skinned women in the Mexican dives that cater almost solely to Mexicans. Many of the "Spanish" girls in this stratum of society are negroid or Indian, in reality; wherefor a truly fair-skinned woman commands a money premium. It is never a good idea for an American girl to roam about the darker streets of a border Mexican town, unescorted.

but fearless girl—who ... Her more timid mother remaine... room in El Paso.

It happened, however, that ... ing into the United States cl... p. m., and when the young la... to return to her hotel, she cou... faced the necessity of spending ... the foreign border town!

"Many a girl would have ... about it," the officers tell. "... presence of mind. She kne... good hotel, where she would ... But just to make sure, sh... mother, and the elder lady c... night in Juarez, too. The ... did not close at 9 o'clock; ... traffic was halted at that ho...

ONE of the aspects of ... has given officers fre... months is counterfeit money...

When a man or wo... drunk on liquor and exc... ance, feel or weight of mo... Sly dealers in the border ... a fake $20 bill with shoc...

It is in Mexico, in ... counterfeiting American ... highest approach to perf... also that the effrontery ... reached a new height.

"I caught one Mexic... over the river with $20 ... said Sergeant Billy M... city detective bureau. ... with paper money, how...

An increasing use ... has been reported at ... track, where the frenz... lessness.

One entire battalio... stationed near Nogal... month's salary in A... back because they a... do more with it in ... border town.

Wherefor, you c... serted, when they ... was counterfeit.

(This is the seco... on "Two Thousan... third will follow ...

MEXICO CENTRE FOR DOPE RING

An international dope ring which used Mexico City as its base was the hard-hit loser when the Government seized $350,000 in

TREATY HITS ALIENS, DRUGS AND LIQUOR

...America"

Easy to Get, Because It Grows Like a Weed, Marihua... Gathers Addicts With Alarming Swiftness; Recent Shocking Crimes Have Focused National Attention on Its Menace

stared at the wretched rooster, then fixed his drug-dulled eyes upon the laughing dancer.

"No one can laugh at my poor rooster that way, not even you, cara mia," he said in a low, menace-laden voice.

But she broke forth in another wild peal of laughter. The next instant a gun flashed in the man's hand. He pressed the muzzle to her forehead, and sent six slugs into her head.

It is true that the weed does not instill everyone who smokes it with murderous intent. It inspires many to laughter, just as it did the girl in the patio. Others simply fall into a stupor, or dream heavenly dreams. In most cases addicts say that they are usually susceptible to hallucinations while under the weed's spell.

Effect Depends On Smoker's Mood

The nature of these hallucinations depends chiefly upon the mood the person is in at the time of the smoking. A moment's happening may seem to stretch over a period of weeks. An object across the room may seem to be miles away. Even one's sense of sound may become confused to the extent where a coin dropped on the floor may sound like the detonation of a cannon, marihauana addicts claim.

The price of marihuana ranges from three cigarettes for 25 cents to four for 50 cents. In most places in the west a tobacco tin of the leaves and buds (the favorite parts of the plant, although some smoke the stems) may be had from a peddler for 75 cents.

The most unusual manner employed by those cultivating the weed, or hemp, for illicit trade is to plant a patch of it in the center of a cornfield, thus keeping the plants hidden from view. Some plant alternate rows of corn and marihuana. Since the latter grows at about the same rate of speed as the corn the corn tops hide the tops of the illegal plant.

Care is taken to keep the tops of the marihuana plants cut off in cases where the corn does not grow as tall as the former.

Many such fields have been discovered lately throughout the country by local as well as federal authorities, who immediately burned the crops.

The fight to stamp out the weed is handicapped by the fact that there is no federal law controlling it, although 34 states and the territory of Hawaii regulate its sale, and 31 states and Hawaii make its possession illegal.

Progress in the war against the weed was reported recently by Commissioner H. J. Anslinger of the narcotics bureau at Washington, D. C. Anslinger said that numerous investigations and arrests in these cases had been reported to his office from widespread points reaching from the Pacific coast to New York state, and from the gulf to the Great Lakes.

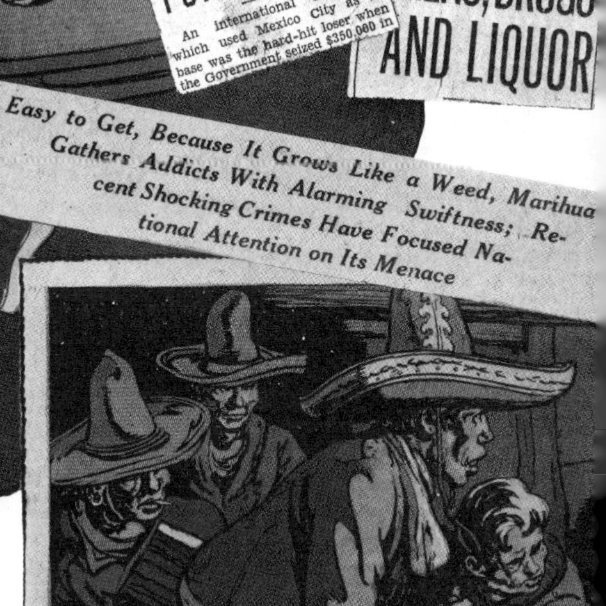

Smoking Marihuana, the Mexican "Loco Weed," Is a Form of Drug Addiction Responsible for Many Suicides and Murders in This Country and Is Especially Prevalent Among Young People. This Photo Is Especially Posed by Models to Show How a "Slick" (Marihuana Decoy) Waits to Contact Students Leaving School.

A Drug Menace

How a Number of Students Became Addicts of the Strangely Intoxicating Marijuana Weed

THE MARIJUANA
IS DRIED AND CURED

IT IS SMOKED IN THE FORM OF CIGARETTES PURE, OR MIXED WITH TOBACCO.

Sunday Magazine—St. Louis Post-Dispatch—April 8, 1934.

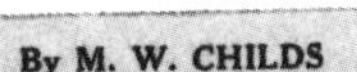

By M. W. CHILDS

Of the Post-Dispatch Sunday Magazine Staff

LAWRENCE, Kansas.

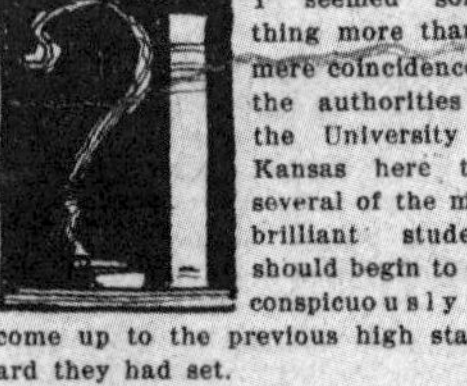

IT seemed something more than a mere coincidence to the authorities of the University of Kansas here that several of the most brilliant students should begin to fail conspicuously to come up to the previous high standard they had set.

Dean Henry Werner, advisor of men, made a few quiet inquiries. The result was a shock that Kansas has not yet recovered from, the beginning of a formal investigation into the development of a drug habit among a considerable number of students. It was shocking, it was incongruous, that this should have happened in the middle of the Middle-West where, by tradition at least, life is healthy and uncomplicated. But Dean Werner and Chancellor E. H. Lindley faced the unpleasant facts and went about it as quietly as possible to stop the practice.

One estimate placed the number of those who had used the drug at roughly between two and three hundred. Chancellor Lindley says frankly there is no way of determining the number with any accuracy whatsoever. The estimate may be too high or it may be too low.

The drug which the Kansas University students used was prepared from the plant known as Indian hemp, commonly called marijuana, and known also as peyote or pellote. There are two kinds of marijuana. One grows in this country, either wild or cultivated. Another type, which produces a stronger effect in the user, is in Mexico. It is said that the person who becomes an habitual user of American marijuana eventually resorts to the stronger Mexican type.

The American plant is often found wild in this part of the country along railroad tracks. It sometimes grows to six feet in height and puts out a yellow blossom. The tender, bud leaves are dried and cured and smoked in the form of cigarettes, either of pure marijuana or of marijuana mixed with tobacco. The smoker takes three deep inhales of the smoke into his lungs and gets an effect which lasts from one to two hours.

From the evidence that has been gathered here, by university authorities and by Will Johns, special investigator for Attorney-General Roland Boynton, various users are effected in various ways, depending possibly upon the person's physical condition or temperament. Some have described the effect as similar to that reputed to be induced by the drugs which are derivatives of opium—that is nirvana, a kind of floating, formless oblivion in which the individual is free from all care and distress. Others have said that they received a stimulation from the drug, as from alcohol, a sense of possessing great brilliance and wit. Again it is reported to have an aphrodisiacal effect. The user who takes alcohol while under the effect of marijuana is for the time being virtually insane. Throughout the Southwest, Mexican railway workers sometimes resort to this kind of jag, affording a serious problem for law-enforcement officials.

It is not definitely established that the drug is habit-forming. Some students have said that they used it two or three times and then gave it up without any further desires.

BUT while it may not be absolutely habit-forming, in the sense that opium derivatives are, the physical attack of marijuana upon the body is rapid and devastating. In the initial stages the skin turns a peculiar yellow color, the lips become discolored, dried and cracked. Soon the mouth is affected, the gums are inflamed and softened. Then the teeth are loosened and eventually, if the habit is persisted in, they fall out. Like all other drugs, marijuana also has a serious effect on the moral character of the individual, destroying his will power and reducing his stamina. To the university authorities perhaps the most shocking fact uncovered by the investigation was that several students of pharmacology, who knew very well the fearful effects of the drug, were among the users of marijuana.

"We regret the publicity that this has received," Chancellor Lindley said to the writer, "because it has inevitably put a stop to our investigation. The situation is not so serious as we at first thought it was. We believe we know how it first came into use and we hope that we shall be able to prevent its use entirely."

When he first learned of the use of marijuana in the university, Chancellor Lindley says he went to Governor Alf Landon at Topeka for help. Governor Landon heard his story and sent him to Attorney-General Boynton. Boynton assigned Investigator Johns, whose home is in Lawrence, to the case. For a month Johns studied this university drug ring without public notice. The facts, as he told them to the writer, are as follows:

Everything points to the introduction of the drug into the university by traveling jazz bands that came to play for large university or smaller fraternity and sorority dances. Johns says that he has learned that many members of jazz bands, not only in this section but generally throughout the country, often resort to marijuana or some other drug to obscure the monotony of their lives, the ceaseless thumping of jazz night after night.

"They take a few puffs off a marijuana cigarette if they are tired," Johns says. "It gives them a lift and they can go on playing even though they may be virtually paralyzed from the waist down, which is one of the effects that marijuana may have."

From traveling jazz bands the use is thought to have spread to local orchestras. A university rule forbade drinking of liquor at dances, and marijuana smoke was a substitute for orchestra members. According to one report, a university orchestra had its own marijuana patch from which it harvested a season's supply.

Once it had been introduced in this way, use of the drug is thought to have spread with some rapidity. A group of students would each put so much money into a pool and send one of their number down to Kansas City in Missouri for a supply of the weed. In the flop-house section of the city, only an hour away from Lawrence, Johns says that marijuana may be purchased almost as readily as illicit liquor before the repeal of prohibition. This was the Mexican marijuana. It was the custom to buy a tobacco tin of it. But it was also obtainable in cigarettes already rolled, the price being three for 50 cents.

The use spread within special groups where one or two persons became users of the drug. Thus, according to Johns, in one rooming house where there were 12 boys, 11 became users of marijuana, either intermittently or habitually. The twelfth boy, showing remarkable will-power and independence of mind, stayed clear of the habit and laughed at the others when they talked in a rambling or foolish way while under the influence.

Johns says that a few girls at the university also used the drug at one time or another. There were slang expressions on the campus for it—"Do you have any hay?"—"Do you have any of the weed?" While the use of marijuana had a quiet, insidious growth, by far the greater part of the student body knew nothing of it at all and went about the usual life of study and sport and "dates."

The investigation might have gone on to completion without attracting any attention—that was the hope of Chancellor Lindley—if it had not been for the suicide of one of the most brilliant students in the university.

at the University of Kansas
IT DESTROYS THE WILL POWER AND REDUCES THE STAMINA.
ONE UNIVERSITY ORCHESTRA HAD ITS OWN MARIJUANA PATCH.

The campus of the University of Kansas, at Lawrence.

At a Friendly After-School Eating Place the "Slick" and His Friend, the Dope Pedler, Smoke "Reefers" as the Drugged Cigarettes Are Called, and Inhalation of the Smoke Weakens Resistance on the Part of the Intended Victims. (Photo Posed by Models)

This young senior not only had maintained a very high average in his work but he had taken a prominent part in many activities on the campus. Chancellor Lindley says that to his knowledge this boy was not a user of marijuana.

BUT nevertheless the local paper, a few days after he had jumped into the Kaw River and had drowned himself, carried a report of the investigation with the reported fact that a number of the young man's friends had been questioned to determine whether they used the drug. This was enough to give the whole story wide currency.

So far the university has not taken drastic disciplinary action against any of those who have confessed to using marijuana. All of them have denied being habitual users and without exception they have professed to be ignorant of the source of supply. They have been cautioned as to the terrible effects of the drug if its use is persisted in and Dean Werner has put them on their honor to try to stop the practice in every way possible. It is this honor policy which the university follows in most disciplinary matters.

Investigator Johns turned up the startling fact that marijuana had even been introduced into certain high schools in Kansas. He found that it was available to and used by certain high school students in Topeka, Concordia and several other towns. Also ... in one Missouri

o. 503 Kansas City, Mo., Lodge No. 26, B. P. O. ELKS

IS TO TIFY THAT

1934-35

'DOPEY' DAN, EX-COLLEGIAN, TRAGIC EXAMPLE OF SLAVERY

Lost Arm 'Over There' and Took to 'Snow.'

By WINIFRED BLACK.

"Dopey" Dan is in jail.

They caught him the other night, selling "dope" down on the docks.

Strange fellow—"Dopey" Dan.

As white as a bleaching bone—thin as a man can be and still not be a skeleton—furitive, nervous, shivering—it is terrible to look at "Dopey" Dan.

It wouldn't be so bad if you'd never known him when he was different.

Eight years ago he was a handsome young fellow—up and coming—gay, and good-humored.

Gave Arm for Country.

He came back from "over there" with his regiment—but he couldn't march up Broadway with them.

They carried him ashore on a stretcher.

Gassed, shellshocked, one arm gone—but still gay and still ready to laugh.

He had a lot of friends and he didn't have to wait long to get a job. The minute he was able to ... up and out, he went to work, ...t there was something wrong— ... had a terrible pain in the chest, ...ke a knife in his lungs, and one ...y he met a "buddy" in a cheap restaurant and the "buddy" had a pain in his lungs, too, but he know ... little white powder that would ... through the day, he said.

WINIFRED BLACK.

"Dopey" Dan twisted his ragged old cap in his hands. "I know," he said; "I know." And he trembled like a little boy who is ill and frightened and alone and doesn't know what to do about it.

Strange Fellows.

"Strange fellows, these "dope" peddlers.

There's an old Chinese down Salinas Way in California. He has a laundry close by the high- ... and on Sunday and Satur-

Chancellor Lindley sought to check the supply of the drug at its source through the aid of the Federal authorities. But he found that the Federal narcotic law does not cover marijuana and that therefore Federal agents were more or less powerless to help him.

Kansas has felt the menace of marijuana to be so real that a year ago the Legislature amended the law regarding the use of the drug. It was formerly only a misdemeanor to peddle it or use it, punishable by a fine of $100 or 30 days in jail. The amendment made it a felony, with penalties of $1000 or a year in prison or both. The law as it now stands says "That it shall be unlawful for any person, firm or corporation or association to plant, cultivate, protect, harvest, cure, prepare, barter, sell, give away or use, or offer to sell, furnish or give away or to have in his or its possession" any of the drug.

SINCE the facts brought to light at the university, Attorney-General Boynton has moved to secure a Federal law or an amendment covering the use of the drug. The response he has received indicates that there will be considerable pressure in Washington for such a law. Senator Arthur Capper has said, "I shall be glad to introduce such an amendment and am asking the Commissioner of Narcotics to suggest its form and where it should be included in the statutes." Representative Harold McGugin has appealed to Attorney-General Cummings for some action.

"Of course, we don't want to put any college students in jail for using marijuana," says Attorney-General Boynton. "That was not the object of the law. We want to check the source of it.

"I have hoped that other and particularly neighboring states, Missouri and Oklahoma, would see the need of a law similar to ours. It is difficult or impossible as it is to keep it out of Kansas."

Kansas is not the only state where outbreaks of marijuana have occurred. In California some months ago in the course of an exposure of the use of narcotics, it was discovered that considerable plots of Mexican marijuana were raised and sold to smokers. In the East, too, it has at times arisen as a danger to the immature.

"I can imagine," says Chancellor Lindley, "some young people who might seek to experiment with this drug, out of bravado or a sense of adventure. But I cannot believe that it would take a very deep hold on them when they are made to understand the very serious consequences. In general I believe that the young people of today are too realistic for this. One sees that in the way in which they have accepted repeal of prohibition. That is, with a perfectly realistic view of the potentialities of alcohol. I cannot believe that the present experimentation is anything more than a passing phenomenon of very limited scope."

JANUARY 31, 1923

GANG RUNS MURDER-B

MARIHUANA MAKES FIENDS OF BOYS IN 30 DAYS: HASHEESH GOADS USERS TO BLOOD-LUST

Physicians Called On to Urge Harding Bid All Nations Meet to Throttle Dope At Its Source; United States Laws Too Lenient

"The Federal Government, operating under the Harrison Act, and the amending Jones-Miller bill, employs one hundred and seventy-three narcotic enforcement agents. For their year's labors Congress appropriates the sum of $750,000. The country is divided into thirteen districts under as many district chiefs, and their agents must cover the country. It is a feeble appropriation and a woefully light brigade."—Sidney Howard in current issue of Hearst's International.

By ANNIE LAURIE
ARTICLE X.

Strange old story—the story of Medusa.

It's come such a long way down to us from the bright old days when "all the men were brave—and all the women beautiful."

Medusa, the beautiful woman, half mortal and half goddess, with the hair that was not hair at all, but a coiling mass of hissing serpents.

And he who followed the soft wooing of Medusa's voice and looked upon the twining serpents that were her hair was turned to stone—and never knew again the delight of human communication with human kind.

Medusa—if we believed in her existence today—we should call her the patron saint of "dope."

Morphine, cocaine, heroin, hasheesh, marihuana—these are the snakes that curl about the head of this modern Medusa.

Where is the Perseus to look with unblinking eyes at this horror and put an end to it once and for all?

COMES BY TONS.

By the tons it is coming into this country—the deadly, dreadful poison that racks and tears not only the body, but the very heart and soul of every human being who once becomes a slave to it in any of its cruel and devastating forms.

Which is the worst of the five evils?

Who can say?

Marihuana is a short cut to the insane asylum.

Smoke marihuana cigarettes for a month and what was once your brain will be nothing but a storehouse of horrid specters.

Hasheesh makes a murderer who kills for the love of killing out of the mildest mannered man who ever laughed at the idea that any "habit" could ever get him.

Morphine shrivels the body to skin and bone, atrophies the will and turns a normal human being into the sick shadow of a man who will sell his own flesh and blood, no matter how young and tender, to the horrible bondage of the streets to get his drug.

Cocaine stifles reason, chokes all sense of responsibility and sets loose upon the world a dangerous "Frankenstein" with neither reason nor conscience to control him.

Heroin combines morphine and cocaine and is stronger and more deadly than either.

Every new "dope" slave means new money in his pocket.

Arrest such a man under the city ordinance in New York City and what can you do with him?

Try him for a misdemeanor—not for a crime—and send him to the island for a few days and make him pay a few dollars' fine, which means just about as much to him as one or two street car fares would mean to you or me.

PUNISH AS CRIME.

Change the city ordinances, make "dope" selling not a misdemeanor but a crime, and punish it as crimes are punished.

In some States the State laws make it about as serious to be caught selling "dope" as it is to be caught throwing a torn envelope into the street instead of into the corner trash box.

The Harrison narcotic law is a good law as Federal laws go, but it does not go far enough.

The Jones-Miller law, which was passed last May, is an excellent law. It makes the penalty for "dope" selling or "dope" buying or "dope" possession ten years in the penitentiary and $5,000 fine.

It gives the power to deport immediately any foreigner caught selling "dope," and it lays a fine upon any ship caught bringing "dope" into American ports.

How is the Jones-Miller law carried out?

As far as the fining of ships goes it is a farce.

The Nanking comes into the port of San Francisco voyage after voyage alive with "dope."

The Collector of the Port estimates the value of the "dope" seizure and fines the ship.

FINE NOT PAID.

The Secretary of the Treasury telegraphs from Washington and reduces the fine to less than one-fourth of the sum which has been set by the Collector of the Port, and not one penny of that even is collected.

This same story can be told of half a dozen ships which are known to the whole Pacific fleet to be "dope" carriers.

Whether this sort of thing goes on in other ports or not the records of those ports will tell. It certainly goes on in San Francisco and goes on week in and week out, month out and month in—and the law is a byword and a laughing stock from one end of

Rich Chinese Silk Merchant Arrested As Head of Huge State Dope Ring

Code Records Indicate Big Consignments Mailed Minor Peddlers in 22 Counties

SACRAMENTO, Jan. 30. — Tung, wealthy Chinese silk ma[...] facturer of this city, character[...] by the police as "king of the nor[...] ern California dope traffic," was [...] rested today by narcotic agents [...] the federal government and t[...] State Board of Pharmacy.

Tung is said to be the source [...] supply for minor narcotic peddle[...] in twenty-two counties of northe[...] California, [...] has morphin[...] between $20[...] in this city.

Code recei[...] been sendin[...] cotics from [...] section of C[...] ered at his [...] in a fashion[...]

Thousands [...] narcotics w[...] Chinese thr[...] mails, it is a[...] to state and [...] placed again[...] prosecuted b[...]

After evadi[...] for three ye[...] against him, [...] of narcotic [...] drove in an [...] chine to a p[...] where he wa[...] package of [...] girl. T. J. M[...] the State Bo[...] Stanley Hals[...] agent, who too[...] into custody, were obliged to [...] escape at the [...]

Conducting a [...] silk factory i[...] the city, Tung [...] traffic for yea[...] Inerney, and w[...] peddlers and a[...] Sacramento [...] Charlie," with property valued at thousands of dollars, he was able to maintain a luxurious home in a fashionable district of the city, where he lived with his wife, a white woman, and their three children.

INDICTMENT HITS OAKLAND DOCTOR IN BARKER DOPE CASE

(Continued from P[...]

with agents of the S[...] macy Board and the U[...] narcotic squad, and wa[...] that they did not think [...] plicated.

It is true that I se[...] number of my patien[...] Barker Sanitorium, but [...] because of certain facilities that were offered, of which a practicing physician might avail himself. I don't see how they got me into this.

Grand jury hearings that preceded today's indictments have extended over a period of two weeks.

WOMAN DETECTIVE.

The principal witness was Mrs. V. P. Merrill, employed as a detective by the State Board of Pharm-

MUSK HASHISH AND BLOOD

BY

HECTOR FRANCE

It was white and smooth, giving somewhat to the touch, soft and sweet to look at and of fine satiny texture, a young, healthy woman's belly.

LONDON AND PARIS

PRINTED FOR SUBSCRIBERS ONLY

MDCCCC

HENRY DE MONFREID

ÉDITIONS
BERNARD GRASSE
61, RUE DES SAINTS-PÈRES, 6
PARIS (VIe)

BOOKS BY VICTOR ROBINSON

AN ESSAY ON HASHEESH (1912)
An historical and pharmacological study of Cannabis Indica, including observations and experiments.

PATHFINDERS IN MEDICINE (1912)
Biographic sketches of Galen, Aretæus, Paracelsus, Servetus, Vesalius, Paré, Scheele, Cavendish, Hunter, Jenner, Laennec, Simpson, Semmelweis, Schleiden and Schwann, Darwin.

DON QUIXOTE OF PSYCHIATRY (1919)
A chapter in the history of American medicine, containing information not elsewhere available.

PIONEERS OF BIRTH CONTROL (1919)
The first volume dealing with the history of Neo-Malthusianism in England and America.

[...] HENLE (1921)
[...] the English language of [...] modern medicine.

AN ESSAY ON HASHEESH

E. H. RINGER
PUBLISHER
136 WEST 71 STREET
NEW YORK
1925

[...] Marijuana—they raise it [...] Mexico and make it into cig[...] ettes. You can buy Marijua[...] cigarettes in Galveston and [...] Dallas and in Fort Worth a[...] in New Orleans and in Bat[...] Rouge, Shreveport, La., and [...] San Diego, Cal., and Los Angel[...]

Marijuana is made from a s[...] ond cousin to the loco weed th[...] drives horses crazy out on t[...] southwestern ranges.

Once let a horse get a taste [...] loco weed and he is worthless [...] long as he lives.

Marijuana is a short cut to [...] insane asylum for men a[...] women. It is sure death f[...] children.

Hashish Trade Thrives In New York and Detroit.

In New York and in Detr[...] there is a trade in hashish—t[...] Indian hemp which drives m[...] mad.

Out in Detroit, where the ci[...] has grown like a huge mushroo[...] in the last two or three yea[...] there are rows of little bungalow[...] all built just a little while a[...] for hopeful young newlyweds.

The newlyweds are all go[...] from those bungalows now. T[...] factories have crowded up arou[...] them, and the once quiet litt[...] homes for quiet simple people a[...] crowded to the doors wi[...] swarthy strangers with gleamin[...] eyes and strange and subtle look[...]

These are Assyrians, Turk[...] Armenians, Lascars, and it is [...] these streets that hashish is sol[...]

Keep away from such a stre[...] at night, a hashish eater [...] smoker kills for the mere love [...] killing.

It is from that word—hashish—that we get our word assassin.

Who plants these things ar[...] where?

Who reaps and harvests th[...] baleful crop?

To what mysterious profit ar[...] to whose material benefit is th[...] earth polluted in this siniste[...] fashion?

Who raises the crops to beg[...] with? Who buys them and [...] whom high up in the seats of th[...] mighty do they sell the drug?

What's behind the cruelty [...] this whole blood-sucking, mone[...] getting, soul-wrecking traffic?

Who are those who prote[...] them?

How is this traffic ringed abou[...] with power

Into what dark and secret fas[...] ness does it hide when justice [...] on its trail

Why is it so hard to catch vi[...] lators of the narcotic law an[...] when they are caught, who, an[...] what is it that so often step[...] in to protect them

And how about those of ou[...] own people who manufacture the[...] narcotics and send them out ove[...] the world, not by the grain, no[...] by the ounce, not by the pound—but by the ton?

To be smuggled back again t[...] our own very door steps.

One big American factory sen[...] 4,000 ounces of narcotics to on[...] small eastern retail druggist—every month.

Into Whose Hands Does The Remainder Fall?

What did those who kept trac[...] of the shipments from that fac[...] tory think was going to happe[...] to those 4,000 ounces of deadl[...] drugs?

Three and one-half tons of nar[...] cotics will take care of the legit[...] mate practice of medicine for th[...] whole world for one year.

DECEMBER 13, 1932

parole to insure the permanency of cures and prevent addicts from becoming criminals.

WARNS OF HASHISH.

Dr. Lichtenstein pointed out he had been physician at Tombs prison eighteetn years, and had treated 60,000 addicts, 40 per cent of them between eighteen and twenty-two. Quoting figures indicating there were 1,000,000 addicts in the country in 1919, he expressed belief the number of addicts had increased.

He stressed a warning against marihuana, a form of hashish. Telling of its spread to New York, he declared certain jazz orchestra leaders smoke one or two "reefers" of the drug before performing.

Dr. Lichtenstein's suggestions [...] by Federal Attor[...] At[...] [...]ond [...] In[...] As-

SMOKE POT
SMOKE POT
2 PCS
WARNING FLAMMABLE
USE ONLY UNDER CLOSE ADULT SUPERVISION. FOR OUTDOOR USE ONLY. DO NOT HOLD IN HAND. LIGHT FUSE AND GET AWAY.

FEBRUARY 27, 1930

NEW DOPE LURE, MARIJUANA, HAS MANY VICTIMS

Called 'Silly Smoke,' Winifred Black Says, It Soon Becomes Murder Smoke in Cigarettes

By WINIFRED BLACK

SAN FRANCISCO, Feb. 26.—So it's the old, old, story over again. A woman of position and reputation sinking into the mire of dope slavery.

This time the scene of the tragedy is Oakland, California.

A year or so ago the very same thing happened in New England.

And everybody in Chicago of any consequence knew the two highly educated clubwomen who went through the same hideous torment—and died in disgrace.

SOME OF ITS VICTIMS.

One of the best know actresses in the world, one of the most popular story writers in America, the young wife of a very popular and successful musician, one of the most brilliant lawyers in California, a lawyer close to the top of the profession in Chicago—oh, it doesn't stay down in the slums, this dope.

"Silly smoke."

What do you know about "Silly Smoke?"

Nothing at all!

I wouldn't be too sure about that.

How about that seventeen-year-old boy that was so good-natured and easy going, and full of boyish tricks, and fun a year ago? What's turning him so sullen and so irritable and ill-natured all of a sudden?

MARIJUANA SMOKERS.

How about that girl, the pretty little girl you are all so fond of? The color is going from her cheeks, her eyes look strange. She forgets things, she's "too tired" to go dancing, and she's always smoking.

The boy is also smoking, too—cigarettes!

Yes, but what kind of cigarettes?

They make Marijuana into cigarettes nowadays, didn't you know that?

Oh, yes, plenty of Marijuana cigarettes on the market. They call them "Silly Smokes," when they sell them.

Marijuana is really hasheesh—an American hasheesh.

In India and in the Malay Peninsula they call hasheesh the "Murder Drug," and we are beginning to hear the American Hasheesh, Marijuana, called "murder smoke" here in police circles.

The police know all about murder smoke.

RAISED IN CALIFORNIA.

Whenever a particularly cruel crime is committed and the criminal gets away the police start hunting for the "murder smoke" users.

They raise marijuana up on some of the delta farms right here in California.

Marijuana is sometimes brewed into a tea, sometimes it is snuffed from the crown of the thumb like cocaine; more often these days it is rolled into a cigarette.

The first "murder smoke" cigarette brings strangs and weirdly beautiful dreams; but after the first few cigarettes it takes more and more smoking to produce the dream, and suddenly the tortured nerves give way and the "murder smoker" must cut and stab and beat and shoot to satisfy the tortured hunger created by the drug.

"Silly smoke"—how much do you know about it?

And how do you know when it is going to turn into "murder smoke?"

Queen of Sweden Shows Improvement

7, 1935

Peddlers' Dope
ROWS IN BACK YARD

aining enough of the narcotic weed to make cigarettes for unfortu- dope users, a field of can marijuana was de- ed by police yesterday e back yard of a desert- rooklyn house.

pe peddlers would have d a retail value of $5,000 on contents of the field of vio- y narcotic weeds, police said. nbers of an emergency squad royed it completely. he field evidently had been vated with care, in the rear 9 Hazel st., in the Brownsville n. A passerby, Samuel Le- itz, 1580 Pitkin ave., noticed strange growth and notified police.

OLICE SEARCH

The weed was identified by City hemist Edward Kelly as that om which the Mexican dope garettes are made. Captain Jos- ph Mooney, of the Narcotic quad, supervised the destruction f the field.

A wide circulation of marijuana cigarettes in the Brownsvill recently alarmed caused a widesp dope sellers.

A 'BULLY' GOES TO JAIL

Called a "bully" Harris in West day, a burl found guil for beati of the The dant 94th June office severe man's newsp Boar

THE BEE'S SUPERIOR CALIFORNIA NEWS — Tuesday, September 11, 1934

Destroying Marijuana Supply

Undersheriff Forrest Monroe of Woodland and two aides are seen in the picture destroying a field of Indian hemp plants destined for use as marijuana, a narcotic. Following a raid on the place by Monroe, Deputy Sheriff Walter Leinberger of Broderick and Detective Sergeant Ed J. Cox and Detective W. A. Thomas of Sacramento, guards were stationed on the place and the plants chopped down. They will be burned when sufficiently dry. Julio Pena and Joseph Soldi, arrested in Sacramento by Officers Cox and Thomas are being held pending their arraignment before justice of the Peace W. H. Scott in Davis.

—Photo by J. L. Hearn, Jr., Bee's Davis Correspondent.

Placer Hunter Is Killed By Falling

TRIAL OF YUBA

Yolo U... Sheriff Retur...

WINERY AT ELK GR... S...

Delay Is Granted In Arraignment Of

DOPE FOUND GROWING IN BROOKLYN GARDEN

Sergeant Bernard Boylan (left) and Capt. Joseph Mooney, of the police Narcotic Squad, inspect marajuana they destroyed after it was found growing in the yard of a vacant Brooklyn house.

HURSDAY, OCTOBER 18, 1934 — CLASSIFIED AD PHONE, DRydock 4-8000 — 23

Brooklyn's Narcotic Farm
Marajuana Field

BURNING FIELD OF DOPE PERILS CITY OFFICIALS

Geoghan and Others Escape in Blast of Gasoline at Brooklyn 'Marajuana Patch' Fire

Flames leaping suddenly from gasoline-soaked loco weeds imperiled District Attorney Geoghan and other officials of Brooklyn last night when he applied the torch to the "marajuana patch" found in that borough.

Accompanied by other officials and reporters, Geoghan went to the field of loco weeds (cannabis indica), a narcotic, in a block bounded by Washington, Adams, Nassau and Concord sts., discovered by police.

SUDDEN BLAST.

Since the arrest of Robert Arnold, 29, and Louis Kelly, 26, charged with growing, possessing and selling a narcotic, the weeds had been uprooted and prepared for the fire.

First efforts to fire the weeds failed, and it was decided to spray gasoline over them. As the District Attorney applied a burning paper to the pile there was a sudden blast and a sheet of flame leaped toward the group. All jumped to safety. The field was burned without further mishap.

HELD WITHOUT BAIL.

Arnold and Kelley, who both gave their address as 17 Concord st., Brooklyn, were held without bail for hearing Oct. 25 by Magistrate Rudich in Downtown Court yesterday.

Detectives Thomas Mason and Arthur McCloskey posed as rookies from Governors Island for four weeks in their search for the marajuana field.

The Mexican narcotic, which has become increasingly popular among addicts and thrill-seekers in the metropolitan area is sold in cigarette form. Hawkers charge from 50 cents to $1 for eight.

AMAZING DISCOVERY NEAR BRIDGE

POLICE RAID

CRAFTY DETECTIVE WORK; 2 ARRESTS

Hidden by buildings in Brooklyn's "jungle," almost a stone's throw from Brooklyn Bridge, a whole flourishing field of Cannabus Indica, the weed from which is made marajuana, Mexican narcotic, was discovered by detectives yesterday.

The discovery followed a raid on an apartment at 17 Concord st., where two men were arrested. The raid, conducted by the police narcotic squad, came as a result of four weeks of clever detective work by police with the co-operation of the U. S. Army.

Two members of the 16th Infantry were taken into custody by military authorities at the same time.

The Cannabus Indica field, 125 by 100 feet, is in the center of a group of ramshackle buildings on the block bounded by Washington, Nassau, Adams and Concord sts.

Largest Area

Police said it is the largest cultivated area of the weed found in the East in recent years. They believe it has been one of the big local sources of the narcotic from which marajuana cigarettes are made.

In recent months marajuana has been for sale almost openly in Harlem and Greenwich Village, and has been found among soldiers on Governors Island.

The men arrested in Brooklyn on charges of possessing and selling the narcotic said they were Robert Arnold, 29, alias Nicholas Mack, and Louis Kelly, 26.

Back of the raid is a story of a patient investigation. When officials at Governors Island noticed that many soldiers showed the symptoms of having smoked marajuana, they communicated with the War Department. New York police were asked to help.

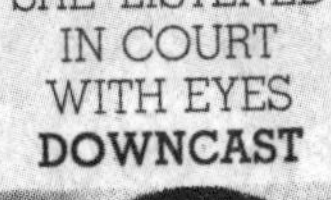

SHE LISTENED IN COURT WITH EYES DOWNCAST

REMEMBER... sive Marquita ... her purported ... N. Y. Ame...

'I FIR...

LOPEZ ...

Alleged S... Accus...

Marquita Lo... yesterday with... and her should... listened to wo... have told po... murder. of ... Costa.

For the firs... on trial charg... she failed to ... person on th...

Marijuana Spray Spoils Dope Ring's $5,000,000 Dream

200 Workmen, with Chemicals, Cover Areas Where 1936 Seizures Were Made

WEEDS GO

Behing the commonplace activities of 200 Works Progress Administration workers who, to all outward purposes, are only uprooting ragweed for relief of hayfever sufferers, the New York American yesterday uncovered a carefully devised plan by the Federal narcotics bureau and city officials to thwrat a $5,000,000 marijuana harvest on borough lots by an organized ring of dope peddlers.

While they work with grub hooks and spraying tanks in weed-choked lots, the gangs of workmen are after bigger plan-game than ragweed, golden rod and those grasses whose noxious pollen play havoc with their sneezing victims.

DANGEROUS DRUG.

The real objective is the habit-forming marijuana, grown here on deserted patches of ground by the underworld, to be harvested in early August and then ground up for "reefers"—marijuana addicts' cigarettes, which are peddled for prices ranging from 25 cents to a half-dollar apiece.

That this is no idle pursuit is emphasized by figures obtained yesterday from William Paxton, local superintendent of operations. He told The American that last year in Brooklyn they found 941,420 pounds of the drug, which, it is said, induces many smokers to commit violent sex crimes.

At present values in the illegal drug market, marijuana commands the high price of $60 per pound. If this year's yield in Brooklyn equals last year's seizure, the total will thus go far beyond the $5,000,000 mark.

WEEDS SCREEN DOPE.

Wide open spaces in the outlying parts of Brooklyn are chosen by the marijuana planters as their best fields for operation. Here, under cover of darkness, they do their planting and harvesting. Outer fringes of ordinary weeds are left standing to act as a ... for the ...

Hashish Hideouts Doomed

Chemical Shower Nip Drug Supply

BROOKLYN, SUNDAY, JUNE 6, 1937

SALINE SPRAYS KILL LURKING MARIJUANA
WPA Men Destroy Makin's For Dope Addicts' 'Reefer' Butts as They Start Out to Destroy Every Weed Patch in Borough

N. Y. American Staff Photo.

Relief Chiseler Must Pay Back

Freeport Man, Who Listed 6 Dependents, Discovered

Diphtheria Deaths Stir Rice

Lack of Immunization Blamed for Fatalities

'Girls Take Dope to Be Fashionable'

Proper Treatment Will Bring Cure

Let us clear up the marihuana situation. Amend the Harrison Act to include this drug. This pernicious weed is a stimulant to assault. Let us give Anslinger more men and money to carry on. If this is impossible, then let all the law-enforcing agencies act in concert with the Federal authorities.

The District Attorney of New York County is willing. The city's police department at all times has cooperated.

Let us instruct the adolescent boy and girl about the evils of addiction.

Under proper conditions and with proper treatment, narcotic addiction can be cured.

Discourage, drive out the pedlar.

Revoke the license of the dope-dispensing doctor.

Addiction is responsible for at least 15 per cent of crime. Remove this cause and you will not only decrease crime but also prevent the creation of innumerable mental cripples.

Police revealed at the same time they are preparing for an extensive campaign against Autumn sale of marijuana. This weed is grown in vacant lots on outskirts of the city and usually harvested at night. It is rolled into cigarettes or brewed as tea for addicts. Captain John J. Mooney, of the New York Narcotics Bureau, said his department has two tons of confiscated weed awaiting destruction.

It is particularly alarming that in New York State little or nothing is being done, outside of Greater New York, to stop the sale and use of insanity-breeding marihuana.

There is as yet NO FEDERAL LEGISLATION against this poisonous weed, of which school children are among the victims.

The Narcotic Bureau of the New York City Police Department, with the co-operation of the City Health Department, has accomplished major results. The destruction of 208 tons of marihuana in 1936 was entirely an achievement of Greater New York City.

HARRY ANSLINGER

VICTIM'S STORY

Revelations of Narcotic World

How girls, in order to be "fashionable," are led to take up the dope habit and the results of such addiction, were graphically detailed here yesterday by Shirley Urkov, 18, beautiful daughter of a wealthy Chicago doctor.

The girl was arrested in a raid on an apartment at 60 W. 68th st., and will appear in West Side Court tomorrow on a charge of possessing narcotics.

Her boarding-school girl friend, Miss Muriel Franklin, niece and ward of a wealthy Chicago matron, attempted to end her life during the raid by stabbing herself with a paring knife. Thomas Murelle, said to be the husband of Miss Franklin, also was arrested.

First Experience

Miss Urkov, known on the stage as Libby Lorraine, is step-daughter of Barney Balaban, Chicago's movie house magnate.

The girl told of attending the fashionable boarding schools of Chicago. She said:

"Nearly two years ago I met some musicians and they introduced me to Marihuana cigarettes. They gave me quite a jag. But I didn't know at the time they contained dope. I finally told my father for he is a doctor. He decided I was in bad company."

The girl then told of taking theatrical training, appearing in Chicago at the Terminal Theatre and then coming here to seek work. She lived at the St. Moritz and at the Ansonia, she said, and mingled with the theatrical crowd. But she declared she could not make the proper connections and so last April returned to Chicago.

'Very Fashionable'

"Back in Chicago I picked up the old crowd again. My father didn't approve of them and sent me to a Stony Lodge Sanitarium at Ossining, N. Y., to be treated. I spent several months there and felt fine and then went back to Chicago again. There I kept hearing about dope all over the city. I was told it was fashionable and I was assured that numbers of my friends, nice girls, were strong for the stuff. I saw these friends and they looked very badly. It disheartened me to see how dope could get them down while I was trying to climb up."

Miss Urkov then told of coming back here a few months ago, living quietly and seeing practically no one. She told of her girl friend. Muriel, calling her one day on the telephone and telling her that she had married Murrelle. She added:

"Muriel said she was off dope. She said she had an extra room in her apartment to rent and I was lonely, so I moved in. I saw no signs of dope around the apartment, however, although they say they found heroin, morphine and opium during the raid."

SHE'LL TELL ALL IN FRENCH SCANDAL

Madame Stavisky, now ready to talk.

Widow to Tell on Paris Police

PARIS, Jan. 2 (AP).—Her readiness to reveal "political and police maneuvers" in connection with the Stavisky scandal, which has shaken France for the last year, were expressed by Madame Arlette Simon Stavisky today in a letter to the president of the Chamber of Deputies' investigating committee.

This is the first time the widow of Serge "Handsome Alex" Stavisky has expressed willingness to talk. Hitherto she has insisted she was not familiar with the details of her husband's business affairs, matters which cost investors in the Bayonne Municipal Pawnshop and other Stavisky enterprises millions of francs.

Crusade Against Marihuana

A NATIONWIDE crusade of American women against the menace of marihuana smoking has been launched by the Women's National Exposition of Arts and Industries in New York City.

H. J. Anslinger, head of the Federal Narcotics Bureau, explained to the group the urgent necessity of NATIONAL ACTION.

Declaring that marihuana smoking is "taking our youth like wildfire," Mr. Anslinger said:

"If the hideous monster Frankenstein came face to face with the monster marihuana he would drop dead of fright."

This is not overstatement. Users of the marihuana weed are committing a large percentage of the atrocious crimes blotting the daily picture of American life.

It is reducing thousands of boys to CRIMINAL INSANITY.

And ONLY TWO STATES have effective laws to protect their people against it.

The marihuana weed, according to Mr. Anslinger, is grown, sold and USED in every State in the Union.

He charges, and rightly, that this is not a responsibility of one State, but OF ALL—and of the Federal Government.

American women, aroused to this DANGER, will GET ACTION.

In New York State organized groups of women are GETTING ACTION by demanding enactment of the McNaboe bill creating a State Narcotics Bureau. That Bureau would replace the existing one-man Narcotics Division, which is powerless to cope with the fact that eighty per cent of New York's criminals are narcotic addicts.

Conciliation, Not Strife

Editorial Page—APRIL 6, 1937

U. S. Ban Sought On Marihuana

Chicago Civic Leaders Commend Hearst for Fight on Dope

Special to the New York American.

CHICAGO, Feb. 20.—Chicago moved to end the deadly narcotic menace of marihuana cigarettes today when a group of judges, lawyers and civic leaders agreed to sponsor Federal legislation outlawing the weed.

Spurred by reports from Miss Ethel Schiller, sociologist of Women's Court, who said 60 per cent of all juvenile delinquents are victims of the drug, the conference agreed to finance an extensive anti-narcotic educational campaign.

Resolutions commending William Randolph Hearst and the Hearst newspapers "for pioneering the national fight against dope" were adopted unanimously.

The meeting was called by Irving S. Roth, president of the Lawyers Legislative League of America.

Declaring Sen. Minton of Indiana has indicated he will introduce in Congress an anti-marihuana bill to be prepared by the league, Secretary Thomas J. McCormick added:

"Marihuana is not covered by present Federal laws. It is often referred to as the 'kid catcher' because of its convenient form in cigarettes and its wide sale by illicit peddlers around high schools.

"Yet, when police seize the fiends who prey upon youth with this deadly drug, their only weapon is a city ordinance with insignificant penalties."

'Cut-de-Grass' Does Bad Job

Beer Dispenser's License Imperiled

An allegedly intoxicated man, ...lified only as "Cut-de-

The Pot Begins To Simmer

The Narcotic Invasion Of America

AMERICANS will pay close attention to the charge by the Council of International Affairs at Nanking that the Japanese concession in Tientsin is world headquarters for the narcotic industry.

Narcotics are reaching the United States in alarming volume.

We are deeply interested in their SOURCE.

America is only indirectly concerned in the Council's belief that "narc... ...eing employed by Japan as an i... ...nal policy designed to ... ...hinese race."

But A... ...in the further charge that ... ...gaged chiefly in exportin... ...States and that:

"The ... ...oney market, and ha... ...n perfect its lines to ...

The Coun...

"This i... ...tentacles throughout th... ...direct connections with the ... rings in Europe and the Americas."

2. Indentification of Marihuana in Cigarettes:

a. Attach a suspected cigarette to a small test tube, or cylinder, with an ordinary paper clip, and with the aid of a small funnel pour 5 c.c. (1 thimbleful) of petroleum ether into one end of the cigarette, so that the fluid flows through the interior of the cigarette, extracting the filler on its way.

b. Pour about half of this extract into a small white porcelain dish, and evaporate; add to the evaporated portion a few drops of Solution No. 1 (1 per cent KOH in alcohol). The residue in the dish should become purple in a minute or so, the color deepens gradually on standing.

* * *

TO THE extent these charges are true, the effect is to "weaken and debauch" not the Chinese but the AMERICAN race.

The evidence that they are LARGELY TRUE contained in this recent statement in the *Journal the American Medical Association:*

"The problems of greatest menace in the United States seem to be the rise in use of Indian hemp [marihuana] with inadequate control laws, and the oversupply of narcotic drugs available in the Far East which threatens to INUNDATE THE WESTERN WORLD."

—JUNE 29, 1934

Protect Youth Against Dope

THE Hearst newspapers, which have crusaded unceasingly against the NARCOTIC EVIL in all its vicious forms, are gratified to know that Narcotic Education Week is centering attention upon the MARIHUANA PROBLEM.

Legal authorities, while increasingly vigilant against other habit-forming drugs, have permitted the marihuana cigarette to become a NATIONAL MENACE.

One of the consequences, according to Ethel Schiller, sociologist of the Chicago Women's Court, is that SIXTY PER CENT of all juvenile delinquents are victims of the drug.

* * *

ADMIRAL RICHMOND P. HOBSON, President of the World Narcotic Defense Association, says:

"The warfare on the dope ring has made much progress. At the same time the enemy has developed a very dangerous new field, the exploitation of marihuana cigarettes, which is especially menacing and destructive for our youth."

The marihuana cigarette is one of the most INSIDIOUS of all forms of dope, largely because of the failure of the public to understand its fatal qualities.

The nation is almost defenseless against it, having no Federal laws to cope with it and virtually no organized campaign for combatting it.

The result is tragic.

High school boys and girls buy the destructive weed without knowledge of its capacity for harm, and conscienceless dealers sell it with impunity.

* * *

THIS is a NATIONAL PROBLEM, and it must have national attention.

The fatal marihuana cigarette must be recognized as a DEADLY DRUG and American children must be PROTECTED AGAINST IT.

The New Narcotic Menace

AS THE State Department's representative at the Opium Advisory Committee's sessions Stuart J. Fuller is a recognized expert on the international narcotics problem.

Both Government and the public should therefore receive with alarm the warnings with which Mr. Fuller returned this ... than Geneva. He said:

... of forged government certificates Honment and the various States ... sufficient morphine in the last own defenses against smuggled dope from whatever source ... legitimate needs for a ... to the

Also, Mr. Fuller reminds us, some drastic action is needed at home.

This country, he reports, is now producing more marihuana, or Mexican hasheesh, than any other area in the world.

Obviously, besides guarding our own shores against foreign narcotics, it is an imperative duty to ourselves and the world that we prevent America from becoming a depot of soul-destroying, habit-forming drugs.

THE PROHIBITION POLL

IF THE first 320,000 votes in the Literary Digest's poll may be taken as significant, then the dry law is decidedly unpopular.

Over 270,000 want to kill it, and only 51,285 wish to see it enforced. The tally has just begun, but 85 per cent of the voters have registered a swift and violent protest against the present law. To realize the growing distrust in this law we have only to recall that in the 1928 poll those who wanted repeal were in the minority of 40 per cent.

Dry sentiment was overwhelmed in the previously arid States of North Carolina, Georgia and Virginia. Indiana, touchstone of the Prohibitionists, now urges repeal by the majority of 64 per cent.

Though the Middle West, stronghold of the Drys, has hardly responded, Indiana's change indicates that something is in the air that will greatly worry the commissars of the Dry League. And the last thing the politicians expected was that the leading bone-dry States south of Dixie would join the moist parade of Massachusetts, Illinois, New York and Connecticut.

THE MARIHUANA TAX ACT OF 1937

Public—No. 238—75th Congress
Chapter 553—1st Session; H. R. 6906

AN ACT

To impose an occupational excise tax upon certain dealers in marihuana, to impose a transfer tax upon certain dealings in marihuana, and to safeguard the revenue therefrom by registry and recording.

Be it enacted by the Senate and House of Representatives of the United States of America in Congress assembled, That when used in this Act—

...

(b) The term "marihuana" means all parts of the plant *Cannabis sativa L.*, whether growing or not; the seed thereof; the resin extracted from any part of such plant; and every compound, manufacture, salt, derivative, mixture, or preparation of such plant, its seeds, or resin; but shall not include the mature stalks of such plant, fiber produced from such stalks, oil or cake made from the seeds of such plant, any other compound, manufacture, salt, derivative, mixture, or preparation of such mature stalks (except the resin extracted therefrom), fiber, oil, or cake, or the sterilized seed of such plant which is incapable of germination.

(c) The term "producer" means any person who (1) plants, cultivates, or in any way facilitates the ...

SEC. 9. (a) Any marihuana which has been imported, manufactured, compounded, transferred, or produced in violation of any of the provisions of this Act shall be subject to seizure and forfeiture and, except as inconsistent with the provisions of this Act, all the provisions of internal-revenue laws relating to searches, seizures, and forfeitures are extended to include marihuana.

(b) Any marihuana which may be seized by the United States Government from any person or persons charged with any violation of this Act shall upon conviction of the person or persons from whom seized be confiscated by and forfeited to the United States.

(c) Any marihuana seized or coming into the possession of the United States in the enforcement of this Act, the owner or owners of which are unknown, shall be confiscated by and forfeited to the United States.

(d) The Secretary is hereby directed to destroy any marihuana confiscated by and forfeited to the United States under this section or to deliver such marihuana to any department, bureau, or other agency of the United States Government, upon proper application therefor under such regulations as may be prescribed by the Secretary.

SEC. 10. (a) Every person liable to any tax imposed by this Act shall keep such books and records, render under oath such statements, make such returns, and comply with such ...

(1) To a transfer of marihuana to a patient by a physician, dentist, veterinary surgeon, or other practitioner registered under Section 2, in the course of his professional practice only: *Provided*, That such ...

(2) To a transfer of marihuana, made in good faith by a dealer to a consumer under and in pursuance of a written prescription issued by a physician, dentist, veterinary surgeon, or other practitioner registered under ...

(3) To the sale, exportation, shipment, or delivery of marihuana by any person within the United States, any Territory, the District of Columbia, or any of the insular possessions of the United States, to any person in any foreign country regulating the entry of marihuana, if such sale, shipment, or delivery of marihuana is made in accordance with such regulations for importation into such foreign country ...

(4) To a transfer of marihuana to any officer or employee of the United States Government or of any State, Territorial District, county, or municipal or insular government lawfully engaged in making purchases thereof for the various departments of the Army and Navy, the Public Health Service, and for Government, State, Territorial, District, county, or municipal or insular hospitals or prisons.

(5) To a transfer of any seeds of the plant *Cannabis sativa L.* to an...

The Literary Digest

NEW YORK — MAY 16, 1936

RISING TIDE OF NARCOTICS OVER WORLD

Smugglers Baffle Officials After Curb Placed by Geneva

... flow of poppy "mud" (opium) from China, Turkey, and Yugo-slavia increased; "snow" (cocain) from the coca plants of Java, Peru, and Bolivia sifted over the world; "reefers" (cigarettes of marihuana made from hemp) bobbed up to supply the craving of their 2,000,000 users, the hemp drawn from half the States of the Union.

The mad hunger of ten million "junkers"—"snowbirds," "hopheads," and "muggles"—seemed stronger than all the combined forces of ...

Heavy Confessions—Spurred on by ... "whiskers" (Federal agents) seized 21,000 antiasthma cigarettes made of crushed poppy-heads, took 52,000 shots of morphin from a ship in Seattle Harbor, confiscated 1,000,000 doses of cocain.

Typical of the legal difficulties in the peculiarly American war against marihuana is the case of a Florida youth who became a hopeless addict after a chance peddler had supplied him with a "simple" cigarette.

One night he became obsessed with the idea that people were trying to cut off his arms and legs. Seizing an ax, he killed his father, mother, two brothers, and a sister as they slept.

In only thirty-three States is there a law against the sale of narcotics. Since there is no national statute, the Federal ...

SOWING AND REAPING

"For they have sown the wind; they shall reap the whirlwind."—Hosea 8:7.
"The fathers have eaten a sour grape, and the children's teeth are set on edge."—Jeremiah 31:29.
"Whatsoever a man soweth, that shall he also reap."—Galatians 6:7.

Assassin of Youth! Marihuana

"REEFERS" or "MUGGLES"

It is exceedingly difficult for the forces of righteousness to keep up with the enemies of God and humanity. Scarcely is one evil thing calculated to ruin and curse our young people, brought out into the light, so that it can be fought in the open, before another undercover method of corruption is in vogue. The curse of Indian hemp or marihuana is one of Satan's latest methods of attack. It is well that teachers and ministers should be advised concerning it. In ... recent book by Robert James Devine this has been ... singly and with full proof of the wide... young people to take up its pernici... be forearmed." There ...

MARIHUANA

AMERICA'S NEW DRUG PROBLEM

A Sociologic Question with Its Basic Explanation Dependent on Biologic and Medical Principles

BY

ROBERT P. WALTON

...SOR OF PHARMACOLOGY, SCHOOL OF MEDICINE
UNIVERSITY OF MISSISSIPPI

35) College. White, some Negroes and Latin-Americans. This college is located near one of the famous "tea-pads" of Harlem. Many of the students pass the house regularly. Continued observation did not reveal any student attendance.

36) Junior High School. Negro. Most of the boys of this school were familiar with the subject of marihuana. The pupi... school are incessant smokers of ordinary cigaret... able to obtain any information which would indi... "reefers." Some students were observed entering ... there was a "tea-pad," but we never found an... of this "tea-pad" to be pupils of the school. ... the school stated that during the previous te... picions regarding the use of marihuana.

CONCLUSIONS

From the foregoing study the following conclusions are drawn:

1. Marihuana is used extensively in the Borough of Manhattan but the problem is not as acute as it is reported to be in other sections of the United States.
2. The introduction ...
3. The cost of marihuana is low and therefore within the purchasing power of most persons.
4. The distribution and use of marihuana is centered in Harlem.
5. The majority of marihuana smokers are Negroes and Latin-Americans.
6. The consensus among marihuana smokers is that the use of the drug creates a definite feeling of adequacy.
7. The practice of smoking marihuana does not lead to addiction in the medical sense of the word.
8. The sale and distribution of marihuana is not under the control of any single organized group.
9. The use of marihuana does not lead to morphine or heroin or cocaine addiction and no effort is made to create a market for these narcotics by stimulating the practice of marihuana smoking.
10. Marihuana is not the determining factor in the commission of major crimes.
11. Marihuana smoking is not widespread among school children.
12. Juvenile delinquency is not associated with the practice of smoking marihuana.
13. The publicity concerning the catastrophic effects of marihuana ... New York City is unfounded.

... September 13, 1938, The New York Academy of Me... was informed of Mayor LaGuardia's concern about the mari... problem and of his desire "that some impartial body such a... New York Academy of Medicine make a survey of existing k... edge on this subject and carry out any observations requir... determine the pertinent facts regarding this form of drug addi... and the necessity for its control." The Mayor's request was ref... to the Committee on Public Health Relations of the Acad... which Committee on October 17, 1938 authorized the appoint... of a special subcommittee to study the Mayor's ...

... undertaking would have been impossible w... help and cooperation of Dr. Peter F. Amoroso, of the D... of Correction, who, aside from his services as a mem... Committee, was responsible for arrangements for vol... among the prisoners at the Riker's Island Penitentiary. ... due also to the entire medical staff of the Riker's Island H... their assistance in the narcotic addiction study.

The Subcommittee therefore came to the conclusion th... of the possibility that marihuana smoking might consti... portant social problem, it was time that a study of i... made based upon well-established evidence, and prepa... ne of methods of procedure for the study of the proble... ended that such a study should be divided into two ... logical study dealing with the extent of marihu... and what relation there is between its use and cri... ocial acts; and (2) a clinical study to determine by ... olled experiments the physiological and psycholog... arihuana on different types of persons; the question... causes physical or mental ...

... the City of New York, it is my duty to foresee a... revent the development of hazards to the heal... fare of our citizens. When rumors were recen... ning the smoking of marihuana by large segme... ... and even by school children, I sought adv... from The New York Academy of Medicine, as is my custom w... confronted with problems of medical import. On the Academ... recommendation I appointed a special committee to make a thorou... sociological and scientific investigation, and secured funds fr... three Foundations with which to finance these studies.

My own interest in marihuana goes back many years, to the t... when I was a member of the House of Representatives and, in ... capacity, heard of the use of marihuana by soldiers stationed ... Panama. I was impressed at that time with the report of an A... Board of Inquiry which emphasized the relative harmlessness of ... drug and the fact that it played a very little role, if any, in prob... ... in the Canal Zone.

LaGuardia Demands Congress Probe Dope

By KENNETH CLARK.

WASHINGTON, Feb. 3.

A MOVEMENT to strike a death blow at the illicit dope traffic, which is taking a toll of thousands of lives and millions of dollars annually, was started today by Representative La Guardia, Republican of New York.

He announced he would introduce in the House tomorrow a joint resolution calling for a sweeping investigation of the narcotic menace.

Under La Guardia's plan the inquiry would be conducted by two Senators and three members of the House. Vice President Dawes and Speaker Longworth would appoint the committee.

An effort will be made to secure prompt, favorable action on the resolution.

A fund of $50,000 would be available to the committee, which would be authorized further to hold meetings during the recess and adjournment of Congress this summer.

La Guardia's resolution provides that a report containing specific recommendations for "such legislation as may be necessary to wipe out this terrible menace throughout the American nation" must be submitted by the committee by December 31, next.

La Guardia said:

"A most comprehensive investigation is necessary because of the startling increase in the use of habit-forming drugs in this country. I think a survey first should be made to determine the maximum amount of narcotics required for the medical profession and for legitimate purposes.

"Next, the committee should investigate smuggling operations, through which the nation is being flooded with a poisonous flow of morphine, cocaine, heroin and other vicious drugs.

"Finally, recommendations should be made to enable the Federal Government to cut straight to the root of the 'dope' evil and suppress the illicit traffic."

Every Death from Poisoned Alcohol 'Official Murder' to La Guardia.

REP. FIORELLA LA GUARDIA.

LAGUARDIA.
...merican Staff Photo.

...dia was 52 years ...

THE MARIHUANA PROBLEM IN THE CITY OF NEW YORK

MAYOR'S COMMITTEE ON MARIHUANA

CLICK
PHOTO-PARADE
10¢
MAR.193
WEIRD forms when marijuana fumes are pounding
Subtlety disappears and the most depraved brutalities
Erotic pain seems unusually thrilling to drug-sodden senses
Photos Posed by Professional Models
NO APHRODISIAC, marijuana does remove ordinary inhibitions. After half of one cigarette, the novice smoker is open to almost any suggestion. The drug is classified as a malevolent hypnotic by research scientists
-DOZEN "REEFERS" addicts are "high," "leaping." wobbly, they find even the most commonplace things up- imaginations run wild, sex repressions are forgotten
addicts try vainly to stay "high" by smok
juana users start in their teens, investiga
shocking statistics about U. S. high sch
higher nerve centers weake
ours may pass before victi
Addicts trying to remember
NS BRUTE when under the deadly influence of marijuana, If capable of anything, probably will be totally unable to re- hat he has done. He may even kill, then entirely forget it
WHERE MARIJUANA AND MURDER MAKE A THRILLING STORY IN "IT AIN'T HAY"
MARIJUANA:
HOW A ROADSIDE WEED HAS BECOME A NATIONAL MENACE
Most vicious of drugs plaguing the United States today is not opium, heroin, or cocaine—all of them imported, all of them expensive—but marijuana, which is so common it may well be growing wild in your own backyard!
Its use and history
Being cheap, easily cultivated, and easily concealed, requiring no elaborate apparatus for use, marijuana is giving U. S. narcotic agents the hardest fight they've ever had. The world knows it by many names: as hashish, bhang, charras. It has long grown wild in our Southwest, is called loco weed by men who have watched cattle go mad and die after feeding on it. Unlike the other widespread narcotics, marijuana has almost no medicinal value
Effects vary widely
In some addicts marijua
duces a high exhilaration,
stimulates the imagination,
mood may change to one o
savagery. Brutal mass mu
perhaps of close friends, or e
members of the addict's o
family, is a fairly frequent res
IT AIN'T HAY
List of Thrilling Chapters—
I. A Hypothetical Client
II. Quickest Road to Insanity
III. Dope and Homicide
IV. Two Stiffs for One
V. "You're Stinking Up My Office
VI. Business After Hours
VII. "You Are the Damndest Man."
VIII. Reliable as a Dollar Watch
IX. Webster Makes a Deal
X. "Pighead!"
XI. A Messy Job
XII. Cut Up Like Corned Beef Ha
XIII. Better Than a Drink
XIV. Undressing the Inner Man
XV. A Girl Who Won't Screa
XVI. A Dirty Assignment
XVII. Neat Knife Work
XVIII. Very, Very Risky
XIX. Whenever Ladies Scre
Just a Cheap Floozie
High as a Kite
it's Fifteen Minut
Brought Home in a Baske
IT AIN'T HAY
DAVID DODGE
DOWN AND DOWN...
You start it almost as a joke just for the laughs, just to be sociable. That's your first reefer cigarette. Then do it again, to show the no hard feelings about first one. Then you start ing around on your own, even without your "pals" to
TAKEN FOR A RIDE
ON MARIHUANA'S TRAIL
A ROADSIDE WEED BECOMES A
MARIHUANA, THE LIAR
FANCIES AND FOLLIES
MADNESS FOR PROFIT
HOW DOPE PEDDLERS OPERATE
HOW MARIHUANA DIFFERS FROM OTHER NARCOTICS
DOPE'S MISSING LINK
HOW SHALL WE TEACH OU
WHAT OF THE FUTURE?
ON THE TRAIL OF MARIHUANA
The WEED OF MADNESS
B-107. STABLE BOY. Adam Robe
B-108. GUTTER GANG
ST-201. HILL BILLY IN HIGH HEELS. Jeff Bo
She was sixteen, ripe for love. Passion runs rampan this delightfully unusual novel of backwoods feudin' sinnin'.
ST-202. MALE VIRGIN. Jack Woodford and John B. Thompson
The frank, intriguing story of the search for an answer
WARPED WOMEN. Janet Pritchard
MARIJUANA GIRL. N. R. de Mexico
Here is a pitiless study of a young girl enslaved by the dope habit, revealing her every thought, every facet of her warped life, her disturbed relations with other kids—with older men.
TRAMP GIRL. Thomas Stone
Missy had the morals of an alley cat because men taught her that love was a jungle, and her own lovely body was fair game.
THE QUEER SISTERS. Steve Harragan
DOPE DOLL
STEVE HARRAGAN
I'LL GET MINE
APPING, MUR
TREMENDO
OMAHA WORLD-HE
CHAS
The MARIJUANA MOB
Marijuana Girl
SHE TRADED HER BODY FOR DRUGS—AND KICKS!
WILLIAM IRISH
A cheap and evil girl sets a hopped-up killer against a city
MARIHUAN

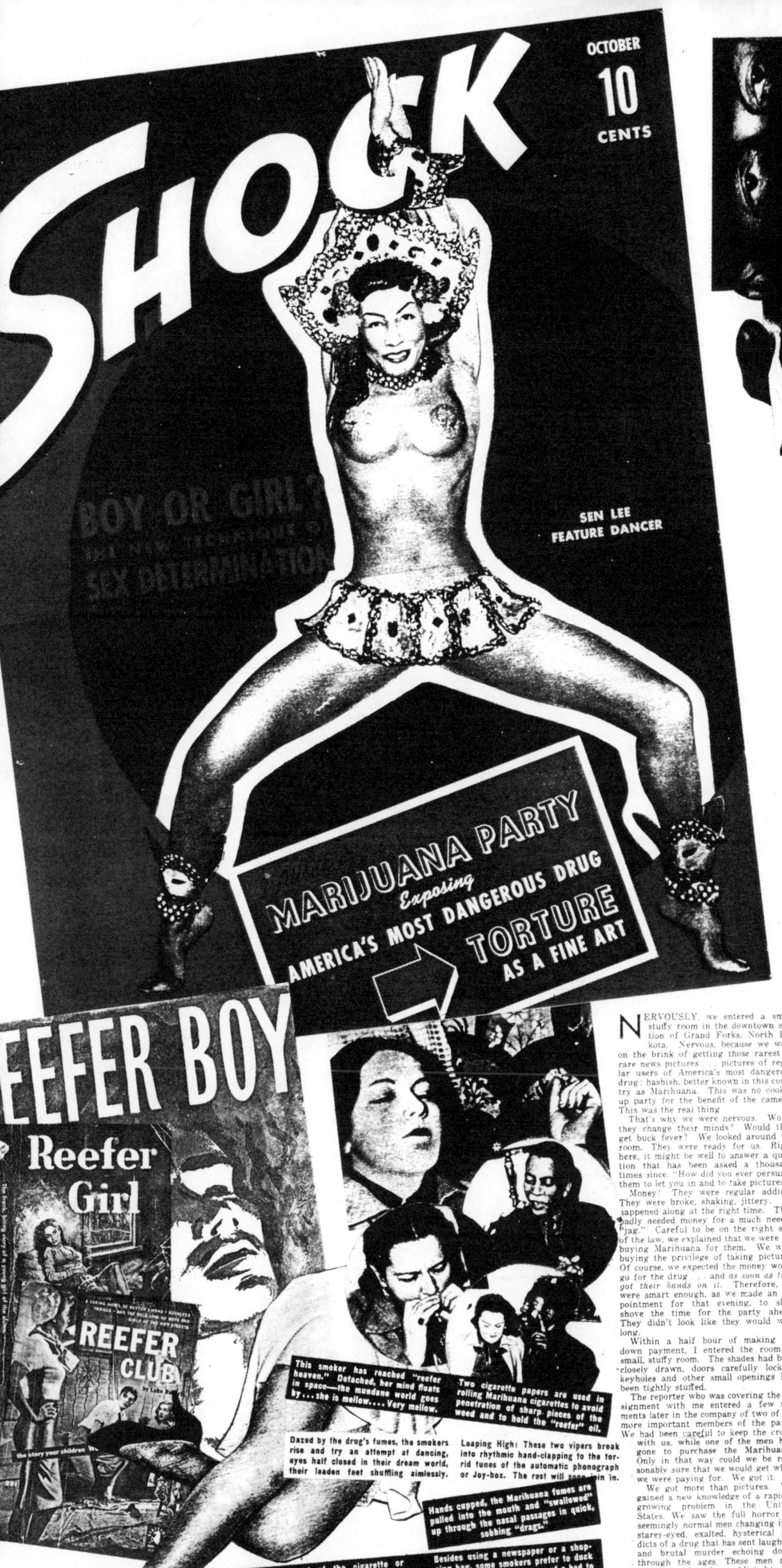

This smoker has reached "reefer heaven." Detached, her mind floats in space—the mundane world goes by . . . she is mellow. . . . Very mellow.

Two cigarette papers are used in rolling Marihuana cigarettes to avoid penetration of sharp pieces of the weed and to hold the "reefer" oil.

Dazed by the drug's fumes, the smokers rise and try an attempt at dancing, eyes half closed in their dream world, their leaden feet shuffling aimlessly.

Leaping High: These two vipers break into rhythmic hand-clapping to the torrid tunes of the automatic phonograph or Joy-box. The rest will soon join in.

Hands cupped, the Marihuana fumes are pulled into the mouth and "swallowed" up through the nasal passages in quick, sobbing "drags."

The butt end of the cigarette or "roach" is the part which packs the real wallop. Often a split match,

Besides using a newspaper or a shopping bag, some smokers prefer to duck their head under the covers of a bed to get all the terrific bang from the reefer.

NERVOUSLY, we entered a small stuffy room in the downtown section of Grand Forks, North Dakota. Nervous, because we were on the brink of getting those rarest of rare news pictures . . . pictures of regular users of America's most dangerous drug: hashish, better known in this country as Marihuana. This was no cooked up party for the benefit of the camera. This was the real thing.

That's why we were nervous. Would they change their minds? Would they get buck fever? We looked around the room. They were ready for us. Right here, it might be well to answer a question that has been asked a thousand times since. "How did you ever persuade them to let you in and to take pictures?"

Money! They were regular addicts. They were broke, shaking, jittery. We happened along at the right time. They badly needed money for a much needed "jag." Careful to be on the right side of the law, we explained that we were not buying Marihuana for them. We were buying the privilege of taking pictures. Of course, we expected the money would go for the drug . . . and *as soon as they got their hands on it.* Therefore, we were smart enough, as we made an appointment for that evening, to slyly shove the time for the party ahead. They didn't look like they would wait long.

Within a half hour of making the down payment, I entered the room—a small, stuffy room. The shades had been closely drawn, doors carefully locked; keyholes and other small openings had been tightly stuffed.

The reporter who was covering the assignment with me entered a few moments later in the company of two of the more important members of the party. We had been careful to keep the crowd with us, while one of the men had gone to purchase the Marihuana. Only in that way could we be reasonably sure that we would get what we were paying for. We got it.

We got more than pictures. We gained a new knowledge of a rapidly growing problem in the United States. We saw the full horror of seemingly normal men changing into starey-eyed, exalted, hysterical addicts of a drug that has sent laughter and brutal murder echoing down through the ages. These men and women had long been addicted to the use of Marihuana. This party was made possible by a purchase of a drug made in our quiet, law-abiding little town of Grand Forks—a purchase that required only minutes for those "in the know" to consummate. We saw every step of the procedure, from the opening of the bindle to the final collapse of the last member o[f] the party.

ONCE started, the initial fear
the smokers soon vanis
Throughout the process of "th
ing," rolling and the smoking o
first reefer, we were compelled
peat again and again our pled
secrecy and our pledge that we
close our ears to anything e
might slip out while they we
the influence of the drug.

As a rule, Marihuana is
form of cigarettes already
cause in that way the tr
greater profit. That the
cured a package of "ha
form was a good indication th
had close access to the sour
for Marihuana vary grea
ferent communities in
portion to the amount
the law. At this t
cigarettes were
Forks at three fo
select few coul
bulk and the p
Immediately
taken prices
spite the
secrecy on
grape-vine
had word
hours of it
clean-up by
high price
made it ne
pants of ou
escape the
well as th

The pa
locking an
small stuf
the purp
spread on
feverishly
the weed.
closely rese
is much coa
threshing is
tate rolling
cigarette pap
papers are used
First, because the roug
of the weed penetrate the thin
whereas two sheets provide s
strength. Second, two pape
wetted, help retain the Mar
oil. It is the oil that give
Bang.

The cigarettes rolled, the u
were ready to start smoking. Eve
one seemed highly nervous at this stage. Shaky hands lighted the cigarettes. At this point we learned a very important lesson about using this particular drug. To get a jag from smoking Marihuana, a special smoking technique is required. Marihuana is not smoked like tobacco.

How then, we asked, could it be true that boys and girls came home to their parents under the influence of Marihuana with the explanation that a "friend" had given them a cigarette under the pretext that it was a different kind of tobacco, and that they didn't know what they were smoking?

Impossible, we learned. The boy or girl who gets a Marihuana jag knows what he is doing. He has to. And we saw the reason why. Smoking Marihuana has to be learned. The cigarette is held close to the lips and the inhaling is done in a hissing way that draws the fumes mixed with air along the outside as well as the inside of the cigarette directly into the lungs with no stopover in the mouth.

But it is from the very last part of the cigarette that the real kick comes. It is the "butt" or "roach" that really packs the wallop. As the cigarette is smoked the butt end accumulates a more concentrated supply of the Marihuana oil. When it gets to be very short, a split match called a "crutch" is used to hold the "roach" and a hissing, sucking inhale of that portion of the cigarette produces an immediate effect.

AS this technique was being demonstrated, one of the men who had been sitting quietly on the floor beside a table burst into an hysterical laugh. We were startled by his apparently insane outburst, but were reassured by the casual explanation given us by another smoker.

"Laughing jag," he explained. "It won't last long. No telling how he will feel when he comes out of it."

The laugh stopped as abruptly as it had started. As if nothing unusual had taken place, the fellow who had just had such a good belly laugh got up, crossed the room, lay down in a corner and placed a shopping bag over his head.

That was to keep the fumes close to the smoker, we were told. That was one way of doing it. The trick is used for the purpose of inhaling the same fumes over and over again. The smoker who was explaining this to us said that she would just as soon use a newspaper folded into the shape of a cone. She picked up a paper, went into a corner where she lay down and folded the paper across her face. She was there for a few minutes, then got up and crossed the room to sit on the bed. As she seated herself we couldn't help but notice the obvious feeling of superiority it gave her to be be able to sit there and explain things to us.

Suddenly she jumped up, scooped up the remaining Marihuana, rushed over to a sink and washed it all down the drain.

"I don't want any of that stuff around me," she exclaimed.

No one else stirred. They just sat and watched her. A man near us said quietly, "Bull horrors . . . stay quiet."

That was just another example of the effects of hashish. It hits the addict in waves. And all waves seem highly exaggerated. If he is afraid, he is extremely afraid. If he is brave, nothing in the world can scare him. It is that peculiar exaggeration, we learned, that explains so many Marihuana-inspired attacks on

hey all look alike, we
an under the in-
girl becomes a
ssion becomes ex-
est degree. Killing
brutal.
quieted down and
n the bed, we ven-
why she had de-
She seemed puz-
stion; but meekly
to thinking some-
in here. Say! Do
north with me?"
passed into the

about the north
e room to an-

aved.

One
athly
erous
mped

A shopping bag or paper over the head keeps all the fumes near the smoker. This technique speeds up the oncoming jag.

bells?" the
A man side
in a low voice,
Perhaps they did
may have been a de
the "big ear." Senses,
are also greatly exagg
tensified by smoking
The sense of hearing
acute that faint sounds r
in their ears. There may ha
church bells ringing in the dis
but we couldn't hear them.

A man jigged across the room to us.

"So you're a reporter, huh? You want to know how I feel, huh? I'm goofier'n a pigeon . . . goofier'n a pigeon. I'm floatin' on high."

He looked it. Never had we seen a human face take on such a hideous vacuous expression.

"What if you were to take a drink now?" I asked.

The answer was simple and to the point. "You blow your top. You go nuts. That's all."

In this section of the country, we learned, wine and Marihuana were commonly used by those addicts who were seeking the most vicious kind of jag. It also leaves the worst kind of hangover, whereas Marihuana alone does not leave the addict with a hangover at all.

AS the party wore on, smokers grew groggy, collapsed on the bed and on the floor. As the last man passed out, we took one final picture and left, grateful for the lung-filling draughts of fresh air once we were out of that room.

While doctors can predict the effect of other drugs such as opium, morphine, cocaine, they never know from one experiment to another how Marihuana will strike the user. It doesn't hit the same person twice any times. Apparently harmless at first, producing scarcely any hangover effect, Marihuana gives a big kick. But, Marihuana has been responsible for some of the most brutal crimes in history.

Medically speaking it affects the central nervous system, paralyzing the normal restraint centers, releasing the user from either the desire or the power to reject suggestions. It often produces hallucinations.

The use of Marihuana has led to the most revolting sex crimes against children. It has been the cause of brutal massacres of entire families by crazed addicts. Yet novice users are enthralled by the knowledge that when they smoke Marihuana they may experience any one of a countless number of sensations.

They may feel that they are gods floating . . . floating on clouds. On the other hand the drug may affect them worse than the most terrible nightmare, nightmares in which they are falling, falling into a bottomless pit. Whatever they feel, it is different from normal experience. They forget that under its influence they may commit gruesome crimes otherwise entirely foreign to their nature.

Gradually, the casual smoker becomes addicted, although not in the same sense as addiction to other drugs. A user can break away from Marihuana with sufficient effort while breaking with other drugs has been known to kill the person trying to escape. Constant users of Marihuana face another danger . . . the danger of going crazy. The drug affects the mind and nervous system. To what degree depends upon individual conditions.

MY JOB IS SAVING 'flaming youth' of '43

(All photos posed by Miss Livingston (in dark hat) and professional models.)

IN THE MARIHUANA PARLOR you see them . . . 14 and 15-year-olds, masquerading as older girls and picking up soldiers, civilians, anything in pants . . . But, too often, the "fun ends in tragedy."

1—NIGHT AFTER NIGHT Miss Livingson seeks them out . . . the 'teen-agers with a superficial air of sophistication which fools many a service man into believing they are much older . . .

—HE'S USUALLY ASTONISHED—and she resentful—when he's given proof of her age. But despite the fact that Miss Living-n devotes herself mainly to the problem of the young girl . . .

3—SHE'S TREMENDOUSLY concerned that the visiting service man shall not find himself inadvertently in trouble. He leaves when warned—though the "cute number" begs him to stay.

WHETHER it's Papa or Mama who wears the pants in the home has been a favorite subject for humorists since time immemorial. But there is no humor whatsoever in the fact that today, all too frequently, it's daughter who wears the pants. And a 'teen-age daughter, at that!

It's daughter who all too often decrees how the home shall be run; daughter who decides on the household furnishings and on the clothes the family shall wear; daughter who decides whether she will go to school or not; daughter who passes [illegible]he social contacts. And, finall[illegible]er who sets her own hours [illegible]t, staying out or de[illegible] she'll come home at [illegible]es with tragic consequen[illegible]ave learned over a long period [illegible]escue work.

Sociologists, educators and jurists are tremendously concerned over the growing problem of delinquency among young girls; attribute it to changing economic conditions, wartime hysteria and a dozen other factors. But I have come to the conclusion that, despite the fact that economic conditions and wartime hysteria play their part, in general it is the utter futility of parents as parents which is too often responsible.

Parents seem to have lost all control over their youngsters. The kids come as they please, go as they please and meet all demands for explanation with sullenness and downright defiance. Today, as never before, in my experience, I find them—the girls particularly—convinced that, at fourteen and sometimes even younger, they are their "own bosses."

Watch the big movie houses along "Main St." any morning at eleven o'clock—and see the stream of young girls, with school books under their arms, many of them using their lunch money for admittance. Just playing "hookey?" Often worse than that. Once inside, some will pick up any strange man who comes along—as I've learned from my own experiences in routing them out and sending them either back to school where they belong, or home.

Watch some jive palaces, the dingy bars, some juke parlors—and see them, in slacks and scarves, posing as older girls, picking up soldiers, sailors, civilians, anything in pants. And hear their resentment when you spot them, inform their "escorts" that they're under age and take them, unwillingly, to their homes.

It doesn't matter whether it's eight in the evening or two in the morning, large cities like New York are over-run with 'teen-age girls who are "running wild" as they never have before. The "flaming youth" period which followed World War I definitely was nothing like this.

"If I try to restrain her, she tells me I'm old-fashioned; that she's old enough to do as she pleases and that her affairs are 'none of my business.' When her father comes home he says he's 'too tired to listen to arguments,' and that 'bringing up the kids' is my job. What can I do?"

And there, I believe, is the crux of the problem . . . the indifference of fathers and the "helplessness" of mothers, on the one hand and, on the other, too great severity in upbringing and lack of understanding to insure our modern daughters a normal happy life.

There are some mothers—thank God they're in the minority—who actually don't care what their daughters do or refuse to believe you when you try to warn them, such as the mother of a girl whom I shall call Mary K.

For several months now I have been watching Mary K— with great distress. She happens to live in my own neighborhood and I've seen her grow up—not happily, I may add. The companions she chooses are of the worst, the social environment no better. Her "hangouts" are the dingy little bars and grills which dot the sordid byways of a big city's tawdry night life. Until two and three in the morning Mary has been frequenting these places, picking up strange men, drinking, raising Cain generally. And, mind you, she's not fifteen yet!

Repeatedly I have warned her mother that Mary was heading for trouble. Repeatedly, kindly police officers on the beat have spoken to her, too. But the results have always been the same—a torrent of abuse and an insistence that "My Mary is all right. She knows what she's doing and you quit picking on her."

Last week Mrs. K. was frantic when a doctor told her that pretty soon her fourteen-year-old Mary would have to be entered in a maternity hospital.

If the case of Mary K. were an isolated one, there would be no particular cause for alarm, but unfortunately it is all too common. Sociologists are appalled at the amazing increase in the number of illegitimate births, not only in our larger cities but in smaller ones, where the rapid growth of war industries or proximity to army camps has mushroomed the population. And they are appalled even more at the youth of the mothers involved.

Cooperating with the Federal authorities are State and City officials who, also shocked at the situation, are particularly aware of local conditions and, therefore, in better position to cope with them. During the past year many conferences have been held by health authorities and dismaying indeed are the statistics they reveal. Just the other day at one such conference held in Trenton, N. J., Dr. Glenn S. Usher, of the State Health Department, revealed that 40 out of every 1,000 Navy men stationed in New York City were becoming infected by social disease every year and that reports at the close of last Summer indicated that 300,000 man days per year were being lost within the Second Service Command of the Army for the same reason.

Dr. Usher and his associates blamed the "misguided sense of patriotism" of the young women in the vicinity and stressed the unhappy fact that he did not mean the old offenders. This may have surprised his hearers, but it certainly surprised no metropolitan social worker.

The delinquency problem among young girls which is always more acute during wartime is aggravated by a number of other factors in this particular period—factors of which social workers have been aware for some time, but which are just now coming to the attention of the public.

The marihuana menace, for instance.

When reports from San Francisco reveal that a famous band leader has been arrested and charged with contributing to the delinquency of a minor by sending a 17-year-old to buy marihuana for him, the public begins to sit up and take notice.

When police report that in midtown New York several women with names well known to the theatrical profession have been taken into custody for running a "pad joint" (or reefer parlor) for the benefit of service men, the public is shocked.

But suggest to this same public that 'teen-age youngsters are indulging in the deadliest of vices and one is met with mingled scorn, disbelief and actual hostility. Yet social workers have known for some time that the "reefer habit" was spreading insidiously among children of school age; that peddlers linger outside schoolyards and playgrounds, plying their nefarious trade and making addicts of the youth[illegible]lly susceptible. They have known [illegible] the "cellar clubs" where older boys and girls initiate youngsters into the "delights" of marihuana and they have observed for themselves the morally degrading effects of the weed upon children scarcely out of the lollypop age. Yet until recently their warnings have been unheeded and their voices as of those crying in the wilderness.

How the twin evils of drugs and vice combine to give even experts on juvenile psychology some of their biggest headaches

ORDIALLY INVITED TO THE
SAILORS' AND SOLDIERS' CLUB
BROADWAY, NEAR 76TH STREET
Manhattan Congregational Church
OPEN DAILY FROM 4 TO 10.30 P. M.
FOR
Sociability · Comfort · Entertainment
SHOWERS MUSIC · POOL LIBRARY · CANTEEN GAMES
FACILITIES FOR WRITING TO THE FOLKS AT HOME
DANCING MONDAY AND THURSDAY EVENINGS
SUNDAY SUPPER FROM 6 TO 7.30, 25 CENTS

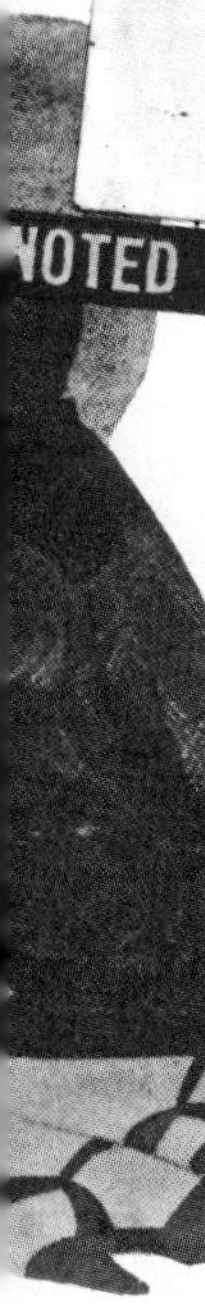

O2 · P2 · 25 SPARE

NOTED WOMAN'S BATTLE WITH ONE OF THE NATION'S GREATEST WAR-TIME PROBLEMS

Tokyo Voices Hint Drugs

U. S. Prisoner Talk Declared Dulled

SAN FRANCISCO, Jan. 23 (INS)—Numerous persons who have listened to Tokyo broadcasts expressed belief Friday that American war prisoners were under the forced influence of drugs while delivering radio messages to this country.

This condition, San Francisco listeners said, was especially evident Wednesday night when a United States naval surgeon and a marine aviator spoke over the Tokyo radio, thereby producing an effect opposite from that intended by Jap propagandists.

31 SUGAR · 43 COFFEE · 37 SPARE

1—'TEEN-AGE GIRLS are particularly susceptible to a uniform and, for some reason, a sailor's garb is especially appealing, according to Miss Livingston. Hence the "come-hither" glance which so often meets the lonely tar in barroom or grill . . .

2—MEN ARE EASILY DECEIVED by a girl's appearance, so the serviceman rarely guesses that the "cute number" he's picked up is still of high school age and ought to be home. All he knows is that he's likely to be away a long time, and . . .

3—FEMININE COMPANIONSHIP is very desirable. But not if it's going to cause a lot of trouble . . . and Miss Livingston's job is to see that it doesn't. She spots the 'teen-agers immediately; tips off the lads they've picked up. In most cases . . .

For over three decades I made Chinatown the focal point of my activities and know only too well the tragedies which were enacted daily—and nightly—beyond the murky curtains of its underground labyrinths. Fortunately I was able to rescue literally thousands of young girls who had fallen into the hands of the procurers and vice panderers of the day and, all too frequently, found them kept in the most degrading of all slavery through the medium of drugs. At the time, the conditions were undeniably shocking and when, finally, that particular quarter of the city had been rid of its last reeking hole of iniquity, I breathed a sigh of relief. Never again, I thought, would the combination of drugs and vice prove such a menacing threat to the young girls of a great metropolis like New York.

But I was wrong.

Today it is marihuana which is contributing to moral delinquency and, if anything, its influence is more deadly than opium ever was. The danger lies in its insidiousness. For, smoked in the form of "reefers" which are far more easily procured than opium ever was, it is comparatively easy to acquire the "habit."

The number of 'teen-age youngsters who have acquired the "reefer" habit in the last few years is not only dreadful to contemplate but is appalling in its significance as a factor in the problem of wartime morale.

Not so long ago the public was shocked to learn that in the very heart of New York, Federal officers rounded up a group of young women who were making it their business to introduce the "delights" of marihuana to the men in the armed services. The "tea pad," as these drug parlors are called, was doing a thriving business, with soldiers, sailors and others in uniform arriving in endless stream to taste "thrills" of which most of them had never even heard in the small towns from which they came. Fortunately, such concentrated centers of vice are few and far between and the FBI has always a wary eye open. But the habit spreads just the same through the proselytism of confirmed addicts.

One of the few quarters in New York where the "tea pads" still flourish despite official watchfulness is the fringe of Harlem, around the teeming colored district which, for some reason, has always proven a lure to thrill-hunting whites. There, despite the fact that its great proportion of decent-living citizens frown upon the fact, are any number of resorts which pander to the worst in man—and in woman. How vicious is the circle which operates under any conditions but in wartime particularly may best be illustrated by a recent case which came to my attention.

It is to this small "borderland" community that the vice-panderers bring unfortunate girls, initiating them into the twin evils of drugs and prostitution. And it is here that I have been working for the past two years

I would like to point out, first, that the fringes of Harlem are inhabited by a conglomeration of races. There are, besides the colored folk, a large sprinkling of other races and colors, too, but of the most underprivileged class.

For many years sociologists and others interested in the public welfare have been trying to warn the public about the dangers of marihuana, but until recently with little success.

Today they are beginning to be heard. But only because the menace is increasing and what were once mere whispered rumors, as far as the public is concerned, are becoming dreadful facts to be shouted from the housetops. Jive, curiously enough, has been responsible. The jazz-mad kids of the early twenties have given way to the hep-cats and rug-cutters. But there's a woeful difference between the two generations. Oldsters shook their heads when the flapper and her boyfriend took a slug of gin from a flask and went "wild" to the syncopated rhythms that passed for dance music immediately following the last war. But the jazz mania of that era and the flask-toting kids of that generation would bore today's boys and girls to distraction. For the combination of jive and marihuana is so potent, so insidious in effect that its lure is irresistible to the initiate.

For a long time it has been whispered that some of the exponents of jive and boogie-woogie relied upon the illicit drug for their best effects and it was inevitable that their young votaries should try it, too, "just for fun." That's how the evil spread. But, too, that's how it's dangers came out into the open at last.

Reefer-smoking kids used to hide their butts; used to deny their addiction. Today they flaunt both. Just as the flapper used to "show off" the flask she slipped down into the top of her rolled-down stocking. I've taken the "butts," as they call them, from hundreds of 'teen-age girls. It's not hard to spot them. You'll notice that the reefer-smoker never has a package of cigarettes. He—or she—usually has just one or two—sometimes just half of one. They're pretty expensive. And, besides, they're usually sold just a few at a time. Risky business, reefer peddling. But not risky enough. For marihuana is one of the most dangerous of drugs.

Marihuana breaks down all moral restraint, releases its victims from every inhibition and is, therefore, in large part responsible for the promiscuity which is making the youngsters of today not only a menace to themselves but to the servicemen on leave. But with or without drugs, sociologists and other interested welfare workers are aware, promiscuity is on the increase—particularly among the very young.

4—SAILOR IS USUALLY GLAD to be warned, listens to Miss Livingston's advice a makes a hasty farewell. It's then Miss L. tackles the girl—frequently fac a torrent of abuse. "I'm old enough to be my own boss," is the usual tirade . . .

A VICTIM OF MARIHUANA . . . "It was two o'clock in the morning when I first spotted Rita. Half led and half carried out of a dingy doorway by two sinister and swarthy youths, the girl swayed uncertainly . . . obviously under the influence of drugs . . ."

5—AFTER QUESTIONING, Miss Livingston personally escorts the girl home. girls, she says, respond to sympathetic understanding, but too few of them it at home. Parents too lax or strict are responsible for much juvenile delinqu

DRUG-CRAZED GUNMEN, CAR TRACED TO S. F. UNDERWORLD

Mexican Narcotic, Marihuana, Inciting With Lust to Slay, Blamed for Death Cruise

Police... men, p... Francisc... sudden ... would h... crazed b... way thr... alternate... Saturday...

Police ... tectives ... the drug... day of r... murderous work last night or else disappear.

SOURCE IS TRACED.

Marihuana — a crazing Mexican narcotic — was definitely established yesterday as the inciting cause of the blood lust under the spell of which the two young bandits worked.

Their source of supply—if not their headquarters—has been traced by the police to a resort in Harrison street, long under suspicion.

TWO DISAPPEAR.

Men answering the description of the killers have been seen frequenting this place within the past few days. The taxicab of Walter Swanson, slain driver, in which the bandits started their series of murders on Monday night, was seen in front of this place a few minutes before he was killed and robbed of his cab and uniform.

Two men answering the description of the bandits have recently occupied a furnished room in this neighborhood, but have now disappeared.

Veteran highwaymen, desperate criminals and strangers in San Francisco, according to the police theory, the two bandits are believed to have been introduced to the Mexican drug by underworld associates and to have gone berserk under its influence. Although quite commonly used by a certain class of Mexicans, marihuana is said to have the effect of exciting a blood-craving in the case of new addicts.

It was in front of this sinister resort that the taxicab of Walter Swanson was recognized by a friend at 5:40 o'clock on Monday evening. There was a man in the rear seat of the cab, according to this witness, and the blinds were pulled down so as to conceal his features.

TRACE BEGINNING.

This hidden figure in the cab was joined after a moment by another man who emerged from the resort and entered the cab, with a brief word of instruction to Swanson, who drove away. Within twenty minutes after that, Swanson had been murdered on the Sixteenth street viaduct and the murder cruise had begun.

This much of the beginning of the tragic night has been reconstructed by Lieutenant George McLaughlin of the robbery detail.

The Yellow-Checker Taxicab Company has been able to throw little light upon Swanson's movements just before he was killed. His last recorded trip was to 7 Twenty-seventh street, where he received $1.70 for taking two persons. There was a later call on which he was sent to 2665 Franklin street, the address of an elderly couple, who deny that they called a cab or that Swanson ever arrived there.

The police have a theory that one of the bandits gave this address over the telephone and flagged the cab outside the house to drive to the marihunana rendezvous. The meter shows a trip calling for a fare of $3.85, which is unaccounted for.

"CLUES" FAIL.

Police yesterday found in the taxicab a pawn ticket and a bank book, which were at first believed to have been left there by the bandits and perhaps have been the reason for the return of the bandits to the spot where they had murdered Swanson.

The pawn ticket was found later to be for Swanson's watch, which he had pawned for $5 with the Remedial Loan Association on March 29. The bankbook was found to be the record of a closed account in the name of Joseph Noiel, a negro seventy years of age, formerly living at 489 Buena Vista avenue, who is said to have spent much money riding about in taxicabs.

Neither of these documents is believed by the police to have any bearing upon the bandits or upon their night of murder and robbery.

ANOTHER MISTAKE.

Another clue to the movements of the bandits is believed to have been exploded yesterday, when Corporal Charles Mangeto and Patrolman J. Kenny discovered the stolen sedan car of F. S. McGinnis, passenger traffic manager of the Southern Pacific Railway at Fifteenth and Utah streets. This car, in which the bandits were thought to have fled after they had wrecked Swanson's cab, was reported on Tuesday as passing through Petaluma at a high rate of speed.

Captain of Detectives Duncan Matheson stated yesterday that it would have been impossible for this car to re-enter the city from Sonoma county without observation by police officers at the ferries. He was of the opinion that a mistake had been made in its identification at Petaluma.

The speedometer on the McGinnis car shows that it had been driven about 206 miles after it was reported stolen. Oakland Levy, negro chauffeur for the railway official, has been ordered to report at police headquarters for questioning.

OCTOBER 14, 1926—

Student Dope Sales Charged

Reports of asserted peddling of marijuana cigarettes to school children were brought to the attention of San Francisco's educational chiefs yesterday by Municipal Judge Twain Michelsen.

The jurist said that three members of Parent-Teacher groups had informed him that the weed was being sold to children in stores near the schools. He also said he had trailed the suspected peddler's car, obtained a description of the men and the license number of their automobile.

State Narcotic Chief W. G. Walker, invited to the conference by J. P. Nourse, superintendent of schools, said an investigation would be made immediately...

Feb. 17, 1944

10 ARRAIGNED ON DOPE COUNT

Ten Negroes accused of selling marijuana cigarettes to servicemen were arraigned before United States Commissioner Harry M. Westfall and bound over to the grand jury under $3,000 bond each yesterday.

The arraignments followed a roundup of alleged sellers of the narcotic weed in Seattle Sunday by federal agents and police. Six Negroes were bound over to the grand jury Tuesday.

Eight of the ten yesterday denied federal agents' charges that they had sold marijuana cigarettes to ... $1 a "stick." Two...

Hotel Clerk Identifies Marihuana Smoker As 'Wild Gunman' Arrested for Shootings

A hungry-looking transient picked off the street was linked Friday to the strange shootings two week ends in a row of two elderly hotel clerks.

He was identified as John Kelly Stephens, 30, a onetime state hospital inmate and admitted marihuana user.

He was held on two charges under $15,000 bail; assault with intent to rob and assault with intent to kill.

Detectives said he admitted trying to rob a downtown drug store Wednesday night and "remembered" being in the Grove hotel, 421 W. Burnside street, at the time a 69-year-old night clerk was sho...

...tives Bob McKeown and Joseph Blewitt, Stephens admitted he had been drinking heavily, used marihuana, and could not remember all his actions.

A foot patrolman, Fred Sutterfield, plucked Stephens off the street Thursday afternoon as a likely suspect in the attempted holdup Wednesday night of Powers & Estes drugstore, 724 S. W. Washington street.

Sutterfield told detectives he was convinced Stephens "fitted closely enough to be brought in and checked."

Witnesses 'Pick' Him

Shortly after two witnesses to the drug store attempt pick... him...

BANDITS' DOPE DEN

POLICE SEIZE BIG DOPE STOCK

100 Pounds of Loco Weed Taken by Officers in Raid on Cigar Stand.

One hundred pounds of mariguana, known as "loco weed," a drug which the authorities claim is fast becoming a menace in Northern California, was seized yesterday by detectives of the police department and the State Board of Pharmacy.

The narcotic was found in a cigar store conducted by Rosendo Fernandez at 34 Salmon alley. Fernandez was arrested and charged with violating the state poison law. The poison is said to be valued at more than $4,000 and is the biggest seizure of the kind ever made in San Francisco.

Detective Henry Carmack of the Board of Pharmacy and Police Detectives John Floyd and Michael Mitchell found a score of cans of the drug hidden under the counter of the store.

According to the authorities the use of mariguana, sometimes known as Indian hemp or as loco weed, is fast becoming of common use among drug addicts in this community, especially in the Latin quarter.

Its effect is said to be even more harmful than cocaine or opium. Carmack said after the arrest:

"Recently mariguana has been smuggled into Northern California in large quantities. The State Board of Pharmacy has had trouble for a long time trying to keep it out of Southern California, but only recently has it made an appearance here. It is used ... smoke in cigarettes. Some...

September 14, 1936

'MONA LISA' GIRL WARNED

Beauty Told Narcotic Danger

"If you use these narcotics, your Mona Lisa beauty will go," Chicago's Judge Robert Dunne told Eileen Tortoriello, caught with marihuana cigarettes. She begged mercy, won six months' probation. —International News Photo.

Aqueduct—Drug Raid-

HELD IN DRUG HAUL—Jose Bernardez, thirty, proprietor of sailors' boarding house at South street and the East River, who was held yesterday after raid disclosed a $25,000 cache of hasheesh.

JUNE 20, 1923

Marihuana
Mariguana
Marajuana
Matakwane }
Mnoana }
Mutokwana
Opishnu
Penek

Penek
Pienka
Penka
Penka
Rongoyne
Sejav
Ahets-mangha
Fasuka
Vijaya

Teriaki
Tekrowia
Takrousi
Takruri
Takrouri }
Tekrouri }

Gard
Rup
Taghalim
Ganja
Gabza
Momea

Shahjehani
Mashak, Bhā
and Dust

Chastry }
Chatzraki }
Chastry

Hachich
Hafiou }
Hafioun }
Hashish

Hashish Oil

Cooked Hashish

Maju

Majum
Tadhal
Majoon
Madjoon

Majoom

Madjun

Madjoun

Madjoun
Magi-oun
Majoan

Mapuchari

Mapouchari
Mapouchair

Maslac

Nasha

Guaza

Haschischa
Hasheesh
Hashish
Haschisch

Hasheesh

Hachache
Hachaichi
Hadschi
Haschisch
Hashish

Assis

Berch

Bernavi
Bernaouy

Bers
Bhang

El Mogen
Malach

Mosjusck
Maconha
Marihuana

Chiras

Churus }
Churrus }
Chira

Chinty
Dawamesc

Kif or Kief

Kerp
Kharaneq
Sharâneq
Shanâreq
Sjarank
Sheera
Ma
Ma-yo

Ma
Ta-ma }
Si-ma }
Tse-ma }
Maguen

Canappa
Cañamo
Canhamo
Cañamazo
Kanas

Kanas
Kas
Hon-neb
Hen-nab
Hennip
Hennup
Hampa
Hampa
Hamp
Kamp
Kemp
Hemp
Hanf

Ma'goungy

Hachaichi

Ganja

Guaza

Guaza

Kunubu

Kunnapu
Cannabis }
Kannabis }

Konnab
Kinab
Kon-nab
Kannab
Kanub
Kinnab
Quinnab
Konneb
Quonnab
Quinnaq
Qinnab
Kenneb

Alcanque

Kinnabis
Kinnub
Kannab
Kanop
Kanaq
Ranob
Canapa
Kanep
Canep
Konopj
Konople
Konopli
Konoplia
Canapa

Tabannaj
Chillum
Narghile

Maschechel
Maschicheh
Poddar
Ganja-doct...

PORTLAND, OREGON, SATURDAY, JANUARY 5, 1[illegible]

Jury Urges Gun School For Police

Lack of Training Held Responsible In Shooting Melee

Portland...

Dope Raids Net 500 Suspects

★ ★ ★ ★ ★ ★ ★ ★ ★ ★ ★

Four Arrested in Portland Drug Cleanup

(inset) believed to contain marijuana. ...possession of narcotics and her hus... ...ged with illegal sale of marijuana.

FOUND

...ited States

Muggles, Mooter, Reefers, Greefa, Griffo, Mary Warner, Mary Weaver, Mary Jane, Indian Hay, Loco Weed, Love Weed, Joy-Smoke, Giggle-Smoke, Bambalacha, Mohasky, Mu, Moocah, The Weed, Grass, Tea. In New Orleans "Pig Latin" is used as a sort of code, as Ea-Tay for Tea; Eed-Way for Weed; also, "Eed-Waggles." "Specials" are cigarettes which cost more and are more potent than "singles," sometimes "gold-leaf specials."

Muggle head—An habitual user of marihuana.
Crutch —Holder made with a split match for short butt.
Roach —Short cigarette butt.
Manicuring —Trimming the stalks of leaves and tops.
Foxy —The condition obtained after smoking marihuana. "apprehensive and intuitive."
Floating —Refers to the feeling of lightness and unreality.

Bhanga
Bangue
Banga
Bhang
Bhanga
Banga
Bang
Beng
Benghin
Benj
Bendj
Bangue
Bhanga
Bhanga
Bhang

Bhang
Bhang

Ganja
Ganjica
Gangika
Ganga
Ganga
Ginji
Ginjeh
Gunjeh
Gindsche
Ganja

Azallu

Assis

Assis
Axis
Assyuni
Asarath
Nasha
Anascha

Asa
Dakka
Dakha
Dacha
Dakka
Dakkan
Dagga
"

Dakkan
Djamba
Diamba
Jamba
Riamba
"

Damba

Kanedir
Kanabira
Kendir
Kender
Kennevir
Kenevir
Kenryr
Bust
Cadaneh
Cansjava
Chanvre
Chènevis
Chènevis

Chutsao
Chu-Tsao
Chu-Tso
Hursuni
Indrasans
Jia
Intsangu

Keif

Kif
Kief
Kif
Kinif

250 Agents Spring Trap Over Nation

Top Racket Bosses Face Jury Probe; Purchases Traced

WASHINGTON, Jan. 5 (AP) Government narcotics agents snapped a giant trap on the drug underworld Friday and seized more than 500 suspected dope peddlers. Every big city in the nation was involved.

Harry J. Anslinger, narcotics commissioner in the treasury department, told reporters the mass mop-up operation by 250 undercover agents in his bureau will continue throughout the night. He predicted it will deal a staggering blow to the illicit drug traffic.

The roundup of peddlers, Anslinger said, is by far the biggest ever staged.

A few underworld giants were arrested Friday, he added, but more top racket bosses will be captured when a grand jury investigation, now under way, is completed within three weeks.

Chief Guards Locale

Asked where the jury probe is centered, Anslinger told a news conference, "If we even mentioned the name of the city, some of the men who are talking will be killed."

The commissioner said the raids were aimed at peddlers who have supplied dope for an alarming increase in teen-age addiction, and at veteran offenders who face stiffened penalties under a new narcotics law which makes prison terms mandatory.

Anslinger said the arrested peddlers "are the most dangerous type of criminals," but that the raids were so thoroughly prepared and secretly staged there was no violence.

Agents Make Purchases

Each of the arrests, the commission said, represents an actual purchase of heroin or marijuana by treasury agents who have worked undercover in the midst of narcotic rings for more than a month.

Anslinger predicted "a very sharp drop" in drug addiction and illicit dope traffic. He said he couldn't estimate mathematically how crippling the blow will be.

The raids started before dawn Friday in San Antonio, Tex., and spread throughout the nation to more than 18 states. Up to 100 alleged peddlers were seized in Texas alone, 50 in New York, 50 in Philadelphia and 30 in Washington.

Chief Lauds Italians

Anslinger said the crackdown is tied to a drive to close huge European sources for drugs sent to the United States.

He said Italian secret service agents are doing "a magnificent job" in prosecuting drug shippers. Anslinger said Charles (Lucky) Luciano, deported U. S. underworld king, is under investigation in Italy in connection with the crackdown.

Secretary of the Treasury John W. Snyder, under whose supervision the narcotics bureau falls, told Anslinger he and President Truman "want to congratulate you and your agents for a fine day's work."

Well-heeled agents worked three to four months, spending thousands of dollars to buy drugs and establish contact with peddlers. One young agent in Dallas, Tex., posed as an underworld marijuana peddler to collect evidence.

"Through tireless and relentless enforcement, the trend toward an increase in teen-age drug addiction has been halted," Anslinger said.

Prison Terms Mandatory

Dispute of Dope Peddlers Leads to Big Haul; Marijuana Worth $18,000, Two Men Seized

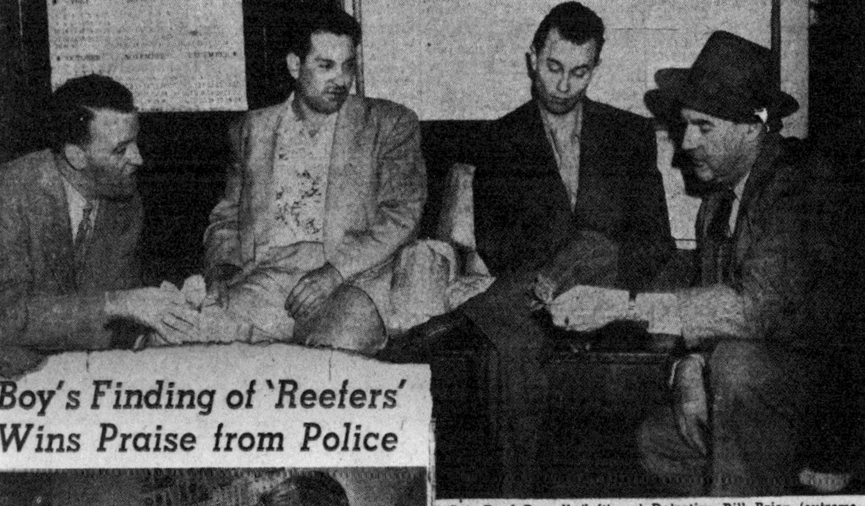

Sgt. Bard Purcell (left) and Detective Bill Brian (extreme right) hold part of 12 pounds of marijuana seized from (left to right) Alfred Diaz and Meredith Nickens, shown seated on bench at police headquarters with rest of marijuana in two-pound paper bags, stacked between them. Below is closeup of marijuana—leaves of Mexican hemp, Cannabis sativa.

Tavern Argument Tips Off Police; Drug Concealed in Auto Upholstery

BY GEORGE SPAGNA
Staff Writer, The Oregonian

A "hopped-up" argument between two California dope peddlers early Sunday led police to the surprising recovery of some $18,000 worth of pure marijuana.

Detectives, glowing over the catch, believed it to be the biggest load of the drug weed ever seized in the Pacific Northwest.

From one of the two men in custody, a slender admitted peddler from Stockton, Detective Bill Brian and Sgt. Bard Purcell learned an amazing story.

Meredith E. Nickens, 29, who said he was a son of a retired California policeman, talked freely of how the two had been running the weed out of Mexico the last 18 months "without a hitch."

Whole Coast Sales Area

Together with Alfred Diaz, 24, a Los Angeles Mexican, Nickens confessed having made at least 30 trips out of Tijuana, Mexico, with the stuff in their car and pedding it all up and down the coast.

Two prowl officers, Fred Teed and John Lindholm, picked up the pair for disorderly conduct in a St. Johns tavern after a waitress complained they were arguing "loudly and profanely and threatening to fight it out right here."

Nickens, admittedly woozy from a "reefer" smoked just before they hit town, sought help from the two policemen.

"I was afraid he (Diaz) was going to kill me for the load," he said in protective custody of two detectives Sunday morning.

The load, it proved, was some 180 ounces of marijuana, dried and packaged in two-pound paper sacks.

The bags, six of them, were found concealed in the door paneling of Nickens' car, but he readily stripped off a section of the upholstery to prove he "really had it."

A bag, like those recovered, Nickens said, was bought for $70 "at a place I know in Mexico."

Lot Valued at $18,000

"We've been peddling it—he knows the outlets—in skid roads all up and down the coast," he told Detective Brian. "We get as high as $400 a bag for it—wholesale.

"A hoppie," he continued, "can break down the stems and seeds and get at least 1800 'joints' from a bag."

On the market today, a federal narcotics agent called in said, a "joint" or single "reefer" goes for $1.

The whole lot, seized from Nickens and Diaz, he said, would bring about $18,000 if made up into cigarets.

Nickens said he hadn't held a legitimate job since 1946 when he was turned out of the army with a medical discharge. He had been living with his mother in Stockton for most of the time when not on the road, he said.

He hasn't seen his father, the retired policeman, for ten years, he said. "Guess he doesn't want to see me now."

He named Los Angeles, Santa Barbara, San Francisco and Seattle as the biggest outlets for the weed. Nickens and Diaz had been in Portland only a few times before but were certain they would dispose of their whole load here, Nickens said.

Prisoner Fears Reprisals

As to his source and outlets for the drug, Nickens frankly said he wouldn't talk.

"My life wouldn't be worth a dime if I did," he said.

Detectives admitted they were surprised the pair hadn't been caught before this.

Nickens stated frankly he had gone across the California-Mexico border "at least 30 times," but "acting like a businessman" had never before been caught.

Border guards had stopped his car many times, but never really given it a thorough search, he said.

Pressed for proof that his accomplice, Diaz, might have intended to kill him, he would only assert:

Stockton Agents Alerted

"I got real high on that smoke—thought he was going to kill me because I felt like I wanted to kill him—if I'd had a gun—you know how 'teaheads' get."

In the trade a "teahead" is a user of marijuana. Nickens kept insisting his "stuff" was of fine quality.

"The top flowered cuts," he put it.

Federal narcotics agents in Stockton were alerted immediately of the arrest here and directed to pick up a car Diaz admitted leaving behind in that city.

Boy's Finding of 'Reefers' Wins Praise from Police

Newsboy David Griffin, 2715 S. E. 141st avenue, paid a call at police headquarters Friday to examine the loot he came across Thursday while delivering his route—33 marihuana cigarets. Holding some of the cigarets here, David is congratulated for his work by Vice Squad Lt. Howard W. Russell.

*Muggle-smoking was the offense ouis Armstrong served a jail term last win Muggles (also called "Reefers" or "Mary Warners") are shorter, thinner than ordinary cigarets, cause a temporary, happy jag, cost 25¢ in Harlem. The drug in Muggles comes from a variety of hemp called Marijuana (TIME, Sept. 7, 1930).

FILM STARS IN DOPE

ACTOR MITCHUM HELD IN MARIJUANA RAID

SEPTEMBER 1948

MITCHUM IN MARIJUANA ARREST

By RUTH BRIGHAM
Staff Correspondent International News

HOLLYWOOD, Sept. 1 (INS). Movie Hero Robert Mitchum, Actress Lila Leeds and two other persons were arrested early today when narcotic agents broke up a marijuana smoking party.

Mitchum, 31 year old idol of the bobby-sox brigade, calmly admitted to police as he was booked with the other three on suspicion of violating the state narcotic law:

"I'm ruined. I've been smoking reefers for years. I knew I would get caught sooner or later."

DANCER ARRESTED

Arrested with Mitchum and the beauteous Miss Leeds were Dancer Vickie Evans, 25, who came to Hollywood several weeks ago from Philadelphia, and Robin Ford, 31-year-old real estate man.

The film actor and the two women were released at 10 a. m. on writs of habeas corpus and posting of $1,000 bond each.

Ford, apparently the "forgotten man," remained in jail in lieu of bail.

The arrests climaxed nearly a year of intense investigation by authorities in the local movie capital.

Narcotics agents managed to gain entrance into Miss Leeds' sumptuous Laurel Canyon home by first making friends with her three boxer dogs.

ENTERED BY RUSE

The officers said they peeked through windows at the reefer party for nearly two hours before finally scratching on a rear screen door, imitating a dog which wanted into the house.

A. M. Barr, one of the arresting officers, disclosed that Mitchum—a $3,000 a week screen star—had been under surveillance for the past eight months.

Miss Leeds, a shapely blonde who recently had been treated for an overdose of sleeping pills, had been closely watched by investigators for six months, Barr added.

HAD PREMONITION

The actress, once the wife of Orchestra Leader Little Jack Little, told officers at Los An[geles C]ounty jail—where all four were held on suspicion of violating the state narcotics law:

"I had a premonition of this. About 10 o'clock last night I wondered what if police were to break in here? I figured I would try to run to the bathroom before they got in.

"Well, this is it. I'm glad it's over — even though I'm probably ruined now."

Miss Evans, who allegedly was not actually smoking marijuana when police stormed into the luxurious living room, was held for assertedly visiting a place where narcotics were used.

She told officers:

"Sure, I smoked marijuana —but you didn't catch me. I'm lucky, I guess, and I hope it will teach me a lesson."

Ford was practically noncommittal. He insisted that he had been showing Mitchum apartments and merely dropped in at Miss Leeds' rented mansion as they happened to pass by.

MITCHUM WISECRACKS

Mitchum, garbed in a red-checkered shirt and a brown jacket, wisecracked with newsmen in a pre-dawn conference at the jail.

The husky actor—who rode the rods, worked as a stevedore, was an aircraft worker and an Army enlisted man during the war before hitting stardom — did seem worried, however, about his family.

He declared:

"This is really going to hurt my family. This is the bitt[er] end."

The Mitchums separated s[ev]eral months ago, and Mrs. Mitchum—his childhood sweetheart — took their two young children to the East for the summer.

Arresting officers represented federal and state narcotic bureaus.

They said that while they petted the dogs, they heard a telephone ring. Miss Leeds and Miss Evans, who lived together in the rented house, were smoking in the living room.

Police said they heard Miss Leeds answer the phone and say, presumably to Mitchum:

"You got white ones and brown ones. I want some of the white ones.

"Vickie and I are waiting for you. We'll leave the front light on."

Barr said that Miss Leeds then turned to Miss Evans and remarked:

"The boys are loaded."

Five minutes later Mitchum and Ford arrived.

Mitchum asked Lila to turn down the lights. They were all seated in the front room. Then Barr related:

"Lila lit up one and handed it to Bob. Bob was smoking when we entered."

When police scratched on the back door, Miss Leeds innocently opened it for them.

Officers Break Up 'Reefer Party' In Girl's Home

Film Actor Robert Mitchum (left) and Robin Ford, real estate agent, landed in Hollywood jail garb after arrest in raid on alleged marijuana smoking party at of Screen Actress Lila Leeds. Also jailed Miss Leeds and Dancer Vickie Evans.

Narcotics Raid Nets Actor For Smoking Marijuana

Pictures on Wirephoto Page

HOLLYWOOD, Sept. 2 (AP)—Handsome Robert Mitchum, screen player, and two attractive actresses, left jail under $1000 bond each Wednesday after their arrest earlier in a narcotics raid on a Laurel Canyon home.

Mitchum, along with Actress Lila Leeds, 20; dancer Vickie Evans, 25, and Robin Ford, a real estate man, were booked on suspicion of violating state and federal narcotics laws after police said they broke in on a marijuana smoking party in the girls' home. Ford, 31, remained in jail temporarily.

The 31-year-old actor and th[e] two girls were freed after th[ey] had posted bond on their pe[ti]tions for writs of habeas corpu[s]. The writs will be heard in su[]perior court September 8.

Two Men Smoking

Detective Sgt. A. M. Barr of the Los Angeles narcotics detail said both men were smoking marijuana cigarets when the officers broke into the home after a long vigil, during which they made friends with Miss Leeds' three boxer dogs.

They said they took from Mitchum a package with 13 of the "reefers" and that the blond Miss Leeds gave up several more.

The officers said Miss Evans was not observed smoking, but was arrested on suspicion of visiting a place where narcotics were used.

Barr said the raiding party viewed proceedings 2½ hours through a rear bedroom window after "bribing" the dogs with food.

Robert Mitchum, Starlet Nabbed in Dope Case

...Sun, ...reer as a western actor, but in the last two years has been playing starring roles in high-budget productions. Miss Leeds has played a number of smaller parts, and Miss Evans, a dancer, told police she arrived here recently from Philadelphia.

Probably Mitchum's best-known film was "G. I. Joe." Among his other efforts were "Undercurrent," "Pursued" and "The Locket."

ACTRESS LILA LEEDS
Arrested in Narcotics Raid

FILM ACTOR ROBERT MITCHUM
Shown in Jail Clothing After Dope Raid Arrest

His first pictures were in the Hopalong Cassidy series.

DANCER VICKIE EVANS (LEFT) AND FILM ACTRESS LILA LEEDS
In Jail After Arrest With Actor Robert Mitchum and Another Man in Dope Raid

HIDDEN BEAUTY

For Candy Barr was the victim of circumstances—convicted of possessing marijuana, but not of smoking it: betrayed by her loyalty to a lover for whom she was carrying a cigaret, along with some of the weed in a small bottle she had hidden deep in the snug caverns of her bra.

So while real criminals—creeps who make a care[er] out [of] ...ing marijuana and dope, vultures who prey on

RAID

Gene Krupa Takes Plea

San Francisco—Gene Krupa pleaded guilty in court here on April 19 to a charge of using his 17-year-old valet to transport marijuana from his hotel to his theater dressing room. He will be sentenced on May 10.

MAY 1, 1943

NAB ACTOR

Hair Raising

Robert Mitchum, screen hero, has been pretty busy the past few weeks raising the foliage shown here, while serving a 60-day term for violation of the narcotics laws. He's due out March 30. (AP Wirephoto)

FEBRUARY 17, 1949

Prison Farm Due Mitchum

HOLLYWOOD, Feb. 15 (INS) Film Actor Robert Mitchum was informed Tuesday that he will serve out the remainder of a 60-day jail term on marijuana charges at the sheriff's honor farm.

Chief Jailer Charles Fitzgerald said that the husky actor passed his physical examination "with flying colors."

At the honor farm Mitchum will work on farming and road projects until his 60 days are up early in April.

When Mitchum swapped his tweeds for faded blue jail garb he said that he hoped they would transfer him to the farm. The actor said that he wanted to keep in shape and to keep his tan.

He said, however, "everything is fine" at the Los Angeles county lockup and that he was "enjoying" his duties as assistant trusty.

Mitchum is due to make a brief appearance in court on March 8 at the trial of Dancer ...

MARCH 31, 1949

Film Star Mitchum Free After 50-Day Term in Jail

Picture on Page 8

LOS ANGELES, March 31 (AP)—Robert Mitchum went home Wednesday, ending 50 days as a ward of the county.

The $3250-a-week film hero trimmed the mustache from his tanned face, donned a natty pin stripe in lieu of jail denims and boarded a taxi for his home in the Hollywood hills.

"I'll go back to making pictures Monday after a few days ... my wife and two ...

Mitchum, several shades darker and several pounds lighter from his work at the county honor farm, presents a problem for his studio. His current film "The Big Steal," was about half finished when he was jailed and his changed appearance may mean retakes, or at least some rewriting, studio sources said. They won't know until he faces the camera next week.

Ranch Preferred to Cell

...ncho is a good ...man's rehabili...or, 31, confided ...ost men get into ...selfishness and ...escence. So the ...ter place to put ...il cage."

...ss Leeds, Dancer ...nd Real Estate ...ord were arrest...t 31 when nar...raided a secluded ... rented by Miss ...Miss Evans were ...sentenced to jail. ...tted by a jury. ... in jail. He was ...ch 16 to a 60-day ...ced on probation

Drop at Box Office Shown By Robert Mitchum Pictures

BY JIMMIE FIDLER

Distributed by McNaught Syndicate, Inc.

HOLLYWOOD, March 1—Ever since Robert Mitchum's arrest on that dope charge, Hollywood's "smart guys" have predicted that the sensational publicity attending his case would help, not hurt, his box office standing. To support their contention, they are able to cite half-a-dozen other cases in which Holly... had

Robert Mitchum

the two big local theaters which booked Mitchum's new picture, "Red Pony." They'll find that John and Jane Public didn't rush to buy tickets. In fact, "Red Pony" played to less than 50 per cent of the business normally expected in those theaters.

It may just be that the American public is getting fed up with Hollywood scandals. If that proves to be true, there are apt to be some astonishing changes in Filmville.

There has never been a time when studio heads couldn't have prevented a considerable percentage of the uncomplimentary headlines caused by stellar misdemeanors had they chosen to do so. They haven't enforced the morality clauses in players' contracts for the good and logical reason ... haven't ...

Mitchum, Actress Put In Lockup

FEBRUARY 10, 1949

Bobby Soxers' Idol To Serve 60 Days, 2-Years' Probation

Mitchum and Lila Shocked When They Hear 60-Day Jail Sentence

Actor Robert Mitchum, $3250-a-week hero of bobby soxers, turned in his Hollywood tweeds Wednesday for jail denim. He was sentenced to 60 days in the county lockup on a charge of conspiring to possess marijuana.

The handsome film star and Actress Lila Leeds, convicted on the narcotics count, growing out of an alleged doped cigaret smoking party, steadily eyed Superior Judge Clement D. Nye as he passed similar sentences on each.

He placed them on probation for two years and ordered another charge—of actually possessing marijuana—put off the calendar, but not dismissed. This means that anytime during the probation period they can be tried on the other count.

Eloquent Plea Delivered

... sentence followed an elo... ...Mitchum's attor... ...legal...

Mitchum, 31, rising young ex-truck driver from Rising Sun, Del., appeared only slightly affected by the sentence.

"This is the last time you fellows will see me up here," he jauntily told jailers as they fitted and fingerprinted him.

"The first thing I want to do is get out to the honor farm as soon as I can," the actor told newsmen. "I want to be outdoors."

He added: "I think the sentence is fair."

The blond Miss Leeds, retaining her composure, said: "I ... will... ...nces." ...tence, ...or for ...bilities ... hun... ...e idol... To the

REUNION Movie Actor Robert Mitchum and his wife, Dorothy, reunited Friday for the first time since he was arrested two days ago in a narcotics raid. She was driving across country with their two young boys at the time of his arrest with Starlet Lila Leeds. (AP Wirephoto).

IN COURT Actor Robert Mitchum bends an attentive ear to Robin Ford, arrested with him and two girls a week ago on narcotics charges, as they appeared in court Wednesday for hearing on writ of habeas corpus. (AP)

SEPTEMBER 19, 1948

Dope Scandal Hands Studios Hot Issue As to How to Overcome Public Revulsion

BY HAROLD HEFFERNAN

North American Newspaper Alliance

HOLLYWOOD, Sept. 18—Now that the ugliest and most devastating of all scandals—dope—once more has ...peared ... the ... pic... ...stry, ...curi... the ...

thing else. Exposures of this type cause public revulsion that time never will heal. We're in for it now. We might as well face it."

This sober-minded executive opinion is reflected privately in the plush corridors of the screen tycoons from Burbank to Culver City and, judging by the number and length of ...

...tory" public reaction to t... Mitchum case, one trade pape... said that a trailer advertisin... one of the accused star's fu... ture pictures was "roundly ap... plauded" in local theaters.

This semiofficial attempt to whitewash violations against public decency is pretty hard to digest, even though it is ...

Dancer Jailed As Fugitive

Woman Involved In Mitchum Case

NEW YORK, Jan. 12 (AP)—Dancer Vicki Evans, a defendant in the west coast narcotics trial in which Screen Actor Robert Mitchum was found guilty, was arrested Wednesday as a fugitive.

She was picked up in her hotel room by detectives acting on a California bench warrant. The warrant was issued Monday when she failed to appear for trial along with Mitchum and two others.

Miss Evans was booked at the West 30th street police station and taken to the women's lockup for the night. She is scheduled to appear in felony court Thursday.

Mitchum, Actress Lila Leeds and Robin Ford, a real estate salesman, were found guilty Monday in California of conspiracy to possess marijuana.

They were arrested with Miss Evans last September 1.

The 25-year-old dancer said she could not go to the coast for trial Monday because she had no funds. She ad... that she wa... and "clear ...

Miss Eva... Benjamin, ... will fight ... fornia. He ... was telegra... office in L...

Held in Gambling Raid

OCTOBER 2, 1948

APRIL 1, 1949

Vickie Evans ... identified herself as a dancer at Earl Carroll's, were among a number of persons arrested Friday in a gambling raid on a Hollywood club. They were booked on suspicion of vagrancy. Miss Evans already faced narcotics charges as a result of a recent raid in which Robert Mitchum, actor, was among those arrested. (Associated Press Wirephoto)

A story of life's greatest adventure...

the growth of a boy into manhood, the love of a man and a woman!

Starts TODAY

A GREAT STORY BY CALIFORNIA'S GREATEST STORY TELLER . . . Now One of the Year's Outstanding Motion Pictures . . . Capturing All the Beauty of Life in the Magic of Technicolor . . . !

ROBERT MITCHUM

in His New 1949 Role!

MYRNA LOY

in JOHN STEINBECK'S

The Red Pony

MAY 18, 1934

A Perfect Combination of Screen Entertainment!

Murder set to music... a thrilling mystery in the spectacular setting of a world-famous revue with death and "the most beautiful girls in the world" walking side by side

EARL CARROLL'S MURDER at the VANITIES

Pathos in a great heart story

Music in dance and lilting song!

What Songs! "Marihuana" "Ebony Rhapsody" "Live and Love Tonight" "Cocktails for Two" "Lovely One"

"GRASS"

Is the Kind of a Story that Mad Nature Stages Once in a Millennium to Mock the Minds of Men Who Write

Written by an Angry God and enacted by

50,000 Human Beings & 500,000 Beasts

ON THE FROZEN PATHS OF A FORGOTTEN WORLD WITHERED BY THE BLASTS OF A SUN THAT LAUGHED IN CYNICAL GLEE

Decreed that 50,000 humans and 500,000 beasts furnish photographic evidence that THE GREATEST DRAMAS IN THE WORLD ARE NOT WRITTEN BUT HAPPEN!

Let your startled eye and dazed mind travel across blasted plains that frost the blood, stun the imagination, over mountain chains covered with age old snows, across glacial rivers that race like maddened locomotives—Barefooted—Hungry—

PROVING THAT IT CAN BE DONE NO MATTER WHAT IT IS

BEGINS FRIDAY IMPERIAL A PARAMOUNT PICTURE

"Romola" Ends Thursday "BUT SCRIP BOOKS" TIME IS SHORT—HURRY—COME TODAY

Picture Tells Of Narcotics

Taken from actual case histories in the files of the anti-narcotics bureau, "Cairo Road," the new film opening Thursday at the Paramount theater, is one of the most unusual and interesting screen hits of the year.

In addition to being based on real-life cases, the film was also photographed in the actual locales where the story takes place—Cairo, Suez and Kantara.

Hailed as an exciting thriller, the story is concerned with the unceasing war against the international traffic in drugs and narcotics.

For the first time on the screen, the inside of an institution devoted to the cure and rehabilitation of addicts is shown.

Eric Portman, Maria Mauban and Laurence Harvey are starred.

1938

IT Dares TO EXPOSE THE EVILS OF MARIHUANA

ASSASSIN OF YOUTH (MARIHUANA)

REEFER

MARIHUANA Weed from the Devil's Garden!!

"Dangerous as a coiled rattlesnake" —Courtesy Riley Cooper in Readers' Digest Magazine

Plus Another FIRST-RUN HIT!!

THE PRIVATE LIFE OF A PRIVATE UNDERWORLD

"NUMBERED WOMAN" with SALLY BLANE LLOYD HUGHES

MOST DARING EXPOSE EVER SHOWN IN PORTLAND!! Every parent—every youth should see it!

Starts TODAY! NEW RIVOLI

1938

Rivoli Opens 'Reefer' Film

'Assassin of Youth' Shows Evil Results From Marihuana Use

While doing research work preparatory to filming "Assassin of Youth," the feature picture exposing the evils of marihuana opening today at the Rivoli theater, Leo McCarthy, the producer came upon a national crusade aimed to stamp out the reefer smoking evil.

Marihuana is found growing wild in every state in the country and in many places the owners of the property where it is grown are unaware of what they have in the common looking weed. Because of the ease of production and unlimited supply the cost to the smoker is small.

Narcotic officials have found that ordinary dope such as cocain, heroin, morphine are used by criminals to gain courage to execute maniacal plans made in advance. But with marihuana it is said the victim smokes the weed solely for a ...

"THE MAGNIFICENT DOPE"

1 "Tell Your Children," a new movie exposes one method of selling marijuana ... caused by smoking them. Jack (left) is a peddler. His customers are high school boys and girls, whose friendship he gains with ... at the Varsity Club.

3 Blanche, an older girl and a marijuana addict, and Jimmy, Mary's kid brother who also has become a victim of the drug, ... lure Bill to Jack's apartment. As usual, a hot party is in full ... Bill is induced to smoke a marijuana cigaret ...

4 The Sensual Dancing and marijuana smoking make a weakling of Bill, who once took pride in his strong will power. Before realizing what he is doing, he becomes an addict of the habit-forming drug. He craves its strange, stimulating effect. Seduced by Blanche, he quits going with Mary. She wonders why ...

8 Blanche Commits Suicide after a lengthy grilling in which she tells the whole story. Previously, Ralph, breaking under the strain, had overpowered and killed Jack in the hide-out. The noise of the fight attracts police. Ralph is adjudged hopelessly insane. Blanche's confession frees Bill, but his life is wrecked. He cannot forgive himself for Mary's tragic death.

Alpha Beta Tau chapter of ... will entertain Sunday at Battle Ground lake.

... the "Girls' State" to be conducted this year by the Oregon department.

Dope Picture Held for Run

1934

Tragic results of constant use of marihuana, one of society's most evil drugs and source of much crime, features the theme of "Assassin of Youth," current attraction at the Rivoli theater.

"Assassin of Youth" tells the tale of young persons who fall into the habit of smoking marihuana, how their parties are held, the results and society's attempt to wipe out the practice. A definite message of warning to parents is carried in the story.

"Numbered Woman," a story of the underworld, accompanies as major feature. Sally Blane and Lloyd Hughes play the principal roles.

1940 Starts TOMORROW! CAPITOL

"DOPED YOUTH"

The most daring picture ever made of America's Newest Narcotic Menace!

A puff of smoke changed their lives

MARIHUANA

Cock your ears for such songs as "Cocktails for Two", "Lovely One", "Live and Love Tonight"! Keep your eyes peeled for "Marihuana", "The Sea of Mermaids" and "The Human Powder Box".

Exotic

Maria Mauban plays Camelia in "Cairo Road," story of world-wide traffic in narcotics opening at the Paramount Thursday.

... discusses the unfortunate aspects of the marihuana problem and other wartime evils which complicate the problem of juvenile delinquency.

Dope Cases Spark Film

Paramount Theater Has 'Cairo Road'

Taken from actual case histories in the files of the anti-narcotics bureau, "Cairo Road," is now being shown at the Paramount theater.

In addition to being based on real-life cases, the film was also photographed in the actual locales where the story takes place—Cairo, Suez and Kantara.

Hailed as an exciting thriller, the story is concerned with the unceasing war against the international traffic in drugs and narcotics.

For the first time on the screen, the inside of an institution devoted to the cure and rehabilitation of addicts is shown. ... Portman, Maria Mauban ... Harvey ...

'GRASS' COMING TO IMPERIAL

"Yo Ali!" A nation on the march. That is the cry of the wild Bakhtiari tribe as they trek over snow-clad mountains 10,000 feet high and through icy torrential rivers twice a year in search of grass for their flocks and herds. On one side of these barriers the grass grows in the summer and on the other side pasturage is plentiful in the winter.

Three intrepid explorers traveled last year right with the tribe during their spring migration and captured with the motion picture camera a mighty human drama. The film is entitled "Grass," and will be shown at the Imperial beginning next Friday.

This picture is now the sensation of New York and Philadelphia.

A special music score composed of ancient tribal music accompanies the picture.

CURRAN POPULAR MATINEE TOMORROW LOUIS O. MACLOON JANE

1st Portland Run CAPITOL

IT'S VIVID! IT'S DARING!... IT'S POWERFUL! BUT IT'S TRUE!

"DOPED YOUTH" See the TRUTH about America's NEWEST NARCOTIC MENACE!

Five Big Acts of VAUDEVILLE

No Advance in Prices 15c

TOMORROW!

The stark, searing, shocking story behind the traffic in narcotics!

CAIRO ROAD

PARAMOUNT

Youngsters plan "hot jazz" parties during which recordings of their favorite bands are p... ed. But such occasions ... turn into drinking sessions or marijuana and cocaine ...

Marihuana—The Evil Weed

MEN VOL. 3, NO. 10

MAN to MAN THE STAG MAGAZINE

REEFER RENEGADE

... very pretty, but the dope ... her money and her life

These teen-age delinquents light up reefers to put them in mood for the desperate acts that may lie ahead.

Homosexuality is another vice that is on the increase in Los Angeles and in Hollywood area.

... paneled room ... with smoke. There is ... —and marijuana—in the heavy air.

I "JOINED" A Teen-Age DOPE GANG

... vice of smoking marijuana is most serious menace among the California teenagers. Vivid scene is from film "Wild Weed," Franklin Productions.

COLUMBIA
25c
STARTS TODAY!
SEE FOR YOURSELF
It will hold you spellbound!
NOTE:
ADULTS ONLY!
1934
"NARCOTIC"
EXTRA!
PROF. HOWARD D. YOUNG, D. S.
Famous Dietician and Health Specialist Lecturing in Person at Each Performance
Just a needle mark on her arm . . but it reached her SOUL!
New STAR
6TH & BURNSIDE OPEN ALL NIGHT!
A FIFTH COLUMN SOWING DESTRUCTION IN THE YOUTH OF AMERICA . . . .
1943
VICE DENS EXPOSED
"DEVIL'S HARVEST"
ALWAYS ENTERTAINING! ALWAYS REVEALING!
A VICIOUS RACKET WITH IT'S ARMS AROUND YOUR CHILDREN!
OPEN ALL NIGHT TILL 6 A.M.
LAST STAGE SHOW
12:30 A.M.—Sat. 1:30 A.M.
STAGE
BEAUTIFUL EXOTIC
"ROSANNE"
FIRST PORTLAND SHOWING
SPEED
VICTORY!
New STAR
6TH & BURNSIDE OPEN ALL NIGHT!
STARTS TODAY FOR ONE BIG WEEK
A VICIOUS RACKET WITH IT'S ARMS AROUND YOUR CHILDREN!
SIN
DEGRADATION
VICE
INSANITY
DEBAUCHERY
ADULTS ONLY
1944
"DEVIL'S HARVEST"
PARAMOUNT
STARTS TODAY!
"The war against Narcotics! can never stop!"
For the first time the screen rips aside all conventions to bring the world the stark searing shocking story behind the vile traffic in dope!
1952
CAIRO ROAD
. . . the double-crossroad of the world!
With ERIC PORTMAN
Laurence Harvey • Maria Mauban
COMPANION FEATURE
BREAKDOWN
EXTRA! COLOR CARTOON
JAMES CAGNEY
"The Mayor of Hell"
EPIC OF THE OLD WEST
AMERICAN
FREE MARINOFF BEER!
MID-TOWN BALLROOM
S. W. FOURTH AND TAYLOR ST.
MIDNIGHT SHOW TONIGHT
4STAR FOLLIES
SENSATIONAL EXPOSE OF THE DOPE RACKET
1949
NARCOTIC
JUVENILE DELINQUENCY EXPOSED!
Youth Aflame
WHAT HAPPENS TO 500,000 TEEN-AGERS YEARLY!
SHOCKING DRAMA OF FLAMING YOUTH
ONE WEEK ONLY
STARTS TODAY
4STAR FOLLIES
ONE WEEK ONLY
SENSATIONAL!
"NARCOTIC"
IT MAKES BEASTS OF MEN AND WOMEN!
ON OUR STAGE
BURLESQUE
HELD OVER—TERRY
STAGEFUL OF GIRLS
3:30—7:30—9:30—12 MIDNIGHT
CAN THEY CHANGE BACK?
What's Wrong With Modern Youth?
1949
Youth AFLAME
A DARING EXPOSE of JUVENILE DELINQUENCY!
"REEFER" MADNESS
It's VIVID It's DARING
It's POWERFUL BUT It's TRUE
PARAMOUNT
"CAIRO ROAD"
"BREAKDOWN"
MARIHUANA
DEVIL'S GARDEN!
Reefer MADNESS
HUNTING A THRILL, THEY INHALED A DRAG OF CONCENTRATED SIN!
THIS PICTURE WILL BE SHOWN TO ADULTS ONLY
"TWO GALS AND A GUY"
with JAMES GLEASON
JOHN HAMRICK'S
MUSIC BOX
TOMORROW!
DARING-THRILLING-DRAMATIC EXPOSE OF THE INTERNATIONAL DOPE RACKET!
First Portland Showing!
1952
"THE MARIHUANA STORY"
A vice of weaklings, the smoking of marijuana is a crutch to give fancied superiority to those who know they've nothing on the ball but day dreams
EDNESS—THE
TEST SEX FEAR
WEIRD EFFECTS OF MARIJUANA SMOKING
WAS MYSTERIOUSLY MURDERED AS SHE SOUGHT RIP KIRBY'S HELP.
MONTGOMERY, THE PHOTOGRAPHER, MONOPOLIZED CHIP FARADAY'S MODELING TALENT. HE IS RHODA'S FRIEND AND A DRUG ADDICT.
MUSHY, OWNER OF THE CLUB PENGUIN, SUPPLIES MONTY WITH DRUGS.
Marijuana 'Kingpin' Guilty; 'Sanitary Sam' Hill Breaks; Wife Testifies for State
IT NEVER BOTHERED ME TO THINK YOU MADE YOUR DOUGH GAMBLING, "SANITARY SAM"!.. BUT I WON'T BE MARRIED TO ANOTHER MARIJUANA PEDDLER!
"THE ROLLED REEFERS WENT TO SMALLER CUSTOMERS HIDDEN UNDER CORSAGES!"
I'M NOT KIDDING, SCOTTY! I TRIED IT ONCE, FOR A LAUGH...IT DIDN'T END FUNNY, THOUGH! WENT TO MY HEAD, I DID CRAZY THINGS...BEFORE MY DELIRIOUS ADVENTURE WAS OVER...
WHAT BROUGHT THIS ON ? SOUNDS LIKE DOUBLE-TALK OR COPE!
—HE WAS UNDER THE INFLUENCE OF A CHEAP, BUT POWERFUL NARCOTIC!
"YOU SEE, WHEN MEATBALL BURNED UP HIS WHOLE MARIJUANA CROP, I THOUGHT HE MEANT TO QUIT THE DIRTY RACKET!"
ME DOPE! ME DOPE! ME DOPE!
?
... I HAD ENDANGERED MY FRIENDS' LIVES AND A SKY-PILOT MET HIS DEATH! NOT A PRETTY SITUATION, EH ?
YEAH... BAD THINGS, REEFERS!
JOHNNY HAZARD
EVER SMOKE A REEFER, SCOTTY ?
HUH ? OH, NO... NOT ME! I'M THE SIMPLE TYPE... JUST GO IN FOR STRONG STUFF!
BUT WHO DID YOU EXPECT TO ROB HERE, YAQUI JOE ?
QUIEN SABE, BUT MANY GRINGOS COME WEETH AMERICAN DOLLARS TO BUY SMALL PACKAGES!
WITH A GLEAM OF ANTICIPATION IN HER EYES, SHE GENTLY REMOVES A SMALL TISSUE ENVELOPE CONTAINING A WHITE POWDER
MARSHAL, HERE'S TH' RINGLEADER OF TH' NARCOTIC SMUGGLERS!